The Country Justice

The Country Justice:

CONTAINING

The PRACTICE, DUTY and POWER

OF

The Justices of the Peace,

As well in as out of

THEIR SESSIONS.

By MICHAEL DALTON of Lincolns-Inn, *Esq;*
And one of the Masters in Chancery.

WHEREIN

All the STATUTES in Force and Use from *Magna Charta* 9 *Hen.* III. to 15 & 16 *Geo.* II. and also All the CASES in LAW, relating to the Jurisdiction and Authority of Justices of the Peace, are carefully collected and digested under proper Titles.

AND

For the better Help of such JUSTICES of PEACE as have not been much conversant in the Study of the LAWS of this REALM, there is added,

An APPENDIX;

BEING

A Compleat Summary of all the Acts of Parliament, shewing the various Penalties of Offences by STATUTE, and the particular Power of **One, Two, Three,** or more Justices, in their Proceedings and Determinations, under several distinct Heads, in Alphabetical Order.

With **Four Tables,**

The First, of the Heads of the Chapters. **The Third,** of the Divisions and Sub-divisions
The Second, of All the Statutes relating to contained in the Appendix: And,
Justices of the Peace. **The Fourth,** of The Principal Matters.

And **The Precedents** Translated into *English.*

ALSO

ADDENDA, containing

The Statutes of 16, 17, 18 & 19 *Geo.* II. with all the Modern Cases of Authority published since the Year 1742, down to the Present Time.

Justice is the Staff of Peace, and the Maintenance of Honour.   Cic.

In the SAVOY:

Printed by HENRY LINTOT (Assignee of *Edw. Sayer,* Esq;) and Sold by S. Birt, at the *Bible* and *Ball* in *Ave-Mary-Lane*; D. Browne, at the *Black Swan* without *Temple-Bar*; and J. Shuckburgh, at the *Sun* next the *Inner Temple-Gate* in *Fleetstreet.* M.DCC.XLVI.

Sir *HENRY MOUNTAGUE*, Kt.

Lord Chief Juſtice of the Pleas, holden before the KING'S MAJESTY.

My Honourable good Lord,

AFTER I had ſpent many Years in the Study of the Laws of this Realm, and was called to the Miniſtration of *Juſtice* in my Country, I thought it not ſufficient to apply my ſelf only to the Precepts and Directions of former Times, but to obſerve ſuch new Accidents as daily happened within my Experience, the better to perform the Duties of my Place. Whilſt I thus endeavoured my ſelf, I obſerved that *Juſtices* of Peace in their Places grew in Neglect, and many Times were overſwayed by ſuperior Sollicitations, and ſometimes ſo diſgraced, that I could have been content rather to have ſat down in Quiet, than with Study and Pains to incur ſuch Hazards and Diſcontentments. But again, whilſt I ſtood thus doubtful, it pleaſed the Fountain of Juſtice (I mean, His *Royal Majeſty*) ſo to grace, and to ſhew his high Eſteem of the Authority of *Juſtices* of Peace, not only (in his Majeſty's late Speech in the *Star-Chamber*,) valuing them with the neareſt employed about him, but (to the great Honour of this Realm, and of the Government thereof) alſo eſtabliſhing this Country Government by Juſtices of Peace in his Majeſty's Native Country of *Scotland* ; ſo as I ſaw the Current of Juſtice to run clear through the Land, and my ſelf to receive new Vigour and Encouragement : Whereupon I began to recollect my confuſed Notes and Obſervations, willing, for my private Help, to digeſt them into ſome Order and Method, ſuch as my Underſtanding could beſt contrive. Thus prepared, I yet queſtioned with my ſelf, whether it were better to adventure the Publiſhing of theſe my Labours, or to keep them for my private Uſe. In this unſettled Conſultation,

being

The Epiſtle Dedicatory.

being brought unto your Lordſhip by my good Friend, (who alſo difcovered to your Lordſhip this my Labour) and finding your Lordſhip favourably to reſpect me and it, I took Encouragement to put
the ſame in Print, after I had obtained (according to my humble
Suit) your Lordſhip's Favour for Allowance and Patronage thereof.

Now it remaineth farther, to crave of your Lordſhip, not only
for my ſelf, but for all that ſhall uprightly labour in this juſticiary
Courſe, that we may receive from your Lordſhip ſuch Encouragement, as that we may undergo the Charge impoſed upon us, without Fear of Oppoſitions, or other Diſturbances. So by your Lordſhip's Favour and Means ſhall Juſtice be the more duly adminiſtred,
and his Majeſty's Peace be the more firmly maintained, to the
Honour and Safety of the King's Majeſty, and the good and peaceable Government of all his Subjects. And ſo his Majeſty will no
Doubt proceed (as he hath begun) ſtill to increaſe your Honour,
for your Care in honouring him, and his Royal Throne thereby;
and the People, who ſhall feel the Benefit of your Zeal for Juſtice,
will heartily pray for your Happineſs; and God, beholding how you
make Juſtice and Peace go together, will, according to his abundant
Mercies, give you the everlaſting Reward of Juſtice and Peace: For
all which I will continually pray, and beſides, reſt

Your Lordſhip's in all Humility

And Duty ever to be commanded,

MICHAEL DALTON.

To

To the RIGHT WORSHIPFUL

Sir *JAMES LEE*, Kt.

The King's Attorney of his Court of *Wards* and *Liveries*; and to the Right Worſhipful, and my very good Uncle, *Thomas Spencer*, Eſq; and to the Reſidue of my Maſters of *Lincoln's Inn*.

*I*T *may ſeem ſtrange, that after ſo many learned Writers in this Kind, I (a Man of ſo weak Parts) ſhould preſume to offer to the View of the World a Work of this Nature: Yet my Reaſons being conſidered with indifferent Favour, I hope to be excuſed not only with you, but with all others who are Lovers of their Country, and ſeek the Peace thereof. I confeſs my ſelf a long, yet an unprofitable Member of your Honourable Society; but ſeeing that my Calling is to a Country-Life, and conſidering that he who is of the meaneſt Condition, and hath the ſmalleſt Talent, may not (without juſt Reprehenſion) retire himſelf ſo to his private Pleaſure or Profit, as that he ſhould neglect to ſhew ſome Fruit and Token of his Love to his Country, (leſt therein the Heathen Philoſopher might juſtly condemn him, who ſaid,* Non ſolum nobis nati ſumus, ſed partim Patriæ, &c.) *I have been the bolder, according to my ſmall Power and Capacity, to offer this my Mite into the Treaſury of my Country; this Work (whatſoever it be) being written firſt as private Notes for my particular Help in this Buſineſs, wherewith my ſelf and many others are daily employed, without yielding any Pleaſure or Profit at all to us, otherwiſe than for the publick Good.*

The Sweet of like Labours you, my great Maſters, (which I do moſt gladly behold) do from Time to Time reap more fully, riſing daily to great Honour and Wealth, through your Wiſdoms, Deſerts, and great Pains. That which remaineth to us Country-Juſtices (for the moſt part) is the Wearying of our ſelves, the Spending of our Time, and Eſtates, ut alii inde pace fruantur, *being requited many Times not only with much evil Will from or by the Means of ſuch as we have in Juſtice to deal withal, but oftentimes alſo rather diſgraced than encouraged by ſome in higher Place.*

I ſpeak not this without acknowledging it to be both juſt and meet, that the Actions and Proceedings of the Juſtices *of* Peace *ſhould be well and duly looked into, and themſelves puniſhed, when through Malice, or other Corruption, they ſhall do unjuſtly: But if through unwilling Ignorance they happen to err, they are rather to be better informed than ill intreated.* Nemo naſcitur ſapiens, & humanum eſt errare.

I am bold to write unto you, my worthy Maſters and Friends, and the reſt of this Honourable Fellowſhip, knowing that there are many among you riſing to great Places, whoſe Honour it will be to maintain the Life of the Law, and Juſtice of the Realm, in cauſing due Execution thereof to be had and done; redreſſing the Abuſes and Defects thereof,

2 *and*

The Epiftle.

and encouraging fuch as fhall carry themfelves jufte, fideliter, & fincere: *Again, that there are many among you of great Learning and Judgment; by whom this my unperfect Work may, and I hope fhall be more publifhed and perfected. And feeing fome others amongft you whofe Fortunes prove (as mine doth) to withdraw themfelves into their Countries, I would gladly encourage them to employ their better Talents to the common Good.*

I acknowledge there are divers Books in this Kind more Learned *and* Methodical; *but withal I obferve the Bufinefs of the* Juftices of Peace *to confift partly in Things to be done by them out of their* Seffions, *(and fometimes privately, and upon a fudden, without the Advice or Affociation of any other) and partly at their* Seffions *of the Peace. Of Things of this laft Kind I purpofe not in this* Treatife *to meddle, for that at fuch publick Meetings and Affemblies they are far more able to direct themfelves: But for the private and fudden Help of fuch* Juftices *of* Peace, *who have not read over the former* Writers, *and if they have, yet the Multiplicity of* Statutes *(whereupon the Office and private Practice of* Juftices *of* Peace *doth principally confift) is fuch, and at every* Parliament *fo altered, by Expiration, Difcontinuance, and otherwife, as that it is a Work very hard and laborious for Gentlemen not converfant in the Study of the Laws (although otherwife very induftrious) to proceed as by the Commiffion they ought and are prefcribed,* &c. *fecundum* Leges & Statuta Regni; *upon thefe Confiderations, and for their Eafe principally, I have publifhed this Work; knowing that there are divers, both Honourable and Worthy Perfons in the Country, fome of whom for want of Knowledge of the many particular* Statutes *in Force, and Tedioufnefs of the Study of them, do feek to be exempt out of the* Commiffion *of the* Peace; *others being in, do forbear to meddle, or medling do not that good Service therein which they are defirous to do. I have herein endeavoured to fet down Things fo plainly and briefly as I could, with Reference to the* Statutes *abridged, whereby the* Reader *may the better refolve and fatisfy himfelf, what he ought to do in every particular almoft that fhould come before him, or them, out of their General* Seffions *of the* Peace. *And yet for that in Cafes of Ambiguity,* Satius eft fontes petere quam fectari rivulos, *I could wifh all* Juftices *of the* Peace *to have ready by them the* Statutes *at large, as well as the* Abridgments, *and to ufe this Book or the* Abridgments *of the* Statutes, *as* Tables *and brief Memorials, but to truft and ground themfelves upon the* Books *at large.*

I am now only to intreat your Favours: And although I might reft confident by the honourable Patronage *I have obtained of him, whofe high Place and Prefidency for Matters of* Juftice *and judicious Underftanding drew me to covet the fame, (and not a little induced thereto, in Regard of the near Alliance by Marriage into the honourable Houfe of the* Spencers;) *yet withal I could not, out of that Duty and Love which I owe to this Honourable Society, (my firft Breeder in the Studies of the Law) and Hope of your tender Refpect, to uphold the Credit of an affectionate Member of your Society, but be bold alfo to crave your farther Countenance in thefe my Labours; and that you would be pleafed to accept this loving Remembrance as a thankful Gratuity to you, to whom I muft ever acknowledge my felf deeply obliged, and ever to reft at your Commands.*

MICHAEL DALTON.

THE

THE
EDITOR's
PREFACE.

IN this Edition Abſtracts of the Statutes relating to the Authority and Juriſdiction of Juſtices of Peace, down to the ſixteenth Year of his preſent Majeſty, incluſive, and ſeveral References have been added. Many Errors, Typographical and others, which had crept into former Editions, have been Corrected ; and Expired or Repealed Statutes and frivolous Repetitions ſtruck out. The *Latin* Precedents are now Tranſlated. The Statute Table in an Alphabetical Order of Heads, inſerted by Mr. *Nelſon*, was thought ſuperfluous, the Statutes being found in that Order in *Dalton* and in the Appendix; in its ſtead the Reader will find a Table of Statutes in the Order of Time, with the Chapters where they are abſtracted in this Book.

To diſtinguiſh the Additions from *Dalton*'s Text, the Marks (*a*) and (*d*) are uſed inſtead of the *Italicks* and inverted *Comma's* which disfigured the Edition of 1727 ; the Mark (*a*) after the Number of a Chapter, as in *Page* 89 *Chap.* XLI. (*a*) ſignifies that the whole Chapter is an Addition to *Dalton* ; in any other Place (*a*) ſhews all that follows to be an Addition, either to the End of the Chapter or to the Mark (*d*) where *Dalton* begins again. This Diſtinction could not be regularly made before the Preſs was advanced to *Chap.* XLI. becauſe the firſt Edition of 1618, the only one we thought we could truſt in this Reſpect, did not come to Hand ſooner.

A TA-

A
TABLE
OF THE
HEADS of the CHAPTERS.

Chap.
1. OF the Common Law, and of such as had and still have Conservation of the Peace by the Common Law. Page 1
2. The first Ordaining of Justices of the Peace. 4
3. Of Peace. 7
4. Justices of Peace, their Oaths. 10
5. The Form of the Commission of the Peace. 12
6. The Power and Authority of Justices of Peace. 16
   Accessaries, see c. 161
7. Alehouses. 20
8. Affray. 28
   Apprentice, see Labourers, c. 58
   Arrest, see c. 170
9. Armour. 30
   Artificers. 31
   Badger, see c. 46
   Bakers, see c. 112
10. Barrator. 31
11. Bastardy. 32
12. Bailment. 39
13. Bankrupt. 40
14. Blasphemy. ibid.
15. Brewers and Bakers. 41
16. Bridges. 42
17. Buggery. 45
   Burglary, see c. 40, 151
18. Burials. ibid.
   Bullion. 46
19. Butchers. 46
20. Butter and Cheese. 47
   Buttons and Button-holes. 49
   Cards and Dice. ibid.
21. Carriages, Coaches, Chairs and Carts. 50
22. Cattle. 52
   Certiorari, see c. 195
   Challenge to Jurors, see c. 186
23. Churches and Church-yards. ibid.
   Clerk of the Peace. 53
24. Cloth, Clothiers and Drapery. 54
   Coals. 59
   Coin, see High Treason, c. 140
25. Common Prayer. 60
26. Coffee, Tea and Chocolate. ibid.
   Conformity. 61
27. Corn. ibid.
   Conies, see c. 46, 55

Chap.
28. Constables. Page 63
29. Conspiracy. 65
30. Conventicles. 66
31. Cottages and Inmates. 68
32. Counterfeiters. ibid.
33. Customs. 69
34. Custos Rotulorum. 71
   Dissenters. 72
35. Dyers. ibid.
36. Egyptians. 73
   Escape and breaking Prison, see c. 158, 159
37. Estreats. 73
   Evidence against Felons, see c. 164
38. Excise. 74
   Brandy. 78
   Brewers. 80
39. Extortion. 82
40. Felony. ibid.
   Fairs, see c. 62
41. Fees. 89
42. Fish. 91
43. Fire. 96
44. Forcible Entry. ibid.
45. Forestallers, Regrators, and Ingrossers. 100
   Forest, see c. 55.
   Forfeiture for Felony, see c. 163
   Forgery, see c. 160.
46. Games and Plays. 103
   Game. 107
47. Guns. 110
   Gunpowder, see the Appendix.
   Gaol, see c. 78
   Hats and Caps.
   Hawkers and Pedlars. 111
48. Hawking. 112
49. Hearth-Money and Chimney-Money. ibid.
   Hedges, see c. 101
   Hides, see c. 59
50. Highways. 112
   Highwaymen. 123
51. Particular Highways. 124
52. Horses. 125
53. House of Correction. 127
54. Hue and Cry. 128
55. Hunting. 129
   Husband and Wife, see c. 157
   Indictments, see c. 184

b

A Table of the Heads of the Chapters.

Chap.

Informer and Informations, see c. 191
56. Innholders. Page 132
57. Inrolment. 133
 Journeymen Taylors, see c. 58
 Judgment, see c. 188
 Jury, see c. 186
 Justice of Peace, see c. 173, 189
58. Labourers. 134
59. Leather. 145
60. London. 151
61. Malt. 152
 Manufactures, see c. 196
62. Markets and Fairs. 153
63. Marriages. 154
64. Mariners and Seamen. ibid.
65. Night-walkers. 156
66. Nusances. ibid.
67. Oaths. 157
 Orchard, see c. 101
 Papists, see c. 81
 Partition of Lands. 158
 Parliament, see the Appendix.
68. Partridges and Pheasants. 158
69. Pasture-Land. 160
70. Peace. ibid.
 Perjury. 161
71. Petitions. 162
 Pewter. ibid.
72. Plague. 163
73. Poor. 164
 Posse Comitatus, see c. 171, 172
74. Post-Office. 189
75. Preachers. ibid.
76. Printers and Printing. 190
 Probate of Wills, see c. 41
 Process, see c. 193
77. Prophecies. ibid.
78. Prison. 191
 Pretended privileged Places. 192
79. Purveyors. ibid.
80. Quakers. 193
 Rape, see c. 160
 Rates, see c. 96, 196
 Recognisance, see c. 168
81. Recusants. 194
82. Riots, Routs. 211
83. Rogues and Vagabonds. 219
84. Robbery. 220
85. Sacraments. 223
86. Sabbath Day or Sunday. 224
 Salt. 225
 Scavenger. 226
 Servants, see c. 58
87. Schoolmaster. 226
 Seaman, see c. 64
 Sessions, see c. 185
88. Sewers. 226
89. Sheep. 228
90. Sheriffs. 229
91. Ships. 231
 Shoemakers, see c. 58
92. Silk-throwing. 232
93. Skinners. ibid.
 Smugglers. 223

Chap.

94. Soldiers. Page 233
95. Spices. 235
 Squibs. ibid.
 Stamp-duties. ibid.
 Starch and Hair Powder, see the Appendix.
96. Stock of the Shire. 236
 Stolen Goods, see c. 155
97. Subsidy. 238
 Surety of the Peace, see c. 116
98. Swearing. 238
 Tanner, see c. 59.
 Taxing, see c. 73, 96, 196
 Timber, see c. 111.
99. Tobacco. 239
 Toll, see c. 112.
100. Transportation, Importation, Exportation and Transportation of Felons. 240
 Trees, see c. 101
101. Trespass. 242
 Trial, see c. 187
102. Tythes. 245
103. Tyle. 246
 Vagabonds, see c. 83
 Waggoners, see c. 21.
104. Watch. ibid.
105. Watermen. 247
106. Wax. 249
107. Wears. ibid.
108. Weavers. 250
109. Wine. ibid.
110. Wild Fowl. 251
111. Wood. ibid.
112. Weights and Measures. 254
113. Wool. 263
114. Words, News. 264
115. Some particular Statutes that give Power to one or two Justices of Peace out of the Sessions. ibid.
116. Surety for the Peace. 267
117. For whom, and of whom Surety of the Peace may be granted. 269
118. How this Surety may be demanded, and how the Commandment may be executed. 272
119. Concerning the Recognisance of the Peace. 276
120. What Things shall discharge the Recognisance of the Peace, or the Party of his Appearance at the Sessions. 278
121. What Acts shall be a Forfeiture of the Recognisance of the Peace. 280
122. Concerning the Writ of Supplicavit. 284
123. Surety for the Good Behaviour. 287
124. For what Cause this Surety for the Good Behaviour shall be granted. 288
125. Forcible Entry, and Forcible Detainer. 292
126. What is a Forcible Entry or Holding within these Statutes. 293
127. Lawful Force. 299
128. Where Forcible Detainer of Possession is lawful. 301
129. The

4

A Table of the Heads of the Chapters.

Chap.

129. *The several Remedies the Party hath for Forcible Entry or Detainer.* Page 302
130. *Of Restitution to be made to the Party put out.* 304
131. *Who shall award Restitution.* 305
132. *To whom Restitution shall be made.* 306
133. *Causes of staying Restitution.* 307
134. *Restitution, when to be made.* 309
135. *Riots.* 310
136. *What shall be said a Riot, Rout, or unlawful Assembly.* ibid.
137. *Concerning the Lawfulness, or Unlawfulness of the Act.* 312
138. *For the Manner and Circumstances.* 313
139. *What Persons may commit a Riot.* 314
140. *High Treason.* ibid.
141. *Misprision.* 321
142. *Petty Treason.* 323
143. *Of Felonies by the Common Law.* 325
144. *Felo de se.* 327
145. *Murder.* 328
146. *Manslaughter.* 333
147. *What Persons are chargeable with Homicide, and who not.* 334
148. *Misadventure or Chance.* 335
149. *Casual Death.* 336
150. *Homicide upon Necessity.* 337
151. *Burglary.* 340
152. *Theft.* 344
153. *Robbery.* ibid.
154. *Larceny.* 346
155. *Of the Manner of Larceny.* 347
156. *Of what Things Larceny may be committed, of what not.* 349
157. *What Persons be chargeable with Larceny.* 352
158. *Other Felonies by the Common Law.* 354
159. *Felonies by Statute.* 355
160. *Felonies by Statute.* 359
161. *Accessaries.* 367
162. *Rules concerning Felony.* 373
163. *The Forfeiture of Felony.* 375
164. *Examination of Felons, and Evidence against them.* 377

Chap.

165. *Whether Information, Evidence or Proof of Witnesses shall be taken against the King.* Page 381
166. *Causes of Suspicion.* ibid.
166. *Part 2d. Bailment and Mainprise.* 384
167. *Where Bailment is taken away by Statute.* 390
168. *Recognisance.* 399
169. *Warrants.* 401
170. *Arrest and Imprisonment.* 406
171. *Posse Comitatus.* 411
172. *What Persons may take Posse Comitatus, and in what Cases.* 412
173. *Advice to Justices of Peace.* 413
174. *Warrants and Precedents.* 415
175. *Supersedeas.* 427
176. *Recognisance.* 430
177. *Licences and Testimonials.* 438
178. *Warrants.* 440
179. *Mittimus and Records.* 443
180. *Bailment.* 444
181. *Releases of the Peace.* 446
182. *Forcible Entry, and Records thereof.* 448
183. *Riots, and Records thereof.* 452
184. *Indictments* 455
185. *Sessions.* 456
186. *Jurors and Challenges to them.* 462
187. *Trial.* 464
188. *Judgment.* 465
189. *How Justices and other Officers may defend themselves against Suits.* 466
190. *Clergy.* ibid.
191. *Informations, Actions popular.* 468
    Informations 470
192. *Mayor or Magistrate, where he may act as a Justice of Peace by some particular Statutes.* 470
193. *Process.* 471
194. *Traverse.* 474
195. *Certiorari.* ibid.
196. *Of the Powers given to Justices of the Peace by several late Statutes.* 479

For

For the better finding out of the Authors herein alledged, observe that,

F signifies *Fitzherbert.*

Br. Brook.

Dir. Certain Directions or Resolutions of all the Judges of Assizes, *Anno* 1663. and imprinted for *William Coke, Ann.* 1636.

Fi. Finch.

Raft. Raftall's Abridgment of the Statutes, printed *Anno Dom.* 1583.

Lib. Intr. The Book of Entries, Impreff. 1596.

Lbt. or *Lambt. Lambert's* Juftice of Peace, Impr. 1559.

P. Poulton's Abridgment of the Statutes, Impr. 1606.

Cro. or *Crompt. Crompton's* Juftice of Peace, Impr. 1606.

P. R. Poulton de Pace Regis.

Ba. Sir *Francis Bacon's* Elements of the Common Law.

Ba. V. His Ufe of the Law.

Refol. Refolutions of the Judges of Affifes *Ann.* 1633. to certain *Quæres.*

Mo. Moor's Reports.

Hawk. P. C. Hawkins's Pleas of the Crown.

1, 2 *H. H. P. C. Hale's Hiftoria Placitorum Coronæ* Vol. 1ft, 2d.

The other References are as ufual in Law Books.

A Table

A TABLE of all the STATUTES in Force and Use relating to Justices of the Peace, from *Magna Charta* 9 *Hen.* III. to 16 *Geo.* II. inclusive.

The first Column shews the Years of the several Reigns, the second the Chapters of the Statutes, and the third the Chapters of this Book where the Statutes are respectively abstracted. Where App. *is referred to, it signifies the Appendix.*

Henry III.

Anno	Cap.	Chap. of Dalton.
9	25	112
51	Stat. 1.	Ibid

Edward I.

Anno	Cap.	Chap. of Dalton.
3	9	162
	15	166 part 2, 167
	20	160
13	11(ft.1)	167
	47	42
	Stat. 2	84, 104
27	3 (St.1)	166 part 2

Edward III.

Anno	Cap.	Chap. of Dalton.
1	16(ft.2)	2
2	3	9, 44
	15	62
5	5	62
	14	104
14	10	160
25	2 (ft. 5)	140, 142
	10	112
27	10(ft.2)	112
34	1	2, 82
	22	160
37	19	160

Richard II.

Anno	Cap.	Chap. of Dalton.
7	13	9
12	10	185
13	8 (ft. 1.)	42
	19	112
	1 (ft. 2)	145
14	11	185
15	2	44, 125
16	3	112
17	9	42
20	1	9

Henry IV.

Anno	Cap.	Chap. of Dalton.
5	5	160
	10	170
13	7	82, 135

Henry V.

Anno	Cap.	Chap. of Dalton.
2	4(St. 1)	4, 185
	8	82, 135
	9	82
	1(St. 2)	2

Henry VI.

Anno	Cap.	Chap. of Dalton.
8	7	167
	9	44, 128, 130
	12	160
	29	125
9	8	20
18	17	112
	19	160
23	10	12, 39, 166 pt. 2
	15	167
33	1	40

Edward IV.

Anno	Cap.	Chap. of Dalton.
1	2	90
3	4	20
17	4	103

Henry VII.

Anno	Cap.	Chap. of Dalton.
1	7	55, 160
3	1	162, 186
	2	160
	14	159
	23	167
4	3	19
	20	191
11	4	112
	15	90
	17	68
	21	167
12	5	112
19	6	71
	11	55
	13	135

Henry VIII.

Anno	Cap.	Chap. of Dalton.
14 & 15	6	51

Henry VIII.

Anno	Cap.	Chap. of Dalton.
14 & 15	10	55
21	7	58, 155
	11	164
22	5	16, 167
	7	102
	10	36
	11	160
23	1	190
	4	112
	5	88
25	6	17, 160
	11	110
	13	89
	17	111
26	7	51
	13	141
27	16	57
	20	167
	24	3
28	1	190
	15	160
32	3	190
	13	52
	27	167
33	1	34
	6	47
	9	46, 167
	17	66
	39	176
37	1	34

Edward VI.

Anno	Cap.	Chap. of Dalton.
1	1	85
	5	100
	12	160, 190
2	10	61
2 & 3	2	94, 160
	15	29
3 & 4	19	19
	21	20, 45
5 & 6	4	23

Anno

A Table of all the Statutes relating to Justices of Peace.

Edward VI.

Anno	Cap.	Chap. of Dalton.
5 & 6	6	24
	9	160
	14	22, 27, 45
	25	7
7	5	109

Mary.

Anno	Cap.	Chap. of Dalton.
1	3 (St. 2)	75
	6	140
	8	90
	9	167

Philip and Mary.

Anno	Cap.	Chap. of Dalton.
1 & 2	4	36, 160
	5	100
	10	140
	11	140
	13	12, 40, 166 pt.2
2 & 3	3	69
	7	52
	8	50
	9	46
	10	40
	16	105
4 & 5	3	94, 160
	5	24

Elizabeth.

Anno	Cap.	Chap. of Dalton.
1	1	81
	2	23, 81
	12	24
5	1	81
	4	58
	5	64, 160
	9	70
	11	140
	12	45
	13	50
	14	160, 167
	15	77
	20	36, 160
	21	55, 101, 124, 167
8	2	167
	3	89, 160
	4	153
	8	52
	9	112
	11	167
	12	24
13	2	81, 140
	5	167
	9	88
	25	111
14	3	140
18	1	140
	3	11
	5	191

Elizabeth.

Anno	Cap.	Chap. of Dalton.
18	10	50
23	1	23, 81, 87, 140
	5	111
	8	106
	10	48, 55, 68
27	2	81, 140
	7	90
	12	90
	13	54, 84
	17	24
29	4	90
	6	81
31	4	160, 165
	5	46, 191
	7	31
	11	128, 133
	12	52, 160
35	1	81
	2	81
	10	24
39	5	53
	14	24
	15	160
	17	73, 94, 160
	19	51
	20	24
43	2	31, 73, 96
	3	94
	6	167
	7	101
	10	24
	13	160

James I.

Anno	Cap.	Chap. of Dalton.
1	4	87
	6	24
	8	145
	9	7, 167
	11	160
	22	19, 45, 59, 111
	25	24, 58, 73
	27	47, 68, 160
	31	72, 124, 160
3	4	23, 81, 140, 160
	5	81
	9	93
	10	78, 170
	12	42, 107
	13	47, 124
4	2	24
	5	7
7	1	187
	3	73
	4	11, 53, 124, 178
	5	11, 166
	6	67, 81
	7	24, 155
	8	69

James I.

Anno	Cap.	Chap. of Dalton.
7	11	68
	12	189
	16	24
21	4	191
	6	157, 188
	7	7
	8	118, 122, 195
	12	189
	15	126
	18	24
	20	98
	21	56
	22	20
	26	160
	28	52

Charles I.

Anno	Cap.	Chap. of Dalton.
1	1	46
	4	7
3	2	86
	4	7, 11
	5	73
16	19	112

Charles II.

Anno	Cap.	Chap. of Dalton.
12	19	33
	23	38, 63, 195
	24	38, 79
	25	109
	32	113
	34	99
13	5 (St. 1)	71
13 & 14	1	67, 80
	4	25
	7	59, 66
	11	33
	12	11, 28, 73
	13	20, 100
	15	92
	18	113
	19	24
	22	160
	26	20
	28	42
15	2	101, 111
	7	99, 100
	8	19
	11	26, 28
16 & 17	2	24
17	3	23
18	2	42, 66, 100
	3	160
19	3	60
	4	78
20	7	100
22	1	30
	5	160
	8	112

Charles

Anno	Cap.	Chap. of Dalton.	Anno	Cap.	Chap. of Dalton.	Anno	Cap.	Chap. of Dalton.
Charles II.			**William III.**			**Anne.**		
22	12	50	7	30	38	9	11	19, 59, 160
	13	27		31	86		14	46
22 & 23	5	38		32	187		15	111
	7	40, 160		34	80, 102		16	160
	11	160	8	16	50		18	21
	20	78, 170		19	38		23	20, 21, 160
	22	37		20	160		25	46
	25	42, 55		26	40, 140, 160		26	42
	26	99		30	58, 73	10	2	26
25	2	4		31	67		16	24
29	7	86		33	195		18	34
9 & 30	2	160		36	92		19	20, 95, 160
30	3	18		37	86 See App. Tit. Scavenger.		26	59, 160
	8	24	9	4	32	12	7 (St.1)	40, 58, 151
	9	42		6	86		18	73
	Stat. 2.	81		7	66, 95		14 (St.2)	81
31	2	78		11	73		18	91, 160
32	2	20, 100		25	160	**George I.**		
James II.				27	47	1	5 (St.2)	82, 160
1	17	73		32	14		11	21
	19	27		40	113		13	4
William and Mary.				43	92 See App. Tit. Alamodes and Lustrings.		15	24
1	8 (St.1)	4, 67	10	2	20		18	42
	12	27		10	113		23	33, 64
	15	81		17	66		26	15
	18	30, 34, 75, 81		23	23, 40, 160		46	99
	21	23, 34		25	42		48	101, 160
	24	24, 38	11	4	81		52	50, 86. See App. Tit. Scavenger.
	26	81		7	160		55	81
	33	59		15	7, 112		57	21
2	8 (St.2)	51, 86. See App. Tit. Scavenger.		19	78	3	11	46
3	9	40, 151, 190	13	3	140		15	41, 90
	10	55, 195		6	4		18	81
	11	73	**Anne.**			4	6	47
	12	21, 50, 195	1	8 (St.1)	3		7	20
4	4	160		9 (St.2)	40, 160, 161		11	113, 155
	7	20		12	23		12	160
	10	20		17	140	5	4	34
	18	191		18	16		8	73
	23	46, 68, 195	2	6	64		12	21
	24	186	3	4	47		15	55
5	4	4		18	186		18	55
	11	195	4	19	64		26	App. Tit. Gunpowder.
	21	160		21	42		27	9
6	1	33,	5	6	159		28	55
	10	24, 112		14	46, 68, 195	6	6	21
	11	98		31	40, 104		11	160
	16	21, 107		34	19		16	101
	17	18, 140	6	7	140		18	66, 160
William III.				29	21		19	83
7	3	140		31	43		21	7, 20, 33, 38, 74, 95, 160
	6	102, 195,	7	6	19		23	23, 40, 50, 100, 160
	21	64	8	6	20	7	12 (St.1)	20
	29	50	9	10	74			George

A Table of all the Statutes relating to Justices of Peace.

George I.

Anno	Cap.	Chap. of Dalton
7	13	58
8	6	80
	18	33, 93
	19	46, 68
	22	160
9	3	61
	7	6, 73
	12	160
	22	32, 42, 55, 160
	27	58
	28	78, 160
10	10	26
11	22	78, 160
	23	App. tit. *Gunpowder.*
	29	160
	30	26, 38
12	4	61. See App. tit. *Malt.*
	12	7
	28	33
	32	160
	34	160
	36	160
13	24	35

George II.

Anno	Cap.	Chap. of Dalton
1	17	109
	19	50, 160
2	1	61. See App. tit. *Malt.*
	18	27
	21	143
	25	70, 160
	26	105
	28	7, 38, 46
	31	67
	36	64
3	11	107
	20	86

George II.

Anno	Cap.	Chap. of Dalton
3	25	186
	26	24
	29	15, 73
4	9	160
	16	160
	18	160
	26	184
	32	160
	33	74
5	12	27
	18	2
	19	195
	30	13, 46, 160
6	17	38
	30	160
	31	11
	37	160
7	10	2
	21	84, 153, 160
	22	160
8	16	84
9	20	60
	23	38, 160
	25	160
	26	67
	29	160
	30	160
	33	42
	35	33
10	28	46
	31	105, 160
	32	46, 160
11	1	61
	19	81
	22	27, 160
	26	38
	34	160
12	21	160, 196
	25	59
	28	46

George II.

Anno	Cap.	Chap. of Dalton
12	29	196
13	8	196
	18	195, 196
	19	46
	24	28, 196
	29	196
14	6	160'
	33	16, 196
	42	50
15 & 16	2	196
	13	Ibid.
	24	Ibid.
	27	Ibid.
	28	Ibid.
	32	Ibid.
	33	Ibid.
	34	Ibid.
16	8	197
	15	Ibid.
	18	Ibid.
	26	Ibid.
	29	Ibid.
	31	Ibid.
17	3	Ibid.
	5	Ibid.
	8	Ibid.
	17	Ibid.
	29	Ibid.
	30	Ibid.
	35	Ibid.
	37	Ibid.
	38	Ibid.
18	10	Ibid.
	20	Ibid.
	27	Ibid.
	33	Ibid.
	34	Ibid.
	36	Ibid.
19	——	Ibid.

E R R A T A.

Page 26 *Margin, for* 6 Geo. 1. c. 22. §. 54. *read* 6 Geo. 1. c. 21. §. 56. *p.* 27 *Line* 47 *read* 12 Geo. 1. c. 12. *p.* 30. *lin. ult. dele* Army Debentures, &c. *p.* 39 *marg. for* 6 Geo. 2. c. 33. *read* 6 Geo. 2. c. 31. *ib. marg. for* 1 & 2 P. & M. c. 3. *read* 1 P. & M. c. 13. *p.* 52 *marg. for* 5 Ed. 6. c. 4. *read* 5 Ed. 6. c. 14. *p.* 54 *marg. for* 33 El. 20. *read* 39 El. 20. *ib. for* 43 El. 20. *read* 43 El. 10. *p.* 58 *marg. for* 10 Ann. c. 6. *read* 10 Ann. c. 16. *p.* 62 *marg. for* 2 W. & M. *read* 1 W. & M. *p.* 65 *line* 24, *and in marg. for* 12 Ann. Stat. 2. c. 23. *read* 13 Geo. 2. c. 24. *ib. for* upon View of a Justice of Peace or Oath of one Witness, *read* On Oath of one Witness before a Justice of Peace. *ib. for* 20 s. *read* any Sum not exceeding 5 l. or less than 10 s. *p.* 69 *dele l.* 3 & 4 the Statute 9 & 10 W. 3. c. 4. being expired. *ib. marg. for* 13 & 14 Car. 2. c. 6. *read* 13 & 14 Car. 2. c. 11. *ib. line* 37 *for* 12 Car. 2. c. 14. *read* 12 Car. 2. c. 19. *p.* 74 *line ult. for* Gallon *read* Barrel. *p.* 91 *line* 14 *for* 13 E. 47. *read* 13 Ed. 1. 47. *p.* 92. *marg. for* 4 & 5 Ann. c. 12. *read* 4 & 5 Ann. c. 21. *p.* 93 *marg. for* 9 Ann. c. 2. 6. *read* 9 Ann. c. 26. *p.* 117 *marg. for* 22 Car. 1. *read* 22 Car. 1. *p.* 120 *marg. for* 1 Geo. 1. c. 22. *read* 1 Geo. 1. c. 52.

p. 128 *marg. for* 27 El. 17. *read* 27 El. 13. *p.* 152 *line* 2 *for* 13 Geo. 2. c. 21. *read* 13 Geo. 2. c. 8. *p.* 155 *marg* *for* 2 Geo. 1. c. 36. *read* 2 Geo. 2, &c. *p.* 190 *marg. fo* 1 W. & M. Stat. 1. c. 88. *read* 1 W. & M. Stat. 1. c. 18 *p.* 191 *line* 39 *for* 11 & 12 W. c. 9. *read* 11 & 12 W. 3 c. 19. *p.* 192 *line* 24 *for* shall be guilty of Felony, and transported, *read* shall be guilty of Felony without Benefit o Clergy, and all concealing such disguised Persons shall b guilty of Felony, and transported, *See* Cap. 160. *p.* 23 *marg. for* 4 El. c. 2. *read* 43 El. *&c. p.* 242 *marg. for* 4 El. c. 1. *read* 43 El. c. 7. *p.* 245 *marg. for* 32 H. 7. 8 *read* 32 H. 8. 7. *ib. for* 7 & 8 W. 3. c. 35. *read* 7 & W. 3. c. 34. *p.* 255 *marg. for* 27 El. 3. c. 10. *read* 27 Ed 3. c. 10. *p.* 343 *marg. for* c. 107. *read* c. 160. *p.* 352 *lin* 41 *for* 33 H. 1. *read* 33 H. 8. *p.* 364 *marg. for* 11 & 1 W. 3. c. 23. *read* 10 & 11 W. 3, *&c. p.* 366 *line* 14 *fo* cap. 6. *read* cap. 7. *p.* 377 *marg. for* 2 & 3 P. & M. 13 *read* 1 & 2 P. & M. *&c. p.* 391 *line* 31 *for* 12 H. 7. c. 21 *read* 11 H. 7, *&c. p.* 392 *line* 7 *for* West. 1, cap. 5. *rea* West. 1. cap. 15. *p.* 393 *marg. for* 5 El. 2. *read* 5 El. 21.

CHAP. I.

Of the Common Law, *and of fuch as had, and ftill have, the Confervation of the Peace by the* Common Law.

T HE Common Laws of this Realm of *England*, receiving principally their Grounds from the Laws of * God and Nature ; (which Law of Nature, as it pertaineth to Man, is alfo called the Law of † Reafon) and being, for their Antiquity, thofe whereby this Realm was governed many hundred Years before the Conqueft ; the Equity and Excellency whereof is fuch, as that there is no human Law fo apt and profitable for the Peaceable and profperous Government of this Kingdom, and fo neceffary for all Eftates, and for all Caufes, concerning Life, Lands or Goods, as thefe Laws are. And to that Purpofe, at the Common Law (long before Juftices of the Peace were made) there were fundry Perfons to whofe Charge the Maintenance of this Peace was recommended, and who with their other Offices, had (and yet ftill have) the Confervation of the Peace annexed to their Charges, as a Thing incident to and infeparable from their faid Offices. And yet they were and are called by the Names of their Offices only, the Confervation of the Peace being included therein.

Margin notes: ʰ *The Law of God is the Law of the Land.* 34 H. 6. 40. Doct. & St. lib. 1. cap. 6. Fitz. 3. Co. 340. † *Common Law is common Reafon.* Vide Plo. 36.a. 67.a. 107. b. & 465. a. Co. L. 142. 9 *Part, Pref.* Fortefcue, c. 17. Lit. 209.

Firft, The King (by his Dignity Royal) is the Principal Confervator of the Peace within his Dominions, (and is *Capitalis Jufticiarius Angliæ*) in whofe Hands the Adminiftration of all Juftice and all Jurifdiction in all Caufes firft was ; and afterwards by and from him only was this Authority derived and given to others.

Margin notes: King. 20 H. 7. 7. a: Co. 11, 85.

And yet fo, as that whatfoever Power is by him committed unto other Men, the fame remaineth ftill in himfelf ; infomuch that he may himfelf in Perfon fit in Judgment, as in ancient Times Kings here have done, and may take Knowledge of all Cafes and Caufes, unlefs they concern himfelf ; for in fuch Cafes wherein the King is a Party, he cannot properly fit in Judgment, but muft perform that by his Juftices, or Commiffioners, as in Cafes of Treafon and Felonies. The King alfo, as he is the principal Confervator of the Peace, fo he may command all others, and may award Procefs againft them to conferve the Peace ; but he cannot take a Recognizance for the Peace, becaufe it muft be made to himfelf, &c.

The Lord Chancellor, or Lord Keeper of the Great Seal, the Lord High Steward of *England*, the Lord Marfhal, and High Conftable of *England*, the Lord Treafurer of *England*, and every Juftice of the King's Bench, as alfo the Mafter of the Rolls, as fuch, have the Confervation of the Peace over all the Realm ; and they may award Precepts, and take Recognizances for the Peace, as incident to their Offices ; and upon Prayer of Surety of the Peace made to them, or any of them, againft any Perfon, they have Authority to grant their Warrant to the Sheriff, Conftables, or other the King's Officers, to arreft the Party, &c. and when he is come before them, may take a Recognizance for the Peace. And if the Party fhall refufe to find fuch Surety, they may commit him to Prifon. And yet for the Mafter of the Rolls, it is held that he maketh Procefs and taketh Recognizance, not as incident to his Office, (as all the other may) but by Prefcription.

Margin notes: Officers. Lamb. 12.

The Chamberlain of *Chefter* is Judge of the Court of Exchequer there, which hath the Jurifdiction of a Court of Chancery, and is by Virtue of his Office a Confervator of the Peace there, as was amongft other Things certified by Sir *James Dyer*, and the Juftices of the Court of the Common Bench to Queen *Elizabeth*.

Confervators of the Peace are now out of Ufe ; and in lieu of them there are ordained Juftices of Peace, affigned by the King's Commiffion in every County. Sir *Fr. Bacon* his *Ufe of the Law*, pag. 12.

There

Judges.
Lamb. 13.
2 H. 7. 2.
Br. Peace 12.

There be others who, by Virtue of their Offices, have the Confervation of the Peace, but yet only within the Precinct of their feveral Courts: As namely, the Juftices of the Court of the Common Pleas, the Barons of the Exchequer, and the Juftices of Affize and Gaol-Delivery. And any Perfon may pray the Surety of the Peace before any of thefe in their Courts: And if the Party be prefent, or within the Place or Precinct of their Court, or within their View, they may fend the Warden of the Fleet, or other Officers attending their Court, to bring the Party before them, and they may take Surety of him; and if he fhall refufe to find fuch Surety, they may commit him to Prifon. See *Sir* F. Bacon, *pag.* 12.

Alfo the *Juftices of Affize*, if the Peace happen to be broken in their Prefence and Precinct of the Court, may command the Offender to Prifon. And if Complaint be made to them that *A.* is minded to break the Peace, or elfe if they do perceive the fame in their Prefence, they may command the Parties upon a certain Pain to keep the Peace, and that Weapons be taken from the Jurors or Witneffes that appear before them. But as they be meerly Juftices of Affize, they may not award any Procefs or Warrant for the Peace, neither may they take Sureties of the Peace. *Lamb.* 13.

Stewards.
Lamb. 14.
Br. Leet 36.

Alfo the *Steward of the Sheriff's Turn*, the Steward of a Leet, and the Steward of a Court of Piepowder, are Confervators of the Peace within their feveral Courts; for every of them may commit him that fhall make an Affray in their Prefence whilft they be in Execution of their Offices; for thefe are Courts of Record; and fo in all other Courts of Record. But none of thefe may grant any Warrant for the Peace.

13 H. 4. 12.
21 E. 4. 21.
Crom. 7.
Br. Leet 39.
F. N. B. 12.

And the Steward of the Sheriffs Turn, as alfo the *Steward of a Leet*, (during their Courts) may by Recognizance bind him to the Peace, that fhall make an Affray in their Prefence, fitting the Court; and may commit him until he hath found Surety for the Peace; and may alfo take Examination of Felons, and commit them to the Gaol; and may alfo take the Prefentment of any Felony at the Common Law, committed within their Precinct, or of any other Offence againft the Peace, except the Death of a Man. See *Br. Leet* 1, 2, 14, 18, 22, 26.

Fine.
Co. 8. 38. *b.*

And fo if any other Contempt or Difturbance to the Court fhall be committed in any of the faid Courts, or in any other Court of Record, the Judge (or Steward) there may impofe upon fuch Offenders a reafonable Fine. See *Br. Leet* 14, 36.

Sheriff.
F. N. B. 81.
d. & 82.
Br. Peace 13.
Lamb. 186.

The *Sheriff*, by the Common Law, is a principal Confervator of the Peace in every Place within his County. And (upon Requeft to him made) may command another to find Surety of the Peace, and may take the fame Surety by Recognizance, and that *ex Officio*, and without any Writ of *Supplicavit* to him directed: And this feems to be by Virtue of his Commiffion, which faith, *Commifimus vobis cuftodiam Comitatus, &c. Vide Br. Judges* 11. *& Recogn.* 5, 14, 16, & 18.

Coroner.
Stamf. 48.

Coroners alfo (by the Common Law) are Confervators of the Peace within the County where they are Coroners: But they (as alfo all other the Confervators of the Peace by the Common Law) have Power for the Keeping of the Peace only as the Conftables have at this Day; *viz.* they may take Surety for the Peace by Obligation. *Vide hic infra,* 3 *E.* 4. 9. & 10 *E.* 4. & Tit. *Forcible Entry,* & *Cromp.* 6.

Conftables.

The *High Conftables* of the Hundreds are Confervators of the Peace within their feveral Hundreds and Limits by the Common Law. *Cromp.* 6 & 222. 12 *H.* 7. *fol.* 18.

And therefore thefe High Conftables, at their petty Seffions, for any Affray made in Difturbance of their Court, may imprifon the Offenders. *Co.* 11, 43, 44.

Br. Peace 13.
Fitz. 127.

Every *Petty Conftable* within the Limits of their feveral Towns are Confervators of the Peace (at the Common Law) by Virtue of their Office. *Vide Tit. Affray* and *Forcible Entry.*

And thefe Petty Conftables may do what they can to keep the Peace; but they cannot take Surety of the Peace *at the Requeft of any Man.* Yet *ex Officio* they may caufe fuch as in their Prefence are about to make an Affray, to find Sureties to keep the Peace; and that as well before the Affray as after. See *Cromp.* 6 & 222, & 12 *H.* 7. *fol.* 18. *a.* & *hic poftea.*

There be other Officers of like Authority to our Conftables: As the *Borfholders* in *Kent;* the *Thirdborough* in *Warwickfhire;* and the *Tithingman,* and *Borowhead,* or *Headborough,* or Chief Pledge in other Places. But yet the Office of a *Conftable* is diftinct, and of greater Authority and Refpect than thofe other; as you may fee by the Statute of 39 *Eliz.* 4. where the Tithingman or Headborough is to be affifted in the Punifhment of Rogues, with the Advice of the Minifter, and one other of the Parifh, whereas the Conftable alone of himfelf, as well as the Juftices of the Peace may appoint or caufe

Rogues

Rogues to be puniſhed.   And *M. Lambard* of the Duty of Conſtables; *p.* 51, *&c.* holds Lamb. 51,52, that theſe *Borſholders, Thirdboroughs, Tithingmen, Headboroughs,* and other ſuch, being 53, 54, 55. in any Town or Pariſh where a Conſtable is, cannot meddle, becauſe Conſtables are (in Compariſon of them) Head-Officers, and that the *Tithingmen, &c.* are but as Aſſiſtants to the Conſtables in their Office ; and that there are many other Things which the Conſtables may do, and wherewith the Borſholders and the Reſt cannot meddle at all.   And yet in Towns where there are no Conſtables, the *Borſholders, Thirdboroughs, Tithingmen, Headboroughs* or ſuch other, are there the only Officers for the Peace ; as alſo in ſuch Caſes where the Power or Authority of the *Borſholders, &c.* is declared to be equal with the Power of the Conſtable ; in all ſuch Caſes their Office and Authority are in a Manner all one.   See *Lambard Office del' Conſt.* 4, 6, 9.

There are alſo divers *Statutes* which appoint Offenders to be puniſhed by the Conſtable or other *inferior Officer.*   Now who be theſe inferior Officers, if not the Tithingmen, *&c.?*

And now, becauſe theſe Petty Conſtables are often abſent from their Houſes, being Advice. for the moſt part Huſbandmen, (and ſo moſt of the Day in the Fields ;) it would prove very ſerviceable, if, by a Law to be made in Parliament, every Town and Village were to have a Tithingman, or ſuch other Officer, to attend the Service of the Conſtable, in his Abſence at the leaſt, for that for want of ſuch Aſſiſtance, Rogues, Vagabonds, and the like, knowing their Times, now travel up and down more boldly.

And yet Mr. *Crompton, fol.* 222. ſaith, That a *Conſtable* may make a *Deputy* to exe- Deputy Conſta cute his Office in his Abſence, for that he may be ſick, *&c.* And it hath been reſolved, ble. that he may make a *Deputy,* becauſe it is but a Miniſterial Office. *Mich.* 13 *Jac.* Moor's Rep. *B. R. Phillips* and *Winſcome's* Caſe.   But ſome. have held, that the Making a Deputy p. 845. is rather by Toleration, than by Law.   *Reſol.* 29. *   * According to 2Hawk.p.62.

it is not ſettled that a Conſtable can make a Deputy without ſpecial Cauſe, as Sickneſs, &c.   In 2 H. H. P. C. p. 88. it is generally ſaid he may make a Deputy, and he is within 7 Jac. 1. 5. to plead the General Iſſue, Moor 845. Pl. 1141.   Yet in 1 H. H. P. C. 581 it is ſaid, that if a Warrant be directed to the Conſtable he muſt execute it himſelf, and may not ſubſtitute another.   Ideo quære.

If any Man ſhall make an Affray or Aſſault upon another in Preſence of the Conſta- Affray. ble or Borſholder ; or if any Man in the Preſence of the Conſtable ſhall threaten to kill, 3 H. 4. 9. a. beat or hurt another, or ſhall be ready to break the Peace ; in every of theſe Caſes the 9 Ed.4. 26. a. Conſtable or Borſholder may commit the Offenders to the Stocks, or to ſome other ſafe p. 137. Cuſtody for the Preſent, (as his or their Quality requireth) and after may carry them be- Hic. cap. 8. fore ſome Juſtice of Peace, or to the Gaol, until they ſhall find Surety for the Peace ; Stocks. which Surety the Conſtable himſelf may alſo take by Obligation, to be ſealed and delivered to the King's Uſe : And if the Party will not find ſuch Surety to the Conſtable, he may be impriſoned until he ſhall do it.   3 *H.* 4. 9, 10.

I have ſeen the Report of *Skarret's* Caſe, *Termino Trin. Anno* 35 *Eliz. Rot.* 1458, where *Skarret* brought his Action of falſe Impriſonment againſt one *Hanmer,* for arreſting and impriſoning him, *&c.*   The Defendant to the Impriſonment pleaded, that he was High Conſtable of the Hundred of *E.* in the County of *S.* and that the Plaintiff made an *Affray* within the ſaid Hundred upon one *H. W.* who preſently came to him and Affray. told him thereof, and ſwore upon a Book that he was in fear of his Life by the other ; whereupon the Defendant came to the Plaintiff, and arreſted and impriſoned him, until he had found ſufficient Sureties for the Peace ; upon which the Plaintiff demurred.   And it was adjudged, that the Plea of the Defendant was inſufficient ; firſt, for that he was not preſent at the Aſſault and Affray ; ſecondly, for that he was the High Conſtable of the Hundred, and not Conſtable of the Town.   In the Argument of which Caſe *Anderſon* Conſtable. *Ch. Juſtice,* held Conſtables to be Conſervators of the Peace at Common Law, and ſtill ſo to be, and that they ought to preſerve the Peace as much as in them lieth ; but that (ſaid he) was by parting of Men which they ſhould ſee breaking of the Peace, and to carry them before a Juſtice to find Sureties for the Keeping thereof : But to take Sureties himſelf the Conſtable cannot.   And thoſe, which hold that he may take Surety, cannot tell what Surety that ſhould be ; for he cannot take a Recognizance nor Bail, for he is no *Officer of Record* ; and if he ſhall take an *Obligation,* how the ſame ſhall be certified, and into what Court, he ſaid he knew not ; and that it would be very inconvenient to give ſuch Authority to every Conſtable.   But by three other Judges, namely, *Walmſley, Owen,* and *Beamond* ; although a Conſtable cannot take Surety for the Peace by Recognizance or Bail, yet he may take an *Obligation,* according to the Book of 10 *E.* 4.   And if the Affray be in their Preſence, they are Conſervators of the Peace, and therefore may uſe ſuch Means for Keeping it by taking Surety by *Obligation.*   And that before Juſtices of

Peace

Peace were, the Peace was preſerved, and that by the Conſtables. And that the *Statute* which ordained Juſtices of the Peace, did not take away the Authority of the Conſtable. But the Conſtable hath no Authority to take an Oath of the Party that is in Fear, &c. Whereunto *Anderſon* Ch. Juſtice replied, ſaying, I doubt not but that at the Common Law the Peace was kept, but that was to be done in ſuch Manner as the Law appointed, and that is, by Writ out of the Chancery or King's Bench.

Bacon V. 5. And yet I have ſeen another Author, ſuppoſed to be Sir *Tho. Egerton*, after Lord Chancellor; who writeth in theſe Words, By the Common Law the Conſtable's Office was, to arreſt the Parties that had broken the Peace, or were (*in a Fury*) ready to break the Peace; ſc. if either he had ſeen it himſelf, or were truly informed thereof by others, or upon the Confeſſion of the Party who had freſhly broken the Peace: And that all 10 E. 4. 18. 21 E. 4. 35. ſuch Offenders the Conſtable might impriſon in the Stocks, or in his own Houſe, as the Quality required, until they had been bound by *Obligation* with Sureties to the King to keep the Peace from henceforth; which Obligation was to be ſealed and delivered to the Conſtable to the Uſe of the King; and the Conſtable was to ſend it into the Exchequer, or Chancery, from whence Proceſs ſhould be awarded to levy the Debt, if the Peace be broken. *Quod nota.* Vide etiam *Finch, fol.* 127. agreeing herewith, for ſuch as the Conſtable *findeth* breaking the Peace.

Every of theſe Conſervators of the Peace are (by the Common Law) to imploy their own, and may alſo command the Help of others, or arreſt and pacify all ſuch who in their Preſence and within their Juriſdiction and Limits, by Word or Deed, ſhall go about to break the Peace.

Affrays. Now theſe Conſervators of the Peace are only to meddle with *Affrays, Aſſaults* and *Batteries,* or *Threatnings to break* the Peace, done in their *Preſence*; but not with *Riots,* or *Forcible Entries,* or *Detainers.*

And if a Conſervator of the Peace, being required to ſee the Peace kept, ſhall be negligent therein, he may be indicted and fined for the ſame.

Alſo every of theſe Conſervators of the Peace, if they have committed or bound over any ſuch Offenders, they are then to ſend to, or be preſent at, and attend the next Seſ-ſions of the Peace or Gaol-delivery, there to object againſt them.

But for the High Conſtables and Petty Conſtables, although they have (by the Com-mon Law) the Charge of the Peace, as incident to their Office; yet their Offices and Authority began not long before the Time that Juſtices of the Peace were ordained: (See here Title *Conſtable.*) Whereas the Sheriffs, Coroners, Stewards of the Sheriff's Turn, of the Leet, and of the Court of Piepowders, and the Juſtices of all higher Courts, were long Time before the Conqueſt. See *Co.* 9 *Part,* the Preface.

There were other Perſons who (by the Common Law) had the ordinary Keeping of the Peace, and were named *Cuſtodes pacis;* whereof ſome were by Election (in full County) and ſome by Tenure, as you may ſee in *M. Lambard* 16, 17. There were others which were called to this Office by the King's Writ, to continue for the Term of their Lives, or at the King's Pleaſure, but theſe are now all ceaſed.

CHAP. II.

The firſt Ordaining of Juſtices of the Peace.

See this Oath at large, *Brac.*lib.3.*and* *Dr. Cowel* 235. KING *Edward* the Firſt, (according to the firſt Article of the Oath taken by him, and ſince by other Kings and Queens of this Realm at their ſeveral Coronations, in theſe Words, *Servabis Eccleſiæ Dei, Clero & Populo, Pacem ex Integro, & Concordiam in Deo ſecundum vires tuas. Quibus Rex reſpondet, Servabo.*) in his firſt Parliament holden *An.* 3. of his Reign, *Cap.* 1. did eſtabliſh, that the Peace of Holy Church and of the Land ſhall be well kept and maintained in all Points: Which *Peace of the Church* is (and always hath been by the antient Laws of this Land) protected by the King, the Arch-biſhops and Biſhops of this Realm; and the *Peace of the Land* is, and always hath been, defended and maintained by the ſame King, and his temporal Juſtices or Officers lawfully appointed for the ſame, &c. which *Temporal Juſtices*, at the firſt, were the Conſerva-tors of the Peace, as aforeſaid. But more eſpecially in thoſe Times there were alſo in every County Juſtices of *Oyer* and *Terminer*, and alſo there were *Juſtices Itinerants*, which had Power not only to determine all Manner of Quarrels, (as well Real and Per-

2   ſonal)

fonal) but alfo all Offences againft the Peace, &c. as may appear in our Law Books, and efpecially in M. *Fitz.* Tit. *Corone*, amongft the *Iter North' & Canc'.*

For although in our Annals, it is reported that *William* the Conqueror ordained Jufti- ces of the Peace about *An. Dom.* 1070. *An. quarto* of his Reign; yet the Juftices of Peace had not their Being till almoft Three hundred Years after, *viz. An. Dom.* 1327. at which Time Juftices or Commiffioners of the Peace were firft created by the Statute 1 *Ed.* 3. *c.* 16. By which Statute it was ordained, That in every Shire of the Realm certain Perfons fhould be affigned (*fc.* by the King's Commiffion) to keep the Peace. And their Authority was after enlarged by the Statutes 4 *Ed.* 3. *c.* 2. 18 *Ed.* 3. *c.* 2. and 34 *Ed.* 3. *c.* 1. And by many other Statutes made fince in every King's Reign. And by the faid Statute of 34 *Ed.* 3. 1. were they firft enabled to hear and determine (at the King's Suit) all Manner of Felonies and Trefpaffes: And each County had now its proper Commiffioners for the Peace, whereas before the Commiffions to the Juftices of the Peace were not made feverally into one Shire, but fometime jointly to fundry Perfons over fundry Shires.

Their Begin-ning.
Holinfh. 8.
1 Ed.3. cap. 16.

And by the Statute 2 *H.* 5. *c.* 1. *Stat.* 2. Juftices of Peace fhall be made of the moft fufficient Perfons dwelling in the fame Counties, by the Advice of the Chancellor and King's Council.

But the Statute of 36 *E.* 3. *c.* 12. is the firft Statute that nameth them Juftices of the Peace. For the Statutes of 2 *Ed.* 3. *c.* 6. and 25 *Ed.* 3. *c.* 6, 7, 8. fpeaking of Juftices, feem not to be of our Juftices of Peace; but that of 2 *Ed.* 3. as alfo the *Statute of Win-chefter, cap.* 1. therein mentioned, to be meant of *Juftices Itinerants,* or *Juftices in Eyre*; and the other of 25 *Ed.* 3. to be meant of Juftices or Commiffioners fpecially af-figned for Servants and Labourers. See for this laft, *Lamb.* 24. & 577, 578. and the Statutes of Labourers made 25 *E.* 3. *c.* 6, 7, 8. and of 42 *Ed.* 3. *c.* 6. *Raftal. fol.* 233. *a. b. d.*

Their Name.

They be called Juftices becaufe they be Judges of Record, and withal to put them in Mind, (by their Name) that they are to do Juftice, which is, to yield to every Man his own according to the Laws, Cuftoms, and Statutes of this Realm, without Refpect of Perfons. See 2 *Car.* 19. 6, 7.

Juftice of Peace is a Judge of Record.

They are named alfo Commiffioners of the Peace, becaufe they have their Authority by the King's Commiffion.

The Name in *Latin, Cuftodes pacis,* is equivalent to that of *Jufticiarii pacis,* as was refolved *Pafch.* 10 *Jac. B. R.* the King againft *Litle,* where upon a *Certiorari,* it was returned *quod ad general', &c. coram* A. & B. *cuftodibus pacis, Dom. Regis, &c.* an In-dictment was found, and this taken for an Exception that fome were *Cuftodes pacis,* that were not *Jufticiarii pacis,* yet the Exception was difallowed. *Rolls* 2. *p.* 95 *.

* *It hath alfo been refolved, That the De-*

fcription of Juftices of Peace by the Name of Jufticiarii Domini Regis ad Pacem confervandam, &c. *is good without faying* ad Pacem Domini Regis, *for that is neceffarily implied.* The King *and* Hawkins, *Mich.* 3 *Geo.* 1. 2 Hawk. *P. C.* 38.

And here it fhall not be amifs fhortly to put our Juftices of Peace in mind, how Ju-ftice may be perverted many Ways, (if they fhall not arm themfelves with the Fear of God, the Love of Truth and Juftice, and with the Authority and Knowledge of the Laws and Statutes of this Realm.) As namely,

1. By *Fear*; when fearing the Power of another, they do not do Juftice. *Deut.* 1. 17. *Ye fhall not fear the Face of Man, for the Judgment is God's,* who is *Capitalis Jufticiarius totius Mundi,* Chief Juftice of Heaven and Earth, and they are his Lieutenants.

2 Chron.19.6.

2. *Favour*; when they feek to pleafe their Friend, Neighbour, or other, *Deut.* ibid. *Ye fhall have no refpect of Perfons in Judgment. Thou fhalt not favour the Perfon of the Poor, nor honour the Perfon of the Mighty, but judge juftly.* Levit. 19. 15.

3. *Hatred* or *Malice* againft the Party, or fome of his. *Levit.* 19. 18. *Thou fhalt not avenge, nor be mindful of wrong.*

4. *Covetoufnefs*; when they receive or expect Fee, Gift or Reward; for as the wife Man faith, *Rewards and Gifts do blind the Eyes of the Wife, and make them Dumb, that they cannot reprove Faults.*

Eccl. 20. 28.

5. *Perturbation* of Mind; as Anger, or fuch like Paffion. *James* 1. 20. *The Wrath of Man doth not accomplifh the Righteoufnefs of God.*

6. *Ignorance,* or want of true Underftanding of what is to be done. *Ignorantia mater Erroris.*

7. *Preſumption*; when without Law they (preſuming of their own Wits) proceed according to their own Wills and Affections. *There is more hope of a Fool, than of him that is wiſe in his own Conceit.* Prov. 26. 12.

8. *Delay*; which in Effect is a Denying of Juſtice. *Negligentia ſemper habet comitem infortunium, & mora trahit periculum.*

9. *Precipitation*, or too much Raſhneſs; when they proceed haſtily; without due Examination and Conſideration of the Fact, and of all material Circumſtances, or without hearing both Parties: For *the Law judgeth no Man before it hear him.* John 7. 15. And

Seneca. the Philoſopher could ſay, *Qui aliquid ſtatuerit, parte inaudita altera, Æquum licet ſtatuerit, haud æquus eſt*; He that ſhall judge or determine of a Matter, the one Party being unheard, although he ſhall give juſt Judgment, yet he is not a juſt Judge. And again, *Omnia non properanti clara certaque fiunt, Feſtinatio autem ſemper improvida ac cæca eſt*; all Things are plain and certain to him that is not raſh nor heady; but Haſte is always improvident and blind. See *Deut.* 17. 4. *Eccleſiaſticus* 11. 7, 8. and *Prov.* 18. 13.

His Majeſty's Speech in the Star-Chamber, An.1616. All theſe, King *James* hath ſhortly, yet fully obſerved in his Charge given to the Judges, ſc. charging them *that they do Juſtice uprightly and indifferently, without Delay, Partiality, Fear or Bribery, with ſtout and upright Hearts, with clean and uncorrupt Hands; and yet not to utter their own Conceits, but the true Meaning of the Law, not making Laws, but interpreting the Law,* (and that according to the true Senſe thereof, and after deliberate Conſultation,) remembring that their Office is jus dicere, and not jus dare.

Judg. 19. 3. According to this laſt alſo is the Rule given in the Book of *Judges,* ſc. *In all Cauſes doubtful, firſt to conſider of the Matter, to conſult, and then to give Sentence :* Which Sentence muſt be agreeable to the Merits of the Cauſe and Crime, elſe it is not equal.

Yea, God himſelf hath given us Precedents of ſuch deliberate Proceedings; as you Gen. 3. 8, 9, 11. may ſee in *Geneſis, chap.* 3. *ver.* 8, &c. and *chap.* 18. *ver.* 21.

Theſe are worthy Directions for all Juſtices of Peace, and other Magiſtrates, that they carry themſelves in their Places uprightly and indifferently, not uttering their own Conceits, nor upon the ſudden to over-rule Things, but after deliberate Conſideration and Conſultation, then to proceed to execute the Authority committed to them.

Properties of Juſtices. Now there be four eſſential Properties required in Magiſtrates and Juſtices, *viz.*.

1. They muſt be Men of *Ability, of Body and Eſtate,* and of Courage for the Truth, and in the Truth.

2. They muſt be Men *fearing God*; not ſeeking the Place for Honour or Commodity, nor reſpecting Perſons, but the Cauſe.

3. They muſt be *Men dealing truly,* ſearching out all the Truth, and hating Covetouſneſs.

4. They muſt *judge the People at all Seaſons,* uſing all Diligence in hearing and ending Cauſes; and not to neglect the Publick, for private Employments, or Eaſe. See *Exodus* 18. 21, 22. and *Job* 29. 12 ad 17. *For they bear not the Sword in vain.* Rom. 13. 4.

Their Deſcription or Definition. Juſtices of Peace are Judges of Record, appointed by the King to be Juſtices within certain Limits for the Conſervation of the Peace, and for the Execution of divers Things comprehended within their Commiſſion, and within divers *Statutes* committed to their Charge.

9 E. 4. 3. 14 H. 8. 16. Now, firſt, that the Juſtices of Peace are Judges of Record, (yea, that every Juſtice of Peace by himſelf is a Judge of Record, and one upon whoſe ſole Report and Teſtimony the Law repoſeth itſelf very much). appeareth more plainly, if you obſerve theſe Things following :

1. He is made under the Great Seal of *England,* which is a Matter of Record.

2. Every Juſtice of Peace hath judicial Power given unto him by the Commiſſion, ſc. in the firſt *Aſſignavimus.*

Force. 3. Alſo by ſome *Statutes* they have judicial Power given them; for they may make a Record of a *Force* by them viewed, and may thereupon fine and impriſon the Offenders; yea, one Juſtice of Peace in ſome Caſes, may alſo hear and determine Offences, and puniſh an Offender as convict upon his own View, or upon the Confeſſion of the Offender, or upon Examination and Proof of Witneſſes. *Vide Tit. Forcible Entry.*

Lamb. 67, 94. 14 H. 8. 18. Co. 10. 76. 4. His *Warrant* (tho' it be beyond his Authority) is not diſputable by the Conſtable, or other inferior Miniſter, but muſt be obeyed and executed by them. But this muſt be underſtood when the Juſtice of Peace hath Juriſdiction of the Cauſe, for or concerning which he hath granted his *Warrant*; for otherwiſe the Conſtable or other Officer executing their Warrant, ſeemeth to be puniſhable. *Vide* Tit. *Warrants.*

5. He may take a Recognizance (for the Peace, &c.) which is a Matter of Record, Lamb. 67. and which none can do but a Judge of Record. See *Br. Recog.* 8, & 14.

6. His Record (or Teſtimony) in ſome Caſes is of as great Force as an Indictment up- on the Oath of twelve Men, and in ſome other Caſes of greater Force than an Indict- ment. See hereof Tit. *Force, Highways, Peace* and *Riot.*

7. He alſo may make out Proceſs upon Indictments, or Informations againſt Offen- ders, &c. and that out of their Seſſions, (in ſome Caſes) as you may ſee hereafter, Tit. *Proceſs.*

Great Cauſe therefore have the Juſtices of the Peace to take heed that they abuſe not their Authority, either to the Oppreſſing of the Subject, by making untrue Records, or Defrauding of the King, by ſuppreſſing the true Record.

By the *Statute* of 12 *R.* 2. *cap.* 10. there ſhould be but ſix Juſtices of Peace (in every *The Number.* Commiſſion of the Peace) with the Juſtices of Aſſiſe.

After, by the *Statute* 14 *R.* 2. *cap.* 11. it was ordained, That there ſhould be eight Juſtices of Peace aſſigned, beſides the Lords.

And *two Lawyers* (at leaſt) ſhall be aſſigned in every County, to hear and determine Felonies and Treſpaſſes done againſt the Peace. 18 *E.* 3. *c.* 2. 34 *E.* 3. *c.* 1. & 17 *R.* 2. *c.* 10.

Alſo Juſtices of Peace ought to be reſiant and dwelling within the ſame County, (ex- cept Lords and Judges, &c.) 2 *H.* 5. *c.* 4. & 2 *H.* 5. *Stat.* 2. *c.* 1.

Authority given to Juſtices of Peace ought to be purſued, and ſo it ought to appear in their Orders.   2 *Salk.* 475.

Their Orders being judicial Acts, are only voidable, for they continue Orders till avoid- ed. 2 *Salk.* 674.

By the *Statute* 5 *Geo.* 2. *c.* 18. No Perſon ſhall be capable of being a Juſtice of Peace 5 Geo. 2. c. 18. for any County in *England* or *Wales,* who ſhall not have an Eſtate of Freehold §. 1. or Copyhold in Poſſeſſion, for Life, or ſome greater Eſtate, or for Years determina- ble upon Life; or for a certain Term originally created for Twenty-one Years or more, in Lands or Hereditaments in *England* or *Wales,* of the yearly Value of 100 *l.* above Incumbrances.

No Attorney, Solicitor or Proctor, ſhall be capable to be a Juſtice of Peace in *England* Ib. §. 2. or *Wales,* during ſuch Time as he ſhall continue in Practice.

If any Perſon not qualified by this Act, ſhall do any Act as a Juſtice of Peace, he ſhall, Ib. §. 3. for every Offence forfeit 100 *l.* one Moiety to the King, the other to him that will ſue.

This Act ſhall not extend to any City, Town or Liberty, having Juſtices of Peace Ib. §. 4. within their Limits; nor to Lords of Parliament, their eldeſt Sons, nor Perſons qualified to be Knights of a Shire by *Stat.* 9 *Annæ,* *c.* 5. See alſo *Sect.* 6 & 7. of this Act, Ib. §. 5. ſome other Exceptions, with reſpect to the *Green Cloth,* Commiſſioners of the Navy, the two Under Secretaries of State, and the Heads of Colleges.

And by 7 *Geo.* 2. *c.* 10. *ſect.* 3. the Act of 5 *Geo.* 2. *c.* 18. ſhall not extend to de- 7 Geo. 2. c. 10. prive the Vice-Chancellor of the Univerſity, or the Mayor of *Cambridge,* from being Ju- §. 3. ſtices of Peace in the County.

C H A P. III.

Of Peace.

PEACE, in Effect, (ſaith M. *Fitzb.*) is the Amity, Confidence, and Quiet that is *Peace what.* between Men; and he that breaketh this Amity or Quiet, breaketh the Peace.   Fitz. Juſt. of

Yet Peace (in our Law) is taken for an Abſtinence from actual and injurious Force; P. 13. and ſo is rather a Reſtraining of Hands, than an Uniting of Minds. And for the Main- tenance of this Peace chiefly were the Juſtices of Peace firſt made.

The Breach of this Peace ſeemeth to be any injurious Force or Violence moved againſt *Breach of it.* the Perſon of another, his Goods, Lands, or other Poſſeſſions, whether it be by threat- ning Words, or by furious Geſture, or Force of the Body, or any other Force uſed *in terrorem.*

The Office of the Juſtices of Peace is principally to be exerciſed to the Keeping of the Peace, and ſuppreſſing and bringing to Puniſhment Perſons uſing ſuch injurious and unlawful Force or Violence. And yet (the Commiſſion of the Peace being *pro bono*

bono Pacis, ac pro conſervatione ejuſdem, & pro quieto regimine & gubernatione populi,) I ſee not why the Juſtices of Peace ſhould be reſtrained from preventing and repreſſing ſuch other Offences, Miſbehaviours and Deceits, as may break the Amity, Quiet and good Government of the People, and whereof Diſcords, and ſo Breaches of the Peace do

Latch p. 48. often ariſe, (though there appear neither Force nor Violence in the Offence itſelf;) as *Li-bellings, Cozenages,* and ſuch other Offences. *Vide* Tit. *Good Behaviour.*

But it is no Part of the Office of the Juſtice of Peace to forbid lawful Suits; albeit they ſhall do well to be Mediators of Peace in ſuch Suits and Controverſies as ſhall ariſe among their Neighbours. Neither ſhall any Man be puniſhed for Suing any Writ in the King's Courts, *ſoit ceo de Droit ou de Tort.* Co. L. 61.

Conſervation of Peace. The Conſervation of this Peace (and therein the Care of the Juſtice of Peace) conſiſteth in three Things, *viz.*

1. In *Preventing* the Breach of the Peace, by taking Surety for the Keeping of it, or for the Good Behaviour of the Offenders, as the Caſe ſhall require.

2. In Pacifying ſuch as are Breaking of the Peace. See *poſtea,* Tit. *Affray.*

3. In Puniſhing (according to Law) ſuch as have broken the Peace.

But of the Three, the preventing Juſtice is moſt worthy to be commended to the Care of the Juſtices of Peace.

Who may make them. The Conſtituting Juſtices of Peace is inherent, and inſeparable from the Crown, and

Stat. 27 H. 8. c. 24. becauſe this amongſt others had been ſevered therefrom, to the great Diminution and De-triment of that Royal State, and the Hindrance and Delay of Juſtice, as ſpeaks the *Sta-tute* of 27 *H.* 8. It was thereby enacted, That no Perſon ſhould have Authority to make any Juſtices of Peace, but only the King, his Heirs and Succeſſors, by their Letters Patent; nor was, nor is, his Power to be delegated, for the King cannot grant a Man Power to make Juſtices of the Peace, as is the Book of 20 *H.* 7. 7. *a.*

Three Sorts of Juſtices. Juſtices of Peace (at this Day) are of three Sorts, and are appointed or created by three Means.

Ely. 1. Firſt, By Act of Parliament; as the Biſhop of *Ely* and his Succeſſors, and their

27 H. 8. 124. P. Juſt. 2. temporal Stewards of the *Iſle of Ely* (for the Time being) ſhall be Juſtices of Peace with-in the ſaid Iſle, and ſhall uſe and have within the ſaid Iſle all ſuch Power as doth belong to any Juſtice of Peace within any County.

York and Durham. And ſo of the *Archbiſhop of York,* and the *Biſhop of Durham,* and their Succeſſors, and their temporal *Chancellors, &c. ibidem.*

Mayors.
By Grant.
Lamb. 26.
Br. Com-miſſ. 5. 2. Secondly, By Grant made by the King by his Letters Patent under the Great Seal, as Mayors, and the chief Officers in divers Corporate Towns: And ſuch the King can-not diſcharge again at his Pleaſure, but they ſhall continue and enjoy their Juriſdiction according as their Letters Patent do enable them; and therefore if the King granteth to a Mayor, or other Head Officer of a City or Corporate Town, and to their Succeſſors, to be Juſtices of Peace in their City or Town, and after maketh out Commiſſion of the Peace to others there, yet the Authority and Juriſdiction of the Mayor, *&c.* remaineth good, for that it was granted to them and their Succeſſors, and is not revocable at the King's Pleaſure, as the Commiſſion of the Peace is.

Which Grants and Charters may notwithſtanding for ſome great and general Defect of, or Miſcarriage in the Execution of the Powers and Authorities herein granted, be repealed, and the Liberties ſeized, ſo alſo may the King's Majeſty upon reaſonable Cauſe moving him, *ne deeſſet populo in Juſtitia exhibenda,* grant concurrent Commiſſions of the Peace within ſuch Incorporations.

And ſuch Juſtices of Peace by Grant or Patent have thereby the ſame Power as the Conſervators of the Peace had by the Common Law; and ſuch Power alſo is given to the Juſtices of Peace (or to any one Juſtice of Peace) by expreſs Words in any Statute: But none of them have thereby the whole Power which is ordinarily given to the Com-miſſioners of the Peace by their Commiſſions. And ſo of the firſt Sort of Juſtices of Peace by Act of Parliament, ſc. the Archbiſhop of York, and the Biſhops of *Durham* and *Ely,* and their temporal Chancellors and Stewards.

Lawyers. Alſo concerning ſuch Juſtices of Peace by *Grant or Patent,* if the *Grant* be made to ſuch as be not learned in the Law, yet if it be *Ad Pacem conſervandam, &c.* or *Ad in-quirendum tantum,* this is a good Grant: But if the Grant be made, *Ad audiendum & terminandum,* this is a void Grant, (*ut dicitur*) unleſs ſome one learned in the Laws be alſo joined with the other in the Commiſſion; and then ſuch a Commiſſion made *Ad au-diendum & terminandum* is good in Law. For in all Caſes where the Commiſſion or Grant is *Ad audiendum & terminandum,* it is meet that ſome, or one of them at the leaſt,

                                      ſhould

fhould be learned in the Laws of this Realm. See the *Statutes* 18 E. 3. *cap.* 2. &
13 R. 2. *cap.* 7. & 17 R. 2. *cap.* 10.

3. The third Sort of Juftices of Peace are by Commiffion (made of common Courfe *By Commiffions.* under the Great Seal of *England:*) And thefe are appointed by the Difcretion of the Lord 18 H. 6. Chancellor, or Lord Keeper of the Great Seal. And yet the Juftices of Peace within the *cap.* 11. County Palatine of *Lancafter* are to be made by Commiffion under the Seal of the fame Raft 184. d, Dutchy, by the *Statute* 27 H. 8. *c.* 24. *Lancafter.*

But thefe Commiffioners of the Peace their Authority doth determine by divers Means, *How they determine.* yet more ufually by three Means.

Firft, By the *Death of the King*, or by his Refignation of his Crown : For by the Commiffion he maketh them *Jufticiarios noftros*, fo that he being once dead, or having given over his Crown, they are no more his Juftices, and the Juftices of the next Prince they cannot be, unlefs it fhall pleafe him afterwards fo to make them. *Lamb.* 71. *Dyer* 165. *a.*

After the Death of a King of *England*, his Succeffor by Proclamation fignifies, that all in Judicial Places, as Juftices of Peace, &c. fhall continue and exercife their Offices, yet it is not fafe for them to act without a new Commiffion, as was done 1 *Ca. primi* touching the Juftices at *Weftminifter. Cro. Car.* 1.

2. At the King's Pleafure, and that in two Sorts.

1. Either by the King's Pleafure expreffed, (as the King in exprefs Words may dif- *§ E. 4. 32.* charge them by his Writ under the Great Seal) or by *Superfedeas*; but the *Superfedeas* *Br. Coron. 18.* doth but fufpend their Authority, which may be revived by a *Procedendo*. *12 Aff. 21. Br. Com. 13.*

2. Or by Implication; (as by making other Commiffioners of the fame Kind, and *Br. Com. 20.* within the fame Limits, leaving out the ancient Commiffioners Names.) 10 E. 4. 7. *14.* & 3 *Mar.* 1.

But the ancient Commiffioners muft have Knowledge of fuch new Commiffion; for *Br. Com. 26.* this Determination of the old Commiffion groweth not immediately by making the new *18.* Commiffion, but either by giving fpecial Notice of the new Commiffion unto the old Commiffioners; or elfe by and after the Reading (or Proclaiming) of the new Commiffion at the Affifes, Seffions of the Peace, or at the full County; or elfe by holding of *More's Rep.* fome open Seffions by Virtue of the new Commiffion, (in which two laft Cafes the old *Pl.* 187. Commiffioners muft take Notice of the new Commiffion :) And in all thefe Cafes, if the ancient Commiffioners do fit by Virtue of their ancient Commiffion, and after fuch Notice or Publifhing of the new Commiffion, all, whatfoever fuch ancient Commiffioners fhall fo do, is void : And contrariwife, until fuch Notice or Publifhing of the new Commiffion, whatfoever mean Acts fuch ancient Commiffioners fhall do, by Virtue of their ancient Commiffion, are good in Law. See 34 *Aff.* 8. *B. c.* 14.

Alfo in all Places where any ancient Commiffion of the Peace is determined by a New, *11 H 6. 6.* yet no Procefs or Suit depending before the old Commiffioners fhall be difcontinued there- *P. Difc. 6.* by; neither fhall any other Thing done by the Juftices of Peace by force of their ancient Commiffion be made or become void thereby.

3. By the Acceffion of another Office; as when a Juftice of Peace is chofen to be She- *Sheriff.* riff of the fame County, his Authority of a Juftice of Peace there is fufpended during his *1 Ed. 6. 7.* Sheriffwick,; but after that another is chofen and fworn Sheriff of the fame County, then *1 M. 8.* this Authority as a Juftice of Peace remaineth as it was before; without any renewing of *P. Difc. 4.* the Commiffion, and without any of the Oaths newly to be taken by him; except his Name be then left out of the Commiffion, as fometimes had been ufed to be done; and perhaps only to get new Fees.

The Reafon why his Authority of a Juftice of Peace is fufpended during his Sheriff-wick feemeth to be, for that the Sheriff is a Minifter, and a Juftice of Peace is a Judge; and the one is as neceffary as the other. And befides the Office of a Judge being to command, and of a Minifter to execute the Commandment; if one Man fhall be both Judge and Minifter, it would follow, that the Sheriff ought to command himfelf, or that he fhould, as an Officer, ferve his own Precept made as Juftice or Judge, which cannot be.

Alfo if a Juftice of Peace be made a Coroner of the County, this by fome Opinions is a Difcharge of his Authority of Juftice of Peace; otherwife where he fhall be made an Efcheator, Under-Sheriff, Bailiff, or the like. *Lamb.* 72. *Quære.*

But if a Juftice of Peace be made a Knight, or Serjeant at Law, or hath any greater *1 E. 6. c. 7.* Name or Office of Honour or Dignity given him, this taketh not away his Authority *P. Difc. 4.* of a Juftice of Peace. *Br. Commiff.* 4 & 22. See alfo the Statute of 1 E. 6. *c.* 7.

Demiſe of the King.
Dyer 165.
Co. 7. 30.
B. Com. 5.
Br. Com. 19.
21. B. Offic.
15.

Note alſo, that although by the Death of the King, or by his Reſignation, the Authority of all Juſtices of the Peace, which are by Commiſſion (yea, and of all Judges, Commiſſioners of *Oyer* and *Terminer*, Commiſſioners of Gaol-Delivery, Sheriffs, Eſcheators, and other Officers that are by Commiſſion) doth ceaſe; yet Mayors and chief Officers in Cities and Corporate Towns, (which have the Authority of Juſtices of Peace, or of the Conſervation of the Peace, by Grant under the King's Letters Patent to them and their Succeſſors) their Authority ſtill remaineth.

So alſo the Office and Authority of the High Conſtables and Petty Conſtables ſeemeth to remain, notwithſtanding the Death of the King, *&c.* for that their Authority is by the Common Law, and to their ſaid Office the Conſervation of the Peace remaineth, as a Thing incident and inſeparable from the ſame.

Coroners.
4 E. 4. 44.
B. Offi. 25.
Dyer 165.

Coroners alſo do remain Conſervators of the Peace (within the County where they are Coroners) notwithſtanding the *King's Death, &c.* for they are made by the *King's Writ,* and not by *Commiſſion*; and their Office and Authority doth remain until they be removed by the King's Writ; and their Office remaining, the Conſervation of the Peace remaineth as incident thereto. They are elected by the Freeholders, and are returned of Record into Chancery; and therefore being judicially made, muſt be judicially diſcharged.

1 An. c. 8.

By Statute 1 *An. c.* 8. *ſect.* 5. No Commiſſion of Aſſiſe, *Oyer* and *Terminer,* general Gaol-Delivery, or of Aſſociation, Writ of Admittance, Writ *Si non omnes,* Writ of Aſſiſtance, or *Commiſſion of the Peace,* ſhall be determined by the Death of any King, or Queen of this Realm; but every ſuch Commiſſion and Writ ſhall continue in full Force for *ſix Months* next enſuing ſuch Demiſe, unleſs ſuperſeded and determined by the next Succeſſor.

C H A P. IV.

Juſtices of Peace : Their Oaths.

P. Juſt. 4.
1 El. 1.

EVERY Juſtice of Peace (before he ſhall take upon him to exerciſe the Office of a Juſtice of Peace) ſhall take two corporal Oaths; the One concerning the Office of a Juſtice of Peace, the Other concerning the King's Supremacy.

The Oath concerning this Office ſeemeth to be by Force of the Statute made 13 *R.* 2. *c.* 7. And yet ſee the Oath of the Juſtices made *Ann.* 18 *E.* 3. much to the like Effect that now it is; in which Year alſo M. *Marrow* taketh it that Juſtices of Peace were firſt made, they having then firſt Power given them to hear and determine Felonies and Treſpaſſes againſt the Peace, as appeareth by the Statute of 18 *E.* 3. *c.* 2.

The Form of the Oath is at this Day as followeth.

Their Oath.

YE ſhall ſwear, that as *Juſtice of the Peace in the County of* Cambridge, *in all Articles in the King's Commiſſion to you directed, you ſhall do legal Right to the Poor and to the Rich, after your cunning Wit and Power, and after the Laws and Cuſtoms of the Realm, and Statutes thereof made: And ye ſhall not be of Counſel of any Quarrel hanging before you: And that ye hold your Seſſions after the Form of the Statutes thereof made: And the Iſſues, Fines, and Amerciaments that ſhall happen to be made, and all Forfeitures which ſhall fall before you, ye ſhall cauſe to be entered without any Concealment (or imbezelling) and truly ſend them to the King's Exchequer. Ye ſhall not let for Gift, or other Cauſe, but well and truly you ſhall do your Office of Juſtice of the Peace in that Behalf: And that you take nothing for your Office of Juſtice of the Peace to be done, but of the King, and Fees accuſtomed, and Coſts limited by the Statute. And ye ſhall not direct, nor cauſe to be directed, any Warrant (by you to be made) to the Parties, but ye ſhall direct them to the Bailiffs of the ſaid County, or other the King's Officers, or Miniſters, or other indifferent Perſons, to do Execution thereof. So help you God, &c.*

The Parts of this Oath are ſhortly Six.

Part of the Oath.

1. That they ſhall do *equal Right to Rich and Poor,* according to the Laws and Statutes of the Realm.

2. That they ſhall *not be of Counſel with any Perſon* in any Matter depending before them.

I

3. That they ſhall keep their *Seſſions according to the Statutes*, which (by the *Statute* 2 *H.* 5. *c.* 4.) ought to be in the firſt Week after the Feaſt of St. *Michael*, after the *Epiphany*, after the Clauſe or Feaſt of *Eaſter*, and after the Tranſlation of S. *Thomas* the Martyr, being the third Day of *July*, and accordingly the Quarter-Seſſions of the Peace ought ſtill to be holden throughout the Realm. See *Lamb.* 579, 580. And yet by the Statute of 14 *H.* 6. *c.* 4. the Juſtices of Peace of *Middleſex* are to keep their Seſſions but twice in the Year. ^{*Time when th'}

> *Time when the Quarter-Seſſions ſhall be kept.*
> 2 H. 5. 4.
> P. Juſt. 5.

4. That all *Iſſues*, *Fines*, *Amerciaments*, and *Forfeitures*, which happen before them, be by them truly entered, and ſent into the Exchequer.

5. That they *take nothing for doing their Office*, but of the King, and the accuſtomed Fees appointed by the Statutes.

6. That they ſhall *not direct any of their Warrants* to the Parties but to the Bailiffs of the County, or to other of the King's Officers, as to the Sheriff, High Conſtable, Petty Conſtable, &c. or other indifferent Perſons.

Now farther concerning the Times of the Quarter-Seſſions, it ſeemeth to be the Intent or Meaning of the afore recited Statute, 2 *H.* 5. *c.* 4. that the Weeks wherein the aforeſaid Feaſts of S. *Michael*, the *Epiphany*, and S. *Thomas* fall, muſt be firſt ended before the Seſſions can begin. So that if any of theſe three Feaſt-Days ſhall fall upon the *Sunday*, *Monday*, *Tueſday*, or *Wedneſday*, then ſhall the Seſſions (in our County of *Cambridge*) be upon *Thurſday* ſeven-night after ; but if any of thoſe Feaſts ſhall fall upon *Thurſday*, *Friday*, or *Saturday*, then ſhall our Seſſions be upon the next *Thurſday* after ; and for our *Eaſter* Seſſions, upon the *Thurſday* ſeven-night after *Eaſter* Day.

> *Seſſions.*
> *At what Times Seſſions ſhall be kept.*
> 36 E. 3. 12.

The other Oath concerning the King's Supremacy, is by Force of the Statute made *primo Eliz. c.* 1. But that is now abrogated *, and inſtead of that Oath this is now injoined.

> P. Crown. 4.
> * 1 W. & M.
> c. 8.

ſ. **I** DO ſincerely promiſe and ſwear, that I will be faithful, and bear true Allegiance to his Majeſty King George. So help me God.

> *The Oath of Allegiance.*

I M. D. do ſwear, that I do from my Heart deteſt and abjure as impious and heretical, that damnable Doctrine and Poſition, that Princes excommunicated may be deprived by the Pope, or any Authority of the See of Rome, may be depoſed by their Subjects or any other whatſoever. And I do declare, that no Foreign Prince, Perſon, Prelate, State or Potentate, hath or ought to have any Juriſdiction, Power, Superiority, Pre-eminence or Authority, Eccleſiaſtical or Civil within this Realm. So help me God.

> *The Oath of Supremacy.*

All Perſons who ſhall bear any Office Civil or Military, ſhall within three Months afterwards take the ſaid Oaths, and the Oath of Abjuration, as followeth.

> 13 & 14 W. 3.
> c. 6.
> 1 Geo. 1. c. 13.

ſ. **I** M. D. do truly and ſincerely acknowledge, profeſs, teſtify and declare in my Conſcience, before God and the World, that our Sovereign Lord King George is lawful and rightful King of this Realm, and all other his Majeſty's Dominions and Countries thereunto belonging. And I do ſolemnly and ſincerely declare, that I do believe in my Conſcience, that the Perſon pretended to be Prince of Wales during the Life of the late King James, and ſince his Deceaſe pretending to be, and taking upon himſelf the Stile and Title of King of England, by the Name of James the Third, or of Scotland by the Name of James the Eighth, or the Stile and Title of King of Great Britain, hath not any Right or Title whatſoever to the Crown of this Realm, or any other the Dominions thereunto belonging : And I do renounce, refuſe, and abjure any Allegiance or Obedience to him. And I do ſwear, that I will bear Faith and true Allegiance to his Majeſty King George, and him will defend to the utmoſt of my Power, againſt all traiterous Conſpiracies and Attempts whatſoever, which ſhall be made againſt his Perſon, Crown or Dignity. And I will do my utmoſt Endeavour to diſcloſe and make known to his Majeſty and his Succeſſors, all Treaſons and Traiterous Conſpiracies which I ſhall know to be againſt him or any of them. And I do faithfully promiſe, to the utmoſt of my Power, to ſupport, maintain, and defend the Succeſſion of the Crown againſt him the ſaid James, and all other Perſons whatſoever, which Succeſſion, by an Act, intituled, An Act for the farther Limitation of the Crown, and better ſecuring the Rights and Liberties of the Subjects, is, and ſtands limited to the Princeſs Sophia, Electreſs and Dutcheſs Dowager of Hanover, and the Heirs of her Body being Proteſtants. And all theſe Things I do plainly and ſincerely acknowledge and ſwear, according to theſe expreſs Words by me ſpoken, and according to the plain and common Senſe and Underſtanding

> *The Oath of Abjuration.*

derſtanding of the ſame Words, without any Equivocation, mental Evaſion, or ſecret Reſervation whatſoever. And I do make this Recognition, Acknowledgment, Abjuration, Renunciation, and Promiſe heartily, willingly and truly, upon the true Faith of a Chriſtian. So help me God.

And all Perſons who are required to take the ſaid Oaths, ſhall at the ſame Time repeat and ſubſcribe the Declaration againſt Tranſubſtantiation :

The Declaration.
25 Car. 2.
cap. 2.
13 & 14
W. 3. c. 6.

ſſ. I M. D. do declare, that I do believe there is not any Tranſubſtantiation in the Sacrament of the Lord's Supper, or in the Elements of Bread and Wine, at or after the Conſecration thereof by any Perſon whatſoever.

Wales,
5 Will. 3.
cap. 4.

The King by his Commiſſion under the Great Seal may conſtitute ſuch Number of Juſtices of Peace in *Wales* as he ſhall think convenient ; and the Perſons thus conſtituted ſhall have as full Power to execute the Office of a Juſtice of Peace as any other Juſtice might have done before the Making that Act.

Yet it is moſt uſual that both of theſe Oaths are taken by a ſpecial Commiſſion, (*viz.* by a Writ of *Dedimus poteſtatem,* directed out of the Chancery to ſome ancient Juſtice of Peace to take the ſame Oaths) which by them is to be certified into the ſame Court, at ſuch Day as the Writ commandeth. *The Form of which Certificate,* ſee *hic poſtea.*

The Juſtice of Peace (or other Perſon) to whom a *Dedimus Poteſtatem* ſhall be directed, to take the Oaths of a new Juſtice of Peace, if he ſhall return the Commiſſion, and the Oaths to be taken, when they were not taken, he is fineable in the Court of King's Bench.

So if the new Juſtice of Peace ſhall exerciſe this Office before he hath taken both theſe Oaths, he ſhall be diſabled to ſue, to be Guardian, Executor or Adminiſtrator, and be incapable of any Legacy, or Gift, or to be in any Office, and ſhall forfeit 500*l.* to him who will ſue for the ſame.

Crom. 11.
Co. 11. 98.

Alſo if a Juſtice of Peace ſhall not perform his Oath, (concerning his Office) it ſeemeth he is fineable, &c. Yet ſee *Co. 11. 98. a.* That a Man ſhall not be charged in any Court Judicial for the Breach of a general Oath, which he taketh when he is made an Officer or Miniſter, &c. But if he do a Thing contrary to his Oath, that aggravates his Offence.

Nota, quod Juramentum debet habere comites, Veritatem, Judicium, & Juſtitiam. Jer. 4. 2. Et ſi iſta defuerint, non Juramentum, ſed Perjurium erit. Nemo ſe ſeducat ; qui enim per lapidem falſo jurat perjurus eſt. Quacunque arte verborum, vel mentis reſervatione jurat aliquis, Deus ita accipit ſicut ille cui juratur intelligit : Et minus malum eſt per Deum falſum jurare veraciter, quam per Deum verum jurare fallaciter.

Now for that all the Authority and Power of theſe Commiſſioners or Juſtices of the Peace ariſeth partly out of their Commiſſion, and partly out of the *Statutes,* I will firſt ſet down the Form of the Commiſſion itſelf, ſhortly conſidering the Parts thereof.

CHAP. V.

The Form of the Commiſſion of the Peace.

1.
Ad pacem conſervandam.

GEORGIUS, &c. *Prædilecto & fideli* King, *Domino Cuſtod. Mag. Sigilli Angliæ,* — *Comiti Theſaurar' Angliæ,* &c. *Salutem.*

Sciatis, quod aſſignavimus vos, conjunctim & diviſim, & quemlibet veſtrum Juſticiarios noſtros, ad Pacem noſtram in Comitatu noſtro Cantabrigiæ conſervandam, ac ad omnia Ordinationes & Statuta pro bono Pacis noſtræ, ac pro conſervatione ejuſdem, & pro quieto regimine & gubernatione populi noſtri edita, in omnibus & ſingulis ſuis Articulis, in dicto Comitatu noſtro (tam infra Libertates quam extra) juxta vim, formam & effectum eorundem cuſtodiendum, & cuſtodiri faciendum ; Et ad omnes contra formam Ordinationum vel Statutorum illorum, aut eorum alicujus, in Com' præd' delinquentes, caſtigandum & puniendum, prout ſecundum formam Ordinationum & Statutorum illorum fuerit faciendum ; & ad omnes illos, qui alicui, vel aliquibus de populo noſtro de corporibus ſuis, vel de incendio domorum ſuarum, minas fecerint, ad ſufficientem ſecuritatem de Pace vel bono geſtu ſuo erga nos & populum noſtrum inveniendam coram vobis, ſeu aliquo veſtrum, venire facien-

I   *dum ;*

dum; & *si hujusmodi securitatem invenire recusaverint, tunc eos in prisonis nostris (quousq; hujusmodi securitatem invenerint) salvo custodire faciendum. Assignavimus etiam vos, & quoslibet duos vel plures vestrum, (quorum aliquem vestrum* A.B.C.D.E.F. &c. *unum* ^{Ad Inquiren-}
esse volumus) Justiciarios nostros ad inquirendum per Sacramentum proborum & legalium ^{dum}
*hominum de Comitatu præd', (per quos rei veritas melius sciri poterit) de omnibus &
omnimodis Feloniis, Veneficiis, Incantationibus, Sortilegiis, Arte magica, Transgressionibus, Forstallariis, Regratariis, Ingrossariis, & Extortionibus quibuscunq; ac de omnibus
& singulis aliis malefactis & offensis (de quibus Justiciarii Pacis nostræ legitime inquirere
possunt, aut debent) per quoscunq; & qualitercunq; in Comitatu præd' factis sive perpetratis,
vel imposterum ibidem fieri vel attemptari contigerit: Ac etiam de omnib' illis qui in Comitatu præd' in Conventiculis contra Pacem nostram, in perturbationem populi nostri, seu vi
armata ierint vel equitaverint, seu imposterum ire vel equitare præsumpserint; ac etiam de
omnibus his qui ibidem ad gentem nostram maihemandum vel interficiendum in insidiis jacuerunt, vel imposterum jacere præsumpserint: Ac etiam de Hostelariis, & aliis omnibus &
singulis personis, qui in abusu Ponderum vel Mensurarum, sive in venditione Victualium,
contra formam Ordinationum & Statutorum, vel eorum alicujus, inde pro communi utilitate
Regni nostri* Angliæ *& populi nostri ejusdem editorum, deliquerunt, vel attemptaverunt,
seu imposterum delinquere vel attemptare præsumpserint in Com' præd': Ac etiam de quibuscunq; Vicecomitibus, Ballivis, Seneschallis, Constabulariis, Custodibus Gaolarum, & aliis
Officiariis, qui in executione Officiorum suorum (circa præmissa seu eor' aliqua) indebite se
habuerunt, aut imposterum indebite se habere præsumpserint, aut tepidi, remissi vel negligentes fuerunt aut in posterum fore contigerint, in Comitat. prædicto: Et de omnibus &
singulis articulis & circumstantiis & aliis rebus quibuscunq; per quoscunq; & qualitercunq;
in Com. præd. factis sive perpetratis, vel quæ in posterum ibid' fieri vel attemptari contigerit, qualitercunq; præmissorum vel eor' alicujus concernentibus plenius veritatem: Et ad in-*
*dictamenta quæcunq; sic coram vobis seu aliquibus vestrum capta, sive capienda, aut coram
aliis nuper Justiciariis Pacis in Com' præd' facta sive capta (& nondum terminata) in-* ^{Indictamenta}
spiciendum: Ac ad Processus inde versus omnes & singulos sic indictatos, vel quos coram ^{capere.}
vobis in posterum indictari contigerit, (quousq; capiantur, reddant se, vel utlagentur) fa- ^{Processus}
ciend' & continuand'. Et ad omnia & singula Felonias, Veneficia, Incantationes, Sorti- ^{facere.}
*legia, Artes magicas, Transgressiones, Forstallarias, Regratarias, Ingrossarias, Extortiones, Conventicula, Indictamenta præd' cœteraq; omnia & singula præmissa, secund' Leges
& Stat' Regni nostri* Angliæ, *(prout in hujusin' casu fieri consuevit aut debuit) Audiendum & Terminandum; & ad eosdem Delinquentes, & quilibet corum, pro delictis suis, per
Fines, Redemptiones, Amerciamenta, Forisfacturas, ac alio modo (prout secundum Legem
& Consuetudinem Regni nostri* Angliæ, *aut formam Ordinationum vel Statutorum præd'.
fieri consuevit aut debuit) castigandum & puniendum.*

Proviso semper, qd' si casus difficultatis sup' determinatione aliquor' præmissor' coram vo- ^{Adaudiendum}
bis, vel aliquib' duob', vel pluribus vestrum evenire contigerit; tunc ad judicium inde red- ^{& terminan-}
dend', nisi in præsentia unius Justiciariorum nostrorum de uno vel de altero Banco, aut ^{dum.}
*Justiciarior' nostrorum ad Assisas in Com' præd' capiendas assignatorum, coram vobis, vel
aliquibus duobus, vel pluribus vestrum, minime procedatur.*

Et ideo vobis & cuilibet vestrum mandam', qd' circa custod' Pacis, Ordination', Statu- ^{Charge to the}
tor', & omnium & singulorum cœteror' præmissor', diligenter intendatis. Et ad certos dies ^{Justices.}
& loca, quæ vos vel aliqui hujusin', duo vel plures vestrum (ut' præd' est) ad hæc provide- ^{Exceptio.}
*ritis, sup' præmissis faciatis Inquisition', & præmissa omnia & singula audiatis & terminetis, ac ea faciatis & expleatis in forma præd' inde quod ad Justitiam pertinet, secundum
Legem & consuetudinem regni nostri* Angliæ: *Salvis nobis Amerciamentis, & aliis ad nos
inde spectantibus.*

Mandamus etiam tenore præsentium Vicecomiti nostro Cantabrigiæ, *qd' ad certos dies &* ^{To the Sheriff.}
*loca (quæ vos vel aliqui hujusmodi, duo vel plures vestrum, ut præd' est, ei, ut præd' est,
sciri feceritis) venire faciat' cor' vobis, vel hujusin' duobus vel pluribus vestrum (ut dict'
est) tot' & tales probos & legales homines de Balliva sua, (tam infra Libertates quam extra) per quos rei veritas in præmissis melius sciri poterit & inquiri.*

Assignavimus deniq; te præfatum Johan. Cutts *Militem, Cust. Rot. Pacis nostræ in dicto* ^{To the Custos}
Com. nostro. Ac propterea tu, ad dies & loca præd', Brevia, Processus, & Indictamenta ^{Rotulor'.}
præd', coram te & dictis sociis tuis venire facias, ut ea inspiciantur, & debito fine terminentur, sicut præd' est. In cujus rei testimonium, &c. Datum, &c.

E   *The*

The ſame in Engliſh.

'GEORGE, &c. To our Wellbeloved and Faithful *King*, Lord Keeper of the Great
' G Seal of *England*, and ―――― Treaſurer of *England*, &c. Greeting. Know ye,
' that We have aſſigned you, and every one of you, jointly and ſeverally, our Juſtices to
' keep our Peace·in the County of *Cambridge*; and to keep, and cauſe to be kept all Ordi-
' nances and Statutes made for the Good of the Peace, and for Conſervation of the ſame, and
' for the quiet Rule and Government of our People in all and every the Articles thereof, in
' our ſaid County, (as well within the Liberties as without) according to the Force, Form,
' and Effect of the ſame; and to chaſtiſe and puniſh all Perſons offending againſt the Form
' of thoſe Ordinances, or Statutes, or any of them, in the County aforeſaid, as according
' to the Form of thoſe Ordinances and Statutes ſhall be fit to be done; and to cauſe to
' come before you, or any of you, all thoſe Perſons who ſhall threaten any of the People
' in their Perſon, or in Burning their Houſes, to find ſufficient Security for the Peace, or
' for the good Behaviour towards Us and the People; and if they ſhall refuſe to find ſuch
' Security, then to cauſe them to be kept ſafe in Priſon until they find ſuch Security : We
' have alſo aſſigned you, and every Two or more of you (whereof any of you the ſaid *A*.
' *B.C.* ſhall be one) our Juſtices to inquire by the Oath of good and lawful Men of the
' County aforeſaid, by whom the Truth may be better known, of all and all Manner of
' Felonies, Witchcrafts, Inchantments, Sorceries, Magick Art, Treſpaſſes, Foreſtallings,
' Regratings, Ingroſſings, and Extortions whatſoever; and of all and ſingular other Miſ-
' deeds and Offences, of which Juſtices of Peace may or ought lawfully to inquire, by
' whomſoever and howſoever done or perpetrated, which hereafter ſhall happen howſoever
' to be done or attempted in the County aforeſaid; and of all thoſe who in the County
' aforeſaid have either gone or ridden, or hereafter ſhall preſume to go or ride in Compa-
' nies with armed Force againſt the Peace, to the Diſturbance of the People; and alſo of
' all thoſe who in like Manner have lain in wait, or hereafter ſhall preſume to lie in wait,
' to maim or kill our People; and alſo of Inn-holders, and of all and ſingular other Perſons
' who have offended or attempted, or hereafter ſhall preſume to offend or attempt in the
' Abuſe of Weights or Meaſures, or in the Sale of Victuals, againſt the Form of the Ordi-
' nances or Statutes, or any of them, in that Behalf made for the common Good of *Eng-*
' *land*, and the People thereof in the County aforeſaid; and alſo of all Sheriffs, Bailiffs,
' Stewards, Conſtables, Gaolers, and other Officers whatſoever, who in the Execution of
' their Offices about the Premiſſes, or any of them, have unlawfully demeaned themſelves,
' or hereafter ſhall preſume unlawfully to demean themſelves, or have been or hereafter
' ſhall be careleſs, remiſs or negligent in the County aforeſaid. And of all and ſingular
* Note:
Here is neither
Perſon, Time,
nor Place ex-
cepted.' Articles and Circumſtances, and all other Things whatſoever, * by whomſoever and
' howſoever done or perpetrated in the County aforeſaid, or which hereafter ſhall happen
' howſoever, to be done or attempted in any wiſe more fully concerning the Truth of the
' Premiſſes, or any of them : And to inſpect all Indictments whatſoever ſo before you or
' any of you taken or to be taken, or made or taken, before others, late Juſtices of the
' Peace in the County aforeſaid, and not as yet determined; and to make and continue the
' Proceſs thereupon againſt all and ſingular Perſons ſo indicted, or which hereafter ſhall
' happen to be indicted before you, until they be apprehended, render themſelves, or be
' outlawed : And to hear and determine all and ſingular the Felonies, Witchcrafts, In-
' chantments, Sorceries, Magick Arts, Treſpaſſes, Foreſtallings, Regratings, Ingroſſings,
' Extortions, Unlawful Aſſemblies, Indictments aforeſaid, and all and ſingular other the
' Premiſſes, according to the Laws and Statutes of *England*, as in like Caſe hath been uſed
' or ought to be done : And to chaſtiſe and puniſh the ſaid Perſons offending, and every of
' them for their Offences, by Fines, Ranſoms, Amerciaments, Forfeitures, or otherwiſe,
' as ought and hath been uſed to be done according to the Laws and Cuſtoms of *England*,
' or the Form of the Ordinances and Statutes aforeſaid.

    ' Provided always, That if a Caſe of Difficulty upon the Determination of any of the
' Premiſſes ſhall happen to ariſe before you, or any two of you, or more of you; then you,
' nor any Two or more of you do proceed to give Judgment therein, except it be in the
' Preſence of one of the Juſtices of the one or the other Bench, or Juſtices of Aſſiſe in the
' County aforeſaid.

    ' And therefore We command you and every of you, That you diligently intend the
' Keeping of the Peace, Ordinances, Statutes, and all and ſingular other the Premiſſes;
' and at certain Days and Places which you, or any ſuch Two, or more of you, as is

    I   ' afore-

' aforefaid, ſhall in that Behalf appoint, ye make Inquiries upon the Premiſſes, and hear
' and determine all and ſingular the Premiſſes, and perform and fulfil the ſame in Form
' aforefaid, doing therein that which to Juſtice apperteineth, according to the Law and
' Cuſtom of *England :* Saving to us the Amercements, and other Things to us thereof
' belonging.

' And we command, by Virtue of theſe Preſents, the Sheriff of the ſaid County of *Cam-*
' *bridge,* that, at certain Days and Places which you, or any ſuch Two or more of you,
' as aforefaid ſhall make known to him, as aforeſaid, he cauſe to come before you, or
' ſuch Two or more of you, as aforeſaid, ſuch and as many good and lawful Men of his
' Bailiwick (as well within Liberties as without) by whom the Truth in the Premiſſes may
' be the better known and inquired of.

' Laſtly, We have aſſigned you the ſaid *John Cutts* Knight, Keeper of the Rolls of the
' Peace in the ſaid County. And therefore you ſhall cauſe to be brought before yourſelf
' and your ſaid Fellows, at the ſaid Days and Places, the Writs, Precepts, Proceſſes, and
' Indiĉtments aforeſaid, that the ſame may be inſpeĉted, and by a due Courſe determined,
' as aforeſaid. In Witneſs whereof, *&c.'*

Note; By this laſt Clauſe the Keeper of the Rolls ſhall have the Cuſtody of Indiĉtments,
Preſentments, Bills, Recognizances, and ſuch like Records of Seſſions; but not the Cuſtody
of Records of Riots, Precepts of Peace, or other ſpecial Records, or other Records not per-
taining to the general Seſſions.

The Commiſſion of the Peace was, when Juſtice *Fitzherbert* and ſome others wrote, · *Correĉtion of*
incumbered with many Statutes, and ſtuft with vain Repetitions, and many Corruptions *the Commiſſion.*
crept therein by the Miſtaking of Clerks: For Amendment whereof all the Judges of 4 Inſtit.
England were aſſembled, *Mich.* 32 & 33 *Eliz.* and upon Peruſal of the former Commiſ- p. 171.
ſion of the Peace, and often Conference within themſelves, reſolved upon a Reformation
of the former, with divers Additions and Alterations as it ſtandeth at this Day both in
Matter and Method.

This Commiſſion hath two Parts, containing the Power of the Juſtices of Peace.

The firſt *Aſſignavimus* of the Commiſſion doth give Power to any one Juſtice of the
Peace (more, or all) to keep, and cauſe to be kept the Peace, and all Ordinances and
Statutes made for the Conſervation of the Peace, and for the quiet Government of the
People: As namely the Statutes made for *Hue and Cry after Felons;* and the Statutes Stat. Win.
made againſt *Murtherers, Robbers, Felons, Night-Walkers,* and *Affrayers, Armour worn* 13 E. 1.
in terrorem, Riots, Forcible Entries, and all other Force and Violence; all which are 5 E. 3. 6.
directly againſt the Peace. The Particulars whereof you ſhall find more fully hereafter, 2 E. 3. 3.
and moſt of them under their proper Titles.

By this firſt Clauſe in the Commiſſion, the Juſtices of Peace have as well all the anci- Lamb. 49.
ent Power touching the Peace which the Conſervators of the Peace had by the Common
Law, as alſo that whole Authority which the *Statutes* have ſince added thereto.

The Means which the Juſtices of Peace muſt uſe for the Keeping of the Peace, and
for the Execution of theſe *Statutes,* are as followeth.

To prevent the Breach of the Peace, he may ſend his *Warrant* for the Party, and *Warrant.*
may take ſufficient Sureties of him (by Recognizance) for Keeping the Peace, or for the
Good Behaviour, (as the Caſe ſhall require:) And may ſend the Party to the G..ol for
not finding ſuch Sureties.

But for theſe Statutes made for the Peace, they are to be executed according to ſuch Lamb. 47.
Order as themſelves do deliver; wherein if no Power at all be expreſly given to any one
Juſtice of Peace alone, then can he not otherwiſe compel the Obſervation thereof than by
Admonition only: In which Behalf if he ſhall not be obeyed, he may prefer the Cauſe
at the Seſſions, and work it to a Preſentment upon the *Statute,* and ſo (by the Help of
his Fellow Juſtices) to hear and determine thereof as Law requireth.

And here note, That whereas before the Making the *Statute* 1 *Ed.* 3. *cap.* 11. there 1 Ed. 3.
were no *Juſtices,* but only *Conſervators of the Peace,* (as is before ſhewed:) And where- cap. 11.
as by the Commiſſion of the Peace, preſently after, and to this Day, the Juſtices of Peace
had, and ſtill have, the Statute of *Wincheſter* given them in Charge, to execute the
ſame; which Statute of *Wincheſter* (being made 13 *Ed.* 1.) was long before there were
any Juſtices of Peace. By this it may appear, that the King by his Commiſſion, may
commit the Execution of the Statutes and Laws to whom he ſhall pleaſe. And ſo alſo a
Juſtice of Peace, by Virtue of the Commiſſion, may execute any *Statute* whereunto he
ſhall

shall be enabled by the said Commission, although there shall be no such express Power given to him so to do by the Words or Letter of the same *Statute*.

2. Assigna-
vimus.

The second *Assignavimus* in the Commission doth give Authority to any two Justices of the Peace (or more, the one being of the *Quorum*) in these five Things following:

Jury.

1. To inquire (by a Jury) of all Offences mentioned within the Commission.

2. To take and view all Indictments or Presentments of the Jury.

3. To grant out Process against the Offenders, thereby to cause them to come and answer.

4. To hear and try all such Offences (upon any former or future Indictments taken before themselves, or before any other Justices of the Peace) after the Offenders are come in.

5. To determine thereof, by *giving Judgment*, and inflicting Punishment upon the Offenders according to the Laws and Statutes; (*viz.*) By Fine, Imprisonment, or otherwise according to Law: But not to award any Recompence to the Party wronged, otherwise than by Perswasion.

But all the Business included within the second *Assignavimus* belongeth to the Sessions of the Peace.

Note also, That there are divers *Statutes* which be not specified within the Commission, and yet are committed to the Charge and Care of the Justices of Peace; but all such *Statutes* which do give expresly any Power or Authority to the Justices of the Peace, are to them a sufficient Warrant and Commission of themselves, although they be not recited in the Commission; and all such *Statutes* are also to be executed by them, according as the same *Statutes* themselves do severally prescribe and set down.

And for that most of the Business of the Justices of Peace doth consist in the Execution of such Statutes as are committed to their Charge, (whether they be specified in the Commission, or not specified there) the Numbers of which Statutes are exceedingly increased of late, therefore to give some little Help to such Justices of Peace who (being destitute of the Assistance of such as are learned in the Laws) are daily to administer Justice, and to execute their Office at home, and out of their Sessions; I have for their better Ease herein, endeavoured to set down particularly the several Parts and Branches of every such Statute by itself, under their proper Titles, with farther References to the Statutes themselves at large, or to the Abridgments.

C H A P. VI.

The Power and Authority of Justices of Peace.

Their Power.

THE Power and Authority of the Justices of Peace as well by the said Commission as by the Statutes, is in some Cases ministerial, and in other Cases judicial.

Ministerial, when he is thereunto commanded by an higher Authority.

As upon {

A *Supplicavit*, out of the Chancery or King's Bench, for the taking of Surety for the Peace, or good Behaviour. See hereof Tit. *Surety of the Peace.*

A Writ upon the Statute of *Northampton*, upon a Forcible Entry. See hereof Tit. *Forcible Entry.*

In the Execution of which two Writs, the Justice of Peace is to proceed no farther, or otherwise, than he is authorised by such Writ; and is also to return the Writ, and to certify his Doings therein, into the Court whence the Writ came.

So upon a *Certiorari* out of any of the Higher Courts at *Westminster*, directed to the Justices of Peace (or to any of them) to certify any Recognizance, Indictment, or other Record taken before him, or them, or any of them; or in his or their Hands; of which see more *postea*.

But in all other Cases the Power of the Justices of Peace seemeth to be absolute, so as they, and every of them may proceed *ex Officio*, and as a Judge.

Discretion.

And yet for that all considerable Circumstances can neither be comprehended in the Commission, nor foreseen at the Time of the Making of the Statutes, therefore some Things are referred to the Consideration of the Justices of Peace, and left to be supplied by them in their Discretion.

I

The

The Commiſſion of the Peace (in itſelf) doth leave little or nothing to the Diſcretion of the Juſtices of Peace, but doth limit them to proceed *ſecundum Leges, conſuetudines, Ordinationes & Statuta :* And indeed to leave too much to Diſcretion, were to open a Gap to Corruption.

But by ſome late Statutes ſome Things are referred to the Diſcretion of the Juſtices of Peace ; ſome out of Seſſions, and ſome at their Seſſions.

I will here only ſet down ſome Particulars of ſuch Things as are referred to their Diſcretions out of their Seſſions.

Some Things referred to the Diſcretion of one Juſtice of Peace out of the Seſſions, which you may more fully ſee hereafter in this Book, in the ſeveral Titles here under written.

ONE Juſtice may compel any Perſon meet *in his Diſcretion* to be bound an *Apprentice.*

One Juſtice of Peace may cauſe all ſuch Perſons as be meet to labour, *by his Diſcretion* to work in *Harveſt and Hay-Time.*　　　　　　　　　　*Labourers.*　5 El. 4.

Malts that be deceitful may be ſold, &c. at ſuch reaſonable Prices as one Juſtice of Peace in his Diſcretion ſhall think expedient.　　　　　　　　*Malt.*　2 E. 6. 10.

Treſpaſſers in Corn, Orchards, Hedges, or Woods, which *in the Diſcretion* of the Juſtices are not thought able to give Satisfaction, ſhall be *whipped.*　*Treſpaſs.*　43 El. 7.

One Juſtice of Peace may hear and determine by Examination, or otherwiſe, *by his Diſcretion,* the Offences committed in *Tile-making.*　　　*Tiles.*　17 E. 4. 4.

Some Things referred to the Diſcretion of two Juſtices of Peace out of the Seſſions.　*Alehouſe-Keepers.*

TWO Juſtices may allow and diſcharge *Alehouſe-Keepers,* as they ſhall think meet, but they ought to allow none but ſuch as be capable and needful for the Place.　5 E. 6. 25. but vid. inf. Ch. 7.

Two Juſtices may take Recognizance of Alehouſe-Keepers for keeping good Orders, &c. according *to their Diſcretions.*　　　　　　　　　　　　5 E. 6. 25.

Clothiers, their Work-folks imbezilling any Part ſhall be puniſhed, &c. by the *Diſcretion of two Juſtices.*

Two Juſtices may grant their Warrant to call before them any Perſon or Perſons which *in their Diſcretions* ſhall be thought fit to diſcover any Offence in the Making of deceiveable Woollen Cloth, &c. 21 *Jac.* 1. c. 18.

Servants, &c. aſſaulting their Maſter, may be impriſoned for one Year, or leſs, at the *Diſcretion of two Juſtices.*　　　　　　　　　　　　　*Labourers.*

Two Juſtices may (*by their Diſcretion*) compel Women to ſerve, and for ſuch Wages, and in ſuch ſort, as they think meet.　　　　　　　　*Servants.*

Two Juſtices may tax others of the County, *by their Diſcretions,* towards the Relief of Places infected, &c.　　　　　　　　　　　*Plague.*

Two Juſtices may tax any in the Hundred (*by their Diſcretions*) towards the *Relief of* the Poor of any Town that is overcharged.　　　　　　*Poor.*　43 El. 2.

Two Juſtices may diſpoſe of all Forfeitures to grow upon the Statutes of Rogues, *at their Diſcretions,* &c.　　　　　　　　　　　　*Rogues.*

Two Juſtices may aſſeſs (*according to their Diſcretions*) proportionably all the Pariſhes within the Hundred, towards a Contribution for the Parties charged upon a Robbery, &c.　　　　　　　　　　　　　　*Robbery.*

Two Juſtices ſhall take Order (*by their Diſcretions*) to ſet *poor Soldiers,* &c. to Work that cannot get Work ; and for want of Work, may tax the Hundred (*by their Diſcretions*) for the Relief of ſuch Soldiers, &c.　　　　　*Soldiers.*

Two Juſtices may fine (*by their Diſcretions*) the head Officers in Boroughs and Market-Towns that do not view, &c. all *Weights and Meaſures,* or do not break and burn the defective.　　　　　　　　　　　　*Weights.*

Two Juſtices may fine (*by their Diſcretions*) all Buyers and Sellers with unlawful *Weights and Meaſures.*

There be ſome other Statutes, and ſome other Caſes, wherein the *Diſcretion of the Juſtices of the Peace* out of their Seſſions is tolerated : But the Counſel of *Cicero* herein is to be obſerved, *Sapientis eſt Judicis cogitare tantum ſibi eſſe permiſſum, quantum ſit commiſſum ac creditum.*

Alſo the Sayings of the Reverend Judge, in his fifth Part, in *Rook*'s Caſe, and in his tenth Part in *Knightley*'s Caſe, are worthy of Obſervation : ſc. That *Diſcretion* is a Knowledge or Underſtanding to diſcern between Truth and Falſhood, between Right and Wrong, between Shadows and Subſtance, between Equity and colourable Gloſſes and　　*Diſcretion defined.*　Co. 5. 101, & 10, 140.

　　　　　　　　　　　　F　　　　　　　　　　　Pretences,

Pretences, and not to do according to our Wills and private Affections, for *talis difcretio difcretionem confundit.* And therefore in both the recited Cafes it was holden that though the Word in the Commiffion of Sewers do give Authority to thofe Commiffioners to do *according to their Difcretions,* that yet their *Difcretion* ought to be limited and bounded with the Rules of Reafon, Law, and Juftice, and their Proceeding muft be *fecundum Legem & Confuetudinem* Angliæ; and fo of other like Commiffioners. Again, *Difcretion,* faith he, is *fcire vel difcernere per Legem quid fit juftum; viz.* to difcern by the right Line of Law, and not by private Opinion. *Co. L.* 227. And therefore every Judge, Juftice, (or Commiffioner) ought to have *duos Sales, viz. Salem Sapientiæ ne fit infipidus; & Salem Confcientiæ, ne fit diabolus.*

And (as *M. Lambard* well faid) no way better fhall the *Difcretion* of a Juftice of Peace appear, than if he (remembring that he is *Lex loquens*) fhall contain himfelf within Law, and fhall not ufe his Difcretion, but only where both the Law permitteth and the prefent Cafe requireth.

In all Cafes therefore where the Statutes refer the Trial of Offenders (or Hearing and Determining of Offences) to the *Difcretion of the Juftice* or Juftices of Peace, out of Seffions, it is very requifite, that the faid Juftices take due Examination (of the Offenders themfelves, and alfo of credible Witneffes) as well concerning the Fact itfelf as the Circumftances thereof; and upon Confeffion, or other due Proof of the Offence, then to proceed according to Law and Juftice.

But not to denounce or give Sentence before the Party be cited, and heard to anfwer for himfelf: For this Defence is allowed by God's Law. *Gen.* 3. 9. Adam, *Where art thou?* and *Gen.* 4. 9. *Where is thy Brother* Abel? And in the Cafe of the five Cities, *I will go down and fee. Gen.* 18. 21.

Note, That in all Cafes where the Statute referreth the Trial, *&c.* to the *Difcretion of the Juftices,* the faid Statutes themfelves feem alfo to enable the faid Juftices of Peace to take the Examination of Witneffes, and that upon Oath.

Note farther, That the Juftices of Peace out of their Seffions, are now armed with far more ample Authority and Power than the ancient Confervators of the Peace were: For the Juftices of the Peace have double Power given them; the one of Jurifdiction to convene the Offenders before them, (by their Warrant, and in divers Cafes out of their Seffions) to examine, hear and determine the Caufe; the other of Coercion (*fc.* after the Caufe heard) to conftrain them to the Obedience and Obfervance of their Order and Decree, (which notwithftanding muft be according to the Rules of Law and Juftice, as is aforefaid:) Whereas the ancient Confervators of the Peace had no Jurifdiction or Authority at all, either to convene the Offender before them, or to examine, hear or determine the Caufe; but had only Coercion, or Punifhment of an Offender in fome few Cafes, as you may fee before, *chap.* 1.

Have no Authority out of their County, nor in Corporations.
Plo. 37.
Corporate Towns.
Lamb. 48.19.
Crom. 8. & 181.
20 H. 7. 6. 7.
Crom. ib.

And here I muft farther put the Juftices of Peace in Mind, that their Authority and Power is limited, to be exercifed only within the County or Counties where they are in Commiffion; but they muft not intermeddle in any City there, which is a County of itfelf, nor in any City or Corporate Town there, (though it be no County of itfelf, but within the County) which have their proper Juftices of Peace within themfelves by the King's Charter or Commiffion, efpecially if in fuch Charter there be any fpecial Words of Prohibition, that the Juftices of the Shire *non fe intromittant, &c.* except fuch Juftice fhall alfo be in Commiffion in fuch City or Town Corporate.

But in other Corporate Towns which have not their *proper Juftices of Peace,* as alfo in all Liberties and Franchifes (within the County) which have the Return of the Writs, but have not their proper Juftices, there the Juftices of the Peace of the County ought to execute their Authority, and that by the Words of their Commiffion.

See hic Tit. Poor.

Again, if a Parifh fhall extend into two or more Counties, or if Part thereof fhall lie within the Liberties of any City or Town Corporate (which have their proper Juftices) and Part without; then as well the Juftices of the Peace of every County, as alfo the Juftices (or Officers) of fuch City or Town Corporate, fhall intermeddle only within their own proper and diftinct Limits and Bounds, (*fc.* within fo much of the faid Parifh, *&c.* as lieth within their feveral Liberties and Limits) and not in other Jurifdictions: For it would be againft Law and Reafon, where Officers and Jurifdictions are feveral, that the one fhould intermeddle within the Jurifdictions of the other.

Co. 4. 46.
Ubi quis delinquit, ibi punitur. See *hic* Tit. *Homicide.*

Neither fhall any Juftice of Peace deal in, or punifh any Trefpafs, or other like Offence, committed in any other County againft any penal Statute, though fuch Offender fhall be brought before him, (fee the Commiffion the firft *Affig.* & *poftea,* Tit. *Guns, Labourers*

2
bourers

bourers and *Partridges*) except the Statutes ſhall eſpecially enable them thereto, as the Statutes 1 *Jac.* & 7 *Jac.* which do enable the *Juſtice of the County where the Offence ſhall be committed, or the Offender apprehended,* (See Tit. *Partridges*) and the like; or that it be for Matters of the Peace, or in Caſe of Felony. (See Tit. *Affrays* and *Felony*.) 33 H. 8. c. 6.
9 El. p. 12.
23 El. c. 10.

By the Statute of 2 H. 5. 4. *Juſtices of Peace may ſend their Writs for fugitive Labour- ers to every Sheriff* of England. 2 H. 5. 4.

Neither ſhall any Juſtice of Peace for the Time that he ſhall be out of the County (where he is in Commiſſion) take any Recognizance, or any Examination, or otherwiſe to exerciſe his * Authority in any Matter that ſhall happen within the County, where he is in Commiſſion ; neither can he cauſe one to be brought before him out of the County where he is in Commiſſion, into the other County; for being out of the County where he is in Commiſſion he is but as a private Man. *Vide hic* Tit. *Affray, Impriſonment, Robbery and Warrants,* and *Plo.* 37. & 13 *F.* 4. 8. * *This muſt be intended by Virtue of his Office.*

In the Caſe of *Helier* againſt the Hundred of *Benhurſt,* it was reſolved, That where a Perſon robbed in one County, and made Oath before a Juſtice of the Peace of the ſame County being in *London,* that he might well take the Oath where he was, although out of the County, for he acted therein not *virtute officii,* but as a Perſon deſigned to a particular End and Purpoſe, and the Plaintiff had his Judgment : But they held, that if he acted or did any Thing *virtute officii* out of his County it was void. Cro. Car. 211.

And yet a Sheriff being out of his County may make a Panel, or may make Return of any Writ. 9 *H.* 4. 1.

But now by *Stat.* 9 *Geo.* 1. *c.* 7. *ſect.* 3. for the greater Eaſe of Juſtices of Peace for Counties, it is enacted, That if any Juſtice of Peace ſhall happen to dwell in any City, or other Precinct, that is a County of itſelf, ſituate within the County at large for which he ſhall be appointed Juſtice of Peace, although not within the ſame County, it ſhall be lawful for any ſuch Juſtice to grant Warrants or Orders, at his own Dwelling-Houſe, though out of the County where he is authoriſed to act as a Juſtice of Peace, and in ſome City or Precinct adjoining, that is a County of itſelf; and that all ſuch Warrants or Orders, and the Acts of any Conſtable, Overſeer of the Poor, Surveyor of the Highways, &c. in Obedience to ſuch Warrant or Order, ſhall be good and effectual in Law. Provided, that nothing in this Act ſhall extend to give Power to the Juſtices of Peace, in Cities or Towns, which are Counties of themſelves ; nor to impower Juſtices of Peace, Sheriffs, Conſtables, or other Peace-Officers, to act in any Matters ariſing within ſuch Cities or Towns, but that all ſuch Actings ſhall be of the ſame Effect, and no other, as if this Act had never been made. 9 Geo. 1. c. 7.

Now my Purpoſe is to ſet down more particularly what Things the Juſtices of Peace may do in the Execution of their Commiſſion, or of the Statutes wherewith they are charged. And herein you muſt obſerve, that ſome Things are permitted to be executed by any one, two, or more Juſtices ; and ſome other Things are more eſpecially appointed and appropriated (by ſome Statutes) to ſome one certain Juſtice of Peace, or two, or more Juſtices ; either in regard that ſuch Juſtice or Juſtices is or are next the Place, or are of the *Quorum,* or the like. *Authority.*
One Juſtice.

And here Note, that whatſoever any one Juſtice of Peace alone may do (either for the Keeping of the Peace, or in other Execution of the Commiſſion or Statutes) the ſame alſo may lawfully be done and performed by any two or more Juſtices.

But where the Law giveth Authority to two, there one alone cannot execute this : For *Una perſona non poteſt ſupplere vicem duarum* ; & *plus vident oculi quam oculus.* See Co. 5. 94. & Plo. 393. *a. b. Co. L.* 181. *Two Juſtices.*
Co. 4. 46.

And yet where a Statute appointeth a Thing to be down by two Juſtices of Peace (or more) if the Offence be any Miſdemeanor or Matter againſt the Peace, there, upon Complaint made (of the Offence) to any one of thoſe Juſtices of Peace, it ſeemeth that one of thoſe Juſtices may grant his Warrant to attach the Offender, and to bring him before the ſame Juſtice or any other Juſtice, to find Sureties for his Appearance at the next general Seſſions, there to make Anſwer to ſuch his Offence ; or elſe he may bind the Offender to the Good Behaviour, and ſo to appear at the next Seſſions, if the ſaid Juſtice ſhall ſee any juſt Cauſe ſo to do. But one Juſtice of Peace alone may not hear and determine the ſame.

Alſo when Things by Statute are appropriated to one certain Juſtice or more, there ſuch Juſtice or Juſtices are to purſue their Authority accordingly: And yet if ſuch Juſtice or Juſtices ſhall therein join with any other Juſtice of the ſame County, it may ſeem no leſs lawful and warrantable ; *tamen quære,* & *vide* Co. 11. 92. Where an Authority is given to *Authority.*

four,

four, or to one of them; if two of them fhall execute this, it feems they have not purfued their Authority. So if an Authority be given to three *conjunctim & divifim*, if two
of them do it in the Abfence of the Third, it is void, *Dyer* 62. for that the Authority is

Sheriff. not purfued. But Co. L. 181. b. *taketh a Difference where the Thing is* pro bono publico, *and where* pro privato; *as if a Sheriff upon a Capias maketh his Warrant to three or
four jointly or feverally to arreft the Defendant, two of them may arreft him, for that it is
for the Execution of Juftice, which is* pro bono publico, *and therefore fhall be more favourably expounded than when it is only for private.*

Plo. 205.
See Co. 11.59, Befides, there is a general Rule put in *Stradling*'s Cafe (in *Plo.*) That when a Thing
& 64. is appointed by any Statute to be done by or before one Perfon certain, that fuch Thing
cannot be done by or before any other, but that it ought to be done as the Statute hath
appointed; and by fuch exprefs Defignation of one, or Power given to one, all others
are excluded.

Baftard Child. And yet whereas by the 18 *Eliz.* the Order to be taken for a *Baftard Child* is appropri-
18 El. 3. ated to *two Juftices of the Peace* (one being of the *Quorum*) in or next unto the Parifh
where fuch Child fhall be born; if *two fuch Juftices* cannot agree upon the reputed Father (or in making fuch Order as the Statute requireth, or in other Execution of that
Statute) *Quære* what is to be done. I have known the Cafe lately moved to the Judges
of Affife, who thought it fit, that fuch Difference between the two Juftices of Peace fhould
be referred to the Hearing of the whole Bench, and the Matter to be re-examined by
them; and what Order fhould be therein fet down by the Bench, the fame to ftand good.
Vide Tit. *Baftard.*

But in fuch Things appropriate *to fome one or more Juftices of the Peace,* if without
fuch Juftice or Juftices, all (or any of) the Refidue of the Juftices of that County fhall
intermeddle therein, fuch their Doing feems no ways warrantable, but their Proceeding
to be *Coram non Judice,* and that there is no Neceffity to obey therein, as being no lawful Judges of the Caufe.

Acceffaries. See Chap. 161.

C H A P. VII.

Alehoufes. See *Innholders,* and Chap. 176. in *Conditions of Recognizances.*

Of the Authority of Juftices of Peace touching Alehoufes.

*Inns and Ale-
houfes, their
Ufe.* THE true and principal Ufe of *Inns, Alehoufes* and *Victualling-houfes,* is twofold;
fc. either for the *Relief* and *Lodging* of Wayfaring People travelling from Place to
Place about their neceffary Bufinefs, or for the neceffary Supply of the Wants of fuch
poor Perfons as are not able by greater Quantities to make their Provifion of Victuals:
And is not meant for Entertainment and Harbouring of lewd or idle People, to fpend or
confume their Money or Time there, (as appeareth by the Preamble of the Statute made
1 *Jac.* 1. *c.* 9.)

But Abufes crept in, and Diforders multiplied, by the Increafe of them, as was per-
ceived fo long fince as 11 *H.* 7. *c.* 2. whereby Power was given to *two Juftices of the
Peace* to leffen their Number; yet the Mifchief arifing by their Increafe, and Licentiouf-
nefs growing every Day more confiderable, a good and profitable Law was made 5 & 6
E. 6. *c.* 25. for the Redrefs of that general Inconvenience, without working that Reformation that was defired and intended.

And therefore to prevent the Mifchiefs and great Diforders happening daily by the
Abufes of fuch Houfes, divers good and profitable Laws are made for the Redrefs thereof, as followeth:

Tavern. Every Keeper of a Tavern (keeping alfo an Inn or Victualling in his Houfe) and eve-
1 Jac. 1. c. 9. ry *Alehoufe-keeper, Inn-keeper,* and *Victualler,* which fhall fuffer any Townfman, or any
21 Jac.1. c.7. Handicraftfman, or Labourer, working in the fame City or Town, to remain and con-
1 Car. 1. c. 4. tinue Drinking in their faid Houfe, (except fuch as fhall be invited thither by a Traveller, and fhall accompany him during his neceffary Abode there; and except Handi-

craftfmen,

craftfmen, Labourers and Workmen, in Cities, Towns Corporate and Market-Towns upon the Working-day, for one Hour at Dinner-time to take their Diet there, or fojourning or lodging there; or except they be allowed by two Juſtices of Peace) the ſaid Offence being ſeen by any Juſtice of Peace within his Limits, or being confeſſed by the Offender before the Juſtice of Peace, Mayor or Bailiff, or Head-Officer, or being proved before any Juſtice of Peace by one Witneſs upon Oath; every ſuch Taverner, Alehouſe-keeper, &c. ſhall forfeit for every ſuch Offence 10 s. to the Uſe of the Poor.

And note, that the voluntary Confeſſion (before the Juſtice of Peace, or other Perſon authoriſed to miniſter the Oath) of any Offender againſt either of the Statutes of 1 *Jac.* c. 9. or 4 *Jac. c. 9.* ſhall ſuffice to convince the Perſon ſo offending; and after ſuch Confeſſion, the Oath of the Party ſo confeſſing ſhall be taken, and be a ſufficient Proof againſt any other offending at the ſame Time.　21 *Jac. cap.* 7.

1 Jac. 1 c. 9.
1 Car. 1. c. 4.

And yet note, That whereſoever any Conviction ſhall be before the Juſtice of Peace, by or upon the Oath or Teſtimony of any other Perſon than the Delinquent himſelf, there the Juſtice of Peace muſt firſt ſend for or convene the Delinquent before him, to make anſwer, &c. and to hear and examine him of the Offence, &c. for it may be, that he can make ſufficient Defence or Excuſe of the Fact.　And this was the Direction of Sir *Nicholas Hide,* Lord Chief Juſtice of the King's Bench, and well agreeth with the Rule here before, *Chap.* 2. *Qui aliquid ſtatuerit, parte inaudita altera, æquum licet ſtatuerit, haud æquus eſt judex.*

Every Perſon who ſhall continue Drinking in any Inn or Alehouſe, &c. *in the Town where he then dwelleth,* (contrary to the former Statute made *primo Jac.*) the ſaid Offence being ſeen by any Juſtice of Peace, or being proved before him, as aforeſaid, ſuch Perſon ſhall forfeit for every ſuch Offence *three Shillings and four Pence.* Tiplers.
4 Jac. 1. c. 5.
21 Jac. 1. c. 7.

If any other Perſon (*whereſoever his or their Habitation or Abiding be*) ſhall be found (by View of any Juſtice of Peace, or by his own Confeſſion, or Proof of one Witneſs) to be *Tipling* in any Inn, Alehouſe, or Victualling-houſe, every ſuch Perſon ſhall be adjudged to be within the ſaid Statutes of 1 *Jac.* 1. c. 9. and 4 *Jac.* 1. c. 5. as if he inhabited and dwelt in the City, Town Corporate, or other Town or Village, where the ſaid Inn, Alehouſe, or Victualling-houſe is or ſhall be, where he ſhall be ſo found Tipling, and ſhall incur the like Penalty; and the ſame to be in ſuch Sort levied and diſpoſed as in the ſaid Act is expreſſed concerning ſuch as there inhabit.　And the voluntary Confeſſion of ſuch an Offender ſhall ſuffice to convince himſelf; and, after his Oath, ſhall be a ſufficient Proof againſt any other offending at that Time.　21 *Jac.* 1. *cap.* 7. 1 Car. 1. 4.;
21 Jac. 1. 7.

Now theſe Statutes prohibit, not only the continuing Drinking in thoſe Inns and Alehouſes, &c. for longer Time than for the neceſſary Abode; but alſo all Tipling there, *viz.* the vain Uſe of drinking Healths there, &c.　For theſe Houſes were not ordained, neither are they to be ſuffered, for any ſuch Uſes; but only for the neceſſary Relief of Travellers, and to ſupply the Wants of the Poor, as aforeſaid.

Every *Taverner* (keeping alſo an Inn or Victualling in his Houſe,) and every *Innkeeper, Alehouſe-keeper,* and other *Victuallers,* who ſhall ſuffer any Perſon (whereſoever his Dwelling or Abiding be) to tipple in the ſaid Houſe, contrary to the true Intent of any of the ſaid former Statutes, ſhall be adjudged within the Statute 1 *Jac. c.* 9. 1 Car. 1. 4.
1 Jac. 1. 9.

So that now by theſe Statutes, no Perſon may tipple in any ſuch Tavern, or in any Inn, Alehouſe, or Victualling-houſe, in the ſame Town where he dwelleth, nor Dwelling within two Miles thereof, except he be a Traveller.　And ſo Sir *Francis Harvey* Knight delivered it in his Charge at *Cambridge* Summer Aſſiſe, *An.* 1629. *But the Statute* 21 Jac. & 1 Caroli, *forbids all Tipling in ſuch Houſes, whereſoever they be dwelling or abiding, and by whomſoever it be.*

Any Juſtice of Peace in any County (and any Juſtice of Peace or other Head-Officer in any City or Town Corporate, within their Limits) ſhall have Power (upon his own View, Confeſſion of the Party, or Proof of one Witneſs upon Oath) to convict any Perſon of Drunkenneſs, whereby ſuch Perſons ſo convict ſhall incur the *Forfeiture of five Shillings* for every ſuch Offence, to be paid within one Week next after ſuch Conviction into the Hands of the Church-wardens of the Pariſh where the Offence ſhall be committed, &c.　And if the Offender be not able to pay the ſaid Sum of *five Shillings,* then he ſhall be *committed to the Stocks* for every ſuch Offence, there to remain by the Space of *ſix Hours.* Drunkenneſs.
4 Jac. 1. 5..
21 Jac. 1. 7.

And for the *ſecond Offence of Drunkenneſs,* every Perſon convict thereof, as aforeſaid, ſhall be bound with two Sureties in the Sum of ten Pounds, with Condition for the Good Beha- 2d Offence.
4 Jac. 1. 5.
21 Jac. 1. 7.

Behaviour, by any one Juſtice of Peace, or other Head-Officer aforeſaid, by 21 *Jac. c.* 7. and for Want of ſuch Sureties to be ſent to the Gaol.

Every Conſtable, Church-warden, Headborough, Tithingman, Aleconner and Sideſman ſhall, in their ſeveral Oaths incident to their ſeveral Offices, be charged to preſent the Offences contrary to that Statute 4 *Jac.* 5. and ſo likewiſe to preſent Offences againſt 1 *Jac.* 9. and 4 *Jac.* 5. 21 *Jac.* 7.

No Perſon ſhall be impeached or moleſted for any Offence againſt that Statute, unleſs he ſhall be thereof preſented, indicted, or convicted within *three Months* after the Offence, and ſhall be once puniſhed for each Offence. 4 *Jac.* 5.

Now, to know a drunken Man the better, the Scripture deſcribeth them *to ſtagger and reel to and fro.* Job 12. 25. Iſa. 24. 20. And ſo where the ſame Legs which carry a Man into the Houſe cannot bring him out again, it is a ſufficient Sign of Drunkenneſs.

1 Jac. 1. 9.
p. 6.   Every Juſtice of Peace (within his Limits) hath Authority to miniſter the ſaid Oath to ſuch Witneſſes. 21 *Jac.* 1. *cap.* 7.

The Forfeitures.
Diſtreſs.
4 Jac. p. 5.
21 Jac. 1. 7.
1 Jac. 1. 9.   All and every the *Forfeitures* aforeſaid ſhall be to the *Uſe of the Poor of the Pariſh where ſuch Offence ſhall be committed;* and the ſaid Forfeitures are to be levied by *Diſtreſs and Detainer of the Offender's Goods,* (and after *ſix Days by Sale* thereof, &c.) by the Conſtables or Church-wardens of the ſame Pariſh, upon a *Warrant* from any one or more Juſtices of Peace, under his or their Hand and Seal.

The ſaid Forfeitures of the *Taverners, Alehouſe-keepers, Inn-keepers* and *Victuallers,* being diſtrained for, as aforeſaid, if within ſix Days next enſuing they ſhall not pay the ſaid Forfeiture, then may the Conſtables or Church-wardens, by virtue of the ſaid Warrant, appraiſe and ſell the ſaid Diſtreſs; but they muſt deliver the Surpluſage to the Party of whom the Diſtreſs was taken. 1 *Jac.* 9. P. 7.

Commitment for Want of Diſtreſs.
1 Jac. 1. 9.
P. 7.   For every Offence aforeſaid, the *Alehouſe-keeper, Inn-keeper,* and other *Victualler,* for Want of ſufficient Diſtreſs to be taken for ſuch Forfeitures, ſhall (by any one Juſtice of Peace) be committed to the common Gaol, there to remain until the ſaid Penalty be paid.

Stocks.
4 Jac. 1. c. 5.
§. 4.
1 Jac. 1. 9.
21 Jac. 1. 7.   Every Townſman, or other Perſon whatſoever, &c. that ſhall continue Drinking, or be found Tipling in any Inn, Alehouſe, or other Victualling-houſe, contrary to the Statute, and he being convicted of it according to the Statute of 1 *Jac.* 9. (for Want of ſufficient Diſtreſs, and not being able to pay the ſaid Forfeiture of three Shillings four Pence) ſhall be ſet in the Stocks for every ſuch Offence four Hours, (upon Warrant or Commandment from any one ſuch Juſtice of Peace.)

Default or Neglect of Officers.
1 Jac. 1. 9.   If the Conſtable and Church-wardens ſhall neglect to levy, or ſhall not levy the ſaid ſeveral Forfeitures of *Alehouſe-keepers,* &c. ſuffering Tipling in their Houſes, or for their Meaſure of Ale or Beer; or in Default of Diſtreſs ſhall neglect by twenty Days to certify the ſame Defaults of Diſtreſs to the Juſtice of Peace; then every ſuch Conſtable and Church-warden ſhall forfeit for every ſuch Default 40 *s.* to the Uſe of the Poor, to be levied by Diſtreſs (of the Offender's Goods) by like Warrant to any other indifferent Perſon, from any one (or more) Juſtices of Peace, &c. under their Hand and Seal: The ſaid Diſtreſs to be taken and detained for the ſaid Forfeiture for the Space of ſix Days; within which Time, if Payment be not made, then the ſame Goods to be preſently appraiſed and ſold, and the Surpluſage to be delivered to the Party, &c. And for Want of ſufficient Diſtreſs, ſuch Conſtables and Church-wardens to be (by any ſuch Juſtice of Peace, &c.) committed to the common Gaol, there to remain until they have paid the ſame Forfeiture. And,

Alſo if any Conſtable, or other inferior Officers of the Pariſh, ſhall neglect to execute the Juſtices Warrant for the due Correction of, or for the Levying of the Penalties of Offenders in Drunkenneſs; ſuch Conſtable, &c. ſhall forfeit 10 *s.* to the Uſe of the Poor, &c. to be levied as aforeſaid. 4 *Jac.* 5.

Refuſing to lodge.
Br. Acc.
Sur. 92. & 76.
5 E. 4. 3.   If a *common Innholder* or *Alehouſe-keeper* will not lodge a Traveller, any Conſtable (or Juſtice of Peace) may compel him thereto; but how the Officer ſhall compel him *Quære:* It ſeemeth that all the Officer can do, is, either to cauſe ſuch Alehouſe-keeper to be ſuppreſſed; or elſe to preſent ſuch Offence at the Aſſiſes or Seſſions of the Peace, that ſo ſuch Offender may be thereupon indicted. See the Commiſſion.

And at a Lent Aſſiſes, *Anno Domini* 1622. Sir *James Ley* (Knight and Baronet, Lord Chief Juſtice of the King's Bench) delivered it in his Charge, that an *Inn-keeper,* or *Alehouſe-keeper, offending herein, might be indicted, fined and impriſoned for the ſame;* or elſe, that the Party grieved might have his Action *ſur le Caſe* againſt the Inn-keeper or Alehouſe-keeper refuſing to lodge him. *Vide Cro.* 50. and 4 *H.* 7. 22.

I   But

But no *Innholder*, *Alehouſe-keeper*, or *other Victualler*, ſhall be compelled to ſell, or let any Traveller or other have any Victuals or Lodging, except the Party ſhall firſt tender and pay ready Money for the ſame, if it be required. 10 H. 7. 8. 5 E. 4. 3. *Co.* 9. 87. *b.*

Any two Juſtices of the Peace (the one being of the *Quorum*) may allow the Keeping *Two Juſtices.* of any *common Alehouſe*, or *Tipling-houſe*, and ſhall (from Time to Time) take Bond *Licenſe.* with Surety by Recognizance of ſuch Alehouſe-keepers, as well againſt the Uſing of un- 5 Ed. 6. 25. lawful Games, as alſo for the Keeping of good Rule and Order in their Houſes, accord- P. 2. ing to the Diſcretions of the ſame Juſtices.

And yet note, that the Words of the Statute do not warrant the Juſtices of Peace to al-low Alehouſe-keepers at their Pleaſure; but the Words are thus: None ſhall be admitted to keep a common Alehouſe, &c. but ſuch as ſhall be allowed in open Soſſions, or by two Juſti-ces, the one of the Quorum, &c. And therefore if two ſuch Juſtices out of the Seſſions ſhall allow more than are needful, or ſuch as are diſabled, or ſuch as have been ſuppreſſed; the Juſtices may be puniſhed, the rather for that the Number of unneceſſary Alehouſes are Cauſes of much Diſorder, poor labouring Men and Servants reſorting thither, and there miſſpending both their Money and Time.

There ſhall be paid for ſuch Recognizance but 12 d. and the ſaid Juſtices ſhall certify *Recognizance.* the ſame Recognizance at the next Quarter-Seſſions (upon Pain of five Marks.) *Ibidem.*

Any two Juſtices of Peace (the one being of the *Quorum*) may remove, diſcharge, and *Put down Ale-* put down any *Alehouſe* where they ſhall think meet. *houſes.* 5 E. 6. 25.

The Juſtices of Peace in their Seſſions by Preſentment, Information or otherwiſe at their 5 & 6 E. 6. 25. Diſcretion, may inquire of Perſons as be allowed to keep Alehouſes, and that be bound by Recognizances, if they have done any Acts whereby they have forfeited their Recognizance, and upon ſuch Preſentment or Information ſhall award Proceſs to ſhew Cauſe why they ſhould not forfeit the ſame, and ſhall hear and determine the ſame in ſuch Manner as by their Diſcretion ſhall be thought fit.

The Alehouſe-keeper put down and diſcharged by any two ſuch Juſtices of Peace can-not be allowed again by any other Two or more Juſtices of Peace, except it be in open Seſſions, as Sir *Peter Warburton* delivered in his Charge at *Cambridge* Aſſiſes, *Anno Do-mini* 1613.

Any two Juſtices of the Peace (the one being of the *Quorum*) may commit to Priſon *Selling Ale* in the common Gaol (for three Days without Bail) thoſe that keep common Alehouſes, *without a Li-* or that uſe common Selling of Ale or Beer, obſtinately of their own Authority, without *cenſe.* Allowance by two ſuch Juſtices, or contrary to the Commandment of two ſuch Juſtices. 5 E. 6. c. 25. And the ſaid two ſuch Juſtices (before the Delivery of ſuch Offenders) ſhall take Recog-nizance of them with two Sureties, that he or they ſhall keep no more a common Ale-houſe, or uſe commonly Selling of Ale or Beer, according to the Diſcretion of the ſame Juſtices; and ſhall certify ſuch Recognizance, Diſcharge and Offence, at their next Quarter-Seſſions: Which Certificate ſhall be a ſufficient Conviction in Law of the ſame Offence, without any farther Trial thereof to be had: *And for ſuch Offence the Fine of* 20 s. *ſhall be aſſeſſed in open Seſſions. In Places where Fairs are kept, any Perſon may uſe common Selling of Beer as hath been uſed.* 5 & 6 E. 6. 25. 3 Car. 1. c. 4.

But for that this former Law made 5 *Ed.* 6. hath not wrought ſuch Reformation as 3 Car. 1. c. 4. was intended, it is farther enacted by another Statute made 3 *Car.* 1. *cap.* 4. That if any Perſon ſhall upon his own Authority (not being thereunto lawfully licenſed) take upon him, or her, to keep a *common Alehouſe*, or *Tipling-houſe*, or ſhall commonly uſe *Sell-ing of Ale, Beer, Cyder*, or *Perry*, that every ſuch Perſon for every ſuch Offence ſhall forfeit *twenty Shillings*, to the Uſe of the Poor of the Pariſh where ſuch Offence ſhall be committed; the ſame Offence being viewed by any Juſtice of Peace, Mayor, or other *One Juſtice.* Head-Officer of any City or Town Corporate, within their Limits, or confeſſed by the Offender, or proved by the *Oath* of two Witneſſes.

Every ſuch Juſtice of Peace (or other Head-Officer aforeſaid) hath Power to miniſter 3 Car. 1. an *Oath* to ſuch Witneſſes.

Alſo every ſuch Juſtice (and other Head-Officer aforeſaid) within their ſeveral Limits, 3 Car. 1. may make their *Warrant* to the Conſtables or Church-wardens of the Pariſh where the ſaid Offence ſhall be committed, to levy the ſame *twenty Shillings* by Diſtreſs of the Of-fender's Goods; and for Default of Satisfaction, within three Days next enſuing, the ſaid Diſtreſs to be appraiſed and ſold, and the Overplus to be delivered to the Offender: And this to be only for the firſt Offence. *Ibidem.*

If

1. *Offence*.
3 Car. 1. c. 4.
§. 2.   If fuch Offender fhall not have fufficient Goods whereby to levy the faid *twenty Shil-lings by Diftrefs*, or fhall not pay the faid *twenty Shillings* within fix Days after fuch Conviction, then the faid Juftice (and other Head-Officer aforefaid) fhall commit the faid Offender to the Conftable where the Offence fhall be committed, or the Party appre-

Whipped. hended, to be openly whipped.

Ib. §. 3.   If the Conftable, *&c.* fhall neglect to execute the faid Warrant, or do refufe, or do not execute upon the Offender the faid Punifhment of Whipping, the faid Juftice (or Of-ficer) may commit the Conftable, *&c.* to the common Gaol without Bail, until the faid Offender fhall be by him punifhed, as aforefaid, or until the faid Conftable, *&c.* fhall pay forty Shillings to the Ufe of the Poor of the Parifh.

2. *Offence*.
Ib. §. 4.   The unlicenfed Alehoufe-keeper, for fuch his fecond Offence, fhall be committed to the Houfe of Correction for one Month.

3. *Offence*.
Ib.   And for every fuch Offence after, he fhall be committed to the Houfe of Correction, there to remain until he be delivered by Order from the General Seffions.

   Provided that fuch Offender fhall not be punifhed twice for the fame Offence, *fc.* fhall not be punifhed both by the Statute made *An.* 5 *E.* 6. and by the Statute of 3 *Caroli*.

Feme Covert.   If a *Feme Covert*, againft the Will of her Hufband, fhall keep an Alehoufe, or fhall ufe common Selling of Ale or Beer without Licenfe, *&c.* the Hufband is punifhable there-fore, and it feemeth the Wife alfo (by the Difcretion of the Juftices of Peace) may be im-prifoned for fuch her perfonal and wilful Offence, until fhe fhall find Sureties for her good Behaviour, and that fhe fhall no more Ufe the fame.

5 E. 6. c. 25.
P. 1. 4.   Alfo it feemeth (by the Letter of the Statute) that the Alehoufe-keeper put down or difcharged by two fuch Juftices, if (contrary to their Command) he fhall ufe common Selling of Beer or Ale again, though allowed by two other Juftices of Peace out of the general Seffions, yet the two Juftices that firft difcharged him may put him down again, and may commit him to the Gaol, for felling contrary to their Command.

5 E. 6. c. 25.
§. 5.   And yet the Statutes allow common Victualling, and Selling of Ale or Beer in Fairs, though unlicenfed, *&c.*
3 Car. 1. c. 4. § 6.
Brewers.   *Brewers uttering or delivering any Beer or Ale to any unlicenfed Alehoufe-keeper, fhall forfeit for every Barrel* 6 s. 8 d.   4 Jac. 1. c. 4.

Not licenfed.   If any Alehoufe-keeper which is *not licenfed*, fhall fuffer Townfmen or any other Per-fons to tipple in his Houfe, or fhall break the Affife, *&c.* he is punifhable for the fame by the Statute made *primo Jac. c. 9.* and befides he may alfo be *committed* to Prifon for three Days by Force of the Statute 5 *Ed.* 6. c. 25. or 3 *Car.* 1. 3. for felling Beer, *&c.* without Licenfe. Alfo if any Townfman, or other Perfon, fhall be found to be Tipling in any unlicenfed Alehoufe, fuch Perfons are alfo punifhable by the fame Statute, made *primo Jacobi, cap.* 9.

1 Jac. 1. c. 9.   Any two Juftices of Peace may give Allowance to Labourers, *&c.* for urgent and ne-ceffary Occafions to remain in an Inn, Alehoufe, or Victualling-houfe.

Inn-keepers
that fuffer
Tipling.
Co. 8. 32.   *Common Inns* are appointed for Travellers and Wayfaring Men, and therefore if any Inn-keeper fhall fuffer Perfons inhabiting in the fame Town, or any other Perfons (con-trary to the Statutes) to be ufually Tipling in his Houfe, fuch an Inn-keeper may be ac-counted as well an Alehoufe-keeper as an Inn-keeper; and fuch Inn-keepers may be bound by Recognizance with Sureties for Keeping of good Order, and obferving Affife, as Alehoufe-keepers are: And fo Judge *Warburton* delivered it in his Charge at *Cambridge* Affifes, *An. Dom.* 1613. And therewith alfo agreed Sir *James Ley* and Sir *John Dodde-ridge*, in their feveral Charges at *Cambridge* Affifes, *An. Dom.* 1621. for that fuch Inn-keepers (faid they) do pervert the End for which they were firft appointed. Or elfe it feemeth they may be punifhed, or committed, as Alehoufe-keepers without Licenfe, (by two Juftices of Peace, as aforefaid:) Or they may be indicted thereof at the Affifes or Seffions of Peace, as it feemeth by the Commiffion of the Peace.

   Jo. Brakey *de, &c. Innholder, &c. convicted for letting his Beer to farm to his Tapfter for fourteen Shillings the Barrel, he paying but eight Shillings to the Brewer.* Ord. 2. Sept. 9. Jac. Seff. Pac. Mid.

   It was the Opinion of the Court in the Cafe of one T. Jennings, *That the Keeping of an Inn gave no Warrant to fell Beer without other Licenfe.* Ord. 6 Jan. 1 Car. lib. Seff. Pa. Mid.

Crom. 77.   Alfo it hath been agreed for Law, That fuch Inns as have been erected fince the Sta-tute of 5 *Ed.* 6. *cap.* 25. and were not Inns before, ought to have Licenfe; and that fuch Inn-keepers are to be bound by Recognizance, with Sureties, for keeping of good Orders, as Alehoufe-keepers are.

And yet at *Lent* Aſſiſes, *Anno Dom.* 1621. Sir *James Ley* delivered his Charge, That Inns were Hoſteries by the Common Law, and that every Man might erect and keep an Inn or an Hoſtery, ſo as they were *probi homines*, Men of good Converſation, Fame and Report, dwelling in meet Places: But yet that they were not worthy of any Allowance or Licence under the King's Great Seal, *&c.*

And he delivered farther in his ſaid Charge, That if ſuch Inns or Hoſteries be uſed *ad nocumentum populi Dom. Regis, &c. ſc.* do keep any diſorderly Houſe contrary to the Law, or be more in Number than are needful, and to the Hindrance of other antient and well governed Inns; that then they may be thereof indicted at the Aſſiſes, or Seſſions of the Peace, and there may be either fined or ſuppreſſed. And Sir *James Ley* told me after at his Lodging in *Trinity College*, That this was the Opinion of all the other Judges, upon a late Conference had among themſelves.

But ſuch Inns or Hoſteries, if they ſhall be inconvenient or diſordered, in reſpect either of the Inn-keeper, or of the Reſort thither, or that the Place be unmeet, they are to be ſuppreſſed, upon an Indictment found at the Aſſiſes or Seſſions.

And if they ſhall ſuffer Townſmen or other Perſons (uſually) to tipple there, they   An. 1616. are to be puniſhed as Alehouſe-keepers without Licence: For theſe Inns or Hoſteries are to be allowed only for Travellers.

His Majeſty, in his Speech in the Star-Chamber, hath juſtly excepted againſt the *What Perſons* Abundance of Alehouſes, and more ſpecially againſt the infamous and blind Alehouſes, *are fit to be allowed.* as being Haunts for Robbers, Thieves, Rogues, Vagabonds, and other idle, looſe and ſturdy Fellows, *who loiter and enquire in theſe Places where they may have a Booty, or do a Miſchief to the neighbouring Inhabitants:* And therefore here I thought good to put the Juſtice of Peace in Mind, that in allowing of Alehouſes they have Regard as well to the Perſon as the Place; for all Perſons, eſpecially infamous or defamed, are not fit to be allowed for Alehouſe-keepers, neither are all Places meet for an Alehouſe.

And therefore Alehouſes to be allowed are meeteſt to be about the Midſt of the Town; Places fit for *but not to be in any Blind or By-Corners (much leſs in Woods or Places remote from* Alehouſes. *Towns) where Thieves and Rogues may be harboured: Nor in Places out of or diſtant* 7 E. 6. 5. *from the Town; except upon the River-ſide and where there is great Need, and the Perſons well known.* Reſol. 34.

The Keeping of Taverns, Alehouſes or Tipling-houſes, by Bailiffs, Serjeants *or other* Bailiffs. Miniſter, *is found generally miſchievous, for when they Arreſt any Perſon, upon Pretence of Favour they carry them to their own Houſes, and there lodge and entertain them ſo long Time as their Money laſts, and then and not before carry them to Priſon; whereby both the Party arreſting is many Times defrauded of his Debt, and the Perſon arreſted under Colour of Liberty cheated of his Money, and at laſt left to periſh in a Gaol, and therefore have I known many of theſe ſuppreſſed in the King's Bench; and, as I remember, a Rule of Court was made that none ſuch ſhould be licenſed, which is a worthy Example for other Juſtices of Peace to obſerve,* to prevent which Inconveniencies an Act of Parliament was made 22 & 23 Car. 2. whereby is provided, if any Under-Sheriff, Bailiff, Serjeant, or 22 & 23 C. 2. other Officers ſhall by Virtue or Colour of any Writ, Proceſs or Warrant, have any Perſon in Cuſtody, ſuch Officer ſhall not carry, or convey or cauſe, &c. the ſaid Perſons to any Tavern, Alehouſe, or Victualling, or Drinking-houſe, without his voluntary Conſent, ſo as to charge him with any Sum or Sums of Money for any Thing there, but what he ſhall call for, nor take any Reward for Keeping ſuch Perſon out of Gaol than the Party will freely give, nor take any more for each Night's Lodging or Expences than is reaſonable, or ſhall be adjudged by the next Juſtice of Peace, or at the Quarter-Seſſions, to pay for any Thing elſe than what the Party calls for.

As if the Party be in a Livery, or a Retainer to any Man, Bailiff of a Hundred or *The Perſon.* Liberty, Conſtable, *&c.* or be one that is not of good Fame, Converſation or Government; ſuch Perſons are not fit to be allowed to be Alehouſe-keepers. See *Fitz. N. B.* 172. That no Victualler ought to ſell Victual ſo long as he is in Office, *&c.* Statute 12 E. 2. cap. 6.

Again *dicitur*, that no Perſon, uſing any Trade, ought to be allowed to keep an Alehouſe, for that were to take away the Means, and ſo the Life of another: *Tamen quære inde,* for that by the Common Law no Man is prohibited to uſe divers Trades. *Vide hic* Tit. *Labourers.*

T. Byworth *ſuppreſſed from keeping an Alehouſe, for that it appeared to the Court that he is a Steel-forger, which is a good Trade, ſufficient for him to live by.* Ord. Seſſ. Pac. Mid. 26 Jul. 8 Car. *which ſee to reſolve the* Quære *aforeſaid.*

         Alſo

Alſo there are ſome Perſons that by Law are diſabled to keep an Alehouſe (at leaſt for a certain Time;) as,

7 Jac. 10.
21 Jac. 7.

1. The Alehouſe-keeper convicted for any Offence againſt 1 *Jac.* 9. and 4 *Jac.* 5. or being convicted (according to the Statute *viceſimo primo Jac.* 7.) for ſuffering Townſmen, &c. (or any other Perſon) to continue Drinking in his Houſe, contrary to the ſaid Statute, (which ſee here before) ſuch Alehouſe-keeper is diſabled to keep an Alehouſe for three Years after ſuch Conviction. 21 *Jac. cap.* 7.

4 Jac. 5.
7 Jac. 10.
21 Jac. 7.

2. The Alehouſe-keeper that ſhall continue Drinking in another Alehouſe or Inn in the ſame Town where he dwelleth, (the ſaid Offence being ſeen by any Juſtice of Peace within his Limits, or being proved before him by two Witneſſes upon Oath) every ſuch Alehouſe-keeper alſo is diſabled for three Years after ſuch Conviction to keep any Alehouſe, as it ſeemeth upon comparing thoſe Statutes of 4, 7 & 21 *Jac.*

3. So the Alehouſe-keeper that ſhall be drunken, and thereof lawfully be convicted, (by Indictment at the Aſſiſes, Seſſions of Peace, or in a Leet, or otherwiſe before the Juſtice of Peace) is diſabled for three Years to keep an Alehouſe.

4 Jac. 3.
7 Jac. 10.
21 Jac. 7.

4. An Alehouſe-keeper convicted and ſuppreſſed for any of the former Offences, if he ſhall be licenſed or allowed again by two or more Juſtices of Peace within three Years, ſuch Licence is void, and he is to be puniſhed as one Victualling without Licence. And ſo it was delivered by Sir *Nic. Hide*, at *Cambridge* Aſſiſes, *An.* 3 *Caroli Regis*. And ſo it ſeemeth, if he were convicted, though he were not ſuppreſſed, if he be after licenſed again within three Years after ſuch Conviction, ſuch Licence is void, &c.

5. The Alehouſe-keeper that is diſcharged or put down by any two Juſtices of Peace, the one being of the *Quorum*, &c. is alſo diſabled, ſo as he cannot be allowed again, except in open Seſſions. See *hic antea*.

Alſo in Towns which are no Thorough-fare, the Juſtices ſhall do well to be ſparing in allowing any Alehouſe, except it be at the Suit of the chief Inhabitants there, and to ſupply the neceſſary Wants of their Poor.

11 & 12 W.3.
c. 15.
* *Or in the City of London.*
Pots not marked.

By the Statute 11 & 12 *Will.* 3. 'tis enacted, That Ale and Beer ſhall be ſold by the Ale-quart or Pint, according to the Standard in the * *Exchequer*, and in a Veſſel ſtamped or marked with *W. R.* and a Crown; and if ſold in a Veſſel not ſtamped as aforeſaid, or if an Inn-keeper or Alehouſe-keeper refuſes in bringing in the Reckoning to give the particular Number of Quarts and Pints, he ſhall not detain any Goods of the Gueſts if they refuſe to pay the Reckoning, but may bring his Action at Law.

Beſides, ſelling Beer or Ale in *Pots* not marked, according to the ſaid Standard, forfeits not above 40 *s.* nor under 10 *s.* to be levied by Diſtreſs and Sale of the Goods of the Offender; one Moiety to the Uſe of the Poor where the Offence was committed, and the other to the Proſecutor; the Conviction is to be by the Oath of one Witneſs, before one or more Juſtices; and the Proſecution muſt be within thirty Days after the Offence.

And if any Action ſhould be brought for putting the aforeſaid Statute in Execution, it ſhall be laid in the proper County where the Fact was done, and *not elſewhere*; and if the Plaintiff ſhall be caſt, the Defendant ſhall have *treble Coſts*.

The *Collectors of the Exciſe* muſt provide a *full Ale-Quart* and Pint in every Market-Town within their reſpective Diviſions, or they forfeit 5 *l.*

The Chief Officer of every Town ſhall cauſe the Pots to be marked as aforeſaid, for which he may take one Farthing for every Veſſel; and if he neglect or refuſe to mark the Veſſel, he forfeits 5 *l.* and treble Damages ſhall be had by the Party grieved and full Coſts.

Before this Statute was made a Man was indicted for Selling Ale in black Pots *unſealed*, and the Indictment concluded *contra pacem*, without ſaying *contra formam Statuti*, for there was a former Statute which directed the Sealing of Meaſures; and upon a Motion to quaſh the Indictment, becauſe it did not conclude *contra formam Statuti*, it was adjudged that this Indictment was good at *Common Law*, becauſe Meaſures were by that Law, and the Statutes only direct the Manner of aſcertaining them.

1 Vent. 13.
S. C.

Sid. 409. *The King* verſus *Burgoine*.

Brandy.
12 & 13 W.3.

By the Statute 12 & 13 *Will.* 3. 'tis prohibited to ſell *Brandy* or other diſtilled Liquors by Retail, to be drunk in Houſes without a *Licence* in the ſame Manner as common Alehouſe-keepers are licenſed, and the Offender is made ſubject to the ſame Penalties and Forfeitures as thoſe are who ſell Ale or Beer without Licence.

Licences.
6 G. 1. c. 22.
ſect. 54.

And by the Statute 6 *Geo.* 1. 'tis enacted, that all Mayors, Town-Clerks, and other Perſons whom it may concern, ſhall make or cauſe to be made out *Ale Licences* duly

ſtamped

ftamped before new *Recognizances* are taken, and this under the Penalty of 10 *l.* for every Offence.

Now as to Selling Ale without *a Licenfe*, it hath been a Queftion, Whether an Indictment will lie for that Offence? Thofe who argue for the Affirmative tell us, That where a Thing is prohibited by any Statute which is of a general Concern; and the Method of Recovering the Penalty is in *affirmative Words*, in fuch Cafe the general Method of Proceeding by Indictment is not taken away, for that muft be by *negative Words*.

That in 1 *Saund. Rep.* 248. there is a Precedent of an Indictment for felling Ale *with-* Sid.409. S. C. *out a Licenfe*, which is very true, but it was never objected in that Cafe, that the Indictment would not lie for that Offence, for it was quafhed, becaufe it concluded *in contemptum Domini Regis nunc legumq; fuarum ac contra pacem, &c.* whereas it was no Offence at Common Law to keep an Alehoufe without a Licenfe, for it was made fo by a * 5 & 6 Ed. 6. * particular Statute, and therefore it fhould have concluded *contra formam Statuti, &c.*

This Queftion was fome Years afterwards formally debated in the Cafe of the *King and* 4 Mod. 144. *Queen* againft *Mariott*, where it was held, that felling Ale without a *Licenfe* is an Of- Show. Rep. fence created by a *Statute*; and fince a particular Method of Profecution is appointed by 393. S. C. the Statute itfelf, (*by which the Juftices of Peace have Power in their Seffions to inquire thereof, either by Prefentment or Information,* &c.) that Method muft be followed and no other; but an Indictment is another Method of Profecuting, not fo much as mentioned in the Statute, and therefore it would not lie; and two Judges declared, that they never yet heard of an *Indictment* againft any Perfon for Keeping an Alehoufe without *Licenfe*, which feems very ftrange, for certainly they muft have heard of *Falkner*'s Cafe, reported by the Chief Juftice *Saunders*, as aforefaid; however they were of Opinion, that the Indictment would not lie, and the rather becaufe by the Statute the Offender might be convicted by the View of the Chief Officer within his Limits, or by his own Confeffion, or by the Oath of two Witneffes; and then the Penalty is to be levied by Diftrefs.

However in the principal Cafe, the Chief Juftice *Holt* being of Opinion, that the * In- * See 2 Salk. dictment being a fummary Way of Proceeding, was more beneficial for the Subject, and 45. S. P. therefore that Method ought to be purfued: Nothing was done upon this firft Motion, but only to ftay the Proceedings on the Indictment; but it being afterwards moved again, the Indictment was quafhed for the Reafon beforementioned.

The Defendant was convicted upon the Statute 3 *Car.* for felling Ale, *fine aliqua licentia & contra formam Statuti*; and upon a Motion to quafh this Conviction it was objected, that the Selling without Licenfe is punifhable by former Statutes, particularly by the Statue 5 & 6 *Ed.* 6. by which 'tis enacted, That none fhould keep Alehoufes without Licenfe granted either in Seffions, or by two Juftices; and it doth not appear but that the Defendant might be licenfed by two Juftices according to that Statute. *Sed per Curiam*, it being alledged, That he fold *fine aliqua licentia quacunq*; that is fufficient. *Trin.* 9 *Geo.* 1.

The Defendant was found Guilty upon an Indictment for felling Ale without paying the Excife, but upon a Motion in Arreft of Judgment it was quafhed, becaufe it did not fet forth to whom, or at what Time it was to be paid, nor what Quantity of Ale he fold, fo that a Conviction upon fuch an incertain Indictment cannot be pleaded to any other for the fame Offence; befides in Criminal Cafes the utmoft Certainty is required, therefore the Quantity of the Offence ought to be fet forth in this Indictment. *Mich.* 1722. B. R. *The King* verfus *Gibbs*.

By the Statute 12 *Geo.* 1. *fect.* 1. as to felling Ale and Beer within the Bills of Mortality only, 'tis enacted, That after 24 *June* 1726. not lefs than one Pound, nor more than fix Pounds, fhall be paid yearly by every Victualler and Retailer of Beer and Ale, within the Bills of Mortality.

That Commiffioners fhall be appointed by the King or the Treafury, to manage the faid Duty, who may fubftitute fuch Officers as they fhall think neceffary, which Commiffioners, or the major Part of them, fhall grant Permiffions for retailing Beer and Ale.

That no Victualler, &c. within the Bills of Mortality fhall fell Beer or Ale without a Permiffion firft obtained, under the Hands and Seals of fuch Commiffioners, or the major Part of them; and in order to obtain fuch Permiffion, the Victuallers, &c. fhall every Year, within twenty Days after the 24th of *June*, or fome Perfon for them, make Application to the Commiffioners, &c. and then compound with them for a Sum of Money, to be paid for one Year; one Moiety of which Compofition-Money fhall be paid down at the Signing of the Permiffion, and the other Moiety at the End of fix Months next enfuing

enfuing, which Permiffions at the Expiration of one Year, fhall be fent to the Commif-fioners to be cancell'd, and new Compofitions made, and the like Permiffions granted for the next Year.

Provifo, That an Inn-keeper, Victualler, &c. leaving off retailing Ale and Beer, and difcharging all Compofition-Money, and giving Notice thereof at the Office, &c. fuch Permiffion and Compofition fhall ceafe.

The Commiffioners, &c. fhall make Compofitions, according to the beft Intelligence they can get of the Trade of the Compounder, and fhall demand no more than two Shil-lings and fix Pence for each Permiffion, which fhall be yearly accounted for and paid with the other Money, to be rais'd by Compofitions.

That no Victualler, &c. fhall fend Beer or Ale out of their Houfes to drink, in any Pot, Cup or Veffel, lefs than a Gallon, in Ale Meafure; but Beer or Ale may be drunk at the Door of the Houfe, or in any Out-houfe, Shed or Arbour, Garden or Yard, be-longing to the Houfe, in lefs Meafures.

Victualler, &c. neglecting or refufing to take out a Permiffion, or to pay the Compo-fition-Money as it fhall become due, fhall for every Neglect, &c. forfeit 20 l. to be le-vied by the Laws of Excife.

That the Commiffioners fhall have the fame Power as the Commiffioners of Excife.

Provifo, this Statute fhall not alter or diminifh any Power of the Juftices of the Peace, in licenfing and regulating Victuallers.

Any Perfon fued for putting this Act in Execution may plead the General Iffue, and give the Statute and the Special Matter in Evidence; and if the Plaintiff be Nonfuit, or the Defendant obtain Judgment on a Demurrer, or a Verdict, he fhall have treble Cofts.

2Geo.2.c.28. §.11. *By Stat. 2 Geo. 2. c. 28. fect. 11. No Licence fhall be granted to keep a common Inn or Alehoufe, or to retail Brandy, but at a general Meeting of the Juftices acting in the Di-vifion where the Perfon dwells; and all Licenfes granted to the contrary fhall be void.*

Ib. §. 10. *And by the fame Statute, Sect. 10. Retailers of Brandy, &c. fhall be licenfed in the fame Manner as Alehoufe-keepers, and Juftices of Peace fhall have the fame Jurifdiction* Ib. §. 12. *over fuch Retailers as over Alehoufe-keepers. But by the fame Statute, Sect. 12. Nothing herein fhall alter the Method of granting Licenfes of keeping common Inns, Alehoufes, or Brandy-fhops, in any City or Town Corporate.*

C H A P. VIII.

Affray.

What and whence. AFFRAY *is in our Law a Skirmifh or Fighting between two or more; and is* derived of the *French* Word *Effrayer*, which fignifieth to terrify, and which the Law un-derftandeth to be a common Wrong. And therefore I will fhew you what every Man may do in fuch Cafes.

Every private Man. Every *private Man* being prefent *before, or in and during the Time of any Affray*, ought to ftay the Affrayors, and to part them, but may not hurt them if they refift him; nei-ther may he imprifon them, becaufe he is but a private Man.

An Affray being in the Street, if any other fhall come with Arms or Weapon to join with either Party, every Perfon prefent, or that feeth it, may ftay them till the Affray be over.

Alfo *every private Man* (being prefent) may ftay the Affrayors until their Heat be over, and then may deliver them to the Conftables to imprifon them till they find Surety for the Peace: But yet the Conftable may not imprifon the Parties, except the Affray was in his Prefence. *Hic, cap.* 1.

Lamb. 134. If any Perfon be dangeroufly hurt in an Affray, every Perfon may arreft the Offender, and carry him to the Gaol or to a Juftice of Peace, (who is either to bail him until the next Gaol-Delivery, or to commit him until it be known whether the Party hurt will live or die.) *Br. Faux Imprif.* 35, 44.

The Conftable. 3 H.7.c.1. Br. Coron. 225. 10 H.7.20. The Conftable in fuch Cafes is armed with a more large Authority within his Jurif-diction; for he may and ought in the King's Name to command the Affrayors, or fuch as are about to make an Affray, to depart (upon Pain of Imprifonment:) And if the Con-ftable (being prefent at an Affray) doth not his beft Endeavour to part them, it being presented by Enqueft at the Seffions of the Peace, such Conftable shall be fined for it. *See more chap.* 1.

But where the Affray is made out of the *Prefence or Sight* of the Conftable, and one telleth him of it, and wifheth him to go and fee the Peace kept, and the Conftable doth nothing, but neglecteth his Duty therein, he fhall be fined by the Juftices at their Seffions, upon Prefentment thereof by the great Enqueft. *Cro.* 146. *Quære tamen & vide hic, cap.* 1. *&* 5. the Commiffion, *&* 121 the Form of the Conftables Oath. *3 H. 7. 10. Lamb. 135.*

If the Affrayors will not depart, but shall draw Weapon, or give any Blow, the Conftable may command Affiftance of others for the pacifying the Affray, and may juftify the Hurting of them, if they make Refiftance.

The Conftable may in the King's Name make Proclamation (if the Affray be great or dangerous) that the Affrayors shall keep the King's Peace and depart, &c. *Lamb. 135.*

Alfo if the Affray be great and dangerous, then the Conftables may command the Affrayors to Prifon for a fmall Time, till their Heat be over ; yea, they may imprifon the Affrayors till they find Sureties for the Peace. And if any of the Parties have received any dangerous Hurt in the Affray, the Conftable ought to arreft and carry the Offenders to the Gaol, (or to a Juftice of Peace) that they may find Sureties to appear at the next Gaol-Delivery ; and the Conftable may juftify the Beating, &c. of fuch an Offender, if he will not obey the Arreft, but make Refiftance, or flieth. *Lamb. 139. 38 E. 3. 8. & 11. Br. Faux Imp. 6.*

Note, that it is no Affray unlefs there be fome Weapons drawn, or fome Stroke given, or offered to be given, or other Attempt to fuch Purpofe; for if Men shall contend only *in hot Words,* this is no Affray : Neither may the Conftable for *Words only* lay Hands upon them, unlefs they shall threaten to kill, beat, or hurt one another, and then he may arreft fuch Perfon, to go before fome Juftice of Peace, to find Sureties for the Keeping the Peace ; and yet fuch Threatning is no Affray. But yet a Challenge by Word or Meffage to fight was held an Affray, and *Anno* 16 *Car.* 2. one *Collins* was fined 100 *l.* and committed for a Month without Bail, being convicted on an Indictment for carrying a Challenge, knowing the Contents thereof. *Sid.* 186. *Hic. cap. 1.*

If the Affray be in an Houfe, and the Doors fhut, the Conftable may *break into the Houfe,* to fee the Peace kept, though none of the Parties have taken any Hurt. *Purfuit.*

If the Affrayors flie into *another Man's Houfe,* the Conftable *(in frefh Suit) may break* into the Houfe, and apprehend the Affrayors. *7 E. 3. 19.*

If the Affrayors fly into another County, the Conftable (or Juftice of Peace) feeing this, may in *frefh Suit purfue,* or caufe them to be purfued, and to be taken there; but they can meddle no farther but (as every *private Perfon* may do) to carry them before fome Juftice of Peace of the County where they are taken, to caufe them to find Surety for the Peace. *Plo. 57. Cromp. 146. b. & 172. b.*

But if the Affrayors fly into a *Franchife* within the fame County, the Conftable (or Juftice of Peace) feeing this, may in *frefh Suit purfue* and take them out of fuch *Franchife.* *Cromp. 246.*

After the Affray the Conftable, without a Warrant, cannot arreft the Affrayors, except fome Perfon be in Peril of Death by fome Hurt there received. *38 H. 8. Br. F. Imp. 6.*

Every *Juftice of Peace* may do that which every Conftable or private Man may do by the Common Law herein. *The Juftice. 9 Ed. 4. 3.*

Befides every Juftice of Peace (within his Limits) may prefently after the Affray commit the Offenders, until they have found Surety for the Peace, if the Affray *were in his Prefence.* And if not in his Prefence, yet upon Complaint, or upon his *own Difcretion* he may after make his Warrant to take or commit fuch Offenders, until they have found Surety for the Peace. *Vide* Tit. *Peace and Surety for the Peace.* *Cromp. 195, 196.*

If an Affray be made in the Prefence of a Juftice of Peace, he may lay Hands upon and arreft the Offenders to find Sureties for the Peace, and may take away their Weapons. 21 *H.* 7. 22. *b. Moor.* *Br. Faux Imp. 12. & 33.*

And yet by the fame Opinions, the Juftices of Peace in Cafes of an Affray, hath no farther Authority than every private Man hath : For though the Juftices of Peace (fitting in their Seffions, or out of their Seffions) may command a Man to be attached, who shall make an Affray in their Prefence, and may make a Record, and certify the fame, which shall be a Conviction of the Offender; and the Juftice of Peace may prefently upon the Fact command or fend fuch Offenders to the Gaol; yet the Juftices cannot themfelves attach or arreft any Man for an Affray, or other Thing done in their Prefence, (no more than a Stranger or private Perfon may do;) but after the Affray they may make or grant out their Warrant to attach or arreft the Offenders, and may then commit them to the Gaol, except they shall find Sureties for the Peace.

Every

Every Juftice of Peace (in his *own Difcretion*, and *ex Officio*) may bind all fuch to the Peace as *in his Prefence* fhall ftrike another, or fhall threaten to hurt another, or fhall contend only in *hot Words. Vide* Tit. *Sureties for the Peace.*

Dangerous Hurt.
P. Juft. 173.
10 H. 7. 20.
Cromp. 154.

If any Perfon be dangeroufly hurt in any Affray (or otherwife,) every Juftice of Peace, within *the Year and Day* after fuch Hurt, may commit to the Gaol fuch Offender, there to remain until the *Day and Year* be expired, or that the faid Offenders fhall find Sureties to appear at the next General Gaol-Delivery, to anfwer to the Felony, if the Party hurt happen to die within a Year after the Hurt. *Vide Stat.* 3 *H.* 7. *c.* 1. *And by God's Law, Exodus* 21. 18, 19. *If the Party happen to recover, the Offender fhall pay to the Party hurt for lofing his Time, and alfo for his healing.*

But where the Hurt fhall be dangerous, or Wound *mortal*, although the Juftice may bail the Offender, *living* the Party fo hurt; yet it fhall be better *Difcretion* for him to commit the Offender to the Gaol, there to remain, until there fhall appear fome Hope of Recovery in the other : And fo Sir *Nicholas Hyde* advifed at *Cam.* Lent *Affizes, Ann.* 5 *Car.* 1. *Regis.*

And by the Stat. de officio Coronatoris, 3 *or* 4 *E.* 1. *upon Appeal of Wounds, and fuch like, efpecially if the Wounds be mortal, the Parties appealed fhall be taken immediately, and kept till it be known perfectly whether the Party hurt fhall recover or not; and if he die, the Offender fhall be kept ; and if he recover, he fhall be attached by four or fix Pledges, as the Wound is great or fmall: And if it be for a Main, the Offender fhall find no lefs than four Pledges; if it be for a fmall Wound or Maim, two Pledges fhall fuffice.*

5 H. 7. 6.
Br. Faux
Imp. 41.

If an Affray or Affault be made upon a *Juftice of Peace or a Conftable*, they may not only defend themfelves, but may alfo apprehend and commit the Offenders, until they have found Sureties for the Peace : The Juftice of Peace may prefently caufe them to be arrefted, and carried before another Juftice, who may fend them to the Gaol : And the Conftable muft commit them to the *Stocks* for the prefent, and after carry them before a Juftice of Peace, or to the Gaol. *Vide hic poftea.*

Apprentice. See *Labourers*, cap. 58.

Arreft. See *cap.* 170.

C H A P. IX.

Armour.

2 E. 3. c. 3.
P. 1.
7 R. 2. 13.
20 R. 2. c. 1.

IF any Perfon fhall ride or go armed offenfively before the King's Juftices, or any other the King's Officers or Minifters doing their Office, or in Fairs, Markets, or elfewhere, (by Night or by Day) in Affray of the King's People, (the Sheriff, and other the King's Officers) and every Juftice of Peace (upon his own View, or upon Complaint thereof)

One Juftice.

may caufe them to be arrefted, and may bind all fuch to the Peace or Good Behaviour, (or, for Want of Sureties may commit them to the Gaol): And the faid Juftice of Peace (as alfo every Conftable) may feize and take away their Armour and other Weapons, and fhall caufe them to be apprifed, and anfwered to the King as forfeited. And this the Juftice of Peace may do by the firft *Affignavimus* in the Commiffion. See hereof *antea.*

Lam. Offic. of
a Conft. 13.

So of fuch as fhall carry any Guns, Daggs, or Piftols that be charged, or that fhall go apparelled with privy Coats or Doublets, the Juftice may caufe them to find Sureties for the Peace, and may take away fuch Weapons, &c. *Vide* Tit. *Surety for the Peace.*

2 E. 3. c. 3.
Co. 5. 72.
20 R. 2. 1.

And yet the King's Servants in his Prefence, and Sheriffs, and their Officers, and other the King's Minifters, and fuch as be in their Company affifting them in executing the King's Procefs, or otherwife in executing of their Office, and all others in purfuing *Hue and Cry*, where any Felony or other Offences againft the Peace be done, may lawfully bear Armour or Weapons.

Any Perfon may arm himfelf to refift or fupprefs thofe who difturb the Peace; but 'tis moft difcreet to be affiftant to fome minifterial Officer in this Matter; fo refolved by all the Judges. *Anno* 39 *Eliz. Poph.* 121.

Army Debentures. See *Felony*, by Stat. cap. 160.

4

Artificers.

By the Statute 5 *Geo.* 1. *c.* 27. one Juſtice may bind over to the Aſſizes or Seſſions, any Artificer about to go beyond Sea; and thoſe who endeavour to withdraw him thither.

And the Seſſions may fine a Perſon contracting with, enticing or perſuading any Artificer in Exciſe, Wool, Iron, or Steel, or any other Metal, Clock-maker, Watch-maker, or any other Artificer to go out of the Kingdom, 100 *l.* for the firſt Offence, and three Months Impriſonment, and until ſuch Fine paid; and if any Perſon having been once convict, ſhall offend again, he ſhall be fined at the Diſcretion of the Court, and impriſoned twelve Months, and till the Fine be paid: The Proſecution muſt be within twelve Months.

Artificer convicted by one Witneſs of any Promiſe or Contract, or Preparation to go beyond Sea, muſt find Sureties not to depart out of the King's Dominions as the Court ſhall think fit, and for want of Sureties, to be committed until he find them.

If an Artificer ſhall go out of the King's Dominions to exerciſe, or teach his Trade to Foreigners, and ſhall not return within ſix Months after Warning given by the Miniſter or Conſul of *Great Britain,* ſuch Artificer ſhall be incapable of any Legacy, or of taking by Deſcent or Purchaſe, *&c.* and ſhall be deemed an Alien.

Badger. See *cap.* 46.

Bakers. See *Weights.*

C H A P. X.

Barrator.

BArrator *cometh from the French* Barrat, *id eſt,* aſtutia, *in Engliſh, a Deceiver. In our Law a Barrator is a common Wrangler that ſetteth Men at odds, and is himſelf never quiet, but at Braul with one or other.* Dr. Cow. *&* Minſh.

Every Juſtice of Peace (*upon his Diſcretion*) may bind to the Peace or good Behaviour, ſuch as are common Barrators.   *E. 4. 5. Lamb.* 79.

Alſo a common Barrator is he who is either a common Mover and Stirrer up (or Maintainer) of Suits of Law in any Court, or elſe of Quarrels or Parties in the Country. *Co. Lit.* 368.   *Co. 8. 36. 9 E. 4. 3. 2.*

As if in any Court of Record, County-Court, Hundred, or other inferior Courts, any *In Courts.* Perſon by Fraud or Malice under Colour of Law, ſhall themſelves *maintain* (or ſtir up others unto) Multiplicity of unjuſt and feigned Suits or Informations (upon penal Laws,) or ſhall maliciouſly purchaſe a ſpecial *Supplicavit* of the Peace, to force the other Party to make Compoſition; all ſuch are Barrators.

In the Country; and theſe are of three Sorts.   *In the Country.*

1. *Diſturbers of the Peace, viz.* ſuch as are either *common Quarellers or Fighters* in their own Cauſe; or common Movers or Maintainers of Quarrels and Affrays between others.

2. *Common Takers or Detainers* (by Force or Subtilty) the Poſſeſſions of Houſes, Lands or Goods, which have been in Queſtion or Controverſies.

3. *Inventors and Sowers of falſe Reports,* whereby Diſcord ariſeth, or may ariſe between *Co. 8. 36.* Neighbours. All theſe are Barrators.

Yea, if one be Communis Seminator litium, *he is a Barrator.* Weſt. Indict. 75, 76.

Or if any Man of himſelf be Communis oppreſſor vicinorum, *either by unjuſt or wrangling Suits, or other Oppreſſions or Deceits, he is a Barrator.*

Or if one be Communis Pacis Perturbator, Calumniator, & Malefactor, *he is a Barrator.* Crom. 257.

But all ſuch Perſons muſt be *common Barrators, ſc.* not in one or two, but in many *Co. 8. 37.* Cauſes.

A Feme Covert cannot be indicted of common Barratry, and an Indictment againſt one for that Offence was quaſht. T. 16. Jac. Roll's Rep. Part 2. p. 39. *   * *But this is queſtionable, according to* 1 Hawk. P. C. 243.

1. *A*

Puniſhment.   1. *A Man convicted of common Barratry ſhall be puniſhed by* Fine and Impriſonment, *and may be bound to the good Behaviour.* 34 E. 3. c. 1.

Indictment.   2. *An Indictment was* Communis Barrector, *where it ſhould have been* Barrectat', *and quaſhed for that Fault,* &c. 20 Jac. Alport's *Caſe.*

3. *And although Barratry be an Offence made up of ſeveral Acts, yet a Place muſt be laid where the Offence was committed for the Neceſſity of Trial.* Roll's Rep. 1 Part, p. 295. *The King againſt Wells.*

Certiorari.   4. *Barratry is of a mixt Nature, and the Juſtices of Peace cannot take an Indictment and Fine, and puniſh the Offender barely by Virtue of the Commiſſion of the Peace,*
* But ſee *but in reſpect of the Clauſe therein to hear and determine Felonies,* &c. ** And a Caſe*
1 Hawk. P. C. *was* H. 17. Jac. *Where a Man being indicted of Barratry at the Seſſions, brought a Cer-*
244. & 2 *tiorari, and an Indictment was certified* capta coram, *&c.* Juſtic. Dom. Regis ad pacem,
Hawk. 40. *but* necnon ad diverſa, *&c. was left out, and for that Cauſe the* Certiorari *was quaſhed.*
ſect. 39. con- Roll's Rep. 2 Part, p. 151.
tra.

Suing in an-   5. Suing one in another's Name *is a Species of Barratry, and there by* 8 El. c. 2.
other's Name. *He that cauſeth or procureth another to be arreſted or attached in any Action at the Suit, or in the Name of another, where there is no ſuch Perſon known, or without his Conſent, upon Conviction by two Witneſſes, ſhall be impriſoned ſix Months without Bail, and before Delivery ſhall pay ten Pounds with treble Coſts and Damages to the Party, to be recovered by Action of Debt,* &c. *in any Court of Record.*

It was formerly held that the Words *Communis Barrectator* ought to be in every Indictment for a Barratry, and therefore to ſet forth that a Man is a Promoter of Suits, or *Communis vicinorum oppreſſor,* was not ſufficient to ſupport the Indictment. *Vide* 1 *Hawk. P. C.* 244. accord.

But now 'tis ruled otherwiſe, for where the Defendant was indicted that he was *quotidianus perturbator pacis,* the Indictment was held good. *Hill.* 8 *Will.* Rex verſus *Gregory.*

But 'tis eſſential to conclude the Indictment *contra pacem.* 2 Cro. 527. 2 Roll. Abr. 82.

It was likewiſe formerly thought not neceſſary to ſet out in what Place the Defendant was a *Barrator,* becauſe he who is a Common Barrator is ſo in every Place; but 'tis of late ruled otherwiſe, for if the Fact is traverſed, and no Place alledged, there cannot be any *Venire facias* to try it where the Fact was alledged to be. *Anno Regni Domini noſtri,* leaving out the Word *Regis;* the Indictment was quaſhed. 1 *Sid.* 214. *Godb.* 557.

Upon an Indictment of Barratry, the Evidence was that *T. S.* was arreſted at the Suit of another in an Action of 4000 *l.* when in Truth he owed the Proſecutor nothing; and coming before the Chief Juſtice to give Bail, the Defendant appeared there and ſollicited againſt the Proſecutor; *ſed per curiam,* this is not Barratry but *Maintenance.*

But where a Man is arreſted by another only to oppreſs him, and not to recover any Right, this is Barratry; and ſo in lending Money to ſtir up or promote Suits; and in this Caſe the Defendant did entertain the Proſecutor in his Houſe, and brought ſeveral Actions in his Name; and it was held to be Barratry, there being nothing due. 3 *Mod.* 97.

Where the Defendant is indicted for Barratry, he muſt have a Note of the particular Fact, that he may know for what he is charged, otherwiſe the Proſecutor ſhall not proceed. 5 *Mod.* 18.

C H A P. XI.

Baſtardy.

BAſtardus eſt qui naſcitur ante matrimonium. Co. L. 243. *It cometh of the* French *Word* Baſtard, *i. e.* Nothus; *and yet* Baſtardus eſt triplex; Manſer, inceſtuoſe natus. Co. L. 244. Nothus, natus ex patre nobili & matre ignobili, ſc. Concubina; Spurius, natus ex matre nobili & patre ignobili. *A Baſtard is* Terræ filius, *tho' his Mother be known.*

      Cui pater eſt populus, pater eſt ſibi nullus & Omnis.
      Cui pater eſt populus, non habet ille patrem.

Much more of Foundlings, where neither Father nor Mother are known.

                                                     Every

Every Juſtice of Peace (upon his Diſcretion) may bind to the Good Behaviour him *Lam.* 122. that is *charged or ſuſpected to have begotten a* Baſtard-child, that he may be forth-coming *Crom.* 196. when the Child ſhall be born; otherwiſe there will be no *putative Father*, when the two Juſtices (after the Birth of the Child) ſhall come to take Order according to the Statute of 18 *El. c.* 3. The like may be done after the Birth of the Child, and before ſuch Order taken.

Alſo if the putative Father of any ſuch Child, either before the Birth of the Child or after, ſhall, by any Perſwaſion, Procurement or other Practice, be conveyed or ſent away, or ſhall run away, ſo as the Juſtice of Peace cannot come by him, or ſo as the Order of the Juſtices, by Means thereof, ſhall not be performed; every Juſtice of Peace, *upon his Diſcretion*, may bind to the Good Behaviour, and ſo over to the next General Gaol-delivery, (before the Judges of Aſſiſe) or to the next Quarter-Seſſions, ſuch as ſhall have any Hand in ſuch Practice, &c. *And ſuch Offenders may by the Diſcretion of the Juſtices,* (at their *General Seſſions*) *be ordered to contribute towards the Maintenance of the ſaid Baſtard-child. And ſo of Conſtables, which having received a Warrant from the Juſtice to apprehend the reputed Father, ſhall willingly or negligently ſuffer him to eſcape; or fine them.* So ſuch as by Practice, &c. ſhall cauſe the *Mother of the Child* to be conveyed or ſent away, or to run away, whereby ſhe leaveth her Child to the Charge of the Town, &c.

Two Juſtices of Peace (one being of the Quorum) *in or next to the Limits where the* *Two Juſtices.* *Pariſh-Church is, in which Pariſh any Baſtard-child (begotten and born out of lawful* 18 El. c. 3. *Matrimony) ſhall be born, upon Examination of the Cauſe and Circumſtances, ſhall and* P. 2. *may take Order by their Diſcretion, as well for the Relief of the Pariſh (in Part, or in* *Order.* *all) and Keeping of the Child, (by charging the Mother or reputed Father with the Pay- ment of Money weekly, or other Relief,) as alſo for the Puniſhment of the Mother and re- puted Father.*

But ſuch a Baſtard-child muſt be one that is left to be kept at the *Charge of the Pariſh*, or one likely to be (or which may be) chargeable to the Pariſh. See the Stat. of 18 *Eliz.* and the Stat. 7 *Jac. cap.* 4.

The Juſtices of the Peace in Seſſions could not before the Statute of 3 *Car.* 1. *c.* 4. *Where Seſſions meddle with the Settlement of, or Proviſion for a Baſtard-child, according to* 18 *Eliz.* *may make an c.* 3. *until the two next Juſtices had made ſome Order therein, and after ſuch Order* *Order. made by the two next Juſtices, the Seſſions might proceed therein to make a new Order;* Cro. 13. Ca. *but now by* 3 *Car.* 1. cap. 4. *the Juſtices in Seſſions have Power originally to make an* Slater's Caſe, *Order therein, but this is ſeldom or never done.* 18 E. 3.

3 Car. 1. 4.
And if the two next Juſtices of Peace make an Order according to 18 *Eliz. c.* 3. *and* Cro. Car. p. *the Party appeals from that Order to the next Seſſions, and they alter, or diſcharge, or* 248. & 225. *confirm that Order, any other Seſſions cannot order any Thing contrary thereto; for the* Pridgion's *Order upon the Appeal is final, as in Appeal upon the Statute of Charitable Uſes, and the* Caſe. *Statute of* 3 *Car.* 4. *The giving Authority to Juſtices of Peace in Seſſions, is to be under-* 3 Car. 1. 4. *ſtood where the next Juſtices have made no Order therein.*

A Man is charged to be the reputed Father of a Baſtard, by Order of two Juſtices, he *Appeal next appeals to the Seſſions, and prays a Day to another Seſſions to bring in his Proofs; beſides* *Seſſions. giving Day, nothing is done; and if the Court might hear him, and give Relief at an- other Seſſions, was the Doubt; and it was referred to the Juſtices of Aſſiſe.* And Walter, *Chief Baron, upon Conſideration of the Statute of* 18 *Eliz. Reſolved, That the next Seſſions after, the two Juſtices Order muſt relieve him, or none elſe could.* Gittens and Edwards's *Caſe. Summer Aſſiſe in* Sar. 5 Car. *And ſo it was reſolved* B. R. Mich. 6 Car. 1. *in* Smith's *Caſe againſt the Pariſh of* Blackthorne *in Com.* Oxon.

The reputed Father, by the Law of God, was to give unto the Maid's Father fifty Shekels of Silver, *and he alſo was to take her to Wife.* Exod. 22. 16. *and* Deut. 22. 28, 29. *wherewith agreeth the* Canon 67. Apoſtol. Quam quis violaverit virginem, ducat in uxorem.

If the two Juſtices cannot agree upon their Order, what is then to be done, ſee *Hic* 7 Jac. 5. *antea, c.* 6. But by ſome Opinions the Words of this Statute being (in the Diſjunctive) if the two Juſtices of the Peace in that Diviſion or Limits cannot agree, then the two Juſtices of Peace next to that Diviſion or Limits, (being in the ſame County, and one of them of the *Quorum*) have Power to take Order therein.

Alſo the Mother may be examined upon Oath concerning the reputed Father, and of the Time and other Circumſtances; for that in this Caſe, the Matter and Trial thereof

K   dependeth

dependeth chiefly upon the Examination and Teſtimony of the Mother.   *Vide Lic cap.* 66. and *Lamb.* 512.

By the Statute 7 *Jac.* it appeareth that the Juſtice of Peace ſhall commit ſuch lewd Woman to the Houſe of Correction, there to be puniſhed, &c. And therefore *quære* if the Juſtices of Peace may puniſh the Mother by corporal Puniſment by force of this Statute of 18 *Eliz. c.* 3. and then ſend them to the Houſe of Correction : For the Rule of Law is, *Nemo debet bis puniri pro uno delicto* ; and the Divine ſaith, *Deus non agit bis in id ipſum.* Co. 4. 43, & 8. 118.

Corporal Pu-
niſment. But ſuch corporal *Puniſment* or Commitment to the Houſe of Correction, is not to be until after the Woman is delivered of her Child, neither are the Juſtices of Peace to meddle with the Woman until the Child be born (and ſhe ſtrong again) leſt the Woman being weak, the Child wherewith ſhe goes happen to miſcarry ; for you ſhall find that about 31 *Eliz.* a Woman great with Child, and ſuſpected for Incontinency, was commanded (by the Maſters of *Bridewell* in *London*) to be whipped there, by Reaſon whereof ſhe travelled, and was delivered of her Child before her Time, &c. And for this the ſaid Maſters of *Bridewell* were in the Star-Chamber fined to the Queen at a great Sum, and were farther ordered to pay a Sum of Money to the ſaid Woman.

And as for the reputed Father, the two Juſtices ſhall do well, (as I conceive) *if he be of Ability, to charge him more deeply ; which if he refuſe, then with Puniſment according* *Ch.* 174. *to the Statute of* 18 Eliz. *See for this Purpoſe an Order in ſuch Caſe here.* ·Chap. 174. *And if the reputed Father be of ſmall Ability, and ſhall not find Friends to yield ſome reaſonable Allowance, then to undergo the more Puniſment.*

Not performing
the Order.
18 Eliz. 3.
P. 1. After ſuch Order by two ſuch Juſtices ſubſcribed under their Hands, if the ſaid Mother or reputed Father, upon Notice thereof, *ſhall not perform the ſaid Order,* then ſuch Perſon ſo making Default ſhall be committed to the Gaol, there to remain without Bail or Mainpriſe ; except ſuch Parties ſhall put in ſufficient Sureties to perform the ſame Order, or elſe perſonally to appear at the next General Seſſions of the Peace in that County, and to abide ſuch Order as the Juſtices of Peace, or more Part of them, then and there ſhall take in that Behalf, (if they ſhall take any) or in Default thereof, then to abide and perform the Order before made.

Note, That according to *Co. Lit.* 123. *Legitimum tempus mulieribus conſtitutum,* is nine Months or forty Weeks ; and that a Child born after that Time was, *Trin.* 18 *Ed.*1. adjudged not to be legitimate ; ſo it ſeems, a Child born above forty Weeks after a Wo-* *A Child born*
nine Months
and twenty man has charged a Man with having had carnal Converſation with her, ſhould not be adjudged the Child of that Man *.

Days after the Death of the Father has been allowed legitimate ; but if the Child is born eleven Months after the Death of the Huſband, and it is proved he could not enjoy his Wife within a Month before his Death, it was adjudged a Baſtard. Vide New Abridg. V. 1. p. 312.

7 Jac. 4. Every lewd Woman who ſhall have a Baſtard which may be chargeable to the Pariſh, the Juſtices of Peace ſhall commit her unto the Houſe of Correction, there to be puniſhed daily, and ſet on Work for one Year, and to live of her own Labour ; and if ſhe ſhall offend again, then to be committed to the Houſe of Correction, as aforeſaid, and there to remain until ſhe can put in good Sureties for her Good Behaviour not to offend ſo again. See *c.* 118.

Now ſuch Commitment to the Houſe of Correction ought to be by *two Juſtices* at the leaſt, (by the Words of this Statute ;) and by comparing theſe two Statutes (of 18 *Eliz.* and 7 *Jac.*) it ſeemeth fitteſt for the two next Juſtices authoriſed by 18 *Eliz.*

Alſo (by the Words of this Statute 7 *Jac.*) ſuch a Woman ſhall not be ſent to the Houſe of Correction till after the Child be born, and that it be living ; for it muſt be ſuch a Child as may be chargeable to the Pariſh.

18 El 3. Alſo a Baſtard Child is not to be ſent with the Mother to the Houſe of Correction, but rather that the Child ſhould remain in the Town where it was born, (or ſettled with the Mother) and there to be relieved by the Work of the Mother, or by Relief from the reputed Father. See to this Purpoſe the Reſolution of the Judges, *Reſol.* 6. in the Title *Rogues.* And yet the common Opinion and Practice is otherwiſe, ſc. to ſend the Child with the Mother to the Houſe of Correction ; and this may alſo ſeem reaſonable where the Child ſucketh the Mother. *Vide plus cap.* 6. *fine, & cap.* 40. *Reſol.* 7. *& Quære.*

A Maid-ſervant gotten with Child, where ſhe ſhall be ſettled. See *Chap.* 40. *& Reſol.* 12, *&* 21.

14 Car. 2.
cap 12. *Putative Fathers and lewd Mothers of Baſtard-Children leaving their Children upon the Pariſh, the Church-wardens and Overſeers for the Poor of the Pariſh where the Child was*

1   *born,*

born, may ſeize and take ſo much of the Goods and Chattels, and of the Rents and Profits of the Lands of ſuch reputed Fathers or Mothers, as ſhall be ordered by two Juſtices of the Peace, for and towards diſcharge of the Pariſh, for providing for ſuch Baſtard; and by Order of the Seſſions may ſell the ſaid Goods, or ſo much thereof as the Court ſhall think fit, and to receive ſo much alſo of the Rents and Profits of the Lands, for the ſaid Purpoſes, as ſhall be ordered by the Seſſions. The Puniſhment of ſuch as ſhall kill their Baſtard-Children, ſee poſtea Tit. Felony by Statute.

And firſt concerning the Order of the two Juſtices.

1. It muſt directly adjudge who is the putative Father.

2. It muſt be made by two Juſtices *Quorum unus.*

3. They muſt reſide next the Place where the Pariſh Church is, and which Pariſh is to be relieved.

4. It muſt be made concerning a Baſtard-Child, and ſo expreſſed, and the Child muſt be adjudged to be chargeable to the Pariſh, (*vide infra*) and it muſt appear how long the Father is to maintain it.

5. The Place of Birth muſt be ſet forth in the Order, becauſe it may be born in a Pariſh where the two Juſtices who made the Order had no juriſdiction, and that it was born in that Pariſh to which Relief is ordered.

6. It muſt be made purſuant to the Act for the Relief of the Pariſh, in Part or in all, and for Relief of the Child by a weekly Maintenance.

Rules concerning the Order.

As to the ſecond Rule abovementioned, the Order is ill, if it doth not appear that one of the Juſtices is of the * *Quorum*; and ſo 'tis if the Money is ordered to be paid till the Child is fourteen Years old, for it ought to be ſo long as 'tis *chargeable to the Pariſh*; and ſo 'tis if the reputed Father ſhould be ordered to give ſuch Security to indemnify the Pariſh as the Overſeers or Church-wardens ſhall think fit, becauſe by ſuch an Order the Juſtices delegate their Authority to another. [Sid. 222. *Salk. 477.]

So it is if the Order is, that *T. S.* ſhall contribute half the Charge, for that he ſuffered a Soldier to get his Servant with Child.

It hath been a Queſtion, whether the Juſtices could order the Payment of a Sum in Groſs by the putative Father. 1 *Vent.* 336. But as to that Matter 'tis now ruled, that they may.

Two Juſtices made an Order, that the putative Father ſhould pay 9 *l.* for the Maintenance of a Baſtard, and adjudged good, for it may be to indemnify the Pariſh from the Charges ſuſtained before the Father was taken; and by the Statute the Juſtices have Power to take order for Payment of Money weekly, for the Relief of the Pariſh, or other *Suſtentation of the Child.* [*Orders good.* 1 Salk. 134.]

Upon a *Certiorari* to remove an Order made by two Juſtices for Keeping a Baſtard-Child, it was moved to quaſh it, for that it was *ad Seſſionem pacis in Com. præd.* and did not ſay *pro Com*', but this was over-ruled; 'tis true, the Objection had been proper to an Indictment, but in Orders there is not ſo much Strictneſs required; then it was objected, that it doth not appear that the Child was likely to *become chargeable to the Pariſh.* [1 Vent. 37.]

But that was ſufficiently ſet out in the Order, for it was for the Father to pay ſuch Charges which the Pariſh had ſuſtained, which ſhews that the Child was chargeable.

The like Objection was made to another Order, but adjudged, that it was ſelf-evident that a Baſtard Child is likely to be chargeable to the Pariſh. [2 Salk. 475.]

An Order to keep a Baſtard-Child was quaſhed, for that it was that *T. S.* ſhould keep his reputed Baſtard-Child, becauſe he had kept it before; but it did not ſet forth, that this Child was his Baſtard. See *poſtea hic.* [*Orders quaſh'd.* Style 134.]

An Order to pay Money *Weekly* to a Pariſh towards Keeping a Baſtard-Child quaſhed, becauſe it did not appear that the Child was *born in that Pariſh* to which the Money was to be paid. [Style 368.]

Upon a *Certiorari* to remove an Order, *&c.* there were two Objections made to it; firſt, becauſe it was, that the putative Father ſhould allow 4 *s.* to the *Midwife*, when it did not appear that ſhe was procured by the Pariſh, or that they paid her: Secondly, For that by the Orders 7 *s. per* Week was allowed for the Nurſing and Clothes, and until it ſhould be able to get its Living by Working, which was both exceſſive in the Sum and incertain in the Time; it ſhould have been for ſo long Time as the Child is chargeable to the Pariſh, and for theſe Reaſons the Order was quaſhed. [1 Vent 212.]

Another

2 Sid. 365.

Another Order was quaſhed, becauſe there was no *Adjudication*, that the Perſon againſt whom the Complaint was made was the reputed Father of the Baſtard.

1 Salk. 121, 468.
1 Mod. 20.
S. P.

Another Order quaſhed, for that it was to pay ſo much Money by the Week till the Child was fourteen Years old, becauſe the Power of the Juſtices extends no farther than to indemnify the Pariſh, and that is only to compel the putative Father to pay ſo much as long as the Child ſhall be chargeable.

2 Sid. 363.

Another Order quaſhed, for that it was the reputed Father ſhould pay 2 *d. per* Week for the Maintenance of the Child, becauſe it was too little ; 'tis true, the Juſtices of Peace have Power to adjudge who is the Father, yet if they are unreaſonable in ordering what Sum he is to pay for the Maintenance of his Child, the Court may judge of that Matter.

Caſes adjudged on Appeals.
1 Bulſt. 341.

The Seſſions muſt either affirm the Order of the two Juſtices, or diſallow it; and if they diſallow it, they may refer it back to the ſame Juſtices (if in the ſame County) to conſider farther of the Proof, for the Matter is then before them as *Res integra*.

1 Sid. 149.

Reſolved, That the Words of the Statute 18 *Eliz. cap.* 3. (*next Quarter-Seſſions*) muſt be intended, that the Order made by the two Juſtices muſt be confirmed or diſcharged at the next Quarter-Seſſions of that *Part* of the County where it was made, and not at the next Seſſions in the County, for that would be miſchievous in many Counties where there are ſeveral Seſſions in diſtinct Parts of the County. See alſo *Slaw's* Caſe in *Carth.* 455.

2 Sid. 325.

An Order was made by two Juſtices, that *T. S.* ſhould pay 8 *l.* for Relief of a Baſtardchild of which he was the reputed Father, and afterwards ſo much every Week; but it appearing that he had no *Notice of this Order*, till the Time of Appeal limited by the Statute was paſt, (which is the next Seſſions after the Order made) the Court made a Rule, that the next Seſſions in *Middleſex* (where the Matter was) ſhould hear it, and make an Order to diſcharge or charge the ſaid *T. S.* and that ſuch Order ſhould be final.

1 Vent. 48.

Two Juſtices made an Order for *T. S.* to keep a Baſtard-child, and upon an Appeal that Order was vacated, and it was referred back to the two Juſtices, who would make no other Order ; but afterwards at the next Seſſions, *B. B.* was adjudged the putative Father, and ordered to pay ſo much *per* Week to the Pariſh-Officers till the Child ſhall be twelve Years old, which Order being removed by *Certiorari*, the Seſſions Order was quaſhed, for that they had no Authority to refer the Matter back to the two Juſtices. *Note,* This is contrary to the Caſe before-mentioned.

1 Salk. 121.
S P.

A Woman big with Child was removed from *Weſtbury* in *Gloceſterſhire* to *Corſham* in *Wiltſhire*, where ſhe was delivered of a Baſtard-child, *Corſham* appealed to the next Seſſions, and there that Order was reverſed, but then the Child was ſent by an Order of two Juſtices to the Pariſh of *Corſham*, becauſe there it was born, when it ſhould be ſent to *Weſtbury* ; but on an Appeal by *Corſham*, that Order was reverſed, becauſe the Birth of a Child under an illegal Order ſhall make no Settlement. *Trin.* 3 *Ann. in B. R.*

Carth. 397.
Cro.Car. 248.

By the Order of two Juſtices, *Pridgeon* was adjudged the putative Father of a Baſtardchild, which Order was diſcharged upon an Appeal to the next Seſſions ; afterwards, at another Quarter-Seſſions the Matter was re-examined, and then he was adjudged the putative Father according to the original Order of the two Juſtices ; and for not giving Security to obey this laſt Seſſions Order, he was committed ; and being brought into Court by *Habeas Corpus*, it was adjudged, that he being diſcharged upon the *Appeal,* according to the Statute 18 *Eliz.* the ſecond Seſſions had no Power to alter what was done by the firſt and next Seſſions after the Order made.

* 18 Eliz. c. 3.
3 Car. 1. c. 4.

It hath been a Queſtion, whether the Seſſions can make an original Order in Caſes of Baſtardy ; 'tis plain by the Statute * 18 *Eliz.* they could not; but by the Statute * 3 *Car.* 1. Power is given to the Juſtices of Peace *within their ſeveral Limits and Precincts, and in their ſeveral Seſſions,* to do and *execute all Things concerning that Part of the Statute touching Baſtards, that by Juſtices of Peace in the ſeveral Counties were by the ſaid Statute limited to be done.*

But this was but a temporary Law, for it was to continue till the next Seſſions of Parliament, which happened *Anno* 16 *Car.* 1. and not before; and that Parliament being diſſolved without any Notice taken of the aforeſaid Statute 3 *Car.* 1. by Conſequence that Statute muſt be expired.

16 Car 1.
cap 4.

Afterwards by another Statute made the very next Year, (*viz.*) *Anno* 16 *Car.* 1. and by another Parliament, it was enacted, that all Statutes which were continued by the Statute 3 *Car.* 1. or were to continue to the End of the firſt Seſſions of the next Parliament, ſhould ever ſince that Seſſion have the ſame Force and Effect as on the *laſt Day of that Seſſion,* and *from thence till ſome farther Act of Parliament* be made about the Continuance or Diſcontinuance of the ſaid Statutes.

Now the Statute 3 *Car.* 1. was to continue *till the End of the firſt Seſſion of the next Parliament*, and that Seſſion being ended without any Notice taken of that Statute, it muſt therefore be expired; but by Virtue of the Statute 16 *Car.* 1. 'tis to have ſuch Force and Effect as it had on the laſt Day of that Seſſion, and *from thence till ſome farther Act of Parliament ſhall continue or diſcontinue the ſame*, which was never yet done by any ſubſequent Act, and by Conſequence that Clauſe in the Statute 3 *Car.* 1. by which the Juſtices in their Seſſions have Power to execute all Matters concerning Baſtard-children, as the two Juſtices might do by the Statute 18 *Eliz.* muſt now be in Force.

But there is no Caſe where it hath been adjudged to be in Force; and as often as this hath been made a Queſtion, the Judges have been doubtful of it; ſo was the Chief Juſtice *Holt, Anno* 4 *Annæ,* in the Caſe of *The Queen* verſus *Weſton*; and the Practiſe all over *England* is for the two Juſtices to make the Order, and not the Quarter-Seſſions, for otherwiſe the Seſſions Order would be final, and the Party deprived of the Benefit of an Appeal. *

* *The Stat. 3 Car. 1. is certainly in Force by 16 Car. 1. c. 4. but for the Reaſon here given the original Order is commonly made by two Juſtices.*

'Tis true, in *Slater's* Caſe it was adjudged, that the Quarter-Seſſions have Power to make original Orders in Caſes of Baſtardy, but that is no Authority that they may do ſo now, becauſe that Caſe was adjudged when the Stat. 3 *Car.* 1. was in Force and not expired; for it was adjudged in *Eaſter Term,* * *Anno* 13 *Car.* 1. The Caſe was thus: The two next Juſtices making no Order where *A. B.* was charged with a Baſtard, the Seſſions, upon Proof that *T. S.* was the putative Father, made an Order to diſcharge *A. B.* and that *T. S.* ſhould pay for the Keeping the Child; afterwards, at the Aſſizes, the Judges ordered that the two next Juſtices where the Child was born ſhould conſider the Matter, who thereupon made an Order that *A. B.* was the putative Father, and that he ſhould pay 18 *l.* to the Overſeers, *&c.* and 14 *s.* weekly, which he refuſed; and thereupon the two Juſtices committed him; and this being removed into *B. R.* by *Certiorari,* it was reſolved, that before the Statute 3 *Car.* 1. the Juſtices in Seſſions had no Authority to meddle in Caſes of Baſtardy, till the two next Juſtices had made an Order according to the Statute 18 *Eliz.* but that by the Statute 3 *Car.* the Juſtices in Seſſions had Power to make original Orders in Caſes of Baſtardy, and therefore the Order made in this Caſe by the Seſſions was good, and the Order made by the two Juſtices void, and could not alter the Seſſions Order. *Cro. Car. 470.*

But before the Reſolution in the laſt Caſe, and likewiſe before the Statute 3 *Car.* 1. was expired, there was a contrary Reſolution in *Eaſter-Term, Anno* 8 *Car.* 1. in the Caſe of *Bowler* verſus *Painter,* (*viz.*) that Juſtices of Peace, nor yet Juſtices of Aſſiſe have Power to meddle in Caſes of Baſtard-Children, upon the Statute 18 *Eliz.* but upon Appeal. *2 Bulſt. 343.*

The ſame Point was adjudged in *Watkyns* and *Edwards's* Caſe; 'tis true, it was not the Point in Queſtion; however, the Judges declared, that the Seſſions could not make an original Order for Keeping a Baſtard-child, but upon an Appeal, and certainly they could never be of that Opinion if it had been clear that the Statute 3 *Car.* was then in Force. *1 Vent. 175.*

Appeal to the Seſſions from an Order of two Juſtices, by which *T. S.* was adjudged to be the putative Father of a Baſtard, and ordered to pay ſo much Weekly to the Overſeers of the Poor, *&c.* and the Seſſions confirmed the Order, and committed *T. S.* for Non-payment of the Money; it was objected, that the Seſſions had no Power to commit, but the Recognizance ought to be put in Suit; but it was held, that they might commit by Virtue of the Statute 3 *Car.* 1. but not by the Statute 18 *Eliz.* if ſo, then that Statute 3 *Car.* is ſtill in Force. *Of the Juſtices Power to commit in Caſes of Baſtardy.* *Salk. 122.*

But there hath been a contrary Reſolution in this very Point; it was an Order made by two Juſtices for the putative Father to pay ſo much *per* Week for ten Years, *&c.* which Order was confirmed upon an Appeal to the Seſſions, and they committed him for not giving Security; it was objected, that the Seſſions had not Power to commit, but that the two Juſtices before they allowed the Appeal, ſhould have taken a Recognizance (as is uſual) to appear at the next Seſſions, and to abide ſuch Order as the Juſtices ſhould make, and for diſobeying ſuch Order, then the Pariſh muſt proceed upon the Recognizance, but the Seſſions cannot commit. 2 *Ann. The Queen* v. *Chaffry.* 12 *Will.* 3. *The King* v. *James.* See 2 *Bulſt.* 341.

The Husband, who was ſettled in the Pariſh of St. *Margaret Weſtminſter,* was divorced *a Menſa & thoro cauſa adulterii,* and afterwards ſhe and the Adulterer went into the Pariſh of St. *George, Southwark,* where ſhe had three Children by him, all chriſtened there, and regiſtred by his Name; but an Order was made by two Juſtices to remove them to the *Who ſhall be Baſtards by our Law. Salk. 123.*

L

the Pariſh of St. *Margaret*, where the Husband was ſettled, for that the Juſtices were of Opinion the Children were born in lawful Wedlock notwithſtanding the Divorce, which Order was confirmed upon an Appeal, the whole Matter being ſpecially ſet forth therein; and both Orders being removed by *Certiorari*; it was inſiſted for the Pariſh of St. *Margaret*, that theſe were Baſtards, and ought to be ſettled where born; but on the other Side it was ſaid, that theſe Children were legitimate, for tho' there was a Divorce *a menſa & thoro*, the Marriage ſtill continues, and the Orders do not ſet forth, that the Husband had no Acceſs to the Wife after the Divorce, and therefore where he is *infra quatuor maria*, an Acceſs ſhall be preſumed; but the Court held that theſe Children were Baſtards, and

‣ Becauſe the Court will intend a due Obedience to the Sentence of Divorce, unleſs the contrary appear. that * Acceſs ſhall not be preſumed; but it muſt be proved on the other Side to make them legitimate; but one begotten and born after a voluntary Separation ſhall not be a Baſtard.

5 Mod. 419.
Carth. 470.   Upon a Special Order of Seſſions, the Queſtion was, if the Husband was beyond Sea during the whole Time the Wife went with Child, whether this Child will be a Baſtard by the Statute 18 *Eliz. cap.* 3. and adjudged that it will; but the Order was quaſhed, becauſe it did not appear that the Husband was abſent all that Time, it being in the Disjunctive, that he was not here *at the Begetting or Birth of the Child*, for if he was here at either of thoſe Times, 'tis ſufficient.

Seiſure of the putative Father's Goods.   By the Statute 13 & 14 *Car.* 2. *c.* 12. *ſect.* 19. the Pariſh-Officers where a Baſtard is born, may ſeize ſo much of the Goods, and receive ſo much of the Rents of the Lands of the putative Father and Mother as ſhall be ordered by two Juſtices, which Order muſt be confirmed at the Seſſions, and this is to diſcharge the Pariſh. And it ſhall be lawful for the Seſſions to make an Order for the Church-wardens or Overſeers to diſpoſe of the Goods, as the Court ſhall think fit.

Where the Child is to be ſettled.
2 Bulſt. 350.   A Baſtard was born in the Pariſh of *C.* ten Years paſt, and *T. S.* the putative Father took the Child from the Mother, and placed it out at Nurſe, and then married and cohabited with his Wife in the Pariſh of *B.* and thither he brought the Child, where he maintained it for ſeveral Years, and died, leaving ſeveral Children by his ſaid Wife; adjudged, that this Baſtard-child is to be ſent to his Mother, if ſhe be of Ability, but if not, then 'tis to be ſent to the Pariſh of *B.* becauſe there it was ſettled with the putative Father.

5 Mod. 204.
1 Salk. 121,
532. S. P.   An Order to remove *A. B.* late of the Pariſh of *C.* ſingle Woman, and *W. B.* her Son, from the Pariſh of *L.* to the Pariſh of *M.* for that by Fraud of the Pariſh of *L.* ſhe was delivered of the ſaid *W. B.* her Baſtard-Son in the ſaid Pariſh of *M.* and it was inſiſted, that where a Baſtard is born, there 'tis ſettled, unleſs ſome other Settlement appears; now this Baſtard was born in the Pariſh of *M.* therefore it ought to be ſettled there; and it did not appear by the Order, that the Mother was ſettled in *L.* 'tis true, 'tis ſaid *that* A. B. *late of L. ſingle Woman*, but that is only a Deſcription of her Perſon and an Allegation of the Place, and it doth not prove that ſhe was legally ſettled there.

An Order was made by two Juſtices many Years ſince, that the Pariſh of *B.* where a Baſtard-child was born, ſhould maintain the ſaid Child, which Order being removed by *Certiorari*; it was adjudged, that an Order made upon the Overſeers of the Poor of a Pariſh for raiſing Money towards the Maintenance of a Baſtard or poor Perſon, doth not determine the Settlement to be in that Pariſh, becauſe the Right of Settlement is not conteſted, but preſumed.

By an Order of two Juſtices, *Glegg* was adjudged the putative Father of three Baſtard-Children, and he was ordered to pay 10 *l.* to the Overſeers of the Poor, &c. for the Charges that the Pariſh had ſuſtained by Reaſon of the ſaid Children, and 2 *s.* 6 *d. per* Week for ſo long Time as they or either of them ſhould be chargeable to the Pariſh, which Order was confirmed on an Appeal; and both the Orders being removed into *B. R.* by *Certiorari*, it was objected againſt the original Order.

(1.) That it did not appear that *Glegg* was duly ſummoned to appear before the Juſtices; 'tis true, the Order ſet forth that he had Notice to appear, but not for what Cauſe.

(2.) By the Order the Father was charged to pay 10 *l.* whereas the Juſtices have not Power to charge him with a Sum in Groſs.

(3.) He was charged by one Order to be the Father of three Baſtard-Child, when there ſhould be as many Orders as there were Baſtards.

The Court was of Opinion, that if the Defendant was not duly ſummoned to appear, and for what Cauſe, the Order ought to be quaſhed; but as to the ſecond Objection, a putative Father may be charged with a Sum in Groſs, tho' this is ſeemingly againſt the Statute 18 *Eliz. cap.* 3. by which the two Juſtices have Power to charge the Mother or reputed

puted

puted Father with the Payment of *Money Weekly*; but by the same Statute they have likewife Power *to take Order for the Relief of the Parish,* which muft be intended Relief againft that Charge which it hath fuftained, as well as againft the Charge which it may fuftain.

As to the third Objection, the Court gave no Judgment, but that the Parifh fhould have Time to fhew Caufe whether the Defendant was duly fummoned. *Mich.* 1721. *&c.* 4. B. R. *The King verfus Glegg.* Cafes in Law,

By the Stat. 6 *Geo.* 2. *cap.* 31. if a fingle Woman be delivered of a Baftard, likely to become chargeable to any Parifh, or fhall declare herfelf with Child, and that fuch Child is likely to be born a Baftard, and to be chargeable to any Parifh, and fhall in an Examination to be taken in Writing upon Oath before one Juftice of Peace, charge any Perfon with having got her with Child; it fhall be lawful for fuch Juftice, upon Application by the Overfeers of the Poor of fuch Parifh, or by any fubftantial Houfeholder of an extra-parochial Place, to iffue his Warrant for apprehending fuch Perfon fo charged, and for bringing him before any of his Majefty's Juftices of Peace of fuch County; and the Juftice before whom fuch Perfon fhall be brought, is required to commit him to the common Gaol or Houfe of Correction, unlefs he give Security to indemnify fuch Parifh, or fhall enter into a Recognizance with fufficient Surety, to appear at the next Quarter-Seffions, and to perform fuch Order as fhall be made in Purfuance of 18 *Eliz. cap.* 3. 6 G. 2. c. 33.
fect. 1.

If the Woman die or be married before fhe be delivered, or mifcarries, fuch Perfon fhall be difcharged. Ib. §. 2.

Upon Application of the Perfon committed to any Juftice, fuch Juftice is to fummon the Overfeers to fhew Caufe why fuch Perfon fhould not be difcharged; and if no Order be made within fix Weeks after the Woman's Delivery, fuch Juftice fhall difcharge him. Ib §. 3.

It fhall not be lawful for any Juftice to fend for any Woman till one Month after her Delivery, in order to her being examined concerning her Pregnancy. Ib. §. 4.

C H A P. XII.

Bailment.

BY the Common Law, the Sheriff and every Conftable (being Confervators of the Peace) might have bailed one fufpected of Felony: But this Authority is taken from them, and given to the Juftices of Peace, by the Statutes following. Lamb. 15.

Firft, By the Statute 1 *R.* 3. *cap.* 3. every Juftice of Peace had Authority (*by Difcretion*) to let to Bail Perfons imprifoned for Sufpicion of Felony, *&c.*

But becaufe after the Making that Statute, divers not being bailable were notwithftanding let to Bail, and fo many Felons efcaped; therefore this Statute was repealed by the Statute of 3 *H.* 7. and thereby any two Juftices of Peace (the one being of the *Quorum*) were enabled to let any Prifoners (mainpernable by the Law) to Bail, to the next General Seffions of the Peace or Gaol-delivery, as the Cafe fhould require. After, for that one Juftice of Peace, in the Name of himfelf and of one other of his Fellow-Juftices, (not making the other Juftice privy unto the Caufe, whereof the Prifoner fhould be bailed) did oftentimes by finifter Means fet at large great Offenders, fuch as were not bailable, and yet, to hide their Affection therein, did fignify the Caufe of their Apprehenfion to be but only for Sufpicion of Felony, whereby the faid Offenders have efcaped unpunifhed; for Reformation thereof, by the Statute 1 *& 2 P. & M.* it was enacted, That if it be for Manflaughter or Felony, or Sufpicion of Manflaughter or Felony, (*being bailable by Law,*) then the fame Juftices muft be prefent together at the Time of the faid Bailment; and that they muft certify (in Writing fubfcribed with their own Hands) the faid Bailment at the next General Gaol-delivery, to be holden within the County where the Perfon fhall be arrefted or fufpected, upon Pain to be fined by the Juftices of Gaol-delivery. 3 H. 7. c. 3.
Fitz. N. B.
251. F.
Two Juftices.

1 & 2 P. & M.
c. 3. P. Juft.
107.

Now by the Preamble of both the laft recited Statutes, the Mifchief feemeth to be the Efcape of Felons; and therefore if it be not in Cafe of Felony, any one Juftice of Peace alone may bail a Prifoner, (fee the Titles *Affray, Dying,* and *Surety for the Peace*) except where fome particular Statute fhall otherwife prefcribe, as *in titulo Counterfeitors.* See more of *Bailment hic poftea, cap.* 166. One Juftice.

Sheriffs, Under-Sheriffs, Coroners, Stewards, Bailiffs, Keepers of Prifons, and other Officers, fhall let out of Prifon all Perfons by them arrefted, or being in their Cuftody by One Juftice.
23 H. 6. 10.

Force

Force of any Writ, Bill or Warrant in any Action perfonal, or by Caufe of any Indictment of Trefpafs, upon reafonable Sureties of fufficient Perfons within that County to keep their Day, as fuch Writs, Bills or Warrants require; except Perfons arrefted by Cap. Utlagat. *or Excommunication or Surety of the Peace, or committed to Ward by fpecial Command of any Juftices, or Vagabonds, or fhall pay the Party treble Damages and forfeit forty Pounds, a Moiety to the King, the other to the Profecutor, and the Juftices of the Peace have Power to hear and determine.*

Refolved by all the Judges, and agreed to be put in Execution in all Circuits, that where a Felon is examined by a Juftice, and it appears he is not bailable by Law, and that the Juftice commits him on Sufpicion of Felony, not mentioning any other Caufe, and afterwards he is bailed by two Juftices, for that no Caufe was fet forth in the Warrant of Commitment, why he fhould not be bailed; thofe Juftices ought to be fined by the Statute 1 & 2 *Ph. & Mar. cap.* 13. becaufe they offend if they bail him who by the Statute of *Weftm.* 1. *cap.* 15. is not bailable by Law. *Poph.* 96.

A Man was committed for Forging an Endorfement on a Bank-Bill, and he was bailed, for this is only a Mifdemeanor, but Forging the Bill itfelf is Felony. 1 *Salk.* 104.

See more on this Head, Chap. 166. Part 2.

CHAP. XIII.

Bankrupt.

5 Geo. 2. c. 30.

BY Stat. 5 *Geo.* 2. *c.* 30. *feft.* 1. If any Bankrupt fhall not within forty-two Days after Notice in writing left at the ufual Place of Abode of fuch Perfon, or perfonal Notice in cafe he be in Prifon, and Notice in the *London Gazette,* furrender himfelf to the Commiffioners, and fubfcribe fuch Surrender, and fubmit to be examined, and difcover all his Effects, and how he hath difpofed of them, and all Books and Writings relating thereto; and alfo deliver to the Commiffioners all fuch Effects in his Power, with his Books, &c. (neceffary wearing Apparel of himfelf, Wife and Children, excepted): Then the Bankrupt in cafe of not furrendring, &c. as aforefaid, or in cafe of Concealment or Imbezilment to the Value of 20 *l.* or any Books of Account, &c. with Intent to defraud his Creditors, and being convicted, fhall be deemed guilty of Felony without Benefit of Clergy; and fuch Felon's Goods and Eftate fhall go among the Creditors feeking Relief under the Commiffion.

Sect. 3.

Every fuch Bankrupt, after Affignees fhall be appointed, is to deliver upon Oath or Affirmation before one of the Mafters in Chancery, or Juftice of Peace, unto fuch Affignees all his Books of Accounts and Writings, not feifed by the Meffenger of the Commiffion, or not before delivered up to the Commiffioners, then in his Power, and difcover fuch as are in the Power of any other Perfon that may concern his Eftate; and every fuch Bankrupt not in Prifon fhall after fuch Surrender be at Liberty, and is required to attend fuch Affignees upon Notice in Writing, in order to affift the making out the Accounts of the Eftate.

Sect. 14.

Upon Certificate under the Hands and Seals of the Commiffioners that fuch Commiffion is iffued, and fuch Perfon proved a Bankrupt, it fhall be lawful for any of the Juftices of his Majefty's Courts, &c. and the Juftices of Peace, and they are required, upon Application made, to grant their Warrants for apprehending fuch Perfon, and commit him to the common Gaol of the County where apprehended, to remain till removed by Order of the Commiffioners.

CHAP. XIV.

Blafphemy.

BY Stat. 9 & 10 *W.* 3. *c.* 32. *feft.* 1. If any Perfon having been educated in, or having made Profeffion of the Chriftian Religion within this Realm, fhall by Writing, Printing, Teaching, or advifed Speaking, deny any One of the Perfons of the

     Holy

Holy Trinity to be God, or affert that there are more Gods than One, or fhall deny the Chriftian Religion to be true, or the Holy Scriptures to be of divine Authority, and fhall be convicted by Indictment, &c. upon the Oath of two Witneffes, fuch Perfon fhall be incapable to enjoy any Office, and being a fecond Time convicted fhall be difabled to fue in Law or Equity, or be Guardian, Executor, &c. and fhall fuffer three Years Imprifonment, without Bail.

No Perfon fhall be profecuted by Virtue of this Act for Words fpoken, unlefs the Information be given upon Oath before fome Juftice of Peace within four Days, and the Profecution be within three Months after fuch Information. *Sect. 2.*

Perfons convicted of any of the faid Crimes fhall for the firft Offence, upon renouncing fuch erroneous Opinions in the Court where convicted, within four Months after Conviction, be difcharged from all Penalties and Difabilities. *Sect. 3.*

C H A P. XV.

Brewers and Bakers.   See alfo Chap. XXXVIII.
Excife.

A Baker that obferveth not the Affife of Bread, fhall be put into the Pillory, and fhall not be redeemed thence for Silver or Gold.   31 *H. 1. cap. 7.*

A Brewer that breaks the Affife of Ale or Beer, fhall for the firft and fecond Offence be amerced, and for the third Offence put in the Pillory without Redemption. 31 *H. 1. cap. 7.*

There is a good Law made 23 *H.* 8. *c.* 4. that no Brewer fhall be a Cooper, and for fetting the Prices: But the Juftices of Peace have nothing to do therein, as is refolved *Cro.* 4 *Car.* 1. *p.* 112. as to fuing for the Penalties; but Juftices of Peace out of Corporations, and in them the Mayor and fecond Officers may affefs the Price of Ale and Beer.

See the Penalty of a Brewer felling Beer to an unlicenfed Alehoufe, *Tit. Alehoufe,* & 1 *Jac.* 18.

A Brewer that brews Beer with corrupt Hops, or mix'd with Powder, Duft, or other Soil, forfeits the Value of the Hops.   1 *Jac.* 18.

By the Stat. 8 *Annæ, c.* 18. one Juftice of Peace may iffue out his Warrant to levy 40 *s.* by Diftrefs and Sale of the Goods of any Baker or other who bakes or expofeth to Sale any Bread, not obferving the Affife, or which is under Weight, or not duly marked, or who breaks fuch Regulations and Orders as from Time to Time fhall be made by the Juftices. *This Claufe is repealed by Stat.* 1 G. 1. *c.* 26. fect. 5. *See hic poftea.*

The Profecution muft be within three Days after the Offence committed, and the Conviction may be by Confeffion of the Party, or the Oath of one Witnefs, and muft be certified to the Quarter-Seffions, to which there lies an *Appeal* from fuch Conviction, and what the Seffions order fhall be *final.*

He who bakes or fells any Bread, and puts any Mixture into it of any Grain than what fhall be appointed by the Affife, fhall forfeit 20 *s.* to be recovered as aforefaid; and any Magiftrate neglecting his Duty in the Execution of this Act, forfeits 10 *s.* to be recovered in the Courts at *Weftminfter.*

Any Juftice of the Peace may in the Day-time enter the Houfe, Shop or Stall, or Out-houfe of any Baker, and weigh and try the Bread there; and if 'tis defective either in Goodnefs, Weight, or Baking, he may feife it and give it to the Poor; and every Baker or other refifting or oppofing fuch Search, forfeits 40 *s.* to be recovered by Diftrefs and Sale of Goods, &c. to the Informer.

Perfons profecuted for acting in Purfuance of this Statute, may plead the General Iffue, and give the fpecial Matter in Evidence; and if the Plaintiff is nonfuit or caft in the Action, he fhall pay double Cofts.

By the Statute 1 *Geo.* 1. *c.* 26. *fect.* 5. 'tis enacted, that the Claufe in the Statute 8 *Annæ,* which gave the Penalty of 40 *s.* for Bread not being Weight or not marked (and for no other Thing) fhall be repealed; and that if any Baker make Bread wanting an Ounce Weight, or more, he forfeits 5 *s.* for every Ounce, and if lefs than Ounce is wanting, then he forfeits 2 *s.* 6 *d.* being weighed before a Magiftrate, or any Perfon appointed by him, within twenty-four Hours, if within the Bills of Mortality, and *1 Geo. 1. c. 26. §. 5.*

M   within

within three Days in any other Part of *England*; the said Forfeitures to the Informer, and to be recovered by Distress and Sale, &c.

Every Baker may make Peck, Half-peck, Quartern and Half-quartern Loaves, so as the same be made and sold both as to Weight and Measure in Proportion to the Assise-Table in the Act 8 *Annæ*.

And when the Bread shall be altered according to the Powers in that Act, the Price of Grain, Meal and Flower in the next Markets adjacent, where such Assise shall be set, shall be certified upon Oath before the chief Magistrate or Justices respectively, by the Clerks of the Markets, or such other Persons as the Magistrate shall appoint ; and the Assise within the Bills of Mortality (*Westminster*, *Southwark*, and within the Weekly Bills in *Surrey* excepted) shall be set by the Lord Mayor and Aldermen of *London*, &c.

The Statute 8 *Annæ*, with what Alterations are made by this Act, are, by the Statute
12 Geo. 2.
c. 13. 12 *Geo.* 2. *c.* 13. continued to the 24th *June* 1748. and to the End of the then next Session of Parliament.

3 Geo.2.c.29. By Statute 3 *Geo.* 2. *c.* 29. *sect.* 2. Any Person selling Bread at an higher Price than shall be set by the Court of the Lord Mayor and Aldermen of *London*, or the Mayor, &c. of any other City or Burrough, or by two Justices of Peace where there shall be no such Mayor, shall forfeit 10 *s.* to the Informer, to be levied by Distress and Sale of Goods.

C H A P. XVI.

Bridges.

Four Justices.
22 H. 8. 5.
P. 2, 3, 4. WHERE a decayed Bridge is, and that it cannot be proved who nor what Lands be chargeable to the Repairing thereof, four Justices of Peace (whereof one to be of the *Quorum*) within the Shire or Riding wherein such decayed Bridge is, (out of Cities and Towns Corporate ; and if it be within a City or Town Corporate, then four such Justices of Peace there) may within the Limits of their several Commissions call before them the Constables, or two of the most honest Inhabitants of every Town and Parish within the Shire, Riding, City or Town Corporate, wherein such Bridge or any Person thereof shall happen to be; and the said Justices (upon the Appearance of such Constables or other Inhabitants, and with their Assent) may tax every Inhabitant in any such City, Town, or Parish (within their Limits) to such reasonable Sum of Money as by their Discretions they shall think convenient, as well for the Repairing of such Bridge, as also for the Making and Repairing of any Highways lying next adjoining to the End of any such Bridge within this Realm, distant from either of the Ends of the Bridge by the Space of three Hundred Foot.

Taxes.
P. 2. After such Taxation made, the said Justices of Peace shall cause the Names and Surnames of every particular Person, so by them taxed, to be written in a Roll indented.

Collectors.
P. 3. Also the said Justices shall make two Collectors of every Hundred, for the Collecting of all such Sums of Money, by the said Justices set and taxed ; which Collectors receiving the one Part of the said Roll indented under the Seals of the said Justices, shall have Power thereby to collect all the particular Sums of Money therein contained, and to distrain such as shall refuse to pay the same, and to sell such Distress, delivering to the Owner the *Overplus* of the Money, if there be any.

P. 4. Also the said Justices shall appoint two Surveyors, which shall see such decayed Bridges and Ways repaired and amended from Time to Time, as often as need shall require; to whose Hand the said Collectors shall pay the said Sums of Money by them received.

Ibid. The said Collectors and Surveyors, and their Executors and Administrators, and every of them, shall from Time to Time make a true Account to the said Justices of Peace of the Receipts, Payments and Expences of the said Sums of Money ; and if any of them refuse so to do, then the said Justices of Peace from Time to Time (by their Discretions) may make out Process against the said Collectors and Surveyors, their Executors and Administrators, by Attachments, Precept, or Warrant, under their Seals, returnable at their General Sessions of the Peace.

Ibid. Also the said four Justices of Peace may allow such reasonable Costs and Charges to the said Surveyors and Collectors, as by their Discretions they shall think convenient.

If

If any fuch Bridge fhall lie wholly in a City or other Corporate Town, the Inhabi- P. 1.
tants of the Shire or Riding fhall not be charged therewith, but fuch Bridge fhall be *Who fhall be*
made and repaired by the Inhabitants of fuch City or Town Corporate. *charged.*

If any fuch Bridge be without a City or Town Corporate, the fame fhall be made and *Ibid.*
repaired by the Inhabitants of the Shire or Riding within which the fame Bridge fhall be.

If Part of any fuch, Bridge be in one Shire, Riding, City or Corporate Town, and *Ibid.*
Part in another, then every of them fhall be charged to make and repair fuch Parts as
fhall lie and be within their Limits, &c.

But otherwife no Village or Freemen fhall be compelled to make any Bridge, but fuch Magna Char-
as of old Time, and by Right, they had wont to make, and that they and their Anceftors ta. 15. P.
have ufed Time out of Mind to make the fame, or that they hold certain Lands to make Tit. Wears 1.
the fame: For though a Man of his own accord hath made or amended a Bridge, yet 41 E. 3. 31.
fhall he not be thereto conftrained at another Time; and yet if a Man and his Anceftors, 21 E. 4. 46.
or a Corporation, &c. have Time out of Mind ufed to do fuch Things, although they
did it of their own free Mind and Accord, and not of Right, nor have any Land by Reafon whereof they may be tied, yet fuch Continuance fhall conclude them and their
Heirs or Succeffors.   And fo of Highways, 21 Ed. 4. 46.

*Alfo there is a Writ in the Regifter directed to the Sheriff, willing him to caufe
fuch to whom it belongeth, to repair a Bridge, or repair Highways,* &c. Reg. Orig.
fol. 153, 154.

Where a Man and his Anceftors or Predeceffors have ufed Time out of Mind to repair
a Bridge, the King cannot acquit or difcharge them thereof. *Fitz. Grants* 94.

Where it is prefented that *J. S. ratione tenuræ fuæ* hath ufed to repair fuch a Bridge,
this implieth a Prefcription.   21 E. 4. 38. *Crom.* 176.

But a Prefentment that *J. S.* and his Anceftors have ufed to repair fuch a Bridge, *Prefcription.*
this is no good Prefcription to charge the Heir (by the Act of his Anceftor) without any
Profit to be taken therefore.   27 Aff. 8. *Cromp.* 187.   *See the next Cafe but one.*

Otherwife it is of a Corporation Spiritual or Temporal: They by Reafon of Ufage
Time out of Mind, &c. may be charged at this Day to repair a Bridge, although they
have no Land by Reafon whereof to be charged, for that fuch a Body never dies.
Ibidem.

Alfo where a Man hath once repaired a Bridge, and that afterwards the fame was not
repaired within the Memory of Man, by fome Opinions, he or they which have his
Eftate in Land, fhall be bound to repair the Bridge; for that it fhall be fuppofed to have
been done at the firft, by Reafon or Caufe of his Tenancy, except fome other particular
Caufe of the Doing thereof fhall be proved: But where the Caufe fhall appear, there *cef-
fante caufa, ceffabit effectus.*

He that hath his Land adjoining to fuch a Bridge, is not chargeable to make or repair B. Bridges 1.
the Bridge, except where they have made it by Prefcription.   8 H. 7. fol. 5. b.

By common Right, Bridges fhall be amended by the whole County, for 'tis for their Cro. 186. b.
common Good and Eafe; and yet if any have Fifhings or other Profit in that River, & 137. b.
they in Reafon and * Law are chargeable; and therefore the Juftices of Peace may tax * 37 Aff. pl.
fuch proportionably to their Profit. 10. per Gran

Where Men are charged by their Tenure or Lands, every Owner or Occupier of fuch
Lands are to be charged proportionably to their faid Lands.   *Vide* Tit. *Sewers*, and *Fitz.*
N. Br. 235. B.

Such as are chargeable to Repair a Bridge, may enter upon any other Man's Lands or Co. 11. 32.
Soil adjoining, and may lay their Stone, Lime, Timber, or other Things neceffary for
the Repairing and Amending thereof, and the Owner of the Lands fhall have no Action
therefore; for it is for the common Profit, &c. 43 Aff. 37. *Fitz. Affize* 353.

Where one is chargeable to Repair a Bridge, he muft alfo maintain the Way at each
End thereof, (though the Soil be to another;) and if the Ends be broken by the Water-
Courfe, he muft follow the Water-Courfe, and repair the Way, &c. *Crompt.* 186. b.

If a Man maketh a Bridge for Eafement to his Mill, and that decayeth, the Party Co. 187.
nor any other fhall be charged to repair this; for it is no common Paffage.   *Fitz.*
Bar. 276.

Defects of Repair of Bridges fhall be prefented in the County only where they lie,
and no Prefentment nor Information fhall be removed before Traverfe and Judgment
thereupon.   22 *Car.* 2. fect. 4.

Where Lands are given to the Maintenance of Bridges, the Feoffees and Truftees fhall *Ufu.*
let the fame at the moft improved Rent without Fine; if fuch Truftees make Default,
the

the Juftices of Peace in their open Seffions may inquire of the Value thereof, and may order the Improvement and Imployment thereof, except Lands given to any College or Hall in the Univerfities, which have Vifitors. *22 Car. 2. fect. 2.*

Ann. St. 1. By the Statute 1 *Ann. Stat.* 1. *cap.* 18. *fect.* 1. all Claufes in the Act 22 *H.* 8. are con-
.18. firmed, which are not altered by that Act.

And for the more eafy Taxing, and better applying the Money to be raifed for Repair-ing decayed Bridges, it is enacted, *Sect.* 2. That the Quarter-Seffions upon Prefentment that any Bridge is out of Repair, fhall make an Affeffment upon every Parifh or Place with-in their Limits, in fuch Proportions as they have been formerly affeffed; and the Money fhall be levied by the refpective Conftables of each Parifh, or by other Perfons as the Ju-ftices fhall direct; and fhall be paid by the Conftables, &c. to the High Conftable within fix Days after 'tis received, and the High Conftable within ten Days after fhall pay the fame to the Treafurer appointed by the Seffions to receive it; which Money fhall be applied and accounted for as the Seffions fhall direct, which Affeffment fhall be levied by Diftrefs and Sale of Goods, if not paid within ten Days after Demand.

Every High Conftable, Church-warden, Overfeer, Petty Conftable, or other Perfon, neglecting to affefs, collect, or to pay the Money as before directed, fhall forfeit 40 *s.* and the Treafurer paying Money without Order of the Seffions forfeits 5 *l.* for every Offence.

All Fines and Penalties incurred for not Repairing Bridges, fhall be paid to the Trea-furer, and applied towards the Repairs of the Bridges, and fhall not be returned into the Exchequer.

Matter concerning Repairs of Bridges, fhall be determined only in thofe Counties where they lie, and no Prefentment or Indictment fhall be removed by *Certiorari* out of the County into any other Court.

The Seffions may allow any Perfon concerned in the Execution of this Act, any Sum not exceeding 3 *d. per* Pound.

Thofe who are fued for acting in Purfuance of this Statute, or of that of 22 *H.* 8. *c.* 5. may plead the General Iffue, and give the faid Acts in Evidence, and if the Plaintiff is Nonfuit, &c. he fhall pay double Cofts; and this Act fhall not difcharge particular Per-fons Eftates and Places from Repairing fuch Bridges as heretofore they did repair.

And where an Indictment or Information is brought againft any particular Perfon, Body Corporate or Politick, for not Repairing, &c. the Inhabitants of the Town, Cor-poration, County, Riding, or Divifion, where the Bridges lie, fhall be admitted to give Evidence at the Trial, &c.

And laftly, by this new Act the Statute 23 *Eliz.* for Rebuilding *Cardiff Bridge* is re-pealed, and that for ever hereafter that Bridge fhall be reputed a common Bridge; and repaired by the County of *Glamorgan.*

And that the Wardens and Affiftants of *Rochefter* Bridge, fhall be chofen every Year on the *Friday* in the Week next after *Eafter Week.*

Before the Making this Statute, the Courfe was to charge every Hundred with a Sum-mons in Grofs, and to fend it to the High Conftable of each Hundred, who fend their Warrants to the Petty Conftables to collect the Money, by Virtue of which Warrant they affefs the Inhabitants in particular Sums, and then they collect it and pay it to the High Conftables, who bring it to the Seffions.

But becaufe this Way of Taxing was illegal, and becaufe in many Places more Money was levied than was really neceffary for Repairing, and alfo becaufe the Money when le-vied was mifimployed, therefore by this Statute 1 *Annæ* thefe Matters were remedied, and the Manner of levying it is thus:

The Headborough muft demand it of the Party, and if not paid within ten Days after Demand, he may levy it by Diftrefs and Sale of Goods, rendring the Overplus, the ne-ceffary Charges of diftraining being deducted.

And if any Officer neglect to affefs, collect, or pay the Money, he forfeits 40 *s.* for every Offence.

See the Statute 11 *Geo.* 1. *cap.* 10. For the Power is given to Juftices of the Peace with-in the Eaft Riding of *York,* in relation to the Rebuilding of *Stamford Bridge* over the *Darwent* in the Road from *York* to *Burlington.* As to the Statute 12 *Geo.* 1. *c.* 36. and 1 *Geo.* 2. *Stat.* 2. *c.* 18. in relation to *Fulham Bridge;* and Statute 9 *Geo.* 2. *c.* 29. 10 *Geo.* 2. *c.* 16. 11 *Geo.* 2. *c.* 25. about *Weftminfter Bridge.* See *Chap.* 160. *Of Felony by Statute.*

I The

The Juſtices of Peace in any County, City, &c. at their general Seſſions, or general 14 Geo. 2. Quarter-Seſſions, or the major Part, may purchaſe or agree with any Perſons or Bodies c. 33. Politick, for any Piece of Land joining, or near any County Bridge within their ſeveral Limits, for inlarging, or more convenient Rebuilding the ſame; which Pieces of Land ſhall not exceed one Acre in the Whole for any ſuch Bridge, and ſhall be paid for out of the Money raiſed by Virtue of an Act made 12 *Geo.* 2. *c.* 29. intitled, *An Act for the more eaſy Aſſeſſing, Collecting, and Levying of County Rates* * ; the Treaſurers being * *See* Chap. authoriſed by Orders under the Hands and Seals of Juſtices at their General or Quarter- 196. *infra.* Seſſions; which Lands ſhall be conveyed to ſuch Perſons as the ſaid Juſtices ſhall appoint in Truſt, for Inlarging or Rebuilding ſuch Bridges.

CHAP. XVII.

Buggery.

THIS is an Offence committed by one Man with another againſt the Order of Nature, or by a Man with a Beaſt; 'tis made Felony without Benefit of Clergy; by the Statute 25 *H.* 8. *cap.* 6. See the Form of the Indictment in *Nelſon's* Juſtice. Tit. *Buggery.*

See this Article treated of in 1 *Hawk. P. C. ch.* 4. 3 *Inſt. fol.* 58. and 12 *Co. fol.* 36.

Burglary. See *cap.* 151. and *Felony,* cap. 40.

CHAP. XVIII.

Burials.

NO Perſon ſhall be buried in any Shirt, Shift, or Sheet, made of, or mingled with 18 Car. 2. Flax, Hemp, Silk, Hair, Gold or Silver, or any other, but ſuch as ſhall be made c. 4. of Wool only, or be put into any Coffin lined or faced with Flax, Hemp, Silk or Hair, upon Pain to forfeit 5 *l.* to the Poor, for raiſing a Stock to ſet them on Work, to be levied by the Church-wardens and Overſeers, or any of them, by Warrant from any Juſtice of Peace, Mayor, Alderman, or Head Officer, by Diſtreſs and Sale of the Goods of the Party interred, or in Default thereof, of the Goods of any having a Hand in putting the Party thereinto. 18 *Car.* 2. *cap.* 4.

But the ſaid Statute of 18 *Car.* 2. proving ineffectual, the ſame was repealed by the 30 Car. 2. Statute of 30 *Car.* 2. *cap.* 3. *ſect.* 3. whereby it is enacted, That no Corps ſhall be bu- c. 3. ried in any Shirt, Shift, Sheet or Shroud, or any Thing whatſoever made or mingled with Flax, Hemp, Silk, Hair, Gold or Silver, or in any Stuff or Thing, other than what is made of Sheep's Wool only, or be put into any Coffin lined or faced with any ſort of Cloth, Stuff, or other Thing that is made of any Material but Sheep's Wool only, upon Pain to forfeit five Pounds. *Forfeiture.*

Sect. 4 & 5. An *Affidavit* under the Hands and Seals of two Witneſſes (and under *Affidavit.* the Hand of the Magiſtrate or Officer before whom it was ſworn, for which nothing ſhall be paid) muſt be brought to the Miniſter within eight Days after the Party is interred, that he was not buried contrary to the ſaid Act of 30 *Car.* 2. which ſhall be taken before ſome Juſtice of Peace, Maſter of Chancery, Ordinary or Extraordinary, Mayor, Bailiff, or other chief Officer of the City, County, Borough, &c. where the Party was buried: And if no ſuch *Affidavit* be brought, the Miniſter ſhall give Notice thereof under his Hand to the Church-wardens or Overſeers of the Poor, who within eight Days after ſhall repair to the chief Magiſtrate in any Town, &c. if buried there, elſe to a Juſtice of Peace, who upon Certificate thereof from the Miniſter, &c. ſhall grant a Warrant for levying the Forfeiture by Diſtreſs and Sale of the Goods of the Party deceaſed; *Forfeiture* or in Default thereof, of the Perſon's Goods in whoſe Houſe the Party died, or the *levied.* Goods of any that had a Hand in putting ſuch Party into any Shroud, Coffin, &c. contrary to the ſaid Act, or that ordered the ſame: And if ſuch Perſon was a Servant and died in his Maſter's Family, the Maſter's Goods to be liable; and if ſuch Perſon died in his

Parents

Forfeiture levied.   Parents Family, the Parents Goods to be liable; one Moiety of which Forfeiture shall be to the Poor of the Parish where the Party is buried, the other to him that will sue for the same.

Forfeiture by Justices of Peace, &c.   Sect. 6. Ministers, Church-wardens, and Overseers, Justices of Peace or chief Magistrates neglecting their Duty aforesaid, shall forfeit five Pounds for every Offence, to be recovered by Action of Debt, Bill, Plaint, &c. wherein the Prosecutor shall recover his full Costs, so as the Suit be commenced within six Months after the Offence committed; one fourth Part of the Forfeitures to the King; two fourth Parts to the Poor of the Parish where the Offender dwells, and one fourth Part to the Informer.

Register.   Sect. 7. Every Minister shall keep a Register of all Burials and Affidavits, and where no Affidavit is brought as aforesaid, shall enter a Memorial thereof against the Name of the Party interred, and of the Time when he notified the same to the Church-wardens or Overseers of the Poor.

Overseers Accounts.   Sect. 8. And the Overseers, when they give up their Accounts at the Sessions, or to any two Justices at their Monthly Meetings, shall give an Account of the Name and Quality of every Person interred since their former Account; and of such Certificates, and of their levying the Penalties, and of their Disposal thereof, on Pain of 5 l. to be levied by Distress and Sale of Goods, by Warrant from the said Justices or two of them: And their Accounts shall not be allowed till they have accounted for the Burials.

Plague.   Sect. 9. No Penalty shall be incurred where the Party died of the Plague.

Sect. 10. Judges at their Assises, and Justices of Peace at their Quarter-Sessions, shall give this Act in Charge.

Sect. 11. Persons prosecuted for what they shall do in pursuance of this Act may plead the General Issue, Not Guilty; and if the Prosecutor be Nonsuit, &c. the Defendant shall have treble Costs.

Affidavit.
32 Car. 2. c. 1.   And now by the Statute of 32 Car. 2. cap. 1. sect. 3. where no Justice of Peace shall reside, or be to be found in any Parish where any Party shall be interred, such Oaths or Affidavits may be administer'd by any Parson, Vicar or Curate in the same County, other than of the Parish or Chapel of Ease where the Party is interred, and they are to attest the same under their Hands *Gratis.*

Bullion.

6 & 7 Wil. 3. c. 17.   BY the Statute 6 & 7 *Will.* 3. *cap.* 17. *sect.* 8. It shall be lawful for the Warden of Goldsmiths, with two of the Court of Assistants, within the Bills of Mortality, and for any two Justices without the Bills, to enter the House, Room, &c. of any Person suspected of Buying and Selling unlawful Bullion, to search; and in Case the Occupier shall refuse to permit such Search, such Justices, &c. with a Constable, may break open any Door, Box, &c. in order to search for such Bullion: And in case they find any, they are to seize as well the Bullion as the Persons in whose Possession the same is found, who shall be brought before a Justice within the Bills of Mortality, and before two Justices without, to be examined upon Oath, Whether the Bullion was lawful, and not the current Coin of this Realm; and in case the Person shall not prove by his Oath, or by the Oath of one Witness, that the Bullion is lawful, the said Justice or Justices shall commit such Person to Prison, and shall secure the Bullion, and shall oblige the Persons that can give Evidence concerning the Sums, to enter into a Recognizance to prosecute the said Offender; and in case he shall not upon his Trial, on an Indictment, prove by the Oath of one Witness, the Bullion so found to be lawful, such Offender shall be found guilty, and suffer Imprisonment for six Months.

C H A P. XIX.

Butchers.

Ordinance for Butchers, incerti temporis, c. 7.   A Butcher that sells Swines Flesh measled, or any Flesh that dies of the Murrain, shall be fined the first Time; and for the second Offence put into the Pillory; and the third Time be imprisoned and make Fine; and the fourth Time forswear the Town.

Butchers forfeit 12 *d.* for every Ox, and 8 *d.* for every Cow or other Beaft, by them 4 H. 7. c. 3. flain in any wall'd Town, except *Berwick* and *Carlifle.*

A Butcher that flits or cuts an Ox-hide, or any Hide, forfeits 20 *d.* He that fells a pu- 1 Jac. 1. c. 22. trified Hide, or fhall water any Hide, except in *June, July* and *Auguft,* forfeits 3 *s.* 4 *d.* by 1 *Jac.* 1. *cap.* 22. *fect.* 2.

The Penalty for killing or felling Victuals on the Sabbath-day, *vide* Tit. *Sabbath.*

He that buys fat Oxen, *&c.* and fells them again alive, forfeits every Ox, *&c.* fo 3 & 4 Ed. 6. bought. 3 *& 4 Ed.* 6. *cap.* 19. *fect.* 3. c. 19.

No Perfon ufing the Trade of a Butcher, fhall fell any fat Oxen, Steers, Runts, Kine, 1 Car. 2. c. 8. Heifers, Calves, Sheep, or Lambs alive, on Pain to forfeit double the Value of the Cattle, fect. 2. one Moiety to the King, the other to him that will fue.

By the Statute 5 *Annæ, cap.* 34. *fect.* 2. no Butcher in *London* or *Weftminfter,* or within 5 Ann. c. 34. ten Miles thereof, fhall fell or expofe to Sale any fat Cattle or Sheep, alive or dead, to fect. 2. any other Butcher, on Pain of forfeiting the Value; one Moiety to the Crown, and the other to the Informer with full Cofts,

But by the Statute 7 *& 8 Annæ,* 'tis declared that the faid Claufe fhall not extend to 7 & 8 Ann. the Selling of Calves, Sheep, or Lambs dead, by one Butcher to another. c. 6.

By the Statute 9 *Annæ,* 'tis enacted that the raw Hide of any Ox, Bull, Steer, or 9 Ann. c. 11. Cow, or the Skin of any Calf, fhall wilfully or negligently be gafhed, or cut in Fleaing, fect. 11. or being gafhed or cut fhall be expofed to Sale by any Perfon ; he who cut or gafhed it, or offered fuch Hide to Sale, fhall forfeit 2 *s.* 6 *d.* for every Hide, and one Shilling for every gafhed Calf's Skin; one Moiety to the Poor of the Parifh where the fame fhall be found, and the other to the Informer. Such Offences to be heard and determined by two Sect. 37. neighbouring Juftices, refiding near the Place where the Forfeitures fhall be incurred, which Juftices may upon Complaint made within three Months after the Seifure or Offence done, fummon the Party accufed and the Witneffes, and, upon his Appearing or Con- tempt to appear (upon Proof of Notice given) may examine the Witneffes on Oath, and give Sentence accordingly ; and upon Conviction, may iffue a Warrant to levy the Penalty on the Goods of the Offender by Diftrefs and Sale thereof; if not redeemed within fix Days, the Party grieved may appeal to the Seffions, who may fummon and examine the Witneffes on Oath, and finally determine, and in Cafe of Conviction may iffue Warrants to levy the Penalty.

C H A P. XX.

Butter and Cheefe.

BY Stat. 9 *Hen.* 6. *cap.* 8. A Weigh of Cheefe fhall contain thirty-two Cloves, and each 9 H. 6. c. 8. Clove feven Pounds.

By Stat. 3 *& 4 Edw.* 6. *cap.* 21. *fect.* 1. None except Innholders or Victuallers are to buy 3 & 4 Ed. 6. Butter or Cheefe to fell again, except by Retail in open Shop, Fair or Market, and not c. 21. above a Weigh of Cheefe or Barrel of Butter at one Time, on Pain to forfeit double the Value, one Moiety to the King, and the other to him that will fue.

By Stat. 21 *Jac.* 1. *cap.* 22. *fect.* 6. the Act of 3 *& 4 Edw.* 6. *cap.* 21. nor any other Law 21 Jac. 1. concerning the Sale of Butter and Cheefe in open Shop, Fair and Market, fhall extend to c. 22. Cheefemongers or Tallowchandlers free of the City of *London,* and having been brought up as Apprentices feven Years, trading in Butter and Cheefe, for fuch Butter and Cheefe as they fhall fell in *London, Southwark* or *Weftminfter,* for the victualling of Ships of his Majefty or his Subjects, or to Butter or Cheefe which they fhall fell at one Time to one Perfon, not exceeding four Weigh of Cheefe, or four Barrels of Butter, fo as they fell the fame in open Shop, *&c.*

Provided that if the Juftices of Peace of any County fhall declare in open Seffions, that Sect. 7. the Traders in Butter and Cheefe fhall forbear to buy Butter or Cheefe for any Time with- in the fame County, that then during the faid Reftraint the faid Traders fhall not be freed from the Penalties of the faid Acts.

The Kilderkin muft contain 112 *l.* neat, of fixteen Ounces to the Pound, befides the 14 Car. 2. Cafk ; every Firkin fifty-fix Pounds, befides the Cafk ; every Pot of Butter fourteen c. 26. fect. 2. Pounds neat, befides the Pot.

Mixtures.   No old or corrupt Butter fhall be mixed with new or found Butter, nor Whey-Butter mixed with Cream-Butter, but each Sort by it felf; and every Cask or Pot fhall be of the fame, good throughout. No Butter fhall be falted with great, but with fmall Salt; nor more Salt mixed than is neceffary, upon Pain for every Offence in Quantity or Quality, the Value of the Butter fo falfe packed; and where the Kilderkin, Firkin, or Pot, is not of Meafure, fix Times the Value of every Pound wanting.

Sect. 3.   Every Perfon felling Veffels of Butter, fhall deliver the Quantities aforefaid, or elfe make Satisfaction to the Buyer according to the Price it was fold for.

Packing.
Sect. 4.   Every Perfon repacking any Butter to fell the fame again, fhall for every Cask or Pot fo repacked, forfeit the double Value thereof.

Casks.
Sect. 5.   Every Perfon packing Butter in Casks, fhall put it into good Casks, of dry, found and well feafoned Timber; and fhall put upon the fame a Mark of the juft Weight thereof, and when filled, put thereon the firft Letter of his Chriftian Name, and his Surname at Length, with an Iron-brand, upon Pain for not fetting the Weight or Name 10 *s.* for each C. Weight, and fo proportionably.

Marks.
Sect. 6.   Every Potter fhall fet the Weight of the Pot when burnt, and the firft Letter of his Chriftian Name, and his Surname thereon, or forfeit twelve Pence for every Pot fold for packing of Butter. No Perfon fhall pack any Butter in any Pot, but fuch as is fo marked, upon Pain to forfeit 2 *s.* for every Pot. And the faid Offences fhall be determined at the Seffions of the Peace or Court of Record of the City, &c. where committed, by Action of Debt or Prefentment, one Moiety of the Forfeitures to the Poor, the other to the Informer, befides his double Cofts.

Sect. 7.   Every Suit or Information fhall be within four Months after Sale of fuch Butter.

4 & 5 W. &
M.c.7. fect. 2.   By the Statute 4 & 5 *W. & M. c. 7. fect.* 2. after the Factor or Buyer of Butter hath bought and contracted for the fame, and approved thereof at the Place of Sale, by fearching and weighing the fame, if he thinks fit, the Seller fhall not afterwards be liable to any Penalties of the forefaid Act of 14 *Car.* 2. upon any Pretence of Want of Weight, or falfe packing, or mouldy Butter, or the Tare and Weight not being fet on the Cask.

Sect. 3.   After the Factor or Buyer hath approved the Butter, he fhall fet his Seal or Mark upon the faid Butter. And if the fame fhall afterwards be exchanged or opened, and the Cask wherein the fame is put be changed, or bad Butter packt up and mixed with good, or any Fraud be committed by the Seller, the Offender being convicted upon Oath, before one or more Juftices of the Peace, or upon his own Confeffion, fhall forfeit 20 *s.* to

Penalty on ex-
changing But-
ter, &c.   be levied by Diftrefs, &c. reftoring the Overplus. And Conftables of Parifhes, &c. are hereby authorized to levy the fame accordingly by Warrant under Hand and Seal of the faid Juftice or Juftices.

Sect. 4.   *Warehouse-keepers, Weighers, Searchers,* or *Shippers* of Butter and Cheefe in any Port, refufing to receive the fame, or to take Care thereof, or to fhip the fame fucceffively, as it fhall come to their Hands, without undue preferring one Man's Goods before another's, being convicted thereof as before mentioned, fhall forfeit 10 *s.* for every Firkin of Butter, and 5 *s.* for every Weigh of Cheefe, to be levied by Diftrefs and Sale, &c.

Sect. 5.   *Warehouse-keeper,* not keeping Books, and making Entries of Butter and Cheefe, or making undue Entries, (by undue preferring one Man's Goods before another's) or refufing in the Day-time to produce the Books to be infpected, fhall forfeit 2 *s.* 6 *d.* for every Firkin of Butter, and every Weigh of Cheefe, and the like for every other Offence, to be levied by Diftrefs and Sale as aforefaid, and for Want of Diftrefs, to be committed till paid.

Sect. 6.   *Masters of Vessels,* coming to lade Butter or Cheefe, or their Servants refufing to take on board any Butter or Cheefe as fhall be tendred to be fhipped by any Warehoufe-Man before their Veffels are loaded, fhall forfeit 5 *s.* for every Firkin of Butter, and 2 *s.* 6 *d.* for every Weigh of Cheefe, to be levied as before, &c.

Sect. 7.   Half of all the Penalties within this Act fhall be to the Ufe of the Poor of the Parifh where fuch Offence fhall be committed, the other Half to the Informer.

Sect. 9.   This Act doth not extend to the Counties of *Chefter* and *Lancafter,* nor to the County of the City of *Chefter.*

Sect. 10.   Perfons aggrieved may appeal to the next Quarter-Seffions; the Appellant entring into a Bond of 20 *l.* with one or more Sureties, to the Liking of the Juftice of Peace, to pay fuch Cofts as the Court fhall award, within one Month after the Appeal is heard, and he not relieved: The Determination of the Seffions fhall be final.

See the 8 *Geo.* 1. *c.* 27. for the better preventing Abufes committed in weighing and packing of Butter in the City of *York.*

2   By

By Stat. 32 *Car.* 2. *cap.* 2. *sect.* 9. No Butter or Cheese shall be imported for Sale from *Ireland*, under the like Penalties as Importation of Bacon, Beef or Pork.

Buttons and Button-holes.

BY the Statute 14 *Car.* 2. the Importing and Exporting of Buttons made of Hair, Silk, or Thread, is prohibited, and they who sell or expose such imported Buttons to Sale, forfeit 50 *l.* for every Offence. ^{13 & 14 C. 2. c. 13.}

The Importer forfeits 100 *l.* besides the Buttons; one Moiety of these Forfeitures to the Crown, the other to the Informer.

Justices may issue out Warrants to seise foreign Buttons.

By 4 & 5 *W.* 3. *cap.* 10. *sect.* 2. The Importation of all foreign Buttons is prohibited under the like Penalties. ^{4 & 5 W. 3. c. 10.}

Selling or setting on Clothes any Buttons made of *Cloth, Serge, Drugget, Frize, Camlet,* or other Stuffs of which wearing Garments are usually made; the Forfeiture is 40 *s.* for every Dozen of Buttons or Button-holes, to be divided as aforesaid, and to be recovered by Action of Debt, or upon a Complaint to two Justices, who are to summon and examine the Witnesses on Oath, and levy the Penalty, returning the Overplus. ^{10 W. 3. c. 2.}

By 8 *Ann. cap.* 6. The Penalty is 5 *l.* for every Dozen of Buttons or Button-holes; and two Justices by Warrant may levy the Penalty, upon Conviction of the Offenders by one Witness; but the Party aggrieved may appeal to the next Quarter-Sessions, and shall have Costs. ^{8 Ann. c. 6.}

And in order to make this Act more effectual, 'tis enacted by a subsequent Statute 4 *Geo.* 1. *cap.* 7. that no Buttons or Button-holes made of Cloth, *&c.* shall be made or set on wearing Apparel, the Forfeiture is 40 *s.* for every Dozen, and so in Proportion for a less Number; one Moiety to the Informer, the other to the Poor of the Place, after the Charges of the Conviction are deducted; and if not paid within fourteen Days after Demand, then the Justice may issue his Warrant to distrain, and if no Distress can be found, then to commit the Offender for three Months to Labour. But nothing in this Act shall extend to Clothes made of Velvet. ^{4 Geo. 1. c. 7.}

The Prosecution must be within three Months after the Offence committed or discovered.

Conviction must be by one Justice not concerned in the Matter, and on the Oath of one Witness; but the Party may appeal to the next Quarter-Sessions, and shall have Costs, *&c.*

But if the Prosecution is at Law, the Defendant may plead the General Issue, and give the Act in Evidence, and if he recover, shall have treble Costs.

All wearing Apparel with Buttons or Button-holes made of the same Cloth, Serge, *&c.* and exposed to Sale, shall be forfeited, and applied to the Uses aforesaid.

Any Taylor or other Person causing his Servant to make Clothes contrary to this Act shall be subject to the like Forfeitures and Penalties.

This shall be taken for a publick Act.

Every Person who shall wear or use Clothes with Buttons or Button-holes made of, or bound with Cloth, Serge, *&c.* shall forfeit 40 *s.* for every Dozen, and so in Proportion for a less Quantity. ^{7 Geo. 1. c. 12.}

One Justice of Peace upon the Oath of one Witness may convict the Offender, and grant his Warrant to levy the Penalty by Distress, *&c.* one Moiety to the Informer, the other to the Poor.

Persons aggrieved may appeal to the next Quarter-Sessions, giving eight Days Notice, and their Judgment shall be final.

Offences against this Act must be prosecuted within one Month. And Persons sued may plead the General Issue, and on a Verdict, *&c.* shall recover treble Costs.

This Act shall not extend to Clothes made of Velvet.

Cards and Dice.

BY the Statute 3 *Ed.* 4. playing Cards and Dice are prohibited to be imported from beyond Sea, on Pain of Forfeiture of one Moiety to the Crown, and the other to the Person seising. ^{3 Ed. 4. c. 4.}

The aforesaid Act, so far as it relates to the prohibiting the Importation of Cards and Dice, is revived, and declared to stand in Force in every Part of *Great Britain.* ^{10 Ann. c. 19. §. 167.}

9 Ann. c. 23.
§. 41.
All Makers of Cards and Dice, before they begin to make them, fhall fend Notice in Writing of the Place where they intend to make the fame, to the Commiffioners of the Stamp-Duties, or their Officers next adjoining, and the like Notice fhall be given as often as they change the Places of making them; and as often as any Perfon fhall fet up the Trade of making Cards or Dice, he fhall give the like Notice, on Pain of 50 *l.*

6 G. 1. c. 21.
§. 59.
One Juftice of Peace may take the Affidavit of any Perfon, declaring his Knowledge or Sufpicion, that playing Cards or Dice are caufed to be made in any Place, without Notice thereof in Writing given to the Commiffioners of the Stamp-Duties at their head Office.

And after fuch Affidavit made he may iffue out his Warrant directed to an Officer of the Duties on Cards or Dice, giving him Power in the Day-time, and in the Prefence of a Conftable, to break open any Door where the Cards or Dice are fufpected to be made or making, and to feife all fuch Cards, Dice, Tools and Materials for making the fame, and to detain and keep the fame in fuch Houfe or Place as the Commiffioners fhall think fit; all which are forfeited, unlefs claimed and replevied by the Owner within five Days after the Seifure, and to be fold by the Direction of the Commiffioners, one Moiety of the Money arifing by fuch Sale to the King, and the other to the Informer.

CHAP. XXI.

Carriages, Coaches, Chairs and Carts.

3 & 4 W. 3.
c. 12.
The Act of 13
Car. 2. c. 8.
for providing
Carriages for
his Majefty,
and the Act of
13 & 14 Car. 2.
c. 20. *for pro-*
viding Carriages by Land and Water for the Ufe of his Majefty's Navy and Ordnance, revived 1 Jac. 2. *and continued by* 11 & 12 W. 3.
from 29 Sept. 1700 *for feven Years; as alfo the Act of* 1 Jac. 2. c. 10. *inferted in the laft Edition of this Book in* 1727 *are expired.*

BY the Stat. 3 & 4 *W.* 3. *cap.* 12. *fect.* 24. The Juftices of Peace of every County, *&c.* are required, at their Quarter-Seffions after *Eafter* yearly, to affefs the Prices of Land-Carriage of Goods to be brought into any Place within their Jurifdictions, by any common Carrier; and the Rates to certify to the Mayors and other chief Officers of the Market-Towns, to be hung up in fome publick Place. And no common Carrier fhall take above the Rates, upon Pain of 5 *l.* to be levied by Diftrefs, *&c.* by Warrant of any two Juftices where fuch Carrier fhall refide, to the Ufe of the Party grieved.

6 & 7 W. 3.
c. 16. §. 3.
By the Stat. 6 & 7 *Will.* 3. *cap.* 16. *fect.* 3. The Juftices of Peace of *Wilts, Gloucefter, Oxford, Berks* and *Bucks,* or any five of them, in their Quarter-Seffions next after *Eafter* yearly, are required to affefs the Prices of Carriage of Goods from any Place in their Counties, to any other Place upon the *Thames* and *Ifis* in Boats, and fhall give Notice thereof in Writing to the Mayor or head Officer in every Market-Town within their Counties: And if any Owner of any Barge fhall take above the Prices fet, he fhall forfeit 5 *l.* to the Party grieved, with double Cofts.

This *Act* is continued by the 13 Geo. 2. cap. 18. *till the* 1 June 1747.

6 Ann. c. 29.
§. 3.
By the Statute of 6 *Ann. cap.* 29. *fect.* 3. No travelling Waggon or Carriage wherein any Goods fhall be carried (except about Husbandry, Manuring of Land, carrying Hay, Straw, or Corn, Coal, Chalk, Timber, Materials for Building, Stones or Artillery) fhall go in the Highways, or be drawn with more than fix Horfes, Oxen, or Beafts, upon Pain that the Owner of fuch Waggon fhall forfeit for every Offence 5 *l.* one Moiety to the Surveyor of the Highways of the Place where the Offence was done, to be employed in Repairing the fame, the other Moiety to the Difcoverer or Profecutor, fo as he be an Inhabitant of the Town, Village, or Place.

This Penalty is to be levied by Diftrefs of the Horfes or Oxen of the Owner of the Waggon, by a Warrant under the Hand and Seal of one Juftice; and if not paid within five Days after the Diftraining, then to fell the Diftrefs, rendring the Overplus, after Charges deducted.

9 Ann. c. 18.
By the Statute 9 *Annæ,* any Perfon may difcover and profecute another drawing with more than fix Horfes, contrary to the Statute 6 *Annæ,* and may feife or diftrain all or any of the Horfes, and deliver the fame to the Surveyors of the Highways, or other Officer of the Place where the Offence was done; and if the 5 *l.* is not paid within three Days, then the Diftrefs is to be fold, and the Money delivered to the Juftice to be diftributed as by the faid Statute 6 *Annæ* is directed.

2

The

The Perfon *feifing*, &c. and neglecting to deliver the Cattle to the Surveyor, &c. or to other Parifh-Officers, forfeits 20 *l.* to be levied by Diftrefs and Sale, &c. by a Warrant of one Juftice ; and if no Diftrefs can be had, then to be committed to the common Gaol till paid : One Moiety to the Informer, the other to be laid out for Repairing the Highway. _{9 Ann. c. 18.}

Any Perfon employed by a Carrier, or another, and fubject to the Penalties of that Act, and driving or affifting to drive any travelling Waggon or Cart, with more than fix Horfes, forfeits 5 *l.* to be levied and difpofed as before, &c.

When the Horfes allowed fhall not be fufficient to draw the Waggon, &c. up any fteep Hill, or out of any foul Place, Horfes from another Waggon travelling that Road may be added, with the Confent of the Driver, to help up fuch fteep Hill, &c. _{Ib. §. 4.}

By the Statute 1 *Geo.* 1. *cap.* 11. *fect.* 2. The Exception in the 6 *Ann. cap.* 29. or in any other Acts, fhall not extend to the Carriage of threfhed Corn or Coal. _{1 G. 1. c. 11. §. 2.}

By the Statute 5 *Geo.* 1. *cap.* 12. 'tis enacted, that no travelling Waggon for Hire fhall be drawn with more than fix Horfes at length, in Pairs or fideways, nor a Cart with more than three Horfes, on Forfeiture of all the Horfes above Six in a Waggon, and all above Three in a Cart, with all Geers, Bridles, Halters and Accoutrements, to the fole Ufe and Benefit of any Perfon who fhall feife the fame. _{5 G. 1. c. 12. §. 1.}

The Perfon feifing, &c. muft deliver the Horfes, &c. to fome Conftable or Parifh-Officer next the Place where the Scifure was made, who is to receive and keep them till the *Seifor* fhall prove the Offence on Oath before a Juftice, &c. and then the Juftice is to make a Precept directed to fuch Parifh-Officer, to deliver the Horfes to the Seifor, paying reafonable Charges, fuch as the Juftice fhall appoint for Keeping the fame. _{Ib. §. 2.}

He who with Force, or otherwife, attempts to hinder the Seifing and Carrying away, &c. or fhall refcue the fame, or ufe any Violence to the Seifor, fhall be committed by one Juftice to the common Gaol for three Months without Bail, and fhall likewife forfeit 10 *l.* to be levied by Diftrefs and Sale, &c. by a Warrant of one Juftice ; and if not paid within three Days after the Diftrefs taken, then the Perfon feifing may fell the Diftrefs, rendring the Overplus, the Charge of Diftraining and Selling being deducted. _{Ib. §. 4.}

No travelling Waggon for Hire, having the Wheels bound with Streaks of a lefs Breadth than two Inches and an half when worn, or being fet on with rofe-headed Nails, fhall be drawn with more than three Horfes. _{Ib. §. 3.}

This Act doth not extend to Waggons, Wains, Carts or Carriages employed in Hufbandry, nor to carrying of Cheefe, Butter, Hay, Straw, Corn unthrefhed, Coals, Chalk, or any one Tree or Piece of Timber, or any one Stone or Block of Marble, nor to Caravans, and the covered Carriages of Noblemen and Gentlemen for their private Ufe, or fuch Timber, Ammunition or Artillery, as fhall be for his Majefty's Service. _{5 G. 1. c. 12. §. 5.}

By the Statute 6 *Geo.* 1. *cap.* 6. he who carries at one Load in the Cities of *London* or *Weftminfter*, or within ten Miles thereof, in Waggons or Carts having their Wheels bound round with Tire of Iron, more than twelve Sacks of Meal, each Sack containing five Bufhels and no more, or any more than twelve Quarters of Malt, or more than 700 and an half of Bricks, or more than one Chalder of Coals, forfeits one of the Horfes, together with the Geers, Bridles, &c. to any Perfon who fhall feife the fame in fuch Manner, and to fuch Ufes, as in the Stat. 5 *Geo.* 1. *cap.* 12. the Penalties and Forfeitures are to be levied and applied. _{6 G. 1. c. 6.}

See alfo Tit. *Highways*, chap. 50.

The Crown may nominate Commiffioners under the Great Seal for licenfing Hackney Coaches and Chairs. _{9 Ann. c. 23. Made perpetual by 3 G. 1.}

The Commiffioners may make By-Laws to bind the Perfons who have Licences, and annex Penalties for the better putting in Execution of this Act, and for the good Government of the Perfons licenfed. Thefe By-Laws fhall be approved of by the Lord Chancellor, the two Chief Juftices and Chief Baron, or any three of them, and then printed ; and the Breach of fuch By-Laws fhall be punifhable by any Juftice of Peace, Mayor or head Officer, where the Offence fhall be committed. _{c. 7. §. 1. Ib. §. 16, 17.}

One Moiety of the Penalties belong to the Crown, the other to the Informer. _{Ib. §. 13.}

That Part of the Penalties which belongs to the Crown, fhall be tranfmitted to the Receiver General of the Revenues of Hackney Coaches, and certified to the Commiffioners within ten Days after levied, upon Forfeiture of double the Sum, two Thirds to the Crown, and one Third to the Informer. _{Ib. §. 18.}

If

§. 13.
If any one refuse to pay a Coachman or Chairman his juft Hire, or fhall cut or break any Coach or Chair wilfully, a Juftice of Peace may grant a Warrant againft the Offender, and upon Proof on Oath award Satisfaction; and upon Refufal to make Satisfaction may bind him over to the next Seffions, which fhall finally determine; and for Non-payment levy by Diftrefs.

Ib. §. 49.
A Coachman or Chairman demanding more than his Fare, or giving abufive Language, being convicted by the Oath of one Witnefs before the Commiffioners, or one Juftice for *London, Weftminfter, Middlefex,* or *Surrey,* fhall forfeit not exceeding 20 s. to the Poor; and if not able to pay fhall be fent to the Houfe of Correction for feven Days.

Ib. §. 8.
Hackney Coachmen or Chairmen exacting more than their Fare (for which fee the Act) or refufing to go at that Rate forfeit 40 s. but by 1 *Geo.* 1. *cap.* 57. *fect.* 2. he fhall forfeit a Sum not exceeding 3 l. nor lefs than 10 s.

1 Geo 1. c. 57. §. 2.

Ib. §. 3, 4.
See alfo this Statute of 1 *Geo.* 1. *cap.* 57. *fect.* 3 & 4. about Coaches and Hearfes attending Funerals without Licenfe, which is a Forfeiture of 5 l.

Ib. §. 7.
Every Juftice of Peace of the faid Cities and Counties, may inflict and levy the like Penalties for any Offences contrary to this Act, as the Commiffioners may; provided no Perfon be punifhed Twice for the fame Offence.

Ib. §. 8.
By this Act alfo, If any Perfon driving any Cart, Dray or Waggon, in the Streets of *London* and *Weftminfter, Southwark,* and other Streets and Lanes within the Bills of Mortality, fhall ride upon fuch Cart, &c. not having fome other Perfon on foot to guide the fame, fuch Offender being convicted before the Alderman of the Ward, or a Juftice of Peace, by Oath of one Witnefs, fhall forfeit 10 s. to be levied by Diftrefs, &c. one Moiety to the Informer, the other to the Poor; and in Default of Payment to be fent to the Houfe of Correction for three Days.

C H A P. XXII.

Cattle.

Selling live Cattle.
5 E. 6. c. 4. §. 9.
NO Perfon fhall buy any Oxen, Ronts, Steers, Kine, Heifers, Calves, Sheep, Lambs, Goats, or Kids alive, and fell the fame again, unlefs he keep the fame five Weeks in his own Grounds; or where he hath Herbage by Grant or Prefcription, upon Pain to lofe double the Value of the Cattle; one Moiety to the King, the other to the Informer.

Drovers.
5 E. 6. 14. §. 15.
Drovers licenfed in Writing by three Juftices of Peace (*Quorum unus*) may buy Cattle and fell them again in Fairs and Markets, at reafonable Prices, diftant from the Place where bought, forty Miles at leaft. So that fuch Cattle be not bought by Foreftalling;

Ib. §. 17.
And provided, That fuch Licenfe of Juftices of Peace fhall not endure above one Year.

See the Statute 2 & 3 *Ph. & M. cap.* 3. & 7 *Jac.* 1. *cap.* 8. in *Chap.* 69. of Pafture Land. As to the Statute 18 *Car.* 2. *cap.* 2. 20 *Car.* 2. *cap.* 7. 32 *Car.* 2. *cap.* 2. See Chap. 100. *Tranfportation,* &c.

Certiorari. See *cap.* 195.

Challenge to Jurors. See *cap.* 186.

C H A P. XXIII.

Churches and Church-yards.

Uniting.
17 C. 2. c. 3.
THE Bifhop of the Diocefe, where two Parifhes lie in a Corporation, with the Confent of the Mayor, Aldermen, and Juftices of Peace, Bailiff or Bailiffs, or other chief Officers, or the major Part of them and the Patrons, may by due Order of Law, unite the two Churches or Chapels, and may appoint where God's Worfhip fhall be performed; and to that the Parifhioners fhall refort, and pay their Tithes.

If any fhall ftrike another in a Church or Church-yard, or draw a Weapon in a *Striking.* Church or Church-yard, with an Intent to ftrike; and being thereof convicted by Verdict, or Confeffion, or Oath of two, Witneffes, before (amongft others) the Juftices of *5,6, E.6. c 4.* Peace in their Seffions, fhall be adjudged to have one of his Ears cut .off; and having no Ears, then fhall be burned in the Cheek with an hot Iron, having the Letter *F.*

But an Indictment alone with an Outlawry upon it, is not fuch a Conviction as to in- *Conviction.* flict the corporal Punifhment required by this Act. *Crom. 15. b.*
Dy. 275. q.

A Man takes up a Stone in a Church-yard, and offers to throw at another; or, having a Hatchet or Ax in his Hand, offers to ftrike another; this is not within *5 E. 6.* By two Juftices; for thefe are not fuch Weapons as are drawn, as a Sword and Dagger.

An Indictment at the Seffions for Striking with a Weapon in the Church-yard was removed into *B. R.* and moved, that the Defendant might be admitted to a Fine, but it was denied, becaufe the Statute appoints Lofs of an Ear as well as a Fine. *Palm.* 344.

By the Statute 1 *Eliz.* all Perfons above the Age of fixteen Years muft repair to their 1 Eliz. c. 2. Parifh-Church, Chapel, or to fome Place where the Common Prayer is ufed, and abide there foberly during the Time of Service; the Forfeiture is 12 *d.* for every Offence, to be levied by the Church-wardens, for the Ufe of the Poor of the Parifh; and the Party may likewife be punifhed by Ecclefiaftical Cenfures, having no reafonable Excufe to be abfent.

By the Statute 23 *Eliz.* Perfons not coming to Church, according as appointed by the 23 Eliz. c. 1. Statute 1 *Eliz.* fhall forfeit 20 *l. per* Month, and if he forbear for twelve Months, after *By Stat.* 1 W. 3. a Certificate thereof made by the Ordinary into *B. R.* then one Juftice of the County *c. 18.* where the Party dwells, may bind him with two Sureties in 200 *l.* to be of the Good *This Act is not* Behaviour till he come to Church; the * Informer is to have the third Part of the *Proteftant* Forfeiture.
Diffenters.
* *The other two*

Thirds to the Crown, one to its own Ufe, the other to the Poor; Conviction muft be at Quarter-Seffions.

By the Statute of 3 *Jac.* 1. a Perfon not coming to fome Church or Chapel, forfeits 3 Jac. 1. c. 4. 12 *d.* to the Poor, to be levied by Diftrefs and Sale of Goods, and in Default of Diftrefs *§. 27.* to be committed; the Profecution muft be within a Month, and the Conviction may be *By Stat.* 1 W. 3. made by Confeffion, or Oath of one Witnefs. *This Act is not to extend to*

He who keeps any Servant in his Houfe, or other Perfon not coming to Church for *Proteftant* one Month together, forfeits 10 *l. per* Month. *Diffenters.*

No Woman fhall be charged with any Penalty by this Act, for fuch Offence which *Ib. §. 40.* fhall happen during her Marriage.

See 1 *Hawk. P. C. cap.* 10, and 11. *Of Offences of not coming to Church, and of fuffering others to be abfent from Church.*

The Defendant was indicted on the Statute 5 *Ed.* 6. for Striking in St. *Paul*'s *Church-* *Striking.* *yard;* it was objected, that it being the Church-yard of a Cathedral, it was not within the Statute; but adjudged to the contrary. *Cro. Eliz.* 234. *Dethick*'s Cafe.

Indictment for Drawing his Dagger in a Church againft *T. S.* not fetting forth, that it was with an Intent to ftrike him, for which Caufe it was adjudged void. 2 *Leon.* 188. *Perchall*'s Cafe. *Cro. Car.* 464. *Cholmley*'s Cafe. S. P.

Any Buildings erected on any Part of St. *Paul*'s *Church-yard, London,* except a Place for 1 Ann. Stat. 2. the Meeting of the Chapter, and for keeping Stores for Repairs of the Church, fhall be *c. 12. §. 4.* deemed common Nufances.

Claufes are commonly inferted in the feveral Acts of Parliament for making Provifions for the Rectors of New Churches, which Claufes give certain Powers to Juftices of Peace -in relation to the Affeffments to be made for that Purpofe, for which fee the feveral Acts in the *Statutes at large.*

Clerk of the Peace.

THE *Cuftos Rotulorum* is to nominate the Clerk of the Peace, who for his Mifmanage- *Clerk of the* ment may be fufpended or difcharged by the Juftices of Peace; and if the *Cuftos* *Peace.* *Rotulorum* refufe or neglect to put in another, the Juftices may nominate one at their ge- 1 W. & M. neral Quarter-Seffions. *c. 21.*

The *Cuftos Rotulorum* is to be appointed as directed by a Statute made in the 37th of *Ibid.* *H.* 8. *cap.* 1. And the *Cuftos Rotulorum,* or other Perfon to whom of Right it doth belong, fhall from Time to Time nominate the Clerk of the Peace.

Clerk of the Peace mifdemeaning himfelf in his Office, the Juftices of Peace in their *Ibid.* general Quarter-Seffions, or the major Part of them, upon Complaint in Writing, may

fufpend

suspend or discharge him. And in such Case the *Custos Rotulorum*, or other Person to whom of Right it doth belong, shall appoint another Person residing within such County, &c. in his Room; and in case of Neglect or Refusal to make such Appointment before the next general Quarter-Sessions after such Refusal, the Justices of Peace at their general Quarter-Sessions may appoint one, who shall be liable to all the Penalties, Conditions, &c. hereby mentioned, and may be discharged by the said Justices as aforesaid.

By the Statute 1 *Will. & Mar.* it was enacted, That the *Custos Rotulorum* shall appoint the Clerk of the Peace for so long Time as he behaveth himself well in the Office, so that now he hath an Estate for Life, determinable only upon his Misbehaviour. But before this Statute his Estate was very incertain, for he was removeable with the *Custos*, whose Power is not so large since this Statute was made as it was before; for now he cannot be removed by the *Custos*, but by the Justices in Sessions, upon Complaint exhibited in Writing of his Misbehaviour, and due Proof thereof made; and in such Case if the *Custos* doth not appoint another before the next Sessions, the Justices themselves may appoint one; but in both Cases the Person thus appointed must be resident in the County.

His Business is to draw up the Process of the Sessions, to draw and read Indictments, and to record the Proceedings of the Sessions; and if he draws an insufficient Indictment, he must make another without Fee, or forfeits 5 *l.* to be recovered by him who will sue for it in any Court of Record.

10 & 11 W. 3.
c. 23.
§. 7.
He must not take any Thing of a Witness who shall give Evidence against a Felon, nor more than 2 *s.* for Drawing an Indictment, upon Pain of 5 *l.* Forfeiture, with full Costs.

§. 8.
And if any Clerk of the Peace, or of the Excise, or his Clerk or Deputy, draw a defective Bill of Indictment, they shall draw a new one *gratis*, or forfeit 5 *l.* with full Costs; and all the said Forfeitures shall be recovered by him or them who shall sue for the same by Action of Debt, &c.

6 G. 1. c. 23.
§. 1.
All Securities for Transportation shall be by Bond in the Name of the Clerks of the Peace; which Clerks and their Successors shall prosecute such Bonds in their own Names, to which Purpose they shall be deemed a Body Corporate; and shall be paid all such Costs as they shall sustain in any such Suit, as the Justices at their Quarter-Sessions shall direct, out of the publick Stock, by the Treasurers: And all Monies recovered on such Bonds shall be for the Use of the County, &c. and paid to such Treasurer, to be Part of the Publick Stock.

C H A P. XXIV.

Cloth, Clothiers and Drapery.

One Justice.
Searching.
39 Eliz. c. 20.
43 El. 10.
P. Drap. 118,
127.
EVERY Justice of Peace may enter in and upon any Houses, Land, or Grounds, and search for any Tenters, Wrinches, or other Engines whatsoever, whereby any Deceit may be used in or about the Stretching of woollen Cloth; and may deface the same Tenters, &c. and for the second Offence may sell them to the best Value thereof. *But the Disposing of such Money shall be by two Justices.* See *hic post.*

Penalty.
And if upon Information made to any Justice of Peace, of any such Tenters, &c. he shall not make Search and execute this Law within seven Days, he shall forfeit for every such Default five Pounds.

P. Drap. 115,
127.
3 E. 6. 2.
33 El. 20.
43 El. 20.
P. Drap. 45,
115, 118.
Also one or two of the Justices of Peace of the Shire next adjoining to any City, Borough, or Town Corporate within *England*, may join with them of such City, Borough, or Town Corporate, in appointing the yearly Overseers for such Cloths, &c. *Ibid.*

Two Justices.
Overseers.
Any two Justices of Peace within their Limits may once every Year appoint Overseers or Searchers for that whole Year following, or for a shorter Time (at their Discretions) of any woollen Cloth, to be made or sold in any Town not being Corporate, and may charge them upon their Oaths, and bind them in Recognizance of forty Pounds a-piece, to do their best Endeavours by all lawful Ways and Means, for their Time, to see the Statutes of 3 *Ed.* 6. *cap.* 2. and of 39 *Eliz. cap.* 20. in all Points truly observed and kept within their Limits, (*sc.* within the Town or Parish where the said Overseers shall be dwelling.) The Particulars seem to be these.

Duty of Overseers.
P. Drap. 114.
1. That the Weights, Lengths and Breadths, of all woollen Cloths, be according to the Statute 39 *El.* See the Statutes 4 *Jac.* 1. *cap.* 2. 21 *Jac.* 1. *cap.* 18.

2. That

2. That every fuch Cloth have a Seal of Lead, containing the juft Length and Weight. 39 *Eliz.*

3. That fuch be not ftretched or ftrained. *Ibid.*

4. Where there be any Tenters, Wrinches, or fuch other Engine for the Stretching of 21 Jac. 18. Cloth. *Ibid.*

5. That no Iron Cards or Pickards, be occupied in any woollen Cloths.   3 *Ed. 6. c. 2.*

6. That Cloths or Wools be not falfly died or coloured. *Ibid.*

7. That no Hair, Flocks, Thrums, Yarn made of Lambs Wool, Chalk, Flower, or Starch, or other deceivable Thing, be put in or upon any woollen Cloth, *upon Pain to forfeit for every Offence five Pounds, to the Ufe of the Poor of the Parifh where fuch Cloth is made.* See 3 *Ed.* 6. and 43 *Eliz. cap.* 10. and 4 *Jac.* 1. *cap.* 2. and 21 *Jac.* 1. *cap.* 18.

8. That no Cloths be in any deceivable Manner preffed, to be put to Sale, 3 *Ed.* 6. See alfo of the Statutes of 5 *Ed.* 6. *cap.* 6. and 21 *Jac.* 1. *cap.* 18.

The Statute of 5 Edw. 6. *fpeaks of Hot-preffes, which is a deceitful Way of preffing Cloths, and is much to its Damage, and makes them feem fair to the Eye, when they are full of Faults, and are dangerous alfo for Fire.   As was attefted by Cloth-workers in the* King's Bench.   13 *Jac. Roll's Rep.* 2 *Part. p.* 312.

Any two (or more) Juftices of Peace within the County, City, Borough, or Town *Conviction.* Corporate, where deceivable Cloth fhall be made, or fufpected to be made, (upon Com- 21 Jac. 18. plaint or Information of any Overfeer, Searcher, or any other, of any fuch Offence) may grant their Warrant to call before them any Perfon or Perfons that in their Difcretion fhall be thought fit to difcover any fuch Offence, and may examine upon Oath any fuch Per- fons for the Trial and better finding out of the faid Offence.   And if upon fuch Examina- tion it fhall be found by Teftimony of two Witneffes (or more) or by the Confeffion of the Offender, that any fuch Offence hath been committed, the fame fhall be a fufficient Conviction of the Offence ; and then the faid Juftices fhall or may certify fuch Offence un- to the Church-wardens and Overfeers (for the Time being) of the Poor of the Parifh where fuch deceivable Cloth fhall be made, under the Hands and Seals of the faid Juftices ; and upon fuch Certificate, and a Warrant made by the faid Juftices to the faid Overfeers and Church-wardens for the levying of the Forfeiture, the faid Overfeers and Church-war- dens, or any of them, or their, or any of their Succeffors, immediately from and after fuch Certificate and Warrant delivered to them, or any of them, may levy the Sum or Sums of Money, which by the faid Certificate and Warrant fhall appear to be forfeited, by Way of Diftrefs and Sale of the Offender's Goods, rendring to the Offender the Over- plus, &c. and in Defect of fuch Diftrefs, the faid two Juftices may commit the Offender to the common Gaol, there to remain without Bail, until Payment fhall be made of the Sums fo forfeited, to the faid Overfeers and Church-wardens, or fome, or one of them, &c. 21 *Jac.* 1. *cap.* 18.

Thefe Overfeers, or two of them, fhall (or may) from Time to Time, or once every *The Overfeers* Month, at leaft, go into all or any Houfes, Shops, or other Rooms of any Clothier, *Duty.* Draper, Cloth-worker, or other Perfon where fuch Cloth fhall be, or fhall be fufpected to be, and there make due Search and Trial, &c. 39 *Eliz. cap.* 20. and 21 *Jac.* 1. *cap.* 18.

Alfo the fame Overfeer fhall fix on every Cloth (by them viewed) a Seal of Lead, con- 39 Eliz. taining the Length and the Weight of every fuch Cloth, together with this Word *Searched*, 21 Jac. 18. or *Faulty*, if there be Caufe, and fhall be viewed, fearched, or weighed by none other, upon Pain to forfeit to the Party grieved five Pounds, to be recovered in the Quarter- Seffions.

Alfo every Overfeer of Cloth, appointed by any former Law (now in Force), to fix un- P. 15. to any Kind of Cloth a Seal of Lead, fhall ingrave or fet upon every their Seals of Lead (which they fhall fix upon any Cloth by them to be fealed) his Chriftian and Surname : And no Cloth to be fealed with any Seal of Lead which fhall want fuch Ingraving or Print, fhall be allowed to be fufficiently fealed. 21 *Jac.* 1. *cap.* 18.

Alfo the faid Overfeers fhall feife and carry away as forfeit all fuch Cloth as upon their Search they fhall find not to be fealed with a Seal, containing the juft Length and Weight, and fhall prefent the fame Cloth to the Juftices of Peace at the next Quarter-Seffion of the Peace. 39 *Eliz.* 20.

And if the faid Overfeers fhall find any falfe Seal fet upon any Cloth, or any Cloth to be ftretched or ftrained, they fhall prefent fuch Defaults at the faid next Seffions, toge- ther with the Names of the Owners of fuch Cloths. *Ibid.*

But Cloth once lawfully fearched, viewed, weighed, and fealed by the Overfeers and Searchers of the Parifh, Town, or Place, where the faid Cloths be made, fhall not after- wards

wards be viewed, searched, or weighed by any other Person or Officer whatsoever. 4 *Jac.* 1. *cap.* 2. and 21 *Jac.* 1. *cap.* 18.

39 Eliz.

And if the said Overseers shall find any such Tenters, Wrinches, or Engines (for the stretching of Cloth) they shall deface the same; and for the second Offence therein, they shall take away the said Tenters, &c. and shall sell the same to the best Value thereof, and by the Consent of two Justices of Peace shall dispose the Money thereof to the Poor of that Parish. *Vide* 21 *Jac.* 1. *cap.* 18.

21 Jac. 1.
c. 18. sect. 10.

If any Person whose Tenters shall be once defaced, shall *eftsoons* offend, he shall forfeit forty Shillings, to the Use of the Poor.

If any Person, commanded by two Justices of Peace to appear to be made an Overseer according to this Statute, do (without reasonable Excuse) refuse to come and take upon him that Office, he shall forfeit for every such Refusal. five Pounds, the one Half to the King, and the other Half to those two Justices: And shall remain in Ward to the Sheriff, until he hath paid the same Forfeiture, or put in Sureties for the same. 39 *Eliz. cap.* 20.

P. Drap. 118.

The Money that shall be made upon the Sale of any Tenters, Wrinches, and other such Engines, shall be disposed of to the Poor of the Parish where the said Tenters, &c. shall be found, by the Consent of any two Justices of Peace within the same County.

7 Jac. 1. c.16.

But by Statute 7 *Jac.* 1. *cap.* 16. certain Cloths made within the County of *Cumberland, Westmorland* and *Lancaster,* shall not be subject to Search, &c. Also by the Statute of

1 Jac. 1. c.25.

1 *Jac.* 1. *cap.* 25. *sect.* 28. no Person shall incur any Penalty for Want of Length, Breadth or Weight of *Welsh* Cottons, under the Price of 15 *d.* the Yard, or 2 *s.* the Yard, so as they be not mixed with Hair or other deceitful Stuff; nor for any others above that Price, except they be mixed as aforesaid, or shall shrink above Half a Yard in twelve Yards, or weigh less than 14 Ounces the Yard, or hold not full three Quarters of a Yard broad.

The Forfeitures.
21 Jac. 1.
c. 18.

All Penalties and Forfeitures for Want of Length, Breadth, and Weight of Cloth, limited by any Statute now in Force, shall be distributed into three Parts equally; whereof one third Part shall be unto the Searchers, finding and certifying the same, &c. To be recovered by them, at, or in the Quarter-Sessions of the County, City, or Town Corporate, where the Offence is committed, by Action of Debt, Bill, Plaint, or Information. And the other two Parts shall be to the Poor of the Parish where the said Cloth shall be made: The said two Parts to be levied by Way of Distress, and Sale of the Offender's Goods, &c. upon a Warrant from two Justices of Peace, &c.

And because by the Statute of 21 *Jac.* all Penalties and Forfeitures, for Want of Length, Breadth, and Weight of Cloths, are under the Power of Justices of Peace, for their Direction therein, I shall set down the same as they are mentioned in the Statutes of 5 & 6 *Ed.* 6. *cap.* 6. 4 & 5 *Ph.* & *Mar. cap.* 5. 27 *Eliz. cap.* 17. and 4 *Jac.* 1. *cap.* 2.

4 Jac. 1. 2.
5, 6 Ed. 6.
c. 6.
4, 5 Ph. &
Ma. c. 5.
Ibid.

1. Broad Cloths, and Cloth of died Wool and mingled Colours, shall contain between 30 and 40 Yards, every Yard and Inch of the Standard, and no more; and in Breadth, 6 Quarters and a Half of a Yard within the Lift, and shall be in Weight 86 Pounds.

2. Long Worcesters, and Cloth of like Making between 30 and 33 Yards; and in Breadth 7 Quarters; and shall weigh 78 Pounds.

Ibid.

3. Long coloured Cloths called Plunkets, Azures, and Blues, and long white Cloths, and Cloths of like Make, shall be in Length between 29 and 32 Yards; and in Breadth, 6 Quarters and an Half, and weigh 86 Pounds.

4, 5 Ph. &
Ma. c. 5.

4. Short Cloths coloured, and short white Cloths called Sorting-Cloths, in Length between 23 and 26 Yards; and in Breadth, 6 Quarters within the Lift, and weigh 64 Pounds.

Ibid.

5. White short *Suffolk,* or Cloth of the like Make, shall contain in Length between 23 and 26 Yards; and in Breadth 6 Quarters and a Half, and weigh 64 Pounds.

Ibid.

6. Every white Cloth of like making, called Handy-warps, shall contain between 29 and 32 such Yards in Length; and in Breadth 6 Quarters, and weigh 76 Pounds.

Ibid.
6 E. 6.
35 El. c. 9.

7. Broad Plunkets, Azures, Blue, and other Cloth of like Make, shall contain in Length between 26 and 28 Yards, and in Breadth 7 Quarters and an Half, and weigh 68 Pounds.

Ibid.

8. Short Cloths made of died or mingled Colours in *Yorkshire,* or of like Make, between 23 and 25 Yards in Length; and in Breadth 6 Quarters and a Half, and weigh 66 Pounds.

Ibid.
27 Eliz. c. 17.
5, 6 Ed. 6.
c. 1.

9. Broad-lifted Whites and Reds, called Sorting-Pack broad-lifted Cloths, in Length between 26 and 28 Yards, in Breadth 6 Quarters and a Half, and weigh 64 Pounds.

10. Narrow-

10. Narrow-lifted Whites and Reds, called Sorting-Pack Cloths, Length between 26 and 28 Yards, Breadth 6 Quarters and an Half, and weigh, being white, 61 Pounds, and being red, 60 Pounds. *4 Jac. 1. c. 2. §. 5.*

11. Fine Cloth with plain Lifts, between 29 and 32 Yards, Breadth 6 Quarters and a Half, and weigh 72 Pounds. *Ib. §. 6*

12. Cloths having ftop Lifts, and not plain Lifts, Length between 30 and 33 Yards, Breadth 7 Quarters, and weigh 78 Pounds. *Ib. §. 7.*

13. Broad-Cloth called *Tauntons, Bridgwaters,* and *Dunfters,* between 12 and 13 Yards, Breadth 7 Quarters, and weigh 30 Pounds. *Ibid.*

14. Narrow Cloth of that Sort, Length between 24 and 25 Yards, Breadth one Yard, weigh 30 Pounds, the Half-cloth to be proportionable. *Ibid.*

15. All fuch Broad Cloths and Narrow Cloths, made into White and Red in *Yorkfhire;* the Broad to hold the like Weight, Length, and Meafure; but the Narrow to contain between 17 and 18 Yards of like Meafure, Breadth and Weight proportionable. *Ibid.*

16. All *Devonfhire* Kerfies called *Dozens,* Length between 12 and 13 Yards, Weight 13 Pounds. *Ib. §. 8.*

17. *Check* Kerfies, ftrait and plain Grays, between 12 and 18 Yards, Breadth one Yard, Weight 24 Pounds. *Ibid.*

18. Ordinary Penniftones or Foreft Whites, Length between 12 and 13 Yards, Breadth five Quarters and an Half, Weight 28 Pound. *ibid.*

19. Sorting Penniftones, Length between 13 and 14 Yards, Breadth 6 Quarters and an Half, Weight 35 Pounds. *Ibid.*

20. Kerfies called *Wafhers* or *Wafhwhites,* Length between 17 and 18 Yards half-thicked, and between 18 and 19 Yards quarter-thicked, Weight 17 Pounds. *Ib. §. 10.*

21. If longer than as before directed, the Seller to forfeit for every Yard and Inch, ten Shillings. If of lefs Weight, fhall forfeit 10 s. for every Pound above two Pounds fo wanting; and if failing in Breadth, to forfeit for every Cloth falling narrow throughout 20 s. half Way 10 s. a Quarter of it 5 s. *Ib. §. 17, 18 & 19.*

22. A Cloth found in the Party's Prefence, or upon Notice in his Abfence to be of lefser Length than the Seal fixed imports, the Seller fhall forfeit to the Buyer 6 s. 8 d. for every Yard wanting, and the Value of fo much as is wanting. *Ib. §. 20.*

23. Every raw *Devonfhire* Kerfey, or Dozen, being a Rudgewafh Kerfey, fhall in the Market weigh 17 Pounds raw, as it comes off the Weaver's Loom, and without Racking, fhall contain between 15 and 16 Yards; and if of lefs Weight or Meafure, the Weaver fhall forfeit for every Quarter of a Pound twelve Pence; and for every Quarter of a Yard twelve Pence. *35 El. 10. §. 3 & 4.*

24. Several Forfeitures by the Statute of 35 *Eliz.* 10. may be fued for in any Court of Record, (as the Seffions, &c.)

25. Every Cotton fhall weigh 11 Pounds at leaft, and in Length 20 Goads at leaft, and in Breadth three Quarters of a Yard, or within one half Nail thereof. Every Frize and Rugg fhall weigh 43 Pounds, and in Length between 35 and 37 Yards, and in Breadth at moft 3 Quarters, and at leaft within a Nail thereof; and if longer, it fhall weigh as it ought to weigh, proportionably, upon Pain, for every Yard not fo weighing, twelve Pence; and if of lefs Weight, the Seller to forfeit for every Pound under three Pounds, twelve Pence; and for every Pound lacking above three Pounds 5 s. one Half to the King, the other Half to the Informer. But nothing in this Act fhall be prejudicial unto any Liberty, Borough or Town Corporate within the County of *Lancafter.* *8 El. 12. §. 6 & 7.* *Ib. §. 9.*

If any Perfon (which fhall retail any of the Cloths, Kerfies, Frizes, Rugs or Cottons, of the feveral Makings fpecified in the Statute 5 *Ed.* 6. *cap.* 6.) do prefent any fuch woollen Cloth which is defective or faulty unto the two Juftices of Peace next adjoining, (out of a City, Borough, or Town Corporate) where fuch Cloth fhall be found faulty; the fame Juftices fhall caufe the fame Cloth to be cut into three equal Pieces, whereof the King fhall have one, the Prefenter another, and the Third the faid Juftices fhall retain to themfelves. *5 & 6 Ed. 6. c. 6. fect. 31.*

And two Juftices of Peace may take Order between the Clothier and his Spinfters, Carders, Kembers, Sorters and Weavers, which fhall unjuftly or deceitfully convey away, imbezil, fell or detain any Part of the Wool or Yarn delivered to them: And as well every fuch Spinfter, &c. fo offending, as alfo the Buyers and Receivers, (knowing the fame to be imbezilled) being thereof convicted by the Confeffion of the Party, or by one fufficient Witnefs upon Oath, before two fuch Juftices, fhall give fuch Recompence to the Party grieved, for fuch their Lofs and Damage, as by the faid Juftices fhall be ordered; and if fuch Offender fhall not be thought (in the Difcretion of the faid Juftices) able, or do not make Recompence according to fuch Order, then fuch Offender is to be whipped, or fet *Spinfters, &c. imbezilling.* *7 Jac. 1. 7.*

Q in

in the Stocks (in or near the Place where the Offence was committed) at the Difcretion of the faid Juftices. For the fecond Offence he is to undergo the like, or fuch other Punifhment of Whipping, or being put in the Stocks, as fhall be thought fit. And fuch two Juftices have full Power to minifter the Oath to fuch Witneffes, and finally to hear, end, and determine the faid Offences.

Wages.
1 Jac. 6.
P. Juft. 66.

Clothiers and other Mafters that fhall refufe to pay fuch Wages (to their Spinfters, Weavers, or other Workmen whatfoever) as fhall be affeffed at the Seffions by the Juftices of Peace, and fhall be thereof convicted before any two Juftices of Peace, (one being of the *Quorum*) upon their own Confeffion, or upon Proof by two fufficient Witneffes, fhall forfeit for every fuch Offence ten Shillings to the Party grieved, the fame to be levied by Diftrefs and Sale of the Offender's Goods, by Warrant from the fame Juftices.

Linen Cloth.
1 Eliz. 12.
Raft. 249.

Two Juftices of the Peace (one being of the *Quorum*) may take the Information of Stretching, or other deceitful ufing of Linen-Cloth, (by him that feifed it) and of his Seifure thereof; and may bind the faid Seifor to give in Evidence, and to purfue the fame Matter with Effect (at the next Seffion, &c.) And alfo to pay the Moiety of all that he fhall recover, to the Ufe of the King's Majefty, &c.

The Juftices of Peace of the Weft-Riding of *York*, and others, are to be a Corporation, and to have a common Seal, and have Power to appoint Searchers of Cloth, and to make By-Laws, 14 *Car.* 2. *cap.* 32. Such By-Laws, Rules and Ordinances, as fhall be made by the Warden and Affiftants of Weavers in *Norwich*, touching the well making of *Norwich* Stuffs, fhall be ratified and confirmed by the Mayor, and two Juftices of the City, and County of *Norfolk*, and three Juftices of the County of *Norfolk* (*Quorum unus.*)

The Power of the Juftices of Peace of the Town of *Kidermifter*, in Execution of the Statute made 22 & 23 *Car. cap.* 8. Touching *Kidermifter*-Stuffs. See that Statute.

Importing Wool-Cards.
14 Car. 2.
c. 19.
39 Eliz. c. 14.

No Foreign Wool-Cards, or Foreign Card-wire, or Iron-wire, for making of Wool-Cards, fhall be imported into *England*, nor ufed there; nor any Card-wire taken out of old Cards, be put into new Leather, or new Card-boards, nor fuch Wool-cards made thereof, be put to Sale, upon Pain, That every Perfon importing, or making, or putting to Sale, fhall forfeit the fame, or the Value thereof, if the fame be not feifed. A Moiety to the King, the other Moiety to him that fhall firft feize or fue by Action of Debt, Bill, Plaint, Information, or Indictment, in any of the King's Courts at *Weftminfter*, or in the County, City, Borough, or Town Corporate, 14 *Car.* 2. *cap.* 19. It feemeth by this Statute, that it may be profecuted by Information or Indictment in the Seffions.

10 Ann. c. 6.

By the Statute 10 *Annæ*, mix'd or medley Broad-cloth muft be meafured at the Fulling-Mill, after 'tis mill'd by the Mafter or Occupier of the Mill, who is firft to make Oath before fome neighbouring Juftice, that he will truly perform fuch Meafuring; the Juftice is to give him a Certificate thereof, and then the Meafurer is to fet a Seal to each Cloth, with his Name ftamped in Lead, mentioning in Letters the Length and Breadth, for which the Owner is to pay him one Penny; and the Number fo ftamp'd fhall be a Rule of Payment to the Buyer.

If the Mafter of the Mill refufe or neglect to fix fuch Seal, or any Perfon fhall afterwards take it off, or deface or alter the Figures before the Cloth is fold; and if the Buyer refufe to accept the fame, according to fuch Meafure, the Offender being convicted on Oath, forfeits 20 s. but by the Statute 1 *Geo.* 1. *cap.* 15. he forfeits 20 l.

1 Geo. 1.
c. 15.

And by the fame Statute the Mafter of the Fulling-mill refuſing to make fuch Oath, forfeits 20 l.

10 Ann. 16.
fect. 3.

Clothier or Fuller, after fuch Cloth is fully wetted and ftamped, fhall not ftretch a Cloth above one Yard in 20 Yards Length, or above one Nail in a Yard in Breadth, on Forfeiture of 20 s.

Sect. 4.

Every Mill-man fhall keep in his Mill a Table or Board, in Length 12 Foot, and in Breadth 3 Foot, on which the Cloth fhall be creafed and laid plain, and one Inch more inftead of a Thumb's Breadth, (*viz.*) 37 Inches, to prevent any Difpute in refpect of Meafuring by the Yard.

Sect. 5.

Clothiers, or others concerned in the woollen Manufactures, fhall pay in Money all Perfons concerned in the faid Work, and not impofe or deliver any Goods or Ware for fuch Work, on Forfeiture of 20 s. for every Offence.

Offences againft this Act, as alfo againft the 1 *Geo.* 1. *c.* 15. are to be heard and determined by one Juftice not concerned in the Matter of Complaint, and upon the Oath of one Witnefs.

1 Geo. 1.
c. 15. §. 7.

The Penalties of 1 *Geo.* 1. *cap.* 15. are to be diftributed, one Moiety to the Informer, and the other, if in *London*, to the Ufe of *Chrift's-Hofpital*; if in any other Place, to the

2   •   Poor

Poor of the Parifh, &c. and the Offehder refufing Payment for thirty Days after Con- 1 Geo. 1.
viction, the Juftice may grant his Warrant to levy it by Diftrefs and Sale, &c. rendring c. 15.
the Overplus, &c. and if no Diftrefs can be had, then to commit the Offender to the
Gaol, or Houfe of Correction, for three Kalendar Months.

The Profecution muft be within forty Days after the Offence difcovered.   Sect. 8.

The Defendant may plead the General Iffue, and if the Plaintiff be nonfuit, &c. the Ib. §. 9.
Defendant fhall have treble Cofts.

See the fame Act of 1 *Geo.* 1. *cap.* 15. *fect.*14, 15, & 16. relating to *Yorkfhire* Cloths;
as alfo the 11 *Geo.* 1. *cap.* 24. for the better regulating the Manufacture of Cloth in the
Weft-Riding of the County of *York,* which Act is explained and amended by 7 *Geo.* 2.
cap. 25. See alfo the farther Regulations by 11 *Geo.* 2. *cap.* 28; and 14 *Geo.* 2. *cap.* 35.

An Appeal lies to the Quarter-Seffions, which fhall be final, and the Juftices there Ib. §. 10.
fhall allow Cofts.

Coals.

ALL Sea-Coals brought into the *Thames* and fold fhall be fold by the Chalder, con- 16 & 17 C.2.
taining thirty-fix Bufhels heaped, according to the Bufhel at *Guildhall.* Coals fold c. 2. §. 1.
by Weight fhall be fold after the Proportion of 112 Pounds to the Hundred *Avoirdupois,*
upon Pain of Forfeiture of Coals otherwife fold, and double the Value thereof, to be
recovered in any Court of Record, or by Complaint to the Lord Mayor and Juftices of
Peace of *London,* or any two of them, or to the Juftices of Peace of the Places where
fuch Coals fhall be expofed to Sale, who upon due Proof are to convict the Offenders,
and give Warrant for levying the Forfeitures; Half to the Profecutor, and Half to the
Poor, or Repairing the Highways within the fame, or any adjoining Parifh. And the
Lord Mayor and Court of Aldermen, and the Juftices of Peace of the feveral Counties,
or three of them, one of the *Quorum,* are to fet the Prices of Coals fold by Retail from
Time to Time.

If any Retailer fhall refufe to fell accordingly, the Lord Mayor, &c. taking a Con- Ib. §. 2.
ftable may force Entrance into any Place where fuch Coals are ftored, and fell them at
fuch Rates, rendring to fuch Retailer the Money, Charges deducted. This Act is made
perpetual by 7 & 8 *Will.* 3. *cap.* 36. *fect.* 2.

The Bowl Tub of *Newcaftle* upon *Tine* for meafuring of Coals, is to contain twenty- Coals.
two Gallons and a Pottle, *Winchefter* Meafure, and one and twenty fuch Bowls heap 30 C. 2. c. 8.
Meafure, are allowed to a Chalder: The Contents of each Wain for Carriage of Coals
there, fhall be feven Bowls; and of each Cart, three Bowls and one Bufhel heap Meafure; and three fuch Wains, or fix fuch Carts, fhall be allowed for a Chalder.

All Keels and other Boats, Carts and Wains for Carriage of Coals there, are to be Ibid.
meafured and marked by Commiffioners to be appointed by the King for that Purpofe;
and if they carry any Coals before they be meafured and marked, they are forfeited together with the Coals laden upon them.

Every Perfon having a Hand in removing or altering fuch Mark, according to 6 & Forfeiture.
7 *Will.* 3. *cap.* 10. upon Proof thereof by one Witnefs before a Juftice of Peace, fhall for- 6 & 7 W. 3.
feit ten Pounds, to be levied by Diftrefs and Sale of Goods, by Warrant of fuch Juftice; c. 10. §. 7.
and for want of fuch Diftrefs, to be committed to Gaol for three Months without Bail.

By the Act of 3 *Geo.* 2. *cap.* 26. *for the better Regulation of the Coal Trade,* all the 3 G. 2. c. 26.
Penalties thereof under 5 *l.* fhall be recovered by Complaint made to the Lord Mayor of §. 16.
London, or one Juftice of Peace within *London,* or one Juftice of the feveral Places where
the Offenders live; upon Proof made, the Lord Mayor or Juftice may grant Warrant to
levy the Forfeiture, &c. one Moiety to the Informer, the other to the Poor of the
Parifh. For want of fufficient Diftrefs the Offender fhall be committed to the Houfe of
Correction for any Time not exceeding thirty, and not lefs than fourteen Days, to be
kept to hard Labour. The Penalties above 5 *l.* are to be recovered with double Cofts
within fix Kalendar Months after the Offence committed, by Action of Debt, &c. in
any of his Majefty's Courts of Record; one Moiety to the Crown, the other to the Informer. As to the various Cafes in which the feveral Penalties are incurred, fee the Statute at large, or Mr. *Cay's Abridg.* Tit. *Coals* and *Coal Trade.*

Coin. See *High Treafon,* Chap. 140.

C H A P.

CHAP. XXV.

Common Prayer.

13 & 14 C. 2. EVERY Incumbent of a Benefice with Cure refiding on his Benefice, and having a
c. 4. §. 7.   Curate, fhall in Perfon (not having a lawful Impediment to be allowed of by the
Ordinary) once in every Month openly read the Common Prayers and Service, and (if
there be Occafion) adminifter the Sacraments and other Rites in the Parifh-Church, or
elfe forfeit 5 *l.* to the Ufe of the Parifh, upon Conviction by Confeffion or Proof of two
Witneffes, before two Juftices of Peace of the County; and if not paid within ten Days,
to be levied by the Church-wardens or Overfeers, by Warrant of the faid two Juftices by
Diftrefs and Sale, rendring the Overplus.

Ib. §. 21.   If any Perfon difabled by 14 *Car.* 2. *cap.* 14. To preach a Sermon or Lecture, fhall,
during that Difability, preach a Sermon or Lecture, he fhall fuffer three Months Imprifonment without Bail; and two Juftices of the Peace of the County, or Mayor, or
Chief Magiftrate of any City or Town Corporate, upon Certificate from the Ordinary
fhall commit him to the Gaol.

A Curate was indicted and convicted for refufing to Ufe the Common Prayer, and
for depraving it; and Judgment given, that he fhould be deprived; but it was fet afide,
becaufe a Temporal Judge cannot give Sentence of Deprivation; for 'tis a Spiritual Act.
Gouldsb. 162.

CHAP. XXVI.

Coffee, Tea and Chocolate.

15 Car. 2. NONE fhall fell or retail Coffee, Chocolate, Sherbet, or Tea, without Licence obtained
c. 11.   at the General Seffions of the County, or from the chief Magiftrate of the Place;
firft fhewing a Certificate that he hath given good Security for Payment of his Duties
* This is not of Excife to the King by Recognizance; for which Licence, Security and Recognizance,
in Force as to he fhall pay 12 *d.* and no more, upon Pain to forfeit 5 *l.* for every Month he fhall re-
Coffee, Choco- tail without Licence. ***
late or Tea.

Chocolate.   No Chocolate ready made, or ready made Cocoa-Paft, fhall be imported, on Pain of
10 Geo. 1.   forfeiting the fame, together with double the Value, and the Package..
c. 10. §. 2.
Ib. §. 4, 5, & 6.   The new Duties are 2 *s. per* Pound on Coffee †, 4 *s. per* Pound on Tea, and 1 *s.* 6 *d.*
† But if the *per* Pound on Chocolate, to be paid by the Makers or Sellers.
Coffee be of the
Growth of the Englifh *Plantations* in America, *the Duty is but* 1 s. 6 d. per Pound, *by* 5 Geo. 2. cap. 24. fect. 1.

Ib. §. 7.   The King or the Treafury may appoint Commiffioners for the Receipt and Manage-
ment of thofe Duties, the major Part of which Commiffioners may fubftitute proper
Officers requifite for fuch Purpofes, which Commiffioners and Officers fhall have fuch
Salaries as the Treafury fhall appoint; and fhall pay the Money arifing out of fuch
Duties diftinctly into the Exchequer, from all other Branches of the Revenue.

Ib. §. 8.   All the Powers by any Law now in Force, relating to the Revenue of Excife on Beer,
&c. fhall be put in Execution for managing thefe Duties.

Ib. §. 10.   Every Perfon who fhall be a Seller or Dealer in Coffee, Tea, or Cocoa-Nutts, or
Maker, or Seller of Chocolate, fhall make a true Entry in Writing of the Places ufed
for keeping or making the fame, on Forfeiture of 200 *l.* and the Coffee, &c. found
therein.

Ib. §. 13.   Upon Sufpicion of Concealments in any Place, and Oath made thereof, two Commiffioners within the Bills of Mortality, or a Juftice of Peace in any other Part of *Great
Britain,* may by Warrant authorize an Officer by Day or Night; but if by Night, then
in Prefence of a Peace Officer, to enter fuch Place, and to feife and carry away the Coffee,
&c. fraudulently concealed, as forfeited for the King's Ufe. Perfons hindring the Officers from entring, &c. forfeit 100 *l.*

2   Perfons

Perfons counterfeiting the Marks of Chocolate directed by this Act, or felling Choco- Sect. 22. late with such counterfeit Mark knowingly, shall forfeit 500 *l.* and be committed to the next County Gaol for twelve Months.

If any Perfon shall affault or hinder Officers in the feifing of Coffee, &c. or by force Sect. 40. refcue any of the faid Commodities after Seifure, or ftave, break, deftroy or damage any Veffel or Package wherein the fame shall be contained, he shall forfeit 50 *l.*

The Judgments given in Purfuance of this Act by the Commiffioners and Juftices of Sect. 42. Peace shall be final, and not removed by *Certiorari.*

By Stat. 11 *Geo.* 1. *cap.* 30. *sect.* 12. Juftices of Peace may fummon and examine Per- 11 Geo. 1. c. fons fufpected of making untrue Entries upon Oath or Affirmation, touching the Entries; 30. §. 12. and any Dealer in Coffee, &c. who shall neglect to make fuch Oath or Affirmation, or to attend fuch Summons, shall forfeit 20 *l.*

If any Perfon shall, on Chocolate for which the Inland Duties have not been duly Sect. 13. paid, fix any Paper having the Impreffion of the Stamps provided to inclofe Chocolate, with Intent to defraud his Majefty, the Offender shall be liable to the Penalties in 10 *Geo.* 1. *cap.* 10. *sect.* 22. for counterfeiting the faid Stamps. *Vide fupra.*

All Perfons who shall work their Chocolate over again, if out of the Limits of the Sect. 15. Bills of Mortality, shall make Proof before two Juftices of Peace, that the Duty for the Cocoa-Nuts have been paid, and that all the Chocolate fo to be re-worked has been duly entred.

Conformity.

BY the Statute 10 *Annæ,* the Quarter-Seffions may take the Oath of Perfons having 10 Ann. c. 2. Offices, and who have been convicted of Non-conformity, that they have conform- ed for a Year laft paft, and that they have received the Sacrament three Times in that Year.

Oath muft be made of the Offence before one Juftice, and within ten Days after 'tis committed, and the Profecution muft be within three Months afterwards, and the Con- viction is to be by Oath of two credible Witneffes.

C H A P. XXVII.

Corn.

THE Certificate of one Juftice of Peace (joined with the Cuftomer of the Place) 5 E. 6. of the Unlading and Selling of Corn or Cattle, carried by Water from one Place 13 El. 25. to another of this Realm, unto the Cuftomer and Controller of the Place where the P. Foreftal. 6. fame was imbarked, is fufficient upon the Statute of *Foreftalling.* See more of Corn, Tit. *Tranfportation.*

By the Statute 1 & 2 *Ph.* & *Mar. Stat.* 2. *cap.* 5. Corn could not be tranfported without Licence, unlefs it were under thefe Prices by the Quarter, Wheat 6 *s.* 8 *d.* Bar- ley 4 *s.* Rye 3 *s.* and every Juftice of Peace might inquire of it by the Statute 13 *El.* 13. Certain Perfons may determine when Corn shall be tranfported, when not, which they may afterwards alter, or the Juftices of Peace in Seffions may alter till the Affifes; and the Queen by Proclamation may controul all of them. See there the Poundage of Corn.

By 1 *Jac.* 1. 25. Corn may be tranfported, when of or under thefe Prices by the Quarter; Wheat twenty-fix Shillings and eight Pence, Rye, Peafe and Beans fifteen Shillings, Barley or Malt fourteen Shillings. See there the Poundage.

By 21 *Jac.* 1. 28. It may be tranfported, when not exceeding thefe Prices by the Quarter; Wheat thirty-two Shillings, Rye twenty Shillings, Beans and Peace fixteen Shillings, Barley or Malt fixteen Shillings. See there the Poundage.

By 3 *Car.* 1. 4. It may be tranfported, not exceeding thefe Prices by the Quarter, *viz.* Wheat thirty-two Shillings, Rye twenty Shillings, Peafe and Beans fixteen Shillings, Barley or Malt fixteen Shillings. See there the Poundage.

By 12 *Car.* 2. *cap.* 4. Corn may be tranfported, not exceeding thefe Prices, by the Quarter, *viz.* Wheat forty Shillings, Rye, Beans and Peafe twenty-four Shillings, Barley and Malt twenty Shillings, Oats fixteen Shillings.

R

By

15 Car. 2.
c. 7.

By 15 *Car.* 2. *cap.* 7. Corn not exceeding thefe Prices may be tranfported, *viz.* Wheat forty-eight Shillings, Barley or Malt twenty-eight Shillings, Buck-wheat twenty-eight Shillings, Oats thirteen Shillings and four Pence, Rye thirty-two Shillings, Peafe and Beans thirty-two Shillings. See there the Poundage.

But by 22 *Car.* 2. *cap.* 13. Any Perfon, Native or Foreigner, may tranfport any Sort of Corn or Grain, although the fame exceed the Prices mentioned 15 *Car.* 2. *cap.* 7. *See the Statute at large.*

This Statute of 22 *Car.* 2. *cap.* 13. is made perpetual by 3 *Geo.* 1. *cap.* 7.

5 & 6 E. 6.
c. 14. §. 12.

Any Perfon allowed by three Juftices of Peace, may buy Corn or Cattle to carry by Water from one Place to another within this Realm, if he fhall without Fraud, within forty Days after he fhall have bought the fame, as foon as the Weather will permit, carry the fame to fuch Place as his Cockets fhall declare, and there unlade and fell the fame, and bring a Certificate from one Juftice of Peace, Mayor, or Bailiff, and of the Cuftomer of the Port, of the Day and Place of the Unlading thereof, to the Cuftomer of the Port where the fame was laden.

Foreign Corn.
1 Jac. 2. c.19.
§. 3.

The Juftices of Peace at their Quarter-Seffions next after *Michaelmas* and *Eafter* yearly, by the Oaths of two fubftantial Perfons of the refpective Counties, being neither Merchants nor Factors for importing Corn, not interefted in the Corn imported, and having a Freehold Eftate of 20 *l.* per Annum, or a Leafe of 50 *l.* per Annum, above all Charges, &c. (which Oaths the Juftices are impowered to adminifter) and by fuch Ways as to them fhall feem convenient, to examine the Prices of midling *Englifh* Corn and Grain, as they fhall be fold, and certify the fame with two fuch Oaths made as aforefaid, in Writing annex'd, unto his Majefty's chief Officer or Collector of the Cuftoms, refiding in the refpective Ports where fuch Corn fhall be imported, to be hung up in the Cuftom-Houfe for publick Information ; and the Cuftom and Duty of all fuch Foreign Corn fhall be collected according to the Price in fuch Certificate. Provided, that whatfoever is done by the Juftices of Peace at their Quarter-Seffions in their feveral Counties, may be done in like Manner in *London*, in *October* and *April* yearly, by the Mayor, Aldermen and Juftices of the Peace there ; the Perfons making fuch Oaths being no Corn-Chandlers, Mealmen, &c. but fubftantial Houfe-keepers, qualified as before.

2 W. & M.
Stat. 1. c. 12.
§. 2.

When Malt or Barley *Winchefter* Meafure is 24 *s.* per Quarter, or under, and Rye 32 *s.* per Quarter, and Wheat 48 *s.* per Quarter, any Perfon may fhip on an *Englifh* Veffel, whereof the Mafter and two Thirds of his Mariners are *Englifhmen*, any Sort of Corn to tranfport, bringing a Certificate under his Hand to the Commiffioners of the Cuftoms of the Port, of the Quantity and Quality of fuch Corn, and upon Proof of fuch Certificate by the Oath of one Perfon, and a Bond of 200*l.* given by the Tranfporter for every hundred Ton fo fhipped, and fo in Proportion, that the faid Corn fhall be exported, and not relanded in *England*, &c. fuch Tranfporter fhall receive from the faid Commiffioners for every Quarter of Barley or Malt 2 *s.* 6 *d.* Rye 3 *s.* 6 *d.* and Wheat 5 *s.* without paying any Cuftom, Fee, or Reward.

1 W. & M.
Stat. 1. c. 24. fect. 18.
§. 18.

The Benefit of this Act is extended to *Berwick* by 1 *W. & M. Stat.* 1. *cap.* 24.

2 Geo. 2.
c. 18. §. 3.

If the Juftices of Peace fhall neglect to determine the Prices of Corn at their Quarter-Seffions after *Michaelmas* and *Eafter* yearly, and to certify the fame to the chief Officer and Collector of the Cuftoms, refiding in the Parts where foreign Corn may be imported, to be hung up in the Cuftom-Houfe as is directed by 1 *Jac.* 2. *cap.* 19. in fuch Cafe the Collector of the Cuftoms at the Port of Importation is impowered to receive the Duties of the Corn imported, according to the loweft Price of the fame Sort of Corn, mentioned in 22 *Car.* 2. *cap.* 13.

5 Geo. 2.
c. 12. §. 1.

Juftices of Peace at their Quarter-Seffions may give in Charge to the Grand Jury, to make Prefentment of the Market Prices of midling *Englifh* Corn of the Sorts mentioned in 22 *Car.* 2. *cap.* 13.

§. 2.

Such Prefentment fhall be certified by the Juftices to his Majefty's chief Officers of the Cuftoms in every Port where fuch Corn fhall be imported, and be hung up in the Cuftom-Houfe.

§. 4.

Nothing in this Act fhall prejudice the Authority given by the Act of 1 *Jac.* 2. *cap.* 19. to the Mayor, Aldermen, and Juftices of Peace of the City of *London.*

§. 5.

No Perfon fhall tranfport any foreign Corn, or foreign Corn mixed with *Englifh*, under Penalty that all fuch Corn fhall be forfeited, and every Offender fhall forfeit 20 *s.* for every Bufhel of fuch Corn, and the Ship upon which fuch Corn fhall be laden fhall be forfeited ; one Moiety to the King, the other to him that will fue, and the Mafter and

Mariners

Mariners of fuch Ship, knowing fuch Offence, and affifting thereunto, fhall be imprifoned three Months.

If any Perfons fhall beat, wound, or ufe other Violence to any Perfon, with Intent to 11 Geo. 2. hinder him from buying of Corn ; or fhall ftop or feize upon any Carriage or Horfe loaded c. 22. §. 1. with Wheat, Flour, Meal, Malt, or other Grain, in the Way to or from any City, Market-Town, or Sea-port, and break, cut, or deftroy the fame, or any Part thereof, or the Harnefs of the Horfes ; or fhall take off, drive away, kill or wound fuch Horfes, or beat or wound the Drivers, in order to ftop the fame, or fhall fcatter, fpoil or damage fuch Wheat or other Grain ; every fuch Perfon being convicted before any two Juftices of Peace, fhall be fent to the common Gaol or Houfe of Correction, to be kept to hard Labour for any Time not exceeding three Months, nor lefs than one Month ; and fhall by the Juftices be ordered to be once publickly whipped, on the firft convenient Market-Day, at the Market-Place, between the Hours of eleven and two.

The fecond Offence is Felony. See *Chap.* 160. *Felony by Statute.*   §. 2.

Hundreds are to make Satisfaction to the Perfons injured. See the *Statute.*   §. 5, &c.

Conies. See *Game,* Chap. 46. *Hunting,* Chap. 55.

C H A P. XXVIII.

Conftables.

CONSTABLE, this Word is derived from two old *Saxon* Words, *Cunning,* or *Their Name.* *Kinning,* which fignifieth *King,* and *Stable, Stability* ; fhewing, that thefe ancient Officers were reputed to be as the Stability or Stay of the King and Kingdom. *Lamb.* 5. *Dodd.* 73.

Every Juftice of Peace may caufe two Conftables to be chofen in each Hundred, *High Confta-* *Lamb.* 190. This feemeth to be meant of the High Conftables of Hundreds, and to in- *bles, how to be* clude the Swearing of them ; and this by Virtue of the Statute of *Winchefter,* made *chofen.* 13 *E.* 1. and of the Commiffion, the firft *Affignavimus* or Claufe.

And by the Statute of 34 *H.* 8. *cap.* 26. two Juftices of Peace, the one being of the *Quorum,* may appoint the High Conftables in *Wales.*

And yet the ufual Manner is, that thefe High Conftables of Hundreds are chofen either at the Quarter-Seffions of the Peace ; or if out of the Seffions, then by the greater Number of the Juftices of Peace of that Divifion where they dwell ; and likewife that they be fworn either at the Seffions, or by Warrant from the Seffions ; which Courfe hath alfo been often allowed and commended unto us by the Judges of Affife.

Alfo in fuch Manner as they are to be chofen, in the fame Manner, and by the like *How to be re-* Authority, they are to be removed ; for *eodem modo, quo quid conftituitur, diffolvitur :* *moved.* So if there fhall be Caufe to remove an High Conftable, it hath not been thought fit that one or two Juftices of Peace fhould do it upon their Difcretion, but that it fhould be done by the greater Part of the Juftices of that Divifion, and that for fome juft Caufe ; or elfe that it be done at and in the General Seffions of the Peace ; and fo was the Direction of Sir *John Doderidge* at Summer Affifes at *Cambridge, Anno Dom.* 1620.

By the Opinion of Mafter *Lambard* and others, the Conftables of Hundreds were firft *When firft* appointed to be chofen by the faid Statute of *Winchefter, tempore Ed.* 1. And they were *made. appointed for the Keeping of the Peace,* and to view Armour twice every Year, and to 13 E. 1. c. 6. prefent before Juftices Defaults of Armour, of Watches, of Highways, and of Hue and Cry ; and alfo all fuch as lodged Strangers for whom they would not anfwer. See *Raftal* 379. *c. d.* Lamb. *Duty of Conft.* 5. *Minfh.* verbo *Conftable.*

Petty Conftables (in Towns and Parifhes) were after devifed (for the Aid of the Con- *Petty Confta-* ftables of the Hundred,) *viz.* about the Beginning of the Reign of King *Ed.* 3. as it ap- *bles.* *See Stat.*4 E.3. peareth by Mr. *Lambard* in his Book of *The Duty of Conftables,* pag. 9.   *cap.* 3 & 10.

But it appeareth by *Fineux,* 12 *H.* 7. *fol.* 18. *a.* that whereas the Sheriffs at the firft *Hundreds* had the Government of their Counties committed to them, afterwards, by reafon of the *when firft* Multitude of the People, and for that it was too great a Thing for one Perfon (*fc.* the She- *made.* riff) to undertake, therefore *Hundreds* were divided and derived out of the Counties ; and in every Hundred there was ordained a Confervator of the Peace, who was called the *High Conftable* ; and after, Boroughs or Towns were made, and within every of them alfo alſo was ordained a Conſervator of the Peace, who is called the *Petty Conſtable*, (and in ſome Places the Borough-Head:) And this was long before the Times that Mr. *Lambard* ſpeaketh of, *ſc.* long before King *Ed.* 1. or King *Ed.* 3. which alſo may appear by the Derivation of *the Word Conſtable* hic ſupra, *and that they were in the Time of the* Saxons : So that it may ſeem, that as well the High Conſtables as the Petty Conſtables, and their Authorities, were by the Common Law; and that the old Statutes concerning them are but a Recital of the ancient Common Law.

Deputy Con-
ſtable.   The Authority which High Conſtables and Petty Conſtables have by the Common Law for keeping the Peace, ſee *Chap.* 1. And the Conſtables Power to make a Deputy. *Ibid.*

Conſtables may make their Deputies, and ſuch Deputies are within the Statute of 7 *Jac.* as was reſolved in *Felp*'s Caſe, *M.* 13 *Jac. B. R.*

Co. 5. 59.   If a Juſtice of Peace make a general Warrant to bring a Man before him, or any other,
Foſter's Caſe. *&c.* It is not at the Choice of the Delinquent, but of the Conſtable, before what Juſtice to carry him; but a Juſtice of Peace may make a Warrant to bring an Offender before him-ſelf, and it is good.

I have ſeen a MS. ſaid to be a Collection of Sir *Nicholas Hide*'s of the Office of a Juſtice of Peace; wherein it is ſaid, That it was reſolved by all the Judges of *England*, *Trin.* 5 *Car.* 1. That Juſtices of Peace at Seſſions may not compel the Conſtables of Hundreds to at-tend at the Quarter-Seſſions, and to preſent Offenders upon Oath, otherwiſe it is at the Aſſizes, *&c.*

Petty Con-
ſtables, how   The Chuſing and Swearing of theſe *Petty Conſtables* properly belongs to the *Court-Leet:*
choſen and re- Yet we find it uſual and warranted by common Experience, that every Juſtice of Peace
moved. doth alſo ſwear them, and upon juſt Cauſe doth and may alſo remove them. See the Title *Warrants and Precedents,* Chap. 174.

Sheriff.   But in antient Time both the High Conſtable of Hundreds, as alſo the Petty Conſtable
Ba. U. 5. 6. of every Town, were yearly appointed by the Sheriff in his Torn, and were there ſworn, and they may ſtill be choſen or appointed, and ſworn in the Sheriff's Torn, as well as in the Leet.

Conſtables lawfully choſen, if they ſhall refuſe to be ſworn, the Juſtice of Peace may bind them over to the Aſſizes or Seſſions of the Peace. And for ſuch his Contempt, he is there to be indicted, and thereupon fined and impriſoned. *Dyer* 29.

But he cannot commit them, until they will take on them the Office: For ſuch a Commitment was adjudged void, *M.* 1652. And it was there reſolved, that they could not chuſe Conſtables, but might ſwear them, or if unfit Perſons were choſen, might re-move them.

Conſtables,   And here, for the better chuſing them, the Law requireth that every Conſtable be *Ido-*
their Ability. *neus homo,* that is, apt and fit for the Execution of the ſaid Office; and he is ſaid in Law to
Co. 8. 41. be *Idoneus,* who hath theſe three Things, Honeſty, Knowledge and Ability.

Honeſty, to execute his Office truly, without Malice, Affection or Partiality.

Knowledge to underſtand what he ought to do.

Ability, as well in Subſtance or Eſtate, as in Body, that ſo he may intend and execute his Office diligently, and not through Impotence of Body, or Want, to neglect the Place.

For Conſtables choſen out of the meaner Sort, they are either ignorant what to do, or dare not do what they ſhould, or are not able to ſpare the Time to execute this Office:
They are therefore to be able Men, and to be choſen of the abler Sort of Pariſhioners; and
Sid. 333. are not to be choſen either by the Houſe, or other Cuſtom: But the Uſage is otherwiſe.
Co. 8. 42.   And if any ſhall be choſen Conſtable who is not thus inabled and qualified, he may by Law be diſcharged of his ſaid Office, and another fit Man appointed in his Place.

Leets chuſing unable, or unfit Petty Conſtables, is Cauſe of Forfeiture of the Leet, and ſuch Choice is void. And two Juſtices of Peace may remove ſuch a Conſtable; or rather the Lord of the Leet ſhould be dealt withal to chuſe fitter Conſtables; and upon his De-fault, Complaint is to be made at the Aſſizes or Seſſions of the Peace, from thence a War-rant to be granted to the Juſtices of Peace to chuſe and ſwear others more fit. And ſo was the Direction of the Judge of Aſſize at *Cambridge,* *Anno* 8 *Caroli Regis.*

December, 4 *Car. William Stockdale* elected Conſtable was diſcharged, for that his Dwelling was not convenient for the well Execution of the ſaid Office. *Ex libr. Seſſ.* *Middleſ.*

If a Conſtable die, or remove out of the Pariſh, his Place is to be ſupplied at the Leet, if that Time fall near; otherwiſe by the Seſſions: But if that be too far off, then by the next Juſtices. *Dyer* 30.

If

If a poor weak Man be chosen a Constable, the Justices of the Peace must help this. *Dyer* 31.

A Man for his Quality otherwise fit to be a Constable, &c. procuring himself to be the King's Servant Extraordinary, may notwithstanding be chosen a Constable, and may well perform his ordinary Service in the Country. *Dyer* 38.

For the Duty of a Constable, see their Oath. *Chap.* 174.

Two Justices of the Peace may appoint and swear new Constables, Headboroughs, &c. in Case of Death or Removal of such Officers out of the Parish. They to continue till the Lord hold a Leet, or until the next Sessions, who shall approve of them, or appoint others as they shall think fit. And if, in Default of holding Court-Leets, they continue above the Year, they may be discharged at the Sessions, and others put in. *13 & 14 Car. 2. c. 12. §. 15. Made perpetual by 12 An. 6. 1. c. 18.*

And by the same Statute, Constables, Headboroughs, and Tithing-men out of Purse, with the Church-wardens and Overseers of the Poor, and other Inhabitants of the Parish, may take Rates upon all Occupiers of Lands, and Inhabitants, and all others chargeable by the Statute 43 *El.* to the Poor; which being confirmed under the Hands and Seals of two Justices of the Peace, may be levied by their Warrants, by Distress and Sale of the Refuser's Goods; for the Re-imbursing themselves their Charges in relieving, conveying with Passes, and in carrying Rogues, Vagabonds, and sturdy Beggars to the House of Correction. *Poor Rates. Ib. §. 18. See in Carthew 293, an Indictment on this Clause.*

Attornies, Clergymen, Justices of Peace, Infants, Lawyers, Physicians, poor and old Persons were exempted from being Constables, but not Tenants in Antient Demesne. *Exempted.*

As to Persons privileged from being Constables, see 2 *Hawk. P. C. p.* 63 & 64, as also *p.* 65, for the Power of Justices of Peace, in Relation to these Matters.

Constables neglecting their Duty, according to 12 *Ann. Stat.* 2. *cap.* 23. shall, being convicted upon View of a Justice of Peace, or Oath of one Witness, forfeit 20 *s.* to the Use of the Poor, to be levied by Distress, &c. by Warrant of one Justice. *12 Ann. Stat. 2. c. 23. §. 27.*

C H A P. XXIX.

Conspiracy.

IF any Butchers, Brewers, Bakers, Poulterers, Cooks, Costermongers, or Fruiterers shall conspire, covenant, make Promise or Oath, not to sell their Victuals but at certain Prices; or if Artificers, Workmen, or Labourers, conspire, covenant, or promise, or make Oaths that they will not do their Work but at certain Prices, or Rates, or shall not work but at certain Hours and Times, or shall not take on them to finish what another hath begun, or shall do but a certain Work in a Day; such Person convicted by Witness, Confession, or otherwise, shall forfeit ten Pounds to the King, and if he have not sufficient to pay, or do not pay it within six Days after Conviction, shall have twenty Days Imprisonment, and shall only have Bread and Water. And for the second Offence shall forfeit twenty Pounds, and shall pay it within sixty Days, or else have the Pillory. And for the third Offence forfeit forty Pounds, and if he pay it not within six Days shall be set in the Pillory, and have one of his Ears cut off and be infamous. *2 & 3 E. 6. c. 15. §. 1.*

And if such Conspiracy be made in a Society, Company of any Craft, Mystery or Occupation of the Victuallers above-mentioned by the more Part of them, then over and besides the particular Punishment above-mentioned, the Corporation shall be dissolved. Justices of Peace, Mayors, &c. at their Sessions and Courts shall hear and determine the Offences, and punish the Offenders. * *Ib. §. 2.*

This Act was revived, continued and confirmed by 22 & 23 Car. 2. c. 19. which is now expired; so quære, if this of the 2 & 3 Ed. 6. be in Force.

Several Journeymen Tailors in *Cambridge* were indicted for a Conspiracy to raise their Wages, and being found guilty, they moved in Arrest of Judgment,

That the Fact was laid in the Town of *Cambridge*, without setting forth in what County; and it shall never be intended, that the Town of *Cambridge* is within the County of *Cambridge*, because this is a criminal Case, wherein Intendments are never allowed.

Besides, this Indictment ought to conclude *contra formam Statuti*, because by the Statute 7 *Geo.* 1. *cap.* 13. Journeymen Tailors are prohibited to enter into any Agreement for the Advancement of their Wages.

S   But

But adjudged, that the Fact being laid within the Town of *Cambridge*, it fhall be intended, that the Town is within the County, and this in order to fupport all inferior Jurifdiction; and this being an Indictment for a Confpiracy, 'tis not material to conclude it *contra formam Statuti*, becaufe Confpiracy is an Offence at Common Law. *Mich.* 1721. The King verfus *Journeymen Tailors of* Cambridge.

CHAP. XXX.

Conventicles.

By Stat. 1 W. & M. 3. c. 18. §. 8. *The Preachers or Teachers of diffenting Proteftants are exempted from the Penalties of this Act.*

THE Stat. 17 *Car.* 2. *cap.* 2. *apud Oxon.* enacts, That all Parfons, Vicars, Curates, Lecturers, and other Perfons in Holy Orders, or pretended Holy Orders, or pretending to Holy Orders, and all Stipendaries, and other Perfons who have been poffeffed of any Ecclefiaftical or Spiritual Promotion, and who have not declared their Affent, and fubfcribed the Declaration mentioned in the Act of 14 *Car.* 2. for Uniformity of publick Prayers, &c. and fhall not take and fubfcribe the Oath following :

Preachers.

I A. B. do fwear, That it is not lawful upon any Pretence whatfoever, to take Arms againft the King : And that I do abhor that traiterous Pofition of taking Arms by his Authority againft his Perfon, or againft thofe that are commiffioned by him, in Purfuance of fuch Commiffions; and that I will not at any Time endeavour any Alteration of Government, either in Church or State.

And all fuch Perfons who fhall take upon them to preach in any unlawful Affembly, Conventicle, or Meeting, under Colour or Pretence of any Exercife of Religion, contrary to the Laws and Statutes of this Kingdom, fhall not at any Time after the 24th of *March* 1665, unlefs in paffing upon the Road, come or be within five Miles of any City or Town Corporate, or Borough that fends Burgeffes to the Parliament, within *England, Wales,* or Town of *Berwick* upon *Tweed,* or within five Miles of any Parifh, Town or Place where-in he or they have, fince the Act of Oblivion, been Parfon, Vicar, Curate, Stipendary or Lecturer, or taken upon them to preach in any unlawful Affembly, Conventicle or Meeting, under Colour or Pretence of any Exercife of Religion, contrary to the Laws and Statutes of this Kingdom, before he or they have taken and fubfcribed the faid Oath before the Juftices of the Peace at their Quarter-Seffions, to be holden at the Divifion next to the Corporation, City or Borough, Parifh, Place, or Town, in open Court (which the faid Juftices are impowered to adminifter) upon Forfeiture for every fuch Offence of the Sum of forty Pounds, one third Part thereof to his Majefty and his Succeffors, the other third Part to the Poor of the Parifh where the Offence is committed, the other third Part to the Perfon that will fue for the fame by Action of Debt, Plaint, Bill, or Information, in any Court of Record at *Weftminfter,* or before any Juftices of Affize, *Oyer* and *Terminer,* or Gaol-delivery, Juftices of the Counties Palatine of *Chefter, Lancafter,* or *Durham,* great Seffions in *Wales,* or Juftices of the Peace in their Quarter-Seffions; no Effoin, Protection, or Wager of Law herein to be allowed.

It fhall not be lawful for any Perfon or Perfons reftrained from coming to any City or Town Corporate, Borough, Parifh, Town or Place, as aforefaid, or for any other Perfon or Perfons who fhall not firft take and fubfcribe the faid Oath, and fhall not frequent Divine Service eftablifhed by the Law of this Kingdom, and carry him or herfelf reverently there, to teach any publick or private School, or take any Boarders or Tablers to be taught or inftructed by him or herfelf, or any other, upon Pain of Forfeiture of forty Pounds for every Offence, to be recovered and diftributed as aforefaid.

And any two Juftices of the Peace in their refpective County, upon Oath to them of any Offence againft this Act, (which Oath they are impowered to adminifter) may commit the Offender for fix Months without Bail; unlefs before fuch Commitment he fhall before the faid Juftices of the Peace fwear and fubfcribe the faid Oath and Declaration.

Provided, That Appearance to any *Subpœna,* Warrant or Procefs, whereby perfonal Appearance is required, fhall not be conftrued an Offence within this Act.

There was an Act made 16 *Car.* 2. *cap.* 6. Touching the fuppreffing Seditious Conventicles, but the fame being Temporary is expired, as by the fame Act appeareth.

4   If.

If any Subject of sixteen Years of Age shall be present at any Meeting under Pretence of 22 Car. 2. c. 1.
Exercise of Religion in any Place, at which are present five Persons, besides those of the §. 1.
House, if it be in a House inhabited, or if in a House, Field, or Place where no Family Nota, *That*
is, then if above five Persons be present, any one or more Justices of that Liberty, or the *ProteſtantDiſ-*
Chief Magiſtrate upon Proof of the Offence by Confeſſion, or two Witneſſes, or notorious *ſenters are ex-*
Evidence and Circumſtance of the Fact, to make a Record, which ſhall be a Conviction, *the Penalties*
and to impoſe five Shillings Fine on every Offender, which ſhall be certified at the Quar- *in this Act by*
ter-Seſſions; and for the ſecond Offence ten Shillings, which Fines ſhall be levied by Diſtreſs c. 18. §. 4.
and Sale, and if poor, on any Perſon preſent at ſuch Conventicle, and convicted at Diſcretion, ſo as ſuch Sum to be levied on any other, exceed not ten Pounds at one Meeting.

The Conſtable, Headborough, Tithingman, Church-warden, or Overſeer to levy it by Sect. 2.
Warrant, under the Hand and Seal of ſuch Juſtice, or Chief Magiſtrate, and to deliver it
to the Juſtice, or Chief Magiſtrate, one Part to the King, ſo paid to the Sheriff, *viz.* to
be delivered into Seſſions, and they to deliver it to the Sheriff, and to make a Record of
it, and to certify it into the Exchequer; another third Part to the Poor, and the other third
Part to ſuch Informer, or other Perſon as the Juſtices ſhall appoint, having reſpect to their
Induſtry thereabouts.

Every Preacher in ſuch Conventicle ſhall forfeit for the firſt Offence twenty Pounds, to Sect. 3.
be levied by Diſtreſs and Sale, and if he be a Stranger, or unknown, or is fled, or cannot *This doth not*
be found, or the Juſtices ſhall judge him unable to pay, the Juſtice may levy the ſame on *extend to a*
the Goods of any Perſons then preſent, to be diſpoſed of as aforeſaid. And for the ſecond *ProteſtantDiſ-*
Offence the Preacher to forfeit forty Pounds, to be levied and diſpoſed of, as aforeſaid. *ſenter.* 1 W.
c. 18. §. 8.

The Perſon that ſuffers ſuch Conventicle in his Houſe, *&c.* ſhall forfeit twenty Pounds, *The like.*
to be levied and diſpoſed of as aforeſaid. No Perſon ſhall be liable to pay above ten Pounds Sect. 4.
at any one Meeting, in reſpect of the Poverty of other Perſons. Sect. 5.

Where any Sum charged on ſuch Offender exceeds ten Shillings, he may within a Week Sect. 6.
after it is levied, appeal in Writing to the Seſſions, and leave it with the Juſtice, whether
the Party convicting ſhall return the Money, and the whole Record and Evidence under
Hand and Seal, to which the Appellant may plead, and it ſhall be tried by a Jury; and if
he do not proſecute, or ſhall not be acquitted, or Judgment ſhall not paſs for him, the
Juſtices ſhall give treble Coſts, and no other Court ſhall meddle with Appeals, and the
Appellant is to enter into a Recognizance before the Perſon convicting to proſecute his Appeal, which ſhall be alſo certified to the Seſſions.

The Juſtices, or Conſtables, Tithingmen, and Headboroughs by Warrant from them, Sect. 9.
with what Aid they think fit, upon Refuſal, may enter the Houſe or Place, and may ſeize the *This doth not*
Perſons, and upon a Certificate under a Juſtice's Hand and Seal of his Information or Know- *extend to Pro-*
ledge of a Conventicle, and that he cannot ſuppreſs it, any commiſſioned Officer of the *teſtant Diſ-*
Militia, or other the King's Forces, and other Miniſters of Juſtice with Soldiers or other *ſenters.* 1 W.
Aid may prevent or diſſipate them. But no Lord's Houſe ſhall be ſearched, but by War- c. 18.
rant under the King's Sign Manual, or in Preſence of the Lord Lieutenant, or Deputy Lieu- Sect. 10.
tenant, or two Juſtices, *Quorum unus.*

Any Conſtable, *&c.* knowing of a Conventicle, and not giving Information, but they Sect. 11.
or any other being called, refuſing to go in Aid of them, and thereof convicted in Form
aforeſaid, ſhall forfeit five Pounds to be levied by Diſtreſs and Sale, and a Juſtice of Peace,
or chief Magiſtrate neglecting his Duty, forfeits one Hundred Pounds, one Moiety to the
King, the other to the Informer by Action, *&c.*

The Act ſhall be taken beneficially for ſuppreſſing Conventicles, and no Proceeding Sect. 13.
ſhall be revers'd for Form. If any Perſon convicted live in another County or Corporation,
upon Certificate under Hand and Seal of the Perſon convicting, to the Juſtices or Chief
Magiſtrate, he or they ſhall levy the Penalty.

The Party convicted being a Feme Covert, living with her Husband, Penalties of 5 *s.*
and 10 *s.* ſhall be levied on his Goods: Every Offender muſt be preſented within three
Months.

See the 1 *W. & M. ſtat.* 1. *cap.* 18. (confirmed by 10 *Ann. cap.* 2. *ſect.* 7.) which ex-
plains that of the 22 *Car.* 2. and makes divers Exceptions with reſpect to Proteſtant Diſſenters.

CHAP.

CHAP. XXXI.

Cottages, and Inmates.

Erecting Cottages.
31 El. 7.
See for the Exposition of this Statute 2 Inft.
736.
Continuing Inmates.
* *This must be presented by the*

NO Perfon fhall make, build or erect, or caufe, &c. any Cottage for Habitation or Dwelling, nor convert any Building to be ufed as a Cottage, unlefs he affign and lay to it four Acres of Land, being his Freehold and Inheritance, lying near it, to be continually ufed with it, upon Pain to forfeit to the King 10 *l.* Every Perfon that fhall uphold or continue any fuch Cottage to be erected or convicted, fhall forfeit 40 *s.* for every Month. There fhall be no Inmate, or more Families, or Houfehold, than one dwelling in any Cottage, made or to be made, upon Pain that the Owner, or Occupier wilfully fuffering it, fhall forfeit to the Lord of the Leet * 10 *s. per menfem.*

Jury upon their own Knowledge, or they muft find Indictment upon Evidence, and then and not before the Lord hath a Title to the Penalty.

Ibid.

This Statute fhall not extend to Cottages in any City, Town Corporate, or ancient Borough, or Market-Town, nor to Cottages erected for Habitation of Workmen in Minerals, Cole-Mines, or Quarries of Stone, or about making of Brick, Lime, or Cole, fo as the fame be not above a Mile from the Work, nor to a Cottage within a Mile of the Sea, inhabited by a Sailor, nor to a Cottage for a Keeper or Warrener, nor to a Cottage heretofore erected and ufed for the Habitation of a Shepherd, or poor Perfon, fo allowed to continue by the Seffions.

Ibid.
* *Directed by his Steward to the Bailiff of the Manor.*
43 El. 2.

The Juftices of Peace in their Seffions (*inter alia*) may hear and determine Offences againft that Act by Indictment, or by Prefentment or Information, and to award Execution by * *Fieri facias, Elegit, Capias,* or otherwife, as the Cafe fhall require.

The Church-wardens and Overfeers, by Leave of the Lord in Writing, under the Hand and Seal of the Lord, or by Order of the Seffions with the Lord's Leave, may erect Cottages for poor People.

See alfo *Highways,* Chap. 50.

CHAP. XXXII.

Counterfeiters.

Two Juftices.
33 H. 8. 1.
P. Juft. 54.

TWO Juftices of Peace, the one being of the *Quorum,* may grant their Warrant to attach and bind over to the next General Seffions of the Peace or Affifes, any Perfon that is fufpected of any deceitful getting into his Hands any Money, Goods, or other Thing of any other Perfons, by Means or Colour of any falfe Tokens or counterfeit Letter made in another Man's Name, there to be examined and ordered.

Henry *Jones* for a counterfeit Pafs was adjudged to the Pillory, and fined. *Lib. Delib. Gaol. Newgate* 5 *Dec.* 8 *Car.* The like for counterfeiting a Butcher's Licence, 30 *March,* 7 *Car. eod. Lib.* Alfo the faid Juftices may call before themfelves the Offenders, and after due Examination, &c. may imprifon fuch Offenders, or bail them until the next General Seffion or Gaol-Delivery. And in this Cafe the faid Juftices of Peace fhall do well to take Examination of the Offence, and to certify the fame to the faid Seffions or Gaol-Delivery; and withal to bind over the Informers and Witneffes to give Evidence therein.

Cheaters.

One Juftice of the Peace may bind fuch Offenders, as Cheaters, to their Good Behaviour, and fo to the next Affifes or Seffions of the Peace, there to be examined and ordered; or elfe, by Force of the Statute 7 *Jac.* 1. *cap.* 4. may fend fuch Offenders, as idle and diforderly Perfons, to the Houfe of Correction, there to be continued until the next Affifes or Seffions, and then and there to be forth-coming, &c. yet *Quære* of fending them to the Houfe of Correction: And it feemeth more warrantable, if they be fent to the Houfe of Correction by Order of the Seffions. *Richard Freed* had Judgment to be fet in the Pillory with a Paper written, *A common Cheater and Coufener,* and thence to be had to *Bridewel,* and kept at Work till he paid twenty Nobles for a Fine, and

2   put

put in Sureties for his Good Behaviour. *Lib. Delib. Gaol. Newgate,* 10 *July* 7 *Jac.* 1. *fol.* 77.

Perſons perſonating Seamen, *&c.* in order to receive their Wages, forfeit 200 *l.* over 9 & 10 W. 3. and above the other Penalties inflicted by Law. c. 4. ſ. 3.

Perſons counterfeiting the Hand of the Treaſurer, Controller, Surveyor, Clerk of the i Geo. 1. c. Acts, Commiſſioners of the Navy, or of the vouching Officers of his Majeſty's Navy, 25. ſ. 6. *&c.* to any Bill, Ticket or other Papers, by Virtue whereof his Majeſty's Naval Trea- *Made perpe-tual* 9 Geo. 1. ſure may be diſpoſed of, or ſhall knowingly produce any ſuch counterfeit Ticket, *&c.* c. 8. ſhall be committed to Priſon till he find Sureties for his Appearance at the next Aſſiſes or Quarter-Seſſions. * * *Note ; the Stat.* 22 &

23 *Car.* c. 23. *relating to this laſt mentioned Offence, Inſerted in the former Editions of this Book, is expired. See the Statute at large.*

'Tis Felony without Benefit of Clergy, for any Perſon knowingly to ſend any Letter Or forcibly to another with a fictitious Name, demanding any valuable Thing, *per* Stat. 9 *Geo.* 1. *Reſcuing one in Cuſtody for this Offence.* *cap.* 22.

See more in Tit. *Felonies by Statute,* Chap. 160.

C H A P.   XXXIII.

Cuſtoms.

WHERE any Officers of the Cuſtoms are, by any Perſon armed with a Club or 13 & 14 Car. other Weapon, forcibly hindred, affronted, abuſed, beaten or wounded in the 2. c. 6. ſ. 6. Execution of their Truſts and Services, either on Board a Veſſel, or by Land or Water, the Perſon refiſting, *&c.* ſuch Officers, or their Deputies, ſhall by the next Juſtice of Peace, or other Magiſtrate, be committed to Priſon until the next Quarter-Seſſions.

If any Carman, Porter, Waterman, or other Perſon, ſhall aſſiſt in the taking up, Ib. ſ. 7. landing, ſhipping, or carrying away any Goods, Wares or Merchandizes, either from the Shore outwards bound, or out of any Ship or Veſſel arriving from Parts beyond the Sea, without a Warrant and Preſence of one or more Officers of the Cuſtoms, the Per- ſon ſo offending, being apprehended by a Warrant from a Juſtice of Peace, and the ſame proved by the Oaths of two Witneſſes, for the firſt Offence the Juſtice may commit him to Gaol, until he ſhall find Sureties for the Good Behaviour, for ſo long Time, until he ſhall be thereof diſcharged by the Lord Chancellor, Under-Treaſurer, or Barons of the Exchequer. And for the ſecond Offence, being ſo convicted, the Juſtice may commit him to Gaol for two Months without Bail, or until he ſhall pay the Sheriff five Pounds, or until he ſhall be diſcharged by the Lord Treaſurer, Chancellor, Under- Treaſurer or Barons.

All Juſtices of Peace, *&c.* ſhall be aſſiſting to the Officers of the Cuſtoms and their Ib. ſ. 32. Deputies in the due Execution of every Thing by this Act injoined.

If any Perſon ſhall cauſe any Goods, for which Cuſtom, Subſidy, or other Duties are *To enter a Houſe for Goods conceal-ed.* due by Virtue of one Act of 12 *Car.* 2. *cap.* 14. to be landed or conveyed away, with- out Entry firſt made, and the Cuſtomer, Collector or his Deputy firſt agreed with, upon Oath made before (amongſt others) the chief Magiſtrate of the Port or Place where the 12 Car. 2. c. 19. ſ. 1. Offence ſhall be committed, or the Place next adjoining, he may iſſue out a Warrant to any Perſon or Perſons, enabling them, with the Aſſiſtance of a Sheriff, Juſtice of Peace, or Conſtable, to enter any Houſe in the Day-time, where the Goods are ſuſpected to be concealed, and in caſe of Reſiſtance to break the Houſe and ſeiſe the Goods ; but no Houſe ſhall be entred, but within a Month after the Offence committed ; and if upon ſuch Information a Houſe be ſearched, and the Information prove falſe, the Party ſhall recover his full Damage and Coſts againſt ſuch Information.

All Officers of the Cuſtoms in the Out-Ports, or elſewhere, ſhall before the 25th of 6 W. 3. c. i. *March* next take an Oath before two Juſtices of the Peace, that they will not receive ſ. 5. any Reward or Gratuity other than their reſpective Salaries, or the regular Fees eſtabliſh- ed by Law : And for neglecting or refuſing to take the ſaid Oath, ſhall forfeit their Office or Employment.

The Perſons adminiſtring the ſaid Oath, ſhall certify the ſame to the next General Quarter-Seſſions of the Peace of the proper County, there to be recorded.

6 Geo.1.c.21.
§.34.

By the Stat. 6 *Geo.*1. Perſons armed with Clubs, or any Manner of Weapon, and tumultu-ouſly met together in the Day-time, or in the Night, to the Number of eight or more, their Aiders and Aſſiſters forcibly Hindring, Wounding, or Beating any *Cuſtom-houſe Oſ-ficers* in the due Execution of their Office, and being convicted thereof, ſhall be tranſ-ported by the Order of the Court, and for ſuch a Term of Years not exceeding ſeven Years, as the Court ſhall think fit, in the ſame Manner as Felons are tranſported by 4 *Geo.* 1. *cap.* 11.

Ib. §. 35.

And if the Perſon thus tranſported ſhall return into *Great Britain* or *Ireland*, be-fore the Expiration of the ſaid Term, he ſhall be a Felon without Benefit of Clergy.

8 Geo. 1.
c. 18. §. 6.

All Perſons found paſſing knowingly with foreign Goods, landed from any Ship with-out due Entry and Payment of Duties, in their Cuſtody, from any of the Coaſts of this Kingdom, or within the Space of twenty Miles of any of the ſaid Coaſts, and ſhall be more than five Perſons in Company, or ſhall carry any offenſive Arms, or wear any Maſk or other Diſguiſe, when paſſing with ſuch Goods, or ſhall forcibly hinder or reſiſt any Officers of the Cuſtoms or Exciſe in ſeiſing any Sort of Run Goods, ſhall be deemed and taken to be Runners of foreign Goods within the Meaning of this Act; and being convicted ſhall be adjudged Felons, and tranſported for ſeven Years. And ſuch Offenders returning to *Great Britain* or *Ireland* before the Expiration of the ſaid Term, ſhall be guilty of Felony without Benefit of Clergy.

Ib. §. 10.

If any Perſon ſhall receive or buy any Goods clandeſtinely Run, before the ſame be condemned, knowing the ſame to be ſo clandeſtinely Run, and ſhall be thereof convict-ed, upon Appearance or Default, on the Oath of one Witneſs, or by Confeſſion before one Juſtice of the Peace of the County, *&c.* where the Offence ſhall be committed, or the Offender found; he ſhall forfeit 20 *l.* one Moiety to the Informer, the other to the Poor of the Pariſh; to be levied by Diſtreſs, *&c.* and for Want of Diſtreſs he ſhall be committed to Priſon for three Months.

Ib. §. 16.

All Seiſures of Veſſels, of the Burden of fifteen Tons, or under, made by Virtue of any Act relating to the Cuſtoms, for Carrying uncuſtomed or prohibited Goods from Ships in-wards, or for Relanding Certificate or Debentur Goods from Ships outwards; and all Seiſures of Horſes, Cattle or Carriages, for being uſed in the Removing ſuch Goods, ſhall be heard and determined by any two Juſtices of Peace reſiding near the Place, in

See the Act at large.

ſuch Manner as by 6 *Geo.* 1. *cap.* 21. (except as excepted by this Act) and their Judg-ments ſhall be final, and not liable to any Appeal or *Certiorari.*

Ib. §. 17.

Any two Juſtices for *London* or *Weſtminſter* ſhall have the like Power relating to Seiſures made within thoſe Cities.

This Act is continued by 8 *Geo.* 2. *cap.* 21. to 29 *Sept.* 1742.

12 Geo. 1.
c. 28. §. 16.

One Juſtice of Peace ſhall have Power to adminiſter an Oath to Perſons ſkilled in the Value of the Goods, Veſſels, Boats, *&c.* mentioned to have been ſeiſed in the Informa-tion exhibited before any Juſtice of Peace to view the ſame, and to make a Return of the Value and Quality thereof, to ſuch Juſtices in a limited Time; and after the Goods, Veſſels, *&c.* ſhall have been condemned by ſuch Juſtices, they ſhall be publickly ſold to the beſt Bidder, at ſuch Places and Times as the Commiſſioners ſhall think proper.

9 G. 2. c. 35.
§. 1.

By the Statute 9 *Geo.* 2. *cap.* 35. all Subjects of *Great Britain*, who before the 27th of *April* 1736. incurred any Penalty for Running of Goods, ſhall be indemnified.

Ib. §. 7.

But if any Perſon liable to be tranſported for ſuch Offences ſhall take the Benefit of this Act, and ſhall afterwards commit any ſuch Offences, he ſhall ſuffer Death as in Ca-ſes of Felony, without Benefit of Clergy.

Ib. §. 10.

Upon Information upon Oath, before any one Juſtice of Peace, that any Perſons to the Number of Three have been aſſembled for Running of Goods, and have been armed with offenſive Weapons; ſuch Juſtice ſhall grant his Warrant to the Conſtables and Peace-Officers, to take to their Aſſiſtance as many of his Majeſty's Subjects as may be thought neceſſary for the Apprehending every Perſon againſt whom any ſuch Information ſhall be given, and ſuch Juſtice ſhall (if upon Examination he find Cauſe) commit all the ſaid Perſons to the next County Gaol, without Bail, until they be diſcharged by Law; and every ſuch Perſon, upon Proof of his being aſſembled and armed, in order to run Goods, upon Conviction, ſhall be adjudged guilty of Felony, and tranſported for ſeven Years.

Ib. § 13.

All Perſons, who, to the Number of Two in Company, ſhall be found paſſing with-in five Miles from the Sea-Coaſts, or any navigable River, with Horſe or Carriage, whereon there ſhall be laden more than ſix Pounds of Tea, or Brandy exceeding five Gallons, not having paid the Duties, and not having a Permit; or any other foreign

I   Goods

Goods above the Value of 30 *l.* landed without due Entry, and Payment of Duties, and ſhall carry offenſive Arms, or wear any Diſguiſe, or ſhall forcibly reſiſt any Officers of the Cuſtoms or Exciſe, in the Execution of their Office, ſhall be deemed Runners of foreign Goods within 8 *Geo.* 1. *cap.* 18. And the Proof of Entry, and Payment of Duties, and of the Manner how the ſaid Perſons ſo found with the Goods came by the ſame, ſhall wholly lie on ſuch Perſons; and all Perſons convicted of the ſaid Offence ſhall be guilty of Felony, and ſhall be tranſported for ſeven Years.

Any Officers of the Cuſtoms and Exciſe wounded, *&c.* by the Offenders laſt men- Ib. §. 15. tioned, upon their Conviction, ſhall have 50 *l.* And the Executor or Adminiſtrator of any Perſon killed in apprehending ſuch Offenders, upon Certificate of the Juſtice of Aſſiſe, or the two next Juſtices of Peace, ſhall have 50 *l.* over and above any other Reward.

Upon Information upon Oath before one Juſtice of Peace, of Perſons loitering within Ib. §. 18. five Miles from the Sea-Coaſt, or from any navigable River, and of Reaſon to ſuſpect an Intent of running Goods, ſuch Juſtice may cauſe ſuch Perſons to be brought before him, and grant Warrants for apprehending them, and if they do not give a ſatisfactory Account of themſelves, they ſhall be committed to the Houſe of Correction, to be whipp'd and kept to hard Labour, any Time not exceeding one Month.

If the Perſon brought before the Juſtice deſires Time to make it appear, that he is not Ib. §. 19. concerned in ſuch fraudulent Practiſes, he ſhall not be puniſhed, but the Juſtice may commit him to the common Gaol until he gives ſuch an Account, or gives Security not to be guilty of the ſaid Offences.

Perſons offering Tea, Brandy, *&c.* to Sale, without Permit ; or if any Pedlar ſhall Ib. §. 20. offer Tea, *&c.* to Sale, though with a Permit, the Perſon to whom ſuch Tea, *&c.* is offered, may ſtop it, and carry it to the next Warehouſe of the Cuſtoms or Exciſe, and bring the Offender before any Juſtice of Peace, to be committed to Priſon and proſecuted, as if the Goods had been ſeiſed by an Officer. The Seiſor is intitled to one Third of the groſs Produce of the Sale of ſuch Goods ; or if he deſire it, the Commiſſioners in the mean Time ſhall cauſe 1 *s.* for every Pound of Tea, or Gallon of Brandy ſo ſeiſed, to be paid him, upon Certificate by the Juſtice of the Commitment of ſuch Offender, and after Sale the Money ſo paid ſhall be replaced.

Perſons imployed in knowingly carrying Goods run, in whoſe Cuſtody the ſame ſhall Ib. §. 21. be found, upon Conviction before one Juſtice of Peace, ſhall forfeit treble the Value of the Goods, one Moiety to the Informer, the other to the Poor, to be levied by Diſtreſs, and for want of ſuch the Offender ſhall be committed to the Houſe of Correction for any Time not exceeding three Months.

Perſons forcibly hindering or beating any Officer of the Cuſtoms or Exciſe, on board Ib. §. 28. any Veſſel in Port, ſhall be tranſported (by Order of the Court before whom convicted) for any Term not exceeding ſeven Years, and returning, *&c.* ſhall ſuffer as Felons without Benefit of Clergy.

On all Trials of Seiſures, the Seiſure ſhall be taken to have been made as ſet forth Ib. §. 34. in the Information, without any Evidence ; and all Judges and Juſtices of Peace are to proceed to the Trial of the Merits of the Cauſe, without inquiring into the Seiſure.

Officers of the Cuſtoms and Exciſe may oppoſe Force to Force; and if any Perſon Ib. §. 35. reſiſting the Officers ſhall be killed or wounded, the Officers and their Aſſiſtants being proſecuted, may plead the General Iſſue ; and all Juſtices of Peace are required to admit ſuch Officers, *&c.* to Bail.

C H A P. XXXIV.

Cuſtos Rotulorum.

NO Perſon ſhall be appointed or aſſigned *Cuſtos Rotulorum,* but ſuch as have a Bill 37 H. 8. 1. ſigned with the King's Hand for the ſame, which Bill ſigned ſhall be a ſufficient Warrant for the Lord Chancellor, or Lord Keeper, to grant a Commiſſion to that Purpoſe, until the King in like Manner ſhall aſſign another.

Every *Cuſtos Rotulorum* ſhall nominate and appoint every Perſon who ſhall be Clerk of 37 H 8 1 the Peace, and to grant ſuch Offices to ſuch able Perſons inſtructed in the Laws, as ſhall be able to uſe the ſame, for the Time the *Cuſtos Rotulorum* ſhall continue in his Office.

1 W. & M. Stat. 1. c. 21. §. 4.
By 1 *Will. & Mar.* the Appointing of the *Cuftos Rotulorum* through all the Counties fhall be as directed by 37 *H.* 8. *cap.* 1.

See *Clerk of the Peace*, in *Chap.* 23.

Diffenters.

THOSE who refufe to make and fubfcribe the Declaration 30 *Car.* 2. and to take the Oaths which came in the Room of the Oaths of Allegiance and Supremacy when tendered, are to enter into a Recognizance with two Sureties of 50 *l.* conditioned to procure a Certificate under the Hands of Six of that Proteftant Congregation (whereof the Refufer is one) or under the Hands of four Church of *England* Proteftants, that he is a Proteftant. 1 *Will.* 3. *cap.* 18.

10 Ann. c.18.
One Juftice may require a diffenting Minifter preaching in a County where he is not qualified according to the Act of Toleration, to take the Oath and Declaration of Allegiance and Fidelity.

1 Will. 3. c. 2.
He who difturbs a Proteftant Diffenter, and being convicted at the Seffions by the Oath of two Witneffes, forfeits 20 *l.*

5 Geo. 1. c. 4.
By the Act 5 *Geo.* 1. *cap.* 4. *fect.* 1. Part of the Statute of 10 *Annæ, cap.* 2. and the *Schifm Act* of 12 *Ann.* Stat. 2. *cap.* 7. excluding Diffenters from Offices, are repealed; but Magiftrates knowingly or willingly being at any Meeting for Religious Worfhip, other than the Church of *England*, in the Gown or Habit of, or attended with the Enfigns belonging to their Office, fhall be difabled to hold fuch Office, and adjudg'd incapable of any Publick Office.

CHAP. XXXV.

Dyers.

13 & 14 Car. 2. c. 11. §. 26 & 27.
IN the former Editions of this Book there was inferted the Act of 39 *Eliz. cap.* 11. againft Perfons ufing *Logwood* or *Blockwood* in Dying. But by 13 *& 14 Car.* 2. *cap.* 11. *fect.* 26. any Perfon may import Logwood, and ufe the fame in Dying, provided fuch Importation be according to the Act of Navigation. 12 *Car.* 2. *cap.* 18.

13 Geo. 1. c. 24. §. 1.
By 13 *Geo.* 1. *cap.* 24. If any Perfon fhall dye Black any Bays, or other woollen Goods, as Mather Blacks, the fame not being dyed throughout with Woad, Indigo and Mather only; or fhall dye Black any Cloths, Long Ells, Bays, *&c.* for woaded Blacks, the fame not being woaded throughout, he fhall forfeit for fuch falfe Mathered Blacks as follows:

For every long *Bocking* Bays, containing 70 Yards 44 *s.*

For every *Colchefter* Bays, or fhort Bays, containing 35 Yards, 22 *s.* and fo in Proportion for Bays, or other woollen Goods.

For every Cloth dyed Blacks, without being woaded throughout, containing 44 Yards, 40 *s.*

For every Piece of Bays falfly dyed, as aforefaid, containing 70 Yards, 30 *s.*

For every *Colchefter* or fhort Bays, containing 35 Yards, 12 *s.*

For every *Perpetuana* or Stuff, falfly dyed, 4 *s.* and fo in Proportion for other woollen Goods deceitfully dyed for woaded Blacks.

Ib. §. 2.
All woollen Goods which fhall be truly Mathered Black, fhall be marked with a red Rofe, and a blue Rofe; and all woollen Goods which fhall be truly woaded Black throughout, fhall be mark'd with a blue Rofe; and if any Perfon fhall counterfeit the faid Marks, or fhall affix fuch Mark to Goods falfly dyed, fuch Offender fhall forfeit 4 *l.* for every Piece of Goods to which the faid Mark fhall be affixed.

Ib. §. 3.
If any Perfon fhall ufe Logwood in dying of Blue, he fhall forfeit 40 *s.* for every Piece of Cloth fo dyed, containing 44 Yards; and 22 *s.* for every long Piece of *Bocking* Bays, containing 70 Yards; and 12 *s.* for every *Colchefter* or fhort Bays, containing 35 Yards; and 4 *s.* for every *Perpetuana* or Stuff, containing 24 Yards; and fo in Proportion.

Ib. §. 4.
Dyers of woollen Manufactures within *London*, or within ten Miles compafs of the fame, fhall be fubject to the Infpection of the Company of *Dyers*, and the Mafter, Wardens, and Court of Affiftants of the faid Company, may appoint Searchers within the

I   *faid*

faid Limits; and out of the faid Limits, the Juftices of Peace at their Quarter-Seffions may appoint fuch Searchers, who, taking a Conftable or other Peace-Officer, in the Day-time, may enter the Shops or Work-houfes of Dyers of woollen Goods, to fearch for fuch Goods to be dyed Black or Blue ; and Perfons oppofing fuch Search, fhall forfeit 10 *l.*

Forfeitures by this Act exceeding 5 *l.* to be recovered in Courts of Record at *Weft-* Ib. §. 5. *minfter*, but not exceeding 5 *l.* the Matter fhall be determined by two or more Juftices of Peace of the County, City, &c. where the Offence fhall be committed. And For-feitures by this Act in *London*, and ten Miles Diftance, go one Moiety to the Informer, the other to the Company of Dyers ; beyond fuch Compafs the Whole goes to the Infor-mers. Offenders refufing to pay the Forfeitures not exceeding 5 *l.* for the Space of twen-ty Days, the Juftice may iffue his Warrant to levy the fame by Diftrefs, &c. and where no Diftrefs can be found, to commit the Offenders to the Houfe of Correction to hard Labour, not exceeding three Months.

Profecutions for Offences againft this Act fhall be commenced within forty Days after Ib. §. 6. the Offence committed. Perfons aggrieved by Order of the Juftices may appeal to the next Quarter-Seffions, giving reafonable Notice, the Determination of the Seffions fhall be final ; and they may allow Cofts.

Defendant may plead the General Iffue, and upon Nonfuit, &c. fhall have treble Cofts. Ib. §. 7.

C H A P. XXXVI.

Egyptians.

EVERY Juftice of Peace, Sheriff, and Efcheator, within one Month after their Ar- One *Juftice.* rival, may feife all Goods of any outlandifh Perfons calling themfelves *Egyptians,* 22 H. 8. 10. that fhall come into this Realm, and may alfo keep the one Moiety thereof to his own Raft. 135. Ufe, making Account to the King in the Exchequer for the other Moiety. And every Perfon that can prove by two credible Witneffes (before the faid Juftice or other Officer that fo feifeth the faid Goods) that any of thofe Goods were craftily or felonioufly taken from him, fhall incontinently be reftored thereto (by the Party that fo feifeth them) upon Pain of the double Value thereof to be forfeited by fuch Seifor to fuch Prover.

But note, That after the Month the Offence is made Felony by the Statute of 1 & 2 5 El. 20. *Ph. & Mar. cap.* 4. and 5 *Eliz. cap.* 20. *p.* 2. And then it feemeth the King is to have the Goods wholly. And *Quære* whether the Statute of 22 *H.* 8. be ftill in Force, or be altered by the faid Statutes of 1 & 2 *Ph. & Ma. cap.* 4. and 5 *Eliz. cap.* 20.

Alfo note, That by the Statute of 1 & 2 *Ph. & Ma.* and 5 *Eliz.* the Word *Egyptian,* is now extended to fuch *counterfeit Rogues and Vagabonds*, as being *Englifh* or *Welfh* People, do call themfelves *Egyptians* ; or do accompany themfelves together, difguifing themfelves by their Apparel, Speech, Countenance, or other Behaviour, like unto *Egyptians,* or like unto fuch Vagabonds as call themfelves, or are commonly called *Egyptians* : And fo they are all Felons, or at leaft they are all incorrigible Rogues; therefore the Juftice muft fend all fuch to the Gaol, and they are not bailable by Law, becaufe they are all deemed Felons without Clergy.

Efcape and Breaking Prifon. See *Felony*, Chap. 158, 159.

C H A P. XXXVII.

Eftreats.

EVERY Clerk of the Peace fhall deliver to the Sheriff within twenty Days after the 22 & 23 Car. 29th Day of *September* in every Year, a perfect Eftreat of all Fines, Iffues, Amer- 2. c. 22. §. 7. ciaments, Recognizances, Monies and Forfeitures impofed, fet, loft or forfeited in any Seffions of the Peace, before *Michaelmas*, by any Perfon due to his Majefty.

And the faid Clerk fhall, on or before every fecond Monday after the Morrow of Ib. §. 8. *All-Souls*, deliver into the Exchequer a perfect Schedule of all fuch Eftreats and Sche-dules by him delivered to the Sheriffs, on Pain to forfeit 50 *l.* one Moiety to the King,

U the

Ib. §. 9. the other to the Informer. 22 & 23 *Car.* 2. 2. No Juftice of Peace, or Clerk of the Peace, fhall fpare, difcharge, or conceal any Indictment, Fine, Iffue, Amerciament, forfeited Recognizance, or Forfeiture, fet, loft, or forfeited, or Money paid in Satisfaction of Fine or Forfeiture, unlefs by Order of Court, nor mifcertify any of the fame, whereby the Procefs of Exchequer may be made invalid, upon Pain to forfeit the treble Value thereof, one Moiety to the King, the other to the Informer.

Ib. §. 10. Where any Fine or Forfeiture fhall be paid to any Clerk of the Peace, and be eftreated into the Exchequer, the Summons or Procefs of Green Wax fhall go to the Sheriffs againft him.

Quære, Where a Sheriff demands Money on the Green Wax, he ought to fhew the fame to the Party, and that which is paid fhall be totted, or elfe he fhall pay treble Damage to the Party, and be fined to the King, and the Party may bring his Suit before Juftices of Peace.　Statute 42 *E.* 3. 9.　Statute 7 *H.* 4. *cap.* 3.

Evidence againft Felons.　See *Chap.* 164.

C H A P. XXXVIII.

Excife.

12 Car. 2. c. 23. BY Act of 12 *Car.* 2. *cap.* 23. is fettled upon the King for Life, thefe Duties.
For every Barrel of Beer or Ale, above 6 *s.* the Barrel, brewed by a common Brewer, or any other that doth fell Beer publickly or privately, 15 *d.*
For every Barrel of 6 *s.* or under 3 *d.*
For every Hogfhead of Cyder or Perry by the Retailer, 15 *d.*
For every Gallon of Metheglin by the Maker, to be fold, one Halfpenny.
For every Barrel of Vinegar Beer, brewed by a common Brewer, 6 *d.*
For every Gallon of ftrong Water, or *Aqua Vitæ,* by the Maker 1 *d.*
For every Barrel of Beer or Ale imported from beyond the Sea, 3 *s.*
For every Ton of Cyder or Perry imported, 5 *s.*

By 22 Car. 2. Brandy is declared to be Strong Water within this Act. For every Gallon of Spirits, made of Cyder or Wine imported, 2 *d.*
For every Gallon of Strong Water imported, perfectly made, 4 *d.*
For every Gallon of Coffee, by the Maker, 4 *d.*
For every Gallon of Chocolate, Sherbet, and Tea, 8 *d.*

Excife to the King and his Heirs. The like Excife is given to the King and his Heirs by the Statute of 12 *Car.* 2. *cap.* 24. in lieu of the Court of Wards and Liveries; and the Provifions of both Acts being the fame in Subftance, and for the moft part in Words, are abridged as followeth :

12 Car. 2. c. 24. 1. The Excife of foreign Liquors fhall be paid by the Merchant Importer in ready

Who fhall pay it. Money, and before Landing, and by 15 *Car.* 2. *cap.* 11. there is a Penalty of the Forfeiture of the Goods.

Entries. 2. All common Brewers once a Week, and all Retailers once a Month, fhall make Entries of what they fhall brew or make in that Week, or Month, or elfe the Brewer to forfeit 5 *l.* Inn-keeper 5 *l.* other Retailer 20 *s.*

Payment. 3. A common Brewer within a Week, and other Retailer within a Month after they make, or ought to make their Entry, fhall pay the Duty, or pay double the Duty to be levied of their Goods.

Office. 4. No Perfon living in a Market-Town, fhall go out of that Town, or if he live out of a Town fhall go farther than the next Market-Town on the Market-Day.

Gaugers. 5. The Commiffioners and Sub-Commiffioners in their Divifions may appoint Gaugers under Hand and Seal, which Gaugers may by Night or Day, if by Night in the Prefence of a Conftable, or other lawful Officer, upon Requeft, be permitted to enter any Houfe or Place of Brewers and Retailers, and to take Account of fuch Liquors, and make Return to the Commiffioners, or Sub-Commiffioners, leaving a Copy of fuch Return with the Brewer, Maker, or Retailer, under his Hand, which Return fhall be a Charge upon the Brewer, Maker, or Retailer; and if fuch Brewer, Maker, or Retailer, fhall refufe fuch Gauger Entry, or to Gauge or take Account, the Gauger may forbid him to fell or carry out the fame; and if he fhall fell or carry out the fame, not having paid the Duty, fhall over and above the double Value pay five Pounds.

Veff.s. 6. Every 36 Gallons of Beer, and 32 Gallons of Ale to be taken by the Ale-quart, fhal make a Gallon of Beer or Ale, and other Liquors by the Wine-quart.

7. No Brewer or Retailer fhall upon Sale take more than the ufual Prices, faving that common Brewers may take the Excife. *Prices.*

8. Every common Brewer fhall out of twenty-three Barrels of Beer, be allowed one; and fo out of twenty-two Barrels of Ale. *Allowance.*

9. Every common Brewer wittingly making a falfe Entry, and convicted as by the Act is directed, fhall forfeit as aforefaid; and fo for fix Months next following. *Falfe Entry.*

10. No Beer or Ale is to be delivered by the common Brewer to the Retailer, until the Duty be paid. If any brew only to fell in a Fair, and fhall pay the Day before Sale, he fhall be difcharged.

11. The Commiffioners and Sub-Commiffioners may compound with the Brewer or Retailer, as may be for moft Advantage of the Receipts thereof. *Compofition.*

12. The Lord Treafurer or Commiffioners of the Treafury, or fuch as the King fhall appoint, may let to farm the Duty for three Years. *Farming.*

13. All Forfeitures and Offences to be determined within the Limits of the chief Office in *London*, by the Commiffioners or Governors of Excife, or the Commiffioners of Appeal, in cafe of Appeal. And in other Places, by two or more Juftices of Peace, near the Place; and in Cafe of Neglect or Refufal of fuch Juftice, within fourteen Days after Complaint and Notice to the Offender, then by the Sub-Commiffioners; and if any Perfon find himfelf grieved with the Judgment of fuch Sub-Commiffioners, he may appeal to the Quarter-Seffions, whofe Judgment fhall be final. Which Commiffioners and Juftices are required, upon Complaint, to fummon the Party, and upon his Appearance or Contempt, to examine the Matter; and upon Conviction by Confeffion or Proof, by one or more Witneffes, to give Judgment, and to grant Warrants to levy by Sale of Goods; if not redeemed within fourteen Days, and for Want of Diftrefs, to imprifon until Satisfaction. *Appeal.*

14. The Juftices and Commiffioners may mitigate fuch Forfeitures, but not below the double Duty, befides Cofts and Charges of fuch Officers, which the Juftices fhall allow them. Which Forfeitures (Charges deducted) the King fhall have three fourth Parts, and the Informer one. *Forfeiture.*

15. There fhall be a Head-Office in *London*, or ten Miles of it, to which all other Offices fhall be fubordinate and accountable, as long as the King pleafes, to be managed by fuch Perfons as his Majefty fhall appoint; and *London* and *Weftminfter*, and Places within the Limits of the weekly Bills of Mortality, fhall be within the Care of that Office; (and that the King fhall appoint Commiffioners and Sub-Commiffioners in all other Places) which Office, in all Places where it is appointed, fhall be kept open, from Eight till Twelve, and from Two till Five; and the chief Commiffioners fhall pay all Monies collected into his Majefty's Receipt of the *Exchequer*. *Head Office.*

16. No Perfon fhall be capable of fuch Office or Imployment, relating to the Excife, until he fhall, before two Juftices of the Peace, take the Oaths of Allegiance and Supremacy, and this Oath. *Oath.*

YOU fhall fwear to execute the Office of   truly and faithfully, without Favour or Affection, and fhall from Time to Time true Account make, and deliver to fuch Perfon and Perfons as his Majefty fhall appoint to receive the fame, and fhall take no Fee or Reward for the Execution of the faid Office, from any other Perfon than from his Majefty, or thofe whom his Majefty fhall appoint in that Behalf.

Which Oath every Juftice of Peace fhall certify at the next Seffions, there to be recorded.

17. No Writ of *Certiorari* fhall fuperfede Execution, or other Proceedings, upon any Order made by the Juftices in Purfuance of this Act.

Thus far go thefe two Acts of Parliament; and 15 *Car.* 2. *c.* 11.

An explanatory Act was made as followeth,

Firft, No common Brewer or Retailer of Beer and Ale fhall, without Notice to the next Excife-Office, or to the Commiffioners, Farmers, or Sub-Commiffioners of that Divifion, erect, alter, or inlarge any Tun, Fat, Back, Cooler or Copper, or ufe them for Brewing; or fhall ufe or make any private Store-houfe, Cellar, or Place, other than fuch as were then opened and ufed in his common and ufual Brew-houfe, upon Pain to forfeit fifty Pounds. And every Perfon in whofe Occupation the fame fhall be found fhall forfeit fifty Pounds. And fuch Tun, Fat, Cooler, Back or Copper, with the Beer or Wort therein, may be feifed and delivered to the Overfeer of the Poor, to be fold for the Ufe of the Poor, and diftributed amongft them. *Meafures altered. 15 Car. 2. c. 11.*

Secondly,

Commissioners nor Farmers. Secondly, No Commissioner for regulating the Excise, shall directly or indirectly farm it by Patent to himself, or any other in Trust; nor Farmer be capable of being a Commissioner: And if he act, shall lose the Benefit of his Farm, and be disabled to be Farmer or Commissioner; and all Acts made void; and Persons troubled may bring their Actions.

Gauger. Thirdly, Every Gauger shall weekly, after a common Brewer hath or ought to make his Entry, deliver to him, at his House or some of his Servants a Copy of his Return, or forfeit forty Shillings. And a Brewer, if he certify his Entry, or discharge the same within a Week after such Note delivered, shall not incur any Forfeiture.

Fourthly, Two able Gaugers in every City shall be appointed, one by the Commissioners, the other by the Brewers, and shall take an Oath before one Justice, to gauge all Tuns, Fats, Coppers and Vessels; and deliver one Copy to the Commissioners, and another to each Brewer.

Officer no Justice. Fifthly, No Commissioner, Sub-Commissioner, Farmer of Excise, common Brewer, or Inn-keeper, shall act as a Justice of Peace; if he do, all Acts done by him are void.

Deputies in Towns. Sixthly, The Commissioners, Farmers, or Sub-Commissioners, shall under their Hand and Seal, depute some Person in each Market-Town, to be there every Market-day in some publick Place, to receive Entries; and the next Market-day it shall be published, who shall attend each Market-day from Nine to Twelve, and from Two till Five. And if such Office be not so attended, the Commissioners, Farmers, or Sub-Commissioners for each Market-day forfeit ten Pounds to be recovered by Action, one Moiety to the King, the other to the Informer: And the Person coming, and being able to prove a Tender by one Witness, shall be excused of all Penalties.

Delivery of Beer. Seventhly, No common Brewer shall deliver out Beer, without Notice to the Excise-Office, but between *Michaelmas* and *Lady-day*, between Seven in the Morning and Five at Night; and between *Lady-day* and *Michaelmas*, from Three in the Morning till Nine at Night, or else forfeit twenty Shillings for every Barrel.

Mixing. Eighthly, If a Brewer or Retailer shall, after any Account taken by the Gaugers, of the Quantity and Quality of Beer, Ale, or Wort, mix his small Beer with strong Beer or Ale, and shall deliver out, or retail the same without giving Notice to the Gaugers, or shall hide or conceal his Beer or Ale from the Gaugers, shall for every Barrel so mingled or concealed, forfeit twenty Shillings.

Utensils. Ninthly, The Utensils or brewing Vessels, whosesoever they be, shall be liable to the Duty and Penalties; and the Duty and Penalties may be levied thereof.

Brewing for other. Tenthly, If any common Brewer, that is under a Composition, shall, during that Time, suffer any Beer or Ale to be brewed in his House for another common Brewer, without first giving Notice to the Commissioners, Farmers, or Sub-Commissioners of that Division, of how much is to be brewed, and the Quantity and Quality thereof; and forthwith paying down the Duty: As well the Brewer by whom, as for whom, shall pay for every Barrel five Pounds; one Moiety to the King, the other Moiety to the Informer, to be sued for in any Court of Record.

Bribe. Eleventhly, No Person shall give a Bribe, Money, Fee, or Reward to any Gauger or Officer, to make a false Report or Return; no sworn Gauger, or other Officer, shall so take upon Pain of ten Pounds: And upon Proof by two Witnesses before two Justices, by Warrant to levy of the Goods; for Want of Goods, Imprisonment for three Months.

Appeal. Twelfthly, No Appeal shall be admitted, unless the Appellant lay down in the Hands of the Commissioners, or Sub-Commissioners, the single Duty of Excise, and give Security to the Commissioners of Appeal or Justices, for the Fine and Penalty: And if the Judgment be reversed, the Commissioners shall restore the Duty, or so much thereof as shall be adjudged. And the Party, originally presented, shall pay double Costs; and if affirmed, the Party appealing shall pay the Commissioners complained of like Costs. *Note*; The Words are not intelligible, but, as I conceive, some Mistake is in the Print; for, it seems the Words should be *prosecuting* for *prosecuted*, or some other Words to that Sense.

Vinegar. Thirteenthly, Excise shall be paid for Vinegar-Beer, made to sell in any other Place, as well as in a common Brew-house.

Colleges. Fourteenthly, Colleges and Halls of Universities excepted.

County. Fifteenthly, All Differences, Appeals and Complaints, touching Excise, shall be determined in the proper County.

Receipts. Sixteenthly, No Officer of Excise shall take any Money, Fee, or Reward, for any Bond, Note or Receipt, touching the Excise, if he do, shall pay for every Offence ten Shillings.

Seven-

Seventeenthly, The Juftices, or any two of them, of chief Magiftrates in all Counties and Places, fhall meet once a Month, or oftner, if Occafion be, to hear and adjudge Matters of Excife.

Eighteenthly, One third Part of all Forfeitures (not thereby difpofed of) fhall be to the *Forfeiture.* King, another to the Poor, a Third to the Informer: And all Fines and Forfeitures, for the Recovery whereof no Remedy is ordained by that Act, fhall be recovered by Action of Debt, Bill, Plaint or Information, in any Court of Record in the County, City, or Corporation, where the Offence is committed ; or by fuch other Ways and Means, and in fuch Manner as is by the faid former Act ordained. 15 *Car.* 2. *cap.* 11.

Nineteenthly, In *London* no Appeal to be received, unlefs commenced within two *Time of Appeal.* Months after the Judgment ; and in the County, within four Months after the Judgment.

Twentiethly, No Commiffioner, Farmer, Sub-Commiffioner, or other Perfon, to be *Oaths.* employed in the farming, collecting, or taking Accounts for the Duty of the Excife, fhall take upon them that Office, or proceed in the Execution of that Employment, until they have taken the Oaths appointed by 12 *Car.* 2. *cap.* 23. As is appointed by that Act, and have entred his Certificate of taking the faid Oaths with the Auditor of the Excife, under the Penalty of fifty Pounds the Month, if he fhall neglect it.

By the Statute of 16 & 17 *Car.* 2. *cap.* 4. Farmers of Excife may put in Execution fuch *Farmers.* Powers and Authorities, as Commiffioners, and Sub-Commiffioners may do by 12 *Car.* 2. *cap.* 23. and 15 *Car.* 2. *cap.* 11. Except the judicial Part of hearing Differences, and mitigating Fines and Penalties.

By an Act of 22 & 23 *Car.* 2. *cap.* 5. A Duty of Excife is laid upon Liquors for fix Years, from 24 *June,* 1671. in thefe Proportions.

For every Barrel of Beer and Ale brewed, to be fold, above fix Shillings the Barrel, 9 *d.* *22 & 23 Car.*
2. c. 5.
For every Barrel of fix Shillings, or under, 3 *d.*

For every Hogfhead of Cyder and Perry, made and fold by Retail, to be paid by the Retailer, 1 *s.* 3 *d.*

For every Gallon of Mead by the Retail, *ob.*

For every Barrel of Vinegar-Beer, 6 *d.*

For every Gallon of Strong-Water, 1 *d.*

For every Barrel of Beer or Ale imported, 3 *s.*

For every Tun of Cyder or Perry imported, 4 *l.*

For every Gallon of low Wine of the firft Extraction made of Wine, Cyder, or other Materials imported, 2 *d.*

For every Gallon of Coffee, 2 *d.*

For every Gallon of Chocolate, Sherbet and Tea, 8 *d.*

Which Duty is thereby declared to be ordered in all Things as in the former Act, with thefe Additions.

1. For Wafte and Leakage in every twenty-three Barrels of Beer fhall be allowed three, *Wafte.* and in twenty-two Barrels of Ale fhall be allowed two.

2. Penalties for all Offences againft this Act, fhall be thus employed. One Moiety to the King, the other to the Informer ; but the Penalties may be mitigated, as in former Acts.

3. All Liquors imported, fhall be firft entred before landed, and Duties paid, and *Liquors im-* every Warrant for the landing fhall be figned by the Collectors of Excife, before the fame *ported.* fhall be put a-fhore, or elfe it is forfeited, or the Value of it ; one Moiety to the King, the other to the Informer.

4. No private Perfon fhall lend his Veffels to be brewed in, in his Houfe or elfewhere, *Mixing.* upon Pain to forfeit fifty Pounds.

No Retailer of Beer fhall after the Receipt thereof, from a common Brewer, mix Beer, Ale or Wort, of an extraordinary Strength with Small Beer, in any Tub containing three Gallons, or more ; and if he do, to forfeit for every Barrel double the Duty of Excife, to be heard before the Juftices and Commiffioners, and they to fummon Witneffes : And any Perfon refufing or neglecting to teftify, to forfeit any Sum under forty Shillings, to be recovered and difpofed, as other Penalties by former Laws.

6. No Inn-keeper or Retailer to be troubled for felling at greater Prices than formerly *Prices.* during this Act.

As well Juftices of Peace as Commiffioners of Excife or Appeals have Power to hear and *Excife.* determine Complaints between the Brewers and Gaugers. 1 *W. & M.*
Seff. 1. c. 24.

X No

Forfeitures.   No Commiffioners, or other Perfons employed about the Duty of Excife, fhall receive from any Collectors, Surveyors, Gaugers, &c. any Fee or Reward upon Pain of forfeiting their Office, upon Proof by two or more credible Witneffes, before two Juftices of the Peace.

Over-charge of Gauger.   Commiffioners of Excife or Appeals, or Juftices of Peace upon Complaint made to them,
Ibid.   on Behalf of the Brewers, &c. of any Over-charge returned by the Gaugers, fhall hear and determine the fame, and examine Witneffes upon Oath, on both Sides.

Brandy exported.   Diftillers, &c. upon Oath made before two Commiffioners of Excife, or Juftices of the
2 W. & M.   Peace, that any Brandy, &c. intended to be exported, was drawn from Drink brewed
Seff. 2. c. 9.   from malted Corn, and not mixed with any low Wines, or any other Spirits made from
& 7 & 8 W.   other Materials, and that the Duties of the fame are entered and paid, and that the fame
3. c. 30.   are exported for Merchandize, may export fuch Spirits or Brandy; and upon Certificate from the Officer, &c. fuch Exporter fhall be paid by the Commiffioners of the Port 3 d. for every Gallon fo fhipp'd off.

The Authority given to Juftices of the Peace by feveral Statutes concerning the Excife, extends to thefe Particulars following, *viz.*

To {
 Brandy and Spirituous Liquors.
 Brewers.
 Cyder-Makers.
 Diftillers.
 Gaugers.
 Inn-Keepers and Victuallers.
}
   To {
 Makers of Mead, Vinegar,
   Methlegin and Sweets.
 Low Wines.
 Malt.
 Retailers of Beer, Ale, Cyder,
   Perry, Methlegin, &c.
}

Brandy.

6 Geo. 1. c. 21.   AND firft as to Brandy; all Diftillers, Dealers, Makers, or Sellers of *Brandy, Arrac,*
§. 12.   *Rum, Strong-Waters* or *Spirits,* by Wholefale or Retail, are injoined by the Statute 6 *Georgii,* to make true Entries in Writing of all Warehoufes, Cellars, Rooms, Shops, Store-houfes, or Vaults, which they ufe for keeping Brandy, &c. for Sale, which Entries are to be made at the next Excife-Office.

The Forfeiture is 20 *l.* for every Warehoufe, &c. fo ufed without making fuch Entry; to be fued for, recovered, and levied or mitigated, as any Forfeitures may be by any of the Laws of Excife; one Moiety to the King, the other to the Informer.

Ib. §. 13.   No Brandy, &c. fhall be brought into fuch Warehoufe, &c. without Notice firft given to an Officer of Excife, and without producing and leaving with him a Certificate, that the Duties of fuch Brandies have been paid, or that they were condemned as forfeited, or that they were Part of the Stock of fome Importer, Diftiller, or Maker who paid the Duty.

The Penalty is the Forfeiture of the Brandy, &c. fo brought in, *without Notice,* or Certificate, together with the Cask and Veffel.

Ib. §. 14.   Any Diftiller or Dealer in Brandy, hindering or refufing an Officer of Excife to enter into their Ware-houfes, &c. to take an Account of Brandy, &c. or fhall lett, hinder or obftruct Officers in executing the Powers given them by this Statute, fhall forfeit 50 *l.* for every Offence, to be fued for, levied, mitigated and divided as before.

Ib. §. 15.   No Brandy fhall be fold, uttered, or expofed to Sale by Wholefale or Retail, but when the fame fhall be in one of the faid Ware-houfes, &c. and entered as before mentioned, upon Pain of forfeiting 40 *s.* for every Gallon of Brandy, &c.

Ib. §. 21.   And no Brandy, &c. exceeding a Gallon, fhall be removed or carried from one Place to another, either by Land or by Water, without a Permit or Certificate, from one of the Officers of Excife, on Penalty of forfeiting the Brandy fo removed, together with the Veffel in which 'tis contained.

Ib. §. 18.   Perfons who fhall have in their Cuftody any Brandy above 63 Gallons, fhall be accounted Sellers of Brandy, and fubject to be furveyed by the Officers of Excife.

Ib. §. 20.   *Juftices of Peace* refiding near the Place where any *Seizure of Brandy,* &c. fhall be made, and which hath *clandeftinely been imported,* may fummon the Perfon, in whofe Poffeffion it fhall be found, to appear before them; and upon his Appearance, or in Cafe he makes Default after a Summons, the Juftices may in a fummary Way proceed to examine, and give Judgment to condemn the Brandy, and iffue out their Warrant for Sale thereof, together with the Veffel; which Judgment fhall be final, without any Appeal or *Certiorari* to be brought.

When

When Brandy is feifed, and no Claim made in 20 Days, the Officers muft, after the Ib. §. 21. faid 20 Days, give publick Notice by Proclamation the next Market-Day, of the Day and Place when and where the *Juftices* will proceed to examine the Caufe of fuch Seifure, and to give Judgment of Condemnation of the Brandy fo feifed, which Judgment fhall be final, and not controuled by an Appeal or *Certiorari.*

But in both thefe laft Cafes, the *Juftices of Peace* have no Jurifdiction within the Limits of the Excife-Office in *London*; nor in any Cafe where the Seifure is made for an unlawful Importation, and where the whole Quantity of Brandy, &c. at any Time feifed doth exceed 63 Gallons.

The Mafter or Purfer of any Ship, fuffering Brandy, &c. or other uncuftomed or pro- §. 32. hibited Goods, to be put out of his Veffel into any *Hoy, Lighter, Boat* or *Bottoms* to be laid on Land, if convicted, fhall (befides the Forfeitures to which they are liable by any Law now in Being) fuffer fix Months Imprifonment, without Bail.

No Arrack, Brandy, &c. fhall be expofed to Sale, but in one of the Warehoufes, 11 Geo. 1. &c. in Purfuance of 6 *Geo.* 1. *cap.* 21. on Pain of forfeiting fuch Arrack, &c. together c. 30. §. 3. with the Cafks, &c. over and above the Penalty of 40 s. impofed by that Act.

Sellers of Brandy, and other fpirituous Liquors by Retail, fhall be licenfed in the fame 2 Geo. 2. Manner as common Alehoufe-keepers. See Tit. *Alehoufes.* c. 28. §. 10.

Any Perfon may export Spirits drawn from Corn of *Great Britain,* upon Oath made c. 17. §. 7. before two Commiffioners of Excife, or two Juftices of Peace, that the fame are drawn from Corn in *Great Britain,* without Mixture of other Materials, and that the Duties are paid, and that the fame are exported to be fpent beyond Sea.

As to the Manner of paying the Bounty of 4 *l.* 18 *s. per* Ton, fee the Act.

None fhall fell any Brandy, or other diftilled fpirituous Liquor, in lefs Quantity than 9 Geo. 2. two Gallons, without taking out a Licenfe ten Days before, for which they fhall pay c. 23. §. 1. 50 *l.* The Licenfe to be renewed Annually, paying 50 *l.* for every new Licenfe: Selling §. 2. without fuch Licenfe is a Forfeiture of 100 *l.* Every Gallon retailed is liable to a Duty §. 3. of 20 *s.*

The Powers of the 12 *Car.* 2. *cap.* 24. or any other Law relating to Excife upon §. 4. Beer, Ale, or other Liquors, fhall be exercifed for managing the Duties hereby granted. One Moiety of the Penalties to the King, the other to the Informer.

Officers may by Day or Night enter Warehoufes defcribed in the Act; by Night it §. 9. muft be in the Prefence of a Peace-Officer, Oath being made before any Juftice dwelling near the Place, of probable Caufe of Sufpicion, that fpirituous Liquors are there concealed, and Perfons hindring fuch Officer to enter, &c. forfeit 50 *l.*

Perfons felling fpirituous Liquors about the Streets, &c. or in other Places, but fuch as §. 13. are allowed by this Act, forfeit 10 *l.* and any Juftice of Peace, upon View, Confeffion or Oath of one Witnefs, may convict the Offender. The Money forfeited fhall be for the Ufe of the Poor, if there be no Informer, but if there be, one Half goes to him. If the Offender neglects to pay the faid Forfeiture, he fhall be committed to the Houfe of Correction for two Months.

Nothing in this Act fhall enable any Perfons to fell fpirituous Liquors by Retail, un- §. 14. lefs he be licenfed by two Juftices of Peace, for which Licenfe 2 *s.* 6 *d.* is to be paid to the Clerks of fuch Juftices, and no other Reward to the Clerk of the Peace, or on any other Account, on Pain of forfeiting 5 *l.* and if the Licenfe is not found by the Juftices Clerks, no Fee fhall be due.

It fhall be fufficient for any Juftice, who fhall convict any Perfon of felling ftrong Li- §. 15. quors without Licenfe, to draw up fuch Conviction in the following Form, or any other Form, to the fame Effect.

Middlefex. **A** B. *is convicted on his* or *her own Confeffion* (or on *the Oath of*   ) *of*
A. *having fold Beer, Ale or ftrong Waters, in the Parifh of*
in this County, on the   *Day of*   *without being duly licenfed thereto by two*
Juftices of the Peace.
Given under my (or our) Hand and Seal, or Hands and Seals this   Day of
      or of keeping a Diforderly Houfe.

And if Occafion requires, to add, that the fame is the firft, fecond, or third Conviction, which Convictions fhall be effectual, fubject to Appeal to the next Quarter-Seffions.

Any Juftice of Peace may call before him any Excife-Officer within their refpective §. 20. Divifions, and to examine the faid Officer upon Oath, touching the Entry of any fpirituous

tuous Liquors, Ale, Beer, Cyder or Perry, made by any Perfon fufpected to fell the fame without Licenfe; and every Perfon making fuch Entry fhall be deemed a Seller of fuch Liquors.

11 Geo. 2.
c. 36. §. 2.   This Act is farther enforced by 11 *Geo.* 2. *cap.* 26. by which, If any Perfons, to the Number of Five, fhall in a tumultuous and riotous Manner affemble, to refcue any Offender againft the faid Act, or to Affault, Beat or Wound any Perfon, who fhall have given, or be about to give any Information or Evidence againft, feife or bring to Juftice, any Perfon offending againft the faid Act; all Perfons fo affembling themfelves, and their Aiders and Abettors, being thereof convicted, fhall be guilty of Felony; and the Courts before whom they fhall be convicted, fhall have Power of Tranfporting fuch Felons for feven Years to the Plantations.

§. 3.   Juftices of Peace, or others, upon Actions brought againft them for any Thing done by Virtue of this Act, or the faid Act of 9 *Geo.* 2. may remove fuch Action to any of the King's Courts of Record at *Weftminfter*, fo that the Writ for Removing the fame be delivered to the Judge of the inferior Court before Iffue joined; and fuch Defendant may plead the General Iffue; and if the Plaintiff be Nonfuited, &c. the Defendant fhall recover treble Cofts.

§. 4.   One Juftice of Peace may iffue his Warrant to any Peace-Officer for apprehending, and bringing any Hawker or Seller of fpirituous Liquors, contrary to the Act, before fome Juftice of Peace.

§. 5.   Any Perfon may feife and detain fuch Hawker and Seller, &c. for fuch Time as he may give Notice to a Conftable or other Peace-Officer, who are required to carry fuch Offender before fome Juftice of Peace to be examined, &c.

§. 7.   Conftables neglecting the Execution of this Act, forfeit 20 *l.* upon Conviction before any Juftice of Peace; to be levied by Diftrefs, &c. one Moiety to the Poor, the other to the Informer.

§. 8.   No Diftiller fhall Act as a Juftice of Peace in any Thing concerning the Execution of this Act, or of the forementioned.

Brewers.

15 Car. 2.
c. 11. §. 7.   BY the Statute 15 *Car.* 2. any Juftice of the Peace hath Power to adminifter an Oath to two able Artifts, to complete the Contents and Gage of all Brewing Veffels.

12 Car. 2.
c. 23, 24.
1 Will. 3.
c. 24.
* Upon the
Warrant it
muft be return-
ed, that there was no Diftrefs, before another Warrant can iffue to commit.   And by the Statute 12 *Car.* 2. Brewers not making true Entries once every Week, forfeit 5 *l.* And if they do not pay the Duty within a Week after Entry made at the Office of Excife, they forfeit 10 *l.* to be levied by Diftrefs, and Sale of their Goods, if not redeemed within 14 Days after the Diftrefs made; and for want of * Diftrefs, then to be committed till Satisfaction made.

This Forfeiture may be mitigated by the two Juftices, fo as it be not lefs then double the Duty of Excife, befides Cofts and Charge.

The Conviction muft be before two Juftices, and by one Witnefs or Confeffion of the Party; and the Profecution muft be within three Months after the Offence, and three Parts of the Forfeiture go to the King, and one to the Informer, after Charges deducted.

Brewers not permitting Gagers to enter, and being forbid by Gagers to fell or deliver out any Liquor without paying the Duties, forfeit 5 *l.* and 10 *l.* more, over and above the double Value, to be levied, mitigated and divided, *ut fupra.* And the Profecution and Conviction muft be as before.

Brewers making falfe Entries fhall, over and above the faid Penalties, forfeit their Allowance for their Wafte and Leakage for fix Months; the Profecution and Conviction muft be as before.

15 Car. 2.
cap. 11.
1 Will. 3.
cap. 24.
* By the Stat.
8 Will. 3.
cap. 19. §. 8.
'tis 200 l. one Moiety to the King, the other to the Informer.   A Brewer or Retailer not giving Notice at the next Excife-Office of fetting up, altering, or enlarging any Ton, Vat, Back, Cooler or Copper, and ufing them; or keeping any private Store-houfe for laying fuch Liquors in Cafks, forfeits * 50 *l.* for every Ton, Vat, &c. to be levied by Diftrefs, and Sale of Goods, &c. and for want thereof to be committed to the County Gaol for three Months.

The

The Conviction muft be by two Witnefles, and the Informations muft be brought in three Months, and Notice muft be given within a Week after the Information is brought.

Any Perfon in whofe Occupation the Houfe is, where a concealed Ton, Vat, &c. fhall be difcovered, forfeits 50*l.* to be levied and divided, *ut fupra*; and for want of a Diftrefs, to be committed, *ut fupra*; and the Ton, Vat, &c. together with the Beer, fhall be feifed and delivered to the Overfeers of the Poor, to be fold for the Ufe of the Poor, or to be diftributed amongft them.

The Profecution and Conviction muft be, *ut fupra*; but before the Sale or Diftribution, the Juftices muft make an Adjudication of this very Forfeiture.

Brewers delivering or carrying out Ale or Beer, before Notice, &c. unlefs between 3 in the Morning and 9 in the Evening, from the 25th of *March* to the 29th of *September*; and between 5 in the Morning to 7 in the Evening, from the 29th of *March* to the 25th of *September*, forfeit 20 *s. per* Barrel, to be levied and employed, and the Party to be committed, *ut fupra*.

The Profecution and Conviction muft be, *ut fupra*.

Brewers converting fmall Beer into ftrong, by mixing it after the Gage is taken, without giving Notice to the Gager; or hiding or concealing Drink not gaged, forfeit 20 *s. per* Barrel, to be levied and employed, and the Profecution and Conviction to be, *ut fupra*.

By the Statute 1 *Will.* Brewers who neglect, or refufe to fhew Gagers, all the Beer, Ale, or Worts of every Guile, are to have no Benefit of the Provifio in the Statute 15 *Car.* 2. concerning Mif-entries, and fhall incur all the Penalties impofed by any former Acts. 1 W. 3. c. 24.
§. 10.

Brewers or Victuallers cleanfing before the whole Guile is brewed, forfeit 40 *s. per* Barrel, to be recovered and employed, *ut fupra*. 7 W. 3. c. 30.
§. 21.

And refufing Gager to enter, and to ftay in the Brewhoufe to fee the Guile brewed off, forfeit 20 *l.* to be recover'd and employed, *ut fupra*. §. 22.

Carrying out any Drink, or after 'tis carried out mixing any fmall with ftrong upon the Dray, or in the Cellar of the Victualler, forfeits 5*l.* to be employed and levied, *ut fupra*. §. 23.

Brewer, or any other, obftructing the Officer in fearching for private Tun, Back, Cafk, &c. forfeits 20*l.* to be recovered and employed, *ut fupra*. §. 27.

Every common Brewer fhall tell the Gager how much ftrong Beer or Ale he intends to make of a Guile, and how much fmall, before any Part of the Guile is removed; and upon Refufal of fuch Difcovery, the Gager fhall return the whole Guile to be ftrong; and befides the Brewer fhall forfeit 20*s.* for every Barrel; and if after the Brewer hath declared how much is in the Guile, any Increafe be made thereof, the Brewer forfeits 5*l. per* Barrel; and the Servant affifting him forfeits 20*s.* and if not able, fhall be committed for three Months. 8 W. 3. c. 19.
§. 2.

If fuch Increafe is made by adding Ale or Beer of a former Brewing, the Brewer fhall incur all the faid Penalties, unlefs 'tis proved on Oath that it was done in the Prefence of the Gager.

If it appears to the Gager, that the Quality of ftrong Beer or Ale remaining of a former, and added to a new Guile, hath been alter'd fince it was brewed, he fhall return all that is added to the new Drink, as if then brewed, and the Brewer fhall pay the Duties accordingly.

No common Brewer fhall keep a Pipe or Stop-Cock under Ground, or any private Convenience, by which Worts may be conveyed from one Veffel or Place to another: Penalty is 100*l.* for every Offence.

Gager, or Officer of Excife, may in the Prefence of a Conftable, after Requeft made, break up the Ground in the Day-Time, or any Ground joining to the Brewhoufe, or any Wall, to fearch for fuch Pipes; and if none are found, the Gager fhall make good the Damage. Any Perfon oppofing the Gager in fuch Search forfeits 50*l.*

As to the other Heads relating to the Authority given to Juftices by feveral Statutes concerning the Excife, fee the Appendix, Tit. Excife.

CHAP. XXXIX.

Extortion.

Fees for Arrest.
23 H. 6. 10.
'NO Sheriff, Under-Sheriff, and their Clerks, Coroners, Stewards of Franchifes,
' Bailiffs, Keepers of Prifon, or other Officers or Minifters, by Colour of their
' Office, fhall take any other Thing by them, or by any other Perfon, to their Ufe
' and Profit, of any Perfon to be by them arrefted or attached, nor of any other, for
' the permitting any Arreft or Attachment, or of any Perfon to be arrefted or attached
' for Fine, Fee, Suit of Prifon, Mainprife, or fhewing Eafe or Favour to any Prifoner
' but as followeth: Sheriff 20 *d.* Bailiff 4 *d.* Gaoler 4 *d.*

Ibid.
Panel.
' No Sheriff, Under-Sheriff, Sheriff's Clerk, Steward, &*c.* or Coroner, fhall take for
' making any Return, Panel and Copy, but 4 *d.*

Fees for War-
rant.
' The Sheriffs fhall take no more than 4 *d.* for making any Obligation, Warrant or
' Precept.

Ibid.
Forfeitures.
Fees.
' He that offends fhall lofe to the Party his treble Damages and forty Pounds, *viz.*
' a Moiety to the King, and the other Moiety to the Informer.
' Juftices of Peace have Power to inquire, hear and determine of Office without
' fpecial Commiffion.

See 1 Hawk.
P.C. 170, 171.
' Extortion is an Offence by the Common Law, and is punifhable by Fine and Im-
' prifonment ; and generally Fees fhall not be taken at the Common Law : And where
' any are given by Statute, they may not be increafed or inlarged, and that not only in
' the Court belonging to the Common Law, but in the Ecclefiaftical Courts: Concerning
' all which, how neceffary it is that they be looked into and moderated, any one may
' judge, who hath any Thing to do in either Jurifdiction, who muft needs fee, if not
' feel, they are much increafed, to the great Oppreffion of Suitors, beyond the moft
' large Pretences and Demands of more fober Times.
' For all which Extortions Bills of Indictment will lie at the Seffions of the Peace,
' as it is an Offence at Common Law ; and where fpecial Penalties are provided by Sta-
' tutes, thefe muft be recovered in the Method and Courts by fuch Acts directed.
' And where any Act is either by the Common Law or Statutes appointed to be done
' by any publick Officer, he ought, in Virtue of his Place, do what is fo required with-
' out taking any Thing therefore, unlefs by lawful and reafonable Ufage he hath a
' Fee belonging to him, or by Statute any be given him.
' A Juftice of Peace was convicted of Extortion, and fined 100 Marks, and com-
' mitted during the King's Pleafure, and bound to his good Behaviour for a Year, and
' ordered to acknowledge his Offence publickly at the next Affifes, to be held for the
' County where he lived, and was turned out of the Commiffion of the Peace.

CHAP. XL.

Felony.

EVERY Juftice of Peace (by Force of the Commiffion, the firft *Affignavimus*) may
caufe frefh Suit, Hue and Cry, and Search to be made by the Sheriff, Bailiffs,
Conftables and others, upon any Robbery or Theft : And alfo may caufe the Conftables
to arreft and to imprifon all fuch as fhall be fufpected to be Thieves, Murderers, or
Felons. *Lamb.* 190.

2 & 3 Ph &
M. c. 10.
Alfo every Juftice of Peace may and muft take the Examination of all fuch Felons,
or Perfons fufpected for Felony, as fhall be brought before him. See *hic cap.* 164.

2. And muft take Information againft them (of thofe that bring them) *fc.* of the
Fact, and Circumftances of the Felony and Fact.

3. And muft put in Writing fuch Examinations and Informations, or fo much thereof
as fhall be material to prove the Felony, and muft certify the fame to the next General
Gaol-delivery.

I

4. And

4. And after such Examination and Information taken, then the Justice must commit *1 & 2 Ph. & M. c. 13.* such Felons to the Gaol, or may bail them, if they be bailable; but then there must be two Justices together, and the one of them of the *Quorum.* See *postea* Tit. *Bailment.*

5. And must bind over (by Recognizance) the Informers to appear, and all such as so declare any Thing material to prove the Felony, and to give Evidence against the Felon at the next General Gaol-delivery to be holden within the County, City or Town Corporate, where Trial of the said Felony shall be. 2 *Ph. & M. cap.* 10. See *hic cap.* 164.

' If such Informer be unable to travel, *&c.* then the Justice of Peace may take his Information upon Oath, and may certify the same, *ut supra, &c.* and may forbear to bind such Informer to appear personally before the Justices at the Gaol-delivery, *&c.*

' Note, That in Case of Treason or Felony, the Party accused may require reasonable Time to answer any Interrogatories, and having answered, ought to have Copies of his Examination, if he desire it. *Co. Inst.* 2 *Part, p.* 51. The Cases of *Just. Richil,* 1 *Hen.* 4. And the Lord *Carew,* 16 *Jac.*

' If the Justice of Peace shall not certify such Examinations and Informations to *3 H. 7. 1.* the next Gaol-delivery, or shall not certify their Bailment, or shall not bind over the Informers to appear, and to give Evidence against the Felon at the next General Gaol-delivery, as aforesaid; he shall be fined (for every such Default or Offence) at the Discretion of the Justices of Gaol-delivery. 1 *& 2 & 3 Ph. & M.*

But if it be for *Petty Larceny*, or other small Felonies determinable at the Sessions, *Petty Larceny.* the Justices of Peace may bind over the Informers, and may certify the Examinations and Informations to the next Quarter-Sessions of the Peace: And this was the Advice and Direction of Sir *David Williams* Knight, (late one of the Justices of the *King's Bench*) at the Assises at *Cambridge.* For, said he, it was not meet to keep poor Prisoners in the Gaol for small Matters of Felony from one Assises till another; and therefore he gave Order, that the Justices of Peace (at their General Session of the Peace) should try and deliver Offenders for small Felonies.

Besides, the Justices of Peace, as well by Virtue of their Commission, as also by *Felony.* Force of the Statutes of 18 *Edw.* 3. 2. 34 *Edw.* 3. 1. *& 17 Rich.* 2. 10. have Autho- *P. Just. 1. 18.* rity to proceed to the Delivery of Felons, and to hear and determine, and to give Judg- *Stamf. 58.* ment upon all Felonies whereof any Person shall be indicted before them, and are not *Co. 9. 118.* restrained by the Statutes of *Ph. & M.* but that they may proceed therein before the Coming of the Justices of Assise and Gaol-delivery, the Words of the Commission to that Purpose are, *Assignavimus vos Justiciarios nostros ad Pacem, &c. Ac etiam ad inquirend. de omnibus & omnimodis Feloniis, &c. Et ad omnes, & singulas Felonias, &c. — audiendum & terminandum; & ad delinquentes castigandum & puniendum. Vi. Plo.* 485. *b.*

' And for that Purpose also the aforesaid Statutes of 18 *Ed.* 3. 34 *Ed.* 3. *& 17 Rich.* 2. *Lawyers.* ' have ordained, that some learned in the Laws shall be put into the Commission of the ' Peace in every County within this Realm.

Also there be divers Statutes which by special Words did ordain, that the Justices of *P. Inst. 14.* Peace should have Authority at their *General Quarter-Sessions,* to inquire of, hear and *P. Sher. 13.* determine certain Felonies. As the Statutes,

18 *Hen.* 6. 19. *& 3 H.* 8. 5. * of Soldiers departing without Licence. *By this Stat. of 3 H. 8. c. 5.*

the Stat. 7 H. 7. c. 1. was re-enacted, and it seems questionable if these two Acts were more than temporary. See Cay's Abridg. Tit. *Soldiers.*

1 *Ed.* 4. 2. Felonies presented before Sheriffs in their Turns or Law-Days.
22 *H.* 8. 11. Cutting down of Powdick.   *P. Just. 11.*
25 *H.* 8. 6. Against Buggery.   *P. Just. 32.*
8 *Eliz.* 3. Transporting of Sheep.   *P. Just. 15. P. Just. 74.*
* 39 *Eliz.* 4. *& 1 Jac.* 7. Incorrigible Rogues.   *P Mariners 6.*
39 *Eliz.* 17. Wandering Soldiers and Mariners.   *P. Robbery.*
43 *Eliz.* 13. Carrying Men forcibly out of *Cumberland, &c.*   *Repealed by 12 Ann. 23.*

So that the Justices of Peace at their Sessions may safely proceed to try all Petty Larcenies and small Felonies whereto they are authorized by these last recited Statutes: And in such Cases also the Justices of Peace that shall take the Examination of such Felonies, may safely bind over the Informers, and certify the Examination and Informations to their next General Sessions of the Peace.

And for Petty Larcenies, and other Petty Felonies, after an Indictment preferred at the Quarter-Sessions, if an *Ignoramus* be found by the Great Inquest, here the said Sessions, fions, in good Difcretion, may deliver the Gaol of fuch Petty Felons; otherwife for all Homicides, Robbery, or other Felonies. *Dyer* 29.

Murder.   For in Cafes of Murder, or other Homicide, (by Misfortune, or in his own Defence, or other Manner) the Offenders by the Statute of *Gloucefter* (made 6 *Ed.* 1. *cap.* 9.) are to abide in Prifon until the Juftices of Gaol-Delivery fhall come into the County to deliver the Gaol. And by the Statute of 4 *Ed.* 3. *cap.* 2. two Juftices of Peace might take Indictments, &c. but the Perfons fo indicted were to be delivered by the Juftices of Gaol-Delivery.

But after by the Statutes of 18 *Ed.* 3. *cap.* 2. beforementioned, Juftices of Peace were affigned to hear and determine Felonies, &c. and to inflict Punifhment according to Law, and the Manner of the Deed. And by the Statute of 34 *Ed.* 3. *cap.* 1. Juftices of Peace had Power given them to hear and determine, at the King's Suit, all Manner of Felonies done in the fame County according to Law, &c. And by the Statute of *Lawyers.* 17 *Rich.* 2. *cap.* 10. in every Commiffion of the Peace, two Men of Law (amongft others) are to this Purpofe to be affigned, *fc.* to go and proceed to the Deliverance of Felonies as often as they fhall think it expedient.

Felons not to be dealt with by Juftices of Peace. See Lamb. 529. Cromp. 56. *and the Title* Felony by Statute *infra.*

And yet there are fome Felons which the Juftices of Peace cannot try at all, neither can they inquire thereof, ' As Namely :

' 1. Firft, If any Man being the King's fworn Servant, (and his Name in the *Check-* ' *Roll* of his Houfhold) under the Degree of a Lord, fhall confpire with another to de- ** This is High Treafon. See poftea.* ' ftroy the * King's Majefty, or any Lord of this Realm, or any other fworn to the *3 H. 7. c. 14.* ' King's Council, or the Steward, Treafurer or Comptroller of the King's Houfe; every ' of thefe Offences are made Felony by the Statute made 3 *Hen.* 7. But fuch Offences are ' by the fame Statute appointed to be tried by a Jury of the *Check-Roll* of the fame ' Houfhold, and before the Steward, Treafurer or Comptroller of the King's faid Houfe.

' 2. All Murders or Manflaughters committed or done within any the King's Palaces ' or Houfes, or within the Limits or Bounds thereof, or within any other Houfe where ' his Majefty fhall happen to be then abiding in his Royal Perfon, fhall be inquired of, ' tried, heard and determined before the Lord Steward for the Time Being, of the ' King's Houfhold; and in his Abfence, before the Treafurer and Comptroller of the ' fame Houfhold, and the Steward of the *Marfhalfea*, or two of them, &c. And fuch ' Trial to be by the Inquifition and Verdict of his Majefty's Houfhold Servants in the ' *Check-Roll.* 33 *Hen.* 8. *cap.* 12.

Records im-bezil'd. ' 3. Imbezilling of any Record, Writ, Return, Panel, Procefs, or Warrant of At- ' torney, in the *Chancery*, *Exchequer*, the one Bench or the other, or in the Treafury, ' whereby any Judgment fhall be reverfed; every fuch Offence is made Felony in fuch ' Imbezillor, Stealer, or Taker away, and in their Procurers, Counfellors and Abettors, *8 H. 6. c. 12.* ' by the Statute of 8 *H.* 6. But fuch Offences are by the fame Statute appointed to be *Co. 11. 34.* ' tried by a Jury of twelve Men, whereof the one Half to be of the Men (*fcil.* of ** P. Fel. 18.* ' the Officers and Attornies) of the fame * Courts, who fhall be fworn before the ' Judges of the faid Courts, *fcil.* of the one Bench, or of the other, to inquire of that ' Offence: And if they fhall indict the Imbezillors of fuch Record, &c. they fhall be ' arraigned thereupon before the fame Judges, as in Cafes of other Felonies.

Records rafed. ' 4. Rafing of any fuch Record is alfo Felony within the faid Statute of 8 *H.* 6. and ' to be tried as aforefaid. *Br. Coron.* 174.

' Note; The Entring of a falfe Will Nuncupative is not properly Forgery, but it *2 R. 3 fol. 10.* ' muft be of a Will in Writing. *Miller's Cafe*, 2 *Jac.* C. B.

Forging a Deed. ' 5. Forging any Deed or Writing fealed, or of any Court-Roll, Will or Acquittance, ' or to caufe or affent to be made any fuch forged Writing, to publifh or fhew forth ' in Evidence any fuch forged Writing, knowing the fame to be forged; if any Perfon ' being once lawfully convicted of any of the faid Offences, fhall afterward commit any ' the faid Offences again, every fuch fecond Offence is made Felony by the Statute of ' 5 *Eliz.* But by the fame Statute fuch Offences are to be inquired of, heard and de- ' termined by and before Juftices of *Oyer* and *Terminer*, and Juftices of Affife.

Not indictable at the Seffions. ' And therefore whereas one *R. Smith* was indicted at the Seffions of the Peace in the *5 El. c. 14.* ' County of *Oxford*, upon the faid Statute of 5 *Eliz.* for forging of a falfe Deed; it *2 Salk. 406,* ' was adjudged by the whole Court in the *King's Bench*, 30 *Eliz.* that the fame Indict- *680. S. P.* ' ment was not well taken: For though the Juftices of Peace by their Commiffion have ' Power (of *Oyer* and *Terminer*) to hear and determine Felonies and Trefpaffes, &c. and *Co 9. 118.* ' have in their faid Commiffion an exprefs Claufe, *Ad audiendum & terminandum*, and fo *Cro. 120.*

I   ' are

' are Juftices of *Oyer* and *Terminer*; yet it was refolved by the Court, that forafmuch as
' there is a Commiffion of *Oyer* and *Terminer* known diftinctly by that Name, and the Com-
' miffion of the Peace is known diftinctly by another Name, the faid Indictment taken be-
' fore the Juftices of the Peace at their Seffions, was not well taken; therefore it was
' quafhed.

' The Reafon of this laft Cafe and Judgment feemeth to hold in the former Cafes, and in
' all other like Cafes, where any Statute doth fpecially give Authority to any other diftinct
' Court, or to other Juftices or Commiffioners, (leaving out the Juftices of Peace) to in-
' quire of, hear, and determine, or to try Felons, &c. There the Juftices of the Peace (at
' their Seffions) cannot inquire thereof, &c.

' 6. *Servants imbezilling* or taking away the Goods of their deceafed Mafter, the Execu- *Servants im-*
' tors of the Party deceafed may have a Writ directed to the Sheriff, to make Proclamation *bezilling their*
' two Market-Days, that fuch Offenders fhall appear in the *King's Bench* at a certain Day. *Mafter's*
' And if fuch Writ be returned, that Proclamation was thereupon made accordingly, then, if *Goods.*
' the faid Perfons do not appear in the *King's Bench* at the Day fpecified in the faid Writ,
' they fhall be attainted of Felony, by the Statute of 33 *H*. 6. * So that fuch Offence begin- 33 H. 6. c. 1.
' neth firft to be Felony upon their Default of Appearance in the *King's Bench* after Procla- Raft. pl. fo.
' mation; of which Default the Juftices of Peace cannot take Notice, becaufe they have * Qu. if 33 H.
' not before them the Record of fuch Default, or not appearing, &c. *Cromp.* 56. *Lamb.* 6. c. 1. be in
' 529.   Cay's Abridg.
                                   Tit. Servants.

' But in the former Cafes, if fuch Offender fhall be brought before any Juftice of Peace,
' and charged with any fuch Felony; *Quære*, what he is to do therein, confidering the
' Juftices of Peace are no Judges of fuch Felonies; neither have they any Jurifdiction given
' them by the Statutes in fuch Cafes: And yet for that, they are by their Commiffion au-
' thorifed to deal with all Felonies, as alfo with all Offences againft the Peace of the King
' and Realm, of which Sort all thefe laft recited Offences are. *Quære*, If the Juftice of Peace
' fhall not do well to examine the Offence, and then to certify his Examination to fuch
' Perfons as by the Statute are made Judges of the Caufe; and alfo to commit fuch an Of-
' fender to Prifon, to bind over the Informer, and to take their Information upon Oath.

' Again, If a Man had been felonioufly ftricken in one County, and after died thereof in *Wound in one*
' another County, (by the Common Law) no Indictment could be taken in either of the faid *County, Death*
' two Counties, for that the Jurors of the County where fuch Perfon died (of fuch Stroke) *in another.*
' could not take Knowledge thereof, (being in a Foreign County,) nor the Jurors of the Co. Inftit. 3
' County where the Stroke was given, could not take Knowledge of the Death in another part. p. 135.
' County. But now by the Statute of 2 & 3 *Ed*. 6. an Indictment thereof found by Jurors Raft. fol.
' of the County *where the Death* fhall happen (whether it fhall be found before the Coro- 2 & 3 Ed. 6.
' ner, or before Juftices of Peace, or other Juftices, &c.) fhall be good and effectual in Law: c. 24.
' And that the Juftices of Gaol-Delivery, and *Oyer* and *Terminer* in the fame County where
' fuch Indictment fhall be taken, fhall and may proceed upon the fame, as if fuch Stroke
' and Death had been in one and the fame County.

' Alfo where Felons had robbed or ftoln Goods in one County, and after conveyed Goods *Stealing or*
' fo ftoln, into another County, to their Adherents there, who knowing of fuch Felony, *Robbing in one*
' received the fame Goods. In this Cafe, although the *Principal* were after attainted, the *Flying into ano-*
' Acceffary notwithftanding efcaped by Reafon that he was Acceffary in another County, *ther.*
' and that the Jurors of the faid other County (by the Common Law) could take no Know-
' ledge of the principal Felony in the firft County. But now by the faid Statute, 2 & 3
' *Ed*. 6. it is enacted, that where any Murder or Felony fhall be committed and done in
' one County, and other Perfons fhall be *Acceffary* (in any Manner) to any fuch Murder Acceffary.
' or Felony in any other County, that an Indictment thereof found or taken againft fuch
' *Acceffary* before the Juftice of Peace, or other Juftices, &c. *in the County where fuch Of-* Co. 9. 117.
' *fence of Acceffary fhall be committed*, fhall be good and effectual in Law; and that the
' Juftices of Gaol-Delivery, or *Oyer* and *Terminer*, of or in fuch County where the Offence
' of any fuch Acceffary fhall be committed, fhall write to the *Cuftos Rotulorum* where fuch
' Principal fhall be attainted or convict, to certify them whether fuch Principal be attainted,
' convicted, or otherwife difcharged of fuch Felony; and thereupon the *Cuftos Rotulorum*
' fhall make Certificate in Writing under his Seal to the faid Juftices accordingly: And
' then the Juftices of Gaol-Delivery, or *Oyer* and *Terminer*, fhall proceed upon every fuch
' *Acceffary in the County where fuch Acceffary became Acceffary*, as if both the principal
' Offence and Acceffary had been committed and done in the County where the Offence
' of the Acceffary was committed.

         Z   ' So

‘ So as by the Letter of this laft recited Statute, the Jurifdiction over thofe Felons, and
‘ over, fuch Acceffaries, is not committed to the *Juftices of Peace*, to proceed to the Trial
‘ of them ; but this Authority is remitted to the Juftices of Gaol-Delivery, or of *Oyer* and
‘ *Terminer :* Yet the Juftices of Peace may examine thefe Offences, and take Information
‘ againft the Offenders, and certify the fame to the next General Gaol-Delivery, and may
‘ bind over the Informers, and commit the Offenders : Alfo the Juftices of Peace may
‘ inquire thereof, and take Indictments againft them, as in other Cafes of Felony.

‘ 8. Laftly, the Juftices of Peace (at their Seffions) cannot try fuch as are indicted of
‘ Felony before *Coroners*, or before the Juftices of Gaol-Delivery, or of *Oyer* and *Termi-*
Lamb. 530. ‘ *ner*, unlefs the fame Perfons (*fcil.* the faid Coroner, Juftices of Gaol-Delivery, or of *Oyer*
‘ and *Terminer*) were alfo Juftices of the Peace in the fame County, fo as the Indictment
‘ may be underftood to be taken by them, as before Juftices of the Peace. For the Com-
‘ miffion of the Peace, and the Authority of Juftices of the Peace, extendeth only to try
‘ fuch as ftand indicted before themfelves, or before former Juftices of the Peace, or before
‘ the Sheriff in his Turn, or the *Steward in a Leet.* See *Lamb.* 486. *& Stat.* 1 *Ed.* 4.
‘ *cap.* 2. *& Stamf.* 87. for Indictments taken in the Sheriffs Turn. And for Indictments
‘ taken in Leets, fee *Br.* Tit. *Leet* 1. And yet by the Book 8 *H.* 4. *fol.* 18. it feemeth,
‘ that Indictments or Prefentments of Felony taken in the Leet fhall be delivered over to
‘ the Juftices of Gaol-Delivery. *Br. Frank.* 5.

Treafon. ‘ Alfo in fome Cafes of *Treafon and Mifprifion of Treafon*, the Juftices of Peace may in-
‘ quire, and take Indictments, but cannot proceed to Trial, or to hear and determine the
‘ fame.

5 Eliz. 1. ‘ As to *Maintainers of the Authority of the Bifhop or See of* Rome, and of their Procurers
23 Eliz. 1. ‘ and Maintainers, *&c.* the Juftices of Peace in their Quarter-Seffions may inquire of fuch
‘ Offences ; but they muft certify every Prefentment thereof made before them into the
‘ *King's Bench* (within forty Days, upon Forfeiture of an Hundred Pounds by every Juftice
‘ of Peace there prefent, not making Certificate accordingly). *5 Eliz. cap.* 1.

'13 Eliz. 2. ‘ 2. So of fuch as fhall *obtain from* Rome, &c. *any Bulls or Abfolutions*; or fhall publifh,
23 Eliz. 1. ‘ or put in Ure any fuch Bull ; or fhall give or take *Abfolution* by Colour of any fuch *Bull.*
‘ And their *Procurers* and *Maintainers*, &c.
‘ And the *Concealers of fuch Bull or Abfolution* offered to them.

23 Eliz. 1. ‘ 3. So of fuch as fhall *withdraw any Subject from the Religion now ufed to the* Romifh *Re-*
‘ *ligion*; or from their Obedience to the King's Majefty, or to the Obedience of the Pope, *&c.*
‘ And of fuch as fhall be fo *withdrawn.*
‘ And of their *Procurers and Maintainers*, &c.
‘ And of the *Concealers* of fuch Offences.

13 Eliz. 2. ‘ 4. So of fuch as fhall bring into this Realm any *Agnus Dei*, or other *Superftitious Pic-*
21 Eliz. 1. ‘ *tures, or Beads*; or fhall deliver, or offer any fuch to any Subject.
‘ And of the Receivers of fuch *Superftitious Things.*
‘ For all thefe laft recited Offences againft the Statutes of *5 Eliz.* 1. 13 *Eliz.* 2. and
‘ 23 *Eliz.* 1. fee more fully *poftea* Tit. *High Treafon.*
‘ And if any fuch Offender againft any of thefe laft mentioned Statutes fhall be brought
‘ before any Juftice of Peace, and charged with any fuch Offence, the Juftices muft take
‘ the Examination of fuch Offenders, and bind over the Accufers and Informers to appear)
‘ and to prefer a Bill of Indictment, and thereupon to give Evidence to the Inquirors againft
‘ fuch Offenders) at the next Quarter-Seffions, or rather at the next Affizes, or General
‘ Gaol-delivery, or elfe in the *King's Bench*, whenfoever (upon reafonable Warning) they
‘ fhall be thither called ; and then to commit the Offender to Gaol ; and after to certify
‘ the faid Examinations, Informations, and Recognizances (by him taken) to the faid
‘ Seffions of Gaol-delivery, or into the *King's Bench, &c.*
‘ In other Cafes of *High Treafon, or Mifprifion of Treafon*, what the Juftices of Peace,
‘ out of their Seffions, fhall do with fuch Offenders brought before them, fee *poftea* Tit.
‘ *Mifprifion.*’

But now to return to the Bufinefs of the Juftices of Peace out of their Seffions.

Refufes to If one fhall bring a Man, fufpected of Felony, before any Juftice of Peace, *but refufetl*
give Evidence. *to be bound to give Evidence* againft the Prifoner (either at the General Gaol-delivery, or
Quarter-Seffions, as the Cafe fhall require;) if fuch Bringer hath given Evidence before the
faid Juftice againft the Prifoner, or can declare any Thing material to prove the Felony
and will not be bound to give Evidence upon his Trial, the Juftice of Peace (upon his Difcretion) may commit to Prifon fuch Perfon fo refufing, or may bind him to his Good Behaviour.

2

haviour, *and to appear at the next Gaol-delivery or Quarter-Seſſions.* But if the Bringer Crom.101.b.
of a Perſon ſuſpected of Felony cannot declare any Thing material to prove the Felony,
nor any other Perſon then preſent, it ſeemeth the Juſtice ought not to commit the Priſoner.
And ſo was the Direction of Sir *David Williams* at the Aſſizes of *Cambridge* aforeſaid; yet
the Juſtices ſhall do well to *examine the Priſoner,* and if he ſhall not confeſs the Felony,
then to commit him; or if upon his Examination there ſhall appear any juſt Cauſe of Suſpicion, or if the Priſoner be a Man of evil Fame, and that there be a Felony committed.
In theſe Caſes, the Juſtice ſhall do well not to let him go, but at leaſt to bind him over to
the next Gaol-delivery, and in the mean Time to take farther Information againſt him. See
the other Title *Felony, poſtea, cap.* 160.

  ' As to the Value of the Goods ſtolen, it muſt be above 1 *s.* for if under 'tis not * Felony *Petty Larceny,*
but *Petty Larceny,* but ſtealing ſeveral Things at ſeveral Times, which in the whole *what.*
amount to the Value of 1 *s.* or more, is Felony; ſo if two or more ſteal together above * *Petty Lar-*
that Value, 'tis Felony in all of them; but the Jury may find under that Value, and *ceny is Felony.*
 See Hal.Hiſt.
then 'tis *Petty Larceny.*' P. C. 530.

  'Tis Felony maliciouſly to *burn, or cauſe in the Night-time* to be burnt or deſtroyed, *Barns burning.*
any *Ricks* or *Stacks of Corn, Hay,* or *Grain, Barn,* or other Houſes or Buildings, or *Kilns,* 22 & 23 Car.
or to kill or deſtroy any Horſes, Sheep, or other Cattle. 2. c.7.

  The Offender ſhall be tranſported, and if he return within ſeven Years, he ſhall ſuffer
Death as a Felon.

  But this Conviction works no Corruption of Blood, Loſs of Dower, or diſinheriting
the Heir.

  A Man may be guilty of Felony in ſtealing Goods, *tho' he came lawfully to the Poſſeſſion* *Carrier who*
thereof, as if a Trunk is delivered to a *Carrier,* directed to a certain Perſon to be carried *hath a lawful*
 Poſſeſſion.
to a certain Place, and he carries it to another Place, and there breaks it open and takes *See* hic poſt.
away the Goods, this is Felony.

  So 'tis where a Shepherd ſteals Sheep out of a Flock which he was to look after, or a *Servant.*
Butler ſtealing Plate delivered to his Care; for he being a Servant, hath neither a general
or ſpecial Property in it, for that remains ſtill in his Maſter.

  Where Goods were delivered to *B. B.* and ſtolen from him by *T. S.* 'tis Felony, for
which *B. B.* may maintain an Indictment.

  Where the Wife ſteals Goods with her Husband, or by his Compulſion or Command, *Husband and*
'tis not Felony; but if ſhe receives ſtolen Goods, knowing them to be ſtole, and her Huſ- *Wiſe.*
band doth not know it, 'tis Felony in her.

  If an Infant, before he is of Age of Diſcretion, ſteal Goods, 'tis not Felony. *Infant.*

  He who comes into a Fair or Market, or Shop, and cheapens Goods, as if he cheapens *Felony, tho' the*
an Horſe, and the Owner gives him Leave to ride to try his Paces, and he rides away, this *Party had a*
 lawful Poſſeſ-
is Felony. *ſion.*

  Delivering Goods to a Workman to manufacture, and afterwards he ſteals them, this is
Felony notwithſtanding the Delivery, becauſe the Property ſtill remained in the Deliverer, and the Workman had only the Poſſeſſion to a particular Purpoſe, (*viz.*) to manufacture.

  Taking out Execution upon a Judgment in Ejectment, where the Party had no Colour *Felony by other*
of Title, and breaking open the Houſe and taking away Goods, Felony; for 'tis *in frau-* *Acts.*
 Taking out
dem Legis; this was *Farr*'s Caſe, who was convicted and executed. *Sid.* 254. *Execution,* &c.

  Breaking down a Copper fixed to a Freehold and carrying it away at the ſame Time, no *Breaking down*
Felony. *Kelynge* 29. *a Copper,* &c.

  Breaking a Dwelling-houſe in the Day-time, and taking and removing Goods from one *Breaking a*
Room to another, Felony; for by the taking he had the Poſſeſſion, and this was Steal- *Houſe in the*
 Day-time.
ing, and by Conſequence Felony.

  A Gueſt in a common Inn ariſing in the Night-time, and carrying Goods out of his *Gueſt in an*
Chamber into another Room, and from thence to the Stable, intending to ride away with *Inn.*
them, Felony.

  By a late Act of Parliament it was enacted, that the Stealing Goods, which by any *Stealing Goods*
Contract or Agreement between him and the Owner he is to uſe, or which is let to him to *which he had*
 by Contract.
uſe in *Lodgings,* Felony. 3&4 W.3.c.9.

  Forging Stamps on Indentures denoting the Duties on the Money for putting out *Ap-* *Forging*
prentices, Felony without Benefit of Clergy. *Stamps.*
 8 Ann. c. 9.

  Tearing, burning, cutting, defacing, or ſpoiling Cloaths or Garments in the Streets, *Spoiling*
Felony and Tranſportation for ſeven Years. *Cloaths.*
 6 G. 1. c. 23.

Stealing

Stealing out of a Coach-houfe.
10 & 11 W.3. cap. 23.

Stealing Goods out of a Coach-houfe, tho' not broke open, to the Value of 5 *s.* or affifting in it by Night or Day, Felony.

Coin.
8 & 9 W. 3. c. 26. §. 6.
1 Hawk. P. C. 46.

Blanching Copper for Sale, or mixing blanched Copper with Silver, or knowingly Buying or Selling, or offering to fell it, or Buying or Selling any malleable Compofition or Mixture of Metals or Minerals which fhall be heavier than Silver, and look and wear like ftandard Gold, but be manifeftly worfe than Standard, or receiving, paying, and putting off any counterfeit milled Money, or milled Money unlawfully diminifhed and not cut in Pieces, at a lower Rate than the fame by its Denomination fhall import, Felony; but without Corruption of Blood or Lofs of Dower. The Profecution muft be within three Months after the Offence committed.

This Act was at firft temporary, (*viz.*) to continue to the End of the next Seffions of Parliament, and continued by the Statute 1 *Annæ, cap.* 9. and afterwards by the Statute 7 *Annæ, cap.* 25. it was made perpetual.

Robbery.

Robbing one to the Value of a Penny is Felony, if the Party is *put in fear.*

So if *T. S.* is threatned to be murdered, unlefs he will fwear to bring fuch a Sum to *J. L.* at fuch a Place, which he brings accordingly, this is Robbery.

Apprehending a Felon.
10 & 11 W. 3. c. 23.

He who apprehends a Felon ftealing to the Value of 5*s.* out of a *Coach-houfe, Stable,* or *Warehoufe,* fhall upon Conviction have a *Certificate* under the Hand of the Judge, before whom he was convicted, certifying the fame; and alfo within what Parifh the Felony was committed; and if feveral fhall affift in Taking fuch Felon, and a Difference fhould arife touching their Right to the Certificate, the Judge may direct fo many Shares to be divided amongft the contending Parties, which may be affigned once and no more; and by Virtue thereof the original Proprietor or Affignee fhall be difcharged of all Parifh or Ward Offices within the Parifh where the Felony was committed, which *Certificate* muft be inrolled by the Clerk of the Peace, who fhall have for his Fee one Shilling and no more.

And if the Perfon is killed in taking Houfe-breakers, Horfe-ftealers, or other Felons, his Executor or Adminiftrator fhall have a Right to the Certificate *gratis.*

Felon difcovering others.

A Felon out of Prifon difcovering Two of his Accomplices in any Burglary, Houfebreaking, or Felony in ftealing Horfes, Money, Wares or Goods, from whom the Benefit of Clergy is taken away, and fuch Accomplices being convicted thereof, the Difcoverer fhall have his Pardon for any Felony committed before the Difcovery, which Pardon fhall be a good Bar to an Appeal.

Refcuing a Felon.

He who refcues a Felon from the Sheriff, who was carrying him to Execution, is guilty of Felony; and fo is he who voluntarily fuffers him to efcape.

A Perfon was convicted of Murder, and being in the Place where Prifoners ftand at the *Old Baily, T. S.* came thither pretending fome Bufinefs with him, and watching the Keepers, he took an Opportunity of going out and the Prifoner followed him, but they were foon retaken, and then *T. S.* faid he had done what he ought to do to help his Friend, who was in Danger of his Life; this was adjudged Felony.

Burglary.

A Chamber in *Somerfet-houfe* was broke open, and the Offender was indicted for breaking *Domum manfionalem*; adjudged not good, becaufe the whole Houfe is *Domus manfionalis,* and this is not like Breaking open a Chamber in the Inns of Court, for every Perfon hath a feparate Intereft in thofe Chambers, and therefore each Chamber may properly be called *Domus manfionalis.*

Outhoufes adjoining, &c.

Barns and Outhoufes adjoining to the Dwelling-houfe are reputed Part of the Manfionhoufe, and 'tis Burglary to break them open.

Apartment in the Houfe of another.

So where a Man hires an Apartment in the Houfe of another, if 'tis broke open, fome are of Opinion the Offence may be laid in the Indictment to be *in Domo manfionali* of him who hires it; but the better Opinion is, that the Offender ought to be indicted for Breaking open *Domum manfionalem* of the Proprietor *.

* *See* Hal. P. C. 237, 238. 1 H. H. P. C. 522, 523. 2 H. H. P. C. 354. *and* 2 Hawk. P. C. 355.

Servant opening the Door.

A Thief finding the Door of a Dwelling-houfe faft lock'd, pretended to have fome Bufinefs with the Mafter, and defired to fpeak with him, and thereupon the Servant opened the Door, and the Thief entered and robbed the Houfe, this is Burglary; for the Event fhews, that he intended at firft to commit a Robbery, and the Door being opened upon a falfe Pretence, made the Fact Burglary, though there was no actual Breaking.

2

And

And to this Purpofe it was enacted, that if any Perfon felonioufly take away Goods *Breaking open* out of a Dwelling-houfe, the Owner or other Perfon being therein and put in Fear, or *an Houfe, or* fhall rob any Dwelling-houfe *in the Day-time*, any Perfon being therein, or fhall be ac- *houfe in the* ceffary to the fame, or fhall break any Dwelling-houfe, Shop, or Wharehoufe thereunto *Day-time.* belonging *in the Day-time*, and felonioufly take away Goods to the Value of 5 s. though 3 & 4 W. 5. no Perfon therein, or fhall counfel, hire, or command another to commit Burglary, fhall c. 9. §. 1. not have the Benefit of Clergy.

He who hath committed Burglary, and being out of Prifon, fhall difcover Two or *Difcovering* more Burglars, who fhall be convicted thereof, fuch Difcoverer fhall have his Pardon for *Burglars.* any Burglary which he fhall have already committed, which Pardon fhall be a Bar to an 10 & 11 W.3. Appeal.

He who fhall apprehend another guilty of Burglary, or felonious Breaking open an *Apprehending* Houfe in the *Day-time*, and profecutes him to Conviction, fhall within one Month after *a Burglar.* fuch Conviction, receive of the Sheriff 40 l. upon tendring to him a Certificate under the 5 Ann. c. 31. Hand of the Judge who convicted the Offender, certifying fuch Conviction; and if the Sheriff fhall not pay it, he fhall forfeit double to the Party grieved, to be recovered in the Courts at *Weftminfter*, with treble Cofts.

And where any Perfon is killed in Taking an Houfe-breaker, then his Executor or Adminiftrator fhall be intitled to the 40 l. upon the Certificate of the Juftice of Affife in the County where the Fact was done, or of the Two next Juftices of Peace, that fuch Perfon was killed.

He who enters into the Dwelling-houfe of another, either by Day or Night, tho' without *Entring an* breaking it, with an Intent to commit Felony, or being in the Houfe, commits Felony, *Breaking it.* and in the Night-time breaks the Houfe to get out, Burglary without Clergy. 12 Ann. c. 7.

Stealing Money or Goods to the Value of 40 s. being in a Dwelling-houfe or Outhoufe *And Taking* thereunto belonging, though it was not actually broken, and though no Perfon was there- *more than the* in, Burglary without Clergy; and fo 'tis in the Aider and Affifter. *Value of 40 s.*

By another Paragraph in the fame Statute 10 & 11 *Will.* 3. 'tis enacted, That if any Ib. §. 1. Perfon fhall fteal out of a Shop, Warehoufe, &c. any Goods privately and felonioufly, of the Value of 5 s. or more, though fuch Shop, &c. be not broke open, &c. or that fhall affift in committing fuch Offence, &c. fhall not have the Benefit of Clergy; now the Cafe at a Seffions in the *Old Baily* 9 *Geo.* 1. was thus:

A Shirt, which was the Property of *W. R.* was left in the Shop of *T. S.* to be fent to a Sempftrefs to mend, and it was ftolen by the Prifoner out of the Shop, for which he was indicted and convicted; and the Queftion was, whether he fhould have his Clergy; and adjudged that he might, for this was not a Felony within that Statute which was made as a Remedy for the Owners of Shops to preferve their own Goods there by Way of Trade, and therefore did not extend to Goods cafually loft there, and confequently Stealing fuch Goods to the Value of 5 s. was not Felony within that Statute, and without Benefit of Clergy.

See alfo the Titles *Felony* by Common Law and by Statute, *Chap.* 158, 159, and 160.

Fairs.   Vide Tit. *Markets.*

C H A P. XLI. (a)

Fees.

GENERALLY, as I have faid elfewhere, any publick Officer fhall take no other *Where due.* Fees or Rewards, for doing any Thing relating to his Office, than fome Statute in Force gives him; or elfe, as hath been anciently and accuftomably taken. And if he do otherwife, he is faid to do it *colore officii*, and he is therein guilty of Extortion. I fhall therefore, for the Juftices of Peace Direction herein, take Notice of fome Fees, they and others are to take, and leave them to inquire for the Reft in fome proper Titles in this Book.

Sheriff taking more than 12 d. for every 20 s. of the yearly Value of Lands above 100 l. *per Annum*, and 3 s. 6 d. if under that Value, for executing a *Writ of Poffeffion*, or taking *Poundage* for executing a *Ca. Sa.* or charging one in Execution for a greater Sum than really due, this is Extortion; and being convicted, fhall forfeit treble Damages to

A a   the

the Party grieved, and double the Sum extorted, and 200*l.* more to be divided between the King and the Profecutor. 3 *Geo.* 1. *cap.* 15.

Seſſions Fees.
12 R. 2. 10.   Every Juſtice of Peace may for every Day they keep their Seſſions (which by that Statute may be three Days) take four Shillings, and their Clerk two Shillings *per Diem,* of the Fines and Amercements coming of their Seſſions by the Sheriff's Hands; but by

14 R. 2. 11.   14 *Rich.* 2. 11. no Duke, Earl, Baron, or Baronet (ſo is the Print in *Pulton,* but the Original is Banneret) albeit they be aſſigned Juſtices, and hold their Seſſions with other, ſhall take any Wages for their Office.

Inrolments.
27 H. 8. 16.   Where Inrolments are to be made of Deeds, if the Lands exceed not the yearly Value of forty Shillings, the Juſtice and Clerk ſhall take two Shillings, *viz.* One Shilling the Juſtice, and one Shilling the Clerk. And if it exceed forty Shillings *per Annum,* then five Shillings, *viz.* the Juſtices two Shillings ſix Pence, and Clerk two Shillings ſix Pence. *Vide poſtea* Inrolment.

Fees of Sheriffs, Bailiffs, and Gaolers, about Arreſts. See before Tit. *Extortion.*

Alehouſe.
5 & 6 E. 6. 25.   The Party licenſed to keep an Alehouſe, ſhall pay for the Recognizance directed by 5 & 6 *Ed.* 6. *cap.* 25. but twelve Pence.

Licenſe.
5 Eliz. 12.   Every Licenſe to be a Badger, Drover, Lader, Kidder, Carrier, or Buyer of Corn, &c. ſhall be made by the Clerk of the Peace only; for which he ſhall take twelve Pence, and no more.

Labourers.
5 Eliz. 4.   Juſtices of Peace, Mayors, and Head Officers, for every Day they ſit in Execution of the Statute of Labourers (not exceeding three Days at one Time) ſhall take five Shillings *per Diem* each, out of the Fines and Amercements happening by that Statute.

Gun.
1 Jac. 27.   The Clerk of the Peace ſhall take for a Licenſe to ſhoot in a Gun for Hawk's Meat, twelve Pence and no more.

Wills and Adminiſtration.
21 H. 8. 5.   Where the Goods amount not to 100*s.* nothing ſhall be taken for the Probat of a Teſtament, ſaving ſix Pence to the Scribe for Writing, and ſo for an Adminiſtration, the Teſtament being exhibited to him with Wax; and if the Goods exceed 100*s.* and not forty Pounds, the Party ſhall pay for the Plea but three Shillings ſix Pence, *viz.* two Shillings ſix Pence to the Ordinary, &c. and twelve Pence to the Scribe. And if the Goods exceed forty Pounds, then to pay five Shillings, whereof two Shillings ſix Pence to the Ordinary, and two Shillings ſix Pence to the Scribe, or elſe the Scribe may refuſe two Shillings ſix Pence, and take one Penny for every Line containing ten Inches: And the Party ſhall pay for Adminiſtration where the Goods exceed 100 *s.* and not exceeding forty Pounds, two Shillings ſix Pence, and not above. And if any Perſon require a Copy of the Teſtament or Inventory, the Ordinary, &c. ſhall deliver it, taking only ſuch Fee as is to be taken for Probat, or elſe the Scribe may take one Penny for every Line being ten Inches: But as to Seamens Eſtates and Adminiſtration thereof granted, there are certain Fees appointed by a Statute made 22 & 23 *Car.* 2.

22 & 23 Car. 2.

Teſtimonial.
5 Eliz. 4.   The Parſon, Vicar, or Curate of a Pariſh, ſhall take for the Making of a Teſtimonial of a Servant, &c. but two Pence.

Citation.
23 H. 8. 9.   No Ordinary ſhall take for the Seal of any Citation above three Pence.

Coroner.
3 H. 7. 1.   No Coroner ſhall take above thirteen Shillings four Pence for his Fee, upon View o the Body, of the Goods of the Slayer or Murderer of any; or elſe of the Amercia ments, upon any Pariſh for an Eſcape, and nothing where the Perſon is dead by Miſ adventure.

1 H. 8. 7.   As for the Fees in Seſſions, for traverſing, trying, or diſcharging Indictments, diſ charging Recognizances of the Peace and Good Behaviour, &c. Theſe vary according t the Cuſtom of the Country, and in that Caſe *Conſuetudo loci eſt obſervanda.*

See the Oath.
c. 1. §. 2.   As to the Juſtice of Peace himſelf touching Fees or Profit by him to be taken, hi Oath ought to direct him, which is as to that Purpoſe, That you take nothing for you Office of Juſtice of Peace to be done but of the King, and Fees accuſtomed, and Coſt limited by the Statute.

2

CHAP. XLII.

Fiſh.

Conſervators
Welt. 2. 47.
13 R. 2. 19.
P. Fiſh, 1.
P. Juſt. 14.
17 R. 2. c 9

EVERY Juſtice of Peace by 17 R. 2. *cap.* 9. is a Conſervator of Rivers, and of the Statutes made in that Behalf, (*ſc.* of the Statutes of 13 Ed. 1. *cap.* 47. 13 R. 2. *cap.* 19. and 17 R. 2. *cap.* 9.) within this County where he is a Juſtice, and may appoint and ſwear Under-Conſervators ; and (when he may attend it) ought to ſurvey all the Wears in the Rivers, that they be of a reaſonable Wideneſs, and all other Defaults done againſt the aforeſaid Statutes.

Every Juſtice of Peace may burn the Nets and other Engines put or caſt into Waters, wherewith the Fry or Breed of any Fiſh may be taken or deſtroyed ; ' And this ſhall be · for the firſt Offence : And for the ſecond Offence the ſaid Juſtice of Peace may (as · it ſeemeth) impriſon ſuch Offenders for a Quarter of a Year ; and for the third Offence, one whole Year : And as the Treſpaſs or Offence increaſeth, ſo may the Juſtice of Peace increaſe the Puniſhment of ſuch Offenders. See the Statute 13 E. 47. 13 R. 2. 19. and 17 R. 2. 9.

Nets.

' To ſpeak it once for all, where a Penalty is appointed upon Conviction of a third
: Offence, it muſt be intended (if not expreſſed in that Statute) that there be, and ought
' to be Convictions for the firſt Offence, and ſo for the ſecond, before the Perſon ſhall
' incur or bear the Penalty for the third Offence ; and the third Offence muſt be com-
' mitted after the ſecond Offence, and Conviction thereof, that is, lawful Judgment
' given for the ſecond, and ſo the ſecond after the firſt.

2 Inſt. 468.

By Warrant of any one or more Juſtices of Peace, the Conſtables and Church-wardens (where any Offence is committed in deſtroying the Spawn or Brood of Sea-fiſh, againſt the Statute 3 *Jac.* 1.) may levy the Forfeitures of the Offenders by Diſtreſs and Sale of the Offenders Goods, rendring to the Offenders the Surpluſage.

3 Jac. 1. 12.

(*a*) The Particulars of the ſaid Statute 3 *Jac.* 1. are as followeth :

1. No Perſon in any Haven, Harbour or Creek, or within five Miles of the Mouth of any Haven, Harbour or Creek of the Sea, ſhall fiſh with any Draw-net, or Drag-net, under three Inches Meaſh, (*viz.* one Inch and an half from Knot to Knot) except for Taking of Smoulds in *Norfolk* only ; and except for Taking of Herring, Pilchards and and Spicots.

2. No Perſon in any Haven, Harbour or Creek, or within five Miles of the Mouth of any Haven, &c. ſhall fiſh with any Net with Canvas, or other Engine or Device, whereby the Spawn, Fry or Brood of any Sea-fiſh may be deſtroyed.

And for every ſuch Offence the Offenders ſhall forfeit their Nets, and ten Shillings in Money ; the one Half thereof to be to the Uſe of the Poor of the Town or Pariſh where the Offence ſhall be committed, and the other Half to him that will ſue for the ſame ; and to be levied by the Mayor or other Head Officer of every City, Borough or Town Corporate, or by Warrant from one or more Juſtices of Peace, *ut ſupra.*

3 Jac. 1. 12.

Touching the Fiſhing for Pilchards, &c. in *Cornwal* and *Devon,* ſee the ſaid Act ; and for general Fiſhing the Act of 15 *Car.* 2. *cap.* 14.

If any Ling, Herring, Cod or Pilchard, freſh or ſalted, dried or bloated, or any Salmons, Eels or Congers taken by any Foreigners, Aliens to this Kingdom, ſhall be imported, ſold, uttered or expoſed to Sale in *England,* any Perſon may ſeiſe it ; one Moiety to the Seiſor, the other to the Poor where ſeiſed. 18 *Car.* 2. *cap.* 2. Made perpetual 32 *Car.* 2. *cap.* 2.

*Imported.
18 C. 2. c. 2.*

But now by the Statute 32 *Car.* 2. Stock-fiſh and live Eels may be imported into *England,* notwithſtanding 18 *Car.* 2.

No ſuſpicious or idle Perſon ſhall in the Night-time aſſemble or gather together about the Boats, Nets or Cellars belonging to any Pilchard-Craft upon the Coaſts of *Devon,* and having no Buſineſs there, and having Notice by the Company to be gone ; every Perſon ſo refuſing, upon Complaint to a Juſtice of Peace, ſhall pay five Shillings to the Poor, or be ſet in the Stocks five Hours. 14 *Car.* 2. *cap.* 28. *ſect.* 5.

*Aſſemblies.
13 & 14 C. 2.
c. 28.*

If any Perſon ſhall uſe any Caſting-net, Chief-net, Drag-net, Tramel-net, Shove-net, or other Net whatſoever ; or any Angle, Hair-nooſe, Troll or Spear, or ſhall lay any Wear, Pots, Nets, Fiſh-hooks, or other Engines, or ſhall take any Fiſh by any other

*22 & 23 C. 2
c. 25.*

Means or Device whatſoever, in any River, Stew, Pond, Mote, or other Water ; or ſhall be aiding and aſſiſting thereunto, without the Conſent of the Lord or Owner of the Water, and be convicted by Confeſſion or Oath of one Witneſs before one Juſtice of Peace of the County, Diviſion, Riding or Place, ſhall recompence the Party ſuch Damages, and within ſuch Time as the ſame Juſtice ſhall think fit, not exceeding treble Damages, and pay to the Overſeers for the Uſe of the Poor ſuch Sum of Money as the Juſtice ſhall think fit, not exceeding ten Shillings, and in Default of Payment to be levied by Diſtreſs and Sale of Goods ; and for Want of Diſtreſs to commit the Offender to Priſon for ſuch Time as the Juſtice ſhall think fit, not exceeding one Month, unleſs he ſhall by Bond with one competent Surety or Sureties be bound to the Parties injured, not exceeding ten Pounds, never to offend in like Manner. 22 & 23 *Car.* 2. *cap.* 25. *ſect.* 2.

If a Fiſhmonger ſell Fiſh at unreaſonable Prices, he is puniſhable for it by Indictment. So likewiſe if a Malſter buy Barley, and ſell the Malt at unreaſonable Prices, he is puniſhable for the ſame by Indictment. *P.* 12 *Jac.* Rolls, *Part* 15. 11.

Severn.
30 *C.* 2. *c.* 9.
If any Perſon ſhall in the River of *Severn* fiſh with, or make uſe of any Engine or Device whereby any Salmon, Trout or Barbel under the Length appointed by the Statute of 1 *Eliz.* ſhall be taken or killed, or ſhall fiſh with any Net for Salmon, Salmon-mart, Salmon-peal, Pike, Carp, Trout, Barbel, Chub or Grayling, the Meſh whereof ſhall be under two Inches and· an half Square from Knot to Knot, or above twenty Yards in Length, and two Yards in Breadth, or above fifty Yards in Length, and ſix Yards in Breadth in the Wing of the Net in the ſaid River, from *Rippleſtock-lake* to *Glouceſter-Bridge,* or above ſixty Yards in Length below *Glouceſter-Bridge,* and ſix Yards in Breadth in the Wing of the Net, or ſhall fiſh with more than one of thoſe Nets at once, or ſhall uſe any Device for Taking the Fry of Eels, he ſhall forfeit five Pounds for every Offence, and the Fiſh ſo taken, and the Inſtruments uſed in Taking them ; and ſhall alſo forfeit five Pounds for every Time he or they ſhall water any Hemp or Flax in the ſaid River.

Spawn.
Ibid.
If any between the firſt of *March* and the laſt of *May* ſhall do any Act whereby the Spawn ſhall be deſtroyed, they ſhall forfeit forty Shillings for every Offence, and the Inſtruments imployed for the ſaid Purpoſe.

Conſervators.
Ibid.
The Juſtices of Peace of the Counties of *Worceſter, Salop* and *Glouceſter,* ſhall be Conſervators of the ſaid River in their reſpective Counties, and make one or more Under-Conſervators in their reſpective Limits, to whom or to any Conſtable, Tithingman or Headborough, upon their own Knowledge or Information of any ſuch Offence, they ſhall iſſue Warrants under the Hands and Seals of any two of them, to ſearch in all ſuſpected Houſes, &c. for ſuch unlawful Inſtruments, and ſeiſe them, and bring them to the Quarter-Seſſions to be deſtroyed.

Puniſhment.
Ibid.
None ſhall be puniſhed for the ſaid Offences but by Information or Indictment before the Juſtices of Aſſiſe and *Niſi prius, Oyer* and *Terminer* and Gaol-delivery, or the General Seſſions of the Peace ; the one Moiety of the Forfeitures ſhall be to the Uſe of the Poor of the Pariſh where the Offence ſhall be committed, the other to the Proſecutor, to be levied by *Fieri facias* or *Capias ad ſatisfaciendum.*

10 W 3 c.25.
§. 13.
In the Edition 1727 of this Peck, 6 & 7 W. 3. c. 16 which has no Relation to this Place, was here inſerted. See an Abſtract of it Tit. Carriages.
By Stat. 10 *W.* 3. *cap.* 25. *ſect.* 13. All Robberies, Murders, Felonies, and other capital Crimes committed upon Land in *Newfoundland,* or any of the Iſlands thereunto belonging, may be inquired of, tried, heard and determined in any County of *England,* by Commiſſion of *Oyer* and *Terminer* and Gaol-Delivery, according to the Laws of this Land for Puniſhment of ſuch Crimes committed within this Realm.

Salmon.
4 & 5 Ann.
c. 12.
An Act was made 4 & 5 *Ann.* for the Increaſe and better Preſervation of the Salmon and other Fiſh in the Rivers in the Counties of *Southampton* and *Wiltſhire.*

By the aforeſaid Statute 'tis declared, that the Statute 13 *Ed.* 1. ſhall extend and be in Force as well to Rivers, Creeks and Waters in the ſaid Counties, as to the Waters of *Humber, Owſe, Trent,* in that old Act mentioned, and under the ſame Penalties as therein are ſet forth.

And 'tis farther enacted, That the Juſtices of Peace reſiding within ſix Miles of any Rivers, &c. in *Hampſhire* or *Wilts,* may under their Hands and Seals appoint Overſeers of the ſaid Statute 4 & 5 *Ann.* who ſhall be ſworn before the ſaid Juſtices, and then they may take Offenders and deſtroy their Nets or Engines, which are kept or uſed contrary to any Statute relating to Fiſhing.

1

And

And such Overseers of the said Statute may bring Offenders, &c. before a Justice of Peace, and every Offender shall for the first Offence forfeit not under 20 s. nor above 5 l. and double for the second Offence; and as that shall increase, so the Penalty shall be doubled by the Justice before whom convicted, which is to be upon the Oath of one or more Witnesses, or the Confession of the Party offending; one Moiety to the Informer, the other to the Poor of the Parish where the Offence was done; and if not paid on Demand, or if not able to pay it, then the Justice before whom the Party was convicted shall send him to the House of Correction for three Months.

After the 30th of *June* till after the 11th Day of *November*, Salmon shall not be taken or offered to Sale under the like Forfeiture and Penalty.

This Clause is repealed by the Stat. 1 G. 1. c. 18. §. 11. as to Owners of Fishery, &c. See the Proviso infra.

And if any Salmon shall swim into Ditches, Cuts or Water-carriages of Meadow-Grounds, within the Time restrained by this Act; then the Owners or Tenants of such Grounds shall suffer them to pass into the main Rivers, and not wilfully destroy them, under the like Penalties.

Those who are Owners or Tenants of Mills in *Hampshire* or *Wilts*, upon any of the Waters or Rivers there, must keep open a small Hatch of a Foot square in the direct Stream; and where there is no Wheel for the Salmon to pass and repass, from 11th Day of *November* to the last Day of *May*, and shall not during that Time use any Devices for killing or taking Salmon in that Hatch, under the like Penalties.

If Pots are laid to catch Eels between the 1st of *January* and the 10th of *March*, Racks must be set before them to keep out the old Salmon, and after the said 10th of *March* to the 30th of *May*, no Pot shall be laid but such as shall be wide enough to let the young Salmon pass thro' to the Sea, and shall not take or keep, or offer to Sale any of the young Fry during that Time, under the like Penalties.

Sea Trouts shall not be taken in any of the said Rivers, Creeks, or Arms of the Sea, *Sea Trouts.* in either of the said Counties, after the 30th of *June* to the 11th of *November*, under the like Penalties.

To be levied by a Warrant of the Justice, &c. before whom the Conviction is made by Distress and Sale of the Goods of the Offender; and for Want of Distress to be sent to the House of Correction. *

* This Act only extends to the County of Southampton, and Southern Part of Wiltshire.

The Court of Assistants of the Fishmongers Company, or the major Part of them, may *By-Laws.* make By-Laws for the Government of the Company, to be approved by the Lord Mayor and *9 Ann. c. 2. 6.* Aldermen, and allowed and confirmed according to the Statute, &c. and every Year there shall *§. 1.* be a fit Person chosen out of the six Wardens of that Company, after the 10th of *June*, by the Lord Mayor and Aldermen, to be a Master of the Art of Fishery, and out of the twelve Assistants six fit Persons to be Wardens of that Art, whereof the Water-Bailiff of *Court of Assistants.* *London* shall be one; and out of Sixty of the Commonalty, thirty Persons to be Assistants; which said Master, Wardens and Assistants, or any sixteen of them, with three Wardens, are constituted the Court of Assistants, and shall meet on the first *Thursday* in every Month in their Common Hall to form a Court, and keep it for regulating Abuses in Fishery. The Water-Bailiff shall be summoned to attend the Court, and the major Part of them may *Water-Bailiff.* call before them any Person who shall fish or drudge as common Fishermen, within the Limits of the Fishery, and cause every Person duly qualified, or who have served on board the Navy two Years, to register their Names there, together with the Place of his Abode, and the Name of every Servant or Apprentice he hath, using the Trade of Fishing or Drudging within the said Limits; and shall cause a Mark to be set on every Boat, not to be de- *Boats to be* faced, changed or altered, that Offenders, &c. may be found out, and that the Crown *marked.* may know what Number of able Seamen that Company can furnish; and if any Person duly summoned shall neglect to appear at the said Court, he shall be sent on board the Navy, and disabled from Fishing in the *Thames* for two Years.

The Lord Mayor, upon Application to him made by the Court of Assistants, may or- *Ib. §. 2.* der Stakes to be driven in any Place within the River, between the *London* Mark-stone above *Stains-Bridge* and *London-Bridge*, so as it be not prejudicial to the Navigation of the River, and no Person shall remove or loosen them.

Fish shall be sold once and no more within *Billingsgate*, or 150 Yards of the Dock, and *Billingsgate-* no Person shall sell or expose to Sale any Fish in *Billingsgate* Market, or within 150 *Market.* Yards, *Ib. §. 3.*

Yards, &c. except free Fishmongers in their Houses and Shops, and Fishermen and the first Importers thereof, &c.

Water-Bailiff. The Court of Assistants shall pay the Water-Bailiff every Year 30 *l.* clear of all Taxes,
Ib. §. 4. on *Easter* and *Michaelmas*, by equal Portions; and he may grant Licenses to fish in their several Seasons, according to Custom.

Ib. §. 5. No Fish shall be sold or exposed to Sale in *Billingsgate Market*, or within 150 Yards of the Dock, before Three of the Clock in the Morning, from *Lady-day* to *Michaelmas*, and before Five in the Morning from *Michaelmas* to *Lady-day*, and the proper Officer shall ring a Bell for that Purpose.

Ib. §. 6. The Lord Mayor and Aldermen of *London*, and the Justices of Peace of the respective Counties, or one of them, for all Offences committed out of the Jurisdiction of the Conservator, in wilfully killing or exposing to Sale any Brood or Fry of Fish, or any Spawn or Spat of Oysters, or any unwholsome Fish, or in catching, killing, or destroying any Fish out of Season, or by exposing such Fish to Sale, or by wilfully buying, harbouring, or receiving, or using as Food for Hogs, or otherwise, any Spawn or Fry of Fish, or catching Salmon between the 24th of *August* to the 11th of *November* every Year, may either upon View or Complaint made, examine and determine the same upon Oath; and upon Conviction set a Fine not exceeding 10 *l.* nor under 5 *s.* to be levied by Distress as aforesaid, unless the Fine be forthwith paid, or good Security given to abide the Order of the Court of Conservancy, if the Conviction be before the Lord Mayor, or at the Quarter-Sessions by the Justices, in Case the Offender shall appeal to either; and for Want of Distress, then to be committed to the House of Correction, without Bail, for any Time not exceeding two Months. And if the Offence is committed within the Jurisdiction of the Lord Mayor, then one Moiety of the Fine shall be paid to him, the other to the Informer; and if elsewhere, then to the Poor of the Parish, &c. and the Prosecutor.

Ib. §. 10. This Act shall be taken as a publick Act; and if an Action is brought for putting it in Execution, the Defendant may plead the General Issue, and give the Statute in Evidence together with the Special Matter, and if he recover shall have full Costs.

1 Geo. 1. No flat or fresh Fish whatsoever shall be imported, which were taken, bought, or re-
c. 18. §. 1. ceived of any Foreigner, or out of any Stranger's Bottom (except Protestant Strangers dwelling here) nor shall any Person give or exchange Goods for such Fish so taken.

Ib. §. 2. Master, &c. of a Smack in which any Fish shall be brought to Shore contrary to this Act, being lawfully convicted upon his Appearing, or after, or Default to appear, being summoned before one or more Justices, &c. where the Offender resides or shall be found, and this upon the Oath of two credible Witnesses, shall forfeit 20 *l.* for every Offence, to be levied by Warrant of such Justices, by Distress, &c. and for Want thereof to be committed to Gaol for 12 Months.

Ib. §. 3. Nothing in this Act shall extend to prevent the importing or buying Anchovies, Botargo, Cavear, Eels, Stockfish, or Sturgeon.

Nets. Any Person using at Sea, upon the Coast of *England*, any Sea-net for catching Fish (ex-
Ib. §. 4. cept Herrings, Pilchards, Sprats and Lavidnian) with a Mesh in his Net less than three Inches and an half from Knot to Knot, or any false or double bottom Cod or Pouch, or shall put any Net, tho' of a legal Size, upon or beyond the other, in order to destroy the small Fish, the Forfeiture is the Nets and 20 *l.* for every Offence, to be recovered as the Penalty above inflicted on the Master, &c. and in Default of Payment or Distress, to be committed to Gaol for twelve Months.

Ib. §. 5. The Penalties in this Act (except for illegal Nets) shall be one Moiety to the Informer, the other to the Poor of the Parish where the Offence shall be committed, necessary Charges being deducted.

Ib §. 6. Where any illegal Nets shall be proved to be forfeited, they shall be publickly burnt by Virtue of a Warrant of a Justice, &c. for that Purpose.

He who brings on Shore in *England*, or sells or exposes to Sale, or exchanges for other Goods any unsizable Fish, which shall not be of the several Lengths from the Eyes to the Extent of the Tail,

	Inches.		Inches.		Inches.
ss. Bass	12	Dab	8	Plaice	8
Bret	16	Flounder	7	Sole	8
Brill	14	Mullet	12	Turbot	16
Codlin	12	Pearl	14	Whiting	12

shall

ſhall forfeit the Fiſh, and 20 *s.* for every Offence, one Moiety to the Informer, the other to the Poor of the Pariſh, to be levied by Warrant of a Juſtice, by Diſtreſs, &c. and for Want thereof to be ſent to the Houſe of Correction and whipp'd, and kept to hard Labour for ſix Days, and not longer than fourteen Days.

The Proſecution muſt be within one Month after the Offence.

Any Perſon may import and ſell any Quantity of Lobſters or Turbots, in the ſame Manner they might have done before the Statute 10 & 11 *Will.* 3. *cap.* 24. was made.

It ſhall be lawful for Owners of Fiſheries at any Time from 11th of *June* till 1 *Auguſt* every Year, to take or kill any Salmon, or Salmon-Peal or Salmon-Kind, or expoſe them to Sale within the Times aforeſaid. *Salmon.* Ib. §. 11.

Provided, that ſuch Owners, &c. or their Servants, ſhall not, between the 1ſt of *Au-guſt* and the 12th of *November*, take, kill, or wilfully hurt any Salmon by *Angles, Gins, Hawks, Nets, Racks*, or other Devices, or offer to Sale any of the ſaid Fiſh ſo taken, under the like Penalties as in the Statute 4 & 5 *Annæ*. Ib. §. 13.

Laying or drawing any Nets or Engines, or doing or cauſing to be done, any other Act in the Rivers herein mentioned, *viz. Air, Calder, Derwent, Dee, Dunn, Eure, Mercy, Ouze, Ribble, Severn, Swaile, Team, Tees, Trent, Ware* and *Wye*, or any of them, whereby Salmon, &c. not eighteen Inches long, from the Eye to the Middle of the Tail, may be taken or killed, or hindered by any Bank, Dam, &c. from going up the ſaid Rivers to ſpawn; and being convicted before one Juſtice, either upon View, Confeſſion, or Oath of one Witneſs, forfeits 5 *l.* for every Offence, &c. And ſo ſhall he, who from the laſt Day of *July* to the 12th of *November*, hurts any Salmon, or who ſhall after that Day fiſh in any of thoſe Rivers with Nets not allowed by the Statutes 1 *Eliz.* and 30 *Car.* 2. beſides the Fiſh and Nets; one Moiety to the Informer, the other to the Poor of the Pariſh where the Offence was done, to be levied by a Warrant of a Juſtice, and by Diſtreſs and Sale, &c. and for Want of a Diſtreſs, to be committed, for not leſs Time than one Month, nor for more Time than three Months; and to be held to hard Labour, and to ſuffer ſuch other corporal Puniſhment as the ſaid Juſtice before whom convicted ſhall think fit, who ſhall order ſuch Nets to be ſeiſed and cut to Pieces, or deſtroyed in his Preſence, and ſhall cauſe ſuch Banks to removed at the Charge of the Offender, which, if not paid upon Conviction, &c. ſhall be levied in the ſame Manner as aforeſaid. *Nets.* Ib. §. 14.

Salmon ſhall not be ſent from any of the ſaid Rivers to Fiſhmongers in *London*, or their Agents, weighing leſs than ſix Pounds each Fiſh; he who is convicted of buying, ſelling, or ſending Salmon of leſs Weight, ſhall forfeit 5 *l.* beſides the Fiſh ſo bought and ſold; one Moiety to the Informer, the other to the Poor, &c. and if not paid upon Conviction, then to be levied by Warrant, &c. by Diſtreſs and Sale, &c. and for Want of Diſtreſs to be committed and kept to hard Labour for three Months, unleſs the Forfeiture be paid in the mean Time. *Salmon to weigh ſix Pounds.* Ib. §. 15.

Offenders puniſhed by this Act ſhall not be proſecuted, nor incur the Penalty of any other Law for the ſame Offence. Ib. §. 16.

An Appeal lies to the Quarter-Seſſions, who are finally to determine, &c. Ib. §. 17.

This Act ſhall not extend to any antient Locks or Wears, but that the Proprietors may repair, rebuild, remove, or take them down, &c. Ib. §. 18.

By *Stat.* 9 *Geo.* 2. *cap.* 33. *ſect.* 1. every Perſon offending againſt the 1 *Geo.* 1. *cap.* 18. *ſect.* 1. againſt importing Fiſh by Foreigners, ſhall forfeit 100 *l.* to be recovered in any Court at *Weſtminſter-Hall*, one Moiety to the Informer, the other to the Poor, &c. and the Maſter of the Veſſel forfeits 50*l.* The Proſecution muſt be within 12 Months. 9 *Geo.* 2. *c.* 33. §. 1.

Perſons killing Lobſters on the Coaſt of *Scotland*, from the 1ſt of *June* to the 1ſt of *September*, forfeit 5 *l.* for each Offence, to be recovered upon a ſummary Complaint before any two Juſtices of Peace. Ib. §. 4.

The Rates allowed for *Fiſh* exported are as follows.

For every Caſk of Pilchards or Scads, containing 50 Gallons, 7 *s.* 5 Geo. 1.
For every Hundred of Codfiſh, Ling or Hake (except Haberdine) in Length fourteen Inches from the Bone in the Fin to the third Joint in the Tail, 5 *s.* *c.* 18.
For every Barrel of wet Codfiſh, Ling or Hake, containing thirty-two Gallons, 2 *s.*
For every Hundred of dried Codfiſh, Ling or Hake, called Haberdine, 3 *s.*
For every Barrel of Salmon, containing thirty-two Gallons, 5 *s.* 6 *d.*
For every Barrel of white Herrings, containing thirty-two Gallons, 2 *s.* 9 *d.* And of Red Herrings, 1 *s.* 9 *d.* And of ſhotten Herrings, 1 *s.*

For

For every Laſt of dried red Sprats, 1 *s.*

And ſo in Proportion for a greater or leſſer Quantity, which Allowances ſhall be paid by the Collector of the Duties on Salt in the Port from whence exported, within thirty Days after Demand, &c. See the Statute, and alſo the Statutes 8 *Geo.* 1. *cap.* 4. & 16.

Black Facts.
9 Geo. 1. c. 22.
He who ſhall be armed and have his Face black or diſguiſed, and ſhall unlawfully take away or ſteal any Fiſh out of a River or Pond, or break down any Head or Mound of a Fiſh-pond, whereby the Fiſh ſhall be loſt, is a Felon without Benefit of Clergy. See *Felony by Statute.*

C H A P. XLIII. ^(a)

Fire.

6 Ann. c. 31.   SErvant firing any Dwelling-houſe or Out-houſe, thro' Negligence, forfeits One hundred Pounds, to be paid to the Church-wardens, to be given to the Sufferer; or to be committed to the Houſe of Correction, as two Juſtices ſhall think fit.

C H A P. XLIV.

Forcible Entry.

One Juſt.
WHAT is Forcible Entry, and what is a Forcible Holding or Detainer; ſee the other Title, *Forcible Entry, hic poſtea cap.* 125.

15 R. 2. 2.
8 H. 6. 9. P. 2.
Dyer 210.
Lam. 150.
Every Juſtice of Peace, upon Complaint to him made, or upon other Notice to him given, of any Forcible Entry into, or Forcible Holding or Detainer of Poſſeſſion of any Lands, Tenements, or other Poſſeſſions (or of any Benefices or Offices of the Church) contrary to theſe Statutes, without any examining, or ſtanding upon the Right or Title of either Party, ought in convenient Time (at the Coſts of the Party grieved) to do Execution of theſe Statutes in Manner and Form hereunder following.

View.
15 R. 2. 2.
Lamb. 152.
1. Firſt, he ought to go to the Place where ſuch Force ſhall be.

2. He may take with him ſufficient Power of the County or Town, by his Diſcretion; and the Sheriff alſo, if need be, to aid him, as well for the arreſting of ſuch Offenders, as alſo for removing the Force, and for conveying them to the next Gaol. (*a*) And whoſoever (of that County) ſhall refuſe to attend and aſſiſt the Juſtice of Peace herein, ſhall be impriſoned, and fined to the King. 15 R. 2. *cap.* 2.

Arreſt.
3. (*d*) He ought to arreſt and remove all ſuch Offenders, as at his coming he ſhall ſee or find continuing the Force; and may take away their Weapons and Armour, and cauſe them to be praiſed, and after to be anſwered to the King as forfeited, or the Value thereof.

Break open Doors.
If the Doors be ſhut, and they within the Houſe ſhall deny the Juſtice to enter, it ſeems he may break open the Houſe to remove the Force.

But if ſuch Offenders, being in the Houſe at the coming of the Juſtice, ſhall make no Reſiſtance, nor make Shew of any Force, then the Juſtice cannot arreſt or remove them, except upon the Enquiry, a Force be found. See *Cromp.* 73. and the other Title, *Forcibly Entry.*

Two Counties.
Cromp. 71.
Alſo if the Houſe or Land which is holden with Force, ſhall extend into two Counties, and the Offenders remove their Force into that Part of the Houſe or Land which is in the other County, when the Juſtices do come, they cannot then remove the Force.

Reſtitution not without Enquiry.
And if the Juſtice at his coming ſhall ſee or find a Force, and ſhall remove the Offenders, yet he may not upon his own View reſtore the Party ouſted to his Poſſeſſion again, without Enquiry firſt made of the Force by a Jury, as appears hereafter.

Record.
14 H. 7. 8.
4. Alſo the Juſtice ought to make a *Record of ſuch* Force by him viewed; which Record ſhall be a ſufficient Conviction of the Offenders, and the Parties ſhall not be allowed to *traverſe* it.

4

And

And this Record (being made out of the Seſſions by a particular Juſtice) may be kept Lamb. 152, by him; or he may make it indented, and certify the one Part into the King's Bench, or 163 & 375. to leave it with the Clerk of the Peace, and the other Part he may keep himſelf. 21 H. 6. 5.

The Form of the Record, ſee the other Title, *Forcible Entry*, and *Precedents.*

5. Alſo he ought to commit (immediately) to the next Gaol all ſuch Perſons as he *Impriſon con* ſhall find and ſee continuing the Force at his Coming to the Place; the ſaid Offenders *victed on* there to remain convict by his own View, Teſtimony and Record, until they have paid *View.* a Fine to the King: For this *View of the Force by the Juſtice*, being a Judge of Record, Br. Peace. 4. maketh his Record thereof, in the Judgment of the Law, as ſtrong and effectual, as if Co. S. 120. the Offenders had confeſſed the Force before him; and touching the Reſtraining of P. 2. Traverſe, more effectual than if the Force had been found by a *Jury* upon the Evidence of others.

And yet the Words of the Statute ſeem more large; ſc. *And if he do find any that made* P. 2. *any ſuch Forcible Entry, or that hold the Place with Force,* &c. *he ſhall commit the Offenders to the Gaol,* &c. But ſuch Force muſt be in the Preſence or View of the Juſtice of Peace, or elſe he can neither record it, nor yet commit the Offenders. 13 H. 7. Crom.195. b. Crook 41.

The Form of the *Mittimus*; ſee the other Title, *Forcible Entry.*

6. Alſo the ſame Juſtices of Peace, or ſome of them that ſhall ſee the Force, as having Fint. beſt Knowledge of the Matter, and having the Cuſtody of this Record, are the proper Co. 8. 41. a. Judges of this Offence; and therefore may aſſeſs the * Fine upon every ſuch Offender; 597. Lam. 193. but it muſt be impoſed ſeverally, and not upon them jointly: And the Juſtice ought to Co. 11. 43. a. eſtreat the ſame Fine, and to ſend the Eſtreat into the Exchequer, that from thence the * If the Fine is Sheriff may be commanded to levy it for his Majeſty's Uſe. But upon the ſame Fine ſet, the Convic- to aſſeſſed and eſtreated, the Juſtice is to deliver the Offenders. *Lamb.* 554. tion cannot be quaſhed on Mo-
Defendant muſt bring his Writ of Error. 2 Salk 450. tion, but the

Alſo upon Payment of the Fine to the Juſtice, or upon Sureties found (by Recog- Lam. 162. nizance) for the Payment thereof, he may deliver the Offenders out of Priſon again at 555. his Pleaſure, by ſome Opinions: But *quære* whether the Juſtice of Peace ſhall meddle with Br. Imp. 10. receiving the Fine, for that the Sheriff is accountant for all Fines. *Lamb.* 555.

Or the Juſtices of Peace, by ſome Opinions, may record ſuch Force, and commit Cromp. 161. the Offenders, and after certify the Record to the Juſtices of Aſſiſe and Gaol-delivery, Lam. Ed. as it was done at *Stafford* Aſſiſes, *Ann.* 26 *Eliz.* by the Report of Mr. *Crompton*;) or 1582. elſe to certify it to the General Seſſions of the Peace, (as it ſeemeth to Mr. *Crompton*) and there the Offenders may be fined: For, ſaith he, the Statute doth not ſay, that the Fine ſhall be aſſeſſed by them that record the Force, more than by other Juſtices.

Or rather the Juſtice of Peace may certify or deliver the Record by him made (and Lamb. 163. refer the Fine and farther Proceedings therein) to the King's Bench (in regard of their ſupreme Authority in ſuch Caſes.) And this Mr. *Lambard* thinketh to be the ſafeſt Courſe.

7. Alſo the Juſtice of Peace, notwithſtanding his own View of the Force, may, and Enquiry. ought in ſome Town or Place, near where the Force was, to inquire by a ſufficient Jury Sce the Stat. of the ſame County, to be returned by the Sheriff, as well of thoſe who made ſuch For- 8 H. 6. c. 9. cible Entry, as of thoſe who made ſuch Forcible Detainer. & Plo. 86.

And here note, that any Juſtice of Peace alone out of the Seſſions may make an Inquiry Br. Peace 14. being ſo appointed by the Statute;) whereas otherwiſe there muſt be two Juſtices at the leaſt, to make an Inquiry, or to hold a Seſſions, and one of them of the *Quorum.*

And this Inquiry ought to be made, whether the Offenders be preſent or gone, at the Br. Forcib.27. Coming of the Juſtice of Peace; and though he go not to ſee the Place where the Force is; for without this Inquiry there can be no Reſtitution. See more concerning this In- quiry in the other Title, *Forcible Entry,* &c.

(*a*) Alſo by the Words of the Statute of 8 H. 6. *cap.* 9. (*maintenant meſme les Juſtices ſoient inquirer,* &c.) the Juſtices are to make this Inquiry immediately after the Force committed, and Complaint made to them by the Party griev'd; and yet they may make this Inquiry at any convenient Time after. *Crom.* 124.

If the Sheriff ſhall not duly execute the Juſtices Precept directed to him for returning a Jury, he ſhall forfeit 20 *l.* And the Juſtice of the Peace may proceed to hear and determine ſuch Default of the Sheriff. See 8 H. 6. *cap.* 9. *hic poſtea.*

(*d*) The Form of a Precept to the Sheriff to return a Jury, ſee the Title *Precedents.*

C c   The

The Form of the Inquiry, Prefentment or Verdict, fee as before.

Reftitution.
* P. R. 41. b.
36. b. See the
Words of the
Stat. 8 H. 6.
c. 9. §. 3.

8. And if upon fuch Inquiry, fuch Forcible Entry, or * Forcible Detainer, fhall be found by the Jury, then the faid Juftice of Peace fhall refeife the Lands or Tenements fo entered upon or holden, and put the Party in Poffeffion again, who was put or holden out. See the other Title of *Forcible Entry.*

But the putting out, muft of Neceffity be found, and that by exprefs Words in the Indictment. *See as before.*

(*a*) And fo note, that the Juftice or Juftices of Peace, recording only the Force by his or their View, may not put the Party into his Poffeffion again, but the Juftice muft firft make Inquiry thereof by a Jury of the County at a fpecial Seffions by the faid Juftices to be holden; and then the Force being found by the faid Jury, the faid Juftice or Juftices may put the Party into his former Poffeffion.

(*d*) And this Reftitution the Juftice of Peace may make himfelf; or he may make his Warrant to the Sheriff to do it: Or elfe he may certify fuch Prefentment or Indictment taken before him, into the King's Bench, and fo leave the Reftitution to be awarded out of that Court. *See as before.*

Co. 9. 118.
Co. 11. 65.
7 E. 4. 18.

But the Juftices of Affife and Gaol-delivery, nor the Juftices of Peace at their General Seffions, cannot, it feems, make or award Reftitution, except the Indictment were found before them; but the Juftices of Peace only, or fome of them, that were prefent at the Inquiry, and when the Indictment was found, they only have Power to make Reftitution; except the Juftices of the King's Bench, who have a fupreme Authority in all Cafes of the Crown.

And therefore if the Record (*fc.* the Prefentment of fuch Force,) fhall be certified by the Juftices of Peace into the King's Bench, or that the fame Prefentment or Indictment fhall be removed thither by *Certiorari,* there the Juftices of the King's Bench may award a Writ of Reftitution to the Sheriff of the fame County, to reftore Poffeffion to the Party fo expelled.

Break open the
Houfe.
P. R. 41. b.

After it is found by fuch Inquiry, that fuch Forcible Entry or Detainer is made, the Juftices of Peace may break open the Houfe by Force, to refeife the fame, and to put the Party, fo put out, in Poffeffion again. And fo may the Sheriff, having the Juftice's Warrant.

The Form of fuch Warrant from the Juftice of Peace to the Sheriff, to make Reftitution, fee in the other Titles, *Forcible Entry,* and *Precedents.*

* But now in
the King's
Bench.

But the Juftice of Peace may not (in any Cafe) make a Reftitution without fuch an Inquiry firft had, and fuch Force thereby found: For if the Juftice fhall make Reftitution without Inquiry, it feems to be punifhable in the Star-Chamber *.

Alfo this Reftitution ought to be made to none, but to him only that was put out; fo that if the Father be put out by Force, and dieth (after Inquiry, and before Reftitution) his Heir fhall not have Reftitution.

To whom Reftitution fhall be made, fee the other Title, *Forcible Entry.*

Alfo fuch Reftitution muft be made only, where a Man is put out, or holden out, *&c.* of *Houfe* or *Land,* and is not to be underftood of a *Rent, Common, Advowfon,* or fuch like. See the other Title, *Forcible Entry.*

Traverfe.

Alfo the Juftice may make Reftitution, notwithftanding any Offer of *Traverfe;* but yet upon *Traverfe* tendred, the fafeft Way for the Juftice of Peace feems to be to deliver or certify the Prefentment into the King's Bench, and fo to refer the farther Proceedings therein to them. See the other Title, *Forcible Entry.*

Default of the
Juftices.

And although thefe Statutes do inflict no Penalty upon the Juftices of Peace, if they fhall not execute them; yet if upon Complaint (or other Notice given of fuch Force) they fhall not at leaft remove the Force, record it, and commit the Offenders, they are punifhable in the Star-Chamber.

(*a*) In the Cafe of *Drayton Baffet* (in the County of *Stafford*) *Ann.* 22 *Eliz.* certain Juftices of Peace of that County, (although they dwelt not near the Place) where a great Riot was committed by a Forcible Detainer, were for their Default fined in the *Star-Chamber,* upon the Statute 17 *R.* 2. *cap.* 8. (as Mr. *Crompton* reporteth) which Statute is, that the Sheriff, and all other the King's Officers, fhall fupprefs Rioters who fhall affemble themfelves in outragious or great Numbers. See *Cromp. Author. des Courts, fol.* 32.

Fine and com-
mit.

(*d*) Although the Juftice of Peace ought to *commit to the Gaol,* and may *fine* all fuch as he fhall fee continuing their Force at his Coming to the Place; yet upon Force found by the Inquiry only, and not viewed and feen by the Juftice, (although this Prefentment of the Jury be a Conviction of the Offenders) the Juftice of Peace may neither *fine,* nor *fend o the Gaol* the faid Offenders, by the Statute of 8 *H.* 6. which appointeth the Inquiry: Cromp. 161. ⌐or the Juftice hath Power by the faid Statute to make Reftitution only, as faith Mr. b. 162. a. *Lambard* 162. yet Mr. *Crompton* holdeth the contrary. contra.

But howfoever, the Juftice of Peace (upon Force found by the Jury) is to remove the Offenders that be prefent, that fo he may reftore the other, and may bind the Offenders o their good Behaviour ; and if the Offenders be gone, yet the Juftice may make his War- ant to take them, and may after fend them to the Gaol, until they have found Sureties or their good Behaviour.

Note, That if fuch Forcible Entry or Detainer fhall be made by *Three Perfons, or* Riot. *tore,* then it is alfo a *Riot ;* and then if there be no former Inquiry thereof made, he two next Juftices of Peace, upon Notice thereof, ought to inquire thereof, as a Riot, y a Jury, within one Month, upon Pain to either of them making Default, to for- Cro. 68. b. ⌐it 100 *l.*

Alfo one Juftice of Peace may hear and determine the Defaults of Sheriff and Bailiffs, Defaults of n not returning fufficient Jurors (whereof every one fhall have Lands, &c. to the Va- Sheriffs in not ue of forty Shillings by the Year at the leaft) before him, to inquire of fuch Forcible returning a Jury. Entry or Detainer : And the faid Juftice of Peace may proceed therein as well by Bill, at 8 H. 6. 9. he Suit of the Party grieved for himfelf, as alfo by Indictment only for the King ; and the P. Juft. 8. 9. ame Procefs fhall be made againft fuch Perfons indicted or fued by Bill in this Behalf, as Raft. 174. c. hould be made againft Perfons indicted or fued by Writ of Trefpafs, with Force and Arms againft the King's Peace. What the Procefs in fuch Cafe is, *vide* Tit. *Procefs.*

And though any one Juftice of Peace may proceed in every of the former Cafes of *For-* Two Juftices. *ible Entry or Detainer,* as aforefaid ; yet if two or more Juftices fhall join therein, it ⌐ better ; for *Plus vident oculi quam oculus ; & fecurius expediuntur negotia commiffa plu- ibus.* Co. 4. 46.

Alfo the *Mayors, Juftice or Juftices of Peace, and the Sheriffs and Bailiffs* of Cities Corporate *nd Boroughs having Franchife,* fhall have in the faid City, Towns and Boroughs, like Towns. Authority to remove fuch Entries, and to inquire thereof, and of *putting or holding out,* 8 H. 6. 9. s the Juftices of Peace and Sheriffs in Counties and Shires have. Raft. 174. d.

Alfo every Juftice of Peace, to whom a Writ upon the Statute of *Northampton* con- The Statute of erning the removing a Force fhall be delivered, ought to execute the fame Writ, *fc.* he Northampton. ⌐ught to remove the Force, and to certify his Doings therein to the *Chancery.* 2 Ed. 3. 3.

And for that the Juftice of Peace, to whom this Writ fhall be delivered, is herein but . Minifter, and is to certify that which he fhall do therein, I will here fet down the Manner how he fhall proceed to execute this Writ.

Firft, When the Juftice of Peace fhall come to the Place where the Force is fuppofed, ⌐y this Writ, he may caufe Three *Oyes* for Silence to be made, and then he may make *Proclamation in the King's Name, to this Effect :*

The King's Majefty's Juftice of Peace ftrictly chargeth, and in his Majefty's Name com- Lam. 173. *nandeth, all and every Perfon to keep Silence, whilft his Majefty's Writ,* &c. *be read, and Proclamation be thereupon made accordingly.*

Secondly, Then may he read, or caufe to be read, the Writ, or may declare the Ef- ⌐ect thereof.

Thirdly, Then let Three other *Oyes* be made ; and thereupon make Proclamation gain, as followeth.

His Majefty's faid Juftice doth, by Virtue of his Majefty's Writ, ftrictly Charge and Fitz. 249. *Command, that no Manner of Perfon, of what Eftate, Degree or Condition foever, now ⌐eing within the Houfe of B. &c. (named in the faid Writ) fhall go armed, or keep Force of Armour or Weapon, nor do any Thing there, or elfewhere, in Difturbance of his Majefty's Peace, or in Offence of the Statute made at* Northampton *in the Second Year of King* ⌐dward 3. *upon Pain of lofing his faid Armour and Weapons, and of imprifoning his Body* 2 Ed. 3. c. 3. *it his Majefty's Pleafure.*

God fave the King.

Fourthly, Then the Juftice of Peace may enter and fearch whether there be any Force of Armour or Weapon worn or born, againft this Proclamation : Or otherwife he may inquire ⌐hereof by a Jury, for fo the Writ itfelf doth warrant him. And if after Proclamation my fuch be found, he ought to imprifon the Offenders, and to feife to the King's Ufe,
ar.d

and prize (by the Oaths of ſome preſent) the Armour and Weapons ſo found with them; and the Offenders ſo impriſoned are to remain there until ſome other Command be given concerning them from his Majeſty, or his Juſtices. See the Writ, *Fitz.* 249. and the Title, *Bailment, poſtea.*

But if, upon the Proclamation made, they do depart in peaceable Manner, then hath the Juſtice no Authority by the Writ to commit them to Priſon, nor to take away their Armour.

Crom. 74, 162.

But when the Juſtice hath removed the Force, (upon this Writ) he may not put the Party that was put out in Poſſeſſion again; if he do, he and the Party alſo are puniſhable in the Star-Chamber, for the Writ doth authorize the Juſtice only to remove the Force, and not to make Reſtitution.

The Form of this Writ upon the Statute of *Northampton,* you may ſee in *Fitz. N. B.* 249.

The Form of a Certificate, or Return of this Writ into the *Chancery,* ſee in the other Title, *Forcible Entry.*

Without Writ.
P. Armor 1.
2 Ed. 3. 3.

Alſo every Juſtice of Peace (*ex officio,* and without any Writ) may do Execution of this Statute of *Northampton,* and that as well by Force of the Commiſſion, as of the ſaid Statute.

Lam. 176.

The Manner to execute this Statute by the Juſtice of Peace (*ex officio*) ſeemeth to be all one as before, *where he hath a Writ delivered him*; ſaving that when he doth this *ex officio,* and *without Writ,* he needeth not make any Proclamation, nor to ſend any Certificate into the *Chancery:* But the Juſtice may go to the Place where the Force is, and (if it be in a Houſe) he may enter and ſearch, if any Force of Armour or Weapon be worn or born againſt this Statute; and if any ſuch Offenders be found, he may commit them to Priſon, and may ſeiſe and prize the Armour and Weapon ſo found with them. And he ought to record all that which he ſhall do in this Behalf, and to ſend ſome Eſtreat into the Exchequer, that the King may be anſwered of the Armour, or of the Value thereof.

But here again the Juſtice muſt not make any *Reſtitution of the Poſſeſſion* to the Party ouſted, but muſt *only remove the Force.*

Fine.
Cro. 160.
Lam. 176,
516.

And concerning the Offenders ſo found, and committed by the ſaid Juſtice of Peace, he (at his Diſcretion) may fine them, and upon Payment thereof, or upon Sureties found for the ſame, that the ſaid Juſtice may deliver the Offenders, even as in the former Statutes of 15 R. 2. & 8 H. 6. or elſe he may record ſuch Force, and commit the Offenders, and after certify the Record into the King's Bench, or to the Juſtices of Gaol-delivery, or to the General Seſſions of the Peace, as here in this Title a little before. *Vide* Tit. *Bailment.*

* 15 Ric. 2.
c. 2.

(*a*) The Defendant was convicted for a Forcible Detainer, upon the * View of a Juſtice of Peace ſetting forth that he held a *Chamber in a Houſe,* in ſuch a Street and Pariſh by Force; but did not ſhew whoſe Houſe it was, nor whether the Chamber was backward or forward, or how many Pair of Stairs high, and the Commitment was to Newgate; but it did not ſet forth that Newgate was the County Gaol; and the Statute expreſly requires that the Commitment ſhould be thither.

But the Court would not intend that there were two Chambers on one Floor, for they held the Chamber was ſufficiently deſcribed: However the Conviction was quaſhed, for though they would intend that Newgate was the County Gaol, yet the Words in the Record being all in the preterperfect Tenſe, when they ſhould be in the preſent Tenſe, for that Reaſon it was quaſhed.

See the Form of Records *and* Warrants *on this Head,* Chap. 182.

C H A P. XLV. (*a*)

Foreſtallers, Regraters, Ingroſſers.

Butter, Cheeſe.
3 & 4 Ed. 6.
c. 21.

NO Perſon ſhall buy to ſell again any Butter or Cheeſe, unleſs he ſell the ſame in open Shop, Fair or Market; and not in Groſs upon Pain of Forfeiture of the double Value, to be recovered in any of the King's Courts of Record, one Moiety to the King, the other to the Informer.

The

The Word *Retail* ſhall be expounded, where a Weigh of Cheeſe or Barrel of Butter, 3 & 4 E. 6. or leſs, and not above, ſhall be ſold at any Time without Covin.   c. 21.

The Statute ſhall not extend to *Inn-keepers or Victuallers*, where the ſame is ſpent in Ibid. their Houſes.

Any Perſon who ſhall buy any Merchandize, Victuals or other Thing whatſoever coming *Foreſtaller*. by Land or Water to a Market or Fair to be ſold, or coming towards any City, Port, 5 E. 6. c. 14. Haven, Creek, or Rode of *England* from beyond Sea, to be ſold, or make Promiſe, or §. 1. contract for the ſame, before the ſame ſhall be in Market, Fair, City, &c. to be ſold, or ſhall make any Price or dearer. Selling of any ſuch Things, or diſſuade, move or ſtir any Perſon not to come thither, ſhall be accounted a Foreſtaller.

Any Perſon that doth regrate, or get into his Hands in any Fair or Market, any *Regrater*. Corn, Wine, Fiſh, Butter, Cheeſe, Candles, Tallow, Sheep, Lambs, Calves, Swine, Ib. §. 2. Piggs, Geeſe, Capons, Hens, Chickens, Pigeons, Conies, or other dead Victuals what- ſoever brought thither to be ſold, and ſhall ſell the ſame again in the ſame Fair or Market, or any other within four Miles thereof, ſhall be taken for an Ingroſſer.

Any Perſon that ſhall get into his Hands by Buying, or Promiſe-taking, other than *Ingroſſer*. by Demiſe, Grant, or Leaſe of Land; or Tithe any Corn growing in the Fields, or Ib. §. 3. any other Corn, Grain, Butter, Cheeſe, Fiſh, or other dead Victuals, with Intent to ſell the ſame again, ſhall be taken for an unlawful Ingroſſer.

Any Perſon thereof convicted by Law of the Realm, or in Form preſcribed by that *Penalty.* Act, ſhall for the firſt Offence ſuffer Impriſonment for two Months without Bail, and 1 *Offence*. ſhall forfeit the Value of the Goods ſo bought.   Ib. §. 4.

For the ſecond Offence, being thereof attainted, ſhall ſuffer Impriſonment by Half a 2 *Offence*. Year, without Bail, and ſhall loſe double the Value of the Goods ſo bought.   Ib. §. 5.

And for the third Offence ſhall be ſet on the Pillory where he inhabits, and forfeit all 3 *Offence*. his Goods and Chattels, and be committed to Priſon, there to remain during the King's Ib. §. 6. Pleaſure.

Firſt, *buying Barley* or *Oats*, to be made into *Malt* or *Oatmeal*, not by foreſtalling ; *Exception*. or Secondly, *buying*, (not by foreſtalling) by *Fiſhmongers, Butchers* or *Poulterers*, Things Ib. §. 7. belonging to their Trades, being ſold again by Retail at reaſonable Prices. Thirdly, *Taking Corn, Cattle, Butter, Cheeſe*, upon Reſervation in Leaſe. Fourthly, *Inn-holders, buying Wine or Victuals*, and ſelling them by Retail in their Houſes, or to their Neigh- bours for Suſtenance, at reaſonable Prices. Fifthly, *Buying of dry'd Fiſh*, &c. not fore- ſtall'd, and ſold at reaſonable Prices. Sixthly, a *Badger, Lader, Kidder* or *Carrier*, being licenſed by three Juſtices where he dwells, *buying Corn, Fiſh, Butter* or *Cheeſe*, he ſelling the ſame within one Month in Fair or Market, or to a Victualler or other Perſon for Proviſion for the Houſe, the ſame being bought without foreſtalling. Seventh- ly, Proviſion for a *City, Town Corporate*, or *Victualling for Ships* or *Forts*, without foreſtalling, ſhall not be adjudged Offences.

A Man *buying Corn for Change of Seed*, and not bringing ſo much to the Market, Ib. §. 8. ſhall forfeit the double Value thereof.

The Juſtice of Peace at Seſſions ſhall inquire, hear and determine theſe Offences by *Who may in-* *Inquiſition, Bill, Preſentment* or *Information* before them exhibited, and by Examination *quire*. of *two lawful Witneſſes*, or by any other Ways or Means in their Diſcretion, and to Ib. §. 10. make Proceſs, as if they were indicted by Inquiſition or Verdict, and upon Conviction, by Information or Suit at any other Proſecution, to make *Eſtreats* of the King's Part, as in other Caſes, and to award Execution for the Plaintiff, or Informer, by *Fieri fa- cias*, or *Capias*, as the King's Juſtices may do ; and if the Conviction be for the King, then the whole Forfeiture to be eſtreated.

Foreſtalling of Corn, Vide *Corn*, Chap. 27.   Ib. §. 12.

No Perſon ſhall be impeached on this Act, if not ſued within *two Years* after the Ib. §. 14. Offence.

Any Perſon living within a *Mile of the Sea*, may buy *Fiſh*, freſh or ſalted, ſelling Ib. §. 15. the ſame again at reaſonable Prices.

Foreſtalling Cattle, Vide *Cattle*.   Ib. §. 16, 17.

So much of this Statute of the 5 & 6 *Ed.* 6. *cap.* 14. and all other Statutes againſt Regrators, &c. as concerns the Buying of Sea-fiſh unſalted, or Mud Fiſh, or Wine, Oil or Salt, bought at Sea, and brought in *Engliſh* Ships, and diſcharg'd in any Harbour within the Realm, is repealed by 5 *Eliz. cap.* 5. *ſect.* 13.

London.
21 Jac. 1. c.
22. §. 6.

The Statute of 3 & 4 E. 6. 21. & 5 & 6 E. 6. 14. ſhall not extend to Freemen of *London* buying *Butter* and *Cheeſe*, and ſelling the ſame again in *London* Liberties, *Southwark* and *Weſtminſter*.

Ib. §. 7.

If Juſtices of Peace ſhall declare in their open Seſſions the Traders in *Butter* and *Cheeſe* ſhall forbear to buy; if they ſhall not forbear during ſuch Reſtraint, they ſhall not be exempted from the Penalties of theſe Laws.

Licences.
Badger.
5 El. 12. §. 4.

No *Drover, Badger, Lader, Kidder, Carrier, Buyer* or *Tranſporter* of *Corn* or *Grain, Butter* and *Cheeſe*, ſhall be allowed but in the open and general Quarter-Seſſions of the Peace of the County where the Party dwells, and dwelt three Years together before the Teſte of his *Licence*; and none but ſuch as *are or have been married*, and ſuch as are at the Time of their Licence *Houſholders*, and not *Servants* or *Retainers*, and of the Age of *thirty Years* at leaſt, and ſhall be *licenſed only for one* Year.

Crom. 72.

Note; a *Woman* can have no ſuch Licence, for the Statute ſpeaks only of a Man, and he that hath ſuch Licence ſhall not ſell by his Servant.

5 El. 12. §. 5.

The Licences ſhall bear Date the Day and Place of the Seſſions, and ſhall be ſigned and ſealed with the proper Hand and Seal of *three Juſtices* then preſent, *Quorum unus*, upon Pain that he that takes a Licence contrary to that Statute, ſhall forfeit 5 *l.* to the King.

Ib. §. 6.

The Juſtices in Seſſions ſhall take *Bond and Surety* by their Diſcretion; that the Perſons licenſed do not *foreſtal, ingroſs*, or do any Thing contrary to 5 *E.* 6. 14. The Clerk or his Deputy, and none other, ſhall write them, for which Licence he ſhall pay 12 *d.* at moſt, for the Recognizance 4 *d.* at moſt; for which Fee the Clerk ſhall keep a Regiſter of the Names, &c. and bring it to the Seſſions.

Ib. §. 7.

No Perſon ſhall by Authority of ſuch Licence buy *Corn* or *Grain* out of open Fair or Market, unleſs he be thereunto licenſed, and that by ſpecial Words in his Licence ſo to do, or forfeit 5 *l.*

Hear and de-
termine.
Ib. §. 8.

The Juſtices of Peace in their Quarter-Seſſions ſhall hear and determine the Offences againſt that Act, by Inquiſition, Preſentment, Bill or Information, before them exhibited; and by Examination of two Witneſſes, or by any other lawful Means by their Diſcretion, and may make Proceſs, as if they were indicted: And upon Conviction, by Information of any other than the King, they may extract the King's Moiety as in other Caſes, and to make Execution for the other Moiety for the Informer by *Fieri facias* or *Capias*, as in the Courts at *Weſtminſter*; and if the Conviction be at the King's Suit only, he ſhall have the whole Forfeitures.

Ib. §. 9, 10.

This Act ſhall not prejudice *Corporations* in their Purveyance, nor extend to the Counties of *Weſtmorland, Cumberland, Lancaſter, Cheſter*, nor *York*.

Bark.
1 Jac. 1. c. 22.
§. 19.

No Perſon ſhall *regrate* or *ingroſs* any Oaken *Bark*, before it be ſtripped or after, to the Intent to ſell the ſame again, upon Pain to forfeit the Bark.

Hides.
Ib. §. 7.

No Perſon ſhall foreſtal any *Hide* coming to a Fair or Market, or buy any Hide but in a Fair or Market, except of the Owner who killed the Beaſt, to be ſpent in his own Houſe, upon Pain to forfeit for every Hide 6 *s.* 8 *d.*

Where a Man buys Meal and converts it into Starch, he is no *Engroſſer*, becauſe 'tis not the ſame, but altered by a *Trade*; but if he buys Corn and converts it into *Meal* with an Intent to ſell it again in the ſame Market, he is an *Engroſſer*, becauſe it remains Corn ſtill.

Fiſhmongers, Poulterers and Butchers, are not within this Law, if they buy what belongs to their reſpective Trades; but if they buy with an Intent to ſell again contrary to Law, they are puniſhable; nor Inn-holders nor Victuallers buying Wine or any Thing for the Suſtenance of Man. *Cro. Car.* 381. 1 *Rol. Rep.* 134.

See 1 *Hawk. P. C. Chap.* 80. *p.* 234, &c. of *Foreſtalling*, &c.

Foreſt. See *Hunting*, Chap. 55.

Forfeiture for Felony. See *Chap.* 163.

Forgery. See *Felonies by Statutes*, Chap. 160.

CHAP. XLVI.

Games and Plays.

(a) THERE shall be no Meeting of People out of their own Parishes on the Lord's Sunday. Day (or *Sunday*) for any Sport or Pastimes whatsoever; nor any Bear-baiting, 1 Car. 1. c. 1. or Bull-baiting, Interludes, Common Plays, or other unlawful Exercises or Pastimes, used by any within their own Parishes, upon Pain that every Person offending in any the Premisses do forfeit for every Offence three Shillings and four Pence, to be imployed to the Use of the Poor of the same Parish where the Offence shall be committed. And any one Justice of Peace of the County (or the Chief Officer of any City, Borough or Town Corporate) upon his or their View, or Confession of the Party, or Proof of any one Witness by Oath, shall give Warrant under his Hand and Seal to the Constables or Church-wardens of the Parish where the Offence shall be committed, to levy the said Penalty by Distress and Sale of the Offenders Goods, rendring them the Overplus; and in Default of Distress, the Offenders to be set in the Stocks by the Space of three Hours; provided that none be impeached by this Act, except he be called in Question within one Month next after the said Offence committed. 1 *Car.* 1. *cap.* 1. Continued indefinitely by 3 *Car.* 1. *cap.* 4. & 16 *Car.* 1. *cap.* 4.

King *James, Anno* 1618. publickly declared to his Subjects, these Recreations or Exercises hereunder mentioned to be lawful; that is to say, Dancing of Men or Women, Archery, Leaping, Vaulting, May-games, Whitson-Ales, Morris-Dances, and set up May-Poles, and other Sports therewith used: And commanded that no such honest Mirth or Recreation should be forbidden to his Subjects upon the *Sunday* or Holy-days, after Divine Service (*sc.* Evening Prayer) ended. Restraining and barring notwithstanding from this Liberty any Recusants, and all such as absent themselves from Church upon those Days; commanding each Parish by itself to use these Recreations, and only after Evening Prayer ended: And prohibiting all unlawful Games to be used upon *Sunday*, Bear-baiting, Bull-baiting, Interludes and Bowling by the meaner Sort.

All which King *Charles* the First, by publick Declaration, *Anno* 1633. confirmed; allowing farther the Feasts of the Dedication of Churches, commonly called Wakes, and all Manlike Exercises to be there used with all Freedom, yet so as none bring any Weapons thither: Commanding all Justices of Peace to look that no Disorder be at such Wakes, but to be prevented or punished, &c.

The Statute of 12 *R.* 2. *cap.* 6. is repealed by 21 *Jac.* 1. *cap.* 28. and by the Statute of 33 *H.* 8. *cap.* 9. all Statutes for the Restraints of unlawful Games, as touching the Penalties and Forfeitures of the same, are repealed; so that now the Statute of 33 *H.* 8. *cap.* 9. is to any Penalties in force, and such Games as be prohibited by 11 *H.* 4. *cap.* 4. & 33 *H.* 8. *cap.* 9. are unlawful, *viz.* Tables, Tennis, Football, Coits, Dice, Bowls, Cloysh-cales, half Bowls, Cards, Logats; so that the Offences relating to Games are upon these Accounts: First, Games are by those Statutes said to be unlawful in Respect of the Condition of the Persons playing; such are Servants and Labourers in Husbandry, &c. by 12 *R.* 2. *cap.* 6. 11 *H.* 4. *cap.* 4. & 33 *H.* 8. *cap.* 9. Secondly, Persons keeping Houses or Places for those Games for Lucre, Gain or Living. Thirdly, Persons haunting such Houses for those Games sake, out of which Cases Gaming is lawful, and not only the Games before mentioned are in Cases and Circumstances aforesaid unlawful, but any new Game to be invented, if used by Persons of the mean Condition aforesaid; or used and kept by Persons for Game, Lucre and Living, are unlawful by 33 *H.* 8. *cap.* 9. that is, as to some Persons using them, and the Places where used, as being to such Persons, and in such Places, Means of Idleness, Debauchery, and other grievous Mischiefs.

The Punishment of Players at Dice, &c. by the Civil Law, besides Infamy, avoiding of the Contract and Security for any Money so won, and Restitution of the Thing so obtained, was and is Arbitrary. See *Althusius Dicæologice, p.* 417. *l.* 26.

(d) Every Justice of Peace may from Time to Time (as well within Liberties as without) enter into any common House or Place where any Playing at Dice, Tables, Cards, Search.
33 H. 8. c. 9.
§ 64.
P. Just. 64.
Plays, 5.
* 12 R. 2. c 6.
Lamb. 196. Bowls, Coyts, Cailes, Logats, Shove-groat, Tennis, Casting the Stone, * Foot-ball, or other unlawful Game now invented, or hereafter to be invented, shall be suspected to be used; and may arrest the Keepers of such Places, and imprison them till they

they find Sureties by Recognizance no longer to occupy any such House, Play, Game, Alley, or Place.

Places.　　　(*a*) Yet it was resolved in 3 *Jac.* That if the Guests in any Inn or Tavern, call for a Pair of Dice or Tables, and for their Recreations play with them, or if any Neighbours play at Bowls for their Recreations, or the like, that these are not within the Statute of 33 *H.* 8. *c.* 9. for the Statute confists of two Parts. 1. That no Person shall for his or their Gain, *&c.* So that although these Games are used in any Inns, Taverns, or other Houses, if the House be not kept for Gaming, Lucre or Gain, but they play only for Recreation, and for no Gain to the Owner of the House, this is not within the Statute, nor is such Person, that plays in such House that is not kept for Lucre or Gain, within the Penalty of that Law.

33 *H.* 8. *c.* 9.　(*d*) Also he may arreft and imprison the Players there, till they be bound by them-
§. 14.　selves, or with Sureties, by Recognizance to the King's Use, no more to play at, or to haunt any of the faid Places or Games.

Ib. §. 13.　(*a*) The faid Statute of 33 *H.* 8. prohibited all Manner of Persons to play at any unlawful Game in any *common House, Alley,* or Place; except the Keeper of fuch House or Place have a *Placard,* containing what Games fhall there be used, as alfo what Persons fhall play thereat; and then fuch Persons may play there, *&c.*

Ib. §. 16.　Also the faid Statute prohibiteth all *Artificers, Husbandmen, Labourers, Mariners, Fishermen* and *Watermen,* and all *Apprentices* and *Servants* whatfoever, to play at any un-lawful Game, in any Place, or at any Time, except in *Chriftmas Time* only and in their Houfes, or Servants in their Mafters Houfes, and by their Mafter's Licence; or Serving Men within the Precinct of their Mafter's Houfe, Garden, or Orchard, and by their Mafters Licence. Alfo no Manner of Perfon fhall at any Time play at *Bowls* in any open Places out of his Garden or Orchard, under Pain to forfeit 6 *s.* 8 *d.*

Bowls.　· And the faid Statute makes all Games almoft unlawful, fave Shooting in the long Bow, that being a great Defence for the Realm, and a meet Exercife for all Manner of Perfons to ufe, and a Means to prevent or divert Men from other unlawful, crafty and deceitful Games, and from the inordinate and common Haunting of Alehoufes and Tipling.

Ib. §. 16.　(*d*) Every Juftice of Peace finding or knowing any Perfon to exercife or ufe any of the aforenamed unlawful Games (contrary to this Statute of 23 *H.* 8. *cap.* 9.) may commit him to Gaol, there to remain without Bail, until he become bound (in fuch Sum of Money as he the faid Juftice fhall think reafonable) that he fhall not from henceforth ufe fuch unlawful Games.

Penalties.　(*a*) The Penalties for Artificers, Husbandmen, Labourers, Apprentices, Servants at Hus-
33 *H.* 8. *c.* 9.　bandry, Journeyman, or Servant of Artificers, Mariners, Fifhermen, Watermen, or Serving Men, Playing at Tables, Tennis, Dice, Cards, Bowls, Clafh, *&c.* out of *Chrift-mas,* is twenty Shillings, and in *Chriftmas* Time, to play in their Mafter's Houfe or Prefence.

Ib. §. 11.　The Penalty for keeping an Houfe of unlawful Games, is forty Shillings *per diem.*
Ib. §. 12.　The Penalty for reforting thither, or playing there, is fix Shillings and eight Pence for every Time.

Ib. §. 15.　Mayors, Sheriffs, Conftables, and Head Officers, *&c.* fhall once a Month fearch Places fufpected, or forfeit for every Month forty Shillings.

Ib. §. 19, 20.　All Mayors, *&c.* and Head Officers, fhall four Times every Year proclaim this Statute in the Market. And all Juftices of Peace fhall proclaim the fame in their Seffions.

31 Eliz. c. 5.　All Suits upon the Statutes of unlawful Games, fhall be heard, fued, and profecuted,
§. 7.　at the Affizes or Seffions of the County where the Offence is committed, or in the Leet.

2 & 3 Ph. &　Every Licenfe, Placard, or Grant, made to any Perfon for having or keeping any
Ma. c. 9.　Bowling-Alley, Dicing-Houfes, or other unlawful Games, prohibited by the Laws of the Realm, fhall be void.

Although thefe Games aforenamed, are by Statute prohibited as unlawful for fome Places, Perfons, and Times; yet they are not unlawful or evil of themfelves, but are Matters of Recreation and Pleafure, (though fome of them more vain and more idle than others:) And the King by his Prerogative may tolerate and licenfe the moderate Ufe of all fuch Games. *Co.* 11. 85. *b.*

Cards and　(*d*) Note alfo, that playing at *Cards, Dice,* and the like are not prohibited by the Common
Dice.　Laws of this Realm (except one be deceived by *falfe Dice,* or *falfe Cards;* * and then he that is
* *According to*　deceived may have his Action of the Cafe for fuch *Deceit*; neither are they *malum in fe,* or
† Rol. Abr.　of their own Natures, for then none might be tolerated or licenfed to ufe them; whereas
78. *a Player*
at Hazard ufing falfe Dice may be indicted and fet in the Pillory.

I　　　　　　　　　　　　　　　　　　　　　　　the

he Statute doth except and tolerate certain Perfons, Places and Times.   And yet good
Divines do hold divers of thefe Recreations to be altogether unlawful, as being Actions • B. *Baily.*
vherein we neither blefs God, nor look to receive a Bleffing from God ; nay, fuch as we 400.
are not pray to God for a Bleffing on them, nor on our felves in the Ufe thereof. (*a*) But Dr. *Willet,*
fpecially on the Sabbath Day all fuch Recreations and Games are holden unlawful.   For M. *Perkins.*
flawful Works be forbidden on that Day, much more unlawful Sports, (yea, fuch Sports
nd Games, which otherwife, and at other Times are lawful.)   See *Ifai.* 58. 13.

For the preventing deceitful and exceffive Gaming, a good Law was made 16 *Car.* 2.
ap. 7. but the Juftices have nothing to do therein.

(*d*) But inquire what Games fhall be faid to be unlawful, other than thofe aforenamed.
Quære of dancing the Morrice, or other open Dancings, Bear-baitings, Common Plays,
nd Fencings.   All thefe feem to be prohibited by the Statute of 39 *El.* 4.

(*a*) Two or more Juftices may caufe any Perfon to come before them, whom they fhall *Perfons who*
iave Reafon to fufpect hath no vifible Eftate, Profeffion, or Calling, to maintain himfelf, *live by Ga-*
ut doth for the moft part fupport himfelf by Gaming : And if he cannot make it appear *ming may be*
hat the chief Part of what he expends is not got by Gaming, the Juftices may require him *good Beha-*
o find Sureties for his good Behaviour for twelve Months ; and if he cannot find fuch *viour.*
fureties, they may commit him till he can. *9 An. c. 14.*
§. 6.

And if he doth. give Security, *&c.* and afterwards play for more than 20 *s.* at one Sit- *Playing for*
ing, this is a Breach of his good Behaviour, and he fhall forfeit his Recognizance. *more than 20s.*
is a Breach
of Good Behaviour. 9 An. c. 14. §. 7.

This Act fhall not extend to hinder any Perfon from Gaming in any of the King's Pa- *King's Palace.*
aces during his Refidence there, fo as fuch Gaming be not in any Houfe, Lodging or *Ib. §. 9.*
other Part of the Palace, the Freehold whereof is not in the Crown, and fo as fuch play-
ng is for ready Money.

And no Bankrupt fhall be difcharged or receive any Benefit by the Statute 5 *Geo.* 2. who *Bankrupts.*
hall have loft in one Day 5 *l.* or 100 *l.* in twelve Months before he became a Bankrupt, ei- 5 *G.* 2. c. 30.
her at Play, or in Racing or other Paftimes, or by bearing a Share in the Stakes, Wagers,
or Adventures, or by betting on the Sides of fuch as fhall play, ride or run.

The Defendant was convicted for keeping a Cock-pit fix Days ; this was adjudged an *Cockpit.*
inlawful Gaming within the Statute, and he was fined 12 *l.* being 40 *s. per diem,* according to the Statute 33 *H.* 8. tho' the Indictment was at Common Law. 3 *Keb.* 510.

All Securities for Money won at Play, or which fhall be lent at that Time and Place of *Securities for*
Money won at
fuch Play to any Perfon gaming or betting, fhall be void.   And where fuch Securities fhall *Play void.*
be a Charge on any Lands, they fhall enure and be to the fole Ufe of the Heir at Law, or *9 Ann. c. 14.*
§. 1.
o the Reverfioner, as if they had been made to him, and the Grantor had been actually *Such Securities*
lead ; and all Conveyances made for preventing fuch Lands from devolving upon fuch *fhall be to the*
Perfon, fhall be void. *Ufe of the*
Heir at Law.

Any Perfon, who at one Time fhall lofe by playing or betting to the Value of 10 *l.* and *Lofing above*
hall pay or deliver it or any Part thereof, may within three Months then next following *10 l. may be*
ecover what was fo loft, or any Part thereof, from the Winner by Action of Debt, with *recovered of the*
Winner within
Cofts in any Court of Record ; and if the Lofer fhall not within that Time without Col- *three Months.*
ufion fue for the fame with Effect, any Stranger may fue for it, and recover it with treble *Ib. §. 2.*
A Stranger
he Value, together with Cofts ; one Moiety to the Profecutor, and the other to the Poor *may fue for it*
of the Parifh where the Offence was done. *if the Lofer*
will not.

Every Perfon, who is liable to be fued for Money or other valuable Thing won at Play, *The Winner*
hall anfwer upon Oath any Bill which fhall be exhibited againft him for the Difcovery *muft anfwer a*
Bill of Dif-
hereof, but upon Difcovery and Repayment of the Money or other Thing, the Perfon *covery on Oath.*
hall be difcharged from any farther Punifhment he may have incurred by Playing. *Ib. §. 3.*

If any Perfon fhall by Fraud or Deceit at any Games, or bearing a Share in the Stakes *Ib. §. 4.*
Cheating at
or Wagers, or betting on the Side of the Players, win any Sum or valuable Thing, or *Play, or win-*
hall at one Time win above the Value of 10 *l.* and being convicted of *either the faid Of-* *ning above 10l.*
at one Time,
ences, upon an Information or Indictment he fhall forfeit five Times the Value of the Sum *forfeits five*
or Thing fo won, to the Informer, *&c.* and fhall be deemed infamous, and fuffer corpo- *Times the Va-*
lue.
al Punifhment as if he was guilty of Perjury. *Ib. §. 5.*

Affaulting or Beating, or Challenging another to fight for Money won at Play or Bet- *Challenging*
ing, and being convicted thereof upon Indictment or Information, forfeits to the Crown *another for Mo-*
ll his Goods and Chattels, and perfonal Eftate, and fhall fuffer Imprifonment for two *ney won at*
Play.
Years without Bail. *Ib. §. 8.*

E e   The

The Court was moved for Leave to file an Information againſt the Defendant upon an Affidavit of the Proſecutor, that he had loſt 15 *l.* to the Defendant at one Sitting ; but this was oppoſed, becauſe the Proſecutor had indicted the Defendant for the ſame Offence, and the Bill was found ; 'tis true, the Indictment was quaſhed, and the Defendant was never tried upon it, but the Court would not give Leave to file an Information, becauſe the Jury might find another Bill for the ſame Offence. *Mich.* 9 *Geo.* 1. *B. R.*

2 Geo. 2.
c. 28. §. 9.

Where it ſhall be proved on the Oath of two Witneſſes before any Juſtice of Peace, as well as where ſuch Juſtice ſhall find upon his own View, that any Perſon hath uſed any unlawful Game, contrary to the Statute 33 *H.* 8. *cap.* 9. the Juſtice ſhall have Power to commit ſuch Offender to Priſon, unleſs he enter into Recognizance with Sureties, or without, at the Diſcretion of the Juſtice, that he ſhall not play at ſuch unlawful Games.

10 Geo. 2.
c. 28. §. 1.

Any Perſon repreſenting any Interlude, Play, or other Entertainment of the Stage, or acting any Part therein, for Gain, (in caſe ſuch Perſon ſhall not have any legal Settlement in the Place where the ſame ſhall be acted) without Authority of a Patent from his Majeſty, or without Licenſe from the Lord Chamberlain, ſhall be deemed a Rogue and a Vagabond within the Act 12 *Ann. ſtat.* 2. *cap.* 23. See Chap. 83. of *Rogues and Vagabonds.*

Ib. §. 2.

If any Perſon, with or without a legal Settlement, ſhall act without Licence for Gain, he ſhall forfeit 50 *l.* and in Caſe the ſaid 50 *l.* be paid or recovered, he ſhall ſuffer no other Penalty of the ſaid Act.

Ib. §. 4.

Acting any Play, &c. unleſs a Copy be ſent to the Lord Chamberlain fourteen Days before repreſenting, or contrary to his Prohibition, is a Forfeiture of 50 *l.* each Offender, and the Licenſe by which the Managers ſet up the Play-houſe or Company ſhall ceaſe.

Ib. §. 5.

No Patent or Licence ſhall be granted to act, &c. in any Part of *Great Britain* but in *Weſtminſter,* or in the Place of the King's Reſidence during ſuch Reſidence only.

Ib. §. 6.

The pecuniary Penalties of this Act, may in any Part of *Great Britain* be recovered in a ſummary Way before two Juſtices of Peace, by the Oath of one Witneſs, or Confeſſion of the Offender, to be levied by Diſtreſs and Sale of Goods, and for Want of Diſtreſs the Offender to be committed to the Houſe of Correction, for any Time not exceeding ſix Months, to be kept to hard Labour, or to the common Gaol of ſuch County, &c. for the like Time. Perſons aggrieved may appeal to the next Quarter-Seſſions : The Penalties ſhall belong one Moiety to the Informer, the other Moiety to the Poor of the Pariſh.

Ib. §. 7.

If any Interlude, &c. be repreſented in any Place where Wine or other Liquors are ſold, the ſame ſhall be deemed to be repreſented for Gain.

Ib. §. 8.

Proſecutions muſt be in ſix Kalendar Months. If a Verdict be for a Juſtice or other Perſon, upon an Action for any Thing done in Purſuance of this Act, ſuch Juſtice, &c. ſhall recover treble Coſts.

12 Geo. 2.
c. 28.

By the Statute of 12 *Geo.* 2. *cap.* 28. it is enacted, That if any Perſon ſhall erect any Office or Place, under the Denomination of a Sale of Houſes, Land, &c. Plate, Jewels, Ships or other Goods, by Way of Lottery, or by Lots, Tickets, Numbers or Figures, Cards or Dice, or ſhall publiſh Propoſals for advancing ſmall Sums of Money by ſeveral Perſons, amounting in the whole to large Sums, to be divided among them by Chances of the Prizes in ſome Lottery allowed by Parliament, or ſhall deliver out Tickets to Perſons advancing ſuch Sums, to intitle them to a Share of the Money ſo advanced, or ſhall expoſe to Sale any Houſe, &c. by Device of Chance of any Kind, whether by Cards, Dice, or any Machine, ſuch Perſon upon Conviction before any Juſtice of the Peace, or Mayor of any City, &c. by Oath of one credible Witneſs, or View of ſuch Juſtice, &c. or by Confeſſion of ſuch Perſon accuſed, ſhall forfeit 200 *l.* to be levied by Diſtreſs and Sale of the Offender's Goods, by Warrant from any Juſtice of Peace of the County or Place where the Offence ſhall be committed ; One Third to the Informer, and Two Thirds to the Poor, except within the City *Bath,* where the Two Thirds ſhall go to the Infirmary there, after deducting the Charges of Conviction.

The Games of the *Ace of Hearts, Faro, Baſſet* and *Hazard,* are declared to be Lotteries ; and Perſons ſetting up ſuch Games ſhall be liable to the Penalties of this Act.

Every Adventurer in ſuch Games, Lotteries or Sales, ſhall forfeit 50 *l.* to be recovered as aforeſaid.

All ſuch Sales of Houſes, &c. are declared void, and the Houſes and Goods forfeited to thoſe who ſue for the ſame.

Perſons aggrieved by the Judgment of any Juſtice or Mayor, may appeal to the next Quarter-Seſſions, giving reaſonable Notice, and entring into a Recognizance with two ſufficient Sureties to try ſuch Appeal ; and in Caſe the Conviction be affirmed, the Party appealing ſhall pay the Proſecutor treble Coſts.

No Conviction shall be set aside for want of Form or removed by *Certiorari*, until such Proceeding have been first determined by the Quarter-Seffions.

Nor shall any Writ of *Certiorari* issue to remove the Record of any Conviction, or Order from the Quarter-Seffions, until the Party convicted find two sufficient Sureties to become bound to the Profecutor in the Sum of 100 *l.* to profecute the fame with Effect within six Months, and to pay treble Cofts, in case such Order or Conviction be affirmed.

And if any Perfon convicted of erecting any of the said Lotteries or Games, or of being an Adventurer in such, shall not have sufficient Goods whereon to levy the Penalties, or shall not pay, or give Security for the fame, the Juftice may commit such Perfon to the common Gaol for any Time not exceeding six Months.

Juftices or Mayors refusing to do what is required by this Act, shall forfeit 10 *l.* for each Offence; one Moiety to the Perfon who fues, and the other to the Poor, to be recovered with full Cofts; such Profecution being commenced within six Months after such Refusal.

Actions againft any Perfon for any Thing done in purfuance of this Act, shall be brought within three Months after the Fact committed, and shall be laid in the County or Place where the Caufe of Action shall arife. The Defendant may plead the General Iffue, and if the Plaintiff be nonfuited, &c. the Defendant shall recover treble Cofts.

By 13 *Geo.* 2. the Game called *Paffage*, and all other Games with Dice (*Backgammon*, 13 Geo. 2. and Games with the Backgammon Tables only excepted) shall be deemed Lotteries by c. 19. Dice within the Meaning of the Act of 12 *Geo.* 2. and the Keepers of any Office or Table for, and the Players at fuch Games shall be liable to the Penalties of the said Act; and the Plaintiff, befides the Penalties recovered, shall have double Cofts.

See also the Appendix, *Tit.* Lotteries.

Game. (*a*)

BY the Statute 4 & 5 *W.* 3. 'tis enacted, that inferior *Tradefmen*, *Apprentices*, and *Trefpaffers and* other diffolute Perfons, neglecting their Trades and following *Hunting*, *Fifhing*, *to pay full* and other Game, if fued for a wilful Trefpafs, and found Guilty, shall pay full Cofts as *Cofts.* well as Damages.   4 & 5 W.
                                                                                        c. 23. §. 10.
All Statutes in Force for the Prefervation of the Game not altered or repealed by the Ib. §. 1. aforesaid Statute 4 & 5 *Will.* shall be put in Execution.

Conftables, &c. may by Warrant of a Juftice enter and fearch (in Manner as by the *Search.* Act 3 & 4 *Will.* 3. *cap.* 10. againft Deer-ftealers) the Houfes of *fufpected Perfons* not qua- Ib. §. 3: lified, and if any *Game* shall be found, then to carry the Offender before a Juftice, to whom he muft give an Account how he came by the fame, or if not, or doth not produce the Party of whom he bought it, or fome credible Witnefs to make Oath of whom he bought it, the Juftice shall convict him of the Offence, and he shall forfeit for every Hare, Partridge, &c. or other Game, not under 5 *s.* nor exceeding 20 *s.* one Moiety to *Hare and* the Informer, and the other to the Poor of the Parish where the Offence was done, to *Partidge.* be levied by Warrant, &c. by Diftrefs and Sale, &c. and for Default of a Diftrefs, to be fent to the Houfe of Correction for any Time not exceeding a Month, nor lefs than 10 Days, there to be whipt and kept at hard Labour. He who is not qualified and doth keep or ufe any *Bows*, *Greyhounds*, *Setting-Dogs*, *Coney-Dogs*, *Ferrets*, *Lurchers*, *Fer- Dogs, Nets,* *rets*, *Hays*, *Nets*, *Tunnels*, *Low-bells*, *Hare-pipes*, *Snares or other Inftruments* to deftroy *&c.* the Game, and shall be convicted as aforesaid, shall fuffer the Penalties as aforesaid, and if the Perfon charged doth not give Evidence to the Juftice of his Innocence, he shall be convicted thereof in Manner as the firft Perfon charged therewith, and fo from one Perfon to another till the firft Offender is found.

Lords of Manors, and thofe to whom they give Authority, may refift Offenders in the Ib. §. 4. Night-time, in their refpective Manors and Royalties, as if the Fact had been done in any ancient Chafe, Park or Warren.

No Perfon shall keep any Net, &c. or other Engine for taking Fish, other than the *Nets to take* Makers for Sale or Owners or Occupiers of a Fifhery; if they do, fuch Owners, &c. *Fifh.* may either feife, or give Authority to others to feife and keep to their Ufe any fuch En- Ib. §. 5, gine of any Perfon fifhing in a River, without the Confent of the Owner or Occupier. Any Perfon by Warrant from a Juftice, in the Day-time, may fearch the Houfes and *Search.* other Places of Perfons prohibited and fufpected to have fuch Engines, and feife and keep them to their Ufe, or deftroy them.

This

Ib. §. 6.	This shall not extend to abridge Fishermen or their Apprentices to fish in navigable Rivers with lawful Nets and Engines.
Certiorari. 4 & 5 W. & M. c. 23. §. 7.	No *Certiorari* shall be allowed, unless the Party convicted shall, before the Allowance, enter into a Bond to the Prosecutor in the Sum of 50 *l.* with Sureties to be approved by the Justice before whom convicted to pay the Prosecutor his full Costs, on Oath, within a Month after Conviction confirmed, or *Procedendo* allowed, and in Default thereof, it shall be lawful to proceed for the Execution of the Conviction, as if no *Certiorari* had been awarded.
Ib. §. 8.	Offenders punished by this Act shall not incur the Penalty of any other Law for the same Offence.
Ib. §. 9.	He who is prosecuted for doing any Thing in Execution of this Statute may plead the General Issue, and give this Act and any Special Matter in Evidence; and if the Plaintiff is cast, or discontinue, or is nonsuit, the Defendant shall have treble Costs.
Heath and Furze. Ib. §. 11.	For Preserving the red and black Game of Grouse, called Heath-Cocks, or Heath-Polts, no Person shall burn on any Hills, &c. or Waste, between the 2d of *February* and 24th of *June*, any Greg, Ling, Heath, Furze, &c. if he doth he shall be sent to the House of Correction for any Time not exceeding a Month, nor less than ten Days, there to be whipp'd and kept to hard Labour; this is for the better Preservation of Heath-Cocks, &c.
Hare, Pheasant, Partridge, Grouse, Heath-Game or Moor. 5 Ann. c. 14. made perpetual by 9 Ann. cap. 25. Certiorari.	Any *Higler, Chapman, Carrier, Alehouse-keeper, Innkeeper* or *Victualler*, having in their Custody any *Hare, Partridge*, &c. (unless sent by the Carrier by some Person qualified) shall be brought before a Justice where the Offence was done; and upon View of the Hare, &c. or Oath made of the Fact, shall forfeit for every Hare, &c. 5 *l.* to the Informer and to the Poor, to be levied by Distress, by Warrant of a Justice before whom the Offender was convicted, and for Want of such Distress to be committed to the House of Correction for three Months without Bail for the first Offence, and four Months for every other Offence. The Conviction must be within *three Months* after the Offence, and before a *Certiorari* shall be allowed, the Offender shall be bound in 50 *l.* to the Prosecutor, with sufficient Sureties conditioned to pay him full Costs, to be ascertained on Oath, within fourteen Days after Conviction confirmed, or *Procedendo* granted; and in Default thereof the Justice, &c. may proceed to execute the Conviction.
Destroying and discovering a Hare sold to a Higler. Ib. §. 3.	Any Person who shall destroy, sell, or buy a *Hare, Pheasant*, &c. and shall within three Months discover any *Higler, Chapman, Inn* or *Alehouse-keeper*, who hath bought, sold, or had the same in his Possession, so as one may be convicted of the said Offence, shall be discharged himself of the Penalties, and have the same Benefit as the other Informers.
Persons not qualified. Ib. §. 4. Who may take away any Hare, &c. Game-Keeper.	Person not qualified, and keeping *Greyhound, Lurcher, Setting-dog*, &c. or any Engine to destroy the Game, and being thereof convicted before a Justice, &c. shall forfeit 5 *l.* Half to the Informer, and the other to the Poor, to be levied by Distress and Sale, by Warrant of the Justice before whom convicted, and for Want of Distress, to be sent to the House of Correction for three Months for the first Offence; and for every other Offence four Months. Justices within their Jurisdiction, and Lords of Manors within their respective Manors, may take away any *Hare, Pheasant*, &c. or other Game, from such Higler, &c. or from any one not qualified to kill it, and also to take away the Dogs, Nets and Engines to their own Use. And any Lord or Lady of a Manor may, under his Hand and Seal, impower a Game-keeper to kill any Game; but if under Colour of such Power he kill and sell, or dispose of it without Consent of his Lord or Lady, and shall upon his Complaint be convicted thereof before a Justice, he shall be sent to the House of Correction for three Months, and kept to hard Labour.
Heath in Sherwood Forest. 5 Ann. c. 14. §. 5.	No Person shall cut Ling, Heath or Brakes, to burn them to Ashes in *Sherwood Forest*, or in any Waste or Land in the County of *Nottingham*, without License from the Owner of the Soil, under the Penalty of 10 *s.* and the Person buying such Ashes, forfeits 10 *s.* per Peck to the Poor and the Informer; and the Offender being convicted before a Justice, upon Oath, and not paying the Penalties, shall be committed to the House of Correction for a Month, and there kept to hard Labour, unless the Penalties are sooner paid: And the Officers of the Forest, or the Owners of Lands, &c. may take away to their own Use the Instruments used for Cutting, &c.
Game-Keeper. 9 Ann. c. 25. §. 1.	By this Statute that of 5 *Annæ*, which was temporary, is made perpetual; and it is further enacted, that a Lord of a Manor shall appoint but one Game-keeper in one Manor, with Power to kill the Game, and his Name shall be entered with the Clerk of the Peace without Fee, who shall give him a *Certificate* thereof, paying 1 *s.* and if his Name is not entered, and he kill Game, and is not qualified by Law so to do; or

if

if any other, not being qualified, shall sell or expose to Sale any Hare, Pheasant or Partridge, Moor-heath, Game or Grouse, he shall for every Offence incur such Forfeiture as inflicted by the Statute 5 *Anne*, against * Higlers, *&c.* for buying or selling Game, and to be recovered in such Manner as provided by that Act. *Hare sold by one not qualified. Pheasant, Partridge.*
* viz. 5 l.

If a Hare, *&c.* shall be found * in the Shop, House, or Possession of a Person not qualified in his own Right to kill the Game, or being intitled to do it by some qualified Person, the same shall be adjudged an Exposing to Sale. *What shall be exposing to Sale.* Ib. §. 2.

* *This is seems*

must be understood of Proof made that it was found. 6 Mod. 57. Queen and George.

He who kills or destroys a Hare, *&c.* in the Night-time, shall for every Offence incur such Forfeitures as aforesaid, and to be recovered as aforesaid. *Hare killed in the Night-time.* Ib. §. 3.

Any Person between 1 *July* and 1 *September*, in any Year, driving by *Hayes, Tunnels* or *Nets*, and taking *Wild-duck, Teal, Widgeon*, or any other *Water Fowl*, in Places of Resort for Wild-Fowl in the Molting-time, and being convicted thereof before one Justice where the Offence was done, and by the Oath of one Witness, shall forfeit 5 s. for every Fowl to the Informer, and to the Poor, *&c.* to be levied by Warrant, *&c.* by Distress and Sale, *&c.* and for Want of Distress to be committed to the House of Correction, not exceeding one Month, nor less than fourteen Days, to be whipp'd and kept to hard Labour, and the Justice shall cause such Nets, *&c.* to be seised and destroyed in his Presence. *Wild Fowl.* Ib. §. 4.

No Lord or Lady of a Manor shall appoint any Game-keeper with Power to take or kill any Hare, *&c.* or other Game, unless such Person is qualified so to do by Law, or be truly a Servant to such Lord or Lady, or be immediately employed by them to kill the Game for their sole Use; and no Lord of a Manor, *&c.* shall give Authority to any Person not qualified by Law, to keep or use any *Greyhound*, Setting-dog, Hayes, Lurchers, *&c.* Guns, or other Engines, to kill the Game; and any Person not being qualified, or not being truly a Servant to the Lord of the Manor, or not immediately employed to take or kill the Game for his sole Use, who under Pretence of any Deputation, *&c.* to him granted by such Lord, shall take or kill any Game, or use any Greyhounds, *&c.* being convicted thereof, shall for every Offence incur such Forfeitures, and to be recovered and employed, as are appointed by the Statutes 5 *Ann. cap.* 14. and 9 *Ann. cap.* 25. the which said Acts, and all other Laws now in Force for the Preservation of the Game, not hereby altered, shall remain in Force. *Game-Keeper.* 3 Geo. 1. cap. 11.
Dogs, Guns.
Ib. §. 2.

Where a Person shall for any Offence to be committed hereafter against any Law now in Being for the better Preservation of the Game, be liable to any *pecuniary Penalty* upon a Conviction before a Justice, it shall be lawful for any other Person whatsoever to proceed to recover the said Penalty, by Information before a Justice, *or to sue for the same by Action of Debt*, in any Court of Record; and if the Plaintiff recover, he shall have double Costs. 8 Geo. 1. cap. 19. §. 1.

Such Suit must be brought before the End of the *next Term* after the Offence done; but the Offender shall not be doubly charged for the same Offence; if he is, he may plead the former Prosecution pending, or the Conviction and Judgment thereon. Ib. §. 2.

The Defendant was convicted upon the Statute 5 *Annæ*, for Keeping a Greyhound and killing four Hares, not being qualified; but it was by his own Confession, and not upon the Oath of one credible Witness, as that Statute directs; now the Forfeiture of 5 l. relating to the Conviction, if that is not according to the Statute, then nothing is forfeited; and the Justice of Peace having no Power in this Case but what he derives from the Statute, therefore it ought to be pursued, especially where 'tis Penal.

But adjudged, that the * Confession of the Offender is within the Intention, though not within the Letter of the Act; and 'tis the strongest Evidence against the Person confessing, therefore where a Justice convicts upon a stronger Evidence than is required by the Statute, such Conviction must be good. *Hil.* 9 Geo. 1. B. R. *The King* versus *Gage*. * *See Tit. Perjury.*

Another was convicted for keeping Dogs, Nets, Ferrets, *&c.* to catch Conies, not being qualified, and by Virtue of a Warrant his Goods were distrained for the Forfeiture, and a Town-Clerk granted a Replevin to take them out of the Possession of the Constable; the Court would not set aside the Replevin, but made a Rule for the Town-Clerk to shew Cause why an Attachment should not go. *Mich.* 9 Geo. 1.

If any Person between the first of *June* and first of *October*, by Hayes, Tunnels, or other Nets, drive and take any Wild-Ducks, Teal, Widgeon, or other Water Fowl, in Marshes, or other Places of Resort for Wild-Fowl, and shall be thereof convict, as 10 Geo. 2. c. 32. §. 10.

F f

by

by 9 *Ann. cap.* 25. he ſhall be liable to the Penalties of the ſaid Act for taking Water Fowl.

See alſo the Titles Hunting, *Chap.* 55. Partridges and Pheaſants, *Chap.* 68. Wild-Fowl, *Chap.* 110.

C H A P. XLVII.

Guns.

One Juſtice.
Dyer 254.
Co. 11. 87.
33 *H.* 8. 6.
Co 5. 72.
P. 1, 2, 6.

Hoſoever ſhall ſhoot in, carry, keep, uſe, or have in his Houſe, or elſewhere, any Guns, Croſs-bows, (* Dags, Piſtols, or Stone-bows, contrary to the Statute of 33 *H.* 8. 6. every Perſon ſeeing or knowing this, may arreſt or attach the Offenders, and bring or convey them to the next Juſtice of Peace in the ſame County (where they were found Offending;) which Juſtice, upon due Examination and Proof thereof, before him had or made, by his Diſcretion, may commit the Offenders to the Gaol, there to remain until they have paid the Penalty of the Statute, *ſcil.* Ten Pounds.

The Effect and Particulars of which Statute be as followeth.

33 H. 8. c.6.
§. 1.
Co. 5. 72.
1. No Perſon may ſhoot in, or keep any Gun, Dag, Piſtol, Croſs-bow, Hagbut, Demi-hake, or Stone-bow, except he hath *per Ann.* 100 *l.* in Lands, Tenements, Fees, Annuities, or Offices, *in his own Right, or in the Right of his Wife, or any other in Truſt for him, or forfeit ten Pounds for every Time.*

§. 2.
2. No Perſon may ſhoot in, carry, keep, uſe, or have any Hand-Gun under one whole Yard in length, in the Stock and Gun, nor any other Gun (* Dag or Piſtol)
* Co. 5. 72. that ſhall be under three Quarters of a Yard in length, *or forfeit ten Pounds for every Time.*

Every Perſon having in Land, *&c.* 100 *l. per Annum*, may ſeiſe and take from the Offender every Gun (Dag and Piſtol) ſhorter than is before limited, and every Croſs-bow (or Stone-bow) from him that hath not 100 *l. per Annum*, and may keep ſuch Bow; but muſt break ſuch Guns within twenty Days next after ſuch Seiſure, *or forfeit forty Shillings for every Gun not broken, and may keep the Gun ſo broken.*

3 Jac. 1. c. 13.
§. 5.
(*a*) But now, by the Statute made 3 *Jac.* 1. *cap.* 13. if any Perſon, not having Lands, *&c.* of the yearly Value of forty Pounds, or not worth in Goods Two hundred Pounds, ſhall uſe any Gun, Bow, or Croſs-bow, to kill any Deer or Conies, or ſhall keep any Buck-ſtall, or Engine, Hays, Gate-nets, Purſe-nets, Ferrets, or Coney-dogs, (except ſuch Perſons ſhall have any Ground incloſed, uſed for the Keeping of Deer or Conies, *&c.* or be Keepers or Warreners) any Perſon having in Lands an hundred Pounds by the Year in Fee, or for Life, may take from ſuch Malefactors, and to his own Uſe for ever keep ſuch Guns, Bows, Croſs-bow, Buck-ſtalls, or Engines, Hays, Gate-nets, Purſe-nets, Ferrets and Coney-Dogs.

33 H. 8. c. 6.
§. 3.
Lamb. 462.
(*d*) 3. No Perſon may carry in his Journey any Gun (Dag, or Piſtol) charged, or Bow bent, (but only in Time and Service of War, or in going to or from Muſters) except he hath *per Annum* 100 *l.* in Lands, *&c.* or ſhall forfeit ten Pounds.

§. 4.
4. No Perſon may ſhoot in any Gun, *&c.* within any City, Borough or Market-Town, nor within one Quarter of a Mile of any City, Borough or Market-Town, except for the Defence of his Perſon, or Houſe, or at a But, or Bank of the Earth, and in a Place convenient : *Or if he do, ſhall forfeit ten Pounds.*

§. 4.
§. 5.
5. The Maſter may not command his Servant to ſhoot in any Gun or Croſs-bow, *&c.* except at a But, or Bank of Earth, or in Time of War : *Or if he do, ſhall forfeit ten Pounds.*

§. 7, 8, 9.
Except notwithſtanding out of this Statute, Shooting at a But or Bank of Earth by Serving-Men, whoſe Maſters are inabled by Statute, and by Inhabitants of Cities, Boroughs and Market-Towns; except alſo all Lords, Knights, Eſquires, and Gentlemen, and the Inhabitants of every City, Borough and Market-Town; as alſo all Perſons dwelling alone, or near the Sea, and Makers and Sellers of Guns, *&c.* Theſe may keep Guns, *&c.* of the Length aforeſaid, in their Houſes, (yet only to uſe and ſhoot therein at a But, or Bank of Earth :) And Perſons having lawful Placards, they may ſhoot according to ſuch Placard or Licenſe. See other Exceptions there.

2

Any

(*a*) Any Perfon keeping Hawks, having Licence from the Seffions to fhoot at Crows, *Hawks-meat.* &c. for Hawks-meat only, may kill Hawks-meat, fo as he do at the fame Quarter- 1 Jac. 1. c. 27. Seffions become bound by Recognizance in twenty Pounds, not to fhoot at any Fowl §. 7. prohibited by that Law, nor within fix Hundred Paces of a Hernery or Pigeon-houfe, nor in any Foreft, Chafe or Park, whereof his Majefty is not Owner.

(*d*) But forafmuch as in thefe former Cafes the Juftice of Peace hath the whole Matter committed to himfelf, and that fuch Offenders remain convict upon his Examination and Proof or Witnefs made before him; therefore he ought to be circumfpect in his Examination, as alfo in his *Mittimus*. And farther, to make a Record of the Matter, (in Writing under his Hand) and alfo to fend the *Eftreat* of it into the *Exchequer*, whereby the King's Duty may be levied. *

* *The* 2 & 3 Ed. 6. c. 14.

againft Perfons under the Degree of a Lord of Parliament, and not having 100 l. *per Ann. fhooting with Hail fhot,* &c. *which was left inferted in the former Editions of this Book, is repealed by* 6 W. 3. c. 13. §. 3.

The Form of a *Mittimus, vide hic poftea,* Chap. 179.
The Form of the *Record* fee there alfo.

Any two Juftices of Peace may commit to the Gaol for three Months, &c. every fuch *Two Juftices.* Perfon as fhall fhoot with any Gun, or Bow, at any Partridge, Pheafant, Houfe-Dove, *P. Pheafants.* Mallard, or fuch Fowl, or at any Hare. See more in the Title *Partridges,* Chap. 68. and *Wild Fowl,* Chap. 110.

(*a*) But Note, That the Sheriff, or any of his Officers, for the better executing of their Office, may carry with them Hand-Guns, Dags, or other Weapons, (invafive or defenfive) notwithftanding the Statute of 33 *H.* 8. *c.* 6. *Co.* 5. *fol.* 72.

All Juftices of Peace in their Seffions may hear and determine thefe Offences, fo as no 33 H. 8. c. 6. lefs Fine than ten Pounds be affeffed for any fuch Offence; which Fine fo affeffed in Seffions, fhall be to the King's Ufe only.

Any Perfon feeing, finding, or perceiving any Perfon to offend againft the Act, may 33 H. 8. c. 6. attach and arreft, and bring him before the next Juftice of Peace, who fhall upon due Examination and Proof, by his Difcretion, commit him to the next Gaol, there to remain till the Penalties be paid; one Moiety to the King, the other to fuch Bringer.

If any Jury conceal the Offence, the Juftices may impanel Twelve or more; who, f they find the Concealment, every one of the firft Jury fhall pay twenty Shillings to he King.

An Indictment will lie on the Statute 33 *H.* 8. *cap.* 6. before the Seffions, tho' this *Indictment.* hath been formerly doubted, becaufe tho' the Juftices have Power by the general Words of their Commiffion to punifh Offences againft the Peace, yet Shooting is not fuch an Offence, for 'tis only a Defect of the Qualification of the Perfon who fhoots in a Gun.

There are feveral Inftances of fuch Indictments, tho' they have been quafhed for Infufficiency, as an Indictment for Keeping *diverfa Tormenta* (*Anglice,* Guns) *carentia ongitudine fecundum formam Statuti,* not good. 4 *Mod.* 49.

The Defendant was convicted upon the aforefaid Statute for carrying a Gun, not being qualified; but upon a *Certiorari* to remove it into *B. R.* he was difcharged, and he Conviction quafhed, becaufe it was *coram nobis,* &c. *jufticiariis Domini Regis ad acem-confervand'*, but did not fay *Affignatis.* 1 *Vent.* 39. *Sid.* 419. *S. C.*

The Defendant being convicted before a Juftice of Peace for Shooting with Hail-fhot n an Hand-Gun, was committed until he paid the Fine of 10 l. one Moiety to the King, the other to the Informer; and the Juftice having recorded the Conviction, it was certified upon the Return of an *Habeas Corpus* into *B. R.* and there upon Debate in he Court it was adjudged, that the Statute being purfued, no Court could difcharge the Defendant without paying the Forfeiture inflicted by that Act.

Gunpowder. See the *Appendix* under this Title.

Gaol. See *Prifon.*

Hats and *Caps.* See 8 *El.* 11. and 1 *Jac.* 17. 5 *Geo.* 2. 22.

Hawkers and Pedlars. (*a*)

PETTY Chapmen trading without a Licence forfeit 12 l. one Moiety to the In- 8 & 9 W. 3. formers the other to the Poor, to be levied by a Warrant by Diftrefs and Sale, &c. c. 24. being convicted by Confeffion, or by one or more Witneffes, before one Juftice on Oath. 9 & 10 W. 3. c. 27.

Any

Any Perfon fo trading and refufing to fhew a Licence to one Juftice, on Demand, forfeits 5 *l.* to the Ufe of the Poor, being convicted as before; and upon Non-payment fhall, as a Vagrant, be committed to the Houfe of Correction.

Conftables or other Officers refufing or neglecting on due Notice to aid or affift in the Execution of thefe Laws, forfeit 40 *s.* to the Poor and the Informer, to be levied by Diftrefs, &c.

Any Perfon may feife and detain a Hawker, &c. till he fhall produce his Licence, and if he hath none, then till Notice is given to fome Parifh-Officer, who fhall carry the Offender before a Juftice, who fhall levy the Penalty on the Goods and Wares, &c. with reafonable Charges.

3 & 4 Ann.
c. 4. §. 1.
Any Perfon trading as an Hawker, &c. and who hath not a Licence ready to be produced on Demand, forfeits as one trading without a Licence, and may be committed, and the Forfeiture levied by Diftrefs and Sale.

4 G. 1. c. 6.
§. 1.
Makers and wholefale Traders in *Englifh* Bone-lace, and felling the fame by Wholefale, are not Hawkers. And they may go from Houfe to Houfe to their Cuftomers, who fell again, without being liable to the Penalties againft *Hawkers.*

C H A P. XLVIII.

Hawking.

P. Pheafants 4.
P. Juft. 38.
EVERY Juftice of Peace may examine the Offences for Hawking or Hunting with Spaniels in eared or codded Corn, and may bind the Offenders with good Sureties to appear at the next General Seffions of the Peace, to anfwer their faid Offences. *23 Eliz.* 10. It feemeth requifite alfo that the Juftice do bind over the Witneffes which fhall difcover the Offence.

Againft Hawking at Pheafants or Partridges between the firft Day of *July* and laft of *Auguft,* fee 7 *Jac.* 1. 11. Tit. *Partridges,* Chap. 68.

Hawks that be found fhall be delivered to the Sheriff. See Tit. *Felonies by Statute,* Chap. 160.

Hawks, where the Taking or Concealing them is Felony. See there alfo.

(*a*) If any Perfon fhall take any Hawk, or the Eggs of them, out of the Woods or Ground of another, not having Licence fo to do, he fhall be imprifoned three Months, and pay the Party his treble Damages, and give Securiy to be of the Good Behaviour feven Years, or elfe lie in Prifon feven Years. 5 *Eliz.* 2. *fect.* 3. *See more largely in* Tit. Hunting.

C H A P. XLIX. (*a*)

Hearth-Money and Chimney-Money. The Statute 14 Car. 2. cap. 10. *which gave this Duty, is repealed.*

Hedges. See *Trefpafs,* Chap. 101.

Hides. See *Leather.*

C H A P. L.

Highways.

(*a*) MAxima prifcis temporibus Senatus diligentia fuit faciendis farciendifque viis tam intra quam extra urbem, faith *Rofinus, Antiq. Rom. l.* 7. *p.* 300. And the Care of them was firft committed to the *Cenfors;* but they having other Imployment, they
chofe

chofe Men whom they called *Quatuor viros viarum curandarum*; but the Number of their Ways increasing, particular Ways had particular Citizens appointed, who were called *Curatores viarum*, which *Cæsar Auguftus* made an ordinary Office. *Ibid. p.* 301. to which our Surveyors now exactly anfwer.

V I A, a Way, is defined to be *Tranfitus à loco in locum.*　　　*Definition.*

Note, That there are three Kinds of Ways, *fcil.*　　　*Co. 1. 56.*

1. A Foot-way called *Iter, quod eft jus eundi vel ambulandi hominis.*　　*Kinds.*

2. A Foot-way and an Horfe-way called *Actus, ab agendo*; and this vulgarly is called a Pack or Drift-way, and is both a Foot-way and Horfe-way.

3. The Third, a Cart-way, &c. called *Via* or *aditus*, (and containeth the other Two, and alfo a Cart-way) for this is *Jus eundi, vehendi, & Vehiculum & Jumentum ducendi :* And this is twofold.

Viz. { *Via Regia,* the King's Highway for all Men : With this only, The Juftices of Peace are to meddle. *Communis Strata*; belonging to a City or Town, or between Neighbours.

Minfh. out of *Ulpian* maketh alfo three Kinds of Ways, *Publicam, Privatam, & Vicinalem.*

Via Publica, quam Latini Regiam appellant.

Vicinalis, quæ in vicis eft, vel quæ in vicos ducit : Ways between Street and Street, Neighbour and Neighbour, and Houfe and Houfe in Cities and Towns.

Privata eft, quam agrariam dicunt; And thefe are of two Sorts.

Vel ea quæ ad agros ducit, per quam omnibus commeare licet.

Vel ea quæ eft in agris, cui impofita eft fervitus, ita ut ad agrum alterius ducat.

(d) Every Juftice of Peace may caufe the Highways to *Markets,* where any *Woods, Bufhes,* or *Ditches* be, to be *enlarged and cleanfed* of Bufhes and Trees, (fo that there be neither *Bufh, Ditch,* or *Tree,* within Two hundred Foot of either Side of the Way. *The* Statute 13 E. 1. excepteth *Afhes* and *great Trees*; but by the Statute 5 *El.* 13. all *Trees* and Bufhes therein are to be cut down, *&c.* And this the Juftices of Peace may do by Force of the Commiffion, the firft *Affignavimus,* (*Lamb.* 190.) But how the Juftice fhall compel the fame to be done, I fee not, otherwife than by Admonition ; and if they be not obeyed, then to prefent it, or caufe it to be prefented at the Quarter-Seffions, *&c.* *Vide* Tit. *Commiffion of the Peace.*　　*One Juftice.*　*Ways enlarged ?*　*Woods.*　*5 El. 13.*　*See poftea Tit. Robbery.*

(a) Alfo by the Articles of Inquifition upon the Statute of *Winchefter,* (made about 34 E. 1.) it is appointed, That if the *Highways be not inlarged* accordingly, Inquiry fhall be made where the Ways be, who ought to inlarge them, and of fuch as do hinder fuch In-largements, as well in Parks as in other Woods. See *Poulton's* Statutes at large, *fol.* 93.

The Highway is not only the common Tract, where Carts, Carriages and People have gone ; but if the Way be foundrous, that People cannot pafs in the common Tract, and there be Outlets out of it into the Soil of another adjoining, the People may in fuch Extremity ufe thofe Outlets upon another's Soil, altho' it be fown with Corn, which in fuch Cafe as the King's Highway as well as the other ; for the King's Subjects muft have a convenient Paffage, as was refolved in a Trial at Bar againft Sir *Henry Dun-comb, T.* 10 *Car. Roll's* 1 *Part of Abridgment, fol.* 390. Therefore where a Way goes thro' a Man's Land, and the Owner of the Land fences it on both Sides, he by fo doing hath made himfelf liable to repair the Highway, and keep it paffable; and it is not fuffi-cient for him to keep it in as good Repair as it was at the Time of the Inclofure, for by fo doing he hath ftraitned the Highway.　　*Highway, What it is.*　*Inclofure.*

(d) Every Juftice of Peace (upon his own Knowledge) may prefent in open General Seffions any Highway not fufficiently repaired and amended within the County and Li-mits of his Commiffion.　　*Prefentment.*　*5 Eliz. 13.*　*P. Juft. 69.*　*Cromp. 31.*

Every Juftice of Peace (upon his own Knowledge) may *prefent* in open General Sef-fions, any other Default or Offence committed (within the County and Limits of his Commiffion) contrary to the Statutes of 2 *&* 3 *P. & M.* 8. and 5 *Eliz. cap.* 13. concern-ing the Amendment of Highways; and every fuch *Prefentment* fhall be of the Force of a Prefentment of twelve Men, (*fcil.* fhall be a good Indictment againft the Offenders;) fo that upon fuch Prefentment the Juftices at the faid Seffions may affefs the Fine upon fuch Offenders, and that in the Abfence of the Party, and without calling them to it by any Procefs, faving to every Offender their lawful Traverfe.　　*5 Eliz. 13.*　*Cromp. 131.*　*Fine.*

So that every Juftice of Peace may prefent, as aforefaid, all and every thefe Defaults following, being all contrary to the faid Statutes, *&c.*　　*2 & 3 Ph. & M. c. 8.*　*5 Eliz. 13.*　*29 Eliz. 5.*

G g　　　　　　　　　　　　　　1. If

Surveyors.
P. 1.

1. If the Conſtables and Church-wardens of every Pariſh yearly, upon the *Tueſday* or *Wedneſday* in *Eaſter* Week, do not call together the Pariſhioners, and do not then alſo chuſe Surveyors, for the amending of Highways in their Pariſh leading to Market-Towns, according to the Statute 2 & 3 *P. & M.* 8.

Workers.
P. 2.
4 Raſt. 199.
Lamb. 459.
2 P. & M.

2. If every Perſon having in his Occupation a *Plough-land in Tillage* or Paſture in the ſame Pariſh, or keeping there a *Plough*, or a *Draught*, do not ſend at every Day and Place appointed, &c. for every Draught or Plough-land, in Tillage or Paſture, one Cart furniſhed with neceſſary Tools, and two able Men with the ſame; and that they do ſuch Works as they ſhall be appointed (by the Surveyors) by the Space of eight Hours, every of the ſaid * ſix Days.

* *Indictment*
ſetting forth,
that ſix Days inter ſuch a Time and ſuch a Time were limited; and that the Defendant did not work on any of the Days, was held ill; for *the particular Days ought to be ſet forth.* 1 Salk. 357.

Chargeable in the Pariſh where they live.

But by the Statute 18 *Eliz.* 10. he that ſhall occupy a *Plough-land* in Tillage or Paſture, lying in ſeveral Pariſhes, ſhall be chargeable only in the Pariſh where he dwelleth; and he that occupieth ſeveral Plough-lands as aforeſaid, in ſeveral Pariſhes, ſhall be charged in each Town or Pariſh where ſuch Land lieth, *ſcil.* To find in each Town or Pariſh one Cart furniſhed as aforeſaid.

(*a*) In Places where there is no Uſe of Carts and Teams, but the Uſage is to carry Materials on Horſes Backs, or by other Kind of Carriages, then the Inhabitants uſing ſuch Kind of Horſes or Carriages, ſhall ſend in the ſame with able Perſons, to work under ſuch Directions, Forfeitures and Penalties, as by former Statutes is appointed for Carts and Teams. 22 *Car.* 2. *ſect.* 8.

P. 13, 14.
P. 3.

(*d*) 3. If any of the Carriages ſhall not be thought needful by the Surveyors upon any the ſaid Days, if then every ſuch Perſon ſhall not ſend two able Men for every Cart of theirs ſo ſpared. 2 & 3 *P. & M.*

P. 4.

4. If every other Houſholder, Cottager, or Labourer, (able to labour, and being no hired Servant by the Year) do not by himſelf, or one ſufficient Labourer, work every of the ſaid ſix Days by the Space of eight Hours, as they ſhall be appointed by the Surveyors. 2 & 3 *P. & M.*

Cottage.

(*a*) A Cottage one deſcribeth to be, *Caſa ruſtica ex leviore materia excitata, arundine aut ulva paluſtri tecta.* Minſh.

And he is a Cottager that dwelleth in ſuch Cottage or Houſe without Land belonging to it. 4 *E.* 1. *Stat.* 1.

P. 12.

(*d*) 5. Note, That all Perſons being chargeable but as Cottagers, yet if they be in the Subſidy five Pounds in Goods, or forty Shillings in Lands, or above, they ſhall find two

18 El. 10.

able Men to work every of the ſix Days by the Stat. 18 *El. cap.* 10. But it ſeemeth the Juſtice cannot preſent ſuch Default upon his own Knowledge.

Hedges and Ditches.
P. 7.

6. If all Fences, Hedges and Ditches, next adjoining on the other Side any Highway, be not from Time to Time diked, ſcoured, repaired and kept low by the Owners of the Ground. 5 *El. cap.* 13. and 18 *El. cap.* 10.

7. If all Trees and Buſhes growing in the Highways be not cut down by the Owners. 5 *El. cap.* 13. 18 *El. cap.* 10.

(*a*) And now it ſeemeth, that if (according to theſe laſt mentioned Statutes of 5 *El. cap.* 13. & 18 *El. cap.* 10.) all the Hedges and Fences be kept low, the Trees and Buſhes cut down, and the Ditches ſcoured and repaired, it ſufficeth though the Ways be not Two hundred Foot wide on each Side.

Whoſe the Soil is.

Note, That the King's Highway (or *Regia via*) leading either to the Market, or from Town to Town, the Freehold and Soil thereof, and the Intereſt of all the Trees, and other ſuch Profits thereupon growing, do belong to the Lord of the Soil, or the Lord

Roll's 1 Pt. p.
392.

of the Manor. 17 *E.* 3. *fol.* 43. and 8 *E.* 4. *fol.* 9. *Br. Chemin* 10, 11. and 27 *H.* 6. *fol.* 9. *Br. Leet* 3. And therefore ſuch Lords are chargeable to cut down the Trees and Buſhes growing in ſuch Highways; and yet by the Opinion of *Keble*, 8 *H.* 7. *fol.* 5. the Freehold of the Highway, and the Trees thereupon growing, are belonging to him

2 Leon. 148.

(*ſcil.* to any Freeholder) that hath the Land next adjoining. *Br. Nuſance* 28. But it ſeemeth this muſt be underſtood of common Field-ways, or other private Ways, and not of the King's Highway. See 2 *Ed.* 4. *fol.* 9. *Britton, fol.* 111.

Yet generally he that hath the Soil, or both Sides the Highway, ſhall have the Trees growing on the Highway; as was held 18 *El. B. R.* Cited *P.* 11 *Jac. Roll's* 1 *Part* 392. Yet the Lord of a Rape that hath ſeveral Hundreds in it, may preſcribe to have the Trees growing in any Highway, within that Rape, for the Uſage, to take the Trees as a Badge of Ownerſhip; as was adjudged 11 *Jac. B. R.* in the Caſe of Sir *John Pelham.*

Note alſo, that he who hath Land adjoining next to the King's Highway, by the Common Law (before theſe Statutes) was and is chargeable, and bound of common Right, to cleanſe and ſcour the Ditches adjoining to the ſaid Way, *ſcil.* Between his Land and the Highway, *without any Preſcription ſo to do*; *but if another's Land lie next the Highway, then he that lies not next is not bound, but by Preſcription.* 8 H. 7. 5. Br.
Nuſance 28.

At *Lent* Aſſiſes at *Cambridge, Anno* 1622. Sir *Ja.* Ley delivered it in his Charge, that if any Perſon hath made, or ſhall make any Incloſure next the King's Highway, that ſuch Perſon ſhall be charged to amend the Highway adjoining to his ſaid Incloſure; eſpecially where he hath incloſed on both Sides, he ſhall be charged with mending the whole Way between his Incloſures. And if one Man hath incloſed on the one Side or Part, and another Man on the other Side, they ſhall both be charged to amend the ſame Way; and the Pariſh is to be diſcharged. *Incloſure.*
Style, p. 364.
per Roll.

1 Roll's Abr.
390.

Otherwiſe Highways muſt be ſufficiently amended at the Charge of the whole Town; and it is not enough for the Inhabitants to do their full *ſix Days Work yearly*, except their Ways be all well and ſufficiently repaired: For if all their ſaid Ways be not ſufficiently amended, the whole Town may be indicted therefore.

Where a Highway lies out of a Pariſh or Hundred in a County, the County ought of Right to repair it; and Proceſs ſhall go againſt the whole County.

Becauſe every Town regularly is to maintain and amend the Highways within their own Pariſh, except it can be proved to have been uſually amended by any other Perſon or Town, or by the Hundred, or County, &c. Therefore if ſix Days Work in the Year will not ſerve to amend them, the Surveyors may, yea muſt, appoint more Days, &c.

And in the Caſe of *Mile-end Green*, it was reſolved *M.* 1649. that a *Hamlet* is not bound of common Right to repair the Highways, unleſs it be by ſpecial Cuſtom; but a Village or Town is, as I have it in a *MS.* and you may ſee to the ſame Purpoſe, *Style Rep. p.* 163.

Alſo concerning the *Cauſey* (near *Cambridge*) called Doctor *Harvey*'s Cauſey, towards the Repair whereof Doctor *Harvey* hath given eight Pounds *per Annum*, (payable by the Maſter and Fellows of *Trinity-Hall* in *Cambridge*.) Sir *James Ley* ſaid, That if this eight Pounds *per Annum* were not ſufficient to repair the ſaid *Cauſey*, that then the Towns adjoining, within which that Cauſey or Way doth lie, ought to help to repair the ſame. *Cauſey.*

It is called the *King's Highway*, for that the King at all Times hath therein Paſſage for himſelf and his People, and may puniſh all *Nuſances* therein; though otherwiſe the Intereſt thereof be in the Lord, to take all the *Trees*, and ſuch other Profits there growing, and to bring his Action for digging therein, or for any other like Treſpaſs there done. *Highway.*
12 E. 4. 9.
9 E. 4. 9.
2 E. 4. 9.
8 E. 4. 9.
F. N. B. 113. a.

And the King (by the Common Law) may award his *Commiſſion* for the amending the Highways and Bridges throughout his Realm, ſo as his People may have ſafe Paſſage thereby. P. 1.

(*d*) 8. If any choſen to be Surveyor ſhall * refuſe the Office, or will not take upon him the Execution thereof, 2 & 3 *P. & M.* every Juſtice of Peace may preſent this, as aforeſaid. * By Stat. 3
& 4 W. 3. he
forfeits 5 l. to
be levied by
Warrant and
Diſtreſs, &c.
P. 8.

9. So if the Surveyors ſhall not within one Month after any of the former Offences committed, preſent every ſuch Offence to the next Juſtice of Peace. 5 *Eliz.*

10. Alſo if the Bailiff or High Conſtable (who hath received an *Eſtreat* for the levying of any Forfeiture upon theſe Statutes) ſhall not levy the ſame, or ſhall not (between the firſt Day of *March* and the laſt of *April* yearly) make a true Account and Payment of all Sums as he hath levied to the Conſtables and Church-wardens of every Pariſh, wherein the Offence was committed; or if the Conſtables and Church-wardens have not employed the ſame upon their Highways; it ſeemeth every Juſtice of Peace may (upon their own Knowledge) preſent every of theſe Defaults, as aforeſaid. *Eſtreats and*
Levies.
P. 10.
Raſt. 199. c. z.
P. & M.

And if the Surveyors ſhall preſent any of the former Offences (by them to be preſented) to the next Juſtice of Peace, within one Month next after the Offence committed; the ſame Juſtice ought to certify ſuch Preſentment at the next General Seſſions, *ſub pœna* 5 l. But if the Surveyors do not make their Preſentment to the Juſtice till after the Month, and the Juſtice certifieth it, this ſeemeth not good againſt the Offenders. P. 3.

(*a*) Every ſuch Surveyor (for the better Amendment of the Ways within the Pariſh) may by their Diſcretion take and carry away *the Rubbiſh or ſmalleſt Stones of any Quarry* within their Pariſh, *ſcil. ſuch Rubbiſh as* they ſhall find there *ready digged* by the Owners of the ſaid Quarry, or otherwiſe by their Licenſe. *The Surveyors*
Authority.
5 Eliz. 13. P. 3.

Every

Materials.
Ibid.
Every such Surveyor may also (for the Use aforesaid, dig for and take) or cause to be digged for and taken (in the several Grounds of any Person within the Parish, near adjoining to the Way to be amended) any *Gravel or Sand*; so as they dig in no Man's Garden, Orchard, or Meadow, and but one only Pit, and not above ten Yards over at the most, and the same within one Month to be filled up again with Earth at the Charge of the Parish.

Ibid.
Every such Surveyor may likewise cause Stones to be gathered upon any Man's Ground within the Parish, and the same to carry away for the Use aforesaid.

Ib. §. 6.
Every such Surveyor may cause any Water-course or Spring of Water (being in the Highway within their Parish) to be turned into another Man's several Ditch (or Ground) next adjoining to the said Way, in such Manner as by the Discretion of the said Surveyors shall be thought meet.

Two Justices,
Accounts.
2 P. & M. c. 8.
§. 4, 5.
(d) Also any two Justices of Peace, (the one being of the *Quorum*) upon Complaint to them made by the Church-wardens of any Parish, may convene before them the Bailiff and High Constables, (to whom the Clerk of the Peace or Steward of any Leet hath delivered any Estreats for the collecting of the Fines, Forfeitures, or Amercements for the Defaults aforesaid) and may take their Accounts; and may compel them to pay all such Arrearages, as they shall adjudge, to the Constables and Church-wardens of the Parish where the Offence was committed; or may imprison them until they have paid such Arrearages.

(a) Every Bailiff and High Constable upon their said Accounts shall have allowed for every Pound he shall collect and pay 8 d. for his own Pains, and 1 2 d. for the Fee for the Estreat delivered him.

Also it seemeth any two such Justices of Peace, upon Complaint to them made by the succeeding Church-wardens or Constables, may convene before them the precedent Constables and Church-wardens, and may take their Accounts, and may compel them (as aforesaid) to pay all Arrearages in their Hands 2 & 3 *P. & M.* 8.

(d) Note, That all such Fines or Forfeitures arising in the Sessions, shall be levied by Estreats indented, made by the Clerk of the Peace, who shall Seal and Sign such Estreats, and shall deliver the one Part thereof so sealed and signed to the Bailiff or High Constable of the same Hundred, and the other Part thereof to the Constables or Church-wardens of the Parish where such Default was made; and to be delivered by the Clerk of the Peace within six Weeks after *Michaelmas* yearly; the which Estreats shall be a sufficient Warrant to the said Bailiff or High Constable, to levy such Fines and Forfeitures by Distress: And all such Fines and Forfeitures shall be bestowed by the Church-wardens on the Highways in the same Parish.

18 Eliz. 10.
Also two Justices of Peace (by the Statute 18 *El.* 10.) may take the Account of the Surveyors of the Ways, and of the Petty Constables and Churchwardens, for all such Forfeitures (within the Statute) as they have levied. 18 *El. cap.* 10.

Here I thought good to move some Doubts, and desire that some Resolution may hereafter be given, for better Satisfaction, for that they be so ordinarily questioned.

Queries.
Co. 9. 124.
Co. L. 69.
What, and how much a Plough-land is, Sir *Ed. Coke* in his Ninth Part, in *Low's* Case, and upon *Littleton*, telleth us, and saith, That a *Carue or Hide of Land, or a Plough-land*, which is all one, is not of any certain Content, but so much as one Plough may plough in one Year; and so in some Countries it is more, and in some other it is less, according to the Heaviness of their Soil: And herewith agreeth Mr. *Lambard*, verbo *Hide.*

35 H. 6. 9.
And of the same Opinion was Judge *Prisot*, 35 *H.* 6. 29. where he saith, That a *Carue of Land* is greater in one Country than in another, for that a Plough may plough more Land in the Year in one Country than in another.

(a) And yet some others do make a Difference between an *Hide of Land*, and *a Carue or Plough-land*: For they say that an *Hide of Land doth contain four Plough-lands, sc.* 480 *Acres*; whereas a *Carue or Plough-land containeth but sixty Acres*; and every Plough-land or Carue is four Yard-lands, (in *Latin* called *Quatrona terræ*) every *Yard-land containeth thirty Acres*). But a Plough-land or Carue of Land, is called in Latin *Carucata terræ*, that is *quantum aratrum arare potest in æstivo tempore*: For which see M. *Skene, Minsh.* and the *Surveyors Dialogue* made by *John Norden, p.* 59. And yet this Definition or Description of *Carucata terræ* sheweth, that it is not of any certain Content.

Co. 4. 37. b.
& 9. 124.
(d) Also a Carue of Land (or a Plough-land) may contain House, Meadow, Pasture and Wood.

A Plough-land
is 50 l. *per*
Annum. post.
7 & 8 W.
1. Now a Man with one Plough and five or six Horses will plough and dress seven or eightscore Acres of Land yearly, (as many do with us in the East Parts of *Cambridgeshire*) and

4

and will in Summer go ufually with two Draughts or Carts; yet fuch Perfon is ufually charged to the amending of the Highways but with one Cart furnifhed. And another Man dwelling in the fame Town, occupieth but 40 or 50 Acres, or not fo much, and keepeth but three Horfes, and one Draught or Cart, and he likewife is ufually charged as the former, with one Cart furnifhed. Whether fhould their two Charges for Carriages for the Highways be alike? For mine own Opinion, I think it both reafonable and warranted by the Words of the Statute, that he that for his own private Bufinefs fhall fet up two Draughts or Carts, fhall alfo for the King and Country's Services be chargeable with two Draught, or Carts, though he occupy all his Land but with one Plough.

(a) This Matter came in Debate in *B. R. M.* 27 *Ca.* 2. upon Order made by the Juftices of Peace in *Middlefex*, for charging feveral Brewers and Brickmakers living there, and ufing feveral Draughts or Carts, to fend fo many as they kept for the repairing of the Highways, and the Order being removed in *B. R.* a *Procedendo* was awarded by *Hale* Juftice, and the whole Court, who were ftrongly of Opinion, that fo many Draughts as they kept, fo many they ought to fend, for fo the Service they do will anfwer the Wrong and Damage by them occafioned.

(d) 2. Again, what a Draught for Carriage fhall be, *fc.* with how many Horfes; and *Carriage.* whether he that keepeth but two Horfes and a Cart (as many with us do) be chargeable or no: I find that a Draught for the King's Carriages heretofore hath been fometimes with two Horfes, as by the Statute of *Magna Charta, cap.* 21. (the Words of the Statute are, *No Sheriff, &c.* fhall take the Horfes or Carts of any Perfon for Carriage, except he pay for one Cart with two Horfes 10 *d.* by the Day, and for a Cart with three Horfes 14 *d.* by the Day: And therefore I fhould think him who ufually goeth to Cart (for his own Bufinefs) with two Horfes, to be chargeable to find a Cart and two Horfes for the amending of the Highways, and to carry fuch Loads as his two Horfes are well able to draw.

3. Again, if one occupieth a Plough-Land in Pafture, *viz.* fix or eightfcore Acres or more of Pafture for feeding of Cattle, but keepeth neither Cart nor Plough, how fhall he be charged to find a Cart or Draught that keepeth none? and yet the Words of the Statute feem to charge him. *Raftal* 199. (a)

4. Again, he that fhall keep a Draught for Carriage, or a Plough, though he occupy little or no Land or Pafture in his own Hands, but only carteth or plougheth for other Men, whether he is not chargeable to find a Cart for the amending the Highways. It feemeth he is: But *quære* whether he be chargeable to find two able Men with his Cart, 2 & 3 P. & M. except he hath in his Occupation a Plough-land: Perhaps alfo he keepeth no Man. c. 8. §. 3.

(a) Any Conftable or Surveyor not putting the Acts, touching the Repair of Highways, in *Officers Ne-* Execution, or fuffering Carts to pafs through their Limits, otherwife than as aforefaid, *glect.* fhall upon Complaint to any Juftice of Peace of that Place, or Divifion, and Proof of fuch 22 Car. 1. Neglect, by Oath of one credible Witnefs, or upon View of fuch Juftice, incur fuch Fine c. 12. §. 1. as fuch Juftice fhall impofe, not exceeding 40 *s.* to be levied by Diftrefs, *&c.*

If any Perfon fhall refift or oppofe any Perfon employed in the due Execution of the *Refifting.* Acts, touching Highways, or make Refcue of any Goods diftrained, being convicted in Ib. §. 3. Form aforefaid, fhall forfeit forty Shillings, which if he pay not within feven Days after Notice of fuch Conviction, any Juftice of Peace refiding near the Place of fuch Refcue or Oppofition, may commit him to Gaol till he pay the Forfeiture to the Surveyor.

Where Lands are given for Maintenance of Caufeways, Pavements, Highways or *Gifts.* Bridges; the Feoffees and Truftees fhall let them to Farm at the beft improved Value 22 Car. 2. without Fine: And the Juftices of Peace in their Quarter-Seffions may inquire into the c. 12. §. 2. Value thereof, and if they find a Neglect or Fault in the Truftees, may order the Improvement and Employment thereof (except where there be proper Vifitors.)

Where the Highways cannot be repaired before *Midfummer-day*, the fame may be repair- *Time.* ed before St. *Luke's* Days yearly, without incurring any Penalty. Ib. §. 3.

All Defects of Repairs of High-ways, Caufeways, Pavements or Bridges, fhall be pre- *Where pre-* fented only in the County where they lie, and not elfewhere; and that no fuch Prefent- *fentable.* ment or Indictment fhall be removed by *Certiorari*, or otherwife out of the faid County, Ib. §. 4. till Traverfe and Judgment given.

A Bridge lying between two Counties, and not known in which of thefe two Counties Part lies, nor who ought to repair the fame, an Indictment for the fame feems to be removeable by *Certiorari*, notwithftanding this Statute: So likewife if a Perfon in Refpect of Lands in one County, ought to repair a Bridge or Highway in another County; *ne deficeret juftitia.*

The Juſtices of Peace have alſo Power in their Seſſions by Indictment, to puniſh by Fine all Nuſances, Encroachments and Purpreſtures in the Highways, as namely,

1. The building and erecting of Gates on the Highways, where none have ancient'y been, and theſe as every private Perſon may pull down and break, in Order thereto, if it cannot be done otherwiſe, as was reſolved in the Caſe of *Jones* and *Harward, P. 6. Ca. B. R. Jones Rep. p. 221. & Cro. 1 Part, p. 133.* So the Perſons ſo doing may by Indictment being found guilty be fined therefore, and injoined to remove the ſame.

12 E. 4. 9.
8 E. 4. 9.
2. The Encroaching on any Part of the Highway by Building, or other Incloſure, the King ſhall have the Puniſhment of it, although the Soil be another's.

3. Another's annoying thereof, by laying Carrion on the ſame.

4. The Overflowing the ſame with Water ſtopp'd in thoſe Ways, or in any Man's private Grounds; whereby the publick Ways are overflowed.

5. Digging Pits in the Ways, or near them, by which Paſſage becomes dangerous.

27 H. 8. 26.
6. The Laying Loggs, or any Things obſtructive of their Uſe, for which although none can have an Action but he that hath particular and ſpecial Damage, yet any one may indict, and ſo procure to be reformed.

3 & 4 W. &
M. c. 12. §. 3.
Conſtables, Headboroughs, &c. and other the Inhabitants of every Pariſh, ſhall on the 26th Day of *December* yearly, make a Liſt of the Names of the moſt ſubſtantial Inhabitants, and ſuch as are legally qualified, and return it to two or more Juſtices of the Peace, at a ſpecial Seſſions to be held for that Purpoſe on the 3d of *January* next following, or within 15 Days after: Out of which ſaid Liſts the Juſtices are, by Warrant under their

Surveyors nominated, and by whom. Penalty on Refuſal.
Hands and Seals, to nominate one, two or more to be Surveyors of the Highways for the Year enſuing. Which Nomination ſhall be notified by the Conſtables, &c. to the Perſons nominated within ſix Days: And if Perſons ſo nominated ſhall refuſe, &c. they ſhall forfeit 5 l. to be levied by Diſtreſs on their Goods, and Sale thereof by Warrant of two Juſtices of the Peace, which Warrant the Juſtices are to make upon Information of one credible Witneſs upon Oath; one Moiety of ſuch Forfeiture to the Informer, and the other to the Repair of the Highways: And in ſuch Caſe the Juſtices ſhall nominate ſome other fit Perſon to execute the Office, who ſhall upon like Notice take upon him the Office, under the ſame Penalty. And Conſtables, &c. neglecting to return ſuch Liſt of Names ſhall forfeit each 20 s. to be levied and employed as aforeſaid.

Obſtructions to be removed.
3 & 4 W. & M.
c. 12. §. 4, 5.
No Perſon ſhall lay in any Highway not 20 Foot broad, any Matter whereby the ſame may be obſtructed, on Pain to forfeit 5 s. to be levied and diſpoſed as aforeſaid. And ſhall clear the Highways and cleanſe their Ditches within ten Days after Notice given by any of the Surveyors, on Pain of forfeiting 5 s. to be diſpoſed as before.

Roads to be viewed.
Ib. §. 8.
Surveyors ſhall view the Roads, &c. and within every four Months preſent upon Oath to ſome Juſtice of Peace, in what Condition they find them, or incur the Penalty as in Caſe of refuſing to execute their Office, except they have ſome reaſonable Excuſe allowed by two Juſtices of Peace. If any Offender, after 30 Days Notice given by the Surveyors, neglect to amend the ſame, the Surveyors amending the ſame ſhall be allowed ſuch Charges by the Defaulter as the Juſtice ſhall think fit, to be levied as aforeſaid.

Preſentment.
Ib. §. 9.
Juſtices of Peace ſhall once in four Months hold a Special Seſſions, and ſummon all the Surveyors of Highways, and declare to them what they are to do by Virtue of this or any other former Act. And the Surveyors ſhall upon Oath make Preſentment of what Offences any are guilty. And before any Surveyor ſhall be diſcharged of his Office, he ſhall at ſome Special Seſſions give an Account upon Oath of all Monies come to his Hands concerning the Highways, and how diſpoſed; and if any be remaining in his Hands, he ſhall deliver it to the next Surveyors, and upon Failure ſhall forfeit double the Value, to be levied and diſ-

Ib. §. 10.
poſed as aforeſaid. Surveyors neglecting their Duty, ſhall forfeit 40 s.

Juſtices neglecting.
Ib. §. 11.
Juſtice of Peace neglecting or refuſing his Duty, ſhall forfeit five Pounds, one Moiety to the Proſecutor, the other towards amending the Highways, to be recovered in any of his Majeſty's Courts of Record, by Action of Debt, &c.

Surveyors to be reimburſed.
Ib. §. 13.
The Surveyors giving Notice to the Juſtices at their Special Seſſions upon Oath, of what Sums they have expended in repairing the Highways, the Juſtices (or any two of them) may by Warrant cauſe an equal Rate to be made to reimburſe them, according to an Act of 43 *Eliz. cap. 2. for Relief of the Poor*; and if any refuſe, the ſame to be levied by Diſtreſs, &c.

Fines levied into the Hands of Surveyors.
Ib. §. 14.
No Fine, Forfeiture, &c. for not repairing the Highways ſhall be returned into the Exchequer, or other Court; but levied into the Hands of the Surveyors, to be employed for the Amendment of ſuch Highways: And if any Fine, &c. be levied, on one or more

2　　　　　　　　　　　　　　　　　　　　　　　　　particu-

particular Inhabitants, upon Complaint to the Justices at their Special Sessions, or any two of them by their Warrant, may cause a Rate to be made for their Reimbursement.

If Justices at their Quarter-Sessions shall be satisfied, that the Highways, &c. cannot *Assessments.* be sufficiently amended without the Help of this Act, Assessments upon Persons usually 3 & 4 W. & rateable to the Poor, shall be made and levied by such Persons, and in such Manner as the M. c. 12. Justices at such Sessions shall appoint; the Money so raised to be employed according to §. 17. their Orders, for repairing the Highways, &c. The said Assessments, if not paid within ten Days after Demand, to be levied by Distress, rendring the Overplus, Charges deducted.

No such Assessments in one Year shall exceed 6 d. in the Pound of Lands, nor 6 d. for Ib. §. 18. 20 l. personal Estate.

If any Persons shall find themselves agrieved by such Assessments, or by any Act of *Appeal.* the Justices of Peace, the Justices of Peace at their General Quarter-Sessions shall take Ib. §. 19. Order therein, which shall conclude all Parties.

All Prosecutions for Offences against this Act shall be within six Months; nor shall *Six Months.* any be punished by this Act, being punished for the same Offence by any former Law. Ib. §. 20.

Justices at their Quarter-Sessions shall assess the Prices of all Land-carriage of Goods. *Rates for Car-* See Tit. *Carriages,* Chap. 21. *riage.* Ib. §. 24.

Where any Liberty, Precinct, or Village, have used to repair their own Highways, 7 W. 3. c. 29. and have levied 6 d. in the Pound towards the Repairs, &c. and yet they are not well re- §. 4. paired, the Justices in their special Sessions, for Consideration of the Highways, may order the *whole Parish* to contribute to the Repairing.

He who hath in his Occupation *Woodland,* or other Land to the Value of 50 l. per An- *Plough-Land* num, shall be accounted to have a Plough-Land within the several Statutes for Repairing *what.* Highways. Ib. §. 9.

He who pulls up, cuts down, or removes any Post, Block or Stone, Bank of Earth, *Removing* or other Security, set up for securing Horse and Foot Causeways from Carts, shall forfeit *Posts, &c. for* for every Offence 20 s. to the Surveyors; one Moiety for the Use, and to repair the High- *securing Ways.* ways, the other Moiety to the Informer; the Conviction is to be by one Witness, before Ib. §. 6. one Justice of the Peace or Division, &c. or upon his View, the Forfeiture is to be levied by Distress and Sale.

The Justices at their Quarter-Sessions, or the major Part of them, being at least five, *Sessions may* shall have Power to enlarge or widen any Highways in their respective Limits, so that *enlarge High-* the Ground to be taken in do not exceed eight Yards in Breadth; and that they do not 8 & 9 W. pull down any House, or take away the Ground of any Garden, Orchard, Court c. 16. §. 1. or Yard.

The Sessions may impanel a Jury on Oath to assess Damages to the Owner of the *And impanel a* Ground taken in, not exceeding twenty-five Years Purchase, and for making Satis- *Jury to give* faction for any new Ditch or Fence, and to any Person that may be injured by enlarging *Owner of any* the Highways. *Ground taken in.* Ibid.

Upon Payment of the Money to the Owner of the Land, or leaving it with the Clerk *Which shall* of the Peace for his Use, he shall for ever be devested of the Land, and it shall be then *a Highway.* taken to be a publick Highway. 8 W. 3. c. 16. §. 1.

The Money to be paid for the Land, shall be raised by an Assessment on the Pa- *The Purchase* rishioners, who ought to repair the Highways by the Order of the Justices, and by the *Money to be* Overseers, &c. by Distress and Sale, &c. if not paid within ten Days after Demand. *Assessment.* Such Assessment shall not exceed 6 d. per Pound in one Year. Ib. §. 2.

The Justices, at the Request of any Person for putting the Powers of this Act in Exe- *The Owners* cution, may issue out their Precepts to the Owners of such Ground, or to others in- *directed to them* trusted in the same, to appear at the next Quarter-Sessions, and shew Cause why the *may appear at* Highway should not be enlarged. *the next Sessi-* *ons.* Ib. §. 3.

The Owner shall have Liberty within eight Months after the Ground is taken, to cut *And may cut* down the Wood or Timber growing thereon; and for Neglect thereof it shall be sold by *down any Wood* the Justices, the Money to be paid to the Owner. *or Timber.* Ib. §. 4.

There lies an Appeal to the Judges at the next Assises, who may affirm or reverse the *An Appeal lies* Session's Order; and if affirmed, may award Costs against the Appellant for Vexation *to the Judges* and Delay, to be levied by Distress and Sale, &c. *at the next* *Assises.* Where Ib. §. 5.

An Appeal from an Inclosure by Writ Ad quod damnum, lies to the next Sessions.
Ib. §. 6.

Where a Highway shall be inclosed after a Writ *Ad quod damnum* issued, and Inquisition thereon taken, any Person agrieved may appeal to the next Quarter-Sessions after such Inquisition taken, whose Determination shall be final; and if no Appeal be made, then the Inquisition and Return, entered and recorded by the Clerk of the Peace at the Quarter-Sessions, shall be for ever binding.

Surveyors may set up a Stone where two Cross-ways meet.
Ib. §. 7.

Justices in their Special Sessions held every four Months, by Virtue of 3 & 4 *W. & M. cap.* 12. may direct their Precepts to Surveyors in any Parish, where two or more Cross-ways meet, requiring them to fix a Stone or Post where such Ways join, with an Inscription in large Letters of the next Market-Town to which each of the Ways lead, they to be reimbursed as by the Statute 3 & 4 *Will.* is directed.

Neglecting to set up a Stone, &c. forfeits 10 s.
Ibid.

Surveyor neglecting to erect such Post or Stone three Months after a Precept directed and delivered to him, forfeits 10 s. to be levied by Distress and Sale, by a Warrant of one Justice, which Sum shall be employed in erecting the same; and if there be any Overplus, then in mending the Cross-ways.

Surveyors to view the Roads.
1 Geo.1.c.52. §. 1.

All Laws and Statutes concerning Highways, not hereby altered or repealed, shall be put in Execution.

Ib. §. 2.
And give to the Justices an Account in Writing and on Oath of the Condition thereof, and of the Defect of Labourers and Teams.

Surveyors appointed according to the Statute 3 & 4 *Will.* shall, within fourteen Days after the Acceptance of their Office, view the Roads every four Months, or oftener, if required, by the Warrant of two Justices, together with all Nusances and Encroachments thereon in their respective Parishes, and give an Account in Writing on Oath of the State and Condition of the Highways, and the Neglect of Labourers or Teams, &c. to the Justices, at their next *Special Sessions* to be holden for the Amendment of the Highways, and for neglecting to give such Account shall forfeit 5 l. to be levied by Distress and Sale, by Warrant of two Justices, which they are to grant on the Oath of one Witness; one Moiety to the Informer, the other to Repair the Highways.

The Special Sessions may order the Reparation of the Highways to be repaired. 1 Geo. 1. cap. 22. §. 3.

Justices in their Special Sessions may, by Writing under their Hands and Seals, order the Reparation of such Roads as in their Division most want to be amended, and at what Time, and in what Manner it shall be done.

Surveyors must see the Ways repaired before Harvest.
Ib. §. 4.

Surveyors must take the first and most convenient Time of the Year for Repairing, &c. and, if possible, perfect it before Harvest; and summon the Teams and Labourers to come in upon such early and seasonable Days as the Year shall afford to Repair, &c. as the Justices in their Special Sessions shall direct; and if they make no Direction or Order, then to repair such Highways as need it most.

Misapplying Fines or any Forfeitures, the Penalty is 5 l.
Ib. §. 5.

Fines or Forfeitures laid upon any Surveyor, or other Person, for not doing his Duty, and being misapplied, upon Oath thereof made before the Justices at their Special Sessions, the Person misapplying them shall forfeit 5 l. to the Informer, to be levied by Distress and Sale; and Justices may examine upon Oath all Persons who can give an Account of any Money which ought to be applied to amend the Highways, and levy the Penalties and Forfeitures, and employ them as aforesaid.

Quarter-Sessions may assess 6 d. per Pound, tho' the six Days Work hath not been done. Ibid. §. 6.

The Quarter-Sessions may cause Assessments to be made, and Money raised, not exceeding 6 d. *per* Pound for one Year, for Repairing Highways, tho' the six Days Work hath not been performed.

Justices in Towns Corporate and Boroughs.
Ib. §. 7.

Justices in Cities, Corporations and Boroughs, are impowered to put this Act in Execution, and all former Acts relating to Highways within their respective Jurisdictions.

Neglecting to scour Ditches after 30 Days Notice, forfeits for every Yard 2 s. 6 d.
Ib. §. 8.

He who ought to scour Ditches and Water-courses near Highways, and neglecting to do it after thirty Days Notice given him by the Surveyors, or leaving the Earth of the Ditches scoured in the Highway for eight Days, and Oath being made thereof by the Surveyors at the Special Sessions for the Hundred, or Division, &c. shall forfeit for every eight Yards of Ditch not scoured 2 s. 6 d. and for each other Offence not exceeding 5 l. nor under 20 s. to be levied by Distress and Sale, and applied by the Surveyors to mend the Highways.

Justices in Cities, &c. may appoint Scavengers.
Ib. §. 9.

Justices in Cities and Market-Towns, may at their Quarter-Sessions appoint Scavengers for Cleansing the Streets, and Repairing them, &c. and order Assessments not exceeding

2   6 d.

6 d. *per* Pound to defray the Charge, to be levied on the * *Occupiers* and *Owners* of Houfes, Lands, *&c.* in fuch Cities, *&c.* and the Money thereby raifed, fhall be employ-ed and accounted for according to the Order and Directions of the Juftices; and the Af-feffments being allowed by them, may be levied by Warrant, *&c.* by Diftrefs and 'Sale, f not paid within eight Days after Demand.

marginal: * *Tho' the Sta-tute mentions Owners or O-cupiers, yet if he will not ufe the Lands him-felf, nor let them, it fhall*

be charged on them ; for the Publick ought not to fuffer for his Negligence. Palm 389. 2 Rol. Rep. 412. N. Abr. V. 3. p. 59.

Surveyor neglecting his Duty is to forfeit 40 s. to be levied and difpofed as aforefaid.

marginal: *Surveyor neg-lecting, &c.* Ib. §. 10.

Clerk or Servant of a Juftice fhall not take any Thing of a Surveyor for the Oath, or Accounts given in at fuch Special Seffions, on Pain of 10 l. to be recovered in any Court of Record.

marginal: *Juftice's Clerk muft take no-thing of a Sur-veyor for his*

Oath. 1 Geo. 1. cap. 52. §. 11.

He who is agrieved by any Thing done in Execution of this Act may apply to the Sef-fions, whofe Order fhall be final, except it be for a Neglect in Scouring Ditches, and carrying away the Earth, or for not carrying away Stone, Timber, Straw, or Dung left n the Highway, or for not removing Annoyances by Water-courfes.

marginal: *Appeal to the Seffions.* Ib. §. 12.

He who is fued for any Thing done in Purfuance of this Law, may plead the General Iffue, and give the Act and the fpecial Matter in Evidence ; and if the Plaintiff is caft, he Defendant fhall have double Cofts.

marginal: *General Iffue.* Ib. §. 13.

Offenders muft be prefented within fix Months, *&c.* and Perfons punifhed by this Act hall not be punifhed by any former Law.

marginal: *Profecution muft be within fix Months.* Ib. §. 14.

Lord Mayor and Juftices in *London*, may execute their Authority in paving and clean-ing the Streets as before.

marginal: *Lord Mayor, &c.* Ib. §. 15.

Note, That by 9 *Geo.* 2. *cap.* 18. *fect.* 3. the Claufe in 1 *Geo.* 1. *cap.* 52. *fect.* 9. im-powering Juftices of Peace to make Affeffments in Cities and Market-Towns, is extended o Towns Corporate.

marginal: 9 G. 2. c. 18. §. 1.

By Statute of 7 *Geo.* 2. *cap.* 9. If the Surveyors of the Highways fhall find any High-way deep and foundrous, and the Hedges adjoining to be fo high, as to prevent the Be-nefit of the Sun and Winds; fuch Surveyors may make Prefentment of fuch Hedges to he Juftices of Peace, who live in or near the Divifion where the Highway is, at their Spe-cial Seffions ; which Juftices, or two of them, are impowered to fummon the Occupiers of the Lands, whofe Hedges are prefented, to appear at the next Publick Meeting of the Juftices, to fhew Caufe why fuch Hedges fhould not be new made or cut low ; and if it ppear that the Way is damaged by the Height of fuch Hedges, the Juftices, or any two of them, are required to iffue out a Precept to the Surveyors, to leave Notice in Writing t the Place of Abode of fuch Perfons, that they are required to new make, or cut low he faid Hedges, within thirty Days of fuch Notice (provided the Notice be given be-ween the laft of *September* and firft of *February*) and in Cafe of their Neglect to do the ame, the Surveyors are required to caufe the Hedges to be new made, or cut low, fo as uch Hedges be left three Feet high above the Bank. And the Perfons fo neglecting fhall epay the Surveyors their reafonable Expences, which if neglected for fourteen Days after the fame fhall have been demanded, the Juftices, at their monthly Meeting, may iffue a Pre-cept to the Conftable, to levy fuch Sums of Money for Repayment of the Surveyors, as heir faid Expences fhall amount to, upon the Goods of the Perfons who have neglected o pay the fame.

marginal: 7 Geo. 2. c. 9. §. 1.

marginal: Ib. §. 2.

But nothing in this Act fhall alter the Law in relation to Timber Trees in Hedges ad-oining to Highways.

marginal: Ib. §. 3.

See the Statutes 6 *Ann. cap.* 29. 9 *Ann. cap.* 18. 1 *Geo.* 1. *cap.* 11. *fect.* 2. 5 *Geo.* 1. *ap.* 12. 6 *Geo.* 1. *cap.* 6. about Waggons, *&c.* travelling for Hire, in Tit. *Carriages*, Chap. 21.

By the Statute of 14 *Geo.* 2. *cap.* 42. For the Prefervation of the Publick Roads of Eng-land, It is enacted, That the Truftees appointed by the feveral Acts of Parliament for Repairing Highways, may caufe Cranes, or weighing Engines to be erected at any Turn-pike, and caufe all Carriages paffing the Turnpike to be weighed, and take over and above the Toll, 20 s. for every Hundred Weight, fuch Carriage with the Loading fhall

marginal: 14 Geo. 2. c. 42.

I i   weigh

weigh above 6000 Pounds weight ; and the Money so raised shall go towards Mending the Highways.

Farmers or others may carry Goods in Wheel-Carriages, bound with Streaks or Tire of any Breadth.

The Collectors may levy the additional Duty by Distress and Sale of the Person's Goods refusing to pay the same.

And if any Person attempt to hinder the Weighing, or the Seizing or Carrying away any Distress, as aforesaid, or use any Violence to the Persons concerned, on Oath made thereof by one Witness before the next Justice, the Offender shall suffer three Months Imprisonment, and forfeit 10 *l.* to be levied by Distress of his Goods after three Days.

Carriages employed only about Husbandry, *&c.* (as in 5 *Geo.* 1. *cap.* 12. *supra* Tit. *Carriages*) shall not be weighed, and the Act of 5 *Geo.* 1. *cap.* 12. shall extend to all Waggons, *&c.* whether travelling for Hire or not ; and all Offenders against these two Acts shall be liable for every Offence (being convicted on Oath, within three Days, before a Justice of the County, *&c.* where the Offence shall be committed, or the Offender shall be) to the respective Forfeitures and Seizures of 5 *Geo.* 1. for the Space of three Days after the Offence, as they would have been had they been seised in the Fact.

N. Abr. Vol. 3. P. 57. And as to Nusances on the Highways, or any other Injuries, by digging Ditches, making Cross-hedges, laying Logs of Timber, or any other Thing, which in some Measure may obstruct the Passengers ; any Person may remove them at Common Law, but cannot *But it is no* convert the Materials to his own Use : * But in such Cases no one Person can have an *Nusance for an* Action for obstructing the Highway, but the Remedy is by Presentment at the Leet, or by *Inhabitant of* Indictment, unless any Man hath a particular Damage for them, he may have an Action *a Town to un-* on the Case, *&c.* 1 *Inst.* 56. *lade Billets,* *&c. in the* *Street before his House, by Reason of the Necessity of the Case, unless he suffer them to continue an unreasonable Time.* 2 Rol. Abr. 137.

Indictment. Now all *Indictments* relating to this Matter ought to be *certain,* both as to the Place *from which the Way doth lead, and to the Place* where it doth lead ; but there is not any Necessity to shew that it leads to a Market-Town, because every Highway leads from one Market-Town to another.

Nusance. But 'tis necessary to shew in what Place the Nusance was done, and to what Parts of the Highway it did extend, shewing how many Foot in Length and Breadth it contained ; because without such Certainty the Defendant cannot make a Defence, nor the Court judge of the Greatness of the Offence, that they may the better set a Fine ; therefore an Indictment for stopping a great Part of the Highway at *C.* is not good, because 'tis uncertain, for the Place is not sufficiently set forth.

Common High- 'Tis likewise necessary to set forth, that the Way wherein the Nusance was done, is a *way.* common Highway, or that it is a Footway to a Church ; but then it must not set forth that 'tis a Footway for all the Parishioners of *H.* but a Foot-way generally leading to the Church of *H.*

Repairing. As to Repairing, *&c.* where one is indicted for not repairing a Highway, which he ought to do by Reason of his *Tenure* ; 'tis not sufficient to set forth that he is to repair, *&c.* *ratione tenuræ terræ* generally, but the Word *suæ* must be added.

N. Abr. V. 3. p. 58. 1 Mod. 112. If a Parish is indicted for not repairing, upon Not guilty pleaded, this shall be intended that the Way is in Repair, but does not go to the Right of Reparation. And if a private Person be bound to repair, the Parish must plead it specially, and cannot take Advantage of it on the General Issue.

If a particular Person is indicted, he may give in Evidence that another is to repair, *&c.* *Quære.*

Presentment. A Presentment, that an Highway in such a Place is in Decay thro' the Default of the Parishioners of *H.* is good, tho' no particular Person is named ; but in an Indictment all of them must be charged, and not *eorum uterque.*

Indictment An Indictment against the Inhabitants of *Mile-end* in the Parish of *S.* was quashed, be-*quashed.* cause *Mile-end* is not a Parish, but an *Hamlet* ; and of common Right, every * Parish * Vent. 183. where the Way lies unrepaired, is bound to repair, unless any particular Person is to do it, by Reason of Tenure, Enclosure or otherwise.

Indictment against several Defendants for not repairing a common Footway, they all confessed the Indictment, and submitted to a Fine : But that did not end here, for a *Distringas* shall issue against them, and so *in infinitum,* 'till 'tis certified that the Way is repaired as formerly it had been when at the best. 1 *Salk.* 358.

2   The

The Defendant was prefented at the Seffions by a Juftice of Peace, *upon his View*; for not repairing a Highway which he ought; for that he held fome Lands inclofed which were Parcel of that Way, on which he had *incroached*, to judge that he ought not to be charged for both, *viz.* for holding Lands inclofed, and for *incroaching* but fingly for each; becaufe he is to be charged for incroaching, fo long as the Incroachment continues, and no longer; for if he lays it open, he is no longer liable to repair; but where he is charged *ratione tenuræ, viz.* in Refpect of his holding the Lands there, tho' he lay them open, the Charge ftill continues. *(margin: Prefentment on a Juftice on his View. Encroachment. 2 Saund. 260. Sid. 464.)*

The Parfon is liable to the Charge of repairing the Highways, in Refpect of the Lands and Tenements which he holds of the Church, as refolved by all the Judges; for he is liable to all publick Charges impofed by Statutes, unlefs particularly excepted. *(margin: Clergymen liable. 1 Lev. 139.)*

Juftices ordering a Man to work towards Repairing the Highways, muft not appoint the Time generally, as fix Days between fuch a Time and fuch a Time, but muft fet forth the Days particularly. An Indictment for not working, &c. in fuch a Cafe, was held naught. *(margin: Salk. 357.)*

An Indictment for fuffering a Houfe on the Highway to be ruinous, and likely to fall down, will lie againft a Tenant at Will, and the Words *ratione tenuræ* are Surplus. See alfo on this Subject of Highways, 1 *Hawk. P. C. chap.* 76. *p.* 200. *of Nufances relating to Highways.* *(margin: Salk. ib.)*

Any Perfon who fhall break down or deftroy any Turnpike-gate, or any Poft, Rail, Wall, or other Fence belonging to fuch Turnpike or Gate erected by Act of Parliament, fhall, upon Conviction by the Oath of one Witnefs before two Juftices of Peace (who may fummarily determine the fame) be fent to the Common Gaol or Houfe of Correction for three Months; and on the firft convenient Market-day fuch Offender fhall be publickly whipt between the Hours of Eleven and Two, by the Keeper of fuch Gaol, &c. at the Market-place of the City or Town near which the Offence was committed. *(margin: 1Geo.2.c.19. §. 1.)*

If any Perfon fo convicted fhall fo offend a fecond Time, or if any Perfon fhall pull down or demolifh any Houfe erected for the Ufe of a Turnpike-gate, or fhall break down any Lock, Sluce or Floodgate erected by Authority of Parliament upon any navigable River, fuch Offenders being convicted, upon Indictment before the Juftices of Affife, *Oyer* and *Terminer*, or Gaol-delivery, fhall be guilty of Felony; and the Court may tranfport them for feven Years, *(margin: Ib. §. 2.)*

The Action muft be commenced within fix Months after the Fact. The Defendant may plead the General Iffue, and if the Plaintiff be nonfuited, &c. fhall recover treble Cofts. *(margin: Ib. §. 3.)*

This Act fhall be publickly read at every Quarter-Seffions, and at every Leet or Law-day. *(margin: Ib. §. 4.)*

Continued by 13 *Geo.* 2. *cap.* 18. to 1ft of *June* 1747.

By the 5 *Geo.* 2. *cap.* 33. the firft Offence of pulling down Turnpikes, &c. was made Felony, &c. and returning from Tranfportation Death without Benefit of Clergy. And by 8 *Geo.* 2. *cap.* 20. the firft Offence of this Nature was Felony without Benefit of Clergy, but thefe two Acts were to continue only five Years, from the 12th of *May* 1735, and to the End of the next Seffions of Parliament.

Highwaymen.

HE who apprehends and profecutes an Highwayman, fo as he is convicted, fhall within one Month after fuch Conviction, receive of the Sheriff of the County where the Robbery was committed 40 *l.* producing a * Certificate under the Hand of the Judge, before whom the Highwayman was convicted. *(margin: Taking a Highwayman 40 l. * That the Highwayman was taken by the Perfon claiming it, &c. 4 & 5 W. c. 8.)*

If any Perfon is killed in taking or purfuing a Highwayman, he or they who have a Right to adminifter, fhall have the * 40 *l.* and he who takes, profecutes and convicts him, fhall have his Horfe, Furniture, Money and other Goods; the King's Title, or that of the Lord of the Manor, or other Perfon who lent the fame to the Highwayman, in any wife notftanding, but the Right of the Perfon from whom they were felonioufly taken is faved. *(margin: Ib. §. 2. * Producing a Certificate from the Judge, or from the two next Juftices,)*

and if not paid then, the Sheriff forfeits double the Sum, with treble Cofts.

A Highwayman being not in Prifon, and difcovering two or more Robbers, fo as they may be convicted, fhall have the King's Pardon for all Robberies committed before that Time; which Pardon fhall be a good Bar to any Appeal. *(margin: Ib. §. 8.)*

The Streets of *London* and *Weftminfter* fhall be deemed Highways, and of all other Cities, Towns and Places: And all Certificates hereafter to be figned for Convictions of Robberies, fhall be * figned without Deduction or Fee, except 5 *s.* for Writing thereof; the Perfon taking *(margin: 6 Geo. 1. c. 23. §. 8. * And the Money paid.)*

taking more fhall forfeit 40 *l.* to be recovered by Action of Debt, to the Ufe of the Perfon intitled to the Certificate.

CHAP. LI.

There be alfo certain particular Statutes concerning Highways and Streets, as followeth.

One Juſtice.
39 El. 19. §. 3.
Ibid.

THE Occupier of any Iron-works, for every three Loads of Coal or Mine, and alfo for every Tun of Iron that he fhall caufe to be carried in Winter-time by the Space of one Mile in the Highways within the Wilds of *Suffex, Surrey,* or *Kent,* fhall pay to the Juftices of Peace dwelling near to the Places in that County where the Highways fhall be moft annoyed, or to his Affigns, 3 *s.* in Money; the fame, in Default of Payment, to be levied by Diftrefs by fuch Juftice, or his Affignee, of the Goods of the Party in the faid County.

Ib. §. 4.

Alfo fuch Occupier, for every thirty Loads of Coal and Mine, and for every ten Tuns of Iron carried in the faid Highways, *&c.* fhall lay one Load of Cinder, Gravel, Stone or Chalk, in Places to be appointed by fuch Juftice, or elfe within eight Days after Demand, fhall pay 3 *s.* for every fuch Load to the Hand of fuch Juftices, who, upon Default of Payment, fhall levy the fame by the Diftrefs, *&c.*

The faid Juftice of Peace fhall beftow all fuch Sums of Money upon the amending of the fame Highways, at his Difcretion.

Two Juſtices.
Ibid.

Two Juftices of Peace, whereof one to be of the *Quorum,* which were prefent at the Seffions wherein any Perfon was convicted for any Offence againft the Statute of 39 *Eliz.* may make Warrant for levying the Forfeits thereof to any Conftable, or other Officer: And they may alfo appoint fuch Ways and Means as they fhall think meet, to levy the double Sums for not paying thofe Forfeits within twenty Days next after lawful Demand of the fame by fuch Officer.

New-ways.
14 & 15 H. 8.
c. 6.
26 H. 8. c. 7.
§. 3.

By the Affent of two Juftices of the Peace, and twelve difcreet Men of the Hundred and Hundreds adjoining, any Perfon may make and lay out, in and over his own Land in Fee-fimple, in the Wild of *Kent,* as alfo in the County of *Suffex,* a new Highway more commodious than the old; and inftead thereof may retain the Ground of the old Way in Severalty to him and his Heirs: And the fame Juftices and twelve Men fhall within three Months certify under their Seals fuch new Way into the Chancery, *fc.* the Length and Breadth of the fame new Way, and other Things adjoining or concerning the fame, accord-

* *The* Stat. 13 ing to their Difcretion. *
& 14 Car. 2.

c. 2. *for repairing the Highways,* &c. *and paving the Streets in and about* London, *inſerted in former Editions of this Book, is expired.*

London New-ways paved.
2 W. & M.
ft. 2. c. 8. §. 7.

(*a*) Where any new Streets fhall be made in *London, Weftminfter,* or the Suburbs, *&c.* Juftices of Peace may view the fame: And if they judge them fit to be paved, may certify the fame to the next Quarter-Seffions, to do therein as they fhall think fit.

Scavengers.
Ib. §. 9.

Scavengers, *&c.* refufing or neglecting their Duty, incur a Penalty, to be levied by Diftrefs and Sale of Goods, by Warrant from a Juftice of Peace; and fhall account to two or more Juftices for what Money remains in their Hands, and be imprifoned for not accounting.

Dirt lodged.
Ib. §. 12.

Scavengers may by Order of the Juftices at their Petit Seffions lodge their Dirt in convenient Places near the Street, giving Satisfaction to the Owners: And in Cafe of unreafonable Demand, the Juftices may moderate the fame. And Perfons aggrieved by any Tax by Virtue of this Act, or by the Determination of the Juftices, *&c.* may have Recourfe to the General Quarter-Seffions, whofe Determination herein fhall be final.

Affeffment.
Ib. §. 13.

If Common Highways in the faid Parifhes cannot be fupported without the Help of this Act, then one or more Affeffments fhall be made on the Inhabitants, *&c.* to be allowed by fuch Perfons as the Juftices at their Quarter-Seffions fhall direct; fuch Affeffments in Cafe of Non-payment, to be levied by Diftrefs, *&c.*

Lamps.
2 W. & M.
ft. 2. c. 8.
§. 15.

Houfholders within the Weekly Bills of Mortality, from *Michaelmas* to *Lady-day,* to hang out Lights, or agree to make Ufe of *Lamps,* to be placed at fuch Diftances as fhall be approved by two or more Juftices of the Peace.

Ib. §. 16.

Hay wanting Weight, to forfeit 18 *d. per* Trufs: All Carts loaden with Hay, Straw, *&c.* within the Weekly Bills of Mortality, ftanding at irregular Hours, fhall forfeit for

2   every

every Offence 5 *s.* Juſtice of Peace upon View, Confeſſion, or Proof by one Witneſs, may convict ſuch Offender, and grant his Warrant for levying the Penalty.

No Swine ſhall be kept on the Backſide of any paved Street, where the Houſes are con- *Swine.* tiguous, upon Pain of forfeiting the ſame. And the Churchwardens, Conſtables, &c. may Ib. §. 23. in the Day-time, by Warrant from the Lord Mayor or any Juſtice, ſearch for Swine, and drive them away to ſell and diſtribute the Money to the Poor.

See Tit. *London,* Chap. 60.

C H A P. LII.

Horſes.

EVERY Juſtice of Peace (after Sale in open Fair or Market of any ſtoln Horſe, *Claim.* &c.) at any Time within *ſix Months* next after the ſaid * Sale, (or rather next *Stoln Horſe.* after the Felony done) may take and hear the Claim and Proof of the right Owner, 31 Eliz. c. 12. (from whom the ſame was ſtoln, or of his Executors or Adminiſtrators, or other Per- * Lamb. 205. ſons by their Appointment;) which Proof muſt be by two ſufficient Witneſſes upon *See the Stat.* Oath, to be made *within forty Days next enſuing ſuch Claim.* §. 4.

Alſo the ſame Juſtice of Peace may miniſter an Oath to the Party who *bought* P. Fairs 8. *the ſaid Horſe,* or who had the Poſſeſſion and Intereſt thereof, what Money he paid 31 Eliz. c.12. for the ſame *bona fide,* ſo as the right Owner repaying it may have his ſaid Horſe §. 4. again.

(*a*) Note, that in every *Fair or Market* where any *Horſes, Geldings, Mares* or *Colts* are *Toll-taker.* to be ſold, there ought yearly to be appointed out one certain and ſpecial open Place 2 & 3 P. & M. where the ſaid Horſes, &c. ſhall be ſold; and one ſufficient Perſon or more to take *Toll,* c. 7. who ſhall continue in the ſaid Place from the Hour of *Ten before Noon until Sun-ſetting* every Day of the aforeſaid Fair.

(*d*) Alſo Note, every *Sale,* or other Putting away, in any *Fair or Market,* of any *ſtoln Market.* *Horſe,* &c. not being according to the Statute, in every of theſe Particulars following, is 2 & 3 P. & M. void, to take away the Property of the Owner from whom ſuch Horſe was ſtoln, *ſcil.* c. 7. 31 El. 12.

1. If the Horſe be not, in the Time of the ſaid *Fair or Market* between Ten of the *Sale.* Clock and Sun-ſetting, *one Hour together* (at the leaſt) in the open Place of the Fair, &c. where Horſes are commonly ſold, 2 *P. & M.* the Sale is void, &c.

2. If all the Parties to the *Bargain,* being, in the Fair, ſhall not come together with the Horſe to the *Book-keeper* to the open Place appointed, 2 *P. & M.* the Sale is void, &c.

3. If the *Book-keeper, Toll-taker, Bailiff,* or other chief Officer of the ſame *Fair or Voucher.* *Market,* ſhall not take perfect Knowledge of the *Seller* or of the *Voucher, ſc.* of their 31 Eliz. true *Chriſtian Name, Surname, Myſtery* and *Place of Dwelling,* or ſhall not enter all the ſame into his Book, the Sale is void, &c. And one Voucher is enough, if he be a ſuffi- cient and credible Perſon.

4. But if the Voucher be not a ſufficient and credible Perſon, or if the Voucher ſhall 31 Eliz. not know the Seller indeed, or ſhall not truly declare to the Book-keeper, &c. the *Chriſtian Name, Surname, Myſtery* and Place of *Dwelling, as well of himſelf as of the Seller,* the Sale is void, &c.

5. If the *Book-keeper,* &c. ſhall not make *Entry* into his Book of the true Price that *Entry of the* the Horſe is ſold for, with the Colour, and one ſpecial Mark at the leaſt of the ſame *Price.* Horſe, &c. 2 *P. & M. & 31 Eliz.* the Sale is void, &c.

6. So, if a true and perfect Note in Writing, of the Name of the Seller or Voucher, *Book-keeper* and of their Dwelling, &c. and of the Price, be not given to the Buyer by the Book- *muſt give a* keeper, &c. and ſubſcribed with his Hand. *Note to the* *Buyer.* 31 Eliz.

7. And laſtly, if Toll be not paid where Toll is due, or the Book-keeper not paid 2 P. & M. for the Entry, &c.

(*a*) If the Thief which ſtealeth an Horſe ſhall ſell the ſame Horſe in Market overt or *Thief ſelling a* Fair by a *falſe Name,* and it is ſo entred into the Toll-Book, ſuch Miſnaming of the Seller *Horſe by a* maketh the Sale void againſt the right Owner of the Horſe. And this was the Opinion *falſe Name.* of *Windham* and *Rhoads* Juſtices, (upon this Statute 2 & 3 *P. & M.*) *Anno* 30 *El.* in a

K k   Caſe

Caſe between *Gibbs* Plaintiff againſt *Baſtel*, the Caſe being thus: One *Potter* did ſtea the Horſe of the Plaintiff, and ſold him to the Defendant in Market overt, by th Name of *Lyſter*, and ſo it was entred into the Toll-Book, that *Lyſter* ſold the Horſe whereas his Name was *Potter*; whereupon *Gibbs* the Plaintiff brought his Action of th Caſe *ſur Trover* againſt the Defendant *Baſtel*, &c. See *hic poſtea.*

(*d*) Note alſo, that every *Contract for any ſtoln Horſe, &c.* made out of open *Fair* i void, though they be after book'd. *Dyer* 99.

Co. 3. 78, 83.
7 H. 7. 12. Alſo a Sale in a *Fair or Market* overt ſhall not take away the Owner's Property where the *Buyer* doth know that the Property was to another Man, or where the *Buye* knoweth that the Horſe or other Goods were ſtolen.

Co. 5. 83. Alſo to alter the Property of a Stranger who hath Right, the Horſes and all othe Goods are to be ſold in ſuch a Place, or Shop, as is commonly uſed for the Selling o Goods of the ſame Kind or Nature.

Sunday. (*a*) Alſo a Sale upon a *Sunday*, though in a *Fair or Market* overt, ſhall not be a goo Sale to alter the Property of the Goods, by *Brian* 12 *E.* 4. *fol.* 1. *b.*

And indeed *Fairs and Markets* kept upon the *Sabbath* Day are prohibited by the Sta tute of *Winch. cap.* 6. and of 27 *H.* 6. *cap.* 5. And now by the Statutes 1 *Eliz. cap.* 2 & 3 *Jac.* 1. *cap.* 4. all Perſons reſorting upon the *Sabbath* Day to any *Fair or Market* and by the Means thereof abſenting themſelves from the Church, or not abiding at th Church orderly during all the Time of Prayer, Preaching, and other Divine Service, ar to be puniſhed by any Juſtice of Peace, according to the Form of the ſaid Statute 3 *Jac* (which ſee *hic poſtea* Tit. *Recuſants*) or by the *Ordinary*, or Biſhop of the Dioceſe, b the Statute 1 *Eliz.* Or otherwiſe the Offender may be indicted (for ſuch his Abſenc from Church) at the Quarter-Seſſions of the Peace, or General Gaol-Delivery.

Alſo the *Lord of ſuch a Fair or Market* kept upon the *Sabbath Day*, contrary to th Statute, may be therefore indicted, either at the Aſſiſes and General Gaol-delivery, o at the Quarter-Seſſions of the Peace within that County.

But yet for that by *Nonuſer* of a Franchiſe, Fair or Market, they may be forfeite and ſeiſed; therefore Fairs anciently holden upon *Sundays*, or upon other Principa Feaſt-Days, might be holden and kept within three Days before or after any of the ſai Feaſts, after Proclamation firſt made, what Day the Fair ſhall be holden, though th Lord of the Fair hath otherways no Power to keep his Fair but upon ſuch Day. Sta tute 27 *H.* 6. *cap.* 5.

What Horſes may be put in- to Commons.
32 H. 8. c. 13.
§. 2. No *Commoner* in any *Foreſt, Chaſe, Moor, Marſh, Common* or waſte Grounds; no any Officer thereof in *Norfolk, Cambridge, Buckingham, Huntington, Eſſex, Kent South-Hampſhire, North-Wiltſhire, Oxfordſhire, Barkſhire, Worceſter, Gloceſter, Somerſet- ſhire, North-Wales, South-Wales, Bedford, Warwick, Northampton, Yorkſhire, Cheſhire Staffordſhire,* County of the City of *York,* Town of *Gloceſter* and Liberties, *Kingſto upon Hull, Lancaſter, Salop, Leiceſter, Herefordſhire* and *Lincolnſhire,* ſhall put t Paſture there any ſtoned Horſe or Horſes above the Age of two Years, and under th Height of fifteen Handfuls, to be meaſured from the loweſt Part of the Hoof of th Forefoot unto the higheſt Part of the Wither, every Handful to contain four Inche by the Standard, to feed or depaſture there, upon Pain of Forfeiture of the Horſes found there. 32 *H.* 8. *cap.* 13.

Seizure.
Ib. §. 3. Theſe Perſons finding ſuch Horſes therein, ſhall go to the Keeper of ſuch Foreſt o Chaſe, his Deputy or Deputies, or to the Conſtable, Bailiff, Headborough, Borſholde or Tithingman of any Town next adjoining, and command them to go and bring ſuch Horſes to the Pound, there to be meaſured by ſuch Officer or Officers, in the Pre ſence of three honeſt Perſons to be named and appointed by the Officer, and if he be once found contrary, ſuch Perſon challenging him may take him to his own Uſe.

Neglect.
Ib. §. 4. If any of the ſaid Officers or Perſons to be appointed ſhall refuſe to meaſure, or not meaſure juſtly, every of them ſhall forfeit for not doing, or refuſing, 40 *s.*

Drift of Com- mons.
Ib. §. 6. All Foreſts, Chaſes, Commons, Moors, Marſhes, Heaths and Waſte-Grounds in *England* and *Wales,* ſhall be driven yearly by the Owners or Officers of the ſame, and by the Conſtables, Headboroughs, Bailiffs, Borſholders and Tithingmen, within whoſe Limits they lie, upon Pain that every of the ſaid Officers not ſo doing at *Michaelmas* every Year, or fifteen Days after, ſhall forfeit 40 *s.* for every Time, and the Lords, Owners and Poſſeſſors may by the Officers aforeſaid make ſuch Drift at any other Time in the Year.

If upon fuch Drift there fhall be found any Mare, Filly, Fole or Gelding, that fhall Killing fit. not then be thought able or likely to grow to be profitable for Labour, in the Difcre- Ib. §. 7. tion of the Drivers, or the greateft Number of them, the Drivers fhall caufe the fame Beaft to be killed.

The Juftices of Peace and Stewards of Leets may inquire of all Defaults, Contempts, Who may de- Omiffions and Offences againft this Act, and the Prefentments in the Leet fhall be certi- termine it, and how. fied to the next Seffions, or to the *Cuftos Rotulorum* within forty Days after it is made; Ib. §. 8. and the Juftices may determine the fame by Examination, or otherwife; and if the Steward imbezil, conceal, or do not certify, he fhall forfeit 40 s. for every Offence; a Moiety to the King, the other Moiety to the Profecutor that fues for it in the Seffions by Bill or Information.

This act as to the Marfhes, Fens, Seggy Ground in *Ely, Cambridgfhire, Huntingdon-* 8 El c. 8. §. 2 *fhire, Northampton, Lincoln, Norfolk* and *Suffolk,* fhall be repealed; but none fhall put & 3. into thefe Grounds any ftoned Horfe above two Years old not of the Height of 13 Handfuls, to be meafured as aforefaid.

Nor fhall this Act extend to the County of *Cornwall,* by 21 *Jac.* 1. *cap.* 28. 21 Jac. 1. c. *fect.* 12.   28 § 12.

Concerning Tranfporting of Horfes, Geldings and Mares, *vide* Tit. *Tranfportation,* Chap. 100. *&c.*

Clergy is taken from Acceffaries in Horfe-Stealing both before and after the Fact.

Selling a Horfe in Fair or Market by a wrong Name, tho' all the Circumftances in the Statute are purfued, makes the Sale void: As for Inftance,

A Horfe was *loft* and fold by *T. S.* in *Smithfield* by the Name of *W. H.* when there Palm. 486. was no fuch Man: Adjudged that the Property was not altered, becaufe it did not ap- W. Jones 163. S. C. pear that the Horfe was ftole, and probably the Owner could not prove that it was ftole.

C H A P. LIII. [a]

Houfe of Correction.

EVERY Perfon feifed of an Eftate in Fee-fimple, may by Deed inrolled in Chancery Charities. erect, found and eftablifh one or more Hofpitals, abiding Places or Houfes of Cor- 39 El. 5. rection, as well for Suftentation of Poor, as to fet Poor on Work, *&c.* See this Sta- tute well explained, 2 *Inft.* 720. And that Act is made perpetual by 21 *Jac.* 1. * * The 39 El. c. 4. inferted in former Editions, is repealed by 12 Ann. ft. 2. c. 23.

By 7 *Jac.* 1. *cap.* 4. it was enacted, that a convenient Houfe or Houfes fhould be Erection. provided, with a Backfide adjoining, with Mills, Turns, Cards, and neceffary Imple- 7 Jac. 1. 4. ments to fet idle Perfons on Work in fome convenient Place or Town of the County, which fhall be purchafed, conveyed and affured to fuch Perfons as the Juftices of Peace in Seffions fhall think fit in Truft to be employed, *&c.* or elfe every Juftice of Peace was to forfeit 5 *l.* to be employed for the Erecting, Procuring, *&c.* fuch Houfe.

The Juftices of Peace in their Seffions may elect and appoint one or more Perfons to Governor. be Governor or Mafter of the Houfe of Correction, who fhall have Power to fet Rogues, Ib. §. 4. Vagabonds, and idle and diforderly Perfons to Work and Labour, being able; and to punifh them by putting Fetters or Gives on them, and by moderate Whipping of them; which Perfons fhall not be chargeable to the County, but fhall have fuch Allowance as they deferve by their Labour.

The Juftices of their Seffions may appoint a yearly Allowance to the Mafter of the Allowance. Houfe of Correction, to be paid Quarterly beforehand by the Treafurer appointed by Ib. §. 6. 43 El. 2. The Mafter giving Security for Continuance and Performance of the Service, which if the Treafurer fhall not do, the Mafter may levy it, as the Treafurer might have done by that Statute.

If the Governor fhall not every Quarter-Seffions yield a true and lawful Account to Governor's the Juftices of all Perfons committed to their Cuftody, or if the Perfons committed be Duty. troublefome to the Country by going abroad, or fhall efcape away before they be law- Ib. §. 9. fully delivered, the Juftices may in Seffions fet down fuch Fines and Penalties on the Mafter as they fhall think fit, which fhall be paid to the Treafurer.

The

Mittimus.
2 Inft. 730.
* *See this Sta-*
tute well ex-
pounded and
explained by my Lord Coke. 2 Inft. 728.

.The Juftices Mittimus to the Houfe of Correction may be moft fafely made upon this Statute, *Quia otiofa & inordinata perfona,* for that he is an idle and diforderly Perfon, or for that he is an idle Perfon, or that he is a diforderly *. *Vide poftea* in *Mittimus,* Chap. 178.

See alfo Chap. 83. *Rogues and Vagabonds.*

C H A P. LIV.

Hue and Cry.

When, and
how to be
made.

(a) **H**UE *and Cry* fignifieth a Purfuit of one or more that have committed Felony, and fly for the fame.

(d) Every Juftice of Peace may caufe Hue and Cry, frefh Suit and Search to be made, upon any *Murder, Robbery, Theft,* or other Felony committed: And this he may do by Force of the Commiffion, the firft *Affignavimus.*

(a) The Party robbed, or fome one of the Company of one murdered or robbed, muft fpeedily come to the Conftable of the next Town, or to fome other Habitant dwelling near the Place where the Felony was committed, and muft give Notice of the faid Felony, and will him to raife Hue and Cry, or to make Purfuit after the Felon: And the Conftable muft forthwith make Search in his Town; and if the Felon be not there found, then to give Notice to the next Towns, &c.

28 Ed. 3.
cap. 11.
27 Eliz. 17.
§. 10 & 11.

(d) Note, That all *Hues and Cries* ought to be made *immediately* after Notice given of the Felony done, from Town to Town, and from County to County, and by Horfemen and Footmen; otherwife it is no lawful Purfuit.

Note alfo, When *Hue and Cry* is levied upon any Robbery or other Felony, the Officer of the Town where the Felony was done (as alfo the Officer whence Hue and Cry fhall be after levied) ought to fend to every other Town round about him, and not to one next Town only: And in fuch Cafes it is needful to give Notice in Writing (to the Purfuers) of the Things ftolen, and of the Colour and Marks thereof; as alfo to defcribe the Perfon of the Felon, his Apparel and Horfe, &c. and fhew which Way he is gone, if it may be.

(a) Sir *Nickolas Hide,* in his Charge at *Cambridge* Affifes in Lent, 1622. delivered, That Hue and Cry muft be made or purfued with Horfemen and Footmen; and that not only a private Search is to be made in every Town, but that they muft raife the Country as they go, and all ftill to follow the Hue and Cry, as againft a common Enemy.

Alfo the Officers of every Town to which Hue and Cry fhall come, ought to fearch in all fufpected Houfes and Places within their Limits: And as well the Officers, as all other Perfons which fhall purfue the Hue and Cry, may attach and ftay all fuch Perfons, as in their Search or Purfuit they fhall find to be fufpicious; and thereupon fhall carry them before fome Juftice of the Peace of the County where they are taken, to be examined where they were at the Time when the Felony was committed, &c.

1 Leon. 323.

Where a Perfon is robbed, and the Juftice refufeth to take his Examination, an Action on the Cafe lieth againft him, becaufe in this Cafe he doth not act as a Judge of Record, but as a Minifter appointed by the Statute; for which Reafon he may take the Examination of a Perfon robbed, though the Juftice is not in the County where the Robbery was done, becaufe he taketh the Oath, not by Virtue of his Office, but by Virtue of the Statute, as aforefaid.

Cro. Car.211.
W Jones
239. S. C.

Owen 7.
Goldf.58.S.P.

'Tis not material in what Parifh the Robbery was done, but there muft be a Certainty of the Hundred.

Goldf. 86.

Goods delivered to a Carrier were feifed in one Hundred, and the Horfe and Goods were led into another Hundred, and there they were taken away; adjudged, that the Hundred fhall be charged where the Horfe and Goods were feifed, becaufe at that Inftant of Time they were in the Poffeffion of the Offenders; but it was no Robbery till he came into the fecond Hundred, if the Carrier himfelf had led his Horfe thither, for then it had been ftill in his Poffeffion.

But

But if a Man is affaulted in one Hundred, and he efcapes into another Hundred, and Hutt. 125. is purfued and robbed there, in fuch Cafe the fecond Hundred is liable.

The Servant was robbed, and he ought to take the Oath, and not the Mafter, becaufe Cro. Eliz. the Servant might know fome of the Robbers, but the Mafter could not, becaufe he was 142. not at the Time in Company of his Servant. 1 Leon. 323.
S. C.

So where a Servant was robbed of his Mafter's Goods, and brought an Action againft the Hundred, in which he declared, that he was poffefs'd, &c. *ut de bonis fuis propriis,* 4 Mod. 505. &c. and the Jury found, that he was robbed of 20 *l.* of his Mafter's Money, and 20 *s.* of 2 Salk. 614. his own Money ; adjudged, that this Action was maintainable by the Servant ; for by the bare Poffeffion he is intitled to the Money as his own againft all Perfons but the right Owner.

There is another Cafe where the *Servant* was robbed, and the *Mafter* brought the 2 Salk. 613. Action againft the Hundred ; the Jury found that the *Mafter* was a *Quaker,* and would not take an Oath to anfwer whether he did know any of the Robbers ; adjudged, that the *Mafter* might bring the Action, and that the Oath of his *Servant* was fufficient, efpecially if he was not robbed in the Company of his *Mafter,* but if robbed in his Prefence, then the *Mafter* muft make the Oath ; which the *Quaker* refufing, he could not recover againft the Hundred, becaufe the Statute 27 *Eliz.* was made in Favour of the Inhabitants, to prevent Combination amongft Robbers and thofe who were robbed.

See the Stat. 8 Geo. 2. *of* Hue and Cry *in the* Title Robbery, *Chap.* 84.

See alfo 2 Hal. Hift. P. C. p. 98, &c. *and the* New Abrid. *under this* Title.

C H A P. LV.

Hunting.

UPON Information given to any Juftice of Peace of the County where any unlaw- Hunting in Vizards. ful Hunting of Deer or Conies (by Night, or with painted Faces, or other Difguifing) in any Foreft, Park, or Warren fhall be had, of any Perfon fufpected thereof ; fuch Juftice may make a Warrant to the Sheriff, Conftable, Bailiff, or other Officers, to take the Party, and to bring him before him, or before any other Juftice of Peace of the fame County, who may examine him of that Hunting, and of the Doers thereof : And if he conceal that Hunting, or any Offender with him therein, then the faid Con- 1 H. 7. c. 7.
P. Juft. 16. cealment fhall be * Felony in fuch Concealer. But if he then confefs the Truth of all * Quære, that he fhall be examined of and knoweth in that Behalf ; then his Offence of Hunting If they kill nothing. fhall be but Trefpafs, and fineable : The Fine to be affeffed at the next General Seffions Dy. fo. 50. of the Peace, by the Juftices there. See *poftea* Tit. *Felony by Statute,* Chap. 160. pl. 5.

Alfo to difobey fuch a Warrant, or to make *Refcous* thereupon ; fo that the Execution thereof cannot be had, is Felony. *Vide ut fupra.*

(a) If any fhall by Night or Day, unlawfully break or enter into any Park impaled, or In Parks. feveral Grounds clofed with Wall, Pale, or Hedge, and ufed for the keeping, breeding, 5 El. 21. and cherifhing of Deer ; and being thereof convicted at the Suit of the Queen, or Party, fhall be imprifoned three Months, and pay the Party treble Damages ; and be bound with Sureties to the Good Behaviour for feven Years, or elfe continue in Prifon feven Years.

This Act extends not to Parks, or inclofed Grounds, then after to be made and ufed for Deer, without the Grant or Licenfe of the Queen, her Heirs, Succeffors or Progenitors.

The Juftices of Peace in their Seffions, may hear and determine the Offences of Taking, Hawking, Fifhing and Hunting againft that Statute ; and the Party may have his Remedy before them there, and may make out Procefs as well upon Indictments, as by Bill of Complaint, Information, or any other Action.

The Party grieved, upon Satisfaction to him made of his Damages ; and upon Confeffion by the Offenders in open Seffions, may releafe the Suretifhip for the Good Behaviour, at any Time, within the feven Years : And if the Party be bound, if he fhall come in open Seffions, and confefs the Offence, and be forry for it, and pay the· Party his treble Damages, may in the fame, or any other Seffions, releafe the Recognizance. 5 *El.* 21. But it feems, that no other Juftices, but thofe before whom fuch Confeffion is made,

can

can in the fame, or any other Seffions, releafe or difcharge the Recognizance. And it feemeth alfo, if the Party lie in Prifon for Want of Sureties for the Good Behaviour, after the three Months; neither the Party grieved, nor Juftices, upon Confeffion, can difcharge him.

And forafmuch as many Grounds ufed for the Keeping of Deer, were altered or incl ofed fince 5 *El.* 21. a Statute was made 3 *Jac.* 1. 13. with the fame Provifions touching Deer, but extended to the Killing of Conies alfo; but this Statute of 3 *Jac.* 1. 13. extends only to the Killing, Hunting, and Chafing of Conies in the Night, and not in the Day-time; nor to any Park, or inclofed Grounds, after to be ufed for keeping Deer and Conies, without Grant.

Hunting in Corn.
23 Eliz. c. 10.

No Perfon fhall Hawk, or with his Spaniels hunt in any Ground, where Corn or other Grain fhall then grow (except in his own Ground) at fuch Time as any eared or codded Corn or Grain, fhall be ftanding; nor before it be cocked, fhocked, &c. upon Pain to forfeit for every Time he fhall fo hawk or hunt, without the Confent of the Owner, forty Shillings to the Owner: Which, if he pay not within ten Days after Conviction, he may be imprifoned a Month, without Bail, or may be recorded by Action; and the Juftices of Peace may hear and determine the fame in their Seffions: And every Juftice of Peace may examine the Offender, and bind him to the Seffions to anfwer the Offence, and to pay the Penalties, and receive the Punifhment.

(*d*) The Juftice of Peace that fhall take the Examination of an Offender for unlawful Hunting in Parks, &c. as aforefaid, may after fuch Examination bind the Offender to his Good Behaviour, that he may be forth-coming, till the Offence and Refidue of the Offenders be fully examined: Otherwife, if it fhall after appear, that the Offender hath concealed any Thing whereby the Offence becomes Felony, then the Offender perhaps will not be found.

1 Jac. 1. c. 27.
P. Pheafant 7.

Alfo all fuch unlawful Hunting, if it be by Three or more, will prove a *Riot*.

Greyhound.

Whofoever fhall have or keep any Greyhound or Setting-dog, (not having fufficient Living according to this Statute;) or fhall trace or courfe any Hare in the Snow, or

Hare.

otherwife deftroy, kill, or take any Hare; the faid Offences being proved, &c. before two Juftices of Peace, the faid Offenders fhall be by them committed to the Gaol, &c. *Vide* Tit. *Partridges* more fully hereof.

Co. 11. 86, 87.

And yet Hunting and Hawking, and fuch other Paftimes, every Man may ufe upon his own Lands at his Pleafure, fo far as they be not reftrained by Act of Parliament. But no Man may make a Park or Warren within his own Ground, without the King's Grant or Licenfe; and therefore fuch a Park or Warren (made without Licenfe) is not within the Stat. of 1 *H.* 7. 7. See *Br. Warren* 1. *Co. Lit.* 233.

What a Park is, and the Difference between a Park, a Foreft, and a Chafe, and what be Beafts or Fowls of Park, Chafe and Warren, *vide Co. L.* 233.

There be divers other Statutes made againft *Hunting*, &c. which be very Penal, but not to be dealt withal by Juftices of Peace, except at their General Seffions. See more of them *hic poftea*, Tit. *Bailment*, & *Stat.* 3 *Jac.* 1. *hic antea* Tit. *Guns.*

This Stat. extends to all Perfons of whatever Eftate.

If any fhall hunt, deftroy, and kill a *Hare* in the *Snow*, and being thereof convicted, fhall forfeit fix Shillings eight Pence for every one. 14 *H.* 8. 10.

Search.
22 & 23 Car. 2. c. 25. §. 2.

One Juftice of Peace, by Warrant under his Hand and Seal, may authorize any Game-keeper (which any Lord of a Manor, of the Degree of an Efquire, may appoint under his Hand and Seal) or any other Perfon or Perfons, to fearch in the Day-time the Houfes, Outhoufes, and other Places of Perfons thereby prohibited, as upon good Ground fhall be fufpected to keep Guns, Bows, Greyhounds, Setting-dogs, Ferrets, Coney-dogs, or other Dogs, to deftroy Hares or Conies, Hayes, Tramels, and other Nets, Lowbels, Hare-pipes, Snares, and other Engines; and them to feife and keep for the Lord of the Manor, or to deftroy them.

Ib. §. 3.

All Perfons are thereby prohibited, except fuch as have Lands and Tenements, or fome other Eftate of Inheritance in his own or his Wife's Right, of One hundred Pounds *per Annum*; or for Term of Life, or have Leafe or Leafes for ninety-nine Years, or a longer Term of One hundred and fifty Pounds *per Annum*, the Son and Heir of an Efquire, or other Perfon of higher Degree. The Owners and Keepers of Forefts, Parks, Chafes and Warrens, being ftocked with Deer and Conies for their neceffary Ufe in refpect thereof.

Warren.
Ib. §. 4.

Any Perfon that fhall enter any Warren, or Ground ufed for the Breeding and Keeping of Conies (although the fame be not inclofed) and there fhall chafe, take, or kill any Conies, being convicted thereof by his Confeffion, or by the Oath of one fufficient

Witnefs,

Witnefs, before any Juftice of Peace, within one Month after the Offence, fhall pay to the Party grieved treble Damages and Cofts, and be imprifoned for three Months, and after, till he find Sureties for the Good Behaviour.

If any Perfons in the Night-time fhall kill or take any Conies upon the Borders of any *Ib. §. 5.* Warrens, or other Grounds, lawfully ufed for the breeding or keeping of Conies, except the Owner or Occupier of the Soil, or other Perfons imployed by them, whereupon they are killed or taken, and be thereof convicted as laft aforefaid, they fhall give the Party fuch Satisfaction, and within fuch Time as fhall be appointed by the Juftice before whom fuch Conviction is, and fhall pay to the Overfeers for the Poor's Ufe, fuch Sums of Money, not exceeding ten Shillings, as the Juftice fhall think fit : And in Default of fuch Payment, fuch Juftice may commit the Party to the Houfe of Correction for fuch Time as he fhall think fit, not exceeding one Month.

Any Perfon that fhall be found or apprehended, fetting, or ufing any Snares, Hare- *Ib. §. 6.* pipes, or like Engines, and fhall be thereof convict as aforefaid, fhall be punifhed as in the faid laft Claufe is mentioned.

Any Perfon grieved by any fuch Judgment, may appeal to the next General Quarter- *Ib. §. 9.* Seffions, who fhall give fuch Relief as is agreeable to that Act: Which Judgment fhall be final, if no Title to any Land or Royalty be concerned.

If any Perfon having no Chafe, Park or Foreft of their own, keep, or caufe to be *19H. 7. c. 11.* kept any Nets, called Deer-Hayes, or Buck-ftalls, by the Space of a Month after Procla- mation made of that Statute, he fhall forfeit forty Pounds a Month for keeping of them.

No Perfon fhall ftalk, or caufe to be ftalked, with Bufh or Beafts to any Deer in any Park, Chafe, or Foreft, but in his own Ground, Park, Chafe or Foreft, without Licence of the Owner, Mafter, or Keeper, on Pain of Forfeiture of ten Pounds.

Two Juftices of Peace in their Seffions may call the Perfon fufpected before them, and examine him ; and if upon Examination the Party be found in Default, then to commit him to Prifon, till he find Sureties to pay the Fine ; and thefe Juftices that examine him, fhall have the tenth Part of the Forfeiture.

Any one that fhall unlawfully courfe, hunt, &c. any Red or Fallow-Deer in any Foreft, *Deer-ftealers.* Chafe, &c. or other Ground inclofed, where Deer are or fhall be ufually kept, or fhall be *3 & 4 W. &* aiding therein, and fhall be convicted by Confeffion, or the Oath of one Witnefs, before a *M. c. 10. §. 2.* Juftice of Peace of the County where the Offence fhall be committed, or the Party appre- hended, within twelve Months after the Offence done, he fhall forfeit for every fuch Of- fence twenty Pounds, and for every Deer wounded, taken or killed thirty Pounds, to be *Penalty.* levied by Diftrefs and Sale of Goods, by Warrant from the Juftice before whom the Con- viction fhall be made; one third Part to the Informer, another third Part to the Poor of the Parifh where the Offence fhall be committed, and the other third Part to the Owner of the Deer. And for Want of Diftrefs fhall be imprifoned a Year, and fet in the Pillory an Hour, on fome Market-day in the Town next adjoining to the Place where the Offence was committed.

Conftables, &c. by a Juftice's Warrant, may enter and fearch for ftolen Goods, the *fearch.* Houfes or other Places of fufpected Perfons; and if any Venifon or Skins of Deer or Toils *Ib. §. 3.* be found, fhall carry fuch Offender before a Juftice of Peace ; and if he do not give a good Account how he came by them, or produce the Party of whom he bought them, or prove fuch Sale upon Oath, he fhall be convicted of fuch Offence, and be fubject to the Penalties inflicted for killing of Deer.

No *Certiorari* fhall be allowed to remove any Conviction, or other Proceeding upon *Certiorari.* this Act, unlefs the Party convicted fhall before it be allowed, become bound to the Profe- *Ib. §. 6.* cutors in fifty Pounds, with Sureties to be approved by the faid Juftice, to pay within a Month after Conviction confirm'd, or a *Procedendo* granted, their full Cofts to be afcer- tain'd upon Oath.

Any Perfon that fhall in the Night-time pull down or deftroy any Pails or Walls of any *Deftruction of* Park or Foreft, where Red or Fallow-Deer fhall be kept, fuch Perfon being convicted by *Pails.* Oath of one Witnefs before a Juftice of Peace, fhall by fuch Juftice's Warrant fuffer three *Ib. §. 9.* Months Imprifonment.

By 5 *Geo.* 1. *cap.* 15. fuch Offender fhall be fubject to the Forfeitures by the Act 3 & *5Geo. 1. c. 15.* 4 *W. & M. cap.* 10. inflicted for killing one Deer. *§. 6.*

Any Profecution for any Offence againft the Statute 3 & 4 *W. & M. cap.* 10. may be *9 G. 1. c. 22.* commenced within three Years from the Offence committed. *§. 13.*

5 G. 1. c. 15.
§. 1.

No *Certiorari* shall be allowed to remove the Proceedings concerning any Matter in the Act 3 & 4 *W. & M. cap.* 10. unless the Party convicted shall before Allowance of such *Certiorari*, and at the same Time that Security is given for Payment of Costs, become bound to the Justice before whom such Conviction was made, with Sureties to be approved of by the Justice, in the Penalty of 60 *l.* for each Offence, with Condition to prosecute such *Certiorari* with Effect, and to pay such Justice the Forfeiture due by such Conviction, to be distributed as the Statute directs, or to render the Person convicted to such Justice in one Month after the Conviction shall be confirmed, or a *Procedendo* granted; and in Default the Justice may proceed to Execution, as if no *Certiorari* had been awarded.

Ib. §. 2.

After delivering the Rule to the Justice, whereby such Conviction has been confirmed by a Superior Court, the Justice may proceed as if a *Procedendo* had been granted.

Ib. §. 4.

Every Person convicted by Virtue of the said Statute, shall, before he be discharged out of Custody, become bound to the Person against whom the Offence was committed, in 50 *l.* with Condition for his good Behaviour, and not to offend in like Manner; and on Refusal to enter into such Bond, he shall be committed to the County Gaol till such Bond be given: And if such Person after his becoming bound, be convicted for any Matter in the said Statute, the Bond shall be forfeited, and the Penalty recovered with Costs in any Court at *Westminster*, which Penalties shall be distributed in the same Manner that the Forfeitures are to be by the said Statute; and the Party convicted shall be likewise liable to the Penalties therein.

Ib. §. 5.

If the Keeper or other Officer of any Forest, *&c.* where Deer are usually kept, shall be convicted on the Statute of 3 & 4 *W. & M. c.* 10. for killing or taking away any Deer, or being aiding therein, without Consent of the Owner or Person chiefly intrusted with the Custody of such Forest, *&c.* he shall forfeit 50 *l.* for each Deer so killed, *&c.* to be levied by Distress, and distributed as the Forfeitures of the said Act are to be; and for Want of Distress he shall be imprisoned three Years, and be set in the Pillory two Hours on some Market-day in the Town next the Place where the Offence was committed, by the Chief or Under-Officers of such Town.

5 G. 1. c. 28.
§. 1.

By 5 *Geo.* 1. *cap.* 28. Persons entring any Park, *&c.* and wilfully wounding or killing Deer, being convicted thereof on Indictment before any Judge of Gaol-delivery of the County wherein such Park, *&c.* lies, shall be transported to the Plantations for seven Years.

9 G. 1. c. 22.
§. 13.

By 9 *Geo.* 1. *cap.* 22. *sect.* 13. if any Venison or Skin of a Deer be found in the Custody of any Person, and it shall appear that he bought it of one that might justly be suspected to have unlawfully come by the same, and does not produce the Party of whom he bought it, or prove upon Oath the Name and Place of Abode of such Party, then the Person who bought the same shall be convicted of such Offence by any one Justice of Peace, and shall be subject to the Penalties for killing a Deer by *Stat.* 3 & 4 *W. & M. cap.* 10.

See more in *Chap.* 160. *Felony by Statute.*

Husband and Wife. See *Chap.* 157.

Indictments. See *Chap.* 184.

Informer and Informations. See *Chap.* 191.

C H A P. LVI. (*a*)

Innholder.

Horse-bread.
21 Jac. 1.
c. 21. §. 2.

NO Hostler or Innholder shall make his Horse-bread within his Hostery, but Bakers shall make it; and the Assize shall be kept, and the Weight be reasonable, after the Price of Corn in the Market adjoining; and they shall sell their Horse-bread, Hay, Oats, Beans, Pease, Provender, and all Kind of Victuals, both for Man and Beast, at reasonable Gain, having respect to what the same shall be sold for in the Market adjoining, without taking any Thing for Litter.

2   · II

If an Innholder live in a Town or Village, which is no City, Town Corporate, or Ib. §. 3.
Market-Town; yet being a Thorow-fare and common Paſſage, and no Baker dwelling
there, he may make Horſe-bread in his Houſe of lawful Aſſiſe and Price.

Juſtices of Peace (amongſt others) may hear and determine Offences againſt this Act; *Penalty.*
and the Party offending ſhall be fined according to his Offence, and being once convicted, Ib. §. 4.
for the ſecond Offence he ſhall ſuffer Impriſonment for a Month, and for the third Offence
ſhall be ſet upon the Pillory without being redeemed for Money. And if after ſuch Judgment of Pillory, he ſhall offend again, he ſhall be forejudged of keeping an Inn any more.
Where Innholders are within the Statutes of Alehouſes and Tipling, ſee Tit. *Alehouſes.*

Every Man may erect an Inn, that can and will; for it is not a Franchiſe, as was reſolved in Parliament, 20 *Jac. Roll's Abridgment, Part* 2. p. 84.

It was reſolved by all the Judges, that any Perſon might erect an Inn to lodge Travel- Hutt. 99.
lers, without any Licenſe or Allowance ſo to do.

But if an Inn uſeth the Trade of an Alehouſe, as almoſt all Inkeepers do, it ſhall be 1 Bulſt. 109.
within the Statutes made about Alehouſes.

An Innkeeper ſhall not be liable to make any Satisfaction for a Robbery done in his Inn Moor 876.
and in the Chamber of any of his Gueſts hired for ſome Time; but if he leaves Goods in his 2 Brownl.
Chamber, and returns again the ſame Night, the Innkeeper ſhall be liable for ſuch Goods 254. S. C.
ſtolen.

Latch 88. S.P.
Bendloe 173.
S. C.
Noy 126. 2 Cro. 188. S. C.

If an Innkeeper bids his Gueſt take the Key of his Chamber and lock the Door, and that Moor 78.
he will not take the Charge of the Goods, yet if they are ſtolen, he ſhall be anſwerable, becauſe he is charged by Law for all Things which come to his Inn, and he cannot diſcharge
himſelf by ſuch or the like Words.

Innkeepers are bound by the Law to receive Gueſts, and for that Reaſon they may detain 1 Salk. 388.
their Goods till they are paid; but *Holt* Chief Juſtice doubted, whether a Man is a Gueſt
by ſetting up his Horſe at an Inn, becauſe the Horſe muſt be fed, by which the Innkeeper
hath ſome Gain, tho' the Owner never lay in the Inn; but if he had left a Trunk or a Box
there, he is a Gueſt.

The Queſtion was, whether Houſes kept for Lodgings in *Tunbridge* or *Epſom*, and dreſſing Meat for Lodgers, and finding Hay and Oats for their Horſes, were properly Inns for
quartering Soldiers, according to the Statute 4 & 5 *W.* 3. *cap.* 13. it was inſiſted that they
were, being common and publick Houſes kept for Gain, and therefore within the equitable
Conſtruction of that Statute; but adjudged that they were not, becauſe the Soldiers are
quartered againſt a Man's Will; but in Inns Perſons are quartered willingly and upon Acceſs; and an Innkeeper is indictable if he refuſe a Gueſt, but the Owner of one of thoſe
Houſes is not, if he refuſe a Lodger; nor a Livery-ſtable is not properly an Inn, becauſe
the Accommodation is for Horſes only.

C H A P. LVII.

Inrolment.

ANY one Juſtice of Peace may join with the Clerk of the Peace, in taking the Inrol- 27 H. 8. 16.
ment of any Indenture of Bargain and Sale of Lands, &c. lying in that County where
he is a Juſtice, and it is good.

(*a*) Now the ſaid Juſtice of Peace, and the Clerk of the Peace, are to take for the inrolling
f the ſame Deed indented in Parchment, &c. theſe Fees following, *viz.* where the Lands *Fees.*
exceed not the yearly Value of forty Shillings, they are to take two Shillings, *ſcil.* twelve
Pence for the Juſtice, and twelve Pence for the Clerk. And where the Lands exceed the
yearly Value of forty Shillings, there they are to take five Shillings, *ſcil.* two Shillings ſix
Pence for the Juſtice, and two Shillings ſix Pence for the Clerk. *Ibid.*

(*d*) But ſuch Deed (and all other Deeds, to be inrolled according to this Statute) muſt be Co. 5. 29. b.
indented *revera*, and muſt be inrolled within ſix Months after the Date of the ſame In- Co. 5. 1. b.
denture: And if it have no Date, then within ſix Months after the Delivery of the Deed; Daliſon.
or if it be inrolled the very Day of the Date of the Deed, or the very laſt Day of the ſix Dyer 218.
Months, it is ſufficient.

M m   Note;

Computation,

Note; Herein you muſt account twenty-eight Days to every Month, and not above, (ſcil.) Four Weeks to the Month.

Co. 6. 62.

Note alſo the Difference when a Statute accounteth by the Year, Half-Year, or Quarter, and when by the Month ; for a Year, Half a Year, or a Quarter of a Year, ſhall be accounted according to the Kalendar, and by the Days in the Kalendar, and not after twenty-eight Days to the Month. And a Year, or a Twelve-month (in the ſingular Number) includes the whole Year according to the Kalendar. But twelve Months (in the plural Number) or eight Months, or fix * Months, &c. ſhall be accounted after twenty-eight Days to every Month: For the Month, by the Common Law of *England*, is but eight and twenty Days. And ſo

Co 5. 135.
* Except in a
Quare Imp.
See Co. ib.

$$\text{Whereas}\begin{cases}\text{Three Months}\\\text{Six Months}\\\text{Twelve Months}\end{cases}\text{hath but}\begin{cases}84\\168\\336\end{cases}\text{Days.}$$

$$\text{The}\begin{cases}\text{Quarter of a Year}\\\text{Half-Year}\\\text{Year}\end{cases}\text{hath}\begin{cases}91\\182\\365\end{cases}\text{Days.}$$

Dyer 345.

Ter centum, ter viginti, cum quinque diebus,
Sex horas, neque plus integer annus habet.

And as to theſe fix Hours, the Law giveth no Regard to them; and yet theſe fix Hours every fourth Year make a Day, and ſo make the Leap-Year, and this Leap-year containeth in it Three hundred ſixty and fix Days.

Note alſo for the Year, That the *Julian* Year, (inſtituted by *Julius Cæſar*) beginneth the firſt Day of *January*, and ſo doth the Empire begin; the *Hebrews*, the Firſt of *April*; the Church of *Rome* on the twenty-fifth of *December :* But in all Matters legal with us, the Year beginneth not till the twenty-fifth Day of *March.* And therefore when in an Indictment, or other Writing or Deed, it ſhall be ſet down, (or the Writing ſhall be dated *Anno Dom.* 1617.) it muſt be accounted according to the Computation of the Church of *England*, which beginneth the Year upon the twenty-fifth Day of *March*; upon which Day our Saviour Jeſus Chriſt aroſe from Death, as it is holden, Dr. *White's Def.* 151. and upon which Day Chriſt was conceived in the Virgin's Womb, (as ſome write) and ſo was born in *December* ; and then the Year of Our Lord muſt be accounted rather from his Conception and Incarnation, than his Nativity ; and upon which Day the World, *Adam* our firſt Father, was created, as it is holden by others: But I leave theſe Things to Antiquaries. See the Hiſtory of *Venice*, pag. 4 & 5.

Bible impreſ.
1611.

Journeymen Taylors. See *Labourers.*

Judgment. See Chap. 188.

Jury. See Chap. 186.

The Form of the Precept to return a Jury. See Chap. 115.

Justice of Peace. See Chap. 173, 189.

CHAP. LVIII.

Labourers.

One Juſt.
5 El. c. 4.
§. 22.

EVERY Juſtice of Peace, upon Requeſt, may cauſe all ſuch Artificers and other Perſons fit to labour, to work by the Day in Hay-time, and Harveſt-time, for the Saving of Corn and Hay, and may, upon their Refuſal, impriſon them in the Stocks, by the Space of two Days and one Night.

And

(a) And the Conſtable upon Complaint ſhall have Authority to ſet the Offender in the Stocks, and neglecting ſo to do, ſhall forfeit 40 s.

(d) Any one Juſtice of Peace may licenſe under his Hand and Seal ſuch Labourers as ^{Ib. §. 23.} paſs in Hay-harveſt and Corn-harveſt from one County to another to work.

Any one Juſtice of Peace (upon Complaint to him made) may compel any fit Perſon ^{*Apprentice.*} (in his Diſcretion) to be bound as an Apprentice with any one that ſhall require him to ^{Ib. §. 35.} Husbandry, or any other Art, &c. And upon their Refuſal may commit them to Ward, there to remain until they will be bound to ſerve as an Appretentice, according to the Statute.

(a) No Perſon ſhall be compelled to be an Apprentice, unleſs he be under twenty-one ^{Ib. §. 36.} Years of Age.

Apprentice ſignifieth one that is bound, by Covenant in Writing indented, to ſerve another Man for certain Years, and that his Maſter ſhall in the mean Time endeavour to inſtruct him in his Art or Trade. The uſual Covenants for Apprentices, ſee *Chap.* 181. And note, that in ſuch and other Covenants, *Conventio legem vincit.*

Every Perſon being a Houſholder, and uſing Half a Plough-land, at leaſt, may take ^{5 El. 4. §. 25.} an Apprentice above ten Years of Age, and under eighteen, to ſerve in Husbandry.

Every Houſholder, twenty-four Years old, dwelling in any City, Borough, or Town ^{Ib. §. 26.} Corporate, and exerciſing any Art, Myſtery, or manual Occupation, may retain the Son of a Freeman not occupying Husbandry ; nor being a Labourer, and inhabiting in the ſame, or in any other City, &c. to ſerve and be bound as an Apprentice for ſeven Years, at leaſt, ſo as the Term expire not before the Apprentice be twenty-four Years old. In ^{Ib. §. 28.} Market-Towns not Corporate, they may take the Child of an Artificer.

No Merchant, Mercer, Draper, Goldſmith, Ironmonger, Imbroiderer, or Clothier, ^{Ib. §. 27.} dwelling in a Corporate Town, may take any Apprentice, except the Apprentice or Father have Freehold Lands to the Value of forty Shillings *per Annum*, &c. But if ſuch ^{Ib. §. 29.} Maſter live in a Market-Town not Corporate, his Apprentice, or his Friends, muſt have 3 l. *per Ann.* in Freehold.

But theſe Artificers, *viz.* Smiths, Wheel-wrights, &c. may take the Children of any ^{Ib. §. 30.} Parents as Apprentices.

Every Cloth-worker, Fuller, Shearman, Weaver, Taylor, and Shoemaker, that keep ^{Ib. §. 33.} three Apprentices, ſhall keep one Journeyman ; and for every Apprentice above Three, ſhall keep one Journeyman, upon Pain of ten Pounds for every Default,

(d) If any Maſter ſhall miſuſe his Apprentice, or that he ſhall have juſt Cauſe to com- ^{*Miſuſer.*} plain, or if the Apprentice do not his Duty to his Maſter, upon Complaint thereof made ^{Ib. 35.} by the Maſter, or Apprentice being grieved, to any one Juſtice of Peace of the County where ſuch Maſter dwelleth, the ſaid Juſtice ſhall take order between them, and for want of Conformity in the Maſter, may bind him to appear at the next Seſſions to be holden in the ſaid County, where the Juſtices of Peace, or *four of them*, whereof one of them to be of the *Quorum*, if they ſhall think meet, may diſcharge the ſaid Appren-tice of his Apprenticeſhip and Indentures ; but if there ſhall be Default in the Appren-tice, the ſaid Juſtices (at their ſaid Seſſions) may cauſe due Correction to be miniſtred to him. Alſo it ſeems, that if the firſt Juſtice of Peace, to whom Complaint was made, ſhall find the Default to be in the Apprentice, then he may ſend him to the Houſe of Correction, as an idle or diſorderly Perſon, by the Statute of 7 *Jac. cap.* 4. and needeth not to trouble the Seſſions with him, *tamen quære.*

(a) It ſeemeth by this Clauſe, that for ill Uſage of the Maſter towards the Apprentice, upon Complaint by the Apprentice in the Manner directed by the Act, the Juſtices may diſcharge the Apprentice from the Maſter's Service, and not *è converſo*, but for Miſcar-riage of the Apprentice he may be corporally puniſhed : And this I remember came in Queſtion in the King's Bench, when *Hale* was Lord Chief Juſtice there ; and he and the Court ſeemed to hold accordingly, but ſaid, ſome Things and Queſtions were better ſleep than be ſtirred : By which he diſcovered his Opinion ; but nothing more came thereof.

If an Apprentice ſhall ſteal or purloin any Thing not delivered him to keep, above ^{*Purloining.*} the Value of twelve Pence from his Maſter, the Apprentice, together with thoſe that inticed or perſuaded him thereto, or ſhall receive any of the ſame Goods, knowing they were purloined, after due Examination and Confeſſion or Proof thereof made before any Juſtice of Peace, he may ſend the Apprentice, as alſo the Inticers, Procurers and Re-ceivers of thoſe Goods, to the common Gaol, &c. But if the Goods be not above the

Value

Value of twelve Pence, the Apprentice, with the Procurers and Receivers, may be sent to the House of Correction by the Justices of Peace, or rather by the Justices at their General Sessions.

Difcharges.
5 El. c. 4. §. 5
& 6. No Master, Mistress, or Dame, shall put away any Servant before the End of their Term, unless it be for some reasonable Cause, to be allowed by a Justice of Peace, &c. nor shall put away any Servant at the End of the Term without one Quarter's Warning given before two sufficient Witnesses, &c. *ut postea.* And the Proof of the Sufficiency or Insufficiency of the Cause of putting away of a Servant shall be made at the Quarter-Sessions, &c. *ut postea.* Nor may the Servant depart before the End of his Term, nor at the End of his Term without a Quarter's Warning.

*Servant put
away.* (d) Any one Justice of Peace may allow the Cause of putting away a *Servant,* or of the *Departure of a Servant* within his Term.

5 E. 4.
Br. 27, 30.
Plowd. 259.
Fitz. 143.
Ward. But otherwise it is of an *Apprentice,* who cannot be discharged but by *four Justices of Peace* at the least, and in open Sessions as aforesaid; or else by the *Agreement of the Master and the Apprentice,* and *under his Master's Hand in Writing:* And yet one that is retained as an Apprentice, may be seised by his Lord as a Ward, by Reason the Lord's Title is more antient.

Two Justices.
5 El. 4. §. 8
& 9.
*Servant de-
parting.* Any two Justices of Peace upon Complaint to them made, that any *Servant* (who is retained according to the Statute of *5 Eliz.*) hath departed before the End of this Term, (unless it be for sufficient Cause to be allowed by one Justice of Peace at the least) or at the End of his Term, without *one Quarter's Warning given before two Witnesses;* or that any Person compellable by the Statute to serve in *Husbandry,* or in any other Sciences in the said Statute named, upon Request made, hath refused to serve for the Wages appointed (by Proclamation in that County, &c. according to this Statute; or hath promised or covenanted to serve, and doth not according to the Tenor of the same, the said Justices may examine the Matter; and if they shall find such Servant or Person faulty therein, they may commit him to remain without Bail until he shall be bound to the Party offended, to serve and continue with him for the Wages limited according to this Statute, and then to be discharged without paying any Fee to the Gaoler.

And yet any one Justice of Peace may make his Warrant to attach a Servant departed out of Service, or refusing to serve, to be before the Justices at their Sessions, there to answer their Defaults. See *postea* Tit. *Warrants.*

*Who compel-
lable to serve.*
Ib. §. 4. Now by the Statute *5 Eliz.* every Person unmarried, and every other Person (married) being under the Age of thirty Years, having been brought up in any of the Arts, Sciences, or Trades in the Statute mentioned, is compellable to serve in any the said Trades, upon Request made by any Person using the same Trades, except such Persons be lawfully retained with some other; or have 40 s. in Land, &c. or 10 l. in Goods, and so allowed by two Justices of Peace under their Hands and Seals; or have some Farm in Tillage, whereupon to imploy themselves.

Ib. §. 7. Also every Person between the Age of twelve Years and threescore (not being lawfully retained according to the Statute, nor being a Gentleman born, nor a Scholar, nor having Means of 40 s. *per Annum,* or in Goods 10 l. as aforesaid, nor Parents living, having 10 l. yearly in Lands, or 40 l. in Goods, and being their Heir apparent) shall be compellable to serve in Husbandry by the Year, upon Request, &c. See *hic postea.*

(a) As for Servants Wages generally, they are grown so excessive at this Day (in many Countries) that the poor Farmers are thereby much disabled; for Remedy wherein, the Justice of Peace shall do well to take it into better Consideration, and give Remedy.

P. Just. 66.
& Lamb. 4.
5 Eliz. c. 4.
§. 18 & 19. (d) Any two Justices of Peace may imprison without Bail the Master for ten Days, and the Servant, Workman, or Labourer, for twenty-one Days, that shall give, or shall take or receive excessive Wages, *scil.* Any greater Wages, or other Commodity, contrary to the Rates or Wages assessed by the Justices of Peace at their *Easter* General Sessions, and Proclamation thereof made in that County.

Ib. §. 15. (a) Now concerning the Wages of Servants, &c. the Justices of Peace (at every *Easter* Quarter-Sessions) shall do well to call some discreet Persons of that County, and they together respecting the Plenty or Scarcity of the Time, and other necessary Circumstances, to assess the Wages as well of Servants, as of all Artificers, Handicraftsmen, and Labourers, &c. according to the Statute, at their Discretions, and yet in such Manner, as that Servants, &c. may reasonably maintain themselves therewith; and that their Masters should in no wise exceed or give above such Wages by Way of Contract.

4.

But

But yet Mafters may reward a well-deferving Servant, *&c.* (over and above his Wages) according as he fhall deferve; fo that 'tis not by Way of Promife or Agreement upon his Retainer. See the Preamble of the Statute 5 *Eliz.* 4. that confidering the Advancement of Prices of all Things belonging to Servants and Labourers, if more reafonable Wages and Allowances be not given than is limited by former Statutes, it would be too great a Grief and Burden to the poor hired Servants and Labourers.

Of which Rates Proclamations fhall be made, and the Juftices may every Year alter Ib §. 16, 17. and reform the fame, as in their Difcretions fhall feem meet. And every Juftice of Peace fhall be prefent at the Taxing fuch Wages, unlefs reafonable Caufe of his Abfence upon Oath, to be allowed by the faid Juftices, or forfeit 10 *l.*

By the Law of God, *Thou fhalt not opprefs an hired Servant, that is needy and poor ; but thou fhalt give him his hire fpeedily, for therewith he fuftaineth his Life.* Deut. 24. 14, 15.

Two Juftices made an Order for the Defendant to pay 40 *s.* Wages generally : Adjudged this fhall be intended Wages in Husbandry. 2 *Salk.* 484, 442.

And the hire of Labourer kept back, crieth and entreth into the Ears of the Lord. Jam. 5. 4.

(*d*) Note, That every Retainer, Promife or Payment of Wages, or other Thing whatfo- Ib. §. 20. ever, contrary to the true Meaning of this Statute, and every Writing or Bond made for that Purpofe, fhall be utterly void.

Alfo any two Juftices of Peace may imprifon without Bail the Mafter who fhall re- *Retainer for* tain or keep any Servant, Workman, or Labourer, contrary to the Statute, *fc.* In any *one Year.* the Particulars following : 1. Either in giving Wages contrary to the Statute, *ut fupra.* 5 El. c. 4. 2. Or retaining or hiring a Servant for lefs Time than *one whole Year* ; but this feems to extend to Artificers or Tradefmen, and not to Husbandry. *Quære.* 3. Or that fhall retain any Servant that is departed out of Service, without fhewing before his Retainer, a Teftimonial of his lawful Departure. *Quære.*

(*a*) The Arts and Trades mentioned in the Statute 5 *Eliz.* are thefe following : *Arrow-* *The Trades* head-makers, Bakers, Brewers, Butchers, Bowyers, Cappers, Clothiers, Cloth-workers, *mentioned in* Cooks, Cutlers, Curriers, Dyers, Ferrors, Felt-makers, Fletchers, Fullers, Glovers, Hat- *the Stat.* 5 El. makers, Hofiers, Millers, Pewterers, Sadlers, Shearmen, Shoe-makers, Smiths, Spurriers, Taylors, Tanners, Tuckers, Turners, and *Woollen-cloth Weavers.*

And yet no Retainer of any Servant for lefs Time than for *one whole Year* is good, or according to Law. See *Fitz.* 168. *b. Co. L.* 42. *b.*

(*d*) Any two Juftices of Peace of the County where the Offence hereunder mentioned *Affault his* fhall be committed, may imprifon by the Space of one Year or lefs, by their Difcretion, *Mafter.* any fuch *Servant,* Workman, or Labourer, as fhall wilfully make any *Affault or Affray* Ib. §. 21. upon his Mafter, or upon any other having the Charge or Overfight of him, or of his Work, the faid Offence being proved before the faid Juftices by Confeffion of the faid Servant, *&c.* or by the Oath of two honeft Men.

(*a*) And yet upon Complaint thereof made to any one Juftice of Peace, he may bind the Offender to his Good Behaviour, and fo to the next Seffions, and there he may be convicted and punifhed according to the Statute.

(*d*) Any two Juftices of Peace may compel any Woman (being of the Age of *twelve Woman.* Years, and under *Forty, and unmarried*) and whom they fhall think meet to ferve, to Ib. §. 24. be retained in Service by the Year, Week, or Day, for fuch Wages, and in fuch Sort as they fhall think meet. And if fuch a Woman fhall refufe, they may commit her, until fhe fhall be bound to ferve as aforefaid.

For Clothiers which will not pay their Workmen fuch Wages as fhall be affeffed by *Clothiers.* the Juftices at their Seffions, fee the Title of *Cloth, &c.*

The Certificate which is to be made to the Head Officer of any City or Town Cor- *Three Juftices* porate, where a Child is to be bound Apprentice, That the Father and Mother of fuch *Certificate.* Apprentice have Lands of Freehold of the Value of 40 *s.* yearly, muft be under the Ib. §. 27. Hands and Seals of three Juftices of the Peace of the Shire where the Land lieth.

(*a*) The Reafon of this Law feemeth to be, for that fuch as are to be bound Apprentices in Corporate Towns, *&c.* if their Parents be of a competent Livelihood, then their Mafters fhall not only be the better fecured, *&c.* but fuch Apprentices alfo in Likelihood fhall have the better Means to fet up their Trades after their Time expired. And concerning fuch whofe Parents have not forty Shillings *per Annum,* they are fitter to be bound Apprentices to Husbandry, *&c.* in the Country.

But concerning this Certificate, 'tis not much in Use at this Day; neither is it material, that for Want thereof, the Indentures for the Binding of such an Apprentice shall be void, (for the Justices of Peace cannot be compelled to certify,) &c. but if the Parents have forty Shillings *per Annum*, it sufficeth: And so were the Opinions of Sir *Humphry Winch* and Sir *William Jones*, in the Court of *Common Pleas*, *Termino Pasch.* 21 *Jac. Regis.* But Sir *Henry Hobart* Lord Chief Justice of the *Common Pleas*, did not then deliver his Opinion directly; yet he seemed to me to hold, That the Parents of such an Apprentice ought to have forty Shillings *per Annum*, and also ought to procure such a Certificate from the Justices of Peace.

(*d*) Here I think it not amiss to set down certain Cases, some of them being by Way of Exposition of this Statute 5 *Eliz. cap.* 4. And other some at the Common Law, or grounded upon former Statutes; yet such as may give Light and Help to our Justices of Peace in this Business.

Trades, what lawful.
Co. 11. 53.

First, By the *Common Law*, no Man may be prohibited to work in any *lawful Trade*, for the Law abhorreth Idleness, as the Mother of all Evil.

Co. 11. 86.

A Man cannot be restrained to use the *Trade of making Dice, Cards, Bowls*, or the like, (except it be by Parliament) for all *Trades*, which do avoid Idleness, and exercise Men in Labour for the Maintenance of them and their Families, and to increase their Substance, and to serve the King, when Need shall be, are profitable for the Commonwealth; and therefore the Restraining of them is against the Law, &c.

(*a*) So necessary are Trades to a Kingdom, That if a Man be bound not to use a Trade that he hath been brought up in, that Bond is void: But a Man may bind himself not to use a Trade in a particular Place. 3 *Mod.* 128.

Co. 11. 54.

(*d*) Also by the Common Law no Man is prohibited to use *divers Mysteries or Trades* at his Pleasure: And although this was prohibited by the Statute 37 *Ed.* 3. *cap.* 6. yet at the next Parliament (that Restraint of free Trade being found prejudicial to the Commonwealth) it was enacted, That all Persons should be as free as they were at any Time before the said Statute. *Co.* 11. 54. See the Statute of 38 *Ed.* 3. *cap.* 2.

Ibid.

So that without an Act of Parliament, no Man may be restrained, either to work in any lawful Trade, or to use divers Mysteries or Trades; therefore Ordinances made to restrain any Person therein are against the Law: And yet Ordinances made for the good Order and Government of Tradesmen, &c. are good. *Co. ibid.*

Apprentice seven Years.
5 El. c. 4.
§. 31.

(*a*) None shall use any Art, Mystery, Craft, Trade, or Occupation, except he hath been brought up therein *seven Years as Apprentice.* By 15 *Car.* 2. *cap.* 15. *Hempdressers*, and Makers of *Cloth of Hemp or Flax, Nets, and Tapestry* are excepted.

Co. 11. 54.

(*d*) And it is lawful for any Person to use privately any Trade (as of a *Cook, Brewer, Baker*, or *Taylor*, &c.) in his own House, or in the House of any other, for the private Use of the Family, although such Person were never *Apprentice* to the Trade. *Co. ibid.*

(*a*) If a Man use the Trade of *Tallow-Chandler, Baker, Brewer*, or any other lawful Trade or manual Occupation, for his own Use, or for the Use of his Family, without selling any for Lucre and Gain, he may lawfully do it. *Co.* 8. 129, 130.

But yet he which useth any *Trade*, or other *manual Occupation*, for the Use of himself, or of his Family only, (without Selling) cannot retain any Apprentice within the Statute of 5 *Eliz. Co.* 8. 129. But he may hire one to be his Servant, who is skilful in that Trade or Occupation.

Not an Apprentice.

One purchased a *Mill*, and hired a *Miller* to be his Servant, who ground the Grists of his Neighbours, and the Wife of the Owner of the Mill took Money of the Neighbours for their Grist so ground; and for this the Husband (who was Owner of the Mill) was indicted at *Cambridge* Summer Assises, *An. Dom.* 1619. by reason that he was never himself Apprentice to the Trade. It was the Case of *T. P.* Yeoman.

The Intent of this Statute 5 *Eliz. cap.* 4. was, that no Person should take upon them any *Art, Mystery*, or *Trade*, &c. but such wherein they had *Skill and Knowledge*, according to the Rule, *Quod quisque norit, in hoc se exerceat.* Co. 8. 130.

And therefore none may keep a *Common Brewhouse, Bakehouse, Cook's Shop*, &c. to sell to others, except they have been Apprentice thereto by the Space of seven Years, &c. *ibid.*

Note, That these Words Mystery, Trade, and Craft, do all bear one Sense or Signification. See *Plow.* 537. *b. Co.* 11. 54.

(d) Note next, That this Statute, 5 *Eliz. cap.* 4. extended not to *Serving Men,* but to Cromp. 185.
Servants in Husbandry, and *Handicrafts :* And yet where the Words of any Statute be
Servant in general, there it seems to extend to all.

(a) Any Imployment which requireth no extraordinary Skill to exercise is not within this
Statute ; and it hath been adjudged and affirmed in a Writ of Error, that a Pippinmonger
s not within this Statute, for it requireth no Skill to use it ; so *Ploughing* or *Digging*
s not within it ; for in those Trades Strength is more required than Skill. *Quære,* Of
Upholsters. Roll's 2d Part. Rep. p. 10. The *King* against *Tollin.*

Every one bound an Apprentice according to that Statute, although under Age, yet is *Apprentice be-*
compellable to serve his Time out, as if he were of Age when he was bound, 5 *Eliz.* 4. *ing an Infant.*
But that is to be underſtood of a Compulſion, by the Means preſcribed by that Statute ;
for the *Covenant* is not good, so as to inable the Maſter to bring an Action upon it, as
was reſolved, *H.* 5 *Car.* 1. *Cro. p.* 129. *Gilbert* verſ. *Fletcher.*

(d) An Apprentice muſt be retained by *Indenture,* and by the Name of an Apprentice *Who be compel-*
expreſly ; or elſe he is no Apprentice, though he be bound. *lable to serve.*
Who are compellable to serve, see in this Title before and after. Crom. 185.
P. 15.
Every Juſtice of Peace may command vagrant Perſons to Priſon, if they will not Fitz. 168. b.
ſerve.

Every Perſon who hath not ſufficient Lands to occupy, or live upon, nor other Art, Fitz 178. a.
s compellable to serve. 168. 1.
Fitz.167. d. e.
If an Infant, Man or Woman, of twelve Years of Age, or Gentleman, Chaplain, or Br. Ley 67.
other Perſon, who is not compellable to serve ; yet if they ſhall make a *Covenant* to P. 3. 14.
ſerve in Husbandry, they ſhall be bound by their Covenant, and are puniſhable, if they
then ſhall depart, *&c.*

Yet by the Common Law such a Covenant or Retainer of an Infant under twelve *Infant.*
Years of Age was void, they neither having Ability of Body nor Years to conſent : For an 7 H. 4. 5.
Infant (by the Common Law) is not of Age to bind itſelf by *Covenant, ante annos nu-* 2 H. 4. 18.
biles, which is twelve Years in a Woman, and fourteen Years in a Man Child. *Co.* 7. Br. 19, 20.
43. *& 9.* 72. Neither before that Age are they accounted *Potens in corpore,* which are
the Words uſed in the Statute 23 *Ed.* 3. though theſe Words are now left out of the
Statute of 5 *El.* and thereupon *Markham* in 21 *H.* 6. and *Brooke* abridging that Caſe, 21 H. 6. 32.
ſeem to hold fourteen Years to be the Age for Retainer of an Infant, but there the Caſe Br. 30.
was of a Man Child that was retained.

But now by the Statute of 5 *Eliz. cap.* 4. any Perſon above the Age of ten Years, by
their own *Conſent and Agreement,* may by Indenture be bound as an *Apprentice to Huſ-*
bandry, or any other Trade or Art.

Alſo ſome of twelve Years of Age by the ſame Statute, are compellable by the Juſtice
to ſerve in Husbandry : So alſo it ſeemeth of other Trades, Arts, or Occupations.

Such Children, whoſe Parents are not able to maintain them, though they be under
Twelve, may be bound Apprentices by the Overſeers of the Poor, with the Aſſent of any
two Juſtices of Peace, by the Statute of 43 *Eliz. cap.* 2. See *poſtea* Tit. *Poor.*

(a) All Perſons to whom the Overſeers of the Poor ſhall, according to *Stat.* 43 *Eliz.* 1 Jac. 1. c. 25.
cap. 2. bind any Children Apprentices, may keep them as Apprentices. §. 23. re enacted by 21 Jac.
1. c. 28. §. 1.
(d) If a Woman who is a Servant, ſhall *marry,* yet ſhe muſt ſerve out her Time, and *Married Per-*
her Husband cannot take her out of her Maſter's Service. *ſons.*

(a) A married Man and his Wife do bind themſelves to ſerve, they ſhall be compelled 2 H. 4. f. 13.
to ſerve according to their Covenant or Agreement. *Fitz.* 168. Fitz 168. a.
Br. 13.
One under the Age of thirty Years, and brought up in Husbandry ; or a Maid-ſervant
brought up in any of the Trades mentioned in the Statute of 5 *Eliz.* 4. and not inabled
to live (according to that Statute) at his or her own Hands, ſuch Perſons living out of
Service ; and not having viſible Means of their own to maintain themſelves without their
Labour, and refuſing to ſerve as an hired Servant by the Year, may be bound over to the
next Seſſions, or Aſſiſes, and to be of Good Behaviour in the mean Time ; or may be
ſent to the Houſe of Correction. *Dyer* 17.

But a Man that holdeth Land of his Lord, to do certain Days Works yearly ſhall not
be compelled to ſerve. 40 *E.* 3. 39. *Cromp.* 185.

(d) If a Man who is not able nor ſufficient to keep a Servant, ſhall retain one, ſuch Fitz. 168. b
Retainer is void.

(a) If a Man retaineth a Labourer or Servant, to ſerve him according to the Statute, tho' *What Retain-*
no Wages be ſpoken of upon the Retainer, yet 'tis good, and they ſhall have ſuch Wa- *er is good.*

ges

ges as are affeffed and appointed by Proclamation, for that Wages are certain. See to this Purpofe the Book 3 *H.* 6. *fol.* 23.

If a Man retaineth another, except the Retainer be according to the Statute, 'tis void; without it be by Indenture, and then being by Deed, he is bound by his *Covenant*. See *Fitz. N. B. fol.* 168.

If a Man retaineth upon Condition, 'tis a good Retainer. See 11 *H.* 4. 42.

A Man retaineth a Servant to ferve him generally, not expreffing in what Office, or in what Bufinefs, (as to ferve him in Hufbandry or in the Office of a *Book, Butler, Horfe-keeper, &c.*) yet fuch Retainer is good. 21 *H.* 6. 9. *Br. Labor* 29.

A Man is retained to ferve during his Life, 'tis a good Retainer. *Br.* 44. 2 *H.* 4. *fol.* 15. . And fo for three Years or more. *Fitz.* 168.

A Man is retained for one Year, to ferve at any Time when he fhall be thereto required; this is no good Retainer. See 23 *H.* 6. 30. *Br.* 31.

Fitz. 169. h.   (*d*) Retainer of a Servant generally, without expreffing *any certain Term*, fhall be for *one*
P. 1.   *Year* (in Conftruction of Law) for that Retainer is according to Law. And this is now
C. L. 42. b.   by 5 *Eliz. cap.* 4. made void, unlefs it be for a Year, to certain Trades therein named.

Fitz. 169. f.   *A.* retaineth a Servant for forty Days, and after *B.* retaineth the fame Servant for one Year; the firft Retainer by *A.* is become void. *Br.* 51. See 11 *H.* 6. 1. *Br.* 46.

Departure.   If a Servant, who is retained, fhall depart out of his Service, and wander, he may be
Fitz. 168.   compelled to ferve another Man; but yet the firft Mafter may take him again. But it is fafe to get the Confent of his firft Mafter; for now by the Statute, 5 *Eliz. cap.* 4. the
5 El. c. 4.   Mafter retaining a Servant that is departed out of Service, without fhewing (before his
§. 11.   Retainer) a Teftimonial, fhall forfeit five Pounds.

(*a*) A Man that retaineth a Servant, ought to take Notice of every former Retainer within the fame County; otherwife it is of a Retainer in another County. 17 *E.* 4. *fol.* 7. *Br. Notice* 20.

Fitz. 168. b.   (*d*) And yet Mr. *Fitzh.* Opinion was, that if one retaineth another Man's Servant (gene-
Br. 7, 29, 33.   rally) not knowing that he was another Man's hired Servant, he was not punifhable, ex-
Dr. St. 149.   cept he fhould detain him after Notice thereof, but now the Mafter may and muft take Notice whether he hath a Teftimonial or no.

Departure of a   If one taketh an *Infant*, or other Servant out of another Man's Service, this is punifh-
Servant.   able, though the Infant or Servant was not retained; but if an Infant, being retained as
Fitz. 168. d.   an Apprentice or Servant, fall to be a Ward, the Lord may take him from his Mafter,
Fitz. 143, 1.   for the Lord's Title is more ancient; yet here the Lord ought firft to give Notice there-
Plo. 259.   of to his Mafter. 50 *E.* 3. 22. *Br. Labor* 17. See *Br. Notice* 24.

5 El. c. 4.   (*a*) If a Servant or Apprentice depart into another County, the Juftices of Peace may iffue
§. 47.   out a *Capias* againft him into the County or Place whither he is fled; and being taken thereon, fhall be imprifoned till he give Surety to ferve as he ought.

Teftimonial.   If a Servant depart, and be retained without a Teftimonial, he fhall be imprifoned un-
Ib. §. 11.   til he procure it; and if he procure it not, within twenty Days, he fhall be ufed as a Vagabond; and the Perfon that Retains him without fuch Teftimonial fhewed, fhall forfeit five Pounds. And if any Perfon be taken with a counterfeit Teftimonial, he fhall be whipped as a Vagabond.

Note, That by the Retainer, the Servant is in Service prefently by Law, although he cometh not into his Mafter's Service indeed. 41 *E.* 3. 20. 46 *E.* 3. 4. 47 *E.* 3. 14 *Br.* 9. 11.

Fitz. 168.   (*d*) If a Servant depart from his Mafter, he may take him again, and keep him whether he will, or no. See the Title *Surety for the Peace.* (*a*) And the Conftable may take and bring fuch Servant to his Mafter again. *Fitz. Labor* 56.

Task Work.   Any Artificer or Labourer that fhall take any Piece of Work *in Great, in Task, or in*
5 El. c. 4.   *Grofs*, or that fhall take on him to make or finifh fuch Work, fhall not depart from the
§. 13.   fame (unlefs it be for Non-payment of his Wages, or Hire, or otherwife taken to ferve the King, or for other lawful Caufe) without Licenfe, upon Pain of Imprifonment for one Month without Bail, and five Pounds; for which the Party may have his Action and Cofts.

Putting away   (*d*) The Mafter cannot difcharge his Servant, during his Term, *&c.* without the *Agree-*
a Servant,   *ment of his Servant.* And now by the Statute 5 *El.* 4. it muft be for fome reafonable
vide antea.   Caufe to be allowed by one Juftice, at leaft, *&c.* otherwife the Mafter fhall forfeit forty
Ib. §. 8.   Shillings. (*a*) *Tamen quære.* For where the Departure or putting away the Servant, is by
16 *H.* 6. 30.   the joint Confent of both, 'tis not within the Statute of 5 *Eliz.* neither is the Allowance of
Br. 27.   the Juftice of Peace requifite therein.

I

The

(d) Before 5 *El. cap.* 4. the Mafter might have difcharged his Servant by Word; but an *Apprentice* cannot be difcharged, except it be by *Writing*; for that an Apprentice cannot be but by Writing.

If a Servant fhall be put away by his Mafter, he fhall have his *Wages* for the Time he ferved. And yet in this Cafe, if the Servant agree thereto, the Servant fhall have no Action to recover any Part of his Wages, but muft crave the Help of the Juftice of Peace herein. But if fuch Servant be within Age, it feemeth fuch Agreement fhall not prejudice the Servant.

But if a Servant of his *own Accord fhall depart* from his Mafter before his Time expired, he fhall lofe all his Wages.

(n) If a Servant be retained according to the Statute, and the Mafter dieth, his Executors fhall be chargeable to pay fuch Servant his Wages; otherwife it is where the Retainer was not according to the Statute, except it were by Indenture. See 2 *H.* 4. 15. *Br. Labor* 49. and *Fitz. Nat. Br.* 168. *f.*

An Infant of five Years of Age, or other Perfon which is not *Potens in corpore*; yet if they fhall be retained, and fhall ferve indeed, their Mafter muft pay them their Wages. See 38 *H.* 4. 22. *Br. Labor* 46. and *Ley Gager* 67.

If a Servant retained for a Year, happen within the Time of his Service to fall fick, or to be hurt or lamed, or otherwife to become *Non potens in corpore*, by the Act of God, or in doing his Mafter's Bufinefs; yet the Mafter muft not therefore put fuch Servant away, nor abate any Part of his Wages for fuch Time.

If a Servant fhall refufe to do his Service, that is a Departure in Law, although he ftay ftill with his Mafter.

If the Mafter fhall detain from his Servant his *Wages, Meat* or *Drink*; this is a good Caufe of Departure: But yet this Caufe is now by the Statute of 5 *Eliz.* to be allowed of by the Juftices of Peace, before the Servant may lawfully or fafely depart.

So if the Mafter fhall *licenfe* his Servant to depart, or if the Mafter, or Wife of the Mafter fhall *beat the Servant*; thefe were good Caufes for the Servant to depart, before the Statute 5 *Eliz.* 4. But now the Allowance of the Juftice of Peace, is requifite as forefaid. And yet Note, That the Mafter by Law is allowed with Moderation to chatife his Servant or Apprentice. See 33 *H.* 8. 12. and in the Title, *Surety for the Peace.*

But now that by the Statute of 5 *Eliz.* the Caufes of putting away and departing of Servants, are referred to the Confideration and Allowance of the Juftices of Peace: It behoveth them to have good Care, left by their giving too much way therein, either to the Mafter or Servant, many, which might by due ordering have proved good Servants, turn Rogues and Vagabonds.

(a) Now for the better rating of Servants Wages, and for the better Placing, Beftowing, fetling, and Ordering not only of Servants, but alfo of all fuch idle People (Men and Women) as being fit and able to labour and ferve, do neverthelefs refufe to labour, or feek to get themfelves Services, or (rather living idle at home with their Parents) perhaps cannot get themfelves any Services, the Statute made 5 *Eliz. cap.* 4. *fect.* 48. hath enabled the High Conftable of Hundreds in every Shire, to hold, keep and continue their Petit or Statute Seffions in all Shires wherein fuch Seffions have been ufed to be kept, and fter the ancient Manner: And as to thefe Seffions, both Houfholders, Servants, and others fit for Service, do or ought to come; fo if one or two of the next Juftices of Peace in every Divifion, would take the Pains to be there alfo to affift the High Conftables, it would both add Force to their Proceedings, as well for the Placing of Servants, as alfo for Affeffing the Wages: And alfo for the preventing many other the Abufes and Diforders both in Mafters and Servants.

Juftices of Peace fhall meet twice in the Year to inquire of the Breaches of the Statute of 5 *Eliz.* 4. And fhall have five Shillings *per Diem* for their Wages.

A Moiety of all Forfeitures to the King, the other Moiety to the Informer. And the Juftices may hear and determine the Offence, as well by Indictment and Information, as Action of Debt or Bill; and may make Procefs according to Law; and in *Michaelmas* Term fhall certify the Eftreats. But in Cities and Corporate Towns, all Forfeitures fhall be levied to the Ufe of the fame City, &c. as other Forfeitures have been.

By the Statute 5 *Eliz.* one Juftice may reconcile any Difference between the Mafter and his *Apprentice* if he can, and if he cannot, and the Fault be in the Mafter, he may bind him over to the Quarter-Seffions, and then four Juftices under their Hands and Seals may difcharge the Apprentice; and if the Fault be in him, then to fend him to the

6 E. 4. 2.
2 E. 6. 35.
Br. 30, 38.

6 E. 4. 33.
Br. 30, 38.

Br. 48.
10 H. 6. 3.

Executor.
10 Ed. 4. 2.
49 H. 6. 19.
Br. 40.

Appr. 26.

Infant.

Sicknefs.

3 H. 6 37.

Fitz. 1. 68.
Br. 51.
P. 6.

Fitz. 169.
Br. 51.

Wages.

Conftables Seffions.

5 El. c. 4.
§. 38.

Ib. §. 39.

Ib. §. 43.

Apprentices to Trades.
5 Eliz. c. 4.
§. 35.

O o   Houfe

House of Correction, if he will not give Security to appear at the next Seſſions; and if he doth, then four Juſtices may make ſuch Order as they ſhall think juſt.

But the Maſter and Apprentice may, by Agreement between themſelves, leave each other; and if ſo, then the Maſter may give Leave under his Hand for the Apprentice to depart; and then one Juſtice out of Seſſions may diſcharge him, allowing the Cauſe of his Departure.

Mod. Ca. 70.

Where the Maſter gives Leave under his Hand for his Apprentice to depart, he can-not afterwards recal it: Therefore where an Action of Covenant was brought by the Maſter, for that the Apprentice left his Service at ſuch a Time, the Defendant may juſti-fy by Virtue of a *Licenſe* from the Plaintiff at ſuch a Time; and at the Trial the Maſter ſhall not give Evidence of his Apprentice leaving him at any other Time, becauſe the Time is not tranſitory, as in an Action of Treſpaſs, but very material upon ſuch a Declaration.

2 Salk. 471.

Apprentices to Trades.

A *Mountebank* took an Apprentice in *Yorkſhire* where he had a Stage, and cove-nanted in the Indenture to teach him the Art of Surgery; afterwards being in *Middle-ſex*, the Apprentice complained to the Juſtices, that his Maſter did not teach him the ſaid Art, and obtained an Order to be diſcharged, but it was quaſhed: 'Tis true, the Words in the Statute 5 *Eliz.* which relate to the *Service* of an Apprentice, are very Ge-neral, *viz. Arts and Sciences*, under which Words a *Surgeon* may be comprehended; but the other Words, which relate to the *diſcharging Apprentices*, extend only to the *Trades* mentioned in that Statute, but neither a *Surgeon* or *Mountebank* are therein mentioned.

After one Juſtice hath endeavoured to compoſe the Matter between the Maſter and his Apprentice, four Juſtices, upon the Appearance of the Maſter, may diſcharge the Apprentice; ſuch an Order was made, but it did not ſet forth that the Maſter appeared, which is required by the Statute; but adjudged that the Statute muſt have a reaſonable Conſtruction; for admitting the Maſter run away, yet the Apprentice ſhall be diſcharged: But in the principal Caſe the Maſter was a *Collar-Maker*, which is not a Trade men-tioned in that Part of the Statute which relates to the *diſcharging Apprentices.*

1 Rol. Rep.1.
2 Bulſt. 186,
187. Sid.361.
1 Lev. 243.

It was the Opinion of my Lord *Coke*, that an *Upholſter* is not a Trade within the Sta-tute, but the later Opinions are otherwiſe.

Noy 133.

Information againſt the Defendant for exerciſing the Trade of a *Dyer*, not having ſerved ſeven Years Apprenticeſhip to that Trade; it appeared at the Trial that the De-fendant was a *Felt-maker* and *dyed* Hats, which being Part of his Trade, he was ac-quitted.

Raim. 385.

Indictment againſt the Defendant for uſing the Trade of a *Barber*, and againſt ano-ther for uſing the Trade of a *Saleſman*, not having ſerv'd an Apprenticeſhip for ſeven Years: Adjudged that both theſe Trades are within the Statute; this was upon a De-murrer to the Indictment.

Indictment againſt the Defendant for exerciſing the Trade of a *Merchant-Taylor* is not within the Statute, becauſe not uſed here before that Statute 5 *Eliz.* was made, for which Reaſon it was quaſhed.

2 Cro. 178.
8 Red. 129.
1 Sand. 311.
Sid. 427.
S. P.

A *Brewer* is a Trade within the Statute, ſo adjudged upon a Writ of Error.

Indictment againſt the Defendant for exerciſing the Trade of a *Woollen-Draper*, who pleaded that he was a Freeman of *London*; and upon Demurrer to this Plea there was Judgment againſt him.

Of Indentures of Apprentice-ſhip, and Co-venants there-in.

An *Infant* may bind himſelf Apprentice, *Cro. Car.* 179. *Hutt.* 63. and by the Statute 5 *Eliz. cap.* 4. *par.* 43. he ſhall be bound by his Indenture notwithſtanding his Non-age. * Owners of Ships or Veſſels, or any Houſholder uſing the *Fiſhing Trade*, may take Apprentices for 10 *Years* or under; but this muſt be by Indenture *inrolled* in the Town Corporate where the Apprentice lives; or if he doth not live in ſuch Towns then in the next Corporation: + Therefore where a *Mariner* took an Apprentice by Indenture, with a Bond for Performance of Covenants, and after he ran away, the Bond was put in Suit, and the Defendant pleaded this Statute, and that the Indenture was not *inrolled, &c.* the Court inclined againſt the Plaintiff.

* *Yet neither at Common Law, nor by any Words of the Stat.* 5 *El.
a Covenant or Obligation of an Infant for his Apprenticeſhip ſhall bind him.* Cro. Car. 179. + 1 Lutw. 474.

2 Roll. Rep.
305.

The Indentures of an Apprentice in *London* muſt be inrolled within a Year, *&c.* and if the Default is in the Maſter, then the Apprentice may ſue them out, and ſhall be diſ-charged;

I

charged; but if the Fault is in the Apprentice for not coming before the *Chamberlain*, he fhall not be difcharged.

A Bond given by an Apprentice to deliver up a juft and true Account, is good, be- 3 Bulft. 179. caufe 'tis for a collateral Matter, and not within the Words of the Statute 5 *Eliz. cap.* 4. which makes all Covenants and Bargains, for having, taking or keeping an Apprentice, void.

An Order of two Juftices confirmed at Seffions for putting a poor Boy Apprentice in *Poor Apprentices in Hufbandry.* Hufbandry was quafhed, becaufe by the Statute he is to be put out by the Churchwardens and Overfeers of the Poor, with the Approbation of two Juftices; and the Churchwardens 3 Mod. 269. were not named in the original Order.

The *Churchwardens*, &c. have Power to place out poor Children, therefore they are proper Judges of Perfons who are fit to be their Mafters; and thofe are all Perfons who by their Profeffion or Manner of Living have Occafion to keep Servants: And it was ufual *formerly*, that if a Mafter refufed to take fuch Apprentice, he was bound over to the Af- *8 & 9 W. c. 30.* fizes, &c. but now by the * Statute, *upon the Oath of one Churchwarden*, before two Juftices, that the Mafter refufed, he is to forfeit 10 *l.* to be levied by Virtue of a Warrant of thofe Juftices, to the Ufe of the Poor, &c. but an Appeal lies to the Seffions, whofe Order is final.

Therefore where a poor Girl was put out to a *Merchant* by the Order of two Juftices, 2 Salk. 241. who appealed, that Order was difcharged, becaufe the Seffions did not think it proper to place out fuch a Girl to a Merchant; and thefe Orders being removed into *B. R.* the Court confirmed the Order of Seffions, becaufe an Appeal being given to them from the Order of the two Juftices, they are now the proper Court to determine who is fit to receive, or not to receive Apprentices.

It has been held that there is no exprefs Authority given by any Law to fend a bad Apprentice to the *Houfe of Correction*, nor to difcharge him from his Mafter, if the Fault is in him (the Apprentice), as there is, if the Fault is in the Mafter; but the fending a bad Apprentice to the Houfe of Correction, feems to be warranted by the Statute 7 *Jac.* 1. *cap.* 4. made for the erecting fuch Houfes to fet idle People to work, which is rather an Enlargement than a Reftraint of the Power of the Juftices, for they cannot punifh a bad Mafter; 'tis true, they may difcharge the Apprentice from him, but they may either punifh or difcharge a bad Apprentice; and the Seffions have originally difcharged many bad Apprentices, without any previous Application to one Juftice.

An Apprentice being chargeable to a Parifh, and his Mafter being dead, two Juftices Show. Rep. made an Order to fend him to the *Adminiftrator*, charging him to provide for him; and 165. upon an Appeal that Order was confirmed, and both the faid Orders being removed into *B. R.* it was objected that the Power of the Juftices extended only to the Mafter, and not to his *Adminiftrator*; for the Juftices cannot try whether the Adminiftrator hath Affets or not, neither can they fend the Apprentice to the Adminiftrator, if he lives in another County; and if the Adminiftrator fhould happen afterwards to be poor himfelf, the Parifh muft be charged with this Apprentice, if fent to him by fuch Order: 'Tis true, if there were Covenants in this Indenture to oblige the Adminiftrator, it might be otherwife, but there being no fuch, the Order was quafhed.

Adjudged that the Mafter * affigning, and the Apprentice himfelf confenting, will not *But by the Cuftom of London he may be turned over to another.* make him an Apprentice to the *Affignee* within the Statute 5 *Eliz. cap.* 4.

A *Turkey Merchant* trading in Cloth thither, employed Cloathworkers in his Houfe *What fhall be exercifing a Trade.* who had been Apprentices to that Trade for feven Years, and he provided Materials for them to make Cloth, and conftantly paid their Wages every Week, but was never Ap- 3 Mod. 315. rentice to that Trade; the Chief Juftice *Holt*, and two more Judges againft the Opinion of the fourth, held this was Exercifing a Trade within the Statute: 'Tis true, the private exercifing a Trade is not within that Law, but where 'tis ufed for Profit and Gain, and not confined to a particular Family, that is an Exercifing a Trade within the Statute.

The Defendant was found Guilty upon an *Indictment for enticing an Apprentice* to leave *Enticing Apprentices.* his Mafter's Service; but the Judgment was fet afide, becaufe this is a private Injury, for which an Indictment will not lie, but an Action of the Cafe, *per quod fervitium amifit.*

'Tis true, an Indictment will lie for *enticing* a Servant or Apprentice to *imbezil his* Mod. Ca. 88. *Mafter's Goods*, but a Conviction for that Offence was fet afide, becaufe it was not fet forth in the Indictment that the Apprentice did *imbezil* any of the Goods, for there muft be fome Fact done in Purfuance of the Enticing.

By

Felony in Servants to go away with their Masters Goods.
21 H. 8. c. 7.
By the Statute 21 *H.* 8. 'tis Felony in a Servant to go away with his Master's Goods, to the Value of 40 *s.* with an *Intention to imbezil, or to steal them*; this Statute extends only to Servants above 18 Years old, and not to *Apprentices.*

But in such Case the Goods must be delivered to him to keep by the actual Delivery of the Master; therefore if the Master delivers to him a Bond to keep, and the Servant afterwards receives the Money, this is not Felony, because he did not receive the Money by the actual Delivery of the Master.

3 Inst. 105.
The Law is the same if the Master delivers Cattle to his Servant to look after, and he sells them, *&c.* and runneth away with the Money; this is not Felony, for he had not the Money by the Delivery of the Master.

12 Ann. c. 7.
But now by a late Statute, 'tis Felony in a Servant to imbezil or make away his Master's Goods above the Value of 40 *s.* and this without Benefit of Clergy; but this Statute doth not extend to Apprentices under the Age of fifteen Years.

Salk. 68.
Adjudged that what an Apprentice gains is for the Use of his Master, tho' he is only an Apprentice *de facto*, and not actually bound by any Writing.

Journeymen Taylors.
7 G. 1. st. 1.
c. 13. §. 1.
All Contracts by or between any Persons who shall exercise the Art of a Taylor, or Journeyman Taylor, within the Bills of Mortality, for advancing their Wages, or for-lessening their usual Hours of Work, are declared void; and if they enter into, or, knowingly are concerned in any such Contract, the Offender being convicted thereof, upon the Oath of one Witness before two Justices, they may commit him to the House of Correction, there to be kept at hard Labour not exceeding two Months, or to the common Gaol, as they shall see Cause, there to remain, without Bail, for two Months.

The Information must be exhibited, or the Prosecution must be within three Months after the Offence.

Ib. §. 2.
* *The Words of the Statute are,*
One Penny Halfpenny a Day for Breakfast.
The Hours of Working shall be from Six in the Morning till Eight at Night, except that *there shall be allowed Half an Hour for Breakfast,* * and an Hour for Dinner; and the Wages shall be from the 25th of *March* till the 24th of *June* 2 *s. per Diem*, and for the rest of the Year 1 *s.* 8 *d.*

Ib. §. 4.
Two Justices, upon Complaint, *&c.* for Wages, may summon the Plaintiff offending, *&c.* and by their Warrant may levy it by Distress, *&c.* and for Want thereof may commit, *&c.* to the Common Gaol without Bail, till he shall pay.

Ib. §. 6.
Journeymen Taylors within the Limits aforesaid being retained to work, and departing before the End of the Term for which they are retained, or before the Work is finished; or who shall refuse to work after Request by any Master Taylor, for the Wages and Hours before mentioned (without some reasonable Cause to be allowed by two Justices) and being lawfully convicted thereof, shall be sent to the House of Correction, there to be kept to hard Labour for any Time not exceeding two Months.

Ib. §. 7.
A Taylor, or any Person professing that Trade, giving greater Wages than as aforesaid, and being lawfully convicted, as aforesaid, of the said Offence, shall forfeit 5 *l.* one Moiety to the Informer, the other to the Poor, *&c.* And the Servant or Journeyman taking greater Wages, and being thereof convicted as aforesaid, shall be sent to the House of Correction, there to be kept to hard Labour for any Time not exceeding two Months; all Retainers, Promises or Securities for greater Wages shall be void.

Ib. §. 8.
But where an Agreement is made for more Wages, to work before or after the said Hours limited, or to be limited, in such Case more Wages may be paid and received.

Ib. §. 9.
An Appeal lies to the next Quarter-Sessions from the Order of the two Justices, giving six Days Notice, whose Determination shall be final, and they may give Costs to either Party.

Shoemakers.
9 Geo. 1. c. 27.
§. 1.
Journeyman Shoemaker, or any Person hired as such within the Bills of Mortality, being accused by his Master employing him of having fraudulently purloined, sold, pawned or exchanged any Boots, Shoes, Slippers, Leather cut, Lace, Lasts, or other Materials for making Boots, *&c.* not being the proper Goods of the Person accused, shall by a Justice of

* *Complaint being made on Oath.*
the County where the Offence shall be done, or where the Party accused doth reside, be * summoned, or by Warrant commanded to be brought before him; and on his Appearance or Default to appear, the Justice may examine the Fact with which the Party is charged

Justice may award Satisfaction to the Party.
and upon Confession, *&c.* or Proof on Oath by one Witness, he may convict the Offender and award the Party griev'd reasonable Damages for his Loss and Charges, which if no immediately paid, then it may be levied by Warrant by Distress and Sale, *&c.* and so

Wan

Want of fufficient Diftrefs, then to caufe the Offender to be whipp'd in the Parifh where *Juftice may* the Offence was committed; and if afterwards he fhall be convicted of a fecond Offence, *award Satis-* then to be fent to the Houfe of Correction, there to be kept to hard Labour for any Time *faction to the Party:* not exceeding a Month, nor under 14 Days.

He who buys, receives, or takes in Pawn any Boots, &c. or Materials for making them, *He who buys* not being the proper Goods of the Seller or Pawner; or he who offers to fell or pawn them, *or takes Boots, Shoes, &c. at* fhall for every Offence, being convicted thereof in Manner as aforefaid, make Satisfaction *Pawn, fhall* within two Days after it fhall be awarded, otherwife his Goods fhall be fubject to a Diftrefs; *make Satisfaction.* and for Want of Diftrefs, to the like Punifhment as aforefaid. *Ib. §. 2.*

Two Juftices within the Bills of Mortality, may upon Complaint on Oath, iffue out *Juftices may* their Warrant to fearch the Houfes of fufpected Perfons in the Day-time who have bought *grant War-* or taken fuch Goods at Pawn, and on Refufal may break open the Houfe, &c. oppofing *rants to fearch. &c.* fuch Search forfeits 10 *l.* to the Informer fuing for it by Action of Debt, in the Courts in *Ib. §. 3.* *Weftminfter-Hall* within two Months; and if upon the Search, or the Oath of one Witnefs, it fhall appear that fuch Perfon hath the Goods, the Juftice fhall caufe them to be reftored, and Satisfaction to be made to the Owner for detaining and getting them; the Party refufing fhall be fubject to the like Punifhment as aforefaid.

Any Perfon employed by one Shoemaker, and retained by another before he hath finifhed *Ib. §. 4.* his Work, being convicted on Oath before one Juftice, fhall be fent to labour in the Houfe of Correction, not exceeding one Month.

There lies an Appeal to the next Seffions, giving eight Days Notice, whofe Determina- *Ib. §. 5.* tion fhall be final.

C H A P. LIX. (*a*)

Leather.

NO Perfon, by himfelf or other, fhall gafh or cut the Hide of any Ox, Bull, Steer, *Gafhing.* or Cow, upon Pain to forfeit twenty Pence for every Hide. *1 Jac. 22. §. 2.*

No Butcher fhall water any Hide, but in *June*, *July*, or *Auguft*, nor offer to Sale any *Watering.* Hide putrified or rotten, on Pain to forfeit three Shillings and four Pence for every fuch Hide. *Ibid.*

No Butcher fhall by himfelf, or any other, ufe the Trade of a Tanner, while he ufeth *Butcher.* the Trade of a Butcher, upon Pain to forfeit 6 *s.* 8 *d. per Diem.* *Ib. §. 4.*

No Perfon fhall tan any Leather, nor take any Benefit or Advantage by that Craft, ex- *Who may be a* cept he have been brought up and inftructed therein as an Apprentice, or Covenant, or *Tanner.* hired Servant, by feven Years; and except the Wife, and fuch Perfon as fhall marry the *Ibid.* Wife or Daughter to whom he fhall leave a Tan-houfe and Fats; and except fuch Son or Sons as have ufed the Trade four Years, upon Pain to lofe the Leather, or the juft Value thereof.

No Perfon ufing the Trade of a Tanner fhall ufe any Trade exercifed in the Cutting of *Trades.* Leather, upon Pain to forfeit the Leather, or juft Value. *Ib. §. 6.*

No Perfon fhall buy, contract for, befpeak any rough Hide, or Calve-skin, except fuch *Buying.* Perfon as may ufe the Trade of a Tanner, and fhall tan the fame; or fuch Perfons as *Ib. §. 7.* fhall tan the fame, except falt Hides for Ships, upon Pain to forfeit the Leather, or juft Value.

No Perfon fhall foreftal Hides, or buy them, but in Fair or Market, except of the *Foreftalling.* Owner that killed for his own Ufe, upon Pain to forfeit for every Hide 6 *s.* 8 *d.* *Ibid.*

No Perfon may buy, contract for, or befpeak any unwrought Leather, but he that will *Buying* and fhall work out the fame into Wares, upon Pain to forfeit the Leather, or Value *Leather.* thereof. *Ib. §. 8.*

Upon which Claufe a Cafe was *M.* 16 *Car.* 1. inter *Lodge* & *Holkwel*, where a Currier *Currier.* bought Hides, and curried them with Oil and Tallow, and Things neceffary; and after *Cro.Car.588.* fhaved and died them, and fold them to a Shoemaker; and it was adjudged this was an Offence againft this Claufe of the Statute, and is againft the Meaning of 5 & 6 E. 15, & 27 *El.* 16, & 1 *Jac. cap.* 22. For a Currier may not buy and fell by Wholefale.

Perfons ufing to convert Leather into Wares, may buy at *Leadenhall*, and Sadlers and *Ib. §. 9, 10* Girdlers may fell their Necks and Shreds of tanned Leather.

No Perfon ufing Tanning, fhall fuffer a Hide or Skin to lie until it be over limed. *Lime.* *Ib. §. 11.*

Tanner.   Nor shall put any Hide or Skin in Tanfats, before the Lime be well fokened and wrought out of them.

Material.   Nor put or ufe any Stuff about the tanning of Leather, but Afh-Bark, Oak-Bark, Tapwort, Malt, Meal, Lime, Culver-dung, or Hen-dung.

Parching,   Nor fuffer Leather to lie or hang wet until it be frozen.

    Nor dry or parch the Leather with Heat of Fire, or the Summer Sun.

    Nor shall tan a putrefied or rotten Hide.

Woozes.   Nor fuffer the Hides for outer Sole-Seather to lie in the Woozes any lefs than twelve Months.

    Nor the Hides for upper Leather, to lie in the Woozes lefs than nine Months.

Forfeits.   Nor shall negligently work the Hides in the Woozes, but shall renew and ftrengthen their Woozes as often as is requifite, upon Pain to forfeit every Hide of Ox, Steer, Bull, or Cow, otherwife wrought and put to Sale, or the Value.

Raifing with Mixtures. *Ib. §. 13.*   No Perfons shall raife with any Mixtures any Hide for Backs, Bend Leather, Clouting Leather, or other Sole-Leather, except the Hide be fit for that Ufe, for State, Largenefs, or Growth, upon Pain to forfeit it.

Searching. *Ib. §. 14.*   None shall put to Sale any tanned Leather, red, and unwrought, before it be fearched and fealed, in fome open Fair or Market; nor until it be fearched and fealed according to that Statute, upon Pain to forfeit for every Hide or Piece of Leather 6 s. 8 d.. And for every Dozen of Calves Skins, and Sheeps Skins, 3 s. 4 d. and of the fame Hide, Skins, and Leather, or the Value. But this Claufe touching Search and Sealing of fuch Skins, is repealed by 4 *Jac.* 1. *cap.* 6. fo as the fame be made into Wares in *England.*

Skins. *4 Jac. 1. 6. §. 2.*

Not well tanned, or dried. *1 Jac. 1. c. 22. §. 15.*   If any Tanner put to Sale any Leather, not fufficiently tanned or dried, and the fame be found fo by the Triers, he shall forfeit the whole Hide, Back, or Skin, if it be wholly defective, or if Part defective, that Part to be cut by the Triers.

Undue Tanning. *Ib. §. 17.*   No Perfons shall fet their Fats in Tan-hills, or other Places where the Woozes or Leather may take any unkind Heat.

    Nor put any Leather in hot or warm Woozes.

    Nor tan any Hide, Calves Skin, or Sheeps Skin, with warm or hot Woozes; or if he do, shall forfeit for every fuch Offence 10 *l.* and shall ftand in the Pillory three Market Days, in a Market-Town next the Place of the Offence.

Foreftalling. *Ib. §. 19.* *Ib. §. 25.*   The Penalty of foreftalling of Oaken Bark, is the Forfeiture of fuch Bark, or the Value.

    None ufing the Trade of a Currier, shall ufe the Trade of a Butcher, Tanner, Cordwainer, or other Trade ufing cutting of Leather, upon Pain to forfeit 6 s. 8 d. for every Hide or Skin he shall curry.

Currier's Place. *Ib. §. 22.*   No Currier shall curry any Leather in any other than his own Houfe, fituate in a Corporate or Market Town.

    Nor shall curry any Leather, not fufficiently tanned and dried, after its wet Seafon: Nor in its wet Seafon, he shall not ufe any ftale or deceitful Mixture to corrupt or hurt it.

Materials.   Nor curry any Leather meet for outer Sole-Leather, but with hard Tallow, and of that as much as the Leather will receive.

    Nor curry any Leather meet for upper Leather, but with good Stuff, frefh and not falt, throughly liquored till it will receive no more.

    Nor burn or fcald any Hide or Leather in the Currying.

Gafh.   Nor shave any Leather too thin, nor gafh or hurt in the Shaving, or by other Means, but shall work it fufficiently in all Refpects.

Forfeits.   Upon Pain to forfeit for every Offence (except in Gafhing, or hurting in Shaving) 6 s. 8 d. And the Value of every Hide and Skin fo marred, by his evil Workmanfhip; and for every Offence in Gafhing, or hurting by Shaving, double fo much to the Party grieved as the Leather shall be impaired by the Judgment of the Wardens of the Curriers, and Wardens of the Company whereof the Party grieved shall be.

London Cordwainers. *Ib. §. 23 & 24.*   No Cordwainer or other dwelling in *London,* or within three Miles, ufing wet Leather, shall put any Leather to be curried, but to one free of the Company of Curriers of *London,* upon Pain to forfeit the Leather, or the Value, nor ufe any curried Leather before the fame be fearched and allowed by the Wardens of the Curriers, or fuch Perfons as they shall affign, and fealed, upon Pain to forfeit for every Hide or Skin 6 s. 8 d. and the Value of fuch Hide or Skin.

Ib. §. 26.   Every Currier shall curry Leather, brought to him, within eight Days in Summer, and fixteen Days in Winter, the Party bringing good Stuff for liquoring it, and that in the Prefence of the Party bringing it, if he or his Servant will be prefent, and shall not refufe to

curry

curry it, upon Pain of 10 s. for every Hide or Piece not well and fpeedily curried, to the Party grieved.

The Wardens of the Curriers, or fuch as they fhall appoint, fhall try and feal all curried Leather, within a Day after Currying, by any of their Company, and Requeft; taking a Penny for a Dicker, and a Penny for fix Dozen of Calves-skins, or forfeit for every Hide 6 s. 8 d. *Ib. §. 27.*

Cordwainers, &c. fhall make no Shoes, Boots, Buskins, Startups, Slippers, or Pan-tofles of *Englifh* Leather wet curried (other than Deer-skins, Calves-skins, Goat-skins, made and dreffed like *Spanifh* Leather) but of Leather well tanned and curried, or well tanned and well fewed with good Thread well twifted and waxed, and Wax well rofin-ed, and Stitches hard drawn with Hand-Leathers, without mixing the over Leather, *i. e.* Part Neat, Part Calve. *Cordwainers. Ib. §. 28.*

Nor put into any Shoes, &c. Leather made of Sheep-skin, Bull-hide, or Horfe-hide.

Nor into the Upper Leather of any Shoes, &c. nor into the neather Part of any Boots (the inner Part of the Shoe excepted) any Leather called Wombs, Neck, Shank, Flank, Powle, or Cheek.

Nor put into the utter Sole, any other Leather than the beft of Ox, or Steer-hide.

Nor into the inner Sole, any other than Wombs, Neck, Powle or Cheek.

Nor into the Trefwels of any double foled Shoes, other than the Flanks of the Hide.

Nor fhall make or put to Sale in any Year, between the laft Day of *September* and the twentieth Day of *April*, any Shoes fit for one above four Years old, any Boots, &c. wherein fhall be any dry *Englifh* Leather, other than Calve and Goat-Skins drefs'd like *Spanifh* Leather.

Nor fhall fhew with Intent to put to Sale any Shoes, &c. upon *Sunday*, upon Pain to forfeit for every Pair of Shoes, &c. 3 s. 4 d. with the full Value thereof.

The Mafter and Wardens of the Companies of Cordwainers, Curriers, Girdlers, and Sadlers in *London*, upon Pain of 40 l. fhall every Quarter of the Year at the leaft in *London*, and within three Miles thereof, where any Artificers cutting Leather dwell, enter, fearch and feife, if Wares be not made of tanned Leather; and according to that Act, each Company to fearch thofe of their own Trade only. *Companies fearching. Ib. §. 29.*

The Coach-makers of *London*, or three Miles from the fame, fhall be under the Survey of the Mafter and Wardens of the Company of Sadlers. *Ib. §. 30.*

The Mayor and Alderman, upon Pain of 40 l. fhall yearly appoint eight out of thofe four Companies, whereof one fhall keep the Seal, to fearch and feal in *London*, or three Miles next it. *London. Ib. §. 31.*

All Mayors, Bailiffs, and Head-Officers of all Cities, Boroughs and Towns, Lords of Liberties, Fairs and Markets, upon Pain of 40 l. (a Moiety to the King, and the other Moiety to the Profecutor) fhall chufe and fwear two or more Perfons yearly, to fearch and view Leather, who fhall fearch and have a Mark, and therewith mark Leather that is fufficient; who if they find any Leather not well tanned or curried, or Shoes, Boots, &c. not well made, may feife the fame, and retain them until tried by the Triers. *Searchers. Ib. §. 32.*

The Lord Mayor of *London* fhall within fix Days after Seifure choofe fix; two Cord-wainers, two Curriers, and two of the better Sort of Tanners, ufing *Leaden-hall* Market, who fhall be no kin to the Owners, who upon Oath fhall the fecond or third Market-Day, upon the *Monday* * for Leather, next after the Seifure, in the Afternoon, try whether the Leather fo feifed fhall be fufficient or not. *London, Triers. Ib. §. 33.* * By 13 & 13 Car. 2. c. 7. §. 9. the Mar-ket for Leather in Leaden-hall in London fhall be kept on the Tuefday.

Other Mayors, Bailiffs, Head-Officers, and Lords, with convenient Speed fhall elect fix Triers, who upon Oath, upon fome Market-Day within fifteen Days after Seifure, fhall try, &c. *Mayors. Ib. §. 34.*

The Lord Mayor, Mayors, &c. not electing Triers, fhall for every Default forfeit 5 l. and the Perfons elected for Trial of the faid Leather, &c. fhall proceed without Delay, on Pain to forfeit 5 l. *Forfeits. Ib. §. 35.*

Four of the Searchers and Sealers of Leather in *London* fhall be every Year changed, and no Perfon fhall continue above two Years in that Office, and fhall not be chofen again within three Years, upon Pain to forfeit 10 l. for every Month ufing that Office. *Searchers. Ib. §. 36.*

If any Scarcher or Sealer fhall refufe with convenient Speed to feal any Leather fuffi-ciently tanned, wrought and ufed, or allow that which fhall be infufficient, he fhall forfeit 40 s. And if any Searcher fhall receive any Bribe, or exact any other Fee than is *Ib. §. 37.*

4 by

by this Statute limited, for the Searching, Sealing and Regiftring of Leather, he fhall forfeit 20 *l.* And if any Perfon elected to the Office of Searching or Sealing of Leather refufe to execute the faid Office, he fhall forfeit 10 *l.*

Leaden-hall.
Ib. §. 38.
All Leather to be brought into *London,* or within three Miles, fhall be brought to *Leaden-hall* before it be perufed, and there fearched and regiftred, paying half Fees for fuch tanned Leather as fhall be bought out of *London :* But it extends not to Leather brought to *Bartholomew* or *Southwark* Fair.

London.
Ibid. §. 39.
No tanned Leather fhall be fold in *London* before fearched and fealed, upon Pain of Forfeiture thereof, or the full Value.

Oppofition.
Ib. §. 40.
If any withftand or deny any Entry and Search to be made in their Houfes, or of their Goods made of Leather, or will not fuffer a Seifure, he fhall forfeit 5 *l.* every Time.

Regiftry.
Ib. §. 41.
The Searchers and Sealers appointed fhall regifter all Leather bought and fold, with the Names of Parties, Prices, and Particulars, taking of the Seller for every ten Hides, &c. two Pence, and two Pence for every fix Dozen of Calves-skins or Sheep-skins.

Ib. §. 42.
None fhall fell, exchange, or put away any tanned Leather, nor buy or carry the fame out of the Fair before it be regiftered, upon Pain of Forfeiture of the Value.

London Cur-
riers.
Ib. §. 44.
If any Currier in *London,* or within three Miles of it, curry any Leather infuffi- ciently tanned, or do not curry Leather fufficiently, he fhall forfeit the Wares, and the juft Value thereof.

London Arti-
ficers.
If any Shoemaker, Cordwainer, or Cobler in *London,* or within three Miles of it, put any tanned Leather in any Shoes, &c. or other Things made of tanned Leather, that is not fufficiently tanned.

Or put in any curried Leather into any Shoes, &c. not fufficiently curried, tanned and fealed.

Or make any Boots, &c. or other Things made of *English* tanned Leather, in other Manner than as abovefaid.

Or if any Shoemaker, Sadler, or Artificer, ufing, cutting, or working of Leather, make Wares of tanned Leather not fufficiently tanned; or of tanned and curried Leather not fufficiently tanned and curried as aforefaid.

Or do not make their Ware fubftantially and fufficiently. Every Perfon fo offending fhall forfeit the Wares and the Value.

London Mar-
ket.
Ib. §. 45.
No Perfon fhall in *London,* or within three Miles of it, fell any Wares appertaining to any Artificer, ufing cutting of Leather, but in open Shop, Fair or Market, upon Pain of forfeiting the Wares fold, and 10 *s.* for every Time.

Ib. §. 46.
All Perfons ufing cutting of Leather in *London,* or within three Miles, fhall be under the Search of the Mafter, &c. as Freemen of *London* be.

Penalty.
Money.
All Penalties of Money (except what is otherwife difpofed) fhall be divided in three Parts; one Part to the King, another to the Profecutor, in any Court of Record, a third Part to the City, &c. where, &c.

London.
All Wares of tanned and curried Leather in *London,* or within three Miles, forfeited, &c. to be brought into the *Guildhall* of *London,* and paid one Part to the Seifor, the fecond Part to the Chamber, and the third Part to the Poor, as the Mayor and Alder- men fhall think fit.

All Shoes, &c. and other Things made of Leather, in any Place above three Miles from *London;* if in a City, &c. fhall be brought to the Common Hall; if no Hall, to an open Place and prized : One Part to the Poor, and to Works of Charity, the fecond Part to the City, &c. or Lord, the third Part to the Seifor.

Ib. §. 47.
Forfeited Wares fhall not be fold to any that will fell the fame again; or the Seller fhall forfeit for every Part thereof 3 *s.* 4 *d.*

Leather.
Ib. §. 49.
The Hides and Skins of Ox, Steer, Bull, Cow, Calf, Deer Red and Fallow, Goats and Sheep, being tanned or tawed, and every Salt Hide, fhall be reputed Leather.

Judges.
Ib. §. 50.
Juftice of Peace, Mayor, &c. and Head-Officers in their Seffions, Leet, or Law- Day, fhall hear and determine all thefe Offences, and by their Difcretions examine the Perfons fufpected.

Dry Currying.
Ib. §. 52.
Dry currying and frizing fhall be conftrued to be dreffing and currying after the Manner of *Spanish* Leather; and all Artificers (other than Shoemakers, between the laft Day of *September* and the twentieth Day of *April*) may ufe it as before the making of that Act, fo as it be well and fufficiently curried and dreffed.

Officers.
Tranfport.
Ib. §. 54.
Every Controller, Cuftomer, Surveyor, or Collector of Tonnage, Poundage, or their Deputies, or any other Perfons hearing or knowing of any Leather to be tranfported from any Place within his Office, and do not endeavour to feife it; or being tranfported,

do

4

do not difclofe it within forty Days after their Knowledge or Hearing, in fome Court of
Record, fhall for the firft Offence lofe 100 *l.* and for the fecond his Office.

Every Officer that fhall make a falfe Certificate of the Arrival of any Leather in any *Certificates.*
Pórt, Creek or Place, fhall forfeit 160 *l.*   Ib. §. 55.

The Statute 5 & 6 *Edw.* 6. *cap.* 15. *fect.* 1. which enacts, that no Perfons fhall buy
or ingrofs tanned Leather, to fell the fame again, upon Pain to forfeit the Leather or
the Price thereof, was repealed by 1 *Mar. Stat.* 3. *cap.* 8. *fect.* 2. But this Statute of
1 *Mar.* was repealed, and the Statute 5 & 6 *Edw.* 6. *cap.* 15. revived by 1 *Eliz. cap.* 8.
which is repealed by 5 *Eliz. cap.* 8. and 1 *Jac.* 1. *c.* 22. So *Quære* which is in Force,
and fee *Cro. Car.* 588.

None fhall carry or tranfport, or caufe, &c. out of *England* the Skins or Hides *Tranfporta-*
tanned or untanned of any Ox, Steer, Bull, Cow or Calf, otherwife than is by this *tion.*
Act directed.   13 & 14 C. 2.
                                                                                 c. 7. §. 2.
No fuch Hide taken from the Body of fuch Beaft in any Ifland belonging to *England, Importing.*
except *Ireland,* fhall be carried out of that Ifland into any Place but into *England,* upon Ib. §. 3.
Pain to forfeit for every fuch Offence double the Value thereof.

Every Perfon fo tranfporting any Hides or Leather, except Calves-skins and Sheeps- *Penalty of*
skins dreffed in the Wool, and found guilty thereof, fhall be difabled to trade in Leather, *Tranfporta-*
and for every Offence forfeits 500 *l.*   *tion.*
                                                                                 Ib. §. 5.
All red tanned Leather made of any Hides or Skins of the Beafts aforefaid, fhall be *Sale in Mar-*
bought only in open Market for Leather, upon Pain for every Offence to forfeit the *ket.*
Leather, or Value thereof, and the Contract to be void.   Ib. §. 4.

All fuch Leather fhall be fearched and fealed before it be put to Sale, and upon Sale *Searched.*
regiftred, and a true Entry thereof made by the Buyer and Seller, both to be prefent;
and their Names and Places of Abode to be entred, upon Pain that the Buyer or Seller
not doing the fame, fhall for every fuch Offence forfeit the Value thereof.

Boots, Shoes and Slippers, may be tranfported.   *Boots, &c.*
                                                                                 Ib. §. 6.
All Juftices of Peace, Mayors, and Chief Officers of Corporations, may as well by *Searching and*
Land as by Water fearch for and feife all Leather and raw Hides, wrought or un- *Seifing.*
wrought, cut or uncut, packed or unpacked, intended to be tranfported beyond Sea, or Ib. §. 7.
into *Scotland,* except Calves-skins and Sheeps-skins as aforefaid.

Every Tanner who fhall fhave, cut, and rake their Upper Leather Hides all over, *Tanners fha-*
and the Necks of the Backs and Buts, fhall forfeit the fame; and Searchers and Sealers *ving.*
may fearch it.   Ib. §. 8.

The Penalties fhall be recovered by Action of Debt, Bill, Plaint or Information *Penalties.*
(amongft others) in any Court or Courts of Record in the City, Town, County or Place, Ib. §. 10.
where the Offence is committed, wherein no Wager, &c. and fhall not be removed out
of the fame; the Moiety to the King, the other Moiety to the Informer.

All Exportation and Tranfportation contrary to the Act, is declared a common *Nufance.*
Nufance.   Ib. §. 11.

By the Statute 1 *Jac. cap.* 22. 'tis enacted, That no Man fhall buy Leather unwrought, but he who fhall make it into Wares: An * Information was brought on * Jones W.
this Paragraph againft a Currier, for buying and felling Leather tanned and not made 463.
into Wares; and it appeared upon the Evidence at the Trial, that he bought Hides
tanned, which he fhaved, coloured and glazed, and then fold them; and this was adjudged to be an Offence within the Statute, becaufe this Operation was not Making it
into Wares.

By the Statute 9 *Ann. cap.* 11. the aforefaid Act 1 *Jac.* is injoined to be obferved in 9 Ann. c. 11.
every Thing not altered by this Statute.

Now the Alterations made by this laft Act relate to *raw Hides and Calves-skins,* the *One Juftice*
firft muft not be *gafhed,* under the Penalty of 2 *s.* 6 *d. per Hide,* and 1 *s. per Calf- may give an*
skin to the Poor, and to the Seifor or Informer.   *Oath to a*
                                                                                 fubordinate
Officer of Duty on Hides who fhall receive any Salary in refpect of his Office, before he acts, for the faithful Execution thereof.

Shaving fuch Hides or Skins, by which they are impaired, or the Duty diminifhed,
Forfeiture of the Hides and Skins to the King and the Informer.

Thofe who drefs Hides and make *Vellum,* muft give Notice in Writing to a proper
Officer of their Names and Places of Abode, and of their *Tanhoufes, Warehoufes, Yards,
Mills, Pits, Fats,* and they muft if they change their Tan-yards, &c. Penalty is 50 *l.*
one Third to the King, and two Thirds to the Informer.

10 Ann. c. 26. Several additional Duties are laid on Hides, &c. See both the said Statutes at large, for the Justices may hear and determine Offences against both, by Summoning the Offender and Witnesses on either Side, and examining them on Oath: The Prosecution must be within three Months after the Seisure or Offence, and an Appeal lies to the Quarter-Sessions, and no *Certiorari* shall be allowed, but the Justices may mitigate the Forfeitures, so as the Penalty is not reduced to less than a fourth Part, and so as the Charges of the Prosecution be allowed over and above such Mitigation.

9 Ann. c. 11. §. 47. , No Information shall be brought in the Courts of *Westminster* for any of the Offences in 9 *Ann. cap.* 11. in Cases where such Offences are cognisable by the Justices, &c.

By the said Stat. 9 *Annæ*, one Justice may give an Oath to Tanners and Dressers of Hides, that they did within two Days after the Taking the Hide out of the Liquor, &c. make a true Entry with the proper Officer, of the Number and Quality of the Hides, &c. so taken out to be dried, and that they gave Notice to the proper Officer two Days before the Removal of the Hides.

Ib. §. 17. Owners or Occupiers of Tan-yards refusing a proper Officer to enter, forfeit 10 *l.* to the King and the Informer.

Tanners, &c. using any private Tan-yard, or not giving timely Notice of taking the Hides out of the Liquor, or carrying them away, or concealing, or causing them to be concealed, forfeit 20 *l.* and the Hides, &c. or the Value thereof, &c. to be mitigated, *ut supra*: Prosecution must be within three Months, and an Appeal lies to the next Quarter-Sessions.

Tanners, &c. not paying the Duties with which Hides are charged, forfeit double the Duty; and sending, delivering, or carrying away Hides, &c. before the Duty is paid, forfeit likewise double the Value.

Tanners not keeping just Scales and Weights, or not permitting Hides, &c. to be weighed, or removing them before the Duty is charged and the Skins marked forfeit 50 *l.*

Collar-makers, Bridle-cutters, Glovers, and others who dress Skins in Oil, Allom, Salt or Meal, and make them into Wares, are Tawers and Dressers within this Act.

Officer taking Fee or Reward for any Entry, Permissions, Certificates or Marks, forfeits 5 *l.* to the Party grieved for every Offence.

Ib. §. 36. The Judgment of the Justices at their Quarter-Sessions is final.

There was an Act made 1 *W. & M. cap.* 33. for explaining the Statute 1 *Jac.* 1. *cap.* 22. Some Doubts having arisen upon the Construction of this Act of *W. & M.* it 12 Geo. 2. was farther enacted by 12 *Geo.* 2. That all Persons whatsoever who deal or work in c. 25. Leather, may freely buy all Sorts of tanned Leather in any Fair or Market, whether curried or uncurried, being first searched and sealed according to Law; and may cut, and sell the same in small Pieces, in their Shops, to any Person whatsoever.

Provided, That this Act shall not extend to give Liberty to any Person to exercise the Shoe-makers Trade; other than Cordwainers or Coblers.

Nor, to give a Right to any Person to exercise his Trade in any Place, where by Law he cannot now exercise the same.

If any Currier shall not curry any Leather brought or sent to him by a Dealer in Leather, within sixteen Days, between 28 *September* and 25 *March*, and within eight Days the remaining Part of the Year, after the Leather is delivered to him; he shall, upon Conviction before a Justice, by Oath of a credible Witness, forfeit 5 *l.* to be recovered by Distress and Sale, &c. to go Half to the Informer, and Half to the Poor of the Parish.

The Trustees may mitigate Penalties at their Discretion. If any Person think himself agrieved by the Determination of the Justice, he may appeal to the next Quarter-Sessions, whose Determination shall be final, and not removeable by *Certiorari*.

The two Clauses in the Act 1 *Jac.* 1. which prohibit any Persons dwelling in *London* or the Liberties thereof, or within three Miles of the City, occupying wet curried Leather in their Business, to put forth such Leather to be curried, but to Freemen of the City; and to put into any made Wares any curried Leather before searched and sealed by the Wardens of the *Curriers* of *London*, shall be repealed.

This Act shall not extend to lessen the Privileges of the said Curriers Company.

I

CHAP

CHAP. LX.

London *.

* The 35 Eliz.
c. 6. (*inferted*
by Dalton)
*enacting that
no new Build-
ing fhall be
erected within
three Miles of
London and
Weftminfter
is expired.*
19 Car. 2.
c. 3. §. 3.

1) NO Building fhall be erected within the City and Liberties, but fuch as fhall be purfuant to fuch Rules of Building, and with fuch Materials, as are by this Act appointed, and according to fuch Scantlings as are fet down in a Table in this Act fpeci- fied. And if any Perfon fhall build contrary, and be convicted by the Oaths of two Witneffes, before the Lord Mayor, or any Two Juftices for the City, the Houfe fo ir- egularly built fhall be deemed a common Nufance, and the Builder fhall enter into a Recognizance for demolifhing the fame, or otherwife to amend the fame; and in Default of entering into fuch Recognizance, the Offender fhall be committed to Gaol till he have demolifhed, or otherwife amended the fame; or elfe fuch irregular Houfe fhall be demolifhed by Order of the Court of Aldermen.

See the Statute at large; as alfo the 22 *Car.* 2. *cap.* 11. For other Matters relating to Building, fee the *Appendix*, Tit. *Fire.*

9 Geo. 2.
c. 20. §. 17.

If any Perfon fhall wilfully break or extinguifh any Lamps (fet up in purfuance of this Act) to light the Streets, or damage the Pofts or Furniture thereof, every Perfon fo of- fending, and convicted by Oath of one Witnefs before a Juftice of Peace for *London*, fhall for the firft Offence forfeit 40 s. for each Lamp, and for the fecond Offence 50 s. and for the third Offence 3 l.

Ib. §. 22.

It fhall be lawful for the Lord Mayor, or any two Juftices for the City, to hear and determine the Offences punifhable by pecuniary Penalties by this Act; and fuch Juftices are required within ten Days after fuch Offence committed, to fummon the Parties and Witneffes, and after Oath of the Facts by one Witnefs, to iffue Warrants for apprehend- ing the Party offending in *London*, and upon Appearance or Contempt of the Party, to proceed to the Examination of the Witnefs, and to give fuch Sentence as fhall be juft. And where the Party fhall be convicted, it fhall be lawful for fuch Juftices to iffue War- rants for levying the Penalties on the Goods of the Offender, and to caufe Sale to be made in cafe they be not redeemed in five Days; and if no Goods of any Perfon con- victed of breaking or extinguifhing a Lamp can be found, the Juftice before whom he was convicted may commit him to the Houfe of Correction to hard Labour, not exceed- ing three Months, or until fuch Penalty be paid.

Ib. §. 23.

The Juftices may mitigate Penalties, fo as not to remit above one Moiety.

Ib. §. 24.

An Appeal lies to the next Quarter-Seffions.

Ib. §. 25.

One Moiety of the Penalties by this Act, goes to the Informer, the other Moiety to the Alderman of the Ward, to be paid over into the Chamber, as Part of the Fund for maintaining fuch Lights.

Ib. §. 26.

Actions muft be brought within fix Months after the Fact, and laid in *London*. De- fendants may plead the General Iffue, and fhall have treble Cofts if Judgment be againft the Plaintiff.

Ib. §. 9.
Ib. §. 12.
Ib. §. 20.

The other pecuniary Penalties in the Act, befides the abovementioned are, that Collec- tors chofen at the Wardmote according to the Act, refufing to ferve, forfeit 10 l. and continue liable to be chofen the Year following, *toties quoties.* And a Collector retaining more than 50 l. in his Hands for ten Days, forfeits 5 l. Alfo if any Collector fhall neglect to bring in his Accounts to the Alderman at the Wardmote on St. *Thomas's* Day, he fhall forfeit 5 l. and in like Manner 5 l. for every twenty Days.

For *Repairing and Enlarging Streets in and about* London, *fee* Tit. Private Highways.

CHAP. LXI.

Malt.

One Justice.
2 Ed. 6. c.10.
§. 4. continued
indef. by 3 Car.
1. c. 4.
16 Car.1. c.4.

THE Conſtables or Bailiff of any Town, where any deceitful Malts ſhall be made or mingled, to be ſold contrary to the Statute 2 *Ed.* 6. may from Time to Time view and ſearch all ſuch Malt, as ſhall be made or put to Sale within any of their Towns and if thereupon they ſhall find any Malt put to Sale, being evil made, or mingled with evil Malt contrary to this Statute; then the ſaid Conſtable or Bailiff, ſo finding any ſuch deceitful Malt, with the Advice of any one Juſtice of Peace, may cauſe the ſame to be ſold to ſuch Perſons, and at ſuch reaſonable Prices, as to the Diſcretion of the ſame Juſtice ſhall ſeem expedient.

(*a*) Theſe deceitful Malts be of three Sorts, *ſcil.* ſuch as be not well made, or no well dreſſed or mixed. As,

1. Firſt, If any Barley-Malt ſhall be made (in the Months of *June, July* and *Auguſt* only excepted) if the ſame Malt ſhall not have in the Making thereof (*ſcil.* in the Fat Floor, Steeping and Drying thereof) three Weeks at the leaſt; and in the Months of *June, July* and *Auguſt,* ſeventeen Days at the leaſt. For under ſuch Times the Mal cannot be well made, nor wholſome for any Man's Body; and Malt not ſufficiently dried, cannot be kept long, but will be muſty, and full of Wevils.

2. Secondly, If any Malts ſhall be put to Sale which be not well trodden, rubbed and well fanned.

* The Stat.
39 Eliz. c.16.

3. Thirdly, if any Malts be mingled, *ſcil.* Malt not well made as aforeſaid, or made Mow-burnt, or ſpired Barley, and mixed with good Malt, and ſo put to Sale*.

to reſtrain the exceſſive Making of Malt, inſerted by Dalton, is repealed by 9 & 10 W. 3. cap. 22.

Malt damaged
after the Du-
ty paid.
9 Geo.1. c.3.
§. 35.
Certificate of
the Amount of
the Duty.

If any Quantity of Malt ſhall be deſtroyed or damaged by Fire after the *Duties* are paid, or ſhall be damaged by the Caſting away, or any inevitable Accident happening to any Veſſel or Barge carrying Malt from Port to Port, or put on board for that Purpoſe the Proprietors proving the ſame by the Oath of one or more credible Witneſſes, before the *Juſtices in Seſſions,* and by the Oath of the Maltſters or Owners, that the *Duty* was paid, they may grant a Certificate of the Amount of the Duty, and upon producing the ſame the Collector of the Duty ſhall repay the Proprietor ſo much Money as the Sum certified to be paid for the Duty of the Malt ſo loſt ſhall amount unto; and when the Malt ſhall not be totally loſt, but damaged only, the Juſtices, *&c.* on Proof

Juſtices may
ſettle the
Quantum of
the Damage.

of the Damage and Payment of the Duty, may ſettle the *Quantum* of the Damage, and give a Certificate under their Hands and Seals of the Sum by them allowed for ſuch Damage; which Allowance where the Malt is *damaged* only, ſhall bear Proportion to the whole Duty of the Malt ſo damaged, as it ſhall bear to the Value of the Malt before it was damaged; and upon producing ſuch Certificate, the Collector ſhall repay ſo much

Notice muſt be
given to the
Collector to
what Quarter-
Seſſions the
Party will
apply.
Ib. §. 36.

Money as the Sum certified will amount to.

The Perſon ſuſtaining ſuch Loſs, or his Agent, muſt give Notice thereof in Writing to the Collector of the Diviſion next to the Place where the Quarter-Seſſions is held (to which he intends to apply himſelf for ſuch Allowance) of ſuch Loſs and Damages, and his Intentions to apply *ſix Days* at leaſt before the Seſſions, and ſhall make his Application for Relief within *one Month* after the Loſs or Damage happened.

Ib. §. 37.

Where the Juſtices have once aſcertained the Damages or Loſs, the ſame ſhall never be aſcertained by any other Juſtices.

For the 12 Geo. 1. *cap.* 4. and 2 Geo. 2. *cap.* 1. ſee the *Appendix,* Tit. *Malt.*

11 Geo.2. c.1.
Ib. §. 12.

Every Diſtiller, that ſhall receive any Cyder or Perry into his Cuſtody, ſhall give Notice in Writing to the proper Officer, forty-eight Hours before he ſhall begin to put any of the ſame into any Still to be drawn into low Wines; and if any Diſtiller neglect to give ſuch Notice; or if any of ſuch Cyder or Perry be made uſe of by ſuch Diſtiller in any other Way but in Diſtillation, he ſhall forfeit 5 *l.* which Sum ſhall be levied and mitigated, as any Penalty by any Laws of Excise, or by Action of Debt, *&c.*

Ib. §. 15.

Makers of Malt for Exportation ſhall keep the whole Quantity of their Corn making into Malt for Exportation of one Steeping, when the ſame ſhall be on the Kiln, ſeparate

I

rate

ate from any former Steeping, until the fame fhall have been meafured by fuch Malt-
ters in the Prefence of fome Officer, on Pain of forfeiting 50 *l.*

Makers of Malt for Exportation, fhall give Notice in Writing to fome Officer of the *Ib. §. 16.*
Duties, or leave Notice at the next Office of Excife where the Journal is kept, of the Hour
when they intend to take the Malt off the Kiln; and after fuch Malt has been meafured,
the fame fhall be carried on Shipboard, or elfe immediately locked up in fome Store-houfe
belonging to fuch Malfters, in Prefence of the Officer, on Pain of 50 *l.*

If any fuch Malfter, after any Steeping fhall have been locked up, fhall open the Locks, *Ib. §. 17.*
or make any Entrance into fuch Storehoufe or other Place, or fhall remove any Part of
the Partition between any fuch Storehoufe, or any other Place adjoining, or fhall remove
out of the Storehoufe any of the Malt fo locked up, without the Confent of, or without
having given Notice to fome Officer for the faid Duties, he fhall forfeit 100 *l.*

All Perfons that fhall become Makers of Malt for Exportation, fhall within nine Months *Ib. §. 19.*
after the Beginning to make Ufe of any fuch Storehoufe, clear out to be exported all Malt
that fhall have been put into fuch Place within nine Months after they fhall have begun to
make Ufe of fuch Place, and fhall always clear out of fuch Storehoufe to be exported, all
Malt that within every nine Months after the laft Clearing fhall be locked up for Exporta-
ion, on Pain of 50 *l.*

All Penalties for any Offences againft this Act, fhall be levied or mitigated as any Penalty *Ib. §. 20.*
by any of the Laws of Excife, or by Action of Debt, *&c.* and one Moiety fhall be to his
Majefty, and the other Moiety to him that fhall difcover or fue for the fame.

See *Manufactures*, 13 *Geo.* 2. *cap.* 21. infra. *Chap.* 196.

C H A P. LXII. (*a*)

Markets and Fairs.

FAIR feemeth to be derived from the Latin, *Feriæ, Nundinæ enim femper inftar Fefti *Name.*
funt,* faith *Skinner's* Lexicon.

Market feems to be derived from the Latin, *Merces* or *Mercari,* faith *Skinner's* Lexicon. *Privilege.*

Fairs were antiently Places of great Refort and Privilege; for by the Civil Law, *Nundinæ
habent publicam fecuritatem, ut nemo privati debiti caufa ibidem poffit interpellari, non de-
iicti;* which muft be underftood of Debts and Offences preceding the Fair; for as to Con-
racts there made the Law hath provided a Court of *Piepowders,* which is incident to a
Fair; and is a Court of Record for the fpeedy determining of Differences there arifing upon
Contracts.

Fairs are accounted Things of Franchife and Privilege, as well as of Profit; and whether *Time of Con-*
they be held and claimed by Charter of the King, or by Prefcription, which fuppofes a for- *tinuance.*
mer Charter, they ought to be holden for no longer Time, than fuch Grant or Ufe will
warrant: And after fuch Time, what is done there, is not warranted or juftifiable, nor
amounts to more than a private Tranfaction, and the Sheriff ought to make Proclamation, *2 E. 3. c. 15.*
that thofe that have Fairs keep them no longer than they ought to do; and every Lord of
a Fair, fhall at the Beginning thereof make Proclamation how long the fame is to continue,
upon Pain to be grievoufly amerced to the King: And if they hold them longer than they
ought, they fhall be feifed into the King's Hands, until they make Fine for the Offence; *5 E. 3. c. 5.*
and if a Merchant fell Ware after the Time the Fair ought to end, he fhall forfeit to the
King double the Value of what is fold, and the Profecutor fhall have the fourth Part.

Fairs and Markets on the principal Feafts, *viz. Afcenfion-day, Corpus Chrifti-day, Whit-* *Feftival.*
funday, Trinity Sunday, and all other Sundays, the *Affumption* of our *Lady, All-Saints* *27 H. 6. 5.*
and *Good-Friday,* fhall ceafe from all fhewing of Goods and Merchandifes, neceffary Victuals only excepted, upon Pain of Forfeiture of their Goods fhewed, the four *Sundays* in
Harveft excepted, and the Fairs or Markets which are granted to be holden on thofe Fefti-
vals, may be holden within three Days, before or after.

No Fairs or Markets fhall be kept in Church-yards, for the Honour of the Church. *Place.*
13 E. 1. c. 5.
Winch.

Buying and Selling again in the fame Fair or Market of Cattle forbidden. See 3 *&* 4 *Cattle.*
Ed. 6. 19. Tit. *Cattle.*

　　　　　　　　　Touching

Horses.   Touching Sale of Horfes in Fairs and Markets, and the Duty of the Lord or Owner of the Fair thereabouts, fee 1 *P. & M.* 7. and Tit. *Horfes,* and 31 *El.* 12.

Country.   That fuch as live in the Country, fhall not fell divers Merchandifes there named in Towns, except in open Fairs. See 1 & 2 *P. & M.* 7. But the Juftice of Peace hath nothing to do therein.

For the Office of Clerk of the Market, fee afterwards Tit. *Weights and Meafures.*

Rules.   And becaufe Juftices of Peace have often to do with Property, and how far it may be devefted by Sale in a Market-Overt, it will be neceffary to add fome few Cafes touching the fame.

London.   1. That in *London,* every Day in the Week is a Market-day, except Sunday, and a Sale *bona fide* in a Shop therein any Day of the Week, is good.

2. The Sale in fuch a Shop muft be of Things proper to the Trade of the Shop-keeper, and fo a Sale of Plate in a Scrivener's Shop, is not good; and fo of every other Trade.

3. If a Sale be of Plate in a Goldfmith's Shop (where it is properly to be fold) it muft be publickly and open: For if a Sale be there of Plate in an inner Shop, or behind a Curtain, or a Cup-board, or the Windows be fhut, or any Thing elfe hides it; fo that he that paffes by cannot fee what is done there, it will not alter the Property. All this was re-folved H. 38 *El.* Co. 5. 83. *Moor's Rep. p.* 360. *Evefq; de Worcefter's* Cafe. *Moor's Rep. p.* 624.

4. If a Sale in a Market Overt be covinous, or the Party that buys the Goods knows they were ftoln, this Sale alters no Property. 33 *H.* 6. 5. *Co.* 3. 78.

5. The King cannot grant to one, that his Shop fhall be a Market to alter the Property of a Stranger's Goods, for it is againft Law.

6. In a Market or Town where feveral Things are fold in diftinct Places, the Sale ought to be in every Part of the Town, of what is there faleable, as Horfes in *Smithfield.* *Moor's Rep.* 360.

7. He that pleads a Sale in Markets, muft plead it to be done *Pleno Mercatu,* elfe it is not good. *Moor's Rep. p.* 360.

Kelynge 50.   Sale to a Pawn-broker, tho' in his Shop, alters no Property, for 'tis not a Market Overt.

CHAP. LXIII.

Marriage. (*a*)

1: Car. 2.   A LL Mariages made fince One thoufand fix hundred forty and two before any Juftice
c. 33.   of Peace, or otherwife confirmed and made good; and Iffues upon Baftardies, or otherwife touching the fame, to be tried by Juries.

See *Felony by Statute,* Chap. 160.

CHAP. LXIV.

Mariners.

5 El. 5. §. 43.   N O Fifherman ufing the Sea, fhall be taken to ferve as a Mariner by the King's Com-miffion, but by the Choice of two Juftices of Peace next adjoining to the Place where he is taken.

2 Ann. c. 6.   (*a*) Two Juftices, or the Chief Magiftrate of any City or Town corporate, with the
§. 1.   Confent of two Juftices, and the Church-wardens and Overfeers of the Poor may put Boys
* *To Mafters*   Apprentices to the * Sea Service, who are above † ten Years old, and likely to be charge-
or Owners of   able to the Parifh, and whofe Parents are already chargeable, and thofe who beg.
Ships till the
Age of 21 Years.   † *By* Stat. 4 & 5 Ann. c. 19. §. 16. *the Mafter fhall not be obliged to take him under the Age of* 13 *Years.*

The Age muft be
inferted in the   The Church-wardens, &c. muft pay the Mafter 2 *l.* 10 *s.* when the Boy is bound, for
Indenture.   Clothing, &c. which the Parifh muft allow in their Accounts.
Ib. §. 2.
Ib. §. 5.   Church-wardens, &c. muft fend the Counterpart of the Indenture to the Collector of the Cuftoms of the Port to which fuch Mafter fhall belong, who fhall enter it, and indorfe

     I   the

he Regiſtry without Fee; the Collector neglecting forfeits 5 *l.* to the Poor of the Pariſh from whence the Boy was bound.

The Collector ſhall ſend Certificates to the Admiralty of the Names and Ages of ſuch Apprentices, and the Ships to which they belong; and they ſhall not be preſſed or liſted *Ib. §. 4.* n the King's Service till Eighteen.

+ Maſters of Apprentices, according to 43 *Eliz. cap.* 2, may, with the Conſent of two *† Or their Exe-* Juſtices, or chief Officer of the Place where ſuch Boy was bound Apprentice, turn over the *cutors or Admi-* Apprentice to a Maſter of a Ship or Owner, during the Remainder of his Apprenticeſhip; *aſſign the Ap-* which Indenture ſhall be regiſtred and certified as aforeſaid, and Protection given till *prentices.* Eighteen. *Ib. §. 6.*

Every Apprentice ſo bound ſhall be conducted to the ſaid Port by the Church-wardens *Ib. §. 10.* and Overſeers, the Charge thereof to be provided as the Charges for ſending Vagrants.

Two Juſtices, and all Mayors and chief Officers, *&c.* adjoining to ſuch Port to which *Ib §. 12.* ſuch Veſſel ſhall arrive, ſhall have Power to determine Complaints of hard Uſage of Apprentices to Sea-Service.

All Regiſters of Seamen, before their Entrance into ſuch Office, ſhall take an Oath be- *7 & 8 W. 3.* fore the Judge of the Admiralty, or two Juſtices of the Peace, for their true and faithful *c. 21.* Execution of the ſaid Office. And at the Time of his Regiſtring ſhall bring a Certificate of *ſee the Act at* he Place of his Abode, under the Hands of two Juſtices of the Peace of that County, and *large.* ſo often as he changes the Places of his Abode, under the Penalty of loſing the Benefit of his being regiſtred.

See more for Mariners Tit. *Counterfeiting,* Chap. 32. *Rogues and Vagabonds,* Chap. 83. *Soldiers,* Chap. 94,

Diſturbances often happening in the King's Yards by the Turbulency of Seamen, *&c.* *1 Geo. 1. c. 25.* the Treaſurer, Comptroller, Surveyor, Clerk of the Acts, and the Commiſſioners of the *made perpet.* Navy, may puniſh the Offenders by Fine not exceeding 20 *s.* or by Impriſonment not ex- *9 G. 1. c. 8.* ceeding one Week, and for Nonpayment of ſuch Fine may ſend the Offenders to the _ _ . Houſe of Correction for two Months. And where greater Puniſhments are needful, the ſaid Officers may bind the Offenders to their good Behaviour, and to anſwer at the next *Ib. §. 2.* Aſſiſes or *Quarter-Seſſions;* and in Default of ſuch Security may commit to the County Gaol, in order to their being proſecuted.

Convictions and Judgments in Purſuance of this Act ſhall be final, and not ſubject to *Ib. §. 13.* any Appeal or *Certiorari.*

It ſhall not be lawful for any Maſter of a Ship bound beyond the Seas, to carry any *2 Geo. 1. c. 36.* Mariner, except his Apprentices, from the Port where he was ſhipt, to proceed on any *§. 1.* Voyage beyond the Seas, without firſt coming to an Agreement with ſuch Mariners for their Wages, which Agreement ſhall be made in Writing, declaring what Wages each Seaman is to have for ſo long Time as they ſhall ſhip themſelves for, and alſo to expreſs in the Agreement the Voyage for which ſuch Seaman was ſhipt: And if any ſuch Maſter ſhall carry out any Mariner, except his Apprentice, upon any Voyage beyond the Seas, without firſt entring into ſuch Agreement, and he and they ſigning the ſame, he ſhall forfeit 5 *l.* for every ſuch Mariner, to the Uſe of *Greenwich* Hoſpital, to be recovered on Information on the Oath of one Witneſs, before one Juſtice of Peace, who is required to iſſue his Warrant to bring before him ſuch Maſter; and in caſe he refuſes to pay the Forfeiture, to grant his Warrant to levy it by Diſtreſs and Sale of Goods; and if no Diſtreſs can be found, to commit him to the common Gaol till he pay the ſame.

If any ſuch Seaman ſhall deſert, or abſent himſelf from ſuch Ship, after he hath ſign'd *Ib. §. 4.* ſuch Contract, upon Application made to any Juſtice of Peace by the Maſter or other Perſon having Charge of the Ship, it ſhall be lawful for ſuch Juſtice to iſſue his Warrant to apprehend ſuch Seamen; and if he ſhall refuſe to proceed on the Voyage, and ſhall not give a ſufficient Reaſon for ſuch Refuſal, to the Satisfaction of the Juſtice, to commit him to the Houſe of Correction, to be kept to hard Labour not exceeding thirty Days, nor leſs than fourteen.

C H A P.

CHAP. LXV.

Night-walkers.

Lam. 46,122.
13 H. 7. 10.
See Tit. Watch.

EVERY Juſtice of Peace (*Ex officio*, and by the Commiſſion, the firſt *Aſſignavimus*) may cauſe to be arreſted all Night-walkers, be they Strangers or other Perſons that be ſuſpected, or that be of Evil Behaviour, or of Evil Fame; and more particularly all ſuch ſuſpected Perſons as ſhall ſleep in the Day-time, and go abroad in the Nights: And all ſuch as ſhall in the Night-ſeaſon haunt any Houſe that is ſuſpected for Bawdery, or ſhall in the Night-time uſe other ſuſpicious Company; or ſhall commit any other Outragers or Miſdemeanors; and may force them to find Surety for their Good Behaviour. See the Title *Surety for the Good Behaviour.*

Pſal. 104.

For as one ſaith, Such Night-walkers (or Night-birds) are ominous, like the Whiſtler, *&c.* And ſuch Night-walkings are unfit for honeſt Men, and more ſuiting to the Thief (the right Whiſtler) and to Beaſts of the Prey, which come forth of their Dens when Man goes to his Reſt.

CHAP. LXVI.

Nuſances. (a)

Hemp.
33 H. 8. c. 17.

FOR Nuſances in Highways, *vide* Tit. *Highways.*

If any Perſon ſhall water any Hemp or Flax, in any River, running Water, Stream, Brook, or common Pond, where Beaſts be uſually watered, he ſhall forfeit twenty Shillings; a Moiety to the Party grieved, or any that will ſue; the other Moiety to the King, to be ſued for in any Court of Record.

Leather.
14 Car. z. c. 7.
Cattle.
18 Car. z. c. z.

Tranſporting of Leather contrary to 14 *Car.* 2. *cap.* 7. is declared a common Nuſance. Importing Cattle from *Ireland*, declared to be a common Nuſance.

What are common Nuſances.

Alehouſes diſorderly kept,	Highways, Annoyances in them,
Bawdy-houſes,	Inmates,
Brew-houſes,	Melting-houſes for Candles,
Bridges, Annoyances in them,	Rivers, Annoyances in them,
Cottages unlawful,	Scolds, common,
Eves-droppers,	Stages for Mountebanks or Rope-
Gaming-houſes,	dancers.

* Indictment, it muſt conclude ad commune nocumentum omnium ligeorum, &c.

All theſe are publick Nuſances, for which an Action on the Caſe will not lie, but an *Indictment againſt the Offender, who being convicted, ſhall be fined and committed till he pay it.

What are private Nuſances.

Stopping another Man's *Lights*, or building an Houſe ſo near to another that the Water falls on it when it rains; but this is juſtifiable by the Cuſtom of *London*, if upon an old Foundation; ſetting up a Brick-kiln or Hogſty ſo near the Houſe of another as to offend with the ill Smell, *&c.*

Theſe and the like are *private Nuſances*, for which an Action on the *Caſe will lie*, but no Indictment; and both for common and private Nuſances the Party grieved may *enter on the Ground* of the Offender, and with proper Inſtruments remove them; and if he is indicted, either for a Treſpaſs or a Riot, he will only be fined in a ſmall Sum, if convicted.

Where a Man is indicted for a Nuſance, the Court never admits him to a ſmall Fine till the Nuſance is removed, which muſt be proved by Oath, or by the Certificate of *two Juſtices*; and the Defendant ſhall never be allowed to make any Objections againſt the Indictment till he hath *pleaded to it.*

19 Car. 2.
c. 3. ſ. 3.
10 & 11 W. 3.
c. 17. ſ. 1.

Buildings erected contrary to 19 *Car.* 2. *cap.* 3. ſhall be deemed common Nuſances. See Tit. *London*, Chap. 60.

All Lotteries are publick Nuſances.

I

Making,

Making, Selling, Throwing or Firing Squibs, or other Fireworks, in any Street, 9 & 10 W. 3.
Highway or Paſſage, or into any House or Shop, ſhall be adjudged a common Nuſance. c. 7. §. 1.
See *Chap.* 95. Tit. *Squibs.*

. Undertakings by publick Subſcriptions, relating to Fiſheries and other Affairs of Trade 6 Geo. 1. c. 18.
contrary to the 6 *Geo.* 1. *cap.* 18. are declared publick Nuſances. And the Offenders §. 18 & 19.
being convicted in the King's Courts of Record at *Weſtminſter, Edinburgh* or *Dublin,*
are liable to the Pains of *Præmunire,* 16 *Ric.* 2. *cap.* 5. beſides the Puniſhments to which
Perſons convicted of publick Nuſances are liable.

C H A P. LXVII.

Oaths.

(*a*) **N**O Judge, Commiſſioner or Subject, is compellable to take any Oath but what 2 Inſt. p. 479.
hall is warranted by the Common Law, or directed by Statutes : And therefore you
hall always find Clauſes in the Statutes, directing Oaths, and inabling Juſtices of Peace to
adminiſter them.

(*d*) Any one Juſtice of Peace may compel ſuch as are between the Age of fifteen Years *Peace.*
and Threeſcore, to be ſworn to keep the Peace.   Lamb. 190.

If any Perſon of the Age of eighteen Years, and under the Degree of a Baron, ſhall 7 Jac. 1. 6.
land and be preſented, indicted or convicted, for not coming to Church, or not re- §. 26.
ceiving the Communion before the Ordinary, or any other having Power to take ſuch
Preſentment or Indictment ; or if the Miniſter, Petty Conſtable and Church-wardens, or
any two of them, ſhall complain to any Juſtice of Peace, near adjoining to the Place
where the Offender dwells, and he ſhall find Cauſe of Suſpicion ; any Juſtice of Peace of
that County, *&c.* or to whom Complaint ſhall be made, ſhall require him to take the
Oath ; and if the Party refuſe, the Party authoriſed to give the Oath may commit the
Party refuſing to Priſon without Bail, until the next Seſſions or Aſſiſes, where the Oath
hall be again tendred him, and the Party refuſing ſhall incur a *Præmunire,* except
Femes Coverts, who ſhall be committed until they take the Oath.

Two ſuch Juſtices, *&c.* may take the Oaths of the Under-Sheriffs, and their Officers,
&c. See the Title *Sheriffs.*

(*a*) Swearing prophanely. See more *Chap.* 98.

No Perſon may maintain, That the Taking of an Oath in any Caſe whatſoever 13 & 14 C. 2.
though before a lawful Magiſtrate) is unlawful, and contrary to the Word of God ; nor c. 1. §. 2.
may wilfully refuſe to take an Oath, by the Laws of the Land being duly tendred, nor
may perſuade any other to refuſe and forbear the Taking the ſame ſo tendred ; nor go
bout by Printing, Writing, or otherwiſe, to maintain, That the Taking of an Oath in
any Caſe whatſoever, is unlawful, upon the Penalties in the ſaid Act, as upon Quakers.
For which, ſee *Quakers,* who by a late Statute are exempted from the Penalties of the
aid Act 13 & 14 *Car.*

By 1 *Will.* & *Mar. Stat.* 1. *cap.* 8. The Oath of Supremacy required by Stat. 1 *Eliz.* 1 W. & M. ſt. 1.
cap. 1. and the Oath of Allegiance required by Stat. 3 *Jac.* 1. *cap.* 4. & 7 *Jac.* 1. c. 8. §. 2.
cap. 7. are repealed.

See the Stat. 1 *Geo.* 1. *cap.* 13. * For the Oaths to be taken by all Perſons bearing 1 Geo. 1. ſt. 2.
any Office Civil or Military, *&c.*   c. 13.
                                                                                  * Et ſupra c. 4.
By Statute 2 *Geo.* 2. *cap.* 31. ſo much of the Act of 1 *Geo.* 1. *cap.* 13. as requires 2 Geo. 2. c. 31.
Perſons to take the Oaths within three Months, *&c.* ſhall be repealed.   §. 3.

And by Stat. 9 *Geo.* 2. *cap.* 26. Perſons that ſhall be admitted into Offices Civil or 9 Geo. 2. c. 26.
Military, ſhall take the Oaths appointed by 1 *Geo.* 1. *cap.* 13. within ſix Kalendar §. 3.
Months after their Admiſſion.

Serjeants at Law, Barriſters, Attornies, Proctors, *&c.* practiſing in any Court in Ib. §. 4.
England, ſhall take the Oaths appointed by 1 *Geo.* 1. *cap.* 13. in the Chancery, King's
Bench, Common Pleas or Exchequer, at any Time before the End of the next Term
after their Admiſſion, or before the End of the next Quarter-Seſſions, where ſuch Perſons ſhall reſide.

Orchard. See *Treſpaſs.*

Papiſts. See *Recuſants.*

S ſ   *Partition*

Partition of Lands. (a)

8 & 9 W. 3.
c. 31. §. 4.
Made perpetual 3 & 4
Ann. c. 18.

WHEN the High-Sheriff, by reason of Distance, Infirmity, or other Hindrance, cannot conveniently be present at the Execution of any Judgment in Partition, the Under-Sheriff, in Presence of two Justices of Peace, may proceed to Execution by Inquisition; and the High-Sheriff thereupon shall make the same Return as if he were personally present; and the Tenants of the Lands shall be Tenants for such Part set out severally to the respective Owners, under the same Rents and Reservations; and the Owners of the several ·Purparts shall make good under their respective Tenants the said Parts severally, as they were bound to do before Partition made.

Ib. §. 5.

The Sheriff, their Under-Sheriffs and Deputies, and in Case of Disability in the High-Sheriff, all Justices of Peace, shall give due Attendance to the executing such Writ of Partition (unless reasonable Cause be shewn to the Court upon Oath) or otherwise be liable to pay unto the Demandant such Costs and Damages as shall be awarded by the Court, not exceeding 5 *l.* for which the Demandant may bring his Action in any of his Majesty's Courts at *Westminster*; and in Case the Demandant doth not agree to pay unto the Sheriffs or Under-Sheriffs, Justices and Jurors, such Fees as they shall demand, the Court shall award what each Person shall receive, having Respect to the Distance of the Place from their Habitations, for which they may severally bring their Actions.

Parliament. See the *Appendix* under this Title.

C H A P. LXVIII.

Partridges.

11 H. 7. 17.
With Nets.

(a) IF any Person (shall out of his own Warren, and upon the Freehold of another, without the Consent and Licence of the Owner or Possessor) take Pheasants or Partridges by Nets, Snares, or other Engines, he shall forfeit 10 *l.* a Moiety to the Prosecutor, and the other Moiety to the Owner or Possessor. And the Justices of Peace have Authority to hear and determine it, as well by Inquisition as by Information and Proof.

In the Night.
23 Eliz. 10.
P. Pheasants 2.
P. Just. 38.

(d) Every Justice of Peace (by the Statute of 23 *Eliz.*) may examine all Offenders, for the destroying or taking of Partridges or Pheasants in the Night-time; and for Hawking or Hunting with Spaniels, in any eared or codded Corn; and may bind by Recognizance the Offenders with good Sureties to appear at the next General Sessions of the Peace to answer their said Offences, &c. (a) Which Justices in Sessions have Power

Forfeits. —
* By 1 Jac. 1.
c. 27. 'tis 20 s.

thereby to hear and determine the same: The Forfeiture for a Pheasant is 20 s. and for a Partridge * 10 s. And if not paid within ten Days after Conviction, then to have one Month's Imprisonment without Bail; the one Moiety of the Forfeitures to the Lord of the Liberty, the other Moiety to the Prosecutor by Action, &c. But if the Lord of the Liberty shall license, dispense with, or procure such Taking, the whole Forfeiture shall go to the Poor, to be recovered by one Church-warden, &c.

(d) But now by the Statute made 1 *Jac.* 1. 27. and 7 *Jac.* 1. 11. the Offences of Destroying, &c. of Partridges and Pheasants (generally) is referred to two Justices of Peace, to examine, hear and determine out of Sessions. *Vide hic infra.*

23 Eliz. 10.

Also after the Conviction of any such Offender (according to the Statute of 23 *Eliz.*) for taking and destroying any Partridges or Pheasants in the Night-time, any one Justice of Peace of that County, may bind such Offenders with good Sureties, that for the Space of two Years, they shall not take or destroy any Partridges or Pheasants contrary to that Statute.

1 Jac. 1. 27.
P. Pheasants
6, 7.
21 Jac. 1. 28.
3 Car. 4.

1. By the Statute made 1 *Jac.* 1. every Person which shall shoot at, kill or destroy (with any Gun or Bow) any Partridge, Pheasant, House-Dove or Pigeon, Hearn, Mallard, Duck, Teal, Widgeon, Heathcock, or any House-Dove, or ·any such Fowl, or any Hare.

2. Or shall take, kill or destroy any Partridge, Pheasant, House-Dove, or Pigeon, with Setting-Dogs and Nets, or with any Manner of Nets, Snare, Engines, or Instruments.

4

3. Or

3. Or shall take out of their Nests, or willingly destroy, or break in the Nest, the Eggs of any Pheasant, Partridge, or Swan.

4. Or shall trace or course a Hare in the Snow.

5. Or shall at any Time take or destroy any Hare with Cords, or any such Instruments.

6. Or shall have or keep any Greyhound for Deer, or Hare; or Setting-Dog or Net, to take Pheasants or Patridges, except they have Land, &c. of Inheritance of the clear Yearly Value of 10 *l.* or 30 *l. per Annum* for Life, or Goods worth 200 *l.* or be the Son of a Knight, or Baron of Parliament, or of some Person of higher Degree, or the Son and Heir Apparent of an Esquire.

The said Offences being proved by the Confession of the Party, or by the Oath of two 1 Jac. 1. 27. sufficient Witnesses, before any two Justices of Peace of the County where the Offence §. 2. shall be committed, or the Offenders apprehended, every of the Offenders shall by the said Justices, for every such Offence, be committed to the common Gaol for three Months without Bail, unless the said Offenders shall forthwith, upon the said Conviction, pay to the Church-wardens for the Use of the Poor there, 20 *s.* for every Hare, Fowl, and Egg, so taken or destroyed; and 40 *s.* for having such Greyhound, Setting-Dog, or Net. Or after one Month after his Commitment, become bound by Recognizance with two sufficient Sureties in 20 *l.* a-piece, with Condition not to offend hereafter in any the Particulars aforesaid; which said Recognizance shall be taken by two Justices of Peace of the County where the Offender is imprisoned, and by them shall be returned to their * *This Clause* next Quarter-Sessions *. So that any two Justices of Peace may examine, hear and de- *relates only to* termine all Offences against this Statute made 1 *Jac. Regis,* and may perform every *killing of Hare,* other Thing requisite for the due Execution thereof. *Fowl, or Egg, and not to set-* *ting Dogs and Nets.*

(a) If any shall sell, or buy to sell again, any Deer, Hare, Partridge or Pheasant, 1 Jac. 1. c.27. except Partridges and Pheasants brought up in Houses, or brought from beyond Seas, he §. 4. shall forfeit for every Deer 40 *s.* for every Hare 10 *s.* Partridge 10 *s.* Pheasant 20 *s.* the one Moiety to the Prosecutor, the other to the Poor.

(d) By the Statute made 7 *Jac. Regis,* every Person which shall take, kill or destroy 7 Jac. 1. c.11. any Pheasant or Partridge with Setting-Dogs and Nets, or with any Manner of Nets, §. 8. Snares, or Engines, (it being proved by the Confession of the Party, or by the Oath of one sufficient Witness before any two Justices of Peace) shall by the said Justices be committed for three Months without Bail, unless the said Offender shall forthwith pay to the Use of the Poor there 20 *s.* for every such Pheasant or Partridge. And further, to become bound by Recognizance in the Sum of 20 *l.* before any one Justice of Peace, never to take, kill or destroy any Pheasant or Partridge any more; which Recognizance shall be taken by any one Justice of Peace of the County where the Offence shall be committed, and shall be returned to the next Quarter-Sessions.

Every Person which shall hawk at, kill or destroy any Pheasant or Partridge, with 7 Jac. 1. c.11. any kind of Hawk, or Dog, (by Colour of Hawking) between the first of *July* and §. 2. the last Day of *August,* (the same being proved by the Confession of the Party, or by the Oath of two sufficient Witnesses, before any two Justices of Peace of the County where the Offence was committed, or the Offender apprehended) shall by the said Justices be committed to the common Gaol, there to remain for one Month without Bail; unless the said Offender shall forthwith upon the said Conviction pay to the Use of the Poor there (where the Offence shall be committed, or the Party apprehended) 40 *s.* for every such Hawking at Pheasant or Partridge, and + 20 *s.* for every Pheasant or Partridge, + *By the Sta-* which any and every such Offender by himself, his Hawk or Dog, shall take, kill or *tute 8 Geo. 1.* destroy, contrary to the Intent of this Statute. *c. 19. §. 1.* *the Party may bring an Action of Debt for this pecuniary Punishment, and if he recover shall have double Costs.*

But no Offender punished by Virtue of this Law, shall be punished by Virtue of any 7 Jac. 1. c.11. other Law for the same Offence: Also such Offences must be complained of to the Justices of Peace within six Months after the Offence.

Any two Justices of Peace may make their Warrant under their Hands to any Con- 7 Jac. 1. c.11. stable or Headborough, to enter into and search the Houses of any Person (other than §. 9. such as have free Warren, or are Lords of any Manor, or have Freehold of 40 *l.* by the Year, or more, of Estate of Inheritance, or have 80 *l.* by the Year for Term of Life, or be worth in Goods 400 *l.*) being suspected to have any Setting-Dogs, or any manner of

Nets

Nets, for the Taking of Pheafants and Partridges: And wherefoever they fhall find any fuch Dog or Nets, the fame to take, carry away, detain, kill, deftroy, and cut in Pieces.

Qualifications. By the fame Statute 7 *Jac.* 1. *cap.* 11. every fuch Perfon as hath Free Warren, or
Ib. §. 7. is Lord of a Manor, or hath other Eftate as aforefaid, is allowed (on their own Freehold) to take Pheafants and Partridges in the Day-time only, and between *Michaelmas* and *Chriftmas.*

4 & 5 W. & M. (a) One Juftice may grant a Warrant to fearch the Houfes of Perfons fufpected to
c. 23. §. 3. have Partridge or other Game, and if any are found, and the Perfon doth not give a good Account how he came by it, or of whom he bought it, he fhall forfeit not under 5 s. nor above 20 s. to be levied by Diftrefs and Sale, to the Informer and the Poor, and in Default of Diftrefs, to be committed to the Houfe of Correction not exceeding a Month, or lefs than ten Days, to be whipp'd and kept to hard Labour.

5 Ann. c. 14. Higlers, Chapmen, Carriers, Innkeepers, Victuallers, or Alehoufe-keepers, having in
§ 2. made per- their Poffeffion any Pheafant, Partridge, Hare, &c. or who fhall buy or offer to fell the
pet. by 9 Ann. fame, fhall forfeit 5 l. to be levied by Warrant, by Diftrefs and Sale, to the Poor and
cap. 25. the Informer ; and if no Diftrefs, then to be fent to the Houfe of Correction for three Months without Bail for the firft Offence, and four Months for the next Offence ; Conviction may be upon View or Oath of one Witnefs within three Months.

The Laws in Force for the Prefervation of the Game, are continued and inforced by the Statute 3 *Geo.* 1. *cap.* 11. *fect.* 2.

See alfo Tit. Game, *Chap.* 46. Hunting, *Chap.* 55.

CHAP. LXIX. (a)

Pafture Lands.

2 & 3 P. & M. HE that fhall keep or feed above 120 Shear-fheep, for the moft Part of the Year,
cap. 3. §. 2. upon his feveral Paftures, Lands, Feedings, or Farms, apt for Milch Kine, wherein no other hath Common, fhall, fo long as he fhall keep thefe 120 Sheep, for every 60 Sheep, keep a Milch Cow ; and for every 120 Sheep, rear up one Calf, or forfeit 20 s. for every Month's not keeping a Cow, and 20 s. for not rearing a Calf.

2 & 3 P. & M. Every Perfon that fhall upon fuch his Paftures, keep or feed above the Number of
cap. 3. §. 3. twenty Oxen, Rounts, Schrubs, Steers, Heifers, or Kine, fhall for every ten Beafts, keep one Milch Cow, and rear yearly ; and keep for a Year one Calf for every two Milch Cows, upon the Pains aforefaid, except the Calf fhall die within the Year ; one Half of the Forfeitures to the King, the other to the Party fuing in any Court of Record, or before the Juftices of Peace at the General Seffions.

Ib. §. 4. The Act not to extend to Cattle kept to be fpent in a Man's Houfe. The faid Act is made perpetual by 13 *Eliz. cap.* 25.

7 Jac. 1. c. 8. The Act of 2 & 3 *P. & M. cap.* 3. fhall extend to Lands fit for Kine inclofed fince
§. 2. that Act, or hereafter to be inclofed.

See Title Cattle, *Chap.* 22.

CHAP. LXX.

Peace.

EVERY Juftice of Peace hath Authority by the firft *Affignavimus*, or Claufe in the Commiffion, to keep and caufe to be kept the King's Peace ; by Force of which Words they have as well the ancient Power touching the Keeping of the Peace, which
Lamb. 46. the Confervators of Peace had by the Common Law ; as alfo all Authority which the Statutes fince have added thereto : And fo they may caufe to be kept all the Statutes and

Laws

Laws now in Force, which have been made for the Peace, or Keeping thereof; and more especially they may arreft, or caufe to be arrefted and fent to the Gaol, all Murderers, Robbers, and Felons, and all Perfons fufpected of fuch Things.

They may alfo fupprefs, and bind to the Peace, or good Behaviour, all *Affrayors*, and *Affrayors* ill Perfons unlawfully and riotoufly affembled, or unlawfully *wearing Armour*, or any *Weapons*, by Night or by Day, or otherwife putting the People in Fear, and all unlawful *Night-Walkers* and the like. All which may be faid to be Difturbances or Breaches of the Peace. See more for thefe under their particular Titles.

(a) If any *Affray*, *Forcible Entry*, or other Thing in Difturbance of the Peace, be made or committed in the Prefence, or within the *View of a Juftice of Peace*, he hath Power to record it, and to certify the fame; and alfo to commit the Parties to Ward, prefently upon the Fact done. But if there be any mean Space, or Time, then he cannot commit them to Ward, but he may record the fame, and may (at any Time after) make his Warrant to take them, and bind them with Sureties, to their good Behaviour, and for want of Sureties may fend them to the Gaol. *Cro.* 41. *per Curiam.*

If the Juftice of Peace fhall certify unto the King's Bench, that *I. S.* hath broken the Peace in his Prefence, upon this Certificate *I. S.* fhall be there fined, without allowing him any *Traverfe* thereto. *Marr. Lect.* 3. *Cromp.* 131.

Perjury. (a)

WHERE an Oath is adminiftred by a Perfon who hath a lawful Authority, and *See* 1 Hawk. in a *judicial Proceeding*, and the Witnefs fweareth falfly in a Thing material to P. C. 171, the Caufe, this is Perjury. &c.

It muft be wilful, deliberate, and what is affirmed muft be falfe to make it Perjury at Common Law, and it muft be abfolute and direct, and not as the Witnefs believes or remembers.

It muft likewife be in fome judicial Proceeding, either in a Court of Law or Equity, or before Perfons in the Country having Authority to adminifter an Oath, or by making an Affidavit where the Fact is either falfly affirmed or denied.

It muft be in a Matter material to the Iffue, for if 'tis in a Thing immaterial, and not tending to the Caufe, 'tis not Perjury.

Subornation of Perjury is likewife an Offence at Common Law, and this is by procu- 1 Hawk. ring another to take a falfe Oath, and if he doth not take it, the Perfon fuborning is pu- P. C. 177. nifhable by Fine; but the Punifhment for Perjury and Subornation is Fine, Imprifon-ment, and Pillory, and the Offender is for ever afterwards difabled to be a Witnefs.

Perjury is alfo punifhable by the Statute 5 *Eliz. cap.* 9. by which 'tis enacted, That 5 El. c. 9. if any Perfon fhall unlawfully and corruptly procure a Witnefs to commit wilful and §. 3. corrupt Perjury in any Action concerning Lands or Goods in any Court of Record, or in in any Leet, Ancient Demefne Court, Hundred Court, Court Baron, or in the Courts of the Stannary in *Devon* and *Cornwall*, or fhall corruptly procure or fuborn any Witnefs fworn to teftify *in perpetuam rei memoriam*, he fhall forfeit 40 *l.* And if he hath not Ib. §.4. & 5. Lands to that Value, or Goods, he fhall be imprifoned for Half a Year, and ftand in the Pillory one Hour in fome Market-Town, and fhall not be a Witnefs till the Judgment is reverfed.

This Part of the Statute relates only to the Suborner, the other Part extends to the fuborned, and to him who of his own Accord is perjured.

If any Perfon either by Subornation, or by his own Act, fhall wilfully and corruptly Ib. §. 6. commit Perjury by a Depofition in any Court of Record, &c. he fhall forfeit 20 *l.* the one Moiety of the Forfeitures to the King, the other to the Party grieved; he fhall like-wife be imprifoned for fix Months. And if he hath not Goods, &c. to the Value of Ib. §. 7. 20 *l.* he fhall be fet on the Pillory in fome Market-Town, and have both his Ears nailed, &c.

As well the Judges of the faid Courts where fuch Perjury fhall be committed, as al- Ib. §. 9. fo the Juftices of Affifes and Gaol-Delivery, and the Juftices of Peace at their Quarter-Seffions, fhall have Power to inquire of all Offences contrary to this Act, by Inqui-fition, Prefentment, Bill or Information, or otherwife lawfully to hear and determine the fame.

By this Statute a greater Punifhment is inflicted on the Suborner than on the Perjurer, *See* 1 Hawk. but it extends only to Perjury by a Witnefs, and not to Perjury in an Anfwer to a Bill P. C. 179, in a Court of Equity, or to Perjury in an Affidavit by fwearing the Peace, &c. 180.

T t   Neither

Ib. §. 11.

  Neither is a falfe Oath within this Statute, if it is not prejudicial to fome Party in the Caufe. Nor does this Statute extend to Offenders of this Nature in the Ecclefiaftical Courts, if the Matter is Spiritual and not Temporal.

  The fafeft Way to proceed is by Indictment at Common Law, becaufe fo much Certainty is not required in that Profecution, as 'tis upon the Statute.

  One Juftice may bind the Offender over to the Seffions.

  The Defendant having made an Affidavit in *C. B.* and appearing in Court upon a Summons, *confeffed* that he made it, and that it was falfe; whereupon the Court recorded his Confeffion, and ordered that he fhould be taken in Cuftody, and ftand on the Pillory, &c.

  It was objected that his Confeffion was not a Conviction, but only Evidence of his Guilt, and that he ought to be brought before the Court judicially by Indictment, and convicted thereon; befides the Court of *C. B.* hath not Jurifdiction in this Cafe, it being criminal: But *per Curiam,* the Confeffion of a Crime is the ftrongeft Evidence againft the Criminal himfelf; and the Statute *5 Eliz.* gives Power to hear and determine this Offence by Inquifition, &c. or *otherwife,* by which Word the Confeffion of the Party may be intended, and the Punifhment by Pillory is inflicted by this Statute, which fhews that the Court proceeded on the Statute, but 'tis likewife an Offence at Common Law. *Trin.* 9 *Geo.* 1. *B. R.*

2 Geo. 2.
c. 25. § 2.
made perpetual
9 Geo. 2.
c. 18.

  Befides the Punifhment already to be inflicted, it fhall be lawful for the Court or Judge, before whom any Perfon fhall be convicted of wilful and corrupt Perjury, or Subornation of Perjury, to order fuch Perfon to be fent to fome Houfe of Correction within the County for a Term not exceeding feven Years, to be kept to hard Labour; or to be tranfported to his Majefty's Plantations for a Term not exceeding feven Years; and Judgment fhall be given accordingly; and if any Perfon fo committed or tranfported fhall voluntarily efcape, or return from Tranfportation before the Expiration of the Term, fuch Perfon being thereof convicted fhall fuffer Death without Benefit of Clergy; and fhall be tried for fuch Felony in the County where he efcaped, or where he fhall be apprehended.

C H A P. LXXI. (*a*)

Petitions.

Petition to redrefs Grievances.
13 Car. 2.
c. 5. §. 2.

N O Perfon fhall folicit, labour, or procure the Getting of Hands, or other Confent of Perfons above twenty or more, to any Petition, Complaint, Remonftrance, Declaration, or Addrefs to the King, or both or either Houfes of Parliament, for Alteration of Matters eftablifhed by Law in Church or State, unlefs the Matters thereof be firft confented to, by three or more Juftices of the County; or by the major Part of the Grand Jury of that County or Divifion, at the Affifes or Seffions where the Matter arifes; or if in *London,* by the Mayor, Aldermen, and Commons in Common Council. Nor fhall any repair to his Majefty with any Company exceeding ten, upon Pretence of prefenting any Petition, &c. upon Pain to incur a Penalty not exceeding 100*l.* and three Months Imprifonment without Bail, to be prefented at Affife or Seffions, with fix Months after the Offence, and proved by two or more credible Witneffes.

Ib. §. 3.

  But any, not exceeding ten, may prefent any Grievance to a Member of Parliament after his Election, during the Parliament, or to the King; and both or either Houfes of Parliament may addrefs themfelves to the King.

Pewter. (*a*)

19 H. 7. c. 6.
made perpetual
4 H. 8. c. 7.

J USTICES of Peace, at their *Michaelmas* Seffions, fhall appoint two Perfons to be Searchers of Brafs and Pewter.

C H A P.

CHAP. LXXII.

Plague.

IF any Perfon infected, or being, or dwelling in an Houfe infected with the Plague, *Wandering.* fhall be by any Juftice of Peace (or other Head Officer of the City, &c.) commanded to 1 Jac. 1. c 31. keep his Houfe, and notwithftanding fhall wilfully go abroad, and converfe in Company, §. 7. having any infectious Sore upon him, it is Felony; and if fuch Perfon fhall not have fuch Sore about him, yet for his faid Offence he fhall be punifhed as a Vagabond by the Appointment of any Juftice of Peace, and further fhall be bound to his good Behaviour for one whole Year.

It fhall be lawful for the Juftices (and other Head-officers in Corporate Towns) within *Officers.* their feveral Limits, to appoint *Searchers, Watchmen,* Examiners, Keepers, and Buriers, Crom. 122. b. for the Perfons and Places infected; and to minifter unto them Oaths, for the Performance Ib. §. 9. of their faid feveral Offices, and to give them other Direction as to them fhall feem good.

(a) If any Perfon infected, or dwelling or being in a Houfe infected, fhall contrary to Ib. §. 7. the Command or Appointment of the Juftice of Peace (or other Officer) wilfully attempt to go abroad, or to refift fuch their Keepers or Watchmen, then may fuch Watchmen with Violence inforce them to keep their Houfes, and not be impeached for hurting them.

(d) Any two Juftices of Peace (or any two Head-Officers) of any City, Borough, *Tax.* Town Corporate, and Place privileged, may tax all and every Inhabitant, and all Houfes Ib. §. 2: of Habitation, Lands, Tenements, and Hereditaments within the faid City or Borough, &c. or the Liberties thereof, for the reafonable Relief of fuch Perfons as are infected, or inhabiting in Houfes that are infected in the fame City, &c. And may levy the faid Taxes (by Diftrefs and Sale of the Goods of every Perfon refufing, or neglecting to pay the faid Taxes) by Warrant under the Hands and Seals of *two fuch Juftices* or Head-officers, to be directed to any Perfon or Perfons, for the Execution thereof: And in Default of fuch Diftrefs, and that Refufal be made of Payment, upon Return thereof, the faid Juftices Ib. §. 3: by like Warrant may commit fuch Perfons to the Gaol, there to remain without Bail, until he fhall fatisfy the fame Taxation, and the Arrearages.

If the Inhabitants of any fuch City, &c. are unable to relieve their infected Perfons, &c. *Relief.* upon Certificate thereof by the Head-officer, and other Juftices of Peace of fuch City, &c. Ib. §. 4. or by any two of them, to any two Juftices of Peace in the County, of or near the faid City, &c. fo infected, any two of the faid County of, or near-to the faid City may tax the Inhabitants of the County within five Miles of the faid Place infected, at fuch reafonable weekly Rates as they think fit, to be levied by Warrant from any two fuch Juftices of Peace of or near the faid City, by Diftrefs and Sale of Goods; and in Default thereof, by Imprifonment of the Body of the Party taxed, as aforefaid.

If any fuch Infection fhall be in any Borough or Town Corporate where there are no Ib §. 5. Juftices of Peace, or within any Village or Hamlet, within any County; then any two Juftices of Peace of the fame County wherein the faid Place infected fhall be, may tax the Inhabitants of the faid County, within five Miles of the faid Place infected, at reafonable weekly Rates, as they fhall think fit, for the Relief of the faid Place infected, to be levied by Diftrefs and Sale of Goods (upon Warrant of the faid Juftices of Peace of the fame County;) and in Default thereof, by Imprifonment as aforefaid.

All fuch Taxes made by the Juftices of the County, for the Relief of fuch City, &c. fhall be difpofed by the faid Juftices of the faid County, and as they fhall think fit (where there are no Juftices of Peace in fuch City, &c.) And where there are Juftices of Peace, then in fuch Sort as the Head-officer and Juftice of Peace there, or any two of them fhall think fit.

All fuch Taxes made either in City, &c. or County, fhall by the faid Juftices that taxed Ib. §. 6. them (as it feemeth) be certified at their next Quarter-Seffions to be holden within fuch City, &c. or County, refpectively, there to be continued, inlarged, extended to other Parts of the County, or determined, as at their Seffions refpectively fhall be thought fit.

(a) And every Conftable or other Officer that fhall wilfully make Default in levying fuch Money, fhall forfeit 10 s. to be employed on the Charitable Ufes aforefaid.

(d) But no Juftice of Peace fhall do or execute any Thing before mentioned, within ei-Ib. §. 10. ther of the Univerfities of *Cambridge* or *Oxford,* or within any Cathedral Church, or the
Liberties

Liberties thereof, or within the Colleges of *Eaton* or *Winchefter*: But the Vice-Chancellor of the Univerſity, Biſhop and Dean of ſuch Church, and Provoſt or Warden of the ſaid Colleges, ſhall do and execute all Things abovementioned within their ſeveral Precinfts.
This Aft is in Force being continued by 3 *Car.* 1. *cap.* 4. & 16 *Car.* 1. *cap.* 4.

CHAP. LXXIII.

Poor.

What.   (a) POOR are here to be underſtood not vagabond Beggars and Rogues, but thoſe who labour to live, and ſuch as are old and decrepit, unable to work, poor Widows, and Fatherleſs Children, and Tenants driven to Poverty; not by Riot, Expence or Careleſneſs, but by Miſchance, &c.

Not working.
43 Eliz. c. 2.
§. 4.   (d) Any one of thoſe Juſtices of Peace, who may appoint Overſeers for the Poor, may alſo ſend to the Houſe of Correftion, or Common Gaol, ſuch as will not employ themſelves in Work, being thereunto appointed by the Overſeers, according to the Statute 43 *Eliz.*

Ib. §. 1.   The Church-wardens of every Pariſh, and four, three or two Houſholders, to be nominated yearly in *Eaſter* Week, or within one Month after *Eaſter*, under the Hand and Seal of two Juſtices of Peace, whereof one of the *Quorum*, dwelling in or near the Pariſh, ſhall be called Overſeers of the Poor of the ſame Pariſh.

    (a) The Juſtices of Peace, which have the appointing of theſe Overſeers, muſt therein be careful to chuſe ſuch Men as in every Town are fitteſt, ſc. Subſtantial Perſons, having Competency of Wealth, Wiſdom, and a good Conſcience. And they muſt be Houſholders, not Sojourners, however otherwiſe qualified. And indeed, this Name and Office of Overſeers, may beſeem the beſt, and not the meaneſt Men (it being a Name and Office of great Antiquity and Excellency, as you may ſee 1 *Chro.* 23. 4. *Aſts* 20. 28. and *Afts* 6. 3. 5.) And though the Perſons are not dignified according to the Singularity of the Subjeft; yet this is not the leaſt Office to be called Overſeers of the Poor; for as God himſelf hath a ſpecial Reſpeft to the Miſeries of the Poor, ſo they be like God, who provide for the Neceſſities of the Poor.

Large Pariſhes.
13 & 14 Car.
2. c. 12. §. 21.   All poor, needy, impotent and lame Perſons, within every Townſhip and Village in the Counties of *Lancaſhire, Cheſhire, Derbyſhire, Yorkſhire, Northumberland*, the Biſhoprick of *Durham, Cumberland*, and *Weſtmoreland*, and other Counties, where by Reaſon of the Largeneſs of the Pariſhes, they cannot reap the Benefit of the Statute of 43 *Eliz.* ſhall

Cap. 2.   be maintained and ſet on Work in the reſpeftive Townſhip or Village wherein they were inhabiting or ſettled; and that according to the Rules of 43 *Eliz.* ſhall be yearly in every Townſhip and Village choſen two or more Overſeers, who ſhall do and forſeit as in the Aft of 43 *Eliz.* is appointed.

Ib. §. 22.   The Juſtices of the Peace of the ſaid Counties, ſhall do and execute ſuch Authority in thoſe Villages and Townſhips, as is direfted by the ſaid Aft.

* But ſee 2 Sid.
292.
2 Keb. 56 & 69.
2 Lev. 172.   This Aft extendeth not only to the Counties therein named, but alſo to other Counties where ſuch great and large Pariſhes are. *

The Overſeers Duty.
43 El. c. 2.
§. 1.   (d) Such Overſeers and Church-wardens (or the greater Part of them) with the Conſent of two or more ſuch Juſtices, ſhall take Order from Time to Time for ſetting their Poor on Work, putting out Apprentices, and relieving their impotent, as followeth:

Ib. §. 1.   1. Firſt, for ſetting to work the Children of all ſuch, whoſe Parents ſhall not by the greater Part of the Overſeers be thought able to keep and maintain their Children, which Children they, or the greater Part of them, by the Aſſent of two Juſtices, may alſo put out to be Apprentices, ſcil. The Men Children till their Age of 24, and the Women

Ib. §. 5. Children till their Age of 21 Years, or the Time of their Marriage.
1 Jac. 1. c. 25.   And all poor Children of the Age of ſeven Years, or above, ſo bound Apprentices, may be taken and kept as Apprentices by their Maſters, any former Statute to the contrary notwithſtanding.

Work.
43 El. c. 2.
§. 1.   2. For ſetting to Work all ſuch Perſons (married or unmarried) as having no Means to maintain them, uſe no ordinary and daily Trade of Life to get their Living by.

Trade.
3 Car. 1. c. 5.
§. 22.   (a) And note, that the Church-wardens and Overſeers of the Poor may, by and with the Conſent of two or more Juſtices of Peace (whereof one to be of the *Quorum*, &c. (within their reſpeftive Limits, where there are more than one, or if but one, then by his

Confent, fet up, ufe and occupy any Trade, Myftery or Occupation, only for the fetting on work, and better Relief of the Poor of the Parifh, Town or Place where they are Overfeers, &c.

(*d*) 3. To raife weekly, or otherwife by Taxation of every Inhabitant, Parfon, Vicar, *Tax.* and other; and every Occupier of Lands, Houfes, Tithes, Mines or faleable Underwoods *Ibid.* (*proportioning them to an annual Benefit*, &c.) in the fame Parifh, fuch competent Sums of Money as they fhall think fit, therewith to provide a convenient Stock of fome Ware or Stuff, to fet the Poor on work, and alfo competent Sums of Money towards the neceffary Relief of their lame, impotent, old, blind, and other Poor not able to work; and for the putting out of fuch Children (as aforefaid) to be Apprentices.

(*a*) *Toll of Markets* feems alfo taxable, touching which in *Michaelmas* Term 27 *Car.* 2. *Toll taxed.* happened this Cafe in the Town of *Wickham* in *Bucks*, having much Poor, and there be-ing in the Town a confiderable Market; the Toll whereof belonging to the Corporation there, was worth 60 *l. per Ann.* which the Overfeers had taxed, and the Mayor and Juftices refufed to fign, and allow the Tax, pretending it was not taxable. The Overfeers and Juftices, the laft *Trinity* Vacation, attended the Lord Chief Juftice *Hale* for his Opi-nion, who faid he conceived it taxable within 43 *Eliz.* Yet the Juftices would not fign and allow the Tax: Of which Complaint being made to the *King's Bench*, a Rule was for the Mayor, &c. to attend, and he attended accordingly; and he obferving the Court to be angry, promifed to affign and allow the Tax; and the Court ordered him to pay the Over-feers the Charges of their Profecution. And *Hale* faid, For fuch a Refufal a *Quo Warr.* would lie. Which Cafe I have inferted, as well to fhew what is taxable, as to inform Juftices of Peace of their Duty. This Cafe happened *Michaelmas* 27 *Car.* 2.

The Overfeers are likewife to give an Account of the *Burials*, fince their former Ac- *Burials.* count, on Pain of five Pounds: And their Accounts fhall not be allowed till they have ac-counted for the fame. See *Burials*, Chap. 18.

The Office then of thefe Overfeers confifteth principally in two Things.   *Overfeers*
    1. In taxing Contributions of Money for the Relief of the Poor.   *Duty.*
    2. In difpofing thereof according to Law, and good Difcretion.

And in thefe Taxations, there muft Confideration be had, firft to Equality, and then to *Tax.* Eftates.

Equality, that Men may be equally rated with their Neighbours, and according to an equal Proportion.

Eftates, that Men be rated according to their *Eftates of Goods* known, or according to their *known yearly Value of their Lands, Farms, or Occupyings*; and not by Eftimation, Suppofition or Report. Alfo herein the Charge of Family, Retinue, &c. is in fome Mea-fure to be regarded: For if one valued at 500 *l. in Goods*, hath but himfelf and his Wife, and another eftimated at 1000 *l.* hath Wife and many Children, &c. the firft Man by Rea-fon is to be rated as much as the other; and fo of Lands. *Tamen quære*, what the Law is in fuch Cafes.

Touching the Taxation of Mens Eftates, thefe Rules are to be obferved.

1. If a Man live in the Parifh where his Lands lie, and doth demife thofe Lands to *Where to be* others, the Poors Tax in that Cafe ought to be *charged upon the Tenant*, and not on the *taxed, and* Landlord, in Refpect of the Tenant's Occupation thereof.   *how.*

2. A Man having Lands in other Parifhes than where he lives, the fame being in Leafe, or not in Leafe, he is to be taxed in the Parifh where he lives, according to his vifible Eftate there, and not for his Lands or Rent in another Parifh. And both thefe Points were re-folved by *Hutton* and *Crook*, Judges of Affizes, at *Lent* Affizes at *Lincoln*, upon Applica-tion to them made by Sir *Anthony Earby*, againft the Inhabitants of the Town of *Bofton*; and this they faid was agreed upon by all the Judges of *England* upon a Reference to them.

What fhall be faid to be a Parifh within 43 *Eliz.* 2.

If there be an ancient Parifh, and an ancient Village within that Parifh; which *What fhall be* Village had an ancient Church, and thofe within that Village have had parochial Rights, *a Parifh, fee* are chofen Church-wardens and Overfeers of the Poor, and have been feparately taxed ever *hic poftea.* fince 43 *Eliz.* 2. for the Relief of the Poor within that Village; this is a Parifh within 43 *Eliz.* 2. and Taxes may be made and levied within themfelves. And all this was refolved in a Caufe between *Hilton* and *Pawle*, upon a fpecial Verdict between the Parifh of *Hink-ley* in the County of *Leicefter*, and the Village of *Stoke-Goldingham* within that Parifh. *Cro. Car.* 92. And the like was alfo refolved *Trin.* 10 *Car.* 1. between *Nichols* and *Wal-ker*, between the Parifh of *Hatfield* and the Village of *Tatridge*, 1 *Jones* 355. and *Cro. Car.* 394.

The Diſtinction of Pariſhes in *England,* I find attributed to *Theodorus,* Archbiſhop, who died *An. Dom.* 690. (almoſt one Thouſand Years ſince) ; for thus it is written of him, as it is cited out of a *MS. Excitabat fidelium devotionem & voluntatem in quarum-libet provinciarum Civitatibus, necnon villis, Ecclefias Fabricando, Parœcias diſtinguendo, affenſus regios procurando, ut ſi qui ſufficientes eſſent, & ad Dei honorem pro voto habe-rent ſuper proprium fundum Ecclefias conſtruere, earundem perpetuo Patronatu gauderent, &c.* Beda Eccleſiaſt. Hiſtoric. notis Wheel. p. 399.

Compulſion to take. Note alſo, That as the Statute enableth the Church-wardens and Overſeers (with the Conſent of two Juſtices of Peace) to put out Apprentices, ſo it doth enable them to place thoſe Apprentices with the Maſters ; for without Maſters there can be no Appren-* *This is al-tered. See Ap-prentices in Tit.* Labourers. tice. And the ſaid Juſtices may * *compel* all ſuch as be of Ability, to take ſuch Appren-tices (according to their Diſcretion ;) and if any ſuch Maſter ſhall refuſe to take ſuch Apprentice ſo to him appointed, the ſaid Juſtices may bind ſuch Maſter over to the next General Gaol-delivery, there to anſwer ſuch Default. And this was the Direction of Sir *Henry Mountague* Knight, Chief Juſtice of the *King's Bench* at *Cambridge* Aſſiſes, *Anno Dom.* 1618.

8 & 9 W. 3. c. 30. §. 5. This being doubtful, and frequently controverted ; by the Statute 8 & 9 *W.* 3. *cap.* 30. it was enacted, That where poor Children ſhall be appointed to be bound Apprentices, purſuant to 43 *El. cap.* 2. the Perſon to whom they are appointed to be bound ſhall re-ceive and provide for them, according to the Indenture ſigned and confirmed by the two Juſtices, and alſo execute the other Part of the Indentures ; and if he refuſe, Oath being thereof made by one of the Church-wardens or Overſeers, before any two Juſtices for that County, &c. he ſhall forfeit 10 *l.* to be levied by Diſtreſs and Sale of Goods, by Warrant of the ſaid Juſtices, to be applied to the Uſe of the Poor of the Pariſh ; ſaving to the Perſon, to whom any poor Child ſhall be appointed to be bound, his Appeal to the next Quarter-Seſſions.

Lamb. Edit. 1614. p. 360. (d) Two ſuch Juſtices of Peace are to allow the Cauſe or Excuſe of ſuch Overſeers as ſhall not meet every Month to conſider of the Premiſſes, or as ſhall be otherwiſe negligent in their Office.

The Overſeers Account. 43 El. c. 2. Two ſuch Juſtices ſhall take the Account of ſuch Overſeers at the End of their Year, and of the Church-wardens in every of theſe Particulars following :

　　1. Of all Sums of Money by them received, or rated, and not received.

　　2. Of all ſuch Stock of Ware of Stuff as they or any of their Poor have in their Hands.

　　3. What Apprentices they have put out.

　　4. What Poor they have ſet at Work, or relieved.

　　5. Whether they have ſuffered any of their Poor to wander and beg out of their Town, or in the Highways, or in their Town, without their Direction. See for this 39 *Eliz.* 3 & 4. & *Lamb.* 206. *Reſol.* 15.

　　6. Whether they have Monthly met to conſider of theſe Things.

Lamb. 428. 　　7. Whether they have aſſeſſed the Inhabitants and Occupiers of Lands, &c. in their Pariſh, *ſcil.* All ſuch as are of Ability, and with Indifferency.

Ibid. 　　8. Whether they have endeavoured to levy and gather ſuch Aſſeſſments.

　　9. Whether they have been otherwiſe negligent in their Office ; within which Words alſo there ſeemeth to lie included, if they have neglected to execute the Juſtices War-rants to them, or any of them directed, for the Levying of any Forfeiture, according to this Statute.

Charity for Apprentices. 7 Jac. 1. c. 3. §. 2. (a) All Sums given to bind out Apprentices ſhall continue and be imployed to that Uſe, and no other, by the Perſons following, except the Givers otherwiſe diſpoſed of it, *viz.* By all Corporations of Cities, Boroughs, and Towns Corporate ; and in Towns and Pariſhes not Corporate, by the Parſon or Vicar, with the Conſtable or Conſtables, Church-warden or Church-wardens, Collectors and Overſeers of the Poor, or the moſt Part of them ; and they ſhall have the Nomination and Placing ſuch Apprentices, and Guiding and Imployment of ſuch Monies : And if they, or any of them, ſhall wilfully neglect or forbear ſo to do, they and every of them ſhall forfeit five Marks ; one Half to the Poor, the other to the Proſecutor, by Action, &c.

Ib. §. 3. The Maſter, or Miſtreſs or Dame, receiving ſuch Money with ſuch Apprentice, ſhall be bound with two Sureties to the Corporation ; or the Perſon having the Ordering thereof, conditioned to repay the Money at the End of ſeven Years, or three Months after ; and if the Apprentice die, within one Year after his Death ; and if the Maſter, &c. die within ſeven Years, then within one Year after his Death ſuch Money ſhall be put out

　　　　　　　　　　　　　　　　　　　　　　　　　　　　　　again

again and imployed within three Months after it comes in. And if there be no poor
Children to be put out, then the pooreft Children of the Parifh adjoining; and the pooreft Ib. §. 5.
Children fhall always be made choice of, and none to be above fifteen Years of Age.

The Perfons fo intrufted fhall once every Year at *Eafter*, or within a Month after, *Account.*
give to four, three, or two Juftices dwelling in or next the Town, &c. an Account of Ib. §. 6.
all Monies fo imployed, of Securities taken, and what is in their Hands; and at the
Time of their Account, or a Month after, deliver up to fuch as fhall fucceed them the
Obligations and Money.

In Cafe of any Breach of Truft or Mifemployment, the Lord Chancellor may grant Ib. §. 7.
Commiffions, &c.

Quære, What Authority the Juftices have by this Statute, for it feemeth they have
no Authority compulfory over the Perfons accounting, but only to take their Accounts.
And as they find the Money mifimployed, or not imployed, to reprefent the fame to the
Lord Chancellor, &c. that Commiffions may iffue as that Statute directs.

(*d*) Now if the Church-wardens, or either of them, or any of the Overfeers, fhall re- *Refufal to ac-*
fufe to make and yield a true and perfect * Account to the faid Juftices of all fuch Sums *count and pay.*
of Money, and of all fuch Stock as aforefaid, any two fuch Juftices may commit them * *This muft be*
to the common Gaol, there to remain without Bail till they have made a true Account, *within 4 Days*
and fatisfied and paid to the new Overfeers fo much of the faid Sum and Stock, as upon *after the End*
the faid Account fhall be remaining in his (or their) Hands, &c. (*a*) And if they make *and after other*
a falfe Account, they may be bound over to the Affifes or Seffions, and there an Indict- *Overfeers are*
ment may be preferred againft them. *appointed.*
43 El. c. 2.
§. 2, 4.

(*d*) And as for the other Negligences of the Church-wardens and Overfeers in their Ib. §. 2.
Office, or in the Execution of the Orders aforefaid, every of them making Default
fhall forfeit for every fuch Default 20 *s.* (but it feems fuch Default muft be proved either
by the Offender's Confeffion, or by Examination of Witneffes) which Forfeitures fhall
be levied by the new Church-wardens and Overfeers, or one of them, by Warrant from Ib. §. 11.
any *two Juftices of Peace,* by Diftrefs and Sale of the Offender's Goods, &c. or in Defect of fuch Diftrefs, it fhall be lawful for any two Juftices of Peace to commit the Offender to the common Gaol, there to remain without Bail till the faid Forfeitures fhall
be paid; and the fame fhall be imployed to the Ufe of the Poor of the fame Parifh.

Two fuch Juftices may make their Warrant (as well to the prefent as fubfequent *Levy of Taxes.*
Overfeers and Church-wardens, or to any of them) to levy all fuch Sums of Money, *Refufers to pay*
and all Arrearages, (of every one that fhall refufe to contribute according as they fhall *their Rate.*
be affeffed) by Diftrefs and Sale of the Offender's Goods, (rendring to the Party the Ib. §. 4.
Overplus:) And in Defect of fuch Diftrefs, two Juftices may commit him or them to
the common Gaol, there to remain without Bail till Payment be made of the faid Sum
and Arrearages.

If the faid Juftices do perceive that any Parifh is not able to relieve their Poor, then *Parifhes not*
any two Juftices may tax and affefs any other Perfons within the Hundred (where the *able, then to*
faid Parifh is) to pay fuch Sums of Money to the Overfeers of the faid poor Parifh for *tax the Hun-*
the faid Purpofes, as the faid Juftices fhall think fit, according to the Intent of this Law. *dred.*
Ib. §. 3.

If any Perfons find themfelves grieved with any Tax, or other act done by the Over- *Appeal.*
feers, or by the faid Juftices of Peace, they are to be relieved at the Quarter-Seffions. Ib. §. 6.

Head Officers of Cities and Corporate Towns (being Juftices of Peace) have the fame *Corporate*
Authority within their Limits, as herein is limited to Juftices of Peace of the County, *Towns.*
&c. And no other Juftices of Peace are to enter or meddle there. Ib. §. 8.

If any Parifh fhall extend into two Counties, or Part thereof do lie in any City or *Parifh in two*
Corporate Town where they have Juftices, then the Juftices of every County, &c. fhall *Liberties.*
intermeddle only within their own Limits: And every of them refpectively within their Ib. §. 9.
Limits, are to execute this Law concerning the Nomination of Overfeers, binding of
Apprentices, giving Warrants to levy Taxations unpaid, taking Account of Overfeers,
and committing fuch as refufe to account, to pay their Arrearages: And yet the faid
Overfeers fhall, without dividing themfelves, execute their Office in all Places within the
faid Parifh; but fhall give up feveral Accounts.

The *Father* and *Grandfather,* and *Mother* and *Grandmother,* and the Children and *Parents to re-*
Grandchildren of every poor impotent Perfon, or other poor Perfons not able to work, *lieve their*
being of fufficient Ability, fhall relieve fuch poor Perfons in fuch Manner as the Juftices *Children.*
of Peace (of that County where fuch fufficient Perfons dwell) at their General Quarter- 43 El. c. 2.
Seffions fhall affefs, upon Pain that every one failing therein forfeit twenty Shillings for §. 7.
every Month; the faid Forfeiture to be levied by the Church-wardens and Overfeers, or *Forfeiture.*

one

one of them, by Warrant from any two fuch Juftices of Peace (the one being of the *Quorum*) within their Limits, by Diftrefs and Sale as aforefaid; and in Defeft of Diftrefs,

Ib. §. 11. any two fuch Juftices may commit the Offender to Prifon, there to remain without Bail till the faid Forfeiture be paid; and the fame Forfeiture fhall be imployed to the Ufe of the Poor of the fame Parifh.

2 Bulftr. 344. (a) The *reputed Grandfather or Grandmother* feem not to be within this Statute, for a Baftard is *filius populi.* *Reeve*'s Cafe, *M.* 7 *Car.*

Ibid. 346. If the Child live in the County of *Middlefex*, and be maintained by the Parifh there, and the *Grandfather, &c.* live in the County of *Suffolk*, the Juftices of *Middlefex* can make no Order therein; but the Juftices of Peace of the County of *Suffolk* muft make Order to charge, *&c.*

Ibid. 345. If the *Grandmother* be a Perfon of Ability, and then *marries*, the Perfon with whom fhe marries is a *Grandfather* within this Statute; for by the Marriage, all her Goods are given to the Husband, but with this Difference, if *the Grandmother, at the Time of the Marriage, were of Ability*, otherwife not. *Draper*'s Cafe, alfo *Gerrard*'s Cafe. But if the Wife having nothing to bring her Husband in Marriage, but after by her Induftry her Husband becomes a very rich Man, the Husband fhall be charged, by *Whitlock*, but *Crook* to the contrary: But they both agreed, That if an Eftate defcend to the Wife after Marriage, the Husband fhall be charged.

And the Father may be compelled to allow Maintenance to his *Son's Wife*, (the Hufband being abfented) as was done in the Cafe of one *John Ball*, by *Ord.* 2 *Sept.* 15

* And a Fa- *Jac. lib. Seff. pa. Mid.* *
ther-in-Law
has been adjudged within the Meaning of the Act 43 El. c. 2. Style 283.

(d) Now for the better Furtherance of this fo needful and charitable a Service, and for the better Help, as well of the Juftices of Peace as of the Overfeers, *&c.* I thought it not amifs to fet down here certain Refolutions and Advices of the Judges (as I find them in Mr. *Lambard*) together with certain other Obfervations to this Purpofe.

Refolutions. If there be but *one Church-warden* in the Parifh, he with the other Overfeers is fuffi-
Refol. 20. cient.

Parents able. If the *Parents be able* to work, and may have work, they are to find their Children
Refol. 8. by their *Labour*, (and not the Parifh:) But if they be overburthened with Children, it fhall be a very good Way to procure fome of them to be placed *Apprentices*, according to the Statute: And fuch Apprentices would be put out to Husbandry and Houfewifery.

Children, Young Children, whofe Parents are dead, are to be fet on work, relieved and main-
where to be re- tained at the Charge of the Town where they were Dwelling at the Time of the Death
lieved. of their Parents, and are not to be fent to their Place of Birth, *&c.* For if the Parents were not Rogues, we may not make the Children Rogues, except they wander abroad and beg. This was the Direftion of *Flemming* Chief Juftice, in a Cafe between *Wefton* and *Cowledge, Anno* 11 *Jac. Regis.*

Parents dying. If any (not being Rogues) fhall travel with their Children through a Town, and the
Refol. 7. Father or Mother die, or run away, that Town is not bound to keep their Children, nor to fend them away, but only in Charity, except they become wandring Beggars.

(a) A travelling Woman having a fmall Child fucking upon her, is apprehended for *Felony* and fent to the Gaol, and is after arraigned and *hanged*; this Child is to be fent
Birth. to the Place of *its Birth*, if it can be known, otherwife it muft be fent to the Town where the Mother was apprehended, becaufe that Town ought not to have fent the Child to Gaol (being no Malefaftor;) and fo was it delivered by Sir *Nicholas Hide*, at *Cambridge* Lent Affifes, *Anno* 3 *Caroli Regis.*

Refufing to (d) Such Perfons as be of any Parifh, and have able Bodies to work, if they refufe to
work at the work at fuch Wages as are taxed, or commonly given in thofe Parts, are to be fent to
Wages taxed. the Houfe of Correction, and not to their Place of Birth, or laft Dwelling, by the
Refol. 10. Space of a Year. But if they have any lawful Means to live by, though they be of able Bodies, and refufe to work, they are not to be fent to the Houfe of Correction.

Begging. None may be fuffered to take Relief at any Man's Door, though within the fame
Refol. 15. Parifh, unlefs it be by the Order of the Overfeers; neither may any be fuffered to beg by
39 Eliz. 3. the Highway, though in their own Parifh.

Settlement. No Man is to be put out of the Town where he dwelleth, nor to be fent to his Place
Houfes to pro- of Birth, or laft Habitation, but a Vagrant Rogue; nor to be found by the Town, ex-
vide. cept the Party be impotent; but ought to fet themfelves to labour, if they be able, and
Refol 9. can get work: If they cannot get work, the Overfeers muft fet them to labour.

2

(a) One

(a) One *Winde* and his Wife lived' at *Layflas*, and ufed a Houfe and Land which was given the Woman by her Brother, her Brother turned her out of it; and thereupon they went to *Kimmalton*, and took a Houfe there, and lived in it a Year; and at the Inftance of the Parifh of *K.* the Landlord at the Year's End turned him out of the Houfe: He complained to the Juftices, who ordered the Parifh of *K.* to provide him a Houfe; and for not doing it, were in Contempt. And upon Complaint at *Hereford* Lent Affifes, 7 *Car.* 1. *Whitlocke* Juftice of Affife, difcharged the Overfeers of their Contempt, and difcharged the Order made upon *K.* by the Juftices, as being againft Law; for that *W.* was not a poor or impotent Perfon within 43 *Eliz.* 2. And the Juftices had no Power by that Law to compel and to provide a Houfe for him, for he might provide one himfelf. *Inter Parochias de Layflas* & *Kimmalton*, Bulftr. Part 2. p. 347.

(d) And fo of them that have or fhall have Houfes, when their Leafes are expired; *Refol. 9.* and Servants, whofe Times of Service are ended though they cannot get Houfes; for they muft provide themfelves Houfes anew, if they be not impotent.

But fuch Perfons muft not be put out of the Towns where they fo laft dwelt or ferved; Neither are they to be fent from thence to their Place of Birth or laft Habitation, but are to be fettled there to work, being able of Body; or being impotent, are to be there reieved: And yet it feems, that if fuch Perfons fhall wander abroad begging, out of that Parifh, then they may be fent as *Vagabonds* (from the Place where they fhall be taken wandring or begging) to their Place of Birth, &c.

(a) But for the Placing and Settling of thefe poor People (who now for Want of Charity are much fent and toffed up and down from Town to Town, and from Country o Country) it hath been holden by fome, that it is in the Power of the next Juftice of Peace to give Order therein, and that upon Appeal from him, the Juftices of Peace at the Quarter-Seffions may fully take Order therein, and that their Order made in Seffions will not eafily be avoided.

But Sir *Francis Harvey* at Summer Affife at *Cambridge, An.* 1629. did deliver it, *The Practice is* That the Juftices of Peace (efpecially out of their Seffions) were not to meddle, either *now quite con-* with the removing, or fettling of any Poor, but only of Rogues. *trary.*

If a Man *hireth a Houfe in* A. and being there with his Wife and Children, he afterwards fhall bind himfelf as a *Servant* with one dwelling in *B.* yet are not his Wife and Children to be fent to *B.* or placed there, but are to remain ftill at *A.* where they were once fettled. Otherwife if the Hufband hath * *hired a Houfe in* B. *But it muft* *be of the yearly* *Rent of 10 l.*

A Maid-fervant gotten with Child at *A.* by her Fellow-fervant (or by another young Man of the fame Town) after both their Times of Service are expired and they marry, and then the young Man is retained at *B.* then the Woman is delivered of the Child, fhe with her Child are to be fent to the Father at *B.* and there they are to be fettled.

Note; (By an old Law) a Stranger, or he which cometh Gueft-wife to an Houfe, and here lieth the *third Night* is called an *Hogenhyne* (or *Agenhine*) and *after the third Night* he is accounted one of his Family, in whofe Houfe he fo lieth, and if he offend the King's Peace, his Hoft muft be anfwerable for him. *Terms de ley.*

Secundum antiquam confuetudinem dici poterit de familia alicujus qui hofpitatus fuerit cum alio per tres noctes, qui prima nocte dici poterit Uncouth, *fecundo* Guft, *tertia nocte* Hogenhine. *Bract. fol.* 124. b.

And *Minfh.* verb. *Hogenhyne*, and *Uncouth* faith, that *Uncouth* fignifieth *incognitus*, and is ufed in ancient *Saxon* Laws for him that cometh to an Inn Gueft-wife, and lieth there two Nights at the moft; and that by the Laws of *Edward*, and of the Conqueror, *Hofpes trium noctium*, if he did any Harm, his Hoft was anfwerable for the Harm, as for one of his own Family; and that if he tarried any longer, then he was called *Hogenhyne* or *Agenhyne*, that is, *Familiaris.* So it feemeth in thofe Times, that to lodge in a Place for three or four Nights together, was counted a Settling.

(d) Such as fhall remove or put any out of their Parifh, that be not to be put out; *Refol. 11.* this is againft the Statute concerning the Relief of the Poor, and fineable. And if any have been fo fent, they may be fent back again.

Now this *Fine* feemeth to be by Force of the Satute 39 *El. cap.* 4 *, and to amount * *The* 39 *Eliz.* to *five Pounds*, and is to be levied by Diftrefs and Sale of the Offender's Goods, upon a *c. 4. is repeal-* Warrant under the Hands and Seals of any two Juftices of the Peace, either upon the *ed by* 12 *Ann.* Confeffion of the Offenders, or elfe upon the Teftimony of two fufficient Witneffes. *c. 23. §. 28.*

(a) Upon Complaint made to any Juftice of Peace by the Church-wardens or Overfeers, *Removal.* within forty Days, of any Perfon, likely to be chargeable coming to fettle in a Tene- *13* & 14 *Car 2.* ment under 10 *l. per Annum*, two Juftices *Quorum unus* of that Divifion where he comes *c. 12. §. 1.*

to inhabit, may by Warrant remove and convey him to the Parish where he was laft legally fettled, as a native Houfholder, Sojourner, Apprentice, or Servant, for forty Days, unlefs he give Security for the Difcharge of the Parifh, to be allowed by the faid Juftices.

Appeal.
Ib. §. 2.
The Perfons thinking themfelves grieved, may appeal to the next Seffions, who fhall do them right.

Harveft.
Ib. §. 3.
Any Perfon may, for Harveft-work or other Work, travel out of one County into another, fo as they carry with them a Teftimonial under the Minifter's Hand, and the Hand of one Church-warden and one Overfeer, that he hath a Dwelling-houfe there, and hath left a Family there, or otherwife as the Condition of the Perfon fhall require; and if he fhall not return when his Work is finifhed, or fhall become impotent: This fhall not be accounted a Settlement, but two Juftices of Peace may convey him back under the Penalties in that Act.

Not going.
Ibid.
If fuch Perfon fhall refufe to go, or fhall not remain in the Place where he ought to be fettled, but fhall of his own Accord come back to the Place from which he was removed. Two Juftices of Peace may fend him to the Houfe of Correction, to be punifhed as a Vagabond, or to a Workhoufe, in that Act mentioned, to be fet on Work.

Ibid.
If any Church-warden or Overfeers refufe to receive fuch Perfon fo to be removed, and provide for him as an Inhabitant; any Juftice of Peace may bind them to the Affifes or Seffions, to be indicted for their Contempt. This Act to continue to the End of the firft Seffion of the next Parliament.

* This Act is continued by feveral Statutes, and by the Stat. 12 Ann. c.18. 'tis made perpetual.
This * Act being but temporary, but of general and publick Concern, if any future Parliament fhall think fit to continue it, it were good thefe following Matters were alfo provided for, and fo the Queries here made, thereby removed.

1. A Maid-fervant or Man-fervant being fingle, and at Service in one Parifh by the Year, do contract for a Year with a Mafter in another Parifh, and are there fettled; whether upon Complaint they may be removed by this Act. This hath been made a Doubt, but yet, it feemeth fuch Servant is not within the Meaning of the Act: Firft, For that the Act inftanceth in a Perfon's coming to fettle in a Tenement under 10 l. per Annum, and fo aimeth at Perfons keeping Houfe, and having a Family. Secondly, For that it is not likely fuch Perfons can give the Security intended by the Act; fo likewife of Apprentices.

* The Confideration Money muft be 30 l. otherwife he fhall have no Settlement for any longer Time than he dwelleth there,
2. A Man dwelling in *A.* and having a Family, * purchafeth *bona fide* Lands in *B.* under 10 l. per Annum, and cometh to live in it with his Family: Whether he be removeable by this Act. And it feemeth he is not: For that fuch a one cannot well be adjudged likely to be chargeable; nor can it be thought the Mind of the Parliament to prevent fuch Settlements.

but fhall be liable to be removed to the Parifh where laft legally fettled. 9 Geo. 1. cap. 7.

3. As there is a Time limited for Complaint, and no Time limited for the Removal. *Quære,* Within what Time that muft be procured. But it feems reafonable it fhould be before the next Seffions after the Complaint; otherwife a Parifh having complained, may let the Perfon continue with them, and take his Labour, and keep him under Apprehenfions of Removal, which would difcourage Induftry.

Which Cafes and Queries are obvious, as many more are; and it is well worthy Confideration of wife Law-makers to confider, whether notwithftanding the fpecious Allegations in the faid Act's Preamble, it be not prejudicial to the Commonwealth. For that, 1. By the Words *likely to be chargeable,* too great a Scope is given to any Perfon, although never fo juft and prudent, to infpect and to determine another Man's Livelihood and Condition.

* This is now remedied by the Certificate.
2. * A Man without his Offence, is debarred of his natural Liberty, upon a Poffibility remote enough, may be made a Beggar and a Prifoner, at the fame Time deprived of the Company of Friends and Relations, Choice of Air and Place of Trade. 3. It tends to Difcouragement of Ingenuity and Induftry; for why fhould any one learn or indeavour to be excellent in any Handicraft, which he is likely to make fmall Ufe, and fmaller Benefit of? 4. Places and Perfons are deprived of the Labour and Induftry of others. 5. It tends to Depopulation, which is the greateft Inconvenience an Ifland can undergo.

The Authority of the following Refolutions is not great; for fome Country Gentlemen coming to Sir Robert Heath, when Chief Juftice in the Circuits, put to him thefe feveral

Queries,

Queries, to which he fubfcribed his own Opinion, then brought the fame into Serjeants-Inn-Hall, *and propofed the fame to the Reft of the Judges; but they differing in Opinion from him in many Things, they never came to a Refolution, and fo were no more than his private Opinion; which fome Clerk getting, hath publifhed the fame, as Juftice* Twifden *declared in the Court of* King's Bench *in* Eafter Term 28 Car. 2. *as I heard and obferved. And afterwards in* Michaelmas Term 28 Car. 2. *a Gentleman of the Bar ufing thefe Refolutions to the third, fourth, and eighth Queftions touching putting out Apprentices, as an Authority to his Purpofe,* Juftice Twifden *faid, Why do you ufe that as an Authority, which all the Judges difclaimed?* *

* *Thefe Refolutions, though not of Authority, are here inferted, becaufe many of them are confirmed or explained by late Statutes, as will appear by the Marginal Notes. But not to fwell the Book needlefly, Extracts from thefe Refolutions, which in many Places of this Chapter in former Editions were interfperfed with* Dalton's *Text, are omitted.*

Refolutions of the Judge of Affife, 1633.

1. *Queft.* WHether the Church-wardens and Overfeers of the Poor of the Parifh, with Affent of two Juftices of the Peace, one being of the *Quorum,* may by he Statute of 43 *Eliz. cap.* 2. or any Law, inforce a Parifhioner of the fame Parifh to * take a Child of a poor Parifhioner of the fame Parifh, who is not able to keep his faid Child, to be an Apprentice?   ** By Stat. 8 & 9 W. 3. c. 30. be muft take the Child or pay 10 l.*

, *Refol.* The Statute of 43 *Eliz.* which faith, That the Church-wardens and Overfeers of the Parifh fhall put out Children to be Apprentices, neceffarily implieth, That fuch as are fit muft receive Apprentices, and the putting out of poor Children to be Apprentices, is one of the beft Ways for the providing for the Poor.   *Of inforcing Perfons able to take Apprentices. 43 El. c. 2.*

2. *Qu.* If they may, then whether they muft not give Money with him, and who fhall determine what Money fhall be given with him, if the Party that is to take fuch an Apprentice, and the Church-wardens and Overfeers cannot agree thereupon?   *Of giving Money with Apprentices.*

Refol. There is no Neceffity that Money muft be given, but that muft be left to the Difcretion of the Church-wardens and Overfeers, all Circumftances of Age and Ability being confidered; and if they cannot agree with the Party, then the Juftices of Peace near adjoining, or in their Default, the Seffions of Peace are to determine thefe Controverfies.

3. *Qu.* Whether a Knight, Gentleman, Clergyman, or Yeoman, or one that is a Sojourner, ufing Hufbandry, Clothing or Grafing, or the like, may be inforced to take fuch an Apprentice?   *What Perfons are bound to entertain Apprentices.*

Refol. Every Man who is by Calling or Profeffion, or Manner of Living, that entertaineth, and muft have the Ufe of other Servants of the like Quality, * muft entertain fuch Apprentices, wherein Difcretion muft be had upon due Confideration of Circumftances.   ** Or forfeit 10 l.*

4. *Qu.* Whether a wealthy Man keeping few or no Servants, nor wanting a Servant, but living privately, may be forced to take fuch an Apprentice; if not, then whether he may be taxed towards the putting forth of fuch an Apprentice?

Refol. For the receiving of fuch Apprentices, the Anfwer may be referred to the Queftion next before; but out of Doubt every fuch Perfon muft contribute to the Charge, as to other Charges for the Provifion of the Poor.

5. *Qu.* Whether they may inforce a Parifhioner that is of one Parifh, to take fuch a Child Apprentice, that is of another Parifh, but within the fame County or Divifion, if the proper Parifh be not able to provide for the Children of the fame Parifh?   *Apprentices when to be put unto other Parifhes.*

Refol. The Juftices may provide Mafters for them in other Parifhes within the fame Hundred; if the fame Hundred be not able, then out of that Hundred, in the reft of that County; as for other Provifion for the Poor, which muft be at a Quarter-Seffions.

6. *Qu.* If fuch a Parifhioner may be inforced to take fuch an Apprentice, and fhall refufe not only to take fuch an Apprentice, but alfo refufe to be bound to appear at the next Quarter-Seffions or Affifes what fhall be done to him?   *Perfons refufing to take fuch Apprentices, forfeit 10 l.*

Refol. If any refufe, let fuch a one be bound over to the next Seffions or Affifes; if he refufe to give Bond, let him be fent to the Gaol, there to remain until he fhall give fuch Bond.

7. *Qu.* If fuch a Parifhioner who refufeth to take fuch Apprentice, fhall be bound over to the Seffions for not taking fuch an Apprentice, and when he appeareth there, fhall likewife refufe, what fhall be done to him; and what fhall be done to the Parents who

who refuse to suffer their Children to be put out to be Apprentices, themselves not being
* *But by Stat.* able to maintain them* ?
8 & 9 Will. 3..
cap. 30. *the Perfon refufing, upon Oath thereof by one Church-warden or Overfeer before two Juflices, forfeits 5 l. to be levied by Diflrefs,*
&c. *to the Use of the Poor.*

Refusers to take Apprentices at the Quarter-Seffions to be bound to the Good Behaviour, This is altered by the faid Stat. 8 & 9 W. 3.

    Refol. If at the Seffions or Affifes fuch a one refufeth to take an Apprentice, and his Excufe be not allowed, it is fit he be bound to the Good Behaviour; and it will be a good Courfe to indict fuch a Refufer for a Contempt, and thereupon to fine and imprifon him; if he refufe to be bound to the Good Behaviour, let him be imprifoned till he will; and the King's Book of Orders directs, that fuch be bound with good Sureties to appear at the Council-board : And if the Parents of fuch poor Children refufe to fuffer their Children to be bound Apprentices, or being bound, intice them away, themselves not being able to maintain them, let them be committed to the Houfe of Correction.

Fines certain not to be mitigated.

    8. *Qu.* Whether it be in the Power of any General Quarter-Seffions to mitigate any Penalty upon a Statute-Law ; if the Party indicted fhall fubmit himfelf to the Fine of the Court, and wave the Traverfe ?

    Refol. If the Party be convicted, or confefs the Fault, it is not in the Power of the Court to mitigate the Fine, in fuch Cafes where the Statute makes it certain : But if the Party indicted protefting his Innocency, yet *quia noluit placitare cum domino rege* puts himfelf upon the Grace of the Court, they may impofe a moderate Fine, and order to forbear the Profecution.

    9. *Qu.* If any be bound to appear at the Seffions, and fhall tender Submiffion to the Court, whether the Seffions may ftay the Indictment, and mitigate the Fine aforefaid upon the Confeffion of the Fact ?

    Refol. This is anfwered before to the next precedent Article.

No Difcharge of any Forfeiture after Conviction for Drunkennefs, Tippling, &c.

    10. *Qu.* If any Man be convicted for being drunk, tipling, and keeping an unlicenfed Alehoufe, or being licenfed, is convicted for fuffering others to remain Tipling in his Houfe; or for fwearing or driving Cattle upon a *Sunday* contrary to the Statute ; whether the Juftice of Peace, before whom he was convicted, or any other Juftice of the Peace may difcharge him of all, or Part of the Forfeiture or Punifhment appointed by the Statute ?

    Refol. The Juftices have no fuch Power of Mitigation after Conviction, where the Statute appoints the Meafure of the Punifhment.

Conftable break open an Houfe.

    11. *Qu.* Whether a Conftable may upon a Warrant for carrying one to the Houfe of Correction for keeping an unlicenfed Alehoufe, upon the fecond Conviction break open the Houfe, wherein the Party convicted is, to apprehend him ?

    Refol. This Queftion is to be advifed upon, it is put in general Terms, and referred to be confidered in the Particular where it appeareth.

Settlement of a Woman gotten with Child.

    12. *Qu.* If a Woman unmarried be hired from Week to Week, or from Half-year to Half-year, in one Parifh, and there be gotten with Child, and then goeth from thence unto another Parifh, where fhe is fettled in Service by the Space of two or three Months, and then difcover'd that fhe is with Child. The Queftion is, Whether fhe fhall be fettled in the Parifh where fhe was begotten with Child, or in the Parifh where fhe was fettled ?

    Refol. The Place where fuch a Woman was lawfully fettled, is the Direction in this Cafe, not where fhe was gotten with Child.

A Woman gotten with Child, the Mafter to provide for her till her Delivery.

    13. *Qu.* If a Woman-fervant unmarried, be gotten with Child, and then goeth out of her Mafter's Service, before or after it is difcovered that fhe is with Child, and the reputed Father be run away, or is not able to free the Parifh : Whether the Mafter may be inforced to provide for her till fhe be delivered, and for a Month after ?

    Refol. If the Mafter hath legally difcharged his Houfe of fuch a Servant, he is no more bound to provide for her than for any other.

Tenant in Ancient Demefne.

    14. *Qu.* In Cafe a Parifh confift Part of *Ancient Demefne,* and Part of Guildable, an Affefs is made for the Relief of the maimed Soldiers, the Gaol, &c. according to the Statute of 43 *Eliz. cap.* 3. Whether the Tenants in *Ancient Demefne* fhall contribute with the *Guildable* for the Payment of the Affife ?

    Refol. The Statute doth not diftinguifh between the *Ancient Demefne* and the Guildable in thefe Cafes, *Ubi Lex non diftinguit, ibi nec nos diftinguimus.*

Indictment of Forcible Entry removed by Certiorari.

    15. *Qu.* Whether an Indictment of Forcible Detainer be within the Statute of 1 *Jac.* 1. *cap.* 5. and not to be removed by *Certiorari,* unlefs the Party indicted firft find Sureties

1   according

ccording to the Statute; and whether the Party indicted be to be bound in his Abfence
o profecute according to that Statute; and whether an Indictment of Forcible Entry,
&c. found at a private Seffions, be to be removed by *Certiorari* without Sureties, accord-
ng to that Statute?

Refol. This is fitteft to be left unto the Court of King's Bench, to whofe Commif-
ion and Jurifdiction this is moft proper.

16. *Qu.* If one be convicted upon the Statute of 3 *Car.* cap. 2. for driving of Cattle *Driving Cattle*
n the Sunday throughout feveral Parifhes; whether he fhall forfeit 20 s. to every of the *on the Sabbath.*
aid Parifhes, or only to one; if to one, then to which of them?

Refol. The Statute giveth the Forfeiture but of one 20 s. for one Sabbath-day, although
he Driving of that Day be through divers Parifhes. Therefore where the Action is firft
ttached, and the Diftrefs firft taken, that Parifh fhall have the Benefit of the Forfei-
ure, and not the other.

17. *Qu.* If one who is under the Age of thirty Years, and brought up in Hufbandry, *Perfons able*
r a Maid-fervant, or brought up in any of the Arts and Trades mentioned in the Statute *not putting*
f 5 *Eliz.* cap. 4. and not inabled according to that Statute, to live at his or her own *themfelves to*
land, fhall be warned by two Juftices of the Peace to put him or herfelf in Service, *Service after*
y a Day prefcribed by them, and fhall not do the fame accordingly, but fhall after con- *Warning.*
inue living at his or her own Hand; what Courfe fhall be taken with fuch a Perfon,
nd how punifhed?

Refol. Such Perfons being out of Service, and not having vifible Means of their own,
o maintain themfelves without their Labour, and refufing to ferve as an hired Servant
y the Year, may be bound over to the next Seffions or Affifes, and to be of the Good
Behaviour in the mean Time, or may be fent to the Houfe of Correction.

18. *Qu.* Whether the Tax for the Relief of the Poor upon the Statute of 43 *Eliz.* *Taxes for the*
ap. 2. fhall be made by Ability, or Occupation of Lands, or both; and whether the vi- *Poor, how to*
ible Ability in the Parifh where he lives, or general Ability wherefoever; and whether *be made ac-*
is Rent received within the Parifh where he lives fhall be accounted vifible Ability, and *cording to the*
vhether he fhall be taxed for them only, and for any Rent received from other Parifhi- *Stat.*
ners; and what fhall be faid vifible Ability?

Refol. The Land within each Parifh is to be taxed to the Charges in the firft Place
qually and indifferently, but there may be an Addition for the perfonal vifible Ability of
he Parifhioners within that Parifh, according to good Difcretion, wherein if there be
ny Miftaking, the Seffions, &c. or the Juftices muft judge between them.

19. *Qu.* Whether Shops, Salt-pits, Sheds, Profits of a Market, &c. be taxable to *Things taxable*
he Poor as well as Lands, Coal-mines, expreffed in the Statute 43 *Eliz.* *to the Poor.*

Refol. All Things which are real, and a yearly Revenue, muft be taxed to the Poor.

20. *Qu.* Whether the Tax for the County-ftock, Gaol, and Houfe of Correction, is *Tax for the*
o be made by the Statute of 14 *Eliz.* 5. 43 *Eliz.* 2. by Ability, and upon the Inha- *County-ftock,*
itants of the Parifh only, or upon them, or the Occupiers of Lands, dwelling in that *Gaol, Houfe of*
Parifh, or whether fuch as occupy Lands in that Parifh, and dwell in another Parifh *Correction,*
hall be taxed? *how to be made.*

Refol. If the Statute in particular Cafes give no fpecial Direction, it is good Difcretion
o go according to the Rate of Taxation for the Poor: But when the Statutes themfelves
ive Direction, follow that.

21. *Qu.* Whether any Taxes ought to be made for the Charges that Petty Confta- *Tax for the*
les and Borfholders are at, in conveying Rogues from Parifh to Parifh, and relieving of *Charges of*
hem, and how to be rated? *Petty Confta-*
bles.

Refol. It is fit to relieve the Conftable and Tithingmen, in fuch Sort as hath been ufed
n the feveral Places where they live.

22. *Qu.* Whether a Juftice of Peace may difcharge a Servant, being with Child, from
her Service, allowing that as a reafonable Caufe that fhe is thereby made unable to do
he Service, which otherwife fhe might have done; and if he may difcharge her, whether that Parifh fhall provide for her, till her Delivery, if fhe cannot provide for herfelf; and fo alfo, if her Time be expired before her Delivery, who fhall provide for her
after her Time ended?

Refol. If a Woman being with Child, procure herfelf to be retained with a Mafter *A Woman Ser-*
who knoweth nothing thereof, this is a good Caufe to difcharge her from her Service. *vant with*
And if fhe be gotten with Child during her Service, it is all one: But the Mafter in *Child, how it*
neither Cafe muft turn away fuch a Servant of his own Authority. But if her Term *be difcharged.*
be ended, or fhe lawfully difcharged; the Mafter is not bound to provide for her, but

Y y   it

it is a Misfortune laid upon the Parish, which they must bear, as in other Cases of casual Impotency.

23. *Qu.* Whether one being delivered of a Bastard-child in one Parish, and goeth into another with her Child, and becomes Vagrant, and so is sent to the Place of her *Birth*, her Bastard-child being under the Age of seven Years, shall be settled with the Mother, and there maintained; if the Mother be not able, nor the reputed Father known, found; or whether it shall be sent to the Place of its Birth, or being settled with the Mother, whether the Parish where it was born, shall be ordered by the two next Justices, to pay a weekly Sum towards the Maintenance of it?

Bastard children, how to be disposed. *Resol.* The Bastard-child must be placed with the Mother, so long as it is within the Quality or Condition of a *Nurse-child*, which shall be, till seven Years of Age; and then it is fit to be sent to the Place of its Birth to be provided for, the Mother or reputed Father not being able. And the Parish where the Child is born shall not be forced to contribute to the Charge, as long as the Mother lives, and the Child be under seven Years old.

24. *Qu.* A Man with his Wife and Children, takes an House in one Parish for a Year, and before the End of his Term is unlawfully put out of Possession, and after takes Part of an House as an Inmate in another Parish, from whence he is also put out, and then not being able to get any Dwelling, they come to lie in a Barn in a third Parish, where the Husband falleth sick, and the Wife is delivered of another Child, where ought these to be settled?

Illegal Unsettlement not to be allowed. *Resol.* If a Man or Woman having House or Habitation in one Parish, be thrust out; this is an illegal Unsettling, which the Law forbiddeth, and none must be inforced to turn Vagrant, and such one must be returned to the Place where he or she was last lawfully settled, and the Child also born in the Time of his Distraction.

25. *Qu.* Whether an Apprentice put out by the Church-wardens, &c. according to the Statute, to a Master in another Parish, if his Master die and leave no Executor or Administrator fit to keep an Apprentice; or able to place him; he shall be provided for in the Parish where he was Apprentice, or shall be sent back to the Parish from whence he was put out?

Apprentice put out into another Parish, where the Master dies. *Resol.* Servants and Apprentices are by Law settled in that Parish, and if they become impotent there, the Parish must abide the Adventure, after their Term or Time of Service be lawfully ended.

26. *Qu.* What is accounted a lawful Settling in a Parish, and what not?

What is accounted a lawful Settlement. *Resol.* This is too general a Question, to receive a perfect Answer to every particular Case which may happen: But generally this is to be observed, that the Law unsettleth none who are lawfully settled, nor permits it to be done by a Practice or Compulsion; and * *This must be accounted from the Publication of Notice in Writing,* 3 & 4 W. c. 11. every one who is settled as a native Housholder, Sojourner, an Apprentice or Servant for a * Month at the least, without a just Complaint made to remove him or her, shall be held to be settled.

27. *Qu.* A Rogue is taken at *C.* and will not confess the Place of his Birth; neither doth it appear otherwise, but that he confesseth the last Place of his Habitation to be at *S.* Hereupon he is whipped, and sent to *S.* at his coming to *S.* the Place of his Birth is there *A Rogue misconfessing the Place of his Birth or Habitation.* known to be at *W.* and thereupon the Rogue confesseth it to be so, whether he might without any new Vagrancy be sent to *W.*?

Resol. In this Case it is fit to send such a Rogue to the Place of his Birth, for this is but a mistaken, and no legal Settling.

28. *Qu.* If an Indictment be preferred to the Grand Jury of the Quarter-Sessions of the *In what the Goal may be delivered at the Sessions.* Peace, against one for Murder, Manslaughter; for Robbery, Felony, or Petty Larceny, and *Ignoramus* found, whether the said Sessions may deliver the Party by Proclamation, or not?

Resol. Not by Proclamation at all; but for Petty Larcenies, and other petty Felonies, in Discretion the Gaol may be delivered of them.

Constable elect refusing. *Qu.* 29. If a Constable be chosen and refuseth to take his Oath, what shall be done, and whether a Constable may make a Deputy, and by what Means?

Deputy Constable. *Resol.* The Refusal or Neglect to take an Oath in such a Case, is a Contempt worthy of Punishment, and thereupon to fine and imprison him; and the making of a Deputy is rather by Toleration than by Law.

Constable dying, how to be supplied. 30. *Qu.* If a Constable die, or remove out of the Parish where, &c. how is his Place to be supplied?

I

Resol.

Refol. By the Lord of the Leet, if that Time fall near, otherwife by the Seffions; but if that be too far off, then by the next Juftices.

31. *Qu.* If a poor weak Man be chofen Conftable or Tithingman, and be unfit for the Place; how may he be removed, and a fit Man fworn in his Room? *Conftable unfit, how to be removed.*

Refol. The Juftices of Peace muft help this, and if the Lord of the Leet have Power to chufe a Conftable or Tithingman, and perform it fo ill, it is a juft Caufe to feize his Liberty.

32. *Qu.* If a Nurfe-child, a Scholar at a Grammar-School, or in the Univerfity prove to be impotent by Sicknefs, Lamenefs, Lunacy, or Difcovery of Ideocy, &c. how fuch Perfons fhall be difpofed of? *Nurfe-Child, Baftard in a Gaol, Houfes of Correction.*

Refol. A Nurfe-child, or a Scholar at the Grammar-School, or at the Univerfity, or Perfons fent to the Common Gaol, Hofpital, or Houfe of Correction, are not to be :fteemed as Perfons to be fettled there, more than Travellers in their Inns; but their fettling s where their Parents are fettled; and Children born in Common Gaols and Houfes of Correction, their Parents being Prifoners, are to be maintained at the Charge of the County.

33. *Qu.* What Proportion fhall Parfonages or Tithes bear to the Taxation of the Poor of the Parifh? *Parfon, Vicar, how chargeable to the Poor upon the St. 43 El.*

Refol. The Parfon or Vicar Prefentative, fhall bear according to the reafonable Value of iis Parfonage, having Confideration to the juft Deductions.

34. *Qu.* Whether for placing the Poor of the Parifh, not to be removed by Confent of he Parifh, thefe poor Men may not be placed as Inmates for a Time? *In what Cafes Poor may be placed as Inmates.*

Refol. They may by exprefs Words of the Statute of the 43 *Eliz.*

35. *Qu.* If a Parifhioner, or Owner within a Parifh, do bring into the Parifh, (with-out the Confent of the Parifh) a Stranger of another Parifh, which is, or apparently is like .o be burdenfome unto the Parifh; how may they eafe themfelves? *Strangers apparently like to be chargeable to the Parifh brought in, the Bringers in of them to be taxed.*

Refol. By taxing fuch an one to the Charge of the Rates of the Poor, not only having Refpect to his Ability, or the Land he occupies, but according to the Damage and Danger he bringeth to the Parifh by his Folly.

36. *Qu.* For warding in the Day-time, for apprehending of Rogues, whether the Con-table may not inlarge it to a further Time? *Warding in the Day-time for apprehending of Rogues.*

Refol. Warding in the Day-time is of great Ufe, and muft be left to the Difcretion of he Conftables, or Direction of the Juftices to vary according to the Occafion.

37. *Qu.* Whether Alehoufes ought to be allowed only in thoroughfare Towns, and)thers in other Places to be reftrained only to fell to Poor out of Doors? *Alehoufes to be moderated in Number.*

Refol. The Juftices fhall do very well to allow none but in Places very fit for their Si-uation and Ufes, and to moderate the Number.

38. *Qu.* A Man for his Quality otherwife fit to be a Conftable, or of other Office of hat Nature, procures himfelf to be the King's Servant extraordinary, and by that Means vould excufe himfelf to ferve in the Country? *Conftable the King's Servant.*

Refol. A Servant extraordinary may well perform his ordinary Service in the Country, :ccording to his Quality.

The Juftices Opinion touching the Commiffion by which the Juftices fit at Newgate.

THE Juftices at *Newgate* fit by Virtue of two Commiffions, *viz.* Gaol-delivery, and *Oyer* and *Terminer.*

By the Commiffion of Gaol-delivery, they may try all Prifoners in the Gaol, or by 3ail, or fuch as be indicted, and will render themfelves generally for all Felonies; and alfo or fuch other Offences as are particularly affigned to them by Statute.

The Statute of 4 *Eliz.* 3. *cap.* 2. giveth them Power to receive Indictments againft Pri-foners, or fuch as are upon Bail, and to proceed to try the fame, *viz.* Indictments taken before the Juftices of the Peace, and by Equity thereof, all Indictments before Coroners, 3 *Mar. Bro. Commiffion* 24. faith, the Commiffion is, *Ad deliberand. Gaol. de prifon. in 'ifdem exiften'.* But they cannot take Indictments as Juftices of Gaol-delivery, but being Juftices of the Peace, they may take Indictments againft Prifoners, but not againft them .hat be at large; forafmuch as no Power is given them, confequently they muft have Means fo to do, which is by Indictments. *Id quaerend.*

Howfoever it is fo clear, that they may inquire of many Offences, and take Indictments n fuch Cafes where Power by the Statute is given to the Juftices of Gaol-delivery; in fuch Cafes where they have Authority by Law or Statute, there the Title of Indictment is, that

ad

ad gaolom deliberand. tent. before the Commiffioners of Gaol-delivery *J. S.* was indicted, and the Record muft be made up fo.

And whereas by the Statute of 4 *Eliz.* 3. *cap.* 3. Indictments taken before Juftices of Peace or Coroners, or any other againft any Prifoner, then the Entry of the Indictments is returned taken, *Memorand. quod ad generalem Seffionem tent.* before *A. B. C.* Juftices *ad pacem in Com. Middlefex* or *London confervand. J. S.* was indicted, and then tried before Juftices of Gaol-delivery, and by Virtue of the faid Statute, Indictments taken before Juftices of the Peace of *London* or *Middlefex,* are tried before the Juftices of Gaol-delivery.

The Commiffioners of *Oyer* and *Terminer* is *Ad triand. inquirend. audiend. & determinand.* They may inquire of all Offences mentioned in the Commiffion, tho' the Offenders be at large, but they cannot try Prifoners upon Indictments taken before any other than themfelves, as the Juftices of Gaol-delivery may by the aforefaid Statute, unlefs there be a Special Commiffion made, as it was in the Cafe of the Earl of *Leicefter,* mentioned in *Plow. Com.* for the ordinary Commiffion of *Oyer* and *Terminer* is *ad inquirend. audiend. & determinand.* Therefore they cannot determine of Things unlefs they made Inquiry firft; and on the other Side alfo the Juftices of Gaol-delivery may try Indictments taken before Juftices of the Peace; yet if one be indicted before Commiffioners of *Oyer* and *Terminer,* the Juftices of Gaol-delivery cannot try the fame, becaufe the Record of the Commiffion of *Oyer* and *Terminer* is to be return'd in the *King's Bench.* 44 *E.* 3. 31.

The Commiffion and the Records of the Proceedings before the Juftices of Gaol-delivery, are to be returned to the *Cuftos Rotulor.* of the County, when the fame Perfons are Juftices of Gaol-delivery, and of *Oyer* and *Terminer,* they may fit the fame Day and Place, and inquire by the fame Jury, but the Entry of the Records muft be feveral, according as the Indictment is.

At the Affizes in the Country, the Juftices have their feveral Power, as the Juftices of Gaol-delivery, *Oyer and Terminer,* and Juftices of Peace.

But when the Records are made up, they muft be according to the Power they made Election to proceed upon.

This is the regular and legal Courfe. But the Clerks of the Affizes promifcuoufly make Entry thereof; but if a Writ of Error be brought, they muft certify according to Law, or elfe it will be erroneous; and fo upon a *Certiorari.*

The Seffions of *London* may begin at the *Guildhall,* and then adjourn to *Newgate;* if fome Indictments be at *Guildhall,* then thefe muft be fo certified: If others at *Newgate,* then the Adjournment muft be mentioned, and that the Indictment was then taken.

Note, That the Trial of Indictments taken before Juftices of the Peace of *London,* cannot be tried at *Newgate,* as in Nature of a Trial before Juftices of the Peace at *London,* for many of the Commiffioners for Gaol-delivery are not Juftices of the Peace for *London;* but in fuch Cafes the Trial muft be before the Juftices of Gaol-delivery: As upon Indictments taken before the Juftices of the Peace of *London;* as in the Cafe of Indictments taken before the Juftices of the Peace of *Middlefex.*

But if Indictments at *Newgate* are originally taken before them, as Juftices of Gaol-delivery, then it is inquirable how the Jury fworn and impanelled to inquire at the Seffions of the Peace for *London* or *Middlefex,* do ferve to prefent Indictments before the Juftices of Gaol-delivery at *Newgate,* unlefs the Cuftom and Ufage will warrant the two fevera Juries fworn at the Seffions of Peace for *London* or *Middlefex,* are alfo by the fame Oath, and impanelling, to ferve for the Grand Jury for the Commiffion of Gaol-delivery, *Oyer* and *Terminer.*

Upon Conference with the Clerks for *Newgate* of *London* and *Middlefex,* and the Clerks of Affize, and View of the feveral Entries, more certain Refolution may be given, as Occafion may be offered, in any particular Cafe.

3 Mar. Br.
Com. 24.

Poor, three Sorts.

(*d*) Next, here is a Confideration to be had of three Sorts or Degrees of Poor.
    1. Poor by Impotency and Defect.

  1. The Aged and Decrepit that are paft Labour.
  2. The Infant, Fatherlefs and Motherlefs, and not able to work.
  3. The Perfon naturally difabled, either in Wit or Member, as an Ideot, Lunatick, Blind, Lame, &c.
  4. The Perfon vifited with grievous Difeafes, or Sicknefs, though cafually, yet thereby for the Time being impotent.

All thefe (being impotent and not able to work) are to be provided for by the Overfeers o neceffary Relief; and are to have Allowances proportionally, and according to the Conti-

I
                                                   nuance

nuance and Meafure of their Maladies and Needs; and of thefe it may be faid, *Si non pavifti, occidifti.*

2. Poor by Cafualty.

1. The Perfon cafually difabled, or maimed in his Body, as the Soldier, or Labourer, &c. maimed in their lawful Callings.
2. The Houfholder decayed by Cafualty of Fire, Water, Robbery, Suretyfhip, &c.
3. The poor Man overcharged with Children.

All thefe laft (and fuch others) having Ability and Strength of Body, but not fufficient Means to maintain themfelves, are to be holpen, or fet to work by the Overfeers; and being not able to live by their Work, are in Charity further to be relieved in fome reafonable Proportion, according to their feveral Wants and Neceffities.

3. Thriftlefs Poor.

1. The *riotous and prodigal Perfon,* that confumeth all with Play or Drinking, &c.
2. The diffolute Perfon, as the *Strumpet, Pilferer,* &c.
3. The flothful Perfon, that refufeth to work.
4. All fuch as wilfully fpoil or imbezil their Work, &c.
5. The Vagabond that will abide in no Service or Place.

For all thefe laft, the Houfe of Correction is fitteft; and fuch Perfons being able in Body are to be compelled to labour; for the Rule of the Apoftle is, *That fuch as would not work, fhould not eat.* 2 Thef. 3. 10.

(a) And all fuch Perfons fent to the Houfe of Correction, muft there live by their own Labour and Work, without charging the Town or Country for any Allowance. See to that Purpofe the Statute of 7 *Jac. 1. cap. 4.*

But for the Overfeers to fuffer fuch Perfons (or any other Perfons who can live of their Labours or otherwife) to be chargeable to the Town, or to relieve fuch, this is a Means to nourifh them in their Lewdnefs or Idlenefs, and to rob others of Relief who want it, to wrong thofe of their Money that pay it, and to condemn thofe of Overfight who difpofe of it.

And yet if any of thefe laft happen to prove impotent, then according to the Statute 11 *H. 7. cap.* 2. they are to be relieved with *Bread and Water* without other Suftenance: And fo a Reverend Judge delivered it in his Charge at *Cambridge* Affizes. But yet Charity wills us in Cafes of manifeft Extremity, that they are to be relieved by the Town. But I leave that to better Confideration.

(d) Where any Sums of Money are given, to be continually employed for the binding out Apprentices, the Parfon, or Vicar, Conftables, Church-wardens, and Overfeers for the Poor, in Towns not Incorporate, are by the Statute appointed to have the Difpofing of fuch Stocks and Sums of Money: Which Perfons fhall, once every Year, within one Month after *Eafter* Day, make a true and perfect Account before two or more Juftices of the Peace (dwelling in or next to every the faid Towns or Parifhes) of all fuch Sums as they have fo employed, and of all Bonds taken for the Payment thereof, and of all Sums remaining in their Hands, and not employed. *Apprentices. Charity. 7 Jac. 1. 3.*

Two Juftices of Peace may licenfe the poor difeafed Perfons to travel to the Baths for Remedy of their Griefs, fo as they be provided of neceffary Relief (*fcil.* with Money in their Purfes, &c.) for their Travel, and beg not. See hereof *poftea* Tit. *Rogues,* &c. *cap.* 83. * *39 El. 4. 1 Jac. 1. 25. *The 39 El. 4. is repealed.*

The Juftice of Peace dwelling near where any Perfon fuffering Shipwreck fhall land, or where any poor Soldier or Mariner fhall land, may and ought to make a Teftimonial under his Hand to fuch Perfons, of their Landing, &c. and thereby to licenfe them to pafs the next direct Way to their Place of Birth or Dwelling, limiting therein a convenient Time for their paffing thither. See Tit. *Rogues,* Chap. 83. *Teftimonial. 39 El. 17. §. 3.*

But it feems no Juftice or Juftices of Peace can licenfe a poor Man to beg or wander, nor travel but only in the Cafes aforefaid. See Tit. *Rogues,* Chap. 83.

(a) The forty Days Continuance of a poor Perfon in a Parifh, intended by 13 & 14 *Car.* 2. *cap.* 2. to make a Settlement, fhall be accounted from the Time of his Delivery of Notice in Writing of the Houfe of his Abode, and the Number of his Family, to one of the Churchwardens or Overfeers of the Poor of the Parifh to which they fhall remove. *1 Jac. 2. c. 17. §. 3.*

Forty Days Notice of the Continuance of a Perfon to make a Settlement, fhall be accounted from the Publication of Notice in Writing, to be delivered to the Churchwarden, &c. which fhall be read after Divine Service in the Church or Chapel on the next Lord's Day, and the fame to be regiftred in the Poors Book. And the Church-wardens, &c. refufing to read or caufe to be read fuch Notice as aforefaid, or refufing to regifter the *3 & 4 W. & M. c. 11. § 3. Ib. §. 5.*

fame, (upon Proof by two Witneffes before a Juftice of the Peace) fhall forfeit 40 s. to the Ufe of the Party grieved, to be levied by Diftrefs, by Virtue of a Juftice's Warrant to the Conftable, &c. and for Want of a Diftrefs to be committed for a Month.

Settlement.
Ib. §. 7 & 8.

Any Perfon executing any publick Office in a Parifh during a Year, or paying his Share towards publick Taxes; or having no Child or Children fhall be lawfully hired for a Year, or being bound an Apprentice, fhall be accounted a good Settlement without Notice in Writing. And Perfons aggrieved by the Determination of any Juftice of Peace, may appeal to the next Quarter-Seffions, who fhall finally determine the fame.

Ib. §. 9.

Ib. §. 10.

Removal.

Penalty.

Any Perfon removed from one Place to another, by a Warrant of two Juftices of Peace by Virtue of this Act, the Church-wardens, &c. of the Place to which he fhall be removed to, fhall receive him, and upon Refufal (upon Proof by two Witneffes upon Oath, before a Juftice of Peace of the County, &c. to which he fhall be removed) fhall forfeit 5 l. to the Poor of the Parifh from which he fhall be removed, to be levied by Diftrefs, &c. by Warrant from a Juftice of Peace of the County, &c. to which he fhall be removed, to the Conftable of the Place where fuch Offender dwells; and for want of Diftrefs fhall be committed for forty Days. Any Perfon aggrieved by the Judgment of the faid two Juftices, may appeal to the next General Quarter-Seffions of the Place from which the faid Perfon was removed.

Ib. §. 11.
Appeal.

Register Alms.
Ib. §. 12.

Books fhall be kept in every Parifh, to regifter the Names of fuch as receive Alms: And in every *Eafter-week* they fhall be called over, and a new Lift fhall be made, and none allowed to receive Collections, but fuch as are authorized under the Hand of a Juftice of Peace refiding in the Parifh, or in the Parts next adjoining, or by Order of the Juftices of Peace in their Quarter-Seffions, except in Cafes of peftilential Difeafes, in refpect of Families infected only.

What fhall be a Settlement of the Poor, and where.

The Husband ferved an Apprenticefhip in the Parifh of *M.* and there he married, and had feveral Children; afterwards his Wife being dead, he married another Woman, who was poffeffed of Lands for a Term of Years in the Parifh of *H.* where he lived with his faid Wife for a Year, and then returned to *M.* and lived there two Years, and was taxed to the Poor and died; then his Widow and Children were removed by an Order to *H.* The Queftion was, that he returning to *M.* without giving Notice in Writing, &c. whether his being taxed to the Poor there made a Settlement; and adjudged that it would not; but this is not Law.

Shower Rep. 12.
* 1 Jac. 2. c. 17.
3 & 4 W. c. 11.

For it hath been adjudged, that taking a Houfe and being rated to the Poor, and fo obferved by the Overfeers in their Parifh Book, this amounts to Notice, becaufe 'tis plain that the * Acts of Settlement by which Notice in Writing, and Publication of fuch Notice in the Church, is injoined to be given, were made to prevent Clandeftine Settlements, and not publick Removals, where the Parifhioners might of themfelves take Notice of Perfons who come to be fettled amongft them.

Hiring.

A Servant was hired for Half a Year, and when that Time was expired he was hired for a whole Year, and ferved the firft Half-Year, and above Half of the whole Year, for which he was laft hired; and this was adjudged a good Settlement in that Parifh where he was hired, becaufe here was a Hiring for a whole Year at one Time, and a Service for a Year. This is not Law: For the Hiring muft be upon one intire Contract for a Year, and fo muft the Service.

Birth.
2 Bulft. 351, 357.

Where the Place of the Father's laft Settlement is not known, the Children though legitimate may be fent to the Place of their Birth, becaufe it is a Setling them in a certain Place, for that they may not be Vagabonds.

So where a Woman was delivered of a Child in the Houfe of Correction, that Child is to be fent to the Parifh where fhe was laft legally fettled, for that is the Place which by Law is bound to provide for it.

Style 168.

A Servant was hired for a Year in the Parifh of *B.* and being afterwards vifited with Sicknefs, her Mafter turned her away; and fhe going towards *H.* where fhe was born, begged for Relief, and by Reafon thereof was fent as a *Vagrant* to the faid Place of her Birth, who fent her back to the Parifh of *B.* Adjudged, that fhe ought to be fettled in the Parifh of *B.* where fhe was hired, and not in *H.* where fhe was born.

Hiring.
8 & 9 W. 3. c. 30. §. 4.
Birth.

No unmarried Perfon hired into a Place for a Year, fhall be adjudged to have a Settlement there, unlefs fuch Perfon fhall abide in the fame Service for one whole Year.

A Travelling Woman was committed for Felony, having then a fucking Child, and was afterwards convicted and executed: Adjudged, that the Child fhall be fent to the Parifh where it was born, if that can be known, but if not, then to the Place where fhe was apprehended for the Felony.

The

The Wife ought to be fent to the Place where her Husband was laft legally fettled, tho' fuch Settlement was by his being a Servant, &c.

Adjudged that by the Order of two Juftices to remove a Man from one Parifh to another, the Right of Settlement is determined till that Order is reverfed upon an Appeal, therefore without an Appeal the Parifh to which the poor Perfon was fent cannot remove him to a third Parifh, becaufe that would be to falfify the Original Order, which cannot be done but on an Appeal. ^{2 Salk. 488.}

An unmarried Perfon hired for a Year, married before the Year was expired, the Juftices of Peace cannot remove him to the laft legal Place of his Settlement, becaufe they cannot make the Contract between him and the Mafter void; for that muft be done upon the Complaint of the Mafter, and if the married Perfon lives and ferves the whole Year, he gains a Settlement there. ^{2 Salk. 527, 529.}

Adjudged, that paying to a *Scavenger's Rate* in a *Ward in London*, doth not make a Settlement without *Notice*, &c. becaufe this is not a parochial Tax, there being feveral Parifhes in one Ward. ^{What fhall not be a Settlement.}

A Servant was hired for a Quarter of a Year, and when that Time was expired, he was hired again for Half a Year, and after that Time expired for Half a Year more, and ferved all that Time: Adjudged that this made no Settlement within the * Statute, becaufe the Hiring muft be one intire Hiring for a Year, and the Service muft be intire for that Year, and not for a Quarter of a Year and Half-Year, as in the principal Cafe, and for that Reafon the Order was quafhed. ^{Hiring. * 8 & 9 W. 3. c. 30.}

Adjudged that a Hiring *ten Days after Michaelmas*, as from that *Michaelmas* till the following, is no good Settlement; for the Reafon before mentioned. ^{Hiring.}

No Perfon fhall gain a Settlement by a *Purchafe*, where the Confideration-Money doth not amount to 30 *l. bona fide* paid, for any longer Time than the Perfon fhall dwell on fuch Eftate, and then fhall be liable to be removed where he was laft legally fettled before fuch Purchafe made. ^{Purchafe. 9 Geo. 1. c. 7. §. 5.}

It hath been formerly held, that the Statute 3 & 4 *Will.* being an explanatory Law, ought not to be taken according to Equity, but ought ftrictly to be purfued by *Publication of Notice in Writing*, as in the Cafes following. ^{Of Settlement without Notice given.}

ff. The *Banns of Matrimony* were publifhed in the Parifh of *H.* between a poor Man and Woman, who being chargeable to another Parifh where he lived, was by Order of two Juftices fent to the *Parifh of H.* where the faid *Banns* were publifhed, and where he had lived for fome Time; but upon an Appeal that Order was quafhed, becaufe this was not fuch *Notice* as was required by that Statute. ^{Banns of Marriage.}

One who was born in the Parifh of *C.* and ferved an *Apprenticefhip* there for feven Years, went into another Parifh without giving any *Notice*, &c. and there he rented a Shop of the Widow of a Blackfmith, and likewife a Chamber for 50 *s. per Ann.* and this was with the Confent of the *Bailiff of the Manor*, and was publickly employed by the Parifhioners to fhoe their Horfes: Adjudged that this publick Way of Living did not amount to Notice in writing purfuant to the explanatory Statute, tho' it might fatisfy the Statute 1 *Jac.* 2. *cap.* 17. as amounting to the Delivery of Notice in Writing. ^{2 Salk. 476.}

So where a Man was fettled in one Parifh, and clandeftinely came into another, without giving any Notice, and there lived feveral Years, but being chargeable was removed to the firft Parifh by an Order, &c. which was confirmed upon an Appeal, and good; for tho' he had lived in the other Parifh feveral Years, yet Notice ought to be given to make a Settlement; and fince the Statutes before mentioned, Notice fhall not be prefumed. ^{2 Salk. 472.}

But now the Law is held to be otherwife (*viz.*) that thofe Statutes being made to prevent clandeftine Settlements, therefore Notice taken fhall be Notice given; for where the Parifhioners might of themfelves take Notice of a poor Man coming to dwell in their Parifh, by fome open and publick Acts, that fhall amount to Notice given.

There are four Exceptions out of the explanatory Act 3 & 4 *Will.* which make Settlements good without Notice delivered, or Publication of Notice in writing. ^{3 & 4 W. 3. c. 11.}

1. *Where a Man on his own Account executes any publick annual Office during one whole Year.*

Now as to this Matter it was held, that where a poor Man was appointed to be a *Parifh Clerk*, which Office he executed for a Year, this made a good Settlement; and that 'tis not material whether he had the Office by the Appointment of the Parfon, or
by

by the Election of the Parishioners, becaufe he is in for Life; and this is an executing an Yearly Office within the Meaning of that Statute.

2. *Where a Man is charged and payeth the publick Taxes of the Parish.*

Taxes to the King are not comprehended in this Exception, for thofe may be paid by Reafon of the *Refidence* of the Party.

2 Salk. 478.   A poor Man rented an Houfe at 7 *l. per Ann.* and lived therein for a Year, and paid the *Rates and Taxes due for his Houfe*, which were charged on the faid *Houfe*, and not on his Perfon: Adjudged that fuch Payment made a Settlement.

2 Salk. 534.   A poor Man rented Part of an Houfe at 3 *l. per Ann.* but by an Agreement between him and his Landlord he was to *pay no Taxes*; the Apartment which he rented was diftinct from the Dwelling-houfe, but it was *taxed* as an Houfe, and affeffed on the Landlord; the poor Man lived there for fome Time, and was made Free of the Corporation, and voted at an Election of the Chief Magiftrate there: Adjudged that this did not make a Settlement within this explanatory Act, tho' it might within the Statute 1 *Jac.* 2. and the Voting relates to the Corporation, and not to the Parifh.

2 Salk. 523.   It was refolved by the Court, that where a Man is taxed to the Parifh Rates, and lives there forty Days after he is *taxed*, and without giving Notice, &c. this doth not make a Settlement within the Act, becaufe *Taxing* alone is not equivalent to Notice, but

* 3 Salk. 253. *Taxing and * Paying the Tax* is equivalent both to the Delivery of Notice, and to the Publication of that Notice in Writing.

3. *Where an unmarried Perfon, not having Wife or Children, fhall be hired into a Service for a Year, fuch Service fhall be a Settlement without Notice.*

8 & 9 W. 3.   This is explained by a fubfequent Statute, by which 'tis enacted, that an unmarried
c. 30. §. 4.   Perfon hired, &c. for a Year, fhall gain no Settlement unlefs he ferve for a Year.

2 Salk. 478.   The Mafter put his menial Servant to a *Barber* in another Parifh to learn to fhave for which he (the *Barber*) was to have 5 *l.* and the Servant continued with the *Barber* for a Year upon this Agreement, but he himfelf was no Party to it: Adjudged that this did not make a Settlement in that Parifh where he ferved the Barber, becaufe he was no *hired*, but rather continued there as a *Boarder* to learn to fhave.

The Reafon of that explanatory Statute 8 & 9 *Will.* was becaufe of fome Doubt upon thofe Words (*fuch Service*) in the Statute 3 & 4 *Will.* (*viz.*) whether thefe Words fhall relate to a Service where the Perfon continues *unmarried for a Year*, or where the Service was purfuant to a *Hiring for a Year*, and as to that Matter this Cafe happened.

Hiring.   *ff.* A Servant being hired for a Year, continued in that Service for Half a Year, and
2 Salk. 527. then married a Woman in another Parifh: Adjudged that the Words (*fuch Service*) in the Statute 3 & 4 *Will.* fhall relate to a Service where the Hiring is for a Year, becaufe the Marriage is no Hindrance of the Service of the Man; therefore the Hiring fhal not be determined by it, for the Contract ftill continues between the Mafter and the Servant, and not to be diffolved upon the Complaint of the Parifh Officers, tho' it might upon the Complaint of the Mafter, but that muft be at his Election; for if he will fuffer fuch a married Servant to continue in his Service for a Year, no Body elfe can difturb him, and that will make a good Settlement.

Service upon   A Servant continued in his Service for a whole Year, but it was upon two Contracts
two Contracts. each of them for Half a Year: Adjudged this made no Settlement, becaufe the Service
2 Salk. 535. ought to be for a whole Year, upon *one intire Contract*, or Hiring for a Year; for the
* 3 Salk. 257. Statutes require that the Agreement fhall be intire, as well as the Service; * though a Year after the Making the Statute, a Service for a Year and more, upon two Contracts was held a good Settlement.

4. *Where a Perfon fhall be bound Apprentice, and inhabit in any Parifh, fuch Binding and Habitation fhall be a Settlement without Notice.*

Mod.Ca. 190.   The Son of a Man was bound *Apprentice* to his Father, who afterwards gave up the Indentures of Apprenticefhip, but did not *cancel them*; then the Son was hired into another Parifh for a Year, and ferved a whole Year there, and being likely to be chargeable, he was fent by an Order to the Parifh where he lived as an Apprentice, becaufe the Indentures being not cancelled, he ftill continued an Apprentice there.

2

A

A poor Boy was Apprentice for four Years to a Mafter who was only a *Lodger* in the Parifh, and had no Settlement there: Adjudged that this Apprentice having ferved there for fome Time, hath gained a Settlement though his Mafter had none; becaufe his Settlement did not depend on his Mafter, he having gained a Settlement for himfelf within the Statute 14 *Car.* 2. by living in a Parifh forty Days as an Apprentice. The Law is the fame of an hired Servant, though his Mafter had no Settlement, if fuch Servant was hired for a Year, and continued in his Service for a Year. *Servant fettled tho' the Mafter was a Lodger.* 2 Salk. 533.

The Mafter who lived in one Parifh, took a poor Boy Apprentice, where he lived for fome Time, and then *affigned* him to another Mafter who was an Inhabitant in another Parifh: Adjudged that this Apprentice is legally fettled in the fecond Parifh where the Mafter lived to whom he was affigned, for though an Apprentice is not *affignable*, fo as to pafs an Intereft, yet fuch Affignment is not void; for 'tis good by way of Covenant, and fhall amount to a Contract between the Mafter and the Affignee. *Apprentice affigned.*

An Order of two Juftices, &c. was quafhed, becaufe it did not appear that it was made *upon the Complaint of the Church-wardens or Overfeers of the Poor*, befides there was no *Adjudication*. *Orders of Removal quafhed, being informal and not quafhed.*

It was held by the Court for a general Rule, in Cafes of Orders for Removal, that if the Parifh to which a poor Perfon is removed doth not *appeal* in Time, fuch Order is conclufive to the contending Parifhes, and indeed to all Parifhes, except where an After-Settlement can be fixed. *Appeal.*

An Order was quafhed, though it was mentioned to be made upon *due Notice*, and upon hearing the Allegations and Proofs on both Sides, becaufe it ought to be made upon *Complaint of the Church-wardens and Overfeers of the Poor*, which was omitted. *It muft be made upon Complaint of Parifh Officers.*

The Seffions made an Order for the Parifh of *C.* to provide an *Houfe* for *A.* and another Order to relieve *B.* it was held, that if thofe Perfons are not impotent, or if they have Means to live, or are able to work, that fuch Orders are againft Law, and ought to be quafhed.

Upon Complaint to the Seffions, that the Parents did not relieve a poor Child, they appointed two Juftices to examine the Matter, &c. who made an Order for the Parents to relieve it; but it was quafhed, becaufe the Seffions could not delegate their Power to other Juftices, therefore they fhould have made the original Order. *Seffions cannot delegate their Power. Style 154.*

The Order of two Juftices fet forth, that the Perfon removed was *lately fettled* in the Parifh of *C.* &c. it fhould have been *laft legally fettled*, &c. and for that Reafon it was quafhed. *9 Ann.* *It muft be laft legally fettled.*

The Order of two Juftices recites, that they were *credibly informed*, that *T. S.* was laft legally fettled in the Parifh of *C.* for which Reafon it was quafhed, for it muft pofitively be adjudged to be the laft Place of legal Settlement. *And fo pofitively alledged.* 2 Salk. 473.

It was recited in the Order, that the two Juftices were *refiding in the County of* W. for which Reafon it was quafhed, for it muft appear they were Juftices *in and for the County*, &c.

Order for removing a poor Man, and his Wife and *Family*, from fuch a Place, &c. was quafhed, becaufe it did not appear of whom his Family confifted, * probably it might be of fome who are not removeable by Law. *Family.* 2 Salk. 585. * 3 Salk. 260.

A poor Man was removed from the Parifh of *A.* to the Parifh of *L.* and afterwards he went away to the Parifh of *P.* which was a third Parifh, and thereupon this third Parifh got feveral Orders from two Juftices to inforce the Execution of the original Order by which he was fent to *L.* but they were all quafhed, becaufe the Parifh of *P.* ought to have made an original Complaint to two Juftices, and upon that to have got an Order, and not to have grafted it upon the original Order of Removal from *A.* to *L.* 2 Salk. 489.

In every Order of Removal of a poor Perfon, it ought to appear, that he is *removeable by Law*, therefore it ought to be averred, that he is *chargeable, or likely to be chargeable* to the Parifh, and there ought to be an *Adjudication* of that Matter, and of the *laft Place of his lawful Settlement*. *The Party muft be removeable by Law.* 2 Salk. 491. 3 Salk. 255.

An Order made upon *Complaint* generally, &c. is not good, it muft be made upon the Complaint of the *Parifh Officers*; and therefore where that was omitted, the Order was quafhed; and though upon the Return of the *Certiorari*, it appeared to be made upon the Complaint of the *Church-wardens*, &c. yet that fhall not fupply the Defect in the original Order, becaufe the Juftices had executed their Authority before the Return made, and therefore they had no Power to make fuch a Return; they fhould have returned the very Order *in hæc verba*, &c. *3 Salk. 255. 3 Salk. 492. 5 Mod. 149.*

A a a   An

The Party muſt be poor.
3 Salk. 255.

An Order was quaſhed, becauſe it did not ſet forth, that the Perſon removed was *Poor*, or likely to become *chargeable* to the *Pariſh.*

Order muſt be directed to the Pariſh Officers.
3 Salk. 256.

Every Order of Removal ought to be directed to the *Pariſh Officers removing*, and to the *Pariſh Officers to whom removed*, and not to the Officers of that Pariſh alone to which the Perſon is *removed*, and for that Reaſon the Order was quaſhed.

Certiorari returned thereof, good.
3 Salk. 258.

The Return of the *Certiorari* in a Schedule annexed to the Writ was not made by two Juſtices, but by the *Clerk of Peace*; but he not being the Perſon to whom the Writ was directed, it was quaſhed, and a new *Certiorari* granted, which being returned and filed, it was objected, that it did not appear by the Order, that it was made by two *Juſtices of the Diviſion, &c.* purſuant to the Statute 13 & 14 *Car.* 2. but adjudged, that as to this Matter the Statute was only directory and not reſtrictive, as the Words *Quorum unus, &c.* are.

Of Appeals to the next Quarter-Seſſions, and of Orders made at the Seſſions.
1 Vent. 310.

'Tis a ſtanding Rule in *B. R.* that where an Order of two Juſtices is either *affirmed or quaſhed* upon an Appeal, upon the *Merits of the Cauſe* there heard, that this is concluſive between the contending Pariſhes, unleſs there is Error in the Form.

Coſts.
8 & 9 W. 3.
c. 30. §. 3.

The Seſſions upon an Appeal from an Order of Settlement, or upon Proof of Notice of an Appeal given by a proper Officer to the Pariſh Officer of the Pariſh, (though the Appeal is not proſecuted) ſhall award to the Party in whoſe Behalf the Appeal ſhall be determined, or to whom ſuch Notice was given, &c. his reaſonable *Coſts*; and if the Party who is to pay it ſhall live out of the Juriſdiction of the Court; then one Juſtice of the County where ſuch Perſon ſhall live (upon Requeſt to him made, and a Copy of the Seſſions Order produced, and proved by a credible Witneſs) ſhall cauſe the Money mentioned in the Order, to be levied by Diſtreſs, &c. and for Default thereof to commit the Perſon to Gaol for twenty Days.

Appeals, where to be determined.
Ib. §. 6.

All Appeals againſt an Order of Removal of a poor Perſon ſhall be determined at the Quarter-Seſſions in the County or Place from whence the poor Perſon is removed, and not elſewhere.

Notice.
9 Geo. 1. c. 7.
§. 8.

No Appeal ſhall be proceeded on for Removal of a poor Perſon unleſs reaſonable *Notice* be given by a Pariſh Officer of that Pariſh who appeals to a Pariſh Officer from whence the Perſon is removed; and the Seſſions to whom the Appeal is made ſhall determine the Reaſonableneſs of the Notice; and if the Court ſhall be of Opinion, that the Notice was not reaſonable, they may adjourn the Appeal to the next Seſſions, whoſe Determination ſhall be final.

Ib. §. 9.

And if the Court ſhall determine in Favour of the Appellant, they ſhall award ſo much Money as ſhall appear to have been reaſonably paid by the Pariſh appealing, and expended by them in Relieving ſuch poor Perſon from the Time of his undue Removal to the Time the Appeal was determined, to be recovered and levied by Diſtreſs, &c.

Seſſions muſt either affirm or reverſe the Order.
2 Salk. 475.

Upon an Appeal from an Order of two Juſtices, the Seſſions ſent the poor Man by an Order to a third Pariſh, for which Reaſon it was quaſhed; for the Seſſions have only Power to affirm or reverſe the Order of the two Juſtices, and they cannot make an original Order.

Seſſions have no Juriſdiction but on Appeal.

An Order was quaſhed upon an Appeal, but that Seſſions Order was likewiſe quaſhed, becauſe it did not appear that it came before them by Way of Appeal, and they have no Juriſdiction but upon an Appeal.

The Order upon an Appeal is concluſive as to the contending Pariſhes.
2 Salk. 486.

The Order of two Juſtices, by which a poor Man was ſent from *B.* to *K.* was reverſed upon an Appeal, and thereupon he went back to *B.* and that Pariſh ſent him to *D.* a third Pariſh, who moved to quaſh it, for that the Order of Reverſal was concluſive to all Pariſhes, and had actually ſettled the Man at *B.* but adjudged, that the Determination upon the Appeal was concluſive only between the contending Pariſhes, and not to a third Pariſh, who was not concerned in the Order or Appeal.

Affirmance of an Order on an Appeal concluſive is all Pariſhes.
Reverſal is concluſive only to the contending Pariſhes.
2 Salk. 492.
3 Salk. 260, 261.

There is a Difference as to the Place of Settlement, where the Order of two Juſtices is *confirmed*, and where 'tis *reverſed* upon an Appeal, or not appealed from; for where 'tis *confirmed* or not appealed from, there that Pariſh to which the poor Man was removed by the original Order, ſhall never ſay, that it was not the laſt Place of his legal Settlement, becauſe the Affirmance of the Order upon an Appeal is concluſive to all Pariſhes; but where the original Order is diſcharged upon an Appeal, there the Matter is at large again as to all Pariſhes, except that to which the poor Man was removed, which upon the Appeal was determined not to be the laſt Place of his lawful Settlement.

An

An Appeal from the Order of two Juſtices ought to be to the next Seſſions, that is, it ught to be lodged then, but there is no Neceſſity that it ſhould be determined at that Time, becauſe the Seſſions may * adjourn it to another.

The Order of two Juſtices was diſcharged upon an Appeal to the next Seſſions; and pon a Motion to ſet aſide this Order of Diſcharge it was objected, that the Seſſions did ot ſay, whether it was diſcharged for a Defect in Form, or upon the Merits; for if it vas for Want of Form, then the Pariſh from which the poor Perſon was removed, is ot bound; but if on the Merits, then 'tis bound; but adjudged, that the Seſſions are ot obliged to give any Reaſon of their Judgment in the Orders they make, no more han any other of the Courts of Law.

Adjudged, that the Seſſions have no Juriſdiction upon an Appeal, but only to reverſe r affirm the original Order of the two Juſtices made between the two contending Pa- iſhes; therefore where they made an Order to ſend a poor Woman to a third Pariſh, ot concerned before, this Order was quaſhed, for the Reaſon abovementioned.

Adjudged, that where a Village in a Pariſh had a *Church* before the Statute 43 *Eliz.* nd that ſuch Village had been uſed and reputed as a Pariſh, and had all parochial Rights nd Church-wardens, &c. that this is a Pariſh, and chargeable to maintain its own 'oor. *Cro. Car.* 92.

Cro. Car. 394. S. P. W. Jones 355.

There were two Vills in the Pariſh of *H.* one of which Vills had a Chapel of Eaſe, vhere they uſed to *bury, and to chuſe Overſeers of the Poor* amongſt themſelves, and had een reputed a Pariſh : Adjudged, that this was a Pariſh in Reputation, and rateable to he Poor. 2 *Roll's Rep.* 160.

A *Badge* muſt be worn by thoſe who receive Collections, (*viz.*) a *Roman* P. with the irſt Letter of the Name of the Pariſh; this muſt be upon the Shoulder of the right leeve; and the Perſon neglecting or refuſing to wear it, one Juſtice may either abridge r ſuſpend the Relief, or commit the Offender to the Houſe of Correction, to be vhipp'd and kept to hard Labour, not exceeding twenty-one Days.

Any Perſon *leaving his Wife and Children* to the Pariſh, in ſuch Caſe the Pariſh Offi- ers may by Warrant of two Juſtices, &c. ſeiſe ſo much of the Goods and Chattels of he Perſon running away, and receive ſo much of his Rents and Profits as thoſe two Ju- tices ſhall order towards the Diſcharging the Pariſh, which Order being confirmed at he next Seſſions, that Court may order the Pariſh Officers to diſpoſe thereof as they ſhall hink fit, and likewiſe to receive the Rents, &c. for the Purpoſe aforeſaid; but to be ccountable to the Seſſions.

No Juſtice, &c. ſhall order Relief to a poor Perſon without Oath made before him f ſome Matter which he ſhall judge to be a reaſonable Cauſe for giving Relief, and hat the Perſon hath applied himſelf to the Veſtry, or to two Overſeers, &c. and was lenied Relief, and until the Juſtice hath ſummoned the Overſeers, &c. to ſhew Cauſe vhy the Perſon ſhould not be relieved, and they are heard, or refuſe to appear upon ſuch Summons.

If the Juſtice ſhall ſee Cauſe to allow Relief, then the Name of the poor Perſon ſhall e entered in the Pariſh Book as one who is to receive Collection, as long as the Cauſe f ſuch Relief continues; and no Pariſh Officer (unleſs upon ſome extraordinary Occa- ion) ſhall bring to Account any Money he ſhall give to the Poor, who is not regiſtered n his Pariſh Book, on Pain of 5 *l.* to be levied by Diſtreſs, &c. by Warrant from two Juſtices, which ſaid Sum ſhall be applied to the Uſe of the Poor of that Pariſh, by the Direction of the ſaid Juſtices.

The Seſſions made an Order for a *Feme Covert* to keep and relieve her Grandchild; out it was quaſhed, becauſe her Huſband ought to be charged by an Order, and not he Wife.

It was ordered by the Seſſions, that the Son ſhould pay 2 *s. per* Week towards the Relief of his Father, till the Court ſhould order otherwiſe : Adjudged a good Order, tho' t was indefinite, and no certain Time limited how long he ſhould pay the ſaid 2 *s.* but it had been otherwiſe if a certain Time had been limited.

The Father was ordered by the Seſſions to allow his Daughter 2 *s. per* Week, but the Order was quaſhed, becauſe it did not appear that ſhe was not able to work, or that ſhe was ſick, old, or otherwiſe impotent.

The

The Settlement of the Child must follow that of the Parents till 'tis eight Years old, but after that Age it may acquire another Settlement; and if removed from the Place where the Parents were settled, it must appear in the Order that such Child hath gained a Settlement elsewhere.

An Order was made to send an *Ideot* to the Parish where his Father was last legally settled; this was adjudged a good Order.

A Child born in the Parish of *H*. the Father removed from that Parish whilst it was under eight Years old, and gained a Settlement in the Parish of *C*. adjudged that the Child shall likewise be settled there; so where the Father is settled in a Parish, and dies, and the Mother being with Child likewise dies in Child-bed, the Child born shall be settled in that Parish.

The Reason, because it cannot be sent to its Parents where they were last legally settled, because they were both dead; therefore it must be sent to the Place where born.

But if the Parents are living, they must be sent to the Place where they were last legally settled; and as to that Matter this Case happened.

A poor Man, lawfully settled in a Parish, had several Children born there; and afterwards he and his Wife and Children went into another Parish, and he gained a Settlement there; and being likely to be chargeable, his Children under seven Years old were removed

by an Order of two Justices, to the first Parish where they were *born* : But adjudged that 'tis not the Birth of legitimate Children, but the Settlement of the Father which makes a Settlement for them; and the Father in the principal Case having gained a new Settlement in the second Parish, his Children must be settled there, and not as Nurse-Children, but as Part of his Family. 'Tis true, if the Father had been dead, and the Mother had married a second Husband, settled in a third Parish; in such Case her Children by her first Husband must go with her as Nurse-children, and not as Part of her Family; for those Children shall be maintained at the Charge of the Parish where their Father was last legally settled in his Life-time, and thither they may be sent after seven Years old, as to the Place of their lawful Settlement; for this accidental Settlement of their Mother by marrying a second Husband, shall not gain a Settlement of her Children by her first Husband.

A poor Man may remove into any Parish, having a Certificate from the Parish where he was settled, signed and sealed by the Churchwardens and Overseers, or the major Part of them, acknowledging the Person to be an Inhabitant legally settled in their Parish.

But he who comes into a Parish by Virtue of such *Certificate*, shall not have a lawful Settlement there by any Act whatsoever, unless he rent an House, &c. of 10 *l. per Annum*, or execute some annual Office in that Parish.

If any Person shall be an Apprentice, or hired Servant to one who came into the Parish by Certificate, and not having afterwards gained a legal Settlement in the said Parish, such Apprentice or Servant shall not gain any Settlement by Reason of such Apprenticeship, or serving therein, but shall have their Settlement in such Parish, as if they had never been bound Apprentice, or been hired as a Servant.

Anno 9 *Annæ*, The Parish of *H*. gave a *Certificate* to a poor Man and his Children, to the Parish of *A*. where he afterwards becoming chargeable, was sent back to *H*. by the Order of two Justices, which said Parish of *H*. sent him to the Parish of *C*. as the Place of his last legal Settlement, from which last Order the Parish of *C*. appealed, where it was set aside; and these Orders being removed into B. R. the Court held that the Certificate given by the Parish of *H*. is conclusive to them, to remove this poor Man to any other Parish.

Where a poor Man comes into a Parish with a *Certificate*, he cannot be removed, unless he is actually chargeable to that Parish; for 'tis not sufficient to say that he is likely to be chargeable.

A Person who was born in the Parish of *A*. lived some Years in the Parish of *B*. but he had no Settlement there by Law, and yet they gave him a Certificate to remove to *C*. where becoming chargeable, he was sent back to the Parish of *B*. who finding that he was born in *A*. got an Order of two Justices to send him thither : Adjudged, that *B*. who gave the Certificate ought to receive him, and to discharge the Parish of *C*. to whom the Certificate was given, but did not conclude them as to the Sending him to any other Parish, where he was last lawfully settled.

About nine Years after the last mentioned Case there was a Resolution to the contrary, (*viz.*) That before the Statute Certificates were frequently given, but then they were only

4　　　　　　　　　　　　　　　　　　　　Evidences

Evidences of a private Nature between the Parifhes, and in Nature of a Contract; but now Certificate.
fince the Statute they are folemn Acknowledgments that the Perfon is legally fettled with The giving a Certificate
them; and as all other Parifhes are bound to receive him, fo that Parifh which certifies makes a Settlement.
is concluded as to all other Parifhes whatfoever; for 'tis in Nature of an Adjudication, 'tis
figned by the proper Officers, and allowed by two Juftices who are proper Judges, and
who upon lefs Evidence could have adjudged it a Settlement.

Adjudged, that where a poor Man who hath a lawful Settlement in one Parifh, comes But if he gain a Settlement
into another by a Certificate, and gains a Settlement there, he fhall not afterwards be fent after the Cer-
back to the Parifh certifying, becaufe the Certificate being only a private Agreement be- tificate given,
tween the two Parifhes, fhall not alter the Law by which he had gained a Settlement in 'tis good.
that Parifh to which the Certificate was given.　　　　3 Salk. 253.

The *Mother*, who was an Inhabitant legally fettled *in C.* had *two Children* there under Certificate
the Age of 7 Years; and after the Death of her Husband, fhe with her faid Children came fhall not make a Settlement of
by a *Certificate* from *C.* to the Parifh of *D.* afterwards fhe married another Husband, who the Children
was a Parifhioner in *S.* and who lived with * her *at B.* but had no legal Settlement there, not named in the Certificate,
and for that Reafon the Churchwardens of *S.* gave a *Certificate to the Parifh of B.* (where unlefs they live
the fecond Husband and his Wife lived) owning them to be Parifhioners of *S.* but her two with their Pa-
Children by her firft Husband were not named in this laft Certificate : The Mother died, rents.
and the Children were fent *to S.* where their Father in Law and Mother were fettled; but * But it did not appear that her
it was held by the Judges that *C.* was the Place of their Settlement, becaufe that it did not two Children
appear that they ever lived with their Mother after her fecond Marriage. lived with her there.

Where a Parifh is not able to provide for their own Poor, two Juftices of Peace, by Of Rates, &c.
Virtue of the Statute 43 *Eliz.* may tax *any other of other Parifhes, or out of any Parifh* what Parifhes,
within the fame Hundred, to pay fuch Sums to the Parifh Officers, as they fhall think fit; Places and Things fhall be
and if the *Hundred* fhall not be thought able to relieve them, then the Quarter-Seffions rated to main-
may rate any other Parifhes, or out of any Parifh within the *County,* &c.　　　　tain the Poor.

43 El. c. 2.
The Words of the faid Statute, viz. (*Any other of other Parifhes, or out of any Parifh*) 1 Vent. 350.
are general; and therefore it hath been adjudged, that the two Juftices may rate any particular Inhabitants of another Parifh, and are not obliged to lay a general Rate on the
whole Parifh.

The Husband who lived in the Parifh of St. *Botolph* without Aldgate, lying in two Raim. 476.
Counties, viz. in *London* and *Middlefex,* had feveral Children born there, and afterwards
he died; then the Widow married a fecond Husband, and they put thefe Children to Nurfe
in *Enfield* in *Middlefex,* and then the Mother and Father in Law died; afterwards the
Nurfe applied her felf to the Parifh of St. *Botolph* for Money, in which Parifh there is but
one Church-warden, but feveral Overfeers of the Poor for each Part thereof, and the
Parifh Rates are feveral, the Mother living and dying in that Parifh which lies in *Middle-*
fex : The Juftices ordered them to pay the Money, but upon an Appeal and all Orders removed in *B. R.* it was held that each Party of the Parifh fhould be contributory; but
it appearing that each had diftinct Officers, and made diftinct Rates, and Time out of
Mind had made diftinct Accounts to the Juftices of each County, it was adjudged that
each Divifion was a diftinct Parifh; adjudged likewife that the *Birth* of the Children is not
to be regarded, but the laft Place where their Father was fettled.

Refolved by all the Judges of *England,* that the *Rates* for Relief of the Poor ought to Rates how to
be made according to the *vifible Eftates,* both real and perfonal in the Parifhes *where the* be made.
Perfons live, without any Refpect to be had of their Eftates in any other Place; and that
the Occupiers and not the Owners of the Lands there ought to be rated.

Refolved by three Judges againft *the Chief Juftice Holt,* that a Farmer fhall not be 2 Bulft. 154.
rated to the Poor for his neceffary Stock which he ufes on his Farm, for that would be in
Effect to make the Land pay twice for one and the fame Thing, viz. according to a *Pound* Farmer not to be rated for
Rate for his Rent, and according to the Value of his neceffary Stock ufed on his Farm; his neceffary
for what is the Land but the Profits thereof, and how can thofe Profits arife but by the Stock.
Stock ?

The moft reafonable Way of taxing Land, is according to the Pound Rate, and where The Pound
a perfonal Eftate, as Goods, Money, &c. are taxed, it ought to be in the fame Proportion Rate is the moft reafonable
as the Lands, viz. the Value of 100 l. at 5 l. per *Annum,* and the Perfon muft be charg- Rate for Land
ed in that Place where the Goods are when the Rate is made; for if he hath not a perfonal
Eftate to that Value there, and is diftrained for not paying the Rate, he may have an
Action of Trefpafs.　　　　The perfonal

Eftate muft be
By the Statute 43 *Eliz.* every Occupier of Houfes, Lands, Tithes, Woods, Mines or rated in Pro-
other Things out of which an yearly Profit may arife, may be rated. portion to the

Rate on Land.

43 Eliz.

And it hath been refolved, that if two Houfes are inhabited by feveral Families, tho' they had but one Common Door into both, yet they are ratable as two Houfes; fo if one Houfe is divided by a Partition, and inhabited by feveral Families, fuch are feveral Tenements, ratable feverally to the Poor; but if one Family remove, then 'tis but one Tenement again.

Diftrefs for a Quarter's Rate cannot be made till the Quarter is ended.

Adjudged likewife that where *T. S.* took Part of an Houfe in the Parifh of *H.* on the *firft Day of December*, and was rated as an Inhabitant, and diftrained at *Chriftmas* following for a Quarter's Rent, by Virtue of a general Warrant made for the whole Year, that this was illegal, *viz.* that he could not be rated for the whole Quarter, becaufe the Statute directs that the poor Rates fhould be affeffed monthly.

Refolved likewife that *T. S.* could not be diftrained by this Warrant made before the Rate, but there ought to be a Special Warrant for this particular Purpofe; and laftly, that a Diftrefs could not be made for a Quarter's Rate before the End of that Quarter; *per Holt Chief Juftice*, All this was adjudged in Replevin, *&c. Trin. 3 Annæ.*

Hofpital Lands.
2 Salk. 527.

Adjudged that Hofpital Lands fhall be charged in a Rate to the Poor, becaufe no Man by appropriating Lands to an Hofpital fhall exempt them from fuch Rates, for which they were charged before, and by that Means to lay a heavier Burden on the whole Parifh.

Rates.
Who fhall be charged.

One who poffeffes Lands lying in feveral Parifhes, fhall be rated in every Parifh according to the annual Value of the Land lying in each Parifh.

Clergymen.

Every Clergyman is to be rated for his Glebe and Tithes, according to their yearly Value fo long as they are in his own Occupation, becaufe the Statute charges every Occupier of Tithes, *&c.* and the Clergy are contained under thofe general Words, unlefs particularly exempted.

Of Appeals, &c. and of Overfeers Accounts.
Seffions may quafh a whole Rate.
Salk. 483.
43 Eliz. c. 2.

In a Rate for the Relief of the Poor, the Charge was laid on the *real Eftates*; and upon an Appeal to the Seffions that Rate was quafhed, and the Parifh Officers were ordered to make a new Rate, which they did, but very unequal; for they charged the *real Eftates* ten Times more in Proportion than the *perfonal Eftates*; and upon another Appeal that Rate was likewife quafhed by the Seffions: And now thefe Orders being removed into *B. R.* it was infifted that the Seffions could not quafh a whole Rate, for they had only Power to relieve particular Perfons aggrieved; but adjudged that they might fet afide a whole Rate, becaufe the Words of the Statute are, that upon Complaint, *&c.* they may take fuch Order as by them fhall be thought convenient; therefore they may either make a new Rate, or refer it to the Church-wardens, *&c.* to make a new one, which they have done.

Overfeer not bound to lay out his own Money for Relief. If he doth, a Mandamus will not be granted to reimburfe him.
2 Salk. 531.

An Overfeer having laid out his own Money to relieve the Poor, was turned out of his Office before he could make a Rate to reimburfe himfelf; whereupon he moved for a Mandamus to be directed to the fucceeding Parifh Officers to make a Rate for that Purpofe, but it was denied. 'Tis true, it may be granted to raife Money for the Relief of the Poor, but not to raife Money for reimburfing an Overfeer, efpecially fince he is not bound to lay out his own Money to relieve them.

Money in the Hands of an Overfeer, and he refufing to pay it over to his Succeffor, muft be levied on him by Diftrefs, and if that fail, then to commit him. 2 Salk. 533.

Two Juftices took the Account of an Overfeer, *&c.* and allowed it; from which the Parifh appealed to the Seffions, and there it was difallowed, and they ordered him to pay fo much Money over to his Succeffors, which they adjudged to be in his Hands, which he refufing, they committed him; but it was ruled that the Commitment was illegal, becaufe the Money ought to be levied by Diftrefs and Sale, *&c.* and for Default thereof, then to have committed him, but not before.

Churchwarden was committed for refufing to account: it muft appear that he was Overfeer, &c. as well as Churchwarden.

A *Church-warden* was committed by the two next Juftices (as *Churchwarden*) without Bail, for refufing to account for the Money received and disbursed by him; but upon an *Habeas Corpus* he was difcharged, becaufe by the Warrant of Commitment it ought to appear that he was Overfeer of the Poor; for by the Statute 43 *Eliz.* that is annexed to his Office of Church-warden, and the Juftices have no Jurifdiction over him as *Churchwarden*, but as Overfeer. *Mich.* 15 *Car.* 2.

Overfeers are to account before two Juftices, and not to their Succeffors.
2 Salk. 525.

Mandamus was granted to the Juftices to compel the old Overfeers to account *with their Succeffors*, but it was quafhed, becaufe by the Statute 43 *Eliz.* they are to give their Accounts to two Juftices; befides it did not appear by the Writ that all of them therein named were Overfeers.

Mandamus

Mandamus to Overfeers of the Poor to give an Account to the *Juſtices* of what Money
they had received to the Relief of the Poor; they return that they had given an Account,
and that they had diſpoſed ſeveral Sums in ſuch a Manner, ſetting it forth in the Return:
Adjudged that this *Mandamus* was ill, becauſe it was not ſuggeſted that the ordinary Means
could not be had for them to account.

The Defendants were indicted at the Seſſions for that they being duly choſen Overfeers,

&c. and having taken upon themſelves the ſaid Office, they, *& uterque eorum,* did collect and receive ſeveral Sums for the Relief of the Poor, and refuſed to account within
four Days after the End of their Year: It was objected that this Indictment would not lie,
becauſe the not accounting was an Offence created by the Statute 43 *Eliz.* by which 'tis
enacted that they ſhall account of all Things concerning their Office, under the Penalty of
forfeiting 20 *s.* therefore that ought to be purſued. 'Tis true, that is the proper Puniſhment, but refuſing to account was a Contempt of the Law, and therefore an Indictment
will lie.

Two Juſtices made an Order, that *T. S.* being duly elected Overfeer, ſhould take upon
him that Office; it was objected that this Order was not good, becauſe it did not appear
that he was an Inhabitant or Houſekeeper in that Pariſh, and the Court will not intend
that he was; therefore this Order was quaſhed.

The Churchwardens of *Biſhopſgate* made a Tax for the Relief of their Poor for a whole
Year, which amounted to 600 *l.* and upwards, when they ſhould have made only a quar-
erly Tax; and this was confirmed by the Alderman of the Ward, thro' Inadvertency, who
hearing the Churchwardens might collect the whole Sum and make ſome ill Uſe of it, refuſed to grant his Warrant to diſtrain for this Tax, whereupon they moved for a *Mandamus,* and obtained a Rule for the Alderman to ſhew Cauſe why it ſhould not be granted,
who upon another Day ſhewed the Matter before-mentioned for Cauſe; and thereupon a
Rule was made, that he ſhould grant his Warrant to diſtrain quarterly. *Mich.* 1721. *The
Churchwardens of Biſhopſgate* verſus *Alderman Beecher.*

Mandamus to the Juſtices to appoint Overfeers of the Poor in the Town of *Rufford;*
they return, that *Rufford* is an extraparochial Place, and therefore they are not to provide
for their Poor.

It was objected againſt this Return, that admitting it to be extraparochial, yet the
Juſtices are obliged by the Statute 43 *Eliz. cap.* 2. to appoint Overfeers of the Poor, even
in ſuch Places, becauſe in the enacting Part the Words are general, and extend to all Places
viz.) *The Churchwardens of every Pariſh, and two or more Houſholders there to be nominated, &c. by the Juſtices, ſhall be called Overfeers, &c.*

And the Court was of Opinion, that Places extraparochial are within the Words of the
Statute, for by the general Words the Juſtices have Power to name Overfeers in all
Pariſhes, which muſt extend to extraparochial Places as well as to Pariſhes in general; for
where there is the ſame Inconvenience, it ſhould be ſubject to the Controul of the Juſtices,
and moſt of the Foreſts in *England* are extraparochial, but they ought to maintain their
own Poor.

The Husband was born in the Pariſh of St. *Giles* in *Reading,* where his Wife had likewiſe a Settlement before ſhe married, but the Husband was bound Apprentice in the Pariſh
of *Everſly,* where he ſerved two Years, then his Maſter broke, and the Apprentice came
back to *Reading,* and married there and had ſeveral Children, and died, and afterwards
his Widow and Children were by Order of two Juſtices removed to *Everſly,* which Order
was quaſhed on an Appeal, and an Order made to ſend them to the Pariſh of St. *Giles,* becauſe the Mother had a Settlement there before ſhe married; and now both the ſaid Orders
being removed into *B. R.* by *Certiorari,* the original Order of the two Juſtices was confirmed, (*viz.*) That the Widow and the Children ſhould be ſettled where the Husband
and their Father was ſettled, and that his Death made no Alteration in the Caſe; and tho'
the Wife had another Settlement before ſhe married, yet that was loſt by her Marriage.
Trin. 9 *Geo.* 1.

Upon an Order of Removal of a poor Man confirmed on an Appeal, and removed
by *Certiorari,* the Caſe was, (*viz.*) he lived laſt at *B.* at a Place called *Roſcces Tenement,* and paid Taxes by the Name of the *Occupier* of that Tenement, whereas he ought
to be perſonally charged, and not as an Occupier of the Tenement; but it was held,
that paying Taxes as Occupier of a Tenement, and naming him Farmer thereof, is a
ſufficient Deſignation of the Perſon.

No Perſon who ſhall be taxed to the Scavenger, or Repairs of the Highways, and ſhall
duly pay the ſame, ſhall be deemed to have any legal Settlement by Reaſon of ſuch Payment.

Nor ·

Ib. §. 5.   Nor fhall any Perfon have a Settlement by Purchafe of an Eftate of Inheritance in a Parifh where the Confideration-Money was not above 30 *l.* for any longer Time than the Purchafer fhall inhabit on fuch Eftate.

A Servant was hired for a Year in *Chrift-Church* in *Oxford,* and afterwards lived with her Miftrefs three Months of that Year in the Parifh of *Fawley* in *Berks,* where her Miftrefs was a *Vifitor,* and fhe ferved the remaining Part of the Year in *Chrift-Church* where fhe was hired, that being an extraparochial Place; and becoming Poor fhe went into the Parifh of St. *Peter* in *Oxford,* from whence fhe was removed by an Order to *Fawley,* which Order was quafhed upon an Appeal, the Seffions being of Opinion, that her Settlement was in *Chrift-Church* where her *Service determined,* againft which it was objected, that fhe could have no Settlement there, becaufe it was an *extraparochial* Place, it being neither a Town or Parifh, and by Confequence could have no Parifh Officers, and therefore not within any of the Statutes relating to the Settlement of the Poor; for thofe Statutes require, that the *Hiring* fhould be in fome Town or Parifh, where there are proper Officers to take Care that it fhould not be fraudulent to charge the Parifh, and fhe could have no Settlement in *Fawley,* becaufe her Miftrefs was there as a Vifitor.

As to both thefe Points the Court declared, that where a Servant continues forty Days in the Service of a Vifitor as well as of a Lodger, he gained a Settlement, for he could not be removed, unlefs the Parifh fhew fome Caufe, (*viz.*) that he was brought thither on Purpofe to have a Settlement; and as to the Objection, that the Statute requires the Hiring fhould be in a Town or Parifh, and that this Servant was hired in neither, but in an extraparochial Place, fhe may properly be faid to be hired in every Parifh where fhe ferves. *Pafch. B. R.* 1722.

An Appeal from a Removal of a poor Perfon from one Parifh to another, fhall not be proceeded on, unlefs reafonable *Notice* be given by the Parifh Officers, who make the Appeal, to the Parifh Officers from whence fuch poor Perfon fhall be removed the Reafonablenefs of which Notice fhall be determined by the Juftices in the Quarter-Seffions to which the Appeal is made; and if it fhall appear that reafonable Notice was not given, then they fhall adjourn the Appeal to the next Quarter-Seffions, and there finally determine it.

If upon an Appeal concerning any Settlement, the Seffions fhall determine in Favour of the Appellant, that the poor Perfon was unduly removed, then they fhall award the Appellant fo much Money as fhall appear to have been reafonably paid by the Parifh on whofe Behalf fuch Appeal was made, for the Relief of fuch poor Perfon, between the Time of fuch undue Removal and the Determination of the Appeal.

Of providing Workhoufes for the Poor.
9 Geo. 1. c. 7. §. 4.
     The Parifh Officers, with the Confent of the major Part of the Parifhioners in Veftry, or other publick Meeting affembled, may purchafe or hire any Houfes in the fame Parifh, and contract with Perfons for the Lodging, Maintaining, and Employing all fuch Poor as fhall defire to receive Relief, and there keep and employ them and receive the Benefit of their Work and Labour, for their better Maintenance and Relief: And if any Perfon fhall refufe to be lodged or maintained in fuch Houfe, he fhall be put out of the Books where the Names of the Perfons who ought to receive Collection are to be regiftred, and fhall have no Relief from the Parifh Officers.

The Parifh Officers, with the like Confent, may contract with any other Parifh Officers for Lodging, Maintaining and Employing any poor Perfons of another Parifh; and if they refufe fhall be put out of the Collection Book.

3 Geo. 2.
c. 29. §. 8.
     The Witneffes who attefted the Execution of Certificates of Settlements, or one of them, fhall make Oath before the Juftices, who by 8 & 9 *W.* 3. *cap.* 30. are directed to allow the fame, that fuch Witnefs did fee the Church-wardens and Overfeers fign and feal the faid Certificates, &*c.* and the Juftices fhall certify that fuch Oath was made before them; and fuch Certificate fhall be allowed in all Courts as fully proved, and be taken as Evidence without other Proof.

Ib. §. 9.
     When any Overfeers of the Poor, or other Perfons, fhall remove back any Perfons and their Families, fent by Certificate, they fhall be reimburfed fuch reafonable Charges as they have been put to in maintaining and removing fuch Perfons, by the Church-wardens or Overfeers of the Parifh to which fuch Perfons are removed; the Charges being afcertained by one Juftice of the County to which fuch Removal fhall be made; the which Charges fhall, in cafe of Refufal of Payment, be levied by Diftrefs and Sale of the Church-wardens and Overfeers Goods, by Warrant of fuch Juftices.

For expofed and deferted young Children. See *Chap.* 196. *infra.*

Poffe Comitatus. See *Chap.* 171, 172.

                     C H A P.

CHAP. LXXIV. (*a*)

Post-Office.

THE Post-Master General may appoint Persons to measure the Roads *by the Wheel*, _{9 Ann. c. 10.} except such Roads where the Stages are already settled, and the Persons so appoint- _{§. 11.} ed shall make fair Surveys of each Kingdom of *Great Britain* and *Ireland*, and shall leave one with the Post-Master General in *London*, and another at the *Chief Office* in *Edinburgh*, and another at the Chief Post-Office in *Dublin* ; which Surveys shall be signed by the Person who made them, and by the Post-Master General, or his Deputies in each Kingdom, and by the Controllers and Surveyors at the General Post-Offices in *London*, *Edinburgh* and *Dublin*, which Surveys shall determine the Distances on all the said Roads.

He who makes such Survey shall make Oath before some Justice, *&c.* in each King- _{*Who must make Oath before some Justice.*} dom respectively, to perform the same according to the best of his Skill, and the Ju- stice, *&c.* shall certify the same in Writing, to be entered in the three General _{Ib. §. 12.} Post-Offices.

All Money due for Letters not exceeding five Pounds shall be recovered before Ju- _{*Postage of Letters shall be recovered as small Tithes.*} stices of Peace as small Tithes are recovered, and shall be paid before any Debt due to a private Person. _{Ib. §. 50. See c. 102, infra.}

The Post-Master and all his under Officers must take the Oath injoined by the Sta- _{*Post-Master and all his Officers must make Oath.*} tute before some Justice of Peace of the County where resident, *&c.*

See the Form of the Oath in the Statute, and see the Statute at large for the Postage of all Letters.

A Letter, in which there were Bills of Exchange, was delivered at the General Post- _{*Action against the Post-Master for opening a Letter and taking out Bills.*} Office in *London*, to one who was appointed by the Post-Master to receive Letters, and there it was opened, and the Bills taken out ; and in an Action brought against the Post-Master, three Judges against *Holt* Chief Justice held, that it would not lie, because this was an Office of Intelligence and not of Insurance, or of Conveyance of _{Salk. 17.} Treasure ; but the Chief Justice held, that the Action would lie, because the Post-Ma- ster hath a Reward, which is the Reason that Inn-keepers and Carriers are to keep Goods safely, *&c.*

Bills of Exchange wrote on the same Piece of Paper with a Letter, and also Letters _{6 G. 1. c. 21.} to several Persons wrote on the same Piece of Paper, shall be rated as so many di- _{§. 51.} stinct Letters.

The Proviso in 9 *Ann. cap.* 10. *sect.* 13. shall extend only to such Merchants Ac- _{Ib. §. 52.} counts, Bills of Exchange, Invoices and Bills of Lading, as shall be sent to or from the General Post-Office in *London*, to or from any Parts beyond the Seas, not within his Majesty's Dominions ; and all other Merchants Accounts, Bills of Exchange, In- voices and Bills of Lading, shall be rated as so many several Letters.

Nothing in the Act 9 *Ann. cap.* 10. ought to restrain any Messenger of the Penny _{4 G. 2. c. 33.} Post, from taking for every Letter originally sent by the Penny-Post, which shall be delivered at any Place, out of *London*, *&c.* 1 *d.* over and above the 1 *d.* paid upon putting such Letter into the Office.

CHAP. LXXV.

Preachers.

IF any Person shall of his own Authority, willingly disturb any Preacher in the _{*Disturbing.*} Time of his Sermon, or other Divine Service, or shall be aiding, procuring, or _{1 Mar. Stat.} abetting thereto ; or shall rescue any such Offender being apprehended, or shall disturb the _{2. c. 3.} Arresting of any such Offender ; and that any of the said Offenders shall be brought be- _{§ 1, 2, 3, 4, 5 & 6.} fore any Justice of Peace, (within the County where the said Offence shall be committed) then every such Justice of Peace (upon due Accusation thereupon made) shall forthwith

C c c

commit

commit every such Offender (so brought before him) to safe Custody, by his Discretion.

Two Justices Examination. Within six Days (after Accusation had of any the said Offences) and after the Committing of the said Offender to safe Custody by one Justice of the Peace, one other Justice of the Peace of that Shire, must join with the first Justice in the Examination of the said Offence; and if they Two, upon their Examination, shall find the Party accused guilty (and that by two sufficient Witnesses, or by his own Confession) then shall they commit him to the Gaol, there to remain without Bail, for three Month then next ensuing; and further, to the next Quarter-Sessions, &c. But inquire, if this Statute be not repealed by 1 *Eliz. cap.* 2. in general Words at the latter End thereof. *Lamb.* 199.

(*a*) Yet it seemeth not to be repealed in this Matter, *scil.* for Disturbance of Preachers For this Statute containeth several Matters, and so divers Statutes. *Cromp.* 14.

And yet Sir *Nicholas Hide* at *Bury*, *Lent* Assizes, *An.* 1629. delivered it (as I am credibly informed) that this Statute was wholly repealed by the Statute made 1 *Eliz cap.* 2.

1 W & M. Stat. 1. c. 88. Dissenting Preachers taking the Oaths and subscribing the Declaration at the Quarter Sessions where they live, shall not be liable to certain Penalties in former Statutes. *See the Statute at Large*, and 10 *Annæ, cap.* 2. *sect.* 8. *supra, cap.* 26. Tit. *Conformity.*

Such Preachers must declare their Approbation and subscribe the Articles of Religion excepting certain Words in the 20th, 24th, 25th and 36th Articles.

§. 18. Preachers thus subscribing shall not serve on Juries, and shall be exempt from Parish Offices; and he who disturbs them in Preaching shall be bound with Sureties in 50, to appear at the Sessions, and being convicted, shall forfeit 20 *l.* to the Crown; and he will not fine, shall be committed till the next Sessions.

The Proof must be by two Witnesses, on Oath before one Justice.

§. 10. Preachers in *Anabaptist* Meetings subscribing the Articles of Religion, excepting that Part of the 27th Article relating to Infant Baptism, and taking the Oaths, and making and subscribing the Declaration, shall enjoy the same Advantages as other Dissenting Preachers.

CHAP. LXXVI. (*a*)

Printers and Printing.

THE Statute of 13 & 14 *Car.* 2. *cap.* 33. (Entitled *An Act for preventing Abuse in printing Seditious, Treasonable and Unlicenced Books and Pamphlets, and for regulating of Printing and Printing-Presses*) inserted in former Editions of this Book was continued by 1 *Jac.* 2. *c.* 17. for seven Years from 1685, and then expired.

Probate of Wills. See *Chap.* 41. Tit. *Fees.*

Process. See *Chap.* 193.

CHAP. LXXVII.

Prophecies.

(*a*) TOO true is that Saying of the sharp *French* Historian *Comines, lib.* 6. of his Commentaries, *Tribuunt Angli Plurimum vaticiniis*, and great Mischiefs have arisen from the Multitude's too great Credulity to (and others phantastical Publication, and setting on Foot) false Prophecies; against which Evils were the Statutes of 33 *H.* 8. 14. & 3 *E.* 6. 15. made, but they being expired, was made the Statute of 5 *Eliz.* 15. whereby it is provided, that if any shall publish or set forth by Writing, &c. Speech or Deed, any fond phantastical or false Prophecy, upon, or by Occasion of any Arms, Fields, Beasts, Badges, or Things accustomed in Arms, Cognizances, or Signets; or by

4   reason

·reafon of any Time, Year, Day, Name, Bloodfhed, or War, to make any Rebellion or Difturbance in the Realm, and other the Queen's Dominions, he fhall be imprifoned for a Year without Bail, and forfeit 10 *l.* And for the fecond Offence be imprifoned for Life, and forfeit all his Goods; a Moiety to the King, the other to the Profecutor.

Juftices of Peace have Authority to hear and determine thefe Offences, fo as the Party be accufed within fix Months.

(*d*) It feemeth that every Juftice of Peace may imprifon (by the Space of one Year, without Bail) fuch as advifedly fhall publifh any falfe Prophecies (contrary to the Tenor of the Statute 5 *Eliz.* 15.) to the Intent thereby to make any Rebellion, Infurrection, or other Difturbances within the King's Dominions. P. Juft. 24. P. Prop. 1.

(*a*) But *Quære* hereof, for they are fo enabled as Juftices of Affife are, which is in their Courts, and Imprifonment is to enfue Conviction; which muft be in the Seffions.

C H A P. LXXVIII.

Prifon.

'A NY Juftice of Peace, having fent or committed to the Gaol an Offender (for any Offence or Mifdemeanor) if the Offender (having Means or Ability thereto) fhall refufe to bear and defray the Charges of fuch as fhall convey and guard him or them to fuch Gaol, or fhall not at the Time of their Commitment, pay or bear the fame, then the faid Juftice may give his Warrant under his Hand and Seal (to the Conftable of the Hundred, or Conftable of the Town) where fuch Offender fhall be dwelling, or from whence he fhall committed, or where the faid Offender fhall have any Goods within that County or Liberty, to fell fo much of the Offender's Goods, as by the Difcretion of the faid Juftice will fatisfy fuch Charges, &c. the Appraifment to be made by four Inhabitants of the Parifh where fuch Goods be (yielding to the Party the Overplus of the Money:) And where the Offender hath no fuch Goods, then the Charge thereof muft be born by the Town where the Offender was taken, and the Taxation made on the Town for that Purpofe, muft be allowed under the Hand of one Juftice of Peace; and by like Warrant from fuch Juftice, the Goods of the Perfon refufing to pay fuch Taxation, may be diftrained and fold by the Conftable and Church-wardens by Appraifement made by four Inhabitants, rendring the Overplus. 3 Jac. 1. c. 10.

(*a*) The next Juftice of Peace, or the Quarter-Seffions, may adjudge what is fitting to be taken for each Night's Lodging, or other Expences, by any Under-Sheriff, Bailiff, Sergeant, or other Officer that hath any Perfon in his Cuftody, by Virtue of any Procefs or Warrant, while he is under Arreft, and before he is carried to Prifon. *Arreft.* *Fees.* 22 & 23 Car. 2. c. 20. §. 9.

Upon the Prefentment of the Grand Jury at the Affifes or Quarter-Seffions, that the Gaol is out of Repair, the Seffions upon examining Workmen, may agree on a Sum for Building or Repairing it, and levy the fame on the feveral Divifions and Hundreds of the County by a Seffions Warrant to the High Conftables, and may make a Receiver. 11 & 12 *Will. cap.* 9. made perpetual by 6 *Geo.* 1. *cap.* 19.

All Juftices of Peace fhall ufe their Endeavour and Diligence to examine and find out all Legacies and Gifts for the Benefit of poor Prifoners for Debt, and to fend for Deeds, Wills, Writings, and Books of Accounts, and any Perfon concerned therein; and to examine them upon Oath, and to order and fettle the fame. *Charity.* 22 & 23 Car. 2. c. 20. §. 11.

Which Legacies, Gifts, Rates of Fees, and the future Government of Prifons, fhall be figned and confirmed by the Juftice of Peace, and the Judges of the Circuits, and fairly written, and hung up in a Table in every Gaol, and be regiftered by the Clerk of the Peace, and after fuch Eftablifhment, no other greater Fees to be taken. Ib. §. 12.

The Juftices of Peace, at their Quarter-Seffions, may provide a Stock of Materials to fet Prifoners on work, in fuch Manner as other County Charges are levied and raifed: Provided no Parifh be rated above Six Pence a Week; and may provide fit Perfons to overfee them, and make orders therein, and alter or amend them. * *Work.* 19 Car. 2. c. 4. §. 1. * *Vide* 12 G. 2. c. 29. *in Chap.* 196. infra.

The Sheriff or Perfon having the Cuftody of the Gaol, by Confent of four Juftices of Peace (*Quorum unus*) upon emergent Occafions, may provide other fafe Places for Removal of Sick, or other Perfons to be there kept, and conveyed to Gaol-delivery. The like may be done in Corporations. *Sicknefs.* Ib. §. 2.

Perfons

Removal of Prisoners.
31 Car. 2. c.2. §. 9.

Persons Subjects of this Realm committed for any Crime, shall not be removed into Custody of any other Officer unless by some legal Writ; or where the Prisoner is delivered to the Constable, &c. to be carried to Gaol, or sent by any Judge or Justice of Peace his Order to a Work-house, or removed within the County in order to his Trial or Discharge, or in Case of Fire, Infection or Necessity. And Persons signing any Warrant for Removal contrary hereunto, or countersigning the same, and the Officer or Officers that obey or execute such Warrant, shall for the first Offence forfeit to the Party grieved 100*l.* and for the second Offence 200 *l.* and be incapable to hold his Office; to be recovered by Action of Debt, Suit, Bill, Plaint or Information, in any of the King's Courts at *Westminster.*

See the Appendix, *Tit.* Gaol.

Pretended Privileged Places.

9 Geo. 1.
c. 28. §. 1.

IF any Person shall within *Suffolk Place,* or the *Mint,* or their pretended Limits, oppose the Service of any Writ, &c. or any Warrants of Justices of Peace; or Assault any Person serving such Writ, whereby he shall receive any Damage, such Offender shall be guilty of Felony and transported.

Ib. §. 2.

Rescuing any Prisoner taken upon such Writ within the said Place, or concealing any such Prisoner, or such who rescued, or assisting in resisting the Officer, or joining in making any pretended Rule or Ordinance, for supporting any pretended Privilege within the said Place, every Person so offending, convicted on Indictment or Information brought within six Months after the Offence, shall be guilty of Felony and transported.

Ib. §. 3.

Any Person masked or disguised, abetting any Riot in such Place, or opposing Process, &c. shall be guilty of Felony and transported.

Ib. §. 4.

Any Person apprehending any of the aforesaid Offenders shall have 40 *l.*

Ib. §. 5.

And if a Person be killed in endeavouring to apprehend such Offender, the Executors, &c. of such Person killed shall receive 40 *l.*

11 Geo. 1.
cap. 22. §. 1.

If any Number of Persons, not less than Three, shall within the Hamlet of *Wapping-Stepney,* or any other Place within the Bills of Mortality of the Cities of *London* and *Westminster,* wherein Persons shall unlawfully assemble for the Sheltering themselves from their Debts, of which Complaint shall have been made by Presentment of the Grand Jury at a Quarter-Sessions, knowingly obstruct any Persons serving any Writ, Rule or Order of any Court, or other legal Process, and shall assault or abuse any Person serving or executing such Writ, &c. whereby such Person shall receive bodily Hurt, the Offender being convicted shall be guilty of Felony, and transported for seven Years.

Ib. §. 2.

Rescuing, &c. any Prisoner, the Offender shall be guilty of Felony and transported.

C H A P. LXXIX.

Purveyors.

Universities.
13 Eliz. c.21.
1 Jac. 1. c.25.

IF any Person within five Miles of *Cambridge* or *Oxford,* shall refuse reasonably to serve the Provision of the said Universities, then may the Vicechancellor, and any two Justices of Peace within the same University, Town or County, under their Hands and Seals, allow any the King's Purveyors to provide any Corn or Victual of any such Person, to the Use of the King, as they lawfully may in other Places, without the said Precinct.

2 & 3 P. & M.
c. 15.
13 El. 21.
P. Just. 60.
P. Purv. 32.

The Vicechancellor (or his Commissary for the Time being) in either of the Universities, with any two Justices of Peace of the same County, may by the Oaths of Twelve Men, inquire of, and punish the Offences of Purveyors, committed contrary to the Statutes for the Privileges of the Universities, &c. *scil.* in taking or bargaining for any Victual or Grain, within *Cambridge* or *Oxford,* or within five Miles of either of them, without the License of the Chancellor, or Vicechancellor in Writing, under the Seal of their Office; or not according to such License.

23 H. 6. c.14.

(*a*) If any Buyer, or other Officer of any Lord or other Person (but only for the King and Queen, and their Houses) do take any Victual, Corn, Hay, Carriages, or any

            other

other Thing whatfoever, of any of the King's People, in any wife againft their Will (without lawful Bargain between the faid Buyer and Seller made) then upon Requeft made to the Mayor, Sheriff, Bailiff, Conftable, Officer, or other the King's Minifters (under which Word * Minifters, the Juftices of Peace be alfo comprehended) of the Ci-   *Cromp.62 a. ties, Boroughs, Counties, or Places, where fuch Taking fhall happen to be, the faid Mayor, Sheriff, Minifter, and Juftice of Peace, fhall prefently take and arreft fuch Buyer and Officer fo offending, and them fhall fend to the King's next Prifon, there to remain without Bail, until they have re-delivered the faid Goods fo taken, or the Value thereof +.   † *The Stat.*]. 2 & 3 Ph. &

M. 15. 13 Eliz. 21. *mentioned by Dalton, and the Stat.* 23 H. 6. 14. *inferted by former Editors, are obfolete, and therefore omitted in Mr.* Cay's *Abridgment.*

But it being impoffible to regulate thefe Purveyors by the many Laws made againft   *Taken away.* them, and that on the utmoft Penalties: By the Statute of 12 *Car.* 2. *cap.* 24. it is enacted,   12 Car. 2. That no Sum or Sums of Monies, or other Thing fhall be taken, levied, &c. for or in Re-   c. 24. §. 12. gard of any Provifion, Carriages, or Purveyance for the King, his Heirs or Succeffors.

No Perfon by Commiffion, &c. or otherwife by Colour of Purveyance, for the King   Ib. §. 13. or Queen of *England*, or for any Children of any King or Queen, or their Houfhold, fhall take Timber, Fewel, Cattle, Corn, Grain, Malt, Hay, Straw, Victual, Carts, Carriages, or other Thing whatfoever, from any Perfon, without the Owners free Con- fent had without Menace or Inforcement; nor fhall fummon any Carriages for fuch Ufe without the Owners Confent.

. No Pre-emption fhall be allowed or claimed, in Behalf of the King, Queen, or their   Ib. §. 14. Children, in Market or out of Market; but the King's Subjects may fell and difpofe of their Goods as they lift.

If any Perfon fhall make Provifion or Purveyance for the King, Queen, or Children,   *Penalty.* or impofe any Carriages or Things, on any Pretence or Colour of any Warrant whatfo-   Ibid. ever. The Juftices of Peace, or two, or one of them that dwell near; and the Confta- bles of the Parifh or Village, may, and are hereby injoined to commit, or caufe, &c. the Offenders to the Gaol until next Seffions, there to be indicted and proceeded againft for the fame, at the Requeft of the Party grieved; and the Party fhall have his Action for treble Damages, and treble Cofts.

C H A P. LXXX. (*a*)

Quakers.

PErfons fo called, may not affemble themfelves together above five in Number, of the   *Affemblies.* Age of fixteen Years or more, under Pretence of Religious Worfhip, not eftablifh-   13 &14 Car.2. ed by Law, upon Penalty for the firft Offence upon Conviction by Verdict or Confef-   c. 1. §. 2. fion, or by notorious Evidence of the Fact, to pay a Fine not exceeding 5 *l.* for the firft Offence; and after Conviction for the firft, being convicted of a fecond Offence, 10 *l.* to be levied by Warrant of the Parties before whom the Conviction fhall be, and for want of Diftrefs and Non-payment within one Week after Conviction: For the firft Offence Imprifonment in Gaol, or Houfe of Correction, three Months; the fecond Offence fix Months, without Bail, which Penalties fhall be employed for maintaining the Houfe of Correction; the third Offence, the Party offending fhall abjure the Realm, or otherwife the King may give Orders to tranfport the Offender to any of his Majefty's Plantations beyond the Seas.

And Juftices of *Oyer* and *Terminer*, Affife, Gaol-delivery, and Juftices of the Peace in   Ib. §. 3. open Seffions, may hear and determine the fame Offences within their refpective Limits. And any Juftice of Peace, Mayor or chief Officer of a Corporation, may commit to the Gaol, or bind over Perfons with fufficient Sureties, in order to their Conviction.

But this is now taken away by the Act 8 *Geo.* 1. ff. The Quakers fubfcribing the De-   8 Geo.1. c. 6. claration of Fidelity, and the Chriftian Belief, before two Juftices, fhall be intitled to the Benefit of that Act.

No Quaker fhall be a Witnefs in Criminal Caufes, or ferve on Juries, or bear any   7 & 8 Will. 3. Office or Place of Profit in the Government; and their folemn Affirmation is to go   *made perpetual* for an Oath.   *by* 1 Geo.1. c.6.

7 & 8 W. 3.
c. 34.
Declaration.
altered by the
Statute
8 Geo.1.c.6.

Every Quaker fhall, where any Oath is lawfully required, inftead thereof, make a folemn Declaration in thefe Words, *viz.* I A. B. *do declare in the Prefence of Almighty God, the Witnefs of the Truth of what I fay*; which fhall be taken to be of the fame Force in all Courts of Juftice, as an Oath taken in the ufual Form: And upon Condition that he hath declared any Matter or Thing, which if the fame had been in the ufual Form

Penalty.

of an Oath, would have amounted to wilful Perjury, he fhall incur the fame Penalties as in Cafe of Perjury.

Tithes.
Ib. §. 4.

Quakers refufing to pay or compound for great or fmall Tithes, or to pay ChurchRates, the two next Juftices of Peace of the fame County, (other than fuch Juftice as is Patron of the Church, or interefted in the faid Tithes) may, upon Complaint, convene before them fuch Quaker, and examine upon Oath the Truth of the faid Complaint, and afcertain what is due to the Parties complaining, and by Order under their Hands and Seals direct the Payment thereof (not exceeding 10 *l.*) and fuch Quakers refufing to pay according to fuch Order, any one of the faid Juftices may by Warrant under his Hand and Seal, levy the Money fo ordered to be paid, by Diftrefs and Sale of the Offen-

Appeal.

der's Goods. And any Perfons finding themfelves agrieved by any Judgment given by fuch two Juftices may appeal to the next Quarter-Seffions for the County, *&c.* and the Juftices there may finally hear and determine the Matter: And if they continue the Judgment, then to decree the fame by Order of Seffions, and give Cofts againft the Appellant, to be levied by Diftrefs and Sale of Goods. Proceedings upon this Act fhall not

Certiorari.

be removed or fuperfeded by *Certiorari* or other Writ out of the Courts at *Weftminfter,* unlefs the Title of fuch Tithes come in Queftion. The faid Statute is made perpetual by 1 *Geo. cap.* 6.

Rape. See *poftea* Tit. *Felonies by Statute.*

Rates. See *Stock of the Shire,* Chap. 96. and Chap. 196.

Recognizance. See *Chap.* 168.

C H A P. LXXXI.

*Recufants *.*

* This Title is
in the old Edi-
tion of Dalton,
but much al-
tered and in-
larged in fub-
fequent Editi-
ons, we have
here followed
that of 1727.
Recufants,
who.

THIS Word *Recufant* is now become of that Signification, as to defcribe a Perfon on the Account of Adherence to the Church and Court of *Rome,* in her pretended Supremacy over all other Churches in Spiritual Matters, under which Head fhe alfo would comprehend all *Temporal Affairs,* fhe denying to Temporal Princes (claiming under God Imperial Thrones, and juftly poffeffing them, and to the King of *Great Britain* in particular,) That Supremacy that they all lawfully may, and do fome of them actually claim, as their great Charge and Duty; and which by the Statute of 26 *H.* 8. *cap.* 1. is juftly united to the Imperial Crown of this Kingdom.

Supremacy.

The Exactions of that Church and Court being intolerable, and their Ends and Defigns proving Dangerous to Temporal Government, the fame King affifted with his Parliament, did that which other Princes, even in Popifh Times and Countries, fought to redrefs; who, although they cut off fome Branches, yet leaving the Root untouched, the Tree grew even to a monftrous Height. This wife Prince laid the Ax to the Root, by the Statute 26 *H.* 8. *cap.* 1. having by the Statute of 24 *H.* 8. *cap.* 12. difcharged all *Appeals to Rome,* and put the Caufes in a right Channel, to receive a juft and righteous Decifion. And by the Statutes of 25 *H.* 8. *cap.* 20. *&* 26 *H.* 8. 3. prevented the Court of *Rome* from receiving *Firft Fruits for Ecclefiaftical Livings,* and taken Care for a Succeffion of Archbifhops and Bifhops: And alfo by the Statute of 25 *H.* 8. 21. taken off the Payment of all *Impofitions to Rome,* the Clergy having in Convocation recognifed that King to be *Supreme Head of the Church,* and taking Care for the due Management of this afferted Jurifdiction.

Thus ftood the King's Supremacy all the Refidue of the Reign of *Henry* the Eighth, and *Edward* the Sixth, and Queen *Mary,* although a Papift, yet kept *Supremum caput* in her Stile, and thereby fummoned her firft Parliament; but foon after omitted it, and the Statutes made in her Father's Time for afferting the King's Supremacy were repealed.

ealed. But her Authority being fhort, 1 *El. c.* 1. *thofe Statutes of Repeal were repealed,* and confequently the Statutes by Queen *Mary* repealed, were revived. By which, as that Statute recites, *all ufurped and foreign Jurifdiction was put away;* and the ancient Jurif-dictions, Superiorities, and Preheminences of Right belonging to the Imperial Crown of his Realm thereto united, by Reafon whereof the Subjects were kept in good Order, and difburdened of great and intolerable Exactions. And by that Statute of 1 *Eliz.* 1. an Oath was directed for good Subjects to take; the Form you may fee *cap.* 4. *fect.* 5. and a Law made the fame Year, *cap.* 2. for eftablifhing a *Common Prayer-Book in* Englifh, *and Uni-* Common *formity in Divine Service,* and requiring all Perfons to come to Church and hear the *Prayer-Book.* fame, under divers Penalties,

Now although the Common Prayers and Service of the Church were in *Englifh* all *Defection by* *Edward* the Sixth's Time, yet the King's Subjects came to Church and received the Sacra- *the Pope's* ment all his Time, and no open Defection was on that Account. And although the *Means.* Common Prayer-Book and Service, received fome Alteration different from that of *Rome* in 1 *Eliz.* Yet until the eleventh Year of Her Reign, did all her Subjects come to Church promifcuoufly, fo that the Bifhop of *Rome* perceiving his Authority at laft Gafp, by his Bulls *interdicted the Kingdom, abfolved her Subjects from their Obedience to their Prince,* and thereby wrought that Schifm which thofe that profefs Obedience to that See, have ever fince maintained; and had not the Pope then interpofed, it is probable a perfect Union had been in the *Englifh* Church, which will be more reafonable to believe, if we confider how few Perfons quitted their Livings and Dignities, for refufing Communion with the *Englifh* Church, and refufing the Oath prefcribed by 1 *El.* 1. namely, not much above 100 of 9000 and more, as *Camden* witneffeth. *9000 Benefices in England.*

After which Practices, the State thought it neceffary to provide for it felf; and there-upon the Statute of 5 *El.* 1. was made, *that any that maintained the Bifhop of* Rome's *Authority, fhould incur a Præmunire.* And the Statute of 13 *El.* 1. againft fuch as *levied War, or intended bodily Harm to the Queen.* And another 13 *El. c.* 2. *againft fuch Bulls,* and the bringing over and publifhing them; and the Statute of 23 *Eliz.* 1. *againft recon-ciling to* Rome; and the Statute of 27 *Eliz.* 2. for *departing of Priefts and Jefuits;* and the Statute of 29 *Eliz.* 6. *againft Frauds in Conveyances* were made.

Near which Time there rofe another Sort of People, called (by 35 *El.* 2.) *Sectaries Sectariæ.* and Difloyal Perfons, who did oppofe the Queen's Authority in Caufes Ecclefiaftical, but not upon Popifh Defigns, and on that Account forbore to come to Church, againft whom that Statute is made.

The firft Statute I meet with, wherein the Word *Recufants* is mentioned, is that of 35 *Firft Mention* *Eliz.* 1. which mentioned the Statute of 23 *Eliz.* 1. to be made againft Recufants, *of Recufants.* which was againft the Papifts only. And then comes 35 *Eliz.* 2. that mentions a *Popifh Recufant.* Which Word is plainly taken from refufing to take the Oath of 1 *Eliz.* 1. And refufing to read or hear Common Prayers, prefcribed by 1 *Eliz.* 2. And to exprefs the Words of thofe Statutes, is a Refufal with Obftinacy.

So that now there being a twofold Recufancy, Popifh and Sectarian, it will be necef- *Recufants of* fary to obferve and diftinguifh the Laws made againft them. *two Sorts.*

The Statutes now in Force againft *Recufants* of all Sorts, feem to be 1 *Eliz.* 1. *Statutes.* 1 *Eliz.* 2. 8 *Eliz.* 1. 23 *Eliz.* 1. 5 *Eliz.* 1. 13 *Eliz.* 1. And 35 *Eliz.* 2. 1 *Jac.* 4. 3 *Jac.* 4. 3 *Jac.* 5. 7 *Jac.* 2. 7 *Jac.* 6. 29 *Eliz.* 6. 27 *Eliz.* 2. All which are yet in Force, and particularly 33 *El.* 1. is by 16 *Car.* 1. *c.* 4. declared to be in Force: And all the reft, except 35 *El.* 1. againft Sectaries, were per-petual. All which by 1 *Jac.* 1. 4. are ordered to be put in due and exact Execution. I call that of 35 *El.* 1. a Law againft Sectaries, for fo the Preamble mentions it to be; and by an Exception therein contained, Popifh Recufants are excepted. And I obferve fome material Differences between them.

First, The Statute of 35 *Eliz.* 1. requires Conformity from all Perfons, or elfe in-flicts Abjuration. The Statute of 35 *Eliz.* 2. for Nonconformity from Perfons of mean Eftates only, and that the Refidue repair to their Dwellings, Confinement there, and Forfeiture of Goods and Land.

Secondly, The Statute of 35 *El.* 2. is temporary to the End of the next Seffion of Parliament, when it might have expired, had not fome clamorous Perfons Enormities re-vived it: But the Statute of 35 *El.* 1. is perpetual.

Thirdly, No married Women are punifhable by 35 *El.* 1. but are thereout excepted; but by 35 *El.* 2. married Women are declared to be within all Branches and Penalties of it, but Abjuration.

The

Two Points of Recufancy.
1 El. 2.

The Matter of Recufancy ftands in two Particulars, firft, *Abfenting from the Church* fecondly, *refufing the Oath prefcribed* by 1 *El.* 1. and 3 *Jac.* 1. 4.

Abfence from Church.

All and every Perfon, *inhabiting within this Realm, or other the King's Dominions, fhaí* (having no reafonable Excufe to be abfent) *endeavour themfelves to refort to their Parifi Chapel accuftomed, or upon reafonable Let thereof, to fome ufual Place where Common Praye, and fuch Service of God fhall be ufed in fuch Time of Let, upon every Sunday and Holiday and there remain orderly and foberly, during the Time of Common Prayer, Preaching am Service, upon Pain of Punifhment by the Cenfures of the Church; and to pay for every Of. fence* 12 d. *to be levied by the Church-wardens, to the Ufe of the Poor, by Diftrefs.*

By 1 W. & M.
c. 8. *this doth not extend to Diffenters.*
23 El. 1.

The Statute of 23 *Eliz.* 1. faith, *That every Perfon of* 16 *Years of Age, which fhall no repair to fome Church, Chapel, or ufual Place of Common Prayer, but forbear the fam. contrary to* 1 El. 2. *And being thereof lawfully convicted, fhall forfeit for every Mont* 20 l. &c.

If any Subject fhall not refort to Church, Chapel, or other Place appointed, &c every *Sunday*, and hear divine Service, according to 1 *El.* 2. one Juftice, upon Confeffion or Oath of Witnefs, fhall call the Party before him; and if he can make no Excufe, the Juftice fhall give a Warrant to the Church-wardens to levy 12 *d.* for every Default, by Diftrefs; and if no Diftrefs, to commit him till Payment, 3 *Jac.* 4. fo as the Party be impeached within one Month.

Cafes thereupon.
Godb. Rep. 148.

1. Note, that in an Indictment upon 1 *El.* 2. it need not be averred, that the Offender was an Inhabitant; for that ought to come of the other Side. See *Anne Mannock's* Cafe, *M.* 3 *Jac.* 1.

2. That where the Statute of 23 *El.* 1. fays, *being thereof convicted*, does not intend *a* former Conviction, but a Conviction in the fame Action; as is refolved in Dr *Fofter's* Cafe.

Moor's Rep. 606.

3. That where the Statute 23 *El.* fays, *every Perfon of fixteen Years,* &c. an Indictment that faith, *Quod A. B. de,* &c. *Exiftens Ætat.* 16. *Annorum,* &c. This *Exiftens* fhall go to the Time of the Offence, and not to the Time of the Indictment. *Talbot's* Cafe.

Bulft. 3. p. 87.
Hob. p. 179.

4. That *Feme Coverts* are within the Statutes of 1 *El.* 2. & 23 *El.* 1. touching all the Penalties for *Abfence from the Church,* and an Information lies againft the *Husband* for the fame, as was refolved in *Laws's* Cafe. *P.* 13 *Jac.*

Co. 11. 91.
& 63.

5. That the Penalty of 12 *d.* a *Sunday,* by 1 *El.* 2. & 3 *Jac.* 4. and of 20 *l. per menfem,* by 23 *El.* 1. fhall be both paid.

6. That the Statute of 1 *El.* 2. extends to *Holidays* as well as *Sundays;* but the Statutes of 23 *El.* 1. & 3 *Jac.* 4. extend only to *Sundays.*

7. Note alfo, this Repairing to Church every *Sunday,* muft be as well to *Evening Prayers,* as to *Morning Prayers;* for it ought to be an intire Day, and an intire Service. And fo Sir *Richard Hutton,* one of the Judges of the Court of Common Pleas, did deliver it in his Charge at *Cambridge* Lent Affizes, *Anno* 1 *Car. Regis;* and therewith agreed Sir *Robert Bartlet* at Summer Affizes, *Anno* 9 *Car. Regis.*

Holidays.

And becaufe 1 *El.* 2. extends to *Holidays,* it is convenient to obferve which are Holidays: And as to that, I refer you to the Statute of 5 & 6 *E.* 6. *cap.* 3. And the *Rubrick* of our prefent Service-Book, now confirmed by 14 *Car.* 2. *c.* 4.

Oath.
5 El. 1.

The *Oath of Supremacy* muft be taken by Spiritual Perfons, before fuch as have Power to admit them; and fo of Lay Perfons, preferred by the King to any Lay Office, Miniftry, or Service, before fuch as fhall admit them to that Office, or before fuch Perfons as by the King's Commiffion fhall be appointed; and if fuch Perfon refufe, he is difabled to take that Office: But if any Perfon having any Eftate of Inheritance in the Office, fhall firft refufe, and afterwards during his Life take it, he fhall enjoy it. *Vide* the Oath *hic. cap.* 4. *fect.* 5.

Maintaining Foreign Authority.
1 El. 1.

If any fhall by Writing, Printing, Teaching, Preaching, exprefs Words, Deed or Act, maintain, fet forth, or defend the Authority or Jurifdiction, Temporal, or Ecclefiaftical, of any Foreign Prince, Prelate, State, Potentate, formerly claimed or ufurped, or fhall put in Ufe or execute any Thing for Maintenance or Defence of the fame, every fuch Offenders, their Abettors, &c. convicted thereof after the Courfe of the Common

Penalty.

Law, fhall lofe to the King all their Goods and Chattels, real and perfonal; and if the Offender have not 20 *l.* in Goods, over and befides his Goods, he fhall be imprifoned for a Year.

I

And if the Offender be a Spiritual Perfon, he fhall forfeit all his Spiritual Promotions, 1 El. 1.
and the next Patron or Donor may prefent, as if he were dead ; for the fecond Offence,
he fhall incur a Premunire ; and for the third, fuffer as for Treafon, but there muft be
two Witneffes, and they brought Face to Face ; and as touching Aiding, &c. it muft be
proved by two Witneffes, that the Perfon had Knowledge of the Offence.

All Perfons admitted *Ad ordines Sacros*, or taking any Degree in the Univerfity, Oaib.
School-Mafters, and Teachers of Children ; and all Perfons taking any Degree or Learning 5 El. 1.
at Common Law ; and all Attornies, Prothonotaries and Philizers ; and all Perfons admitted to any Miniftry or Office belonging to the Canon Law, or any other Law allowed
in *England*, or that fhall belong to any Court, fhall before Admiffion, in open Court,
or before Commiffioners take the Oath. The Lord Chancellor or Lord Keeper may direct Commiffions to tender the Oath to any Perfons, without further Warrant.

The Perfons compellable to take that Oath, and refufing, fhall incur a *Pramu-* Refufing.
nire. 5 El. 1.

The Perfons having Power to tender the Oath, fhall within forty Days, if the Term 5 El. 1.
be open, or the firft Day of the next Term after the forty Days, return the fame Refufal into the King's Bench, upon Pain of 100 *l.* And the Sheriff of the County,
where the King's Bench is, may impanel a Jury ; and upon the Evidence of that Certificate, and other Evidence, may indict the Party.

If any Perfon *above fixteen Years of Age* that abfents from Church by a Month, Sectaries.
fhall practife, go about, or perfwade any Subject or Perfon, in the King's Dominions, 35 El. 1.
to oppofe his Authority Ecclefiaftical, and fhall move or perfwade any to abftain from Conventicles.
Church, or receiving the Communion, or to be prefent at Conventicles ; or if he fhall
be prefent at Conventicles, being thereof convicted, fhall be committed to Prifon
without Bail, until he conform and make the Submiffion required by that Act, if
within three Months after fuch Conviction, he fhall not conform and fubmit, being
required by the Bifhop of the Diocefe, or a Juftice of Peace, or the Minifter or Curate,
he fhall in open Seffions or Affifes, or Gaol-delivery * abjure the Realm, and depart at * *This is now*
fuch Haven, Port and Time the Juftices fhall affign him, which Abjuration the Juftices *taken away*
fhall record and certify to the Affifes. 35 *El.* 1. *by the Statute*
1 W. 3. c. 1.
upon taking the Oaths and fubfcribing the Declaration.

The Oath of Abjuration may be taken by the Juftices of Peace of fuch Recufants, in *Abjuration.*
this Form, or to this Effect :

Y OU *fhall fwear, That you fhall depart out of this Realm of* England, *and out of all* Oath of Ab-
other the King's Majefty's Dominions ; and that you fhall not return hither or come juration.
again into any of his Majefty's Dominions, but by the Licence of our faid Sovereign Lord 35 El. 1.
the King, or of his Heirs. So help you God. See *Stamf.* 119. *Vide Wilk.* 4c.

And fuch Recufants thereupon fhall depart out of this Realm, at fuch Haven and Departure.
Port, and within fuch Time as fhall in that Behalf be affigned and appointed by the 35 El. 1.
faid Juftices of Peace, unlefs he be letted and ftayed by fuch lawful Means or Caufe
as the Common Law doth allow in Cafes of Abjuration for Felony, &c. 35 *El.* 1.

If any fuch Recufant fhall refufe to make fuch Abjuration, or after fuch Abjuration Not going.
made, fhall not go to fuch Haven, and within fuch Time as is fo appointed him ; and 35 El. 1.
from thence depart out of this Realm, according to this Statute, or after fuch Departure fhall return or come again into any his Majefty's Realms or Dominions, without his
Majefty's fpecial Licence in that Behalf firft obtained, in every fuch Cafe the Perfon fo
offending fhall be adjudged a Felon. *Ibid.*

The Juftices of Peace before whom any fuch Abjuration fhall be made, fhall caufe the Certificate.
fame to be prefently entred upon Record before them, and fhall certify the fame at the 35 El 1.
next General Gaol-delivery to be holden in the fame County. 35 *El.* 1. All this is now
taken away by the Statute 1 *W.* 3. *cap.* 18.

If after Conviction, and before required to abjure, the Party repair to fome Church Submiffion.
or Chapel on fome Sunday or Holiday, and hear Divine Service ; and before the Ser- 35 El. 1.
mon or Reading of the Gofpel, make publick Declaration of his Conformity in the
Form therein expreffed, *viz.* 1 *A. B. &c.* the Party offending fhall be difcharged of
all Penalties, &c.

The Minifter or Curate fhall forthwith enter it into a Book, and within ten Days Certificate.
certify the fame to the Bifhop of the Diocefe. 35 El. 1.

E e e If

Relapſe.
35 El. 1.

If the Party ſhall afterwards relapſe, and refuſe to go to Church, or ſhall go to Conventicles, he ſhall ſtand in the ſame Plight, as if no Submiſſion had been made. *35 Eliz.*

Penalties.
35 El. 1.
Courts.

The Penalties by 23 *Eliz.* 1. and 35 *Eliz.* 1. ſhall be recovered to the Queen's Uſe, by Action of Debt, Bill, Plaint or Information, in the King's Bench, Common Pleas and Exchequer; and a third Part ſhall go to charitable Uſes. 35 *Eliz.* 1.

Popiſh Recu-
ſants confined.
35 El. 2.

Every Perſon born in *England*, or made Denizen, *above ſixteen Years of Age*, having a Place of Abode, and being a Popiſh Recuſant, that ſhall be convicted of Abſence from the Church, and being in *England* at the Time of ſuch Conviction, ſhall within forty Days after ſuch Conviction, if at Liberty; or if reſtrained, within twenty Days after, repair to his Place of Abode, and ſhall not remove five Miles from thence upon Pain to loſe his Goods and Chattels, and all his Lands, *&c.* for his Life. But if he hath no Place of Abode, he ſhall within the Time aforeſaid, repair to the Place where he was born, or his Father or Mother dwells, upon Pain of Forfeiture as aforeſaid: And being come to ſuch Place, ſhall within twenty Days preſent himſelf, and give his Name to the Miniſter or Curate, and to the Conſtable, *&c.* And the Miniſter or Curate ſhall enter his Name in a Book, to be kept in the Pariſh; and the Miniſter and Conſtable ſhall certify the ſame to the next Seſſions, and the Juſtices ſhall enter it in the Rolls.

Abjuration
now tak- by
Statute, as a-
foreſaid.
35 El. 2.

A convicted Popiſh Recuſant of ſmall Ability (not having twenty Marks Freehold *per Ann.* or forty Pounds in Goods, nor being a *Feme Covert*) that ſhall not repair to his Place of uſual Dwelling, or Place of Birth, or where his Father or Mother is dwelling, and there notify himſelf to the Miniſter and Conſtables, according to the Statute of 35 *Eliz.* 1. or ſhall afterwards remove above five Miles from the ſame. If after he be apprehended, and ſhall not conform himſelf within three Months, in coming uſually to Church, and in making ſuch publick Submiſſion, as in the ſaid Statute is appointed, being thereunto required; then any two Juſtices of the Peace, or Coroner of that County, may require ſuch Offender to abjure the Realm, and may aſſign him the Time, and Haven, *&c.* And every ſuch Offender, ſhall upon his corporal Oath, before the ſaid Juſtices, abjure this Realm of *England*, and all other the King's Dominions for ever.

The Abjuration muſt be entred and certified, as herein is directed by 35 *Eliz.* But becauſe that of 35 *Eliz.* 1. was made againſt Sectaries, and this of *cap.* 2. againſt Popiſh Recuſants, I have ſo diſtinguiſhed them; and having obſerved ſome Difference in penning the two Acts, the only remaining Difference is in the Words of Submiſſion in the Acts, that of Sectaries by 35 *Eliz.* 1. being thus:

Submiſſion of
Sectaries.
35 El. 1.

I A. B. do humbly confeſs and acknowledge, *That I have grievouſly offended God, in contemning her Majeſty's godly and lawful Government and Authority, by abſenting my ſelf from Church, and from hearing Divine Service, contrary to the godly Laws and Statutes of this Realm; and in uſing and frequenting diſordered and unlawful Conventicles and Aſſemblies, under Pretence and Colour of Exerciſe of Religion. And I am heartily ſorry for the ſame, and do acknowledge and teſtify in my Conſcience, that no other Perſon hath, or ought to have any Power or Authority over her Majeſty. And I do promiſe and proteſt, without any Diſſimulation, or any Colour, or Means of any Diſpenſation, That from henceforth I will, from Time to Time, obey and perform her Majeſty's Laws and Statutes, in repairing to the Church, and hearing Divine Service, and do my utmoſt Endeavour to maintain and defend the ſame.*

Submiſſion of
Recuſants.
35 El. 2.

THAT of Popiſh Recuſants by 35 *Eliz.* 2. being thus: I A. B. *do humbly confeſs and acknowledge, That I have grievouſly offended God in contemning her Majeſty's godly and lawful Government and Authority, by abſenting my ſelf from Church, and from hearing Divine Service, contrary to the godly Laws and Statutes of this Realm. And I am heartily ſorry for the ſame, and do acknowledge and teſtify in my Conſcience, That the Biſhop or See of* Rome, *hath not, nor ought to have any Power or Authority over her Majeſty, or within any her Majeſty's Realms or Dominions. And I do promiſe and proteſt without any Diſſimulation, or any Colour, or Means of any Diſpenſation, That from henceforth I will from Time to Time, obey and perform her Majeſty's Laws and Statutes in repairing to the Church, and hearing Divine Service, and do my utmoſt Endeavour to maintain and defend the ſame.*

I

Which

Which Submiffion by 35 *Eliz.* 2. is in the fame Manner to be required and made, *35 El. 2.* and to have the fame Advantage, and to be certified in the fame Manner, as by 35 *Eliz. cap.* 1. And the like Provifion touching Relapfe, Women fhall be comprehended in *Women.* and bound by every Branch of that Statute, except thofe of Abjuration.

All fraudulent Conveyances made by Perfons that come not to Church, whether upon *Fraudulent* Power of Revocation, or with any Intent for the Maintenance of himfelf or Family, *Conveyances.* are void. 29 *Eliz.* 6.

Convictions of Recufancy fhall be in the Court of King's Bench, Affife or Gaol-de- *Convictions,* livery, and not elfewhere, and fhall be certified and eftreated into the Exchequer the *where.* next Term, after fuch Conviction, in fuch convenient Certainty for the Time, and other *This Statute* Circumftances, as that the Exchequer may award Procefs for Seifure of the Lands *doth not extend* and Goods of fuch as have not paid the Forfeiture 27 *Eliz.* 6. But fee *Pye* and *Lo-* *Differers.* *vel's* Cafe, *Hob.* 204. It was refolved, That an Information or Action of Debt lay in *1 W. & M.* the Common Pleas, notwithstanding this Statute : For this Statute extends only to In- *c. 18.* dictments for the Queen's Benefit, and not to Informations.

Such as are convicted, fhall pay their Forfeitures into the Exchequer, at two Times *Forfeiture.* in the Year, without any other or further Conviction, having not conformed. 29 *El.* 6. *29 El. 6.* And if they be not paid, the Procefs fhall iffue to feize the Goods, and three Parts of the Lands.

No Indictment fhall be quafhed for not mentioning the Offender to have been in *Indictment.* *England,* nor fhall any Indictment be reverfed for lack of Form, or for other Matter *29 El. 6.* whatfoever, fave only by the direct Traverfe of not coming to Church. 29 *Eliz.* 6. *3 Jac. 4.* 3 *Jac.* 4. But if he go to the Church where he moft abides, or if none fuch, to the Church next adjoining to his Dwelling-houfe, and there hear *Divine Service,* and re- ceive the Sacrament, he fhall be admitted to avoid, difcharge, reverfe, and undo the fame Indictments, and all Proceedings thereupon.

Upon fuch Indictment at Affifes or Gaol-delivery, Proclamation fhall be made, that *Conviction by* the Offender fhall render his Body to the Sheriff before next Affifes or Gaol-delivery. *Proclamation.* And if he do not appear, he fhall ftand convicted as upon Trial ; and now by 3 *Jac.* 4. *29 El. 6.* Juftices of Peace may hear, inquire, and determine of Offences for not coming to *3 Jac. 4.* Church and receiving the Sacrament, as Juftices of Affife may do by former Laws, and *Thefe Statutes* may make Proclamation upon fuch Indictments for the Parties to render themfelves to *do not extend* the Sheriffs, *&c.* Or elfe convict and certify them as is appointed by 29 *Eliz.* 6. But *to Proteftant* the Render muft be to the Sheriff, Bailiff or Gaoler of the Liberty, *&c.* And the *Differers by* Forfeiture muft be paid into the Exchequer, and Certificates of fuch Recufancy, as *1 W. 3. c. 18.* by the Statute of 29 *Eliz.* 6. is directed.

The King may refufe the 20 *l. per menfem,* and take to the two Parts of the Lands, *King's Elect-* and all the Goods, *&c.* And an Advowfon is without that Claufe. *Jones Reports* *on.* *p.* 20, *&c.*   *29 El. 6.* The King fhall feife two Parts only of the Recufant's Eftate to fatisfy the 20 *l. per* *1 Jac 1. 4.* *menfem,* but not the third Part, either in the Hand of the Anceftor or Heir : But after *1 Jac. 1. 4.* the Death of the Anceftor, two Parts fhall remain liable to the Arrears of 20 *l. per menfem.*

Any Popifh Recufant that conforms, fhall within a Year next after receive the Sa- *Conformity.* crament, and fo once every Year after, or forfeit 20 *l.* for the firft Year, 40 *l.* for the *Sacrament.* fecond Year, and 60 *l.* for the third Year, and 60 *l.* every Year after, until he receive *3 Jac. 1. 4.* it ; and if he receive it, and again offend in not receiving a Year, he fhall forfeit for every Year 60 *l. &c.* 3 *Jac.* 4.

A Recufant's Houfe fhall be referved to him, and the King's two Parts fhall not be *Houfe.* demifed to a Recufant.   *3 Jac. 1. 4.*

If a Recufant reform, and be obedient to the Laws and Ordinances of the Church, *Conformity.* and duly go to Church, and continue there during Service and Sermon, he fhall during *1 Jac. 1. 4.* the Time of fuch Conformity, be difcharged of all Penalties. 1 *Jac.* 4.

If a Recufant die, and his Heir be no Recufant, he fhall be difcharged of all Pe- *Heir* nalties, in refpect of his Anceftor's Recufancy ; or if the Heir be a Recufant and af- terwards conform, he fhall be in like Manner difcharged : But if the Heir be within fixteen Years of Age, and at fixteen fhall become a Recufant, he fhall be charged with the Penalties run upon his Anceftors, until he do conform ; but then fhall be dif- charged.

If fuch Offender conform or die, no Forfeiture of 20 *l.* a Month, or Seifure, fhall enfue upon full Satisfaction of all Arrears. 29 *Eliz.* 6.

Any

23 El. 1.

Any Perfon guilty of any Offence againft that Statute, except Treafon and Mifprifion of Treafon, which fhall before Judgment conform before the Bifhop of the Diocefe, or before the Juftices before whom he fhall be indicted, arraigned or tried, having not made the like Submiffion upon his Trial, for the firft Offence fhall upon his Recognition of fuch Submiffion in open Affifes or Seffions of the County where he is refident, be dif charged of all Offences, except Treafon and Mifprifion of Treafon.

Servant.
3 Jac. 1. 4.
This doth not extend to Pro-teftant Diffen-ters. 1 Will. 3. cap. 18.

If any Perfon fhall willingly maintain, retain, relieve, keep or harbour in his Houfe any Servant, Sojourner, Stranger, who fhall forbear for a Month together, to hear Divine Service, not having a reafonable Excufe, fhall forfeit 20 *l.* for every Month, *&c.*

3 Jac. 1. 4.

Any that fhall keep or retain in his, her, or their Service, Fee or Livery, any Perfor that fhall forbear going to Church by a Month, fhall for every Month he fhall fo keep forfeit 100 *l.*

3 Jac. 1. 4.

But a Man may keep his Father, Mother, or Ward, *&c.*

Juftices of Peace.
3 Jac. 1. 4.

Juftices of Peace may hear and determine all Offences of that Statute, except Treafon.

Wives.
3 Jac. 1. 4.

Wives fhall not forfeit for not receiving the Sacrament, during Marriage, nor Huf bands for their Wives not receiving.

Juftice of Peace.
23 El. 1.

By the Statute of 1 *El.* 2. Juftices of *Oyer* and *Terminer,* and of Affife, have Powe to inquire and determine the Offences; but by 23 *El.* 1. the Juftices of Peace have alfo Power to inquire and determine thereof, and of the Offences the Party muft be indicted a the next Seffions by 1 *Eliz.* 2.

1 El. 2.

The Juftices of Peace may inquire of the Offences againft 23 *Eliz.* 1. And the Sta tutes made 1, 5 *&* 13 *El.* touching acknowledging her Majefty's Supreme Government in Caufes Ecclefiaftical, and other Matters touching the Service of God, or coming to Church, or eftablifhing true Religion in this Realm; as other Juftices therein named may do, and may hear and determine all Offences againft this Act, except Treafon and Mif prifion of Treafon.

Forfeitures.
23 El. 1.

All Forfeitures of Money fhall be divided into three Parts, one third Part to the Queen for her own Ufe; another third Part to the Queen for the Ufe of the Poor of the Parifh where the Offence is committed, to be delivered by the principal Officers of the *Exche quer,* without further Warrant; and the other third Part to the Profecutor in any Cour of Record, *&c.*

Juftice of Peace.
5 El. 1.

Juftices of Peace in Seffions, have Power to inquire of all Offences againft 5 *El.* 1 againft fuch as fhall maintain the Authority of the Bifhop of *Rome,* and fhall make Certificates within forty Days after the Indictment into the King's Bench, or every one in Default, forfeits 100 *l.* 5 *El.* 1.

Oath of Obe-dience.
3 Jac. 1. 4.

Any two Juftices of Peace, the one being of the *Quorum,* may out of Seffions, re quire any Perfon of the Age of eighteen Years or above, which is convicted or indicted for any Recufancy, other than Noblemen or Noblewomen, for not repairing to Divine Ser vice; or which have not received the Communion twice the Year paft; or which travel eth the Country, and is unknown (and being examined upon Oath) fhall confefs, or not deny themfelves to be Recufants; or that fhall confefs, or not deny, that he or fhe had not received the Sacrament twice the Year paft, to take the Oath of Allegiance appointed by the Statute 3 *Jac.* 1. *cap.* 4. And if fuch Perfon fhall refufe to anfwer upon Oath, fuch Juftices of Peace examining him as aforefaid, or to take the Oath of Allegiance, then the faid two Juftices fhall commit the fame Perfon to the common Gaol, there to remain without Bail until the next Affifes or Quarter-Seffions; but Noblemen and Noble women are excepted, as not to be dealt withal herein by the Juftice of Peace.

Certificate.

Which Juftices fhall certify under their Hands to the next Seffions, the Names, *&c.* In which Seffions, the Oath fhall be again tendred to them; and if they, or any other

Præmunire.
Women.

fhall refufe, he or they fo refufing, fhall incur a *Præmunire,* except *Femes Covert,* who fhall be committed till they take it. The Oath *vide hic, cap.* 4.

1 Jac. 1. 7.

Alfo any two Juftices of Peace may take the faid Oath of Allegiance of fuch Perfone as have Charge of Caftles, Fortreffes, Blockhoufes, or Garrifons; and of all Captains, having Charge of Soldiers within this Realm, and upon Refufal, may commit the Offen der, being of the Age of eighteen Years, to the common Gaol, there to remain without Bail till the next Affifes or Quarter-Seffions. 7 *Jac.* 6.

7 Jac. 1. 6.

Alfo by the fame Statute 7 *Jac. cap.* 6. any two Juftices of Peace, the one being of the *Quorum,* may require any other Perfon or Perfons Men or Woman, be they Recu-

    A   fants

fants or not, of the Age of eighteen Years or above (under the Degree of a Baron or Baronefs) to take the faid Oath, and may commit them as aforefaid, upon their Refufal.

And by the faid Statute, if any Perfon whatfoever of the Age of eighteen Years, un- *Oath.*
der the Degree of a Baron, fhall ftand and be prefented, indicted or convicted, for not 7 Jac. 1. 6.
coming to Church or receiving the Communion, before the Ordinary or any other, having lawful Power to take fuch Prefentment or Indictment; or if the Minifter, Petty
Conftable and Church-wardens, or any Two of them, fhall complain to any one Juftice
of Peace near adjoining, and the faid Juftice of Peace fhall find Caufe of Sufpicion; then
that Juftice, or any one other Juftice of Peace, within whofe Commiffion or Power fuch
Perfon fhall be, upon Notice thereof, fhall require fuch Perfon to take the faid Oath:
And if any Perfon fhall refufe to take the Oath tendered to him or her as aforefaid,
then fuch Juftice or Juftices fhall commit fuch Offender to the common Gaol, there to
remain without Bail, till the next Affifes or Quarter-Seffions.

The faid two Juftices of Peace fhall certify in Writing, fubfcribed with their Hands, *Certificate.*
at the next Quarter-Seffions, the Names and Place of Abode of fuch Perfons, as have fo 3 Jac. 1. 4.
taken the faid Oath before them, by Force of the Statute of 3 *Jac.* 4.

And it feemeth requifite, That the Juftice or Juftices of Peace do make like Certificate
at the next Affifes or Quarter-Seffions, of fuch Perfons as have taken the faid Oath before them, by Force of the Statute 7 *Jac.* 6.

Such Perfons as have been reconciled to the Pope, if they fhall return into the Realm; *Submiffion of-*
and thereupon within fix Days next after their Return, fhall fubmit themfelves to his *ter Reconciling.*
Majefty, and his Laws, before any two Juftices of Peace, jointly or feverally, of the 37 Eliz. 2.
County where they fhall arrive; the faid Juftices may take fuch Submiffion, and withal
may take their Oath of the Supremacy, and their Oath of Allegiance. And the faid
Oaths fo taken, the faid Juftices fhall certify at the next Quarter-Seffions, upon Pain
of 40 *l.*

Any two Juftices of Peace of the County where any of his Majefty's Subjects (not be- *Seminary.*
ing a Jefuit, or other Popifh Prieft, &c.) brought up in any Seminary fhall arrive, with- 37 El. 2.
in fix Months next after Proclamation to be made in that Behalf in the City of *London,*
under the Great Seal of *England,* may within two Days next after fuch Return, receive
his Submiffion to his Majefty and his Laws, and take his Oath to the Supremacy.

The Juftice or Juftices of Peace, that fhall receive or take any Submiffion or Oath as *Submiffion.*
aforefaid, by force of the Statute 37 *El. cap.* 2. fhall certify the fame into the *Chancery,* 37 El. 2.
within three Months after fuch Submiffion, upon Pain to forfeit 100 *l.* 37 *El. cap.* 2.
. Jefuits 11.

If any married Woman under the Degree of a Baronefs, being lawfully convicted as a *Women.*
Popifh Recufant, fhall not within three Months after fuch Conviction, repair to the 7 Jac. 1. 6.
Church and receive the Communion, &c. Any two Juftices of Peace, (the one being of
the *Quorum*) may commit her to Prifon, there to remain without Bail, until fhe fhall
conform herfelf, &c. unlefs the Hufband fhall pay the King for the Wife's Offence for
every Month 10 *l.* or elfe the third Part of his Lands and Tenements, at the Hufband's
Choice, for fo long as fhe remaining a Recufant convict, fhall continue out of Prifon;
during which Time, and no longer, fhe may have her Liberty.

The Church-wardens and Conftables of every Town, Parifh, or Chapel, or fome or *Prefentment.*
one of them; or if none, then the Conftables of the Hundred, as well in Places exempt 3 Jac. 1. 4.
as not exempt, fhall once every Year prefent the monthly Abfence of all Popifh Recufants from the Church, and the Names of their Children nine Years of Age and upwards,
abiding with their Parents; and their Age, and the Names of their Servants at the Quarter-Seffions, which fhall be received and entered without Fee, by the Clerk of the Peace
or Town-Clerk refpectively; or elfe every Church-warden, Conftable or High-Confta-
ble, fhall for every Default of Prefenting lofe 20 *s.* And every Clerk of the Peace or
Town-Clerk for not Recording 40 *s.* And if upon fuch Prefentment the Party fhall be
convicted (being not before convicted) the Party making fuch Prefentment fhall have
40 *s.* of the Recufant's Goods and Eftate, to be levied in fuch Form as the major Part
of the Juftices, by Warrant under their Hands and Seals, fhall appoint.

Every Perfon going beyond Seas to ferve any foreign Prince, State or Potentate, and *Serving beyond*
not taking the Oath before the Cuftomer or Comptroller of the Port, or their Deputy *Sea.*
or Deputies, fhall be adjudged a Felon, 3 *Jac.* 4. If any Gentleman or Perfon of 3 Jac. 1. 4.
higher Degree, or any Perfon that hath born, or fhall bear any Office or Place of Captain, Lieutenant, or any other Office or Charge in Camp, Army, or Company of Sol- 3 Jac. 1. 4.
diers, or Conductor of Soldiers, fhall go voluntarily out of the Realm to ferve any fo-

                                                                                    reign

reign Prince, State or Potentate, or fhall ferve them before they fhall with good Sureties

3 Jac. 1. 4.
Bond.
become bound in 20 *l.* with Condition not to be reconciled, *&c.* nor to enter into any Practice againft the King or Realm, but fhall difclofe it, fhall be a Felon. Which Bond

Certificate.
fhall be given before the Cuftomer, *&c.* 3 *Jac.* 4. Which Bond and Oath he fhall certify into the *Exchequer* once every Year, or forfeit 20 *s.* for every Oath, and 50 *l.* for every Bond not certified, *&c.*

Reconciling.
3 Jac. 1. 4.
The Branches of Treafon in reconciling, *&c.* or being reconciled, fhall be proceeded upon in the King's Bench, Affife, or Gaol-delivery, as if the Offence had been committed in the County where he is taken. 3 *Jac.* 4.

Sending beyond Sea for Education.
See the Penalties of conveying a Child, or any other, under his Government, beyond the Seas, to enter into any College, *&c.* or to repair to them for Inftruction, or to be refident in any Popifh Family, and be there inftructed by any Popifh Perfon, or to be fent, or to go or continue there for thofe Ends, and to fend any Money, *&c.* to, or for the Maintenance of any there, or under the Name of *Charity,* *&c.* towards the Relief of any Priory, *&c.* 1 *Jac.* 4. 3 *Jac.* 5. 3 *Car.* 1, 2. But of thofe Offences, I take it, the Seifions cannot meddle with or inquire.

3 Jac. 1. 5.
The Penalty of Reconciling, *&c.* and being reconciled, *&c.* See Tit. *Treafon.*

Armor.
All fuch Armor, Gunpowder and Munition, as a Popifh Recufant hath in his Houfe or Houfes, or elfewhere, or in the Hands of any other of his Difpofition, fhall be taken from him by Warrant of four Juftices of Peace at their General Quarter-Seffions (other than neceffary Armor, in the Difcretion of the Juftices, for the Defence of his Perfon and Houfe) and fhall be kept at the Cofts of fuch Recufants, in fuch Place as the Juftices fhall appoint. 3 *Jac.* 5.

3 Jac. 1. 5.
After any Warrant is granted from any four Juftices of Peace in Seffions, for the Taking away the Armor of any Popifh Recufant convict; if any fuch Recufant having any fuch Armor, Gunpowder or Munition, or if any other Perfon having any fuch Armor to the Ufe of any fuch Recufant, fhall refufe to declare unto the faid Juftices of Peace, or any of them, what Armor he or they have, or fhall hinder or difturb the Delivery thereof, to any of the faid Juftices, or to any other Perfon authorized by their Warrant, to take and feife the fame; then every fuch Offender fhall be imprifoned by Warrant of, and from any two Juftices of Peace of fuch County, by the Space of three Months without Bail.

Coming to Court.
3 Jac. 1. 5.
No Popifh Recufant convicted, fhall come to the Court or Houfe where the King or Heir apparent is, unlefs commanded by the King or Warrant from the Council, or any of them, upon Pain to forfeit 100 *l.* a Moiety to the King, another Moiety to the Difcoverer and Profecutor, in any of the King's Courts of Record. 3 *Jac.* 5.

Want of Satisfaction.
Service in Houfe.
He that cannot fatisfy the Money forfeited within three Months, fhall be committed to Prifon, until he have paid, or conform. And a Man having Service in his Houfe, and going four Times a Year to fome Church or Chapel, fhall incur no Penalty.

Child.
Oath.
3 Jac. 1. 5.
Before fome Juftice of Peace of the County, Liberty or Limits, where the Parents of a Child fent beyond Seas, without Licenfe, did dwell; fuch Child muft take the Oath of Allegiance, expreffed 3 *Jac. cap.* 4. And they that were beyond Seas, before the Making of this Act, are to take the fame Oath within fix Months after their Return, before fome Juftice of Peace where fuch Perfons inhabit, before they can take the Benefit of a Gift, Conveyance, Devife, or Defcent, *&c.* of any Lands or Tenements, *&c.* 3 *Jac. cap.* 5.

Books.
Search.
3 Jac. 1. 5.
Any two Juftices of Peace, from Time to Time, may fearch the Houfes and Lodgings of every Popifh Recufant convict, and of every Perfon whofe Wife is a Popifh Recufant convict, for Popifh Books and Relicks of Popery; and they may prefently deface and burn fuch Books and Relicks as they fhall find and judge not convenient for them: Yet if it be a Relick of any Price, the fame is to be defaced at the General Seffions of the Peace, and to be reftored to the Owner.

London.
3 Jac. 1. 5.
Any Popifh Recufant that fhall dwell in *London,* or within ten Miles of it, which be indicted or convicted of Recufancy, or fhall forbear to come to Church three Months, fhall within ten Days after fuch Indictment or Conviction depart thence: And if he live in *London,* or ten Miles, *&c.* fhall give up his Name to the Lord Mayor; and if he live above ten Miles, then to the next Juftice of Peace, upon Pain to forfeit 100 *l.* *&c.*

Bear no Office.
3 Jac. 1. 5.
No Recufant convict fhall practife the Common or Civil Law, as Counfellor (not as Chancellor, as the Print is) Clerk, *&c.* Nor practife Phyfick, nor as an Apothecary, nor be a Judge, Minifter, Clerk, or Steward of any Court, or keep any Court, nor bear any Office in any Camp, Troop, or Company of Soldiers, nor bear any Of-

I   fice

fice in any Ship, Caftle or Fortrefs, but be utterly difabled, and fhall forfeit 100 *l*. *&c.* 3 *Jac.* 5.

A Recufant convict, or having a Wife that is a Popifh Recufant convict, fhall not af- 3 Jac. 1. 5. ter his or her Conviction, exercife any publick Office or Charge in the Commonwealth, except fuch Hufband and his Children nine Years old, and his Servants or Houfhold, fhall once every Month, having no Excufe, at Church hear Divine Service, and his Children and Servants, at Times appointed, receive the Sacrament, and bring up his Children in the true Religion. 3 *Jac.* 5.

A Popifh Recufant convicted fhall be reputed an excommunicated Perfon until Con- *Difability.* formity, and take the Oath of 3 *Jac.* 4. And it may be pleaded in Difability in all 3 Jac. 1. 5. Actions, except for fuch of his Lands, *&c.* as are not to be feifed, *&c.* 3 *Jac.* 5. And the Sheriff and Officer may upon an *Excommunicato capiendo,* break the Houfe to apprehend him. 3 *Jac.* 4.

Any Man being a Popifh Recufant convict, that fhall be married otherwife than ac- *Marriage.* cording to the Orders of the Church of *England*, fhall be difabled to be Tenant by the 3 Jac. 1. 5. Curtefy ; and a Woman otherwife married fhall lofe her Dower, Jointure, Widow's Eftate, and Free Bench, or any Portion of Goods, by the Cuftom of any City, *&c.* And if fuch Man marry a Woman that hath no Land whereof he may be intitled, *As Tenant by the Curtefy*, he fhall forfeit 100 *l.* 3 *Jac.* 5.

If a Popifh Recufant baptife not his Child at Church, or Place appointed for Bap- 3 Jac. 1. 5. tifm by a lawful Minifter, within a Month, if it may be carried thither, otherwife by the Minifter of the Parifh, *&c.* he, if he live a Month after the Birth (or if he die within a Month) the Mother fhall forfeit 100 *l.* a third Part to the King, a third Part to the Profecutor, and a third Part to the Poor.

If a Popifh Recufant not excommunicated, fhall not be buried in a Church or Church- *Burial.* yard, or not according to the Law Ecclefiaftical ; the Executor or Adminiftrator know- 3 Jac. 1. 5. ing the fame, or the Party caufing the fame, fhall forfeit 20 *l.* a third Part to the King, a third Part to the Profecutor, and a third Part to the Poor, *&c.* where he died.

No Popifh Recufant convict, fhall prefent to any Ecclefiaftical Living, Free-School, *Prefentators.* Hofpital, or Donative, but be difabled ; but the Chancellors and Scholars of *Oxford* to thofe in *Suffex*, *&c.* and the Chancellor and Scholars of *Cambridge* to thofe in *Effex*, *&c.* But they fhall not prefent any to any Ecclefiaftical Living, that hath another Living with Cure.

A Popifh Recufant convicted at the Death of the Teftator, or at granting Adminiftra- *Executors, &c.* tion, is difabled to be Executor or Adminiftrator, or to have the Cuftody of a Child, or 3 Jac. 1. 5. be Guardian in Chivalry, Socage or Nurture, and the next of Kin, to whom the Eftate cannot defcend, that comes to Church ufually, and received the Communion three Times that Year before, he fhall be Guardian, *&c.*

Any Juftice of Peace, within the County, in which any Jefuit, or Popifh Prieft, or *Jefuits.* other Ecclefiaftical Perfon, fhall arrive, or land, within three Days after their Landing, 37 El. 2. may take their Submiffion Oath, and Acknowledgment touching their Obedience to the King's Majefty and his Laws, provided in Cafes of Religion ; but if it be any other Subject, who is no Prieft, *&c.* and yet brought up in any Seminary, they muft make their Submiffion, and take the Oath, *&c.* before two Juftices, *&c.* *See more in this Title.*

Every Subject knowing any Jefuit or Popifh Prieft, to be within the King's Domini- *Difcovery of* ons, ought to difcover the fame to fome Juftice of Peace, or other higher Officer, with- *Priefts.* in twelve Days, *&c.* And fuch Juftice of Peace ought within eight and twenty Days, 27 El. 2. after fuch Difcovery made to him, to give Information thereof to one of the King's Privy Council, *&c.* upon Pain of two hundred Marks, and upon fuch Information given by the Juftice of Peace, he fhall have redelivered to him a Note in Writing, fubfcribed by fuch Privy Counfellor, *&c.* with his own Hand, teftifying, that fuch Information was made unto him.

If any Perfon to whom any *Agnus Dei*, Crofs, Picture, Beads, or fuch fuperftitious *Superftitious* Things fhall be delivered or offered, do difclofe fuch Deliverer or Offerer to any Juftice *Things.* of Peace, *&c.* that Juftice of Peace, within fourteen Days, muft declare the fame to one 13 El. 2. of the King's Privy Council, or elfe he fhall incur the Danger of a Premunire.

If any Perfon fufpected to be a Jefuit, Seminary or Mafling Prieft, being examined by *Anfwer.* a Perfon having Authority fo to do, fhall refufe to anfwer directly whether he be fo, 35 El 2. fhall by the Perfon examining him, be committed to Prifon without Bail, till he anfwer directly.

The

Difcovery.
3 Jac. 1. 4.

The Party that doth firft difcover to any Juftice of Peace, any Recufant, or other Perfon, entertaining or relieving any Jefuit, Seminary or Popifh Prieft, or any Mafs to have been faid, or any of them that were prefent thereat, and the Prieft that faid the fame, within three Days after the Offence, and by Reafon of his Difcovery any of the Offenders be taken and convicted, fhall be freed from Danger of the Offence, if he be an Offender therein, and have the third Part of the Forfeiture which fhall be forfeited by fuch Offence. 3 *Jac. cap.* 4. if it exceed not 150 *l.* or if above, he fhall have 50 *l.* and the Difcoverer fhall have a Warrant from the Sheriff or Officer that fhall feife or levy the Forfeiture, to pay him out of the Money levied 50 *l.*

Books.
3 Jac. 1. 4.
3 Jac. 1. 5.

No Perfon fhall bring from beyond the Seas, nor print, fell or buy, any Popifh Primers, Ladies Pfalters, Manuals, Rofaries, Catechifms, Miffals, Breviares, Portals, Legends, and Lives of Saints, containing Superftitious Matter in any Language, nor any Superftitious Books in *Englifh*, upon Pain of 40 *s.* for every Book. A third Part to the King, a third Part to the Profecutor, a third Part to the Poor, where fuch Book fhall be found, (not bound as in the Print) &c.

Mafs.
23 El. 1.

If any Perfon fhall fay or fing Mafs, being thereof convicted fhall forfeit Two hundred Marks, and be committed to the next Gaol for a Year, and from thenceforth til he hath paid the Two hundred Marks. And every Perfon who fhall willingly hear Mafs fhall forfeit 200 *l.* and fuffer Imprifonment for a Year.

Licence.

Recufants confined to five Miles, may be licenfed by any four Juftices of Peace, with the Privity and Affent of the Bifhop, or Lieutenant, or of any Deputy-Lieutenant, refiding in the faid County, under all their Hands and Seals, to travel about their neceffary Bufinefs out of the Compafs of five Miles. But fuch Licences muft certify the particular Caufe of the faid Licence, and the Time of their Abfence muft therein be limited. And the Party fo licenfed muft firft take his Oath before the faid four Juftices, or any of them that he hath truly informed them of the Caufe of his Journey, and that he fhall not make any caufelefs Stays. See the Form of fuch Licence *hic poftea*, Tit. *Precedents.* See more Tit. *Popifh Recufants in the Appendix*, Tit. *Papifts*, &c. and a Licence otherwife is void and going without fuch Licence, fhall forfeit, as by 35 *El.* 2. 3 *Jac.* 5.

Moor's Rep.
836.

In pleading a Licence, he muft fhew that he had taken the Oath of Allegiance, and that the Caufe of his Licence is true, and that it was granted with the Affent of the Bifhop or Lieutenant, &c. And if the fame Perfon be Juftice and Lieutenant, that will not ferve.

Woman.
3 Jac. 5.

A Woman being a Popifh Recufant Convict (her Husband being not convicted) that fhall not conform and remain conformed, which fhall not go to Church, nor receive the Sacrament a Year before her Husband's Death, fhall forfeit to the King two Parts of her Jointure; and two Parts of her Dower, in three Parts to be divided, and be difabled to be Executrix, or Adminiftratrix to her Husband.

Parliament.
30 Car. 2.
ft. 2. §. 2.
Oaths.

No Peer of this Realm, or Member of the Houfe of Peers fhall vote or make his Proxy in the Houfe of Peers, or fit there during any Debate in the faid Houfe; nor any Member of the Houfe of Commons fhall vote or fit there after their Speaker chofen, til he firft takes the Oaths of Allegiance and Supremacy, and fubfcribes and repeats this Declaration between the Hours of Nine in the Morning and Four in the Afternoon, at the Tables in the Middle of the faid Houfes, in a full Houfe, *viz.*

Declaration.

I A. B. *do folemnly and fincerely in the Prefence of God, profefs, teftify and declare, That I do believe that in the Sacrament of the Lords Supper, there is not any Tranfubftantiation of the Elements of Bread and Wine into the Body and Blood of Chrift, at or after the Confecration thereof by any Perfon whatfoever; And that the Invocation or Adoration of the Virgin Mary, or any other Saint, and the Sacrifice of the Mafs, as they are now ufed in the Church of Rome, are fuperftitious and idolatrous: And I do folemnly in the Prefence of God, profefs, teftify and declare, That I do make this Declaration, and every Part thereof, in the plain and ordinary Senfe of the Words read unto me, as they are commonly underftood by Englifh Proteftants, without any Evafion, Equivocation, or Mental Refervation whatfoever, and without any Difpenfation already granted me for this Purpofe by the Pope, or any other Authority or Perfon whatfoever, or without any Hope of any fuch Difpenfation from any Perfon or Authority whatfoever, or without thinking that I am or can be acquitted before God or Man, or abfolved of this Declaration, or any Part thereof, although the Pope, or any other Perfon or Perfons whatfoever, fhould difpenfe with, or annul the fame, or declare that it was null and void from the Beginning.*

I

Every Peer of this Realm, and Member of the Houfe of Peers, and every Peer of *Scot-* | *King's Pre-*
land or *Ireland* of twenty-one Years of Age, or upwards, and every Member of the Houfe | *fence.*
of Commons, not having taken the faid Oaths, and made and fubfcribed the faid Decla- | 30 Car. 2.
ration, and all Perfons convict of Recufancy, that fhall remain in the King's or Queen's | ft. 2. §. 3.
Prefence, or come into any Houfe where they refide, fhall incur and fuffer the Penalties
hereafter mentioned, unlefs fuch Perfon fhall in the next Term after take the faid Oaths,
and make the faid Declaration in the Court of *Chancery*, between the Hours of Nine and
Twelve.

Peers and Members of the Houfe of Commons offending as aforefaid, fhall be adjudged | *Popifh Recu-*
Popifh Recufants convict, and be difabled to hold any Office in *England* or *Ireland*, or | *fants.*
any Iflands or Plantations to them belonging, or to fit in Parliament, or make a Proxy in | *Difability.*
the Houfe of Peers, or to profecute any Suit, to be Guardian, Executor or Adminiftra- | Ib. §. 4.
tor, or to take any Legacy or Deed of Gift, and for every Offence fhall forfeit 500 *l.* to
him that will fue for the fame.

Offenders taking the faid Oaths, and making the faid Declaration after fuch Offence | *Difcharge of*
committed, fhall from thenceforth be freed from all Penalties as Popifh Recufants con- | *Penalties.*
victed as aforefaid, and from all Difabilities incurred thereby: But not to be reftored to | Ib. §. 1.
any Office fupplied upon Voidance, nor to any other till after one Year after taking the
faid Oaths, and making the Declaration aforefaid, nor difcharged of the faid Forfeiture of
500 *l.*

The Lord Mayor of the City of *London*, and every Juftice of Peace of the City of | *Removing of*
London, Weftminfter, and Borough of *Southwark*, and of the Counties of *Middlefex, Surry,* | *Papifts.*
Kent and *Suffex*, may caufe to be arrefted and brought before him every Perfon or Perfons | 1 W. & M.
not being a Merchant-Foreigner within the fame Cities, or within twelve Miles of the | ft. 1. c.9. §. 2.
fame as are, or are reputed to be Papifts, and tender to them the Declaration mentioned
in the Statute of 30 *Car.* 2. intitled, *An Act for the more effectual preferving the King's*
Perfon and Government, by difabling Papifts from fitting in either Houfe of Parliament;
and if fuch Perfon upon Tender refufe audibly to repeat and fubfcribe the faid Declaration,
and fhall after continue to be within the faid Cities, or ten Miles Diftance from the fame,
that the Offender fhall forfeit and fuffer as a Popifh Recufant Convict.

Every Juftice of Peace fhall certify every Subfcription before him by Virtue of this Act | *Subfcription*
taken; as alfo the Names of every Perfon refufing to repeat or fubfcribe as aforefaid upon | *certified.*
Tender, under the Hand and Seal of the faid Juftice, into the King's Bench the next | Ib. §. 3.
Term, or elfe at the next Quarter-Seffions: And if the Perfon refufing and certified fhall
not within the next Term or Seffions after fuch Refufal, appear in the Court of King's
Bench or Seffions, where fuch Certificate fhall be returned, and in open Court repeat and
fubfcribe the Declaration, as aforefaid, and indorfe and enter his fo doing upon the Certificate fo returned, he fhall be from the Time of fuch his Refufal adjudged a Popifh Recufant
Convict.

This Act fhall not extend to any Foreigner that fhall be a menial Servant to any Am- | Ibid.
baffador or publick Agent.

By this Statute it is enacted, That neither the Statute of 23 *Eliz.* intitled, *An Act to* | *Diffenters ex-*
retain the Queen's Subjects in their due Obedience: Nor the Statute of 29 *Eliz.* intitled, | *empted from*
An Act for the more fpeedy and due Execution of certain Branches of the Statute made the | *Penalties.*
twenty-third Year of the Queen's Reign: Nor that Branch or Claufe of a Statute made | c. 18.
1 *Eliz.* intitled, *An Act for the Uniformity of Common Prayer, and Service in the Church* | 23 Eliz.
and Adminiftration of the Sacraments: Nor the Statute made 3 *Jac.* 1. intitled, *An Act for* | 29 Eliz.
the better difcovering and reprefling Popifh Recufants: Nor another Statute made the fame | 1 Eliz.
Year, intitled, *An Act to prevent and avoid Dangers which may grow by Popifh Recu-* | 3 Jac. 1.
fants: Nor any other Statutes made againft Papifts or Popifh Recufants; except the Sta-
tute made 25 *Car.* intitled, *An Act for preventing Dangers which may happen from* | 25 Car. 2.
Popifh Recufants: And except the Statute made 30 *Car.* 2. intitled, *An Act for the more* | 30 Car. 2.
effectual preferving the King's Perfon and Government by difabling Papifts from fitting in either
Houfe of Parliament, fhall be conftrued to extend to any Perfon diffenting from the Church
of *England*, that fhall take the Oaths mentioned in a Statute made this prefent Parliament,
intitled, *An Act for the removing and preventing all Queftions and Difputes concerning the* | 1 W. & M.
affembling and fitting of this prefent Parliament; and fhall make and fubfcribe the Declaration mentioned in a Statute made 30 *Car.* 2. intitled, *An Act to prevent Papifts from*
fitting in either Houfe of Parliament; which Oaths and Declaration the Juftices of Peace
at their General Seffions, are hereby required to tender to fuch Perfons as fhall offer
themfelves to take and fubfcribe the fame, and thereof to keep a Regifter: And no Perfon

fon fhall pay above 6 *d.* to any Officer of the faid Court for entring the faid Oaths, and fubfcribing the faid Declaration : Nor above 6 *d.* for any Certificate figned by the Officer of the faid Court.

Ibid.

All Perfons convicted or profecuted in Order to Conviction of Recufancy by Indictment, Information, &c. or otherwife grounded upon any the aforefaid Statutes, fhall take the faid Oaths mentioned in the faid Statute made this prefent Parliament, and make and fubfcribe the Declaration aforefaid in the Court of Exchequer or Affizes, or at the General or Quarter-Seffions, and to be thence certified into the Exchequer, fhall be from thence exempted from all Penalties and Forfeitures incurred by Force of any of the faid Statutes, without any Compofition or Charge whatfoever.

Perfons exempted.
1 W. & M.

Any Perfon refufing to take the faid Oaths when lawfully tendred, which every Juftice of Peace hath Power to do, fuch Perfon fhall not be admitted to make and fubfcribe the two Declarations in this Act mentioned, though required thereunto, either before any Juftice of Peace, or at the General or Quarter-Seffions before or after any Conviction of Popifh Recufancy, unlefs fuch Perfon can, within thirty-one Days after fuch Tender of the Declarations to him, produce two fufficient Proteftant Witneffes to teftify upon Oath that they believe him to be a Proteftant Diffenter ; or a Certificate under the Hands of four Proteftants conformable to the Church of *England,* or have taken the Oaths, or fubfcribed the Declarations above mentioned; and fhall alfo produce a Certificate under the Hands and Seals of fix or more fufficient Men of the Congregation to which he belongs owning him for one of them. And that until fuch Certificate under the Hands and Seals of fix of his Congregation as aforefaid, be produced, and two Proteftant Witneffes to atteft his being a Proteftant Diffenter, or a Certificate under the Hands of four Proteftants as aforefaid, be produced, the Juftice of Peace fhall take a Recognizance with two Sureties in the penal Sum of 50 *l.* to be levied of his Goods, &c. to the Ufe of the King and Queen for his producing the fame ; and if he cannot give fuch Security, to commit him to Prifon, there to remain until he has produced fuch Certificate, or two Witneffes.

Proteftant Diffenters.

No Congregation or Affembly for Religious Worfhip fhall be permitted by this Act until fuch Place of Meeting fhall be certified to the Bifhop of the Diocefe, or the Archdeacon of that Arch-deaconry, or the Juftices of Peace at the General or Quarter-Seffions of the Peace, and regiftred in the faid Bifhops or Arch-deacons Court, or recorded at the faid General or Quarter-Seffions, and regiftred by the Regifter or Clerk of the Peace, for certifying of which he fhall not have above 6 *d.*

Private Meetings.
Ibid.

Two or more Juftices who fhall know, fufpect or be informed that any Perfon is a Papift, are required to tender fuch Perfon the *Declaration made Anno* 30 *Car.* 2. *cap.* 1 againft *Tranfubftantiation* ; and if he refufe to repeat and fubfcribe it, or to appear before the Juftices (a Summons being left at their ufual Place of Aboad) by one authorized under the Hands and Seals of the faid two Juftices) fuch Perfon fhall be liable to all the Pains and Penalties, Forfeitures, and Difabilities, as follow.

Two Juftices may tender the Declaration to fufpected Perfons.
1 W. & M. c. 15.

He or any other to his Ufe fhall keep no Arms or Gunpowder, other than what fhall be allowed him by the Quarter-Seffions for the Defence of himfelf or Houfe ; and any two Juftices may by their Warrant impower any Perfon in the Day-time, with the Affiftance of the Conftable or his Deputy, or a Tythingman, to fearch for Arms in the Poffeffion of fuch Papift, or reputed Papift, and feize the fame to the King's Ufe, to be delivered at the next Quarter-Seffions for that Purpofe.

And if he refufe to take and repeat it, fhall keep no Arms, & if he doth, they may be feized.

A Papift refufing to fubfcribe the faid Declaration, and not delivering within ten Days after fuch Refufal to fome Juftice, &c. all his Arms, &c. or who fhall hinder any Perfon having Authority as aforefaid to feize, &c. fhall be committed by two Juftices to Gaol for three Months without Bail, and fhall forfeit the Arms, and treble the Value, to the Ufe of the Crown, to be appraifed by the Juftices at the next Quarter-Seffions.

Not delivering his Arms, or hindering the Seizure, fhall forfeit them, and be committed.

The Concealer or being privy to the Concealing fuch Arms, or knowing thereof, and not difcovering to fome Juftice, or hindering any Perfon authorifed to fearch or feife the fame, fhall be committed for three Months as aforefaid without Bail, and forfeit treble the Value of the Arms.

Concealer of Arms fhall be committed for three Months without Bail.

The Difcoverer of concealed Arms, &c. fo as the fame may be feifed, fhall be allowed by the Quarter-Seffions a Sum of Money, amounting to the full Value of the Arms difcovered, the fame to be affeffed by the Seffions, and to be levied by Diftrefs and Sale of the Goods of the Offender.

Difcoverer of Arms fhall have the full Value.

If fuch Refufer fhall defire to fubfcribe and conform, and fhall at the Quarter-Seffions where his Refufal was certified in open Court, make and fubfcribe the faid Declaration

The Perfon informing fhall be difcharged.

4

againft

gainſt Tranſubſtantiation, he ſhall from thenceforth be diſcharged of all Diſabilities and
Forfeitures, &c.

Such Refuſer, &c. ſhall not keep a Horſe above the Value of 5 *l.* if he doth, two *Refuſer ſhall* Juſtices may by Warrant give Power to any Perſon with the Aſſiſtance of the Conſtable, *not keep a* &c. to ſearch for and ſeiſe all Horſes above that Value, which ſhall be forfeited to the Uſe *the Value of* of the Crown, the Concealer or he who aſſiſts to conceal ſuch Horſes, ſhall by Warrrnt 5 *l.* is aforeſaid, be committed for three Months, and forfeit treble the Value of the Horſes, o be ſettled by the Seſſions. *Horſe above*

Every * *Papiſt convict* being diſabled by the Statute 3 *Jac.* 1. *cap.* 5. to preſent to * *See the Stat.* any *Benefice, School, Hoſpital,* or *Donative,* or to grant any *Avoidance* thereof, 'tis now *poſtea.* 12 *Ann.* c.14. by the Statute 1 *Will.* enacted, that the *Refuſer or he who neglects to make and ſubſcribe* 1 W. & M. he *Declaration againſt Tranſubſtantiation* when tendered to him by two Juſtices, or not c. 26. ppearing before them upon Notice, &c. and having his Name certified (as in that Statute *Diſabled to* s required) and recorded at the Quarter-Seſſions, ſhall be diſabled to preſent, collate or *preſent to any* rant any Avoidance of any Benefice, as fully as if he was a *Popiſh Recuſant Convict,* *Benefice.* nd the Univerſity ſhall have the Right of Preſentation to every ſuch Benefice lying with- n their reſpective Limits, as appointed by that Act.

Truſtees of Recuſants diſabled to preſent, &c. by the Statute 3 *Jac.* or by this Act *Truſtees are* Wil. ſhall likewiſe be diſabled, &c. and their Preſentations and Grants ſhall be void, *diſabled.* nd the Univerſities, &c. ſhall preſent.

Truſtee, Mortgagee, or Grantee of any Avoidance who ſhall preſent to any Eccleſiaſti- *Truſtee for a* al Living where the Truſt, &c. ſhall be for any *Recuſant* convict or diſabled, without *Recuſant muſt* iving Notice of the Avoidance in Writing to the Vice-Chancellor of the Univerſity to *give Notice to* vhom it belongs, within three Months after the Avoidance ſhall forfeit 500 *l.* to ſuch *of the next* Univerſity, to be recovered by Action of Debt, &c. *Avoidance.* *the Univerſity*

If a Perſon diſabled, &c. ſhall at the Quarter-Seſſions make and ſubſcribe the Declara- *Perſon diſabled* ion, &c. and take the Oaths appointed by 1 *Will. cap.* 8. he ſhall be diſcharged from all *and conforming* Diſabilities, &c. *charged.* *ſhall be diſ-*

He who apprehends one, or more, Popiſh Biſhop, Prieſt, or Jeſuit, and proſecutes *Apprehending* him ſo as he is convicted of ſaying Maſs, or executing any other Parts of the Office of a *a Popiſh Bi-* Prieſt, ſhall within four Months after ſuch Conviction receive of the Sheriff of the County *Prieſt, ſhall* oo *l.* upon Demand, for every Offender ſo convicted, he tendering a *Certificate* of the *after Convic-* Conviction under the Hand of the Judge or Juſtices before whom the Party was convicted, 500 *l.* nd that ſuch Popiſh Prieſt was taken by the Perſon claiming the ſaid Reward; and the 11 & 12 W. Judge ſhall by his Certificate direct in what Proportions the Reward ſhall be paid among c. 4. he Perſons claiming the ſame. *ſhop, Jeſuit or* *tion have*

The Sheriff dying, or being removed within four Months after Conviction, then the *To be paid by* ſucceeding Sheriff ſhall pay the ſaid Reward within two Months after a Demand, pro- *the Sheriff or* lucing ſuch Certificate as aforeſaid, and if he makes Default in paying it, he ſhall forfeit *his Succeſſor.* o the Perſon to whom 'tis due the Sum of 200 *l.* to be recovered by Action of Debt with full Coſts; and the Sheriff producing the ſaid Certificate, or the Duplicate thereof, ſhall be paid out of the Treaſury.

Popiſh Prieſt being convicted of ſaying Maſs, or exerciſing any Part of his Office in the *Prieſts, &c.* King's Dominions, or keeping School, or taking upon him the Education, Government, *teaching &c &c.* or Boarding of Youth, ſhall be adjudged to perpetual Impriſonment, in ſuch Places within *impriſoned du-* his Kingdom, as the King by Advice of his Council ſhall appoint. *ring Life.* *&c. ſhall be*

This Act ſhall not extend to a Popiſh Prieſt, officiating in the Dwelling-houſe of any *Not to extend* Foreign Miniſter reſiding here, if he is not a Subject of theſe Realms, and ſo as his Name *to a Prieſt of* nd the Place of his Birth, and the Foreign Miniſter to whom he belongs, is entered in *Miniſter.* he Secretary's Office. *any Foreign*

He who diſcovers and convicts another of ſending a Child beyond Sea, to be educated *Sending a* in the Romiſh Religion, ſhall have the 100 *l.* forfeited by the Perſon ſo ſending ſuch *Child beyond* Child. *Sea, &c. for-* *feits 100 l. to* *the Diſcoverer.*

And where a Popiſh Parent ſhall refuſe a fitting Maintenance for a Proteſtant Child *Popiſh Parent* ſuitable to the Ability of the Parent, the Court of Chancery ſhall make ſuch Order there- *muſt allow fit* in as ſhall be agreeable to the Intent of this Act. *for Proteſtant* *Maintenance*

By the former Statutes, the Papiſts diſabled to preſent to a Living, muſt be *convicted* *Child.* of *Recuſancy,* &c. but now by the Statute 12 *Annæ,* 'tis enacted, That every Papiſt or 12 Ann. ſ. 2 Perſon profeſſing that Religion, and every Child not being a Proteſtant (and under 21 c. 14.
　　　　　　　　　　　　　　　　　　　　　　　　　　　　　Years

Years old) of any Papift, and every Truftee or Mortgagee, or Perfon any ways intrufted by or for any Papifh, fhall be difabled to prefent to any Ecclefiaftical Living, &c. and if he doth every fuch Prefentation, and Admiffion, Inftitution, and Induction thereon fhall be void, and the Univerfities refpectively fhall prefent.

When the Prefentation of a reputed Papift or of his Truftee, or of one who is fuf-pected to be fo, fhall be brought to the Ordinary, he is required to tender fuch Perfon the Declaration againft Tranfubftantiation, if prefent, and if abfent, then the Ordinary fhall by Notice in Writing appoint fome Time and Place for the Perfon to appear before him or before fome Perfon commiffioned by him, and upon fuch Appearance fhall tender the Declaration to him, and if he refufeth to make and fubfcribe it, or to appear upon Notice, &c. fuch Prefentation fhall be void, and the Ordinary fhall, within ten Days af-ter, certify fuch Neglect or Refufal, under the Seal of his Office, to the Vice-Chancellor, &c. to whom fuch Prefentation would belong, if the Patron was a Popifh Recufant, which fhall be vefted in the faid Univerfity for that Turn only.

The Ordinary fhall likewife examine the Prefentee on Oath before he gives Inftitution whether the Perfon who prefented him is the real Patron to the beft of his Knowledge or Belief, or whether he made it in his own Right, or as Truftee for fome other, and for whom, &c. and upon his Refufal to anfwer directly, the Prefentation fhall be void

The Univerfities and their Prefentees or Clerks, may exhibit a Bill in Chancery, for the better Difcovery of fecret Trufts created by Papifts againft the Perfon prefenting, and againft fuch Perfons whom they have Reafon to fufpect to be the Truftees of the Ad-vowfon, or againft any other Perfon who may be able to difcover the fame, and if the Defendants fhall not put in their Anfwer according to the Time allowed by the Court, the Bill fhall be taken *pro confeffo*, and may be given in Evidence againft the Perfon neg-lecting to anfwer his Truftees and Clerks.

Provided that the Defendants having fully anfwered, and not knowing any fuch Truft, fhall have Cofts.

Where any *Quare Impedit* fhall be depending, the Chancellor and Scholars of either Univerfity, or their Clerks, being Plaintiff or Defendant, the Court where 'tis depending, fhall upon Motion make a Rule that the Patron and his Clerk who fhall conteft the Right with the Univerfity, fhall give Satisfaction on Oath, being either examined in Court, or by Commiffion under the great Seal, or upon an Affidavit in Order to difco-ver any fecret Truft relating to the Prefentation, and if upon fuch Examination, &c.

it appears that the Patron is but a Truftee, then they fhall difcover who fuch Perfons are, and where they dwell; and upon Refufal to make fuch Difcovery, they fhall be punifhed for a Contempt; and if fuch Patron or his Clerk difcover fuch Perfon for whom he is Truftee, then the Court fhall make a Rule upon a Motion that the Per-fon for whom he is Truftee, fhall in the faid Court or before Commiffioners, make and fubfcribe the Declaration againft Tranfubftantiation, and give fuch farther Satisfaction on Oath, concerning the Truft, as the Court fhall think fit, upon Pain of incurring a Contempt, and if he refufe to make the faid Declaration, &c. he fhall, in refpect of fuch Prefentation, be taken to be a Popifh Recufant convict.

The Anfwer of fuch Patron and of him for whom he is intrufted, and of his and their Clerks, and their Examinations and Affidavits as aforefaid, taken either by the Court or the Ordinary, fhall be allowed as Evidence againft the Perfon prefenting and his Clerk.

No Difcovery made by fuch Anfwer to a Bill exhibited, or to any Examination, fhall fubject the Perfon making the Difcovery, or not anfwering, to any other Penalty, than the Lofs of the Prefentation.

And no Lapfe fhall incur, or Plenarty be a Bar to any Bill exhibited as aforefaid, till after three Months after the Anfwer is put in, or the Bill taken *pro confeffo*, or the Pro-fecution deferted, fo as fuch Bill is exhibited before any Lapfe incurred.

The *Quare Impedit* muft be brought by the Chancellor and Scholars of, &c. or by their refpective Names of Incorporation.

Where any Truft for a Papift is confeffed or difcovered by any fuch Anfwer or Examination, the Court where 'tis made may inforce the Producing the Deeds relating to the faid Truft, by fuch Methods as they fhall judge proper.

Papifts, or he whofe Parent fhall be a Papift, and having an Eftate or Intereft in any Lands, Tenements, &c. and not having taken the Oaths before the laft Day of *Trinity* Names, &c. 1 Geo. 1. c 55.

Term

Term 1716, fhall take the Oaths appointed by 1 *Geo. cap.* 13. and make and fubfcribe the Declaration againft Tranfubftantiation in one of the Courts at *Weftminfter*, or at the Quarter-Seffions where fuch Lands or Part of them lie on or before 20 *January* 1716, and in Default thereof fhall from Time to Time, within fix Months after they, or any Truftees for them or for their Benefit, fhall be in Poffeffion of the Rents and Profits of any Lands, &c. regifter their Names, and all Lands, Tenements, &c. whereof they, or any in Truft for them, fhall be in Poffeffion, or receive the Rents and Profits ; and *Regifter their Lands.* fhall exprefs in fuch Regifter in what Parifh or Place fuch Lands, &c. lie, and who are the Poffeffors thereof, and what Eftate or Intereft the Perfon regiftring hath therein, and if let, then for what yearly Rent, and if let upon Leafe, then by whom fuch Leafe was made, what Rent referved, and what Fine was paid for the fame, if it was made by himfelf ; or by any Perfon in Truft for him, or he was Party or Privy there-unto ; all which he is to do in a Parchment Book, to be kept by the Clerk of the Peace in the County where the Lands lie.

The Perfon whofe Eftate is regiftred, muft take care that his Name is fubfcribed to *Muft fubfcribe* the Regifter, in the Prefence of two or more Juftices, either by himfelf or by any other *his Name to the Regifter.* whom he fhall impower by a Warrant of Attorney, executed in the Prefence of two or more Witneffes, who fhall prove upon Oath at the Quarter-Seffions the Execution thereof.; and two Juftices then prefent, fhall fubfcribe their Names as Witneffes to every fuch Entry, that the fame was duly made, on Pain of 20 *l.* and the Clerk of the Peace fhall keep Parchment Books, or Rolls, and to make Entries therein upon Requeft of the Party defiring it, and delivering to him the Words in Writing which he defires to be regiftred ten Days before the Quarter-Seffions, where the Entries are to be fubfcribed, and paying for fuch Regiftry 3 *d.* for every 200 Words, and no more, and the Clerk of the Peace fhall keep alphabetical Tables of the Names of the Perfons and Lands regiftred, and may take 4 *d.* for every Search for the Name or Eftate of any Perfon.

The Clerk of the Peace fhall give Copies of fuch Regiftry fubfcribed by himfelf or *Clerk of the* Deputy, to any Perfon defiring the fame, and tendring his Fees, and to examine the *Peace fhall give Copies of* fame for which he fhall have 3 *d.* for every 200 Words, and if he neglect or refufe to *the Regiftring.* do it, he fhall forfeit his Office.

A Perfon required to take the Oaths and to fubfcribe the Declaration, or in Default *Neglecting to* thereof, to regifter his Name and Eftate, as aforefaid, and neglecting or refufing fo to *regifter, or fraudulently* do, or fraudulently regiftring it, fhall forfeit the Inheritance of all his Lands, &c. not *regiftring, for-* regiftred or fraudulently regiftred ; whereof he or fhe, or any Truftee for them were *feits the Inhe-ritance of all* feifed in Fee at that Time, and the full Value of all fuch Lands, &c. not regiftred or *Lands, &c.* fradulently regiftred, of which they were not feifed in Fee, &c. Two Thirds to the *not regiftred.* Crown, the other Third to him (being a Proteftant) who fhall fue for the fame ; and the Perfon fo fuing in Chancery, may demand all fuch Difcoveries as if he was a Pur- *The Perfon fu-ing in Chance-* chafer, to which Bill no Demurrer fhall be allowed, but the Defendant fhall fufficiently *ry may demand* anfwer it, and the Perfon fuing for any fuch real Eftate, may bring an Ejectment upon *a Difcovery as* his own Demife, and give this Act in Evidence, together with the Special Matter ; and *if he was a Purchafer,* if the Defendant fhall not prove that he hath taken the Oaths, or regiftred his Name and *and no De-* Eftate, a Verdict fhall be given for the Leffor of the Plaintiff, with Judgment there- *murrer fhall* on, and full Cofts ; and one Third of the Lands recovered fhall be vefted in him, and *be to the Bill.* the other two Thirds in the Crown.

Provifo that a Purchafer *bona fide* for a valuable Confideration, or a * Mortgagee, ** Like Claufe for a Mortga-* not knowing the Default or Fraud in regiftring by the Seller, and before Conviction, *gee, and that* or any Suit brought for the faid forfeited Lands, fhall not be prejudiced in his Eftate or *the Offender fhall forfeit* Intereft therein, but the Defendant fhall forfeit *the Value of the Inheritance* of fuch Lands, *the Value of the Incum-* to be divided as aforefaid. *brance.*

None fhall be obliged to regifter, until he or his Truftee fhall be actually feifed, or *He who regi-fters muft be* be poffeffed, &c. for fix Months, and have Notice thereof. *actually feifed or poffeffed for fix Months.*

And no Tenant at Rack-Rent, or who fhall hold a Leafe whereupon two Thirds of *Tenant at* the full Value fhall be referved, fhall be compelled to regifter. *Rack Rent, &c. fhall not regifter.*

No Action fhall be brought for not regiftring, &c. above two Years after the Offence *Action for not* committed. *regiftring muft be brought*

within two Years, &c. 3 Geo. 1. c. 18.

Manors, Lands or Farms lying in two Counties. And where any Manors or other Lands or Farms lie in two or more Counties, the Regiftring fhall be in the County where the Manor is, or where the Houfe to the faid Farm doth lie, taking Notice that the fame doth extend to other Counties, and that, and no other, fhall be a fufficient Regiftring.

Sale of a Papift's Lands to a Proteftant Purchafer fhall not be void, &c. No Sale of a Recufant's Lands to a Proteftant Purchafer, or for his Benefit, fhall be avoided, by Reafon of any Difabilities or Incapacities in the Acts 1 *Jac.* 1. or 11-*&* 12 *W.* incurred by the Seller, unlefs before fuch Sale the Perfon intitled to take Advantage of fuch Difabilities fhall have recovered fuch Lands, *&c.* or have given Notice of his Title to fuch Purchafer, or have claimed the Lands before the Contract made for fuch Sale, *&c.* and have entered his Claim in open Court at the Quarter-Seffions where the Lands lie, and have *bona fide* with due Diligence purfued his Remedy to recover the fame.

The Claufe in the Act 11 *&* 12 *W.* by which 'tis enacted, That after 10 *April* 1700 every Papift fhall be difabled to purchafe any Lands, and that all Purchafes made to or for his Ufe, or upon Truft for him, fhould be void, fhall remain in Force.

Rents. (a)

11 G.2. c.19. §. 4. IT frequently happening that Tenants or Leffees of Lands or Tenements, fraudulently or clandeftinely carry off their Goods, to prevent the Landlord from diftraining: For Remedy thereof, it is among other Things enacted by 11 *Geo.* 2. *cap.* 19. That, Where the Goods carried off fhall not exceed the Value of 50 *l.* it fhall be lawful for the Landlord, his Bailiff, Servant or Agent, to exhibit a Complaint in Writing againft fuch Offenders before two Juftices of Peace refiding near the Place, not being interefted in the Tenements, who may fummon the Parties, examine the Fact, and all Witneffes upon Oath, or if Quakers, upon Affirmation; and in a fummary way, determine whether fuch Perfons be guilty of the Offence, and inquire of the Value of the Goods by them fraudulently carried off or concealed; and upon Proof of the Offence, by Order the faid Juftices may adjudge the Offenders to pay double the Value of the Goods to fuch Landlord, his Bailiff, Servant or Agent, as the Juftices fhall appoint; and in cafe the Offenders having Notice of fuch Order fhall neglect fo to do, fhall by Warrant levy the fame by Diftrefs and Sale of Goods; and for want of Diftrefs may commit the Offenders to the Houfe of Correction, to be kept to hard Labour for fix Months, unlefs the Money be fooner fatisfied.

Ib. §. 5. It fhall be lawful for any Perfon aggrieved by fuch Order of the two Juftices to appeal to the next Quarter-Seffions, who fhall hear and determine fuch Appeal, and give Cofts to either Party.

Ib. §. 6. Where the Party appealing fhall enter into a Recognizance with Surety in double the Sum ordered, with Condition to appear at fuch Quarter-Seffions, the Order of the two Juftices fhall not be executed in the mean Time.

Ib. §. 7. Where any Goods fraudulently carried away by any Tenant, his Servant or Agent, or other Perfon affifting, fhall be put in any Place locked up or fecured, fo as to prevent fuch Goods from being feifed for Rent, it fhall be lawful for the Landlord, his Steward, Bailiff, Receiver or other Perfon impowered, to feife for Rent fuch Goods (firft calling to his Affiftance the Conftable, Headborough, Borfholder or other Peace-Officer, of the Place where the fame fhall be fufpected to be concealed, who are required to affift; and in cafe of a Dwelling-Houfe, Oath being alfo made before fome Juftice of Peace of a reafonable Ground to fufpect that fuch Goods are there) in the Day-time to break open fuch Houfe, *&c.* and feife fuch Goods for the Rent, as they might have done if fuch Goods had been put in any open Place.

Ib. §. 16. If any Tenant holding Tenements at a Rack-Rent, or where the Rent referved fhall be full three Fourths of the yearly Value of the Premiffes, who fhall be in Arrear for one Year's Rent, fhall defert the Premiffes, and leave the fame uncultivated or unoccupied, fo as no fufficient Diftrefs can be had to countervail the Arrears; it fhall be lawful for two Juftices of Peace (having no Intereft in the Premiffes) at the Requeft of the Landlord, his Bailiff or Receiver, to go upon and View the fame, and to affix on the moft notorious Part, Notice in Writing, what Day (at the Diftance of fourteen Days at leaft) they will return to take a fecond View; and if upon fuch fecond View the Tenant, or fome Perfon on his Behalf, fhall not appear and pay the Rent in Arrear, or there fhall not be fufficient Diftrefs upon the Premiffes, the Juftices may put the Landlord into

into Poffeffion, and the Leafe to fuch Tenant, as to any Demife therein contained only, fhall become void.

Provided, That fuch Proceedings of the Juftices fhall he examinable into in a fummary Ib. §. 17. Way by the next Juftices of Affife; and if they lie in *London* or *Middlefex*, by the Judges of the Courts of King's Bench or Common Pleas; and if in the Counties Palatine, then before the Judges thereof; and if in *Wales*, before the Courts of Grand Seffions; who are impowered to order Reftitution to be made to fuch Tenant, together with his Cofts to be paid by the Landlord, if they fhall fee caufe for the fame; and in cafe they fhall affirm the Act of the Juftices, to award Cofts not exceeding 5 *l.* for the Appeal.

C H A P. LXXXII.

Riots. Routs.

ANY one Juftice of Peace alone, may ufe Means to prevent a Riot or Rout before it *One Juftice* be done, and to ftay it whilft it is in Doing, and may take and imprifon the Riot-*preventing.* ers, or bind them to their Good Behaviour. But being once done, and committed, one Lamb. 184. Juftice of Peace cannot make Inquiry thereof, nor affefs any Fine, nor award any Pro-34 E.3.1. cefs, nor otherwife punifh it in the Nature of a Riot or a Rout, but only as a Trefpafs Crom. 63. againft the Peace, or upon the Statutes of *Northampton*, or of Forcible Entries; whereof 14 H.7.8.9. fee the Title *Forcible Entry.* Br. Peace 7.

And yet, if one Juftice of Peace, fitting in a judicial Place (as in the Seffions) fhall Crom. 65. fee a Riot, he may command them to be arrefted, and may make a Record there-of, and the Offenders fhall be concluded thereby: But if one Juftice of Peace fhall fee a Riot in another Place, and fhall command them to be arrefted, and fhall make a Record thereof, the Offenders fhall not be concluded thereby, but may traverfe it.

(*a*) And yet the Juftice may record it, and certify the fame to the next Seffions, &c. *Cro.* 41.

(*d*) If a Juftice of Peace will commit a Man, pretending untruly that he did a Riot, Ibid. where he did none, the Party may have an Action of Trefpafs againft him.

(*a*) *Fitz. Juft.* 9. *tamen vide Co.* 8. *fol.* 121. *a.* That the Record of a Force made by a Juftice of Peace is not traverfable, for that he doth it as a Judge; and fo the Juftices Record of a Riot is not traverfable. See *hic poftea*; alfo fee *Br. Judges* 2 & 10. That an Action will not lie againft a Juftice or Judge of Record, & 2 *R.* 3. 10. *hic, c.* 120. *fcil. pro re facta judicialiter.*

(*d*) Every Juftice of Peace (being of and in the County, and having Notice of any *Forfeiture.* Riot, Rout, or unlawful Affembly) ought to have a Care of the Execution of the Sta-Dyer 210. tute made 13 *H.* 4. *cap.* 7. (*viz.* that the Rioters, &c. be arrefted and removed) for if Lamb. 521. that Statute be not executed in every Part thereof, by fome of the Juftices, the two next Juftices of Peace fhall forfeit each of them 100 *l.* and every other Juftice of Peace within that County, in whom there fhall be any Default, fhall be finable.

And therefore every Juftice of Peace of the County, hearing of any Rout, or of any 14 H.7.9. b. Intention of a Riot (without making any Precept, or tarrying for his Fellow Juftice, or for the Sheriff) fhall do well to go himfelf (if he be able) with his Servants, or other Lamb. 185. *Power of the County* (if need be) to the Place where fuch Perfons be affembled, and to fupprefs them, and all fuch as he fhall find and fee riotoufly affembled, (and armed) to Br. Peace 7. arreft them, and to force them to put in Surety for the Peace, or for their Good Beha-Lamb. 79. haviour: And for refufing to give fuch Surety, or in Default of Surety, to imprifon 124. them. And alfo he may take away their Weapons and Armor, and feife and prize them for the King. *Vide* Tit. *Armor* and *Forcible Entry.*

(*a*) So that one Juftice of Peace feeing a Riot may and ought to record it, and to at-tach the Rioters, and to commit them, or bind them over to the Good Behaviour; but he may proceed no further therein. For he cannot *Fine* them without *Inquiry*, which *Fine.* Inquiry muft be by a *Jury*, and before two Juftices of Peace, at any Time within the Month; otherwife, for omitting of attaching or arrefting the Offenders at the firft, the Juftice who faw the Riot is punifhable; but the Inquiry by a Jury muft be within one Month, *fub pœna* 100 *l.* to the two next Juftices, &c. See *hic poftea.*

(*d*) And if the Juftice (being come to the Place) fhall not find the Rioters there, he *Servant.* may leave his Servant with his Warrant in Writing, or without Warrant, to reftrain 14 H.7.10. them, Br. Peace 7.

them, or elfe to arreft fuch Offenders when they fhall come, if they fhall offer to commit any Riot, or to break the Peace.

So if the Juftice be fick, he may fend his Servants, or other Power of the County, if need be, to the Place to reprefs it, or to arreft fuch Offenders, and to bring them before him, to find Sureties for the Peace. And all this he may do, and command by Word of Mouth, without any Warrant in Writing, and without expecting the Coming of any his Fellow Juftices, or of the Sheriff, or Under-Sheriff.

Alfo any one Juftice of Peace (by the firft *Affignavimus* in the Commiffion) may caufe to be kept and put in Execution, all other Statutes made for the repreffing Riots Force and Violence: But therein he muft purfue the Form and Order in fuch Statutes preferibed.

Two Juftices.
13 H. 4. c. 7.
P. 5. But the ordinary Power of punifhing Riots belongeth unto *two Juftices of Peace* at leaft; and therefore the two next Juftices of Peace who dwell neareft in the County where any Riot, Affembly or Rout of People fhall be againft the Law, together with the Sheriff or Under-Sheriff of the County, upon Complaint or other Notice of the Riot, Dy. 210. fhall execute the Statute 13 *H.* 4. 7. (*fc.* all and every Part thereof refpectively, as to them is appointed) every one of them, upon Pain of 100 *l.* And in Default of the two next Juftices, the other Juftices of Peace of and within the County (upon Notice of fuch Crom. 63.
Lamb. 322. Riot) ought to do Execution thereof, every one upon Danger to be fined: But the Penalty of 100 *l.* is only to be laid upon the *two next Juftices.*

(*a*) See the Cafe of *Drayton Baffet, hic antea,* Tit. *Forcible Entry;* where certain Juftices of Peace, who did not dwell neareft to the Place where the Riot was committed, yet were fined upon the Statute 17 *R.* 2. *cap.* 1. But that Riot was notorious, for there were a great Number affembled in the Manor-Houfe of *Drayton Baffet,* who did detain the fame forcibly.

Ex Officio.
Dyer 210. (*d*) And if the Riot, *&c. be great and notorious,* whereof by common Intendment every Perfon may take Knowledge, it is not fafe for the Juftice or Sheriff, *&c.* to expect and ftay till Complaint thereof fhall be made unto them, or that they fhall have Information or Notice given them thereof, left they incur thereby the faid Penalty of 100*l.*

If any one other of the Juftices of the Peace of the County (befides thofe two which are next) fhall execute this Statute, that fhall excufe the two next Juftices, for that the Statute giveth Power herein to all Juftices.

Sheriff.
P. R. 30. If one, or the two next Juftices fhall come, and not the Sheriff or Under-Sheriff, fuch Juftices who come fhall be excufed of the Forfeiture of 100 *l.* but yet if there comes but one Juftice of Peace, he ought to arreft the Rioters, and to remove the Force, and commit or bind over the Rioters; otherwife he is finable, *&c.*

Lamb. 322. And if there fhall be two Juftices prefent, and neither the Sheriff nor Under-Sheriff, yet thofe two Juftices are finable, if they fhall not do all which (without the Sheriff or Under-Sheriff) they are authorifed to do by the Statute.

Lamb. 321. But no Juftice of Peace who dwelleth in another County is bound upon the faid Penalty of 100 *l.* to execute the faid Statute of 13 *H.* 4. although he dwelleth next to the Place where the Riot is, and although he be in Commiffion of the Peace for the County where P. 5. the Riot is; for the Words of the Statute are, *The Juftices which dwell neareft in every County where the Riot fhall be,* and not which dwell neareft to the Place where the Riot fhall be; and yet it is fafe, that fuch Juftice dwelling out of the County, upon Notice of fuch Riot do come into the County, and do his Endeavour to fupprefs the fame Riot, and to execute the Statute, for that he is one of the Juftices of the County.

If the Sheriff or Under-Sheriff do not come, the Juftices ought to fend for them, as Mr. *Marrow* thinketh.

P. R. 30. And fome are of Opinion, that if the Sheriff or Under-Sheriff fhall not come to the Juftices, being fent for to affift them, that then all the Juftices of Peace dwelling near or remote, fhall be excufed of the fame Penalty of 100 *l.* or of any other Penalty or Fine; for that the faid Statute giveth the Sheriff or Under-Sheriff equal Authority, and, Lamb. 322.
Cromp. 63. as it were, join him in Commiffion in the Copulative with the Juftices of Peace. But others are of another Opinion, *viz.* That if the Sheriff or Under-Sheriff fhall not come, yet the Juftices of Peace fhall be fined if they come not and arreft the Rioters, and do not moreover proceed to do therein that which (without the Sheriff or Under-Sheriff) they are in any Way authorized to perform.

*What the Ju-
ftices may do
in the Ab-
fence, &c.*
13 H. 4. 7. Now what the Juftices of Peace may or ought to do therein (by Force of this Statute of 13 *H.* 4. *cap.* 7.) without, or in the Abfence of the Sheriff and Under-Sheriff, is worthy Confideration, as being needful for the Juftices of Peace to know, and fafe for

4

them

them to perform, as well for the fpeedy Preventing of fuch prefent Mifchiefs as may happen by fuch dangerous Affemblies, as alfo for their faving the Penalty of the Law.

But herein I dare not determine, finding that others of good Judgment and Experience) who have written hereof, have feemed to doubt. *Lamb. 313, 322.*

And yet there is no Doubt, but that the Juftices of Peace (without the Sheriff or Under-Sheriff) upon all Riots, may and ought firft to go to the Place, and fuch Rioters as they fhall fee or find riotoufly affembled, they may and ought to arreft, and to take away their Armour and Weapons, and to remove and *commit the Rioters,* or may caufe them *to find Sureties for the Peace or Good Behaviour;* and for want of fuch Sureties, may *commit them to the Gaol.* All which any one Juftice of Peace may do.

Alfo *two Juftices* of Peace after the Riot committed (without the Sheriff or Under-Sheriff) may and ought to inquire of the Riot; and if upon fuch Inquiry the Riot be found, the faid Juftices may *fine and imprifon* the Offenders, as hereafter appeareth. *Inquiry. P. Riots 2. Cromp. 67. b.*

But whether two Juftices of Peace *feeing a Riot,* may record the fame upon their own View, without the *Sheriff or Under-Sheriff,* and thereupon (without any Inquiry) may *fine* them for the fame, and may commit them to Prifon till they have paid the fame Fine, is to be confidered. I know the common Opinion to be, that they cannot record the Riot *(without the Sheriff, or Under-Sheriff)* for, fay they (by the Statute) the Sheriff or Under-Sheriff are affociated to the Juftices of Peace, and have equal Authority with them therein; and then confequently the Juftices of Peace alone upon their own View, without Inquiry, can neither fine them, nor imprifon them for their Fine. *View Sheriff.*

Yet *Fineux,* Chief Juftice, faith, that this * Statute of 13 *H.* 4. was made for the common Profit of the Realm, and for a hafty Remedy, and to avoid a prefent Mifchief like to happen; and therefore fhall be conftrued largely for the common Good, and in Furtherance and Advancement of Expedition of Juftice. *14 H. 7. 9. b. See Co. 10. 103. b. fuch a Matter.* * *Mr. Lamb. thinketh it to be*

the Statute of 34 E. 3. 1. that Fineux *meant, rather than the Statute of 13 H. 4.*

Alfo we fee, that any once Juftice of Peace may do all thefe Things, in Cafe of a *Forcible Entry, &c.* he may come with the *Power of the County,* if need be, and may arreft the Offenders, and may *record the Force by him viewed:* And this Record fhall be a fufficient Conviction, fo that he may thereupon commit the Offenders to the Gaol, and may *fine* them. *21 P. 6. f. 5.*

Alfo this Statute of 13 *H.* 4. doth relate to the faid Statute of Forcible Entries, 8 *H.*6. touching the Conviction of Offenders by the Record of the Juftices. *P. 1.*

Alfo by fome good Authorities, if two Juftices of Peace (without the Sheriff) fhall fee a Riot, they may arreft them and make a Record thereof, and the Offenders fhall be concluded by fuch Record, for that the *View of the Riot is not to be traverfed.* Lamb. 313. *Fitz. Juft. 9. 17. 13 H. 7. 3. Cromp. 65, 196.*

Alfo the Statute of 34 *E.* 3. 1. makes *two Juftices of Peace* to imprifon and fine Rioters, and that *without Inquiry,* and then confequently, it feemeth they are to make a Record of the Riot. See *Lamb.* 291, 292. *P. Juft. 11. 34 Ed. 3. c. 1.*

Ideo quære, Whether two Juftices of Peace (upon the Statute of 13 *H.* 4. 7.) without the Sheriff, may not, nay ought not, upon the Penalty of 100 *l.* upon their View of a Riot, record the Riot, and fine the Offenders, and imprifon them till they have paid their Fine (as Convict by their View and Record) which alfo feems to be more for the King's Advantage than to hazard the Fine upon finding it by Inquiry.

(*a*) But it rather feemeth, that the Juftices upon their own View of a Riot, may record it, and commit the Offenders, and then to certify or fend the Record into the King's Bench, where the Offenders fhall be fined. And this I take to be more warrantable, and fafer for the Juftices, if they fhall not inquire thereof.

(*d*) And now to the Particulars of that which the *two next Juftices,* with the *Sheriff* or *Under-Sheriff,* muft do in Execution of this Statute of 13 *H.* 4. 7. every one upon Pain of 100 *l.* *Two Juftices and the Sheriff.*

1. Firft, They fhall go to the Place in *Perfon,* if they be able, where the Riot, *&c.* fhall be. *To go in Perfon with Poffe Comitatus.*

2. And they fhall take the *Power of the County* (if need be) *&c.* they fhall have the Aid of all Knights, and other temporal Perfons under that Degree, that be *above the Age of fifteen Years,* and be able to travel: For all the King's Subjects that are in the County where a Riot, *&c.* fhall be, being able to travel, muft be aiding and affiftant to the *Juftices of Peace, Sheriff, or Under-Sheriff,* (or other Commiffioners) when they fhall be reafonably warned to ride or go with the faid Juftices and the Sheriff, *&c.* in Aid to refift

fuch Riots, &c. upon Pain of *Imprifonment*, and to make Fine and Ranfom to the King; which Ranfom fhall be treble fo much at the leaft as the Fine. *Dyer* 232.

Ranfom.
2 H. 5. 8.
P. 12.
Fine and Ran-
fom.
Lamb. 309.
Cromp. 64.

Lamb. 310.
Cromp. 62.

Arreft.

Mar. Lee. 8.
Cromp. 63.

Record.

Lamb. 312.

Efcape.

Certificate.

Good Behavi-
our.
13 H. 7.
Cromp. 196.

34 E. 3. c. 1.
P. Juft. 18.

Refiftance.
Lamb. 310.
Cromp. 62,
158.

(a) Yet by others, by Ranfom, is intended, that the Party is to make his Agreement with the King, *Ad verum valorem omnium bonorum fuorum mobilium*; but Sir *Edward Coke*, *L.* 127. faith, that in legal Underftanding, a Fine and Ranfom are all one.

(d) But it is referred to the Difcretion of thefe Juftices, how many, or few, they will have to attend them in thefe Bufineffes; and in what Sort they fhall be armed, weaponed, or otherwife furnifhed for it.

Again, it is not good for the Juftices to affemble the *Power of the County*, without certain Information, or Knowledge of fuch riotous Affembly; yet if upon falfe Information of a Riot to be at fuch a Place, the Juftices fhall caufe the *Power of the County* to be affembled, the Juftices fhall be excufed by Reafon of the Information; and if without Information, the Juftices fhall think that fuch a riotous Affembly is made in fuch a Place, and fhall affemble the *Power of the County* to go thither and arreft the Riot-ers, and when they come to the Place they find a Riot there indeed, they muft arreft and imprifon the Offenders, and fhall be excufed of the Affembly made by them: But if they fhall find no Riot there, then fhall they be punifhed for making fuch an Affembly of their own Heads, without Information.

3. All fuch Offenders as they fhall find there prefent, they fhall arreft them, or caufe them to be arrefted, and fhall remove the Force, *&c.* fhall commit to Prifon all the Rioters, and take away their Weapons.

Alfo all fuch as came in Company with fuch Rioters, or in the Company of any of them, if the Juftices fhall find them there prefent, though they do nothing, and though they came without any Intent to commit any Riot, yet they fhall be arrefted, imprifon-ed and fined. See to this Purpofe in the Title *Forcible Entry.*

Alfo all fuch Rioters as the Juftices fhall meet in their Way (riotoufly arrayed, and coming from the Place) they may arreft and imprifon them, for that they found them unlawfully affembled; but they cannot record any Riot by them done, for that they *faw it not*, yet they muft afterward *inquire thereof by a Jury*, that fo the Offenders may be fined, *&c.* See more in this Title.

But if the Juftices do *fee the Riot committed*, and after the faid Rioters fhall efcape at that Time, yet the faid Juftices fhall record it; but they cannot arreft them at any other Time, except it be prefently after, and in frefh Suit; neither can they fine the Of-fenders, nor award any Procefs againft them upon that Record which they fhall make, and yet for that they faw the Riot (and thefe Rioters that be efcaped, committing the Riot) they fhall record it. But that Record fhall not be kept amongft the Records of the Peace, but the faid Juftices fhall fend the faid Record to the King's Bench, that Pro-cefs may from thence be made upon it, againft thofe Rioters that efcaped; where alfo the faid Offenders fhall not be admitted to any *Traverfe*, but muft of Neceffity make Fine for their faid Offences.

(a) If after the Juftices and Sheriff fhall *fee the Riot*, the faid Rioters fhall efcape, and the Juftices and Sheriff fhall record the fame Riot, and then one of the Juftices be put out of the Commiffion; or the Sheriff, or one of the Juftices fhall happen to die, yet fhall that Record be fent or certified into the King's Bench, by the other Juftice and She-riff. *Lamb.* 320.

But if (after the Inquiry, and before the Certificate) the Sheriff, or the Juftices fhall die, or be put out of the Commiffion, or that their Authority doth ceafe by the Death of the King, or otherwife, fuch Record cannot be certified without the King's Writ of *Cer-tiorari*. *Br. Record.* 17. 64. and *Lamb.* 320.

(d) Alfo fuch Offenders, as the Juftices faw committing the Riot, though they fhall efcape from the Juftices, yet the faid Juftices may after grant out their Warrants for them, and fend them to the Gaol, till they fhall find Surety for their Good Be-haviour.

If fuch Offenders fhall depart before the Coming of the Juftices, (yet upon certain Infor-mation of their being there) the faid Juftices may alfo grant out their Warrants for them, and may commit them, till they find Sureties for their Good Behaviour: Or rather the Juftices fhall do well to proceed againft them, by *Inquiry*, and fo to *fine* the Offenders for the King, *&c.* . See more in this Title.

Alfo in the Execution of this Arreft of the Rioters, the faid Juftices, *&c.* may juftify the *Beating*, *Wounding*, or *Killing* of any of the Rioters that fhall refift them, or that will not yield themfelves to them. *Vide* Tit. *Homicide*, bis.

Alfo

Alſo the ſaid Juſtices may take from ſuch Rioters their Armour and Weapons, and *Armour.* ſhall cauſe the ſame to be priſed and anſwered to the King, as forfeited.

4. After the Arreſt made, the ſaid Juſtices, and Sheriff or Under-Sheriff, ſhall make a *Record.* Record in Writing of the ſaid Riot (*ſcil.* of all that which they ſhall ſee, and find done 13 H. 4. c. 7. in their Preſence againſt the Law) without any other *Inquiry.* p. 1.

(*a*) If two Juſtices of Peace ſhall *ſee any making a Riot*, they may command others to *View.* arreſt the Rioters, and then make their Record thereof, and the Offenders ſhall be con- cluded thereby. *Fitz. Juſt. of Peace, fol.* 17.

(*d*) But if the Juſtices of Peace do not themſelves *ſee the Riot*, they cannot make a Record thereof; but then they muſt *inquire thereof.*

If the Juſtices of Peace, *&c.* going to ſee a Riot, another Riot ſhall happen in their Preſence; they may record this, and arreſt and impriſon the Offenders.

So if the Rioters ſhall make a Riot upon the Juſtices (and Sheriff) that do come to ar- *Other Riot.* reſt them for their former Riot, they may record that alſo.

So if two Juſtices of Peace (and the Sheriff or Under-Sheriff) ſhall meet for any other Cauſe, or for any private Buſineſs (as upon an Arbitrament, or other like Matter,) and a Riot ſhall happen to be done upon themſelves, or in their Sight, they may record it, and may arreſt and impriſon the Offenders.

And if the Juſtices of Peace ſhall record a Riot, and upon Examination of the Matter *Concluſion.* after, it ſhall appear to be no Riot; or that they ſaw it not, or that there was no Riot at 9 H. 6. all; yet the Parties ſhall be concluded thereby, and have no Remedy, and therefore the fol. 60. Juſtices ſhall do well to be adviſed what they record. See *9 H. 6. f. 60. Br. Judges* 2. 65. Cromp. 63. *Fitz. Juſt. of P. f.* 17.

And again, for that this *Record of the Juſtices and Sheriff*, is a *ſufficient Conviction in* Lam. 311. *it ſelf* againſt the Offenders, therefore it ought to be formal and certain as well for the *Time and Place*, as alſo for the *Number, Weapons, Manner*, and *other Circumſtances*, be- cauſe the Parties be concluded thereby, and ſhall not be received to *Traverſe*, or deny it in any Point.

The Form of the Record *vide* Tit. *Precedents.*

This Record ought to remain with one of the ſaid Juſtices of Peace; and ſhall not be Lam. 312 & left amongſt the Records of the Seſſions of the Peace, it being made out of the Seſſions, 365, 375. and not appointed to be certified thither.

5. Alſo the ſaid Juſtices of Peace (and none other) ſhall commit ſuch Offenders *to the Impriſonment.* Gaol, there to remain convict *by their View*, Teſtimony and Record, (as in Caſe of *Gaol.* Forcible Entry) until they have paid a *Fine* to the King. P. 1. 11.
Lam. 312.
Alſo ſuch Commitment of the Offenders to the Gaol ought to be done preſently. Co. 8. 120.

And the *Power of the County* ought to be aiding to the Sheriff or Under-Sheriff, for Lam. 310. the conveying of them to the Gaol.

If the Juſtices of Peace, and Sheriff or Under-Sheriff, ſhall record the Riot, and ſhall Cromp. 61. not preſently commit the Rioters to Priſon; or if they ſhall commit them to Priſon, and P. Force 2. ſhall not record the Riot, they ſhall forfeit every of them 100 *l.* by the Statute of 13 *H.* P. Riots 1. 4. for that they have not done Execution of the ſame Statute: For by the Statutes they ſhall record and commit; and again, by the ſame Statutes the Offenders muſt be as well impriſoned as fined.

6. Alſo the ſaid Juſtices of Peace (and none other) ſhall aſſeſs the Fines upon the ſaid *Fine.* Offenders; for they have beſt Knowledge of the Matter, *&c. Co.* 8. 41. *a.* Which Lam. 312. Fines by the Stat. of 2 *H.* 5. 8. ought to be of good Value, that out thereof the Charges 557. Cro. 161. of the ſaid Juſtices and other Officers may be born, *ſc.* their Charges in going, tarrying and returning, *&c.* about the Suppreſſing and Inquiry of ſuch Riots; of which Charges Payment ſhall be made by the Sheriff, by Indenture thereof made between him and the ſaid Juſtices.

And yet ſuch Fines muſt be reaſonable and juſt, and *ſecundum quantitatem & qualita-* *Fines.* *tem delicti*, and not unreaſonable and exceſſive (for *exceſſus in re qualibet jure reprobatur communi, Co.* 11. 44.) And ſo it is commanded by the Statutes 18 *E.* 3. 2. and 34 *E.* 3. 1. *P. Juſt.* 1. *& 18.*

Note alſo, that the Fine aſſeſſed in this, and ſuch like Caſes, muſt not be impoſed up- on all the Offenders *jointly*, but muſt be aſſeſſed upon every Offender *ſeverally. Co.* 11. 43, 44.

(*a*) And yet note, that in ſome Caſes a Fine or an Amercement ſhall be impoſed upon *divers jointly*; (*ſc.* ſometimes upon a *whole County*, ſometimes upon a *Hundred*, and ſometimes *upon a Town*, as for an Eſcape of a Murderer, *&c.* whereof ſee *hic poſt.*) but that

that is by Reafon of the Incertainty of the Perfons, and for the Infinitenefs of their Number. *Co.* 11. 43.

Eftreats.   (*d*) And the faid Juftice fhall caufe the faid Fine to be eftreated into the *Exchequer*, that fo the faid Fines may be levied to the King's Ufe; and then they are to deliver the Offenders again : Or elfe the faid Juftices may record fuch Riot by them viewed, and commit the Offenders, and after certify the Record to the Affizes or Seffions, or into the *King's Bench*, as in Cafe of Forcible Entry.

Inquirers.   7. But if the Riot was not committed in the *Prefence of the faid Juftice* ; or that the
13 H. 4. 7. Offenders be *departed before the coming of the faid Juftices, and Sheriff or Under-Sheriff*,
p. 2. then the faid Juftices, or two of them at the leaft, *within one Month*, immediately after
* *Who fhall re-* fuch Riot, Affembly, or Rout, fhall *inquire* thereof by the Oaths of a fufficient *Jury* to
turn upon every be returned by the Sheriff. * And the fame Riot, &c. being found by fuch Inquifition,
Perfon fo by the Juftices muft make or caufe to be made a Record in Writing, of fuch their Inquiry
him impanelled or Prefentment found before them ; which Record alfo is to remain with one of the faid
in Iffues at the Juftices. *P. R.* 29.
firft Day, 20 s.
at the fecond
40 s.

    The Form of fuch Inquiry or Prefentment. See alfo the Title *Precedents, hic poftea.*

Cromp. 62.   This *Inquiry* fhall not be, but where the *Rioters are gone* before the coming of the Juftices.

    It is not neceffary that one of the Juftices of Peace (which fhall make Inquiry of a Riot) be of the *Quorum.*

Lam. 316.   Although the Words of the Statute are, the fame Juftices (*fc.* which came to fee the Riot) fhall inquire ; yet if any other two Juftices of Peace of that County fhall do it, that will fuffice.

    Alfo the Juftices of Peace although they go not to fee the Riot, yet they may *inquire* thereof *within the Month* after.

Time.   Neither is it of fuch Neceffity, to have the Inquiry within the Month, that for De-
Lam. 317. fault thereof the Prefentment fhall be void; for the Juftices of Peace may inquire thereof at any Time by Force of their Commiffion ; but if it be not within the Month, then every of the two next Juftices are in Danger to lofe 100 *l.* for it. And yet if thefe Juftices do charge the Jury within the Month, and do give Day unto them to yield their Verdict and Prefentment after the Month, the Statute is not offended.

    (*a*) But yet it feemeth that the Juftices of the Peace are not bound upon the Penalty of 100 *l.* to inquire *within the Month* of all *Petty Riots*, but only of fuch Riots as are *notorious and dangerous*, and in the Nature of *Infurrections or Rebellions.*

Sheriff.   (*d*) At this Inquiry, the Sheriff or Under-Sheriff ought to be prefent with the Juftices
Lam. 316, of Peace, as Minifters only for the Returning the Jury, and be not herein affociated
318. with the Juftices, as they were before in arrefting the Rioters, and recording their Dif-
order : But by their Prefence, they may help to efpy the Evil ; and befides, it addeth Force and Credit to the Certificate.

Ex Officio.   If the Juftices do affemble themfelves, the Sheriff and the Jury, to make Inquiry of a
Lam. 317. Riot within the Month, and the Parties be agreed amongft themfelves ; fo as none will
Crom. 62. follicite the Inquiry, nor give in Evidence for the King upon that Riot, yet ought the
P. R. 29. Juftices to proceed (*Ex Officio*) to make Inquiry of that Riot, feeing it may be that fome of the Jury may have Knowledge of it.

Evidence.   And alfo the Juftices ought to make Proclamation, That if any Man will give Evidence for the King concerning that Riot, or (generally) will inform the King's Juftices of any Riots, Routs, &c. And thereupon fome other Perfons may perhaps come forth to inform him therein.

P. R. 29.   But if (at the Party's Requeft) the Juftices fhall difmifs the Jury without Inquiry,
Crom. 62. they are finable.

    And if the Juftices fhall not proceed herein (*Ex Officio*) without fome Evidence for the King ; *quære*, if they fhall not be hereby in Danger to lofe the hundred Pounds upon this Statute, for the Reafons abovefaid.

Complaints   And it feemeth, that the Juftices of Peace may juftly bind to their Good Behaviour,
without Caufe. the Parties that firft complained to them of this Riot, and have caufed them to meet, and now will not profecute the fame for the King, but have agreed it.

Hear and de-   After fuch *Inquiry* had, and the Truth of the Riot found, the faid Juftices have Au-
termine. thority (by the faid Statute) to hear and determine the fame according to the Law, *viz.* They
13 H. 4. c. 7. may make out Procefs againft the Offenders under their own *Tefte* (thereby to caufe the
p. 2.
Lam. 317.   4   Offen-

Offenders to come in and anfwer) and upon their Appearance the faid Juftices may affefs the Fine, and may commit them to Prifon till they have paid it, and may deliver them after Payment, or upon Sureties taken for it (which Sureties ought to be bound by Recognizance;) or otherwife they may receive their Traverfe, and thereupon (if the Matter will fo ferve) to difcharge and difmifs them : But then the faid Juftices fhall do well to fend fuch Indictment or Inquifition found (and fuch Traverfe) to the next Quarter-Seffions, or into the *King's Bench*, and there the Traverfe fhall be tried and determined according to Law. *P. R.* 30.   Br. Imp. 100.

(a) Note, that all *Indictments, Inquifitions* or *Prefentments*, taken and found before *Juftices of Peace*, of any *Riot*, *Forcible Entry*, or other Thing againft the Peace, may be delivered into the *King's Bench*, by the Hands of the fame Juftices of Peace, before whom the fame was found, or otherwife may be removed from the faid Juftices of Peace, before the Juftices of the *King's Bench*, by a *Certiorari :* In both which Cafes the Juftices of the *King's Bench* may proceed to hear and determine the fame.   *Removal.*

Now by the Statute made 2 *H.* 5. *cap.* 8. the King is to bear the Charges of the Juftices of Peace, which fhall execute the Statute of Riots. And therefore,   2 H. 5. c. 8.

Concerning the Fine fo affeffed by the Juftices of Peace, they may thereout pay the Charges of the faid Juftices, and of the Jury (who made the Inquiry, and by whom the Riot was found) *fc.* For their Diet, and the Sheriff's Fees, *&c.* And then they may bring the Record of this Inquiry to the next Quarter-Seffions, and there deliver the fame to the Clerk of the Peace, together with the Refidue of the Money remaining of the Fine, *&c.*   *Charges.*

Alfo the Clerk of the Juftice who maketh up the Record of this Inquiry, may have his Fees out of that Money ; or elfe he may take of every Offender twelve Pence, when they have paid their Fine: For fo the Clerks of the Peace ufe to do.

Or rather the faid Juftices are to be paid their Charges by the Sheriff, by Indentures made between him and the faid Juftices ; whereof the Sheriff, upon his Account in the Exchequer, may have due Allowance. 2 *H.* 5. *cap.* 8.   *The Juftices Charges.*

(d) But when Men are indicted for Riots (or the like) they will ufually yield themfelves, and pray to be admitted to their Fine (in which Cafe the Juftices of Peace commonly do affefs but fome fmall Sum or Fine) and upon the Payment thereof, do difcharge the Offender ; and hereby the Offenders are not imprifoned, (which would work more Fear in fuch Offenders, than fuch Fine) and therefore it is behoveful for the Juftices of Peace to ufe good Care and Difcretion herein ; for by the Statute 2 *H.* 5. *cap.* 8. the Offenders are as well to be *imprifoned as fined*, and this is much more ferviceable, and more agreeing with the Intent of the Law. Befides, this Fine is called in divers Places in the * old Statute, (*Ranfom*, or *Redemptio* in Latin) and feemeth by the Propriety of this Word to imply, That the Offenders ought firft to be imprifoned, and then to be ranfomed, and delivered in Confideration of this Fine.   *Fine.*
Lam. 559.
* Marlb. c. 1,
2, 3, 4.
Ranfom,what.
See Mir. of
Juft. l. 3.

And the Juftices of Peace are injoined by the Statute (2 *H.* 5. *cap.* 8.) to put in greater Sums in thefe Fines than they were wont in fuch Cafes, for the bearing of the Charges of the Juftices and other Officers, *&c.* as is before faid.

At the Common Law, a *Riot* was punifhable as a *Trefpafs*, and as well the *Fine*, as the *Imprifonment* were at the Difcretion of the Judges; and in the fame Manner the Statute of 13 *H.* 4. inabled the Juftices of Peace to punifh fuch Offenders. But now as well the Imprifonment, as the Fine of fuch Offenders are to be increafed by the faid Statute 2 *H.* 5. *cap.* 8.

And therefore where the Juftices of Peace are remifs herein (*fcil.* in not fufficiently punifhing fuch Offenders by due *Fine and Imprifonment*) the Lords in the * *Star-chamber* have often affeffed upon Rioters for the fame Riot (for which the Juftices of Peace have formerly affeffed a Fine in the Country) a greater Penalty, if they fee Caufe: And yet in this Cafe the Offenders are not twice punifhed for one Offence, but that one Part of the due Punifhment is inflicted at one Time, and Part at another.   Crom. 63.
P. R. 34.
* The Court of
King's Bench
hath the fame
Power, the
other Court be-
ing abolifhed.

8. Laftly, if the Truth of a Riot cannot be found by the Juftices of Peace upon fuch Inquiry, being hindred by the *Perverfenefs* of the *Jurors*, or by the unlawful *Maintenance, Countenance*, or *Embracery of others*, then within one Month next after the Inquiry, the fame Juftices, and Sheriff and Under-Sheriff, fhall certify before the King and his Council, or into the * *King's Bench*, the whole Fact and Circumftances thereof, with the Certainty of the Names of the principal Offenders, and of the Names of fuch *Maintainers* and *Embracers*, with their Mifdemeanors; and of the *Time, Place and other Circumftances*, and Impediments, yet the not certifying of the Maintenance or Embracery, is but a Forfeiture   *Certificate.*
13 H. 4. 7.
19 H. 7. 13.
P. 3. 15.
Lam. 319.
* Br. Præmu-
nire 1.
Cromp. 63.

K k k

feiture of 20 *l.* a-piece, to every of the Juſtices and Sheriff; the not certifying the reſt, i:
a Forfeiture of 100 *l. Cromp.* 63. *b. &* 199. *b.*

Lam. 318.

The End of this Certificate is but only to force the Offenders to anſwer thereto before the King and his Council: And though the Words of the Statute make this Certificate to be of the Force of a *Preſentment* of twelve Men againſt the Offenders; yet ſuch

* But ſuch Tra- Certificate is no Conviction, but that the Offenders may * traverſe it, by the Words of the
verſe and Cer- ſame Statute. And ſo this Certificate is in Nature of a *Declaration,* or Indictment at the
tificate ſhall be Common Law; and therefore it ought to comprehend the Certainty of the *Time, Place,*
ſent into the
King's Bench, *Perſons,* and other material Circumſtances.
and there be
tried. P. 3.

If this Certificate be not made within *one Month after the Inquiry,* then it is not according to the Statute, and ſo not good to force the Offenders to anſwer.

If two Juſtices, and the Sheriff, ſhall ſee a Riot, yet any other two Juſtices of the
County *may make the Inquiry,* and then they all together, or the firſt Two; or the laſt
Two (with the Sheriff or Under-Sheriff) may make *Certificate* thereof within the Month
after that Inquiſition taken.

Lam. 320. Where there be ſeveral Certificates made, or that the Certificate and the Inquiry do diſ-
Cromp. 63. agree, then that ſhall be preferred which is beſt for the King.

If there ſhall be twenty Perſons in a Riot, and the Jury ſhall find but ten of them
guilty, yet the Juſtices may certify that twenty committed that Riot; and this Certificate
ſhall ſtand good.

Alſo if any Thing material ſhould be omitted, or left out of the Inquiſition, yet it
may be ſupplied by this Certificate; and it ſhall ſtand good.

Lam. 320. If after the *Inquiry,* and before the *Certificate* made, the Sheriff ſhall die, or one of
the Juſtices be put out of the Commiſſion, no Certificate can then be made, by the Opinion of M. *Marrow.* But *quære,* if the Reſidue ſhall not do well to certify, in Regard of
the Penalty.

For the Form of ſuch Certificate, ſee Tit. *Precedents.*

Commiſſion out Upon the Default of the *two next Juſtices, Sheriff* or *Under-Sheriff* for not executing
of Chancery. the ſaid Satute of 13 *H.* 4. 7. the Party grieved may have *Commiſſion out of the* Chancery
2 H. 5. 8. to inquire as well of the Riot, as of the Default of the ſaid *Juſtices,* and *Sheriff* or
P. 6. *Under-Sheriff.*

2 H. 5. 8. Alſo the Lord Chancellor of *England,* if he ſhall have Notice of ſuch a Riot, ſhall
P. 9. ſend the King's Writ to the Juſtices and Sheriff, commanding them to execute the ſaid
Statute of 13 *H.* 4.

And although that ſuch Writ come not to the ſaid Juſtices, Sheriff or Under-Sheriff,
yet they ſhall not be excuſed of the Penalty of 100 *l.* aforeſaid, if they make not Execution of the ſaid Statute. *Ibid.*

Capias. Alſo, if any Aſſemblies of People in great Number, in Manner of Inſurrection, or other
2 H. 5. c. 9. rebellious Riots, ſhall be done and committed, and that ſuch Offenders ſhall withdraw
8 H. 6. c. 14. themſelves, to avoid the Execution of the Law, then upon Certificate by two Juſtices of
Raſt. 374. Peace, and the Sheriff of that County, by Letters under their Seals to the Lord Chancellor of *England,* of the ſame Riot, and that the common Voice and Fame thereof runneth
in the ſaid County, the Lord Chancellor may make a *Capias* to the ſaid Sheriff, for the
apprehending ſuch Offenders; and after, if need be, a *Proclamation,* That the ſaid Offenders yield themſelves in the *King's Bench,* at a certain Day, upon Pain to be convict
thereof.

Corporation. (*a*) Note, That for Riots in Cities or Corporations which are armed with Power of Government within themſelves, the Franchiſes may be ſeiſed, or the Corporation fined, as it
happened in the Caſe of the Riot where Dr. *Lamb* was ſlain; the City of *London* upon an
Information in the *King's Bench,* was fined 1000 Marks. *Paſch.* 8 *Car.* 1. See more *Chap.*
135, 136.

1 G. 1. c. 5. Where Twelve, or more, are unlawfully, riotouſly and tumultuouſly aſſembled toge-
§. 1. ther to the Diſturbance of the Peace, and being required by a Juſtice, Sheriff or Under-
Sheriff, Mayor, or other Head Officer, by Proclamation in the King's Name (herein after
mentioned) to diſperſe themſelves, and ſhall to the Number of Twelve, or more, unlawfully, riotouſly, and tumultuouſly continue together one Hour, they ſhall be adjudged
guilty of Felony without Benefit of Clergy.

Ib. §. 2. The Juſtice, Sheriff, or other Head Officer, ſhall come as near the Rioters as he can
with Safety, and with a loud Voice command Silence whilſt the Proclamation is making,
and h n read or cauſe it to be read in theſe Words, or to the like Effect.

4　　　　　　　　　　　　　　　　　　　　　　　　　　　ſſ. *Our*

ff. **O**UR *Sovereign Lord the King chargeth and commandeth all Perſons being aſſembled,* *The Proclama-*
    immediately to diſperſe themſelves, and peaceably to depart to their Habitations or *tion.*
lawful Buſineſs, upon Pain contained in the Act made in the firſt Year of King George,
for preventing Tumults and Riotous Aſſemblies.

God ſave the King.

If after Proclamation made the Offenders ſhall continue together one Hour, and not *Ib. §. 3.*
diſperſe themſelves, it ſhall be lawful for any Juſtice, *&c.* or other Peace Officer, and all
Perſons whom they ſhall command, to aſſiſt them to apprehend ſuch Offenders and carry
them before a Juſtice of Peace ; and where any of them are killed in reſiſting the
Perſon endeavouring to apprehend them, that Perſon ſhall be indemnified in ſo doing. *Pulling down*
    Any Rioters demoliſhing or pulling down, or beginning to demoliſh, *&c.* any Church, *any Place of*
Chapel or Building for Religious Worſhip, certified and regiſtred according to the Sta- *Religious Wor-*
tute 1 *W. & M. cap.* 18. or any Dwelling-houſe, Barn, Stable or Out-houſe, ſhall be *ſhip,* &c.
a Felon without Benefit of Clergy. *Ib. §. 4.*
    Any Perſon with Force wilfully obſtructing another to make Proclamation, whereby *Obſtructing the*
ſuch Proclamation ſhall not be made, ſhall be a Felon without Benefit of. Clergy ; and *Reading of the*
Rioters knowing ſuch Hindrance and Obſtruction, and continuing together to the Num- *Proclamation.*
ber of Twelve or more afterwards, for the Space of an Hour, ſhall be Felons without Be- *Ib. §. 5.*
nefit of Clergy.
    Where any Building is demoliſhed in Part or in Whole by the Rioters, the Inhabitants *Buildings de-*
of the Hundred ſhall anſwer the Damages to the Perſons injured, to be recovered in the *moliſhed, the*
Courts at *Weſtminſter* againſt any two or more of the Inhabitants thereof, to be levied *Hundred ſhall*
and paid in ſuch Manner as provided by the Statute 27 *Eliz. cap.* 13. And if the Ac- *Damages.*
tion is brought for Damages done to a Church or Chapel, it muſt be in the Name of *Ib. §. 6.*
the Rector, Vicar, or Curate, and when recovered, it muſt be applied to the Rebuilding
or Repairing ſuch Church.
    This Act ſhall be read at every Seſſion and every Leet. *Ib. §. 7.*
    Proſecutions upon this Act muſt be commenced within one Year after the Offence *Proſecution*
committed. *muſt be within*
    a Year.

See alſo Chap. 183. infra.

Ib. §. 8.

C H A P. LXXXIII.
Rogues and Vagabonds.

(*a*)**T**HE Laws relating to Rogues and Vagabonds, *viz.* 39 *Eliz. cap.* 4. 1 *Jac.* 1.
    cap. 7. and ſo much of the 7 *Jac.* 1. *cap.* 4. as relates to a Privy Search, as alſo
the 12 *Ann. ſt.* 2. *cap.* 23. mentioned in the former Editions of this Book, being now repealed by 13 *Geo.* 2. *cap.* 24. and the Laws relating to Vagabonds reduced into one Act,
and many Doubts and Difficulties being thereby cleared, it will be ſufficient to give an Abſtract of this Statute, for which the Reader is deſired to turn to Chapter 196, where he
will alſo find the 14 *Geo.* 2. *cap.* 33. for providing Houſes of Correction and paſſing
Rogues and Vagabonds.
    Note, That by 6 *Geo.* 1. *cap.* 19. Juſtices of Peace may commit Vagrants and other *6 G. 1. c. 19.*
Criminal Perſons charged with ſmall Offences, either to the Common Gaol or Houſe *§. 2.*
of Correction, as they ſhall think proper.

See alſo Chap. 53. Tit. Houſe of Correction, and Chap. 73. Tit. Poor.

C H A P.

C H A P. LXXXIV.

Robbery.

One Justice.
27 El. 13.
P. Hue &
Cry 8, 10.
Co. 7. 7.

AFTER a Robbery committed, the Party shall not have his Action upon the Statute against the Hundred, except he shall with all Speed convenient give Notice of the said Robbery to some of the Inhabitants dwelling in some Town, Village, or Hamlet, near to the Place where such Robbery was committed; and also except he shall commence his Action within one Year next after such Robbery committed; and also except he shall first be examined upon his Oath within twenty Days next before such Action brought, by some one Justice of Peace (of the County where the Robbery was committed) dwelling within or near to the said Hundred where the Robbery was done, whether he doth know the Parties that committed the said Robbery, or any of them: And if he knoweth any of them, then also (before such Action brought) he shall be bound before the same Justices by Recognizance, to prosecute effectually the said Offenders by Indictment or otherwise, according to the due Course of Law.

27 El. 13.
P. Hue &
Cry 4, 5. After a Robbery committed, and Notice thereof given, as aforesaid, the whole Hundred must answer the Loss, if the Robbers be not taken within forty Days.

Stat. Winton.
13 Ed.1. St.2. (*a*) And if the Robbery be done in the Division of two Hundreds; both the Hundreds, and the Franchises within them, shall be answerable for the Robbery done, and also for the Damages.

Contribution.
27 El. 13. (*d*) And yet because the Party robbed hath his Recovery and Execution against *some one or few Persons of that Hundred,* therefore for Contribution to be yielded from the Residue of the said Hundred, upon Complaint made by the Parties against whom such Recovery and Execution is had; any two Justices of Peace (the one being of the *Quorum*) being of the same County, and inhabiting in or near the said Hundred where such Execution shall be had, may assess and tax according to their Discretions, proportionably all and every the Towns, Parishes, and Hamlets, as well of the same Hundred (where the said Robbery was committed) as also of the Liberties within the said Hundred, towards an equal Contribution to be had for the Relief of the Parties charged: The which Money the Constables of every Town shall levy and deliver over to the same Justices, or to one of them within ten Days after Collection. And which the said Justices shall deliver over (upon Request) to the Parties charged, to whose Use the same was collected.

(*a*) Note, A Person coming to *inhabit after the Robbery and Judgment* given is not chargeable to be taken in Execution; and so was the Opinion of the Court in one *Dean*'s Case, *Mich.* 10 *Car.* in the Common Bench.

But a Person coming *after* thither to inhabit is assessable, because the Country is chargeable at the Time of the Assessment, and not the Persons which were there at the Time of the Robbery committed, as Justice *Barkley* said, and the Court seemed to agree in Sir *Jo. Compton*'s Case, *Pasf.* 15 *Car.* in the King's Bench. *Quære* the Difference.

Note, That the Inhabitants of any other Hundred (within the same County where the Robbery was committed, or within any other County, with the Franchises within the Precincts of such Hundred) wherein Negligence, Fault or Defect of Pursuit, and fresh Suit after Hue and Cry made, shall happen to be, shall answer and satisfy the one Moiety of all and every such Sums of Money and Damages as shall be recovered or had against the Hundred in which the Robbery was done.

And the Recovery of such Moiety shall be in the Name of the Clerk of the Peace, where such Robbery and Recovery is, without naming his Christian or Surname: And such Suit shall not abate by the Death or Removal of such Clerk of the Peace. 27 *El.* 13.

37 El. 13.
P. Hue &
Cry 6. (*d*) And the like Taxation, Assessment, Levying and Payment, as aforesaid, shall be had and made for a *Contribution within every Hundred* where there was any Negligence, Fault or Defect of Pursuit, and fresh Suit after Hue and Cry, *viz.* If upon Suit any Recovery and Execution of any Money, or any Damages shall be had against some one or few Persons of that Hundred where such Default was (towards the Ease of that Hundred where the Robbery was done) upon Complaint made by the Parties so charged, to any two such Justices of Peace, the said Justices may make the like Assessment, *&c.* toward the Relief of the said Parties so charged.

4

Note,

Note, That if any Man be robbed *in his House*, the Hundred fhall not be charged Co. 7. 6.
therewith, whether it were done in the Day or in Night.

Alfo a Robbery done *in the Night* fhall not charge the Hundred; but yet if it be in *When the Hun-*
the Day-time, or by Day-Light, though it be before the Sun-rifing, or after the Sun-fet- *dred is not*
ing, the Hundred fhall anfwer for it. *charged.*
Ibid.

If upon Purfuit any one of the *Offenders be apprehended*, the Hundred fhall not be 27 El. 13.
charged, although the Refidue of the Offenders happen to efcape; but Purfuit without P. Hue &
apprehending fome one of the Robbers is no Excufe. Cry 7.
Co. 7. 7.

If the Party that was robbed fhall himfelf take any of the Thieves after Hue and Cry Cromp. 179.
made, this fhall excufe the Hundred.

(*a*) Although one of the Thieves be taken, yet if Hue and Cry be not duly made, the
Town where the Default is, fhall be amerced: But the Party robbed fhall have no Remedy for his Money (of the Hundred) in regard that one of the Thieves is taken. And
this is by Force of the Statute 27 *Eliz.* whereas the Amerciament is by Force of the Statute of *Winchefter.*

(*d*) It feemeth by my Lord *Dyer*, *Ann.* 22 *Eliz.* that the Statute is fatisfied, if the Dyer 370.
Names of the Offenders be defcribed; fo that they may be indicted and outlawed. *Quære* Pl. 9.
inde, for the Words of the Statute of 13 *Edw.* 1. are that the County muft anfwer for P. R. 155.
the *Bodies* of fuch Offenders.

Nota; The Party robbed muft bring and commence his Action within 20 *Days next*
after his Examination taken before the Juftice of Peace.

Alfo the Juftice of Peace muft be abiding within the County, at the Time of Examination taken by him, as it feemeth. See the Title *Juftices of Peace*, Chap. 6. *fupra.*

(*a*) If a Man be robbed in *Middlefex*, and make Hue and Cry frefhly into *Effex*, if the
Towns adjoining do not according to the Statute of *Winchefter*, the Party robbed may
have his Action of Debt in the one County or the other, by *Fincham.* 15 *Edw.* 4. 18.
Br. *Ditt* 104.

Highways leading from one Market-Town to another, fhall be enlarged, fo that there *Highways.*
be neither Dike, Underwood, nor Brufh, whereby a Man may lurk to do hurt, within
two hundred Foot of the one Side and of the other; and if by Default of the Lord that
will not amend the Ways as aforefaid, any Robberies be done therein, the Lord fhall be
anfwerable for the Robbery: And if a Park be near the Highway, the Lord muft fet his
Park two hundred Foot of each Side from the Way as aforefaid; or elfe muft make fuch
a Wall, Dike, Hedge, or Pale, that fuch Offenders may not pafs to and fro there.
Winch. 13 *Ed.* 1. *cap.* 5.

Every Juftice of Peace may caufe fuch Highways to be enlarged and cleanfed as aforefaid. See *hic antea* Tit. *Highways.*

If any Perfon fhall with offenfive Weapon unlawfully and malicioufly affault, or fhall *Attempt to rob.*
by Menaces, or in any violent Manner, demand Money or Goods from any Perfon, with 7 Geo.2. c 21.
a felonious Intent to rob fuch Perfon, he fhall be guilty of Felony, and fhall be tranf- §. 1.
ported for feven Years.

If any fuch Offender, who fhall be ordered for Tranfportation, fhall break Gaol or Ib. §. 2.
efcape, or fhall return into *Great Britain* or *Ireland*, before the Expiration of feven
Years, he fhall fuffer Death without Benefit of Clergy.

No Perfon fhall maintain any Action againft any Hundred, by Virtue of the Statutes *Hue and Cry.*
13 *Ed.* 2. Stat. 1. and 27 *Eliz.* cap. 13. unlefs he fhall, befides the Notice already re- 8 Geo.2. c. 16.
quired, with as much convenient Speed as may be after any Robbery on him committed, §. 1.
give Notice thereof to one of the Conftables of the Hundred, or to fome Conftable, Borfholder, Headborough or Tithingman, of fome Town, Parifh or Tithing, near the
Place wherein fuch Robbery fhall happen, or fhall leave Notice in Writing at the Dwelling-Houfe of fuch Conftable, &c. defcribing in fuch Notice, fo far as the Circumftances
of the Cafe will admit, the Felons, and the Time and Place of the Robbery; and alfo
fhall within twenty Days caufe Notice to be given in the *London Gazette*, therein likewife defcribing the Felons, and the Time and Place, together with the Goods whereof he
was robbed; and fhall alfo, before Action commenced, go before the chief Clerk or Secondary, or the Filazer of the County wherein fuch Robbery fhall happen, or the Clerk
of the Pleas, of that Court wherein fuch Action is intended to be brought, or before
the Sheriff of the County, and enter into a Bond to the High Conftable of the Hundred
in the Sum of 100 *l.* with two Sureties, to be approved of by fuch chief Clerk, &c.
with Condition for fecuring to fuch High Conftable (who is required to enter an Appear-

ance,

ance, and defend such Action) the Payment of their Costs, in case Judgment shall be against such Plaintiff.

Ib. §. 2.　When such Bond shall be entered into before the Sheriff, such Sheriff shall certify the same to the chief Clerk or Secondary in the Court of King's Bench, or to the Filazer of the County in case the Action be intended to be brought in the Common Pleas; or, if in the Court of Exchequer, to the Clerk of the Pleas; which Certificate shall be delivered by the Party robbed to the said chief Clerk or Secondary, or to such Filazer, or Clerk of the Pleas, before any Process shall issue; and such chief Clerk, &c. shall not take any greater Fee for making such Bond than 5 s. above the Stamp-Duties; nor shall any Sheriff take any greater Fee for making, nor shall such chief Clerk, &c. take any greater Fee for filing such Certificate than 2 s. 6 d. and such chief Clerk, &c. are to deliver over *Gratis* all such Bonds to the High Constables.

Ib. §. 3.　No Hundred shall be chargeable, if one of the Felons be apprehended within forty Days next after Notice in the *Gazette*.

Ib. §. 4.　No Process for Appearance shall be served on any Inhabitant, save only upon the High Constable of the Hundred, who is required to cause publick Notice to be given in one of the principal Market-Towns on the next Market-Day; or if there be no Market-Town, then in some Parish Church immediately after Divine Service on the *Sunday* next after his being served with Process, and he is to enter an Appearance in the Action, and defend the same as he shall be advised; and in case the Plaintiff recover, no Process of Execution shall be served on any particular Inhabitant; but the Sheriff shall upon Receipt of any Execution cause the same to be shewn to two Justices of Peace (one of the *Quorum*) residing within the Hundred, or near the same, who shall cause such Assessment to be made and levied, as by the Statute 27 *Eliz. cap.* 13. in which Assessment there shall be included, over and above the Costs and Damages recovered by the Plaintiff, all necessary Expences which any High Constable hath been at, in having defended such Action, Claim being made thereto by such High Constable before the Justices, upon Notice given him by the Justices; and the Money so levied shall be paid over (by such Officers as by the Statute 27 *Eliz.* are to levy the same) within ten Days, to the Sheriff of the County, to the Use of the Plaintiff for so much as the Costs and Damages by him recovered shall amount to, and to the Use of the High Constable for so much as his Expences shall amount to, of which the High Constable shall give in an Account, and make Proof upon Oath, to the Satisfaction of the Justices, before any Taxation shall be made for reimbursing such High Constable, and shall have no further Allowance toward paying an Attorney, than what such Attorney's Bill shall be taxed at.

Ib. §. 5.　The Money which shall be paid over to the Sheriff, shall (upon Request) be by him paid over to the Parties intitled without Deduction.

Ib. §. 6.　No Sheriff shall be called upon to return such Writ of Execution, until sixty Days after the Writ shall be delivered to the Sheriff, who is to indorse the Day on which he received the same.

Ib. §. 7.　If any Plaintiff, in any Action to be brought against any Hundred, shall be Non-suited, or discontinue, or have Judgment given against him, it shall be lawful for any two Justices (such as are beforementioned) upon Complaint, and upon an Account given in by such High Constable, and Proof made upon Oath to the Satisfaction of the Justices, of Expences necessarily laid out, to make such Taxation, in order to reimburse such High Constable what he shall have necessarily expended in defending such Action, over and above the Costs taxed; and in case it shall appear upon Oath to the Justices, that such Plaintiff and his Sureties are insolvent, it shall be lawful for such Justices to make a Taxation, in the Manner directed by the Statute 27 *Eliz. cap.* 13. to reimburse such High Constable such taxed Costs, as by reason of such Insolvency he shall not be able to recover from the Plaintiff.

Ib. §. 8.　The Money rated for the Reimbursement of the High Constable, in case of Judgment given against the Plaintiff, shall be paid within ten Days after Collection to the Justices, or one of them, to the Use of such High Constable.

Ib. §. 9.　Any Person who shall apprehend such Felons within the Time herein limited, whereby the Hundred hath been discharged, shall upon Proof upon Oath made before such two Justices be intitled to 10 *l.* (which shall be raised upon the Hundred by a Taxation) and such Sum of 10 *l.* shall be paid unto such two Justices, within ten Days after the same shall be collected; and such Justices shall pay over the said Sum to such Persons, in such Shares as the said Justices shall think reasonable; provided that such Person shall not be thereby incapable to be a Witness in such Action.

The

The Juftices, by whom fuch Taxations fhall be made, fhall appoint fome reafonable Ib. §. 10.
Time, within which fuch Taxations fhall be levied, which Time fhall not exceed thirty
Days; and if any Officers, who are to levy fuch Taxations fhall neglect to levy the fame,
or fhall neglect to pay over the Money to the Sheriff and Juftices, fuch Officer fhall for
every Neglect forfeit double the Sum.

Every Conftable, Borfholder, Headborough or Tithingman, to whom Notice fhall be Ib. §. 11.
given, and every Conftable of the Hundred, and every Conftable, &c. within the Hundred or the Franchifes within the Precinct thereof, wherein fuch Robbery fhall happen,
as foon as the fame fhall come to his Knowledge, fhall with the utmoft Expedition
make frefh Suit and Hue and Cry after the Felons; and if any Conftable, &c. fhall offend in the Premiffes, he fhall forfeit 5 l.

Every Forfeiture hereby incurred fhall be recovered with Cofts, and fhall be one Ib. §. 12.
Moiety to the King, and the other Moiety to fuch Perfons as fhall fue for the fame within fix Months after fuch Forfeiture incurred.

If any Action fhall be commenced for any Thing done in Purfuance of this, or either Ib. § 13.
of the recited Statutes, the Defendant may plead the General Iffue.

No fuch Action fhall be brought but within fix Months after the Thing done.   Ib. §. 14.

In any Action againft any Hundred, any Perfon inhabiting within the Hundred fhall Ib. §. 15.
be admitted a Witnefs for the Hundred.

C H A P. LXXXV.

Sacraments.

IT feemeth that three Juftices of the Peace (one of them being of the *Quorum*) may, Three Juftices.
out of the general Seffions, take Information and Accufation (by the Oaths of two 1 Ed. 6. 1.
honeft Perfons) againft fuch as fhall *deprave* the Sacrament of the Body and Blood of our revived 1 El 2.
Lord and Saviour *Jefus Chrift*, againft the Statute, &c. and may bind the Accufers and P. Juft. 8.
Witneffes by Recognizance (in five Pounds apiece) to give in Evidence at the Trial.
But Mr. *Lamb.* maketh a *Quære* hereof.

(*a*) And fuch Perfon, being indicted at the Seffions, and found guilty of depraving, Penalty.
defpifing, or contemning the Bleffed Sacrament, by Words or otherwife, he fhall fuffer Lam. 352.
Imprifonment, and make *Fine and Ranfom* at the King's Pleafure.   1 E. 6. 1.

The Juftices of Peace in Seffions may hear and determine Offences and Contempts Power.
againft that Act, fo as the Parties offending be informed of, or prefented within three Ib. §. 1. & 5 i
Months after the Offence committed.

The Juftices of Peace may make Procefs by two *Capias* and one *Exigent*, and by Procefs.
Capias Utlegatum, into that or any other County, and three of them may bail the Of- Ib. §. 3.
fender in order to his Trial.

The Juftices of Peace in Seffions may award a Writ to this Effect:

THE King to the *Bifhop* of L. *Greeting: We command you, that you, your Chancel-* Writ to the
lor, or other your fufficient Deputy learned, be with our Juftices affigned to keep the Bifhop.
Peace in our County of B. *at* D. *fuch a Day, at our Seffions then and there to be held, to*
give Counfel and Advice to the fame our Juftices of the Peace, upon the Arraignment and
Delivery of Offenders againft the Form of the Statute concerning the Holy Sacrament of the
Altar. Which Writ muft be directed to the Bifhop of the Diocefe.

The Party indicted may purge and try his Innocency by Witneffes.   Ib. §. 6.

Of the Uniformity of Common Prayer and Sacraments, fee the Statute 14 *Car.* 2. 14 Car. 2. c. 4.
cap. 4, at large, and 25 *Car.* 2. *cap.* 4.

See for the Procefs againft fuch as deprave the Sacrament, *hic* Tit. *Procefs.*

CHAP. LXXXVI. (a)

Sabbath-Day, or Sunday.

Penalty.
3 Car. 1. c. 2.
NO Carrier with an Horfe, nor Waggoner, Carter, nor Wainman, with any Wag-gon, Cart, or Wain, nor any Drover, with any Cattle, fhall by themfelves, or any other, travel upon the Sunday, upon Pain that every Perfon fo offending, fhall for-feit twenty Shillings for every fuch Offence.

Butcher.
If any *Butcher*, by himfelf, or any other for him, by his Privity or Confent, fhall kill, or fell any Victual upon the Sunday, he fhall forfeit for every fuch Offence, 6 s. 8 d.

Punifhment.
Any one Juftice of Peace (Mayor, or Head-Officer of any City or Town Corporate) within their Limits, upon their own View of any the faid Offences, or upon Proof there-of upon Oath, by two or more Witneffes, or upon the Confeffion of the Party offend-ing, may make their Warrant to any Conftable or Church-warden (within their feveral Limits, where fuch Offence fhall be done) to levy the fame Forfeitures by Diftrefs and Sale of the Offender's Goods, rendring to the Party the Overplus: Or it may be fued for in any Court of Record, in any City, or in the Seffions.

Every Juftice, and Head-Officer aforefaid, hath Power to minifter an Oath to fuch Witneffes.

Forfeitures.
All the faid Forfeitures fhall be employed to and for the Ufe of the Poor of the Parifh where the Offence fhall be committed.

And yet any fuch Juftice, or other Head-Officer, out of the faid Forfeitures, may re-ward any Perfon or Perfons that fhall inform, or otherwife profecute any fuch Offender according to their Difcretions, fo that fuch Reward exceed not the third Part of the Forfeiture.

Provided, that no Perfon fhall be impeached by this Act, unlefs he be queftioned thereof within fix Months after the Offence committed.

There fhall be no *unlawful Exercifes*, &c. ufed upon the Sabbath-Day. *Vide* Tit. *Games*.

Againft *Fairs*, and Buying and Selling upon the Sabbath-Day, *hic* Tit. *Market*.

Shoemakers.
Any *Shoemaker* that fhall fhew, with an Intent to fell any *Shoes, Boots, Bufkins, Stir-rops*, or *Slippers*, upon the Sunday, fhall forfeit the Goods fhewed, and 3 s. and 4 d. for every Pair fo fhewed. 1 *Jac.* 1. 22.

Working.
29 Car. 2. c. 7.
§. 1.
If any Perfon of the Age of fourteen Years or above, fhall on the Lord's Day, or any Part thereof, do, or exercife any *worldly Labour*, Bufinefs, or Work of his ordinary Calling, (except Works of Neceffity and Charity). he fhall forfeit 5 s. for every Offence.

Selling.
Ib. §. 1. & 3.
No Perfon fhall cry, fhew forth or put to Sale any *Wares, Fruits, Herbs, Goods or Chattels* (except Milk before Nine in the Morning, and after Four in the Afternoon) up-on Pain to forfeit the fame.

Travelling.
Ib §. 2.
No *Drover, Horfe-Courfer, Waggoner, Butcher, Higler*, or any their Servants, fhall travel or come to their Inn or Lodging on the Lord's Day, or any Part thereof, up-on Pain that each Offender forfeit 20 s. for every Offence.

Watermen.
Ib. §. 2.
No Perfon fhall ufe, employ, or *travel* upon the Lord's Day with any *Boat, Wher-ry, Lighter or Barge*, (except upon extraordinary Occafions, to be allowed by fome Ju-ftice of Peace or Head-Officer of the County or Place where the Offence is committed) upon Pain to lofe 5 s. for every Offence.

Conviction.
Ib. §. 2.
The Conviction muft be before any Juftice of the County or Town, or Chief Officer, by View, Confeffion or Proof of one or more Witneffes, who fhall give Warrant un-der Hand and Seal to the Conftables or Church-wardens of the Parifh or Parifhes where the Offence is committed, to feife and fell the Goods fhewed; and to levy the Forfeitures by Diftrefs and Sale, rendring the Overplus; and in Cafe of Want of Diftrefs, or Infuffi-ciency, or Inability to pay, the Party to be put in the Stocks two Hours.

Reward.
Ibid.
Out of the Forfeitures, the Juftices, Mayor, or Head Officer, may reward any Per-fons informing, fo as the Reward exceeds not one Third of the Penalties.

Extent.
Ib. §. 2.
The Act not to extend to dreffing of Meat in private Families, nor in Inns, Cooks Shop, or Victualling-Houfes, for fuch as cannot otherwife be provided for.

No

No Perfon to be impeached thereupon, unlefs prefented for the fame within ten Days *Impeachment.* after the Offence.

If any Perfon travel on the Sunday, and be robbed, the Hundred fhall not be charge- *Robbery.* able to him; but in Default of Hue and Cry made fhall be chargeable to the King for fo *Ib. § 5.* much as might have been recovered againft them.

If any Perfon on the Lord's Day ferve or execute, or caufe, &c. any Writ, Procefs, *Arreft.* Warrant, Order, Judgment or Decree, (except in Cafes of *Treafon*, *Felony* or *Breach of Ib. § 6. the Peace*) fuch Service fhall be void, and the Party liable for Damages, as if no fuch Writ, &c. had ever been made.

All the Laws made for frequenting Divine Service on the Sabbath-day are ftill in Force; notwithftanding the Statute 1 *Wil. cap.* 18. unlefs Perfons go to fome Congregation of religious Worfhip, tolerated by that Act.

Salt.

THE Officers by this Act appointed, may feize all fuch Salt which fhall be conveyed *Taxes.* away before Entry made, without Warrant of the Commiffioners, or other Col- *Salt to be* lectors: And the Salt that fhall be fo feifed, fhall be brought to the Office next the Place *feifed, which* where fuch Salt fhall be fo feized, and there detained: And if the fame be not claimed by *is conveyed a- way before* the true Owner within ten Days after Seizure, it fhall be forfeited, and fold at the next *Entry.* general Day of Sale to be appointed by the Commiffioners or their Officers; one Moiety *5 & 6 W. &* to the Ufe of their Majefties, and the other to him that feifed the fame. And if the *M. c. 7. § 7.* Owner fhall claim the fame within ten Days, and fhall not make it appear before the next Juftice of Peace in the County where fuch Seizure was, by the Oath of one or more Wit- neffes, that the Salt was duly entred, and that there was a Warrant for carrying away the fame, then it fhall be forfeited and difpofed as aforefaid, and he that carried, or caufed it to be conveyed away, fhall forfeit double the Value.

The Lord Mayor and Court of Aldermen in *London*, fhall afcertain the Price of Salt to *Prices of Salt* be fold in *London*, and the Bills of Mortality; and the Juftices of Peace fhall, at their *to be fet by the* General Seffions fet Prices upon Salt fold within the Counties, &c. where they are *Juftices.* Juftices, and fhall from Time to Time alter the Prices of Salt, which Prices are required *7 & 8W.c.31.* to be obferved by Sellers of Salt, under the Penalty of 5 *l.* to be levied by Diftrefs and *§. 92. re- enacted by 9* Sale of the Offender's Goods; and in Default of Diftrefs he may be imprifoned by War- *W. 3. c. 44.* rant from the Lord Mayor, or any Juftice of Peace. *§. 39.*

No Perfon fhall be capable of acting as Chief Commiffioner for collecting the faid *Ib. §. 14.* Duties, till he hath taken, before one of the Barons of the *Exchequer*, the Oaths appoint- ed in the firft Year of King *William* and Queen *Mary*, intitled, *An Act for abrogating Commiffioners the Oaths of Supremacy and Allegiance*, and the Oath following: *You fhall fwear to exe- Oath. cute your Office truly and faithfully without Favour or Affection, and fhall from Time to Time true Account make and deliver to fuch Perfon and Perfons as their Majefties fhall ap- point to receive the fame, and fhall take no Fee or Reward for the Execution of the faid Office from any other Perfon than from their Majefties, or thofe whom their Majefties fhall appoint on that Behalf.* The like to be taken by the other Officers before two of the *Officers Oath.* Chief Commiffioners, or two Juftices of Peace of the Place where he fhall be appointed *Ib. §. 15.* Officer.

No *Certiorari* fhall fuperfede Execution, or other Proceedings, upon any Order made *Certiorari.* by the faid Chief Commiffioners or Juftices of Peace in Purfuance of this Act. *Ib. §. 17.*

If any Merchant, being a Subject of this Realm, fhall fhip any Salt that hath paid the *Ib. §. 21.* Duty, to convey it by Sea to any Part of *England*, and the Veffel fhall happen to be loft or taken, he fhall upon Proof, before the Juftices at the Quarter-Seffions, of fuch Lofs, have a Certificate of it, and upon producing the fame to any Collector of this Duty, the Officer fhall let him buy the like Quantity, without paying any Duty for the fame.

By the Statute 9 & 10 *W*. Salt muft be fold by Weight, after the Rate of 56 Pounds *9 & 10 W. 3.* the Bufhel, and not by Meafure, on Pain of 5 *l.* being convicted by two Witneffes before *c. 6. § 1.* two Juftices, to be levied by Diftrefs, and to be committed till Satisfaction made.

The Offences againft this Act fhall be heard and determined by any two Juftices of *Ib. §. 2.* Peace refiding near the Place where the Offence fhall be committed. There lies an Appeal to the next Quarter-Seffions; and all Juftices of Peace are required, upon Complaint of any Forfeiture made contrary to this Act, to fummon the Party accufed; and upon his Appearance or Contempt, to proceed to the Examination of the Fact; and upon Proof by the Oath of two Witneffes, or the Confeffion of the Party, to give Judgment, and iffue

M m m   Warrants

Warrants for the levying fuch Forfeitures upon the Goods of the Offender, and to caufe Sale to be made, if the fame fhall not be redeemed in fix Days; and for Want of Diftrefs to imprifon the Party until Satisfaction.

For the Salt Duties, &c. fee the Statutes at large, or Mr. *Cay's* Abridgment, Tit. *Salt.*

3 Geo.2.c.20. §. 4.

Note, that by 3 *Geo.* 2. *cap.* 20. the Penalties impofed by former Acts, for Offences in landing of foreign Salt before Entry, or for any Frauds upon the re-exporting the fame, fhall now be fued for in *England*, in the Courts at *Weftminfter*, and in *Scotland* in the Exchequer at *Edinburgh.*

Ib. §. 5.

And where any Provifions are made by former Acts, for recovering any Penalties for Offences in Relation to the faid Duties, before Juftices of Peace, the fame fhall continue in Relation to the Duty of 3 *d. per* Gallon on foreign Salt.

Scavenger.

SEE the Statute 2 *W. & M. ftat.* 2. *cap.* 8. and 8 & 9 *W.* 3. *cap.* 37. in the *Appendix* under this Title. See there alfo a Claufe in 1 *Geo.* 1. *cap.* 52. *fect.* 9. amended by 9 *Geo.* 2. *cap.* 18.

Servants. See 5 El. 2. cap. 4. Tit. *Labourers, fupra* Chap. 58.

CHAP. LXXXVII. (a)

Schoolmafter.

Licence. 23 El. c. 1. §. 6, 7.

IF any keep a Schoolmafter, which fhall not repair to Church, or be allowed by the Ordinary, he fhall forfeit for every Month 10 Pounds. But the Ordinary fhall take nothing for fuch Allowance, and the Schoolmafter, fo teaching, fhall be difabled to be a Teacher of Youth, and fhall fuffer Imprifonment for one Year. It feems by this Act,

1 Jac. 1. c. 4. §. 9.

being in the Disjunctive, that although he doth not come to Church, yet if he be allowed by the Ordinary, it fhall excufe the Penalty. See alfo 1 *Jac.* 1. 4. none fhall ufe or teach a School out of the Univerfities and Colleges, except a Grammar School, or in fome Gentleman's Houfe, or be licenfed by the Ordinary, upon Pain that the Schoolmafter, and he that retaineth him, fhall forfeit 40 Shillings a Day, to be recovered by Action.

Seamen. See *Mariners.*

Seffions. See Chap. 185.

CHAP. LXXXVIII.

Sewers.

SEWER fignifieth fuch Paffages, Gutters or Drains, as carry the Water into or towards the River or Sea; and the Office of the Commiffioners of Sewers, is principally to fee fuch Paffages, Gutters, Drains and Ditches well fcoured, kept and maintained in the Marfh and Fen Counties, for the better Conveyance of the Water into the Sea.

Six Juftices. 13 El. 9. §. 2.

(d) Six Juftices of Peace, (two being of the *Quorum*) within their Limits, may execute the Laws and Ordinances of the Commiffioners of Sewers for one Year after the Expiration of any fuch Commiffion, except a new Commiffion be publifhed in the mean Time.

Co. 5. 100. & 10. 138, 140.

Note, that the Proceedings of the Commiffioners of Sewers ought to be limited and bounded with the Rules of Law and Reafon, and according to the ancient Statutes and Ordinances.

Statutes. Co. 10. 143.

(a) Now thefe ancient Statutes concerning Sewers are many, and are of three Sorts.

The firft Sort confifts in *defending and repairing the Walls*, Banks and Sewers, &c. Of this Sort are the Statutes made 9 *H.* 3. *cap.* 15 & 16. 6 *H.* 6. *cap.* 5. 18 *H.* 6. *cap.* 10. 23 *H.* 6. *cap.* 9. 12 *E.* 4. *cap.* 6. 4 *H.* 7. *cap.* 1. & 6 *H.* 8. *cap.* 10.

The

The fecond Sort confifts in *pulling down and removing Nufances, &c.* As by the Statutes made 9 *H.* 3. *cap.* 23. 25 *E.* 3. 4. 45 *E.* 3. 2. 1 *H.* 4. 12. 9 *H.* 6. *cap.* 9. & 12 *E.* 4. *cap.* 7.

The third confifteth of both Sorts, *fc.* as well in *repairing the Banks, &c.* as in *pulling down Nufances, &c.* And of this Sort are thefe Statutes following, *viz.* 23 *H.* 8. *cap.* 5. 25 *H.* 8. *cap.* 10. 3 *E.* 6. *cap.* 8. 13 *El. cap.* 9.

The Inconveniencies which infue by thefe Nufances, and efpecially by the new levying, or inhanfing of Wears, Mills, Stanks, Fifh-garths, Locks, Stakes, Kidles and Floodgates, are thefe, *fcilicet,* The common Paffage of Ships and Boats in the great Rivers; as alfo Meadows, Paftures, and Arable Grounds adjoining to the Rivers, be greatly difturbed, drowned, wafted and deftroyed, many People perifhed, and the young Fry of Fifh deftroyed. See 1 *H.* 4. *cap.* 12. 2 *H.* 4. *cap.* 11 & 12 *E.* 4. *cap.* 7. See Tit. *Wears.*

The Form of the Commiffion of Sewers; the Authority of the Commiffioners, as alfo the Form of their Oath, you may fee at large in the Statute 23 *H.* 8. *cap.* 5.

Every Commiffioner fhall, before he execute that Office, before Perfons authorifed by *ded' poteftat',* or before the Juftices of Peace in their Quarter-Seffions, take this Oath.

YOU *fhall fwear, that you, to your Cunning, Wit and Power, fhall truly and indifferently execute the Authority to you given by this Commiffion of Sewers, without any Favour, Affection, Corruption, Dread or Malice, to be born to any Manner of Perfon or Perfons. And as the Cafe fhall require, you fhall confent and endeavour your felf, for your Part to the beft of your Knowledge and Power, to the Making of fuch juft, equal, and indifferent Laws and Ordinances, as fhall be made and devifed by the moft difcreet and indifferent Number of your Fellows, being in Commiffion with you, for the due Redrefs, Reformation and Amendmenmt of all and every fuch Things as are contained and fpecified in the faid Commiffion. And the fame Laws and Ordinances to your Difcretion, Wit, and Power, caufe to be put in due Execution, without Favour, Dread, Malice, or Affection. As God you help, and all Saints.* 23 *H.* 8. 5. fect. 5.

And fhall alfo receive the Sacrament, and take the Oaths, and make the Declaration prefcribed by 25 *Car.* 5. which you fhall find *fupra,* Chap. 4.

Note, That the King by the Common Law, may award his Commiffion of Sewers, ^{Power.} for the Amending of the Sea-Banks, and for the Repairing, Amending and Scouring other Banks, Sewers, Gutters, Ditches, Pits, and Trenches, fo as the Frefh-waters may have their direct Courfe. *F. N. B.* 113. *a.* And fee there the Form of that Commiffion, and the Proceedings thereupon.

(*d*) Thefe Commiffioners cannot make any new great River, neither can they make Co. 10. 141. new Inventions (as artificial Mills to caft out the Waters, or fuch like) but fuch new Rivers, and new Inventions (if they be for the publick Good) ought to be made by Parliament: And yet the making new of an antient Bank or a Sewer in a Place more fit, and with fome Alteration and Diftance, and upon Neceffity, feemeth to be warrantable.

Thefe Commiffioners cannot caft down any *Mills, Caufeys* or *Stanks, &c.* erected before the Time of *Edward* the Firft, but only may caufe them to be abated, if they be raifed above their ancient Heights. *Co.* 10. 138.

Thefe Commiffioners ought to tax none towards thefe Reparations, *&c.* but fuch as ^{Tax.} have Prejudice or Lofs by the *Nufances* or Defaults, and which have Benefit by the Amending or Removing them. *Co.* 10. 142.

Alfo thefe Commiffioners ought to *tax* all that be in Danger to be indamaged by the not Co. 5. 100. Repairing, *&c.* (and that according to their Land, *&c.*) And not tax him only whofe Co. 10. 145. Grounds lie next adjoining to the River, *&c.* For, *Qui fentit commodum, fentire debet & onus.*

Note, That in all Cafes of Taxing or Rating by thefe Commiffioners, it ought to be Co. 5. 100. proportionable, and according to the Quality and yearly Value of the Lands, Tenements, Co. 9. 124 a. Rents, Commons, and Fifhings of the Perfons chargeable, and not according to the Quantity or Content thereof. Co. 10. 139.

(*a*) And the yearly Value fhall be accounted as the Lands, *&c.* are of their own Nature, without refpect to the Bettering or Impairing thereof by the good or bad Husbandry of the Owners or Occupiers thereof. See *Co. L.* 171 & 179. to fuch Purpofe.

(*d*) Again, if the Owner of any Land be bound by *Prefcription,* or otherwife, to re- Co. 5. 108. & pair the Bank of a River, Wall, or Sewer, *&c.* he ought to do it; yet if he be not able 10. 139, 140.

to

to repair it, **or** that there be other inevitable Neceffity, **or** that there was no Default in the Party, but that the Banks, **or** Wall, &c. are broken **or** overflown by Tempeft or unufual Overflowing of Waters, or the like, (which be the Acts of God, and which no Providence or Induftry of him that is bound to the Reparations, could prevent). In thefe Cafes the Commiffioners ought not to charge him, only, with the Whole, but may, and in good Difcretion ought to charge and tax all fuch as have any Lands (or other Profits) there, in Danger, or fubject to Lofs.

(*a*) But when one is bound by *Prefcription*, or otherwife, to repair a Bank or Wall, &c. if there be any Default in him, and the Danger not inevitable, but that he alone may well repair it, the Commiffioners may there charge him only to repair this: And if by his Default the Danger become inevitable, or that he alone is not able to repair it, whereby others are charged as aforefaid, every of them may have an Action on the Cafe againft him, &c. and fhall recover their Damages according to their Lofs.

Co. 10. 130. Alfo, where a Man hath any Lands lying between the Sea, the River of *Thames*, or any other River, and his Neighbour's Grounds, and is bound by *Prefcription*, or other-wife, to make or keep certain Banks, or to fcour certain Ditches or Sewers, between his faid Neighbour and the faid River or Sea, and he doth not make, keep, amend, and fcour the fame, as he ought to do, by Reafon whereof his Neighbour's Grounds are drowned, the Party fo damaged fhall have his Action of the Cafe againft the other fo making De-fault, &c. See *F. N. B.* 93. *g.* and 7 *H.* 4. 8, & 41.

Co. 10. 139 (*d*) Alfo, thefe Taxations ought to be particular, *fc.* upon every *Owner or Occupier of*
& 143. *Lands, Tenements, Rents, Commons and Fifhings*, &c. And not to be a general Sum in Grofs upon a whole Town. See more hereafter Tit. *Stock of the Shire.*

(*a*) See Serjeant *Callis's* Reading upon the Statute of 23 *H.* 8. of *Sewers.*

CHAP. LXXXIX. (*a*)

Sheep.

Tranfporting. **I**F any fhall bring, deliver, fend, receive, or take or procure, &c. into any Ship or
8 El. 3. Bottom, any Rams, Sheep or Lambs, or any Manner of Sheep being alive, to be car-ried and conveyed out of *England, Wales*, or *Ireland*, or any the Queen's Dominions; the Party, his Aiders, Abettors, Procurers and Comforters, fhall forfeit all his Goods, a Moiety to the Queen, the other Moiety to the Profecutor in any Court of Record, and fhall fuffer Imprifonment for a Year without Bail; and at the Year's End, in fome Mar-ket-Town, in the Fulnefs of the Market, on the Market-day, have his Left-Hand to be cut off, and nailed up in the openeft Place of fuch Market; and the fecond Offence is Felony.

Juftices of Peace (*inter alios*) have Power to inquire of, hear and determine Offences againft this Act. 8 *El.* 3.

Keeping. No Farmer fhall keep above Two thoufand Sheep at one Time, upon Pain to forfeit for
25 H. 8. 13. every Sheep above, 3 *s.* 4 *d.*
Ibid. It fhall not extend to Lambs under a Year old, nor to Sheep coming by Executorfhip or Marriage; fo as within a Year, he reduce them to Two thoufand, nor to Sheep be-queathed by Will, nor to Sheep kept in a Man's own Demefnes.

The Profecution fhall be within a Year, and Juftices of Peace, as well by Oaths of twelve Men, as by Information of the King's Subjects. And fuch Procefs fhall be made, as in Trefpafs, and the Fines fhall not be lefs than the Forfeitures. 25 *H.* 8. 13.

Sixfcore Sheep fhall be accounted a Hundred. *Ibid.*

For the Offence of Stealing and Deftroying Sheep, &c. *fee* Chap. 160. infra.

C H A P.

CHAP. XC.

Sheriffs.

THE *Cuftos Rotulorum,* or the eldeft Juftice of the *Quorum* (in his Abfence) ought *One Juftice to overfee the County Courts.* 11 H. 7. 15. at the General Seffions after *Michaelmas,* to appoint two Juftices of the Peace (the ne being of the *Quorum*) to have the Overfight and Controlment of the Sheriff, Under-heriff, and other their Officers and Deputies, and the Infpection and Examination of heir Books and Amerciaments, and for making of Eftreats, &c. in their County Courts. ind either of thofe two Juftices of Peace, or any other Juftice of Peace, as fome * think, * Lam. 203. P. 16. pon Complaint of the Party grieved, may examine the Sheriff, Under-Sheriff, Shire-lerk and Plaintiffs, concerning the Taking or Entring of Plaints in their faid County Courts and Books, againft the Statute, *viz.*

1. If any Plaints fhall be entered in their Books, in any Man's Name, unlefs the Party *ShiriffiCourts.* 'laintiff be either prefent in Court in Perfon, or by a fufficient and known Attorney or Deputy.

2. If that the Plaintiff find not Pledges to purfue his faid Plaint (*fc.* fuch Perfons as re known in that County).

3. If they fhall enter more than one Plaint, for one Trefpafs or Contract.

4. If they fhall enter or caufe to be entred any more Plaints than the Plaintiff fuppofeth e hath Caufe of Action for againft the Defendant.

And if the faid Juftices, or Juftice of Peace, upon his or their Examination, fhall find ny fuch Default in the faid Sheriff, Under-Sheriff, or Clerk, it fhall ftand for a fufficient Conviction, without any further Inquiry or Examination; and they fhall forfeit forty hillings to the King for every Default; the fame to be recovered in the *Exchequer.* And he fame Juftice or Juftices who fhall take the Examination, fhall certify it into the *Ex-hequer* within a Quarter of a Year, upon Pain of 40 *s.*

Alfo the faid Juftice of Peace may examine the *Defaults of the Bailiff of the Hundred,* *Bailiff.* or not warning the Defendants (in fuch Plaints) to appear, according to his Precepts re-eived from the *Sheriff or Under-Sheriff.* And if upon Examination, the Juftice fhall ind any Default in fuch Bailiff, in not warning the Defendant to appear, or otherwife in not executing his faid Office, it fhall ftand for a fufficient Conviction; and the faid Bailiff hereupon fhall forfeit to the King for every Default 40 *s.* the fame Examinations to be ertified into the *Exchequer* as aforefaid.

Sheriffs, &c. fhall make no *Eftreats* to levy their *Shire Amerciaments,* until the faid *Eftreat.* Juftices (appointed at the General Seffions as aforefaid) have had the View and Overfight of their Books: And their *Eftreats* fhall be made by Indentures between the faid *Juftices* and the Sheriff and Under-Sheriff, and fealed with their Seals, the one Part to remain with the faid Juftices, and the other Part with the Sheriff.

The Collectors of the faid Amerciaments fhall be fworn by the faid Juftices, that they hall not take more Money than is forfeited, and contained in their faid Eftreats, fealed by he Juftices as aforefaid.

Alfo the faid Juftices of Peace, or one of them, may examine the Default of the faid *Collectors.* Collectors, *Bailiffs,* and other Gatherers of the *Sheriff's Amerciaments,* whether they have taken and gathered any more Money than is forfeited and contained in their *Eftreats* (fealed with the Seals of two Juftices of Peace as aforefaid): And if upon Examination the Juftices or Juftice fhall find any fuch Default, That alfo without further Inquiry, fhall ftand for a fufficient Conviction. And the faid Collectors, Bailiffs, or other Gatherers of fuch Amerciaments, thereupon fhall forfeit to the King for every Default 40 *s.* The faid Examination alfo (whether it be by one or two Juftices) is to be certified into the *Ex-chequer,* as aforefaid.

Alfo the faid Juftices of Peace upon Suggeftion or Information of the Party grieved, *Two Juftices. Procefs.* 11 H. 7. 15. Lam. 349. fhall make like Procefs, as in an Action of Trefpafs againft the faid Sheriff, Under-Sheriff, or other their Officers (offending in any the Particulars aforefaid) to appear before them to anfwer the faid Suggeftion or Information. See what the Procefs is in the Title *Procefs.*

(*a*) 1. No Sheriff, *Coroner,* or other *Officer,* who hath *Return of Writs,* fhall return any *Jurors.* 27 El. 7. §. 2. *made perpetual* 39 Eliz. c.18. §. 32. *Juror* dwelling out of any Liberty, without the true *Addition of his Dwelling* at the Time of his Return, or within a Year before, or fome other fufficient *Addition,* by which he

N n n

he may be known ; nor within any Liberty, without such *Addition*, as shall be certified to him by the Bailiff of his Liberty, or his Deputy, under his Hand.

2. No Bailiff of Liberty, or his Deputy, shall return any Juror, or deliver the Name of a Juror to the Sheriff, his Under-Sheriff, or Deputy, without such *Addition*, &c.

Estreats. 3. No *Extract of Issues against a Juror*, returned as aforesaid, shall be delivered out, renewed, or put in Ure, without the *Addition* put in the original Panel or *Tales.*

4. No *Under-Sheriff, Bailiff,* &c. shall collect any *Issues so extracted* of any other, than of such Person as by the *Extract* is right charged or chargeable with the Payment thereof.

Penalty. Upon Pain that the Clerk writing, &c. And every Person offending against that Act, shall forfeit to the King five Marks, and to the Party suffering Loss, five Marks.

Ib. §. 3. Justices of Peace may inquire, hear and determine thereof, as well within Liberties as without, and make Execution for the Forfeitures.

Jurors.
27 El.c.6.§.1.
4 & 5 W. &
M. c. 24. No Sheriff, &c. shall return a Juror, upon a *Venire*, that cannot dispend 4 *l.* upon Pain to forfeit 20 *s.* By the Statute 4 & 5 *W. cap.* 24. 'tis 10 *l. per Ann.*

§. 15.
Issues.
27 El. c. 6.
§. 2. Upon the first *Distringas* or *Habeas Corpora,* the Sheriff, &c. shall return for Issues upon every Juror 10 *s.* upon the second 20 *s.* upon the third 30 *s.* And upon every further Writ, to double the Issues, or forfeit 5 *l.*

FalseSummons.
Ib. §. 3. If any be returned summoned, where he is not summoned, and lose Issues for not appearing, the Sheriff, &c. in whose Default it is, &c. shall forfeit double his Issues.

Forfeiture for
sparing.
Ib. §. 4. If a Sheriff, &c. shall take or have by himself or any other, any Reward or Profit for sparing, not warning, or not returning a Juror to try any Issue before any Justices ; the Party offending shall forfeit 5 *l.* a Moiety to the Crown, the other Moiety to the Prosecutor in any Court of Record, by Action, &c. or Information.

1 Ma. Stat. 2.
c. 8. §. 2. No Sheriff, for the Year that he is Sheriff, shall exercise the Office of a *Justice of Peace* for that County ; but all Acts done that Year by him, by Virtue of the Commission of the Peace, shall be void.

The Reason seems to be, for that the same Person cannot well exercise two Offices, especially these. For as a Justice of Peace, he is a Judge of Record, and hath Power in many Cases to command the Sheriff, so cannot command himself. But this Statute requires only the Forbearance of the Execution of his Office for that Year ; and he may continue in the Commission of the Peace.

Fees for Exe-
cution.
28 or 29 El.
c 4. Sheriffs, &c. shall take no more for the *Execution of any Extent,* or Execution upon Body, Goods or Lands, than *twelve Pence* in the *Pound for the first hundred Pounds, and six Pence for every twenty Shillings more* ; if he do, he shall lose to the Party his treble Damages : And for every Time he shall offend 40 *l.* a Moiety to the King, the other Moiety for the Prosecutor, by Plaint, Action, Bill, Suit or Information, &c.

By the general Words of which Act, it seemeth, That an Information or Bill lieth before the Justices of Peace in Sessions.

If the Debt be 160 *l.* there shall 100 *s.* Fee be paid for the 100 *l.* and 30 *s.* for the 60 *l.* Residue. *Latch, p.* 19, 51.

Corporation. And the Proviso of the Statute, That it shall not extend to Fees for any Execution in a *Corporation,* shall be intended of *Actions arising within the Corporation :* And for which the Action is brought in the Corporation Court, and Judgment there had, and not where the Sheriff upon any Process out of a Superior Court enters a Corporation, and doth Execution. *Latch, p.* 19, 51. See *hic postea.*

Oath of She-
riff and Bai-
liffs.
27 El. c. 12.
§. 2. Every Under-Sheriff, Bailiff of Franchise, Deputy and Clerk of every Sheriff, and Under-Sheriff, and other Persons that take on them to impanel or return any Inquest, Jury or Tales ; or intermeddle with Execution of Process in any Court of Record, shall before they meddle with the Execution of such Office, or Execution of Process, take this Oath *Mutatis mutandis.*

27 El. c. 12.
By the Statute
3 G. 1. c. 15.
§. 18.
instead of this
Oath there is
another Form
injoined to be
taken by the
Sheriffs, ex-
cept the Under-Sheriffs in Wales and Chester. ¶ A. B. *shall not use or exercise the Office of Under-Sheriff corruptly, during the Time that I shall remain therein ; neither shall or will accept, receive or take, by any Colour, Means or Device whatsoever ; or consent to the Taking of any Manner of Fee or Reward of any Person or Persons, for the Impanelling or Returning of any Inquest, Jury or Tales, in any Court of Record, for the Queen, or betwixt Party and Party, above two Shillings, or the Value thereof ; or such Fees as are allowed and appointed for the same, by the Laws and Statutes of this Realm ; but will, according to my Power, truly and* See *the Statute : But the Under Sheriffs in Wales and Chester shall take the old Oaths.*

I

indif-

indifferently, with convenient Speed, impanel all Jurors, and return all such Writ or Writs touching the same as shall appertain to be done by my Duty or Office, during the Time I shall remain in the said Office.

So help me God.

And if any Person shall intermeddle, &c. not having taken the said Oath, he shall *Forfeiture.* forfeit 40 *l.* A Moiety to the King, and the other Moiety to the Prosecutor. 27 El. 12.

And the Justices of Peace, in their Sessions, have Power to hear and determine the §. 4. Defaults against that Act, as well by Presentment and Information as Indictment; and upon Conviction, to award Execution for the Forfeitures, by *Fieri Facias, Attachment, Capias* or *Exigent.*

(d) The *Custos Rotulorum,* or any two Justices of the Peace, the one being of the *Quorum* 27 El. 12 may take the Oaths of Under-Sheriff of their County, his Bailiffs, Deputies, Clerks and §. 32, 33 other Officers, before they shall exercise their said Offices.

fc. { The Oath of Supremacy.
The Oath for the true Exercising of their Offices. *Vide supra.*

(a) But special Bailiffs made for the serving of Process, are not to be sworn by this Statute, as Mr. *Crompton* reporteth, and saith, *That it was so adjudged in the King's Bench.* And yet the Words of the Statute are, That every Person which shall have Authority, or take upon him to intermeddle with Execution of Process, &c. shall receive and take the said Oaths, *Crompt.* 76, & 103. And so it was resolved *Mich.* 7 *Car.* 1. *Jones's Rep.* 249. And the same Matter was also in Question lately in the King's Bench, but not resolved as I remember.

Sheriffs, Under-Sheriffs, their Bailiffs or Ministers shall not make out any Process on 1 E. 4. c. 2. any Indictments or Presentments in their Leets or Turns, but shall deliver the same to §. 1. the Justices of Peace at their next Sessions; or in Default thereof, shall forfeit 40 *l.* And the Justices of Peace may proceed thereon, as if such Indictment or Presentment were taken before them, and may arraign and deliver the Parties indicted; and such as be indicted of Trespass shall make such Fine as they in their Discretion shall think fit; and the Estreats shall be inrolled and delivered by Indenture. And if the Sheriff, &c. shall arrest, &c. any Person, or levy such Amerciament without such Authority, he shall forfeit One hundred Pounds.

He shall take no more than 12 *d.* Poundage for executing an *Habere facias Possessio-* 3 G. 1 c. 15. *nem* or *Seisinam,* where the whole yearly Value of the Lands doth not exceed 100 *l.* §. 16. and 6 *d.* for every 20 *s.* above that Value.

He shall not take Poundage for executing a *Capias ad Satisfaciendum,* or upon Ib. §. 17. charging one in Execution for any greater Sum than the real Debt, which Sum the Plaintiff shall mark and specify on the Back of the Writ, before it shall be delivered to the Sheriff to execute; he or his Bailiff taking more, are guilty of Extortion, and shall forfeit double the Sum extorted and treble Damages to the Party grieved, upon Proof before the Judge of that Court out of which the Writ issued in such summary Way as he shall think meet, and 200 *l.* to the Crown and to the Prosecutor; to be recovered in the Courts at *Westminster,* so as the Prosecution be within two Years after the Offence.

C H A P. XCI. (a)

Ships.

SEveral of the Penalties given by the Act of Navigation 12 *Car.* 2. *cap.* 18. for Offences against that Statute are and may be recovered by Information in any Court of Record. And it seems the Sessions being so, they may there be recovered: For which see the Statute at large.

Where a Ship is in Distress, and any Person enters without Leave of the Commander 12 Ann. c. 18. (except an Officer of the Customs, or a Constable, or one by his Order) or he who §. 3. *made perpetual* molests Persons assisting, or endeavours to hinder the Saving the Ship or Goods, or when 4 G. 1. c. 12. saved, shall deface the Marks of any Goods before they are entered in a Book, shall, within twenty Days after, make double Satisfaction to the Party grieved, at the Discretion

tion of the two next Juftices, or in Default thereof be fent by the faid Juftices to the House of Correction, there to be kept to hard Labour for twelve Months.

12 Ann. c.18. §. 2. They who affift Ships in Diftrefs, and preferve them or their Cargoes, fhall within thirty Days afterwards be paid a reafonable Reward for their Service by the Commander, and in Default thereof the Ship fhall remain in the Cuftody of the Officer of the Cuftoms, till they be reafonably gratified; and if they cannot agree, then the three next Juftices named by the faid Officer, fhall fettle the *Quantum* to be paid to each Affiftant. And where no Perfon claims the Goods, the chief Officer of the next Port muft make Application to three of the Juftices, who are to put him or fome refponfible Perfon in Poffeffion of the Goods, taking an Account thereof in Writing, to be figned by the faid Officer; and if they are perifhable, then to be fold prefently, or elfe kept a Year.

Ib. §. 5. Any Perfon making or affifting in making a Hole in a Ship in Diftrefs, or ftealing or aiding to fteal any Pump, or wilfully doing any Thing tending to the immediate Lofs of fuch Ship, fhall be guilty of Felony without Benefit of Clergy.

Shoemakers. See *Labourers,* Chap. 58.

C H A P. XCII. (a)

Silk-throwing.

Apprentice. 13 & 14 Car. 2. c. 15. §. 2. NO Perfon fhall ufe, exercife, continue or fet up the Trade of a Silk-thrower, unlefs he is or fhall be Apprentice to that Trade, or have ferved feven Years Apprenticefhip thereunto, upon Pain to forfeit forty Shillings for every Month; one Moiety to the King, the other Moiety to the Profecutor, by Action of Debt, Bill, Plaint or Information; or by other lawful Means (*inter alios*) before the Juftices of the Peace at their Quarter-Seffions.

Imbeziling Silk. Ib. §. 5. If any Silk-winder and Doubler imbezil, pawn or detain any Silk delivered to them to wind or double, every Winder or Journeyman fo offending, and the Buyers and Receivers thereof, being convicted by Confeffion or the Oath of one Witnefs before any *By the Statute 8 & 9 W. 3. c. 36. fect. 6. this extends to all Perfons who fhall imbezil Silk, or pawn, fell or detain it, being delivered ed to any one who manufactures it, their Agents, Journeymen, Warpers or Winders.* Juftice of Peace of the County or Liberty; or if within a Town corporate, before the chief Officer of the fame, who may hear and determine, and give the Party damnified fuch Satisfaction for their Lofs, Damage and Charges, as they fhall order, fo as no more be awarded than the Party is damnified, and hath expended in looking after it. And if the Party be not able, or do not make Recompence in fourteen Days after Conviction he fhall for the firft Offence be apprehended and whipped, or fet in the Stocks in the Place where the Offence was committed, or fome Market-Town of that County, near thereunto; and for the fecond Offence, fhall be punifhed by whipping and putting in the Stocks, as the Juftices and Chief Officers fhall think fit.

Ib. §. 7. The Receivers and Buyers of Silk fhall be fubject to the like Punifhment as the Perfon imbezilling.

Imployment. Ib. §. 8. Any Freeman of the Company of Silk-throwers may fet on work any Native Subject of his Majefty, whether Men, Women or Children, to turn the Mill, tie Threads double Silk and wind Silk, as formerly.

See 9 & 10 *W.* 3. *cap.* 43. *fect.* 5. in the *Appendix,* Tit. *Alamodes* and *Luftrings.*

C H A P. XCIII. (a)

Skinners.

3 Jac. 1. c. 9. § 12. NO Perfons ufing the Trade of Merchandife, or any other Trade, fhall drefs, o caufe, &c. in their Houfes, or by any Workmen not ufing the Trade of a Skinner, any black Coney-Skins, nor tranfport or caufe, &c. Nor pack, fhip or lade, to
tha

that Intent, any black Coney-Skins of the Breed of *England,* unlefs the fame be tawed and perfectly wrought, dreffed and packed, by Skinners or Tawers under them, according to the Science of Artizan Skinners, upon Pain to forfeit the fame, or the full Value thereof.

No Merchant fhall buy, bargain or contract for, or caufe, &c. any Coney-Skins or Ib. §. 3. Lamb-Skins, called *Morkins,* of the Breed of *England,* or being here, under 1000 black Coney-Skins, or 3000 grey Coney-Skins, or 2000 Lamb-Sins, called *Morkins,* at one Time, and not by Parcels, except of Artizan Skinners; nor fhall fell the fame again to any Perfons in this Realm, in fmall Parcels, *viz.* under thefe Numbers of each, unlefs to an Artizan Skinner, upon Pain to forfeit the fame, or the full Value.

No Perfon fhall retain or keep any Servant, Journeyman or Apprentice, to work Ib. §. 4. therein, except the Perfon ufing that Trade hath ferved feven Years therein, and do ufe the Trade of a Skinner, upon Pain to forfeit double the Value of the Skins or Wares wrought.

A Moiety of the Forfeitures to the King, the other Moiety to the Seifor, or that Ib. §. 5. fhall fue for the fame by Action of Debt, Bill, Plaint, or Information in any Court of Record.

See more Tit. Leather, *Chap.* 59.

Smuglers.

ANY Perfons found paffing knowingly with any foreign Goods, landed without 8 Geo. 1. c. 18 due Entry and Payment of the Duties, from any of the Coafts, or within twenty Miles thereof, and fhall be more than five in Company, or fhall carry any offenfive Weapons, or wear any Difguife when paffing with fuch Goods, or fhall forcibly refift any Officer of the Cuftoms or Excife in feifing Run Goods, fhall be guilty of Felony, and be tranfported for feven Years; and if he return before that Time, 'tis Felony without Benefit of Clergy.

Vide fupra Tit. Cuftoms, *Chap.* 33.

CHAP. XCIV.

Soldiers.

EVERY Juftice of Peace of the County, where any Soldier, which hath ferved the *Armor.* King in his Wars, fhall be found, which hath fold, given, purloined, or put away, 2 Ed. 6. 2. &c. any Horfe or Harnefs (wherewith he was fet forth, or which was after appointed P. Juft. 84. to him by the Lieutenant or Captain, &c.) upon Complaint and due Proof of the Offence to be made (by the Owner, his Executors or Adminiftrators) to any fuch Juftice, fhall by the faid Juftice be committed to Ward, there to remain without Bail, until he has fatisfied the Party grieved, his Executors or Adminiftrators; for fuch Horfe or Harnefs, &c. unlefs he bring with him, before the fame Juftice, fufficient Teftimony from his Captain, &c. in Writing under his Seal, teftifying, that the faid Horfe or Harnefs, &c. was loft in the King's Service againft the Will of that Soldier; or was taken by his Captain, &c. from him, and appointed to fome other to ferve withal; except the fame Soldier were imprifoned for the fame Offence before, by his Lieutenant or Captain, &c. and made Reftitution.

The next Juftice of Peace to the Place of Landing of any poor Soldier, Mariner, or *Licenfe.* Seafaring-Man fuffering Shipwreck, may make them a Licenfe to pafs to the Place where 39 Eliz. c. 17. they are to repair, &c. See hereof in the Title *Rogues.* §. 3.

In Default of the Parifhioners, Church-wardens, and Conftables (that fhall not 43 El. c. 3. affefs the Tax impofed upon the Parifhioners by the Juftices at their *Eafter* Seffions; §. 3 & 4. towards the Relief of difabled Soldiers and Mariners) any Juftice of Peace dwelling in the Parifh, or (if none dwell there) in the Parts next adjoining, may affefs the fame: And the fame Juftice of Peace may alfo in Default of the Church-wardens and Conftables, levy the fame by Diftrefs and Sale of the Goods of the Party fo refufing or neglecting, rendring to the Party the Overplus, &c.

O o o   (*a*) Which

Payment.
Ib. §. 5.
Treasurers.

(*a*) Which Church-wardens and Petty Conftables fhall collect it, and pay it to the High Conftable of that Divifion, ten Days before every Quarter-Seffions. Which High Conftable fhall, at the Seffions, pay the fame to two Juftices, or one of them; or to two fuch Perfons, or one of them, as fhall be elected by the more Part of Juftices, who fhall continue only for one Year, and fhall give up an Account the *Eafter* Seffions, or within ten Days, to the next elected.

Failure of Payment.
Ib. §. 6.

If Church-warden or Petty Conftable, or his Executors, or Adminiftrators, fhall fail of Payment, he fhall forfeit 20 s. If High Conftable, &c. fail of Payment, he fhall forfeit 40 s. to be levied by Diftrefs and Sale by the Treafurer.

Treasurers Account.
Ib. §. 7.

If the Treafurer, his Executors or Adminiftrators, fail to give up his Account, or be negligent in his Charge, the major Part of the Juftices in Seffions, may fet a Fine no exceeding 5 l.

To whom Application is to be made.
Ib. §. 8.

Every Soldier difabled, being in the King's Pay, or returning from Sea, fhall, if able repair to the Treafurer of the County, where he was preffed; or if not preffed, to the Treafurers of the County where he was born, or laft inhabited by the Space of three Years, at his Election: And if not able to travel, to the Treafurer of the County where he

The Certificate.

fhall firft arrive, and fhall bring a Certificate under their Hand and Seal of the General of the Camp, or Governor of the Town, under which he ferved; and of the Captain of the Band, or his Lieutenant; and in their Abfence, from the Marfhal or Deputy; or from the Admiral or General at Sea; or from the Captain of his Ship, containing a Particular of his Hurts and Services: Which Certificate fhall be allowed by the General Mufter Mafter, Refident in *England*, or Receiver General of the Mufter-Rolls, the Treafure and Comptroller of the Navy, under his Hand; upon which Certificate the Treafurer fhall give him a proportionable Relief until the Seffions: At which Time, the Juftices under their Hands, to make a Grant of the fame for his Life, if it be not altered, and

The Sum.

the Treafurer fhall pay it; fo as to any one that hath not born Office in the Wars, be not affigned above 10 l. nor to any one that hath born Office above 15 l. nor to a Lieutenant above 20 l.

Alterations.
Ib. §. 9.

The Juftices of Peace may in their General Quarter-Seffions, upon juft Caufe alter diminifh or revoke the Penfions affign'd to Soldiers and Mariners.

Diftance.
Ib. §. 10.

If fuch maimed Soldiers and Mariners fhall arrive in a County, far remote from the Place where they are to have their Penfions, the Treafurers of the County where they arrive, may give them Relief for their Journey, upon their Certificate, with a Teftimonial; and fo the Treafurer of the next County, until they come to the Place where they are to have their Penfion fettled.

Accounts.
Ib. §. 11 & 12.

The Treafurers fhall keep a Book of all Sums they levy, and of the Perfons to whom they give any Relief, and preferve every Certificate: And if any Treafurer fhall wilfully refufe to give or diftribute any Relief according to that Act, the Juftices of Peace in their Seffions, by their Difcretions, may fine fuch Treafurers, to be levied by Diftrefs and Sale, to be profecuted by any two of them whom they fhall authorife.

Begging.
Ib. §. 13.

If fuch Soldier or Mariner be taken begging, or fhall counterfeit a Certificate, he fhall be punifhed as a Rogue.

Surplufage.
Ib. §. 14.

The Surplufage of fuch Stock fhall be ordered and beftowed by the more Part of the Juftices in their Quarter-Seffions, by their Difcretion to fuch charitable Ufes, in fuch Manner as is limited by the Statutes for the Poor, and againft Rogues.

Penalties.
Ib. §. 16.

The Forfeitures of every Treafurer, Collector, Church-warden and other Officers by that Act fhall be employed as the Money to be levied, and the Overplus is directed, or may be referved as a Stock for Soldiers and Mariners.

Corporations.
Ib. §. 15.

Juftices of Peace in the County fhall not meddle as to this Matter in any City, Borough, Place or Corporation, where is any Juftice of Peace; but the Juftices of Peace Mayors, Bailiffs and other Head Officers of Cities, Boroughs, Places and Towns Corporate, where there is any Juftice of Peace, may put in Execution the faid Act in all Things as Juftices of the Peace of the County may do.

Who to be fettled.
Ib. §. 16.

Relief fhall be given to fuch Soldiers and Mariners out of the Stock of the County out of which he was preffed; but if that Taxation fhall be before employed, or they fhall not be preffed Men, then out of the Place where they are born, or laft inhabited by the Space of three Years, at his or their Election.

Continuance of the Act.

This Act was continued indefinitely by 3 *Car.* 1. *cap.* 4. and by 16 *Car.* 1. *cap.* 4.

Mufters.
4 & 5 P. & M.
c 3. §. 2.

If any, commanded to be muftered, fhall abfent himfelf without lawful Impediment; or coming, fhall not bring his beft Furniture, Array or Armor, he fhall be imprifoned ten

I

Days

Days without Bail, unless he agree to pay a Fine of 40 s. to the Queen; which is to be estreated into the *Exchequer* by the Commissioners, &c.

If any Person authorized to muster or levy Men in War, or for the Defence of the *Bribes.* Kingdom, shall take or receive any Money or Reward to spare any Person, he shall forfeit *Ib. §. 3.* ten Times so much as he shall take.

If any Captain or other, having Charge of Soldiers, shall for any Advantage license a *Pay.* Soldier to depart, he shall forfeit ten Times the Thing taken. And if he shall not pay *Ib. §. 4.* the Soldier his Pay within ten Days after he shall receive it, he shall pay the Soldier treble so much. The Moiety of Forfeitures (except Pay) to the Queen, the other Moiety to the Prosecutor, in any Court of Record, by Information or otherwise.

The Justices of Peace in Sessions may by Presentment or Indictment hear and deter- *Ib. §. 5.* mine the Offences, and upon Conviction may award the Party to Prison till Payment of the Forfeitures. A Moiety whereof to the Party that gives Evidence, if Conviction be upon Evidence; otherwise the whole Forfeiture to the Queen.

(*d*) If any poor Soldier or Mariner, coming from or beyond the Seas, shall repair to *Work.* his Place of Birth, &c. and cannot there get Work, then upon his Complaint any two Justices of Peace near the said Place shall take Order (by their Discretion) to set him to work; and, for want of Work, the said Justices shall tax the whole Hundred (by their Discretion) for his Relief till sufficient Work may be had.

(*a*) These Acts concerning Soldiers, though not expired nor repealed, seem to be of little Use at this Time, the several Cases that may arise being provided for by the Statutes relating to the Poor and to Vagrants, or by the annual Act *for punishing Mutiny and Desertion*, &c. Which last see at large.

CHAP. XCV. (*a*)

Spices.

IN the Edition of 1727 of this Book, an Abstract of an Act of 1 *Jac.* 1. *cap.* 19. for well Garbling of Spices, was inserted; but this is repealed by 6 *Ann. cap.* 16.

Squibs.

ALL Persons are prohibited to make, utter, sell, or offer or expose to Sale any Squibs 9 & 10 W. 3. or Fireworks, or to suffer any Squibs to be cast, thrown, or fired out of their *c. 7.* Houses or Lodgings, or any Part thereof, or Places adjoining, into the Streets, or to throw, cast, or fire, or to be aiding or assisting thereunto, if they do, 'tis a *Common Nusance.*

And if any Person make, or cause to be made, give, sell, utter, or offer or expose to Sale any Squibs, &c. he forfeits 5 *l.* to the Poor and the Prosecutor, being convicted before a Justice upon Confession or Oath of two Witnesses, and to be levied by Distress and Sale, &c.

Permitting any Squibs to be cast, thrown, or fired out of their House, Shop, or Habitation into any Street, forfeits 20 *s.* to be levied and divided as afore, &c.

And he who throws them, or is aiding and assisting in throwing them forfeits the like Sum, to be divided as aforesaid; and if not immediately paid to the Justice, upon Conviction, shall be committed to the House of Correction, there to be held to hard Labour for a Month, unless he shall sooner pay the Money.

Stamp-Duties.

EVERY Commissioner and Officer acting in collecting the Stamp-Duties, is to take 10 Ann. c. 19. an Oath mentioned in that Statute before two of the Commissioners, or before one Justice. See the Form of the Oath there; and the Justice is to give the Officer *gratis* a Certificate of his having taken the Oath.

Causing or Procuring to be forged or counterfeited any Stamp or Mark, resembling any 6 Geo.1.c.21. Mark, or Stamp, made or used in Pursuance of this Statute, or any other relating to the §. 60. Stamp-Duties, or Causing or Procuring any Vellom, Parchment, Paper, Cards, or Dice to be marked or ftamped with fuch counterfeit Stamps, this is Felony without Benefi of Clergy.

Surrender of a Copyhold.
10Ann. c. 19.
§. 105.

Writing or Printing any *Surrender* (except to the Ufe of a Will) or *Admittance of* c to any *Copyhold Eftate in Great Britain or Wales* or any Grant or Leafe by Copy of Court Roll, or any Matter directed to be ftamped by the Statute 10 *Annæ, cap.* 19. or fellin or expofing to Sale any Pamphlet or News-Paper, excepting fuch as exceed one whol Sheet of Paper, before the fame fhall be ftamped; the Offender forfeits 10 *l.* with fu Cofts for every Offence to the Crown and the Profecutor.

Steward of a Manor.
Ibid.

Every Steward of a Manor, or his Deputy offending, and being convicted, over an above the faid Forfeiture, fhall lofe his Place; and the Writing fhall not be good, o given in Evidence until 5 *l.* fhall be paid, as alfo the 10 *l.* before mentioned; and a Re ceipt thereof be produced under the Hand of the Receiver General of the Stamp-Duties or his Deputy, and until the Vellom, &c. be ftamped.

Printer of Pamphlets.
Ib. §. 111.

The Printer and Publifher of any Pamphlet exceeding one Sheet, and the Duty not be ing paid, and the Title of it regiftred, and one Copy not ftamped, within the Time limite by that Statute, forfeits 20 *l.* with full Cofts to the Crown and the Profecutor; and th Author, Printer, and Publifher, to lofe the Property of the Copy, though the Title i

Pamphlets muft have the Prin-ter's Name.
Ib. §. 113.

All Pamphlets muft have the Printer's or Publifher's Name printed thereon, or pa 20 *l.* for every Offence, to be divided *ut fupra.*

Two Juftices to determine in a fummary way.
Ib. §. 172.

Two or more Juftices refiding near the Place where any pecuniary Forfeiture, not ex ceeding 20 *l.* upon any of the Statutes relating to the Duties on Stamps, fhall be incurred may hear and determine the fame in a fummary Way within a Year after the Offenc committed, and may iffue Warrants to levy the Penalties on the Goods of the Offender and fell the fame unlefs redeemed within fix Days.

Juftices may mitigate the Penalties.
Ib. §. 173.

The Juftices may mitigate the Penalties, the reafonable Charges, and Cofts of the Offi cers and Informers being firft allowed, and fo as fuch Mitigation doth not reduce th Penalties to lefs than double the Duties over and above the Cofts and Charges.

Appeal to the Seffions.
Ibid.

There lies an Appeal to the Quarter-Seffions from the Order of the two Juftices whofe Determination fhall be final, and they may iffue Warrants to levy, &c.

No Certiorari.
Ib. §. 174.

But no *Certiorari* lies to fuperfede Execution or any other Proceedings upon the afore faid Statute.

Starch and Hair-Powder, fee the *Appendix.*

C H A P. XCVI.

Stock of the Shire.

One Juftice.
To what Ufes they muft be imployed.

IN the Default of the Parifhioners, Church-wardens and Conftables (that fhall no affefs the Tax impofed upon the Parifhioners by the Juftices at their *Eafter* Seffions, towards the Relief of the Prifoners in the *King's Bench* and *Marfhalfea,* and of the He fpitals of that County, and of the Loffes by Fire or Water, and other Cafualties, and Re lief of the Poor within that County) any Juftice of Peace dwelling in that Parifh, or (if none dwell there) in the Parts next adjoining, may affefs the fame: And the fame Juftice, or any other Juftice of Peace of that Limit (in Default of the Church-wardens and Conftables) may levy the fame by Diftrefs and Sale of the Goods of the Party refu fing or neglecting to pay his Part thereof, rendring to the Party the Overplus; and in Default of fuch Diftrefs, any Juftice of Peace of that Limit may commit fuch Perfon to Prifon, there to remain without Bail, till he hath paid the fame.

Levying.
4 El. c. 2.
P. Poor 13.

Soldiers.

(*a*) Alfo in Default of the Parifhioners, Church-wardens and Conftables (that fhall not affefs the Tax impofed upon the Parifhioners by the Juftices at their *Eafter* Seffions, towards the Relief of maimed Soldiers and Mariners) any Juftice of Peace dwelling in that Parifh, or (if none dwell there) in the Parts next adjoining, may affefs the fame: And the fame Juftice of Peace (in Default of the Church-wardens and Conftables) may levy the fame by Diftrefs and Sale of the Goods of the Party refufing or neglecting to pay his Part thereof, rendring to the Party the Overplus. But in Default of fuch Di ftrefs, the Juftices of Peace may not commit fuch Perfon to Prifon, as they might in the former Cafe. 43 *El. cap.* 3. *P. Coptain* 11.

I

(*d*) Now

(d) Now in thefe and other *Rates and Taxations* you fhall obferve thefe Rules following.

1. Firft, That the moft reafonable *rating of Land is by the yearly Value* and Quality *Taxes.* thereof, and not by the *Quantity or Content.* Co. 9. 124.

2. He that occupieth *Lands lying in feveral Parifhes*, fhall be charged *in every Parifh* proportionably for his Land there.

3. The *Farmer fhall be rated for the Lands*, and not *the Leffor* or *Landlord.* Co. 5. 67.

4. The Landlord fhall not be rated or taxed for his *Farm-Rents*, in as much as the Farmer or Occupier of the Land is chargeable for the fame Land. So where my Farmer is affeffed by his *Goods*, I ought not to be affeffed for my Rent of the fame Farm. *Br. Quinz.* 2. 4. 7 *H.* 4. 33. & 11 *H.* 4. 35.

(a) Upon a Complaint to the Judges of Affife in the County of *Lincoln*, it was refolved and ordered, that the *Lands in the Parifh*, and not the *Rent*, neither of that Land nor of the other Lands, could be taxed. Sir *Anthony Irbie*'s Cafe, Affife *Linc.* 1633.

5. (d) By *Goods* in moft Cafes, a Man may be rated as well as *by Lands*, but not both by Goods and Lands, as it feemeth.

(a) The like you may fee in divers Acts of *Subfidies*, wherein there is ufually a fpecial Provifo, that no Perfon fhall be taxed both for his Lands and Goods, nor double rated. See the Acts of Subfidies, 7, 18 & 21 *Jac.* & 27, 29, 31, 35, 39 & 43 *Eliz.* 4 *Car.* and yet fee 44 *E.* 3. *Br. Cuftoms* 6. where a Tax of ten Pounds was made by the Parifhioners for the Amending of their Church, and to be levied of every Plough-Land fix Pence, and of every Cow one Penny, and of every ten Sheep Half-Penny, and *J. S.* for his Lands, Cows and Sheep, was rated at 9 *s.* and was diftrained for the fame; and upon a Replevin, no Exception was taken to the Manner of Rate impofed. But Note, that the faid Tax was made by his Confent; *Et omnis confenfus tollit errorem.* Co. 5. 16, & 40.

So then he that hath both *Lands and Goods* fhall be charged by the beft, but he is not to be double charged, *fc.* by the one and the other; and yet in fome Places they do ufe to charge one Perfon both by *Lands and Goods:* Which if it be warrantable by Law, yet it feemeth to be with this Difference, *fc.* That where a Man occupieth Land, and alfo hath in his Hands a great Eftate or Stock of Merchandize, or be alfo a Clothier, Malfter, or the like, that fuch Perfon may be charged by his Lands, and alfo by fuch his Stocks; but for fuch Goods or *Stock of Cattle, whereby a Man doth occupy, or manure his Lands*, (as Horfes, Sheep, Kine, &c. wherewith he ftocketh his Land) a Man fhall not be charged.

Alfo where a Man is rated by his *Goods*, it feemeth reafonable that fuch Goods be rated *after the Value of Lands to be purchafed, fcil.* one *hundred Pounds in Stock or Goods, to be rated after five Pounds per Annum* in Lands. And fo after the like Proportion for a greater or leffer Eftate in Goods, Stock, Merchandife or the like.

Note; Where a Man is charged by Goods, they muft be *bona notabilia*, as it feemeth; and yet to the Subfidy, Men are rated not only by their Stock of Merchandife or Cattle, Corn, Houfhold-Stuff or other moveable Goods which are *notabilia*, but alfo to their Money and Debts owing to them (deducting fuch Debts as they owe to others, and fuch Debts as be defperate:) But there the Party over-rated, upon his Complaint to the Commiffioners, and his Oath taken before them, that his Goods, Money, or Debts be not of fuch Value (which Oath the faid Commiffioners are authorifed to take by the Statute) they may abate the faid Affeffments according as upon fuch Examination fhall appear to them juft. See the afore-cited Acts of Subfidies.

(d) Alfo for Goods, a Man fhall be charged only in that Town where the Goods be at the Time of the Affeffment. *Br. Quinz.* 4 & 6. See the Statute of 9 *H.* 4. *cap.* 7.

Alfo if a Man be affeffed for *his Goods in D.* when as he had no Goods there, and be diftrained for fuch Affeffment, he may have an Action of Trefpafs. *Br. Quinz.* & 4.

The Conftables (or other Officers) and greater Part of the Parifhioners (upon a gene- *Officers.* ral Warning given in the Church) affembled, may make fuch Taxations by Law. See *like* 5. 67.

The like may be done by the Church-warden and the greater Part of the Parifhioners, or Church Charges.

And if the greater Part of the Parifhioners will not meet upon fuch Warning given, feems the Officers, and fuch of the Parifhioners as will meet, may make fuch Taxations.

(a) Note,

(a) Note, That fuch Taxations being made for a Commonwealth, as for the Making or Amending of a Bridge, Highway, Caufey, Sea-bank or the like, they fhall bind all Perfons (although they affent not). *44 E. 3. 18, 19. Br. Cuftoms 6. Co. 5. 63 Fi. 49.*

And fo of Taxations made to repair the Church, or for other common Town Charges where they are made by the greater Part of the Parifhioners, as aforefaid. See *Co. 5. 36 & 67. & 21 H. 7. fol. 20. b. & 8 E. 1. Fitz. Aff. 413.*

Sewers.   Alfo when Affeffments are made for the Reparation of Bridges, Highways, Sea-Banks Caufeys, and the like, the Sum affeffed upon particular Men, or Towns, ought to be competent and reafonable, having Regard to the Benefit which the Parties affeffed or charged fhall or may have and enjoy, by Reafon of the faid Affeffment, and fo reafonable as that the Party fhall or may have more Benefit than Charge thereby; and then fuch Affeffments cannot be reputed burdenfome or a Charge to the Subject. See *13 H. 4. fol. 14 & Co. 5. 63.*

If a Townfhip be amerced, and the Neighbours do (by Affent) affefs a certain Sum upon every Inhabitant, and do agree that *J. S.* fhall gather it; and that if it be not paid at fuch a Day, that *J. S.* fhall diftrain for the fame; in fuch a Cafe a Diftrefs taken by *J. S.* for fuch Rates behind, is good. *Br. Cuft. 6. Doct. & Stud. 74. b.*

And Iffues eftreated upon the Parifh, may by Order of Seffions be equally rated upon the Inhabitants and levied accordingly. *Ord. 16. May 8. Car. lib. Seff. Pac. Mid. Con fimil. Ord.* for the Inhabitants of *Fulham, 9 Apr. 11 Car.* Inhabitants of *Eling, Ord. 2 Dec. 9 Car.*

See the 12 Geo. 2. cap. 29. for the more eafy Affeffing, Collecting and Levying County Rates, *infra* Chap. 196.

Stolen Goods. See *Theft*, Chap. 155.

C H A P. XCVII.

Subfidy.

THE old Subfidy Acts mentioned by *Dalton* under this Title, are expired.

Surety of the Peace. See Chap. 116.

C H A P. XCVIII. (a)

Swearing.

IF any Perfon or Perfons fhall prophanely fwear or curfe, in the Hearing of any Juftice of Peace in the County, Mayor, Bailiff, or Head Officer of any City or Town Corporate, where fuch Offence fhall be committed; or fhall be thereof convicted by the Oath

Penalty.   of two Witneffes, or by Confeffion of the Party before any fuch Juftice of Peace or Head
21 Jac. 1.   Officer, &c. Every fuch Offender fhall, for every Time fo offending, forfeit and pay to
c. 20.   the Ufe of the Poor of that Parifh where the Offence fhall be committed, the Sum of
3 Car. 1. c. 4.
16 Car. 1. c. 4. 12 *d.*

Ibid.   Every Juftice of Peace, and every fuch Head Officer, may minifter the faid Oath to every Witnefs.

How to be   Every Juftice of Peace, and every fuch Head Officer may make their Warrant to the
levied.   Conftables, Church-wardens, and Overfeers of the Poor of that Parifh where the faid Of
Ibid.   fence fhall be committed; and the faid Conftable, Churchwardens, and Overfeers of the Poor, by Virtue of that Warrant, may levy the fame Sum and Sums of Money by Diftrefs and Sale of the Offender's Goods, rendring to the Party the Overplus.

Ibid.   In Defect of fuch Diftrefs, the Offender, if he or fhe be above the Age of twelve Years, fhall by Warrant from fuch Juftices of Peace or Head Officer, be fet in the Stocks by three whole Hours. But if the Offender be under the Age of twelve Years, and fhall not forthwith pay the faid Sum of 12 *d.* then he or fhe by Warrant of fuch Juftice of Peace or Head Officer fhall be whipped by the Conftable, or by the Parent or Mafter in the Prefence of the Conftable.

But every Offence againft this Law fhall be complained of and proved as aforefaid, Ibid. within twenty Days after the Offence committed.

Any Perfon that fhall prophanely Swear or Curfe, in the Hearing of any Juftice of 6 & 7 W. 3. Peace of the County, or other Head Officer or Juftice of Peace of the City; or fhall c. 11. thereof be convicted by Oath of one Witnefs, or Confeffion of the Party before any *Conviction.* Juftice of the Peace, Mayor, *&c.* The Offender fhall forfeit to the Ufe of the Poor, if he be *Penalty.* Servant, Labourer, Common Soldier, or Common Seaman, one Shilling, and every other Perfon two Shillings: And for every fecond Offence double; and for every third Offence treble.

The Penalties fhall be levied by Diftrefs, by Warrant of one Juftice. If no Diftrefs, Ibid. the Party to be fet in the Stocks one Hour for one Offence; for more than one two Hours, if above fixteen Years of Age; if under, to be whipt.

Juftice of the Peace, *&c.* who wilfully omits the Execution of this Act, forfeits five *Juftice omit-* Pounds. *ting, &c.* Ibid.

None to be profecuted upon this Act, unlefs within ten Days after the Offence. *When profe-cuted.* Ibid.

This Act to be read in Churches by the Parfon the next *Sunday* after every Quarter-day *To be read in* yearly, immediately after the Morning Prayer, upon Pain of twenty Shillings for every *Churches.* Omiffion.

Juftices of Peace, Mayors, *&c.* fhall regifter in a Book kept for that Purpofe, all Con- *Regifter.* victions made before them upon this Act, and the Time, and certify the fame to the Quarter-Seffions, to be there kept upon Record by the refpective Clerks of the Peace, to be feen without Fee.

Vide *Tit.* Oaths.

Tanner. Vide *Leather.*

Taxing. See *Poor, and Stock of the Shire.*

C H A P. XCIX. (*a*)

Tobacco.

NO Perfon may fet, plant, improve to grow, make or cure any Tobacco in Seed, *Penalty of* Plant, or otherwife, upon any Ground in *England, Wales,* Ifles of *Guernfey, Jer- Planting.* fey, Berwick* or *Ireland,* upon Pain of Forfeiture of 40 *s.* for every Pole or Rod of 12 Car. 2. Ground planted, fet or fown; and fo proportionably for any greater Quantity: One c. 34. Moiety to the King, and the other Moiety to him who will fue for the fame in any Court of Record.

And by the Statute of 15 *Car.* 2. *cap.* 7. the Penalty of 10 *l.* for every Pole or Rod of Ground is given, above the 40 *s.* by the faid Act of 12 *Car.* 2. *cap.* 34. And one third Part thereof given to the King, another third Part to the Poor of the Parifh, and the other third Part to the Informer.

And all Sheriffs, Juftices of the Peace, Mayors, Bailiffs, Conftables, and every of *Who may de-* them, upon Information or Complaint made to them or any of them, of any fuch To- *ftroy it.* bacco fown or planted within their Precincts, fhall within ten Days after fuch Complaint caufe the fame to be deftroyed. And any Perfon refifting or oppofing the Execution of the faid Act to forfeit five Pounds for every Offence, to be recovered as aforefaid, and by Diftrefs and Sale of the Offender's Goods; and for Want of Diftrefs the Offender to be imprifoned two Months without Bail. And over and above the Penalties appointed by this Act for fuch as refift; by the Statute of 15 *Car.* 2. *c.* 7. the Party refifting fhall be *Refiftance.* committed to the Gaol without Bail, till he enter into a Recognizance to the King, with two Sureties of 10 *l.* Penalty, not to do fo again; and by the Statute of 22 & 23 *Car.* 2. fhall forfeit 5 *l.* to be levied by Diftrefs and Sale; and if no Diftrefs, by Imprifonment for three Months without Bail, upon Conviction before two Juftices of Peace.

All Juftices of Peace, a Month before every General Quarter-Seffions, fhall iffue War- 22 & 23 Car. rants to the High Conftables, *&c.* requiring them to make Search what Tobacco is fowed, 2. c. 26: § 2. fet, planted, growing, curing, cured or made, and to make a Prefentment in Writing
upon

upon Oath, next Seſſions, of the Names of the Perſons planting, &c. the Quantity of Land, the immediate Tenants or preſent Occupiers, who ſhall be deemed Planters thereof

Inquiry.
Ib. §. 3.

Which Preſentment, filed in Seſſions, ſhall be a Conviction, unleſs the Perſons preſented (having Notice by the Delivery of a Copy of the Preſentment to him, or leaving it at his Dwelling-houſe or uſual Place of Abode, in the Preſence of one or more credible Witneſſes, ten Days before the next Seſſions) ſhall at next Quarter-Seſſions, after ſuch Notice, traverſe the ſame Preſentment, and find Sureties for proſecuting his Traverſe the next Seſſions after ſuch Traverſe.

Ib. §. 4.

All Conſtables, Tithingmen, Bailiffs, and other publick Officers in their Juriſdictions within fourteen Days after Warrant from two or more Juſtices of Peace, calling ſuch Aſſiſtance as they find neceſſary, may deſtroy the ſame Tobacco.

Officers Neglect.
Ib. §. 5.

If ſuch Tobacco ſhall be ſuffered to grow fourteen Days after the Receipt of ſuch Warrant, then ſuch Officers ſhall forfeit 5 s. for every Pole, Perch or Rod, and ſo proportionably for a greater or leſſer Quantity. One Moiety to the King, the other Moiety to the Informer. 22 & 23 *Car.* 2.

Aſſiſtance.
Ib. §. 6.

If any Perſon refuſe or neglect to aſſiſt ſuch Officer, for every ſuch Offence he ſhall forfeit 5 s. upon Conviction thereof before two Juſtices of Peace, to be levied by Warrant from ſuch Juſtices by Diſtreſs and Sale; and if no Diſtreſs, the Party to be committed to the Gaol without Bail for one Week.

Continued for ſuch Time as the Act for Tonnage and Poundage ſhall continue by 5 *Geo.* 1. *cap.* 11.

Cutting Leaves and Plants, &c. reſembling Tobacco.
1 G. 1. c. 46.

Every Perſon who ſhall cut or procure to be cut, any Manner of Leaves, Herbs, Plants or Materials (not being Tobacco Leaves) into the Form or Imitation of any the uſual Sizes or Cuts which Tobacco is uſually cut for Sale, or ſhall colour, or procure to be coloured or cured any ſuch Leaves, &c. to make them reſemble Tobacco, or ſhall ſell or procure to be ſold, or agree or offer to ſell knowingly, any ſuch Leaves, &c. mixed or not mixed with Tobacco, ſhall forfeit for every Pound ſo offered to Sale, and for every Pound of ſuch Mixture 5 s. and after that Rate for a greater or leſſer Quantity ; one Moiety to the Crown bearing the Charge of the Proſecution, and not otherwiſe; the other Moiety to the Informer, to be recovered by Action of Debt in the Courts at *Weſtminſter*, with full Coſts, &c.

Houſe may be opened to ſearch by a ſpecial Warrant from two Juſtices.
Ib §. 4.

No Houſe ſhall be opened to ſearch for ſuch Leaves, or for Engines, Utenſils and Tools, &c. without a ſpecial Warrant from two Juſtices of the Peace, and if ſeiſed above ſix Miles from any Port, ſhall be ſecured by the Order of two Juſtices at the King's Charge, till the Cauſe of Seiſure be determined at the next Seſſions, or the Seſſions after that at fartheſt ; and after Condemnation ſhall be burnt.

Servants and Labourers employed in cutting Leaves, &c.
Ib. §. 5.
5 G. 1. c. 7.

Servants and Labourers employed in cutting ſuch Leaves, or knowingly ſelling the ſame, and being convicted thereof by the Oath of one Witneſs, before two Juſtices, ſhall be by them committed to Gaol, or to the Houſe of Correction, there to be kept at hard Labour for any Time under ſix Months, without Bail.

Enacted, That the Stat. 12 *Annæ, cap.* 8. for encouraging the Tobacco Trade, and all Things therein contained, ſhall be continued and in Force during ſuch Time as the reſpective Duties on Tobacco ſhall continue.

Timber. Vide *Wood.*

Toll. See *Weights and Meaſures.*

C H A P. C.

Tranſportation, (a) *Importation, Exportation, and Tranſportation of Felons.*

One Juſtice.
1 & 2 Ph & Ma 5.
P. Juſt. 27.

(d) IT ſhould ſeem by the Words of the Statute, that any one Juſtice of Peace may inquire, hear and determine (as alſo may examine the Mariners and every other Perſon) of all and ſingular the Offenders againſt the Act 1 & 2 *Phil. & Mar.* provided for the reſtraining of carrying Corn, Beer, Butter, Cheeſe, Herrings and Wood beyond the Sea. But *quære.*

I

And

And it is holden to be great Policy, to provide that Corn be always of a reafonable and *Corn.*
ompetent Value, it being an affured Means to increafe and advance Husbandry and Til-
ige, the antienteft of all Trades and Profeffions, and commanded by God to *Adam,*
Gen. 3. 23. one of the greateft Commodities of this Realm, and much refpected and fa-
oured, as well by the Common Law, as alfo by the common Affent of the King, the
ords and Commons in many Parliaments. *Co.* 4. 39. See 15 *Car.* 2. *cap.* 7. 22 *Car.*
. cap. 13. 1 *Jac.* 2. *cap.* 19. 1 *W. & M. ft.* 1. *cap.* 12 & 24. 2 *Geo.* 2. *cap.* 18.
; *Geo.* 2. *cap.* 12. and 11 *Geo.* 2. *cap.* 22. Tit. *Corn, Chap.* 27.

By 18 *Car.* 2. *cap.* 2. the bringing in of Cattle is declared a Nufance, and if any great *Cattle and*
Cattle, Sheep, Swine, or any Beef, Pork or Bacon, fhall be imported or brought into *Victuals.*
England, any Conftable, Headborough, Tithing-man, Churchwardens or Overfeers, 18 *Car.* 2.
vithin their Limits, may feife the fame, and may keep them for forty-eight Hours in *petual by 32*
ome publick Place; in which Time, if the Owner fhall make it appear by the Oath of *Car.* 2. *c.* 2.
wo Witneffes, unto fome Juftice of Peace, that the fame came not from beyond the Seas,
he fame by Warrant from a Juftice fhall be delivered to the Party : But if he fhall not
nake it fo appear, the fame fhall be forfeited; one Moiety to the Seifor, the other Moiety
o the Poor where the fame are feifed, the *Ifland of Man* excepted, fo as they be of their
wn Breed, and exceed not 600 in one Year, and be landed at *Chefter.*

Not only the Conftables, Tithingmen, Headboroughs, Churchwardens or Overfeers of 20 *Car.* 2.
he Poor, but every Inhabitant, or any other Perfon whatfoever, fhall and may feize any *c.* 7. §. 3.
great Cattle, Sheep or Swine, or any Beef, Pork or Bacon, imported into *England* or
Wales contrary to the aforefaid Statute of 18 *Car.* 2. *cap.* 2. wherefoever the fame fhall be
ound, and fhall within fix Days after Conviction and Forfeiture thereof caufe the faid 32 *Car.* 2.
Cattle, Sheep and Swine to be killed, and the Hides and Tallow fhall be to the Seifor, *c.* 2. §. 5.
ind the Remainder of the faid Cattle, Sheep and Swine fhall be forthwith by the Church-
vardens and Overfeers diftributed among the Poor of the Parifh, upon Notice thereof to
e given by fuch Seifor.

If fuch Seifor, Churchwarden or Overfeer fhall fail in the Execution of his faid Duty, *Forfeiture.*
hey fhall feverally forfeit forty Shillings for every one of the great Cattle, and ten Shil- 32 *Car.* 2.
ings for every Sheep or Swine, which fhould have been fo killed or diftributed; one Moiety *c.* 2. §. 6.
hereof to the Poor of the Parifh, and the other to the Informer, to be levied by Diftrefs
ind Sale of the Offender's Goods, by Warrant of any Juftice of Peace of the County or
Place where the Offence is fo committed, upon Confeffion of the Party, View of the
Juftice, or Oath of one or more credible Witneffes (other than the Informer) the Overplus to the Owners, neceffary Charges of diftraining deducted : And for Want of Diftrefs,
the Offender to be committed to Gaol for three Months without Bail or Mainprize.

If no Seifure fhall be made by the Officers or Inhabitants within the Liberty, Parifh or 20 *Car.* 2.
Place where fuch Cattle or Goods fhall be firft imported, fuch Liberty, Parifh and Place, *c.* 7. §. 4.
and the Inhabitants thereof, fhall forfeit for every Default 100 *l.* for the Ufe of the Houfe
of Correction, within the County or Liberty where fuch Default fhall be.

If any great Cattle, Sheep or Swine fhall be once or oftner feifed, and afterwards by 32 *Car.* 2.
Permiffion, Connivance, Negligence, or otherwife, removed and found alive in any *c.* 2. §. 10.
other Parifh or Place, they fhall be liable to like Seifure, and the Seifor and Poor of the
Parifh or Place to the like Benefit, and the Cattle, Sheep and Swine be forfeited; and
the Proof incumbent upon the Owner, as if fuch Cattle had never been feifed before.

If any *Englifh* or other Cattle, driven or intermixed with *Irifh* Cattle, fhall be feifed *Cattle inter-*
together with them, fuch Cattle fhall be deemed *Irifh,* and fhall be fubject to like For- *mixt.*
feiture, and be ordered and difpofed in all Refpects, as if they were *Irifh.* Ibid. §. 11.

Every Veffel in which any Cattle, Swine, Sheep, Beef, Pork or Bacon fhall be im- *Veffel.*
ported from beyond Sea, and out of which any of them fhall be put on Shore, fhall be 20 *Car.* 2.
forfeited; and any Perfon within a Year after fuch Importation, may feize and fell her : *c.* 7. §. 7.
One Half of the Price to be to the Ufe of the Poor of the Parifh where feifed : The other
Half to him that fhall feife: And any Juftice of Peace of the County, or Chief Officer of
the Port-Town, in or near the Place where fuch Importation fhall be, or where any of
the faid Cattle, &c. fhall be driven or brought, by Warrant under Hand and Seal, may
caufe to be apprehended the Mafters and Mariners of the Veffel, in which fuch Importation fhall be made, and others imployed in landing, driving or taking Care of the fame,
and commit them to Gaol for three Months without Bail.

All Forfeitures by the Acts of 18 *Car.* 2. *cap.* 2. and 20 *Car.* 2. *cap.* 7. are to be *Account.*
accounted for to fuch Perfons, and in fuch Manner, as the Overfeers of the Poor are Ib. §. 4.
appointed to account by the Statute of 43 *Eliz. cap.* 2.

Mutton, Lamb, Butter and Cheese.

No Mutton or Lamb fhall be imported into *England* from *Ireland*, or any foreign Ports; nor any Butter or Cheefe out of *Ireland*; and all fuch Mutton, Lamb, Butter or Cheefe imported or expofed to Sale here, fhall be fubject to the like Seifures, and the Importers and Sellers to the like Penalties as are appointed againft any Importer or Seller on Importation of Beef, Pork or Bacon.

Plantations.
15 Car. 2. c. 7. §. 6.

Suit may be commenced in any Court of Record for any Forfeiture accrued upon any Statute of 15 *Car.* 2. *cap.* 7. whereby is prohibited the Importing any Commodities of the Growth or Make of *Europe*, into any Place in his Majefty's Poffeffion in *Afia*, *Africa* and *America*, but what fhall be fhipped in *England* or *Wales*, and that in *Englifh* fhipping, &c.

Lace and small Wares.
13 & 14 C. 2. c. 13. §. 2.

No Perfon fhall fell or caufe to be fold, or offer to Sale, or export, any foreign Bone-lace, Cut-work, Imbroidery, Fringe, Band-ftrings, Buttons or Needle-work, made of Thread, Silk, or any or either of them, in Parts beyond the Seas, or import, bring in fend or convey, or caufe, &c. into *England*, &c. any fuch foreign Bone-lace, &c. upon Pain, That the Perfon that fhall fell or offer to fale foreign Bone-lace, &c. fhall forfei for every Offence 50 *l.* and the whole Bone-lace, &c. And upon Pain that he that fhal import, &c. fuch foreign Bone-lace, &c. fhall forfeit the whole Bone-lace, &c. and 100 *l.* for every fuch Offence. A Moiety thereof to the King, and the other Moiety to the Profecutor in any the King's Courts of Record, &c.

Search.
Ib. §. 3.

Upon Complaint and Information to any Juftice of Peace at Times reafonable, he fhall iffue out his Warrant to the Conftables, to enter and fearch for fuch Manufactures in Shops, being open, or Ware-houfes and Dwelling-houfes of the Perfons fufpected to have the fame, and feife the fame. 14 *Car.* 2. *cap.* 13.

Horfes.
1 Ed. 6. c. 5. §. 1.

No Perfon fhall give, exchange, fell convey or deliver into any Place beyond the Sea, out of this Realm, or the Dominions thereof, any Horfe, Gelding or Mare, without Licence from the King, under the Great Seal or Privy Signet. No Perfon fhall convey any Horfe, Gelding or Mare into any foreign Parts, without fuch Licence, upon Pain to forfeit the fame to the King, and alfo 40 *l.* for every one. A Moiety to the King the other Moiety to the Profecutor in the King's Court, and Imprifonment for a Year.

Who may inquire.
Ib. §. 2.

Juftices of Peace in their Seffions may inquire of the Offences, and every Subject may arreft the Perfons offending againft that Act. That Act fhall not prejudice any that carry Horfes beyond the Sea, in the King's Service, nor to the Warden of the Cinque Ports, that may give or fend fix Horfes or Geldings beyond Sea in every Year, nor to the Mafter of the Horfe, as to the Duties of his Place.

6 G. 1. c. 23.

'Tis Felony without Benefit of Clergy to refcue an Offender ordered to be tranfported. and likewife aiding or affifting them to efcape.

A Felon ordered to be tranfported, and returning before the Term expired, is guilty of Felony without Benefit of Clergy; and this may be tried in the County where he was taken, or from whence he was ordered to be tranfported; and a Certificate from the Clerk of the Affife, or of the Peace, or their Succeffors, containing the Effect and Tenor of the Indictment and Conviction, and of the Order and Contract for Tranfportation, being produced in Court, fhall be fufficient Proof, that fuch Perfon hath been before convicted and ordered to be tranfported.

Touching exporting Sheep, *vide* Tit. *Sheep.*
Touching exporting Wool, *vide* Tit. *Wool.*
For importing Fifh, *vide* Tit. *Fifh.*

Trees. See *Trespass.*

CHAP. CI.

Trespass.

Orchards. Corn and Fences.
43 El. c. 1. §. 1.

ALL and every lewd and mean Perfons which fhall unlawfully cut or take away any Corn growing, or rob any Orchards or Gardens, or break or cut any Hedge, Pale, Rail or Fence, or dig pull up or take away any Fruit-trees, or fhall cut or fpoil any Woods, Under-woods, Poles or Trees ftanding, (not being Felony) and their Procurers or Receivers, knowing the fame, being thereof convict by Confeffion of the Party, or by the Teftimony of one fufficient Witnefs, upon Oath before any one Juftice of Peace, (where the Offence fhall be committed, or the Offender apprehended) fhall for the firft fault give the Party wronged fuch Recompence (and within fuch Time) as by any one Juftice of Peace (of the County where fuch Offence fhall be done) fhall be appointed. And if fuch Offender fhall be thought (in the Difcretion of the faid Juftice) not able, or do not make Satisfaction accordingly; then the faid Juftice fhall commit the faid Offender to fome Conftable or other inferior Officer (where the Offence fhall be committed or the Offender apprehended) to be whipped.

Alfo for the fecond Fault, and every other Offence whereof fuch Offender fhall be Ib. after convicted in Form aforefaid, fuch Offender fhall be whipped as aforefaid, without any Satisfaction to be taken.

If any Conftable or inferior Officer do refufe, or do not, at the Command of the *Officer's Neg-* Juftice (by himfelf, or fome other by him to be appointed) execute upon the Offender *lett.* the Punifhment aforefaid, the faid Juftice may commit fuch Conftable, &c. to the com- Ib. §. 2. mon Gaol, there to remain without Bail until the faid Offender be by the faid Conftable, or by fome other by his Procurement whipped, as aforefaid.

But no Juftice of Peace fhall execute this Statute for any of the Offences aforefaid Ib. §. 3. alone unto himfelf, unlefs he is affociated and affifted with one or more other Juftices of the Peace whom the Offence doth not concern.

(a) One Juftice of Peace (not being the Party grieved) may fend fuch Offenders for their fecond Fault, &c. to the Houfe of Correction, as idle and diforderly Perfons, there to be detained, &c. at the Difcretion of the faid Juftice; and this by Force of Statute 7 *Jac.* 1. *cap.* 4. efpecially, if they be common Offenders in this Kind; or may bind them to their Good Behaviour, and fo over to the next Quarter-Seffions, and by Order from thence, to be fent to the Houfe of Correction, there to be continued fome convenient Time.

But for the gleaning and leaving of the Harveft, &c. God commandeth, that it be left for the Poor, the Fatherlefs, the Widow, and the Stranger. *Levit.* 19. 9 & 23. *Deut.* 22. 24. And it were worthy the Confideration of the Juftices to take fome Courfe that fuch only might have the Benefit of Gleaning, and not Farmers and Tradefmen, that in many Places in Harveft-Time fet their Servants to that Employment, which is no better than to rob the Poor of what properly belongs to them.

If any fhall by Night or Day unlawfully break, cut down, cut out or deftroy any 5 El. 21. Head or Dam of any Pond, Pool, Mote, Stagne, Slew or feveral Pit, wherein Fifh are or fhall be put, or fhall fifh therein without Authority, and be convicted thereof at the Suit of the King or Party grieved, he fhall be imprifoned three Months, and pay the Party treble Damages; and after the three Months be bound to the Good Behaviour for feven Years with fufficient Sureties, or elfe continue in Prifon for feven Years without Bail. For the Recovery herein, fee Tit. *Hunting.*

No Perfon fhall flay, take or caufe to be taken by Means of any Craft or Engine, Herons, unlefs by Hawking or with Long-Bow, upon Pain to forfeit for every Heron 5 s. 8 d. For the Conviction, fee Tit. *Hunting.* See poftea Tit. *Wood.*

Trees.
1 G. 1. Stat.
2. c. 48. § 1.

Malicioufly
- Barking,
- Breaking down,
- Cutting up,
- Defacing,
- Deftroying,
- Plucking up,
- Spoiling or
- Throwing down

Any
- Fruit-Tree,
- Timber-Tree,
- Or other Tree.

The Party grieved fhall receive Satisfaction from the Inhabitants of the Parifh where fuch Trees fhall be barked, &c. againft whom an Action may be brought to recover the Damages, according to the Statute 13 *Ed.* 1. *cap.* 46.

Any two Juftices where fuch Offence fhall be committed, or the Seffions, upon Com- Ib. §. 2. plaint of the Inhabitants of the Parifh, or the Owner of the Trees, or any other, may caufe the Offenders to be apprehended, and hear and determine the Offence, and on Con- * *And to be* viction may commit them to the Houfe of * Correction, there to be kept to hard La- *publickly whipt* bour for three Months without Bail; and if there be no Houfe of Correction, then *once every* to be committed to the common Gaol for four Months, and to be publickly whipped *Month during* by the common Hangman once every Month during the four Months, on a Market- *in fome Mark-* Day, in fome Town, between the Hours of eleven and two. *et Town and*

Before *Day, &c.*

Ib. §. 3.   Before he is difcharged fhall find Sureties for his good Behaviour for two Years.

Ib. §. 4.   Malicioufly fetting on Fire, burning or caufing to be burnt, any Wood, Underwood or Coppice, or any Parts thereof, is Felony.

6 G. 1. c. 16.

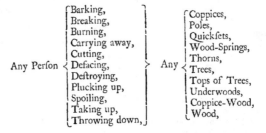

Any Perfon {
Barking,
Breaking,
Burning,
Carrying away,
Cutting,
Defacing,
Deftroying,
Plucking up,
Spoiling,
Taking up,
Throwing down,
}
Any {
Coppices,
Poles,
Quickfets,
Wood-Springs,
Thorns,
Trees,
Tops of Trees,
Underwoods,
Coppice-Wood,
Wood,
}

without the Confent of the Owner, or of him who is intrufted with the Care thereof.

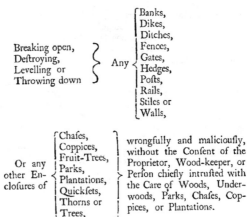

Breaking open,
Deftroying,
Levelling or
Throwing down
}
Any {
Banks,
Dikes,
Ditches,
Fences,
Gates,
Hedges,
Pofts,
Rails,
Stiles or
Walls,
}

Or any other En-clofures of {
Chafes,
Coppices,
Fruit-Trees,
Parks,
Plantations,
Quickfets,
Thorns or
Trees,
}
wrongfully and malicioufly, without the Confent of the Proprietor, Wood-keeper, or Perfon chiefly intrufted with the Care of Woods, Under-woods, Parks, Chafes, Cop-pices, or Plantations.

* Cro. Car.
280, 439.
1 Leon. 108.
Stile 215.
Sid. 107,312.
Raym. 487.
† Weftm. 2.

   He who is damnified fhall have Recompence of the Inhabitants of the Village adjoin-ing, as by the Act * 13 *Ed.* 1. upon which Act † Writs have been founded to diftrain the adjoining Vills, to fatisfy the Damages, where the Offenders cannot be known ; and by the Statute 6 *Georgii* aforefaid, if he be known, and fhall not be convicted by the Parifh within fix Months after the Fact committed.

   Nota ; This laft Statute extends to preferve all Enclofures about Chafes, Coppices, Trees, which the firft Act 1 *Georgii* did not, but the Profecution and the Conviction and Punifhment muft be as by the Statute of *Weftminfter* 2. is injoined.

43 El. c. 7.
15 Car. 2.
c. 2.

   Unlawfully taking or cutting Corn growing, robbing Orchards, and taking away any Fruit-Trees, &c. fhall make fuch Recompence as Juftices fhall direct, and a Sum not exceeding 10 s. to the Poor ; and in Default thereof to be fent to the Houfe of Cor-rection, not exceeding a Month, and be whipped.

15 Car. 2.
c. 2. §. 5.

   Profecution to be within fix Weeks after the Offence, and the Conviction by Confef-fion, or one Witnefs.

   The Defendant was convicted by two Juftices upon the Statute 1 *Geo.* 1. *cap.* 48. for deftroying Fruit-Trees, and it was moved to quafh this Conviction, becaufe it did not fpecify the Punifhment inflicted by that Statute, which is to be fent to the Houfe of Correction for three Months, &c. and the better Opinion was, that this being a fpecial Judgment of the two Juftices, they fhould have fpecified the Punifhment inflicted by the Statute, becaufe it might be different from the Punifhment appointed by them : However there being no Forfeiture in this Cafe, it was held, that *Ideo confideratum eft quod convictus eft* was fufficient without fetting forth the Punifhment. *Trin.* 9 G. 1. B. R.

         Trial. See *Chap.* 187.

I   C H A P.

CHAP. CII.

Tithes.

TWO Juftices of the Peace (the one being of the *Quorum*) upon Complaint by any competent Judge of Tithes, for any Mifdemeanor of the Defendant in a Suit of Tithes (or for other Duties of the Church) may caufe him to be attached and committed to Ward, there to remain without Bail until he find fufficient Sureties (unto the faid Juftices) by Recognizance to the King's Ufe, to obey the Procefs and Sentence of that Judge.

Alfo upon Complaint or Certificate in Writing by any Ecclefiaftical Judge, that hath given definitive Sentence, in the Cafe of Tithes, againft one which wilfully refufeth to pay the Tithes or Sums of Money fo adjudged, two fuch Juftices of Peace may caufe the Party to be attached and committed to the next Gaol, there to remain without Bail, till he find fuch Sureties (as aforefaid) to perform that Sentence. *32 H. 7. 8. P. Juft. 104.*

(*a*) If a Quaker refufe to pay or compound for Tithes, or Church Rates, the two next Juftices may upon Complaint made, fummon him to appear before them (other han fuch Juftices who are Patrons of the Church, or interefted in the Tithes) and they upon Examination of the Matter on Oath, may afcertain what is due to the Perfon complaining ; and if under 10 *l.* may by an Order under their Hands and Seals direct the Payment thereof, and then if he refufe to pay it, one of the faid Juftices may by Warrant, &c. caufe the fame to be levied by Diftrefs and Sale, &c. *7 & 8 W. 3. c. 35. §. 4. made perpetual per 1 Geo. 1. c. 6.*

An Appeal lies to the Quarter-Seffions, and if the Quaker appeals, no Warrant fhall be granted to diftrain till the Appeal is determined. *Ib.*

If the Appeal is determined in Favour of the Appellee, the Seffions may give reafonable Cofts, to be levied by Diftrefs, &c. *Ib.*

No *Certiorari* is to be allowed, unlefs the Title of the Tithes is in Queftion. *Ib. §. 5.*

All Perfons fhall fet out and pay all and fingular their fmall Tithes, Compofitions, &c. to the Rectors, Vicars, or to whom they fhall be due, according to the Rights ufed in the faid Parifhes : And if any Perfon fail, &c. in the Payment, &c. of fuch fmall Tithes, &c. for twenty Days after Demand thereof, then the Perfon to whom the fame are due may make his Complaint in Writing to two or more Juftices of Peace in that County, City, &c. where the fame grows due, neither of which Juftices is to be Patron of the Church where the faid Tithes, &c. arife, nor any Ways interefted in the faid Tithes, &c. *Small Tithes. 7 & 8 W. 3. c. 6. §. 1.*

And if Complaint be hereafter brought to two or more Juftices of the Peace, as aforefaid, the faid Juftices are hereby authorized to fummon in Writing under their Hands and Seals, by reafonable Warning, the Perfon or Perfons againft whom fuch Complaints fhall be made, and after Appearance or Default, the Summons being proved upon Oath, the faid Juftices or any two of them, fhall proceed to examine and determine the faid Complaint, and upon Evidence produced before them, fhall in Writing under their Hands and Seals, adjudge the Cafe, and give fuch reafonable Allowance for fuch Tithes, &c. fo fubftracted, and alfo fuch Cofts, not exceeeing 10 *s.* as they fhall reafonably think fit. *Juftices to determine Complaints. Ib. §. 2.*

If any Perfon fhall neglect or refufe, the Space of ten Days after Notice, to pay the fum fo adjudged, the Conftables and Church-wardens of the faid Parifh, or one of them fhall by Warrant, under the Hands and Seals of the faid Juftices, diftraining the Goods of the Party fo refufing, and after detaining them three Days, in Cafe the Sum adjudged be not paid with reafonable Charges for making the Diftrefs, he fhall make publick Sale of the fame, pay the Sum adjudged to the Party complaining, retain reafonable Charges for diftraining, as the faid Juftices fhall think fit, and return the Overplus. *Charge of Diftrefs. Ib. §. 3.*

The Juftices in their Examination of the Matters offered to them by this Act, may adminifter an Oath or Oaths. *Oath. Ib. §. 4.*

No Complaint to Juftices of Peace for Tithes, &c. hereafter due, fhall be heard and determined by them, unlefs made within two Years after the faid Tithes become due. *Ib. §. 6.*

Parties aggrieved by any Judgment of the faid two Juftices, may appeal to the next Quarter-Seffions, and the Juftices there prefent, or the major Part of them, fhall finally *Appeal. Ib. §. 7.*

finally hear and determine the Matter ; and if they find Caufe to confirm the Judgment given by the faid two Juftices, they fhall decree the fame by Order of Seffions, and give Cofts againft the Appellant, to be levied by Diftrefs, &c. And no Proceedings to be removed by *Certiorari*, unlefs the Title of fuch Tithes, &c. fhall be in Queftion.

Judgment in-rolled.
Ib. §. 9.
Every Perfon obtaining Judgment, or againft whom Judgment fhall be obtained before Juftices of Peace out of Seffions, for fmall Tithes, &c. fhall procure the fame to be in-rolled at the next Quarter-Seffions ; and the Clerk of the Peace upon Tender is to inrol the fame, for which he fhall receive no more than 1 *s.*

Removal of Party.
Ib. §. 10.
If the Perfon againft whom fuch Judgment fhall be had, fhall after fuch Judgment; and before the Levying the Money adjudged, remove out of the County, City, &c. the Juftices who made the Judgment, or one of them, fhall certify the fame under Hand and Seal to any Juftice of Peace of fuch other County, &c. where the faid Perfon fhall inhabit, who is hereby required by Warrant under his Hand and Seal, to the Con-ftables or Church-wardens of the Place to levy the Sum adjudged, in fuch Manner as the other Juftices might have done, in Cafe the Party had not removed.

Ib. §. 12.
The Juftices who fhall hear and determine the Matters aforefaid, fhall have Power to give Cofts, not exceeding 10 *s.* to the Party profecuted, if they fhall find the Complaint falfe and vexatious; to be levied as aforefaid.

This Act is made perpetual by the Statute 3 & 4 *Ann. cap.* 18.

CHAP. CIII.

Tile.

17 Ed. 4. 4.
Lamb. 197.
Cromp. 130.
BY the Words of the Statute, any one Juftice may inquire, hear and determine (by Examination or otherwife by their Difcretion) all and fingular the Offences com-mitted in Tile-making, *fc.* If they be not made good, and of Earth well prepared, and alfo of due Affife in Length, Breadth and Thicknefs ; and may affefs the Fines limit-ted by the fame Statute ; and may call before him fuch as have beft Knowledge in Tile-making, and appoint them Searchers of the faid Defaults ; but Mr. *Lamb.* 197. maketh a Doubt thereof.

(*a*) But the Juftices fo refolved, and accordingly made an Order for licenfing Perfons to be Searchers of all Manner of Tile made within the County of *Middlefex* for four Years. *Ord.* 5. *Oct.* 7. *Jac.* 1. *lib. Seff. pa. Mid.*

Vagabonds. See *Rogues*, &c. Chap. 83.

Waggoners. See *Carriages*, Chap. 21.

CHAP. CIV.

Watch.

13 Ed. 1.
Stat. 2. c. 4.
(*a*) IN great Towns walled the Gates fhall be fhut up from the Sun-fetting until the Sun-rifing ; and no Man fhall lodge in the Suburbs or any Place out of the Town, from nine of the Clock till Day, except his Hoft will anfwer for him.

13 Ed. 1.
Stat. 2. c. 6.
(*d*) Every Juftice of Peace may caufe Night-watch to be duly kept for the arrefting of Perfons fufpect or Night-walkers (be they Strangers or others) that be of evil Fame or Behaviour : And this they may do by Force of the Commiffion, the firft *Affig. Lamb.* 190.

13 Ed. 1.
Stat. 2. c. 4.
This Watch is to be kept yearly from the Feaft of the *Afcenfion* until *Michaelmas,* in every Town, and fhall continue all the Night, *fc.* from the Sun-fetting to the Sun-rifing.

Winch.
13 Ed. 1. 4.
5 Ed. 3. 14.
All fuch Strangers or Perfons fufpected as fhall in the Night-time pafs by the Watch-men (appointed thereto by the Town, Conftable or other Officer) may be examined by the faid Watchmen, whence they come and what they be, and of their Bufinefs, &c. And if they find Caufe of Sufpicion, they fhall ftay them ; and if fuch Perfons will not obey the Arreft of the Watchmen, the faid Watchmen fhall levy Hue and Cry, that the Offenders may be taken, or elfe they may juftify to beat them (for that they refift the Peace and Juftice of the Realm) and may alfo fet them in the Stocks (for the

4

fame)

ime) until the Morning; and then, if no Sufpicion be found, the faid Perfons fhall be
t go: But if they find Caufe of Sufpicion, they fhall forthwith deliver the faid Perfons
o the Sheriff, who fhall keep them in Prifon until they be duly delivered; or elfe the
Watchmen may deliver fuch Perfons to the Conftable, and fo to convey them to the
uftice of Peace, by him to be examined, and to be bound over or committed, until the
Offenders be acquitted in due Manner. See more of *Watch* in the Title *Felony.*

(*a*) Thefe Watchmen are alfo to apprehend all Rogues and Vagabonds, Night-
Walkers, Eve-Droppers, Scouts, and fuch like, and fuch as go armed, &c.

Note, That in an Action of Falfe Imprifonment brought by one *Sm.* againft *Brown* Cro. El. 2.
a Conftable of *Chelmsford* in *Effex*) thefe Things were holden for Law concerning p. 204.
Watches, about 32 *Eliz.*

1. Firft, That no Man is compellable to watch except he be an Inhabitant within
he fame Town.

2. That fuch as are Inhabitants within the Town are not compellable to watch at the
Will of the Conftable, but only when their Turn cometh; and therefore *Gawdy* (Juftice)
iid, That the Statute of *Winchefter* is, That from henceforth Watches fhall be kept as
ath been ufed in Times paft, &c. and fo the Manner of Watching is not referred to the
Will of the Conftable, but only to the Ufe heretofore; which is commonly by Turn, or
y the Houfe.

3. That if a Man who is compellable to watch fhall contemptuoufly refufe, upon Com-
nandment of the Conftable, the Conftable *Ex Officio* may fet him in the Stocks for fuch
is Contempt. *Tamen quære de hoc.* Or elfe the Conftable may prefent fuch his Default
t the Affifes or Seffions of the Peace, &c. or may complain thereof to any Juftice of
Peace who may bind the Offender to the Good Behaviour, and fo over to the next Quar-
r-Seffions, &c.

Note alfo, That both Watching and Warding muft be by Men that be able of Body
nd fufficiently weaponed.

And Note, That Watching is properly intended of the Night, and Warding for the
Day-time; and for the Warding in the Day-time, for the Apprehending of Rogues and
he like idle evil Members, is of great Ufe; it therefore is and muft be left to the Dif-
retion of the Conftable and Directions of the Juftice of Peace to appoint or alter ac-
ording to the Occafion. *Refol.* 36. *fupra,* Chap. 73.

A Certificate under the Hand and Seal of two Juftices, that a Watchman, or other Per- 5 Ann. c. 31.
on, was killed in endeavouring to take a Burglar or Houfe-breaker, intitles his Execu-
or or Adminiftrator to 40 *l.*

C H A P. CV.

Watermen.

EVERY Juftice of Peace (by the general Words of the Statute) within the Shires 2 & 3 P. & M.
next adjoining to the River of *Thames* (between *Gravefend* and *Windfor*) within his c. 16.
P. Boteman.
everal Jurifdiction hath Power (upon Complaint made to him by the Overfeers and Ru- 4.
ers of the Watermen and Wherrymen, or Two of them, or by the Mafters of any fuch P. Juft. 109.
Cromp. 131.
ervants) to examine, hear and determine all Offences againft the Statute, and to fet at Lamb. 205.
arge him that fhall be imprifoned by fuch Overfeers or Rulers, according to this Act (if
here be juft Caufe) and alfo by his Difcretion to punifh thofe Overfeers and Rulers that
hall unjuftly punifh any Perfon by Colour of this Act.

The Offences of Watermen againft this Statute are thefe.

1. No fingle Man fhall be a Waterman there, unlefs he be an Houfekeeper, or an P. Botem. 4.
Apprentice, or retained in Service by the whole Year. See 1 *Jac.* 1. *cap.* 16. P. Ibid. 3.

2. One of the (two) Watermen, rowing together in one Boat, muft be allowed by the
noft Part of the eight Overfeers, by Writing under their Seal, and muft have ufed row-
ng there two Years before.

3. Watermen fhall not hide themfelves in Time of Preffing for the King's Service, &c. P. Ibid. 5.

4. Watermen fhall not take for their Fare and Labour above the Prices affeffed, &c. P. Ibid. 7.
nd fet up in Tables in *Weftminfter-Hall,* &c. But *Quære* whether the Juftice of Peace
e to meddle in this. See the Statute at large.

(*a*) It fhall not be lawful for any Perfon who fhall keep or work any Wherry-Boat, 2 Geo. 2. c. 26.
Tilt-Boat, Barge or other Veffel, for carrying Paffengers or Goods for Hire upon the §. 1.

Thames

Thames between *Gravefend* and *Windfor*, to take or employ any Apprentice or Servant unlefs he be a Houfe-Keeper, or have fome known Place of Abode where he may enter- tain fuch Apprentice, &c. and fhall Regifter with the Clerk of the Waterman's Compan the Habitation, &c. where he fhall refide, upon Pain that every Perfon receiving an' Apprentice, &c. contrary to this Act, and being convicted before the Lord Mayor, o any one Juftice of Peace for the City, or for the County or Place where the Offender fhall be found, by the Oaths of two Witneffes, fhall forfeit 10 *l.* to be levied by Diftref and Sale of Goods by Warrant of fuch Lord Mayor, &c. and for want of Diftrefs, h fhall by like Warrant be committed to the Work-Houfe or Houfe of Correction, to b kept to hard Labour not exceeding one Month, nor lefs than fourteen Days; and th Clerk of the Company fhall regifter the Habitation, &c. of every fuch Waterman, &c without Fee; and in cafe of Neglect, fuch Clerk fhall forfeit 10 *l.* to be levied as an' other Penalty by this Act. And if any Waterman, &c. fhall not Regifter his Habita tion, &c. and every Removal thereof, fuch Apprentice bound to fuch Waterman, &c fhall, on Application to the Rulers at any of their publick Courts, be turned over to an' other Mafter or Miftrefs.

Ib. §. 2.   It fhall not be lawful for any Apprentice to have the fole Care of any Boat within th Liberties aforefaid, till fuch Apprentice fhall have attained the Age of fixteen Years, if h be the Son of a Waterman, and feventeen Years, being the Son of a Landman; and un lefs he fhall have worked on the River for two Years at leaft before his attaining of th faid Ages; and if any Apprentice under the faid Years fhall offend contrary to this Act and be convicted in Manner aforefaid, the Mafter of fuch Apprentice fhall forfeit 10*s.* t be levied, &c. as any other Penalty in this Act.

Ib. §. 3.   In all Cafes where Diftrefs cannot be found to fatisfy the Penalties inflicted by an' Rules, &c. of the Company, Oath being made of fuch Want of Diftrefs before th Lord Mayor, or any Juftice of Peace for the Place where the Offender fhall be found it fhall be lawful for fuch Lord Mayor, &c. to commit fuch Offender to the Work- Houfe or Houfe of Correction, to be kept at hard Labour not exceeding one Month, no lefs than fourteen Days, fuch Offender being convicted according to this Act, or the Ac 11 & 12 *Will.* 3. *cap.* 21.

Ib. §. 4.   If any Perfon, not having ferved feven Years to any Waterman, &c. (except Trinity- men, Fifhermen, Ballaftmen, and Perfons employed in navigating Weftern Barges, Mill- Boats, Chalk-Hoys, Faggot and Wood Lighters, Dung-Boats and Gardeners Boats, ir fuch Manner as hath been accuftomed, and is allowed by 11 & 12 *Will.* 3. *cap.* 21. fhall row any Boat or other Veffel upon the River for Hire, between the Limits afore- faid, every fuch Offender being convicted in Manner aforefaid fhall forfeit 10 *l.* to be le- vied as aforefaid; and for want of Diftrefs, the Lord Mayor, or any Juftice of Peace for the Place where the Offence fhall be committed, is required by Warrant to commit fuch Offender to the next publick Work-Houfe, or Houfe of Correction, not exceeding one Month, nor lefs than fourteen Days.

10 Geo. 7. *c. 31. §. 2.*   Apprentices to Watermen between *Gravefend* and *Windfor*, fhall be bound by Inden- tures to ferve feven Years, upon Pain that every Perfon acting contrary fhall forfeit 10 *l.* upon Conviction, before a Juftice of Peace.

Ib. §. 3.   Apprentices bound contrary to this Act fhall not thereby obtain any Freedom, but fhall be liable to pay for every Time they fhall work any Boat or other Veffel, being con- victed in Manner aforefaid, 10 *l.*

Ib. §. 4.   No Freeman of the Company, nor his Widow, fhall at one Time take more Appren- tices than two, nor fhall take the fecond Apprentice till the Firft hath ferved four Years, under the Penalty of 10 *l.*

Ib. §. 5.   It fhall not be lawful for any Waterman or Lighterman, or his Widow, to keep any Apprentice, unlefs fuch Waterman, &c. be the Occupier of fome Tenement wherein to lodge himfelf and his Apprentices; and fuch Waterman, &c. fhall keep fuch Apprentices to lodge in the fame Houfe wherein he doth lodge, upon Pain of 10 *l.*

Ib. §. 6.   If any Perfon fhall knowingly and wilfully produce any forged or falfe Certificate, and fhall be thereof convicted before the Lord Mayor, or any Juftice of Peace for the City, by the Oath of one Witnefs, he fhall forfeit 10 *l.*

Ib. §. 8.   It fhall not be lawful for any Perfon who fhall work any Tilt-Boat, Row-Barge, or other Boat, for Gain, to carry in any fuch Boat more than thirty-feven Paffengers, and three more Paffengers only, if brought on Board by the Way; nor to carry in any other Boat or Wherry more than eight Paffengers, and two more only if called in by the Way; nor to carry in any Ferry-Boat or Wherry allowed to work on *Sunday* more than eight Paffengers; and if any Perfon fhall carry in any fuch Tilt-Boats, &c. a greater Number,

4   every

every Perfon fo offending, and being convicted by the Oath of one Witnefs, or by Con-feffion before the Lord Mayor of *London*, or one Juftice of Peace for the Place where the Offence fhall be committed, or the Offender found, or on View of any fuch Juftice, fhall for the firft Offence forfeit 5 *l.* and for the fecond Offence 10 *l.* one Moiety to the Informer, and the other Moiety to fuch Ufes as the other Penalties impofed by this Act; and every Perfon who fhall offend in the Premiffes a third Time, fhall be disfranchifed for twelve Months from working any Boat, &c. And in cafe any greater Number of Perfons fhall be carried in any fuch Tilt-Boats, &c. and any Paffenger fhall be drowned, every Perfon who fhall work fuch Boats offending therein, and being convicted, fhall be guilty of Felony, and tranfported as Felons. See the Statute, *fect.* 9, 10, 11, 12. for the Regulations relating to the *Gravefend* Boats.

Penalties by this Act to be levied by Diftrefs and Sale of Goods by Warrant of the Lord Ib. §. 15. Mayor of *London*, or one Juftice of Peace; and for Want of Diftrefs, the Offender may be committed to the Houfe of Correction to hard Labour, not exceeding one Month, nor lefs than fourteen Days.

CHAP. CVI.

Wax.

a) **T**HE 11 *Hen.* 6. *cap.* 12. concerning Wax-Chandlers, and the Price of Candles, and other Wax-Works, inferted by *Dalton*, is repealed by 21 *Jac.* 1. *cap.* 28. *fect.* 11.

By 23 *El. cap.* 8. Mixing Wax for Sale with Rofin, Tallow, or other deceitful 23 El. c. 8. Thing, is a Forfeiture of 2 *s.* for every Pound, Half to the Crown, and Half to the In- §. 1. former, to be fued for in any Court of Record. And Counterfeiting the Marks mentioned Ib. §. 6. in the Statute is a Forfeiture of 5 *l.* to be divided and recovered as above.

CHAP. CVII. *(a)*

Wears.

EVERY Perfon that fhall erect any new Wear along the Sea-Shore, or in any Haven, *Erecting* Harbour or Creek, or within five Miles of the Mouth of any Haven or Creek, or *Wears.* fhall willingly take, deftroy, or fpoil any Spawn, Fry or Brood, or any Sea-Fifh in any 3 Jac. 1. c.12. Wear, Engine or Device whatfoever, fhall forfeit 10 *l.* for every fuch Erecting or Spoil- *Catching Fifh* ing. The one Moiety to the King, the other Moiety to the Profecutor. *with them.*

Any Perfon, which in any Haven, Harbour, Creek, or within five Miles of the *Unlawful* Mouth of any Haven, Harbour or Creek of the Sea, fhall Fifh with any Draw-net or *Nets.* Drag-net, not three Inches Meafh, *viz.* an Inch and a Half from Knot to Knot, except Ibid. for the Taking of Smoulds in *Norfolk* only; or with any Net with Canvas, or any other Engine or Device, whereby the Spawn, Brood, or Fry of Fifh may be deftroyed, fhall forfeit for every Net, and every Time fo doing 10 *s.* a Moiety to the Poor of the Place, &c. the other Moiety to the Profecutor, to be levied by the Mayor, &c. or by Warrant of one Juftice of Peace, by Diftrefs and Sale of Goods, rendring the Overplus, &c.

By 6 & 7 *Will.* 3. *cap.* 16. The Juftices of Peace of *Wilts, Gloucefter, Oxford, Berks,* 6 & 7 W. 3. and *Bucks*, within their refpective Counties, fhall be Commiffioners for putting in Execu- c. 16. §. 2. tion the Powers herein mentioned, *viz.* they, or five of them, fhall have Power at their Quarter-Seffions, upon Examination upon Oath, to make Orders for fettling reafonable Rates to be taken from the Owners of Barges, by the Occupiers of Locks, Wears, Bucks, Winches, Turnpikes, Dams, Floodgates, or other Engines, within their Counties, for the Help which fuch Barges may receive thereby, regard being had as well to the ancient Rates as the Charges of Repairing; and alfo to appoint other neceffary Rules concerning the Navigation, and concerning fuch Locks, &c. and concerning the Behaviour of Barge-men belonging to fuch Barges.

3 Geo. 2.
c. 11.

     This Act was revived and amended by 3 *Geo.* 2. *cap.* 11. By which laft Act the Members of Parliament for the Counties of *Middlefex, Surry, Berks, Bucks, Oxon, Gloucefter* and *Wilts,* and feveral other Perfons therein named, for each of the faid Counties feverally are to be Commiffioners for regulating the Prices to be taken for the Paffage of Barges &c. by Owners of Locks, Wears, &c.

     The Act of 3 *Geo.* 2. *cap.* 11. is by 13 *Geo.* 2. *cap.* 18. continued till the 1ft *Jun.* 1747.

CHAP. CVIII. (*a*)

Weavers.

What Looms they may keep.
2 & 3 P. & M.
c. 11. §. 2.

NONE ufing the Trade of Cloth-working, living out of a City, Borough, Market-Town, or Corporate Town, fhall keep above one Woollen Loom at one Time in his Houfe or Poffeffion, or make Profit by letting or fetting a Loom, or of a Houfe wherein a Loom is, and to be let with it, upon Pain to forfeit for every Week 20 s.

Ib. §. 3.

     No Woollen Weaver living out of a City, &c. fhall keep above two Looms, or make Profit by any other Loom, upon Pain to forfeit for every Week 20 s.

Ib. §. 4.

     None ufing the Trade of a Weaver, and not Cloth-making, fhall keep a Tucking-mill or ufe the Trade of a Tucker, or Fuller, or Dyer, upon Pain to lofe for every Week 20 s.

Ib. §. 5.
What Appren-tices they may take.
Ib. §. 7.

     None ufing the Trade of a Tucker or Fuller, fhall keep or have a Loom, or make any Profit thereby, or forfeit for every Week 20 s.

     No Woollen Weaver living out of any City, &c. fhall have above two Apprentices, upon Pain of 10 l. *

*The Claufe in 5 El. c. 4. §. 32. is repeal'd by 5 W. & M. c. 9.

Ib. §. 8.

     No Perfon fhall ufe the Trade of a Weaver, except he have been an Apprentice, or ufed the Trade feven Years, on Pain of 20 l.

Ibid.

     Of all which Forfeitures, a Moiety to the Queen, and the other Moiety to the Profecutor, in any Court of Record, by Action, &c. or Information.

CHAP. CIX.

Wine.

THE 24 *Hen.* 8. *cap.* 6. mentioned by *Dalton* under this Title, is repealed by 21 *Jac.* 1. *cap.* 28.

Licences.
7 Ed. 6. c. 5.
§. 3.

     (*a*) Note, That no Perfon may fell any Wine in any Town not Corporate, but by the Licence of the Juftices of the Peace in open Seffions by Writing under the feveral Seals of every of the faid Juftices, upon Pain of 5 l. for every Day of fo offending. See *Co. lib. Entr. fol.* 370. *Finch's* Cafe, who recovered 550 l. in an Information upon this Statute, notwithftanding the Queen's Licence there, pleaded in Bar of the faid Action.

Ibid.

     And by the Statute in Towns corporate, no Perfon to Sell but by Licence of the Mayor, Aldermen, &c. and that under the common Seal of the Corporation upon the fame Penalty.

12 Car. 2.
c. 25. §. 1.

     No Perfon unlefs he be authorized in Manner as by this Act, fhall fell by Retail, that is by the Pint, Quart, Bottle or Gallon, or by any other greater or leffer retail Meafure, any Wine to be drank in his Manfion-houfe, or without, upon Pain of 5 l. one Moiety to the King, the other to him that will fue for the fame in any of the King's Courts of Record.

Ib. §. 2.

     Commiffioners to be appointed from Time to Time, under the Great Seal.

Extortion.
Ib. §. 10.

     No Officers to be appointed by his Majefty for carrying on the Duty of Wine Licences by this Statute of 12 *Car.* 2. *cap.* 25. fhall demand or receive any Fees or Rewards, or Sums of Money for, or in Refpect of his Service, other than 5 s. for a Licence, 4 d. for an Acquittance, and 6 d. for a Bond, under the Penalty of 10 l. A Moiety to the King, the other Moiety to the Profecutor.

No Perfon felling or retailing Wine, fhall mingle or utter any *Spanifh* Wine, mingled *Mingling or* with *French* or Rhenifh Wine, Cyder, Perry, Honey, Sugar, Syrups of Sugar or Molaf- *corrupting.* fes, or any Syrups; or put in any Ifinglafs, Brimftone, Lime, Railins, Juice of Railins, Water, or any other Liquor or Ingredient; or Clary, or other Herb, or any Flefh; nor fhall any fuch Perfon mingle or utter any *French* Wines mingled with Rhenifh or *Spanifh* Wines, Cyder, Perry, ftummed Wine, Vitriol, Honey, *&c.* and no fuch Perfon fhall mingle or utter any Rhenifh Wines mingled with *French* or *Spanifh* Wines, Cyder, *&c.* on Pain to forfeit, *viz.* Every Perfon felling Wine in Grofs, mingled or abufed as aforefaid, for every fuch Offence 100 *l.* And every Retailer for every fuch Offence 40 *l.* A Moiety to the King, the other Moiety to the Informer, to be recovered in any Court of Record by Action of Debt, Bill, Plaint or Information, *&c.*

No *Canary* Wines, *Muskadel* or *Alicant*, or other *Spanifh* or Sweet Wines fhall be *Prices and* fold by Retail at above 18 *d. per* Quart. No *Gafcoign* or *French* Wines at above 8 *d. per* *Penalty.* Quart. No Rhenifh Wines at above 12 *d. per* Quart. And fo for leffer or greater Quan- *Ib. §. 12.* tities, upon Pain to forfeit for every Pint, Quart, Pottle, Gallon, or greater or leffer Meafure 5 *l.* A Moiety to the King, the other Moiety to the Profecutor, to be recover-ed as aforefaid : Confirmed by Statute 13 *Car.* 2. *cap.* 7.

No Wines (except of the Growth of the Dominions of the Great Duke, or of *Turky* *1 G.* 2. c. 17. and the *Levant*) fhall be imported in Flasks or Bottles, or in any Veffel containing lefs *§. 7, 8.* than 25 Gallons, on Pain of forfeiting the fame, or the Value thereof, one Moiety to the King, the other Moiety to the Seifor or Profecutor, in any Court at *Weftminfter*, or by any Laws of Excife, for Forfeitures incurred in *England*, or in the Court of *Exchequer* in *Scotland*.

C H A P. CX. (*a*)

Wild Fowl.

NO Perfon fhall between the laft Day of *May*, and the laft Day of *Auguft*, take or *At what Time* caufe, *&c.* any Wild Fowl, as Ducks, Mallards, Widgeons, Teals, wild Geefe, *not to be taken.* or other Kinds of Wild Fowl, with Nets or other Engines, upon Pain of a Year's Im- *25 H.* 8. c. 11 prifonment, and to pay 4 *d.* for every one fo taken. *§. 2.*

The Juftices of Peace have Power to hear and determine the Offences aforefaid, as in *Ib. §. 3.* Cafes of Trefpafs.

A Gentleman that may difpend 40 *s. per Annum* of Freehold, may hunt them with *Ib. §. 4.* Spaniels only, or the Long-bow.

From the laft Day of *March* to the laft Day of *June* in every Year, none fhall take or *Eggs.* convey, or deftroy any Eggs of Wild Fowl from the Place they are laid by the Wild *Ib. §. 5.* Fowl, upon Pain of Imprifonment for a Year, and to lofe for every Egg of a Crane or Buftard 20 *d.* And for the Egg of a Bitton, Heron or Shovelar 8 *d.* And of a Mallard, Teal, or other Wild Fowl 1 *d.* And all Juftices of Peace fhall have Power to inquire, hear and determine the fame.

The Part of the Statute 25 *Hen.* 8. 11. touching taking of Wild Fowl, was repealed by 3 *&* 4 *E.* 6. 7. But it is again revived by 21 *Jac.* 28. *fect.* 9. which is continued by *Car.* 1. 4. and 16 *Car.* 1. 4. and fo is in Force at this Day.

C H A P. CXI.

Wood.

TWO Juftices of Peace (not being of Kindred, Alliance, Counfel or Fee to the *35 H.* 8. 17 Lord or Owner of the Wood) appointed by the more Part of the Juftices of Peace *§. 7.* at their Seffions, upon Complaint of the Lord made unto them, may divide and fet out the fourth Part of the Wood, if the Lord and Commoners thereof (being firft called be-fore them) cannot agree upon it.

(*a*) Whereas the Statute of 43 *Eliz.* doth not fufficiently prevent nor punifh the cut- *Cutting Wood* ting and fpoiling of Woods, by this Statute, it is enacted, that every Conftable and other *15 Car.* 2. *c.* 2. §. 2.

Perfon

Perfon in every County, City, or other Place, where they fhall be Officers or Inhabitants, fhall and may apprehend, or caufe to be apprehended, every Perfon they fhall fufpect having, carrying, or conveying, any Burden or Bundle of Wood, Poles, young Trees, Bark, Maft of Trees, Gates, Stiles, Pofts, Pales, Rails or Hedgwood, Broom or Furzes. See Tit. *Trefpafs.* And by Warrant under the Hand and Seal of any one Juftice, directed to any Officer, he may enter into and fearch the Houfes, Yards, Gardens, and other Places belonging to the Houfes of any Perfons they fhall fufpect to have Trees aforefaid, and finding any fuch Wood, &c. to apprehend the Perfons fufpected for cutting or taking the fame, and as well fuch Perfons apprehended or taken carrying any Kind of Wood or other Premiffes, as thofe in whofe Houfes, or other Places belonging to them, any of the fame fhall be found, to carry before any one Juftice of the Peace of the fame County, City, or Town Corporate. And if fuch Perfons fufpected do not give a good Account how they came by the fame, by the Confent of the Owner, fuch as fhall fatisfy the faid Juftice (or within fome convenient Time to be fet by the faid Juftice) produce the Party of whom they bought the faid Wood, or fome credible Witnefs upon Oath, to prove fuch Sale, then fuch Perfons fufpected, not giving fuch good Account, nor producing fuch Witnefs, fhall be judged as convicted, for cutting and ftealing of Woods, Underwoods, Poles, Trees, Gates, Stiles, Pofts, Pales, Rails, Hedgwood, Broom or Furfe, within the Meaning of the faid Statute of 43 *Eliz.* and liable to the Punifhment therein, and of this Act, *viz.*

Penalty.
Ib §. 3.

Every Perfon fo convicted, fhall for the firft Offence give the Owner Satisfaction for his Damages within fuch Time as the Juftice fhall appoint, and over and above, pay down to the Overfeers of the Poor of the Parifh where fuch Offence is, fuch Sum of Money, not exceeding ten Shillings, as the faid Juftice fhall think fit: In Default of either of which Payments the faid Juftice may commit fuch Offender to the Houfe of Correction for fuch Time (not exceeding one Month) as he fhall think fit, or to be whipt by the Conftable, or other Officer, as in his Judgment fhall feem expedient.

Ibid.

And if fuch Perfon fhall again commit the faid Offence, and be thereof convicted as before, that then the Perfons offending the fecond Time, and convicted, fhall be fent to the Houfe of Correction for one Month, and there to be kept to hard Labour: And for the third Offence, convicted as before, fhall be judged and deemed as incorrigible Rogues.

Buying.
Ib. §. 4.

And whofoever fhall buy any Burdens of Wood, or any the Premiffes, fufpected to be ftoln or unlawfully come by, the Juftices, the Mayor or Chief Officer, or any one of them, within their refpective Jurifdictions, upon Complaint, may examine the Matter upon Oath: And if they find the fame was bought of any fufpected to have ftoln or unlawfully come by the fame, then any one of the faid Juftices or Chief Officer fhall and may award the Party that bought the fame to pay treble the Value thereof to the Party from whom the fame was ftoln or unlawfully taken: And in Default of prefent Payment, to iffue forth a Warrant to levy the fame by Diftrefs and Sale of the Offender's Goods, rendring the Overplus to the Party: And for Want of fuch Diftrefs, to commit the Party to the Gaol, at his own Will, there to remain one Month without Bail.

But no Perfon is to be queftioned for any Offence within this Act, unlefs within fix Weeks after the Offence committed; nor if punifhed by any former Law for the fame.

Quære, If no Owner can claim the Wood as his Own, then it feems, although the fame be fufpected to be ftoln, no Proceedings can be on this Act.

Standels.
35 H. 8. 17.
§. 1.

Every Owner of Coppice-wood (of fourteen Years growing or under) for Inheritance, Life, Copyhold, or for Years, fhall leave ftanding for every Acre, twelve Standels or Storers of Oak; if fo many of Oak; if not, to be made up of Elm, Afh, Afp or Beech, to be left of thofe that were left ftanding at the laft Selling; if fo many; if not, of others, likely to be Timber-trees, which Storers fhall not be cut till they be ten Inches fquare, within three Foot of the Ground, upon Pain of 3 s. 4 d. for not leaving the faid Storers. A Moiety to the King, the other to the Profecutor, by Action, &c. or Information in any Court of Record.

Inclofure.
Ib. §. 2.

All Coppice and Underwoods that fhall be felled at fourteen Years Growth or under, from the twentieth Day of *April* next after the Felling for four Years, fhall be fufficiently inclofed, and the Springs preferved from Cattle by him that hath the lawful Intereft and Poffeffion, upon Pain to forfeit 3 s. 4 d. for every Rod not fo inclofed or preferved by the Perfon fo bounden to it for every Month.

Ibid.

All Coppice above fourteen Years Growth, and not above twenty-four, fhall in like Sort be inclofed or preferved for fix Years, under the like Penalty; and this is inlarged to eight Years, as above.

I

No Perfon fhall convert into Tillage or Pafture any Coppice or Underwoods, contain- *Altering.* ing two Acres or more, being then Coppice or Underwood, and being two Furlongs Ib. §. 3. diftant from the Owner's Houfe, or the Houfe to which it appertains, upon Pain to for- feit for every Acre 40 *s.*

Every Perfon having feveral Woods or Coppice fet with great Trees about twenty-four *Standels.* Years Growth, fhall at the Felling, leave for every Acre twelve Oaks, if fo many Oaks, Ib. §. 5. or elfe fo many Trees of Elm, Afh, Afp, Beech, as make up the Number to be left ftanding, twenty Years after the Felling; and for feven Years next after the Felling, pre- ferve and inclofe it from Deftruction by Cattle, upon Pain that the Owner forfeit for *Inclofing.* every great Tree lacking 6 *s.* 8 *d.* and for every Month for every Rod not inclofed or pre- ferved, 3 *s.* 4 *d.*

But the Owner may take any of them for Repairs and Neceffaries.   Ib. §.6.

The Lord, Owner of the Soil where Woods grow, and others having Common, fhall *Commone s* before Felling, call together the Tenants, and by the Confent of more Part of them, if Ib. §. 7. they can agree, fhall fet out a fourth Part thereof: And if the Lord and Tenants do not agree, then two Juftices to be affigned by the Seffions, at the Requeft of the Lord, being not of his Alliance, Kin, Counfel or Fee, fhall call together Twelve fuch Commoners and Inhabitants, and under fuch Penalties as they think fit; and being met, and the Juftices fhewing the Caufe of their Meeting, if the Juftices, Lord, Commoners and In- habitants, or the major Part of them cannot agree upon a Divifion of a fourth Part, the Juftices may fet out a fourth Part ; and the Lord or Owner may inclofe and fell.

Standels, Storers and Trees, fhall be left upon like Penalties, as before is limited, and *Standels.* the Inclofure maintained, and Springs preferved feven Years from the Felling; and within Ib. §. 8. that feven Years no Beaft be put in or fuffered to feed there, upon Pain to forfeit 4 *d.* for every Beaft.   And the Owner to forfeit for every Tree otherwife felled 6 *s.* 8 *d.*   Ib. §. 9.

After fuch inclofing, the Tenants may ufe and enjoy their Common in the Refidue not *Prefervation.* inclofed ; and the Lord fhall put no Cattle therein for the feven Years.   And after the Ib. §. 10. feven Years it fhall be left open, and ufed as before.

But by 13 *El.* 25. the Woods are to remain inclofed, and Springs to be preferved two 13 El. c. 25. Years longer than by 35 *H.* 8. *cap.* 17. is directed, upon the like Penalties.   §. 18.

No Perfon fhall fell or caufe, *&c.* any Oaken Trees, meet to be barked (where Bark *Bark.* is worth two Shillings a Cart-load above the Charges) except Timber for Houfes, Ships or 1 Jac. 1. c. 22. Mills; but between the firft Day of *April* and the laft Day of *June,* upon Pain of For- §. 20. feiture of the Bark, or double the Value thereof.

No Perfon fhall convert to Fuel, for the Making of Iron, in any Iron-Mills, Furnace *Felling for* or Hammer, any Manner of Wood or Underwood, growing within twenty-two Miles *Iron-works.* about the City of *London,* or Suburbs; or within twenty-two Miles of the River of 23 El. 5. §. 1. *Thames,* from *Dorchefter,* in the County of *Oxford,* downwards; nor within four Miles of the Foot of the *Downs,* betwixt *Arundel* and *Pemfey* in *Suffex* ; nor within four Miles of *Winchelfey* or *Rye*; nor within two Miles of *Pemfey,* or within three Miles of *Haftings,* upon Pain to forfeit for every Load 40 *s.*

This Act fhall not extend to any Woods in any fuch Parts of the Wilds of *Surry, Suffex* Ib. §. 2. or *Kent,* as is diftant above 18 Miles from *London,* and 8 Miles from the *Thames.*

No new Works fhall be fet up within 22 Miles of *London,* nor within 14 Miles of the Ib. §. 3. *Thames,* nor within four Miles of the *Downs,* or of the Towns of *Pemfey, Winchelfey, Haftings* or *Rye,* upon Pain to forfeit 100 *l.*

A Moiety whereof to the Queen, the other Moiety to the Informer, by Action, *&c.* or Information in any Court of Record, *&c.*

The Affize of Tale-wood, Billet, Fagots, and the ordering thereof, and the Penalties therein, fee 43 *Eliz.* 14.

See 27 *Eliz. cap.* 19. *fupra* Chap. 51.

Any Juftice of Peace of the County (or the Mayor, *&c.* of any Town Corporate) fhall 9 Ann. c. 15. have Power to call before him fix good Men of the Town, *&c.* where Billet is expofed §. 2. to Sale, and fhall fwear them truly to inquire and prefent whether the faid Billet be of good Affize ; and if they prefent that fuch Billets are not affized and marked as the Act directs, the Juftice fhall take the Billets not marked, or falfe affized, as forfeited, and de- liver them to the Overfeers of the Poor, to be given to the Poor.

See 1 Geo. 1. cap. 48.   6 Geo. 1. cap. 16. *fupra Tit.* Trefpafs, *Chap.* 101.

CHAP. CXII.

Weights and Measures.

Two Justices.
11 H. 7. 4.
P. Just. 92.
Lamb. 345. TWO Justices of Peace (one being of the *Quorum*) may by Examination or Inquiry; hear and determine the Faults of Head Officers in Cities, Boroughs and Market-Towns, that do not twice every Year view and examine all Weights and Measures in their Towns, &c. and do not break and burn the defective.

Ibid. Also two such Justices may by Examination or Inquiry, hear and determine the Faults of all Buyers and Sellers, which do not buy and sell with Weights and Measures that be Lam. 345.
P. Weight 9. lawful, (*sc.* with such as be marked and sealed, like and equal with the King's Standard.) Also the said Justices may break and burn all defective Weights and Measures.

P. Just. 92.
Lamb. 345. The said Justices may fine all and every the Offenders aforesaid by their Discretion, and make Process against them, as if they were indicted of Trespass against the Peace. For the Process, see hereof in the Title *Process*.

False Weights.
11 H. 7. 4. (*a*) Mayors, Bailiffs, and Head Officers of Cities, Boroughs and Market-Towns, shall cause twice a Year, or oftener, as they think fit, all Weights and Measures there to be brought before them; and such, as upon View and Examination they shall find defective, to break and burn; and the Parties which have offended, and be found defective, shall for the first Offence forfeit 6 *s.* 8 *d.* for the second 13 *s.* 4 *d.* and for the third 20 *s.* to the Mayor, Bailiff, or other having Jurisdiction and Correction; and for further Punishment to be set on the Pillory.

(*d*) Now for the readier Direction of the Justices of Peace herein, I thought good to set down the just and certain Contents of all (or most Sorts of) Weights and Measures, Vera fides,
pondus, men-
sura, moneta
sit una,
Ac status illæ-
sus totius or-
bis erit. that so they may the better judge what be lawful or defective, and what not.

9 H. 3. 25.
P. Weight 1.
P. 7. By the Statute of *Magna Charta*, *cap.* 25. there shall be but one Weight and one Measure of Corn, Wine, Beer and Ale; and one Yard throughout the whole Realm, (*sc.* according to the King's Standard in the *Exchequer*.) And this Statute of *Magna Charta* hath since herein been confirmed by many Parliaments, *viz.* by the Statutes of 14 *Ed.* 3. 12. 25 *Ed.* 3. 10. 27 *Ed.* 3. 10. 34 *Ed.* 3. 5. 13 *Rich.* 2. 9. 8 *H.* 6. 5. 7 *H.* 7. 4. 11 *H.* 7. 4. and 12 *H.* 7. 5. as thereby appeareth.

16 Car. 1.
c. 19. §. 2. (*a*) There shall be one Weight, one Measure, and one Yard, according to the Standard of the *Exchequer*, throughout all the Realm, as well in Places privileged as without, and every Measure of Corn shall be striked without heap. And whosoever shall keep any other Weight, Measure or Yard, whereby any Corn, Grain, or other Thing is bought or sold, shall forfeit for every Offence five Shillings, being thereof convicted, by the Oath of one sufficient Witness, before any Justice of Peace, or Head Officer of City, Town, or Place where the Offence is done, to be levied by the Church-wardens or Overseers of the Poor of the Parish, to the Use of the Poor of the said Parish, by Distress and Sale of the Offender's Goods; and for want of Distress, to be imprisoned without Bail until Pay- Ib. §. 9. ment. And any Justice of Peace, upon Suit against him, for any Thing done upon this Act, to plead the General Issue, and give the Act in Evidence, and to have treble Costs, if unjustly vexed.

The Clerk of the Market, his Duty follows.

Jurisdiction.
Ib. §. 3. The Clerk of the Market of the King's Houshold, shall execute his Office only within the Verge of the King's House, and no where else. And all Mayors, and Head Officers of Towns, Lords of Liberties, according to their Liberties and Jurisdictions, may execute their Offices accordingly.

Standard.
Ib. §. 4. If any Clerk of the Market shall seal or allow any Weights or Measures, other than according to the Standard in the *Exchequer*, or shall refuse to allow such as are according to it, paying only such Fees, as by Statute or Custom are allowed, they, their Deputies, or Agents, shall forfeit 5 *l.* to be levied as aforesaid.

Extortion.
Ib. §. 5. If any Clerk of the Market of the King's Houshold, or others, having Power to execute the Office, shall take, by Colour of his Office, any Fines or Fees, other than such as are allowed by Statute or Custom, or shall take any Fine, Fee, Reward or Consideration for making, signing, or Examination of any Weights or Measures, formerly marked or sealed; or shall set any Fine or Amerciament, without legal Trial of the Offence, or otherwise misdemean himself in his Office, and be convicted, shall for the first Offence

forfeit

forfeit 5 *l.* for the fecond 10 *l.* for the third, and every other Offence 20 *l.* to be levied as aforefaid to the Ufe of the Poor.

The Meafure called *Water Meafure* is thereby continued where the fame was then *Water Meafure. Corn,* ufed. But by 22 *Car.* 2. the fame Claufe, as to the Meafuring of Corn and Salt, is *Salt.* repealed.   *22 Car. 2.*

If any Perfon fhall fell Corn or Grain, ground or unground, or Salt by any other *c. 8. §. 2.* Bufhel than *Winchefter* Meafure, containing eight Gallons ftricken by the Brim, and *See Tit. Salt, this is altered* fealed, he fhall forfeit 40 *s.* to be levied as by the Act of 16 *Car.* 1. is directed.   *Ibid.*

If any Mayor or Head Officer wilfully permit any Perfon to fell by any other Meafure *Neglect to* than as aforefaid; or upon Complaint, fhall not punifh the Breach of that Statute, he *punifh.* fhall, upon Conviction by Prefentment or Indictment at the General Quarter-Seffions of *Ib. §. 3.* the County, forfeit 5 *l.* one Moiety to the Informer, the other Moiety to the Poor, to be levied by Diftrefs and Sale; and for want of Diftrefs, Imprifonment until Payment.

If any Clerk of the Market fhall neglect or refufe to feal or mark any Bufhel, half *Refufal to Seal.* Bufhel, or Peck, duly gaged, he fhall forfeit for the firft Offence 5 *l.* for the fecond, and *Ib. §. 4.* every other Offence 10 *l.* to be levied as aforefaid.

If the Clerk of the Market of the King's Houfe, within the Verge, fhall take more *Fee.* than the lawful and accuftomed Fees; or if any other fhall take above one Penny for the *Ibid.* Sealing and Marking a Bufhel, a Halfpenny for a half Bufhel or Peck: and a Farthing for a Gallon, Pottle, Quart, Pint or half Pint, upon due Proof and Conviction, he fhall incur the Penalties in 16 *Car.* 1. *cap.* 19.

At the Charge of fuch Perfon as hath the Toll and Profit of the Market, fhall be pro- *Providing* vided one Meafure of Brafs, and chained in the Market-Place, or elfe forfeit 5 *l.* to be *Meafure.* recovered as by that Act is directed. One Moiety to the Poor, the other to him that fues. *Ib. §. 5.*

Every Conftable fhall fearch if any ufe any other Meafure, or fhall ftrike the fame *Search.* otherwife than that Act directs, or buy or fell by unfealed Meafures; and if he find *Ib. §. 6.* any unfealed, to break it, and to prefent thofe Offences to the next private or Quarterly Seffions.

(*d*) And yet notwithstanding (the Statutes of *Magna Charta, &c.*) there always hath *Raft. 8.* been, and ftill are two Kinds of Weights ufed in *England*, and both warrantable: The *Diu. fol. 5. 7. b.* one by Law, and the other by Cuftom; but they are for feveral Sorts of Wares or Commodities; for there is *Troy* Weight, and *Averdupois.*

1. *Troy* Weight is by Law; and thereby are weighed Gold, Silver, Pearl, precious *Sorts of* Stones, Silk, Electuaries, Bread, Wheat, and all Manner of Grain or Corn is meafured *Weights.* by *Troy* Weight. And this hath to the Pound 12 Ounces, or 20 *s.* Sterling weight, and *Ibid.* no more. It is called by fome, *Libra medica*; by others, *Libra & uncia Trojana.*

2. *Averdupois* Weight is by Cuftom (yet confirmed alfo by Statute,) and thereby are *Raft. 8. & 14.* weighed all kind of Grocery Wares, Phyfical Drugs, Butter, Cheefe, Flefh, Wax, Pitch, *27 El. 3.* Tar, Tallow, Wools, Hemp, Flax, Iron, Steel, Lead, and all other Commodities not *c. 10.* before named, but fpecially every Thing which beareth the Name of Garble, and whereof iffueth a Refufe, or Wafte. See *Raft.* 8. *fol.* 527. and the Book of Affife, Impref. 1597.

(*a*) The Word *Averdupois* in *French*, is as much as to fay, to have full Weight, *Habere pondus.* *Geo. Agricola* in his learned Tract *De ponderibus & menfuris, pag.* 339. faith thus of both thefe Kinds of Weights, *Medica & civilis libra numero non gravitate unciarum differunt.*

(*d*) And this hath to the Pound 16 Ounces, or 25 *s.* fterling Weight.

Alfo in this *Averdupois* Weight, unto every Hundred is allowed twelve Pounds Weight.

Alfo all Manner of *Averdupois* fhall be weighed by lawful Weights, fealed according *27 Ed. 3. 10.* to the Standard of the *Exchequer.* *P. Weights* 14.

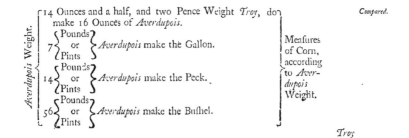

Compared.

14 Ounces and a half, and two Pence Weight *Troy*, do make 16 Ounces of *Averdupois.*

Averdupois Weight.

7 { Pounds or Pints } *Averdupois* make the Gallon.

14 { Pounds or Pints } *Averdupois* make the Peck.

56 { Pounds or Pints } *Averdupois* make the Bufhel.

Meafures of Corn, according to *Averdupois* Weight.

Troy Weight.

Pints or Pounds,	5120	512	256	64	16	8	4	Measures
Quarts,	2560	256	128	32	8	4	2	of Grain
Pottles,	1280	128	64	16	4	2	1	according
Gallons,	640	64	32	8	2	1		to *Troy*
Pecks,	320	32	16	4	1			Weight.
Bushels,	80	8	2	1				
Coombs,	20	2	1	Ten Quarters of				
Quarters,	10	1		Corn is a Last.				

Beer Measures.   Ale Measures.

Pints,	288	144	72	8	4	2		256	128	64	8	
Quarts,	144	72	36	4	2	1		128	64	32	4	
Pottles,	72	36	18	2	1			64	32	16	2	Measures
Gallons,	36	18	9	1				32	16	8	1	of Beer
Firkins,	4	2	1					4	2	1		and Ale.
Kilderkins,	2	1						2	1			
Barrel,	1							1				

See for Corn, Beer, and Ale, more fully in that which followeth.

Troy Weight.

Measures.

Troy Weight, 12 *H.* 7. 5. & 51 *H.* 3.

Thirty-two Wheat Corns, taken in the Midst of the Ear, weigheth one Penny *Sterling.*

Twenty-pence *Sterling,* maketh the Ounce *Troy.*

Twelve Ounces maketh in { Weight one Pound *Troy.* { Measure one Pint.

Two Pints, or Pounds, maketh the Quart.

Two Quarts maketh the Pottle.

Eight Pints } Four Quarts } maketh a Gallon. Two Pottles }

Eight Quarts maketh the Peck.

Troy Weight, 12 *H.* 7. 5. & 51 *H.* 3.

Sixty-four Pints } Thirty-two Quarts } maketh the { Bushel Eight Gallons } { or Four Pecks } { Firkin.

Sixteen Gallons } maketh the { Kilderkin. Two Firkins } { Half Barrel. { Rondlet.

Two Hundred fifty-six Pints } One Hundred twenty-eight Quarts } Thirty-two Gallons } maketh the { Coomb Four Firkins } { or Two Kilderkins } { Barrel. Four Bushels }

Troy Weight.

Five Hundred and twelve Pints } Two Hundred fifty-six Quarts } Sixty-four Gallons } Eight Firkins } maketh the { Quarter Four Kilderkins } { or Two Barrels } { Hogshead. Eight Bushels }

So the { Pint and Pound } { Firkin and Bushel } are of like Content. { Barrel and Coomb } { Hogshead and Quarter }

(*a*) Also

(*a*) Alfo the Statute of 23 *H.* 8. *cap.* 4. doth limit the Weight of every of thefe three 23 H. 8. Veffels here next named, being empty as followeth, *fcil.*
 c. 4. § 6.

1. The Barrel
2. The half Barrel or Kilderkin } muft weigh (being empty) { 26
 13
 6½ } *lb.*
3. The Firkin

(*d*) Meafures of Corn.

All kind of Corn and Grain is meafured by *Troy* Weight.

By the Statute the Bufhel muft contain eight Gallons, or fixty-four Pounds or Pints of Wheat, 31 *Ed.* 1. 12 *H.* 7. 5. *P. Weights.* 2 *Raftal*, 34. *Div.*

And yet by the Book of *Affife*, imprinted *An. Dom.* 1597. the Bufhel is to contain fifty- *See the Book of* fix Pounds (or Pints) of *Averdupois* Weight (which is three Pounds or three Pints and *of Affifes.* eight Ounces *Troy*, more than the Statute or *Troy* Weights.) For fifty-fix Pounds or Pints *Averdupois* Weight, and fixty-feven Pounds eight Ounces *Troy* Weight, do juftly agree.

Alfo eight Bufhels ftricken make the Quarter of Corn. 11 *H.* 7. 4.
Alfo every Meafure of Corn fhall be ftricken without heap. 25 *Ed.* 3. 10.

Corn.
 P. 3.
 15 R. 2. 4.
 P. 1.

Water Meafure, fold within Ship-board, fhall contain five Pecks ftricken to the 34 E. 3. 6. Bufhel.
 P. 9.

No Perfon fhall buy or fell with a Bufhel, except it be fealed and marked by the Offi- P. 9. cer, and according to the King's Standard.

But Note, That in many Places and Countries the Meafure of Corn doth much differ, *Bufhel diffe-* and the Bufhel in one Place is greater than in another: And it feems *Confuetudo loci eft* *rent.* *obfervanda : Tamen quære*, for it is contrary to the Statute of *Magna Charta*, *Chap.* 25. 9 H. 6. f. 56. and divers other Statutes, as you may fee before in this Title: And Cuftom or Prefcription 30 Aff. pl. 38. againft a Statute feemeth not good. See *Bro. Prefcr.* 2, 50.

(*a*) But this Difference of Meafure of Corn comes partly from the Diverfity of Clerks *Clerks of the* of the Market (there being a Clerk of the Market for the King's Houfe, another for the *the Diverfity of* Prince, another for the Dutchy; others in Corporate Towns, and others belonging to the *Meafure.* Lords of Liberties) and partly from the Abufe of divers Corporate Towns and other Privileged Places or Liberties, where they by ufurped Cuftom (without any good Warrant of Law) have ufed to have, and to buy by fuch Meafures. And where the Clerk of the Market for the King hath forborn or neglected to meddle, in regard perhaps of their Corporation, Liberty, or fome other refpect. But this Abufe two Juftices of Peace (the one being of the *Quorum*) may reform, *fc.* Two Juftices of Peace of the County, where there be no Juftices of Peace within that Corporation, *&c.*

Alfo the Clerk of the Market for the King's Houfe may reform this in all Places with- *Clerks of the* in the Verge. 27 *H.* 8. *cap.* 24. *Office.*

And yet by the Words of the Statutes of 25 *E.* 3. *cap.* 10. *& 34 E.* 3. *cap.* 6. the Rents and Farms of Lords, fhall be meafured by the Meafures as they were wont to be, whether it were by heaped Meafure, or greater Meafure than the Statute appointeth.

And Note, that the Clerk of the Market fhall carry with him all his Weights and Meafures figned according to the Standard of the *Exchequer*, 16 *R.* 2. *cap.* 3. And the Juftices of Peace may, yea, ought, to fit with the Clerk of the Market at his Coming into the Country, *&c.*

Sir *Francis Harvey* hath often delivered in his Charge at *Cambridge* Affifes, thefe Directions, *fc.* That one Juftice of Peace at the leaft ought to fit with the Clerk of the Market, to fee that the King's Subjects be not wronged. And that the Clerk of the Market ought to have with him his Directions out of the *Exchequer*. And that he may take no Money for any Bills, *&c.* and that he ought to feal no Bufhel, or other Meafures or Weights, but once (and not yearly as they ufe to do:) And that if after the firft Sealing, he fhall take any Thing for the Sealing thereof again, or for the fhewing thereof, *&c.* it is Extortion; yea, it is one of the greateft Oppreffions (faith he) for that it concerneth almoft all Men.

It was refolved *Nemine contradicente* by all the Juftices, *M.* 39 *& 40 El.* That if the Clerk of the Market claim Fees for examining and feeing any Bufhels or other Things before fealed, the fame was a great Extortion, and no Fee is due unto him therefore, for fuch feeing and examining, is to no other End than to find and difcover Abufes in

Weights

.Weights and Measures. And those that they find false, their Duty is to damn and re-form them, and upon lawful Presentments to punish the Offenders by Amerciaments, which belong to the King. And this agrees with the Statute of 13 *R*. 2. *cap*. 4. And if such Use hath been through Covetousness or Greediness of corrupt Officers, that Use may not make a Law. Which Case you may see *Moor's Rep. p.* 523.

The Clerk of the Market's Duty is to take Charge of the King's Measures, and to keep the Standard of them, that is, the Examples and Patterns of all the Measures that ought to be throughout the Realm, as of Ells, Yards, Quarts, Pottles, Gallons, &c. of Weights, Bushels, and such like, and to see that all Measures in every Place be answer-able to the said Standard or Pattern. *Flet. l.* 1. *cap.* 8, 9, &c. And he is to have with him, when he goeth to assay Weights and Measures signed according to the Standard, and none other but his Weights and Measures. 16 *R*. 2. *cap.* 3.

Bread.

(*d*) For the Assise of Bread, I refer you to the Books made for the Assise thereof, and will only set down some short Observations therein.

1. All Sorts of Bread ought to be weighed by *Troy Weight.*

2. *Post septem dies panis non ponderetur.*

3. The Bakers shall not sell to any Victualler, &c. to be retailed, but only thirteen Pennyworth for twelve Pence, as well Man's Bread as Horse Bread.

(*a*) 4. Every Baker shall have a Mark of his own for his Bread. *Poulton's* Statutes at large, *p.* 111. *& Rast. Weights* 7.

5. Every Sort of Bread shall be weighed according to the Price of the middle Sort of Corn.

6. No Man shall be a common Baker, except he hath been an Apprentice to that Trade by the Space of seven Years at the least.

7. The Statute doth appoint three Sorts of Bread to be made and sold to the Subjects, *viz.* white Bread, Wheaten, and Houshold Bread, besides the Horse Bread.

8. The Bakers of Cities, Boroughs, and Corporate Towns, shall have 6 *s.* Allowance for the baking of every Quarter of Wheat, over and above the second Price of Wheat in the Market.

9. Bakers inhabiting out of Cities, Boroughs, and Corporate Towns, shall have 4 *s.* in Allowance for his Charges in baking of every Quarter, &c.

10. But Foreigners Bread shall weigh six Ounces in the Penny Loaf, more than the Town-dwellers, for that they bear not such Scot and Lot as the others do.

11. Lastly, For Horse Bread, that three Horses Loaves be sold by the Baker for a Penny, 13 *d.* for 12 *d.* and every Loaf to weigh the full Weight of a Penny white Loaf, at what Price soever the Wheat be sold.

Bakers and their Punish-ment.

* Vide supra, Chap. 15.

(*d*) For the Punishment of the Bakers for their unlawful Bread *; *Quære*, Whether they shall only be amerced, &c. after Indictment and Conviction of their said Offence; or that the Justices of Peace (or sworn Officers in Leets) may take away their unlawful Bread, and give it among the Poor, as Officers in Corporate Towns are inabled or appointed to do in the End of the Book of Assise, imprinted *Anno* 1597. And all Justices of the Peace are there willed and required to be aiding and assisting to the said Officers therein.

(*a*) By the Statutes of 51 *H*. 3. & 13 *R*. 2. 8. Bakers and Brewers being convict for not observing the Assise the first, second and third Time, they shall be amerced according to the Offence (if it be not grievous.) But if the Offence be grievous, or often, then shall they suffer Punishment of the Body without Redemption (or remitting of the Offence either for Gold or Silver) *sc.* a Baker to the Pillory, and the Brewer to the Tumbrel (now called *The Cucking Stool*, as it seemeth by Mr. *Lambard* 62. *Minshew* taketh *Tumbrel* for a *Dung-Cart*) or to some other Correction. See another Statute con-cerning Bakers and Brewers, and their Punishments, and to the same Effect, made *incer-to tempore, cap.* 2. & 6. *Poulton's* Statutes at large, *fol.* 111.

Note, That within every Leet or Market there ought to be a Pillory and a Tumbrel to punish the Bakers and Brewers that offend, &c. *Fitz. Leet,* 12. And for want thereof, the Lord of such Leet or Market shall make a Fine to the King. *Cro.* 149.

Also they which have the Keeping and Correction of the Assise of Bread and Beer, if they have not a Pillory and a Tumbrel to punish Bakers and Brewers that are faulty, they shall forfeit their Franchise. *Cro.* 148.

Also a Leet may be seised into the King's Hands, if the Steward there shall take Mo-ney to spare the Punishment of the Tumbrel, where one shall offend in the Assise of Bread or Ale. *Libr. Intr. Cromp.* 181.

The Millers Toll-dish also must be according to the Standard.

Now

Now Millers are to take for the Toll but the twentieth Part, or the twenty-fourth Millers. Part, according to the Strength of their Water, and Custom of the Realm. Statute 3 E. 1. *de Victulariis.* *Rast.* Tit. *Weights, Div. 7.*

And yet in some Places the Millers do claim and take the sixteenth Part ; and where the Custom hath been so used Time out of Mind, it seemeth good and warrantable. *Tamen quære.*

But the Miller ought to take but one Quart for grinding of one Bushel of hard Corn, and if he fetch and carry back the Grist to the Owner, he may take two Quarts of hard Corn ; and this hard Corn is intended of Wheat, Rye, Meslin (which is Wheat and Rye mixed.) And for Malt, the Miller shall take but Half so much Toll as he taketh for hard Corn, (*sc.* one Pint in the Bushel) for that Malt is more easily ground than Wheat or Rye : But if the Miller do fetch to his Mill, and carry back the Malt to the Owner's House, then the Miller also shall have double Toll. See *Cromp. Author des Courts,* 221, & 224.

Note, That Millers are not to be common Buyers of any Corn, to sell the same again, either in Corn or Meal : But ought only to serve for the grinding of Corn that shall be brought to their Mills.

(d) *Measures of Wine, Beer and Ale,* &c.

		Rondlet,	16 and *di.*
Wine,	their Mea-	Barrel,	32 and *di.*
Oil and	sure is all	Hogshead,	63
Honey,	one *sc.* the	Pipe,	126
		Tun,	252

Gallons.

Measures of Liquids.
18 H. 6. 17.
P. Wine, 13.
1 R. 3. 13.

Yet for Honey the Assise is altered to 32 Wine-gallons the Barrel, 16 Gallons the Kilderkin, &c. 23 *El.* 8. P. *Wax,* 6.

Beer ; the Measure thereof is as followeth, *scil.* the	Firkin,	9
	Kilderkin,	18
	Barrel,	36

Gallons.

23 H. 8. 4.
P. Coop. 2.

And so Beer Measure containeth in the Barrel four Gallons more than Wine or any other Vessel.

Ale ; the Measure thereof is as followeth, *sc.* the	Firkin,	8
	Kilderkin,	16
	Barrel,	32

Gallons.

(*a*) No Cooper shall make any other Vessel for Beer or Ale, to be sold within this Coopers. Realm, of any greater or lesser Number of Gallons than is aforesaid, unless he shall cause to be marked upon every such Vessel (of greater or lesser Number of Gallons) the true and certain Number how many Gallons every such other Vessel shall contain. 23 *H.* 8. *cap.* 4.

Also no Brewer of Beer or Ale shall put the Beer or Ale to Sale, to be spent within this Realm, in any other Barrels, Kilderkins, Firkins, or other Vessels of Wood, other than shall be marked by a Cooper, and whereof every Vessel shall contain and hold the Number of Gallons abovesaid, of full and just Measure, or above, and not under that Measure. *Ibid.*

The Wardens of Coopers in all Cities and Boroughs where there be such Wardens, and in all other Boroughs and Towns the Mayor, Sheriffs, Bailiffs, Constables or other Head-Officers, may search and gage all such Vessels (made in such City or Town) whether they bear their true Contents, as aforesaid ; and if they find any Vessel defective, they may mark or amend the same, according to the true Content, or else may cause the same to burned. *Ibid.*

He who shall cause the Marks of Boats, Keels, Wains, &c. to be removed or altered, thereby to frustrate the Intent of the Statute 6 & 7 *W.* 3. shall upon Proof of one Witness, before one Justice, forfeit 10 *s.* to be levied by a Warrant, &c. by Distress and Sale, &c. and for want of Distress to be committed for three Months, and the Boats, &c. to be measured and marked again. *Boats.*
Keels.
Wains.
6 & 7 W. 3.
c. 10.

(*d*) It appeareth by Mr. *Crompton,* that it was agreed by the Justices, that the Measure of Wine and Ale should be all one, but now by the Statute of 1 *Jac.* 1. *cap.* 9. Cromp. 94. b.
P. Alch. 7.

Ale

Ale and Beer fhall be fold by Retail by one and the fame Meafure, *fcil.* by the Ale-quart.

Veffels.
8 El. c. 9.
§. 5.
    (*a*) And for the Prices of all Veffels of Ale and Beer, by the Statute 23 *H.* 8. *cap.* 4 two Juftices of Peace might affefs the Prices thereof, and that no Brewer fhall take for any Barrel, Kilderkin or Ferkin, *&c.* of Ale or Beer, but after fuch Prices and Rates as fhall be affefled by the faid Juftices of Peace in the County, or by the Mayor or their Head-Officers in Corporate Towns, *&c.* But now by the Statute 8 *Eliz. cap.* 9. the Affeffment of the Prices thereof by the Juftices, fhall be by the Juftices, or the more Part of them, being prefent at the *Eafter* Quarter-Seffions, and only of fuch Veffels as fhall be made or fold out of Cities or Corporate Towns.

Soap.
23 H. 8. 4.
P. Soap 1.
    (*d*) Soap, the Barrel, half Barrel and Firkin, fhall be of the fame Content that Ale is, *fc.* the Barrel 32 Gallons or above, and the empty Veffel not to be in Weight above 26 Pounds; the empty Firkin not to weigh above fix Pounds and a half, and to contain eight Gallons or above of full and juft Meafure.

Butter.
See Tit. *Butter.*
14 Car. 2. c. 26.
    Butter alfo fhall be of the fame Meafure that Soap is of.

Cheefe.
P. Weight 6.
    Cheefe: A Weigh of Cheefe muft contain 32 Cloves, and every Clove feven Pounds of *Averdupois* Weight: See the Statute 9 *H.* 6. 8. *Raft.* 28. *diu.* and the Book of Affife, imprinted 1597. And yet by that Book of Affife, the Weigh of *Suffolk* Cheefe muft contain twelve Score and fixteen Pounds of *Averdupois* Weight (and their Barrel of Butter is of like Weight with the firft:) But the Weigh of *Effex* Cheefe or Butter is three Hundred Pounds Weight, after the Rate of five Score and twelve Pounds to the Hundred, which is fixteen Score and fixteen Pounds of *Averdupois* Weight.

Flefh.
    Beef and other Flefh are fixteen Ounces *Averdupois* to the Pound, and eight of them Pounds to make the Stone, except where the Ufage of the Country require more Pounds to the Stone. *Book of Affife.*

Fifh.
    Herrings, the Barrel, half Barrel and Firkin, fhall be the fame Content that Ale is, *fc.* the Barrel 32 Gallons, *&c.* 11 *H.* 7. *cap.* 23, and 13 *El.* 11. P. *Fifh* 9.

    Alfo fix Score Herrings fhall go to the Hundred, ten Hundred to the Thoufand, and ten Thoufand to the Laft.

    Salmon and Eels. See the Contents of their Veffels, Statute 11 *H.* 7. *cap.* 23. P. *Fifh* 8, 10.

Wool.
23 E. 3. 9.
    Wool, 14 Pounds Weight goeth to the Stone of Wool, 28 Pounds goeth to the Tod, and 26 Stone goeth to the Sack. 11 *H.* 7. 4.

Hemp.
    Hemp, 20 Pounds Weight maketh the Stone.

Sugar.
Spices.
Wax.
    Sugar, Spices and Wax eight Pounds maketh the Stone, and thirteen Stone and a half, or 100 Pounds maketh the Hundred. See the Statute *de Comp. ponder. Raft. Weights* 8.

Hops.
    (*a*) Hops, five Score and twelve Pounds maketh the Hundred.

Lead.
    (*d*) Lead, the Content of the Pound, the Stone and the Load. See *Raft. Weights* 8.

Leather.
    Leather, the Content of the Dicker and the Laft. See *Raft. Weights* 8.

Iron.
Glafs.
    The Contents of Iron, Glafs, Linen-cloth, and divers other Things. See the Statute *de Compofit. ponder. Raft.* 8.

    All other Commodities of Tale or Number are fold by the Hundred.

Whereof
    Cattle and Fifh are fold fix Score to the Hundred, and yet the Hundred of Hard-fifh muft contain eight Score. *Raft.* 8.
    Alfo all other headed Things, as Nails, Pins, *&c.* are fold fix Score to the Hundred.

    All other Things have but five Score to the Hundred.

Fuel.
    For the Affife of Fuel, *fcil.* of Cole, Tall-wood, Billet and Fagot, fee the Statute of 7 *Ed.* 6. 7. 43 *El.* 14. A Sack of Coals is four Bufhels.

Timber.
    Timber well hewn, and perfectly fquared, fifty Foot thereof maketh the Load.

Lath.
    Lath fhall contain in Length five Foot, in Breadth two Inches, and in Thicknefs half an Inch.

Tile.
    Tile, fix Score to the Hundred: As for the Affife thereof, (*fcil.* the Length, Breadth and Thicknefs thereof,) fee Statute 17 *Ed.* 4. *cap.* 17. P. 2.

Paper.
* 24 Sheets by
10 Ann. c. 19.
§. 40.
    A Bale of Paper is ten Ream, a Ream is twenty Quires, a Quire * is twenty-five Sheets.

Parchment.
    A Roll of Parchment is five Dozen or fixty Skins.

I

Three

Three Barley-Corns meaſured from End to End (or four in Thickneſs) make one *Meaſures of Length.*
Inch. *P.* Weight 4.
Inch.
Four Inches make a Handful. 27 *H*. 8. 6. *Handful.*
Twelve Inches make a Foot. *Foot.*
Three Foot a Yard. *Yard.*
Three Foot and nine Inches make an Ell. *Ell.*
Five Foot do make a Geometrical Pace. *Pace.*
Seven Foot make a Fathom. *Fathom.*

Five Yards and a half (which is ſixteen Foot and a half) make a Pole, Rood or *Pole.*
Perch. *Ibid.*

And yet by the Uſage of many Countries the *Pole* doth vary, for in ſome Places it Co. 6. 6, 7.
is 18 *Foot*, and in ſome Places 20 *Foot* go to the Pole; and there if a Man ſell a cer- 47 Ed. 3.
tain Number of Acres of Wood, *&c.* it ſhall be meaſured according to the Uſage of f. 18.
Cromp. des
the Country there, and not according to this Statute, for herein *conſuetudo loci eſt* Courts, f. 32,
obſervanda. & 222.

The ſame Reaſon may ſeem to hold of Meaſures of Corn by the Buſhel. See a little *Corn.*
before.

(*a*) Maſter *Osborn* writeth, that the Meaſure of 18 Foot to the Perch (or Pole) is
emmonly called *Wood-land-meaſure* ; 21 *Foot to the Pole is called Church-meaſure*, (*ſc.* of
Land which now doth or formerly did belong to the Church) and *twenty-four Foot to
the Pole is* called (and that rightly) Foreſt-meaſure.

Note, That the Clerk of the Market may inquire of the *Pole or Perch whereby
Land is meaſured,* as well as of other Meaſures. *Cromp. Author. des courts* 221. But
the Juſtices of Peace are not to meddle therewith, eſpecially out of their Seſſions.

Alſo Note, That no Meaſure ſhall be *ſealed* but the *Buſhel, Half-Buſhel,* Peck, *Sealed Mea-
Gallon, Pottle, Quart* and *Pint. Cromp. fol.* 222. *tamen quære.* ſure.*

(*d*) Forty Pole in Length make a Furlong. *Furlong.*
Eight Furlongs (or 320 Pole) make an *Engliſh* Mile. 35 El. c. 6.
Mile.

Note; That our *Engliſh* Mile contains 280 Foot more than the *Italian* Mile.

Forty Pole in Length and four in Breadth (or 160 Pole do make an Acre.) Statute *Acre.*
Compoſit. ulnarum, & Stat. 34 *Ed.* 1.

And (by the Opinions of Mr. *Camden, fol.* 339 and *Hollinſhead, p.* 13. impr. 1586.) *Plow-land is
one hundred Acres is a Hide of Land ; but yet it ſeemeth that a Hide of Land or 50 l. per Ann.*
Plow-land, or Carve of Land, which are all one, are not of any certain Content. See
hereof before, Tit. *Highways.*

(*a*) *Librata terræ* containeth four Oxgangs and every Oxgang 13. Acres *Min.*
A *Yard-land* containeth in ſome Places more, in ſome other leſs. *Yard-land.*

And yet Mr. *Norden,* in his *Surveyors Dialogue,* Page 59. ſaith, that every Plow-
land containeth commonly 120 Acres, and every Plow-land is four Yard-land (in *Latin*
called *quatrona terræ* or *virgata terræ*) every Yard-land containeth thirty Acres; and
yet after ſome Computation, every Yard-land containeth but 20 Acres, and in ſome
Places 24 Acres ; and this is the common Account with us on the Eaſt Part of *Cam-
bridgeſhire.*

(*d*) Now that I have ſet down the Contents of moſt Weights and Meaſures, you
muſt farther obſerve.

Firſt, That in every County (in the Principal or Shire-Town there are) or ought to *Standard in
be Standards of *Braſs for Weights and Meaſures,* (*ſc.* for the Buſhel and Gallon) accord- every Shire-
town.*
ing to the King's Standard of his Exchequer, there to remain with the chief Officers of 11 H. 4.
the ſame Town ; according to the Scantling, of which every City, Borough and Market- 12 H. 7. 5.
Town within the ſame County ought to make them common Weights and Meaſures, to P. 7.
be marked by him that keepeth the Standard.

Alſo in every City, Borough and Market-Town, there ought to be a common Ba- *Market-Town.*
lance, and a common Buſhel, and Weights ſealed, and according to the Standard in 11 H. 7. 4.
their Shire-Town (as aforeſaid) upon Pain to every City 5 *l.* to every Borough 5 *l.* and to 8 H. 6. 5.
every Market-Town 40 *s.* for their Defaults.

Alſo no Man within any City or Market-Town ought to buy or ſell with any Weights 11 H 7. 4.
or Meaſures except they be ſealed and marked in Form aforeſaid (*ſcil.* according to the P. 9. 7.
King's Standard, and by the Officers in whoſe Poſſeſſion the King's Standard remaineth :)
Nor any other Perſon out of a Market-Town, except their Weights and Meaſures be
like and equal with the Standard. See *Raſtall, fol.* 551. *c. diu.* 33.

Weights and Measures sealed.

See Ra. diu. 5, 15, 26, 29, 32, 33. 8 H. 6. c. 5. 15 R. 2. c. 9.

And yet it seemeth by the Statute 31 *Ed.* 1. *& 8 H.* 6. 5. (*Rastall, div.* 3 *&* 26.) that no Man (though out of a Market-Town) shall use Weights or Measures, nor other Thing in the Place of Weights or Measures that is not sealed according to the King's Standard, upon Pain to forfeit the Value of the Goods weighed or measured, and two Years Imprisonment, and to be fined and ransomed, and yield *quadruple* Damages. See *Rastall,* Tit. *Weights, & Cromp.* 94.

11 H. 7. 4. P. 8.

The Officer that keepeth the Standard (in the Shire-Town) shall mark and seal other Weights or Measures to all other the King's Subjects that shall require it; and they shall take for the marking of the Bushel but 1 *d.* and for all other Measures but an Half-penny; and for Weights, for every hundred Weight 2 *d.* and for half an hundred Weight an Half-penny, and for every Weight under, but a Farthing.

11 & 12 W. c. 15. §. 3.

(*a*) The Sub-Commissioners or Collectors of the Excise, not providing or procuring a substantial *Ale Quart* and *Ale Pint* within their respective Divisions, forfeit 5 *l.* to the Use of the Poor, to be levied by Distress.

Ib. §. 5.

The Chief Officer of every City, *&c.* or Market-Town neglecting, or upon Request refusing to stamp and mark the *Quarts* and *Pints,* forfeits likewise 5 *l.* to be levied and employed, *ut supra;* the Conviction may be by one Witness, before a Justice of Peace, and the Prosecution must be within thirty Days, *&c.*

Ib. §. 6.

1 Ann. c. 15.

Selling in any other Water-Measure than according to the Statute 1 *Annæ, cap.* 15. forfeits 10 *s.* to be levied by Distress and Sale; one Half to the Informer, the other to the Poor.

By the said Statute 4 *Annæ* 'tis enacted, that Water-Measure shall be round 18 Inches and an half Diameter, and eight Inches Deep and no more, and so in Proportion for any greater or lesser Measure; and the Measure by which Apples and Pears are sold shall be heaped as usually.

He who buys or sells by any other Measure, forfeits 10 *s.* to the Informer and the Poor, *&c.* being convicted by the Oath of one Witness before one Justice, *&c.* Mayor, *&c.* where the Offence was committed, to be levied by Distress, and Sale, *&c.*

Coals shall be sold by the Chaldron containing 36 such Bushels heaped.

Now follow the Names of the principal Towns in every Shire (or County) appointed to have the Keeping of Standards for the Weights and Measures, according to these Statutes.

BEdfordshire, Town of *Bedford.*	*London,* the same City.
Berkshire, the Town or *Reading.*	*Middlesex,* the City of *Westminster.*
Bristol, the same Town.	*Norfolk* the City of *Norwich.*
Buckinghamshire, the Town of *Buckingham.*	*Northampton,* the Town of *Northampton.*
Cambridgeshire, the University of *Cambridge.*	*Northumberland,* the Town of *Newcastle.*
Cheshire, the City of *Chester.*	*Nottingham,* the Town of *Nottingham.*
Cornwall, the Town of *Lustythiel.*	*Oxford,* the University of *Oxford.*
Cumberland, the City of *Carlisle.*	*Rutland,* the Town of *Upinham.*
Derbyshire, the Town of *Derby.*	*Shropshire,* the Town of *Shrewsbury.*
Devonshire, the City of *Exeter.*	*Cinque-Ports,* the Castle of *Dover.*
Dorsetshire, the Town of *Dorchester.*	*Stafford,* the Town of *Stafford.*
Essex, the Town of *Chelmsford.*	*Somerset* the Town of *Ilchester.*
Gloucestershire, the Town of *Gloucester.*	*Southampton,* the same Town.
Hampshire, the City of *Winchester.*	*Suffolk,* St. *Edmunds-bury.*
Hertfordshire, the Town of *Hertford.*	*Surry,* the Town of *Guildford.*
Herefordshire, the City of *Hereford.*	*Sussex,* the Town of *Lewes.*
Huntingdonshire, the Town of *Huntingdon.*	*Warwick,* the Town of *Coventry.*
Kent, the Town of *Maidstone.*	*Westmorland,* the Town of *Appulbie.*
Lancashire, the Town of *Lancaster.*	*Wiltshire,* the City of *Salisbury.*
Leicestershire, the Town of *Leicester.*	*Worcester,* the City of *Worcester.*
Lincolnshire, the City of *Lincoln.*	*Yorkshire,* the City of *York.*

Stat. 11 *H.* 7.

Levit.

Levit. 19. 35, 36.

Ye shall not do unjustly in Judgment, in Line, in Weight or in Measure : Ye shall have just Balances and true Weights.

Prov. 11. 1. & 20. 20.

False Balances or divers Measures are all an Abomination unto the Lord.

Deut. 25. 13, &c.

Thou shalt not have two Manner of Weights, a great and a small ; nor divers Measures ; but a right, just and perfect Weight and Measure, that thy Days may be lengthened in the Land, &c.

C H A P. CXIII. (*a*)

Wool.

NO Perfon fhall prefs together with Screws, Preffes, or other Engines, into *Preffing in* any Sack, Bag, Pack, or other Wrapper ; or put, prefs, pack or ftrain, any *order to Tranf-* Wool or Yarn made of Wool into any Cafk or Veffel, or fhall lay or carry, or caufe, *porting.* &c. at or near the Shore or Coafts of the Sea or Navigable River, any Wool, Wool- *2. c.18. §.7.* flocks, or Yarn made of Wool, with an Intent to convey the fame out of *England* or *Ireland* into foreign Parts, upon Pain to lofe the fame or Value thereof.

No Bags, Sacks, Packs or Cafk of Wool, Wool-fells, Mortlings, Shorlings, Yarn *Times of Car-* made of Wool, Wool-flocks, Fullers-earth, Fulling-clay or Tobacco-pipe Clay, fhall *riage.* be carried or conveyed to or from any Place or Places in *England*, but from the firft of *Ib. §. 9.* *March* to the Twenty-fourth of *September*, between four of the Clock in the Morning and eight of the Clock in the Evening, and from the Twenty-ninth of *September* to the firft Day of *March*, between feven of the Clock in the Morning and five of the Clock in the Evening, upon Penalty of Forfeiture thereof.

The Moiety of all Forfeitures by this Act to the King, the other to the Profe- *Forfeitures.* cutor. *Ibid.*

Juftices of Peace in their Quarter-Seffions may hear and determine Offences againft *Ib. §. 12.* this Act.

The Exporting, Tranfporting, Carrying or Conveying of any of the Goods, Wares *Ib. §. 11.* or Commodities mentioned in that Act is declared a common Nufance.

Exporting Sheep or Wool of the Breed or Growth of *England* or *Ireland*, or *12 Car. 2. c.* any Woolfels, Mortlings or Shorlings, or any Yarn made of Wool, or any Wool- *32. §. 2, 4.* flocks, or Fullers-earth or Fulling-clay, or loading the fame on any Horfe, Cart or Carriage, or on board any Ship or Veffel, with an Intent to export it, fhall forfeit the fame, and alfo 20 *s.* for every Sheep, and 3 *s.* for every Pound of Wool, *&c.* and the Owners of the Ship or Veffel fhall forfeit their Interefts therein, with all the Apparel and Furniture ; and the Mafter of the Ship knowing the faid Offence, fhall forfeit all his Goods and Chattels and be committed for three Months ; the faid Forfeitures to be divided between the King and the Profecutor, and to be recovered in any Court of Record, by Action of Debt, Bill, Plaint or Information, or before Juftices of Affife, or at the General Quarter-Seffions of the Peace.

The Merchant tranfporting any fuch Goods, fhall be difabled to require any Debt or *Ib. §. 5.* Account of his Factor, or others.

Offenders fhall be tried in the County where the Goods are loaded, or where they are *Ib. §. 6, 7.* apprehended ; the Profecution muft be within a Year after the Offence.

Tobacco-pipe Clay not to be exported, on Pain of forfeiting three Shillings for every *Ib. §. 4.* Pound. *⁕* *⁕ Exporter of*

\ *Fullers-earth or fcouring Clay, forfeit 1. s. for every Pound.* 9 & 10 W. 3. c. 40. §. 2.

10 & 11 W.3. c. 10. §. 1, 2. *By this Act any Person employed in working Wool, Linen, Fustian,*   Wool shall not be transported from *Ireland* to any Place but to *England* or *Wales*, on Pain to forfeit the same, and 500 *l.* for every Offence, and the Vessel with all her Tackle shall be forfeited: And the Master, Mariners, Porters, Carriers, Waggoners, Boatmen, and other Persons knowing the Offence, and assisting therein, shall forfeit 40 *l.* a Moiety to the Informer. *See the Statute.*

Cotton or Iron, and intrusted therewithal, and imbezilling or purloining the same, forfeits double the Value of the Damages to the Use of the Poor: Conviction is to be by the Oath of one Witness, before one Justice, or the Confession of the Party; and if the Forfeiture is not paid, the Justice may send him to the House of Correction; and if not able to pay it, then he shall be whipp'd and kept to hard Labour not exceeding fourteen Days.

Ib. §. 4.   Any Person may seize Wool designed to be exported, and also the Vessel, &c.

Every Offender against this or any other Act, prohibiting the Exportation of Wool, may be prosecuted in any of the Courts at *Westminster*, and thereupon a *Capias* shall issue, the first Process specifying the Sum or the Penalty for which the Suit is brought, and the Defendant shall give Bail to appear at the Return of the Writ, &c.

4 Geo. 1. c. 11.   Any Person being in Gaol for the unlawful Exportation of Wool, and refusing to appear and plead to a Declaration or Information to be delivered to the Gaoler for one whole Term; in such Case Judgment shall be had against him by Default, and where such Judgment is had, or a Verdict be against him, if he doth not pay the Condemnation-Money within three Months after the Entring the Judgment, the Court shall cause him to be transported for seven Years, and if he return before that Time is expired, he shall suffer as a Felon, without Benefit of Clergy.

See 12 Geo. 2. cap. 21. *infra* Chap. 196.

C H A P. CXIV. (a)

Words, News.

JUstices of Peace may by Virtue of their Commission take Cognizance, and punish evil Words, for they tend to the Breach of the Peace, especially if spoken against any publick Person or Officer: And therefore if one say of a Mayor in the Execution of his Office, that he is a Fool, an Indictment lies: But to say of a Mayor playing at Dice, that he is a Fool, no Indictment lies. *Bag's* Case, *Mich.* 12 *Jac.* Roll's *Rep. part* 2. *p.* 79

C H A P. CXV.

NOW for a Conclusion of these Statutes, and of the Services of the Justices of Peace therein, I wish them, that in all Cases where the whole Matter is (by the Statute committed to one alone, or to two Justices, or more, out of their Sessions, *to hear and determine*, &c. as where upon his or their own View, or by Confession of the Offender or upon Examination and Proof of Witnesses; (and without any Indictment found or preferred) they may commit or punish an Offender as convict by such his Confession or Examination and Proof; as also where they may proceed by Inquiry and Indictment; that in every such Case of their judicial Proceeding they be led by no Affection, but advisedly to examine and consider as well the Fact it self as the Circumstances, and then (in the Fear of God, and according to Law) to proceed and to see or cause due Execution of the Punishment to be done upon the Offenders, according to the Quality and Quantity of their Offence, and as the Statutes themselves direct; for Law without due Execution and Punishment of the Offenders, is as a sheathed Sword, without any Use or Profit.

Record.   (a) But in all Cases where the Justices of Peace have Power to *hear and determine* out of their Sessions (*sc.* upon their own View, or upon the Confession of the Offender or upon Proof of Witnesses) if upon such Conviction, the Offender is to be committed to Gaol, the Justices ought to make a Record in Writing under their Hands of all the Matter, and of the Proofs, &c. which Record notwithstanding in many Cases they may keep by them, &c.

Also if upon such Conviction the Offender is to be *fined* to the King, then the Justice of Peace are to *estreat such Fine*, and to deliver or send the Estreat into the *Exchequer* whereby

whereby the Barons of the *Exchequer* may cause the said Fine, or Forfeiture, to be levied to the King's Use.

(*d*) And here I will shortly point out some particular Offences which by the Statutes are referred to the Justices of Peace to hear and determine, *out of their Sessions*, as aforesaid, and will leave the rest to your own Search.

1. Some Particulars where one Justice of Peace upon his own View of the Offence may punish the Offenders.

Alehouse-keepers, &c. suffering Townsmen or any other Person to continue Drinking in their Houses contrary to the Statute 1 *Jac. 1. cap.* 9. and 21 *Jac. 1. cap.* 7. *Vide antea* Tit. *Alehouses.*

Townsmen or Strangers tippling in Alehouses, &c. contrary to the Statute 4 *Jac. 1. cap.* 5. and 21 *Jac. 1. cap.* 7. *ibid.*

Persons that shall ride or go armed, contrary to the Statute 2 *Ed.* 3. *cap.* 5. *Vide antea* T.t. *Armour.*

Persons that shall have any Tenters, &c. for the deceitful Stretching of Cloth. *Vide antea* Tit. *Cloth.*

Offenders in Forcible Entries or Detainers contrary to the Statute. See *antea* Tit. *Forcible Entry.*

Keepers of Places for unlawful Gaming. *Antea* Tit. *Games unlawful.*

Players in such Places. *Ibid.*

Players at unlawful Games, wheresoever, contrary to the Statutes. See as before.

(*a*) *Swearing prophanely, or Cursing,* in the Hearing of any Justice of Peace, &c. *Antea* Tit. *Swearing.*

(*d*) 2. Where one Justice of Peace may punish Offenders as convict, upon their own Confession.

Sheriffs, &c. entring Plaints in their Courts unduly. *Vide antea* Tit. *Sheriffs.*

Persons not repairing every Sunday to Church. *Vide antea* Tit. *Recusants.*

Trespassers in Corn, Orchards or Woods, &c. contrary to the Statute 43 *El.* 7. *Vide antea* Tit. *Trespass.*

Offences in Tile-making contrary to the Statute. *Vide antea* Tit. *Tile.*

Offences in Watermen contrary to the Statute. *Vide antea* Tit. *Watermen.*

3. Where one Justice of Peace may punish Offenders as convict upon Examination and Oath of Witnesses.

Alehouse-keepers, &c. suffering Townsmen or Strangers to be Tippling in their Houses contrary to the Statute 1 *Jac. 1.* and 21 *Jac. 1. Vide antea* Tit. *Alehouses.*

Alehouse-keepers, &c. selling less Beer or Ale than according to the Statute 1 *Jac. 1. ibid.*

Townsmen or Strangers tippling in Alehouses, *&c.* contrary to the Statute 4 *Jac. 1. cap.* 5. *ibid.*

Persons not repairing every Sunday to Church, they may be convicted upon the Oath of one Witness. *Vide antea* Tit. *Recusants.*

Transporters of Corn, &c. *Vide antea* Tit. *Transportation.*

Trespassers of Corn, Orchards or Woods, &c. they also may be convicted upon the Oath of one Witness. *Vide antea* Tit. *Trespass.*

(*a*) And yet here, and in all Cases of Conviction upon the Oath of Witnesses, the Offender himself must also be heard to speak, and be examined by the Justice of Peace, &c. or else it is no lawful Conviction. *See hic, cap.* 6 & 7. & *hic infra.*

(*d*) 4. Where one Justice of Peace may punish Offenders as convict upon Examination generally, the Statutes not shewing what Persons shall be examined; in which Cases the Justices of Peace may thereupon examine as well the Offenders themselves as other Witnesses.

The Defaults of the Collectors of the Sheriffs Amerciaments; as also of Bailiffs of Hundreds. *Vide antea* Tit. *Sheriffs.*

Offences in Tile-making. *Vide antea* Tit. *Tile.*

Offences in Watermen, *Vide antea* Tit. *Watermen.*

5. Where one Justice of Peace may punish Offenders upon Accusation or Proof, generally; which Accusation or Proof must be by Examination of Witnesses only, as it seems.

Offenders in keeping or using Guns or Cross-bows, &c. contrary to the Statute. *Vide antea* Tit. *Guns.*

Disturbers of Preachers. Vide antea Tit. *Preachers.*

Y y y

Soldiers

Soldiers that have purloined their *Horſe or Harneſs. Vide antea* Tit. Soldiers.

Upon Oath.   Note, That in theſe former Caſes, and in all other Caſes where the Juſtice of Peace is to take ſuch Examination of Witneſſes, or ſuch other Accuſation or Proof aforeſaid, though the Statute doth not expreſly ſet down that it ſhall be upon Oath, yet 'tis fit that the Juſtice doth it upon Oath ; for Mr. *Brook* (ſometime Chief Juſtice of the Common Pleas) was of Opinion, that every Examination ought to be upon Oath ; and Mr. *Lamb.* 517. was alſo of Opinion, that theſe Examinations taken by the Juſtices of Peace ought always to be *upon Oath*, the rather, becauſe the Trial in theſe Caſes dependeth wholly upon theſe Examinations. (*a*) Yea, in all other Caſes whereſoever any Man is authorized *Plo.* 12. 2.   to *examine Witneſſes*, ſuch Authority to examine ſhall be taken and conſtrued to be in ſuch Manner as the Law will, which is only by Oath. *Vide poſtea* Tit. *Examination.*

(*d*) Alſo where the Matter is to be *tried by Witneſſes* only, it is fit there be *two Witneſſes* at the leaſt, except where the Statute doth expreſly allow the Oath and Teſtimony of one Witneſs. And ſo was the Opinion of Mr. *Brook*, that in ſuch Caſe there ought to be *two Deut.* 17. 6.   *Witneſſes* at the leaſt ; and agreeable thereto alſo is the Word of God. Otherwiſe it is *& 19. 15.* where the Trial is by a *Jury of twelve Men*, there one Witneſs ſufficeth, yea, there *Matt.* 18. 16. many Times Witneſſes are not neceſſary. See *Plo.* 12. *a.* *2 Cor.* 13. 1.

Where two   Where two Juſtices of Peace (out of their Seſſions for the Peace) may puniſh Offenders *Juſtices may* as convict before them, upon the Confeſſion of the Offender, or upon Examination of *hear and de-* Witneſſes, or upon their own View. *termine out of Seſſions.*

Clothiers refuſing to pay the Wages aſſeſſed, &c. See *antea* Tit. *Cloth.*

Spinſters, &c. which ſhall imbezil any Part of their Wool, contrary to the Statute 7 *Jac.* 1. *cap.* 7. upon Proof of one Witneſs.

(*a*) *Clothiers* making deceivable Woollen Cloth. 21 *Jac.* 1. *cap.* 18. Hic *antea* Tit. *Cloth.* *Servants or Labourers* aſſaulting their Maſter. See *antea* Tit. *Labourers.*

Servants departing, refuſing to ſerve, or taking exceſſive Wages, &c. See Tit. *Labourers.*

(*d*) *Deſtroyers of Partridges* or other Fowl, or of their Eggs, or of Hares, or keeping Hunting Dogs, contrary to the Statute 1 *Jac.* 1. 27. See *antea* Tit. *Partridge.*

Deſtroyers of Pheaſants or Partridges, contrary to the Statute 7 *Jac.* 1. 11. upon Proof of one Witneſs. *Ibid.*

Such as ſhall *put out of their Pariſh*, as poor Perſons, thoſe that be not to be put out. *Vide antea* Tit. *Poor.*

Alſo the Defaults of the *Overſeers of the Poor. Ibid.*

Diſturbers of Preachers. Vide antea Tit. *Preachers.*

Offenders which ſhall diſturb the Execution of the Statute for *Rogues* ; and Officers which ſhall be remiſs or negligent therein, &c. *Vide antea* Tit. *Rogues.*

The *Defaults of Officers* and others touching Weights and Meaſures. *Vide antea* Tit. *Weights.*

But note, that this Manner of Trial by Examination of the Offenders, or Witneſſes is not permitted to Juſtices of Peace, but only in Caſes where either the Statutes do general-ly refer the Trial to their Diſcretions, or elſe do ſpecially authoriſe them to take the Exa-minations.

In all theſe former Caſes where the Juſtices may hear and determine, or may puniſh Offenders as convict upon their own Confeſſion or upon Examination of Witneſſes, the Juſtices may grant out their Warrants againſt ſuch Offenders (or at leaſt ought to ſend for them) to appear before them to anſwer their ſaid Offences : And thereupon may proceed to examine, hear and determine the Offences.

By Indictment   Where one or two Juſtices of Peace may hear and determine, by Inquiry and Indict-*out of Seſſions.* ment taken before them, out of their general Seſſions, as it ſeemeth, *viz.*

Defaults of Sheriffs and Bailiffs, in not returning ſufficient Jurors to inquire of Forcible Entries. *Vide antea* Tit. *Forcible Entry.*

Offenders in Riots. Vide antea Tit. *Riots.*

Tranſporters of Corn, &c. *Vide antea* Tit. *Tranſportation.*

Offences committed in Tile-making. Vide antea Tit. *Tile.*

Defaults as well of Officers as of Buyers and Sellers with unlawful Weights or Mea-ſures. Vide antea Tit. *Weights*, &c.

See L:m. 517,   And in theſe Caſes the Offence being found upon ſuch Inquiry, theſe Juſtices have Au-*and* 496. thority not only to make out Proceſs againſt the Offenders under their own *Teſte*, but alſo to *fine them*, and to commit the Offenders to Priſon till they have paid their Fine, and to deliver them upon Payment of the ſame, or upon Sureties given for it ; Or otherwiſe the

I   *Juſtices*

Juſtices may receive the Traverſe of the Offenders, &c. for to all theſe Effects, the Words in thoſe Statutes, *Hear and Determine*, do ſeem to lead and inable the ſaid Juſtices.

CHAP. CXVI.

Sureties for the Peace.

SUrety for the Peace, is the Acknowledging a Recogniſance (or Bond) to the King, *What it is.* taken by a competent Judge of Record, for the Keeping the Peace : And it is called *Lam. 77.* Surety, of the Word *Securitas*, becauſe the Party that was in Fear, is thereby the more ſecure and ſafe.

This Surety for the Peace every Juſtice may take and command by a two-fold Au- *Two Ways* thority. *Supplicavit.* *F.N.B.79.b.* *Lam. 77.*

1. Firſt, As a *Miniſter* (commanded thereto by a higher Authority) as when a Writ of *Supplicavit*, directed out of the Chancery or King's Bench, is delivered to him : Upon this Writ, that Juſtice of Peace only, to whom ſuch Writ is delivered, is to direct his Warrant, to cauſe the Party to be brought before him *alone* to find Sureties for the Peace. And therein the ſaid Juſtice is to do according as the Writ doth direct him.

See more concerning this Writ of *Supplicavit*, &c. *poſtea, ſub hoc* Tit. *Surety for the Peace.*

2. Secondly, As a *Judge*, and by Virtue of his Office, derived from his Commiſſion, he may command this Surety of the Peace to be found ; and that either of his own *Motion and Diſcretion*, or elſe at the Requeſt or Prayer of another.

The Juſtice of Peace, upon his own *Motion and Diſcretion*, may, if he ſee Cauſe, com- *Upon Diſcre-* mand Surety of the Peace to be found, or may bind a Man to the Peace, and that againſt *tion.* *all the King's Subjects*, if the Juſtice ſhall ſo think meet, in theſe Caſes following :

1. One that maketh an *Aſſault or Affray upon the Juſtice of Peace himſelf*, the Juſtice *For what Act* may commit him to Priſon till he hath found Sureties for the Peace. *done in his* *Preſence.* *5 H. 7. 6.*

2. Such as *in his Preſence ſhall make an Affray upon another*, or ſhall ſtrike or aſſault, *P. R. 18, 19.* or offer to ſtrike another, the Juſtice may commit him to Priſon until he hath found *Bro. Faux* Sureties for the Peace. *Impr.*

3. So of ſuch as *in his Preſence and Hearing ſhall threaten to kill, beat or hurt ano-ther, or to burn his Houſe.*

4. So of ſuch as *in his Preſence ſhall contend only in hot Words*; for from thence often- *P. R. 18.* times do enſue Affrays and Batteries, and ſometimes Maims, yea, Manſlaughters and Murders.

5. So of ſuch as *in his Preſence ſhall go or ride armed* offenſively, or with an unuſual *See Crom. 76.* Number of Servants or Attendants : For theſe are accounted to be an Affray and Fear of *142.* the People, and a Means of the Breach of the Peace : So of Servants and Labourers that *P. R. 4.* ſhall bear any Weapons contrary to the Statute of 12 *R.* 2. *Vide antea* Tit. *Armour.*

6. Alſo he may bind to the Peace any other Perſon, by him ſuſpected to be inclined to *9 Ed. 4. 3.* the Breach of the Peace. *P. R. 4.*

7. If (out of the Preſence of the Juſtice of Peace) any Man ſhall threaten to *kill, maim,* *Out of his* *or beat another*, or do attempt or go about to do it : Then any *Conſtable*, being preſent, *Preſence.* may arreſt ſuch Offender, to come before a Juſtice of Peace, to find Sureties for the Peace, *Crom. 135* and the Juſtice may bind him to the Peace. *and 143.* *P. R. 22.* *F. Bar. 201.*

8. If any Conſtable ſhall perceive any other Perſons in *his Preſence to be about to break* *1 H. 7. 7.* *the Peace*, either by *drawing Weapons*, or by Striking or Aſſaulting one another, or by Aſſaulting the Conſtable himſelf; he may take Aſſiſtance, and carry them all before the Juſtice, to find Sureties for the Peace, and the Juſtice may bind them.

9. If the Conſtable ſhall know that certain Perſons be fighting or quarrelling in a *P. R. 22.* Houſe, he may *break open the Doors, and arreſt them*; and carry them before a Juſtice of Peace, to find Surety of the Peace : And the Juſtice may bind them.

10. Yea, the Juſtice of Peace (either upon his own Diſcretion, or upon any Man's *See Br. Peace* Complaint) may make his Warrant for any ſuch as have made an *Affray* (though out of *41.* *21 Aſſ. 27.* his Preſence) and may bind them to the Peace. *Vide antea* Tit. *Affray.*

11. If

11. If one hath received a Wound, the Juſtice of Peace may take Surety of the Peace of the one and the other, (by his Diſcretion) until the Wound be cured and the Malice be over. *Popham*, late Lord Chief Juſtice of *England* (an honourable and grave Judge) did accordingly between *James* and *Benton*, at *Cambridge* Aſſiſes, 3 *Jac.* 1.

12. All ſuch as ſhall go or ride armed (offenſively) in *Fairs, Markets*, or elſewhere; or ſhall wear or carry any *Guns, Dags* or *Piſtols* charged; any Conſtable, ſeeing this, may arreſt them, and carry them before the Juſtice of Peace, and he may bind them to the Peace; yea, though thoſe Perſons were ſo armed or weaponed for their Defence; for they might have had the Peace againſt other Perſons: And beſides, it ſtriketh a Fear and Terror into the King's Subjects.

2 E. 3. c. 3.
Commiſſion.

See more *hic antea* Tit. *Affray* and *Armor.*

13. Alſo the Juſtice of Peace (upon his Diſcretion) may bind to the Peace a common *Barrator. Vide* Tit. *Barrator.*

14. So of *Rioters. Vide* Tit. *Rioters,* and *Lamb.* 79.

New Sureties.
21 E. 4. 40.

15. He that ſtandeth bound to keep the Peace, if he hath broken (or forfeited) his Recognizance by Breach of the Peace, the Juſtice may and ought to bind him anew; but that muſt not be done, until the Party be convicted of the Breach of the Peace upon his Recognizance; for before his Conviction it reſteth indifferent whether the Recognizance be forfeited or no: But after that he is thereof convicted, and that the Forfeiture be levied, the Recognizance is then utterly determined; and then he is to be compelled to find new Surety, or elſe to be ſent to the Gaol.

Br. Peace 17.
Lamb. 117.
Cromp. 142.

So, though the Forfeiture be not levied, yet if the Party be convict for Breaking the Peace, he ſhall be bound of new. *Cromp.* 141. and *Br. Recog.* 21.

16. Alſo he that ſtandeth bound to keep the Peace, if his Sureties be inſufficient, the ſame Juſtice, or another Juſtice of Peace, may compel him to find better Sureties.

And in many of the former Caſes the Juſtice of Peace ought of Duty (or at leaſt in good Diſcretion) to command this Surety for the Peace, although the ſame be not required by any other Perſon: And if any ſuch Perſon ſhall refuſe to give ſuch Surety, the Juſtice ought to ſend him to Priſon, there to remain until he ſhall find ſuch Surety.

9 Ed. 4. 3.
Br. Peace 8.

If a Juſtice of Peace (upon his own Diſcretion) ſhall cauſe one to be arreſted to find Sureties for the Peace, and ſhall after let him go without taking Surety, or binding him to the Peace, yet the Party hath no Remedy. (a) For an Action will not lie againſt the Juſtice for this, he being a *Judge of Record.* See 9 *H.* 6. *f.* 60. and 9 *E.* 4. *f.* 3. *Br. Judges* 2. 10. and *Br. Faux Imp.* 12.

Lamb. 80.
P. R. 18.

(d) A Juſtice of Peace may perſuade a Man to require the Surety of Peace againſt another, and he himſelf may grant a Warrant for it, becauſe it is no more than he might have granted of his *own Authority*, without any Demand made; and it ſhall be preſumed that he ſaw Cauſe to do all this.

Upon Requeſt.

Alſo at the *Requeſt* or *Prayer* of another, the Juſtice of Peace may command this Surety of the Peace, and may grant his Warrant for it.

Oath, the Form of it.
F. N. B. 79.
H.
Lamb. 84,85.

But here the Juſtice muſt and ought firſt to take an Oath of the Party that demandeth the Peace, which Oath muſt be to this Purpoſe, *ſc. That he ſtandeth in Fear of his Life, or of ſome bodily Hurt to be done to himſelf, or to have his Houſes burnt (and that he doth not crave the Peace for any private Malice, or for Vexation, but of very Fear, and for the needful Safety of his Body or Houſes)* for the Words of the Commiſſion herein are, *Et ad omnes illos qui alicui, vel aliquibus de populo noſtro; de corporibus ſuis, vel de incendio domorum ſuarum, minas fecerint, ad ſufficientem ſecuritatem de pace, &c. inveniendam, &c.*

So he that ſhall be threatned to be hurt in his Body, (*ſcil.* to be beaten, wounded, maimed or killed) the Party ſo threatned may crave and have Surety of the Peace againſt the other.

Alſo if a Man do fear that another will kill, *maim, beat, aſſault*, or hurt him in the Body, he may crave the Peace againſt ſuch other Perſon.

Fitz. 79.
G. H.

So if a Man do fear that another will *burn his Houſe*, or that he will procure or cauſe any ſuch Hurt to be done him by another, *either in his Body or in his Houſes*; for the Words of the Recognizance be, *Non faciet, nec fieri procurabit.*

Cromp. 135 a.

So if a Man *lieth in wait* to beat, kill or hurt another, it is good Cauſe to require the Surety.

Threatning.
Lamb. 84.

If a Man be threatned to have his *Goods burn'd*, by the Opinion of Mr. *Fitz.* he may demand Surety of the Peace for this: *Quære tamen.* (a) Becauſe he may recover Damages for and to the Value of the ſame. *Co. L.* 255.

I

(d) But

(*d*) But where a Man ſhall threaten to *impriſon another*, it is holden, That the Peace ſhall not be granted; for that the Party wronged may have his Action of Falſe Impriſonment, or a Writ *De homine replegiand'*, and ſo ſhall recover Damages for his Impriſonment. 17 E. 4. 4. Br. Peace 22.

Yet inquire hereof, for to threaten Impriſonment is within the Words *minas de corporibus*; and like Harm may happen to a Man by hard Impriſonment, as by cruel Beating of him. (*a*) And to threaten Impriſonment, is a Cauſe to avoid a Deed or Bond, as well as to threaten to kill or maim one, *&c.* 39 H. 6. Br. *Dureſſe* 9. Vide *Co. Lit.* 253. Lamb. 85. F. N. B. 80. G. Lamb. 85.

(*d*) Where a Man is in fear that another will *hurt his Servant or his Cattle or other Goods*; this Surety of the Peace ſhall not be granted by the Juſtice: But in this Caſe Mr. *Fitz.* ſaith, the Party may have a ſpecial Writ out of the *Chancery*, directed to the Sheriff, that he ſhall cauſe ſuch Perſon to find Surety, that he ſhall do no Hurt or Damage to the other Man in his Body, or to his Servants or Goods. And if he will not find Surety, that then he ſhall arreſt and detain him in Priſon until he ſhall find Surety: And that the Sheriff ſhall certify all that he ſhall do thereupon into the *Chancery, &c.* And the Sheriff ought to take ſuch Surety by Recognizance. And yet if a Man ſhall *threaten to hurt my Servant*, or *my Wife or Child*, I ſee no Cauſe but that in their Behalf I may crave the Peace, by the Words of the Commiſſion, and that the Juſtice ought to grant it.

If a Man will require the Peace, becauſe he is *at Variance*, or in Suit with his Neighbour, it ſhall not be granted.

Note alſo, the Surety for the Peace ſhall not be granted but where there is a Fear of ſome *preſent or future Danger*, and not meerly for a *Battery* or *Treſpaſs* that is paſt, or for any Breach of the Peace that is paſt: For this Surety of the Peace is only for the Security of ſuch as are in fear. Now *Metus eſt, præſentis vel futuri periculi cauſa, mentis trepidatio:* And ſo this Surety is, *providere præſentia & futura, & non præterita.* Br. F. imp 42. P. R. 14.

And, as for a Battery, or other like *Treſpaſs that is paſt*, the Party wronged may have his Action of Treſpaſs or Battery, *&c.* or may puniſh the Offender by *Indictment* at the King's Suit: And yet in ſuch Caſe the Juſtice may (if he ſee Cauſe) bind over the the Affrayer. *Vide antea.*

If the Juſtice of Peace ſhall perceive that this Surety for the Peace is demanded meerly of *Malice or for Vexation only*, without any juſt Cauſe of Fear, he may ſafely deny it. As in common Experience we find it, That where *A.* ſhall upon juſt Cauſe come and crave the Peace againſt *B.* and hath it granted to him; when *B.* ſhall come before the Juſtice, *B.* likewiſe will crave the Peace againſt *A.* (and will perhaps ſurmiſe ſome Cauſe) but yet will nevertheleſs be content to ſurceaſe his Suit and demand againſt *A.* ſo as *A.* will relinquiſh to have the Peace againſt him; here the Juſtice of Peace ſhall do well (as I think) not to be too forward in granting the Peace thus required by *B.* but to perſuade him, and to ſhew him the Danger of his Oath which he is to take; but yet if *B.* will not be perſuaded, but will take his Oath, that he is in Fear (where indeed he neither doth fear, nor hath cauſe to fear) this Oath ſhall diſcharge the Juſtice, and the Fault ſhall remain upon ſuch Complainant. *Deny.*

(*a*) And when the Juſtice hath granted the Peace to one, who in his Judgment ſhall crave or require it only out of Malice or for Vexation, he may preſently in good Diſcretion bind him to the good Behaviour that ſo required the Peace.

C H A P. CXVII.

For whom, and againſt whom this Surety for the Peace ſhall be granted.

THE Law hath ſuch an Opinion of the Peaceable Diſpoſition of *Noblemen*, that 'tis ſufficient to take one of their Promiſes, upon his Honour, that he would not break the Peace againſt a Man. Br. *Contempts* 6. 24 E. 3. 3. and 17 E. 4. 4. *Noblemen.*

And therefore if a Man ſhall have Cauſe to have the Surety of the Peace againſt a *Lord of the Parliament*, or ſuch great and noble Perſonage, he ſhall not have a Warrant from the Juſtices of Peace to that Purpoſe; nor yet have a *Supplicavit* out of the *Chancery* Fitz. Subp. 20.

directed

directed to the Justice of Peace: But if there be Cause, he may have a *Subpœna* out of the *Chancery*, (of common Right) and there such *Lord or Nobleman* shall be bound to the Peace. And yet if such Lord will not appear upon the *Subpœna* served, *Quære*, If an Attachment will lie against him upon such his Default; *Cromp. f.* 134. *b.* saith that it was holden in the Case of the Lord *Cromwell* in the *Chancery*, about 18 *El.* that an Attachment will not lie, and *Dyer* 315. seemeth to accord.

Co.65,53,54.
11 H. 4. 14.
Br. Repl. 19.
Co. 9. 49.
Vide 27 H. 8.
f. 22. b.

But though it be true that the Person of a *Baron* (who is a Peer of the Parliament) shall not be arrested in Cases of Debt or Trespass, &c.) first, In respect of their Dignity; secondly, In respect that the Law presumeth that they have sufficient Lands and Tenements whereby they may be distrained; yet in Cases of *Contempt*, they may be arrested by *Capias* or *Attachment*, &c.

Fitz.
Subp 20.
F.N.B.79.g.
Cromp. 134.

Or else he the Party may crave the Peace in the *Chancery* against such Lord or Peer (*sc.* to have a *Supplicavit* directed to the Sheriff) who may and ought to execute the same: And if the Sheriff shall not do his Office therein, an *Alias Plur.* and Attachment lieth against him. And if the Sheriff shall return, that such Lord is so powerful that he cannot arrest him; upon such Return, the Sheriff shall be grievously amerced (for he might have taken the *Posse comitatus, scil.* he might have levied 300 Men by his Discretion, if there had been need, to have aided him. And if such Lord or Peer, who is by the Sheriff so arrested, shall refuse to obey the Arrest, and shall make a *Rescous*, whereupon the Sheriff shall return a *Rescous*, there shall be an Attachment granted out against such Lord, to arrest and take his Body for such his Contempt.

Noblewomen.
Co. 6. 52, 53.

The same Law and Remedy is where a Man hath Cause to have the Surety of the Peace against a *Dutchess, Countess* or *Baroness*; for they are Peers of the Realm, and shall be tried by their Peers, though in respect of their Sex they sit in Parliament: And they are in the same Degree (as concerning their Nobility and the Privileges incident to their Dignities) with Dukes, Earls, and Barons. But here Note this Diversity, *sc.* if such Woman, being a Countess or Baroness, *sc. by Marriage only*, shall marry again under the Degree of Nobility, she hath thereby lost her Name of Dignity (together with the Privileges of her said Nobility also, for in such a Case, *Si mulier nobilis nupserit ignobili, desinit esse nobilis*, and that which was gotten by Marriage may also be lost by Marriage;

Co. ibid.

for *Eodem modo quo quid constituitur, dissolvitur*; but if she be Noble by Birth or Descent, whomsoever she shall marry, yet she remaineth Noble: For Birthright *est Character indelebilis.*

Vide Dyer
79. & Br. Nof-
me de Dignity 31. & 69. & C. l. 168.

And yet by the Curtesy of *England*, if Women have good Estates they never lose by marrying more meanly, but do still take Place according to the Estate of their first Husband.

Knight.

Surety of the Peace may be granted by the Justice against a *Knight*, and all other *Lay Persons* being under the Degree of a Baron or Peer of the Realm, and they shall be bound with Sureties.

* *A Justice of Peace of .*
Surrey.

(a) Sir *Nicholas Stoughton* * in *Surrey* was, upon the Complaint of one *Gilham*, required in Sessions to give Sureties for the good Behaviour for a sufficient Cause; he refused; the Sessions committed him until, &c. he gave Sureties: And afterwards Complaint was made hereof in the King's Bench, and he was compelled there to give Sureties, notwithstanding it was objected that the Justices of Peace were all of equal Power: But it was answered by the Court, that the Sessions made a Court, which Court might require Sureties for the Peace or good Behaviour of any one Justice of Peace.

Parson.
36 H. 6. 73.
Br. Moign.
14 & 15.
See Stat.
1 R. 2. c. 15.
& 1 Mar. c.3.

(d) *Ecclesiastical Persons* (if they be not attending upon Divine Services) may be arrested *for the Peace*, and they shall be bound with Sureties: But whilst they are doing any Divine Service in the Church, Church-yard, or other Place dedicated to God, they may not be arrested. *50 Ed.* 3. 5. *P. Arrests* 1.

Sheriff.

Surety of the Peace may be granted *against the Sheriff, Under-Sheriff, Coroner, Escheator*, and other such Officers of Justice. But Mr. *Marrow* adviseth, that such Persons be not bound *versus cunctum populum*; but only against such Persons as shall demand it, lest otherwise it should argue them unworthy of their Offices.

(a) One Justice of Peace may grant this Surety to any Man against one of his Fellow Justices (and yet the Commission is joint) but great Discretion is herein to be used.

Wife.

Yea, a Justice of Peace, upon Demand, may grant this Surety of the Peace against his own *Wife*: And yet he and his Wife are but one Person in Law.

.4　　　　　　　　　　　　　　　　　　　　　　If

If Surety of the Peace be demanded againſt a *Juror at the Seſſions*, it is grantable; but *Juror.* yet the ſame ſhould not be granted or done before the Seſſions be ended.

(*d*) One Juſtice of the Peace may demand Surety of the Peace of his fellow Juſtice againſt another Man.

If a Man hath Cauſe to have Surety of the Peace againſt one dwelling in the *Cinque* Cinque Ports. *Ports*, he muſt have a Writ out of the *Chancery* directed to the Conſtable of *Dover*, and to the Warden of the *Cinque Ports :* The Form thereof ſee in *Fitz. N. B.* F. N. B. 80.

The Wife may demand this Surety againſt her Huſband, (if ſhe ſhall threaten to kill her, Feme. or outragiouſly to beat her, or if the Wife hath any notorious Cauſe to fear that he will do ſo) and it ſhall be granted her by the Juſtice of Peace, or ſhe may have it by *Suppli-cavit* in the *Chancery*. *Fitz.* 238. *f. Br. Peace* 23.

The Huſband for the like Cauſes may demand Surety of the Peace againſt his Wife. Fitz. 80. f. (*d*) But it was reſolved *T. 9 Car. 1. B. R.* that a Huſband cannot have Sureties of the Peace of the Wife.

Alſo the Juſtice of Peace, upon his own Diſcretion, may in either of the aforeſaid Cauſes between the *Huſband and Wife* (eſpecially happening in his Preſence) grant Surety of the Peace.

An Infant, under the Age of fourteen Years, may demand this Surety, and it ſhall be *Infant.* granted him. Lamb. 81.

Alſo this Surety of the Peace may be granted at the Prayer of any Perſon againſt a Feme Covert, or againſt an Infant, though he be under 14 Years of Age. (For if an Infant under 14 hath Diſcretion to demand the Peace, &c. then hath he Diſcretion to break the Peace.)

But if an Infant and a *Feme Covert* ſhall be bound by Sureties only, they themſelves Co. 10. 43. ſhall not be bound, and if they cannot find Sureties they ſhall be committed to Priſon Cromp.237.b. until they have found Sureties. And yet if an Infant ſhall be bound to the Peace, &c. by Recognizance taken by a Juſtice of Peace, he ſhall be eſtopped to avoid ſuch a Re-cord, if he doth not avoid it during his Minority, for it is not void but voidable, by *Au-dita querela.*

But if a *Feme Covert* ſhall be bound, or acknowledge ſuch a Recognizance (though her Huſband join with her) yet it is merely void as to the Wife, although ſhe overliveth her Huſband.

A Man of *Non ſane Memorie*; this Surety ſhall neither be granted againſt him, nor to Non compos. him upon his *Requeſt*; and yet if there ſhall be Cauſe, the Juſtice of Peace (upon his Diſcretion) ought to provide for his Safety.

A Man that is *Lunatick* (ſc. who at ſome Seaſons hath the Uſe of Reaſon, and at *Lunatick.* other Times not) it ſeemeth this Surety of the Peace may be granted againſt him; and alſo that he may demand the ſame againſt another.

And if one of *Non ſane Memorie*, or a Lunatick, be himſelf bound by Recognizance *See* Co. 4. before a Juſtice of Peace, to keep the Peace, it ſeemeth ſuch Recognizance ſhall bind 1 24. & 11.77. them and all others for ever.

But *Quære*, if there be not a Difference to be taken where a Recognizance by an Infant, or one that is *Non compos Mentis*, ſhall be acknowledged in a Court of Record, or in open Seſſion, and where before a Juſtice of Peace out of the Seſſions.

A Man that is *Deaf, Dumb,* and *Blind,* be it naturally (*ſcil.* that he was ſo born,) *Natural Infr-* or accidentally, he ſhall not have this Surety granted to him, for he hath no Underſtand- *mities.* ing to aſk it, and yet for ſuch a Perſon, (or any other Perſon not having Reaſon to de-mand the Peace) if there be Cauſe, the Juſtice of Peace, upon his Diſcretion, ought to provide for their Safety.

A Man that is born dumb and blind may have Underſtanding; and therefore it ſeem-eth this Surety may be granted to him, or againſt him.

But a Man that is born dumb and deaf can hardly have Underſtanding; for though *See* Stamf. the Sight be the chiefeſt Senſe, yet by Hearing we come chiefly to Knowledge, and de Prærog.fol. therefore it ſeemeth not grantable to him or againſt him. 33, 34. Cro. El. 135.

(*a*) And yet a Man that is *Dumb and Deaf*, or *Blind and Deaf accidentally*, may have Underſtanding, and therefore this Surety may be granted to him, or againſt him.

(*d*) Alſo this Surety of the Peace may be granted againſt an *impotent Perſon*, although *Impotent Per-* he be ſuch a one as is not like to break the Peace himſelf; for he may procure another to *ſon.* kill or beat one : And the common Form of Recognizance is to bind a Man from *pro-curing Hurt*, as well as from doing Hurt.

This

Attaint.   This Surety of Peace may alſo be granted to, or againſt, a Man attainted of Treaſon or Felony.

Excommuni-   A Man *excommunicate* may have this Surety granted to him or againſt him.
cate.

Cromp. 34.   ·So alſo of a Man that hath abjured the Realm ; for notwithſtanding the Abjuration,
Abjured.   he oweth the King his Allegiance, and remaineth within the King's Protection, and the King may pardon and reſtore him again ; *Qui abjurat Regnum, amittit Regnum, non Regem.* Co. 7. 9. b.

Præmunire.   A Man attainted in a *Præmunire,* may (at this Day) require, and ought to have this Surety granted to him. *P. R.* 19. *Cromp.* 133.

Alien.   An *Alien born* who is made *Denizen,* may have this Surety ; and ſo of an Alien born
Crom. 134. who liveth in *England* under the King's Protection (altho' he be not made a Denizen.)
1 R. 19.   And ſo of an Alien whoſe King is in League with our King ; or if there be no Wars
Co. 7. 17. between this Realm and that Realm whereof the Alien is ; for by the Common Law, all theſe may get and have within this Realm any perſonal Goods, and may ſue for the ſame, and ſo have the Benefit of the King's Laws and Protection. But an Alien who
Dyer 2.   is the King's Enemy, (*ſcil.* where there is open War between our King and his King) ſhall not have this Surety granted to him, nor any other Benefit of the King's Laws. Who ſhall be ſaid to be Alien. See *Co.* 7. 16, 17.

Subjects.   In *Calvin's* Caſe, 6 *Jac.* 1. *Reg.* there is a Difference taken between *ante-nati* and
Co. 7. 18. *poſt-nati* in *Scotland,* where it is holden, That *ante-nati* in *Scotland, ſc.* ſuch as were born before the King's Coming to the Crown of *England,* they are Aliens born ; the Reaſon is, for that at the Time of their Birth, they were under the Legiance and Obedience of another King ; and he could not be a Subject born of the Kingdom of *England,* that was born under the Legiance of a King of another Kingdom. And yet it is manifeſt, that *ante-nati,* being the King's Subjects, are herein provided for by the Commiſſion it ſelf ; the Words whereof are, *Et ad omnes illos qui alicui vel aliquibus de popul*, *noſtrô, &c.* of which Number *ante-nati* he : So as they may and ought to have this Surety granted to them, as well as to any other Subjects. See *Dyer fol.* 304 & *Pl.* 306. *a.*

Iriſhman.   An *Iriſhman* born is a natural-born Subject, and capable of, and inheritable to Lands
Co. 7. 23. in *England,* and therefore may have this Surety.

Infidel.   But it may be queſtioned, whether an Infidel, Pagan or Jew, ſhall have this Surety
Co. 7. 17. granted to them. For in Law they are *perpetui inimici* ; there is between Chriſtians and them perpetual Enmity, and can be no Peace : Neither can they get any Thing within this Realm, nor maintain any Action at all. 12 *H.* 8. 4.

CHAP. CXVIII.

How this Surety of the Peace may be commanded, and how the ſame Commandment ſhall be executed.

Parol.   THE Juſtice may command this *Surety of the Peace* either by *Word* only, or by *Writing.*
14 H. 7. 8.   1. By *Word only,* the Party being in his Preſence ; as if in the Preſence and Hearing of the Juſtice, one Man doth threaten another, or ſhall make an *Affray or Aſſault* upon another, or do the like Thing tending to the Breach of the Peace, the Juſtice may command him by Word to find Sureties for the Peace.

14 H. 7. 9.   Alſo if one ſhall demand this Surety againſt another, who is then in the Preſence of the Juſtice, and will be ſworn that he is afraid of him, the Juſtice may by Word command the ſame Party to find Sureties for the Peace.

14 H. 7. 8, 9.   And the Juſtice in ſuch Caſes may (by Word only) command the Conſtable, or any other known Officer, or his own Servant being then preſent, to arreſt ſuch Party to find Sureties for the Peace, and to take the Party into his or their Cuſtody, &c. and if the Party ſhall refuſe to find ſuch Sureties, then the Juſtice of Peace may commit him to the Gaol.

    (*a*) But if the Party (againſt whom this Surety of the Peace is demanded) be *abſent* it is otherwiſe ; for a Juſtice of Peace cannot ſend for or command any Man to be arreſted refted or brought before him, or to be imprifoned, (*who is not in his Prefence*) by Word only, but he muft make his Warrant or Precept in Writing. And *Popham,* Chief Ju-ftice, faid, That the Juftices of the King's Bench, when they fend for any of the King's Subjects, it is either by Writ, or by Warrant, or by a Tipftaff: But the Tipftaff (faid he) is by Prefcription, except that the Party be in *Weftminfter-Hall, &c.* See the Cafe between *Woody* verfus *Bokers & Read-head, Termino Mich. Ann.* 2 *Jac.* 1. *Regis Rotul.* 480. *in Banco Regis.*

(*d*) 2. By Precept or Warrant in Writing, and under the Juftice his Seal; and this *By Writing.* nuft be directed to fome Officer or other indifferent Perfon, and muft contain the Caufe, and at whofe Suit, to the Intent the Party to be bound may provide his Sureties, and ake them with him.

The Form of which Precept, fee *poftea* Tit. *Warrants, cap.* 169.

The Juftice of Peace may make his Warrant to bring the Party *before himfelf,* (to find *Before whom* 3urety for the Peace) by the Opinion of *Wray,* Chief Juftice; for he that maketh the *to be brought.* Warrant, for the moft part, hath the beft Knowledge of the Matter, and therefore he *Co. 5. 59.* s the fitteft to do Juftice in fuch Cafe. And yet the moft ufual Manner is, to make *Br. Peace 9.* fuch a Warrant to bring the Party before the fame Juftice, or fome other of the Juftices *3. P. 78.* of the Peace of the fame County, *&c.* And Judge *Fineux* his Opinion was, That *21 H. 7. 22.* where a Juftice of Peace doth make any Warrant for the Peace *ex officio,* (*fc.* by Force of the Commiffion, and not by Virtue of a *Supplicavit,*) there the Party may chufe to appear before him or any other Juftice in that County: And that the Party may have his Action of falfe Imprifonment againft the Officer, if he do otherwife compel him. Otherwife it is in the Execution of the Writ of *Supplicavit,* as you may fee here *poftea, fub hoc titulo.*

Who may ferve this Warrant, and whether the Officer may make his *Deputy*; and whether they need fhew their Warrant or no; and whether they may break open the Doors, *&c.* See hereof Tit. *Warrants poftea.*

The Conftable (or other Officer) before he arreft the Party upon fuch a Warrant, *How it fhall* ought firft to acquaint him with the Matter, and withal to require or charge the Party *be executed.* in the King's Name, to go (with him) before the Juftices to find and put in Sureties ac- *5 Ed. 4. 13.* cording to the Warrant: And if the Party fhall refufe to do this, *fc.* fhall refufe either *Lamb. 92.* to go before the Juftices, or to find Sureties, then the Officer (by the Words of the *Yet fome Pre-* Warrant) may and ought forthwith to arreft him, and may convey him to the Gaol *cedents are,* without carrying him to any Juftice, and there the Party fhall remain until he fhall vo- *Quod Capia-* luntarily offer and find Sureties. (*a*) And then fuch Officer ought to be at the next *tis, &c.* Seffions of the Peace, there to deliver in his Warrant, and to certify all that he did *P. R. 20. and* thereupon. *Cromp. 2. 5.* *Br. F. Imp. 18.*

(*d*) But if the Party fhall yield to find Sureties, then the Officer may not abfolutely arreft him; but yet the Officer is not bound to go up and down with the Party, to find Sureties, but may keep the Party until he can procure Sureties to come to him: And if afterwards the Party fhall make any Refiftance, or fhall offer to go away, then the Of-ficer may arreft him, and by Virtue of that Warrant may carry him to the Gaol, and may alfo imprifon him in the Stocks, until he can provide Aid to carry him to the Gaol.

When the Party cometh before the Juftices of Peace by Force of this Warrant (or *14 H. 7.* by Force of any other like Warrant for the Peace, Good Behaviour, or a Riot, or the *Br. Peace 7.* like) the Party muft offer Sureties to the Juftice of Peace, or elfe the Juftice may com- *and Mainp.* mit him to Prifon; for the Juftice needeth not demand Surety of him. *39.*

Alfo after that the Party fhall be brought before the Juftice, if he fhall refufe to find *Co. 5. 59.* Sureties, the Officer, without any new Warrant or Command, may carry the Party to Prifon, and that by the Words of the firft Warrant: And if he fhall refufe thus to do that, then, *&c.* See the Form of the Warrant.

If the Officer do arreft the Party, and do not carry him before fome Juftice of Peace, *5 Ed. 46.* to find Sureties, *&c.* or upon the Refufal of the Party, if the Officer fhall arreft him, *P. R. 20.* and do not carry him to the Gaol, in both thefe Cafes the Officer is punifhable by the Juftices of Peace for this Neglect, (by Fine at their Seffions:) And alfo the Party ar-refted may have his Action of falfe Imprifonment for the Arreft. (*a*) For where the Of-ficer doth not purfue the Effect of his Warrant, it will not excufe him of that which he hath done. 21 *H.* 7. 23. *a.* 3 *H.* 7. *fol. b. Brian & Br. Faux. Imp.* 21.

(*d*) And if the Party be imprifoned for Default of Services, and after he who demanded *Dye or releafe.* the Peace againft him happen to dye, or fhall releafe the Peace, in thefe Cafes the Juftice of Peace may make his *Liberate* or Warrant for the Delivery of fuch Prifoner; for after *Liberate.* fuch such Death or Releafe, there is no Caufe to continue the other in Prifon. Alfo any Juftice of the Peace may (upon the Offer of fuch Prifoner) take Surety of him for the Peace, &c. and may thereupon deliver him.

4 E. 3. 16.
2 H. 7. 24.
Br. Privilege
35, 52.
Lamb. 96.

If the Party imprifoned for not finding Sureties hath a Suit depending in the *Common Pleas*, he may by the Courfe of that Court, by a Writ of Privilege, be difcharged of his Imprifonment, if the other Party be not ready in the Court at the Day of the Return of the Writ, to pray there new Sureties of the Peace. But *quære*, for it may be, he which demanded the Peace, hath no Notice of the removing of his Body, and then, how can he be ready in the Court of *Common Pleas* at the Day? And therefore it may feem a hard Cafe fo to be defeated of this Surety.

Execution of Warrant.

If the Party hath gotten Sureties, then if the Warrant proceed *ex officio* (and not upon the *Supplicavit*) and be a general Warrant (*fc.* to *come before me or fome other Juftice*) the Party may go before any other Juftice of Peace to offer his Surety; yet he fhall not inforce the Officer to travel to a Juftice out of the Divifion or Limit where they be dwelling without good Caufe: Nay, it is at the Election of the Officer, who is the Minifter of Juftice, to carry the Party attached to any other Juftice of Peace that he will: For it is more Reafon to give this Election to the Officer, who in Prefumption of Law is a Perfon indifferent, and is fworn to execute his Office duly, than to the Delinquent himfelf, who by Prefumption will feek Shifts, and weary the Officer. (*a*) This hath been fo adjudged.

Co. 5. 59.
B. Faux. Imp.
11.
B. Peace. 9.

Refufing.

(*d*) If the other Juftice of Peace, before whom the Party fo attached fhall come, fhall refufe to take fuch Surety, being offered to him, this is punifhable: For fuch Juftice of Peace ought to take it, and to bind him by Recognizance: But yet that muft be done in all Points, as the Form of the Precept doth require: And thereupon the fame or other Juftice of the Peace, having fo taken Surety for the Peace, may and ought, upon Requeft, to make his *Superfedeas* to all Officers, and to all other Juftices of Peace of the fame County, and thereby the faid Party fhall be difcharged from finding other Surety, and from any other Arreft for the fame Caufe: But by fuch *Superfedeas* the other Juftice can not difcharge the firft Warrant of the firft Juftice, until the Party be bound indeed; nor can give any other Day to the Party to appear at any other Seffions, &c.

Lam. 98.

Superfed. by a Juftice of Peace.
Cromp. 145.

Supplicavit.

Alfo a Juftice of Peace of the County, by a *Superfedeas*, cannot difcharge a Warrant awarded by his Fellow Juftice, by Force of a *Supplicavit* to him directed out of the Chancery or *King's Bench*, to take the Surety of the Peace of one refident in that County.

Alfo when a Man doth fear the Surety of the Peace will be demanded againft him in the Country, or doth hear that fuch a Warrant for the Peace is already granted againft him by a Juftice of Peace; in either of thefe Cafes, he may give Surety of the Peace before any other Juftice of the Peace of the fame County where he dwelleth, and thereupon may have a *Superfedeas* from the Juftice of Peace, &c. But in fuch Cafe it is fit that the Party be urged by fuch Juftice to put in fufficient Sureties, and that he be bound toward the King and *all his People*, and to appear at the next Seffions.

If any Officer, having a Warrant from a Juftice of Peace to arreft a Man to find Surety of the Peace, fhall receive a *Superfedeas*, out of the *Chancery* or *King's Bench*, or from any Juftice of the *King's Bench*, or from any Juftice of Peace of that County, to difcharge the fame Surety of Peace, and yet will urge the Party, by Force of his Warrant, to find new Surety for the Peace, the Party may refufe to give it; and if he be arrefted or im-

Lam. 101.

prifoned for fuch Refufal, he may have his Action of Falfe Imprifonment againft fuch Officer; for fuch *Superfedeas* is a Difcharge of the former Precept or Warrant.

The Form of a *Superfedeas* granted by a Juftice of Peace, fee *poftea*, Tit. *Warrants.*

And this *Superfedeas* is fufficient, though it neither name the Sureties, nor contain the Sums wherein they are bound; but yet it is the better Form to exprefs them both. See 2 *H.* 7. 1.

Lam. 59.

If the Party fhall miflike to be or ftand bound to the Peace, by the Juftices of Peace in the Country, then may he (either before or after that he is bound in the Country) go or fend to *London*, and there give Surety for the Peace, (either in the *King's Bench*, or in the *Chancery*): And thereupon the Party may have a *Superfedeas* (out of the Court where he hath given fuch Surety) to reftrain the Juftices of Peace of the County from taking any Surety of the Peace of him; and then the Juftices of Peace of the Country after the Receipt of fuch *Superfedeas* muft forbear to make any Warrant for the Peace againft the Party. And if any Juftice of Peace have granted out any fuch Warrant againft the faid Party, the faid Juftice muft make his *Superfedeas* to the Officers, thereby commanding

Superfd. from above.
F. N. B. Br.
81.a. &238.e.

I

them

them to furceafe, to put his former Warrant in Execution, and fo to difcharge it, and the Party of an Arreft or Imprifonment thereupon.   See more *poftea, fub hoc titulo.*

The Form of a *Superfedeas* for the Peace or Good Behaviour out of the *King's Bench,* fee *Libr. Intr.* 454.

The Form of a *Superfedeas* for the Peace out of the *Chancery.*   See *Fitz.* 238.

Note, That this *Superfedeas* out of the *Chancery* may be procured at any Time in the Vacation and out of Term.   *F. N. B.* 236. *a.*

(*a*) Thefe Writs of *Superfedeas* from the *Chancery* or *King's Bench,* are Commands to the Juftice of Peace to ftay him from binding the faid Party to the Peace, which otherwife he might not deny.

(*d*) If the Juftices of Peace fhall not furceafe after a *Superfedeas* out of the *Chancery* or **Lam.** 102. *King's Bench,* to them delivered, an *Attachment* will lie againft him or them for fuch *Contempt,* and befides, they may be fined and imprifoned for it.

Yea, fuch a *Superfedeas,* coming out of thofe High Courts to the Juftices of Peace, they ought thereupon to furceafe, although fuch a *Superfedeas* fhould be awarded againft Law.

If fuch a *Superfedeas* fhall be directed to the Juftices of Peace and Sheriff; that Juftice to whofe Hands it fhall be delivered may keep it, and may deliver the Label to the Party.

And in thefe and the like Cafes, the Juftice of Peace fhall do well to fend to the next general Seffions of the Peace, as well the faid *Superfedeas* (if it come to his Hands) as alfo the Recognizance which he had formerly taken of the Party (if he have taken any) for the Recognizance might be forfeited before the *Superfedeas* was purchafed ; or if it were not forfeited, yet the Conufor is not endamaged thereby.

If the Party fhall procure fuch *Superfedeas,* out of the *Chancery* or *King's Bench,* after that he is bound by Recognizance before the Juftice of the Peace to keep the Peace, &c. and to appear at the next Seffions, *Quære* whether the Party fending by his Servant fuch **Lam.** 115, *Superfedeas* to the Juftices of Peace at the next Seffions, be thereby difcharged of his Ap- 116. pearance there, the Recognizance alfo being certified thither by the Juftice.   **Cromp.** 139, 140.

It feemeth to fome, this Difference is to be holden therein, *fc.* if the Party were bound (before the Juftice of Peace) to keep the Peace *againft all Men,* &c. and fhall after procure fuch a *Superfedeas,* teftifying that he hath found Surety in the *Chancery,* &c. *againft all Men for ever,* and fhall fend this to the Seffions, this fhall difcharge his Appearance at the Seffions ; otherwife if the *Superfedeas* fhall teftify that he hath found Surety but till a certain Day (which is after the next Seffions.)   But yet it feemeth fafeft **28 H. 8.** in both Cafes for the Party to appear to fave his Recognizance.   See to the like Purpofe **Dyer 25.** the Cafe in 28 *H.* 8.   *Dyer f.* 25. where a Man being arrefted by the Sheriff upon a **Cromp. 140.** *Capias,* found Sureties for his Appearance at the Day, and there came a *Superfedeas* to the **Lib.Intr.453.** Sheriff; and it was moved, whether it were neceffary for the Defendant to appear, or not, to fave his Bond; or that his Appearance or Surety were difcharged by the *Superfedeas :* And the Opinion of the Court was, That he ought to appear for the faving of his Bond. Alfo the Precedents of Entries are, that the Party bound did fhew his *Superfedeas* in Court, and prayed Allowance thereof; and was thereupon difcharged.

(*a*) But becaufe divers contentious Perfons, defervedly fearing to be bound to the Peace or Good Behaviour by the Juftices of Peace in the Country, do oftentimes procure themfelves to be bound in the *Chancery* or *King's Bench,* upon infufficient Sureties, or upon colourable Profecution of fome Perfon, who will be ready at all Times to releafe them at their own Pleafure ; whereupon his Majefty's Writ of *Superfedeas* is often directed to the Juftices of Peace, &c. requiring them to forbear to arreft or imprifon the Parties for the Caufes aforefaid ; by Means whereof the faid contentious Perfons do greatly difturb their Neighbours, and affront the Juftices of Peace, to the evil Example of others ; therefore **21 Jac.1.c.8.** it is enacted by the Statute made 21 *Jac.* 1. That all Writs of *Superfedeas* to be granted by **Superfedeas.** or out of either of the faid Courts of *Chancery* or *King's Bench* fhall be void ; unlefs fuch Procefs be granted upon Motion in open Court, and upon fuch fufficient Surety as fhall appear unto the Court, upon Oath, to be affeffed at 5 *l.* Lands, or 10 *l.* in Goods in the Subfidy-book at leaft, &c.   And unlefs it fhall alfo appear firft unto the faid Court, that the Procefs of Peace or Good Behaviour is profecuted againft him or them, defiring fuch *Superfedeas, bona fide,* by fome Party grieved, in that Court out of which fuch *Superfedeas* is defired to be fo awarded and directed.

                                                                    C H A P.

CHAP. CXIX.

Concerning the Recognizance for the Peace.

Recognizance. THIS Recognizance which the Justice takes for the keeping of the Peace is rather of Congruence than by any express Authority given him. *Fitz.* 82. *a.* 7 H. 4 34. *accord.*

And this Recognizance for the Peace, if the Justice doth take it by Force of the Writ of *Supplicavit*, then he ought to execute it, and to do in all Things as the Writ directeth him; but where such Writ prescribes not the Sum, &c. that rests in his own Discretion.

Lam. 103. But if he taketh the Recognizance *ex officio*, and by Force of the Commission, *and J as a Judge, and not as a Minister*; then it resteth in the Discretion of the same Justice of Peace wholly to appoint and allow the Number of Sureties, their Sufficiency in Goods of Lands, the Sum of Money wherein they shall be bound, and to limit the Time how long the Party shall be bound, and such other Circumstances.

Sureties and Sum. In the Book 7 H. 4. *f.* 34. *a.* you shall find the Principal to be bound in 1000 *l.* and **7 H. 4. 34.** four Sureties, every of them in one thousand Marks before Justices of Peace, and for the keeping of the Peace.

Br. Im. 18. *Quære*, If Justices of Peace may not examine upon their Oaths the Sureties concerning their Sufficiency; it seemeth to be the Usage in the Courts at *Westminster:* And Mr *Crompton* faith, that the Justices of Peace in their Sessions may do it. *Cromp.* 294.

The most usual Manner and safest Way for the Justice of Peace, is to take two Sureties at the least, besides the Party himself, and to bind them by Recognizance to the King, *viz. Domino Regi :* And it must always be for the keeping of the Peace.

And yet by the Opinion of Mr. *Marrow* (who wrote in the Time of King *H.* 7.) a Justice of Peace might have taken this Surety by a *Pawn* only to him.

Also, by his Opinion, a Justice of Peace might have taken this Surety *by an Obligation made to himself*, by the Name of Justice of Peace.

Fitz. N. Br. 81. D. Yet if a Justice of Peace had injoined a Man upon Pain of 20 *l.* to keep the Peace, this had been nothing worth : But in this Case and the former two Cases, and the like, this one general Reason may be given for all, *sc.* that a Man cannot be bound to the King, but only by Matter of Record, and therefore such Surety taken by Pawn or Obligation, or such Injoining of the Peace, seems nothing worth to bind the Party.

The Form. Besides, by the Statute 33 *H.* 8. *cap.* 39. there is a plain Law made, in these and the **P. Accomp. 1.** like Cases, which willeth, that all Obligations, &c. which shall be taken for the King shall be made in the King's Name, and by these Words *Domino Regi :* And if any Person shall make or take any Obligation or Recognizance to the King's Use in any other Manner, he is punishable by Imprisonment at the King's Pleasure, &c.

Time. A Justice of Peace may take a Recognizance, and thereby may bind the Party to keep **Mar. lect. 6.** the Peace *for one Year*, or for a longer Time, (by his Discretion) yea, he may bind the Party *during his Life* upon reasonable Cause. (*a*) And this the Justice may do either by his own absolute Authority, or upon Complaint to him made, and upon good Cause shewed; as if the Offender be a *common Barrator*, a *Rioter*, or else in the Justice's Conscience a dangerous Person : But if such Surety be so taken during the Offender's Life, the Justice of Peace can never release that afterwards ; and therefore he must be well advised how he granteth such Surety.

(*d*) If the Recognizance be made to keep the Peace generally, without any Time or Day limited, it shall be construed to be during the Party's Life.

Recognizance. A Justice of Peace, intending to take a Recognizance for the Peace, and yet maketh **Lam. 105.** no Mention there, nor in the Condition thereof, that it is for the Preservation of the Peace, it seemeth to be void, as being taken *coram non Judice:* For a Justice hath no Authority to take a Recognizance generally, but for Matters concerning his Office specially.

Lam. 106. If the Recognizance be, that the Party bound shall not *beat nor maim A.* it is not good, because it ought to be for the *Keeping of the Peace* (generally) and the Peace may be broken by *burning the House* of *A.* or the like.

Time. If the Recognizance do not limit *any Time of Appearance* for the Conuzor, but be ge-**Ibid.** nerally to keep the Peace ; yet it is good, for the Time of Appearance is referred to the Discretion of the Justice, and the chief Scope is, the Keeping of the Peace. *Marrow. ib.*

I

Also

Also (by his Opinion) if the Recognizance do limit a Time of Appearance, but no Person named, before whom the Party so bound shall appear, then may he appear, in any Place out of the Sessions where he will, before that Justice of Peace which took the Recognizance. *Ibidem.*

But in the two last Cases, if a Recognizance should be taken in such Manner at this Day, I should think it safe for the Party to appear at the next Sessions for the Peace, and there to record his Appearance. See more *postea, sub hoc titulo.*

(*a*) If the Recognizance be to appear before the Justice of Peace within forty Days, next after the Date or Taking of the Recognizance, and before the End of the forty Days, a General Sessions of the Peace shall be holden, &c. The Party now ought to appear at the same Sessions. *Cromp.* 123. See the like Matter, *Br. Condition* 280.

Also if these Words be in the Recognizance, *sc.* That he shall appear before the same Justice & *sociis suis,* then must he appear at the next Sessions.

(*d*) If the Recognizance be to appear at any other Sessions after (and not at the next Sessions) 'tis good; and yet by the Statute 3 *H.* 7. *cap.* 1. it is enacted, That every Recognizance taken for the Peace, by the Justice of Peace, and *ex Officio* shall be certified, (*sc.* sent or brought in) at the next Sessions of the Peace, and there delivered to the *Custos Rotulorum,* that the Party so bound may be there called; whereby it may seem that every Recognizance taken for the Peace now, ought to be, to appear at the next Sessions. Cromp. 141. P. Just. 106.

If the Recognizance be in twenty Pounds to be levied of his Lands *only,* or of his Goods *only,* yet it is good; and this Word *Only* may seem void: For the Acknowledgment of the Recognizance before a competent Judge, both maketh it a Debt, and implieth the ordinary Means of Law to come unto it. See hereof *postea* Tit. *Recog.* Lam. 107.

If the Recognizance be to keep the Peace towards the King and *all his People,* but not towards any Person certain, 'tis good.

So if the Recognizance be to keep the Peace towards *A. only,* it seems good, or to keep the Peace towards *A. and his Servants,* without being bound *towards the King and all his Subjects,* it seems good. F.N.B.80.G. Cromp. 141.

But the best Form is, to bind the Party to keep the Peace towards the King and all his People; for first the Words of the Commission are to find Surety, *Erga nos & populum nostrum:* And again, the common Usage is so; and besides, it may otherwise prove dangerous to the Party who hath Cause to crave this Surety of the Peace; for the other Party who shall give me just Cause to crave this Surety against him (because he will not be bound to the Peace towards me) he will perhaps pray to bind himself to the Peace to *A.* who is his Companion, and then if the Justice of Peace shall so bind him, then may he and *A.* go before another Justice of Peace (and that within one Week) and there *A.* may release him of the Peace, and so I (trusting that he is still bound) may be after beaten, maimed or slain by him, or his Procurement. *The best Form of a Recognizance.*

So then, though the Recognizance being taken in any Manner as aforesaid, may prove sufficient to bind the Party to the King; yet it will not excuse the Justice of Peace from Blame, and therefore it is safest for the Justice of Peace to follow the received Form.

The Form of the Recognizance for the Peace see *postea,* Tit. *Recognizance, cap.* 168.

The Recognizance for the Peace, being thus taken, if it were by Virtue of the Writ *Supplicavit,* the Justice ought to return-the Writ, and to certify under his Seal his doing therein into the Court from whence the *Supplicavit* proceeded; and he may also send such Recognizance so taken by him, with his Certificate, or else he may keep the Recognizance in his Hands still, until he shall receive a *Certiorari* out of the *Chancery,* directed to him for removing it. See more *sub hoc tit. postea.* *Recognizance to be forfeited. Supplicavit.*

But if this Recognizance for the Peace was taken by the Justice *Ex officio,* then he ought to certify, send, or bring the Recognizance to the next Sessions of the Peace, so that the Party bound may be called thereupon; and that if the Party make Default of Appearance, the same may be then and there recorded. 3 H. 7. 1. P. Just. 106.

If a Man do forfeit his Recognizance (either for Default of Appearance or for Breach of the Peace) the Justices may not award any Process for the Forfeiture, but must certify the Recognizance, with the Cause of the Forfeiture, into some one of the King's Courts at *Westminster, sc.* into the *Chancery, King's Bench* or *Exchequer,* that from thence Process may go out against the Party; and so ought it to be, if it be presented by the Jury, that the Party hath forfeited his Recognizance by Breach of the Peace. *Lamb.* 570. *Process.*

If the Justice of Peace shall not certify such Recognizance at the next Sessions, the said Statute of 3 *H.* 7. 1. limiteth no Penalty; and yet see *Brook,* Tit. *Peace* 11. That the Justice shall forfeit 10 *l.* if he do not *certify the Recognizance of the Peace at the next Sessions;* *Certified.*

fions; but Mr. *Brook* there mentioneth the Statute of 3 *H. 7. cap. 3.* which Statute was only for Bailment of Prisoners, and certifying the fame, and fo feemeth to miftake the Statute.

Cromp. 169.   If he which demanded the Peace fhall *releafe* it, before the faid next Seffions, then, though the Juftice of Peace fhall not certify the Recognizance, the Statute is not tranfgreffed; for the Party fhall not be called in fuch Cafe upon his Recognizance. But it is better to certify the Recognizance, for peradventure it was forfeited before the *Releafe* made.

Recognizance removed.
3 H. 7. 1.
Br. Peace 11.
F. N. B. 81.   Alfo, he that demanded this Surety, or he that is bound to the Peace, may by a *Certiorari* remove fuch Recognizance into the *Chancery* or *King's Bench,* before the Juftice hath certified the fame to the Seffions, in cafe the Juftice fhall not certify the fame thither. *Fitz.* 81. And then the Party bound need not appear. See *hic poftea,* The Form of the Juftice's Return of fuch *Certiorari,* and of the Recognizance.

New Surety.   If the Juftice of Peace was deceived in the Sufficiency of the Sureties, he or any other Juftice, may afterwards compel the Party to find and put in other fufficient Sureties, and may take a new Recognizance for the fame; for that the Precept is *Ad inveniend. fufficientem fecuritatem.* But if the Sureties die, the Party Principal fhall not be compelled to find new Sureties. See more *poftea, fub hoc tit. & poftea tit. Bailment, cap.* 166. Part 2.

C H A P. CXX.

What Things fhall difcharge this Recognizance (of the Peace) or the Party of his Appearance at the Seffion.

Superfedeas.   WHether a *Superfedeas* out of the *Chancery, &c.* fhall difcharge the Party of his Appearance, fee *antea,* Chap. 118.

39 H. 6. 26.
Br. Surety 10.
and Def. 60.   He who is bound to the Peace, and to appear at a *certain Day,* muft appear at that Day, and record his Appearance, although he who craved the Peace, cometh not to defire it may be continued, otherwife the Recognizance fhall be forfeited.

Proclamation.   And if a Man be bound to keep the Peace *towards the King and his People,* but not towards *any Perfon certain,* and to appear at fuch a Seffions, the Court at that Seffions may make Proclamation, That if any Man can fhew Caufe, why the Peace granted againft fuch a one fhall be continued, that he fpeak, *&c.* And if no Perfon cometh to demand the Peace againft him, or to fhew Caufe why it fhould be continued, then the Court may difcharge him. But if a Man be bound as aforefaid, and efpecially to keep the Peace towards *A.* there, tho' *A.* cometh not to defire the Peace may be continued, yet the Court by their Difcretion fhall do well to bind him over till the next Seffions, and that may be to keep the Peace againft *A.* only, if they fhall think good: For it may be that *A.* who firft craved the Peace is fick, or otherwife letted, fo as he cannot come to that Seffions to demand the Continuance of the Peace; and in fome Places in fuch Cafe, they ordinarily ufe to bind him over for two or three Seffions together, by Order among themfelves.

Lam. 112.

2 H. 7. 4.
Br. Surety 13.   And yet by the Courfe of the *Common Pleas,* one that was imprifoned for the Peace (being removed thither by a Writ of Privilege) was there difcharged, for that he which demanded the Peace, came not at the Day (of the Return of the Writ) to pray Continuance thereof. See more *antea,* Chap. 118, 119.

If the Juftice of Peace fhall not *certify the Recognizance* to the Seffions, yet the Party ought to appear, and to record his Appearance. See fuch a Matter of a Sheriff, who took Bond of one to appear in the common Bench, at a certain Day, *&c.* although the Sheriff return not his Writ, *&c.* yet the Party muft appear to fave his Bond. *Vide* 18 Ed. 4. 18. for this laft Cafe.

Appearance.
Crom. 143.   If the Party who is bound to appear, is fo fick that he cannot appear, nor by any Means travel at the Day, yet his Recognizance in Strictnefs of Law is forfeit, and fo it is by the Courfe of the Courts at *Weftminfter, ut dicitur*; yet in this Cafe, upon the due Proof of fuch his Sicknefs, I have known the Juftices of Peace (in their Difcretion) have forborn to certify or record fuch Forfeiture or Default; and that they have taken Sureties for the Peace of fome Friends of his prefent in Court, until the next Seffions; for that the principal Intent of the Recognizance was but the Prefervation of the Peace. But *quære,*

how

how this is warrantable by their Oath ; besides, the Party so bound, might (by a *Certiorari* have removed his Recognizance into the *Chancery* or *King's Bench*, before the Day of his Appearance, and then he should not have needed to appear at the Sessions, for that the Justices there should have no Record whereupon to call him.

(*a*) But the Civil Law in such Cases is more favourable ; for with them the Rule is, *Citatus ad locum non tutum non arctatur comparere* : As if the Plague shall be hot in the Place or Town where the Party is to appear, or where their Court is held. This is a good Excuse in their Law, *ut dicitur*.

So if there shall be any other inevitable Accident, whereby the Party shall be hindred, as by any *great Snow*, Inundation of Waters, or by any Fall, or other Hurt or Sickness, whereby he is in Danger of Death : In these and the like Cases, the Civil Law doth dispense with Default, referring these Things *Arbitrio Judicis*.

See Mr. *Brook*, Tit. *Saver de Default* 17, 28, 45 & 48. and divers other Books, shewing, That the Common Law doth allow divers Cases to save a Default of not appearing in Court, the same being pleaded and proved, as *Imprisonment, Inundation of Waters, Tempest*, and *Sickness*. Vide *Lib. Intr.*

(*d*) If the *Husband* be bound, that he and his *Wife* shall appear at such Sessions, and that they shall keep the Peace in the mean Time, &*c*. and at the Day the Husband doth appear, but not his Wife. Here Mr. *Crompton* saith, the Recognizance is not forfeit ; for if there shall be Cause to continue this Surety of the Peace against the *Husband and Wife*, he shall be bound, and not the *Wife* ; and therefore the Wife's Appearance seems not greatly material. *Baron and Feme.*
Cromp. 144.

If a Man be bound to the Peace during his Life, or generally, without any Time or Day limited, in such Case neither the King, the Justice of Peace, nor the Party, can discharge this Recognizance, during the Life of the Party so bound, by Release or otherwise. *Br. Peace* 17. *Release.*
21 E. 4. 40.
Lamb. 113.

The Justice of Peace, who upon his own Discretion, hath compelled one to find Surety of the Peace upon a certain Day, and hath taken Recognizance for his Appearing, &*c*. may upon the like Discretion release the same before that Day ; and that such a Release will discharge the Recognizance taken by that Justice, if it were not forfeited before, and will also discharge the Party so bound of his Appearance ; for that here all this Business depends only upon the Discretion of the Justice of Peace who bound him. Fitz Just. de
P. 9.
Lamb. 113.
Cromp. 139

If a Justice of Peace shall grant the Peace at the *Request of another* (*sc*. at the Suit of *A*.) and the Recognizance be taken to keep the Peace against *A*. only, then before the next Sessions may *A*. only release it (and none other) and that Release being certified at the next Quarter-Sessions, will discharge the Party so bound of his Appearance, so as he shall not be called upon his Recognizance ; for that Release being so certified, is now become of Record as well as the Recognizance.

If the Recognizance were to keep the Peace *Versus cunctum populum & præcipue versus A*. yet may the same *A*. release it : For although this may seem popular, and that all others shall have Interest therein as well as *A*. Yet as it appeareth, by the Word *Præcipue*, it was specially taken for his Safety : But the contrary was holden by all the Justices, 21 E. 4. 48. *sc*. That the Party at whose Suit the same was granted, cannot release the same. And Mr. *Lambard* alloweth best of that Opinion ; nevertheless the Usage now is, and long hath been, as is first aforesaid. *Br. Peace* 17.

Lamb. 11.

But (in these former Cases) although this Surety of the Peace be released, and the Parties agreed, yet the Recognizance shall not be cancelled by the Justice of Peace, for peradventure it was forfeited before such Release made : And therefore the Justice of Peace shall do best, nay, ought to certify such Recognizance, together with the Release, to the next Quarter-Sessions.

The Form of the Release of the Justice of Peace see *postea* Tit. *Release*.

The Form of the Release of the Party see *ibidem*.

Note, That the Party who first demanded the Peace, may release the same before the same Justice of Peace that took the Recognizance, or before any other Justice of Peace.

Note also, That to release such Surety of Peace by Deed under his Hand and Seal, is nothing worth.

(*a*) But yet it is now holden, That neither the Justice of Peace, nor the Party can discharge the Recognizance of the Peace by their Release out of the Sessions. For first the Recognizance is made to the King, and therefore none but the King can release

or

or difcharge the fame. Secondly, The Recognizance is taken for the Appearance of the Party, &c. (as well as for his Keeping the Peace) and the Releafe of the Juftice, or of the Party, cannot difcharge the Appearance of the Party bound. And therefore notwithftanding that the Juftice of Peace, out of Seffions, fhall make or take any Releafe of the Peace, yet it fhall be fafe for the Party bound to appear to fave his Recognizance; and upon the Certificate made by the Juftice of Peace to the Seffions of fuch Releafe, the Confufor fhall be there difcharged (at leaft) againft the Party who craved the Peace.

And in Truth, the *Appearance* of the Party bound, feemeth requifite notwithftanding any *Releafe* made. Firft, To fave his Recognizance, as aforefaid : Secondly, That others may object againft him (in the open Seffions) if he hath broken the Peace, fo as he may be there indicted, &c.

Difcharge.   (d) Note alfo, The King can in no Cafe releafe or pardon the Surety of the Peace, nor fuch Recognizance (taken in the Behalf of any of his Subjects) until it be forfeited, for the Mifchief that may come to the Party thereby, but being forfeited, then the King, and none other may releafe and pardon the Forfeiture.

Death.   But the Death or Refignation of the King difchargeth this Surety of the Peace taken
1 H. 7. 1.   by his Subject : For the Recognizance is to keep the Peace of the King (*then being*)
Br. Peace 15.   and when he is dead, &c. it is not his Peace.

Lamb. 116.   Alfo the Death of the Recognifor (*fc.* of the Party principal that is bound) difchargeth his Surety of the Peace and the Recognizance.

Forfeited.   Alfo the Death of the Party, at whofe Suit the Peace was taken, difchargeth the Re-
Lamb. 116.   cognizance, if it were to keep the Peace againft him alone.

But yet in thefe three former Cafes, fuch Death fhall not difcharge the Recognizance, if it were forfeited before ; and therefore it fhall be beft for the Juftice of Peace to fend to the next Seffions fuch Recognizance, (notwithftanding fuch Death) elfe the King may be defrauded of a Forfeiture, if any were before.

21 E. 4. 40.   The Death of the *Sureties* fhall not difcharge the Recognizance, neither fhall the Par-
Br. Peace 17.   ty principal be compelled to find new Sureties after their Death ; for if the Peace be broken after their Deaths, their Executors fhall be charged therewith ; and there is no Mifchief by their Death ; yet *alii econtra ibid.* (a) That the Principal fhall be compelled to find new Sureties.

Superfedeas.   Alfo fuch Surety for the Peace may be difcharged by a *Superfedeas* made by another Juftice of Peace of that County, or by a *Superfedeas* out of the *Chancery* or *King's Bench.*

21 E. 4. 40.   (d) If the King and the Recognifor be at Iffue upon the Breach of the Peace, and
10 H. 7. 21.   the King waives the Iffue ; yet is not this Recognizance difcharged, but may be fued
Br. Rec. 21.   again upon a new Breach of the Peace afterwards.

CHAP. CXXI.

What Act fhall be (or makes) a Forfeiture of the Recognizance taken for the Peace.

What is a
Breach of the
Peace.   WHatfoever Act is a Breach of the Peace, the fame is a Forfeiture of this Re-
Lamb. 117.   cognizance.

Words.   And firft, this Breach of the Peace may be committed by ufing any *threatning Speeches*
18 E. 4. 28.   to another ; therefore all *Menacing*, or *Threatning to kill or beat another* to his Face, is
Br. Peace 16.   a Forfeiture of his Recognizance ; otherwife, if the Party fo threatned *be abfent.* And
22 E. 4. 35.   yet if the Party fo bound fhall threaten to kill or beat *A.* who is abfent, and after fhall
Cromp. 135.   *lie in wait* for him to kill, or beat him, this is a Forfeiture of his Recognizance.

Affault.   So *Affaults, fc.* to *ftrike at,* or *offer to ftrike at a Man,* although he never hurt nor hit him ; this is a Forfeiture of this Recognizance. See *Crompt.* 137. *b.* & 40 E. 3. *fol.* 40.

Affray.   Much more all *Affrays,* or violent and malicious Batteries, Strikings, Beatings, Woundings, or other Mifintreatings of the Perfon of another, are Forfeitures of this Recognizance.

The Difference of thefe Three are, Menacing beginneth the Breach of the Peace, Affaulting increafeth it, and Battery accomplifheth it.

I   (a) Or

(*a*) Or thus, Battery is the Wounding or Beating another.

Affault is, when one unlawfully fets upon the Perfon of another, offering to beat him, although he beats him not, or ftriking at him, though he ftrikes him not.

Hither alfo belongeth Lying in wait, Befetting his Manfion-Houfe, and not fuffering his Servants to go in and out, &c.

Menaces are threatning Words to beat another, or the like, for fear whereof he dares not go about his Bufinefs.

(*d*) For Breaches of the Peace, without Word or Blow given, as to go with Weapons, or Company unufual, which be in *Affray de pais.*

If he who is bound procureth another to break the Peace, and that it be done indeed ; Command. this is a Forfeiture of his Recognizance. *Br. Peace* 20.

Alfo Imprifonment, or Arrefting of another without Warrant, is a Forfeiture of this Lamb. 130. Recognizance.

So to thruft another into the Water, whereby he is in danger of drowning.

So to ravifh a Woman againft her Will.

So to commit Burglary, Robbery, Murder or Manflaughter (all which are to the Perfon of another) or to procure the fame.

So to do any Treafon againft the Perfon of the King.

(*a*) This is a Breach of the Peace, and a Forfeiture of this Recognizance: For although the Words of the Recognizance ufually be, *Quod gerat pacem erga cunctum populum Domini Regis, & præcipue erga* A. B. (and is not *erga ipfum Dominum Regem & cunctum populum, &c.*) Yet becaufe this Fact is done againft the Head of the Body of the whole Realm, it is to be adjudged a Prejudice and Hurt *Ad cunctum Populum,* and a Breach of the Peace in the higheft Degree.

(*d*) Note, That the Act which muft make a Forfeiture of a Recognizance for the Peace, muft be *done or intended to the Perfon of another* (by the Opinion of Mr. *Mar-* Mar. left. 7. *row.*) And the Book of 2 *H.* 7. imports as much, faying, that this Surety of Peace is 2 H. 7. 2. b. not broken without an Affray, Fighting, Beating, or the like.

Alfo to be riotoufly affembled, is a Breach of the Peace, and a Forfeiture of this Re- Marr. cognizance. Nay, if two Juftices of Peace fhall record a Riot upon their View (againft Lamb. 311. a Man fo bound to the Peace) although it were no Riot, &c. yet he cannot plead *Not Guilty* in a *Scire facias* upon his Recognizance.

Alfo to wear Armor, or Weapons not ufually worn, or to go with an unufual Number of Attendants, feems alfo to be a Breach, or Means of Breach of the Peace, and a Forfeiture of this Recognizance, for they ftrike a Fear and Terror in the People, and be in *Affray del pais.* See *Br. Surety* 12.

He that is bound to the Peace, ought to carry himfelf well in his Behaviour and Company. See *antea fub hoc tit.*

Yet the having of Weapons or Company unufual, are in fome Cafes allowed and law- *Weapons juft-* ful, and are no Breach of the Peace. See hereof *poftea* Tit. *Poffe Comitatus.* *fiable fome- times.*

Alfo though Affaults and Batteries be for the moft part contrary to the Peace of the Realm, and the Laws of the fame, yet fome are allowed to have a Natural, and fome a Civil Power over others; fo that they may (in reafonable and moderate Manner only) correct and chaftife them for their Offences, without any Imputation of Breach of the Peace; yea, they may (by the Law) juftify the fame.

And therefore the Parent (with Moderation) may chaftife his Child within Age.

So may the Mafter his Servant or Apprentice. Ex. 21.20,21.

So may the Schoolmafter his Scholars.

So may a Gaoler (or his Servant by his Command) his unruly Prifoners.

So may any Man his Kinfman that is Mad, &c. and none of thefe fhall be in Peril Plow. 18. therefore to forfeit any Recognizance of the Peace.

Note, That the Mafter may ftrike his Servant with his Hand, Fift, fmall Staff or Stick *Mafter and* for Correction; and though he do draw Blood thereby, yet it feemeth no Breach of the *Servant.* Peace, as appeareth by the Statute of 33 *H.* 8. *cap.* 12. p. Fighting 1.

And where the Servant fhall be negligent in his Service, or fhall refufe to do his Work, &c. There the Mafter may chaftife his Servant for fuch Negligence or Refufal ; fo as he doth it not outragioufly.

But if the Servant fhall depart out of his Mafter's Service, and the Mafter happen after 38 H. 6. 25. to lay hold of him, yet the Mafter in this Cafe may not beat or forcibly compel his faid Br. Faux Servant againft his Will to return or tarry with him, or do his Service; but either he 5 El. 4. muft complain to the Juftice of Peace for his Servant's Departure, or he may have an P. Labor 6.

Action

Action of Covenant againſt his Servant, if being required to do his Service he ſhall refuſe it. See *antea* Tit. *Labourers.*

38 H. 6. 25.   And as the Maſter without the Breach of the Peace cannot by Beating or Force,
compel his Servant to ſerve him againſt his Will; no more can a Guardian compel his
Ward by Beating or by Force to come unto him, or to tarry with him againſt his Will.

21 Ed. 4. 6.
Lib. Intr. 613.   Alſo the Schoolmaſter, with a Rod, may chaſtiſe his Scholar which is careleſs and
negligent in Learning, or that ſhall abuſe his School-fellows, or for other the like
Occaſions.

21 Ed. 4. 45.
22 Aſſ. p. 56.
Br.F.Imp.35.   Alſo it is lawful for the Parents, Kinſmen, or other Friends of a Man that is Mad or
Frantick (who being at Liberty, attempteth to burn an Houſe, or do ſome other Miſchief, or to hurt himſelf or others) to take and put him into an Houſe, to bind or chain
him, and to beat him with Rods, and to do any other forcible Act to reclaim him, or to
keep him ſo as he ſhall do no Hurt.

An Officer.
Lib. Intr.612.
Stamf. 13,14.
21 H. 7. 39.   Alſo if a Conſtable, Serjeant, Bailiff, or other Officer of Juſtice, or any other being of
their Company, for the better executing of their Office, ſhall be forced to ſtrike any Perſon that will not yield to their Arreſt, or that ſhall reſiſt, or fly from their Arreſt, they
ſhall not be in any Danger to forfeit any Recognizance of the Peace, by any ſuch Aſſault
or Striking, but may well juſtify ſuch Act.

In Defence of
any Perſon.
Lib. Intr.611.
16 Ed. 4. 11.
12 Ed. 4. 6.   Alſo it is no Breach of the Peace for any private Man to beat, ſtrike, or wound another in Defence of his own Perſon, from killing, wounding, or beating, but is a Thing
juſtifiable. And yet, if another ſhall aſſault me, if I may eſcape with my Life, or without being wounded, maimed, or hurt, it is not lawful for me to beat or wound the other
who firſt made the Aſſault, but I muſt firſt flee, or go from him ſo far as I can. *25 E.*
3. 42. 2 H. 4. 8. 33 H. 6. 18. Br. Trn's 28, 71. Cro. 137. hic.

     (a) *Sed vim vi repellere licet, modo fiat moderamine inculpatæ tutelæ.*
Non ad ſumendam vindictam, ſed ad propulſandam injuriam. Co. L. 162.

     By the Civil Law, he ſhall not be ſaid to have done a Wrong, who for his Safe-guard,
after the ſame Manner whereby he is aſſaulted, doth defend himſelf, as when a Man is
aſſaulted by Weapons, he may reſiſt with Weapons: But if he do exceed Meaſure, in re-
pelling an Injury; as if being wronged in Words, he ſhall reſiſt with Weapons, and by
ſuch Reſiſtance do beat or wound the other Party, he which is ſo beaten or grieved, may
have his Action, and ſhall recover Damages, &c.

     And to preſcribe ſome Temper and Moderation in the Reſiſting of verbal or actual In-
juries, one hath theſe Verſes:

> *Res dare pro rebus, pro verbis verba ſolemus,*
> *Pro buſis buſas, pro truſis reddere truſas.*

Things muſt be recompenſed with Things, Buffets with Blows,
And Words with Words, and Taunts with Mocks and Mows.

     Or rather by the Law of God and Nature, we ſhould practice this Leſſon.

> —— *Per te nulli unquam injuria fiat,*
> *Sed verbis aliiſque modis fuge lædere quemquam,*
> *Quod nulli nolles, aliis feciſſe caveto:*
> *Quodque tibi velles, aliis præſtare ſtudeto.*

     If one trained Soldier hurt another by Miſchance, and not willingly, or by Negli-
gence, it is excuſable in an Action of Treſpaſs or Aſſault. *Hobart's Reports, Weaver's*
Caſe, p. 189.

     (d) If two or more do agree together to play at Back-ſword, Foot-ball, or ſuch like,
and one of them doth wound and hurt another, the Party hurt, ſhall not have an Action of Treſpaſs therefore againſt the other; for that it was by Conſent, and to try their
Valour, and not to break the Peace. *Fitz. Bar.* 244.

Lamb. 132.   Yet if ſuch a Man were before bound to the Peace, ſuch Act ſeemeth to be a Forfeiture of his Recognizance. See *Br. Coron.* 229. For although ſuch Sports be ſuffered,
yet they are not lawful.

In Defence of
others.   Alſo it is no Breach of the Peace, for a Man to beat him that doth aſſault and would
beat, wound, or ill intreat his Wife, Father, Mother, or Maſter, but is juſtifiable.

I

So if the Wife shall beat him, that shall assault, and would beat or evil intreat her Husband.

So if the Father or Mother shall beat him that doth assault, and would beat or evil intreat their Child, being then within Age, and not able to defend itself.

But though the Servant may lawfully beat him that doth assault, and would beat *Servant.* or evil intreat his Master or Mistress; yet the Servant cannot justify the Beating of *See Fitz. Bar.* another, in Defence of the Father, Mother, Brother, Sister, Son, or Daughter of his *73. & 102.* Master or Mistress, for he oweth no Obedience or Duty to any of them.

By some Opinions, the Master cannot justify the Beating of him that doth assault and *P. R. 5.* would beat his Servant: But the Master with a Sword, Staff, or other Weapon, may de- *P. Justific. 3.* fend his Servant assaulted from being beaten, in Respect of the Loss of his Service. *Cromp. 136.* Yet Mr. *Lambard* and Mr. *Crompton* are of Opinion, that the Master may beat another *9 E. 4. Fitz.* in Defence of his Servant.   *contra.*

Neither can the Farmer or Tenant justify such an Act in Defence of his Landlord, *Lamb. 132.* nor a Citizen, *&c.* in Defence of the Mayor (or Bailiffs) of the City, or Town Corporate, where he dwelleth.

(*a*) And yet where the Life of any Person is in Danger by beating of another, there any Stranger may lawfully resist it, and that with Force, and beating of him which offereth such Violence. *Vide* 21 *H.* 8. 2. *b. hic.*

(*d*) Also the Law doth tolerate a Man to be at another at for the Preservation of his *In Defence of* Goods; and therefore he that shall attempt by Force to take away my Goods wrongfully, *my Goods.* whether they be Goods whereof I have a lawful Property, or such Goods whereof I *9 E. 4. 21.* have only a Possession by the Bailment of another: I may justify to defend the same *19 H. 6. 31.* by Force; and if I shall hurt or beat such a Person, it is no Breach of my Recogni- *Lib. Intr.611.* zance for the Peace. But if I kill him, it is Felony, and then a Breach of the Recognizance.

(*a*) If another Man will take away my Goods, I must first lay my Hands upon him, and disturb him; and if he will not leave, then I may beat him, rather than he shall have or take away my Goods.

The same Law is in every Case, where another shall attempt by Force to take away, *Possession.* or to put me out of Possession of my Land, Freehold, Copyhold or Lease, or to stop *10 Ed 4. 6.* or turn my lawful Highway, or my ancient River or Water-course leading to my Mill, *3 H. 4. 9* In these, and the like Case, if I shall disturb him therein, whereupon he doth assault, *11 H. 6. 33.* and attempt to beat me, I may justify to beat him again, as well in Defence of my Person, as of my Possessions, but not to kill him.

The same Law is also in every Case, where an Offender is by Order of Law punished *In Execution of* with Whipping, Stocks, Pillory, or otherwise, for any Offence by him committed, *Justice.* contrary to the Laws or Statutes of the Realm: There is no Peace broken, nor any Recognizance of the Peace forfeited by him or them, which shall lawfully execute any such Punishments.

Note farther, that there are divers Things which may be done against the Peace, and *Lamb. 132.* divers Offences, for which an Indictment *contra pacem* will lie; and yet the Committing or doing of such Offence or Act, shall be no Forfeiture of the Recognizance for the Peace: For that the Act that shall be a Forfeiture of such a Recognizance, must be done or intended unto the Person as aforesaid, or *in terrorem populi.*

Therefore to enter into Lands where he ought to bring his Action, or to disseise another of his Lands.

Or to enter into Lands or Tenements with Force, being without Offer of Violence to *Where Things* any Man's Person, and without publick Terror. *Crom.* 136.   *done Vi & Ar-* *mis, break* *not the Peace.*

Or to do a Trespass in another Man's Corn or Grass.

Or to take away another Man's Ward.

Or to take away another Man's Goods wrongfully, so it be not from his Person. *Mar. lect. 7*

Or to steal or take another Man's Horse, or other Goods feloniously, being not from his Person.

All these, and the like, be Breaches of the Peace, and yet these will make no Breach *7 H. 7. 8* of the Recognizance, nor Breach of the Peace, within the Meaning of the Commission of the Peace.

Note, That if a Man be bound in such a Recognizance for himself and his Servants, if any one of them break the Peace, the whole Recognizance is forfeited. *Et sic in similibus.*

                                                                              Note

Note alſo, That the Sureties may plead that the Party Principal hath not broken the Peace, although upon Iſſue the ſame ſhall be found againſt the ſaid Principal; for they are Strangers thereto. *Fitz. Averment* 46.

C H A P. CXXII.

Concerning the Writ of Supplicavit.

Supplicavit.   THE Forms of this Writ, out of the Chancery, are of divers Sorts, as you may ſee, *Fitz. N. B.* 80. *d. & Regiſter* 89.

To whom directed.   By which Forms of the Writ it appeareth, that it may be directed to the Juſtices of Peace, or to one of them; or to the Sheriff, or to every of them, to cauſe the Party that is to be bound, to come before him or them, to find Surety for the Peace. And this Writ may be, that the Principal ſhall be bound in ſuch a Sum, and the Sureties in ſuch a Sum certain, (and that may be in what certain Sums the Demandant will) or the Sums may by the Writ be referred to the Juſtice of Peace, &c. with the Clauſe therein contained, *Pro qua reſpondere volueris.* And the ſaid Writ is farther, that if the Party ſhall refuſe, &c. that they ſhall commit him to the Gaol, *Quouſque,* &c. and that when they have taken ſuch Surety, they do certify the Recognizance (which they have ſo taken) under their Seals, and return the Writ into the Court from whence the ſame was awarded, and that without Delay.

And for that this Writ is of divers Forms, the Juſtice of Peace muſt have a Care that he do execute the ſame in every Behalf, as the ſame ſhall direct and appoint him.

Execution of it.   When the Writ doth refer the Sum (wherein the Principal and his Sureties ſhall be bound) to the Juſtices, &c. then it reſteth in their Diſcretion; but yet it is then ſafe for them to take good Sureties, and to bind them in good Sums, and the rather, when the Clauſe is in the Writ, *Pro qua reſpondere volueris.*

21 H. 7. 20. Br. Peace.   When this Writ is directed to the Sheriff, and to all the Juſtices of Peace of that County, and is delivered to any one of them, he only to whom it is firſt delivered, ought to execute it (in every Behalf,) ſc. He only ſhall make a Warrant, &c. returnable before himſelf, and he only ſhall take Sureties, and make Return thereof (only) without any other.

The Form of a Warrant for the Peace, upon a *Supplicavit,* ſee *poſtea,* Tit. *Warrants.*

Superſedeas.   Alſo the ſame Juſtice of Peace after ſuch Surety taken, may make the Party a *Superſedeas* to diſcharge him from any other Arreſt, or to deliver him being in Priſon for the Peace, (at any other Man's Suit.) *Cromp.* 237. *b.*

The Form of ſuch *Superſedeas* ſee after Tit. *Precedents.*

21 H. 7. Br. Peace, 9.   The Party who is attached upon this Writ of *Supplicavit,* cannot be bound before any other Juſtice of Peace, but only before him from whom the Warrant proceeds; neither can another Juſtice of Peace ·(by a *Superſedeas*) diſcharge ſuch a Warrant made by his fellow Juſtice, by Force of this Writ.

Deputation. 9 E. 4. 32. F. Faux Imp. 4.   The Juſtice or Sheriff, to whom this Writ ſhall be delivered, may make a Deputy herein, ſc. may make his Warrant to the Bailiff, Conſtable, or other Perſon indifferent, to apprehend the Body, or to cauſe the Party to come before him (the ſaid Juſtice or Sheriff) to find Sureties, &c. And that if he ſhall refuſe, that then the Conſtable, &c. ſhall carry him to Priſon, there to remain, until he ſhall find Sureties; and yet the Writ of *Supplicavit* is to commit the Party to the Gaol, if he ſhall refuſe before the Juſtices, (*Si coram vobis, vel te recuſaverit,* &c.) (*a*) But the Juſtice or Sheriff cannot give their Power to another to take this Surety; for that is a judicial Power which cannot be aſſigned over: Neither can they make any Deputy therein, but they muſt take this Surety themſelves; and the Bailiff or Conſtable who apprehended the Body, cannot take this Surety. *Br. Office* 39. *& Faux Imp.* 34.

Roll's Rep. Part 2. p. 348.

A *Supplicavit* is directed to the Sheriff, and four Juſtices of Peace, that they or any Two of them ſhall take a Recognizance; the Writ is executed by two Juſtices which take the Recognizance, and the Sheriff returns it as taken by them, and good. *Leonard's Caſe, Trin.* 21 *Jac.* Roll's *Rep. Part* 2. *p.* 348.

(*d*) If the Party ſhall make Reſiſtance upon the Execution of this Writ, the Officer may take *Poſſe Comitatus,* to aid him to arreſt ſuch Party. See *poſtea* Tit. *Poſſe Comitatus.*

tatus. (*a*) Or elfe the faid Juftice may make his Warrant to the Sheriff, to apprehend the Party, and upon Refiftance, the Sheriff may take *Poffe Comitatus* to arreft the Party.

(*d*) He that is to be bound to the Peace, by Force of this Writ of *Supplicavit* out *F. N. B. 80:* of the Chancery, is to be bound againft him only that fueth out the Writ, as appeareth D. by the Form of the Writ aforefaid.

But yet at this Day it is ufed otherwife, and I once received out of the Chancery a *Recognizance:* fpecial Writ of *Supplicavit*, directed *Cuftodibus pacis, ac vic' & eorum cuilibet*, commanding us to take Sureties for the Party to be bound, *Quod ipfe damnum vel malum aliquod alicui de populo noftro, & imprimis eidem Joh. &c.* (that fued out the Will) *non fac. nec fieri procurabit, &c.*

Alfo by this Writ of *Supplicavit*, the Party (againft whom the Writ is fued forth) *Time:* fhall be bound to the Peace for ever (if he be taken); for the Writ containeth or men- F. N. B. 80: tioneth, not that he fhall be bound to keep Peace until any certain Time, but generally D. (*ad fufficientem fecuritatem inveniendam fub pœna, &c.* And therefore to prevent this, the Party (before he be attached) may come into the Chancery, and there find Sureties, and be bound until a certain Day, that he fhall do no Hurt, &c. unto the Party that fued forth the *Supplicavit*; and thereupon he fhall have a *Superfedeas* out of the Chancery, directed to the Juftices of Peace, and to the Sheriff, or to one of them, commanding them to furceafe to arreft the faid Party, or to compel him to find any Sureties, &c. And that if they have arrefted or imprifoned him, for this Caufe, and none other, that then they deliver him, &c. *Fitz.* 81. *a.* The Form of the *Superfedeas* fee *Regifter* 89.

And if the Party againft whom this Writ is fued forth, cannot travel, (or elfe will *Avoidance:* not travel) to bind himfelf in the Chancery, then he may caufe fome of his Friends to F. N. B. 81. be bound, or to find Sureties in the Chancery for him, according to the *Supplicavit*; a. and thereupon they may purchafe a *Superfedeas* out for him, directed to the Juftices Cromp. 142. of Peace, and to the Sheriff, and by this *Superfedeas*, the Juftices and the Sheriff fhall be commanded to take alfo Surety of the Party himfelf, in the Country (according to the Writ of *Supplicavit*) that he fhall keep the Peace, &c.

Alfo, if the Party happen to be arrefted and imprifoned upon this Writ, yet if he *Superfedeas.* can procure a *Superfedeas* out of the Chancery, it feemeth by the Words in the End of the *Superfedeas*, that this will difcharge him of the Arreft or Imprifonment.

Now after the Party is arrefted and imprifoned (upon this Writ) the Means for him *After the Arreft.* to procure a *Superfedeas* out of the Chancery, muft be:

1. Either to get fome of his Friends to be bound in the Chancery for him, and they to get a *Superfedeas, ut fupra.*

2. Or elfe to get a Certificate to the Lord Chancellor, from three or four Juftices of Peace in his Behalf. (*a*) Signifying, That the Party Plaintiff never demanded the Peace in the Country; and farther, That the Plaintiff is a contentious Man, and the other Party of good Fame: And upon fuch Certificate (*dicitur*) they will either difcharge the Party, or elfe grant him a *Superfedeas*.

(*d*) This Writ of *Supplicavit* is granted (or may be granted) in the Chancery or King's *Where.* Bench, upon great Caufe fhewed and proved there, and is (or ought to be) granted upon F. N. B. 79. Oath, that the Party is in fear, &c. of fome bodily Hurt, &c. Lamb. 86.

But this Writ of *Supplicavit* hath often been procured rather of Malice, and for Co. 8. 37. Vexation, than upon any juft Caufe. And Sir *Edward Coke* fpeaking of fuch as malicioufly fhall purchafe any fpecial *Supplicavit* of the Peace, (and that by Fraud and Malice, to inforce the other Party, *Ad redimendam vexationem*, to give them Money, or to yield them other Compofition) brandeth them as Barrators and Oppreffors of their Neighbours; oppreffing thereby the Poor and Innocent by Colour of Law, which was ordained to protect the Innocent from all Oppreffion. Neither was this a Wrong only to the Party thus malicioufly vexed, but alfo to all the Juftices of Peace in that County, taxing them (*tacite*) as though the Demandant could not have Juftice at their Hands in fuch Cafe, whereas perhaps the Demandant never defired the fame at any of their Hands. And befides, the faid Juftices of Peace (having in all Likelihood, Knowledge of each Party, and their Behaviours) or any one of the Juftices of Peace, might and would, and ought to have yielded the Demandant, upon Requeft and juft Caufe *See more before* fhewed to them, as fufficient and good Security in the Country, every Way for his Safe- *in this Title.* ty; (*viz.*) as many and able Sureties, and better known, and to have been bound in as great Sums, and for as long Time, if the Caufe fhould fo require. So as what fhould

move

move them to feek (with more Trouble, Charge and Delay to themfelves) that Security above, which they may have more fpeedily, and with lefs Charge and Trouble at home, I fee not, but only or chiefly the Vexing and Oppreffion of their Neighbours, as aforefaid.

(*a*) And for that this Manner of Oppreffion grew fo common; therefore by the Statute made 21 *Jac.* 1. *cap.* 8. it is now enacted, That all Procefs of the Peace or Good Behaviour, to be granted out of the *Chancery* or *King's Bench*, againft any Perfon whatfoever at the Suit of any other, fhall be void, unlefs fuch Procefs fhall be granted upon Motion firft made before the Judge or Judges of the fame Court, fitting in open Court, and upon Declaration in Writing upon Oath then exhibited, for the Caufes for which fuch Procefs fhall be granted; and unlefs that fuch Motion and Declaration be mentioned to be made upon the Back of the Writ, the fame Writing to be there entered of Record. And if after it fhall appear to the faid Courts, that the faid Caufes expreffed in fuch Writing, be untrue, then the Court may award Cofts and Damages to the Party grieved, and may alfo commit to Prifon the Offenders, until they pay the faid Cofts and Damages.

(*d*) Now to conclude this Bufinefs: If the Surety of the Peace be taken by Virtue of a *Supplicavit*, then muft the Juftice of Peace make Return of the Writ, and Certificate of his Doings, under his Seal, into the Court from whence the *Supplicavit* did proceed; which may be done in this Manner:

Firft, Let him write upon the Back of the *Supplicavit*, thus:

The Return of the Supp. *The Execution of this Writ appears in the Schedule thereto annext.*

Then may the Certificate or Schedule be thus, and be filed to the Back of the Writ.

I John Cotton Knight, one of His Majefty's Juftices of Peace for the County of Cambridge, *do certify into the* Chancery *of our faid Lord the King, that I, by Virtue of this Writ, firft delivered to me by the within-named* A. B. *have caufed* R. T. *named in the faid Writ, perfonally to come before me on the Day of And I alfo caufed the faid* R. T. *then and there to find fufficient Security of the Peace, according to the Form and Effect of the Writ aforefaid. In Witnefs whereof I have to this Certificate fet my Hand and Seal on the Day of in the Year,* &c.

The Return of a Certiorari. The Juftice of Peace may alfo therewith fend the Recognizance, if he will; or may keep and ftay the Recognizance until a *Certiorari* come to him for it.

And of the Recognizance. And if a *Certiorari* be directed out of the Chancery to the Juftice of Peace, for removing of this Recognizance (becaufe it was not fent up together with the Certificate, as there *Lib. Intr. 435.* was no Neceffity that it fhould) then that Writ alfo may be thus anfwered.

Certiorari. Write upon the Back of the *Certiorari* thus:

By Virtue of this Writ I J. C. *Knight, one of his Majefty's Juftices of Peace for the County of* C. *do certify the Tenor of the Security of the Peace, whereof Mention is made as in the Schedule annext to this Writ.*

And then write the Recognizance *verbatim*, in this Manner here under following, and thereto fet your Seal.

The Schedule or Certificate. *Let it be remembred, that the Day of* (reciting the whole Recognizance to the End). *In Witnefs whereof I the faid* J. C. *have hereunto fet my Hand and Seal,* &c.

And file this Schedule (or Note of the Recognizance) to the Back of the *Certiorari*.

F. N. B. 81. The Form of the *Certiorari* you may fee *F. N. B.* 81, 82, C. *Vide poftea* Tit. *Certiorari.*

F. N. B. 11. B. Alfo this Form of a Certificate may ferve where a *Certiorari* is brought to a Juftice of Peace to remove a Recognizance of the Peace or Good Behaviour taken by him *ex officio, Lamb. 111.* without any Writ of *Supplicavit.* See more *antea, fub hoc* Tit. *Surety,* &c.

And if the Juftice of Peace fhall not return the *Supplicavit*, nor Certificate of his Doings therein, until a *Certiorari* come to him for it, yet 'tis no Danger to him.

Releafe. Alfo if the *Supplicavit* be againft divers, and the Demandant will releafe his Prayer of the Peace againft one of them, then that Releafe ought to be certified for him, and the Writ muft be ferved and executed for the reft: Or elfe *Non eft inventus* may be certified for him, and the Writ executed for the reft.

Peace and Good Behaviour. By the Book 30 *Affifarum plac.* 14. it appeareth, that a Man may be compelled to find Sureties both to the Good Behaviour, and for the Peace: (*a*) For there one that had beaten a Woman in *Weftminfter-Hall*, was bound to the Peace towards the Woman, and was alfo bound to the Good Behaviour towards the King.

Br. Surety 11. (*d*) And yet the Good Behaviour includeth the Peace, and he that is bound to the Good *2 H. 7. 2. b.* Behaviour, is therein alfo bound to the Peace. See the ufual Forms of both Recognizances, & *hic poftea.*

2

But

But if the Recognizance taken for the Good Behaviour, be only *quod bene fe gerat, &c.* *Quære* how far thefe Words will extend. See 2 *H.* 7. 2. *b.* (*a*) where the Juftices held, That the Good Behaviour might be forfeited by the Number of his People, and by the Arms (or Weapons) and the like, although they break not the Peace. And they thought that he who is bound to the Good Behaviour, ought to carry and demean himfelf well in his Carriage, and in his Company, not doing any Thing which fhall be a Caufe of Breach of the Peace, or to put the People in Fear or Trouble; and fo fhall be intended of all Things which concern the Peace; but not in Mifdoing of other Things, which touch not the Peace. See *hic poftea.*

CHAP. CXXIII.

Surety for the Good Behaviour.

THIS Surety for the *Good Behaviour*, is granted by the Juftices of Peace, as well **Nature.** by the Authority of the Commiffion of the Peace the firft *Affignavimus*, as alfo by P. Juft. 18. Force of the Statute 34 *Ed.* 3. *cap.* 1.

And this Surety is of great Affinity with that of the Peace, and is provided chiefly for Lam. 212. the Prefervation of the Peace, as that other is, as you may obferve out of the ufual Forms P. R. 18. of the Recognizances; yea by fome Opinions it differeth little or nothing from that of the Peace; but that there is more Difficulty in the Performance thereof; and the Party fo bound, may fooner fall into the Danger of it, and of his Recognizance. For the Peace Lam. 119. (fay they) is not broken without an Affray committed, Battery, Affault, Imprifoning, P. R. 18. or Extremity of Menacing; whereas the Good Behaviour may be broken, and the Party's Recognizance forfeited without any of thefe : As namely,

1. By the extraordinary Number of People attending upon the Party bound. *Recognizance*
2. Or by his wearing Arms, or other Weapons more than ufually he hath done, or *how broken.* more than be meet for his Degree. 2 H. 7. 2.
3. Or by ufing Words or Threatning, tending or inciting to the Breach of the Peace.
4. Or by doing any other Thing which fhall tend to the Breach of the Peace, or to put the People in Fear, although there be no actual Breach of the Peace.

Yet note, Thefe four laft Matters, as they are the Breaches of the good Behaviour; fo are they alfo Caufe to bind a Man *to the Peace*; yea, they are Breaches of the Peace, and a Forfeiture of the Recognizance of the Peace. *Vide* Tit. *Sureties for the Peace.*

The Book 2 *H.* 7. *fol.* 2. before recited, concludeth, That the Juftices were not all *Peace and* certainly advifed how thofe Words, *de fe bene gerendo*, fhould be taken : Mr. *Brook* *Good Beha-* abridging thereof, Tit. *Surety* 12. faith, that it was holden, That he who is bound to the *viour, how,* Peace, ought to demean himfelf well in his Port, (*fc.* Behaviour) and Company, not *they differ.* doing any Thing that may be the Caufe of the Breach of the Peace, or to put the People in Fear or Trouble; yet the Book feems to mean this of the *Good Behaviour.* *See* Fitz. *Surety* 21.

But though this extraordinary Number of Attendants, and wearing Arms, are *Breaches* *as well of the Peace*, as of *the good Behaviour*; yet the Good Behaviour doth include the Peace, and befides importeth fome greater or other Matters of Misbehaviour, and for which the Surety of the Peace is not to be granted, (although they alfo are againft the Peace and Quiet or good Government of the Land) and you fhall find that this Surety of the *Good Behaviour* is grantable in divers other Cafes, in which the *Surety of the Peace* is not grantable.

The Surety of the *Good Behaviour* is to be granted at the Suit of divers, and thofe be-ing Men of Credit, and to provide for the Safety of many, whereas the *Surety of the Peace* is ufually granted at the Requeft of one, and for the Prefervation of the Peace chiefly towards one.

Alfo this Surety of Good Behaviour, is moft commonly granted either in open Seffions of the Peace; or out of the Seffions, by *two or three Juftices of the Peace*; whereas that of the Peace is ufually granted by *one Juftice*, and out of Seffions.

And yet by the Words of the Commiffion, as alfo by the common Opinion of the 14 H. 7. 8. Learned, one Juftice of Peace alone, and out of the Seffions, may grant this Surety of the Lam. 123. Good Behaviour (and that either by their own Difcretion, or upon the Complaint of others) as they may that *of the Peace.*

But

But this is not ufual, unlefs it be to prevent fome great and fudden Danger; efpecially againft a Man that is of any good Eftate, Carriage or Report.

Alfo this Surety may be granted at the Suit of fome one Perfon.

But the more dangerous this Surety is to the Party bound, the more Regard there ought to be taken in granting it: And therefore, it fhall be good Difcretion in the Juftices, that they do not grant it, but either upon fufficient Caufe feen to themfelves, or upon the Suit and Complaint of others, as aforefaid, and the fame very honeft and credible Perfons.

By Suppli-cavit. Alfo this Security of Good Behaviour, is often taken by the Juftice of Peace, by Virtue of a fpecial Writ in the Nature of a *Supplicavit,* directed out of the *Chancery* or *King's Bench;* and then the Juftice of Peace upon fuch a Writ is to proceed as a Minifter, as in Cafe for the Peace, *mutatis mutandis.* See before Tit. *Sureties for the Peace, and Supplicavit.*

I once received out of the Chancery fuch a Writ directed to the Juftices of the Peace in the County of *Cambridge,* and to the Sheriff of the faid County: And to every of them (and grounded upon the Stat. 34 *Edw.* 3.) commanding us and every of us, to take four Sureties (befides the Party) whereof every one fhould have Lands of fuch yearly Value, or Goods of fuch a Value; and to bind the Sureties every one in fuch a Sum, and the Party in fuch a Sum; That he fhall be of *Good Behaviour* henceforwards towards us and all our People, and fhall attempt nothing contrary to the faid Statutes, &c. and therein I proceeded as a Minifter only.

(*a*) The Party againft whom fuch a *Supplicavit* for the *Good Behaviour* fhall be granted, before he be attached thereupon, may go or fend up, and give Surety above in the *Chancery,* &c. (as here before, for the Peace) and thereupon he fhall have a *Superfedeas* out of the Court directed to the Juftice of Peace and Sheriff, and to every of them, commanding them to furceafe to arreft the faid Party, or to do any Execution of the faid Writ of *Supplicavit;* and that if (before the Coming of the faid *Superfedeas*) they have taken any fuch Security for the *Good Behaviour* of the Party, that then they prefently releafe fuch Surety found by him, the former Writ of *Supplicavit* notwithftanding.

C H A P. CXXIV.

For what Caufe this Surety for the Good Behaviour *fhall be granted.*

Where to be granted. 1. IT is chiefly to be granted (by the Juftices of Peace out of their Seffions) in thefe Cafes following; *viz.* Firft, againft common Barrators, common Quarrellers, and common Breakers of the Peace. See what Barrators be, Tit. *Barrators,* before.

P. Juft. 18. 2. Alfo it is grantable againft Rioters. See hereof before, Tit. *Riots.*

3. Alfo againft fuch as fhall lie in Wait to rob, or fhall be fufpected to lye in Wait to rob, or fhall affault, or attempt to rob another, or fhall put Paffengers in Fear or Peril.

4. Alfo againft fuch as be generally feared, or fufpected to be Robbers, by the Highway.

Cro. 115. b. 5. Alfo againft fuch as are like to commit Murder, Homicide, or other Grievances to any of the King's Subjects in their Bodies.

6. Alfo againft fuch as fhall practife to poifon another.

I lately granted the *Good Behaviour* againft one, for that he had bought Ratsbane, and mingled the fame with Corn, and then wilfully and malicioufly did caft the fame among his Neighbours Fowls, whereby moft of them died; and it was holden to be a good Caufe to bind the Offender over, by the whole Bench. (*a*) And fince I have known it allowed as a good Caufe by the Judges of Affife.

7. The Juftice of Peace alfo upon his own Difcretion (and without Complaint) may bind to the *Good Behaviour* any other Perfon which in his Prefence or Hearing fhall mifbehave himfelf in fome outrageous Manner of Force or Fraud, and may commit fuch Perfon to the Gaol, if he refufe to be bound. Sir *Francis Bacon* 11.

P. Juft. 18. (*d*) It is alfo grantable againft fuch as be of evil Name and Fame, generally, but more
34 E. 3. c. 1. efpecially againft fuch as are defamed or detected in any of thefe Particulars following:

13 H. 7. 10. 1. Firft, againft thofe that are greatly defamed for reforting to Houfes fufpected to maintain Adultery, or Incontinency.

2 2. Alfo

2. Alfo againft the Maintainers of Houfes commonly fufpected to be Houfes of common Bawdery.

One that had fuch lewd Women found in his Houfe, was bound to his good Behaviour, *Crom.* 140. (*by Wray, Anderfon,* and *Manwood*) 28 *El.*

3. Alfo againft common Whore-mongers and common Whores; for Bawdery is an 1 H. 7. 7. Offence temporal, as well as fpiritual, and is againft the Peace of the Land.   27 H. 8. 14.

Upon Information given to a Conftable, that a Man and a Woman be in Adultery or 13 H. 7. 10. Fornication together (or that a Man and a Woman of evil Report, are gone to a fuf- Br.Tiav.432. pected Houfe together in the Night) the Officer may take Company with him; and if he find them fo, he may carry them to Prifon; or he may carry them before a Juftice of Peace, to find Sureties for the Good Behaviour.

4. Alfo againft *Night-walkers* that be fufpected to be Pilferers, or otherwife like to 13 H. 7. 10. difturb the Peace, or that be Perfons of evil Behaviour, or of evil Fame or Report generally, or that fhall keep Company with any fuch, or with any other fufpicious Perfon in the Night.

Againft fuch as by Night fhall *evefdrop* Mens Houfes.

Againft *Night-walkers*, that fhall caft Mens Gates or Carts, *&c.* into Ponds, *&c.* or fhall commit other like Mifdemeanors or Outrages in the Night Time.

5. Againft fufpected Perfons who live idly, and yet fare well, or are well apparelled, having nothing whereon to live; except upon Examination, they fhall give a good Account of fuch their Living.

6. Againft common Haunters of Ale-houfes or Taverns, and common Gamefters; but more efpecially if they have not whereon to live.

7. Againft common Drunkards; but by the Stat. 4 *Jac.* 1. 5. it feems fuch Offenders *Drunkards.* muft be thereof twice lawfully convicted, (*a*) *fc.* by the Prefentment of the Offences at the Affizes, Quarter-Seffions of the Peace, or in the Court-Leet, and thereupon a due Proceeding to Conviction, by the Verdict of another Jury; or by the Confeffion of the Offender in Court.

But now by the Stat. 21 *Jac.* 1. *cap.* 7. any one Juftice of Peace, or any Head-officer in any City, *&c.* hath Power to convict any Perfon of Drunkennefs, *&c.* See *hic antea* Tit. *Alehoufes.*

And for the fecond Offence of Drunkennefs, any one Juftice of Peace may, upon his View, Confeffion of the Party, or Proof of one Witnefs upon Oath, as it feemeth, bind fuch Offender to the Good Behaviour. 21 *Jac.* 1. *cap.* 7.

(*d*) 8. Againft all fuch as ufe to go in Meffage for Thieves, fee Stat. 18 E. 2. P. *Leet.* 1.

For all thefe former Offenders, and the like, are evil Members in the Commonwealth, and fuch their Demeanor and Living is greatly to be fufpected, (and befides, do feem to be more properly faid againft the Peace of the Land, than *Avoutry* in the Cafe before, 1 H. 7. 7.) and therefore it feemeth reafonable, juft and expedient, that the Juftices of Peace, upon their Difcretion, fhould convene fuch Perfons before them, and examine them and their Courfes of Life; and if they cannot give a good Account of fuch their Courfes, then to bind them to their good Behaviour.

Alfo the Good Behaviour feemeth grantable, againft fuch as fhall make falfe Outcries, or fhall raife Hues and Cries without Caufe; for thefe are Difturbances of the Peace. *Cromp.* 179.

If one Man do levy *Hue and Cry* upon another without Caufe, either of them may be *Hue and Cry.* attached, and bound over, as Difturbers of the *Peace, P. R.* 156. (*a*) 29 E. 3. *Fitz.* *Trefpafs* 252. *tamen quære* concerning him upon whom the Hue and Cry is levied: Except that he be either a Man of evil Fame, or that there be fome Felony committed, *&c.*

(*a*) Alfo it feemeth grantable againft Cheaters and Coufeners.

Libellers alfo may be bound to their *Good Behaviour*, as Difturbers of the Peace, whe- *Libels.* ther they be the Contrivers, the Procurers, or the Publifhers of the Libel: For fuch Li- P. R. 1. 2. belling and Defamation tendeth to the raifing Quarrels and Effufion of Blood, and are *See Co.*5. 125. efpecial Means and Occafions tending, and inciting greatly to the Breach of the Peace.

(*a*) *Libellus* literally fignifieth a little Book.

By Ufe it hath alfo two other Significations: Firft, it fignifieth the original Declaration of any Action in the Civil Law.

Secondly, it fignifieth a criminous Report of any Perfon, unlawfully publifhed, and is called an infamous Libel.

Another defcribeth it thus, *Famofus libellus eft qui impingit delictum aliquod notabile.*

4 E   This

This Libelling may be done after divers Manners.

Co. 5. 125. 1. By scandalous Writings, be it in Book, Ballad, Epigram or Rhyme, either in Metre or Prose.

2. By scandalous Words, Scoffs, Jests, Taunts or Songs, maliciously repeated or sung in the Presence of others.

3. By Pictures or Signs, as by hanging of Pictures of Reproach, or Signs or Tokens of Shame, or Disgrace, near the Place where the Party thereby traduced doth most converse: As the Pictures of the Gallows, Pillory, Cucking-stool, Horns, or such like.

And in such Cases it is not material whether the Libel be true or false, or the Party thereby scandalized be living or dead, or be of good Name or evil.

And these Libellers, as also their Procurers, and the Publishers thereof, may be punished in other Manners.

1. Either they may be indicted for the same.

2. Or the Party grieved may have his Action upon the Case, and recover his Damages. *Libr. Intr. fol.* 13. But this it seems, when the Words are actionable.

If therefore any Man shall find a Libel, and would keep himself out of Danger ; if it be made against a private Man, the Finder may either burn it, or else he must presently deliver the same to some Magistrate.

But if it concerns, or be made against a Magistrate, or other publick Person, the Finder ought presently to deliver the same to some Magistrate, to the Intent that by the Examination and Industry of such Magistrate, the Author may be found out.

Causes. (d) Also this Surety of the *Good Behaviour*, is used to be granted against the putative Father of a Bastard-child. See Tit. *Bastardy.*

It seemeth also grantable against unlawful Hunters in Parks, after their Examination taken. See before Tit. *Hunting.*

Also it shall be granted against him that shall *abuse a Justice of Peace,* Constable, or other Officer of the Peace in executing their Office.

(a) *A.* assaulted a Constable in doing his Office, it is a good Cause to bind him to the Good Behaviour. *Fitz. Bar.* 202. *Cromp.* 135.

The Sheriff's Bailiff, upon a Warrant from the Sheriff, to make Execution of the Goods of *A.* went into the House of *A.* finding the Doors open, and *A.* shut the Doors upon the Bailiff, and so detained him a Prisoner in his House ; and Sir *Robert Houghton,* one of the Judges of the *King's Bench,* thought it a good Cause to grant out Process of the *Good Behaviour* against *A.* for thus abusing an Officer of the Law. *Anno* 17 *Jacobi Regis.*

9 E. 4. 3. (d) A Justice of Peace seeth a Man break the Peace, (*sc.* make an Assault or Affray upon *A.*) and he chargeth him to keep the Peace, and the other answereth that he will not, the Justice may bind him to the *Good Behaviour.*

Words.
See Exod. 22, 23. For if (as one saith) Contempt or Contumely, used to the Person of a Man's Better, neither Policy for Example, nor Religion for Peace, may tolerate, much less may any use Contempt towards, or abuse such as are in Authority, especially when they are executing their Office.

Nay, it seems that he who shall use Words of Contempt, or *contra bonos mores,* against a Justice of Peace, though it be not at such Time as he is executing his Office, yet he shall be bound to his Good Behaviour.

(a) But it was adjudged between *Dean* and *Garret,* T. 41 *El.* That *Good Behaviour* is not requirable for unseemly Words spoken of a Magistrate or Justice of Peace, when he is not in the Execution of his Office ; and it was resolved in Sir *William Bruncker's* Case B. R. P. 23 *Car.* 1. That a Justice of Peace cannot commit one, until he find Sureties for the *Good Behaviour,* unless the Party be thereof convicted, or at least indicted, and it seems reasonable so to do, unless for any Offence committed against a Justice of Peace personally : And so also it was adjudged *M.* 29 *El.* That to call a Mayor Fool, unless it be when he is in the Execution of his Office, is not Cause to imprison or bind to the Good Behaviour. *Mo. Rep. p.* 247.

Co. 11. 98. (d) If a Citizen or Freeman of a Town Corporate, shall use Words of Contempt, or *contra bonos mores,* against the Chief Officer of the City or Town, or his Brethren, they are good Causes to commit him to Prison, until he shall find Sureties his Good Behaviour ; for Obedience and Reverence ought to be yielded to the Magistrate, for that they derive their Authority from the King ; and *obedientia est legis essentia.*

Justice of Peace. Also he that shall abuse a Justice of Peace his Warrant, may be bound to the Good Behaviour. See after, Tit. *Warrants.*

2

A Man

A Man complaineth of a Riot, or Forcible Entry, fo that the Juſtices of Peace are ſſembled to inquire thereof; then the Party that complained will not profecute the Matter; it ſeemeth that the ſaid Juſtices of Peace may bind him to the Good Behaviour for hus deluding them.

And fo of fuch as ſhall charge another with Felony before a Juſtice of Peace, and yet vill not give Evidence, &c. See before Tit. *Felony.*

A. is bound to keep the Peace againſt *B.* only, and getteth a *Superſedeas,* and after *B.* Cromp. 134 eleaſeth him; after *A.* is arreſted for Surety for the Peace at another Man's Suit, and heweth his firſt *Superſedeas,* it ſeemeth he ſhall be bound to his Good Behaviour for his Deceit.

(a) Yet, whatſoever Act or Thing is of itſelf a Miſbehaviour, or is againſt the *Good Behaviour,* is Cauſe fufficient to bind fuch an Offender to the Good Behaviour: For the Magiſtrate ought to maintain all Civil Authority.

(d) Alſo by the expreſs Words of the Statutes, the Offenders here under named ſhall e bound to their Good Behaviour. By Statute, who are to be bound to their Good Behaviour.

1. Diſturbers of *Preachers,* 1 M. 3. P. 1.

2. Deſtroyers of *Fiſh-Ponds,* &c. or *Stealers of Fiſh,* after lawful Conviction, &c. viour. ; *Eliz.* 21.

3. Takers of *Hawks* or *Hawks Eggs,* out of other Mens Ground, after lawful Con- 5 El. 21. iction, &c.

4. Unlawful Stealers, Hunters, or Killers of *any Deer* or *Conies* in the Night or Day- 3 Jac. 1. 13. Time, in any Park or Warren, after lawful Conviction, &c. 7 Jac. 13.

But all theſe former Offenders muſt be bound at the Seſſions.

5. *Popiſh Recuſants,* abſenting themſelves from Church twelve Months, ſhall be bound n the King's Bench. 23 El. 1. P. Recuſants 1.

6. He that is *attainted of Felony,* and hath a Pardon for the ſame, ſhall within three 10 E. 3. 3. Months find Sureties for his Good Behaviour; but he ſhall be bound before the Sheriff P. Pardon 5. nd Coroners, who ſhall return the ſame into the Chancery.

Alſo he that is *acquitted of Felony,* if he be of evil Fame, or of evil Behaviour, the Cromp. 135. Juſtices of Peace upon their Diſcretion, may bind him to his Good Behaviour.

7. Such Perſons as ſhall diſturb the Execution of the Statute 39 *Eliz.* 4. concerning 39 El. 4. he puniſhing, or *conveying of Rogues;* any two Juſtices of Peace may bind them to their Good Behaviour. See before, Tit. *Rogues.*

8. So of ſuch as ſhall diſturb the Execution of the Statute for the Relief, Setting on Work, or *Settling the Poor.* See before, Tit. *Poor.*

9. The Mother of a *Baſtard Child* (which may be chargeable to the Pariſh) for her 7 Jac. 1. 4. ſecond Offence ſhall be committed to the Houſe of Correction, there to remain, until ſhe ſan put in Security for her Good Behaviour, &c. See before, Tit. *Baſtardy.*

10. Such as have their *Houſes infected,* or be themſelves infected with the Plague, and 1 Jac. 1. 31. ſeing commanded to keep their Houſes, ſhall diſobey, &c. they ſhall be bound to their Good Behaviour for one whole Year. See before, Tit. *Plague.*

What Act ſhall be a Forfeiture of the Recognizance taken for the *Good Behaviour,* Forfeiture of ſee here before. the Recogni-

Alſo the Party bound to his Good Behaviour for offending againſt any of the Sta- Lamb. 121. ſutes here beforementioned, if he ſhall afterwards offend againſt any the ſaid Statutes, he ſhall thereby forfeit ſuch his Recognizance.

(a) To be drunken is a Breach of the Good Behaviour, as Sir *Nicholas Hyde* did de-iver it in his Charge at *Cambridge,* Lent Aſſiſe, *Anno tertio Caroli Regis.*

One bound to the *Good Behaviour* at the Proſecution of *Stamp,* and he ſaid to him, Words. *Thou art a quarrelſome Fellow, and a Scurvy Knave;* and adjudged theſe Words were no Breach of the Recognizance; but to ſpeak ſuch Words to an *Officer* in the Execution of his Office, is a Breach of the Good Behaviour, for it may be an Impediment and a Diſgrace to him in the Execution of his Office. And to ſay of a Merchant that he is a Bankrupt, is no Breach of ſuch a Recognizance. So one ſaid of a Mayor playing at Ta-bles, *he is a Fool,* this is no Cauſe to impriſon a Man; but if he were in the Execution of his Office, it is otherwiſe. *Stamp's Caſe,* H. 20 *Jac.* 1. B. R. Rol. Rep. Part 2. p. 272. & fo. 200.

A Treſpaſs done, and Indictment and Conviction for the ſame, *quod vi & armis clau-* Moor's Rep. *ſum fregit & averium cepit & abduxit & adhuc detinet,* is not a Breach of the Good P. 249. Behaviour: So likewiſe, for ſaying of another he is a Lyar, a Drunkard, and I will make him a poor Rogue, for they are not Words which menace Battery, and he ought to do such Act as imports an Intention to do Violence to his Body; as to say, I will meet with thee.

(*d*) The Form of a Warrant for the Good Behaviour. *Vide postea* Tit. *Warrants*.

The Form of the Recognizance for the Good Behaviour. See after Tit. *Recognizance*.

Release.
Lamb. 126.   Whether the Surety of the *Good Behaviour* (taken upon Complaint) may be released by any special Person, some do doubt, because it seemeth more popular than the *Surety of Peace*; yet others do hold, that it may be released, either by the Justice of Peace himself that took it, in Discretion, or by the Party upon whose Complaint it was granted even as that for the Peace may.

Superfedeas.
P. R. 22.
Cromp. 237.
Cromp. 146.   It seemeth also a *Superfedeas* of the *Good Behaviour* may be granted by the Justices of the Peace (as well as for the Peace, *mutatis mutandis*) upon good Sureties taken by the said Justices, of the Party to be of the Good Behaviour.

Certiorari.   If a Man be bound to the Good Behaviour (before the Justice of Peace) and to appear at the next Assises or Sessions, yet the Party bound, may by a *Certiorari* remove the Recognizance into the Chancery or King's Bench before the Day, and then he shall not need to appear at the Assises or Sessions; for they shall have no Record whereupon he may be called there.

C H A P. CXXV.

Forcible Entry, and Forcible Detainer.

Common Law.
Lamb. 138.
Cromp. 76.   THE Common Law being the Preserver of the Common Peace of the Land, hath always abhorred Force, *Co.* 3. 12. and yet before the Reign of King *Richard* the Second, any Man might have entred into Lands and Tenements with Force and Arms and also to have kept and detained them with Force, where his Entry was lawful.

And at this Day, if a Man doth enter into any Lands or Tenements with Force, or Multitude of People, where his Entry is lawful, he is not punishable by Action, either at the Common Law, nor by Action upon any Statute; for where the Title of the Plaintiff is not good, there he hath no Cause of Action, although the Defendant doth enter with Force: But in such Case he that entreth with Force must be indicted upon the Statute or otherwise Complaint may be made thereof to the Justices of Peace; and as well upon such Indictment, as upon such Complaint, the Offender shall be punished; yet the Party

15 H. 7. 17.
Br. For. 11.   (ousled) shall not be restored without Indictment, and the Force thereby found. *Vide antea*, Tit. *Forcible Entry*.

Statutes.   And for the better Restraining of such Force and Forcible Entries into Lands and Tenements, and to inflict Punishment upon the Offenders therein, it was first provided by

5 R. 2. c. 7.
Plo. 86. b.   the Statute *5 Rich.* 2. that no Man should enter into Lands or Tenements with Force or Multitude, though he had good Right or Title to enter.

15 Ric. 2. c. 2.   But this Statute provided no speedy Remedy, or extended *to holding with Force*, nor gave any special Power therein to the Justices of Peace, but upon a general Inquiry, in a general Sessions of the Peace, (and not otherwise) and therefore by another Statute made *15 Rich.* 2. it was further provided, that if any Man should detain (or hold) with Force after such Forcible Entry made, upon Complaint thereof made to any Justice of Peace he shall presently take and come with the Power of the County, and shall go and view the same, &c. and if he do find any holding the same forcibly, that then they should be imprisoned in the Gaol by the same Justice, as convict, by the Record of the same Justice; there to remain until they have made Fine and Ransom to the King.

8 H. 6. c. 9.   Yet neither of the former Statutes extended to those that *entred peaceably, and then held with Force*, nor yet doth give any Remedy, if the Parties who made the Entry with Force, removed before the Coming of the Justice of Peace, nor yet ordained any Pain against the Sheriff, if he did not obey the Precepts of the said Justices, to execute the said Statute, when the said Justices would inquire of the same. And therefore the Statute of *8 H.* 6. doth give Remedy, first where any Man shall enter with Force, or shall enter peaceably, and after detain, hold or keep Possession by Force. Also these two last Statutes of *15 R.* 2. and *8 H.* 6. do enable any one Justice of Peace to give present Remedy, *viz.* to remove the Force, and commit the Offenders, in Cases of Forcible Entry, or holding against the aforesaid Statute.

4

And

And the faid Statute of 8 *H.* 6. extendeth further, reaching the Offenders, if they were removed or gone before the Coming of the Juftices; giving an Inquiry and Reftitution, and alfo punifhing the Sheriff that fhall not obey the Precepts of the Juftice in this Behalf.

So that thefe Statutes do now give full Remedy, and do prohibit, and are made againft thefe Degrees or Sorts of Force, *viz.* againft,

1. Such as enter peaceably, and then hold forcibly. Fitz. 248. c.
2. Such as enter with Force, and then hold peaceably. Lamb. 143.
3. Such as do both enter forcibly, and hold forcibly.

I have (here before) already fhewed in fome Meafure how the Juftice of Peace fhall demean himfelf in the Execution of thefe Statutes; now I will proceed to give him fome further Light in this Bufinefs, in thefe Particulars following.

1. Firft, What is a Forcible Entry, and what is a Forcible Holding within the Meaning of thefe Statutes.
2. Who may commit a Forcible Entry, &c. and upon whom.
3. Where a Force, or Forcible Holding, is juftifiable, or lawful.
4. What, and how many feveral Remedies the Party hath, that is fo put out, or kept out of his Poffeffions.
5. The Manner of Proceeding of the Juftice of Peace by Inquiry.
6. Of Reftitution to be made to the Party fo put out, by whom and to whom.
7. What Caufes there may be for ftaying the Juftice of Peace from making Reftitution.

CHAP. CXXVI.

What is a Forcible Entry, or Holding within thefe Statutes.

(*a*) FORCE, in the Common Law, is moft ufually applied to the evil Part, and fignifieth unlawful Violence ufed either to Things or Perfons. *Co. L.* 161. *b.*

(*d*) Our Law taketh Knowledge of two Manners of Force; the one may be termed a Force in Judgment of Law, which accounteth every private Trefpafs to be a Force; fo as if I do but pafs over another Man's Ground without Licenfe, he may have his Action of Trefpafs againft me, why or wherefore with Force and Arms, &c. See *Co. L.* 257.

The other Manner of Force is more apparent, and always carrieth fome fearful Shew and Matter of Terror with it.

This laft Sort of Force is that which is prohibited by thefe Statutes, and therefore Note, that every Force, punifhable by thefe Statutes, muft have one of thefe Badges, *fc.* it muft be either *Manu forti*, with Force or ftrong Hand, or *Multitudine*, with Multitude of People. *Lamb.* 145. and 5 *R.* 2. *cap.* 7.

Manu forti, *viz.* either with apparent Violence (in Deed, or in Word) offered to the Perfon of another, as threatning Speeches, turbulent Behaviour. or Violence, or elfe that they be furnifhed with offenfive Weapons (by them not ufually born) whether they offer Violence or Fear of Hurt to any other there or no, and this may be done by one Perfon only.

Multitudine, *fc.* with Company more than ufually they have attending them, 10 *H.* 7. 12. Now the Law calleth a Multitude when there be three * or more in one Company. * *The Edition of this Book in 1727 has it, Ten or more; and adds, Multitudinem decem faciunt.*

(*a*) And yet Sir *Edward Coke* upon *Littleton* 257, faith, that he never read it reftrained by the Common Law to any certain Number, but left to the Difcretion of the Judges, or Juftices.

(*d*) If therefore one or more Perfons fhall come weaponed (efpecially with Weapons not ufually born) to a Houfe or Land, and fhall violently enter thereinto, this is a Forcible Entry, within the Meaning of thefe Statutes. *Forcible Entry. Lamb.* 146.

Much more, if (being fo entered) he or they fhall there offer Violence, or Fear of Harm to the Perfon of any that is in Poffeffion thereof; moft of all, if he or they fhall forcibly and furioufly expel and drive another out of his Poffeffion.

So it is, if one fhall enter peaceably, (the Door being open, or only latched,) and after he is in the Houfe, he fhall forcibly put another out of his Poffeffion.

So

So it is, if he or they who shall enter peaceably, shall after their Entry offer apparent Violence, Threatnings, or Fear of Harm to the Person of any that is in Possession, to the Intent to get him out, and to make him leave the Possession, though they do not put him out, much more if they get Possession thereby.

If he or they that have entred peaceably, shall after use Words to any in Possession to this Effect, as to say, they will hold it or keep it, though they die for it, or in spite of the other, or such like, or other threatning Words; this maketh it a Forcible Entry.

Lamb. 146.
Cromp. 69.

So it is, if divers Persons shall come with Weapons (not usually born by them) to an House that is open, or to Ground, and shall there enter peaceably without any Disturbance; yet this is a Forcible Entry, for it shall be intended, that they would have used Force if they had been resisted.

So it is, when the Master entreth into an House, or Land, being attended with a greater Number of Servants than usually do wait on him.

Co. L. 257.
10 H. 7. 12.
Br. For. 30.
Lamb. 146.

Note, that though a Man do actually use no Force in his Entry; yet if he do come so appointed either with Weapon or Company, that other Men may be reasonably afraid that he meaneth to make his Way by Force, rather than he will fail of his Purpose, it seemeth to be a Forcible Entry.

(*a*) And if three or more shall enter peaceably (upon another being in Possession) and shall continue there peaceably, though this be no Forcible Entry or Detainer, yet it may prove a Riot in regard of the Number.

Force twofold.

Now there are two Sorts of Forces, as is aforesaid, *sc.*

1. An Actual Force; as with Weapons or Number of Persons, &c. not usual.

2. A Force implied in Law; as every Disseisin, Rescous and Trespass implieth a Force, and is with Force and Arms. *Co. L. 157.*

Trespass.

(*d*) Also every Entry into another Man's House or Ground which is made with Force (*sc. manu forti* or *cum multitudine* either with apparent Violence offered to the Person of any other, or furnished with Weapons or Company, which may offer Fear) though it be but to cut or take away another Man's Corn, Grass, or other Goods, or to sell or crop Wood, or do any other like Trespass, though he do not put the Party out of his Possession, yet this is a Forcible Entry, and an actual Force punishable by these Statutes. See *Lamb.* 145.

(*a*) Breaking into an House, though no Person is in it, this is a Forcible Entry; but not if the Door had been opened with a Key. *2 Roll. 2.*

'Tis Force to put back a Bolt, or draw the Latch. *Ibid.*

Lamb. 145.

(*d*) But if the Entry were peaceable, and they cut or take away any other Man's Corn, Grass, Wood, or other Goods without apparent Violence or Force, though such Acts are counted a Disseisin with Force, yet they are not punishable by these Statutes, *sc.* the Justices of Peace are not to remove, imprison, or fine such Offenders.

Cromp. 70.
11 H. 4. 16.

Also, if one or more shall enter into another Man's House or Land peaceably, and there shall by Force or Violence, cut or take away any Corn, Grass, or Wood, &c. or shall forcibly or wrongfully carry away any other Goods there being; this seemeth to be a Forcible Entry, punishable by these Statutes.

20 H. 6. 11.
Br. Force 1.

So it is, if a Man shall distrain with Force for a Rent (be it due or not due) this doth countervail any Entry with Force. *Lamb.* 147.

By Words.

And in these Cases of Trespass only, the Justice of Peace (upon Complaint to him made) may remove such Force; and upon View thereof, may imprison and fine such Offenders.

If a Disseisor hath entered peaceably, and shall presently threaten to kill the Disseisee (if he re-enter) this seemeth a Forcible Entry in the Disseisor.

2 H. 7. 16.
Br. For. 25.
Cromp. 70.

But Note, that a Forcible Entry cannot be without an actual Entry, for the Words of the Statute be, *Whosoever doth enter*, &c.

Note also, if one that hath Right to enter upon Land, shall go with divers in his Company, and with Weapons, over the Land whereto he hath Right to the Church, Market, or some other Place; this is no Entry with Force, except he shall express his Intent, that he doth enter there claiming the Land.

Note also, That if a Man shall enter with Force (into House or Land) although he obtained not the actual Possession thereby, yet shall he be imprisoned and fined for the only entring with Force; but Restitution is not to be made, but only where there is a Forcible Putting out, or a Holding another out of his Possession.

Lawful.

If by fair Means, a Man (whose Entry is lawful) shall perswade or intice them which are within the House, to come out, and then the Door being open or latched only, he

shall

fhall enter peaceably, without Multitude, offensive Weapons, or other Violence ; this Entry is justifiable.

So it is, if he shall enter peaceably, and then by gentle Perswasions send them out that are within the House, and after shut the Door and keepeth them out ; this is justifiable, so that afterwards he holdeth it not forcibly, nor useth Violence or threatning Speeches.

So it is, if I shall take a Man being out of his House, and then put or send into the House my Servant (or some other) in peaceable Manner, and do hold away the other by Imprisonment of his Person ; this is no Forcible Entry nor Detainer within these Statutes, but a false Imprisonment, punishable by Action only. *Lamb. 149.*

So it is, if he whose Entry is lawful, shall enter peaceably into his House (the Doors being open or latched only) and being so entred, shall continue and abide there peaceably ; this is justifiable. And if they which were before in Possession, shall put him out forcibly, this is a Forcible Detainer of their Parts.

(*a*) Forcible Detainer is a violent Act of Resistance by strong Hand of Men weaponed with Arms, or other Account of Fear in the same Place or elsewhere, by which the lawful Entry of the Justices, or any other is barred or hindred. *Forcible Detainer.*

(*d*) Forcible Detainer must be understood of a forcible With-holding the Possession of Lands or Tenements, and not of the Person of a Man, as before. *Forcible Detainer.*

Note also, Though the Entry were at first peaceable and lawful, yet if there be after a Holding by Force, it is punishable by the Statute, except where there was at the first a lawful and peaceable Entry, and thereupon a lawful Possession, peaceably continued by the Space of three Years together without Interruption : For there a Man may hold and keep such Possession with Force against all others (saving against the King's Officers). *Lamb. 149.* *8 H. 6. c. 9.* *P. Forc. 4.* *Lamb. 164.*

If the Justice of Peace shall come to the House or Place that is supposed to be holden with Force, and there shall find the Doors or Gates shut, and he or they within shall deny, or will not suffer him to enter, this is a Forcible Holding and Detainer, though there be no Weapons shewed or used, and though there be but one Person in the House, or upon the Ground. *Lamb. 148.* *P. R. 4. 1.* *Cromp. 70.*

So it is, if when the Justice of Peace entreth the House or Ground, he shall find there any Persons armed, or having Armour ,or other Weapons (not usually born by them) lying ready by them. This is Forcible Detainer. *Ibid.*

So it is, if the Justice of Peace shall find in the House any great Number of People, other than the ordinary Family or Company. *Ib.*

Also, if a Man shall enter peaceably into a House, and after shall bring into the same more Weapons than he and his ordinary Family do usually wear, or shall make any Use of such Weapons as he doth find in the House, to defend his Possession therewith : These are Forcible Detainers within these Statutes. *P. R. 41.*

If a Man that hath peaceably entred into an House, and will place Men with Force, (*sc.* with Guns or other Weapons) in some other House or Place not far distant, to the Intent that they may be ready to assault such as shall enter upon him : This is a Detainer with Force. *Ib.*

So it is, if the Disseisor of an House or Land, shall forestal the Way of the Disseisee, with Force and Arms, so that the Disseisee dareth not enter, or come near thereto for Fear of Death, &c. *Lamb. 149.* *Cromp. 69.*

(*a*) So if a Man shall distrain for a Rent-Service, or a Rent-Charge, and a Rescous shall be made unto him. This is a Disseisin with Force. *Co. L. 161. b.*

(*d*) So it is, if a Man shall keep his Cattle in another Man's Ground by Force, claiming Common there, where he hath no Common. And in this Case, the Justice of Peace upon Complaint to him made, may remove this Force ; and upon View thereof, may record it, and commit such Offenders to Prison, and may fine them, but cannot award Restitution. *P. R. 39.*

Also there may be a Forcible Detaining the Possession by Word only without any forcible Act.

As if *A.* hath wrongfully, though peaceably entred into the House, or upon the Land of *B.* and hath put out *B.* and shall presently threaten or say to *B.* That if he do come thither again to enter, he will kill him : This seems a Forcible Entry by *A.* And if *B.* shall afterwards come again to make his Entry, and then *A.* shall threaten to kill him, if he entereth there, this is a Forcible Detainer in *A.* *By Words.* *Lamb. 149.* *Cromp. 70.* *P. R. 39.*

And

And to threaten to maim, beat or to do other bodily Hurt to *B.* in the Cafe aforefaid, amounteth to a Forcible Entry or Detainer, for that Death may infue upon fuch Beating or Hurt. See 39 *H.* 6. 50. 7 *E.* 4. 21. But to threaten to burn the Houfe, or to fpoil his Goods therein (if *B.* fhall come thither, to enter again); this feemeth not to amount to any fuch Matter, for that *B.* may afterwards have his Action for the Burning of his Houfe, or Spoiling of his Goods, and fhall thereby recover Damages, to the Value thereof, &c.

39 H. 6. 50.
Br. Drures 12.
116.

Alfo when *B.* fhall come to make his Entry as aforefaid, if *A.* fhall fay to him, that he will not open the Door ; this is no Forcible Detainer.

Cromp. 70.

So it is if *A.* be in Poffeffion of an Houfe, or hath a Leafe thereof at the Will of *B.* and after *B.* entreth into the Houfe, and commandeth *A.* to go out, and leave him in the Poffeffion, and *A.* will not go out, this is no Force; for refuting or denying only to go out, is no Force, unlefs there be withal fome forcible Act or threatning Speeches. *Ubi factum nullum, ibi fortia nulla.* Where there is no Fact, there is no Force. *Co.* 4. 43.

Cromp. 73.

Where nsFact,
no Force.

A. mortgageth his Houfe to *B.* upon Condition, That if *A.* fhall pay to *B.* fuch a Day 40 *l.* then the faid Mortgage and Feoffment to be void, and by Agreement of them both, *A.* the Mortgagor continueth the Poffeffion, until the Day of Redemption, at which Day *A.* payeth not the 40 *l.* and after *B.* cometh to re-enter, and *A.* keepeth the Poffeffion by Force : This is a Detainer by Force in *A.* This was Mr. *Richard Godfrey*'s Opinion between *Willows* and *Turger.*

The Diffeifor maketh a Gift in Tail to *B.* who keepeth the Land with Force, at the Time when the Diffeifee maketh his Claim, which Claim is made within the View fo near as he dareth, for Fear of Death, Battery, or other bodily Hurt, if *B.* after fuch Claim fhall continue the Poffeffion with Force, he may be thereof indicted, &c. for this amounteth to a new Entry, and a Detainer with Force by *B.*

Cromp. 69.
Lit. 429.

And note, that wherefoever my Entry is lawful, if the Poffeffion be detained, or holden from me by Force, I may pray the Aid of the Juftices of Peace to remove fuch Force, as it feems.

If a Man hath a Rent or Common of Pafture out of another Man's Land, and coming to diftrain for his Rent, or to ufe his Common, is fo forcibly refifted by the Tenant of the Land, that he cannot, or dareth not, either diftrain for his Rent, or take the Benefit of his Common; this is a Holding with Force in the Tenant, and punifhable by thefe Statutes.

Lamb. 147.
Cromp. 70.
P. R. 39.

So it is, if the Tenant of the Land fhall foreftal the Way with Force and Arms, or fhall threaten him (who hath the Rent or Common) fo that he dareth not come to diftrain for his Rent, or to take his Common.

Crom. 69.

So it is, if a Man fhall diftrain for his Rent, and the Tenant of the Land fhall make Refcous with Force and Arms.

Ibid.

And in thefe Cafes of a Rent or Common, the Juftice of Peace upon Complaint to him made, may remove fuch Force, and upon View may record it, and may therefore imprifon and fine fuch Offenders, but cannot award Reftitution, *&c.* Cannot reftore the Party to his Rent or Common, which are to be taken, and ufed in another Man's Land, for Reftitution is not to be made, but only of Houfe or Land, as you may fee hereafter.

Br. Imp. 70.

One Perfon alone may commit or make a Forcible Entry or Detainer, if he do it with offenfive Weapons, not ufually born, or do ufe turbulent Behaviour, Violence or Threats, &c. to the Affray or Terror of others; or do refufe to fuffer the Juftice of Peace to enter.

The Perfons.
Lam. 174.
Co. L. 257.

An Infant of the Age of eighteen Years, by his own Act may commit a Forcible Entry or Detainer; and fo he may, though he be under Eighteen, (*a*) if he be of the Age of Difcretion, (*fc.* of the Age of fourteen Years.) See *Perk. f.* 10. *b.* And the Juftices may fine him therefore. But yet it fhall be good Difcretion in the Juftice of Peace to forbear the Imprifonment of fuch Infants. See *Br. Imp.* 43, 45, 75, 101. & *hic poft.* Tit. *Imprifonment.*

Who may be
guilty of it.
Cromp. 69.

For an Infant fhall fuffer no Imprifonment or corporal Pain for any Offence by him committed againft any Statute, wherein an Infant is not exprefly named.

But yet he may forfeit the Penalty of a Penal Statute, and fo by a Penal Statute may forfeit and lofe his Goods, if he be of the Years of Difcretion. See *Doct. & Stud.* 147, 148.

And an Infant of the Age of eighteen Years, may be a Diffeifor with Force, and may be imprifoned for the fame. 22 *Edw.* 4. *Old Nat. Br.* 128.

Infant.

4

(d) But

(*d*) But if an Infant commandeth another to enter, or hold with Force to his Ufe, which is done accordingly; yet the Infant fhall not be punifhed for fuch Offence, for the Commandment therein was void.

Alfo a *Feme Covert*, (by her own Act) may commit a Forcible Entry or Detainer; and upon the Juftice's View of the Force, fhe fhall be imprifoned therefore, (and fhe may be fined in fuch Cafe): But fuch Fine fet upon the Wife, fhall not be levied upon the Hufband; for the Husband fhall never be charged for the Act or Default of his Wife, but when he is made a Party to the Action, and Judgment given againft him and his Wife. *Co.* 9. 72. and *Co.* 11. 61. (*a*) And if upon the Trial it be found to be her only Act, fhe only fhall be taken and imprifoned. *Feme Covert.* Cromp. 69. 16 Aff. 7. Br. Impr. 45. 53. *See more after in the Tit. Riot.*

(*d*) Divers do enter with Force to the Ufe of *A.* who is not then prefent with them, but doth after agree thereto: This Agreement after maketh *A.* to be a Diffeifor, but not to be punifhed for the Force. *Quære*, if *A.* had counfelled, confented or agreed thereto before the Entry. It feemeth, that a Commandment, Confent or Agreement before or after, though it may make one a Diffeifor; yet it is not to be punifhed by the Juftice of Peace upon thefe Statutes, for that a Forcible Entry cannot be adjudged againft a Man, without an actual Entry be alfo made by him, or he at leaft prefent. 2 H. 7. 16. Br. Force 25.

But if *A.* that fhall command or counfel others thereto, fhall alfo be prefent at the Time of the Entry, although he doth then nothing, yet he is now become a Principal, and punifhable by thefe Statutes. *Confent.* Vide 17 Aff. pl. 14.

If divers do come in one Company, to enter into Lands, *&c.* where their Entry is not lawful, and all of them but one did enter, and demean themfelves in peaceable Manner, and one only doth enter with Force, or (after Entry made) doth ufe Force and Violence. This fhall be adjudged a Forcible Entry in them all (though the Force were againft their Will;) for where divers come in one Company to any Place, to the Intent to do any unlawful Thing, be it Robbery, Homicide, Riot, Affray, or any Trefpafs, here the Act of one of them fhall be adjudged the Act of all that are prefent, and every of them fhall be adjudged a principal Doer, altho' they ftand by and do nothing. So, though fome of them came without any Intent of Evil, if they came together in Company with the other Offenders, or if they came after; yet if they be either aiding or countenancing the Offenders, they fhall be alfo adjudged principal Doers, as well as the other. (*a*) And yet *Fineux* Chief Juftice, 2 *H.* 8. made a Difference where their Intent at the firft was to do an unlawful Act, and where not. *Cro.* 161. See *Co. L.* 157. Co.9.67,112, & 115. *See thereof after in Tit.* Fitz. Coron. 314, 350.

(*d*) An Indictment upon the Statute of 8 *H.* 6. for the King, is not good; for the King cannot be diffeifed, nor put out of his Freehold; neither can the King bring any Action upon the Statute of 8 *H.* 6. nor any other Action which might prove him out of Poffeffion of the Land. *P. R.* 39. *b.* *The Perfons put out.* Co. 1. 46. & 10. 112.

And if the King's Termor be put out by Force, he cannot prefer a Bill of Indictment (upon the Statute of 8 *H.* 6.) that he was put out, and the King diffeifed: But he muft have an Information of Intrufion in the *Exchequer*. Cromp. 69.

Yet upon Complaint made to a Juftice of Peace by the King's Termor, of any fuch Force, the Juftice of Peace may, nay ought to amove the Force, and upon his View thereof to record it, and to commit the Offenders to Prifon, and may fine them; and after fuch Force removed, the King's Termor may prefently re-enter (if he can) in peaceable Manner. *The King's Tenant.*

If a Forcible Entry or Detainer fhall be made upon any Leffee for Years, Tenant at Will, or upon a Copyholder, whether it be by a Stranger, or by the Leffor, or by the Lord, the Juftices of Peace upon their View thereof, are to remove fuch Force, and may commit to the Prifon the Parties which made fuch Entry, or which fhall hold it with Force, and may fine them: But whether the Juftice of Peace might make Reftitution, and fet them (*fc.* The Leffee for Years, Tenant at Will, or Copyholder) into their Poffeffions again, hath been much queftioned. *Leffee for Years, Copyholder.*

Some hold Opinion, That the Juftices of Peace might put them in Poffeffion again; and of this Opinion was Mr. *Marrow* and Mr. *Lambard*; and to maintain this Opinion, thefe Reafons may be given. *Reftitution upon View.* Lamb. 159.

Firft, for that the Words of the old Statutes warrant it; for the Statute of 15 *R.* 2. in the Preamble thereof, as alfo the Statute of 8 *H.* 6. in the Body thereof, hath this Word [*Poffeffions*] which Word moft properly doth extend to a Leafe for Years, *&c.*

Again, that Claufe of the Statute 8 *H.* 6. which provideth the Reftitution, is thus: If it be found that any doth contrary to this Statute, then the faid Juftices, *&c.* fhall put the Party fo put out, in full Poffeffion, *&c.*

Now

Now it cannot be denied, but that he which by Force expulfeth a Leffee for Years, Tenant at Will, or a Copyholder, doth contrary to this Statute; alfo they be the Partie put out.

Again, the fame Mifchief and Inconvenience which thefe Laws do labour to remove, is to Leffee for Years, Tenant at Will, and to the Copyholder.

Co. 11. 33, 34.
Plow. 178.
And we may find it ufual, that where Statutes are made for to remedy any common Mifchief, there to help Things in the fame Degree, one Action, Thing, Place and Perfon, hath in Conftruction been taken for another: And a good Expounder, faith Sir *Edw.* Co. 11. 34. maketh every Sentence to have his Operation to fupprefs all the Mifchiefs before the faid Act, and principally thofe that are fpecified in the Act.

Co. 3. 7. &
11. 73.
And again, faith he, It is the Office of the Judges always to make fuch Conftruction of Statutes as may reprefs the Mifchief, and advance the Remedy, and to fupprefs al Evafions which may continue the Mifchief, and to add Force and Life to the Cure and Remedy, according to the true Intent of the Makers of the Statute.

Reftitution.
Others hold the contrary, *fc.* That Leffee for Years, nor Copyholder, or Tenant a Will, could not have Reftitution by the Hands of the Juftice of Peace; and this feemec to be the common Opinion. Their Reafon was,

For that the Words in the Statute of 8 *H.* 6. (in that Claufe which fpecially provideth the Reftitution) are thus. The faid Juftices, *&c.* fhall refeife the Lands or Tenements, and thereof fhall put the Party in full Poffeffion, *&c.* Which Words [*Lands or Tenements*] are only to be underftood of them that have Inheritance, or a Freehold at the leaft. But to this it may be anfwered, That the faid Statute of 8 *H.* 6. (in the Body thereof) hath thefe Words, *Where any do make any Forcible Entry into Lands, Tenements or other Poffeffions, or them hold Forcibly,* &c. Which Word [*Poffeffions*] extendeth to a Leafe for Years, *&c.* And then the Word [*Poffeffions*] being in the fame Statute, we fhall find that a Statute is to be expounded upon all the Parts thereof together, and not upon one Part alone by it felf. To which Purpofe, fee *Lincoln College's* Cafe, and Doctor *Bonham's* Cafe in Sir *Edw. Coke's Reports.*

Raft. 174.

Co. 3. 59. b.
& 7. 118.

But it feems to thofe which held this laft Opinion, That if a Leffee for Years, Tenant at Will, or a Copyholder, be forcibly put out, or held out by any Stranger, if they will have Reftitution, their Indictment muft be made and preferred in the Leffor or Lord's Name; and the Jury muft find that the Leffor or Lord of fuch Copyhold is diffeifed, and the Leffee or Copyholder is put out with Force. And hereupon the Leffor or Lord fhall have Reftitution; and fo by their Reftitution, their Leffee or Copyholder is reftored alfo But fuch Leffee or Copyholder cannot (fay they) prefer an Indictment in their own Name. upon the Statute 8 *H.* 6. for that they have no Freehold.

Cromp. 161.

Indictment.
Cro. 249. a.
And to that Purpofe I find fome Precedents of Indictments in this Form, that is to fay, *into one Meffuage at,* &c. *then being the Freehold of* M. D. *Efq; with Force and Arms,* &c. *with ftrong Hand, and unlawfully upon the Poffeffion of* J. L. *then Farmer of the faid* M. D. *the faid Meffuage did enter, and him the faid* J. L. *with Force and Arms, and ftrong Hand, and unlawfully then did from thence expel and put out, and the faid* M. D. *thereof unjuftly diffeife,* &c. See after *Tit. Precedents.*

Alfo by this Opinion, if a Leffee for Years, Tenant at Will, or a Copyholder, be forcibly put out by their Leffor or Lord, fuch Leffee or Copyholder, hath no Remedy at all by Indictment upon this Statute, for they have no Freehold, and therefore can have no Reftitution upon this Statute.

Alfo by this Opinion, if the Leffee for Years be put out by his Leffor, and after the Leffee putteth out the Leffor again forcibly, the Leffee fhall not be indicted; neither fhall the Leffor have Reftitution upon this Statute, for that the Leffor is not diffeifed of his Freehold; for the Poffeffion of the Leffee is fuch a Seifin of the Leffor, that he may have an Affize, if his Leffee be put out.

Cromp. 72.
And fo of a Copyholder, not having forfeited his Eftate, if his Lord notwithftanding fhall enter upon him, and put him out, and the Copyholder fhall re-enter upon his Lord with Force, the Copyholder fhall not be indicted, nor yet the Lord reftored, for the Reafon aforefaid.

And fo by this laft Opinion, the very Mifchief fpecified and intended to be helped by the Statutes, fhould ftill remain in all Cafes between fuch Leffees and Copyholders, and their Leffors or Lords, fo as there can be no Inquiry, nor Reftitution in Cafes of Forcible Entry or Detainer between them.

But howfoever the Law be taken for the Indictment or Reftitution thereupon, yet in Cafe that Leffee for Years, Tenant at Will, or a Copyholder, be forcibly put out or held

2　　　　　　　　　　　　　　　　　　　　　　　　out,

out, either by a Stranger, or by their Leffor or Lord, the Juftices of Peace, or any one of them, by the Statute of 15 *Rich.* 2. *cap.* 2. might fafely remove the Force, and upon Cromp. 71. View thereof commit the Offenders to Prifon ; and then the Leffee for Years or Copyholder, might prefently re-enter, if peaceably they would, and fo might have his Poffeffion again, without any Reftitution made him by the Juftices.

(a) A Copyholder may bring an Indictment of a Forcible Entry into his Copyhold upon the Statute 8 *H.* 6. *cap.* 9. but the Word *diffeijed* muft not be in, and a Juftice of Peace may remove the Force. *Poph.* 205. *Yelv.* 81.

But now by the Statute made 21 *Jac.* 1. *cap.* 15. it is enacted, That fuch Juftices or 21 Jac.1.c.15. Juftice of Peace, as by Reafon of any Act of Parliament now in Force, are authorized upon Inquiry to give Reftitution of Poffeffion unto Tenants of any Eftate of Freehold, of their Lands, Tenements, which fhall be entred upon with Force, or from them withholden by Force, fhall now have the like and fame Authority (upon Indictment of fuch Forcible Entries, or Forcible With-holdings before them duly found) to give like Reftitution of Poffeffion unto Tenant for Term of Years, Tenants by Copy of Court-Roll, Guardians by Knights Service, Tenants by *Elegit*, Statute Merchant and Staple, of Lands or Tenements by them fo holden, which fhall be entred upon by Force, or holden from them by Force.

Now to fhew fomething more, what the Law accounteth to be Force, and what Wea- *Weapons.* pons be offenfive, in thefe and the like Cafes.

Mafter *Bracton* faith, *Omnes illos dicimus armatos, qui habent cum quibus nocere poffunt.* Co. L. 162. Which have any Thing about them, wherewithal they may ftrike or hurt.

And therefore to have Guns, Bows and Arrows, Crofs-bows, Halberts, Javelins, Bills, Clubs, Pikes, Pitchforks or Swords not ufually born by the Parties, fhall be faid to be *vis armata.*

Again, *Si quis venerit cum armis, & dejecerit, vis tamen armata dicitur, fufficit enim terror armorum.*

Si quis venerit fine armis, & in ipfa concertatione, ligna fumpferit, fuftes aut lapides, Ibid. *vis dicetur armata.*

And fo to ufe cafting of Stones, hot Coals, fcalding Water or Lead, or any other Thing wherewith one may hurt the Perfon of another, fhall be faid to be *vis armata.*

C H A P. CXXVII.

Lawful Force.

WHERE a Force or Forcible Defence is juftifiable, and where not.

Force being oppofed againft the Law, is utterly forbidden ; but being ufed in P. R. 41. the Maintenance of the Law, and with the Warrant of Law, it is allowed, for that it maintaineth the Peace of the Realm: And therefore Force may lawfully be ufed by all the King's Officers, Minifters and Servants thereunto deputed for the Execution or Advancement of Juftice, or of the Judgments of the Law.

And fo firft it is a lawful Force whereby all Offenders in Treafon, Felony and other great Crimes, be purfued, apprehended, carried to Prifon and receive their Punifhments.

It is a lawful Force, whereby the Sheriff and his Officers do apprehend any Perfon by Virtue of the King's Writ.

It is a lawful Force, whereby Juftices of Peace do remove unlawful Entries or Holdings of Poffeffions, and reprefs Rioters, and do arreft and fend to Prifon fuch Offenders.

And in thefe and the like Cafes, the King's Officers (*fc.* the Sheriff, Juftice of Peace 3 H. 7. and Conftable) may take the Help of others (what Number they fhall think meet) to affift Br. Riots 3. them, when Need fhall require. See hereof *poftea in* Tit. *Poffe Comitatus.*

Alfo it is a lawful Force, which Juftices of Peace, Sheriffs, Coroners and Conftables fhall ufe in apprehending or committing to Prifon fuch as within their feveral Jurifdictions, and in their Prefence, fhall in any Sort break, or attempt to difturb or break the Peace, and they may therein take the Affiftance of others, as aforefaid.

Alfo in thefe Cafes following, it is lawful for the King's Officers, by Force to break P. R. 14. open a Man's Houfe to arreft Offenders being therein, if the Doors fhall be all fhut, fo as the Officer cannot otherwife enter the Houfe, *viz.*

1. For the Apprehending of any Perfon for Treafon, Felony or Sufpicion of Felony. Co. 5 91.

2. Where

2. Where one hath dangeroufly wounded another, and then flying into an Houfe, the Conftable or other Officer upon frefh Suit, may break open the Door, and apprehend the Offender.

So may any other Perfon befides the Officer. 7 *E*. 3. 19. *Cromp*. 171.

3. Where there fhall be an Affray made in an Houfe, and the Doors fhut, the Conftable, &c. may break into the Houfe to fee the Peace kept.

4. So upon a Forcible Entry or Detainer found by Inquifition, before Juftices of Peace, or viewed by the Juftices themfelves.

27 Aff. 35.   5. Upon a *Capias Utlagatum,* in any perfonal Action, as alfo upon a *Capias pro fine,* directed to the Sheriff, the Sheriff may break open the Doors, &c.

6. Upon a Warrant or Procefs, for the Apprehending of any Popifh Recufant, being excommunicate, the Officer may break open the Houfe. 3 *Jac.* 1. 4. *P. Rec.* 52.

7. Upon a Warrant for the Peace, or Good Behaviour, the Conftables may break open the Houfe, by the Opinions of *Popham* and *Clerk,* Juftices of Affize, at *Cambridge* Affizes, 3 *Jac.*

8. Laftly, in all Cafes where the King is Party, or hath Intereft in the Bufinefs, the Officers may break open the Doors, as aforefaid: For no Man's Houfe fhall be a Caftle

Co. 5. 91.   againft the King.

Co. 5. 91, 92.   And yet the Sheriff, nor his Officers may not break open any Man's Houfe, to exe-
13 E. 4. 9.   cute the King's Procefs (upon the Body or Goods of any Perfon) at the Suit of any Subject.

But when a Houfe is recovered by any real Action, or by *Ejectione firmæ,* there the Sheriff may break open the Houfe, and deliver Seifin or Poffeffion to the Demandant or Plaintiff, &c. For after Judgment, it is no more (in the Right or Judgment of Law) the Houfe of the Tenant or Defendant.

Co. 5. 91.   But note, that the Officer before he break open the Houfe or Doors of any Perfon, he muft fignify the Caufe of his Coming, and defire that the Doors may be opened unto him.

Forcible De-   Note alfo, although no Man may forcibly keep his Houfe againft the King's Officers in
fence lawful.   the Cafes aforefaid, yet every Man's Houfe is (to himfelf, his Family, and his Goods) as
Co. 5. 91. &   his Caftle, as well for his Defence againft Injury and Violence, as alfo for his Repofe
11. 82.   and Reft. And therefore the Law doth give to Dwelling-houfes divers Privileges.
2 H. 7. 39.

1. Firft, That it is a Man's Caftle for his Defence, as aforefaid.

2. Alfo a Man's Houfe hath a Privilege to protect him againft any Arreft by Force of any Procefs, at the Suit of any Subject, as aforefaid.

Co. 11. 82.   3. A Man's Houfe (in fome Cafes) hath a Privilege againft the King's Prerogative, for it hath been adjudged, that Salpetre-men cannot dig in the Manfion-Houfe of any Subject, without his Affent in Regard of the Danger that may happen thereby, in the Night-time, to the Owner, his Family and Goods, by Thieves and other Malefactors.

Co. 5. 91. &   4. If Thieves fhall come to a Man's Houfe, to rob or murder him, he may lawfully
11. 82.   affemble Company to defend his Houfe by Force; and if he or any of his Company fhall kill any of them in Defence of himfelf, his Family, his Goods or Houfe, this is no Felony, neither fhall they forfeit any Thing therefore.

Crom. 70.   5. Alfo a Man that is in Poffeffion of a Houfe peaceably, and doubteth that another (who indeed hath more Right to the Poffeffion, and who may enter) will enter upon him, here he which is in Poffeffion, may defend it with his ordinary Company, and may juftify to beat the other, which fhall attempt to enter upon him: But if he kill him, it is Felony; nay, he in Poffeffion (in this former Cafe) may not hire any Strangers to aid him, neither may he have his own ordinary Company in Armour, nor otherwife be provided with Bows or Guns to fhoot at the other. *Cromp.* 70. *a.* See after, Tit. *Homicide.*

In Defence of   Alfo, if a Man being in his Houfe, do hear that another will come thither to beat him,
his Perfon.   he may lawfully affemble his Neighbours and Friends, &c. to affift and aid him there in
21 H. 7. 39.   Defence of his Perfon.
Br. Riots 1.
Co. 11. 82.
& 5. 91.

And yet if he, or any of his Company, fhall kill the other (or any of the other Company) in fuch Defence of himfelf or his, this feemeth to be Felony in all of them which be in the Houfe, and in that Action; fo as they fhall forfeit their Goods thereby. See hereof after, Tit. *Homicide.*

21 H. 7. 39.   But if a Man be threatned, that if he come to fuch a Place, that then he fhall be
Co. 11. 81.   beaten. In this Cafe he may not affemble any Company to go thither to fafeguard his
& 5. 91.   Perfon; for there is no Neceffity of his going thither; befides, he may have Surety of the Peace againft fuch as threatned him.

2   *(a)* And

(*a*) And if another shall make any Assault upon me, yet if I may escape with my Life, it is not lawful for me by Law to beat the other who made the Assault, *per Markham*; *Quod tota curia concessit.* 2 *Hen.* 4. *fol.* 7.   *Fitz. Bar.* 72.   *Vide hic* before Tit. *Surety for the Peace.*

(*d*) If there be an Attempt made to beat a Man, his Wife, Father, Mother, or any of his Childen (within Age), he may lawfully use Force to resist it, and may justify the Beating of the other in such Case. *In Defence of others.* 9 E. 4. 28. 16 E. 3. 17.

Also the Servant may justify to beat another in Defence of his Master. *Br. Trn's* 217. 21 H. 7. 39.

(*a*) But yet by the Opinion of *Eliot*, 21 *H.* 8. *fol.* 2. *b.* it is not lawful forcibly to touch the Person of a Man, except that there be so great Peril, that another is like to perish, if he have not Help.   And there I may beat one Man, saith he, to save the Life of another; so that where the Life of another is in Danger, there any Man, though a Stranger, may lawfully resist it, and that with Force and beating of the other.

(*d*) Also a Man may justify to beat another in Defence of the Possession of his Goods. And if another hath taken away my Goods, I may take them again from him by Force. (*a*) But a Man cannot justify the Wounding of another in Defence of his Goods.   And this was the Opinion of *Wray* Chief Justice, *An.* 25 *El.* *In Defence of my Goods.* *Crom.* 65, 69.

And note, that every one may take and detain with Force his own Goods: And the Issue in an Action of Trespass brought therefore shall be, Whether the Party hath Interest or Title to the Goods, or no; and not whether he used any Force in getting them; and if it be found for the Defendant, the Force is excused: But the Force used in an Entry into Lands or Tenements, is the material Matter, and punishable, although the Entry might have been lawful.

(*d*) Also, if there be an Attempt made to disseise me of my Land, or to disturb me of my Highway, or to turn an ancient Water-course from my Mill, I may lawfully use Force to resist it.

A Keeper doth enter and chase upon my Land, pretending this to be within his Purlieu, where it is not.   If I command my Servants to beat him off my Ground, this seemeth justifiable in the Defence of my Possession, against such unlawful Claim.   Yet *quære.* Dyer 327. *Crom.* 68.

C H A P. CXXVIII.

Where Forcible Detainer of Possession is lawful.

THE Statute of 8 *H.* 6. concludeth thus, *Provided that such as keep their Possession by Force, after that they or their Ancestors, or they whose Estate they have in such Lands,* &c. *have continued their Possession in the same three Years or more, shall not be endamaged by Force of that Statute.* 8 H. 6. c. 9. 31 El. 11. P. Force 4.

(*a*) And by Force of this Statute and Proviso, every Heir, and every Feoffee, may justify to keep their Houses and Possessions by Force, where they or their Ancestors, or their Feoffors, or they whose Estates they have, have been in peaceable Possession thereof by the Space of three Years, or more. *Cro.* 187.

(*d*) This Proviso must (as it seemeth) be thus construed, *sc.* That where a Man is seised (of a lawful Estate or Possession) of an House or Lands, and he or his Ancestors, or they whose Estate he hath therein, have continued the Possession of the same peaceably by the Space of three whole Years together without Interruption, and his Estate not ended, there he may hold and keep such Possession with Force, against all others, yea, it seemeth, if he shall hire Strangers to aid him, to keep such Possession, or shall have his Company in Armour, he is not punishable by these Statutes: But he may not resist the Justices of Peace that shall come to view this. 22 H. 6. 6. 1. b. Br. Force 6. 22 & 29. *See the Statute of* 31 El. 11.

And if he shall be indicted for such his Forcible Holding (after three Years such quiet Possession) he may plead such his lawful and peaceable Possession, by the Space of three Years next before such Indictment, and thereby he shall avoid both the Imprisonment and Fine; and also shall debar the other Party of his Restitution.   Neither may the Justices of Peace remove him from his Possession, though it be found by the Inquisition taken before them, that he held that House or Land by Force, after three Years lawful and peaceable Possession, as aforesaid. P. R. 37.

But here it seemeth, that these four Diversities are to be observed:

6 & 7 E. 6.　Firſt, Where the Party in Poſſeſſion did enter peaceably, and where forcibly : For if
22 H. 6. 8.　a Man enter forcibly, and after continue his Poſſeſſion peaceably by the Space of three
Lamb. 65.　Years without Interruption, yet (it ſeems) he ſhall not be aided by theſe Statutes.
Br. Reſt. 12.

Br. Force 22　Secondly, Where the Party in Poſſeſſion hath continued his three Years Poſſeſſion
& 39.　peaceably, and where by Force.

For if after a lawful and peaceable Entry, a Man ſhall continue or hold his Poſſeſſion
by Force, this is a Forcible Holding or Detainer, and puniſhable by the Statute of 8 *H.* 6.
and three Years of ſuch Poſſeſſion ſhall not aid him.

21 H.6.18.b.　Thirdly, Where the Party in Poſſeſſion, is in by Right, and of a lawful State, and
F. Entry 20.　where by Wrong. And therefore if the Diſſeiſor (or other Perſon that cometh in by a
Br. Force 6.　wrongful and unlawful Title) hath continued ſuch his Poſſeſſion peaceably by the Space
Vide 23 H. 8.　of three Years, without Interruption ; he ſhall not be aided by either of theſe Statutes of
p. ſeq.　8 *H.* 6. or 31 *El.*

14 H. 7. 28.　For if a *Diſſeiſor* hath continued his Poſſeſſion forcibly, by the Space of twenty Years
Br. Force 10.　together, yet he may be indicted upon the Statute of 8 *H.* 6. before a Juſtice of Peace, of
the Forcible Detaining of the ſame ; and the ſame being found, the ſaid Juſtice of
Peace is to reſeiſe the ſame, and to award Reſtitution to the Party diſſeiſed, or ſo
put out.

Fourthly, Where the Party hath continued ſuch his Poſſeſſion three Years without Interruption, and where his Poſſeſſion hath been interrupted or diſcontinued.

For if a Man hath been in peaceable Poſſeſſion of Land, *&c.* by the Space of three
Years, and above, by a good Title, and then is diſſeiſed and expelled by Force, and the
Diſſeiſee re-entreth peaceably ; or the Diſſeiſor is therefore indicted upon the Statute of
Br. Force.　8 *H.* 6. and the Diſſeiſſee is thereupon reſtored, and is in Poſſeſſion accordingly ; yet in
Dyer 141.　theſe Caſes the Diſſeiſee cannot juſtify the Detainer of the Poſſeſſion of thoſe Lands by
22 & 29.　Force, becauſe his Poſſeſſion was once interrupted : But after (ſuch Interruption and
Re-entry, or Reſtitution) if he ſhall continue a peaceable Poſſeſſion again for three
Years together, then he may juſtify the Detainer of the Poſſeſſion thereof by Force, by
Virtue of the Proviſo in the Statute of 8 *H.* 6.

23 H. 8.　If a Diſſeiſor hath continued his Poſſeſſion peaceably three Years, and after the Diſſeiſee
Br. Force　doth re-enter, or doth make his Claim ſo near as he dareth, and then the Diſſeiſor re-
c 22.　enters again, or continueth his Poſſeſſion (after ſuch Claim) here the Diſſeiſor cannot
Litt. 429.　juſtify to hold the ſame with Force ; for by the Re-entry or Claim of the Diſſeiſee, the
firſt Diſſeiſin and Poſſeſſion of the Diſſeiſor was determined, and the Diſſeiſor is in of a
new Diſſeiſin.

Dyer 141.　Alſo, if he that hath been a lawful Poſſeſſor of Lands by the Space of twenty Years
together, be once clearly and wholly removed from the Poſſeſſion of the ſame Land, he
cannot come with Force, or Multitude, to put himſelf in Poſſeſſion thereof again, and
to detain the ſame with Force, becauſe his Poſſeſſion was once interrupted : And if he be
indicted (upon the Statute of 8 *H.* 6.) for ſuch Forcible Entry, he ſhall not be relieved
(touching the Reſtitution) by the Statute of 31 *Eliz.* for that he had not the Occupation
of the ſaid Lands, nor had been in quiet Poſſeſſion thereof by the Space of three Years
together, next before the Day of ſuch Indictment found.

C H A P. CXXIX.

How many Remedies the Party hath, which forcibly is either put out or kept out of the Poſſeſſion of his Houſes or Lands, &c. contrary to theſe Statutes.

1. *Action upon*　FIRST, the Party ſo grieved (having an Eſtate for Life, in Tail, or Fee) may have
the Statute of　his Aſſiſe or Action of Treſpaſs of Forcible Entry upon the Statute of 8 *H.* 6. againſt
8 H. 6.　ſuch Diſſeiſor ; and therein if the Defendant be attainted of Force, he ſhall fine to the
4 H. 4. c. 8.　King, and alſo anſwer to the Plaintiff his treble Damages, and treble Coſts of Suit ; and
1 R. 2. c. 9.　alſo the Plaintiff ſhall thereupon have a Writ of Reſtitution to reſtore him to his for-
3 H. 6. c. 9.　mer Eſtate.
P. 2.
F. N. B. 348.
c. & 240. a.
Co. 10. 115. P. R. 39. 9 H. 6. 19. Fitz. 21. 15 H. 7. 17. Co. L. 257.

But

But (this Action being at the Suit of the Party, and only for the Right) is only where the Entry of the Defendant was not lawful: For if a Man entereth with Force, where his Entry is lawful; as if a Diffeifee fhall enter upon the Diffeifor with Force, he fhall not be punifhed by Way of Action: But yet he may be indicted upon the Statute, and upon fuch Indictment found, the Party put out (*fc.* the Diffeifor) fhall be reftored; for the Indictment is for the Force, and for the King. And here the Offender (*fc.* the Diffeifee) fhall make Fine to the King, although his Right be ever fo good. Br. Force 20 & 18.

Secondly, Alfo the Party fo grieved, if he will lofe the Benefit of his treble Damages and Cofts, he may be aided, and have the Affiftance of the Juftices of Peace, and that after divers Sorts. Firft, He may purchafe a Writ out of the *Chancery* (directed to the Sheriff only, or to the Sheriff and Juftices of Peace, and to every of them) for to remove the Force. And this is upon the Statute of *Northampton*, 2 *E*. 3. *cap*. 3. the Form of which Writ you may fee. *F. N. B.* 249. *f*. 2. *Writ upon the Statute of* Northampton.
Lamb. 178.

But upon this Writ, the Juftice of Peace is to proceed only as a Minifter, and to certify his Doings herein; and that Juftice of Peace to whom the Writ fhall be delivered, ought for to execute it, *fc.* he may remove the Force: But here he may not put the Party in Poffeffion again, who was put out. Lamb. 176.
Cromp. 74.
162.

For the Manner of the Juftices proceeding herein, fee in the other Title of *Forcible Entry* before.

Thirdly, Alfo the Party grieved may, at the General Seffions of the Peace within the fame County, prefer his Bill of Indictment, upon the Statute of 8 *H*. 6. for fuch Forcible Entry or Detainer: Which being found there, the Complainant fhall be reftored to his Poffeffion by a Writ of Reftitution, granted out of the fame Court to the Sheriff. 3. *Indictment in Seffions.*
Dyer 187.
Cromp. 165.

Fourthly, Alfo the Party fo grieved, for a more fpeedy Remedy, may complain to any one or more Juftices of the Peace of the fame County, of the faid Force; and thereupon the faid Juftices of Peace may, *ex Officio*, and without any Writ, either do Execution of the Statute of *Northampton*, as aforefaid; or elfe muft go to the Place where fuch Force is, to fee it, and to remove it, and to arreft and commit the Offenders, and fhall alfo keep a Special Seffions to inquire of the faid Force. And if upon fuch Inquiry fuch Force fhall be found, then the faid Juftice fhall reftore the Party grieved to his Poffeffion again; and here no other Juftice of Peace can grant a *Superfedeas* to ftay the fame Reftitution. 4. *By the Juftices of out Seffions.*
Remedium
plus Feftinum.

See more hereof before in the other Title of *Forcible Entry*.

Alfo the Party grieved may remove fuch Indictment, found either at fuch General or Special Seffions, by a *Certiorari* into the *King's Bench*, and the Judges of that Court may award a Writ of Reftitution, to the Sheriff of the County, to reftore the Poffeffion to the Party.

Now when the Juftice of Peace fhall make fuch Inquiry, he fhall direct his Precept or Warrant to the Sheriff, commanding him to caufe to come before the faid Juftice, at fome Town there near, twenty-four fufficient and indifferent Perfons dwelling near to the faid Lands or Tenements (whereof every one fhall have in Freehold Lands or Tenements, forty Shillings by the Year at leaft) to inquire upon their Oaths of fuch Force, &c. See before in the other Title of *Forcible Entry*. *Inquiry.*

Upon Default of Appearance of thofe Jurors, the Juftice of Peace may award an *Alias*, and after that *Pluries infinite*, till they come; but fo that at the Day of the fecond Precept or Writ, the Sheriff muft return forty Shillings in Iffues, upon every one of them, and at the third Writ five Pounds; and at every Day after the double. 8 H. 6. c. 9.
Lamb. 168.

And although any of fuch Jurors fhall not have forty Shillings Freehold Land *per Annum*, yet their Prefentment of fuch Force is good for the King, fo as the Offenders fhall fine therefore to the King; but whether the Party fhall have Reftitution upon fuch a Prefentment, it being pleaded or fhewed at that Time of the Reftitution to be made, feemeth a Doubt. Lamb. 155.

If the Sheriff fhall return fmaller Iffues upon the Inquirors than the Statute doth appoint, yet the Party indicted fhall not impeach the Inquiry therefore. Lamb. 156.

Neither is it Caufe to impeach the Inquiry, though the Juftice of Peace do not go to fee the Place where the Force is. *Marrow*.

And it is convenient upon fuch Inquiry, that the Evidence be given openly to the Jury, to the Intent it may appear to the Juftice of Peace, or Court, whether there fhall be reafonable Caufe to ftay Reftitution or no, after the Indictment found. See Dyer 122.

C H A P.

CHAP. CXXX.

Of Restitution to be made to the Party put out.

Restitution.

I Will here shortly recite the Words of the Statute, which for this Business of Restitution will give the better Light.

8 H. 6. c. 9.

And if upon such Enquiry, it be found before the said Justices that any have done contrary to this Statute (viz. have entred, or held with Force) the said Justices of Peace, &c shall reseise the said Lands or Tenements so entred upon, or holden, and put the Party so put out, in full Possession of the same Lands and Tenements so entred upon and holden as before.

P. R. 35.

Here we see that after such Forcible Entry or Holding so found by Inquiry, the said Justices of Peace, &c. shall reseise the said Lands or Tenements, and shall remove the Force (*sc.* all such Offenders as shall be found in the House, or upon the Lands, that either entred or held with Force) and, upon the Prayer of the Party so put out, the said Justices of Peace shall restore him to his Possession again.

And herein the Justices of Peace need not stay or stand upon the Right and Title of either of the Parties.

Br. Force 27.

But no Restitution shall be made, but where the Forcible Entry or Detainer is first found by Inquisition.

Indictment the Form.
Cromp. 166.

Concerning this Inquisition or Indictment, the Justices of Peace shall do well to peruse and regard the same, to see if it be sufficient ; for the Justices of Peace ought not to award Restitution, where the Indictment shall appear to them to be any way insufficient in the Law, either in Matter or Form.

Lamb. 156,
257.

1. First, Therefore to have Restitution, the Putting out (by express Words) must be in the Indictment, and found by the Inquisition : For another Man may enter upon me and yet not put me out, and then there needeth no Restitution to be made by the Justices.

And this Putting out is to be understood only of House or Land, and not of a Rent Common, and Advowson, and such like, into which an actual Entry cannot be made and therefore none shall have Restitution, but such only as are put out of House or Land.

Sid. 102.

(*a*) And the *Estate* must be set forth, for 'tis not sufficient to alledge generally that *possessionatus fuit*, because Tenant at Will may be *possessed* ; but he is not within either of the Statutes.

2 Roll. Abr.
81.
Raym. 67.

An Entry into two Closes *prati sive pasturæ* not good for the Incertainty.

The Indictment was for a Forcible Entry into a Copyhold, (*viz.*) that the Defendant *ejecit & dissesivit*, void, because Disseisin is applicable only to a Freehold, it ought to be *ejecit, expulit & amovit*.

Lamb. 481.
Br. Force 23.
2 Rol. R. 46.

(*d*) 2. Also the Indictment ought to express the Quality of the Thing entred upon, &c *sc.* Whether it be a Messuage, Cottage, Meadow, Pasture, Wood, or Land Arable : For if the Indictment be, *that by strong Hand they did enter the Tenement, &c.* it is void for the Incertainty, because the Word *Tenement* may extend to either of them.

14 H. 6. 16.
Br. Force 13.

3. Also the Indictment must have these Words, (*viz.*) *yet hold out*, otherwise the Party shall have no Restitution ; and yet these Words be not in the Statute : But without these Words in the Indictment, it may be supposed and thought, that he which put me out, hath left the Possession again, or that I have gotten it again ; and then the Restitution is needless.

So as in every such Indictment, these Words are material, *sc. Expulerunt, & adhuc extra tenent.* And for lack of either of these Words, no Restitution shall be made or awarded.

Lamb. 145.
* But the best Way is not to recite the Statute, for if 'tis misrecited in any Thing, the Indictment will be quashed.

4. Also one of these two Words, *with strong Hand*, or *with Multitude*, seem to be material in the Indictment ; unless they be implied by * reciting the Statute of 8 H. 6 and concluding against the Form of the Statute, or by some other Words in the Indictment. **Cro. Eliz. 93, 96, 106, 307. 1 Bulst. 218**

2

For the Form to be ufed in thefe Indictments, fee more after Tit. *Indictments.*

If a Man fhall be reftored upon an infufficient Indictment taken before the Juftices of Peace, and this be removed into the *King's Bench*, the Court there will caufe the Party to be reftored, that before was put out by the Juftices of Peace. *Cromp. 16*

Alfo if Error or Infufficiency be in the Indictment, taken before the Juftices of Peace, and yet a Precept or Writ of Reftitution is awarded by them, any two of thofe Juftices which were prefent at the Taking of the faid Indictment, upon the Prayer of the Party, may (at another Seffions, or out of the Seffions) grant and award a *Superfedeas* to the Sheriff, to ftay the fame Reftitution, if the Sheriff had not made Reftitution before the *Superfedeas* came to his Hands. *Cromp. 165 & 166. b.*

But no other Juftice of Peace (befides thofe which were prefent at the Taking and Finding of the faid Indictment) can grant a *Superfedeas*, if the Indictment were found at a fpecial Seffions. (*a*) And if it were found at the Quarter-Seffions, yet the *Superfedeas* fhall be granted under the *Tefte* of one of thofe Juftices only which were prefent at the finding of the Force. *Ibidem.* *Dyer 187.*

(*d*) A Man is indicted that he entred with Force, and held with Force, and upon the Traverfe it was found, that he entred with Force, but not that he held with Force; yet this Indictment feems good enough, and the Party fhall be reftored. *Cromp. 165*

So two are indicted of a Forcible Entry and Detainer, and upon the Traverfe it is found, that the one entred with Force, and the other held or detained with Force, yet the Party fhall be reftored. *Ibid.* *Br. Force 15.*

If it be found by one Inqueft, that *A.* put me out by Force, and by another Inqueft, that I did put out *A.* by Force, either of us may pray to have Reftitution againft the other : But he that is firft reftored is in the worfe Cafe; for the other may have Reftitution afterwards, and then he that had Reftitution firft, is without Remedy, by the Hands of the Juftices of Peace; faving that he may re-enter, if he can peaceably, or have his Action. *Cromp. 166.* *Br. Force 6.*

If it be found by one Inqueft, that *A.* put me out by Force, and by another Inqueft taken at the fame Seffions, that *B.* did put me out by Force, I may chufe upon whether of thefe Indictments I will be reftored : And if I have Reftitution againft *A.* and this be returned, I cannot have Reftitution upon the other. But if (upon the Writ of Reftitution) it be not returned that I have Reftitution, then I may afterward have Reftitution againft *B.* upon the other Verdict, if *B.* hath re-entered upon the firft Reftitution made to me. *Marrow.* *Several Indictments.* *Cromp 166.*

A. is diffeifed, or put out with Force by *B.* and after *B.* is put out with Force by *C.* and all this is found by one and the fame Inquifition. Here *B.* may have Reftitution againft *C.* (for *B.* hath more Right to the Poffeffion than *C.*) and then may *A.* have Reftitution againft *B.* But upon this Inquifition, if *A.* have Reftitution firft, then *B.* fhall not have any Reftitution; otherwife, if thefe had been found by feveral Inquifitions.

(*a*) If an Inquifition be removed into *B. R.* by *Certiorari*, there can be no Reftitution, if the Defendant doth not traverfe the Force, or plead three Years quiet Poffeffion before the Force. *1 Vent. 265.* *1 Salk. 260.*

C H A P. CXXXI.

Who fhall award and make this Reftitution.

AFTER the Force is found by the Inqueft, the Juftice of Peace (before whom 'tis found) may himfelf put the Party in Poffeffion again; or he may make his Precept (under his own *Tefte* alone) to the Sheriff to do it. *Dyer 187.*

The Form of the Precept to the Sheriff to make Reftitution, fee *poftea* Tit. *Precedents.*

But no other Juftice of Peace hath any Authority (by the Statute) to grant or award Reftitution, but only he or they before whom the Force was found by Inquifition. Nay the Juftices of *Oyer* and *Terminer*, nor the Juftices of Gaol-delivery cannot grant Reftitution, nor the Juftices of Peace at their General Seffions of the Peace, cannot grant this Reftitution, except the Indictment were found before them. (*a*) And yet by fome Opinions, if it fhall happen that the Juftice of Peace, before whom fuch an Indictment fhall be found, before Reftitution made fhall happen to die or to be removed, then *Dyer 187* *4 & 5 P. & M.* *Dalif. Co. 1.* *59, 65.*

may the Refidue of the Juftices of Peace at their General Seffions, grant a Writ of Reftitution.

Co. 11. 65.
4 H. 7. 18.
(*d*) Alfo the Juftices of the *King's Bench* (in Regard of their fupreme Authority in all Cafes of the Crown) either upon Certificate, or Delivery (to them made by the Juftice of Peace before whom fuch Force was found) of the Prefentment of fuch Force; or if the faid Prefentment or Indictment fhall be removed before them by *Certiorari*, in both

Fitz. Ent. 36.
& Cro. 159.
thefe Cafes the Juftices of the *King's Bench* may award Reftitution. See before in the other Title *Forcible Entry*.

Lamb. 161.
But neither the Juftices of the King's Bench, nor any other (befides him or them that made the Inquiry) can perfonally reftore the Party, but only by way of Precept to the Sheriff.

The Sheriff (if need be) may take the Power of the County, to execute the Precept of the Juftices of Peace herein.

Lamb 160.
And if the Sheriff upon fuch a Precept, or upon a Writ of Reftitution from the Seffions, &c. fhall return that he cannot make Reftitution for Refiftance, &c. he fhall be amerced for making fuch a Return, becaufe in fuch Cafes he might have taken the Power of the County to affift him therein. See the like Cafe, *Fitz. Execution* 147.

See Dyer 123
& 187.
(*a*) *Note*, That the fame Juftice or Juftices of Peace, before whom the Force was found by Inquifition, and which have granted his or their Warrant to the Sheriff, to make Reftitution, may afterwards grant his or their *Superfedeas* to the Sheriff to ftay the fame Reftitution. But no other Juftice or Juftices of Peace, hath or have Authority to grant any *Superfedeas* in fuch Cafe, &c.

Sid. 287.
Indictment for a Forcible Entry into a Meadow, the Defendant tendered a Traverfe, but the Juftices refufed it, and awarded Reftitution; this being removed into *B. R.* the Court declared, that the Juftices ought to have accepted the Traverfe, for the firft Finding is in Nature of a Prefentment, which ought to be tried prefently upon the Traverfe, and if it be found no Force, no Reftitution ought to be awarded.

1 Vent. 308.
Where the Juftices find a Force, and make a Record of it on their own View, they cannot grant Reftitution, but muft commit the Offender.

CHAP. CXXXII.

To whom Reftitution fhall be made.

THIS Reftitution ought to be made to him that was put out, and to none other; for fo are the Words of the Statute.

P. R. 38.
Therefore if the Father be out by Force, and dieth, his Heir fhall not have Reftitution; yet here the Juftices may imprifon and fine the Offenders: For by fuch Forcible Entry they have broken the Peace. See *antea*, in the other Title of *Forcible Entry*.

Lamb. 156.
Alfo, if after the Death of the Father, a Stranger abateth, or entreth into his Land by Force, before the Heir hath gotten actual Poffeffion, the Heir fhall not have Reftitution, becaufe he had but a Poffeffion in Law, defcended upon him.

Fitz. 248. h.
The Diffeifee doth put the Diffeifor out with Force, the Diffeifor fhall be reftored: For the Right or Title is not commonly difputable or material; but by Words of the Statute, he that is in fuch fort (*fc.* forcibly) put out, fhall be reftored.

Dyer 122.
Yet it feemeth in this Cafe, that upon Traverfe tendred by the Diffeifee, and his Right appearing, the Juftice of Peace may ftay Reftitution. See hereof after under this Title.

Br. Force 6.
Fitz. Ent. 20.
Alfo, if the Diffeifor be reftored again, yet the Diffeifee may after re-enter peaceably, or have his Affife.

Cromp. 163.
But if the Diffeifee fhall enter peaceably upon the Diffeifor, and fo they both fhall abide and continue there together for divers Days, and after the Diffeifee doth put out the Diffeifor with Force, and is thereof indicted: Here the Diffeifor fhall not be reftored, for the Diffeifor's Poffeffion was avoided in quiet Manner at the firft Entry of the Diffeifee, and fo the Diffeifor had no Poffeffion in the Eye of the Law when he was put out.

Cromp. 162
& 164.
If the Diffeifee fhall enter peaceably, the Diffeifor and his Family being abroad, and after the Diffeifee fhall keep his Poffeffion with Force, the Diffeifor fhall not be reftored, by Reafon of the eign Title of the Diffeifee, and for that he entred peaceably. See *antea*, in the other Title of *Forcible Entry*.

I

But

But here the Diſſeiſee ſhall be impriſoned and fined for keeping his Poſſeſſion with Force ; for *Forcible Keeping or Detaining* is as well prohibited as *Forcible Entry.*

And here note, That the Being of a Man's Wife, Children or Servants, in the Houſe, or upon the Land, do preſerve his Poſſeſſion ; but his Cattle being upon the Ground, &c. do not preſerve his Poſſeſſion. *Poſſeſſion.*
Cromp. 164.
Aſſiſe 418.

Alſo when two are in Poſſeſſion of an Houſe, &c. and the one claimeth by one Title, and the other by another Title, here the Law ſhall adjudge him to be in Poſſeſſion, who hath the beſt Right. So that if *A.* ſhall wrongfully enter upon *B.* and they both ſhall continue in the Houſe, and after *B.* ſhall put out *A.* with Force ; *A.* ſhall not be reſtored, for *A.* never gained any Poſſeſſion by his Entry. Lit. 140.
Perk. 45.

Two Jointenants, or Tenants in Common, and one of them doth forcibly put the other out of his Poſſeſſion ; he that is ſo expelled, may have an Action of Treſpaſs of Forcible Entry againſt his Companion, upon the Statute of 8 *H.* 6. And thereupon he ſhall have a Writ of Reſtitution to reſtore him to his former Eſtate : But what the Juſtice of Peace can do herein, *Quære*, for that his Entry and Poſſeſſion is lawful through the whole Land, in reſpect of his own Moiety and State. See 8 *E.* 4. 8. Fitz. 249.

P. R. 36.

Two Jointenants be put out by Force and one of them only ſueth to have Reſtitution, Reſtitution ſhall be made unto him. Lamb. 158.

Leſſee for Years, or a Copyholder, &c. may pray, and ſhall have Reſtitution, as well as he in the Reverſion, or the Lord.

If Leſſee for Years be put out of his Term by Force, and die, tho' after his Death this Force be found by Inquiſition, taken by a Juſtice of Peace ; yet his Executors ſhall not be reſtored to that Land (by the Juſtice) for that they are not the ſame Perſon that was put out. P. R. 38.

(*a*) The particular Tenant, as Tenant for Years, or a Copyholder, ſhall be reſtored notwithſtanding the Lord or Leſſor (who have the Freehold) will waive it, or diſagree to it as to themſelves ; and thereupon this Caſe happened. The Lord of a Manor commanded *A. B.* and *C.* to enter with Force upon his Copyholder, which they did, and an Indictment is preferred *quod expulerunt* the Copyholder, and diſſeiſed the Lord with Force, and the Lord laboured that no Reſtitution ſhould be made ; for that, as was alledged, Reſtitution was to be made out of reſpect to the Freehold : Yet the Court granted Reſtitution to the Copyholder. For the Court ought to reform the Wrongs in their ſeveral Degrees ; and that is, to reſtore the Copyholder firſt who is expelled. And ſo was done, as was ſaid by Juſtice *Williams* in the Caſe of the Lord *Norris* who withſtood a Reſtitution to his Leſſee. Sir *Andrew Noel*'s Caſe, *Yelv. p.*81.

The Words of the Statute of 21 *Jac.* 1. 15. are to be ſtrictly taken, and ſhall not be extended by Equity, and to that Purpoſe this Caſe happened ; an Indictment of Forcible Entry was, *Adtunc exiſt. liber. ten. B. ad voluntatem Domini ſecundum conſuetudinem manerii.* The Party in this Caſe could not be reſtored, becauſe it is not ſaid *per Copiam rotulorum cur'.* And it may be ſhe was Tenant by the Verge, and not by Copy. But it was holden, that a Copyholder's Widow that held *per bancum* ſhould be reſtored. *Latch, p.* 182.

C H A P. CXXXIII.

What Cauſes there may be for ſtaying the Juſtice of Peace from granting Reſtitution.

ALthough the Party indicted for a Force ſhall not be heard nor ſuffered to give his Title in Evidence, to excuſe himſelf of his Forcible Entry or Detainer, to ſave his Fine due to the King for ſuch Force (which Fine he ſhall make, tho' his Right be ever ſo good) ; yet to the Reſtitution (which the Complainant ſhall demand, if the Force be found) the Defendant ſhall be heard to diſprove the Title of the Complainant, or what he can ſay otherwiſe for the Stay of Reſtitution. *Quære*, and ſee before in the other Title of *Forcible Entry, contra.* Lamb. 151
Cromp. 162.
Br. Force 11.

Dyer 122

Now the Defendant (or Party indicted) for the Stay of Reſtitution, may at the Time of the Reſtitution to be made, plead or alledge any of theſe Things following.

1. His quiet Poſſeſſion by three Years together.

2. He

2. He may deliver to the Juſtices of Peace, or Court, a *Certiorari.* And this is a *Superſedeas* to them. (*a*) See the Statute 21 *Jac.* 1. 8. hereafter.

Lamb. 162.   (*d*) 3. He may tender his Traverſe ; but Mr. *Lambard* ſeemeth to doubt whether the Party may be admitted to his Traverſe before the ſame Juſtices of Peace. (*a*) And he thinks it ſafer for the Juſtices to make Reſtitution, notwithſtanding the Offer of Traverſe, or rather wiſheth the Juſtices to deliver, or certify the Preſentment into the King's Bench, and ſo to refer the further Proceeding to them, &c.

    (*d*) 4. He may plead the Inſufficiency of the Indictment.

    5. He may plead the Inſufficiency of any of the Jurors, *ſc.* for not having forty Shillings Freehold Land *per Annum,* (*a*) and that muſt not be Antient Demeſne or Copyhold, but Charter Land. (*d*) And in this Caſe Mr. *Marrow* is of Opinion, That the Party ſhall have no Reſtitution. Yet Mr. *Lambard* and Mr. *Crompton* ſeem to be of the contrary Opinion. *Lamb.* 155. *Cromp.* 165. *Ideo quære.*

Lamb. 156.   And it ſeemeth (by the Opinion of Mr. *Lambard*), That the Juſtices of Peace ought not to ſtay Reſtitution, ſave only, either by alledging three Years quiet Poſſeſſion, or by Removing the Record and Preſentment into the King's Bench by a *Certiorari.*

Three Years Poſſeſſion.   For the Firſt, there ſhall be no Reſtitution awarded (upon any Indictment of Forcible Entry, or holding with Force) where the Party indicted hath been in quiet Poſſeſſion by the Space of three whole Years together next before the Day of ſuch Indictment found, if his Eſtate be not ended ; and this the Party indicted may alledge to ſtay the Reſtitution, and the Reſtitution upon this ſhall be ſtaid by the Juſtice of Peace, until it be tried, if the other Party will deny or traverſe the ſame. (*a*) And if the ſame Allegation be tried and found againſt the Party indicted, then ſhall he pay ſuch Coſts and Damages to the other Party, as ſhall be aſſeſſed by the Juſtices before whom the ſame ſhall be tried ; the ſaid Coſts and Damages to be recovered and levied notwithſtanding by the Courſe of the Common Law.

31 El. 11.

Certiorari.   (*d*) Alſo if a Man who hath made Forcible Entry or Detainer, be in doubt that he ſhall be indicted before the Juſtices of Peace, (upon the Statute of 8 *H.* 6.) and that thereupon Reſtitution will be awarded againſt him, he may have a Writ of *Certiorari* out of the King's Bench ready, and when the Bill of Indictment is found, he may preſently deliver it to the Juſtice of Peace or Court. And this is a *Superſedeas* to them for to ſtay the Reſtitution ; for that upon this Writ, the ſaid Indictment ſhall be removed from them into the King's Bench.

Cromp. 164.
P. R. 37.

    And although the Indictment be found after the *Teſte* of the *Certiorari,* it is not material, for they be both the King's Courts, &c.

6 H. 7. 16.   But if a *Certiorari* comes to remove an Indictment of Forcible Entry taken before the Juſtices of Peace in the Country, and the Party will not ſue to remove it, but ſuffereth it to lie ſtill, the Juſtices of Peace may proceed to grant Reſtitution, notwithſtanding the Writ, as *Hobart* the King's Attorney ſaid in 6 *H.* 7. But *Keble* held Opinion againſt him ; and it ſeemeth rather, that the Juſtices of Peace ought *Ex Officio* to ſend the Indictment away, becauſe they are commanded ſo by the Writ. And this Writ is a *Superſedeas* of it ſelf to the Juſtices of Peace, to ſtay their Proceedings. And if they ſhall proceed after, it is erroneous.

Lamb. 498.
Cromp. 166.

Cromp. 162.   After Reſtitution made by the Juſtices of Peace, if the other Party doth remove the Indictment by a *Certiorari* of a more eign Date than the Indictment, the Juſtices of the King's Bench may award Reſtitution back again : For upon the Matter, the Juſtices of Peace had no Power to make Reſtitution, for that the *Certiorari* hath Relation from the Date thereof.

Ibid.   After Reſtitution granted from the Seſſions, and delivered to the Sheriff, the other Party having a *Certiorari,* delivereth it alſo unto the Sheriff after the Seſſions ; the Sheriff ſhall not ſurceaſe thereupon (for he hath no Authority to allow thereof). But if the *Certiorari* were delivered to any Juſtice of Peace, he may thereupon grant a *Superſedeas* to the Sheriff. And if Reſtitution were made by the Sheriff before the ſaid *Superſedeas* came to his Hands, then the other Party ſhall have Reſtitution back again in the King's Bench, upon the Indictment removed thither.

See Tit. *Certiorari,* Chap. 195. *infra.*

    (*a*) A Bill of Forcible Entry was found before Juſtices of Peace, and Reſtitution awarded, but not executed ; a *Certiorari* was delivered to one of the Juſtices, who refuſed to open it without conſulting with his Companions, and Reſtitution is made. This was moved in the King's Bench, and the Reſtitution awarded, and the Juſtice of Peace chid, in the Caſe of *Fitz-Williams. Yelv. p.* 32.

I   (*a*) The

(*d*) The Tender of a Traverfe (to an Indictment of Forcible Entry, upon the Statute *Traverfe.* of 8 *H.* 6.) is no *Superfedeas*, but in Difcretion; fo as the Juftices of Peace or Court Dyer 122 (notwithstanding the Traverfe tendred) may grant or may ftay the Reftitution at their Difcretion, according as the Truth of the Right or Title fhall appear to them: And fo is the Ufe of the King's Bench.

Or elfe the Juftices of Peace (before whom the Indictment was found) may after Traverfe tendred, certify or deliver the Indictment into the King's Bench, or to the Quarter-Seffions, and fo refer the further Proceedings therein to them.

But if the Party indicted fhall tender a Traverfe prefently, whereupon Reftitution is Cromp. 165. ftayed, and after he fhall not purfue his Traverfe with Effect, (but difcontinueth it) and after doth tender another Traverfe upon Reftitution prayed at another Time; the Juftices of Peace or Court, fhall do well to proceed to grant Reftitution, notwithstanding fuch Traverfe tendred.

And it is the Courfe of the King's Bench, that he that tendreth the Traverfe there Cromp. 166. (upon fuch an Indictment) fhall bear all the Charges of the Trial, and not the King, nor he at whofe Suit the Indictment was found: And the fame Reafon feemeth upon an Indictment traverfed before Juftices of Peace.

(*a*) But upon a Forcible Entry found, and a Traverfe tendred, if the Juftices of Cromp. 150, Peace will try the Traverfe, it feemeth they ought to caufe a new Jury to be returned 152. (by the Sheriff before them) to try the fame Traverfe. The which may be done the next Day, but not the fame Day.

Alfo after the Indictment of Force found, if a Traverfe be tendred, or whatfoever *Pardon.* fhall be alledged for the Stay of Reftitution, it ought to be in Writing (and not verbal only), for upon the Traverfe, &c. a *Venire facias* muft be awarded, a Jury returned, the Iffue tried, a Verdict found and a Judgment given, and Cofts and Damages award-ed: And they muft have a Record, which muft be in Writing, to do all this, and not a verbal Plea. *Vide* 14 *H.* 8. 16. *Fitz.* And all this muft be done at the fame Seffion, if it be defired; or elfe Reftitution is to be granted. It feems alfo that the King's Par-don will difcharge the Forcible Entry or Detainer, and bar Reftitution.

And in the Cafe of *Fawcet, H.* 4 *Jac.* the Forcible Entry was pardoned by a Par- Yelv. p. 99. liament-Pardon; and the Court was of Opinion, Reftitution could not be granted: For 2 Cro. 148. by the Pardon, the Strength of the Indictment is gone, but there is a Remedy for the S. C.
Noy 119. Party by Suit, where he may be fure of the Effect of it. And Juftice *Williams* faid, S. C. That *Thynne* being indicted for an Entry by Force, upon the Lands of the Lord *Staf-ford*, got the King's Pardon, and pleaded it in Bar of Reftitution; and it was adjudged a good Plea.

On this Subject of *Forcible Entries and Detainers*, fee alfo 1 *Hawk. P. C. Chap.* 64.

C H A P. CXXXIV. (*a*)

Reftitution, where it fhall be granted.

IT is generally held as the Law and Courfe of the Court of King's Bench, that Re-ftitution is a Thing in the Difcretion of the Court; and they will grant it or deny it, as the Juftice and Reafon of the Cafe fhall require: And therefore they will grant it ordinarily in thefe Cafes.

1. If the Indictment removed, be for any Caufe appearing in the Body of it, or Cap-tion quafhed.

2. If a *Certiorari* hath iffued, and the fame be not allowed, or Proceedings ftayed thereupon; but Reftitution be granted after the Allowance or Tender of it.

3. If any indirect Courfe be ufed to avoid the Effect of a *Certiorari*, as I remem-ber this Cafe happened. One *P.* having made a Forcible Entry upon *L.* of Lands in *W.* And being threatned with an Inquiry of a Force, he imployed one *C.* his Attor-ney, to procure a *Certiorari*, and gave the Names of thofe that were moft likely to be indicted: Which one *R.* the Attorney of *L.* fufpecting, by pretending himfelf to be the Attorney of *P.* fpoke to the Clerk in the Crown-Office, underftood the Names of thofe for whom the *Certiorari* was intended to be made, and procured an Inquiry by the Ju-ftices in the Country, and fuch to be indicted as the *Certiorari* was not for. So when

the

the *Certiorari* came, it was infignificant, and *L.* was reftored.   But this Matter appearing in the King's Bench, *H.* 1658, Reftitution was awarded.
   4. If the Juftices below fhall mifbehave themfelves, and fhall not allow the Plea of
three Years Poffeffion well pleaded.
   But Reftitution being as I faid, a Thing difcretional, the Equity and Reafon of the
Cafe doth often incline the Court, not to grant it where they may do it, efpecially if
the Party in Poffeffion fhall offer to appear, and go to fpeedy Trial of the Right ;
and fo I have often obferved it to be done.

C H A P.   CXXXV.

Riots.

IT may plainly appear to all fuch as have been converfant in our Chronicles, how
   dangerous to this Kingdom, unlawful Affemblies have been in all precedent Ages,
even fuch as at the firft were very fmall, and began upon fmall Occafion; yet not being
repreffed in Time, grew to fuch Greatnefs, that they afterwards put in hazard the State.
And therefore it is Wifdom for all Juftices of Peace, to indeavour to quench the Be-
ginnings and firft Sparks of fuch Affemblies, as knowing, that for Want of timely
Reftraint, they may foon grow to the like Danger again.

Statutes.   Now for the better Suppreffing of fuch unlawful Affemblies, and partly for the better enabling the Juftices of Peace therein, there were three Statutes provided by the Wifdom of the Realm, and are remaining yet in Force ; That is to fay, the Statute of
13 *H.* 4. 7.   2 *H.* 5. 8. & 19 *H.* 7. 13.
13 H. 4. c. 7.   The Statute of 13 *H.* 4. authorifing, nay, upon a great Penalty injoining the Juftices of Peace (together with the Sheriff) to arreft, remove and punifh the Offenders.
2 H. 5. 8.   But for that the aforefaid Statute gave no Remedy to the Party grieved, if the Juftice
of Peace or Sheriff fhould make Default; as alfo for the better Stirring up the Juftices
in this Bufinefs, the Statute of 2 *H.* 5. was made, authorifing the Lord Chancellor of
England (at the Inftance of the Party grieved) to grant a Commiffion, to inquire of
the Defaults of the two next Juftices of Peace and Sheriff, in not executing the aforefaid Statute of 13 *H.* 4.   And withal providing, how the Charges of the Juftices, about
the Suppreffing and Inquiry of fuch Riots, fhould be born ; and alfo limiting what
Punifhment, as well the Offenders attainted of fuch Riots, as alfo fuch as fhould not
be ready to affift and aid the faid Juftice to reprefs fuch Rioters, fhould fuffer.
19 H. 7. 13.   And laftly, for that the two former Statutes did not exprefs of what Sufficiency the
Jurors, impanelled to inquire of Riots, fhould be; nor what Iffues they fhould lofe, if
they appeared not; nor any certain Punifhment was inflicted upon the Maintainers or
Embracers of fuch Jurors: Therefore the Statute 19 *H.* 7. was made.   But fo much of
thefe Things as concern the Juftices of Peace, do appear more particularly here before :
And therefore now I will proceed in this Bufinefs.

C H A P.   CXXXVI.

Firft, What fhall be faid to be a Riot, Rout or un-lawful Affembly, within the Meaning of thefe Statutes.

Br. Riot 5.   WHEN three Perfons or more, fhall come and affemble themfelves together, to the
Cromp. 68.   Intent to do any unlawful Act, with Force or Violence againft the Perfon of ano-
P. R. 25.   ther, his Poffeffions or Goods, as to kill, beat or otherways to hurt, or to imprifon a Man;
to pull down a Houfe, Wall, Pale, Hedge or Ditch ; wrongfully to enter upon or
into another Man's Poffeffion, Houfe or Land, &c.   Or to cut or take away Corn,
Grafs, Wood or other Goods wrongfully ; or to hunt unlawfully in any Park or War-
Br. Riot 4, 5. ren ; or to do any other unlawful Act (with Force or Violence) againft the Peace ; or to
Lamb. 179. the manifeft Terror of the People ; if they only meet to fuch a Purpofe or Intent,
181.
      2   although

although they ſhall after depart of their own Accord, without doing any Thing, yet this *Unlawful Aſ-* is an unlawful Aſſembly. *ſembly.*

If after their firſt Meeting, they ſhall ride, go or move forward towards the Execu- *Rout.* tion, of any ſuch Act (whether they put their intended Purpoſe in Execution, or not) This is a Rout.

And if they execute any ſuch Thing in Deed, then it is a Riot. *Riot.*

And yet by the Opinion of ſome, a Rout is only where ſuch a Company, of three or Br. 4, 5. more, are ſo aſſembled, for their own common or proper Quarrel, and not in the Quarrel of any other Perſon. As where the Inhabitants of a Town do aſſemble together to pull down a Houſe, Wall, Pale, Ditch, or other Incloſure, pretending to have Title of Common, or a Way there; or to beat a Man that hath done them ſome publick Offence. But yet the Word *Rout,* ſeemeth to have a more large and ample Meaning, as appeareth by the Statute of 18 *Ed.* 3. *cap.* 1. ſpeaking of Routs that are brought in the Preſence of the Juſtices; and the Statute of 2 *R.* 2. *cap.* 6. treating of Riding in great Routs.

(*a*) *Finch* deſcribed them ſhortly thus. *Fi. lib.* 2.

An *unlawful Aſſembly* is, when above the Number of two ſhall aſſemble to do any un- Br. 4, 5. lawful Act. Lamb. 180.

A Rout is, when they ſet forward to do it.

A Riot is, when they do it in Deed.

But at the Common Law (before the Making of theſe Statutes) theſe Facts and unlawful Aſſemblies committed or done, were no more than common Treſpaſſes; although ſometimes by the Diſcretion of the Juſtices, a greater Fine was aſſeſſed in ſuch Caſes than was for other common Treſpaſſes.

(*d*) Now in Riots, Routs, and unlawful Aſſemblies, theſe four Circumſtances are to be *Circumſtances.* conſidered.

1ſt, The Number of the Perſons aſſembled.

2d, The Intent and Purpoſe of Meeting.

3d, The Lawfulneſs or Unlawfulneſs of the Act.

4th, The Manner and Circumſtances of doing it.

For the Number, there muſt neceſſarily be *three Perſons* at the leaſt, ſo gathered toge- *The Number.* ther; for elſe it can be no Riot, Rout or unlawful Aſſembly within the Meaning of theſe Statutes.

But an Aſſembly of an hundred Perſons or more (yea, though they be in Armour) yet if it be not in Terror or Affright of the People, and were aſſembled without any Intent to break the Peace, it is not prohibited by any of theſe Statutes, nor unlawful. See *infra.*

For the Intent: It ſeemeth it can be no Riot, &c. except there be an Intent precedent *The Intent.*
Cromp. 62. to ſome unlawful Act, and with Violence or Force. P. R. 25.

And therefore, if divers be aſſembled, and none of them do know to what End or Lam. 184. Purpoſe they are met; this can make no Riot or Rout, till the Intent be known. Cromp. 61.

If the Maſter (intending to make a Riot) taketh with him his ordinary Servants, and maketh an Affray or other Outrage with them: This is no Riot in the Servants, except their Maſter had made them privy to his Intent before, but the Maſter only ſhall be puniſhed for this. (*a*) Yet *quære,* whether this ſhall be adjudged, or puniſhed in the Maſter as a Riot.

(*d*) And in this former Caſe it is not material, though the Number of his Servants that go with him are above his Degree, ſo long as they be his Houſhold Servants. *Lamb.* 184. *P. R.* 25.

If divers being lawfully aſſembled, ſhall quarrel or fall out upon the ſudden, without *Affray.* any former Intent: This is no Riot, but a ſudden Affray. Cromp. 62.

If divers be at an Ale-houſe, and without any Intention of an Affray they ſuddenly Lam. 184. fall together by the Ears: This is no Riot, but a ſudden Affray, becauſe they had no ſuch Intention before.

If a Jury being together, ſhall fall out and fight: This is no Riot, becauſe they were Ibid. lawfully aſſembled.

Alſo where there be three or more gathered together, either to execute the Juſtice of the Law, or for the Exerciſe of Valour, and Trial of Activity, or for the Increaſe of Amity or neighbourly Friendſhip, (and not being met with an Intent to break or diſturb the 3 H. 7. 1.
Br. Riot 2. Peace, or to offer Violence or Hurt to the Perſon of any) ſuch Aſſemblies be not prohibited by any of theſe Statutes, nor unlawful; as if the Sheriff, Under-Sheriff or Bailiff, ſhall take Power (what Number they ſhall think good) to execute the King's Proceſs, &c. it is lawful: So of other Officers. See more thereof *poſtea,* Tit. *Poſſé Comitatus.*

So

So it is a lawful Affembly, which is gathered together to run at Tilt, &c. by the King's Commandment.

So the Affembly of People, and their Ufe of Armour upon *Midfummer* Night in *London*, being only for Sport, is lawful; and though it be with a great Affembly of People, and in Armour; yet it being neither in Affright of the People, nor *malum in fe*, nor to do any Act with Force or Violence againft the Peace, it is lawful.

(*a*) If Stage-players, by their Shows, occafion an extraordinary and unufual Concourfe of People to fee them act their Tricks; this is an unlawful Affembly and Riot: For which they may be indicted and fined, as *Coke* faid, *M.* 12 *Jac.* 1. *Roll's Rep.* 2 *Part*, *p.* 109.

(*d*) Alfo if divers do affemble and gather together, to drink at an Alehoufe; or elfe to play at Football, Bucklers, Bear or Bull-baitings, Dancings, Bowls, Cards or Dice, or fuch like Sports : This is neither Riot, Rout nor unlawful Affembly within thefe Statutes, nor here prohibited : For thefe Meetings are not with any Intent to offer or do Violence or Hurt to the Perfon, Poffeffions or Goods of any other; neither are they *malum in fe*, they are in themfelves neither evil, nor unlawful, nor prohibited by the Common Law, though otherwife fome of them are prohibited by Statute. See before Tit. *Games Unlawful.*

But if any of the Perfons affembled together for any the Sports above mentioned (or for the like) came with any Intent or Purpofe to break or difturb the Peace, or to offer Violence, or Hurt to the Perfon of any, and fhall make an Affray, or do other Outrage; this feemeth to be a Riot, in fo many as came with any fuch unlawful Intent or Purpofe.

And if any of the Perfons affembled together (to drink or play) at an Ale-houfe, or for any the Sports above mentioned, or the like, fhall fall out fuddenly (without any former Intention of an Affray) and in that their Falling out, they fhall betake themfelves to fundry Parts and fhall make an Affray, that this fhall be adjudged a Riot in fo many of both Sides, as fhall be Parties to that Affray or Quarrel. But *quære* hereof, for that it was without any fuch Intent before their faid Affembly, and done only upon the fudden, and upon a fudden Occafion happening after their faid Meeting; and again, their faid Affembly was at the firft lawful, or at leaft not prohibited by any of thefe Statutes, nor yet the Common Law. *Co.* 11. 87.

But otherwife, if by Agreement they fhall meet again, and fight afterwards, that maketh it a Riot, as being a new Affembly upon the former Quarrel; and fo their fecond Meeting was upon an Intent precedent to do an unlawful Act.

(*a*) Where a great Number fhall affemble themfelves, or come into a Houfe, and there detain Poffeffion of the Houfe with Force (though this is neither a publick Fact, or Force, done in the open Sight of the People;) yet this is a Riot, and the Juftices of Peace punifhable, if they fhall not remove fuch Force, and fupprefs fuch Riots. See the Cafe of *Drayton Baffet* before, Tit. *Forcible Entry.*

C H A P.   CXXXVII.

Concerning the Lawfulnefs or Unlawfulnefs of the Act.

NOTE, That the Lawfulnefs or Unlawfulnefs of the Thing done or intended, doth not always excufe or accufe the Parties to a Riot, &c. but fo, that the Manner and Circumftances of the Act muft alfo be confidered.

For every Man may affemble Company to aid him in his Houfe, againft Injury or Violence. But if a Man be threatned, that if he come to fuch a Place he fhall be beaten : In this Cafe, if he fhall affemble any Company to go thither with him (though it be to fafeguard his Perfon) it feemeth to be within the Compafs of thefe Statutes, and unlawful.
Every Man in peaceable Manner may affemble a meet Company (and may come) to do any lawful Thing; or to remove, or caft down any common Nufance.

Every private Man, to whofe Houfe or Land any Nufance fhall be erected, made or done, may in peaceable Manner affemble a meet Company, with neceffary Tools, and
may remove, pull or caft down fuch Nufance, (and that before any Prejudice received thereby) and for that Purpofe, if need be, may alfo enter into the other Man's Ground.
A Man erects a Wear crofs a common River, where People have a common Paffage with their Boats, and divers did affemble with Spades, Crows of Iron, and other Things neceffary to remove the faid Wear, and made a Trench in his Land that did erect the

Wear,

Wear, to turn the Water, fo as they might the better take up the faid Wear, and they did remove the fame Nufance. This was holden neither any Forcible Entry, nor yet any Riot.

But in the Cafes aforefaid, if in removing any fuch Nufance, &c. the Perfons fo affembled fhall ufe any threatning Words (as to fay, they will do it in Spight of the other; or they will do it, though they die for it, or fuch like Words) or fhall ufe any other Behaviour, in apparent Difturbance of the Peace, then it feemeth to be a Riot ; and therefore where there is Caufe to remove any fuch Nufance, or to do any like Act, it is the fafeft not to affemble any Multitude of People, but only to fend one or two Perfons, or (if a greater Number) yet no more than are needful, and only with meet Tools, to remove, pull or caft down the fame, and that fuch Perfons tend their Bufinefs only without Difturbance of the Peace or threatning Speeches.

For the Manner of doing a lawful Thing, may make it unlawful.

Alfo the Manner of doing an unlawful Act, by an Affembly of People, may be fuch as that it fhall not be punifhed as a Riot.

As if I fhall affemble a meet Company to carry away a Piece of Timber or other Thing Lamb. 181. (whereto I pretend a Right) that cannot be carried without a great Number, if the Number be not more than are needful for fuch Purpofe, although another Man hath better Right to the Thing fo carried away ; and that this Act be a Wrong and unlawful : Yet it is of it felf no Riot, except there be withal threatning Words ufed, or other Difturbance of Peace.

C H A P. CXXXVIII.

For the Manner and Circumftances.

AS there muft neceffarily be three Perfons at the leaft affembled together to make a Riot, &c. fo their being together, and their Demeanor muft be fuch, as fhall or may breed fome apparent Difturbance of the Peace ; either by threatning Speeches, turbulent Gefture, Shew of Armour, or actual Force or Violence (to the Terror of the peaceable Sort of People, or the imboldning and ftirring up of fuch as are of evil Difpofition) or elfe it can be no Riot, &c. For, as I faid before, the Manner of doing a lawful Thing, may make it unlawful, & e converfo.

And therefore if divers in one Company, going to the Church, Fair or Market, fhall Lamb. 182. go armed ; or one going to the Seffions, or the like Affembly, fhall go with his Servants in P. Armor 1. Armour (to the Terror of the People) though he or they have no Intent to fight, or to commit any Riot ; yet this is a Rout by the Manner of his or their going, being needlefs, difordered, and againft the Law. See 2 Edw. 3. cap. 3.

But in the former Cafes, if they had gone in privy Coats of Plate, Shirts of Mail, or Crom. 64. the like, to the Intent to defend themfelves from fome Adverfary : This feemeth not punifhable within thefe Statutes, for that there is nothing openly done in Terror of the People.

One N. W. together with fourfcore Perfons, came with Spades, Mattocks, Piftols, 31 Eliz. Swords and Daggers in the Night, to a Piece of Ground (where Sir Tho. St. had made a Crom. 64. great Wear crofs over the River of Trent, in the County of Nottingham, to the great Nufance of Paffengers there, &c.) and there they made one or two little Trenches to let out Water, &c. And though it were lawful to make the Trenches, and to debrufe the Nufance, yet for that they came with fuch Number, and Weapons, they were deeply fined in the Star-Chamber.

Alfo one Kemp, Lord of a Manor, did enter with twenty Perfons, and cut his Copy- 31 & 32 El. holder's Corn with Force, for that his Copyholder would not compound with him for Crom. 64. his Fine ; and although the Entry of the Lord was holden lawful, yet punifhable as a Riot in Regard of his Number and Force.

In all Cafes where three (or more) fhall enter into Lands, &c. with Force, upon the Crom. 64. Poffeffion of another, where their Entry is lawful, yet it is a Riot, by Reafon of Number and Force ; for the Statute of 5 R. 2. prohibiteth the Entry with Force or with Multitude of People, although the Entry be otherwife lawful.

C H A P.. CXXXIX.

What Persons may commit a Riot, &c.

IF a Number of Women (or Children under the Age of Discretion) do flock together for their own Cause, this is no Assembly punishable by these Statutes, unless a Man of Discretion moved them to assemble for the doing of some unlawful Act, as M. *Marrow* held.

Lam. 184.
Crom. 62.
Yet certain Women, that had apparelled themselves in Man's Apparel, and had pulled down riotously a lawful Inclosure, were punished for the same in the Star-chamber.

Tit. Surety for the Peace, and Forcible Entry.
Also Women and Children may commit a Force, may commit Larceny, and may be bound to the Peace, as Breakers of the Peace.

Co. 3. 72. &
11. c. 61.
Also Women Covert are holden to be within the Stat. of *Mert. cap.* 6. for Ravishment of Wards; and within the Stat. of *Westmin.* 1. *cap.* 20. *de Malefactoribus in parcis:* And within the Stat. 8 *H.* 6. of Forcible Entry: And within the Statutes of 1 *El. cap.* 2. and 23 *El.* for Recusancy, although they be not named within any of these Statutes.

Published.
Co. Ibid.
4 E. 4. 26.
Co. 11. 61. b.
Also if a Woman Covert shall commit any Riot, or do any Trespass or other Wrong, she is punishable for it; and for a Trespass done by the Wife, or for a Scandal published by her, the Action lieth against both the Husband and Wife, *&c.* an Action of Trespass, or of the Case, shall be brought against the Husband and Wife, and there the Husband is chargeable to the Damages or Fine, because he is Party to the Action and Judgment. (See *paulo antea*, Tit. *Forcible Entry*.) But if a Woman covert without her Husband be indicted of a Trespass, Riot or any other Wrong, there the Wife shall answer, and be Party to the Judgment only ; and in such Case the Fine set upon the Wife shall not be levied upon the Husband; yet after the Husband's Death, such Damages or Fine shall then be levied of the Wife her self; and as for Imprisonment or other corporal Pain, it shall be inflicted upon the Wife only, and not upon the Husband for his Wife's Act or Default.

22 Ass. 87.
43 E. 3. 18.
Br. Imp. 100.

(*a*) And note, that any Subject of this Realm, for any Injury done to his Person, or done to him in his Lands or Goods, may pursue, and have the Justice of the Law against any other Subject, be he bound or free, be it a Woman or an Infant, be they religious Persons, or be they Persons excommunicate or outlawed, or other Person whatsoever, without any Exception, *&c.* for the King, by the Stat. of *Mag. Chart. cap.* 29. saith, *Nulli vendemus, nulli negabimus, aut differemus justitiam, vel remedium.* Dyer 104.

Lam. 185.
(*d*) But if a Mayor and Aldermen, or Bailiff and Burgesses, or the Fellows of any other Society, do assemble in their common Quarrel, and make a Riot or Rout, this shall be punished in their own private natural Persons, and not in the Body politick.

For Riots, *see also* Chap. 82. *and* 1 Hawk. P. C. Chap. 65.

C H A P. CXL.

High Treason.

Defined.
Glanvil.
HIGH Treason (called in Law, *Crimen læsæ Majestatis*) was always esteemed a grievous Offence, done or attempted against the Estate Regal, (*viz.* against the King the Head, Life and Ruler of the Commonwealth) in his Person, the Queen his Wife, his Children, Realm or Authority; as,

About Life.
25 E. 3. c. 2.
P. 1.
To compass the Death of the King, the Queen his Wife, or of their eldest Son and Heir.

(*a*) To compass the Death of the Father or Mother of the King, or of any of the King's Children, although that such Compassing be not brought to Effect, yet it is Treason, by *Britton* in his Title of *Appeals, fol.* 39. *Stamf. fol.* 1. *p.* Quære, for it was Treason before the Statute, but not since, as *Stamf. fol.* 1. *p.* holds.

To

To compafs the Death of an Ufurper of the Crown is Treafon, for which the Offender Stamf. 2. h.
Co. 8. 28.
Br. 24. 29. may be arraigned in the Time of another King, as appeareth. *Br. Treaf.* 10.

(*d*) To *intend* or *imagine* the Death of the King or Queen, though they bring it not to *Effect* ; *fc.* if they fhall declare this by an *open Act*, whereby it may be known, or to utter it by Words or Letters, is Treafon.

To intend to deprive the King, or to fay, that he will be King after the King's Death, is High Treafon.

(*a*) M. *Glanvil* alfo, and M. *Bracton* fay thus, or to this Effect: *Si quis machinatus fuerit, vel aliquid fecerit in mortem Domini Regis, vel ad feditionem Regis, vel exercitus fui, vel confenferit, confiliumve dederit, vel auxilium procuraverit, feu præftiterit, licet id quod in voluntate habuit, non produxerit ad effectum, tenetur tamen criminis læfæ Majeftatis reus.* See *Glanv. lib.* 14. *fol.* 110. *& Bracton, lib.* 3. *fol.* 118. *Stamf.* 1 *v. x.*

One *Williams* expelled the *Middle Temple* for Religion, wrote two Books, the one he called *Balaam's* Afs; the other *Speculum Regale*, wherein he took on him the Office of a Prophet, and faid the King fhould die *Anno Dom.* 1621. grounding himfelf upon the Prophecy of *Daniel* of Time and Times, and Half a Time; and that now was the Time of *Antichrift*; for Sin was at the Higheft, and that this Land was the Abomination of Defolation, and the Habitation of Devils, *&c.* The Court held this to be High Treafon, and that by the Common Law; for thefe Words import the End and Deftruction of the King and his Kingdom, and that Antichriftianifm and falfe Religion is maintained; which is a Motive to People to commit Treafon and Rebellions. It was alfo refolved, that although he pretended he did it for the King's Information, and as a Caveat and Admonition, becaufe when he had declared the Judgment, he after added (*which God avert*;) yet his good Intention fhall not be refpected, when his Words and Actions appear to the contrary; and when a Man hath fpoken Treafon in the Premiffes, he fhall not qualify it, with a *God fave the King.* Secondly, It was refolved, that although it feems to be his Opinion and Thought only; yet *in atrocioribus delictis punitur affectus licet non fequatur effectus*; and in this Cafe *fcribere eft agere.* Thirdly, It was refolved, That although his Books were inclofed in a black Box, and fent privately to the King; yet it was Treafon becaufe his Intent appeared by his Act. And *Yelverton* the King's Attorney faid, at Common Law, there were four Manner of Treafons, 1. Rebellion. 2. To deny the King's Title or Power Temporal or Spiritual. 3. To maintain or advance Superior Power to the King. 4. To bear the People in Hand, that the King's Government is Erroneous, Heretical, Unjuft. *William's* Cafe, *P.* 17 *Jac.* 1. *Roll's Rep. Part* 2. *p.* 88.

And fo note, that Treafon may be committed by Imagination, and a Refolution to *Intent.* perform or do any Act, although it be not brought to Effect, as in thefe former Cafes. This was the Cafe of * *Bightan* and *Terefh*, who were both hanged, only for that they *The Chamberlain of King Ahafuerus.* had a Will to kill the King *Ahafuerus*, and fought to lay Hands on him. *Efther* 2. 21, 22.

(*d*) If one that is a Mad-man do kill or attempt to kill the King, it is in him High Co. 4. 124. Treafon; whereas Petty Treafon, Homicide or Larceny, fhall not be imputed to fuch a Perfon. (*a*) *Vide Stat.* 33 *H.* 8. *cap.* 20. But *Coke* 3 *Inft.* 6. is otherwife. *Ideo quære.*

(*d*) One *Conftable* pointed to another, faying to his Friends, *Behold King Edward* Dyer 128. Abr. (who was then dead) and for thefe Words he had Judgment and Execution as a Traitor. *Dyer* 128. But *Co.* 7. 10. obferveth, That the Words were accompanied with other Circumftances, which appear not in our ufual printed Books.

(*a*) Treafon may be committed by Words, as to fay, The King being excommunica- *Words.* ted by the Pope, may be lawfully depofed and killed by any Perfon whatfoever; which Killing is no Murder. *P.* 13 *Jac.* 1. *Owen's Cafe.*

To intend the bodily Hurt of the King, or to affirm that the King is not King, or is an Heretick, Tyrant or Ufurper, *&c, Vide Stat.* 13 *Eliz. cap.* 1. To arreft or imprifon the King is Treafon, for that is the Way to kill him. *Roll's Rep.* 2 *Part, p.* 89.

(*d*) Alfo to deflower the King's Wife, his eldeft Daughter being unmarried, or his *P. 1.* eldeft Son and Heir's Wife, is High Treafon. 25 *E.* 3. 2.

(*a*) So it is if any Man fhall deflower any other of the King's Daughters; yea, or the *P. 1.* Nurfes of any of the King's Children, as Mr. *Briton* writeth, *fol.* 43. *Stamf. fol.* 1. *b.*

(*d*) To levy War againft the King, *&c.* in his Realm, is High Treafon. *War.*

(*a*) Note, That to detain or hold a Caftle or Fortrefs, againft the King, is to levy War againft the King. See *Br. Treafon*, 24, 25 *E.* 3. *cap.* 2.

.　(*d*) So

(*d*) So to confpire to levy War againft the King, *&c.* is High Treafon.

Dyer 298.   (*a*) Alfo to detain, keep or with-hold from or againft the King, any of his Ships, or Ordinance, or malicioufly to burn or deftroy any of the King's Ships; or malicioufly to bar any Haven within any of the King's Dominions; all and every of thefe are included within thefe Words, [*To levy War againft the King*] and fo be High Treafon. See *Br. Treafon* 24 *& Stat.* 14 *Eliz. cap.* 1. *& quære.*

To fell any Armor to the Enemy, or to furnifh the Enemy with Weapon or Munition, have been accounted Crimes treafonable. *W. Segar Norroy, of Honour Military and Civil, Page* 14.

If any Perfon having a Charge, fhall yield the fame unto the Enemy, this alfo is a Crime treafonable. *Ibid.*

So all Explorators or Spies, that betray our Secrets, and inform the Enemy thereof, are to be accounted Traitors. *Ibid.*

Dyer 298.   (*d*) To practice with a Governor of another Country to invade this Realm, is High Treafon; although fuch Practice be not put in Ure.

So to kill one that is fent in the King's Meffuage. 22 *Aff. Stamf.* 1.

21 E. 3. 23. **Stamf. 1. 1.**   To encounter in Fight and kill fuch as are affifting to the King in his Wars, or fuch as come to help the King, is High Treafon.

Thefe two laft Cafes were holden to be High Treafon, before the Statute of 25 *Ed.* 3.

P. 1.   To be adherent to the King's Enemies (aiding them, or giving them Aid or Comfort, in his Realm, or elfewhere) is High Treafon.

(*a*) To be of Council with another in levying feditious War.

A Subject.   If a Subject fhall go beyond the Sea, and there fhall adhere, or join himfelf with the King's Enemies, and there (in fuch Enmity) fhall die or be flain, this feemeth to be Treafon, and to be an Attainder in Law, without any more, *&c.* by the ancient Common Law of this Land; as appeareth, 8 *E.* 3. *Fitz. Dower* 106.

So if a Subject fhall join in Battle within the Realm to the King's Enemies, and fhall be flain in the Field; by the ancient Common Law of this Realm he fhall forfeit his Lands, Goods and Chattels, and his Blood fhall be corrupted, without any other Judgment, for that he himfelf is the Caufe that he cannot come to the Trial of Law in his Life-Time. *Pl.* 262. *a. &* 263. *a. Vide Stat.* 34 *E.* 3. *cap.* 12.

Alien Enemy. **Br. Treaf. 32.** **Dyer 145.** **Vide.**   (*d*) But if an alien Enemy come to invade this Realm, and be taken in War, he cannot be indicted of Treafon, but he fhall be put to Death by Martial Law. *Co.* 7. 6. *b.* Otherwife it is of an Alien whofe King is in League or at Peace with our King, or who is in this Realm in the Time of Peace, and hath the Benefit of the King's Peace, he fhall be indicted or arraigned of Treafon, and fhall have Judgment accordingly. An *Englifh* Traitor pleading that he is fubject to a foreign Prince, fhall notwithftanding (upon a *Nihil dicit* recorded) have Judgment as a Traitor. *Dyer* 300.

(*a*) If any Perfon fhall join the Arms of *England* with his own Arms, it feemeth to be High Treafon. See 38 *H.* 8. *Br. Treafon* 2.

If any Perfon fhall counterfeit the King's Arms, or the Arms of this Realm, it is High Treafon, as *M. Kitchin* hath it, *fol.* 12.

Seals. **P. 1. 2. 1 M. 6.** **Br. 3. 17.**   (*d*) To counterfeit the King's Great Seal, Sign Manual, Privy Signet or Privy Seal, is High Treafon. (*a*) But before the Statute 25 *E.* 3. thefe were Petty Treafon by the Common Law. *Fi.*

Vide 1 H. H. **P. C. 181,** **182.**   (*d*) So to take an old Seal from another Patent, *&c.* and put it to a new Patent, *&c.* yet *quære* whether this be Treafon, or but Mifprifion. (*a*) *M. Stamf. fol.* 3. *c.* faith, that it was adjudged to be Treafon in his Time. *Vide ibidem.* And fo faid Sir *H. Yelverton, Roll, Part* 2. *p.* 51.

One counterfeited the Crown in the Signet, and left out divers Words of the King's Stile, and added fome others that were not in the Stile of Purpofe that there might be a Variance between them; yet it was adjudged that this was a Counterfeiting by putting this falfe Seal to the Paper, and thereby getting the Great Seal to a Patent. *Robinfon's* Cafe, *M.* 16 *Jac. Roll's R. Part* 2. 50.

See Bract. lib. **3. f. 119. b.** **1 H. H. P. C.** **183.**   (*d*) Alfo *quære* of fuch, as without Authority fhall fet the King's Seal upon any Writing, or fhall fraudulently thruft a Writing (among others) to the Seal, and fo get it fealed.

Money. **25 Fd. 3. c. 2.** **1 Mar. 6.** **Co. L. 208.**   To counterfeit the King's Money, or any other Coin which is current within this Realm, is High Treafon.

                 (*a*) And

(*a*) And the Juſtices of Peace may inquire thereof, and thereupon may make out Proceſs, by *Capias* only, againſt thoſe which before them ſhall be hereof indicted. 3 H. 5.
cap. 7.

(*d*) So to forge or counterfeit ſuch Coin, though he uttereth it not.   Br. 27.

(*a*) And theſe Counterfeitings are where any common Perſon ſhall Coin any ſuch Money without the King's Warrant.

(*d*) To forge or counterfeit any Coin though not current by Proclamation in this   14 El. 3.
Realm, is Miſpriſion of Treaſon.   1 H. H. P. C. 210.

To clip, waſh, round, file, impair, diminiſh, lighten or falſify any Coin current with-   5 El. 11.
in this Realm, is Treaſon.   18 El. P. 5. 6.

To bring any falſe Money into this Realm, knowing it to be falſe, is High Treaſon :   1 & 2 P. & M.
But to bring ſuch Money into *England*, out of *Ireland*, is but Miſpriſion, though he   P. 3.
knoweth it, and uttereth it, *Quia Hibernia eſt quaſi membrum Angliæ*.   25 E. 3. c. 2. Finch.

If he which by the King's Warrant doth coin Money (either in *England*, *Ireland*,   3 H. 7. f. 10.
or elſewhere) making it much leſs in Weight than the ancient Ordinance; or coineth   Br. Treaſon
falſe Metal, it is Treaſon.   19.

(*a*) So to coin any Money, not having Authority or Warrant to do it, is High Treaſon. *Speculum Juſtic.*

To coin Farthing-tokens is no Treaſon, but is puniſhable; and ſo Sir *Francis Harvey*
delivered it in his Charge at *Cambridge* Summer Aſſiſes, *Ann.* 1631.

(*d*) To utter falſe Money made within the Realm, or other the King's Dominions,   3 H. 7. f. 10.
knowing thereof, is Miſpriſion of Treaſon.   Dyer 266.

(*a*) The Book called the *Mirror of Juſtices*, (or *Speculum Juſticiariorum*, written by
Mr. *Andrew Horn*) divides theſe former Treaſons into two Sorts, *ſc. Le Crime de Ma-
jeſte, & le Crime de Fauſonnerrie.* See alſo *Br. fol.* 118.

Le Crime de Ma-
jeſtie, 3. x.
{ Such as ſhall kill the King, or ſhall compaſs to do it.
Such as ſhall do or procure any Thing, *ad ſeditionem Domini Regis
vel Exercitus ſui.*
Such as ſhall deflower the King's Wife, his Daughter, or the Wife of
the King's Heir. }

Le Crime de Fauſonnerric is { Falſifying the King's Seal,
in two Manners, *ſc.* by { Falſifying his Money. }

(*d*) To kill the King's Chancellor, Treaſurer, Juſtices of either Bench, Juſtices in   25 Ed. 3. 2.
Eyre, Juſtices of Aſſiſe, or Juſtices of *Oyer* and *Terminer*, being in his or their Place,   P. 1.
doing his or their Office, is High Treaſon.

(*a*) But becauſe many other like Caſes of Treaſon might happen, *&c.* it was (by the
Statute 25 E. 3. *cap.* 2.) accorded, That if any other Caſe ſuppoſed Treaſon, which is
not in that Statute ſpecified, doth happen before any Juſtices, the Juſtices are not
to proceed thereupon, until the Cauſe be declared before the King and his Parliament, *&c.*

Alſo by the Statute of 1 *Mar. Parl.* 1. *& Seſſ.* 1. it is ordained, That no Act, Deed or
Offence, made Treaſon, Petty Treaſon or Miſpriſion of Treaſon, by any Act of Parliament or Statute, ſhall be taken, deemed or adjudged to be High Treaſon, Petty Treaſon
or Miſpriſion of Treaſon, but only ſuch as be declared to be Treaſon, Petty Treaſon or
Miſpriſion of Treaſon, in or by the Statute made 25 E. 3. any Statute made before or
after the ſaid Statute of 25 E. 3. or any other Declaration or Matter to the contrary notwithſtanding.

(*d*) Note, That the Counſellors, Procurers, Conſenters, Abettors and Aiders to any   *Acceſſory.*
of the forenamed Treaſons, be all within the Purview of the ſaid Statute of 25 Ed. 3.   Stamf. 5.
cap. 2. for in Treaſon all the Offenders be Principals.   p. 2, 3, 4, 5, 6. 19 H. 6. 476. P. 8.

To conceal or keep ſecret any High Treaſon, is Miſpriſion of Treaſon.   1 & 7 P. & M.
And all Receivers and Acceſſaries (to High Treaſon) after the Offence, ſeem to be   c. 10.
in Caſe of Miſpriſion. *Vide poſtea* Tit. *Acceſſory, cap.* 161.

(*a*) To ſet at large unlawfully, any Perſon that is committed to Priſon or Cuſtody for   1 H. 6. fol 5.
Treaſon, is Treaſon by the Common Law.   Br. Treaſon 11.

If a Man that is *Non compos mentis*, do any Act which if done by a Man of ſound Mind   Roll's Part 2
were Treaſon; it is Treaſon in him alſo.   P. 324.

4 M   If

Prison.
Vide 1 H.6 5.
If one that is in Prison for Felony shall break the Prison, whereby a Traitor being in the same Prison shall escape, this is Treason (in him that broke the Prison) by the Common Law.

Stamf. 32. 1.
So voluntarily to suffer any Person to escape, that is committed to Prison, or but under Arrest for Treason; this is Treason by the Common Law.

Dyer 98.
Co. 1. 28.
(d) If Two or more do conspire to commit High Treason, and some or any one of them after do commit and execute it; this is High Treason in them all by the Common Law.

Co. 8. Præf.
Note also, that the aforesaid Statute of 25 E. 3. *cap.* 2. is but a Declaration of the Common Law, for all the said Treasons in the said Statute mentioned, were Treason by the ancient Common Law of this Realm.

Treason by Statute.
Since which Time of King *Edw.* 3. divers others Offences were made Treason, as appeareth by the Statutes 21 *Rich.* 2. 2 *H.* 5. 6. 3 *H.* 5. 6. 8 *H.* 6. 6. 4 *H.* 7. 18. 22 *H.* 8. 9. 26 *H.* 8. 13. 27 *H.* 8. 2. 28 *H.* 8. 10 & 18. 31 *H.* 8. 8. 32 *H.* 8. 25. 33 *H.* 8. 21 35 *H.* 8. 1. & 1 *Ed.* 6. 12. all which were repealed again by the said Statute made 1 M Parl. 1. or before.

Seal and Money.
Also since the aforesaid Statute of Repeal there have been divers other Offences made or declared to be Treason, whereof some were but as an Addition to, or an Exposition of the Treasons before specified, and mentioned in the said Statute of 25 E. 3. *cap.* 2. *viz.* the Statutes 1 *M.* 6. 1 & 2 *P.* & *M.* 11. 5 *E.* 11. 18 *Eliz.* 1. and 14 *Eliz.* 3. by which five several Statutes last mentioned the Counterfeiting of the King's Seal, or Abusing his Coin, and Bringing in of false Coin, &c. are in some Particulars more fully prohibited than before, as may herein before appear.

There are also other Offences made High Treason (by Statute made since the Beginning of the Reign of Queen *Elizabeth*) and those especially made for the Preservation of the said Queen, her Heirs and Successors, and of the Dignity of the Imperial Crown of this Realm; and for the Avoidance of the Dishonours, Inconveniencies and Dangers growing to the whole State, by Means of the Jurisdiction of the See of *Rome*, heretofore usurped within this Realm, &c. as hereunder appeareth.

The Bishop of Rome.
5 El. 1.
P. Rome 1.
First, The Maintaining or Extolling the Authority of the Bishop or See of *Rome*, within any the King's Dominions; and the Procurers, Counsellors, Aiders and Maintainers thereof and every of them.

For the first Offence they shall incur the Danger of a *Præmunire*; the second Offence is High Treason. (a) But no Person shall be tendred the Oath the second Time, but such as have an Office or Ministry in the Church under a Bishop or Archbishop, or Persons refusing to observe the Offices of Divine Service after Admonition, or Depraving the Rites and Ceremonies of the Church, or that shall hear or say Mass.

Books.
(d) Also the Bringers over of any *Books*, that shall maintain, set forth, or defend any such Authority; and the Readers and Hearers of such Books, that shall justify them;

And such as shall deliver any such Books to others, with Allowance and Liking of the same.

Dyer 282.
Co. 7. Præf.
And the Printers and Utterers of such Books within this Realm; all and every such Offenders are (by the Judges) resolved and construed to be within the Meaning of the same Statute, 5 *El. cap.* 1. and their first Offence to be a *Præmunire*, the second is High Treason.

Oath of Supremacy.
5 El. 1.
P. Crown.
6 & 8.
Again, the Refusal of the Oath for the King's Supremacy (in all Cases, and over all Persons, &c.) after lawful Tender thereof made; the first Refusal is a *Præmunire*, the second is High Treason.

(a) The Justices of Peace, &c. may in their Quarter-Sessions inquire of all Things done against 5 *El.* 1. as of Offences against the Peace, and may certify such Presentment into the King's Bench within forty Days after such Presentment made, if in Term-time; or if not, then the first Day of the next Term, or shall forfeit 100 *l.* and the Justices of the King's Bench may hear and determine the Offence, as if the Person offending had been presented upon any Matter in the Statute of 16 *R.* 2.

3 Jac. 1. 4.
P. Recuf. 45.
(d) The second Refusal of the Oath of Allegiance, being tendred according to the Statute, is a *Præmunire.*

(a) Where the first Tender is before two Justices, and a Refusal thereupon, the Refusal in Sessions after incurs a *Præmunire*, but it seems by 3 *Jac.* 1. 4. a Refusal in Sessions without any precedent Tender makes a *Præmunire.*

I

(d) Again

(*d*) Again, to obtain or get from *Rome*, or from any claiming Authority from *Bulls.* thence, any Bull or Writing, (the Effect whereof is, to absolve and reconcile all those ¹³ El ². that will forsake their due Obedience to the King, and yield themselves to the Bishop of *P. Crown ᵗ & Præm. ;.* *Rome*,) or to give or take Absolution, by Colour of any such Bull ; or to publish, or put in Ure any such Bull ; every such Act shall be High Treason, as well in the Offenders, as in the Procurers, Abettors and Counsellors to the Fact.

And all Aiders, Comforters and Maintainers of any such Offender, after the Fact, *Ibid.* shall incur a *Præmunire*.

To conceal such Bull (or Writing) or such Absolution offered them, and not within ¹³ El ². six Weeks to disclose it to some of the King's Privy Council, is Misprision of Treason. *P. Rome 4.*

(*a*) To purchase or pursue (in the Court of *Rome*, or elsewhere) any Excommunica- *Præmunire.* tion, Bull or other Instrument, against the King, his Crown or Realm ; or to bring them within this Realm ; or to receive them, or to make Notification or any other Execution thereof, within this Realm, or without, every such Offender, their Procurers, Maintainers, Abettors and Counsellors, shall incur the Danger of a *Præmunire*, 16 R. 2. *cap. 5.*

(*d*) To practise beyond the Seas or upon the Seas, or elsewhere within the King's Do- ²³ El. 1. minions, to absolve, persuade or withdraw any Subject, or any within the said Domini- ³ Jac. 1. 4. ons, from their Obedience to his Majesty ; or to reconcile them to the Pope, or to draw *P. Rom. 7.* them to the *Romish* Religion (by Argument, Books or otherwise) for that Intent ; or to ³ Jac. 1. 4. move them to promise Obedience to the See of *Rome*, or to any other Prince, State or Potentate ; every such Person, and their Procurers, Aiders, Counsellors and Maintainers, knowing the same, are all guilty of High Treason.

To be willingly absolved, persuaded, withdrawn or reconciled, as aforesaid, or to pro- ³ Jac. 1. 4. mise any such Obedience, every such Person, and their Procurers, Counsellors, Aiders *P. Recuf. 49.* and Maintainers (knowing the same) shall be adjudged Traitors, except they submit *& Rom. 7.* themselves according to the Statute, within six Days after their Return into this Realm, *&c. Vide antea* Tit. *Recusants.*

To conceal any such Offence, and not within twenty Days to disclose it to some Ju- *P. Rome 8.* stice of Peace or other higher Officer, is Misprision of Treason by the Statute 23 *El.* 1.

Again, for any Jesuit, Priest, or other Ecclesiastical Person (born within any the *Jesuits.* King's Dominions) and made by an Authority from the Bishop of *Rome*, to come into, ²⁷ El. 2. be or remain, in any of the King's Dominions, contrary to the Statute, is High *P. Jesuits 2.* Treason.

To receive, relieve, aid or maintain any such Jesuit, *&c.* (being at Liberty, and *P. Jesuits 103.* knowing him to be a Jesuit, *&c.*) is Felony, (*a*) without Benefit of Clergy, 27 *El.* *cap.* 2. But that Clause relates to such as had before that Time taken Orders. See the Statute.

(*d*) To conceal such a Jesuit, *&c. &c.* not to discover them to some Justice of Peace, or other higher Officer, within twelve Days, is punishable by Fine and Imprisonment.

And the Justice of Peace or other such Officer, to whom such a Person shall be dis- ²⁷ El 2. covered, if within twenty-eight Days they give not Information thereof to some of the *P. Jesuits 4.* King's Council, *&c.* they shall forfeit 200 Marks. *See* Tit. Recusants.

(*a*) The Pope's Bulls in *Latin* called *Bullæ*, are so called, *Quod Bullis plumbeis ob- Bulls* *signentur ; and in which *consilium & voluntas Papæ continentur.*

What the ancient Law was for concealing of High Treason, *Bract. lib. 3. fol.* 418. sheweth us, saying, *Si sit aliquis, qui alium noverit inde esse culpabilem, &c. statim & sine intervallo aliquo accedere debet ad ipsum Regem, si possit, vel mittere (si venire non possit) ad aliquem Regi familiarem, & omnia ei manifestare per ordinem :* And he must not stay in any one Place by the Space of two Nights or Days : And if he be negligent therein, he shall be taken as consenting. See more, Misprision, *cap. seq.*

(*d*) If any of the King's Subjects (not being a Jesuit or Ecclesiastical Person) which *Seminary* are or shall be brought up in any Seminary or College of Jesuits, or Seminary beyond the ²⁷ El. 2. Sea, shall not (within six Months after Proclamation in that Behalf to be made in *Lon- P. Jesuits 4.* *don*, *&c.*) return into this Realm, and within two Days after such Return (before the Bishop of the Diocese, or two Justices of Peace of the County where he shall arrive) submit himself to the King's Laws, and take the Oath of Supremacy, (set forth 1 *El.* 1.) then every such Person which shall otherways return, or come into this Realm, or any other his Majesty's Dominions, without such Submission, shall be adjudged a Traitor.

For (as one faith) it may juftly be feared, not only of all Jefuits and Seminary Priefts. but alfo of all fuch other (jefuited) Perfons whatfoever that fhall come into his Majefty's Dominions, or return into this Realm, contrary to this Statute, That it is not Faith but Faction; not Truth, but Treafon; no Religion, but Rebellion, which is the Caufe of their Coming.

27 Fl. 2.
P. Jefuits 5. To convey, deliver or fend, yield or give any Relief, to or for any Jefuit or Prieft &c. or other Perfon abiding in any Seminary beyond the Seas, &c. is a *Præmunire.*

Agnus Dei.
13 El. 2.
P. Rome 5. To bring into this Realm any *Agnus Dei,* Croffes, Pictures, Beads, or fuch like fuperftitious Things, confecrated by Authority from the Pope, and to deliver them, or to offer or caufe them to be delivered to any Subject of this Realm, is a *Præmunire,* as well in fuch Perfon, as alfo in them that fhall receive any fuch Thing, to the Intent to ufe or wear it.

13 El. 2.
P. Rome 6. The Perfon to whom fuch *Agnus Dei, &c.* fhall be offered, muft apprehend the Party offering the fame, and bring him to the next Juftice of Peace, if he can; or elfe muft within three Days difclofe his Name and Place of Abode, to the Ordinary or fome Juftice of Peace in that County: And if he received any Thing, he muft deliver the fame within one Day to a Juftice of Peace of that County, where the Party fo receiving the fame, fhall then be refident or happen to be; and fo doing fhall be pardoned And that Juftice of Peace within fourteen Days muft difclofe the fame to one of th King's Majefty's Privy Council, upon Danger of a *Præmunire.*

(*a*) The former Offences againft the Statute 5 *Eliz.* 1. and 13 *Eliz.* 2. and 23 *El.* 1 may alfo be inquired of by the Juftices of Peace in the Seffions. *Vide Eliz. cap.* 1. & hi cap. 20.

Copy of the Indictment.
7 Will. 3.
cap. 3. Perfons indicted for High Treafon, or for Mifprifion of Treafon, fhall have a tru Copy of the whole Indictment, but not the Names of the Witneffes, five Days at leaf before the Trial, paying for it not exceeding 5 *s.*

Allowed Counfel and Witneffes on Oath. And they fhall be admitted to make their Defence by Counfel, and by Witneffes on Oath, the faid Counfel not exceeding Two, to be affigned by the Court, and to have Accefs to the Prifoner at feafonable Times.

* No Evidence fhall be given of an Overt Act not expref-ly laid in the Indictment. There muft be two lawful Witneffes to the fame Overt-Act, or one of them to one Overt Act *, and the other of them to another Overt Act of the fame Species of Trea fon, unlefs the Prifoner confefs the fame in Court, ftand mute, or refufe to plead, o challenge above 35 Jurors.

Traitor outlawed. A Traitor outlawed may come in and be tried, and have Benefit of the Act, when by Law an outlawed Perfon comes in.

Two diftinct Treafons in one Indictment. Where two diftinct Treafons are laid in one Indictment, one Witnefs to one, and another Witnefs to the other of the faid Treafons, fhall not be two Witneffes to the fame Treafon.

Profecution within 3 Years. The Profecution muft be within three Years after the Offence committed, unlefs fo a Defign to affaffinate and poifon the King.

Copy of the Panel. The Prifoner fhall have a Copy of the Panel two Days before his Trial, and he fhal have the like Procefs of the Court to compel his Witneffes to appear, as is ufually granted to compel Witneffes to appear againft him.

Indictment fhall not be quafhed for Infufficiency.
Judgment may be reverfed by a Writ of Error. Indictment fhall not be quafhed for mif-reciting, mif-fpelling, falfe or impropes Latin, unlefs the Exception is made in Court before any Evidence given; but a Judg ment may be reverfed by a Writ of Error.

Trial of a Peer. All the Peers who have a Right to fit and vote in Parliament, fhall be fummoned a leaft twenty Days before the Trial of a Peer or Peerefs for High Treafon; and every Perfon fo fummoned and appearing, fhall vote at fuch Trial, firft taking the Oaths of Allegiance and Supremacy, and repeating the Declaration againft Tranfubftantiation.

The Act doth not extend to Impeachments, or to counterfeiting the Coin. This Act fhall not extend to Impeachments or other Proceedings in Parliament, nor to Treafons in counterfeiting the Coin, the Great Seal, &c.

Coining Inftruments. No Perfon fhall buy or fell any coining Inftruments, or make Grainings round the Edges of Money, or gild or plate the Coin under Pain of High Treafon.

Pretended Prince of Wales attainted.
13 W. 3. c 3. The pretended Prince of *Wales* ftands convicted and attainted of High Treafon, and if any of the King's Subjects fhall correfpond with him, either in Perfon, or by Letters or otherwife, or with any Perfon employed by him, knowing the Perfon to be

o employed, or fhall remit any Sum of Money, knowing it to be for his Ufe; this
s Treafon.

And if any Offence againft this Act fhall be done out of *England*, it fhall be tried in
any County here.

Witneffes in a Trial for Treafon or Felony fhall be admitted to give Evidence on Oath. *Witneffes on Oath. 1 Ann. c. 9.*

He who oppofes the Succeffion to the Crown, after the Death of the Queen, accord- *Oppofing the Succeffion after the Death of Queen.* ng to the feveral Acts of Limitation of the Crown, and fhall malicioufly, advifedly, and directly attempt it by any Overt Act or Deed; fuch Offender, his Abettor, Pro- curer and Comforter, knowing the faid Offence to be done, fhall be guilty of High *1 Ann. Stat.2. c. 17.* Treafon.

He who maintains the Pretender's Title, or affirms that the King or Queen, by *Maintaining the Pretender's* Authority of Parliament, cannot limit the Succeffion of the Crown, fhall be guilty of *Title.* High Treafon. *6 Ann. c. 7.*

He who apprehends a Perfon who hath counterfeited the current Coin, &c. or for *Clipping and coining Money.* Gain hath clipp'd, wafhed, filed, or diminifhed the fame, or who hath imported any clipp'd, falfe or counterfeited Money, and profecutes fuch Offender to Conviction, fhall *6 & 7 W. 3.* within a Month after receive of the Sheriff of the County 40 *l.* upon Demand, tendring *c. 17.* a Certificate under the Hand of the Judge who tried the Offender, certifying the Con- *Apprehending a Clipper, &c.* viction of fuch Traitor, and that he was taken and profecuted by the Perfon claiming the *fhall have 40 l.* Reward; and if there fhould be any Difference amongft the Claimants where there are more than one, the Judge, &c. fhall fettle the fame; and the Sheriff failing in Pay- ment of the Reward, fhall forfeit to the Party grieved double that Sum, with treble Cofts to be recovered by Action of Debt in the Courts at *Weftminfter.*

None, (except Perfons employed in his Majefty's Mint, or authorifed by the Trea- *Making or mending any* fury) fhall knowingly make or mend any Die, Puncheon, Counter-puncheon, Matrix, *coining Tools.* Stamp, Pattern or Mould, &c. in or upon which there fhall be impreffed the Figure or *8 & 9 Will. 3.* Refemblance of both, or either Side of the current Coin of this Realm, nor make or *c. 26. made perpetual by* mend, or begin or affift to make or mend any edging Tool, Inftrument, (not of com- *7 Ann. c. 25.* mon Ufe in any Trade) but contrived for marking Money round the Edges with Letters, Gravings, or other Marks of Figures refembling thofe on the Edges of Money coined in the King's Mint, nor any Prefs for Coinage, or any cutting Engine, for cut- ting round Blanks by the Force of Screws, out of flatted Bars of Gold, Silver, or other Metal; nor knowingly buy or fell, hide or conceal, or (without lawful Authority or *Concealing or having them in* juft Excufe) have in his Cuftody any Puncheons, or other the Inftruments before-men- *their Cuftody.* tioned, on Pain that they, their Counfellors, Procurers, Aiders and Abettors, fhall be guilty of High Treafon.

He who (without Authority) fhall convey out of the King's Mints any of the afore- *Conveying Tools out of the Mint.* faid Inftruments; and all Perfons receiving, hiding or concealing them, are guilty of High Treafon.

He who makes Letters or Grainings, or other Marks or Figures like thofe on the Edg- *Making Letters or Grainings.* ings of Money coined at the Mints, and Colouring, Gilding or Cafing over any Coin re- fembling the current Coin of this Kingdom, or any round Blanks of bafe Metal, or of coarfe Gold or Silver of a fit Size and Figure to be coined into counterfeit mill'd Money, refembling the faid Gold or Silver Coin, or fhall gild over fuch filver Blanks, &c. fhall be guilty of High Treafon.

Perfons offending againft the laft mentioned Act, may be profecuted at any Time with- *Profecution* in fix Months after the Offence committed. *within fix Months. 1 Ann. c. 9.*

See more fully of High Treafon *in* 1 Hale's Hift. Plac. Cor. Chap. 10. *and the following*;
And 1 Hawk. P. C. Chap. 17.

C H A P. CXLI.

Mifprifion.

(*n*) **M**Ifprifion fignifieth in our Law, Neglect, Negligence or Overfight, in not re- vealing a Treafon or Felony, when we know it to be committed, or about to be committed; fo making a light Account of fuch capital Offences: See *infra*; and fee *High Treafon*, the Statute 13 *Car.* 2. *cap.* 1.

4 N   (*d*) There

(d) There be certain Offences, which by the Common Law are Mifprifion of Treafon, or at leaft punifhable in the fame Degree, and more. As,

22 E. 3. 19.
Stamf. 38. b.
To draw a Sword to ftrike a Juftice fitting in the Place of Judgment, is Mifprifion of Treafon.

P. R. 117.
Ibid.
Br. Contempts 9. Fitz. Judg. 174. Fi.
To ftrike a Juror in the Prefence of the Juftices, fitting in Place of Judgment.

Stamf. 38. c.
Dyer 188.
Fitz. Cor. 285.
F.
To ftrike another in *Weftminfter-Hall*, fitting in any of the King's Courts there.

Br. Pain 16.
Stamf. 38.
(a) So to draw any Weapon, therewithal to ftrike any Perfon in the Prefence of the Juftices, or to make an Affray in their Prefence.

Ibid.
So to refcue any fuch Offender.

See Stamf. 38.
d.
So to ftrike any Perfon in the King's Court (Palace or other Houfe) the King being then in his Court. And Judgment was given accordingly in fuch Cafe upon a Knight, *Ann.* 33 H. 8. for ftriking another at *Greenwich*, the King being there. *Br. Ibid.* Yet now fee the Statute of 33 H. 8. 12. That fuch an Offender in the King's Palace (although he fhall draw Blood by Striking there) he fhall forfeit neither the Profits of his Lands, nor his Goods, but fhall lofe his right Hand, be imprifoned during his Life, and fhall pay Fine and Ranfom at the King's Pleafure: And fo now fuch an Offence done in the King's Palace, fhall not have fo grievous a Punifhment, as if it be done in *Weftminfter-Hall*.

Stamf. 38. c.
(d) But in the three firft Cafes, the Offender fhall have Judgment as in Mifprifion of Treafon, and befides fhall have his right Hand cut off. *Br. Peine* 16. *Fitz. Forf.* 21. *Dyer* 188.

Ibid.
If one of the King's Juftices do arreft one who made an Affray before him fitting in Place of Juftice, and a Stranger fhall refcue the Prifoner, whereby he efcapeth; this is Mifprifion of Treafon in them both.

Stamf. 37. d.
Cromp. 44.
Note, That every Treafon or Felony does include Mifprifion, fo that where any Perfon hath committed Treafon or Felony, the King may caufe the Offender to be indicted and arraigned but of Mifprifion.

Mifprifion defined.
Stamf. 37.
Stat. 5 R. 6.
c. 11.
Mifprifion is properly, when one knoweth that another hath committed or is about for to commit any Treafon or Felony, but was not, or is not confenting thereto, and will not difcover the Offender to the King or his Council, or to fome Magiftrate, but concealeth the Offence.

Stamf. 37.
(a) Compounding of Felonies is alfo Mifprifion of Felony at the leaft, if it be not Felony.

The Judgment.
Br. Trea. 19.
& Stamf. 38.
For Mifprifion of Treafon, the Offender fhall forfeit to the King his Goods and Chattels for ever, and the Profits of his Lands during his Life, and alfo fhall be imprifoned during his Life.

The Forfeiture.
See Br. Treaf.
25. and Finch,
lib. 2.
For Mifprifion of Felony, the Offender fhall be only fined (and ranfomed) by the Juftices, before whom he fhall be attainted, and fhall be committed to Prifon until he hath paid his Fine.

Judgment in High Treafon.
3 H. 7. t. 10.
Vide Co. L.
133. & 372.
For High Treafon, the Offender fhall be hanged, cut down alive, and quartered, and he fhall forfeit all his Lands and Goods to the King: Yea, at this Day, his Lands intailed fhall be forfeited, and his Wife fhall lofe her Dower, and his Blood fhall be corrupted, (faving in certain Cafes.) *Vide Stamf.* 182 & 187. *Co.* 1. 103. 3. 10. & 7. 33, 34. & *Dyer* 289. & 332. *Plo.* 237. b. 249. b. 554. b. & 559. (a) *Eft enim tam grave crimen iftud quod vix permittitur hæredibus quod vivant : Et fi aliquando forte ad fucceffionem admittuntur tales, hoc magis erit de gratia quam de jure.* Bract. lib. 3. fol. 118.

Woman.
But the Judgment and Sentence of Condemnation upon a Woman in Cafe of Treafon is, that fhe fhall be drawn upon a Hurdle unto the Place of Execution, and there burned. *Stamf.* 182. c.

P. Præm. 1, 5.
6, 19.
Co. 7. pref.
& 11. 63.
Co. 8. 130.
Br. Præm.
6, 19.
(d) In cafe of *Præmunire*, the Offender fhall forfeit all his Lands which he hath in Fee for ever, and all his Goods and Chattels to the King, but his Lands, whereof he hath an Eftate-tail, he fhall forfeit only during his Life; and fhall be imprifoned during his Life. (a) But fome do hold, that if the Offender fhall forfeit nothing, if he appeareth at the Day of the *Præmunire* returned. See the Statute & B. *Præm.* 6. & Cromp. *Autor. des Courts* 97. Yet others do hold, that as upon the Statute of 16 R. 2. *cap.* 5. the Offenders fhall forfeit their Lands and Goods if they be attainted (*Br. Præm.* 6. & 20.) fo upon the Statute of 27 E. 3. if the Offender do appear and plead, and be found Guilty, he fhall have

the

2

the Judgment of *Præmunire, fc.* to be put out of the King's Protection, and fhall for- ^{The Judgment} feit his Lands, Goods and Chattels to the King, and his Body fhall be imprifoned during ^{in Præmunire.} his Life, (or until he hath made fine and Ranfom at the King's Will.) See the Statute and *Co.* 11. 34. and the old *Natur. Bre. fol.* 159. *Co. L.* 130, *&* 391.

(*d*) Now for the Offenders in High Treafon, Mifprifion of Treafon, and *Præmunire,* ^{9 H. 3. 1.} although the Juftices of Peace (by their Commiffion, nor by Statute) cannot meddle with ^{Br. Trea. 5.} them in the very Point of their Offences, faving in fome Particulars, and that by way of ^{Peace 7.} Inquiry only, which you may fee *Lamb.* 496. . Yet for that all Treafons, and fuch other Offences are againft the Peace of the King, and of the Realm, therefore upon Complaint made to the Juftice of Peace, or other Knowledge had by him of any fuch Offenders, it fhall be his Part to caufe them to be apprehended, and to join with fome other Juftice of Peace in taking their Examination, and the Information upon Oath of fuch as bring them, or of others that can prove any Thing material againft them, and to put the fame in Writing (under the Hands of the Informers) and then to commit the Offenders to the Gaol; and alfo to bind over by Recognizance all fuch as do declare any Thing material, to appear and give Evidence againft fuch Offenders, before the Privy Council, or in the King's Bench, or at the Affizes and Gaol-delivery, or elfewhere, when they fhall be called upon reafonable Warning, and after to certify their Doings therein to fome of the Lords of his Majefty's Council.

Note, that all Treafons, Mifprifion of Treafon, and Concealment of Treafon, done or ^{26H. 8.a. 13.} committed out of the Realm, fhall be inquired of, and tried within the Realm, *fc.* in the King's Bench, or elfe before fpecial Commiffioners. See Stat. 35 *H.* 8. *cap.* 2. *&* 5 *E.* 6. *cap.* 11. *P. Treaf.* 10. *& Dyer* 287, 298, 132, 360. *Co.* 7. 23. *& 11,* 63.

See alfo for Mifprifion of Treafon, 1 *Hawk.* Chap. 20. *and* 1 *Hale* Hift. *P. C.* Chap. 28.

C H A P. CXLII.

Petty Treafon.

PETTY Treafon is, when wilful Murder is committed (in the Eftate Oeconomical) ^{Defined.} upon any Subject, by one that is in *Subjection,* and oweth *Faith, Duty and private* ^{25 E. 3. c. 2.} *Obedience to the Party murdered,* as in thefe Cafes following. ^{P. Treaf. 8.}

If a *Servant* malicioufly killeth his or her *Mafter or Miftrefs,* this was Petty Treafon ^{By a Servant.} by the Common Law. ^{Ibid. & 10.}

Stamf. 10. 1. Br. 8. 12. & Co. 11. 34. & ^{21 Aff. 30.} ^{25 E. 3. c. 2.}

A Servant of the Age of thirteen Years killed her Miftrefs; it was adjudged Petty ^{Ibid. Fitz.} Treafon. ^{Cor. 118.} ^{B. Treaf. 12.}

A *Servant* departed out of Service, and a Year after killeth his Mafter upon Malice con- ^{Stamf. 10.} ceived when he was in the faid Service; it is Petty Treafon. ^{B.Treaf. 151.} ^{33 Aff. 1. 7.} ^{Co. 1. 99. b.}

A *Servant* doth procure another to kill his Mafter, who killeth him in the Servant's ^{See Plo. 100. a.} Prefence; this is Petty Treafon in the Servant, and Murder in the other. ^{&Br.Cor.119.} ^{& Quære.}

But if the Stranger doth kill the Mafter in the Servant's Abfence, then the Servant is ^{Dyer 128.} only acceffory to the Murder, but it is no Petty Treafon in him.

A Servant confpireth with a Stranger to rob his Mafter, and at a Time appointed in the ^{Dyer 128.} Night, he letteth in the Stranger into the Houfe, and leads him to his Mafter's Chamber, ^{Vide 1 H. H.} and the Stranger killeth his Mafter, the Servant ftanding by but faying nothing, this is ^{P. C. 378,} Petty Treafon in the Servant, and Murder in the Stranger. (*a*) Yet by fome, this is but ^{379,381,382.} Murder in the Servant. *Ibid. &* 40 *Aff.* Br. *Cor.* 119. For where the Principal is but a Felon, the Acceffary cannot be a Traitor. See *Plo.* 100. *a.* that the Servant is a Principal in this Cafe, and after, Tit. *Acceffary.*

(*d*) A Servant commands one to beat his Mafter, and he killeth him, this is Petty ^{Cromp. 20.} Treafon in the Servant, if he *be prefent.*

A Servant upon Malice prepenfed, fhooteth at a Stranger, and miffeth him, and killeth ^{Cromp. 20.} his Mafter being by; this is Petty Treafon in the Servant, (though he intended no Hurt to his Mafter) becaufe he intended Murder thereby.

The

The Wife.
B.Treaf. 301.

The Wife malicioufly killeth her Husband, this is Petty Treafon.   25 *Ed.* 3. *cap.* 2.
The Husband malicioufly killeth his Wife; this is but Murder.

The Reafon of this Difference is, for that the one is in *Subjection* and oweth Obedience, and not the other.

Dyer 332.

The Wife and a Servant do confpire to kill the Husband, and the Servant killeth him in the Wife's Abfence; this is Petty Treafon in them both.

Dyer ibid.
1 H. H. P. C.
378, 379.

The Wife and a Stranger do confpire to kill her Husband, and he killeth her Husband in the *Wife's Abfence*; this is no Petty Treafon in the Wife, but Murder in the Stranger, and fhe fhall be hanged as acceffary to the Murder.

Crom. 20, 21.

Alfo where the Wife or Servant procuring, confpiring, or practifing fuch Murder, at the Time of fuch Murder is in the fame Houfe, though they be not prefent thereat, but are in another Room, yet it is Petty Treafon in them, as by two Cafes reported by Mafter *Crompton* in 4 & 5 *Mar.*

Plo. 474.
Co. 9. 81.
See more in the Title of Murder.

The Wife poifoneth a Thing, to the Intent to poifon her Husband therewith, the Husband eateth it, and becometh very fick thereof, but recovereth; after a Stranger eateth thereof, and dieth thereof; this is only Murder in the Wife.

Crom. 20.

The Wife poifoneth an Apple, to the Intent to poifon a Stranger therewith, and layeth it to that Purpofe in a fecret Place, and the Husband by Chance eateth it, and dieth thereof within a Year and a Day; this is Petty Treafon in the Wife, for that fhe intended Murder thereby.

Crom. 20.

The Wife poifoneth an Apple or other Thing, and delivereth it to *B.* (knowing nothing of the Poifon) to give to *C.* and *B.* giveth it to the Husband, (without the Affent of the Wife) who eateth thereof in the Wife's Abfence, and he dieth thereof; this is Petty Treafon in the Wife.

(*a*) And yet if *A.* lay impoifoned Fruit for a Stranger, being his Enemy, and his Father or Mother come and eat it, Sir *Fr. Bacon* maketh a *Quære*, whether this be Petty Treafon, becaufe it is not altogether *Crimen paris gradus.* But faith he, *in criminalibus jufficit generalis malitia intentionis cum facto paris gradus.* Regula 15. pag. 65, 66.

The Child.
21 E. 3 17.
Co. 7. 13. b.
B. Treaf. 6.
Vide Ba. 53.

(*d*) The Child malicioufly killeth his Father or Mother, this is Petty Treafon (although the Father or Mother at the fame Time gave neither Meat, Drink, nor Wages to fuch Child:) But it is Treafon in the Child, in Refpect of the Duty of Nature violated.

Crom. 21.

A Baftard killeth his Mother; this feemeth Petty Treafon, for the Mother is certainly known.

(*a*) By the Law of God, he that only fmiteth, or curfeth his Father or his Mother, fhall die the Death. *Ex.* 21. 15 & 17.

Dalifon's Rep.
1 M. 1.

The Son or Daughter-in-Law, killeth the Father or Mother-in-Law, with whom they dwell, and have Meat and Drink; it is Petty Treafon, although fuch Child take no Wages; but the Indictment fhall be by the Name of Servant.

A Clerk.
25 E. 3. c. 2.
P. Treaf. 7.
19 H. 6. 47.

A Clerk, or any *Ecclefiaftical Perfon*, malicioufly kills his Ordinary, or Superior, to whom he oweth Obedience, this is Petty Treafon.

(*a*) Note, that unto the Bifhop of every Diocefe, the Clerks within their Diocefe do owe Faith and Obedience, which is called Canonical Obedience.

Finch 137.

(*d*) Note further, that whatfoever Act will prove Murder between Strangers, the fame will make Petty Treafon from the Servant to his Mafter, from the Wife to the Husband, from the Child to the Father or Mother, and from the Clerk to his Prelate or Ordinary, *Mutatis mutandis.*

1 H. H. P. C.
378.

(*a*) Otherwife it is between thefe Perfons, where it is not wilful Murder: As if the Servant fhould kill his Mafter upon a fudden falling out, without any Malice precedent or by Mif-adventure, or *fe defendendo*, thefe are not Petty Treafon, neither fhall the Indictment be *Proditorie, &c.* And fo of the Wife or Child.

Break Prifon.
1 H. 6. 5.
Stamf. 12. a.

(*d*) Breaking of Prifon, whereby Prifoners that were therein for Treafon do efcape, this is alfo Petty Treafon.

Pirates.
40 Aff. p. 25.
Br.Coro. 119.
& Treafon 16.
Stamf. 11. b.

(*a*) A *Norman* being Captain of an *Englifh* Ship, wherein alfo were certain *Englifhmen*, and they robbed upon the Sea; this was adjudged Felony in the *Norman*, and Treafon in the *Englifhmen*; and they were drawn and hanged.

But at this Day all Felonies, Robberies, Murders, and Pyracies, done upon the High Sea, are to be tried before the Lord Admiral in the Court of the Admiralty, and according to the Civil Law. Or they may be attainted before Commiffioners, by Force of the Stat.

2   of

of 23 *H.* 8. 15. and then they fhall forfeit their Lands, and their Blood fhall be corrupt- *Co. L.* 39.
ed. *Co. L.* 39.

(*d*) Alfo it hath been adjudged Petty Treafon in fome Books, and Felony in fome *Indictor.* others, for an Indictor, in Cafe of Treafon or Felony, to difcover the King's Counfel and *Stamf.* 11.36. their Fellows (*fc.* to difcover to others, what Perfon they have indicted; or if they have *Fitz. Cor.* indicted any, then to fhew to others what they have done therein.) But now that Offence 207, 272. is taken only to be finable to the King. *Br. Cor.* 113.

The Punifhment of Petty Treafon is this; the Man fo offending fhall be drawn and *Punifhment.* hanged; the Woman fhall be burned alive, in Cafe as well for Petty Treafon, as of High 1 R. 3, 4. Treafon, 1 *R.* 3. 4. But in Cafes of Felonies, the Judgment both of Man and Woman *Br. Treaf.* 11, is to be hanged. 30.

(*a*) Alfo no Perfon or Perfons, be they Lay or within Holy Orders, &c. which fhall be attainted, or found guilty of any Manner of Petty Treafon, nor any Acceffory thereto before the Fact, fhall be admitted to have the Benefit of his or their Clergy. See the Stat. 12 *H.* 7. *cap.* 7. 23 *H.* 8. *cap.* 1. 28 *H.* 8. *cap.* 1. 32 *H.* 8. *cap.* 3. 1 *E.* 6. *cap.* 12. & 4 & 5 *Ph.* & *Ma. cap.* 4.

(*d*) The Forfeiture for Petty Treafon is, the King fhall have his Goods, and for his *Forfeiture.* Lands the King fhall have *annum, diem* & *vaftum,* and the Efcheat thereof fhall be to every Lord, of his own proper Fee. (*a*) But for Petty Treafon or Felony, if the Offender hath but an Eftate-tail in his Land, he fhall forfeit them but during his Life. *Stamf.* 186, 187. And for Petty Treafon, if the Husband be attainted, the Wife fhall be barred of her Dower. *Co. L.* 37.

(*d*) The Juftices of Peace may inquire of Petty Treafon, as of Felony; And out of *Plo.* 186. their Seffions, every Juftice of Peace may deal with the Offenders therein, as in Cafe of Felony, by Examination of the Offenders, by taking Information againft them, and binding over the Informers to the General Gaol-delivery, and committing the Offenders to the Gaol.

C H A P. CXLIII.

Of Felonies by the Common Law.

(*a*) **F**Elony; by fome this Word is derived, *Quafi felleo animo factum. L.* & *Co.* 4. 124. *Ideo dicta eft felonia, quia fieri debet felleo animo* (with a Mind as bitter as Gall.) *Minfh. verbo* Felon, faith it cometh of the *French* Word Felon, *id eft, atrox, crudelis: Vel a velando, cum celari* & *occultari femper velit. Felonia eft omne crimen capitale infra læfam Majeftatem.*

Thus generally it feems to be taken in many Statutes, as particularly in the Statute of 3 *Eliz. cap.* 9. where it is faid, that all Perfons fhall be ready and apparelled at the Commandment of the Sheriff, and Cry of the Country, to purfue and arreft Felons: And they that will not fo do, and thereof be attainted, fhall make a grievous Fine to the King; and if Default be in the Lord of a Franchife, the King fhall feife his Franchife. And if any Sheriff, Coroner, or any other Bailiff, for Prayer, Fear, or Affinity, that his Kindred or Relation by Birth, or Marriage, fhall conceal, confent, or procure to conceal Felonies; will not do their Offices, and be thereof attainted, fhall have one Year's Imprifonment, and pay a grievous Fine, and if he hath not whereof to pay, fhall have three Years Imprifonment.

(*d*) Felonies by the Common Law are of divers Sorts; as Homicide, Burglary, Theft, Burning of Houfes, Refcous, and Efcape.

Homicide moft properly is, *Hominis occifio ab homine facta;* for if a Man be killed *Homicide.* by a Beaft (as a Horfe or a Dog) or by any other Thing or Mif-chance, although that be *Hominis cædium,* (of which two Words Homicide is derived) yet in fuch Cafes it is not aptly nor ufually faid, that Homicide is committed, but only a Man is faid to be flain. *Bracton* 120.

Others do thus define or defcribe it, Homicide is the felonious Killing of one Man by another within the Realm, and living under the King's Protection. *Lam.* 233.

But to kill a Man *beyond the Seas,* or to ftrike and give one a mortal Wound beyond the Seas or upon the Sea, whereupon he dieth upon the Land, within this Realm, thefe Homicides are not punifhable as Felony by the Common Law; for that they cannot be inquired of, nor tried here; for in criminal Cafes, the Rule is, *Ubi quis delinquit ibi punietur.*

4 O *tur.*

tur. So *Co.* 2. 93. 6. 47. But in Treafon it is otherwife. See hereof, *Paulo antea.* (*a*) And yet all Appeals to be made of Things done out of the Realm, fhall be tried before the Conftable and Marfhal of *England*, by the Statute 1 *H.* 4. *cap.* 14. So that if any of the King's Subjects fhall be killed by another of the King's Subjects in any Foreign Realm, the Wife or Heir of him which is fo flain, may have an Appeal thereof in *England*, before the Conftable and Marfhal, *&c. Stamf.* 65. *b. Vide Co. L.* 74.

Alfo to kill a Man upon the Sea, although it be not triable by the Common Law, yet it is Felony, and is inquirable and triable in the Admiral Court; for thofe of the Admiralty have Jurifdiction, where both the Stroke and Dying is upon the Sea; otherwife not. And therefore in 25 *El.* it was adjudged in one *Lacy's* Cafe, that where the faid *Lacy* had ftrucken *Peacock*, and given him a mortal Wound upon the Sea, whereof *Peacock* died at *Scarborough* in *Yorkfhire*, the faid *Lacy* was difcharged thereof, for that thofe of the County of *York* could not inquire of the Death without Inquiry of the Stroke; and the Stroke they could not inquire, for that it was not given within any Part of the County. See *Co.* 2. 93. *&* 5. 106, 107, *& Stat.* 15 *R.* 2. *cap.* 3. *& 2 H.* 5. *cap.* 6. But yet by the Statutes made *Anno* 27 *H.* 8. *cap.* 4. *& 28 H.* 8. *cap.* 15. all Offences of Piracy, Robbery, Murder, or other Felony done or committed upon the Sea, (or in any other Haven, River, or Creek, where the Admiral pretends to have Jurifdiction) fhall be inquired of, heard, tried, and determined in fuch Shires and Places within the Realm, and before fuch Perfons as fhall be limited and appointed by the King's Commiffion, and after the common Courfe of the Laws of the Land, ufed for Felonies committed within the Realm; and fuch as fhall be fo convict of any fuch Offence, fhall have and fuffer fuch Pains of Death, and Forfeiture of Lands and Goods, as if they were convict of Murder or Felony done upon the Land.

2 Geo. 2.
c. 21.

And now by 2 *G.* 2. *cap.* 21. if any Perfon be felonioufly ftricken or poifoned upon the Sea, or at any Place out of *England*, and dies in *England*, or ftricken or poifoned in *England*, and dies on the Sea, or out of *England*; in either Cafe an Indictment found by Jurors of the County in which fuch Death, Stroke or Poifoning happened refpectively, fhall be as effectual at Law againft Principals and Acceffaries, and all Courts fhall proceed in the fame Manner, and Offenders have the fame Trial, *&c.* (Challenges for the Hundred excepted) as if the Stroke, Poifoning and Death had happened in the County where the Indictment is found.

Lam. 232.   (*d*) But whether he that is flain, be an Alien, or a Denizen, an *Englifhman* or Stranger, it maketh no Difference, if he live within this Realm under the King's Protection.

Co. 7. 13, 17.   To kill a Man that is attainted of Felony or Treafon, is Felony; for none may kill or
Crom. 24.   put to Death any of thefe, but the Officer of Juftice, and by lawful Warrant.
Doct. & Stud.
133.
Co. L. 128. b.

Co. 7. 14.   Alfo to kill a Man attainted upon a *Præmunire*, is Felony.

(*a*) Alfo to kill a Man that hath abjured the Realm, is Felony.

(*d*) Note, that the King's Protection belongeth by the Law of Nature to all thefe, and the King may protect and pardon them all.

Kinds of
Homicide.

Voluntate; &	Murder, *fcil.* of a malicious Purpofe.
eft duplex.	Man-flaughter, or Chance-medly of a fudden.

Homicide is Threefold:

   Cafu, or Mifadventure; this alfo is confiderable after two Sorts, *fcil.* whether it happpen in doing a Thing   — Lawful, or Unlawful.

   Neceffitate; this is fometimes   — Commanded, *fc.* in Execution of Juftice. Tolerated, For Advancement of Juftice. *Se defendendo.* Prohibited. See *poft.* Tit. *Homicide.*

(*a*) *Bracton* divides *Homicide* into two Sorts, — *Lingua, vel Facto.*

Lingua, tribus modis. — *Præcepto. Confilio. Tuitione.*

Facto, quatuor modis. — 1 *Voluntate.* 2 *Juftitia.* 3 *Neceffitate.* 4 *Cafu.*

2.

CHAP. CXLIV.

Felo de fe.

BUT firſt to write ſomething of *Felo de fe*, (a) who deſtroyeth himſelf by Hanging, *The Faet* Poiſoning, Drowning, or otherwiſe.

For the Heinouſneſs thereof, it is to be obſerved, That it is an Offence againſt God, againſt the King, and againſt Nature. Alſo it is within the Degree or Quality of Murder, *ſc.* pretended and reſolved (in his Mind) to be done, before it be done : Yea, it is holden to be a greater Offence than to kill another Man. *Plo.* 261. *& in hoc caſu Chriſtianæ ſepulturæ interdicitur.*

And yet the Civil Law maketh a Difference of ſuch Offenders, and of their Puniſhment, according to the Quality of their Minds, whereby they were moved to kill themſelves ; for if they kill themſelves through Grief or Impatience of ſome Infirmity, no Puniſhment followeth ſuch their Fact (by the Civil Law) but they are left to the Tribunal of the Almighty Judge : But if they kill themſelves upon any other Cauſe, their Goods are confiſcated, and their dead Bodies (for the Terror of others) are drawn out of the Houſe, *&c.* with Ropes, by a Horſe, unto a Place appointed for Puniſhment or Shame, where the dead Body is hanged upon a Gibbet ; and none may take down the Body but by the Authority of the Magiſtrate, *&c. Vide Fulbeck* 90. and Dr. *Cowell* 249.

But by the Common Law, (d) if a Man kill himſelf (either with a meditate Hatred againſt his own Life, or out of Diſtraction, or other Humour) he is called *Felo* *Forfeiture.* Dyer 262. Plo. 261. *de ſe* ; and he ſhall forfeit to the King all his Goods and Chattels real and perſonal, and his Debts due to him by Specialty (but no Debts due to him without Specialty, or upon Simple Contract. *Dyer* 262. 16 E. 4. 7.)

(a) And their Goods are uſually granted and allowed by the King to the Biſhop *Almoner*, and in ſuch ſort as *Deodands* are, *Ba.* 3. *V.*

(d) But he ſhall not forfeit his Lands, neither ſhall his Blood be corrupt. See *Fitz.* Fitz. Cor. 301. Plo. 261. *Coron.* 362 & 426.

(a) Yet if a Man be guilty of another Man's Death, or manifeſt Theft, *&c.* and be taken, and for fear thereof killeth himſelf ; here he ſhall forfeit his Lands, *ac hæredem non habebit.* Bract. lib. 3. cap. 13.

(d) If a Man do give himſelf a deadly Wound, and dieth thereof within a Year and Plo. 262. a Day after, all his Goods, *&c.* which he had at the Time of the Blow given, or any Time after, ſhall be forfeited to the King.

But the Goods of *Felo de ſe*, be not forfeited till his Death be preſented and found of Co. 5. 110. 21 H. 7. 33. Record, neither can theſe Goods be claimed by Preſcription, (by Lords of Liberties, *&c.*) but by the King's Grant.

(a) And altho' he cannot be attainted of his own Death, for that he is dead before there is any Time to attaint him, yet the Finding of his Death by the Coroner (or other Perſon thereto authoriſed) is by Law equivalent to an Attainder in Deed, as to his Goods. *Plo.* 258. b.

(d) If *A.* ſtrike *B.* to the Ground, and then draweth his Knife to kill *B.* and *B.* 44 E. 3. 44. Fitz. Cor. 94. 286, 295. * See 1 Hale's Hiſt. P. C. 413. contra. lying upon the Ground draweth his Knife to defend himſelf, and *A.* is ſo haſty to kill *B.* that he falleth upon *B.'s* Knife ; and ſo *A.* is ſlain ; here *A.* is *Felo de ſe*, * (a) and yet he ſhall not forfeit his Goods in this Caſe. See 44 *Aſſ. p.* 17. *Br. Cor.* 12 & 14 that *A.* was adjudged not to be *Felo de ſe.*

If *A.* of Malice prepenſed diſchargeth a Piſtol at *B.* and miſſeth him, and throws down his Piſtol and flieth, and *B.* purſueth him to kill him, whereupon *A.* turning falleth down, his Dagger drawn, and *B.* through haſte falleth upon the Dagger, here *B.* is *Felo de ſe*, and *A.* ſhall go quit. 44 E. 3. Sir *Fr. Bacon* 4, 5.

If a Caliver be diſcharged with a murderous Intent at *J. S.* and the Piece breaks, and ſtrikes into the Eye of him that diſchargeth it, and killeth him, he is *Felo de ſe* ; and yet his Intention was not to hurt himſelf : For *Felonia de ſe*, and Murder, are *Crimina paris gradus.* See *ibid. p.* 65.

And in ſuch Caſe he ſhall forfeit his Lands, *quia convincitur.* Bract. lib. 13. cap. 31.

(d) If

Who may be Felo de se.
Stamf. 19.
Fitz. Cor. 324.

(d) If one that wanteth Difcretion, killeth himfelf, (as an Infant, or a Man *Non compos mentis*) he fhall not forfeit his Goods, &c.

If a Lunatick Perfon killeth himfelf, he fhall forfeit his Goods, but this muft be underftood when he killeth himfelf out of his Lunacy : Otherwife it is, if he killeth himfelf during his Lunacy, for then he fhall neither forfeit his Goods, nor be counted *Felo de fe.*

Co. 4. 129.

(a) If one being *Non fanæ memoriæ*, or a Lunatick, giveth himfelf a mortal Wound, and after he becometh of found Memory, and then dieth of the fame Wound, in this Cafe, although he dieth by Reafon of his own proper Stroke, yet for that the original Caufe was committed when he was *de non fana memoria*, he fhall not be accounted *Felo de fe*, neither fhall he forfeit any Thing, for that the Death hath Relation to the original Act, the which was the Stroke or Wound given when he was *de non fana memoria.* Co. 1. 99. b. & 4. 42. a. Fitz. Coron. 244. Pl. 260.

Who fhall inquire of it.
Co. 5. 110.

(d) The Inquiry of fuch a Felony belongeth to the Coroner : And yet if *Felo de fe* be caft into the Sea, or fecretly buried, that the Coroner cannot have the Sight of his Body, and fo cannot inquire thereof ; then the Juftices of Peace, or any other having Authority to inquire of Felonies, may inquire thereof (for that it is Felony) : And a Prefentment thereof found before them, intitleth the King to his Goods.

See alfo 1 Hawk. P. C: *Chap.* 27.

C H A P. CXLV.
Murder.

Stamf. 18.
Plow. 261.

OF old Time every Killing of one Man by another, was called Murder, (of the Effect) becaufe Death enfued of it. Afterwards Murder was reftrained to a fecret Killing only ; and therefore *Bracton* and *Britton* in their Definition of Murder, call it *Occulta occifio nullo præfente præter interfectorem & fuos coadjutores*, &c. But fince Murder hath been, and is taken in a middle Degree, neither fo largely as it firft was, nor fo narrowly as Mafter *Bracton* and *Britton* fpeak of it. For Murder is now conftrued to be when one Man upon Malice prepenfed, (*fc.* forethought) or precedent and with his Will, doth kill another felonioufly, *viz.* with a premeditate and malicious Mind, whether it be openly or privily done, this is Felony of Death, without any Benefit of Clergy. 23 *H.* 8. *c.* 1. & 1 *Ed.* 6. *c.* 12. See *Exod.* 21. 14. he fhall be taken from the Altar and put to Death.

Malice.

This Malice prepenfed or precedent, may be either apparent (as where there was a Precedent Falling out, or where there is a Lying in Wait, or a Time and a Place appointed, &c.) or it may be lefs apparent or manifeft, and yet fhall be implied, to be of Malice precedent, by the Manner and Circumftances thereof.

Co. 9. 67.

As where one killeth another without any Provocation, the Law implieth, and adjudgeth it to have proceeded of Malice prepenfed : Therefore if one fuddenly, and without any fhew of Quarrel or Offence offered, fhall draw his Weapon and therewith kill another.

Co. 23, 27.

Or if one fhall be Reading fome Book, or otherwife bufied, fo as he faw not the Party that fhall ftab or ftrike him (and he dieth thereof) ; or fhall be going over a Stile, &c. and another fhall kill him ; fuch Offenders fhall fuffer Death, as in Cafe of wilful Murder.

Statute againft Stabbing.
1 Jac. 1. c. 8.

And accordingly hath the Statute 1 *Jac.* well provided, That if one fhall ftab, ftrike or thruft another, that *hath not then a Weapon drawn*, or hath not then firft ftriken the other ; and if the Party fo ftabbed, ftriken or thruft, &c. fhall die thereof within fix Months after, altho' it cannot be proved that the fame was done of Malice forethought ; yet the Offender being thereof lawfully convicted, fhall fuffer Death as a wilful Murderer without Benefit of Clergy.

Officers.
Co. 4. 40. & 9. 66, 68.
Co. 9. 69.

To kill the Sheriff or any of his Officers, in their Execution of the King's Procefs, or in doing their Office, is Murder in him that killeth the Officer.

But if he be not an Officer known, he muft fhew his Warrant, before he arreft the Party, or upon the Arreft (if the other fhall demand to fee it) or elfe it feemeth the Arreft is tortious ; and where the Arreft is tortious (be it by an Officer known or by

I   another)

another) there the Killing of him that maketh fuch an unlawful Arreft, is no Murder, but Manflaughter only.

Again, where an Officer hath the King's Writ or other lawful Warrant, though it be erroneous, yet in the executing thereof, if he be flain, this is Murder. Co. 9. 65.

For the Officer is not to difpute the Validity of his Warrant, or the Authority of *Magiftrate.* the Court (or of the Juftice of Peace) that fent the Warrant ; but his Office is to exe- Co. 4. 40. cute it. & 9. 68.

To kill any Magiftrate or Minifter of Juftice, in the Execution of their Office, or in 22 Eliz. Keeping the Peace (according to the Duty of their Office) is Murder, and the Law im- Cromp. 23. plieth it to be of Malice prepenfed. And therefore if the Sheriff, Juftice of Peace, High Conftable, Petty Conftable, Watchmen, or any other Minifter of the King, or any that come in their Aid, be killed in doing their Office, this is Murder.

If the Sheriff or Juftice of Peace come to fupprefs Rioters, and one of their Company is flain by one of the Rioters ; this is Murder in all the Rioters that be there prefent.

A Conftable, with others to aid him, comes to part an Affray, if the Conftable, or Co. 4. 42. any of his Company fhall be flain in doing this his Office, it is Murder to him that killed him, although the Affray were on the fudden, and though it were in the Night: Co. 9. 68. For when the Conftable commands them in the King's Name to keep the Peace, altho' they cannot know him to be a Conftable, yet at their Peril they ought to obey him.

And in thefe Cafes, the Killing of fuch an Officer, or any of their Company, is in Co. 9. 67,68. Law intended to be by Malice prepenfed, *fc.* that the Murderer had a malicious Refolu- tion in him, to oppofe himfelf againft the Law, the Officers thereof, and the Juftice of the Realm.

Alfo a Thief that offereth to rob a true Man, killing the true Man in refifting him, Plow. 474. it is Murder of Malice prepenfed. Co. 9. 67.

A Man carried his Father (being fick, and againft his Will) in a frofty and cold 2 E. 3. 18. Time, from one Town to another, and the Father died thereof ; this was adjudged Mur- der in the Son.

An Harlot delivered of a Child, hid it in an Orchard (it being alive) and covered it 2 Eliz. with Leaves, and a Kite ftruck at it, and the Child died thereof, and the Mother was Cromp. 24. arraigned and executed for Murder.

A Man hath a Beaft accuftomed to do Hurt, and the Owner knowing thereof, *Beaft.* doth not tie him or otherwife keep him faft fhut up, but fuffereth him to go at Liberty, Fit. Cor. 311. and after the Beaft killeth a Man ; this is Felony in the Owner of the Beaft : For by fuch Stamf. 17. Sufferance he feemeth to have a Will to kill. Exod. 21.29. 1 H. H. P. C.

And in thefe three laft Cafes, *voluntas reputabitur pro facto,* Death enfuing thereupon : 430. For it may plainly appear, that they had a Will and Meaning of that Harm which fol- lowed, which Will in them, doth amount to Malice, and fo makes their Offences to be Murder, and in fuch Cafes where Death enfueth, *Nihil intereft, utrum quis occidat, an caufam mortis prabeat.*

(a) If a Man hath an Horfe, that will ftrike fuch as come near him, and his Mafter knowing this, rideth amongft a Multitude of People, *&c.* and the Horfe killeth a Man ; this is Felony in the Mafter. *Lect. M. Cook.*

The fame Law feems of an Officer, who being appointed and authorifed to whip, or with an hot Iron to burn or brand, or otherwife to punifh an Offender, fhall do it with fuch Rigour, or in fuch extreme Manner, as that the Offender by Reafon and Means thereof dieth.

If a Man perfuades another to kill himfelf, and be prefent when he doth, he is a Murderer. *Ba.* 65.

The Book called *Speculum Jufticiar.* fpeaking of *Homicida voluntate,* faith, it may Four Ways be either by Striking, Imprifonment, Famine, or other Pain. committed.

1. By Striking or Stabbing, *&c.* as you may fee by that already faid.

2. By Imprifonment ; as if a Man by Imprifonment fhall detain the Body of another (under the Colour of Law or Right) fo as he dieth thereby. See *hic verbo Gaoler.*

3. By Famine ; as if a Man fhall caft, or leave an Infant, or other Perfon which cannot go, in a Defert or fuch other Place, where no Perfon ufually reforts, by Reafon whereof fuch Infant, or other impotent Perfon dieth for want of Succour, *&c.*

4. By Pain ; as if a Man by Torture (or *Dures*) caufeth another to accufe himfelf, where in Truth he did not the Thing, but to be rid of the Pain (rather defiring Death) he confeffeth himfelf guilty of the Felony, when he is not guilty.

4 P (d) If

P. Cor. 163.
Stamf. 16.
1 H.P.C.
429.

(d) If a Man dieth in the Hand of a Physician or Chirurgion authorised to practise, this is no Felony in the Physician or Chirurgion. (a) And yet if a Physician bearing Malice to one who is under his Cure, shall give him a Medicine contrary to his Disease, whereof the Patient dieth ; this is Felony in the Physician. *Lectur. M. Cooke.*

If a Chirurgion authorised, do through Negligence in his Cure, cause the Party to die, the Chirurgion shall not be brought in Question of his Life ; and yet if he do only hurt the Wound, whereby the Cure is delayed, and Death ensues not, he is subject to an Action upon the Case for his Misfeisance. *Sir Fr. Ba.* 37.

43 E. 3. 33.
Lamb. 236.
See 1 Hawk.
P. C. 87.
1 H.H.P.C.
429. *contra.*
34 H. 8. 8.
P. Surg. 2.

(d) If one which is no Physician or Chirurgion (or which is not allowed to use or practise such Faculty) will take a Cure upon him, and his Patient dieth under his Hand ; this hath been holden to be Felony : But *quære* of this last Case, for it cannot be discerned whether the Patient's Death cometh by any wilful Default, in the Party taking such Cure upon him, or by the Patient's Infirmity ; again, there appeareth in them no Will to do Harm, but rather to do Good ; and then the Statute of 34 H. 8. 8. leaveth so great a Liberty of such Practise to unskilful Persons, that it will be hard now to make it Felony. But if a Smith, or other Person (having Skill only in dressing or curing the Diseases of Horses or other Cattle) shall take upon him the Cutting or letting Blood, or such like Cure of a Man, who dieth thereof, this seemeth to be Felony ; for the Rule is, *Quod quisque norit, in hoc se exerceat.*

Cromp. 23.]

Two playing at Tables, fall out in their Game, and the one killeth the other with a Dagger suddenly ; this was holden Murder, in one *Emery's* Case before *Bromley*, at the Assises in *Cheshire*, about 27 *El.* as Master *Crompton* reporteth.

Provocation.
Cromp. 25.

The Husband, upon Words between him and his Wife, suddenly struck his Wife with a Pestle, whereof she died, and it was adjudged Murder at the Assizes at *Strafford*, before *Walmesley.* 43. *El.*

Quære the Reason why it should be Murder in these two last Cases, considering there appeareth no precedent Malice, and that it was done upon the sudden, and upon Provocation.

(a) The Reason seemeth to be, for that in these two Cases there was no sufficient Provocation to take off the Imputation of Malice ; for it was resolved in my Lord *Morley's* Case (as I heard Mr. Justice *Wild* say in the Common Pleas) that Words were no sufficient Provocation to excuse the Malice intended.

Challenge.

Bird challenges *Taverner* to fight, and appoints a Time or Place, for that *T.* did not pay some Money he owed him, *T.* paid the Money duly, and then to preserve his Reputation, meets at the Place appointed, and *B.* kills *T.* and this was adjudged Murder ; for the Law respects not who gave the first Occasion, if the other accept and undertake the Quarrel ; and such Fights grew from settled Determinations and Purposes to kill ; and all Deaths happening of Fights upon Challenges are Murder. *P.* 14 *Jac. Roll's Rep. Part* 2. *p.* 260.

Lamb. 247.

(d) *A.* hath wounded *B.* in Fight, and after they meet suddenly, and fight again, and *B.* killeth *A.* this is Murder, and Malice shall be intended in *B.* upon the former Hurt ; but now if *A.* had killed *B.* this seems but Manslaughter in *A.* for his former Malice shall be thought to be appeased by the Hurt he first did to *B.*

See 1 H. H.
P. C. 451.
452.

Two were in Suit, and they meet suddenly, and quarrel about the Suit, and the Defendant killeth the Plaintiff ; this seemeth Murder. *Tamen quære.*

(a) If *A.* of Malice prepensed, discharges a Pistol at *B.* and misseth him, and throws down his Pistol and flies, and *B.* pursueth him to kill him, whereupon *A.* turneth, and killeth *B.* with a Dagger : If the Law should consider the last impulsive Cause, it should say, that it was in his own Defence : But the Law is otherwise, for it is but a Pursuance and Execution of the first murtherous Intent : And the first Motive will be principally regarded, and not the last Impulsion. Otherwise, if there had been a full Interruption. Sir *Fr. Bacon* 4.

Poisoning.

(d) Also wilful Killing of another by Poison, was, and is Murder by the Common Law. See *Stam.* 21. *& Br. Indictment* 41.

And the Offenders therein, their Aiders, Abettors, Procurers and Counsellors shall suffer Death, and forfeit in every Behalf, as in other Cases of wilful Murder of Malice prepensed. 1 *Ed.* 6. *cap.* 12. *Speculum Justic.* describeth these Offenders thus, *Qui done al auter a manger, ou auternent chose envenom.*

Plo. 474.
1 H.H.P.C.
431.

The Husband gave a poisoned Apple to his Wife, to the Intent to kill her, and she not knowing it to be poisoned, gave it to her Child, who died thereof ; this is Murder in the Husband, and yet he loved that Child dearly : And so it had been if a Stranger of

4

his

his own Accord had after eaten and died thereof; for the putting of Poifon into the Apple, Co. 9. 81.
&c. upon an evil and felonious Intent maketh it Murder, whofoever be killed thereby.

A. bringeth Drink that was poifoned (knowing of it) to *B.* and advifeth *B.* to drink Co. 4. 44.
it, telling him it would do him much Good; by reafon of which Perfwafion *B.* drunk of
it (in the Abfence of *A.*) and died thereof, this was adjudged Murder in *A.*

If one giveth corrupt Victual to another, to the Intent to poifon him, and he dieth Cromp. 30.
thereof within a Year and a Day, this is Murder.

(a) One layeth Corruption at another Man's Door, to the Intent to poifon him with 1 H. H. P. C.
the Savour thereof, and the other Party taketh Infection by the Savour thereof and dieth; 431.
this is Felony. *Lect. M. Cooke.*

So if one giveth to another Spurge Comfits, or other fuch Things in Sport, and not * *Manflaugh-*
in Malice, and he that fo taketh them dieth thereof; this is Felony. * *Ibid.* *ter according to*
1 H. H. P. C.
431.

(d) But if a Man fhall prepare Ratfbane, &c. to kill Rats, &c. and fhall lay this Co. 9. 81.
in certain Places to that Purpofe, without any evil Intent, *fc.* without any Intent to Plo. 474.
kill any reafonable Creature, and another Man finds and eats this, and dieth thereof, 1 H. H. P. C.
this is no Felony. 431.

The Mafter upon Malice precedent goeth to kill another, and taketh his Servant with Plo. 100.
him, (but he did not know his Mafter's Intent) and the Mafter and his Servant do meet
the other, and the Mafter doth affault him, and the Servant taking his Mafter's Part,
doth alfo affault him and kill him; this is Murder in the Mafter, and but Manflaughter
in the Servant.

Note, That when a Man hath Malice to one, and intending and endeavouring to kill Rules in Mur-
him, he killeth another Man; this is Murder whomfoever he killeth. *Vide Plo.* 101. der.
Dyer 128. *Fitz.* 262. *Stamf.* 16. For his Intent was to murder. Plo. 474.

Nay, if two fight upon Malice prepenfed, and in their Sight a Stranger (that would Lamb. 238.
part them) cometh between them, and is killed; this is Murder in them both, if it cannot be proved which of them did kill him.

A Man upon Malice fhooteth at one, or lieth in Wait to kill one, and killeth another Plo 474
unwittingly, in both thefe Cafes it is Murder.

Note alfo, That in all Cafes where a Man cometh or goeth about to do any Thing
unlawful, as to kill, beat or diffeife another, or to do any other Trefpafs; and in doing
this he killeth any Man, this is Murder. See *Cromp.* 24. *b.*

One ftealing Pears in another Man's Orchard, and the Owner came and rebuked him; Cromp. 24.
and the other killed him; this was adjudged Murder. 4 *Mariæ.* Lamb. 237.

Alfo where a Man commandeth another to beat *A.* and he beateth him fo as *A.* dieth Plo. 475.
thereof; this is Murder in him that gave the Command to beat him, for that he com- F. Cor. 314.
manded him to do an unlawful Act, by reafon whereof the Killing of a Man enfued.

(a) For (as that late Reverend and Learned Judge Sir *John Dodderidge, page* 138.
fheweth) there is an efficient Caufe cafual; as if a Man intend to do any unlawful Act,
and in doing thereof another Hurt enfueth, not intended, but by Chance, yet fhall he
be faid the Author of that Act not intended (and fo happening by Chance) that did intend the firft Act.

(d) Note alfo, That if divers Perfons come in one Company to do any unlawful *Principal.*
Thing, as to kill, rob, or beat a Man, or to commit any Riot or Affray, or to do any Br. Cor. 172.
other Trefpafs, and one of them in doing thereof killeth a Man, this fhall be adjudged F. Cor. 350.
Murder in them all that are prefent of that Party abetting him, and confenting to Co. 11. 5.
the Act, or ready to aid him, although they did but look on, &c. See *Stamf.* 40. *Fitz.*
Indictment 22.

Nay, if they be not prefent, yet if they be in the fame Houfe, or upon the fame
Ground, it is Murder in them all. See the Lord *Dacre's* Cafe, *Cromp.* 25.

(a) Mr. *Bracton, fol.* 121. faith further, *Si plures rixati fuerint inter fe in aliquo*
conflictu, & aliquis fit interfectus, nec appareat ex quo, nec ex cujus vulnere, omnes dici
poffint homicidæ, &c. quære, if their Meeting were upon a lawful Occafion, and if they
fuddenly fall out, and no former Malice may appear.

(d) Note alfo, That all who are prefent, and aiding, abetting or comforting another Plo. 100
to do Murder, are principal Murderers, although they fhall give never a Stroke. See See here.
more, 4 *H.* 7. 18. 13 *H.* 7. 10. *Fitz. Coron.* 309. *Co.* 9. 67. 112. &. 11. 5.

As if *A.* and *B.* fall out, and appoint the Field, and they meet accordingly, each of
them bringing Company with them, *A.* killeth *B.* this is Murder in all thofe that came
with *A.* (a) as his Second, or abetting, comforting, or ready to affift or aid him, for
that

that the Prefence of thefe other that came with *A.* is a Terror to *B.* and an Encourage-ment to *A. Vide ibid. & Plo.* 98.

And yet if *B.* cometh in the Company of *C.* who of his Malice prepenfed doth go to kill *D.* and then *B.* feeth them fighting together, he taketh Part with *C.* fuddenly (not having any former Malice to *D.*) and ftriketh at *D.* with the other, and *D.* is thus flain amongft them; this is but Manflaughter in *B.* for that he had no Malice precedent. *Plo.* 100. See the Cafe of the Mafter and his Servants here before. But note, That the Caufe of the Coming of *B.* being unknown to *D.* his Prefence might, and in Like-lihood did ftrike Terror in *D.* and fo the Prefence of the Servants did or might ftrike Terror in the Party murdered, and gave Incouragement to the Mafter.

(d) Note alfo, That in cafe of Murder it is not material who giveth the firft Blow for if he that is flain give the firft Blow, yet if there were Malice prepenfed in the other it is Murder in him that killeth him.

Death. Alfo in cafe of Poifoning, the Party poifoned muft die thereof within a Year and a Day, after the Poifon received.

Cor. 303. Alfo if a Man do beat or hurt another, whereof he dieth, to make it Murder, or other
Co. 4. 42. Homicide, the Party hurt muft die within a Year and a Day next after the Hurt done or Stroke given. But to have an Appeal, it fhall have relation to the Death and not to the Stroke, fo as the Appeal muft be brought within the Year after the Death, and not afte the Stroke.

In effe. Note alfo; in Murder, or other Homicide, the Party killed muft be in *effe, fc. in re-*
F. Co. 146, *rum natura,* and born into the World: For if a Man hurteth a Woman with Child
263. whereby he killeth the Infant in its Mother's Womb, by our Law (at this Day) this is no
Stamf. 21. c. Felony, neither fhall he forfeit any Thing for fuch Offence: And whether (upon a Blow
See Exod. 21, or Hurt given to a Woman with Child) the Child die within her Body, or fhortly after
22, 23. *It*
was Death by her Delivery, it maketh no Difference. (a) Yet in ancient Time it was holden to be
the Law of Felony; and M. *Bracton* took it to be Homicide, if the Blow were given *poftquam puer-*
God. *perium animatum fuerit.* (d) But if the Mother of the Child die within a Year and a
Lamb. 229. Day after fuch Hurt done to her, and upon that Hurt, this is Felony.
Br. Cor. 68,
91. (a) So if the Adulterer, *&c.* counfelleth the Woman to murder the Child when it fhal be born, and fhe doth accordingly, the Adulterer is acceffary to this Felony, by this his Counfel given before the Birth.

Alfo if a Man killeth a Man unknown, yet it is Felony. *Abr. d' Aff.* 76.

Compulfion alfo is a good Excufe in our Law in fome Cafes, as if any Man's Arms be drawn by Compulfion, and the Weapon in his Hand by Means thereof doth kill ano-ther; this is not Felony in him whofe Arms were fo drawn, *&c. Plo.* 19. *a.*

Involuntary Ignorance excufeth alfo with us: So as if an Infant not having Intelli-gence, or of a Man *non fanæ Memoriæ,* fhall kill another, this is no Felony in them See hereof *hic poftea.*

Intent to do a Felony or Murder is not punifhable, by the Common Law of this Realm, until the Act be done: But in Treafon, and fome other particular Cafes, by Sta-
1 *E.* 6. c. 12. tute the Intent may be punifhed. *Doct. & Stud.* 132. *hic.*

23 H. 8. 1. & (d) In Cafes of Murder the Offenders fhall not have the Benefit of Clergy.
26 H. 8. 12. Note alfo, That by the Law of God no Recompence was to be taken for the Life
*Numb.*35.31. of a Murderer.

Pardon. And by divers old Statutes, no Charter of Pardon ought to be granted to any Perfon
13 *Ric.*2. c.1. in cafe of Murder or other Homicide, fave only where the King may do it by his Oath,
P. Pardon 1, that is to fay, where a Man killeth another in his own Defence, or by Misfortune.
3.
Plow. 502. And by our Law at this Day, a Pardon of all Felonies will not difcharge Murder, ex-cept the Pardon be with a *Non obftante, &c.* or that Murder be exprefly mentioned in the Pardon.

Neither will a Pardon of all Felonies difcharge a Man that is attainted of Felony, except alfo the Attainder and the Execution be pardoned. See 9 *E.* 4. 29. *Co.* 6. 13. *b.*

(a) And this Pardon is twofold; one *ex gratia Regis,* which the King, in fome fpe-cial Regard of the Perfon or other Circumftance, fheweth and affordeth upon his Prero-gative: The other by Courfe of Law, which the Law in Equity affordeth for leffer Of-fences, as of Homicide by Mifadventure or *Se defendendo.*

(d) Note, That he which hath a Pardon for Felony, if he hath not found Sureties for his good Abearing, or if afterwards, during his Life, he fhall break the Peace: Such Pardon fhall be holden for none, but that he may be hanged notwithftanding his Pardon;

for by the Pardon, the Offence *tegitur, non tollitur*. See 18 *E. 3. cap. 3. P. Pardon 5. 3 H. 7. f. 7. & 3 H. 7. 7.* where one was executed upon this Statute; for making an Affray after his Pardon. *Br. Coron*.

None have Authority to pardon any Treaſon, Murder or other Felony, or any Acceſ- 27 H. 8. 25. ſary to the ſame, ſave only the King: It being one of his Royal Prerogatives. P. Prerog. 17.

(a) Two Men were beating another in the Street; and a Stranger paſſing by ſaid, it was a Shame for two to beat one; whereupon one of them ran to the Stranger in a furi= ous Manner, and with a Knife, which he held in his right Hand, gave him a mortal Wound, of which he died; and both the other being indicted at the Seſſions in the *Old Baily, 9 Geo. 1.* as Principals in the ſaid Murder, the Judges were of Opinion, that one of them could be neither Principal or Acceſſary to the Murder, becauſe it did not ap= pear that he intended any Injury to the Perſon that was killed: 'Tis true, both of them were doing an unlawful Act, but the Death of the Party did not enſue upon that Act; ſo one was acquitted, and the other found guilty of Murder.

See alſo 1 Hawk. P. C. Chap. 31. And 1 Hale's Hiſt. P. C. Chap. 36, 37, 38.

C H A P. CXLVI.

Manſlaughter.

MAnſlaughter, in right Signification thereof, implieth all Manner of Homicide, and *Definition.* extends in the General, as well to Murder as to the reſt. Nevertheleſs, for that See 1 H. H. in common Speech it is reſtrained to Manſlaughter by Chancemedly alone, in that Senſe P. C. 466. I will here write of it.

Manſlaughter, otherwiſe called Chancemedly, is when two do fight together upon the 1 Hawk. ſudden, and by meer Chance, without any Malice precedent, and one of them doth kill P. C. 76. the other; this alſo is Felony of Death. Br. Coron. 22.

And yet in caſe of Manſlaughter the Offender ſhall have the Benefit of Clergy for the firſt Time; and by the Law of God there was a City of Refuge appointed for ſuch to fly. unto, *Exod.* 21. 33. *Deut.* 19. 3, 4. *Numb.* 35. 11. 22. (a) For in ſuch Caſes of Chance (as we term it) *ſc.* where the Offender hath not laid wait, nor hated in Time paſt, the ſame Scripture ſaith, That God offered the Party ſo ſlain into the Hands of ſuch Man= ſlayer. *Exod.* 21. 13.

(d) Two fall out upon the ſudden and fight, and the one breaketh his Weapon, and Cromp. 26. a Stranger ſtanding by (yet being none of their Company) lendeth him a Weapon, and therewith he killeth the other: This is Manſlaughter, as well in him that killed the other, as in the Stranger who lent him his Weapon.

A. and *B.* fall out upon a ſudden and fight, and *A.* is ſo fierce, that he runneth upon the other's Weapon, and is ſlain; yet this ſeemeth Manſlaughter in *B.* for he ſhould have fled to ſome Wall or Straight, *&c. quære*.

And if *B.* had fled to a Wall, *&c.* and *A.* purſueth him, and *B.* perceiving that *A.* P. R. 122. b. would aſſault him, holdeth his Weapon between them, and *A.* runneth upon the Wea- Stamf. 16. a. pon and is ſlain; this is Homicide in his own Defence, and for which *B.* ſhall forfeit only his Goods: But otherwiſe it had been if *B.* had fallen, and lying upon the Ground had drawn his Knife or Dagger, and *A.* falleth thereon, and ſo is ſlain, for then *B.* could not fly, nor make any other Defence for his Safety, and therefore here *B.* ſhall not forfeit his Goods, nor be culpable of his Death, but be diſcharged, for *A.* in a Man= ner killed himſelf. See hereof *poſtea*.

Two fight together upon the ſudden, and part, and preſently after meet and fight Cromp. 22. b. again, and one killeth the other; or the one preſently fetcheth a Weapon, and kill- 24. a. 26. a. b. eth the other. This ſeemeth but Manſlaughter, for that it is done all in one continu- 1 H. H. P. C. ing Fury, which was at the firſt without Malice, and could not in ſo ſhort Time be 453. appeaſed or aſſwaged.

So if two have born Malice the one to the other, and be reconciled, and after Meet- Lamb. 240. ing again, they fall out upon new Occaſion, and by Agreement immediately they go in- 1 H. H. P. C. to the Field to fight, and the one killeth the other; this ſeemeth but Manſlaughter, 452. (cauſa qua ſupra) unleſs the Diſtance of Time had been ſuch, that by reaſonable Con- jecture their Heat might be aſſwaged.

(a) And

(*a*) And yet by good Opinions it is lately holden, that in both thefe laſt Cafes, and the like, though it be in a continuing Fury, yet if it be wilfully done it is wilful Murder, for which the Offender ſhall ſuffer Death.

See more of Manſlaughter *before in* Murder, *and after in* Miſadventure, *and* 1 Hale's Hiſt. P. C. Chap. 36 & 38.

C H A P. CXLVII.

What Perfons are chargeable with Homicide, and what not.

Non compos Mentis.
Fitz. N. B. 202.
21 H. 7. 33.
Plo. 19.
Co. 4.124. b.

IF one that is *Non compos Mentis,* or an Ideot, kill a Man, this is no Felony, for they have not Knowledge of Good and Evil, nor can have a felonious Intent, nor a Will or Mind to do Harm; and no Felony or Murder can be committed without a felonious Intent and Purpofe; for it is called *Felonia, quia fieri debet felleo animo.*

(*a*) And again, *Actus non facit reum, niſi mens ſit rea;* and a Madman is *Amens, id eſt, ſine mente,* without his Mind or Difcretion, and is enough puniſhed by his Madneſs. *Co. L.* 247.

Hob. p. 96, 134.
Co. 4. 125.

(*d*) So it is if a Lunatick killeth another during his Lunacy, it is no Felony; for all Acts done by him in Lunacy are as the Acts of an Ideot.

(*a*) If another Man ſhall upon Malice procure a Madman to kill another, though a Madman ſhall be excufed, yet the Inciter or Procurer ſhall be puniſhed as a Principal. *Ba.* 57.

See 1 H. H. P. C. c. 4.

(*d*) Now there be three Sorts of Perfons accounted *Non compos Mentis,* to this Purpofe, and the like.

1. A Fool natural, who is fo (*a nativitate*) from his Birth; and in fuch a one there is no Hope of Recovery.

Co. 124.

2. He who was once of good and found Memory, and after (by Sickneſs, Hurt, or other Accident, or Vifitation of God) lofeth his Memory.

3. A Lunatick, *Qui gaudet lucidis intervallis,* and fometimes is of good Underſtanding and Memory, and fometimes is *Non compos Mentis.*

Infant.
See 1 H H. P. C. c. 3.

An Infant of eight Years of Age, or above, may commit Homicide, and ſhall be hanged for it, *viz.* if it may appear (by hiding of the Perfon ſlain, by excufing it, or by any other Act) that he had Knowledge of Good and Evil, and of the Peril and Danger of that Offence. See 3 *H.* 7. 1. *&* 12. *Stamf.* 27. *Fitz. Coron.* 118, 119. *& Br. Coron.* 133, 136.

(*a*) And yet Sir *Edw. Coke* on *Littleton, f.* 147. faith, That it is with an Infant, until he be of the Age of fourteen Years (which in Law is accounted the Age of Difcretion) as it is with a Man *Non compos Mentis;* and that in Criminal Cafes (as Felony, &c.) his Act and Wrong ſhall not be imputed to him, for that *Actus non facit reum, niſi mens ſit rea,* &c. Sir *Fr. Bacon* 38. accordeth.

3 H. 7. 1. b.

(*d*) But if an Infant (of fuch tender Years, as that he hath not Difcretion or Intelligence,) kill a Man, that is not Felony in him.

Plo. 19.

If one that is dumb killeth a Man, it is Felony; yet *quære,* how he ſhall be arraigned.

Deaf and Dumb.
F. Coro. 193.
Stamf. 16.

A Man born deaf and dumb killeth another, this is no Felony; for he cannot know whether he did Evil or no, neither can he have a felonious Intent, &c. See hereof, Tit. *Surety for the Peace, antea.* (*a*) Otherwife, if he were not fo born, but becometh fo afterwards. See *Br. Coron.* 101. *&* 217. That a Man which can neither hear nor fpeak may commit Felony, and ſhall be impriſoned, &c.

(*d*) Note, in thefe former Cafes of Homicide, committed by Perfons being *Non compos Mentis,* or wanting Difcretion, fuch Things happen by an involuntary Ignorance, and therefore the Law accounteth fuch Act of theirs to be no Felony.

Plo. 19.
Co. 4. 125.

But if a Man that is drunk killeth another, that is Felony; for it is a voluntary Ignorance in him, in as much as it cometh to him by his own Act and Folly. (*a*) Sir *Edw. Cooke, L.* 247. calleth a Drunkard *voluntarius Dæmon,* and faith, That fuch a one hath no Privilege thereby, but what Hurt or Ill foever he doth, his Drunkenneſs doth aggravate it.

4

C H A P.

CHAP. CXLVIII.

Misadventure.

(a) BY the Statute of *Marl. cap.* 25. killing a Man by Misfortune or Adventure only, shall not be adjudged Murder.

Misadventure, in a general Signification, is where a Man is killed partly by Negligence, and partly by Chance, and against the Mind of the Killer; and when the Killer's Ignorance or Negligence is joined with the Chance. — *Misadventure, what it is.*

(d) Homicide by Misadventure or Misfortune, is when any Person doing a lawful Thing, without any evil Intent, happeneth to kill a Man : By the Law of God there was a City of Refuge appointed for such Persons to flie unto. *Numb.* 35. 15. & 22 *Josh.* 20. 3. And by our Law, this is no Felony of Death, for he shall have his Pardon of Course, for his Life and his Lands; yet he shall forfeit his Goods, in Regard that a Subject is killed by his means. — *See Stamf. 16. a. b. Fitz. Cor. 69, 302. & 354. Br. Forf. 9. & Co. 5. 91. b.*

As if a School-master in a reasonable manner beating his Scholar, for Correction only, or a Man correcting his Child or Servant, in reasonable manner; and the Scholar, Child or Servant happen to die thereof; this is Homicide by Misadventure. *Cro.* 136. *Bract.* 121. — *See Exod. 21, 20, 21. Stamf. 12. 21 H. 7. 29.*

So if a Man shooting at Butts, or other lawful Mark, and by the shaking of his Hand, or otherwise against his Will, he killeth one that standeth or passeth by. — *Rede. 6. Ed. 4. 7. Br. Cor. 59. & 148.*

So if a Carpenter, Mason or other Person doth throw or let fall a Stone, Tile or Piece of Timber from an House or Wood, or other Thing from a Cart, &c. (and giveth Warning thereof) and another is killed thereby against his Will. — *21 H. 7. Coron. 59. Bract. 121.*

So if a Labourer that is felling or lopping a Tree, and the same, or Part thereof, falleth and killeth a Man. — *6 Ed. 4. 7. F. Cor. 398.*

So if the Head of his Hatchet or other Tool falleth from him, and happeneth to kill one standing by. *Deut.* 19. 5, 6. & 10. accordeth, *&c.* That he is not worthy of Death, but innocent. — *Plo. 19.*

So if a Man be (in due and convenient Time) doing any other lawful Thing, that may be of Danger to such as pass by, and shall give Warning thereof, so that they may hear and flie the Peril, and yet another passing that Way shall be killed therewith.

And so if Men shall run at Tilt, Just, or fight at Barriers together by the King's Commandment, and one of them doth kill another : In these former Cases and the like, it is Misadventure, and no Felony. — *Hob. 134. 11 H. 7. 23. See Br. Cor. 229. contra.*

(a) And yet in such Cases of Misadventure, as also where one killeth another *Se Defendendo,* by the Common Law these Offences were Felony, and the Offender should have died for the same; but now by the Statute, such Offenders are to have Pardon for their Life and Lands, yet their Goods shall remain forfeit as before, at the Common Law. See these Statutes. 6 Ed. 1. *cap.* 9. & 2 Ed. 3. *cap.* 2. 21 Ed. 3. *fol.* 17. Br. Cor. 40. & Forf. 9. 13. 15. — *Co. 5. 61.*

(d) Also in these Cases of Misadventure, and in the former Cases of Homicide committed by Infants, and other Persons, being *Non compos mentis,* as also where one killeth another in Defence of his Person; they shall be discharged in this Manner, *&c.* If they desire to purchase their Pardon, they must upon their Trial plead *Not Guilty* (and shall give in Evidence the special Matter) and then this special Matter being found by Verdict, they shall be bailed, and then they must sue forth a *Certiorari,* to have this Record certified to the Lord Chancellor of *England,* who thereupon shall make them a Pardon of Course under the Great Seal, without speaking or suing to the King for it. See *Stamf.* 15. — *Se Defendendo. Fitz. 246. & 248 b. Br. Cor. 4 H. 7. f. 22. Reg. f. 309.*

But if a Man be doing of an unlawful Act, though without any evil Intent, and he happeneth by Chance to kill a Man; this is Felony, *viz.* Manslaughter at the least, if not Murder, in Regard the Thing he was doing was unlawful. — *Unlawful Act. Stamf. 162. Finch 75.*

As shooting of Arrows, or casting of Stones into the Highway, or other Place, whither Men do usually resort. — *Stamf. 12. c.*

So of fighting at Barriers, or running at Tilt or Justs, without the King's Command, whereby a Man is slain; and although it were by the King's Command, yet it was holden Felony by the Justices, *tempore H. 8.* — *11 H. 7. 23. Br. Cor. 229. Hob p. 134. contra. See 1 H. H. P. C. 473.*

Play-

11 H. 7. 23.
Crom. 26. &
29. a.
Cor.118.136.
See 1 H. H.
P. C. 472,
473.
P. R. 123.
Fitz. Cor.
304 & 354.
See Num. 35.
13.
Br. Cor. 128,
136.
1 H. H. P. C.
475.
Stamf. 12. c.
16. c.

Playing at Back-Sword, Foot-ball, Wreſtling, and the like, whereby one of them re ceiveth Hurt, and dieth thereof within a Year and a Day. In theſe Caſes, ſome are of Opinion, that 'tis Felony; ſome others are of Opinion, that this is no Felony, but th: they ſhall have their Pardon of Courſe, as for Miſadventure, for that ſuch their Play w: by Conſent: And again, there was no former Intent to do Hurt, or any former Malic but done only for Sport, and Trial of Manhood.

A Man caſting a Stone at a Bird or Beaſt, and another Man paſſing by is ſlain there with, *quære*, whether this be Manſlaughter, or but Miſadventure. The Opinion of F *neux* Chief Juſtice in 11 *H.* 7. *fol.* 23. is, That if a Man caſt a Stone over an Houſe, ar killeth a Man, this is no Felony, but Miſadventure. But Mr. *Brook* abridging this Caſ ſaith, It ſeemeth to be no Law, but where the caſting of a Stone is lawful; as where Maſon is untiling an Houſe, &c. but to caſt it for Pleaſure, and not in lawful Labou ſeemeth to be Felony: And ſo was the Opinion of Mr. *Bracton*, and Mr. *Stamford*, (e eſpecially if the caſting of the Stone be in ſuch Place where Men do uſe to paſs by. Y Mr. *Bracton*, *lib.* 3. *cap.* 17. *De homicidio per infortunium & caſualiter*, giveth the Rules, *Crimen non contrahitur niſi voluntas nocendi intercedat, & voluntas & propoſitu diſtinguunt maleficium, ſecundum quod dici poterit de infante & furioſo, cum alterum inn centia conſilii tueatur, & alterum facti imbecillitas excuſet.* Again, *In maleficiis ſpectati voluntas, non exitus, & nihil interſit, occidat quis, an cauſam mortis præbeat.*

See 1 Hale Hiſt. P. C. *Chap.* 5 & 39.

C H A P. CXLIX.

Caſual Death.

ALSO a Man may be ſlain by other Caſualty, than by Hands or Means of anoth Man, as by the Fall of an Houſe, Pit or Tree, &c. upon him; or be killed by Bull, Bear or other Beaſt, or by an Horſe or Cart, &c. or be killed by ſome Fall, whic he himſelf taketh.

And in theſe and the like Caſes, obſerve theſe Rules.

1. Firſt, if a Man be ſlain in any ſuch Manner, yet if it be by the Means or Procure ment, or wilful Default of another Man; this ſhall be Felony in the Party procuring c cauſing it.

Deodand.

2. The Thing which is the Cauſe of ſuch caſual Death, ſhall be forfeit to the King praiſed and taken for a *Deodand*, and the Price of the Thing ſhall be diſtributed in Aln to the Poor, by the King's Almoner, for *Deodand, eſt quaſi Deo dandum, id eſt, in Eleem ſynas erogandum.* But the Almoner hath no Intereſt in ſuch Goods, but hath only th Diſpoſition of the King's Alms, *Durante beneplacito;* ſo that the King may grant ther to any other.

Co. 1. 50.
Dyer 77.
Plo. 260.

3. The Forfeiture ſhall have Relation from the Stroke given; ſo as the Party or Owne ſelling ſuch Thing as was Cauſe of ſuch Death after the Stroke given, taketh not awa the King's Right, but that he ſhall have it as forfeited, notwithſtanding ſuch Sale.

Co. 5. 110.

4. *Deodands* are not forfeited, until the Matter be found of Record, and therefore the cannot be claimed by Preſcription.

Co. 5. 110.
F. Cor. 298.
Stamf. 21.
P. Cor. 10.
4 Ed. 1.

5. The Jury which find the Death of the Man, muſt alſo find and appraiſe the Dec dand, and the Sheriff ſhall be charged with the Price of ſuch *Deodand*, and ſhall levy th ſame of the Town where it falleth, although it were not committed to the Town t keep: And therefore it behoveth the Town to ſee it forth-coming.

F. Cor. 89.
Stamf. 21.

6. If he that is ſo ſlain be under fourteen Years of Age, nothing ſhall be forfeit to th King as a *Deodand* for him.

F. Indictment
27.
Stamf. 21.

And if a Man that is unknown be found dead in the Field, his Apparel and Mone about him ſhall be given to the Poor, &c. And if he were known, then his Good ſhall be delivered to his Executors or Adminiſtrators, or to the Ordinary; but ſhall not b taken as a *Deodand*, in either Caſe (for they are not the Nature of a *Deodand*) they bein no Cauſe of his Death.

Deodand, quid.
See 1 H. H.
P. C. 420.

Next what ſhall be forfeited and taken for a *Deodand*: The old Rule is, *Omnia que movent ad mortem, ſunt Deodanda;* and yet beſides, *Deodands* may be of ſome Thing

4   tha

hat a Man ſhall move or fall from, though the Thing it ſelf moves not: As to fall from Ship, Cart, Mow of Corn or Hay, &c. So as *Deodands* are any Goods which do cauſe, ir are Occaſion of the Death of a Man by Miſadventure. *Co. ibid.* See more *Fitz. Cor.* ;14, 326, 341, 342, 344, 388, 389, 398, 401, 409.

(*a*) If a Man killeth another with my Sword, or other Weapon of mine, my Weapon ſhall be forfeit, as a *Deodand*; for it ſhall be adjudged my Fault, that I did not keep my Weapon from him. ^{Br. Forf. 112.} ^{Doct. & Stud} ^{f. 156. b.}

If I ſhall lend another Man my Sword or other Weapon, knowing him to be minded o fight, or make an Affray therewith, and he with my Weapon in ſuch Fight or Affray, :illeth one, *quære*, if this be not Felony in me: For you ſhall find that an Abbot that lent ı Bow and Arrows to another, to the Intent to kill the King's Deer, was therefore fined ınd ranſomed. *Cromp. Author. des Courts, fol.* 191.

(*d*) The Inquiry of ſuch caſual Death, belongeth alſo to the Coroner: But if he cannot ıave the Sight of the Body, and ſo cannot inquire thereof, *quære*, how the King ſhall be ıntitled to the Goods.

The Office of Coroner in ſuch Caſes, ſee *Bracton, lib.* 3. *Crompton* 226, and 2 *Hawk. P. C.* Chap. 9.

See alſo 1 *Hale P. C.* Chap. 32. of *Deodands.*

C H A P. CL.

Homicide upon Neceſſity.

SOmetime the Juſtice of Law commandeth a Man to be put to Death, as when the Judge hath pronounced Sentence of Death againſt an Offender attainted by due Courſe of Law, there, in due Execution of Juſtice, an Officer, or other Perſon lawfully deputed, may execute ſuch Judgment or Sentence according to his Warrant; this is called Juſtice, or rather Judgment, which is the lawful Execution of Juſtice. ^{Juſtice commanded.}

But if the Officer or other Perſon, ſhall proceed therein upon his own Authority, without Warrant, or *Non obſervato ordine juris*; as where an Offender hath Judgment given upon him to be hanged, if the Sheriff or other Officer, ſhall behead him, or by other Means put him to Death: This is Felony in ſuch Officer, &c. ^{Stamf. 13.} ^{See Doct. &} ^{Stud. fol. 113.} ^{Co. 7. 14.}

Alſo if a Stranger being not thereto lawfully deputed, ſhall upon his own Authority put to Death an Offender that is condemned to die: This is Felony. ^{Stamf. ib.}

Nay, if the Judge himſelf, who gave the Judgment of Death upon an Offender, ſhall after put the ſame Offender to Death, it is not juſtifiable in him.

(*a*) If the Juſtices of Peace ſhall arraign a Man of Treaſon before them at their Seſſions, who is found guilty, &c. and thereupon is hanged: This is Felony, as well in the Juſtices, as in the Sheriff, or Officer which ſhall hang him: For that the Juſtices of Peace had no Authority therein, but it was *Coram non Judice. Lecture, M.* Cook. See alſo *Co.* 10. *fol.* 76.

If the Juſtices of Peace ſhall arraign a Man of Felony, upon an Indictment of Treſpaſs, whereupon he is hanged; this is Felony in the Juſtices, but not in the Sheriff or Officer. *Lecture M. Cook.* The Difference between theſe two Caſes, appeareth in my Lord *Coke's Reports, lib.* 10. *fol.* 76. *ſc.* For that in this laſt Caſe, the Juſtices of Peace had Juriſdiction of the Cauſe; and therefore, although they proceeded *inverſo ordine*, or erroneouſly, yet the Officer is excuſable.

(*d*) Sometimes alſo the Juſtice of the Law tolerateth and ſuffereth a Man to be ſlain, *ſc.* for the neceſſary Execution and Advancement of Juſtice, which otherwiſe ſhould be left undone: And in ſuch Caſe, the Law of the Land imputeth it not as any Fault to him that ſhall ſo kill a Man, but freely diſchargeth him thereof, without the King's Pardon. ^{Tolerated.}

As a Sheriff, Bailiff, or any other Perſon who hath a lawful Warrant to arreſt a Man indicted of Felony, may well juſtify the Killing of him; if he will not ſuffer himſelf to be arreſted, and yield himſelf, and that they cannot otherwiſe take him. ^{F. Cor. 261.} ^{Stamf. 13.} ^{22 Aſſ. 55.}

And ſo every Perſon whatſoever, without any Warrant, may apprehend a Felon upon Hue and Cry, or otherwiſe. And if he will not yield to be arreſted, but ſhall reſiſt or fly, the Purſuer may kill him without Blame. ^{Hue and Cry.} ^{F. Cor. 261.} ^{Stamf. 13.} ^{Co. 5. 109. b.}

(*a*) Herewith alſo agreeth the *Doctor and Student, lib.* 2. *cap.* 41. ſaying, If any Perſon that is an Officer would arreſt a Man that is outlawed, abjured, or attainted of Murder or any other Felony, and ſuch Offender ſhall diſobey the Warrant, and by Reaſon of that Diſobedience he is ſlain, the other ſhall not be impeached for his Death; for it is lawful for every Man to arreſt and take ſuch Perſons, and to bring them forth, that they may be ordered according to the Law.

F. Cor. 288 & 328.

(*d*) An Offender in Felony is led towards the Gaol, and breaketh away from thoſe that conduct him, and maketh Reſiſtance or flieth; his Conductors may juſtify to kill him, if they cannot otherwiſe take him again.

22 Aſſ. 55.

A Priſoner in the Gaol attempteth to eſcape, and having broken his Irons, ſtriketh the Gaoler (coming in the Night to ſee his Priſoners) and the Gaoler ſlayeth ſuch a Priſoner : This is no Felony.

Cro. 23, 30 & 158.

Rioters, and ſuch as ſhall make any Forcible Entry or Detainer, againſt the Statutes, if they ſhall reſiſt the Juſtices of Peace or other the King's Officer, or ſhall not yield themſelves, but ſhall ſtand on their Defence, when the Juſtices of Peace, or other Officer, ſhall come to arreſt or remove them, if any of them happen to be ſlain : This is no Felony in

Lamb. 310.

the Juſtice of Peace or Officer, or in any of their Company that killeth ſuch Rioters, &c.

Stamf. Prærog. fol. 46. Crom. 24, 30 Doct. & St. 133. b.

The Sheriff, Bailiff or other Officer cometh (by Virtue of the King's Proceſs) to arreſt another for Debt or Treſpaſs, who maketh Reſiſtance, and thereupon is ſlain by ſuch Officer or any of his Company; this hath been taken to be no Felony, *tamen quære:* (*a*) For although the Sheriff (being the King's Officer) ought to ſee the King's Command executed, yet that muſt be underſtood to be executed by all lawful Means and Ways.

Stamf. 13. e, f, g.

(*d*) But in all theſe former Caſes, there muſt be an inevitable Neceſſity; *ſc.* That the Offender could not be taken, &c. without killing of him.

Hob. 134.

(*a*) If two Maſters of Defence, playing their Prizes, kill one another; it is not Felony.

Neceſſity.

Neceſſity of three Sorts, *ſc.*

1. Of Conſervation of Life, &c.

2. Of Obedience, as where the Wife ſtealeth with her Huſband.

3. Of the Act of God, or a Stranger.

Yet in theſe Caſes, Neceſſity privilegeth in Caſes of Homicide only when it is inevitable. *Bracton.*

And in Caſes of Theft only *Quoad jura Privata, ſed non valet contra Rempublicam. Ba.* 52.

For Defence of Perſon, Houſe or Goods.

(*d*) Alſo in an Appeal of Felony, if the Appellant and Appellee do join to try it by Battle, and therein the one doth kill the other; as the Law doth allow ſuch Trial, ſo doth it allow the Event to be juſtifiable, as depending upon the Judgment of God, who giveth Victory according to Truth.

Alſo when one Man killeth another in the neceſſary Defence of himſelf, or his, thereby to deliver himſelf, his Poſſeſſions or his Goods, or ſome other Perſons, which he is bound to defend from Peril, and which cannot otherwiſe eſcape : This is Homicide to-

24 H. 8. 5. P. Forf. 1. Fitz. Cor. 303, 305. Hob. p. 96. Co. 5. 91 & 11, 82. Exod. 22. 2. Stamf. de Prærog. 46.

lerated upon Neceſſity.

To kill an Offender, which ſhall attempt feloniouſly to murder or rob me in my Dwelling-houſe, or in or near any Highway, Cartway, Horſe-way or Foot-way, or that ſhall attempt Burglary, or feloniouſly to break my Dwelling-houſe in the Night: This is juſtifiable by my ſelf, or by any of my Servants or Company.

And this being ſo found by Verdict, they ſhall be all diſcharged without Loſs of Life, Land or Goods, or Pardon.

26 Aſſ. 32. F. Cor. 261. 305. & 330. Br. Cor. 100, 102.

To kill a Thief or Murderer, in the Defence of my Perſon, my Houſe and Goods, was no Felony, but juſtifiable by the Common Law, before the Statute of 24 *H.* 8. *cap.* 5. *Stamf.* 14. See *Co.* 5. 91. & 11. 82. (*a*) And yet at the Common Law there was this Difference, *ſc.* That he which killed a Thief which would have robbed him upon the Highway, ſhould forfeit Goods; but he which killed one who would have robbed or murdered him in his Houſe, ſhould forfeit nothing. *Co.* 11. 82. See *Exod. cap.* 22, 23.

26 Aſſ 23. Br. Coron. 200.

(*d*) And if one or more come to burn my Houſe, I, or any of my Servants may juſtify to ſhoot out of my Houſe at them, or may iſſue forth, and kill them; for ſuch Intent of theirs is felonious.

(*a*) If a Woman kill him that aſſaileth her to raviſh her : This is juſtifiable in the Woman, without any Pardon. Sir *Fr. Ba.* 34.

And in theſe Caſes, *Se defendendo* is a Plea for him, or her that is charged with the Death of another, ſaying, That they were driven to that they did, in their own Defence, the other ſo aſſaulting them, &c.

2   If

If divers be in Danger of Drowning, by the Casting away of a Boat or Barge, and one of them gets to a Plank or on the Boat's Side, to keep himself above the Water, and another to save his Life, thrust him from it, whereby he is drowned : This is neither *Se Defendendo*, nor by Misadventure, yet justifiable. *Idem* 30.

And for this inevitable Necessity *Bracton* giveth this Rule, *Si autem inevitabilis, quia accidit hominem sine odii meditatione, in metu & dolore animi se & sua liberando, cum aliter evadere non posset, non tenetur ad pœnam homicidii, f.* 120.

If a Man imprisoned for *Felony* escape, and the Gaoler pursues him, but he resisteth and refuseth to yield himself, and thereby the Gaoler kills him ; this is justifiable and not Manslaughter. But otherwise it is in Case the Imprisonment were for ,*Debt*. *Per Roll's Rep. Part* 2. *p.* 187.

(*d*) But if a Man shall forcibly get, and keep Possession of a House, and the other *Prohibited*, shall come in the Night and fire this House, they within cannot justify to shoot and kill him, or any of his Company, for that they in the House were there unlawfully.   See *Cromp.* 26. *b.*

If one cometh (in the Day-time) to my House, to beat me, and doth make an As- F. Cor. 305. sault upon me in my House, and fighteth with me, and I kill him in Defence of my Co. 5. 91. Person ; yet in this Case I shall forfeit my Goods, and must have the King's Pardon, except it be found, that the Assailant came with a felonious Intent to kill or rob me.

And if one cometh (in the Day-time or in the Night) to enter into my House, pretending Title thereto, and to put me out of my Possession, and I kill him : This seemeth to be Manslaughter in me.

Note ; If one kill a true Man, in Defence of his Person, there ought to be so great Stamf. 15. a. a Necessity, that it must be esteemed to be inevitable, or otherwise it will not excuse ; Speculum Justic. and therefore he that shall be so assaulted by a true Man, must first fly as far as he can Fitz. Cor.116. and till he be letted by some Wall, Hedge, Ditch, Press of People, or other Impediment ; so as he can fly no further without Danger of his Life, or of being wounded or maimed ; and yet in such Case, if he kill the other, he shall be committed till the Time of his Trial, and must then get his Pardon for his Life and his Lands, (which *The Penalty.* Pardon notwithstanding he shall have of Course) but he shall lose and forfeit his Goods and Chattels ; for the great Regard which the Law hath of a Man's Life. *Co.* 5. 91. *b.* See hereof *Paulo antea*, Tit. *Felony by Misadventure.*

A. maketh an Affray upon *B.* and striketh *B.* and *B.* flieth so far as he can for saving Se Defendenhis Life, before any Stroke given by *B.* and *A.* continueth his Assault ; whereupon *B.* doth do. also strike *A.* and killeth him. This is Homicide in his own Defence ; otherwise it 4 H. 7. 2. seemeth to some, if *B.* had struck the first Blow, or had struck before he had fled ; and 6 E. 1. c. 9. yet by other good Opinions, the first Stroke or who began the Affray, is not material ; Stamf. 15. but the whole Matter will consist upon the inevitable Necessity (*sc.* whether the said *B.* who killeth *A.* could not have escaped with his Life, *&c.* without killing *A.* for otherwise it will not excuse *B.* for *Cuncta prius tentanda:* And as it is a charitable, so it is a safe Principle (in these Cases) not to use an Extremity, till thou hast tried all Means.

Also it is holden in the former Case, if *B.* (before he had fled) had striken *A.* and F. Cor. 284 given him divers Wounds, that yet if he fly to a Streight before he give *A.* the mortal & 286. Wound, and then he giveth his Death's Wound ; this is Homicide in his own De- 1 H.P.C. fence.   479.

But in the former Case, if *B.* upon Malice prepensed had first strucken *A.* and then F. Cor. 387. *B.* flieth to a Streight or Wall, and *B.* pursueth him, and striketh him, and *B.* killeth Cromp.22,28, *A.* thereupon : This is Murder in *B.* for the Malice prepensed was the Ground and Beginning hereof.

Yet if there had been former Malice between *A.* and *B.* and they meet suddenly, and *A.* assaulteth *B.* and *B.* before any stroke by him given, flieth so far as he can ; and *A.* pursueth him, and then *B.* killeth *A.* This seemeth to be Homicide in his own Defence, notwithstanding the former Malice.

Copstone's Case : There was Malice between *Copstone* and one *S.* and they had fought 15 El. divers Times, and afterwards met suddenly in *London-street*, and *C.* told *S.* that he Cromp. 27. would fight with him, and *S.* answered, that he had nothing to say unto him ; and *S.* went 1 H.H.P.C. to the Wall, and after *C.* assaulted *S.* and then *S.* struck and killed *C.* and it was found 487. that *C.* began the Affray, and *S.* was thereupon discharged, without forfeiting any Thing. But that was by Virtue of the Statute of 24 *H.* 8. *cap.* 5.

A Man in Fight falleth to the Ground, there his Flying, *&c.* is not necessary, *&c.* See hereof before.

Also

Stamf. 14.
Alfo if a Thief affaults me to rob or kill me, I am not bound to fly to a Wall, &c. as I muft in cafe a true Man affaults me.

Co. 9. 68.
If an Officer of Juftice or Minifter of the Law, in the Execution of his Office be affaulted, he is not bound to fly to a Wall, &c. as other Subjects are.

Servant.
Br. Coron.63.
Alfo the Servant may juftify the Killing of another, in Defence of his Mafter's Perfon or Houfe, if the Hurt cannot be otherwife avoided.

21 H. 7. 35.
Alfo the Servant may juftify the Killing of him, who robbed and killed his Mafter, fo that it be done prefently.

In the Defence of the Poffeffion of my Goods, I may juftify to beat him that fhall wrongfully take them from me; but I cannot juftify to kill him, except he be a *Thief.*

23 Ed. 1.
P. Forefts 4.
Stamf. 13,14.
See 1 H. H.
P. C. 485,
486, &c.
Hob. 159.
So then, to kill a *true Man in Defence of my Perfon*, in Cafe where there is an inevitable Neceffity, (fc. that I firft fhall fly fo far as I can for faving my Life, &c.) This is no Felony, &c. But otherwife it is to kill a *true Man in Defence of the Poffeffion of my Houfe, Lands or Goods*, that is Manflaughter (at leaft) as it feemeth.

(*a*) In Cafe of killing a Man *Se Defendendo*, there muft be *extrema neceffitas*; for if a Man flying fee a Place, beyond which he cannot go, and before he come there, kill his Purfuer; this is not juftifiable, for he muft go to the utmoft Place before he ftrike.

Sir *Francis Bacon* taketh this Difference in thefe former Cafes of *Se Defendendo*, fc. When the Law doth intend fome Fault or Wrong in the Party that hath brought himfelf in the Neceffity : This he calleth *Neceffitas culpabilis*, and faith this to be the chief Reafon why *Se ipfum defendendo* is not Matter of Juftification, but he muft fue out his Pardon, and fhall forfeit his Goods, becaufe the Law intends it hath a Beginning upon an unlawful Caufe; for Quarrels are not prefumed to grow without fome Wrongs in Words or Deeds, and fo Malice on either Part; and it is hardly triable in whofe Default the Quarrel began : But where I kill a Thief that attempts to rob me (and the like), here there can be no Malice or Wrong prefumed on my Part. *Ba.* 33.

Forefter, &c.
Warrener.
Cromp. 30.
(*d*) If any Forrefter, Park-keeper or Warrener, or any in their Company, fhall kill an Offender in their Foreft, Park or Warren, which (after Hue and Cry levied to keep the Peace, and to obey the Law) will not yield themfelves, but will fly, or defend themfelves by Violence; this is no Felony : Yet *Quære*, if there were any former Malice in fuch Keeper. (*a*) But if any fuch Keeper, by Reafon of any former Malice, will lay to any Man's Charge, that he came to do hurt, whereas he did not, neither was found wandring nor offending, and fo kill him; this is Felony in fuch Keeper.

And fo in the former Cafes, where a Man is flain for the Execution of Juftice, fc. when the Offender fhall difobey the Arreft, refifteth or flieth, and fo is flain; as alfo where a Man fhall be flain by an Officer or other Perfon, in keeping or preferving the Peace; yet if fuch Manflaughter or Killing of fuch an Offender, be committed wittingly, willingly, and of Purpofe, under Colour of Execution of Juftice or Keeping of the Peace; this is Felony. See the Statute of 1 *Jac.* 1. *cap.* 8.

See 1 Hawk. P. C. *Chap.* 28, 29. *of juftifiable and excufable Homicide.* *And* 1 Hale's Hift. P. C. *Chap.* 40.

C H A P. CLI.

Burglary.

Definition.
22 E. 3.
18 El. 6.
* *By Statute*
39 Eliz. if
'tis broke open
in the Day-
time, and the
Value of 5 s.
taken away,
'tis Felony without Benefit of Clergy.
BUrglary (*a*) is derived from two *French* Words, *Burg* (a Village or a Farm-houfe), and *Larron* (a Thief); and fo in the natural Signification, is the Robbing of a Houfe : But in our Law it (*d*) is when one or more in the * Night-time, do break a Dwelling-houfe or a Church, or the Walls or Gates of a City or walled Town, with an Intent to do Felony, although he or they do not execute the fame, or do take or carry away nothing; yet it is Felony, and the Offenders fhall be hanged, and fhall not have the Benefit of their Clergy.

(a) And if the Intent or Fact of this Offender be to steal; this is like Robbery, if to murder, it differeth not much from Murder, and so of other Felonies. *West.*

(d) First for the *Time :* Burglary cannot be committed *in the Day-time,* but only in the *Night*; for all Indictments of Burglary be, *Quod noctanter fregit :* And the *Night* (to this Purpose) beginneth at the Sun-setting, and continueth to the Sun-rising: And therefore to break a House, &c. after the Sun-setting, and before it be dark; or after Day-light in Summer, and before the Sun riseth, is Burglary: The Time.
Br. Cor. 185.
Stamf. 30.
Co. 11. 36.
21 H. 7.
See 1 H. H.

Next, for the Manner : It is holden by some good Opinions, That if a Man break the House to do Felony, and yet entreth not, it is no Burglary; and that the Indictment must be, *Fregit & intravit.* And yet by the Opinion of *Shard.* 27 *Ass.* 38. and of Sir *Anth. Brown,* Sir *Edward Montague,* and Sir *Rob. Brook,* late Chief Justices of the Common Pleas, and others, (as Mr. *Crompton* reporteth) if a Man do but attempt to break or enter into a Dwelling-house by Night, to the Intent to rob, or kill any Person there, though he make no actual Entry, yet it is a full and complete Burglary. P.C. 550. con.
The Manner.
Stamf. 30.
Dyer 99.

Cromp. 31,
32, 33.

1 H. H.P.C.
552.

As to put back the Leaf of a Window with his Dagger.

To draw the Latch of the Door.

To turn but the Key, being on the inner Side of the Door.

So to break the Glass-window, and to draw out any Goods there with an Hook, &c. 26 *El.* at *Staff. Assizes.*

So to break a Hole in the Wall, and to shoot in thereby at any within the House. And. Part 1.

So (the Door being opened by some of the House) if any of the Attempters shall discharge a Dagg against any in the House, holding his Hand over the Threshold, though he set no Foot over. P. 114.
26 Eliz.

(a) But if Thieves come to a House, and some within open the Door, and one of the Thieves shoot at the Man, and miss him, and the Bullet breaks the Wall of the House : This is not Burglary. And. Part 1.
P. 114.

Or, if they have a Hole in the Wall, and perceive a Man to come by with a Purse, or any Thing else in his Hand, and snatch it away : This is Burglary. So one came to a Gentleman's Window, and saw a Cabinet with Money in it, and pulling it to him, took out the Money, he was executed for it. Ibid.

(d) So if upon an Attempt of Burglary, they within the House shall cast out their Money for Fear, and the Attempters take it away.

And yet there is no actual Entry made in any of these Cases.

But if a Thief setteth but his Foot over the Threshold, or into any Part of the House, to commit Felony, or shall for that Purpose but put his Hand in at the Window, or at any Hole in the Wall; this shall convict him of Burglary.

Also one being let down the Chimney in the Night, to commit Felony, it was adjudged Burglary by Sir *R. Manwood,* Chief Baron, and yet he broke not the House. Cromp. 32.
See 1 H H.
P. C. 552.
who seems to
doubt.

So it is to come into the House by the Help of a Key.

So if suddenly one come into the House by *Night,* the Doors being open, and the Owner flieth to his Chamber, and the Offender is taken shoving at the Chamber-door.

So it is, if Thieves pretending they have been robbed, &c. shall come to the Constable, and pray him to make search for the Felons, and going with the Constable into a Man's House to search, they rob the good Man of the House. This is Burglary.

So if a Servant conspiring with another to rob his Master, shall open his Master's Door or Window in the Night, and the other entereth thereat; this is Burglary in the Stranger, by the Opinion of Sir *Roger Manwood*; and the Servant is but a Thief, and no Burglar. 21 Eliz.
Terms 34.
1 H. H. P. C.
553.

And yet the House was not broken in any of these Cases.

(a) If a Thief find a Door open, and cometh in by Night, and robs the House, and be taken with the Manner, and breaks a Door to escape; this is Burglary : Yet the Breaking the Door was without any felonious Intent, but it is one intire Act. Sir *Fr. Bacon* 65.

If a Man in the Night entereth into the House by a Hole, or at a Wall broken before, and taketh away any Thing, or to the Intent to do any Felony, it is Burglary.

(d) But if one cometh into my House in the Day, and there hideth himself till Night, and then robbeth me; or if I shall lodge one in my House, and in the Night he robbeth me (*sc.* goeth out of my House, and taketh away some of my Goods with him), yet this is no Burglary, for that he broke not my House. For the first Case it was so holden at *Derby Ass.* 32 *El. Cromp.* 34. (a) *Quære* of his Opening the Door to go out and escape, if that shall not make it Burglary. Vide 12 Anr.
c. 7. infra.

(d) And

11 H. 4. 13.   (*d*) Alſo if divers come to commit Burglary, and but one of them entreth, and commit it, the reſt ſtanding about the Houſe or not far off, to watch that no Help ſhal come: This is Burglary in all that Company.

The Place.   Now concerning the Place, it may be either publick or private; publick, as the Church or Walls, or Gates of a City, or a walled Town; private, as a Dwelling-houſe: And here commonly it is no Burglary, unleſs ſome Perſon be at that Time within the Houſe.

Co. 4. 40.   And yet if a Man hath a Dwelling-houſe, and he and all his Family (upon ſome Occaſion) are Part of the Night out of the Houſe, and in the mean Time one cometh and breaketh the Houſe to commit Felony; this is Burglary.

And. Part 1.   (*a*) And *An.* 36 *Eliz. Term. Paſch.* at an Aſſembly of all the Juſtices at *Serjeants Inn*
P 302.   it was reſolved, That the Breaking of an Houſe in the Night, with an Intent to commit Felony, is Burglary, although that no Perſon be within the Houſe; for the Law is That every Man ought to be in Security or Safety in the Night; as well for their Goods

See 1 Hawk.   as for their Perſons; and that the ancient Precedents are, *Quod domum noctanter felonice*
P. C. 103.   *& burg. fregit,* without ſaying *Domum manſionalem,* or that any Perſon was in the
and 1 H. H.   Houſe; and that the Reaſon why of late Times theſe Words have been put into the Indict-
P. C. 550.   ment (*ſc.* that ſome Perſon was in the Houſe) was, for that in ſuch Caſes the Benefit of Clergy was taken away; but now by the Statute 18 *Eliz.* 6. Clergy is taken away in all Caſes of Burglary; and therefore the Judges then all agreed from thenceforth to put the ſame in Execution accordingly. I have ſeen it thus reported out of a Book of *Popham* late Lord Chief Juſtice of the King's Bench.

    (*d*) So if a Man hath two Dwelling-houſes, and ſometimes dwelleth in the one, and ſometimes at the other, and hath a Family of Servants in both, and in the Night when his Servants are out of the Houſe, the Houſe is broken by Thieves; this is Burglary Adjudged 38 *Eliz.*

    (*a*) I have alſo ſeen a Report of Judge *Popham,* that *Termino Trin.* 36 *Eliz.* it was reſolved by the Judges, that if a Man had two Houſes, and dwelt ſometimes in the one, and ſometimes in the other; if that Houſe wherein he neither then was, nor had any Servants, were broken, *&c.* That this was Burglary, although no Perſon then dwelt or were therein.

Cromp. 33.   (*d*) If one breaketh a Chamber in *Lincoln's Inn,* (or in any other Houſe of Court or *Chancery,* or in any College in *Cambridge* or *Oxford, &c.*) in the Night, to the Intent to commit Felony there, this is Burglary, although there were no Perſon in the ſame Chamber: For the Colleges and Houſes of Court and *Chancery* be intire Houſes, whereof ſuch Chamber is Parcel; ſo that if any Perſon ſhall be in any other Chamber within the ſame Houſe or College at the ſame Time, it is Burglary.

C. omp. 32.   On *P.* was arraigned of Burglary, 22 *Eliz.* for that he aſſaulted one of his Companions of the *Inner Temple, London,* in his Chamber, there to have killed him in the Evening, *&c.* but had his Pardon.

    (*a*) A Servant who lieth continually within his Maſter's Houſe, openeth the Doors in the Night to rob him; this is Burglary. *Lect. Mr. Cook, tempore H.* 8. See *hic antea.*

    A Man cometh as a Gueſt to eat and drink in the Day-time, and there ſtayeth till Night, and in the Night-time breaketh his Chamber, or any Part of the Houſe to rob his Hoſt; this is Burglary. *Ibid.*

    A Gueſt cometh to a common Inn, *&c.* and the Hoſt appointeth him his Chamber, and in the Night the Hoſt breaketh into his Gueſt's Chamber to rob him; this is Burglary. *Ibid.*

2 Ed. 6.   (*d*) Alſo the Breaking (in the Night) of a Stable, Barn, or other Out-houſe adjoining
Br. Cor. 180.   to, or Parcel of, or near to the Dwelling-houſe, to the Intent to ſteal, is Burglary, tho'
Lamb. 256.   he take nothing.

    At Summer Aſſiſes at *Cambridge, An. Dom.* 1616. two Men were arraigned and condemned for Burglary before Sir *James Altham,* Knt. for Robbing a Back-houſe of *Robert Caſtle,* Eſq; in the Night; which Back-houſe was ſome eight or nine Yards diſtant from his Dwelling-houſe, and only a Pale reaching between them: So that although this Offence be not committed in the very Body of the Dwelling-houſe, but in ſome other Houſe near unto it, and being Parcel of or belonging to the Dwelling-houſe, it is Burglary.

Co. 11. 37.   But a Booth or Tent in a Fair or Market, are not eſteemed in Law for a Dwelling-houſe, nor the Breaking thereof in the Night-time to be Burglary; although the Robbing

bing

bing of them be made as penal as Burglary, if the Owner, his Wife, Children, or Servants were within the same.

Lastly, (To make it Burglary) the Purpose and Intent for which the Offender cometh, *The Intent.* must of Necessity be to kill or rob some Person, (or to commit some other Felony) 22 Aff. 95. otherwise it is neither Burglary nor Felony.   Stamf. 126.   Co. 11. 31.

And therefore to break a House in the Night, to the Intent to kill any Person therein, 13 H. 4. 7. is Burglary, although he never touched him.   Fitz.Cor. 267.

So it is, if the Purpose were to rob, although the Offender taketh away nothing.   Fitz. Cor.185 & 264.

But if a Man break and enter an House by Night, of Purpose only to beat a Man, Stamf. 10. this is but Trefpafs.   Co. 11. 33.

And if the Intent were to commit a Rape, which some think to be no Felony by the *Rape, fee af-* Common Law, but only a Trefpafs, then there is some Doubt, faith Mr. *Lambard*, and *ter here,c.107.* Mr. *Crompton* faith, that if a Man breaketh another Man's House in the Night, and ra-Lamb. 260. vifheth a Woman there, this is no Burglary; for (faith he) Ravifhment is no Felony by Cromp. 32. the Common Law, as Burglary is, although it be Felony at this Day by the Statute. *Tamen quære*; for it may feem by Mr. *Bracton, Glanvile* and *Stamford*, that by the an-*Rape.* cient Common Law it was Felony.   The Words of Mr. *Bracton, lib. 2.* are thus, *Olim* Stamf. 21, 22, *quidem corruptores virginitatis & caftitatis fufpendebantur, &c. modernis tamen tempori-* 23. *bus aliter obfervatur, quia pro corruptione virginis amittuntur membra, &c.* And a little after, *Adelftanus; Raptus mulierum ne fiat, defendit tam lex humana quam divina : Et fic fuit antiquitus obfervatum, quod fi quis obviaverit folam, cum pace dimittat eam, &c. Si autem contra voluntatem fuam, &c. jactat eam ad terram, foris faciat gratiam fuam, &c. Quod fi concubuerit cum ea de vita & membris fuis incurrat damnum, &c.* And with this Mr. *Glanvile* alfo agreeth, *fol.* 112. & *Co. L. fect.* 190. Note, that the Words, *De Felony: vita & membris fuis incurrat damnum*, do imply the Offence to have been Felony of Death. *Br. Cor.* 204. *Vide Co. L.* 391.

Alfo amongft the Laws of S. *Edmond*, fometimes King of this Realm; you fhall find this Law, *Qui cum Nunna vel fanctimoniali fornicetur, convndetur ficut homicida : A multo fortiori*, then, faith Mr. *Stamford,* fhall he be punifhed if he had ravifhed her. So as Rape at the firft (faith *Stamford*) was grievoufly punifhed, until the Time of King *Edward* the Firft, who feemed to mitigate the Pain thereof by the Statute of *Weft.* 1. Weftm. 2. 34. *cap.* 13. which gave two Years Imprifonment and fine; but fpying the Mifchiefs infu-P. Rape 1. ing upon the faid Law, at his next Parliament holden at *Weftminfter*, called *Weft.* 2. Br. Cor. 204. *cap.* 34. he made the Offence of Rape to be Felony again.

Note alfo by *Britton, fol.* 17. it is no Burglary in an Infant under fourteen Years of Cromp. 33. Age, nor in poor Perfons, that upon Hunger fhall enter a Houfe for Victuals under the See Pl. 19. Value of twelve Pence, nor in natural Fools, or other Perfons that be *Non compos Mentis*; but *quære* of Poor entring for Victuals at this Day.

(*a*) If for Prefervation of his Life a Man takes Victuals to fatisfy his prefent Hunger, * *But fee* this is not Felony nor Larceny *; for *neceffitas induct privilegium quoad jura privata.* 1 Hale H. Stamf. Sir Fr. Ba. 29. & hic poftea.   P. C. 54.

He who felonioufly takes Goods out of a Dwelling-houfe, any Perfon being with-*Robbing a* in and *put in Fear*; or he who fhall rob any Dwelling-houfe in the Day-time, any Per-*Dwelling-* fon being therein, or be acceffary to the fame; or he who fhall break any *Dwelling-houfe*, *houfe in the* *Shop*, or *Warehoufe* thereunto belonging in the *Day-time*, and felonioufly take away 3 & 4 W. & any Goods to the Value of 5 s. though *no Perfon be therein*; or he who fhall counfel, M. c. 9. hire, or command another to commit Burglary, fhall not have his Clergy.

He who commits Burglary, or any other Crime, for which the Benefit of Clergy is *Difcovering* taken away by the Statute 3 & 4 *Will.* aforefaid, and (being out of Prifon) fhall difcover *two or more* two or more Offenders, and convict them, he fhall have his Pardon, which fhall be a 11 W.3. c. 23. good Bar to any Appeal.   *Burglars.*

He who apprehends and profecutes an Houfe-breaker to Conviction, fhall within one *Profecuting and* Month afterwards upon producing a Certificate of the Judge before whom he was con-*Burglar fhall* victed, receive 40 *l*. of the Sheriff of the County, * without any Deduction, for every *have* 40 *l*. Offender fo convicted.   5 Ann. c. 32.   * 7 Geo. 1.   c. 23.

He who enters into a Dwelling-houfe, either by Day or Night, *without breaking it,* *Entring a* with an Intent to commit Felony; or being in the Houfe commits any Felony and in *Dwelling-* the *Night-time breaks it to get out*, is guilty of Burglary without Benefit of Clergy. *houfe by Day,* *and not break-* *ing it.*

Stealing 12 Ann. c. 7.

Stealing to the Value of 40 s. out of a Dwelling-house, Out-house, tho' not broke open. Stealing Goods to the Value of 40 s. or more, being in the Dwelling-house, or Out-house, *though it was not actually broke open*; and though any Person or no Body was therein; and likewise the *Aider* and *Assister* shall be guilty of Burglary, without Benefit of Clergy.

See also Chap. 160. infra, 1 Hawk. P. C. Chap. 38. *and* 1 H. H. P. C. Chap. 48.

C H A P. CLII.

Theft.

THEFT is the fraudulent Taking away of another Man's moveable Personal Goods, with an Intent to steal them, against (or without) the Will of him whose Goods they be: And this is of two Sorts, Robbery and Larceny.

C H A P. CLIII.

Robbery.

Definition.
Dyer 224.
Stamf. 27.
1 H. H. P. C.
532. RObbery (in *Latin* called *Rapina*) is properly the *felonious Taking* any Thing from the Person of another, against his Will, and putting him in Fear thereby: And here although the Thing taken be but the Value of an Halfpenny yet it is Felony, for which the Offender shall suffer Death, without Benefit of Clergy.

As if one by the Highway assaulteth me, and taketh away my Purse, Money, or Goods.

What.
9 Ed. 4. 28.
Stamf. 29. But if a Thief assault me to rob me, and biddeth me deliver my Purse, but taketh nothing from me (in regard that I being too hard for him, shall apprehend him, or shall levy Hue and Cry, whereby he is taken) this is no Robbery nor Felony. (*a*) For although Intent may make a Man guilty of Treason (as you may see here before, Title *Treason*) yet in case of Felony there must be an Execution of that which was formerly intended, and resolved to be done, *viz.* to kill the Party, or to steal or take away the Thing, &c. and therefore in *M. Plow. fol.* 259. *b. Walsh* Serjeant saith, *Que intent de faire tort, sans del act fait nest punishable in n're Ley, nec le Resolution, &c. mez le fesans de l'act est le sole point que nostre Ley respect.*

Stamf. 72. (*d*) And yet the Assault (yea, to lie in wait) only to rob me, hath been in former Times holden to be Felony, as appeareth by the Books, 27 *Ass. p.* 38. & 13 H. 4. 7. 24 E. 3. 42. *Fitz. Coron.* 132 & 267. *Br. Coron.* 106, 215.

Taking. And so the Intent to commit Burglary (or Murder) hath been holden to be Felony; for the Will was reputed for the Deed. *Vide* 27 *Ass.* 38. *Fitz. Coron.* 383. & *Stamf. fol.* 17. *a.* But the Law is otherwise at this Day.

7 Geo. 2.
c. 21. §. 1. (*a*) And now by 7 *Geo.* 2. If any Person shall, with any offensive Weapon assault, or shall by Menaces, or in a violent Manner, demand any Money, Goods or Chattels, from any Person, with an Intent to rob such Person, such Offender shall be guilty of Felony, and transported for seven Years.

20 Eliz.
Cromp. 34. (*d*) In this former Description of Robbery, the Word (*Taking*) is largely to be extended against the Offender. So that although the Thief taketh nothing from my Person, yet if he assaulteth me, and upon his Assault he threatneth to kill me, if I deliver him not my Purse; and thereupon I cast my Purse down, and he taketh it away; this is Robbery.

Cromp. 34. So if one draws his Sword upon me, and biddeth me deliver my Purse, and I refuse, and after he prays me to give him a Penny, and I do so, yet it seems this is Robbery; for by the Assault I was put in Fear, and out of that I gave him the Money to be rid of him.

Stamf. 37. c. So if a Thief do only assault me to rob me, and I deliver him my Purse with my own Hand; yet this is Robbery, in regard this Fact of mine proceeded from Fear, or by his Menacing, &c.

So in flying from the Thief, I caſt my Purſe into a Buſh to ſave it, and the Thief Stamf. 37. c. ſeeth me, and taketh it away, this is Robbery; for in this Caſe had he not put me in Cromp. 35. Fear, I ſhould not have caſt my Money from me.

So if one aſſaults me to rob me, and I flying away from him, my Hat falleth off, Cromp. 35. and the Thief taketh it up, and carrieth it away; this is Robbery.

So if a Thief biddeth me deliver my Purſe (without drawing any Weapon, or other 29 Eliz. Force uſed) and I deliver him my Purſe, and he finding but two Shillings therein, deli- Cromp. 34. vereth it me all again; yet this is Robbery.

So if Thieves do take a Man, and by Threats compel him to ſwear to bring them 44 E. 3. 14. Money to ſuch a Place (at another Time) or elſe that they will kill him, and he bring- 4 H. 4. 3.
Stamf. 27. eth the Money accordingly; this is Robbery. (a) *Term. Paſch.* 36 *Eliz.* it was adjudged accordingly.

(d) One came to a Fiſherman, going in the Highway to Market with Fiſh to ſell, Crom. 35. and deſired to buy ſome Fiſh of him, and he refuſed; whereupon the other took away ſome of the Fiſhes againſt his Will, and gave him more Money for them than they were worth; but the Fiſherman was thereby put in Fear: Whereupon the other was in- dicted, and arraigned at *York* about 26 *Eliz.* but Judgment was reſpited, for that the Court doubted whether it were Felony or no.

Alſo, in the former Deſcription of Robbery, the Words *from the Perſon* are not ſo Perſon. nicely to be conſtrued, that (to make up Robbery) the Goods muſt needs be annexed to the Body of the Perſon; for in ſome Caſes it may be Robbery, notwithſtanding the Thief doth neither take the Goods from the *Perſon* of the Owner, nor yet aſſault him.

As if in my Preſence a Felon taketh away my Goods openly againſt my will; this Stamf. 27. is Robbery, though he neither taketh them from my Perſon, nor aſſaulteth me: For Lamb. 265. the Loſs is the ſame, and the Fear alike, as though it had been from my *Perſon.*

And if one or more do take a Horſe out of my Paſture, or drive my Cattle out of P. R. 131. my Ground, I ſtanding by, and looking on at the ſame Time; this is Robbery, though the Felon doth neither make an Aſſault or put me in the Fear.

But to make it Robbery the Perſon muſt be *put in Fear*; for if a Felon doth take Mo- Fear. ney from me in the Highway, and ſhall not put me in Fear; this is no Robbery. Lamb. 266.
Cromp. 35.
P. R. 131.

And you ſhall find a Caſe in my Lord *Dyer*, how a Felon did take Money, to the Dyer 224. Value of forty Shillings, or above, from the Perſon of another in the Highway, and yet for that he did not put his Perſon in Fear by Aſſault and Violence, this was holden no Robbery, and the Offender was allowed his Clergy for the ſame Felony.

Alſo if the Robbery be not committed in or near the Highway, it ſeems the Offender * See alſo may have his Clergy. See 1 *Ed.* 6. *cap.* 12. *Raſtal* 60. *b.* & 61. *d.* *. 2 Hawk. P.C.
c. 33. § 25.

Note alſo, if two Thieves ſhall attempt to rob me, and I fly from them, and one of Crom. 84. the Thieves follow me, and the other eſpying another true Man (but out of the Sight of his Fellow) rides towards him, and robs him; this was adjudged Robbery in both the Thieves; and yet the one was neither in Sight, or knowing of this Robbery: But be- cauſe they both came to rob, and at the ſame Time, this Fact committed by one ſhall be imputed to the other alſo. It was *Pudſey's* Caſe, 28 *El.*

If one ſteal my Purſe, or take or pick my Purſe out of my Pocket ſecretly, or privily Cut purſe. and fraudulently, it is Felony without Benefit of Clergy, if it be above the Value of 8 Eliz. 4. twelve Pence. *Quære,* if it be under twelve Pence, becauſe it is taken from the Perſon P. Cler. 1.
Lamb. 266. of a Man, and the Form of the Indictments are *Inſultum fecit.* See *Fitz. Coron.* 430. Cromp. 34. Alſo the Words (8 *Eliz.* 4.) are, That no Perſon taking any Money or Goods (general- ly) from the Perſon of another, &c. ſhall have his Clergy; and yet by the Opinion of 1 Hawk. P.C. Mr. *Lambard* and Mr. *Crompton,* this is no Felony, unleſs the Thing taken be of more 98. accord. Value than twelve Pence, but Petty Larceny, for which the Offender is not to have Judgment of Death, and therefore needeth not his Clergy.

So if one ſhall take any Money or other Goods from my Perſon, *ſecretly* without my P. Clerg. 1. Knowledge, or by Slight only, I neither being made afraid, nor knowing it (if it be Lamb. 266. above twelve Pence in value) it is Felony of Death.

A Man cutteth my Girdle privily, my Purſe hanging thereat, and the Purſe and 26 Eliz. Girdle fall to the Ground, but he did not take them up (for that he was eſpied) this Cromp. 35.
Dyer 224. is no Felony; for that the Thief never had an actual Poſſeſſion thereof, ſevered from my Perſon: But if he had holden the Purſe in his Hand, and then cut the Girdle (al- though it had fallen to the Ground, and that he took it up no more) then had it been

4 T Felony,

Felony, (if there had been above twelve Pence in the Purse) for he had it once in his Possession: But these secret and privy Takings from my Person, are no Robbery; for he neither assaulted me, nor put me in any Fear.

(a) And in antient Time, the Offender only lost his right Thumb. See *Fitz. Cor.* 434.

C H A P. CLIV.

Larceny.

Arceny (being fetched from the Latin Word, *Latrocinium*) is properly a fraudulent and felonious Taking away another Man's personal Goods, removed from his Body or Person, in the Absence of the Owner, and without his Knowledge. (a) *Bracton, lib.* 3. *cap.* 17. & 32. saith, *Furtum omnino non committitur, sine affectu & animo furandi.*

And Mr. *Finch* (Tit. *Felonies*) saith, That Larceny is the secret Taking the Goods of another, above the Value of twelve Pence, without Pretence of Title.

For the tortious Taking of Goods, with Pretence of Title, is only Trespass.

Grand Lar-
ceny.
(d) Grand Larceny is when the Goods stoln be above the Value of twelve Pence; and this is Felony, wherein Judgment of Death shall be given upon the Offender, except he be saved by his Book.

F. Cor. 451.
And yet if the Goods stoln be to the Value of ten Shillings, if the Jury upon his Trial shall find the Goods did not exceed the Value of twelve Pence, then that Offence shall be taken but for Petty Larceny.

Petty Larceny.
West. 1. c.15.
Br. Cor. 84
& 85.
Stamf. 24.
Petty Larceny is when the Goods stoln do not exceed the Value of twelve Pence. And for this the Offender shall be imprisoned for some certain Time, and after shall be whipped, or otherwise punished by the Discretion of the Justices, before whom he is arraigned, but it is no Felony of Death at this Day.

* But the Law
is settled, that
(a) By good Opinions, the Stealing of Goods to the Value only of twelve Pence hath been held to be Felony of Death. See *Fitz. Coron.* 178. & *Br. Coron.* 84, 85. & *Forf.* 1. *Doct. & Stud.* 17. *
it must exceed 12 d. to make grand Larceny. 1 Hale Hist. P. C. 530.

(d) Yet may not the Justice of Peace, before whom such an Offender shall be brought, out of the Sessions, punish by his Discretion the said Offender for Petty Larceny, and so let him go, but must commit him to Prison, or bail him, to the Intent he may come to his Trial, as in Cases of other Felonies; and if upon his Trial, the Jury shall find the Goods stolen to exceed twelve Pence in Value, the Offender shall have Judgment to die for the Fault.

But if the Indictment be laid twenty Pence, and the Offender arraigned thereof; yet upon his Trial, if the Jury shall find the Goods to be but of the Value of ten Pence; here the Offender shall have Judgment but as for Petty Larceny. 41 E. 3. *Abr. d' Assi.* 70.

27 H. 8. 22.
F. Cor. 218.
Bro. Cor. 54,
88. & 219.
1 Hawk. P.C.
95.
Also, although Petty Larceny be not punishable by Death, yet it is a felonious Taking; for the Indictment of Petty Larceny must be *Felonice cepit:* And he shall forfeit all his Goods and Chattels for such a Felony; and there is no Difference either in the Nature of the Offence, or in the Mind of the Offender, but only in the Value of the Thing stoln, which also maketh the Difference of Punishment.

(a) And yet by some late Opinions, Petty Larceny is but in the Nature of a Trespass, and then where the Principal is convicted but of Petty Larceny, there can be no Accessaries, and the Procurers or Receivers, knowing of the Goods to be stolen, are not to be dealt withal as for Felony: But to be sent to the House of Correction, or to receive some other Punishment, by the Discretion of the Justices at the Quarter-Sessions. *Quære inde.*

F. Cor. 415.
Stamf. 24.
Cromp. 36. c.
(d) If one shall steal Goods to the Value of four Pence at one Time, and six Pence at another Time, and of three Pence at another Time, which together do exceed the Value of twelve Pence; and that these several Goods be all stolen from one and the same Person, then may they be put together in one Indictment; and the Offender being thereupon arraigned and found guilty, shall have Judgment of Death therefore. *
* But this Se-
verity is seldom practised, according to 1 Hawk. P. C. 95.

F. Cor. 404.
Stamf. 24. l.
Again, if two or more together, do steal Goods above the Value of twelve Pence: This is Felony of Death in them all; for the Felony in them is several, though the Stealing be jointly done.

I   (a) By

(a) By the Law of God, for Theft the Offender was to yield at leaft the double Value to the Party robbed; and if he were not able to make full Reftitution, then he was to be fold for the Theft. *Exod.* 22.

Leges etiam Civiles furtum manifeftum judicant per redditionem quadrupli; & furtum non manifeftum per dupli compenfationem expiari. Cow. 199.

Where a Shopkeeper delivers Goods in his Shop to a Cuftomer, pretending to buy them, Raim. 275, and he runs away with them; 'tis Felony, for the Running away fhews his Intention to get the Goods *animo furandi.*

C H A P. CLV.

Theft. Now firft for the Manner.

IN Larceny two Things muft concur, *fc.* to take, and to carry away, or to remove the *The Manner.* Thing taken, with a Purpofe to fteal the fame; for the Indictment muft be, *Cepit & tffortavit,* or *cepit & abduxit*; and yet in thefe Words, the Letter is not fo much to be nfifted upon as the Meaning, and that for the better Suppreffing of Offenders in this Kind.

For although by the Law in *Glanvil's* Time, *A furto omnimodo excufatur, qui initium Delivery. habuerit fuæ detentionis per dominum illius rei*; yet at this Day it may be Felony, though the Offender take not the Thing, but hath it by Delivery from the Owner's own Hand, and fo cometh lawfully to the Poffeffion; as,

If a Taverner do fet a Piece of Plate before his Gueft to drink out of, and the Gueft car- 13 E. 4. 9. rieth it away; this is Felony: For the Taverner gave him no Poffeffion thereof, but only Stamf. 25. the Ufe to drink out of it for the Time.

If I deliver Goods to a Carrier, or other Perfon, and bargain with him to carry them to *Carrier.* a certain Place appointed; if he carrieth them to the Place, and then conveyeth them away Ibid. fraudulently, this is Felony: For the Privity of Bailment was determined when they came at the Place appointed.

So if the Carrier fhall take out Parcel of the Goods; this is Felony. Ibid.

Alfo if the Carrier fhall carry them to another Place, and there breaketh them up, and Ibid. converteth Part, or all, to his own Ufe; this is Felony.

But if the Carrier fhall fell, or give away, or otherwife imbezil the Whole as he re- Stamf. 25. a. ceived them; this is holden to be no Felony, becaufe it was delivered him. Cromp. 36. a.

And yet in this laft Cafe there is befides the Delivery, a Bargain and Agreement to carry the Goods, and the Delivery was only to that Intent; fo that the Property of thofe Goods did always remain in the firft Owner. *Ideo quære.*

But if *A.* lendeth his Horfe to *B.* being a Stranger, who rideth away with the Horfe; 1 H. H. P. C. this is no Felony in *B.* by Reafon of the Delivery. And fo did Sir *John Dodderidge* 504. accord. Knight, give Direction at *Cambridge* Affifes, 1617, upon an Indictment of Felony pre- ferred in fuch Cafe. *Quære,* if the Horfe had been delivered to a Servant, who rideth away therewith. *Vide poftea, fub hoc tit.*

If a Clothier fhall deliver any Wool or Yarn to his Carder, Spinfter, or Weaver, *&c.*, 7 Jac. 1. c. 7. to drefs, and they fhall convey away, imbezil, or fell any Part thereof; this is no Felony, by Reafon of the Delivery, but they fhall be punifhed by the Difcretion of two Juftices of Peace, by Whipping or Stocking, *&c.* *Vide antea,* Tit. *Cloth.*

So if I deliver my Goods to another to keep, and he fraudulently confumeth them, or 13 E. 4. 9. otherwife converteth them to his own Profit; this is no Felony, becaufe of the Delivery.

And fo (it feemeth) if I deliver Money or Goods to *A.* to deliver to *B.* and *A.* flieth away with them, confumeth them, or converteth them to his own Ufe; this is no Felony, by Reafon of the Delivery.

If a Man delivers Money to his Servant to keep, or Plate to his Butler, or Veffel to his *Servants.* Cook, or Horfe to his Horfe-keeper, or Sheep to his Shepherd, and fuch Servant doth go 21 H. 4. 14. away with them, this is Felony by the Common Law in that Servant (for thefe Goods 13 E. 4. 10. were always in the Mafter's Poffeffion, and kept and ufed by the Servant to the Mafter's 21 H. 7. 15. Behoof). But yet there was much Difference of Opinions herein; for the clearing where- *Apprentices* of, in fome Part, the Statute 21 H. 8. *cap.* 7. (which was made perpetual, by the Sta- *and Servants* tute of 5 El. cap. 10.) provided, That all and fingular Servants of the Age of eighteen *fhall be in Cafe* Years, (other than an Apprentice, which muft be underftood of fuch as be bound by In- *as they were* denture, and by the Name of an Apprentice) to whom any Money, Goods or Chattels, *before the ma-* *&c.* *king of this Sta-* *tute.*

21 H. 8. 7.
P. Felon. 10.
Crom. 50.
&c. by his or their Mafter or Miftrefs fhall be delivered to keep of the Value of forty Shillings, or above; if fuch Servant fhall go away with, or fhall imbezil, or fhall convert to his own Ufe, any fuch Money, Goods or Chattels of the faid Value, to the Intent to fteal the fame, or to defraud his Mafter or Miftrefs thereof, it fhall be Felony. But this muft be profecuted within one Year after the Offence.

And now upon the Conftruction of this Statute of 21 H. 8. divers new Queftions and Cafes have fince arofe: As,

Dyer 5.
If a Man delivers an Obligation to his Servant, to go and receive the Money thereupon due; and the Servant receiveth the Money, and then goeth away therewith, or doth convert it to his own Ufe: This is holden to be no Felony within the Meaning of this Statute, for the Mafter did not deliver the Money to his Servant.

Dyer 5.
So if a Man delivers to his Servant Wares or Cattle to fell at the Fair or Market, and he felleth them there, and receiveth the Money, and then goeth away with the Money, or converteth it to his own Ufe: This is no Felony within this Statute; for he had not the Money by his Mafter's Delivery, neither went he away with the Goods of his Mafter delivered him.

28 El.
Crom. 35.
But if the Servant received of his Mafter twenty Pounds in Gold to keep, which he changed into Silver, and then ran away with that; this is Felony, for that Gold and Silver are both of the fame Nature, fc. Money.

21 H. 7. 15.
And if a Man delivers to his Servant a Horfe to ride to Market, or Money to carry to a Fair, or to buy Cattle, or other Things, or to pay to another Man, and the Servant goeth away therewith: This was no Felony by the Common Law, by Reafon of the Delivery thereof to him by his Mafter: But *quære*, if it be not Felony by this Statute, for that he went away with the Thing delivered him.

(*a*) If the Goods delivered to the Servant to keep, be under the Value of forty Shillings, and the Servant goeth away therewith, this is holden to be no Felony at this Day. But if the Servant fhall imbezil, or go away with any Goods of his Mafter's, which were not delivered to him; this is Felony, although they be under the Value of forty Shillings, &c.

If a Man appoint his Servant to take and carry Corn to Market, and to take his Horfe to carry the fame upon, and the Servant goeth away with the Corn and Horfe; this is Felony in the Servant, if the Goods he fo goeth away with, be all to the Value of forty Shillings, &c.

But if a Servant waftefully confumeth the Goods, and returned again to his Mafter; this is no Felony. And thefe were the Directions of Sir *Nicholas Hide* to a Jury of Life and Death, upon the Arraignment of a Servant in fuch a Cafe at *Cambridge* Lent Affizes, *Anno* 2 *Caroli Regis.*

Dyer 5.
(*d*) And if one of my Servants doth deliver to another of my Servants Goods of mine (to the Value of forty Shillings) and he doth go away therewith, or converteth them to his own Ufe; this is Felony within this Statute, for this fhall be faid my Delivery.

5 H. 7. 16.
Br. Property
23.
Crom. 50.
If a Man delivers to his Servant a Piece of Cloth to keep, and the Servant maketh himfelf a Garment thereof, and after goeth away therewith; this is Felony within this Statute: For that the Property is not altered by making a Garment thereof, becaufe the Cloth may be known ftill. Otherwife, it is of Barley turned into Malt, or of Money melted and turned into a Wedge or Piece of Metal, or the like; for that in thefe Cafes the Barly or Money cannot be known again, but are altered in their Nature and Kind. But *quære*, and fee the Words of the Statute.

(*a*) If a Man delivers Goods to one to keep, and after retains the fame Perfon into his Service, who after goeth away with thofe Goods; this is no Felony by 21 H. 8. becaufe he was no Servant at the Time the Goods were delivered to him. *Vide* Sir *Fra. Ba.* 39, 40.

Crom. 50.
If I deliver Goods to the Servant of *A.* to keep, and after I die, and make *A.* mine Executor; and before any new Command of *A.* to his Servant for the Cuftody of the fame Goods, his Servant goeth away with them; this is out of 21 H. 8. *Ibid.*

13 E. 4. 9.
(*d*) If my Receiver of my Rents receive ten Pounds of my Tenants, and run away therewith, it is no Felony; for the Statute is, *where the Mafter delivereth to keep,* &c.

If a Man delivers to his Servant the Key of the Chamber-door, and the Servant taketh away his Mafter's Goods in the Chamber (above the Value of twelve Pence): This is Felony at the Common Law, for the Goods were not delivered.

(*a*) A Man laid and hid a Purfe of Money in his Corn-mow within his Barn, and after his Servant finding the fame, took Part of the Money out of the Purfe, &c. And the Servant was therefore indicted and arraigned of Felony, at *Cambridge* Summer Affizes, *Anno Dom.* 1621. before Sir *John Dodderidge.*

                     If

If an Apprentice or Servant, under the Age of eighteen Years, shall imbezil their Master's Goods, which were not delivered to them, nor committed to their Charge, if the Goods so imbeziled be above the Value of twelve Pence, it is Felony. But if the Goods be under that Value, it seems such Apprentice or Servant, may be sent to the House of Correction.

(d) Another Felony there is by the Statute 33 *H.* 6. *cap.* 1. in the Servant that shall *Servant.* take away or spoil the Goods of his deceased Master : But this Felony groweth upon P. Felony 11. their Default of Appearance in the King's Bench, after Proclamation ; and therefore P. Exec. 51. neither the Trial nor hearing thereof belongeth to the Justices of Peace, because they cannot well take Knowledge of such Default in the King's Bench.

The second Thing which must concur (in Larceny) to make it Felony, is the *Car-* Carrying. *rying away* the Thing so taken ; and yet it is not of Necessity that it be clean carried out of the House or Place where it was ; but sufficeth, that it be so far removed, that the evil and felonious Intent of the Taker may plainly appear. As,

If a Guest will feloniously take the Sheets, or other Goods of the Inn-keepers, out 27 Ass. 36. of the Chamber where he lodges, and then (going to the Stable for his Horse) is taken *See* Stamf. 26. with them, or they be found in some other Room of the House where he had laid Br. Cor. 107. them ; it is Felony in both Cases, although the Possession of those Goods continued in the Owner.

So is it, if one taketh a Horse in another Man's Close, with an Intent to steal Lamb. 277. him, and be apprehended before he hath gotten the Horse out of the same Close ; this Crom. 36. a. is Felony.

(a) Taking Money or Reward directly or indirectly to help another to stolen Goods, 4 G. 1. c. 11. unless he doth apprehend, or cause to be apprehended, such Felon who stole the same, and bring him to Trial, and give Evidence against him, is guilty of Felony, and shall suffer the Penalty according to the Nature of the Felony committed in stealing such Goods, and in the same Manner as if he had stolen the same.

Upon this Clause the famous *Jonathan Wilde* was executed, *Anno* 10 *Geo.* 1.

If one takes a Sheep in my Pasture or Fold, or a Calf in my Pen, &c. and killeth the same, and be found or taken doing it, and then begins to flie ; this is Felony, though he hath not carried the same away out of the Place where he first took it.

For Sheep stealing, see Chap. 160. *infra.*

CHAP. CLVI.

Next, Of what Things Larceny may be committed, and of what not.

Larceny may be committed by taking any of the moveable Goods of any Person, as *Moveable* Money, Plate, Apparel, Houshold-stuff, or Corn, Hay, Trees or Fruit, (that are *Goods.* severed from the Ground) or the like ; the Stealing of them is Felony.

It is also Felony to steal any Horses, Mares, Colts, Oxen, Kine, Sheep, Lambs, *Domestical.* Swine, Pigs, Hens or Geese, Ducks, Turkies, Peacocks, and other domestical Birds or 1 Hawk. P.C. Beasts of tame Nature. (d) For the Nature of these Things being tame, (and not Sa- Ch. 33. § 28. vage) if they shall run or flie away, though out of Sight of the Owner, yet in what Place soever they be found, they cease not to be his, so as whosoever detaineth them from the Owner is punishable by Way of Action.

(d) It is Felony also to take some Things that be of wild Nature : As to take young *Wild.* Pigeons which cannot flie, out of another Man's Dove-house or other House ; or to take Fitz. 86. l. young Hawks, or young Herons, out of their Nests (or Airies) and breeding in a Park 10 E. 4. 17. or other several Ground ; so to take *Fishes* that be kept in a Trunk or several Pond. a. Bingham, (a) For that the Property of such Things shall be always adjudged in the Owner of the & 18 E. 4. f. Dove-house, Ground, Trunk or Pond, in as much as such Things cannot (of them- 8. a. selves) get out thereof, but that the Owner of such Dove-house, Ground or Pond, may take them at all Times at his Pleasure.

(d) *Quære* of old Doves taken in the Dove-coat, or of any other wild Beast or Fowl Br. Cor. 92. being of Value) and taken within a Man's House.   22 Ass. 95.
                                                                              Kit.9.b. 27 b.
                                                      See 1 Hawk. P. C. Ch. 33. § 26.

See Hawk. ib.
§ 27.
22 H. 8. 9. b.
18 E. 4. 8. a. (a) At *Cambridge* Summer Affizes *Anno* 1627, there were two indicted and arraigned of Felony before Sir *Francis Harvey*, for taking Fifh out of a Net lying in the River being the feveral Fifhing of Sir *Ed. P.*

(d) Alfo it is Felony to take any Swans that be lawfully marked, though they be at large. (a) For a Man hath Property in fuch. See *Co. L.* 16. b. 17. a. *Quære*, if they be flying Swans, and not pinioned.

Co. 7. 17. b. Alfo for Swans unmarked, if they be domeftical or tame, *fc.* kept in a Moat, or in a Pond near to a Dwelling-houfe, and fo be *Domui* or *Manui affueta*, to fteal fuch i Felony.

Co. 7. 16. b. So it feemeth of Swans unmarked, fo long as they keep within a Man's Manor, o within his private Rivers; or if they happen to efcape from thence, and be purfued and taken, and brought in again.

But if Swans that be unmarked fhall be abroad, and fhall attain to their natura Liberty, then the Property of them is loft, and fo long Felony cannot be committed by taking of them.

Co. lib. 7. f.
16. a. b. &
18. a. b. And yet fuch unmarked and wild Swans, the King's Officers may feife (being abroad for and to the Ufe of the King, by his Prerogative, they being *Volatilia Regalia* : Alfo the King may grant them, and by Confequence another Man may prefcribe to have them within a certain Precinct or Place; for it may be intended to have a lawful Beginning by the King's Grant.

Alfo young Swans or Cygnets, belong to both the Owners in common Equality, *fc* to the Owner of the old Cock, and to the Owner of the old Hen, and the Cygnets o young Swans fhall be divided between them. *Co.* 7. 17. And to fteal fuch Cygnets i Felony; for they fhall be of the fame Nature with the old Cock or Hen.

Deer.
10 E. 4. 15.
Stamf. 52. (d) Alfo it is Felony to take a tame Deer which is marked and domeftical, efpecially if the Taker knows it to be tame and domeftical, or that it weareth a Bell.

(a) If a Hart, Buck, or other Beaft which hath been wild by Nature, and made tame, and hath at his Neck a little Collar of Leather, or any other notorious Sign, and doth go abroad, and returneth again to the Houfe (of his Mafter or Owner) at his Pleafure, if he be taken by a Stranger and killed by Night, or in other fecret Manner, this is Felony by the Common Law. *Crompt. Author. des Courts* 167.

Fitz. 87. a.
Fi. 45. (d) But by the Common Law, Larceny cannot be committed by taking favage or wild Beafts, Fowls or Fifh, found in their Wildernefs and abroad, or at large; as Deer, Conies, Hawks, Doves, Pheafants, Partridges, Herons, Swans unmarked, or Fifh that are at Liberty, &c. for no Perfons can claim Property in them.

(a) By the Statute *de Forefta, cap.* 10. *Nullus de cætero amittat vitam vel membrum pro Venatione noftra*, (*fc. pur tuer Deere le Roy* :) which Branch is but an Affirmance of the Common Law. *Cromp. Author. des Courts* 166.

P. Felon. 24.
Lamb. 271. (d) Howbeit by Statute it is now made Felony to hunt Deer or Conies (after fome Sort) in a Foreft, Park or Warren; or to take a tame Beaft or other Thing in a Park, by Manner of Robbery. See the Statute 3 *Ed.* 1. 20. & 1 *H.* 7. *cap.* 7. *Vide poftea Felony by Stat.*

Hawk.
P. Felon. 20. Alfo by Statute it is Felony to fteal, take away, or conceal a Hawk. *Ibid.*

Co. 17. b.
Fi. 4. But for the better Underftanding what the Law is in Things that be *feræ naturæ*, obferve thefe Differences.

Property.
Feræ Naturæ. In fome Things that be *feræ naturæ*, a Man hath Right and Property, and in fome of them a Right of Privilege.

There be three Manners of Rights of Property : *fc.*

1. Abfolute. This Property a Man cannot have in any Thing which is *feræ naturæ*, but only in fuch Things as are *domitæ naturæ.*

2. Qualified. ⎫ Thefe Properties a Man may have in Things *feræ naturæ*; and to
3. Poffeffory. ⎭ fuch Properties a Man may attain by two Means :

Property, how gotten. 1. By Induftry : And this may be either by taking them only, or by the making them tame, (*fc. manfueta, id eft, manui affueta*, or *domeftica, id eft, domui affueta*). But in thefe laft a Man alfo hath but a qualified Property, *fc.* fo long as they remain in his Poffeffion, and fo long Felony may be committed by taking them away; but if they attain to their natural Liberty, and have not *animum revertendi*, then the Property of them is loft.

18 E. 4. fol. 8.
Stamf. 25. c.
Fitz. 86. l. &
89. k. 2. *Ratione impotentiæ & loci* : As where a Man hath young Gofhawks or Herons, or the like, which are *feræ naturæ*, and doth breed (or air) in his Ground, he hath a poffeffory Property in them; fo as if one takes them when they cannot fly, the Owner,

2 of

of the Soil may have an Action of Trespass, *Quare bofcum fuum fregit, & tres pullos Efpervorum fuorum*, or *Ardearum fuarum, pretii tanti, nuper in eodem bofco nidificantium cepit & afportavit.* And to take thefe away, is Felony as aforefaid.

(*a*) Alfo note, That my *Hawk* which is flying at a Fowl, and my Deer that is chafed out of my Park, fo long as my Servant or Keeper maketh frefh Suit after them, they ftill remain in my Poffeffion, and the Property is ftill in me: But if they ftray it is lawful for any Man to take them. *Fi.* 45.

(*d*) But when a Man hath Beafts or Fowl (that be favage, and in their wildnefs) *ratione privilegii, fc.* by reafon of a Park or Warren, &c. (as Deer, Hares, Conies, Pheafants or Partridges, or the like, which be Things of Warren) he hath no Property in them: And therefore in an Action, *Quare Parcum*, or *Warrenam*, &c. *fregit & intravit & 3 damas, lepores, cuniculos, phafianos, perdices, &c. ibidem invent' cepit & afportavit*, he fhall not fay *fuos*, for that he hath no Property in them, but they belong unto him *ratione privilegii*, (for his Game and Pleafure) fo long as they remain in the Place privileged. And if the Owner of the Park die, his Heir fhall have them, and not his Executors or Adminiftrators, for that without them the Park (which is an Inheritance) is not compleat: Neither can Felony be committed by taking them. *Co. 8. 138 b. See Doct. & Stud. f. 16.*

Neither can Larceny be committed by taking of Dogs of any Kind, Apes, Parrots, Squirrels, Singing Birds, or fuch like Thing, kept only for Pleafure, and not for any Profit, though they be in the Houfe and made tame. *Dogs. Lamb. 270.*

No not by taking a Blood-hound or Maftiff, although there is good Ufe of them, and that a Man may be faid to have a Property in them, fo as an Action of Trefpafs lieth for Taking them; yet in regard they are Things of fo bafe a Nature, no Felony can be committed by taking them. *Co. 7. 18. 12 H. 8. 3 Br. Tref. 407*

(*a*) But yet to take a Dog of any Kind, or other Thing of Pleafure, from the Perfon of another, or out of the Poffeffion of another, and in his Prefence, if it be done with Force or Violence, it amounteth to the Breach of the Peace. And if it be done with Force, and by the Number of three Perfons or more, it will amount to a Riot.

(*d*) Alfo it is Felony to fteal the Flefh of any tame or wild Fowl, or of any Deer or other Beaft that is dead, out of the Poffeffion of another Man. *Stamf. 25.*

So it is to pull the Wool from the Sheeps Back, or to kill them, and to take the Skin, and leave the Body behind. *Sheep and Wool. Cromp. 36.*

But note, that in all thefe Cafes of Felony aforefaid, the Thing fo taken or ftolen muft exceed the Value of 12 *d.*

Alfo the Taking of any real Chattel or Thing is no Felony: As,

If one cuts down my Tree, or my Corn, and carrieth it away, or pulleth and ftealeth any Apples hanging on the Tree, and carrieth them away; thefe are no Felonies, for thefe Things be Part of my Freehold, till they be fevered. *Things real. Stamf. 25. 10 E. 4. 17.1. Co. 4. 19.*

But if I gather mine Apples, or cut down a Tree or Corn of mine own, then it is Felony if another Man fhall carry them away felonioufly.

And by the Opinion of *Mar.* if a Stranger cuts down my Tree or Corn without Title, and another Time after he fetches it away, that will prove Felony, becaufe it was a Chattel fevered when he took it. *Stamf. 25. Lamb. 272. Cromp. 36. 12 Aff. p. 37 Br. Coron. 76 Cromp. 37.*

Alfo to take Lead from off a Houfe or Church will not amount to Felony, for it is Parcel of the Houfe or Freehold.

(*a*) But this is now altered by Statute 4 *Geo.* 2. *cap.* 32. by which it is enacted, That all Perfons who fhall fteal or rip, cut or break, with Intent to fteal, any lead, iron Bar, iron Gate, iron Palifadoe, or iron Rail, fixed to any Dwelling-houfe or other Building, or fixed in any Garden, Court-Yard, Fence or Out-let belonging to any Dwelling-houfe or other Building, fhall be guilty of Felony; and fuch Offenders may be tranfported for feven Years: And all Perfons who fhall be affifting in ftealing, or in fuch ripping, cutting or breaking, any lead, iron Bar, &c. or fhall buy or receive any fuch lead, iron Bar, &c. knowing the fame to be ftolen, fhall be liable to the fame Punifhment as if he had ftolen the fame. *4 Geo. 2. c. 32.*

(*d*) Alfo to take away the Evidence of a Man's Land, or any Indenture of Leafe, or any Obligation, Deed, Specialty, or other Writings, be they in or without a Box, it is no Felony, becaufe they cannot be valued; and again, becaufe they concern Inheritance, Chattels real, or Things in Action. (*a*) Yet if they be in a Box unfealed, it feemeth that the Taking of the Box felonioufly is Larceny; but if the Box be fealed, and have Writings within it, the Box fhall be of the fame Nature as the Writings that be therein. 10 Ed. 4. *fol.* 16. *Writings. Stamf. 25. Lamb. 271. 10 Ed. 4 16 Br. Cor. 122 Co. 8. 31.*

(*d*) So

Stamf. 25.

(*d*) So to take away an Infant in Ward is no Felony.

The Owner unknown.
Stamf. 27.
F. Cor. 187, 265.
Br. Cor. 176.

Alfo the Taking and Carrying away of fuch Things whereof the Owner is unknown in fome Cafes is no Felony: As the Taking away of Treafure that was hidden or left (be it Money, Bullion or Plate) or of Wreck of the Sea, or Goods that be waived or Strays (before they be lawfully feifed, &c.) (*a*) But the Takers away of fuch Treafure, Wreck, and Waif, fhall be punifhed by Fine and Imprifonment. 22 *Aff. p.* 10 *Br. Coron.* 96. *Fit. Coron.* 187. & 265. *Vide Bract. lib.* 3. *fol.* 119 & 120.

Dyer 99.
Lamb. 272 & 476, 478.
7 E. 4. 14, 15.
Br. Indictment 33.

(*d*) And yet where the Goods be *bona cujufdam hominis ignoti*, or *bona cujufdam mortui & ignoti*, or *bona Parochianorum*, or the Goods of a Church or Chapel, as (Bells Books, Chalices, Surplices, Bell-ropes, &c.) or the Goods of any Corporation in Time of Vacation; in thefe Cafes there be Owners of them to fome Purpofe, and therefore it i Felony to fteal fuch Goods.

Digging up a dead Body.
1 Hawk.
P. C. 94.
contra.

One *Nottingham* digged a dead Body out of his Grave, and took away his Winding fheet; this was holden to be no Felony, but punifhable as a Mifdemeanor, and the Offender was adjudged to be whipped, &c. for it. This was at *Cambridge* Summer Affifes *Anno* 1617.

His own Goods.
7 H. 6. 43.
5 H. 7. 18.
Stamf. 26.
1 Hawk.
P. C c. 33.
§. 30, accord.

Note alfo, That a Man may commit Felony by Taking his own Goods: As,

If *A.* do lend or deliver Goods to *B.* to keep, and after *A.* doth take them away felonioufly, or privily and fraudulently, (to the Intent to charge *B.* or to recover Damage for the fame againft *B.* by an Action of *Detinue*) this is Felony in *A.* and yet the Property of the Goods was in him. (*a*) Yet M. *Brook, Coron.* 142. maketh a *Quær* thereof.

Mar. lect. 12.
Cromp. 37.

(*d*) If I lend my Plate, or deliver my Goods to another to keep, and he melteth my Plate, or changeth the Fafhion of my Goods; now if I fhould take that Metal or thof Goods felonioufly, it were Felony in me, becaufe the Property is altered by altering o the Fafhion. *See a little before.*

If the Party robbed taketh his Goods again from the Thief, and fuffereth him t efcape. *Vide poftea,* Tit. *Acceffaries.*

Cromp. 37.
P. R. 129.

A Man findeth my Purfe in the Highway, and being afked for it, denieth it, thi feems to be no Felony, for he came not thereby at the firft felonioufly. (*a*) But by the *Levitical* Law he was to reftore the Thing found, with an Addition of the fifth Par more thereto. *Levit.* 6. 3, 5. *Numb.* 5. 7.

A Man hath two Chains, the one of Gold, the other of Copper, and he felleth the gold Chain, and delivereth it, and prefently after he fecretly conveys away his gold Chain, and puts the copper Chain in the Place thereof: This is Felony. *Lecture* M. *Cook.*

So if one taketh away my Horfe, and leaveth another of his (which is like unto mine) inftead thereof; this is Felony. *Ibidem.*

Cromp. 37.
P. Juft 54.

(*d*) A Man cometh to my Wife, or to my Servant, with a falfe Meffage, Token o Letter made in my Name, and thereby getteth my Goods: Yet this is no Felony, but i fhall be punifhed by the Statute of 33 *H.* 1. *cap.* 1. See *antea,* Tit. *Counterfeiters.*

CHAP. CLVII.

What Perfons are chargeable in Larceny.

Wife.
27 Aff. 40.
Stamf. 26. 142.
Fi. 12.
Plo. 19.
1 H. H. P. C.
434, 516.

A Feme Covert doth fteal Goods by the Compulfion or Conftraint of her Hufband; this is no Felony in her. *F. Coron.* 160. (*a*) & *Fitz. Coron.* 199. *Br. Coron.* 108. For where the Words of the Law are broken by Compulfion, there the Law is not offended, neither fhall any Perfon be damnified for doing a Thing, whereto he is forced or compelled, but fuch Compulfion fhall be a good Excufe in our Law.

Mar. lect. 12.

(*d*) But if by the Compulfion of her Hufband fhe committeth Murder, this is Felony in them both.

27 Aff. 40.
See Stamf. 26, 27, 142.
P. R. 130.
Br. Cor. 108.
Ibid.

If a Feme Covert doth fteal Goods by the Command or Procurement of her Hufband, (without any Conftraint) this hath been holden to be Felony in her. M. *Bracton* alfo faith it is Felony; for *Licet uxor obedire debeat viro, in atrocioribus tamen non eft ei obediendum.* But M. *Stamf.* and others are of another Opinion.

4   (*a*) If

(*a*) If the Husband and the Wife join in committing Treason, the Necessity of Obe- F. Co. 130.
dience doth not excuse the Wife's Offence, as it doth in Felony, because it is against the Lamb. 257.
Commonwealth; for *Privilegium non valet contra Rempublicam*. Ba. 32.

(*d*) But if the Husband and the Wife together *steal Goods*, this shall be taken to be he only Act of the Husband, and not to be Felony in the Wife. *Vide Stamf.* 26. *a*) *& Lamb. Fitz. Coron.* 160. *& Ba.* 31 *&* 37. that the Wife can neither be Principal or Accessary, in regard of the Subjection and Obedience she oweth to her Husband.

And yet Mr. *Bracton* seems to be of another Opinion herein, saying, *Quid erit si uxor cum viro conjuncta fuerit, vel confessa fuerit, quod viro suo consilium præstiterit & auxilium? Nunquid tenebuntur ambo? Imo, ut videtur.* (And a little after he saith) *Alter orum potest esse malus per se, & alter bonus; ita uterque eorum possit simul & conjunctim esse malus.*

And again, *Sicut sunt participes in crimine, ita debent esse participes in pœna. Ibidem.*

And Mr. *Bracton* seemeth to make this Difference, That although the Wife may conceal her Husband's Offence in case of Felony, (as also she may relieve and keep Company with him, knowing him to be a Felon) *Consentire tamen non debet Feloniæ viri sui, neque esse coadjutrix sed Feloniam & nequitiam viri impedire quantum possit.* And accordingly at *Cambridge*, at Lent Assises, *Anno* 1619. the Wife was in such Case indicted and arraigned with the Husband for robbing a Windmill.

Again at *Cambridge*, Lent Assises, 1620, one *William Hougthon*, and *Katharine* his Wife, were together indicted and arraigned for Stealing certain Apparel: And the Husband and Wife were indicted for the like at Lent Assises, *Anno Dom.* 1624.

Also the Wife is chargeable for Trespass done by her and her Husband together; and therefore it shall be safe for the Justice of Peace, in such Cases, to commit the Wife to Gaol as well as the Husband.

And yet for this Case of a Trespass committed by the Husband and Wife, Sir *Fr. Bacon* giveth this Rule, *Excusat aut extenuat delictum in Capitalibus quod non operatur idem in Civilibus: sc.* In capital Causes, *in favorem vitæ*, the Law will not punish in so high Degree, except the Malice of the Will and Intention appear, *p.* 36, 37.

(*d*) But a Woman Covert alone by herself (the Husband not knowing thereof) may Stamf. 26. commit Larceny, and may be either Principal or Accessary: As if she steal another Man's Goods, or receive the Thief that stealeth them; or shall receive stolen Goods into her House, knowing them so to be; or shall lock them up in her Chest or Chamber, her Husband not knowing thereof: And in such Cases, if her Husband so soon as he Fitz.Cor.383. knoweth thereof, do forthwith forsake his House and her Company, and make his *See* Stamf. 26. Abode elsewhere, he shall not be charged for her Offence; whereas otherwise the Law P. R. 130. will impute the Fault to him and not to her.

(*a*) M. *Bracton* saith farther, *In certis casibus de furto tenebitur uxor, si furtum inve-* Bract. lib. 3. *niatur sub clavibus suis, quas quidem claves habere debet uxor sub custodia & cura sua;* c. 32. *Claves, viz. dispensæ suæ, arcæ suæ, scrinii sui: & si aliquando furtum sub clavibus istis inveniatur, uxor cum viro culpabilis erit, sc. vir si consenserit, vel rem ei Warrantizabit.*

(*d*) Goods are delivered to the Husband to keep, and his Wife stealeth them, it is no Mar. Lect.12. Felony. Otherwise it is, if the Husband had delivered them to a Stranger, and then the Wife had taken them feloniously out of the Possession of the Stranger, this had been Felony in the Wife.

Also the Wife shall not be accounted a Felon for Taking or Stealing the Goods of her F. Cor. 455. Husband: And if the Wife do take her Husband's Goods secretly, and deliver them to Br. Cor 142. a Stranger, knowing thereof, yet this is no Felony in the Stranger. Stamf. 27.
 Abr. d' Ass.
 fol. 71.

But if a Man do take away another Man's Wife with her Husband's Goods against the Br. Cor. 77. Wife's Will, this is Felony by the Statute *Westm.* 2. *cap.* 34. as it seemeth. And so if Cromp. 35. any Man takes another Man's Wife with her Husband's Goods against the Husband's P. R. 130. Will, this also is Felony.

(*a*) If a married Woman shall deliver to her Adulterer her Husband's Goods, this is Fe- *Vide* 1 H. H lony in the Adulterer. *Lecture* Mr. *Cook.* P. C. 514.

(*d*) And if the Husband commit Larceny, and the Wife knowing thereof, do receive or relieve him, *&c.* she is not thereby Accessary to the Felony. *Vide postea*, Tit. *Accessary.*

    4 X   (*a*) Note,

21 Jac. 1. c.6.   (a) Note, That a Woman convicted of or for the felonious Taking of any Money, Goods or Chattels above the Value of 12 d. and under 10 s. or as Accessary to any such Offences, being no Burglary nor Robbery in or near the Highway, nor the felonious Taking of any Goods from the Person of another privily, shall for the first Offence be branded in the Hand, and farther punished by Imprisonment or Whipping, at the Discretion of the Judge or Justice, before whom she shall be so convicted.

Servants.   (d) If a Servant, by the Compulsion of his Master, steal another Man's Goods, this
1 H. H. P. C.   is Felony in them both, notwithstanding such Compulsion. See more of Servants here
516.   before, *sub hoc* Tit.

Ideots and   An Ideot, Lunatick, dumb or deaf Person, and an Infant, are chargeable in Larceny,
Infants.   after the same Sort as they are chargeable in Homicide, which see here before in *Man-*
Lamb. 278.   *slaughter.* And yet if an Infant shall commit Larceny, and shall be found guilty there-
See 1 H. H.   of before the Justices of Peace, it shall not be amiss to respite the Judgment; and so it
P. C. 25, 26,   hath often been done by the Judges. See *Stamf.* 27. & 3 *H.* 7. *fol.* 1. *b.* & 12. *b.* &
&c.   35 *H.* 6. 11. *Br. Covert,* 80.

     (a) At *Cambridge* Assises in Lent 1619. before Sir *Henry Montague* and Sir *John Dodderidge,* Judges of Assise there, they sitting together upon the Prisoners, an Infant about 14 Years of Age was arraigned before them of Felony, and was found guilty, and upon Demand of his Clergy had the same allowed him, and was burnt in the Hand.

     The like was done there at Lent Assises 1624. before Sir *Randal Crew,* Lord Chief Justice. See *Doct. & Stud. fol.* 148.

Lect. M. Cook.   A Bailiff, &c. distraineth secretly for Rent, and after selleth the Distress, and when the Owner demandeth his Goods which were so distrained, the Bailiff denieth them; this is Felony.

Ibid.   If an Escheator or other Officer telleth a Man that he is outlawed, when he knoweth he is not outlawed, and by Colour thereof he taketh his Goods; this is Felony. But if the Party be indeed outlawed, and the Officer cometh to take his Goods, and the other Party sheweth him a *Supersedeas,* and notwithstanding the Officer taketh away his Goods; this is no Felony.

Vide Dalt.   If an Officer shall levy any Duty for the King without Warrant, this is Felony.
Sheriff, c. 126.   So where any Officer shall levy any Duty without sufficient Warrant or Authority, and shall after convert the same to his own proper Use, it seems to be Felony.

C H A P. CLVIII.

Other Felonies by the Common Law.

Burning of   BUrning of a Barn (which is adjoining to a Dwelling-house) in the Night feloniously,
Houses.   is Felony by the Common Law.
11 H. 7. 1.
Co. 4. 20.   So is it to burn a Barn (in the Day-time) having Corn in it, and though it adjoined
Lamb. 262.   not to the Dwelling-house.

3 H. 7. 10. a.   Burning of any Dwelling-house, or other House, Parcel thereof, willingly and felo-
Co. 11. 29.   niously done, is Felony by the Common Law, whether it be done by Night or by Day.
Stamf. 36.
Br. Cor. 135,
155, 226.   Burning of any other House, or of a Stack of Corn, feloniously, seemeth also
Fit. 169. b.   to be Felony by the Common Law: For the Words of the Statute of *Westm.* 1.
Co. 11. 29.   *cap.* 15. (which Statute seemeth to be but a Rehearsal of the Common Law, *Br.*
Stam. 36.   *Mainpr.* 78.) ordain, That such as be taken for House-burning (generally) feloniously done, be not bailed: And of that Opinion seemeth Master *Britton,* who wrote presently after the Making of the same Statute; *Britton, fol.* 16. (a) See Statute *Winchest.* 13 *E.* 1. *cap.* 1. & 28 *E.* 1. *cap.* 17. And it appeareth also by *Britton, lib.* 1. *cap.* 17. that such Offenders were by the Common Law to have been burned. *Fitz.* 269. *b.*

     The Book called the *Mirror of Justice,* amongst other Capital Offences hath this, *Le crime de Arson:* And he describeth the Offenders in this Sort, *Ardours sont qui ardent Citie, Ville, Meason, Home, Beast, ou auters Chattels de lour Felony in temps de Peace, pur pain ou vengeance.*

Vide 1 Hawk.   If a Man will burn his own House willingly, this is no Felony. But if by such Burn-
P. C. c. 39.   ing he burneth his Neighbour's House, this seemeth to be Felony.
§. 3.

I   A

A Man intending to burn another Man's Houſe, caſteth Fire thereupon, and after ^{1 H.H.P.C}
hat is kindled and burnt in part, it is quenched; this is Felony, although the whole ^{568, 369.}
Houſe were not burnt down.

So it ſeemeth, if a Man ſhooteth unlawfully in an Hand-gun, and the Fire thereof ^{*Vide* 1 Hale}
ſetteth another Man's Houſe on fire and burneth it down, this is Felony. *Quære.* ^{Hiſt. P. C.}
^{569. *contra.*}
(d) If an Indictor (or Juror) in caſe of Treaſon or Felony, ſhall diſcover the King's ^{*Diſcovery.*}
Council and his Fellows, it hath been adjudged Felony. *Vide antea,* Tit. *Petty Treaſon.*

Reſcuing, or taking away from an Officer, any Offender, who is attainted, impriſon- ^{*Reſcous.*}
d, or but arreſted for Felony, ſuch *Reſcous* is Felony, as well in him that made the ^{1 H. 7. 6.}
Reſcous, as in him that is reſcued. See more *infra.* ^{Br. Cor. 127,}
^{130.}
^{Stamf. 31 b.}

Alſo when a Man hath arreſted another for Felony, and after letteth him go at Li- ^{*Eſcape.*}
berty, this is a wilful Eſcape, and ſhall be adjudged Felony in him that did ſo let him ^{9 H. 4. 12.}
eſcape. And in Caſe of Treaſon ſuch Eſcape is Treaſon. See *paulo poſtea.*

Breaking of Priſon (before the Stat. *De frangentibus priſonam,* made 1 E. 2.) was ^{*Breaking of*}
Felony by the Common Law, for what Cauſe ſoever he was in Priſon, yea, though he ^{*Priſon.*}
had been impriſoned but for a Treſpaſs. But now that Statute hath changed the Com- ^{Stamf. 30, 31.}
mon Law therein : So that now, if a Man be impriſoned or arreſted, or taken for Treſ- ^{See the Stat.}
paſs, and do make an Eſcape, or be reſcued by a Stranger, this is but fineable at this ^{1 E. 2. & P.}
Day. ^{Priſ. 5.}

(a) If any Offender which is adjudged, or otherwiſe by Law is to abjure the Realm, ^{*Abjuration.*}
ſhall depart, and after ſuch Departure ſhall return again without the King's Licence;
then if the Cauſe for which he did abjure were Felony, the Offender ſo returning ſhall
have Judgment of Life and of Member by the Common Law. But if the Caſe were not
for Felony, then the Offender by the Common Law ſhall be taken, and only make a
Fine to the King. But now ſee the Statute of 35 *Eliz.* 1 & 2. where it is made Felony
alſo for Popiſh Recuſants, or other Sectaries, which are to abjure, if after Abjuration
they ſhall return without the King's Special Licence. See *hic poſtea.*

C H A P. CLIX.

Felonies by Statute.

IF any Man, being the King's ſworn Servant, &c. ſhall confederate, imagine, com- ^{*Conſpiracy.*}
paſs or conſpire with another to deſtroy the King, or any Lord of this Realm, or any ^{3 H. 7. c. 14.}
other ſworn to the King's Council, or the Steward, Treaſurer or Comptroller of the ^{P. Felon. 13.}
King's Houſe, it is Felony : But what the Juſtice of Peace may do herein, ſee *antea* Tit.
Felony.

Breaking of Priſon by one being therein for Felony, or by one being a Priſoner for ^{*Breaking of*}
Felony, is Felony. ^{*Priſon.*}
^{1 E. 2.}
^{P. Felon. 15.}

(a) And yet by the Common Law, if the Priſon had been broken by the Party himſelf, it had been Felony, whatſoever the Cauſe of his Impriſonment were, yea, although
it were but for a Treſpaſs. *Vide Stamf.* 30. c. & *M. Finch, lib.* 2.

But now by the Statute 1 *Ed.* 2. it is no Felony, except the Priſoners were there committed for Felony. *Vide Co. Inſt.* 2 *Part* 589. upon the Statute *de frangentibus Priſonam. Fitz. Coron.* 248. *Eſcape non adjudicabitur verſ. ipſum qui commiſſ. eſt pro
tranſgreſſ.*

(d) Now every one who is under Arreſt for Felony is a Priſoner, and that as well without ^{*Dyer* 99}
the Priſon as within, or in the Stocks in the High Street, or in the Poſſeſſion of any that ^{*Finch, lib.* 2.}
hath arreſted him, or that hath the Keeping of him being arreſted for Felony.

And therefore if any Perſon who is under Arreſt for Felony, or Suſpicion thereof, ^{*Eſcape.*}
(whether he be in the Gaol or out, or but in the Stocks, or but in the Poſſeſſion of any
that hath arreſted him) if he ſhall make an Eſcape, this is a Breaking of Priſon in ſuch
Priſoner, and is Felony.

(a) And yet one committed to the Conſtable, by the Juſtice, for Suſpicion of Felony, ^{1 E. 3 17}
making an Eſcape from the Conſtable, was after taken again, and indicted and arraigned ^{P. R. 147}
for

for that Felony, and by the Jury of Life and Death was found Not guilty of that Felony, and after was indicted for the Escape: But here, considering the Prisoner was found Not guilty of the first Felony, therefore his Escape from the Constable was holden not to be Felony; and so I have known the Jury directed by the Judge of Assize.

Gaol.

Before the Statute of 1 *Ed.* 2. if it had not been the King's Prison which had been broken, it had been no Felony, as it appeared by *Brit. fol.* 17. And with him also agreeth the Book called the *Mirror of Justice, lib.* 2. who saith thus, *Gaole nest auter close que common Prison, & nul avera tiels forsq; le Roy: Private Prison est dauter, dom a chescun list de scaper que poet, si non que il face trespass que escape.*

2 Ed. 3. 1.
Stamf. 31. d.

(*d*) But note, that at this Day there is no Difference whose Prison the Offender both break, whether it be the King's Prison, the Lord's of a Franchise, or any other Person's (*a*) for the Letter of the Statute is, *Prisonam frangentibus,* and not *Prisonam nostram:* So that whose Prison soever it be which is broken, it is within the Compass of this Statute.

Also whether it be a common Gaol, or a private Gaol or Prison, yea or but the Constable's House, or the House of any other Person who hath the Custody of him for Felony, there is no Difference; for these are Prisons for the Time, and so within both the Words and Meaning of this Statute.

Plo. fol. 13. b.
14 H. 7. 29.
Read 15 H.
7. 2.

Also by this Statute the Breaking of Prison is Felony in the Prisoner himself. And yet if the Prison shall be on Fire by Casualty, and they within shall break the Prison for saving of themselves; this is no Felony, but excusable by the Law of Nature.

Rescous by a Stranger.
1 H. 7. 6.
1 Ed. 3. 17.
Dyer 99.

(*d*) And if a Stranger doth break the Prison, or open the Stocks, or make a *Rescous* whereby one imprisoned or arrested for Felony escapeth; this is Felony both in the Prisoner and in the Stranger, although the Prisoner was never indicted of the Felony.

9 H. 4. 1.
F. Co. 333.
Stamf. 33. 2.

By some Opinions, if a Stranger shall disturb the arresting of a Felon, it is no Felony except the Felon were taken and arrested, and after rescued: Yet *Fitz. Just. P. fol.* 114 saith, that such Disturbance before Arrest is Felony.

1 H. 7. 6.

If a Prisoner be rescued at the Gallows, or as he is going to Execution, this is a Breaking of Prison, and Felony within the Statute. (*a*) And yet note this Difference; *sc.* that if a Felon, in going to his Execution, *&c.* be rescued from the Sheriff, this is Felony, if it be presented before the Justices, *&c.* and so found by Inquest: But otherwise it is, if it cometh in by the Return of the Sheriff, there is no Felony. 1 *H.* 7. *fol.* 6. *Fitz. Indictment* 30.

Escape.
P. R. 147.
149.
44 Ass. 18.
Br. Esc. 31.
Stamf. 31.

(*d*) If a Gaoler, a Constable, or any other which hath a Prisoner under Arrest for Felony, or Suspicion thereof, voluntarily suffereth him to go at Liberty; though this be no Breaking of Prison, yet 'tis Felony in the Gaoler, Constable, or him that letteth such Prisoner escape, but it is no Felony in the Prisoner; but if such a Prisoner shall escape by the Negligence of his Keeper, then the Felony resteth in the Prisoner only, and not in the Gaoler, *&c.*

(*a*) If any Man arrest another, and after voluntarily lets him go at large, if the Arrest were for Felony, it is Felony in him that so lets his Prisoner go; if the Arrest were for Treason, it is Treason, and if for Trespass, it is Trespass, *& sic de similibus.*

If the Gaoler or Keeper shall marry a Felon which is in his Gaol, this is an Escape But *quære,* whether it be Felony in the Gaoler or no.

If a Gaoler shall let a Felon to Mainprise which is not bailable, *dicitur* that this is no Felony, but finable: For although it were voluntary, yet it was *per Ignorance del Ley* But *quære* hereof, for that the Gaoler hath no Authority to let any Prisoner to Bail; and the Prisoner being in for Felony, the Sheriff at this Day hath no Authority to bail such a Prisoner, except it be by Virtue of the King's Writ, *&c.*

If the Constable, or other Officer, shall voluntarily suffer a Thief, being in his Custody to go into the Water to drown himself, this Escape is Felony in the Constable, and the Drowning is Felony in the Thief, *quia Felo de se.*

Otherwise, if the Thief shall suddenly (without the Assent of the Constable) kill hang, or drown himself, this is but a negligent Escape in the Constable.

Voluntary Escape.
P. R. 149.
150.
9 H. 4. 1.
Stamf. 32.

(*d*) The voluntary letting of a Felon to escape who is not arrested for Felony, though he knoweth of the Felony, yet it is no Felony; neither can it be an Escape without an Arrest: And yet such an Offender, being an Officer, may for such his Negligence or Default be indicted and fined, as it seemeth by the Words of the Commission. *Quære* if he not accessary to the Felony. See *Br. Escape* 43.

Dyer 44. a.

Note, that a Man is always said to be in Prison, so long as he is within the Sight of the Gaoler, or of him that hath him in Custody, though he do break away or escape.

I

(*a*) For

(a) For an Escape is properly, when a Prisoner shall escape or get out of the View of _{Fresh Pursuit.} his Gaoler or Keeper, and shall be taken again by fresh Suit. _{Stamf. 33.} _{Br. Esc. 4. &}

_{35.}
(d) And if a Prisoner shall make an Escape (of his own Wrong, and without the Con- _{13 E. 4. 9.} sent of the Gaoler, or other Person that hath him in Custody) tho' he escape out of their _{Stamf.33.b.c} Sight, and into another County, yet if he be taken again upon *fresh Suit*, before the Gaoler, &c. be sued, or hath fined for the Escape (though it be seven Years after) yet this is no Escape, as it seemeth, for which the Officer shall be charged; for there is no Prejudice to the King by the Escape, though it be Felony in the Prisoner as aforesaid, and a Breaking of Prison in him, Co. 3. 44 & 52. accordeth in Case of a Prisoner taken in Execution, that shall make an Escape of his own Wrong.

If a Gaoler, or other Officer, &c. shall licence his Prisoner to go abroad for a Time, _{Co. 3. 44.} and to come again ; this is an Escape, because the Prisoner is found out of the Bounds of _{Stamf. 33. c.} his Prison, though the Prisoner return again, according as he shall be prescribed; and so is it, if the Officer shall suffer his Prisoner to go abroad for a Time by Bail, this is an Escape: Yet they are holden in both Cases to be but negligent Escapes in the Officer, and so but finable. But *quære*, for the Gaoler and other Officers ought to keep their Prisoners _{Fitz Cor. 243} in *Salva & arcta custodia*. *Vide post* Tit. *Imprisonment*. _{& 431.}

Note, that the Sheriff of every County shall have the Keeping of, and shall be charge-able and charged with the Common Gaol and Prison of the same County, and with all the Prisoners therein ; and must put in such Gaolers or Keepers for whom they will an-swer, as appeareth by the Statutes, 14 E. 3. *cap.* 10. & 19 H. 7. *cap.* 10. which also seemeth to have been the Common Law before, as you may see by the Preamble of the Statutes of 14 E. 3. & Co. 4. 34. And therefore the High Sheriff himself shall be an-swerable for an Escape of a Felon, suffered by his Gaoler, and may be indicted for the same. (See the Precedents in *Lambard, West, Crompton*). And so the High Sheriff, as _{6 H. 7. 11.} he hath an Office of great Antiquity, Trust and Authority (for the Time,) so withal it is _{Co. 4. 33.} a Place of great Peril and Charge ; and if the Rigour of the Law should be laid upon _{West. M. 1.} _{Co. 4. 98.} them, then should they have a warm Office, and be well rewarded. But in such Cases I _{Lam. 11. 5.} have observed the favourable Exposition and Dealing of the Learned and Reverend Judges. _{Temp. El.} First, you shall find in Sir *Edw. Coke's Reports, lib.* 9. *f.* 98. that the Gaolers who have the actual Possession shall be answerable for Escapes, if they have wherewith : Also *Pop-ham* Chief Justice did cause one *Staver* (a Gaoler at *Cambridge*) to be indicted, arraigned, and hanged, for an Escape of a Felon suffered by him.

(a) In the *Doct. & Stud. dialog.* 2. *cap.* 42. this Difference is taken ; *sc.* that if the Escape were by Default (*sc.* a negligent Escape) of the Gaoler, that the King may charge the Gaoler if he will, or the Sheriff may be charged by Reason of the Statute 14 E. 3. *cap.* 9.

But if it be a wilful Escape in the Gaoler, which is Felony in him, the Sheriff shall _{1 H. H. P. C.} not be bound to answer to the Felony. (See there *fol.* 135. & 147.) But there the _{597.} Sheriff may be fined to the Value of his Goods. *Stamf.* 35. *b.*

(d) Now an Escape is of two Sorts : *Voluntary* and *negligent.*

Voluntary Escape is, where one doth arrest or hath imprisoned another for Felony (or _{Escape is of} other Offence,) and after *voluntarily* letteth him go at Liberty where he will. _{two Sorts.} _{Stamf. 32.}

Negligent Escape is, when the Party arrested or imprisoned doth escape against the _{Stamf. 33.} Will of him that arrested or imprisoned him, and is not freshly pursued and taken again before he hath lost the Sight of him which escaped ; the Penalty whereof seemeth to be only a Fine at the Discretion of the Judges or Justices : Yet see *Stamf.* 35. *k.* a Difference of the Fine : Where the Prisoner is attainted, *le Fine serra C. l.* where but indicted *C. s.* and where only taken upon Suspicion, *semble dispunishable.* *Quære & vide F. Coron.* 224, 316, 454. & *hic infra*, that in Case of a Trespass a *negligent Escape* is finable.

But for *voluntary Escape*, if the Arrest or Imprisonment were for Felony, it shall be _{Stamf. 32.} adjudged Felony in him which did voluntarily suffer the Prisoner to escape; and if the Arrest, &c. were for Treason, it shall be adjudged Treason ; and if the Arrest or Im-prisonment were for a Trespass, it shall be adjudged a Trespass ; and yet see *Fitz. Coron.* 248. Escape, *non adjudicabitur pro transgr.* (a) And in Case of Felony there is no Dif-ference, whether the Felon be arrested by an Officer, or by another. See *Br. Cor.*

Also in Case of a Trespass, or other Offence of what Kind soever, (being neither Treason nor Felony) there seemeth no Difference, whether the Escape suffered by the Officer be voluntary, or negligent ; but that the Officer in both Cases shall be fined for

such

such an Efcape, according to the Quantity of his Fault, by the Difcretion of thofe that fhall be Judges of it.

5 Ann. c. 6.

Any Perfon having the Benefit of Clergy, and being committed to the Houfe of Correction, and efcaping, and being re-taken, fhall be brought before one of the Judges, or two Juftices of the Peace (one of the *Quorum*) of the Place where re-taken, who fhall commit fuch Offender to fome Houfe of Correction in the Place where re-taken, without Bail, for no lefs Time than 12 Months, and not exceeding 4 Years, to be kept to hard Labour: And if the Keeper of the Houfe neglect his Duty above directed, any Judge of Affize or Gaol-delivery, upon Complaint and Proof upon Oath, may remove the Keeper from his Office.

(d) One *Nichols* affaulted *Cholmly* to rob him, and killed him; after Q. *El.* granted *Nichols* his Pardon: But *Cholmly*'s Wife having commenced her Appeal againft *Nichols*, he was ftill detained in Prifon at the Woman's Suit: After the Gaoler fuffered *Nichols* voluntarily to go at large, and fo to efcape. By the Opinion of M. *Plowden*, this was Felony in the Gaoler, although *N.* the Prifoner were now no Felon to the Queen, in Regard he had obtained his Pardon. *Plow.* 476. b.

F. Cor. 430.
& 431.
P. R 150.

A Prifoner, found guilty of Petty Larceny, is adjudged to be imprifoned by the Space of a Month, for his Punifhment, and after the Month he breaketh Prifon, and efcapeth: *Quære* what this is in the Prifoner, and what in the Gaoler. It is holden that the Gaoler fhall be charged with this Efcape. But if the Prifoner be difcharged (by Judgment) paying his Fees, if he efcape, here the Gaoler is not chargeable. The Difference is, the Prifoner in the firft Cafe was by Judgment committed to Prifon; and in the laft Cafe he

21H.7.17.2.
Br. Efcape 16.
Plow. 465.

is adjudged to be acquitted of his Imprifonment, paying, &c. and yet he is a Prifoner until he hath paid his Fees.

11 H. 4. 12.
Plow. 258.
263. & 401.
Br. Efc. 17.

Note, that a *voluntary Efcape* is no Felony, if the Act done were not Felony at the Time of the Efcape made. As if *A.* do ftrike *B.* and hurt him mortally, whereupon the Conftables do arreft *A.* and after willingly fuffer him to efcape, and after *B.* dieth of that Stroke: This Efcape is no Felony, either in the Conftables or in the Prifoner; yet the Conftables fhall make a great Fine, yea, fhall, or may, at the Difcretion of the Judges, be fined to the Value of their Goods, as it feemeth, by 11 *H.* 4. 12. and *Stamf.* 25. h. becaufe this Efcape was voluntary.

Cromp. 39.

The voluntary Suffering him to efcape who hath killed another *fe defendendo*, or by Mifadventure, or of him that hath committed Petty Larceny, feemeth not to be Felony; for that thefe Offences are no Felony of Death; but he that fuffereth fuch an Efcape fhall be fined only. *Cromp.* 39. Yet *quære*, for they that fuffered this Efcape, are not to judge whether thefe Offences be Felony or no. See hereof *poftea*, Tit. *Evidence againft Felons.*

(a) A Man was taken for Sufpicion of Felony, and was delivered to the Conftable of *G.* and after efcaped for Want of good Keeping, and the Conftable was therefore taken and arraigned; and pleaded, That forafmuch as the Felon was not taken with the Manner, nor at the Suit of the Party, nor indicted of Felony, therefore it was no Efcape, &c. And fo was the Opinion of the Court then. See 42 *Aff. P.* 5. Br. *Efcape* 39.

But the contrary was after holden in Cafe where the Efcape was voluntary, although the Prifoner were taken only upon Sufpicion. 44 *Aff. p.* 12. Br. *Efcape* 31. & *Dyer* 99. that it is Felony, although the Prifoner were not indicted of Felony.

P. Efcape 2.
Stamf. 35.

(d) Note alfo, where one is a Prifoner by Arreft only, and he doth efcape, there the Efcape fhall be prefented before the Juftices of Peace, or other Juftices having Authority to inquire of it, before he that fuffered the Efcape fhall anfwer it, fc. before any Thing fhall be taken or levied by the Sheriff or other Officer. *Vide Co.* 11. 64, 65. & *Stat. Weftm.* 1. *cap.* 4.

13 H. 7. 7.
Cromp. 40.
P. R. 151,
152.
Cro. 34.
1 H. H. P. C.
592.

Note alfo, if a Man be arrefted for Sufpicion of Felony by the Conftable or other Perfon, and after they fhall have Intelligence that there was no fuch Felony committed, here they may fet the Party arrefted at Liberty again, and they fhall not be charged with the Efcape; for there can be no Felon where there is no Felony committed.

44 Aff. 12.
Cromp. 40.

But if a Man be flain, or that there be any other Felony committed, and one is arrefted for the fame Felony, or for Sufpicion thereof, though he that made the Arreft fhall after have certain Knowledge that the Party arrefted is not guilty of that Offence, yet he or any other may not fet the Party fo arrefted at Liberty; for now he muft not be delivered by any Man's Difcretion, but by Courfe of Law: Or otherwife it will prove a voluntary Efcape, and fo Felony.

(*a*) And yet if a Watchman fhall take any Man for Sufpicion of Felony, he may inquire of his good Name and Fame; and if he finds him to be of good Name and Fame, he may let him go. See the *Old Juftice of Peace*, imprinted *Anno* 1559. *fol*. 13. But it were more fafe for the Watchman to deliver fuch fufpected Perfon to the Conftable, Juftice of Peace, or to the Sheriff, according to the Statute of *Winchefter*. *See hic antea* Tit. *Watch*.

(*d*) If a Juftice of Peace fhall fend for a Felon out of the Gaol, and fhall deliver him without Bail, this feemeth to be a voluntary Efcape, and fo Felony in the Juftice; otherwife where the Juftice erreth *pro defectu fcientiæ*, as to bail one that is not bailable, this is but a negligent Efcape.

(*a*) If the Juftice of Peace or Sheriff fhall bail one who is not bailable, this is an Efcape. *Fitz. Efcape* 3. *& Cor.* 246. *fc.* a negligent Efcape, if it be in Ignorance, *ut fupra*.

But if one that is brought before a Juftice of Peace for Sufpicion of Felony, fhall confefs the Felony before the Juftice, and yet he fhall fuffer the Prifoner to go at large without Bail, this is a voluntary Efcape, *&c*. *Vide Cromp*. 39. *a*.

Juftice of Peace. 25 E. 3. 39. 1 H. H. P. C. 597.

C H A P. CLX.

Felonies by Statute.

(*a*) **A** *Nnuity Orders :* Counterfeiting or Procuring them to be counterfeited or forged, or knowingly affifting therein, or fraudulently demanding any Annuity by Virtue of fuch forged Receipt: Felony without Benefit of Clergy.

There is a like Claufe in 4 *Geo*. 2. *cap*. 9. *fect*. 9. and in other Acts by which Annuities have been granted.

Affurers of Ships : The Corporations thereof, *&c*. Counterfeiting their Corporation-Seal, or altering any Policy, Bill, Bond or Obligation under their common Seal, or paying fuch counterfeit Policy, or demanding the Money therein, knowing it to be counterfeited: Felony without Benefit of Clergy.

Bail : Perfonating another before thofe who have Authority to take Bail: Felony.

Bank-Bills : Counterfeiting the Common Seal of the Bank of *England*, or any fealed Bank-Bill or Note, or Altering or Erafing fuch Bill or Note: Felony without Benefit of Clergy.

Bankrupt : Concealing his Effects, *&c*. Felony without Benefit of Clergy, and the Goods which he forfeits by fuch Felony, to be divided amongft his Creditors.

Blacks, &c. appearing in any Difguife in Forefts, Parks, *&c*. or Highways, *&c*. and unlawfully hunting Deer, robbing any Warren, deftroying Fifh, maiming Cattle, deftroying Trees in any Avenue, *&c*. firing Houfes, Stacks of Corn, *&c*. malicioufly fhooting at any Perfon, fending threatning Letters, *&c*. is Felony without Benefit of Clergy.

Deftroying any Part of *Fulham* Bridge, or attempting fo to do, is Felony without Clergy.

Attempting to deftroy *Weftminfter* Bridge, is alfo Felony without Clergy.

(*d*) *Buggery* committed with Mankind or Beaft is Felony without Benefit of Clergy, it being a Sin againft God, Nature, and the Law. (*a*) And in antient Times fuch Offenders were to be burnt by the Common Law. *Fitz.* 269. *b*. *Fi. lib.* 2.

(*a*) *Burning of Houfes and Stacks of Corn :* If any in the Night-time, malicioufly or willingly burn, or caufe to be burned or deftroyed any Ricks or Stacks of Corn, Hay or Grain, Barns, Houfes or Buildings, or Kilns, or kill or deftroy any Horfes or Sheep; it is Felony.

If any Perfon that fhall be convict or attaint of that Felony to avoid Judgment of Death, fhall elect to be tranfported to any Plantation, Judgment fhall be entred, That he fhall be tranfported, and there remain feven Years; and the Sheriff fhall convey him, and imbark him for Tranfportation. And if he return within feven Years, he fhall die as a Felon.

If a Man maketh a Bill or Writing, and layeth or cafteth the fame at another Man's Door, therein threatning to burn his Houfe if he giveth not fome Money, *&c*. this hath been taken to be Felony. See 6 *H*. 7. *f*. 13. *a*. And *quære* what Statute it is that the Book meaneth. *Note*; by the Statute of 8 *H*. 6. *cap*. 6. fuch Offence was made Treafon

Annuity Orders. 9 Geo. 1. 12.

4 G. 2. c. 9.

Affurers of Ships. 6 Geo. 1. 18. §. 13.

Bail. 4 W. & M. c. 4. §. 4.

Bank-Bills. 8 & 9 W. 3. c. 20. §. 36.

Bankrupts. 5 Geo. 2. c. 30. §. 1.

Blacks, &c. 9 Geo. 1. 22. §. 1.

12 Geo. 1. c. 36. §. 3

9 Geo. 2. c. 29. §. 5.

Buggery. 25 H. 8. 6. 1 H. H. P. C. 628, 669, *&c*.

Burning Stacks of Corn, &c. 22 & 23 Car 2. c. 7. §. 2.

Ib. § 4.

Br. Cor. 213.

fon

fon, if after the Offender did burn the Houfe ; but that Statute of 8 *H.* 6. ftandeth now repealed.

9 G..1. c.22.   By the Statute 9 *Geo.* 1. *cap.* 22. malicioufly fetting Fire to any Houfe, Barn or
§ 1.   Outhoufe, or to any Hovel, Cock, Mow or Stack of Corn, Straw, Hay or Wood is Felony without Benefit of Clergy.

Coal Pits.   Willfully and malicioufly fetting on Fire, or caufing, *&c.* any Mine, Pit or Delph
10 Geo. 2.   of Coal, is Felony without Clergy.
c. 32. § 6.
6 G. 1. c. 23.   *Clothes :* Wilfully and malicioufly Affaulting a Perfon in the Highway, with an In-
§. 11.   tent to fpoil or deface Clothes, Felony, and to be tranfported for feven Years.

Coin.   *Coin, &c.* Blanching Copper for Sale, or mixing blanch'd Copper with Silver, o
The Inftru-   knowingly Buying or Selling fuch, or any malleable Mixture of Metals or Minerals hea-
ments to be   vier than Silver, and wearing like Gold, or receiving, paying, or putting off any coun-
feifed.   terfeit or unlawfully diminifhed mill'd Money, at a lower Rate than it imports
8 & 9 W. 3.   Felony.
c. 26. §. 6.

Congregation of   (d) *Congregations and Confederacies holden by Mafons,* it is Felony in the Caufers thereof
Mafons.   and fineable in the Mafons that come to fuch Congregations. 3 *H.* 6. *cap.* 1. *
* *This is re-*
pealed according to 1 H. H. P. C. 645.

11 G. 2. c.   (a) *Corn :* If any Perfon convicted of the Offences mentioned 11 *Geo.* 2. *cap.* 22
22. §. 1.   *fect.* 1. (*See* Tit. *Corn* fupra, *Chap.* 27. *p.* 63.) fhall commit the like a fecond Time or fhall wilfully and malicioufly deftroy any Store-houfe or Place where Corn fhall b kept for Exportation, or enter fuch Place and carry away Corn, Meal, *&c.* or fpoil th fame, or enter any Ship or Veffel and damage any Grain, *&c.* for Exportation, fuch Offender fhall be guilty of Felony, and tranfported for feven Years, and returning ·be fore the Expiration of the faid Term, fhall fuffer Death without Benefit of Clergy.

5 H. 4. c. 5.   *Cutting out of* any the King's Subjects *Tongues,* or *putting out* their *Eyes,* of Malic
P. Fel. 19.   prepenfed, is Felony.
See *Maiming,*
infra.

22 Car. 2.   *Cloth :* Such as fhall fteal Cloth, or other Woollen Manufactures from the Tenters in
c. 5. §. 3,4.   the Night-time, and be indicted thereof, fhall lofe the Benefit of Clergy ; but the Judg may order him to be tranfported ; which if he fhall refufe to be, or fhall return within feven Years, he fhall be executed.

Banks.   (d) *Cutting or Breaking* down of Powdike or other Banks in Marfhland malicioufly
22 H. 8. 11.   is Felony. 2 & 3 *Ph.* & *M. cap.* 19.
P. Fel. 36.
See alfo 15 Car. 2. c. 17. §. 13. and infra, *Fens.*

6 G. 2. c. 37.   (a) Unlawfully and malicioufly cutting down the Bank of any River or Sea-Bank
§. 5. Contin.   whereby Lands fhall be damaged, is Felony without Benefit of Clergy.
to 1 Sep. 1744.

Conjuration   *Conjuration,* or *Invocation of any evil Spirit,* for any Intent, *&c.* or to be counfel-
and Witches.   ling or aiding thereto, was made Felony without Benefit of ·Clergy, by 1 *Jac.* 1 *cap.* 12. but this Statute being repealed by 9 *Geo.* 2. *cap.* 5. which enacts, That no Pro fecutions whatfoever fhall be carried on againft any Perfon for Witchcraft, Sorcery *&c.* we fhall here omit the Account and Defcription of Witches and Witchcraft, inferted in the former Editions of this Work.

But note, That by the faid Statute 9 *Geo.* 2. *cap.* 5. pretenders to Witchcraft and Fortune-tellers, *&c.* fhall be imprifoned· for a Year, and once every Quarter of the Year ftand on the Pillory for an Hour, and fhall be obliged to give Security for their good Behaviour in fuch Sum and for fuch Time, as the Court, by which Judgment fhal be given, fhall judge proper.

Cuftoms.   *Cuftoms :* Officer hindered in the Execution of his Office, by Perfons tumultuoufly
6 G. 1. c. 21.   affembled to the Number of eight or more, fuch Offenders, and thofe who aid and af-
§. 34.   fift them, fhall be tranfported for feven Years, and if they return within that Time,
See 8 Geo. 2.   'tis Felony without Benefit of Clergy :
c. 18.
9 G. 2. c. 25.   And Perfons to the Number of three affembled and armed, in order to run Goods, fhall be guilty of Felony, and tranfported for feven Years. See more fully, *fupra,* *pag.* 70, 71.

9 G. 2. c. 30.   *Enlifting Soldiers,* for the Service of Foreign States, without the King's Licence, is
§. 1.   Felony without Benefit of Clergy. The Perfon inlifted is fubject to the fame Penalty, but indemnified if within fourteen Days he makes Difcovery to fome Civil Magiftrate of the Perfon who enticed him.

I

Ex-

Exchequer Bills. See *Forgery, infra.*

(d) *Imbeziling the King's* Ordnance, Armour, Shot, Powder or other Habiliments for *Imbeziling* War, or Victuals provided for Soldiers, *&c.* if it be by any Person having the Charge or *Stores.* Custody thereof, and to the Value of twenty Shillings, though at several Times, it is p. Fel. 33. Felony. ³¹ El. 4.

Imbeziling any Record, or Parcel thereof, Writ, Return, Panel, Process, or Warrant 8 H. 6. 12. of Attorney in the Chancery, Exchequer, King's Bench, Common Pleas, or Treasury, P. Fel. 18. (by Reason whereof any Judgment shall be reversed) it is Felony in the Parties; and in Vide Co. 11. their Counsellors, Procurers or Abettors. 33. b.

(a) Clergy is taken away from such as offend against 31 *Eliz.* 4. As also, if any 22 Car. 2. shall steal or imbezil any of the King's Sails, Cordage, or Naval Stores, to the Value of c. 5. §. 3 twenty Shillings, and be found guilty by Verdict or Confession ; or will not answer directly, or stand mute, or be outlawed ; he shall suffer Death, without Benefit of Clergy.

The Judge may reprieve the Prisoner, and order him to be transported ; which if he Ib. §. 4. shall refuse to be, or shall return in seven Years, he shall be executed.

(d) So the *Razing of such Record,* is Felony (within the said Statute of 8 H. 6.) Yet 1 R. 3. 1. 10. if a Judge do imbezil or raze a Record, this is but Misprision in the Judge. 2 R. 3. See 1 R. 2. *Br. Cor.* 174. *& Treason* 31. c. 4. Lamb. 529. Co. 11. 34.

But the Justices of Peace have not to do with these two last Sorts of Felonies, (*sc.* with imbeziling or razing of Records) for that these Felonies are committed to other Judges to deal with, by the same Statute of 8 H. 6. *P. Records* 4. See before Tit. *Felony.*

Egyptian, sc. if any Person of the Age of fourteen Years or above, shall call himself *Egyptian.* an *Egyptian,* or shall be in the Company of such, or shall disguise himself in Apparel, 1 & 2 P. & M. Speech, or otherwise, like such, and shall be or continue in *England* one Month, at 4. §. 3. one or several Times ; it is Felony without Benefit of Clergy. P. Fel. 26. 5 El. 20. See Egyptians, *Ch.* 36. supra.

(a) *Note,* That these Manner of Persons are besides all of them for the most part Thieves, Cut-purses, Couzeners, or the like ; and therefore the Justice of Peace shall do well to be careful, not only in the examining of them, but also to cause them to be well searched for counterfeit Passes, stolen Goods, and the like.

Every Person which shall acknowledge any *Fine, Recovery, Deed inrolled,* Statute, *Personating* Recognizance, Bail or Judgment, in the Name of any other Person not privy or con- *others in Fines* senting to the same, being thereof lawfully convicted, shall be adjudged a Felon, with- 21 Jac. 1. out Benefit of Clergy, *&c.* c. 26. §. 2. *&c.*

Fens : Maliciously setting Fire to any of the Engines for draining the Fens in *Ely* ; 11 G. 2. c. the first Offence is Imprisonment for three Years ; the second, Felony without Benefit of 34. §. 10. Clergy.

Forestalling or Buying any Merchandize before they come to the Staple, *&c.* was made Felony by 27 *Ed.* 3. *cap.* 11. but see Mr. *Cay's* Abridgment, Tit. *Forestallers,* 3.

(d) *Forging of Evidences, sc.* of any Deed, Charter, Obligation, Bill, Release, or *Forging.* other Writing sealed, or of any Court-Roll, or Will, or of any Acquittance ; or to 5 Eliz. 14. cause or assent to be made any such forged Writing ; or Publishing any such Writing, P. Fel. 26. knowing the same to be false : The second Offence is Felony without Benefit of Clergy. Lamb. 229. But it seemeth also, that the Justices of the Peace have not to deal with this, for that they cannot well take Notice of the former Conviction. See *Co.* 9. 118. *b. & hic antea,* Tit. *Felony.*

(a) *Forging* the Hand of the Accountant General of the Court of Chancery or of 12 G. 1. c. the Register, *&c.* in order to receive any Money of the Suitors, or forging any Certifi- 32. §. 9. cate, *&c.* made by the Accountant General, *&c.*

Or any Bond of the *East-India* Company, or any Indorsement thereon ; or any Bond of the *South-Sea* Company ; Felony without Clergy.

Forging any Deed, Will, Bond, Writing Obligatory, Bill of Exchange, Promissory 2 G. 2. c. 25. Note, Indorsement of any such Bill or Note, or any Acquittance or Receipt for Money §. 1. revive'd or Goods, or uttering or publishing any such with Intent to defraud ; Felony without and made per- Clergy. petual 9 G. 2. c. 18.

Forging, altering or erasing a *Mediterranean Pass* ; Felony without Clergy. 4 G. 2. c. 18. §. 1.

7 G. 2. c. 22.   *Forging* the Acceptance of any Bill of Exchange, or the Number or Principal Sum o any accountable Receipt for any Note, Bill or other Security for Money, or any Warrant or Order for Payment of Money or Delivery of Goods ; Felony without Clergy.

It is made Felony without Benefit of Clergy, to forge *Bank Notes, Exchequer Bill* or *Orders,* by the several Acts of Parliament relating to thofe Securities.

Gaolers.   (d) *Gaolers* (by Durefs of Imprifonment and Pain) inforcing their Prifoner to become ar
14 Fd 3. 10.   Approver, (that is, an Accufer of others as Coadjutors with him in Felony ;) this i:
P. Fel. 17.   Felony in fuch Gaoler, although the Appellee, or Party fo accufed be acquit, or fhal
Stamf. 36. c. happen to die before he be arrefted upon the Appeal.

(*a*) If a Gaoler fhall only procure his Prifoner to appeal, or accufe another of Felony this is Felony, by *Scrope. An.* 18 *Ed.* 3. *Abr. d'Aff.* 75. & *Fitz. Coron.* 272. And ye the Statute of 14 *Ed.* 3. feemeth to extend only where the Gaoler fhall do this by grea Durefs or Pain.

Alfo by *Brit. f.* 18. if the Gaoler fhall keep his Prifoner more ftrait than he ough' of Right to do, by Reafon whereof the Prifoner dieth ; this is Felony by the Common Law in the Gaoler. And herein the Book called *Speculum Jufticiar.* agreeth with *Briton.* And yet by the Statute of *Weft.* 1. *cap.* 12. Notorious Felons, and fuch as be openly of evil Name, or which be rebellious, they fhall have ftrong and hard Imprifonment.

Hawks.   (d) *Hawks :* Whofoever findeth any Hawk that is loft, if he fhall not immediately
34 E. 3. 22. bring the fame to the Sheriff of the fame County to be proclaimed, &c. but doth imbe-
37 E. 3. 19. zil and carry away the Hawk, it is Felony.
P. Fel. 20.

P. Hawks   So it is in him whofoever taketh up any Hawk, and concealeth the fame from the
2. Vide.   Owner, or his Falkner, or that taketh away any Hawk from the Owner, or ftealeth any Hawk and carrieth it away, not obferving the aforefaid Ordinance.

6 G. 2. c. 37.   (*a*) *Hop-binds :* Malicious cutting them, in Plantations of Hops, is Felony without
§. 6. contin.   Benefit of Clergy.
to 1 Septem.
1744, and to the End of next Seffions, by 10 G. 2. c. 32. §. 3.

31 El. c. 12.   *Horfe-ftealing :* The Principal and Acceffaries before and after are Felons, without
§. 5.   Benefit of Clergy.

Hunting.   (d) *Hunting of Deer or Conies* in any Park, Foreft or Warren, unlawfully in the
1 H. 7. 7. Night-time, or with Vizards or other Difguife, and (upon an Examination by a Juftice
P. Felon. 24. of Peace, &c.) to conceal the Offence, or any other Offender therein, is Felony in fuch
Lamb. 271. Concealer : But if fuch Offender (upon his Examination) fhall confefs all the Truth,
Dyer 50. then he is but finable. See hereof, *antea* Tit. *Hunting.*

If any Perfon to be arrefted for fuch Offence fhall difobey the Arreft, or if any Perfon fhall make Refcous, fo that the Warrant (of the Juftice of Peace) &c. for arrefting them be not executed, it is Felony.

Quære, If fuch Hunting and Concealment, or Refiftance, be Felony where the Offenders killed no Deer, &c. it feemeth not ; for all the Precedents do run, *Occiderunt & afportaverunt,* &c. See *Lambard, Crompton & Weft.*

(*a*) Alfo *Quære,* If all fuch Hunting difguifed, or any other unlawful Hunting in the Night-time, be not Felony ; although the Offender be never examined thereof, nor conceal the fame, as abovefaid. See the Statute 1 *H.* 7. *cap.* 7. *in fine,* where it feemeth that all unlawful Hunting in the Night (generally) is Felony. See in this Chapter, *antea Blacks.*

3 Fd. 1. 20.   (d) If any Perfon fhall take a tame Beaft, or other Thing in a Park, by Manner of
P. Fel. 24. Robbery, it is Felony ; and the Statute feemeth to be but an Affirmance of the Common Law in this Point.

Imprifonment.   (*a*) *Imprifoning,* or Taking againft their Wills (without lawful Authority) any Sub-
43 El. 13. ject in *Cumberland, Northumberland, Weftmorland,* and the Bifhoprick of *Durham,* and carrying them away to make a Prey of them.

Or, to be privy, confenting, procuring, aiding or affifting thereto :

Or, to receive, carry, or give any Confideration (called *Blackmail*) for Protection therein.

Or, to burn any Barn or Stack of Corn there ; or to be aiding, procuring or confenting thereto.

Every of thefe Offences is Felony without Benefit of Clergy.

I

Lead fixed to any Houfe, &c. ftealing it, is Felony. See *Chap.* 156. *fupra.*   . 4 Geo.2.c.32.

Leather and Skins : Forging any Mark made in purfuance of 9 *Annæ, cap.* 11. or 9 Ann. c. 11. counterfeiting the Impreffion of the fame on any Skin or Hide, &c. to defraud the § 44. Crown ; or felling fuch Hide with fuch counterfeit Mark, knowing it to be fuch, is Felony without Clergy.

Linen : Counterfeiting any Seal, (or its Impreffion) provided in Purfuance of 10 *Ann.* 10 Ann. c. 19. *cap.* 19. for Marking Linens or Silks, &c. printed in *Great Britain,* is Felony with- § 97. out Clergy.

Stealing out of any Bleaching Croft, Linen or Cotton Cloth, or Thread, Yarn, Tape, 4 Geo.2.c.16. &c. expofed to be whiten'd, to the Value of 10 *s.* or Receiving fuch ftolen Goods know- § 1. ingly, is Felony without Clergy.

Lottery Tickets : Forging or Counterfeiting them, or ftanding Orders made and ex- *Lottery Tickets* changed for them, or Receipts to be given out in Purfuance of the Lottery-Acts; or Al- *and Orders.* tering the Number or principal Sum of any Order, or Counterfeiting the Hand of any Perfon to fuch Order, is, by a Claufe inferted in the feveral Acts, made Felony without . Benefit of Clergy.

Maiming : Malicious Cutting out, or Difabling the Tongue, Putting out an Eye, Slit- 22 & 23 Car. 2. ing the Nofe, Cutting off Nofe or Lip, Difabling any Limb or Member of any of the c. 1. § 1. King's Subjects, with Intention to maim or disfigure, is Felony without Benefit of Clergy.

(d) Marriage : fc. If any Perfon being married, fhall marry a fecond Hufband or Wife, *Bigamy.* the firft Hufband being alive, &c. it is Felony; *(a)* except where the Hufband or Wife 1 Jac. 1. 11. have been abfent feven Years, and the one not knowing the other to be living within P. Fel. 4. that Time; except alfo Perfons divorced, &c. by Sentence in the Ecclefiaftical Court; and except Perfons marrying within the Age of Confent.

Mofs-Troopers : For the Suppreffion of Thieves and Robbers, called *Mofs-Troopers,* *Mofs-Troopers.* fee 13 & 14 *Car.* 2. *cap.* 22. which is continued by 6 *Geo.* 2. *cap.* 37. *fect.* 7. to the 6 Geo.2.c.37. firft of *September* 1744, &c. and the Claufe in the 18 *Car.* 2. *cap.* 3. *fect.* 2. taking away § 7. the Benefit of Clergy from great and notorious Thieves and Spoil-takers in the Counties of *Northumberland* and *Cumberland;* as alfo the Claufes in the 29 & 30 *Car.* 2. *cap.* 2. *fect.* 2 & 3. impowering the Juftices of Peace for the faid Counties refpectively, to take Security from the Perfons by them employed, for the Prefervation of the faid Counties from Theft and Rapine, &c. are likewife revived and continued to the faid firft of *Sep- tember* 1744, &c.

Perjury : Offender may be tranfported for feven Years, and returning before the 2 Geo.2.c.25. Expiration of the Term, fhall be a Felon without Benefit of Clergy.

Piracy : Concerning this Offence, fee the Statute of 28 *H.* 8. *cap.* 15. as alfo 11 & *Piracy.* 12 *W.* 3. *cap.* 7. and by 4 *Geo.* 1. *cap.* 11. *fect.* 7. Pirates are debarred from the Benefit of Clergy.

(d) Plague, fc. If any Perfon being infected with the Plague, and being commanded *Plague.* by an Officer to keep his Houfe, fhall notwithftanding go abroad, and converfe in Com- 1 Jac. 1. 31. pany, having an infectious Sore upon him, it is Felony. § 7. P. Fel. 3.

Poifoning, fc. Wilful killing of any Perfon by Poifon, is wilful Murder in the Offen- *Poifoning.* ders, their Aiders, Abettors, Procurers and Counfellers. 1 *Ed.* 6. 12. *Co.* 11. 31. But P. Fel. 37. the Party poifoned muft die thereof within a Year and a Day after the Poifon received. P. Mur. 5. See *antea,* in the Title *Murder.*

Popifh Priefts : To receive, relieve, aid or maintain any fuch, &c. is Felony. Here *Popifh Priefts* *antea,* Tit. *High Treafon.* *and Recufants.* P. Jefuits 2.

Popifh Recufants : And fuch other Recufants and Sectaries which (by the Statutes of P. Fel. 5. 35 *Eliz.* 1 & 2.) are to abjure, if they fhall refufe to abjure, or after Abjuration fhall 35 El. c. 1. not depart the Realm, according as they fhall be appointed, or after fuch Departure, § 3. fhall return again without the King's fpecial Licenfe in that Behalf firft obtained, it is 35 El. c. 2. Felony without Benefit of Clergy. § 10.

Pretended privileged Places : Any Perfon within the *Mint,* wilfully obftructing any 9 Geo. 1. c. 28 Perfon ferving any Writ, Warrant, or legal Procefs, &c. fhall be guilty of Felony, and tranfported for feven Years.

• And any Perfon difguifed joining in any Riot, or oppofing the Execution of any legal Ib. § 3. Procefs, &c. within the Limits aforefaid, fhall be adjudged guilty of Felony, without Benefit of Clergy. And every Perfon aiding or abetting, concealing or harbouring fuch difguifed Perfon, fhall be adjudged guilty of Felony and tranfported.

The

11 Geo. 1.
c. 22.

The like Provision is made against the said Offences, if committed within the Hamlet of *Wapping, Stepney,* or any other Place within the Bills of Mortality, whereof Presentment shall have been made by the Grand Jury at a General or Quarter-Sessions *Vide supra* Chap. 78. Tit. *Pretended privileged Places.*

9 Ann. c. 16.
§. 1.

Privy Council: Attempting to kill, or striking a Privy Counsellor in the Execution of his Office, is Felony without Benefit of Clergy.

Purveyors.

Purveyors, Purveyance is taken away by 12 *Car.* 2. *cap.* 24. *vide supra Chap.* 79. so the old Learning on this Head is here omitted.

Riot.

1 Geo. 1. c. 5.

Riot, &c. where there are twelve Persons or more unlawfully assembled, and will not depart after Proclamation made for that Purpose, they shall be guilty of Felony without Benefit of Clergy.

6 Geo. 2.
c. 30. §. 53.

Rivers: Destroying or damaging Banks or other Works, to the Prejudice of the Navigation of the River *Dee* is Felony.

Robbing.

39 El. 15.
* Co. 11. 36.
P. Clergy 13.
5 Ed. 6. 9.
Lamb. 405.
23 H. 8. c. 1.

(d) *Robbing* in the Day-time any Dwelling-house, or any Out-house belonging and used to and with any Dwelling-house, or a * Barn or Stable, *&c.* if it be to the Value of five Shillings, or above, although no Person therein; or to rob any House by Day or by Night, any Person being therein, and thereby put in Fear; or to rob any Person in any Part of his Dwelling-place or House, the Owner or Dweller, his Wife, Children or Servants, being therein, or in any Place within the Precinct of the same House or Dwelling-place sleeping or awaking; or to rob any Booth or Tent in a Fair or Market, the Owner, his Wife, Children, or any Servant being there within the same (sleeping or

See 11 Co. 31,
32, 36.
Stamf. 126.

waking;) every of these Offences are now by the Statute made Felony, and as penal as Burglary, by the Loss of the Benefit of Clergy. But to break a House in the Day-time, although he hath a felonious Intent, yet if he carrieth away nothing, this is no Felony; for there must be actual Felony done, besides the Breaking of the House in the

Lamb. 261.
* 23 H.8.c.1.
5 E. 6. c. 9.

Day. And by the Report of Master *Dalison,* the * Statutes shall be strictly construed (in favour of Life) and according to the bare Letter; so that if the Robbery be done by Day, and there be in the House but one Servant only, or there be in the House, Booth or Tent, but a Stranger or Sojourner only, the Fact shall not be adjudged an Offence against these Statutes. *Cromp.* 118. *Co.* 11. 36.

7 Geo. 2. c. 21.

(a) *Assaulting* with an Intent to rob is also Felony.

Servants.

Servants imbezieling their Master's Goods. See hereof *antea,* Tit. *Theft.*

Sheep: Transporting them, when Felony *vide infra Transporting.*

14 Geo. 2.
c. 6.

If any Person shall drive away, or in any other Manner steal any Sheep or other Cattle of other Persons, with an Intent to steal the whole Carcase, or any Part, or shall assist any Person to commit such Offence, such Offenders shall be guilty of Felony without Benefit of Clergy.

Ship.

4 Geo. 1.
c. 12. §. 3.
11 Geo. 1.
c. 29. §. 5.

Ship, &c. The Owner, Captain, Master, Mariner, or other Officer belonging to any Ship, who shall wilfully burn or destroy the Ship, or direct or procure the same to be done, to the Prejudice of any Underwriter of a Policy of Assurance, or of any Merchant who shall load Goods therein, shall suffer Death.

22 & 23 Car. 2.
c. 11. §. 9.

A Mariner laying violent Hands on his Commander, to hinder him from Fighting in Defence of his Ship and Goods, shall suffer Death as a Felon.

Ib. §. 12.
& 1 Ann. Stat.
2. c. 9. §. 1.

Wilfully Casting away, Burning or Destroying a Ship, by the Officers or Mariners belonging to it, is Felony.

12 Ann. c.18.
§. 5.

Making Holes in the Bottom, Sides, or any Part of a Ship, stealing the Pump, or doing any Thing to the Loss of it, Felony without Benefit of Clergy.

Shop, &c.

11 & 12 W. 3.
c. 23. §. 1.

Shop, Warehouse, Coach-house or *Stable:* Stealing Goods out of any of them, by Night or Day, to the Value of 5 s. although the Shop, *&c.* be not broke open, and although the Owner or other Person be not in such Shop, *&c.* or assisting, hiring or commanding such Stealing; is Felony without Benefit of Clergy.

Soldiers.

3 Jac. 1. c. 4.

(d) *Soldiers, scil.* If any Subject shall pass out of this Realm, to serve any foreign Prince, *&c.* not having before their Passing taken the Oath of Allegiance, *&c.* before the Officer thereunto appointed, it is Felony.

Ibid.

If any Gentlemen, or Person of higher Degree, or any Captain, or other Officer in Camp, shall pass out of this Realm to serve any Foreign Prince, *&c.* or shall voluntarily serve any foreign Prince, *&c.* before they shall become bound to the King with two Sureties (before the Officer thereto appointed) with Condition to this Effect, *viz.* not to be reconciled to the Pope, *&c.* nor to make or consent unto any Conspiracy against the King, *&c.* but to disclose all Conspiracies upon Knowledge thereof, *&c.* it is Felony.

I

Soldiers

Soldiers entred of Record, and having taken Preft-Money, or Parcel of their Wages of their Captain, if they fhall not pafs the Sea, or go with their Captain, or being in the King's Service fhall depart without Licenfe, it was made Felony by the Statute of 18 *H.* 6. *cap.* 19. But fee *Co.* 6. 27. that this Statute of 18 *H.* 6. 19. is now of little Force, for that the ancient Manner of retaining Soldiers, to which this Statute hath Reference, is now altogether changed, &c. And yet if a Soldier who is retained, or hath taken any Preft-money, fhall at this Day depart out the King's Service without Licenfe, it is Felony by the Statutes 7 *H.* 7. 1. & 3 *H.* 8. 5. Which two laft mentioned Statutes are yet in Force, and are Acts perpetual *. *Co. ibid.* And by the faid Statute of 3 *H.* 8. *cap.* 5. fuch Licenfe of Departure muft be made by the King's Lieutenant. _{18 H. 6. 19. P. Fel. 23. P. Capt. 3.} _{Co. 6. 27.} _{* But fee Mr. Cay's Abr. Tit Soldiers 4.}

Soldiers, if they fhall depart without Licenfe, after they have ferved in the King's Wars, it is Felony without Benefit of Clergy. None but the Lieutenant fhall give a Soldier Licenfe to depart. See 4 & 5 *Ph.* & *Mar. cap.* 3. _{2 & 3 Ed. 6. c. 2. Co. 6. 27. 4 & 5 P. & M. c. 3.}

If any Mariner or Gunner, having taken Preft-wages to ferve the King on the Sea, fhall not come unto, or fhall depart from his Captain without Licenfe, it is Felony. (*a*) Yet *quære*, and fee the Statute of 5 *El. cap.* 5. at large, for that it doth relate to the aforefaid Statute of 18 *H.* 6. 19. which (as appeareth before) is now of little Force. _{5 El. 5. P. Fel. 23.}

(*d*) Soldiers and Mariners, and all idle Perfons wandering as Soldiers and Mariners, which will not fettle themfelves to fome lawful Courfe of Life, but fhall wander up and down idly, or beg up and down, it is Felony in them without Benefit of Clergy. _{Soldiers. 39 El. 17. §. 2.}

So it is if any idle or wandring Soldier or Mariner, coming from beyond the Seas, or from the Seas, fhall not have a lawful Teftimonial under the Hand of fome one Juftice of Peace near the Place of his Landing, fetting down therein the Place and Time of his Landing, and the Place unto which he is to pafs, and a convenient Time for his Paffage. _{39 El. 17.}

Or having fuch Teftimonial, if they fhall wilfully exceed the Time therein limited above fourteen Days. _{Ibid.}

Or if they fhall forge or counterfeit any fuch Teftimonial; or fhall have any fuch forged Teftimonial, knowing the fame to be forged, &c. _{Ibid.}

Or being retained into Service after his Arraignment, &c. if he fhall depart within the Year without Licenfe of his Mafter. In all thefe former Cafes it is Felony in fuch Soldier, &c. without any Benefit of Clergy.

(*a*) Juftices of Peace may hear and determine thefe Offences by Soldiers, Mariners, and idle Perfons wandering, and fhall execute the Offenders convicted before them, except fome Subfidy-man, or honeft Freeholder, to be allowed by the Juftices, will be content before them, to take him into Service for a Year, and be bound in a Recognizance of 10 *l.* to keep him a Year, and to bring him to the next Seffions after the Year : And if he depart from his Service before the Year ended, he fhall be indicted, tried and judged as a Felon, and not to have his Clergy. _{Ibid.}

And yet fee the Statute of 43 *El.* 3. that Soldiers and Mariners begging, or counterfeiting a Certificate from their Captain, fhall be adjudged and punifhed but as Rogues. See *hic antea*, Tit. *Rogues.*

Offences of Soldiers are now provided for by the annual Act *for punifhing Mutiny and Defertion*, which fee at large.

South-Sea : Forging any Warrant for a Dividend, or any Indorfement or Writing, &c. or tendering the fame, &c. Felony without Benefit of Clergy. _{South Sea. 6 Geo. 1. c. 11. §. 50.}

Spirituous Liquors : Tumultuous riotous Affembling to the Number of five, to refcue Offenders againft 9 *Geo.* 2. *cap.* 23. or to affault, beat, &c. Informers, is Felony ; and Offenders may be tranfported for feven Years. _{9 Geo. 2. c. 23.}

Stamps : Forging them is Felony without Benefit of Clergy. _{Stamps. 5 & 6 W. &}

M. c. 21.   9 & 10 W. 3. c. 25.   9 Ann. c. 23.   10 Ann. c. 19.   10 Ann. c. 26.   6 Geo. 1. c. 21.

Stock, or Share of Company, &c. Forging, or procuring to be forged, or wilfully acting and affifting in forging a Letter of Attorney, or other Inftrument, to transfer or affign any Share in the Capital Stock of any Corporate Body eftablifhed by Act of Parliament, or the Name of any Proprietor ; or to receive any Annuity or Dividend, or falfly to perfonate any Proprietor, Felony without Benefit of Clergy. _{Stock, or Share of Companies. 8 Geo. 1. 22. §. 1.}

6 Geo. 1. c. 23.   The Court, before Felons are convicted, may appoint two Justices of the County, to contract with any Person for transporting them.

Sheep. 8 El. 3. P. Fel. 2.   (d) *Transporting* or sending any live *Sheep* out of the King's Dominions, the second Offence is Felony.

Wools. 27 E. 3. c. 3. 7, 12, & 18.   (a) It was made Felony for any Man to carry or to transport any Wools, Leather, Woolfels or Lead, out of *England* or *Ireland*; but f.e other Statutes since made concerning the same. *Supra* Chap. 113, and *infra* Chap. 196.

1 Geo. 2. c. 19. §. 2.   *Turnpikes :* Destroying them, the second Offence is Felony. See Title *Highways*, *supra Chap.* 50.

10 Geo. 2. c. 31.   *Watermen* carrying more Passengers than allowed by 10 *Geo.* 2. *cap.* 32. if any Passenger shall be drowned, such Waterman shall be guilty of Felony. See *Chap.* 105. *supra.*

Women. *Rape.* 13 E. 1. 34. P. Fel. 14. 6 R. 2. c. 6.   (d) *Women : fc.* To ravish a Woman where she doth neither consent before nor after ; or to ravish any Woman with Force, though she do consent after, it is Felony ; (a) and the Offender shall have no Benefit of Clergy. 18 *El. cap.* 6. *Br. Cor.* 204. *Vide Dyer* 202. That Man shall die by the Law of God, *Deut.* 22. 25.

If a Man take away a Maid by Force and ravish her, and after she giveth her Consent, and marrieth him, yet it is a Rape.

Ravishment is here taken in one and the same Signification with Rape, which is a violent Deflowering of a Woman, or carnal Knowledge had of the Body of a Woman against her Will. 9 *Ed.* 4. 36. *Fl. l.* 2. & *Co. L.* 123.

Stamf. 22. Cromp. 100. 1 H. H. P. C. 632.   (d) A Woman that is ravished ought presently to levy open Hue and Cry, or to complain thereof presently to some credible Persons. *Glanvile* 115. See the Statute *De Officio Coronatoris.* 4 *E.* 1.

(a) *Fleta* faith, That the Complaint must be made within forty Days, or else the Woman may not be heard. *Lib.* 3. *cap.* 5. But in *Scotland*, and some other Countries, this ought to be complained of the same Day or Night that the Crime is committed. The Reason is, *Quia lapfu diei hoc. crimen præfcribitur. Minfb.* and Dr. *Cowel.*

And yet in an Indictment of Rape there is no Time of Profecution neceffary, for *Nullum tempus occurrit Regi.* But in cafe of an Appeal of Rape, if the Woman doth not profecute it in convenient Time, she shall be barred.

Brit. 55. Stamf. 24. Finch, l. 2. 1 H. H. P. C. 631. *is contrary.*   (d) If a Woman at the Time of the fuppofed Rape do conceive with Child by the Ravifher, this is no Rape ; for a Woman cannot conceive except she doth consent.

5 E. 4. 6. Br. Parl. 55. 1 H. H. P. C. 631.   And yet if a Man ravish a Woman, who confenteth for Fear of Death or Durefs ; this is Ravifhment againft her Will, for that Consent ought to be voluntary and free.

All fuch as are prefent, abetting, aiding or procuring another to commit a Rape, are principal Felons.

(a) If a Man and a Woman be prefent, with Purpofe that the Man shall by Violence carnally know the Body of another Woman there alfo prefent, againft her Will, and the Man doth the Fact in the Prefence of the other Woman, she fo prefent (as well as the Man) shall be a principal Ravifher ; the Man the Agent, and the other Coadjutant : And fo one Woman may be a Principal to the Ravifhment of another. *Dod.* 138.

Stamf. 22. * *But according to* 1 H. H. P. C. 629. *this is no Exception at this Day.*   (d) It is a good Plea in an Appeal of Rape, to fay, That before the Ravifhment fuppofed she was his Concubine, as Mr. *Bracton* faith *.

Cromp. 47.   And yet to ravish an Harlot againft her Will is Felony ; for *licet Meretrix fuerit ante, certe tunc temporis non fuit, cum nequitiæ ejus reclamando confentire noluit.* Braĉt. *lib.* 2.

3 H 7. 2. P. Fel. 16. 39 El. c. 9.   Alfo to take any Maid, Widow or Wife (having Lands or Goods, or being Heir apparent to her Anceftor) againft her Will unlawfully, is Felony ; and to receive any fuch Woman fo taken, knowing thereof, or to procure and abet the fame, is Felony ; and they shall all be reputed as Principals : And as well the Principals as Acceffaries before the Offence shall lofe all the Benefit of Clergy, by 39 *El. cap.* 9.

But this Act doth not extend to any Perfon taking any Woman, only claiming her as his Ward.

2   The

The Taking away of a Maid under fixteen Years of Age, without the Confent of her Parents or Governors, or Contracting Marriage with her, or Deflowering, is no Felony; but yet fhall be punifhed with long Imprifonment without Bail, or with grievous Fine. ^{4 & 5 P. & M. P. Women 7, 8. See Co 3. 37, &c.}

But unlawfully and carnally to know and abufe any Woman Child under the Age of ten Years, is Felony; although fuch Child confents before, *Cromp.* 47. and the Offender fhall have no Benefit of Clergy. ^{18 Eliz. 7. P. Pel. 14.}

Alfo to take away a Man's Wife with the Goods of her Hufband, whether it be againft her Will, or againft her Hufband's Will, feemeth to be Felony by the Statute of *Weft.* 2. cap. 34. the Words thereof are, *De mulieribus abductis cum bonis virorum fuorum, habeat Rex fectam de bonis fic afportatis.* ^{13 Aff. 6. Br. Cor. 77. Stamf. 94. Cromp. 35.}

But if the Wife take her Hufband's Goods, and fo goeth away voluntarily with another Man, and with thofe Goods, or delivereth them to another Man; thefe two laft Cafes feem not to be Felony. ^{F. Cor. 455. Stamf. 27.}

(a) If a Woman be delivered of any Iffue of her Body, which, if it were born alive, fhould by the Laws of this Realm be a Baftard, and that fhe endeavour (privately, either by Drowning, or fecret Burying thereof, or any other Way) fo to conceal the Death that it may not come to light, whether it were born alive or not, but be concealed; in every fuch Cafe, the faid Mother fo offending fhall fuffer Death as in Cafe of Murder, except fhe can prove that the Child was born dead. ^{Baftards. 21 Jac. 1. c. 27.}

Now the Mother's Proof that her Child was born dead, muft be by Witneffes: And therefore, if the Mother will call for no Help at the Time of her Labour, but fecretly be delivered, and then the Child be found dead, it is a ftrong Prefumption againft her, that fhe murdered it; and the rather, for that it is a received Opinion, That if the Child were dead in her Body, fhe could not then be delivered without the Help of fome others; which Opinions fome grave Matrons have denied, and that of their own Knowledge.

Woods : Malicious fetting Fire to any Wood or Coppice is Felony. ^{1 Geo. 1. c. 48. §. 4.}

Wool : Vide 4 *Geo.* 1. *cap.* 11. *fupra Chap.* 113.

Affaulting any Mafter Woolcomber, or other Perfon concerned in the Woollen Manufactures, whereby fuch Mafter, &c. fhall receive bodily Hurt, for not complying with illegal By-Laws, &c. or fending Threatning Letters for that Purpofe, is Felony. ^{12 Geo. 1 c. 34. §. 6.}

Entring by Force into any Houfe, with Intent to deftroy Woollen Goods in the Loom, or any Tools employed in making thereof; or deftroying fuch Goods in the Loom, or on the Rack, or deftroying Racks or Tools, &c. without Confent of the Owner, is Felony without Clergy. ^{Ib. §. 7.}

Obftructing or Beating of Officers, &c. in putting the 12 *Geo.* 2. *cap.* 21. in Execution, in feifing Wool, &c. or attempting with offenfive Weapons, or in Difguife, to refcue fuch Goods feifed by any Officer, the Offenders fhall be tranfported for any Time not exceeding feven Years; and returning before the Time for which they fhall be tranfported, they fhall fuffer as Felons without Benefit of Clergy. ^{12 Geo. 2. c. 21.}

C H A P. CLXI.

Accessaries.

a) ONE defcribeth an Acceffary, *Acceffarius, quafi accedens ad culpam, & particeps culpæ*, as knowing it; another, *Acceffarius etiam fecundarius dicitur.*

(d) In *High Treafon* there be no Acceffaries, for the Advifers, Counfellors, Perfwaders and Affiftants therein, as alfo the Receivers knowing thereof, be Principals, and as much as if they were Actors or Doers; yea, all that fhall advife, counfel, perfwade, command, procure or hire another to do any Treafon or Felony, (they being indeed the very Caufe of the Fact) may well feem as culpable, if not more than the principal Actor; for the Rule is, *Plus peccat auctor quam actor.* Examples alfo we have hereof in the Book of God, *Gen.* 3. The Serpent, the Procurer of the firft Sin, by God's own Judgment, had a greater Punifhment than the Woman or Man. Again, 2 *Sam.* 12. 9. *David* is told (from God) that he had killed *Uriah*, whereas he only commanded *Joab* to kill him, &c. Yet in cafe of Felony our Law is otherwife. ^{In Treafon. 3 H. 7. 10. Stamf. 40. Br. Treaf. 19.}

Note;

Stamf. 40.   Note; Whatever Offence doth make a Man Acceſſary *in Felony,* the same or like Of-fence maketh him a Principal in *High Treaſon.*

Br. Cor. 135   But yet this is to be underſtood of *Acceſſaries before the Treaſon;* for Receiving, Aid-
Brian.   ing and Comforting a Traitor after the Offence, knowing the ſame, was holden to be but
But vide 1H. Miſpriſion of Treaſon. 12 & 13 *Eliz. Dyer* 296. * And yet by ſome other Authori-
H. P. C. 233. ties, the Receiving of Traitors after the Offence, knowing thereof, is holden to be Trea-
and 2 Hawk. fon. See 3 *H.* 7. 10. *Br. Treaſon* 19. *Huſſey* Chief Juſtice, and *Cromp.* 42. *b.* who
P. C. c. 29.
§. 3.   alledged the Book called *The Expoſition of the Terms of the Law,* Tit. *Acceſſaries.*

In what Of-   (*a*) Sir *Edw. Coke L.* 57. telleth us, That in the higheſt and loweſt Offences there be no
fences.   Acceſſaries, but all are Principals: As in the higheſt Offence, which is *Crimen læſæ Ma-jeſtatis,* there be no Acceſſaries; and ſo in the loweſt, as in Riots, Routs, Forcible En-tries, and other Treſpaſſes, *Vi & Armis.*

In Caſes of *Præmunire* there may be Principal and Acceſſary. 44 *E.* 3. & 8 *H.* 4. 6. *b. Hulls,* Br. *Præmunire* 4. 6. *Tamen quære,* for theſe Offences ſeem more like a Treſ-paſs than a Felony, &c. And upon the Statute of 27 *E.* 3. the Offenders ſhall forfeit nothing, if they appear at the firſt Day; but if they appear not at the firſt Day, then for their Contumacy they ſhall be out of the King's Protection, and ſhall forfeit their Lands and Goods to the King, which are as a Pain given by the Statute; but it is no Attainder: Alſo, if the Principal appear not, or happen to be dead, yet the other ſhall anfwer; and therefore it ſeemeth that they be all Principals in Caſes of *Præmunire.* Br. *ibid.* *

* *According to* 1 H. H. P. C. 613. *there are no Acceſſaries in* Præmunire, *but* 1 Hawk. P. C. c. 29. §. 6. *this is ſaid not to be agreed.*

(*d*) In Petty Treaſon there is a Principal, and there may be Acceſſaries, as there is in Felonies.

Two Sorts in   In Felony there be two Sorts of Acceſſaries.
Felony.   The one is Acceſſary before the Felony committed.
The other is Acceſſary after the Offence done.

But he that is preſent at the Time of the Felony committed (be it in Caſe of Murder, Robbery, Burglary or Larceny) is a Principal at this Day, if he were either a Procurer, or Mover or Aider, Comforter or Conſenter thereto, although at that preſent he doth no-thing. See before, *Plo.* 100. *a.* 11 *H.* 4. *Br. Coron.* 188 & 228. & *Indictment* 5.

(*a*) And yet concerning Murder, in every Appeal the Count is, that every Principal *Luy coup' & feruſt mortalment,* &c. But theſe Words are but Form, and the Striking of him which killeth the Party, ſhall be adjudged the Striking of all thoſe which command, procure, move, aid, or conſent thereto, when they be preſent; and they which give the Stroke or Wound may be termed Principals in Fact, and the other being preſent, Prin-cipals in Law. See *Plo.* 97. *b.* & 100. *a.*

Stamf. 40. *b.*   (*d*) If one being preſent at the Killing or Robbing of a Man doth nothing, yet would have aided his Companion if there had been Need been, he ſhall be adjudged a Principal. *Fitz Coron.* 309.

Miſpriſion.   But if one be preſent by Chance, and feeth when another is ſlain or robbed, or when
F. Cor. 395. any other Felony is committed, and doth not come in Company with the Felons, nor is
Stamf. 37. of their Confederacy, altho' he doth not make Reſiſtance, or diſturb the Felon, or levy
40. *b.*
Cromp. 44. Hue and Cry, nor diſcovereth the ſame, but concealeth; yet it is no Felony in him, but
14 H. 7. 31. Miſpriſion of Felony, and fineable as a Treſpaſs.
1 H. H. P. C.
439.   (*a*) And he may be impriſoned by the Juſtice of Peace until he ſhall find Sureties to pay ſuch Fine as ſhall be aſſeſſed upon him by the Juſtice, before whom the Cauſe ſhall be heard. See *Fitz. Coron.* 395.

(*d*) Alſo in ſome Caſes a Man may be a Principal, altho' he be not preſent at the Time of the Felony committed; as if *A.* knowing Drink to be poiſoned, perſuades *B.* to drink it, and after *B.* (in the Abſence of *A.*) doth drink it, and dieth thereof, *A.* is here a prin-cipal Murderer. *Co.* 4. 44. See other like Caſes of Poiſoning. *Antea* Tit. *Murder. Et poſtea, ſub hoc* Tit. *Acceſſaries.*

And. Part 1.   (*a*) Two Thieves, *viz. A.* and *B.* ſet upon *C.* and *D.* to rob them, *C.* flieth one
p. 116.   Way, and *A.* purſueth him, but robbeth him not. *D.* flieth another Way, and *B.* pur-ſueth him, and robbeth him: Adjudged by the whole Court of *King's Bench,* that *A.* is Principal in the Robbery of *D.* and was hanged for it. *H.* 26 *El.*

(*d*) Note, that the Acceſſary in Felony, whether before or after, tho' it be another Offence, and diſtinct from the principal Fact; yet it is alſo Felony, and they ſhall have the ſame Puniſhment which the Principal ſhall have.

2   (*a*) Note

(*a*) Note alfo; when a Statute maketh an Offence to be Treafon or Felony, which was not fo before by the Common Law, and yet the Statute faith not that the Abettors, Aiders, Comforters or Confenters to the Doing thereof, fhall be alfo Felons; yet it fhall be Felony in them, for that they were the Caufes of committing the Offence, which, it may be, otherwife had not been committed. See *Lamb. p.* 279, 280. 19 *H.* 6. *fol.* 47. & 11 *H.* 4. *fol.* 13. *Fitz. Coron.* 228.

And fo it feemeth of Receivers, &c. after the Offence. *Lamb.* 281. for where a Statute maketh a Thing Felony, it is made as Felony to all Intents and Purpofes.

The Book called the *Mirror of Juftices* maketh divers Manner of Acceffaries; *fc.*   *Kinds.*

Thofe who command.
Thofe who counfel.   And fo Murder, and other Felonies, may be commit-
Thofe who confent.   ted as well in Words and Heart, as by outward Act.
Thofe who are Partakers in the Gain.
Thofe who know thereof, and do not difturb or hinder the fame.
Receivers knowing thereof.
And thofe who are prefent at the Fact. But thefe laft, at this Day, are Principals as aforefaid.

And now our Books do divide them into two Sorts, *fc.* Acceffaries before the Felony (or Fact), and Acceffaries after the Fact.

(*d*) *Acceffaries before the Felony*, are fuch as command, hire, procure, move, confpire, *Before the Fact.* counfel, abet, *fc.* incourage or fet on, or confent to commit any Petty Treafon, Mur- *Præcipiendo,* der, Robbery, Rape, Burglary or Larceny, but are not prefent thereat; yet all fuch are *Perfuadendo,* thereby Felons, when the Felony is committed. *Confulendo,*
Confentiendo.

But here fome Differences are to be obferved, when the Principal and chief Offender doth not accomplifh the Fact altogether in the fame Sort, as it was before-hand agreed between him and the Acceffary; and therefore if *A.* command *B.* to lay hold upon *C.* and *B.* goeth and robbeth *C.* This is no Felony in *A.* if he abfent when the Robbery is done, for his Command might have been performed without any Robbery.

But if the Command had been to beat *C.* and the Party commanded doth kill *C.* or *F. Co.* 314. beat him fo that he died thereof, *A.* fhall be acceffary to his Felony and Murder; for it is a Hazard in beating a Man that he may die thereof.

A. commandeth *B.* to rob *C.* and in attempting this *B.* killeth *C. A.* fhall be accef- *Plow.* 475. fary to this Murder; for in attempting to rob *C.* the Command of *A.* was purfued, and when in the Execution thereof another Thing falleth out, he which gave the Command fhall be adjudged a Party thereof, for that his Command was the Caufe thereof.

He that commandeth or counfelleth any Evil or unlawful Act to be done, fhall be ad- *Rule.* judged Acceffary to all that fhall enfue upon the fame evil Act, but not to any other di-ftinct Thing. *Ibid.* As if

A. commandeth *B.* to fteal a Horfe, and he ftealeth an Ox, or to fteal a White Horfe, *Plo.* 475. and he ftealeth a Black; or to rob a Man by the Highway of his Money, and he robs him in his Houfe of his Plate; or to burn the Houfe of *B.* and he burns the Houfe of *C.* Thefe be other Acts and Felonies than *A.* commanded to be done, and therefore *A.* fhall not be adjudged Acceffary to them.

But if *B.* fhall commit the fame Felony which *A.* did command or counfel to be done, tho' he doth it at another Time, or in another Place, or in another Sort than *A.* did command or counfel, yet here *A.* fhall be Acceffary thereto; (*a*) for *Mandata illicita recipiunt latam & extenfam interpretationem.* Vide *Ba.* 66, 67.

(*d*) As if *A.* doth counfel *B.* to kill *C.* by Poifon, and he killeth him with his Dag- *Ibid.* ger, or by other Violence; or to kill *C.* by the Highway, and he killeth him in his Houfe; or to kill him one Day, and he killeth him upon another Day: In thefe, and the like Cafes, *A.* fhall be Acceffary to the Murder.

A. counfelleth *B.* to poifon *C.* and to that End, *A.* buyeth Poifon, and delivereth it *Lamb.* 283. to *B.* who tempereth it in an Apple, and delivereth it to *C.* with Intent to poifon him; and *C.* knowing nothing thereof, giveth the Apple to *E.* who eateth it, and dieth there-of. Here *A.* is not Acceffary to the Murder of *E.* yet it is Murder in *B. Plo.* 475, 476.

A. counfelleth or commandeth *B.* to kill *C.* and before he hath killed him, *A.* doth repent, and countermands it, charging *B.* not to kill *C.* and yet after *B.* doth kill *C.* Here *A.* fhall not be adjudged Acceffary to the Death of *C.* for the Law adjudgeth no Man Acceffary to a Felony before the Fact, but fuch as continue in that Mind at the Time that the Felony is done and executed. *Plo.* 475.

But

Dyer 186.
Co. 7. 9. a.
But if *A.* counſelleth a Woman to murder the Child in her Body, when it ſhall be born, and after the Child is born, and then the Midwife or other Perſon, in the Preſence of the Mother, and by her Command killeth the Child, although it be done in the Abſence of *A.* yet he is acceſſary by his counſelling it before the Birth, and not countermanding it. *Dyer* 186.

Miſpriſion.
Lamb. 285.
14 H. 7. 31.
A Man knoweth a Felony intended to be done, and doth conceal it, and ſuffereth it to be effected : This maketh him no Acceſſary to the Felony, except he conſenteth thereto; but ſuch Concealment ſeemeth to be only Miſpriſion of Felony, and fineable. And yet the Rule is, *Qui non prohibet, quod prohibere poteſt, conſentit. Ideo quære. (a)* And *Bracton, fol.* 121. ſpeaking of Murder, ſaith thus, *Ille, qui cum poſſit hominem a morte liberare, non liberabit, immunis eſſe non debet a pœna.*

Co. 4. 44.
(d) Note, That in Manſlaughter there can be no *Acceſſary* before the Fact, for Manſlaughter is upon a ſudden Falling out.

Forgery.
Moor 666.
(a) Alſo in Forgery made Felony by the Statute all are Principals. See *Booth's* Caſe.

Clergy.
Note alſo, That none ſhall have Clergy who maliciouſly command, hire or counſel any Perſon to commit any Petty Treaſon or wilful Murder, or to do any Robbery. 4 & 5 *Ph. & Ma. cap.* 4. See *Dyer* 183, 186. & *Co.* 11. 35.

Burning.
Alſo none who is Acceſſary before the Fact, to any felonious Burning of any Dwelling-houſe, or any Part thereof, or Barn with Corn, ſhall have any Benefit of Clergy. 1 *E.* 6. *cap.* 17. 4 & 5 *Ph. & Ma. cap.* 4. See *Co.* 11. *Poulter's* Caſe.

Horſe-ſtealing.
No Horſe-ſtealer, nor Acceſſary thereto, either before or after ſuch Felony done, ſhall have any Benefit of Clergy. 2 *E.* 6. *cap.* 33. & 31 *El.* 12.

After the Fact.
Stamf. 41.
Br. Indict-
ment 4.
(d) Acceſſaries after the Offence are they, who knowing that another hath committed a Felony, do voluntarily receive, harbour, relieve, aſſiſt, comfort, or aid him, whether it be before the Attainder of the Felon, or after his Attainder.

As to comfort or relieve a Felon, before he is attainted, with Money, Meat, Drink, or Lodging, knowing of the Felony, maketh one Acceſſary. 26 *Aſſ. pl.* 47.

Ibid.
So to lend him a Horſe to go his Way withal, or otherwiſe to be a Means of his Eſcape. *Fitz. Coron.* 427.

Br. Cor. 103.
1 H. H. P. C.
600, 601.
Lam. 286.
Crom. 42.
1 H. H. P. C.
621.
But to relieve him being in Priſon, maketh not a Man Acceſſary : Alſo to aid him by his good Word, or ſue for his Deliverance, or to ſend a Letter for his Inlargement.

A Felon under Bail, and who ſtands bound to appear for his Trial; to receive, harbour, or relieve ſuch a one with Money or Victual, is no Acceſſary, becauſe the Felony cannot be concealed, nor the Trial hindred by it.

A Felon getteth his Pardon; ſuch as ſhall receive or relieve him after ſhall not be accounted Acceſſary; but to receive or relieve him before his Pardon obtained, is Felony. See *Plo.* 476. Yet it ſeemeth upon this Pardon, ſuch Acceſſary before ſhall be diſcharged.

F. Cor. 377.
Stamf. 96.
Dyer 355.
A Felon is attainted by Verdict, Confeſſion, or by Utlary, to receive, harbour, or relieve ſuch a one, by any Perſon dwelling in the ſame County where the Felon is attainted, it maketh ſuch Receiver or Aider, an Acceſſary to the Felony, although ſuch Receiver, &c. did not know of the Felony; becauſe by the Attainder of the Felon, he is ſo of Record; whereof every Perſon dwelling in the ſame County is to take Notice. Yet Maſter *Bracton* requireth a more direct Knowledge in the Parties to make them Acceſſaries; for tho' a Record (and ſpecially the pronouncing of an Utlary in the County Court) be ſo notorious, that every Man may eaſily know the ſame; yet it would be a great Extremity, that every Man ſhould, upon the Peril of his own Life, take certain Knowledge thereof. Which Opinion of Mr. *Bracton*, Mr. *Lambard* alſo holdeth to be very reaſonable.

Lam. 289.

F. Cor. 377.
Vide Stam.41.
But a Felon attainted by Verdict, Confeſſion, or Utlary, in one County, if another doth receive or aid him in another County; this maketh ſuch Receiver or Aider no Acceſſary to the Felony, unleſs he did alſo know of the Felony.

Feme Covert.
F. Co. 383.
Stamf. 26. &
43. f.
If a Feme Covert ſhall relieve, or receive and keep Company with her Husband, knowing him to be a Felon, ſhe is no Acceſſary thereby; for a Woman Covert cannot be Acceſſary in Felony to her Husband, for ſhe ought to relieve him, and not to diſcover his Counſel. *(a)* But *quære*, if this be not underſtood of *Acceſſary after the Fact*; for if the Wife ſhall procure, counſel or conſpire with her Husband to commit any Felony, and he thereupon ſhall execute the ſame, though the Wife be not preſent thereat, yet ſhe may ſeem to be Acceſſary to her Husband in ſuch Caſe; for Mr. *Bracton* ſaith, *Uxor virum*

ccusare non debet, nec detegere Furtum suum neque Feloniam; consentire tamen non debet Feloniæ viri sui, neque esse coadjutrix. Stamf. 26.

(*d*) Also if the Wife receiveth, &c. another Felon, she is an Accessary.

(*a*) A Servant may be Accessary to a Felony, committed by his Master or Mistress, *sc.* Servants: By relieving or aiding them, or otherwise by being a Means of their Escape; for Mr. *Bracton* saith, *Concubina & famula domus non sunt in eodem casu quo uxor; ipsæ enim accusare tenentur, aut recedere a servitio, alioquin videntur consentire.* Stamf. 27. *a.*

A Servant knowing his Master to be a Felon, continueth to do him Service; the Servant is thereby an Accessary. *Lect. M. Cook.*

The Master knowing his Servant to be a Felon, still keepeth him in his Service; the Master is thereby an Accessary. *Ibid.*

(*d*) A Felon fled to the House of his natural Brother, and the Brother shut the `See Stamf. 43. c.` fore-door against the Pursuers, and conveyed the Felon out of his House at a back `such a Matter.` Door, whereby he got to the Church: This Brother was adjudged an Accessary for it, or he was a Means of the Escape.

Quære, If a Felon flieth and cometh to his Friend's House, and his Friend shutteth the Door against him, and yet maketh the Pursuers believe that he is in the House, whereby he escapes; if this make not the Friend an Accessary.

(*a*) A Man hath a Felon in his House, and (knowing of the Felony) suffereth him `9 H. 4. 1.` to go his Way, and so to escape; yet this is no Felony, for that he had not arrested `Br. Cor. 26.` him of the Felony before: Neither can such an Escape make him an Accessary, except `See Br. Esc. 43.` he were any Means of the Escape.

(*d*) If one do rescue him that is arrested for the Felony, he is a Principal Felon, `Rescous.` and not an Accessary, `1 H. 7. 6.` `Stamf. 43. c.`

Receiving or buying of stoln Goods, knowing they were stoln, maketh not a Man `Buying stoln` Accessary to the Felony, unless he receiveth also (or aideth) the Felon himself; yet `Goods.` Mr. *Crompton* maketh a *Quære* thereof, and alledgeth some Cases to the Contrary. `12 Ass. 69.` See *Cromp. fol.* 41, 42, 43. (*a*) But it was adjudged, *T.* 44 *El. B. R. Dawson's* Case, `9 H. 4. 41.` `Stamf. 43. b.` That it maketh no Accessary, *Yelvert. pag.* 4. See at the End of this Chapter, and `1 H. H. P. C.` the Statute 1 *Annæ*, *cap.* 24. `619.`

(*d*) But herein there seems a Difference between a Buyer, being a Stranger to the Felon, and who for valuable Consideration shall buy such Goods, and a Receiver or Buyer who is an Adherent or Companion to the Felon, or that by Covin shall receive or buy such Goods. See the Preamble to the Statute 2 & 3 *Ed.* 6. *cap.* 24.

A Man buyeth stolen Goods for five Shillings, which are worth twenty Shillings, this `Undervalue.` maketh the Buyer an Accessary, by the Opinions of Mr. *Crompton*, *fol.* 43. and of Sir `Cromp. 43.` *Nich. Hyde* in his Charge at *Lent* Assises at *Cambridge*, 1629. For it may well appear by the Price, that the Seller came not truly by them; and therefore it is safe to lay hold upon such Sellers as shall sell any Thing at any great Undervalue.

A Man pursueth and taketh a Felon that hath stolen his Goods, and then taketh his `Taking again` Goods again, and suffereth the Thief to escape; he is not Accessary thereby, for he may `stolen Goods.` `Br. Cor. 122.` *in initio agere civiliter*, or *criminaliter*, at his Pleasure, as Mr. *Bracton* writeth, `Lamb. 286.` Stamf. 28. *Quære tamen.* For Mr. Stamf. *fol.* 40. says, that if he take his Goods again `Cromp. 37,` from the Felon to favour him; this is Theft-boot, (the Punishment whereof, in ancient `41, 42.` `P. R. 131.` Time, was of Life and Member, though at this Day it be punishable only by Ransom `Terms of the` and Imprisonment.) Yet by some it is holden to be Felony at this Day. The like if `Law 184.` `Dyer 50.` he take his Goods again from the Felon, and then favoureth him, and letteth him go. `Fitz. Cor. 355,` See *the Mirror of Justices*, *lib.* 2. & *Fleta*, *lib.* 1. *cap.* 27. `Finch. l. 2.`

But if the Party robbed take Money or other Goods, &c. of the Thief, to the End `6 E. 6.` `Lamb. 286.` he shall favour him, or shall not give Evidence against him, whereby the Thief esca- `Cromp. 41.` peth; now he is an Accessary to the Felony of his own Goods; though some other seem `P. R. 131.` to take this for Theft-boot, and so to be punishable at this Day only by Ranson and Im- `Br. Cor. 1, 2.` prisonment, as aforesaid.

If the Party robbed, or if he that shall have any Goods stoln from him, after Complaint by him made of the Felony (to a Justice of Peace, or to the Constable) shall then take his Goods again, or otherwise be compounded withal, and will not prosecute this Matter against the Felon, but will suffer him to escape after he was once so charged, and perhaps arrested for the same. *Quære*, if this maketh not him an Accessary, for that he did once *agere criminaliter*, by Complaint made to the Officer against the Felon.

I think

I think in ſuch Caſe the Juſtice of Peace ſhall do well (at leaſt) to bind over both the one and the other to the next Quarter-Seſſions, or to the next Gaol-delivery, and then to acquaint the Court with the whole Matter.

27 Aſſ. 62.
Lamb. 285.

But if upon Hue and Cry, a Man do arreſt a Thief that hath ſtoln another Man's Goods, and then take the Goods from the Felon, and ſo let him go; this maketh him an Acceſſary to the Felony, if not a Principal Felon.

Time.
Stamf. 287.

Note ; In all Caſes of an *Acceſſary after the Fact*, it is requiſite that the Fact (to which he is an Acceſſary) be a Felony at the very Time in which he becometh an Acceſſary to it : For if *A.* giveth a mortal Wound to *B.* upon the firſt of *March*, and *C.* knowing thereof, receiveth, &c. *A.* two or three Days together, and letteth him go, and after *B.* dieth of the Wound within the Year ; yet this Receipt, &c. makes *C.* no Acceſſary, becauſe the principal Fact was no Felony at the Time either of the Receipt, or of the letting him go.

P. Trial, 2.
Stamf. 41.
f. 63. h.

By the Statute of 2 *Ed.* 6. *c.* 24. Acceſſaries may be to a Felony done in another County ; whereas before the Statute, the Common Law laid no hold of ſuch Acceſſaries, for that thoſe in another County, upon the Trial, could not have Cognizance of the principal Offence, &c.

But now by the ſaid Statute, there ſhall be a Certificate from the *Cuſtos Rotulorum* of the County, where the Principal ſhall be attainted or convicted, &c. See *antea* Tit *Felony.*

Rules.
Lamb. 285.
Stamf 44.

Note, That if an Offence be made Felony by Statute, though the ſame Statute doth not expreſly mention Procurers, Counſellers, Abettors, Receivers, Conſenters, and Aiders, &c. yet they ſhall be taken as Acceſſaries (within the Compaſs of the ſame Statute) even in the ſame Manner, as if it were Felony at the Common Law.

Acceſſary of
Acceſſary.
26 Aſſ. 52.
F. Cor. 190.

A Man may be an Acceſſary to an Acceſſary ; as if he ſhall receive, relieve, or comfort him who is Acceſſary to a Felon, knowing the ſame. *Br. Cor.* 104.

P. Appeal 3.
Co. 4. 43. &
9. 117, 119.
Plo. 98, 99.
Cro. 33, 107.
* *This is now*
altered by the
Statute 1 Ann.
c. 9. (viz.)
Weſtm. 1. cap. 14.
That where a

Although the Acceſſary ſhall be puniſhed, and ſhall have Judgment of Life and Member, as well as the Principal, which did the Felony ; yet the Principal, (yea, all the Principals) ought * firſt to be attainted (by Verdict, Confeſſion, or Utlawry) before the Acceſſary can be charged, or put to anſwer (as an Acceſſary); and the Acquittal of the Principal, is the Acquittal of the Acceſſary ; for *ubi non eſt Principalis, non poteſt eſſe Acceſſorius* ; but yet the Acceſſary ſhall be attached, and ſurely kept, (and be committed by the Juſtice of Peace, &c.) until the Principal be attached and attainted. See

Man is convicted of Felony, it ſhall be lawful to proceed againſt the Acceſſary, though the Principal had his Clergy, was pardoned or otherwiſe delivered before Attainder ; and ſuch Acceſſary ſhall ſuffer as if the Principal had been attainted.

(*a*) But though the Acceſſary in Felony cannot be proceeded againſt, until the Principal be tried, yet if a Man upon Subtilty and Malice, ſet a mad Man by ſome Device to kill another, and he doth ſo ; now for as much as the mad Man is excuſed, becauſe he can have no Will or Malice, the Law accounteth the Inciter as a Principal, though he be abſent, rather than the Crime ſhall go unpuniſhed. 33 *Eliz.* Ba. 57.

(*d*) And if the Principal be attainted, though erroneouſly, that ſhall not avail the Acceſſary, but he muſt anſwer, &c. *Co.* 9. 68. *b.* & 119.

Co. 4. 43,44.
F. Cor. 116.
& 378.
Vid. Br. Cor.
70, 71,
80, 83, 86,
132, 138.
Cromp. 34. b.

If the Principal die before he be attainted, or if the Principal be found Not guilty by Verdict, or be found by Verdict that he ſlew the other in his own Defence, or if after Conviction by Verdict, Confeſſion or Utlawry, and before Judgment, he hath his Clergy, or getteth his Pardon, the Acceſſary in all theſe Caſes ſhall be * diſcharged : But it is not ſafe for the Juſtice of Peace to diſcharge ſuch Acceſſary out of Seſſions.

* *This is altered by the Statute* 1 Annæ, *c.* 9. *as aforeſaid.*

A Man killeth another *Se Defendendo*, or by Miſadventure, and it is ſo found upon his Trial ; the Acceſſary ſhall be diſcharged. For that in theſe Caſes the Principal ſhall not have Judgment of Death. *Et omne Acceſſorium ſequitur ſuum Principale.* See *Br. Forf.* 13.

1 Ann. c. 9.

(*a*) If any Principal Offender ſhall be convicted of Felony, ſtand Mute, or challenge above 20 of the Panel peremptorily, it ſhall be lawful to proceed againſt the Acceſſary, either before or after the Fact, as if the principal Felon had been attainted, though he had his Clergy, or was otherwiſe delivered before Attainder, and ſuch Acceſſary being convicted ſhall ſuffer the ſame Puniſhment as if the Principal was attainted.

Perſons

Perfons who buy and receive ftoln Goods knowing them to be ftolen, may he profe- Ibid.
uted for a Mifdemeanor, and punifhed by Fine and Imprifonment, tho' the principal
Felon is not convicted; and this fhall exempt the Acceffary from being punifhed again,
f the Principal is afterwards convicted.

C H A P. CLXII.

Rules concerning Felony.

[F a Man committeth Felony in the Time of one King, he may be charged and ar- 1 E. 6.
raigned for it after, in the Time of another King. Br. Cor. 178.

If a Man do commit Murder, fteal Goods, or do any other Felony in one County, 13 E. 4. 9.
nd then flieth into another County, and is taken there, and brought before a Juftice Br. Frefh Suit
f Peace there, he fhall (by the Juftice) be imprifoned in the Gaol in the County where 3.
,e is taken ; and after fhall be removed by the King's Writ into the Gaol of the County
vhere he committed the Felony. And the faid Juftice fhall bind Informers over to ap-
,ear, and to give Evidence againft fuch Felons, at the next general Gaol-delivery, to be
,olden in that County where the Trial of fuch Murder or Felony fhall be ; whither
lfo the faid Juftice muft certify fuch Information taken by him.

If a Man committeth a Robbery, or ftealeth a Horfe, Beaft, or other Goods in one County.
County, and doth carry, lead, or drive the Goods into another County, it is Felony in 4 H. 7. 5.
very County, whither he doth carry or drive them, and the Offender may be indicted or 34 H. 8.
ppealed of Felony or Theft, and arraigned, and have his Judgment in any of thofe Br. Cor. 171.
Counties : But he cannot be appealed or indicted of Robbery, but only in the County Co. 7. 2.
vhere the Robbery was done ; for it is not Robbery in any other County ; for Robbery
nuft be done to the Perfon of a Man. *Br. Cor.* 140. *& Indictment* 26.

If a Man do fteal another Man's Goods, and after another ftealeth the fame from Double.
,im, the Owner of the Goods may charge the firft or fecond Felon at his Choice. 13 E. 4. 5.

Alfo if a Man fhall deliver Cloth to a Taylor to make a Garment, if the Cloth 4 H. 7. 5.
,e ftoln from the Taylor, the Offender may be charged and indicted for ftealing the fame, P.R. 130.
,ither at the Owner's Suit, or at the Taylor's. Cro. 70.

Alfo an Indictment may be, *Quod bona & catalla cujufdam hominis ignoti felonice* Dyer 99.
epit. See here before. And any Man may in fuch Cafe, both inform the Court,
,nd by their Direction may prefer an Indictment againft the Felon, and give Evidence
o the Inqueft therein.

And fo if the Owner be known, but will not charge the Felon therewith, any other Confpiracy.
Perfon (efpecially after Proclamation made in the Court, that if any will inform or 35 H. 6. 15.
give in Evidence for the King he fhall be heard) may fafely come in, and may inform Fitz. Cor. 5.
the Court, prefer an Indictment, and give in Evidence for the King, againft the Felon Stamf. 163.
without any Danger of Confpiracy, becaufe it is for the King's Advantage to have the 173.
Forfeiture of the Felon's Goods : Yea, in the two former Cafes, if the Juftice of
Peace fhall hear of any Perfon that can inform any material Thing againft fuch a Felon,
or againft any Felon, the Juftice in his Difcretion may fend for him, take his Information, and may bind him to give Evidence againft fuch Felon :

(*a*) For every one fhall be admitted to give Evidence for the King. *Stamf.* 163.

(*d*) Alfo if any Robbery or Theft be committed, and the Party robbed, or other Profecution.
Owner of the Goods, will not charge the Felon therewith, yet every Juftice of Peace
may caufe fuch Felon (or any Perfon fufpected for fuch Felony) to be apprehended,
and may examine him thereof ; and alfo may fend as well for the Party robbed, &c. as
for all fuch other Perfons as can inform any Thing material concerning the faid Felony,
and may take their Informations (upon Oath :) And if upon fuch Examination he fhall
find Caufe, the faid Juftice may commit the Offenders, and bind over the Informer.
See *antea* in the other Title of *Felony.*

Note alfo (for the better Prevention and apprehending of Felons) that upon all Ho- Hue and Cry.
micides, Burglaries, Robberies and other Felonies, and when Men are put in great 3 E. 2. c. 9.
Danger, *Hue and Cry* fhall be levied, and every Man fhall follow the Hue and Cry, P. Fel. 38.
and whofoever doth not, and is thereof convicted, fhall be attached to appear before Hue and Cry
the Juftices of Gaol-delivery. Alfo, any Juftice of Peace may bind them over to ap- 1.

pear before the Juftices of Gaol-delivery, and that by Force of the Commiffion in the firft *Affignavimus.*

3 Ed. 1. 9.Yea, upon any Felony committed, all Men fhall be ready (at the Command of the Sheriff, and at the Cry of the Country) to purfue and arreft Felons, upon Pain to be grievoufly fined.

Efcape.
13 E. 1. c. 14.
27 El. 13.
28 E. 3. c. 11.

And fuch Hue and Cry and Purfuit fhall be made from Town to Town, and from Country to Country : And fhall be made by Horfe-Men and Foot-Men : And in Cafe of Robbery, if (after Notice given thereof to fome dwelling near) none of the Felons be taken within forty Days after the Felony committed, then the whole Hundred where the Robbery was done, fhall anfwer for the Robbery and the Damages : But yet the Inhabitants of any other Hundred, wherein Negligence, Fault or Defect of Purfuit and fiefh Suit fhall happen to be, fhall anfwer and fatisfy the one Moiety, and Half of all and every fuch Sums of Money and Damages. See more here before, Tit. *Hue and Cry, and Robbery.*

3 H. 7. c. 1.
Co. 7. 6. b.

And if a Man be flain in the Day-time, (*fc.* fo long as it is full Day-light) in a Town not walled, and the Murderer efcape, the whole Town where the Murder was done fhall be amerced for this Efcape. But if it be in a City or Town walled, then if the Murder, &c. were by Night or by Day, they fhall be amerced for the Efcape. *Fitz Cor.* 238, 293, 299, 302. *Stamf.* 33. 3 H. 7. 1. *P. Coroners* 13.

And if a Man be flain in the Day-time, out of any Town, then the Hundred fhal be charged therewith ; and for the Infufficiency of the Hundred, fhall all the County be charged, &c. *Stamf.* 34. Yet fee *Dyer* 210. *b.* that the Townfhip fhall be amerced for the Efcape, although the Murder were committed in a Field of the Town, or in a Lane, &c. And the Juftices of Peace are to inquire of fuch Efcapes, and to certify the fame into the King's Bench. *P. Juft.* 19.

P. R. 156.

Alfo every Man is a fufficient Bailif and Officer to apprehend him that is purfued by Hue and Cry : And if he be taken with the Thing, fuppofed to be ftolen, tho' he neither be of evil Name, nor a Stranger, yet every Man may commit as well fuch fufpected Perfon, as alfo fuch Goods, to the Town where they be apprehended, to anfwer to the King according to the Law ; and the Conftables of the Town are to carry before fome Juftice of Peace, as well fuch Prifoners, as alfo the Bringers, that the Juftice may take their Information againft fuch Prifoner, and may examine and commit fuch Offender or Perfon fo fufpected.

But if a Man do levy Hue and Cry upon another without Caufe, both the one and the other fhall be attached, and carried before a Juftice of Peace to anfwer it, as Difturbers of the Peace, and be bound to their good Behaviour.

Houfe.
9 Ed. 4. 9.
Co. 5. 92.

Note alfo, That the King's Officers may break open any Man's Houfe, to apprehend any Felon, or any Perfon that is fufpected of Felony, being in the faid Houfe. See hereof *antea,* Tit. *Forcible Entry.*

Town.
13 E. 1. 4.
P. Watch 1.

And for the better Detecting and Apprehending of fuch Offenders in great Towns being walled, the Gates are to be fhut from the Sun-fetting until the Sun-rifing; and no Man fhall be lodged in the Suburbs from nine of the Clock until Day, unlefs his Hoft will anfwer for him. And in all other Towns, Watch fhall be kept from the Feaft of the *Afcenfion* until *Michaelmas,* from the Sun-fetting until Sun-rifing ; and if

Night-walkers.
5 H. 7. 5. a.
Lambard's Office of the Conftable.

any Stranger do pafs by them, he fhall be arrefted until the Morning, &c. And if they will not obey the Arreft, then all Men fhall be ready to follow with Hue and Cry. until fuch Night-walkers fhall be taken : And for fuch Arreft none fhall be punifhed And the Conftables ought to fee thefe Watches duly fet and kept ; and as well the Conftables of Hundreds and of Franchifes, as alfo the Petty Conftables of Towns, ought to make Prefentment to the Juftices of Peace at their Seffions, (and to all other Juftices

Watch.

thereto affigned) of the Defaults of Watches, and of fuch as lodge Strangers, for whom they will not anfwer : And the Juftices of Peace at their Seffions fhall punifh fuch as be

2 H. H. P. C. 97.

found in Default. *P. Watch* 2. See *antea,* Tit. *Watch,* That every Juftice of Peace may caufe thefe Watches to be duly kept.

CHAP. CLXIII.

The Forfeiture of Felony.

(a) THE Punifhment of every Perfon attainted of Felony is fourfold, *fcil.* . . . . . . Co. 4. 124.
1. The Offender fhall lofe his Life, and be hanged between Heaven and Co. L. 41.
Earth, as unworthy of both.

2. He fhall lofe his Blood, as well in Regard of his Anceftry, as of his Pofterity ; for Ibid.
his Blood is corrupted, fo as he hath neither Anceftor, Heir, nor Pofterity. See *Co.* 11.
1. *b. & Littleton* 745. *&c. Co. L.* 391, 392.

3. He fhall forfeit his Fee-fimple Lands (from the Time of the Offence, *&c.*) where- Ibid.
in the King fhall have *Annum, diem & vaftum,* to the Intent that the Offender's Wife Stat. Prær.
and Children fhall be caft out thereof, his Houfes razed, his Trees rooted up, his Meadows ploughed up, and all his Land wafted and deftroyed. And after the Year, Day,
and Wafte, the Land fhall go by Efcheat to the chief Lord of the Fee: (But yet the
Lord may fine with the King for all, *fc.* for the Year, Day, and the Wafte, and fo have
the Land prefently.) *Quære,* if the Lord may enter ; it feemeth he cannot. See
17 *E.* 2. *cap.* 16. *& Stam. de Prær.* 49. *Fitz. Tra.* 48. *Refeif.* 36.

4. The Offender fhall forfeit and lofe all his Goods and Chattels, from the Time of
his Attainder only.

(d) The King fhall have all the Goods of Felons which be condemned, and which be P. Prærog 16.
fugitive, wherefoever the faid Goods be found ; *fcil.* All their Goods moveable and un- Co. 3. 3. a.
moveable, their Corn growing, and the Profits of their Fee-fimple Lands, for a Year and 334. F. Cor. 317.
a Day, and the Iffues and Profits of their other Lands during their Lives ; and all their 19 H. 6. 47.
Debts due to them by Statute, Recognizance, Obligation or Simple Contract, and Mo- Dyer 30.
ney due upon Accounts. And the King, or he to whom the King fhall give fuch Debt,
fhall have an Action therefore in his own Name ; and yet the King fhall not pay fuch
Debts as the faid Felons did owe.

(a) But the Offender fhall not forfeit his Lands for Manflaughter, nor in Cafes of
Homicide by Mifadventure, or in doing a lawful Act, nor in Homicide of Neceffity, or
Se defendendo. Vide Ba. 2, 3. & Co. L. 391.

(d) By the Common Law, after a Felon is found guilty before the Coroner, or that Seizure.
it be found, that he did fly for the Felony, there the Coroner, Sheriff, Under-Sheriff, 22 Aff. 96.
or Efcheator, *&c.* may (for the King) feife the Goods of the Felon, and praife them by Br. For. 33.
an Inqueft, *&c.* before his Attainder ; for by fuch Thing found before the Coroner, the Br. Forf. 7. 43 E. 3. 24.
Goods of the Felon are forfeited without further Inquiry or Trial of the Felon ; and yet 7 H. 4. fol.
the Officer may not in fuch Cafe carry the Felon's Goods away, but (after Appraifement Stamf. 192. ult.
as aforefaid) muft leave them in the Cuftody of the Felon's Neighbours where he dwelt,
or in the Cuftody of the Town where the Goods were, to be anfwered to the King: And
if he were indicted of Felony, yet his Goods fhould not be removed out of his Houfe
until he were attained, but the Officer was to feife and praife them, and to take Surety of
the Party, that they fhould not be imbeziled ; and if the Party would not find Surety,
then the Officer was to deliver them to the Neighbours, and the faid Goods fhould be
kept by his Neighbours all the Time of his Imprifonment : And the Felon muft have
had reafonable Maintenance of his Goods for himfelf and his Family, until he were convicted and found guilty of the Felony ; and then the Remainder was the King's. See
25 *Ed.* 3. *cap.* 14. *P. Indict.* 5. *& Bract. fol.* 123. *& 136. b.*

And now by the Statute made 1 *R.* 3. *cap.* 3. it is ordained, That if any Sheriff, *&c.* P. Sheriff 24.
or other Perfon, do take or feife the Goods of any Perfon arrefted and imprifoned for
Felony, or Sufpicion thereof, before the fame Perfon be convicted or attainted of fuch
Felony, or that the fame Goods be otherwife lawfully forfeited ; he fhall pay to the Party grieved the double Value of the Goods fo taken or feifed, *&c.* which Statute feemeth
to be but a Confirmation of the Common Law, faith Mr. *Stamf. fol.* 193. fave that it P. Indict. 5.
giveth the Party grieved a more ample Recompence, and more fpeedy Remedy than the Stamf. 193.
Common Law before did : So that before Attainder or Conviction, the Goods of the Felon that is in Prifon ought not to be feifed nor committed to the Town, nor taken out
of the Felon's Houfe or Poffeffion. For (a) a Man attainted of Felony fhall forfeit fuch
Goods as he hath at the Time of the Attainder, and not at the Time of the Felony committed ;

Br. Forf. 58.
Co. 8. 171.
Stamf. 162.
mitted; and (*d*) a Felon or Traitor, after the Felony or Treason committed, and before Attainder or Conviction, may sell (*bona fide*) for his Suftenance, &c. his Goods or Chattels, be they real or perfonal. (*a*) But yet they may not diforderly sell or wafte their Goods. Therefore it feemeth, that the Officer may still take Surety that the Goods be not imbeziled; and for want of Sureties may feife them, and praife or value them, and then deliver them to the Town fafely to be kept, until the Offender be convicted or acquitted. See *Br. Forf.* 44. where Mr. *Brook* delivers his Opinion, That this Order ought to be obferved of every one which committeth Felony, until he be attainted.

Relation.
(*d*) Nay, after Attainder, if they shall grant their Goods or Lands, it shall bind all Perfons, except the King and Lord by Efcheat; but againft them fuch Grant is void. (*a*) And as to their Lands, Relation is to be had to the Day of the Felony committed, by the Attainder, by Verdict, Utlary, or otherwife. *Stamf. de Prærog.* 48.

F. Cor. 366.
(*d*) After the Conviction of a Felon, (if the Goods were in the Felon's Poffeffion at the Time of his Conviction) the Town prefently ftands charged therewith, and shall anfwer for the Lofs or Impairing them, though the Goods were never feifed by the Officer, nor delivered to the Town; (except they can shew what other Perfon hath detained thofe Goods, and that they could never have Poffeffion of them; which Exception is by Sta-
Stamf. 193, 194.
tute of 31 *E*. 3. *P. Eftreats* 3.) So that it shall be fafe for the Town to feife fuch Goods, in whofe Hands foever they be found, (*a*) prefently after the Conviction of any Felon; and then it shall be fafe for them to do it by Inventory, taken in the Prefence, and by the Teftimony of fome other honeft Men. Yet *quære*, for, by the Opinion of *Prifot*, none may feife any Goods for the King, but an Officer who is accountable to the King. 49 *H*. 6. 1. *Br. Refeife* 15.

Conviction.
Co. 11. 50. &
58.
P. R. 179.
Dyer 279.
(*d*) *Conviction in Felony* is, where a Man (being indicted of Felony) upon his Arraignment, fubmitteth himfelf to be tried by the Country, and then is found guilty by the Verdict of twelve other Jurors; or shall confefs the Offence upon his Trial, or is outlawed for the fame, (*a*) (*fcil.* is pronounced outlawed of the Felony at the County Court.) Alfo Conviction in all other Offences (by the Common Law) is, where the Of-
Co. 11. 30.
fender is indicted, or the Offence prefented by a Jury, whereto the Offender pleadeth *Not Guilty*, and is found guilty by the Verdict of twelve Jurors.

Recufant.
And yet a Popifh Recufant indicted thereof (at the general Gaol-delivery, or Quarter-Seffions for the Peace) and Proclamation there made, commanding the Offender to render his Body to the Sheriff of the fame County, &c. If at the next Gaol-delivery or Seffions, the fame Offender fo proclaimed, shall not make Appearance of Record, fuch Default recorded shall be a fufficient Conviction in Law of the faid Offence. 29 *El. cap.* 6. & 3 *Jac.* 1, 4. *P. Recufants* 13, 42.

And fometimes (in other Cafes) upon Proclamation made, if the Party shall not appear and yield himfelf, he shall be thereby convicted or attainted of the Fact, &c. See 5 *H*. 4. *cap.* 6. 11 *H*. 6. *cap.* 11. 13 *H*. 6. *cap.* 7.

(*d*) And (by divers Statutes) you shall find that an Offender may be convicted (out of Court) either upon the View and Record of the Juftice of Peace, or by the Confeffion of the Offender, or upon Examination of Witneffes before one or two Juftices of Peace, and that out of the Seffions. See here *antea.*

And fometimes Conviction may be in the Seffions, upon the Certificate or Prefentment of the Juftice of Peace. See Tit. *Alehoufes and Highways.*

And fometimes by Confeffion, or Examination of Witneffes in Court, without any Verdict taken. See *Cromp.* 130, 131. *B. Confeff.* 32.

Attainder.
Co. 11. 58.
Stamf. 138.
& 185. b.
Co. L. 390.
b.
And in fome Cafes, Conviction shall be taken for Attainder. See *Co.* 11. 59, 60.

The Difference between Attainder and Conviction in cafe of Felony, is, The Perfon attainted hath Judgment of Death given upon him: The Perfon convict, before Judgment, prayeth his Clergy, and hath it, and fo preventeth the Judgment, &c. or after Verdict, Confeffion or Utlary, the Felon is faid to be convicted till Judgment be given.

(*a*) And fo a Man is properly faid to be indicted, when the Offence is firft found by the great Inqueft, or other Jury of Inquiry.

2. Convicted, when the Offender having put himfelf upon his Trial, is found guilty by a fecond Jury; here he is Convict before he hath Judgment.

Attainted, when (after fuch Conviction) Judgment is given againft the Offender, and thereby his Lands are forfeited, and his Blood corrupted. *Co. L.* 391.

C H A P.

CHAP. CLXIV.

Examination of Felons, and Evidence againſt them.

WHEN any Perſon ſhall be brought before a Juſtice of Peace for Murder, Man- 2 & 3 P.&M.
ſlaughter, or any other Felony, or for Suſpicion thereof; before the Juſtice 13.
ſhall commit or ſend ſuch Offender to Priſon, he ſhall take, P. Juſt. 108.

1. The Examination of ſuch Offender.

2. The Information of ſuch as bring him, *viz.* he ſhall take their Examination and Information of the Fact, and the Circumſtances thereof, and ſo much thereof as ſhall be material
to prove the Felony, he ſhall put in Writing within two Days after the ſaid Examination.

3. Alſo the ſame Juſtice of Peace ſhall bind all ſuch by Recognizance, as do declare
any Thing material to prove the Felony, to appear at the next general Gaol-delivery, (to
be holden where the Trial of the ſaid Felony ſhall be) then and there to give in Evidence
againſt ſuch Offenders. See *antea*, Tit. *Felony.*

4. And then the ſame Juſtice ſhall make his *Mittimus*, to carry the Offender to
the Gaol.

Or if ſuch Offender be bailable, (and that there be two Juſtices of Peace preſent toge- 1 & 2 P.&M.
ther, the one of them being of the Quorum) after ſuch Examination and Information 13.
taken, and put in Writing, the ſaid Juſtices of Peace may bail ſuch Priſoner. P. Juſt. 107.

5. And the ſaid Juſtice or Juſtices of Peace ſhall certify at the next general Gaol-delivery ſuch Examination, Information, Recognizance and Bailment.

And if any Juſtice of Peace ſhall offend in any Thing contrary to the Intent and Meaning of either of theſe Statutes of 1 & 2, and 2 & 3 *Ph. & M.* the Juſtices of Gaol-delivery,
in their Diſcretions, ſhall fine every ſuch Juſtice of Peace.

And yet for Petty Larcenies, and ſmall Felonies, the Offenders may be tried at the
Quarter-Seſſions, and the Examinations and Informations may be certified thither, and
the Informers bound thither. See hereof *antea*, Tit. *Felony, & 3 H. 7. cap. 3. &
Fitz.* 251. *f.*

The Form of the Recognizance, ſee *poſtea*, Tit. *Recognizance.*

The Form of the Mittimus, ſee *poſtea*, Tit. *Mittimus.*

The Form of the Bailment, ſee *poſtea*, Tit. *Bailment.*

If the Offender, upon his Examination before the Juſtice of Peace, ſhall confeſs the *Confeſſion.*
Matter, it ſhall not be amiſs that he ſubſcribe his Name or Mark to it.

If the Offender confeſſeth the Felony before the Juſtice of Peace, and notwithſtanding
he letteth him go, without committing or bailing of him; this ſeemeth to be a voluntary Eſcape, and ſo Felony in the Juſtice. *Cromp.* 39, 44.

Alſo, if any Perſon ſhall be brought before a Juſtice of Peace, and charged with any *Bailment.*
Manner of Homicide, (other than that which ſhall be done in the orderly Execution Lamb. 229.
of Judgment) as if it were done *Se Defendendo*, or by Caſualty, which are not Felonies,
or done by an Infant, a Lunatick, or the like; yet it is the Juſtice's Part, and ſafeſt for
him, to commit the Offender to Priſon, or at leaſt to join with ſome other in the Bailment of him, (if the Cauſe will ſuffer it) to the End the Party may be diſcharged by a
lawful Trial. See *antea*, Tit. *Homicide.*

The like is to be done where any Felony is committed, and one brought before the
Juſtice of Peace upon Suſpicion thereof, though it ſhall appear to the Juſtice, that the
Priſoner is not guilty: For it is not fit that a Man once arreſted and charged with Felony
(or Suſpicion thereof) ſhould be delivered upon any Man's Diſcretion, without farther
Trial. *Vide Cromp.* 34. *Lamb.* 229.

The Juſtices of Peace have Authority (by the Words of the Statute) to bind by Recog- *Evidence by*
nizance, all ſuch as do declare any Thing material to prove the Felony. And yet the *the Wife.*
Wife is not to be bound to give Evidence, nor to be examined againſt her Huſband; for, 1 & 2 P.&M.
by the Laws of God, and of this Land, ſhe ought not to diſcover his Counſel, or his 13.
Offence, in caſe of Theft, or other Felony. See *Stamf.* 26. *b.* Nay, I have known
the Judge of Aſſiſe greatly to diſallow, that the Wife ſhould be examined, or bound
to give in any Evidence againſt others in the Caſe of Theft, wherein her Huſband was
a Party; and yet her Evidence was pregnant and material to have proved the Felony

5 D

againſt

against others that were Parties to the same Felony, and not directly against the Husband. See *antea*, Tit. *Accessary*.

(*a*) And *Coke Lit.* 6. *b.* saith, That it hath been resolved by the Justices, *Termino Pasch.* 10 *Jac.* that the Wife cannot be produced either against or for her Husband. *Quia sunt duæ animæ in Carne una.*

And yet it was resolved by the Judges (in the Case of the Lord *Audley*) that in Criminal Causes the Wife may be a Witness against her Husband, especially where she is the Party grieved. But that in Civil Causes she cannot. 7 *Caroli Regis.*

But in the Lord *Audley*'s Case before mentioned, who had procured one to ravish his Lady, and was assisting to it himself, it was resolved, That the Wife might in that Case be a Witness against her Husband : But the Reason of that Case will not hold in other Cases of Felony, for there she was *pars læsa*, and the Case was capable of no other Proof.

The Child.
E. 3. *b.* 4. 2.
G. 2, 3, 4.

(*d*) But for Children, I find in the Book of the Discovery of Witches at *Lancaster* Assises, *Anno Dom.* 1612. that the Son and Daughter of *Elizabeth Device*, a Witch, were not only examined by the Justices of Peace against the said Mother, and the said Examination certified and openly read upon the Arraignment and Trial ; but the Daughter also was commanded, and did give open Evidence against her Mother, then Prisoner at the Bar.

By an Infant.
1 H. P. C.
634.

I farther find in the said Book of the Discovery of Witches, that two Children, the one about nine Years of Age, the other of fourteen, did upon their Oaths give Evidence against the Prisoners upon their Arraignment. See the Book, *f.* 4. *lib. b. K.* 4. *a. b.*

(*a*) The like was done at *Cambridge*, at Lent Assises, *Anno Dom.* 1629. before Sir *Henry Mountague*, Lord Chief Justice of the *King's Bench*. And herewith agreeth Mr. *Bract. fol.* 118. *b.* That *Minor infra ætatem* may be a Witness or Accuser, *cum tamen accusatus attachietur usq; ad ætatem accusantis.*

Accusation or Information by one that is decrepid or unable to travel is good, and may be taken by the Justice of Peace upon Oath, and certified at the next general Gaol-delivery, or Sessions of the Peace, as the Cause shall require.

If one be an Accuser upon his own Knowledge, Sight, or Hearing, and he shall utter the same to another, that other may be an Accuser. *Dyer* 99.

Accusation by an Approver. See hereof, Tit. *Bailment.*

And note, That an Offender confessing any Felony (upon Indictment or otherwise) against himself, may also accuse others of the same Felony : And such Accusation may be taken by the Justice of Peace, &c.

By Persons discredited.

(*d*) Two inform against another in Matter of Felony, and they vary in their Tales, (*viz.* in the Day and Place, when and where the Felony was committed) such Information is not much to be credited. See the Story of *Susanna.*

Cromp. 100.

He that is examined, if Part of what he speaketh be proved to be false, he is not to be credited in the Residue of his Information ; and therefore we shall find in 16 *E.* 4. that a Man who was produced as a Witness in the *Chancery*, in his Deposition was found to swear falsly in Part, and thereupon his Testimony was utterly rejected.

(*a*) Mr. *Bracton, lib.* 3. *fol.* 118. saith, That an Accuser or Witness, must be *integræ famæ, & non criminosus, quia criminosi ab omni Accusatione repelluntur : Ut si Accusans fuerit Latro cognitus vel Utlagatus, vel aliquo genere Feloniæ convictus vel convincendus.* Vide Pl. Co. L. 6.

A Man attainted of Perjury, and the King pardons and restores him, &c. *Quære,* Whether such a Person's Information shall be allowed against a Prisoner ; for the old Saying is, *Once forsworn, ever forsworn.*

A Man attainted of Conspiracy or Forgery shall not be received to give Evidence, or be a Witness. See *Cromp.* 127. *b.*

But if one be brought before a Justice of Peace upon Suspicion of Felony, although the Information against the Prisoner shall be by such Witnesses, yet 'tis safest for the Justice to take their Information for the King, and to bind them over to give Evidence, &c. and to commit the Party suspected ; and upon the Trial to inform the Justices of Gaol-delivery, concerning the Credit of those Witnesses.

(*a*) Concerning those Accusers or Witnesses, I have farther seen two old Verses in these Words :

> *Conditio, sexus, ætas, discretio, fama,*
> *Et fortuna, fides ; in Testibus ista requires.*

And yet in Cafe of Felony any Man (though of no Worth) may be allowed for a Witnefs or Proof.

By God's Law one Witnefs fhall not be fufficient againft an Offender, for any Sin, Trefpafs or Fault, *Numb.* 35. 30. *Deut.* 19. 15. And to the fame Purpofe was the Statute 25 *Hen.* 8. *cap.* 14. And yet now by our Law one Witnefs is fufficient, where the Trial is by a Jury ; for they are all fworn to try the particular Matter wherewith the Defendant is charged. So alfo one Witnefs is fufficient to convict an Offender before the Juftice of Peace in divers Cafes, he being exprefly therein enabled by Statute.

And yet in other Cafes where the Matter is to be tried by Witneffes only, it is meet that there be two Witneffes.

But no Man is to be condemned without an Accufer. *John* 8. 10.

(*d*) When a Prifoner fhall be brought before the Juftice of Peace for Felony, or Sufpicion thereof, but they who bring him, or firft complained of him, will not or cannot inform any material Thing againft the Prifoner ; yet the Juftice of Peace ought to commit the Party fufpected after his Examination taken, and to bind over fuch as did firft accufe the Prifoner, or fuch as do bring him before the Juftice to give in Evidence, &c. And if afterwards the faid Juftice fhall hear of any other Perfons that can inform any material Thing againft the Prifoner to prove the Felony, whereof he is fufpected; he may grant his Warrant for fuch Perfons to come before him, and may alfo take their Information, &c. and may bind them to give Evidence againft the Prifoner, for every one fhall be admitted to give Evidence for the King. *Stamf.* 163. See *antea* Tit. *Felony*, and Tit. *Acceffary*.

And the Parties grieved ought to be bound, not only to give Evidence, but alfo to prefer a Bill of Indictment againft the Prifoner ; and the other Perfons who can inform any material Thing to prove the Felony, may be bound to give Evidence only.

And for that Men fhould be the readier and more willing to give Evidence againft Felons, the Statute 21 *H.* 8. *cap.* 11. hath enacted, That if any Man hath Goods ftolen from him, if the Felon be thereof indicted, and after in any Sort attainted or arraigned, and thereof found guilty, by Reafon of Evidence given by the Party robbed, or Owner of the fame Goods, or by any other by his Procurement, (tho' the Thief be not hanged, nor have Judgment of Death) then the Party robbed, or Owner of the Goods, fhall be reftored to his faid Goods by a Writ of Reftitution, though he never made any frefh Suit, or Hue and Cry. Before which Statute the Party robbed could have no Reftitution, without fuing an Appeal againft a Felon, and frefh Suit made. *Reftitution of ftolen Goods.* 21 H. 8. c. 11. P. Reftit. 1. Br. Eftra. 8. Doct. & Stud. 64. Stamf. 165, 166.

(*a*) Alfo if the Felon fhall be outlawed upon the Indictment by Means of the Party robbed, or Owner of the Goods ftolen, he fhall have Reftitution of his Goods by a Writ of Reftitution, *ut fupra. Ba. U.* 76.

And note, That the Juftices, before whom any fuch Felon fhall be found guilty, or otherwife attainted by Reafon of Evidence given by the Party fo robbed, or Owner, or by any other by their Procurement, have Power to award a Writ of Reftitution for the Money or Goods ftolen, directed to the Party in whofe Hands the fame Goods are, &c. 21 *H.* 8. *cap.* 11. *Br. Reftit.* 22.

(*d*) Alfo the Executors of the Party robbed fhall have Reftitution by Force of this Statute, *viz.* Upon Evidence given by them, or by their Procurement againft the Felon, whereby the Felon is attainted or found guilty. *Co. 6. 80. Ben. 3 El.*

If a Thief do rob or fteal Goods from three Men feverally, and he be indicted of the Robbing or Stealing from one of them, and arraigned thereupon ; in this Cafe, though the other Two would give Evidence againft the Offender, yet fhall not they have Reftitution of their Goods, by the Meaning of that Statute; for the Felon is not attainted of any other Felony, faving of that whereof he was indicted. But if he be indicted of all the three Robberies or Felonies feverally, and arraigned upon one of them, and found guilty by the Evidence given by one of the Parties robbed, &c. yet fhall he be after arraigned upon the other two Indictments, to the Intent he alfo may be found guilty by the Evidence of the other two Perfons robbed, and that fo they may have Reftitution of their Goods ftolen, according to the Meaning of the faid Statute. *Stamf. 166. P. R. 162.*

And if a Man fteal Goods at divers Times from feveral Men, and is after attainted at the Suit of one of them only, for the Goods ftolen from him, but is not attainted at the Suit of the other ; by this Attainder the Felon fhall forfeit to the King not only his own Goods, but alfo the Goods ftolen from thofe others at whofe Suit he was not attainted, though the Felon had no Property, but only a Poffeffion of thofe Goods ; and the Property *44 E. 3. 44. 1 H. H. P. C. 545.*

perty

perty of the Goods which remaineth in the right Owner in this Cafe, is forfeited by the Owner to the King, for Default of the Owner purfuing the Felon.

See Stamf. 166. , Alfo if there be divers Thieves, and but one of the Principals attainted as before, yet the Party robbed fhall have Reftitution.

Market. But in thefe and the like Cafes of Reftitution, if the Felon hath fold the Goods in a Fair or * *Market Overt*, and after be attainted of the Felony, (upon Evidence given by the Party robbed, here the Owner fhall not have Reftitution; for by Alienation in a Fair or Market Overt, the Property of the Goods ftoln is altered. 12 *H.* 8. 10. *b.* Yet if he that bought the Goods in Market were privy to the Felony, fuch Sale fhall not alter the Property, *quia particeps criminis.* See 33 *H.* 6. 7. *Co.* 3. 78. *Vide antea* Tit. *Horfes.*

* *The Practice hath been otherwife ever fince 5 Car. 1. for if the Criminal is convicted at the*

Profecution of the Party from whom the Goods were ftolen, he fhall have Reftitution, tho' fold in a Market; and if the Buyer pleads fuch Sale, the Plaintiff upon a Demurrer fhall have Judgment. See alfo 1 H. H. P. C. 543.

See 1 H. H. P. C. 543. (*a*) If any Goods of what Nature foever they be, be ftolen, purloined, &c. and be fold, exchanged or pawned to any Broker, &c. in *London, Weftminfter, Southwark,* or within two Miles of *London,* the fame fhall alter no Property. 1 *Jac.* 1. 21. *fect.* 5.

(*d*) A Man fhall have Reftitution of Money ftolen, &c. though it cannot be known. *Br. Reftit.* 22.

Waifs. But if a Man hath a Horfe or other Goods ftolen from him, and knoweth not by whom; if the Felon waiveth the Goods, flieth and efcapeth, and the King's Officer, or the Lord of the Manor, &c. feifeth them, the Party robbed fhall have no Reftitution, for that he cannot indict and attaint the Felon. And yet if the Felon had not the Goods in his Poffeffion at the Time when he fled, but had formerly left them elfewhere, *fc.* in the Thief's own Houfe, or in any other Man's Houfe, or in the Cuftody of any other, or had hid them, then are they no waived Goods, nor forfeited, but the Owner may take them again wherefoever he findeth them, without any Reftitution awarded. *Co.* 5. 109.

Alfo in the forefaid Book of Difcovery of Witches, I obferve one other Thing, *viz.*

That Examinations taken by Juftices of Peace in one County, may be by them certified in another County, and there read and given in Evidence againft the Prifoner. *Y.* 2. 3.

(*a*) And in fuch Cafes the Examinations fhould be taken upon Oath.

Examination certified. Cromp. 193. (*d*) The Offender himfelf fhall not be examined upon Oath: For by the Common Law *Nullus tenetur feipfum prodere.* Neither was a Man's Fault to be wrung out of himfelf, (nay not by Examination only) but to be proved by others, until the Stat. 2 & 3 *P. & M. cap.* 10. gave Authority to the Juftices of the Peace to examine the Felon himfelf.

Upon Oath. Cromp. 194. But 'tis convenient, in Cafes of Felony efpecially, that the Information (of the Bringers and others) which the Juftices of Peace do take againft the Prifoner, be upon Oath: Otherwife upon the Trial of the Prifoner, fuch Examination fhall not be given in Evidence againft the Prifoner upon his Trial. And fo was the Direction of Sir *Edw. Coke,* late Lord Chief Juftice, (5 *Jacobi* at *Cambridge* Summer Affizes) upon the Trial of a Felon; for, faith he, in Cafe of a Trefpafs to the Value of two Pence, no Evidence fhall be given to the Jury, but upon Oath, much lefs where the Life of a Man is in Queftion. See *Lamb. pag.* 210. that he hath heard the Opinions of other Juftices of Affize delivered accordingly.

Alfo if the Witneffes be examined upon Oath, then though it happen they fhould die before the Prifoner have his Trial, or if they fhall not appear upon the Recognizance, and give Evidence againft the Prifoner (being laboured, perhaps, to abfent themfelves) yet may their Information be given in Evidence, as a Matter of good Credit.

Alfo it is found by Experience, that without Oath many Witneffes will fpeak coldly againft a Felon before the Face of the Juftice; yea, and will alfo fpeak very fparingly and coldly upon their Evidence given before the Judges of Affize; as I have obferved in fome, had they not been urged with their former Information taken upon Oath; for the Labouring (by the Offender and his Friends) to fuch as are to give Evidence, both before the Matter cometh before the Juftice of Peace and after, is now grown very common and ufual.

Lamb. 219. Alfo Mr. *Brook* (Tit. *Examinations* 32.) is of Opinion, That every Examination ought to be upon Oath: And fo alfo is the Practice of the Juftices in the higher Courts at *Weftminfter,* in all the Examinations of Summoners, Viewers, Sheriffs, Clerks, or other Officers, &c.

Oaths. And here let me admonifh all fuch as are Witneffes againft a Prifoner, or any Offender, before a Juftice of Peace, or other Magiftrate, that they be well advifed what they teftify

4

upon

upon their Oaths, knowing that in ſuch Caſes, if either they ſhould not ſpeak the Truth, or ſhould conceal any Part of the Truth, they ſhould offend againſt God, the Magiſtrate, the Innocent, the Commonwealth, and their own Souls, *ſc.* Againſt

God, in deſpiſing of him, taking his Name in vain, and belying the Truth.

Magiſtrate, in miſleading and deceiving him, and cauſing him to do Injuſtice.

Innocent, in ſpoiling him of his Name, Goods or Life.

Commonwealth, *ſc.* If the Party be guilty, and he clears him by falſe Witneſs.

His own Soul; for it is Perjury in him, at leaſt in the Preſence of God and good Men.

(*a*) And though he be not preſently ſenſible of the Sore, yet, as one well ſaith, it will ·feſter, and he ſhall then feel it moſt when no Plaiſter ſhall be found to cure it: Yea, a Hell will come to them, before they come to Hell; for a Conſcience is,

$\left\{\begin{array}{l}\text{1. } \textit{Teſtis, a Witneſs accuſing them.}\\ \text{2. } \textit{Judex, a Judge judging and condemning them.}\\ \text{3. } \textit{Carcer, a Priſon.}\\ \text{4. } \textit{Tortor, an Executioner; ·yea, no Tongue can expreſs the Torture of a troubled Conſcience.}\end{array}\right.$

C H A P. CLXV.

Whether Information, Evidence or Proof of Witneſſes ſhall be taken againſt the King.

IT ſeemeth juſt and right, that the Juſtices of Peace, who take Information againſt a Felon or Perſon ſuſpected of Felony, ſhould take and certify as well ſuch Information, Proof and Evidence, as goeth to the Acquittal or Clearing of the Priſoner, as ſuch as makes againſt the Priſoner; for ſuch Information, Evidence, or Proof taken, and the Certifying thereof by the Juſtice of Peace, is only to inform the King and his Juſtices of Gaol-delivery, *&c.* of the Truth of the Matter.

And Sir *Edw. Coke* (at Lent Aſſizes at *Bury*, 5 *Jac.*) adviſed a Coroner, that he ought to have done accordingly, as I have heard.

But *quære*, if the Juſtices of Peace, or Coroner, may take upon Oath ſuch Information, Evidence or Proof, as maketh againſt the King? It ſeemeth no.

Upon Trial of Felons before the Juſtices of Gaol-delivery, the ſaid Juſtices will often hear Witneſſes and Evidence which goeth to the Clearing and Acquittal of the Priſoner, yet they will not take it upon * Oath, but do leave ſuch Teſtimony and Evidence to the Jury to give Credit or to think thereof, as they ſhall ſee and find Cauſe. Crom. 110. b.
*This is altered
by the Stat. 1
Annæ, c. 9.
That the Wit-
neſſes muſt be
upon Oath.

Popham, Chief Juſtice, (at *Cambridge* Aſſizes *tempore Eliz.*) committed one to Priſon, who, upon the Trial of a Felon, called out, That he could give Evidence for the Queen; and when he was ſworn, he gave Evidence to acquit the Offender.

But by the Statute of 31 *Eliz. cap.* 4. it was enacted, That ſuch Perſons as ſhall be P. Armour. impeached for any Offence made Felony by that Statute (being againſt imbezilling of Armour, *&c.*) ſhall be admitted to make any lawful Proof that they can, by Witneſs or· otherwiſe, for their Diſcharge and Defence.

In 7 *H.* 4. we ſhall find, that one of the Serjeants, as *Amicus Curiæ*, and to inform Stamf. 141. b. the Court, (that they ſhould not err) did ſhew his Opinion to the Benefit of a Priſoner, upon the Inſufficiency of the Indictment. The like is to be ſeen in *Brooks*'s Caſe. 28 *Eliz.* in *Banco Regis.* Co. 4. 39. Co. 4. 39.

C H A P. CLXVI.

Cauſes of Suſpicion.

NOW npon the Examination of Felons, and other like Offenders, theſe Circumſtances following are to be conſidered.

1. His Name, *fc.* if he be called by divers Names. *Duplex nomen malum omen.*

His Parents; if they were wicked, and given to the fame Kind of Fault.

His Education; whether brought up idly, or in any honeft Occupa-tion.

His Ability of Body; *fc.* if ftrong and nimble, or weak or fickly, not like-ly to do the Act.

His Nature; if civil or hafty, witty and fubtil, a Quarreller, Pilferer o bloody-minded, &c.

His Means; if he hath whereon to live or not, (*a*) or *Si folito ditius fe ha-buerit in veftibus & in aliis ornamentis, cibis, & potibus, & hujufmodi.* Br fol. 120, 122.

2. Quali-ty.

(*d*) His Trade; for if a Man liveth idly or vagrant, (*Nullam exercens arten nec laborem*) it is a good Caufe to arreft him upon Sufpicion, if there ha been any Felony committed. 7 E. 4. 20. *Br. Faux Imp.* 22.

His Company; if Ruffians, fufpected Perfons, or his being in Company with any of the Offenders. 7 E. 4. 20.

His Courfe of Life; *fc.* if a common Alehoufe-haunter, or riotous in Diet Play, or Apparel.

Whether he be of evil Fame or Report.

Whether he hath committed the like Offence before, or if he hath had a Pardon, or been acquitted for Felony before: *Nam qui femel eft malus femper præfumitur effe malus in eodem genere mali.*

(*a*) So if he hath been tranfported or outlawed for Felony, although he hath his Pardon.

(*d*) If he hath any Blood about him or his Apparel, or that his Weapon be bloody.

If any of the Goods ftolen be in his Poffeffion.

(*a*) If any of the Apparel of the Party murdered be in his Poffeffion.

(*d*) The Change of his Countenance, his Blufhing, Looking downwards, Silence, Trembling.

His Anfwers doubtful or repugnant.

If he offereth Agreement or Compofition.

3. Marks or Signs.

(*a*) If he hath laboured his Neighbours not to fpeak thereof.

(*d*) The Meafure of his Foot, or his Horfe's Foot.

The Bleeding of the dead Body in his Prefence.

If, being charged with the Felony, or called Thief, he faith nothing. *F. Cor.* 24.

If he fled: *Fatetur facinus, qui judicium fugit.* Co. 11. 60.

(*a*) If he hides himfelf.

If he lies lurking in a Place where he had nothing to do.

If he were the firft that found the Party murdered.

4. The Fact.

(*d*) *Place, fc.* if convenient for fuch an Act, as in a Houfe, in a Wood, Dale, &c.

Time; the Year, Day, Hour, early or late.

Where the Offender was at the Time of the Fact, and where the Day or Night before; his Bufinefs and Company there: And Witnefs to prove all thefe.

Manner; if willingly, by Chance or Neceffity.

5. The Caufe.

If former Malice.

If to his Benefit, or what Hope of Gain.

If for the Efchewing of any Hurt or Danger.

6. The Perfon.

Agens: If Principal or Acceffary, Infant, Lunatick, &c.

Patiens: If againft the King, Commonwealth, Magiftrate, Mafter, &c.

(*a*) Note. That a Man accufing another but upon Sufpicion, is not to be reproved, though the Party accufed be proved innocent. *Numb.* 5. 28, 31.

2

(*d*) A

(*d*) A Felon brought before a Juftice of Peace accufeth others; it is fufficient Caufe for the Juftice to grant out his Warrant for the reft. See *poftea*.

A Man going to Execution accufeth another of Felony; it is fufficient Caufe to ar- F. Cor. 211. reft him.

Communis vox & fama, that he did the Offence, is fufficient Caufe of Sufpicion, *fc.* Br. Faux where fuch a Felony is done, otherwife not. Impr. 16.

But yet for the better conceiving what may give juft Caufe of Sufpicion, mark fome of Mr. *Bracton*'s Rules.

Oritur fufpicio ex fama: Fama vero quæ fufpicionem inducet, oriri debet apud bonas & Fame. graves, (non quidem malevolas & maledicas, fed providas & fide dignas) perfonas, idque Stamf. 97. *non femel, fed fæpius : Vanæ autem voces populi non funt audiendæ.*

And therefore where the common Proverb is, *Vox populi eft vox Dei*, it fhould be, *Vox populi Dei eft vox Dei.*

Si Furtum in manu alicujus inveniatur, vel fub poteftate alicujus, tunc ille in cujus Stamf. 29. *domo vel poteftate res furtiva inventa fuerit, tenebitur, (nifi Warrantum invenerit quod eum inde defendere poffit)* ; for, as another faith, *Cum adfunt teftimonia rerum, quid opus eft verbis ?*

Si quis noctu cubaverit in domo folus cum aliquo qui interfectus fit, vel fi duo aut plures ibi Stamf. 179. *fuere, & Hutefium non levavere, nec plagam a latronibus vel interfectoribus in defenfione facienda accepere, nec oftendunt quis de fe vel de aliis hominem interfecerit ; his cafibus mortem dedicere non poffunt.*

Si quis in domum fuam notum vel ignotum acceperit, qui vivus ingredi vifus eft, vero Ibid. *poftea nunquam nifi mortuus, dominus domus, fi tunc domi fit, vel alii de familia qui tunc interfuerunt, pænam capitalem fubibunt, nifi forte per patriam fuerint liberati.*

Sunt etiam quædam præfumptiones ita violentæ, ut probationem non admittunt in contra- Stamf. 97 & *rium ; ut fi quis cum cultello cruentato captus fit fuper mortuum, vel fugiendo a mortuo,* 179. *vel mortem confitetur : quibus cafibus non admittitur mortem dedicere, nec alio opus eft* Co. L. 6. *probatione.*

(*a*) Sir *Ed. Coke, Lit.* 6. maketh three Sorts of Prefumption, *viz.*   *Prefumption.*

1. *Violenta*, as in this laft former Cafe, which he faith is *plena probatio*.

2. *Probabilis*, which, faith he, moveth little.

3. *Præfumptio levis, feu temeraria*, which moveth not at all.

(*d*) And yet in Cafes of Felony, &c. the Confeffion of the Offender, upon his Exa- *Confeffion of* mination before the Juftice, fhall be no Conviction, except he fhall after * confefs the *the Offender.* fame again upon his Trial or Arraignment, or be found guilty by Verdict of twelve *Co. 11.30 a. vide.* Men, &c.

(*a*) To the like Purpofe alfo is the Rule of the Civil Law, *Si quis in Judicio fponte de feipfo confiteatur, & poftea maneat in Confeffione, fatis eft :* If any Man in Judgment do confefs of himfelf, of his own Accord, and doth perfevere in his Confeffion, it is enough, and fuch Confeffion fhall be taken for an Evidence of the Crime.

But yet at Lent Affizes at *Cambridge, Anno quarto Caroli Regis*, before Sir *Francis Harvey*, upon the Arraignment of a Prifoner for Felony, his Examination, which was taken before the Juftice of Peace, wherein he had confeffed the Felony, was only given in Evidence, no other Evidence then coming in upon his Trial; and the Prifoner upon that his own Confeffion before the Juftice of Peace was found guilty by the Jury of Life and Death, and had Judgment, &c.

(*d*) Alfo in Cafes of fecret Murders, and in Cafes of Poifoning, Witchcraft, and the like fecret Offences, where open and evident Proofs are feldom to be had, there half Proofs or probable Prefumptions are to be allowed, and are good Caufes of Sufpicion, (*a*) and are fufficient for the Juftice of Peace to commit the Party fo fufpected.

!(*d*) But

8 E. 4. 4.
c H. 7. 4.
Br. F Impr.
4. 10.

(d) But note, by the Common Law, That in an Action of Falfe Imprifonment brought againft the Conftable (or other Perfon that fhall arreft another upon Sufpicion of Felony, it is no Plea for them to fay, that the Plaintiff was fufpected of Felony: But they muft alledge, That there was fuch a Felony committed, and that the Plaintiff was fufpected for the fame; for Sufpicion only, without a Felony committed, is no Caufe to arreft another. (a) Yet fee the Statute of 5 E. 3. *cap.* 14. that if any Man have any evil

17 E. 4. 5.
22 H. 7. 29.

Sufpicion of any Perfon for Felony, &c. be it by Day or Night, they fhall be arrefted by the Conftables of the Towns, &c. and kept in Prifon till they be delivered by the Juftices, &c.

Alfo the Defendant muft alledge fome fpecial Matter, in Fact, to prove that he, who was arrefted, was fufpected of Felony, as to fay, that the Party arrefted is a Man of an evil Fame, or a vagrant Perfon, &c. otherwife one Man may arreft any other, yea every Man in the Town may be arrefted, when any Felony is committed.

7 E. 4. 20.

(a) But what is fufficient Caufe of Sufpicion, and what not, fhall be tried by the Juftices. *Fi.* 127.

Br. Exem. 8.
14, 16, 25.

(d) Alfo the Defendant muft plead, That he himfelf had a Sufpicion of the Plaintiff; for if the Conftable, or other Perfon that fhall arreft one that is fufpected, doth not fufpect him himfelf, it feemeth he may not arreft him upon his own Authority. (a) And yet by the Opinions of *Keble, Vavafor,* and *Townfend,* as well the Conftable, as others in his Aid, may arreft one that is fufpected of Felony, upon the Sufpicion and Complaint made to the Conftable, of the Party robbed. 2 *H.* 7. 15, 16. *Br. Faux Impr.* 14. yet *alii econtra ibid. fc.* that the Sufpicion can extend to no other, but only to him that hath the Sufpicion, and *Br.* 14 *H.* 8. 16. *a.* accordeth ; *tamen quære.* For if Felons may not be arrefted or ftayed but only by thofe who fhall fufpect them, and that others, may not aid and affift the Party that fhall fufpect another to have robbed him, many Felons fhall efcape, and go unpunifhed. See *Plo.* 46. *a.* & *Finch* 127.

(d) But now by the Statute 7 *Jac.* 1. 5. the Conftable, &c. in the former Cafes may plead the General Iffue (Not guilty), and give the faid fpecial Matters in Evidence.

Alfo if the Conftable, or other Perfon, fhall arreft another upon Sufpicion of Felony, by Virtue of a Warrant from a Juftice of Peace, fuch Warrant fhall excufe him, it being given in Evidence, &c. *Vide poftea* Tit. *Warrants.*

See 2 Hawk. P. C. Chap. 13. *for Arrefts by Publick Officers.*

C H A P. CLXVI. Part 2.

Bailment and Mainprife.

Definition.

BAilment, Mainprife or Replevin, is the Saving or Delivery of a Man out of Prifon, or the Freeing or Setting at Liberty one arrefted before that he hath fatisfied the Law ; *fc.* by finding Sureties to appear at a certain Day, and to anfwer, and be juftified by the Law.

And to this Purpofe thefe three Terms, *Bailment, Mainprife* and *Replevin,* be indifferently ufed in our Statutes and Books.

Nature of it.
Stamf. 65.
P. Mainp. 18.

He that is bailed is taken or kept out of Prifon, and delivered, as it were, into the Hands of his Sureties, who are reputed his Guardians, and who may keep him with them, and may imprifon him by fome Opinions. See 22 *H.* 6. *Br. Surety* 8. & *Mainp.* 89.

If the Mainpernors or Sureties do at any Time, or in any Cafe, doubt that their Prifoner, or the Party by them bailed, will fly, they may take him, and bring him before any Juftice of Peace; and upon their Prayer the faid Juftice of Peace may and ought to

Crom. 157.

difcharge fuch Sureties, and commit the Party to Prifon, except he fhall find new Sureties, &c.

So if a Prifoner be bailed by infufficient Perfons, the Juftice of Peace *ex Officio,* may caufe him to find better Sureties, and may commit him till he fhall fo do; for the Stat. of *Weft.* 1. *cap.* 15. requireth, That fuch as be bailed be let out by fufficient Surety. *P. Mainp.* 2. *Vide antea* Tit. *Surety for the Peace.*

(a) If the Prifoner cannot find fufficient Sureties, the Juftice of Peace is not bound (nay ought not, knowing their Infufficiency) to let the Prifoner to Bail. See *Co.* 10. 101.

I

(d) And

(*d*) And therefore, altho' the Number of fuch Sureties, their Sufficiency, and the Sum *Sufficiency.* wherein they fhall be bound, refteth in the Difcretion of the Juftices; yet it is fafe for hem to take two Sureties at the leaft, and thofe to be Subfidy-men, and to be bound in ;ood Sums, efpecially if the Prifoner be in for Felony, or Sufpicion thereof; for the riore able the Sureties are, the rather they will caufe him that is bailed to appear. And igain, for Want of taking fufficient Bail the Juftices of Peace are fineable. And at Cam: *ridge* Affizes, *A. D.* 1613. Judge *Warburton* threatned to have fet 40 *l.* Fine upon two Juftices of Peace, who had bailed a Prifoner that was committed for Sufpicion of Felony, ind appeared not, for that the Sureties were not Subfidy-men.

Quære, If the Juftices of Peace may not examine upon their Oaths the Sureties con- *Oath.* :erning their Sufficiency, or whether they be Subfidy-men. (*a*) The Juftices of the Com- non Pleas (7 *H.* 6. 25.) did examine the Ability of the Sureties upon their Oaths, *&c.* And that which the higher Courts do, may be a good Rule for others. *Vide* 2 *H.* 7. *f.* 1.

(*d*) Now Bailment by the Juftices of Peace, in Cafe of Felony, or for any other Mat- *Nature.* er, is always in a certain Sum of Money, (as 40 *l. &c.*) the which Sum the Sureties, *&c.* *Stamf. 77.* hall forfeit to the King, if the Prifoner appeareth not at his Day; 21 H.7. 20. 2 H.H.P.C. 125.

Alfo the Bailment in Felony is, *Ad ftandum rectum de latrocinio prædicto fecundum Le-* *rem, &c.* which feemeth to imply, That they which have taken him to Bail fhall not only caufe him to appear, but alfo to anfwer the Felony: *Stamf. 77. d.*

And in this Bufinefs of Bailment, being a Matter of much Weight, it behoveth the *Danger.* Juftices of Peace to be very circumfpect, as well for Fear of Wrong by denying it to him that is bailable, as alfo for Fear of Danger to the Service it felf, by yielding where it is not grantable; and for Fear of Danger to themfelves in both Cafes;

For whofoever detains Prifoners who are bailable, after they have offered fufficient Sure- 3 E. 1. 15. ies, fhall be amerced to the King: And he that doth take any Reward for the Deliver- *See* 23 H. 6. ince of fuch, fhall be amerced to the King, and pay double to the Prifoner. c. 10.

So on the other Side, if one who by the Law is not bailable, fhall be let to Mainprife, 25 E. 3. f. 39. this fhall be adjudged a negligent Efcape to him or them that do let him at Mainprife; and *Stamf.* 33.77. for fuch an Efcape or Offence, they fhall be fined and punifhed as followeth.

If the Sheriffs, Conftable, or any Bailiff of Fee who hath the Keeping of Prifoners, 3 E. 1. 15. fhall bail any Perfon which is not bailable, and be thereof attainted, they fhall lofe their P. Mainp. 3, Fee and Office for ever. And if the Under-Sheriff, Conftable, or Bailiff, or fuch as have 4. Fee for keeping of Prifoners, do it contrary to their Mafter's Will, or any other Bailiff being not of Fee, they fhall have three Years Imprifonment, and make Fine at the King's *Doct.* & *Stud.* Pleafure. 135.

Note, That the Sheriffs and other Officers which do let to Bail any Perfons forbidden 27 E. 1. c. 3. by the Statute of *Weftm.* 1. to be bailed, fhall be punifhed by the Juftices of Gaol-de- P. Main. 4. livery, according to the Form of the fame Statute; or elfe by the faid Juftices they may 3 E. 1. c. 15. be put to their Fine, as for an Efcape punifhable at the Common Law. 25 E. 3. 39.

(*a*) *Quære,* if it be not Felony for them to bail Felons, or Perfons fufpected for Fe- lony, for that thefe Officers have no Authority at this Day to bail fuch Prifoners..

The Writ of *Mainprife* * lieth properly where a Man is taken for Sufpicion of Felony, * *L. Coke fays* or indicted of Felony, for the which Thing by the Law he is bailable, and he offereth *this is taken* fufficient Sureties unto the Sheriff or others who have Authority to bail him, and he or *away; but this* they do refufe to let him to Bail; then he who is fo kept in Prifon may fue for fuch *is a Miftake* Writ. *F. N. B.* 553. *g.* *according to* 2 H. H. P.C. 142, 143.

What Perfons be forbidden to be bailed by the faid Statute of *Weftm.* 1. fee *poftea fub hoc tit.*

(*d*) Note, that the Sheriff or Conftable might at the Common Law have bailed one 3 H. 7. 3. fufpected of Felony, (becaufe they were Confervators of the Peace;) but now that Power is transferred to the Juftices of Peace only.

If any Juftices of Peace do let to Bail or Mainprife, any Perfon who (for any Offence *By the Juftices.* by him committed) is declared not to be bailable, or forbidden to be bailed by the afore- 1 & 2 P. & M. faid Statute of 3 *Ed.* 1. the faid Juftices of Peace fo offending fhall pay fuch Fines as fhall P. Juft. 108. be affeffed by the Juftices of Gaol-delivery where the Offence fhall be committed. P. Mainp. 4. Fitz. 251. I.

But the Juftices of Peace and Coroners within *London* and *Middlefex,* and in all other 1 & 2 P. & Cities, Boroughs, and Towns Corporate, have Authority to let to Bail Felons and Pri- M. c. 13. foners, as they have formerly accuftomed. *P. Juft.* 107. *See* Co. 10. 100. b.

If the Sheriff, Juftices of Peace, or other Officers, fhall bail one that is not bailable, fuch Bailment being againft Law, *quære* if the Recognizance or Bond taken upon fuch

Bail-

Bailment (for the Appearance of the Prifoner) be not void. See the Opinion of *Moil* 37 *H.* 6. 1. and of the Court there, that fuch a Bond taken by the Sheriff is void. Now to fhew farther the Authority of the Juftices of Peace in this Behalf.

The Manner. *1 & 2 P. & M. c. 13. P. Juft. 107.*   No Perfon arrefted for *Man-flaughter, or Felony,* or Sufpicion thereof, (being bailable by the Law) fhall be let to Bail or Mainprife, by any Juftice of Peace but in ope Seffions, or by two Juftices of Peace at the leaft, whereof one to be of the *Quorum* and the fame Juftices to be prefent together at the Time of the faid Bailment.

Ibid.   And this Bailment the faid Juftices fhall certify in Writing (fubfcribed with thei Hands) at the next Gaol-delivery, &c. *Vide antea* Tit. *Examination of Felons.*

Ibid.   Alfo before the Bailment of fuch Prifoner, the fame Juftices or one of them, fhal take the Examination of the Prifoner, and Information of them that bring him, or o the Fact and Circumftances thereof; and fo much thereof as fhall be material to prov the Felony fhall be put in Writing, before they make the Bailment : Which Examination, Information, and Bailment, they fhall certify at the next general Gaol-delivery *ut fupra.*

But if any Juftice of Peace hath taken the Examination of the Felon, and Informa tion againft him, and after hath fent him to Gaol; now upon Bailment of him by othe Juftices, they need not take any new Examination of the Prifoner or Informatio againft him, but under their Recognizance (or together therewith) to certify by wha Juftice of Peace the Felon was committed, to the End that at his Hands thofe Exa minations and Informations may be required, if he have not certified them.

Cromp. 156.   By the Opinion of Mr. *Crompton,* a Prifoner (*taken for Felony*) before his Commit ment, ought to be examined and bailed by two Juftices of Peace being together, (as be fore) : But after that the Prifoner is examined and once committed, then he may be baile by any one Juftice of Peace. *Quære* thereof.

Mittimus, the Form.   The Juftices of Peace which fhall fend any Prifoner to the Gaol, ought to fhew i their *Mittimus* the Caufe of the Commitment, to the End it may appear whether fuch Prifoner be bailable or no.

Cromp. 153.   And if the Juftices of Peace fhall commit one to the Gaol, with thefe Words i the *Mittimus, fc.* without Bail or Mainprife, (fhewing a certain Caufe in their *Mittimus* yet if fuch Prifoner be bailable by Law, other Juftices of Peace may bail him : (Ye *Quære,* feeing their Authority is equal :) But if the Prifoner were committed withou Bail or Mainprife, and without fhewing Caufe in the *Mittimus,* then other Juftices o Peace cannot (or at leaft fhall not do well to bail him,) without making the other Juftices who committed him, privy thereto; for he might be committed for fuch Caufe, as tha he is not bailable, (as for Treafon, &c.)

Poph. 96.   (*a*) I have feen a Report of a Cafe, *Term. Trin.* 37 *El.* That upon an Affembly o all the Judges and Barons at *Serjeants Inn,* it was refolved and agreed by them to b put in ure in their Circuits, that if a Juftice of Peace fhould commit a Man to the Gao for Felony, for which by the Law he is not bailable, but by his *Mittimus* he commit him generally, not fhewing any Caufe, if any other Juftices of Peace fhall bail him, no knowing the Matter, &c. they fhall be fined for the fame; for they at their Perils ough to inform themfelves of the Truth of the Matter before they bail him.

14H.7. 10. a.   *Note;* where a Man is bailable, yet when he cometh before the Juftices he muft offe Surety to the Juftices, otherwife they may commit him to Prifon. *Br. Peace* 7.

Next it followeth, that I fhew what Perfons be bailable, and what not.

Perfons not bailable. *P. Main.* 1. *Stamf.* 72.   It appears by the Statute of *Weftm.* 1. *cap.* 15. that in thefe four Cafes following, Man was not bailable at the Common Law. *Br. Mainp.* 47. *F. N. B.* 66. *e.*

D. Mainp. 11, *47, 57, 60, 63, 68.* *F. Cor.* 361.   1. No Perfon taken for the *Death of a Man, fc. for Murder,* or any other Homicide, was bailable by the Common Law.

And yet the Juftices of the King's Bench do ufe to bail them; yea, although it be for Murder. *Br. Mainp.* 60, 63, 78, 47. *See* the Statute 3 *H.* 7. *cap.* 1.

P. Juft. 107. *Lamb.* 336.   Alfo the Statute 1 & 2 *P. & M. cap.* 13. feemeth to admit that for *Man-flaughter,* and all other *Homicides* (except Murder only) the Slayer may be bailed by the Juftices of the Peace; which alfo I take to be the common Practice at this Day. But let the Juftices be well advifed herein, *viz.* that the Offence be but *Manflaughter,* and not Murder.

                                                  Alfo

Alfo it feemeth the Juftices of Peace cannot bail him that hath committed Man- P. Main. 11
laughter, if either he hath confeffed the Offence upon the Examination, (*vide poftea*,
Tit. *Bailment*) :

Or that he be taken with the Manner :

Or that it be apparently known that he killed the other. *Vide pag. fequent.*

He that hath dangeroufly hurt another, may be bailed, &c.   See before, & Stat. 3
H. 7. *cap.* 1.

2. Secondly, no Perfon taken by the *King's Command* was bailable by the Common
Law : But this muft be intended of the King's Commandment by his own Mouth * or * *Vide* 2 H.
by his Privy Council, which are incorporate to him.   See *Stamf.* 72. e.   *Br.* Mainp. H.P.C. 131.
57, 47.   contr a.

3. Thirdly, no Perfon taken by the Command of the King's Juftices was bailable by Stamf. 73.
the Common Law : But this muft be intended of their abfolute Command : As if the
Juftice commands one to Prifon without fhewing Caufe why he doth fo command, or
for a Mifdemeanor done in his Prefence, or for fome other Caufe which lieth in the
Difcretion of the Juftice, more than his ordinary Power, &c.

(*a*) And therefore if the *Lord Chancellor of England*, or *Lord Keeper* of the Great
Seal, who have Power to commit one to Prifon wherefoever they are in *England*, fhall
command or commit one to Prifon (by fuch their abfolute Authority) fuch Perfon fhall
not be bailed.

And fo if the *Juftices of the King's Bench* fhall command one to Prifon.

And fo if the *Juftices of the Court of Common Pleas* fitting in their Court.

Or *Juftices of Affife* in their Places ; if thefe fhall commit any to Prifon they are not
bailable.

But where any Juftice or Juftices fhall commit one rather to be fafely kept, than for
a Punifhment, fuch Commitment may be faid to be an ordinary Command ; and the
Party fo committed is bailable.   *Terms de Ley.*

(*d*) 4. Fourthly, *Trefpaffers in the Foreft* were not bailable by the Common Law :
But that was remedied by the Statute 1 E. 3. *ft.* 1. *cap.* 8. & 7 R. 2. *cap.* 4. F. N. B.
67. *c.*

But now, for that by the Statute 1 & 2 P. & M. *cap.* 13. it is provided, that no By Statute.
Juftice or Juftices of Peace fhall let to bail any Perfon contrary to the aforefaid Statute P. Juft. 107.
of *Weftm.* 1. made 3 E. 1. *cap.* 15. and fo the Statute of *Weftm.* 1. is now as a Line,
whereby the Juftices of Peace are to guide themfelves in Cafes of Bailment ; I will fhew
here what Perfons are bailable by that Statute of *Weftm.* 1. and what not.

By this Statute of *Weftm.* 1. no Prifoner fhall be let to Bail which is taken in any of 3 E. 1. 15.
thefe 12 Cafes following.   P. Main. 1.
                                                                                                            F. N. B. 66.

1. Such as have *abjured the Realm*, fhall not be bailed.   Abjured.

2. Nor any *Approver or Appellor*, for that he confeffeth the Felony, and himfelf Approver.
Guilty, before he can accufe another, as Coadjutor or Helper with him in doing the Stamf. 144. b.
fame.   Lamb. 337.

3. Nor he which is *appealed by an Approver*, fo long as the Approver doth live, ex- Fit. 250. d.
cept he be of good Name, or that the Approver doth waive his Appeal. See *Stamf.* Br. Main. 9.
74. (*a*) Or that the Approver be vanquifhed.   25 E. 3. 43.

4. (*d*) Nor he which is taken for *burning a Houfe*, &c. felonioufly. *Vide antea Felony Burning a*
by the Common Law.   *Houfe.*

5. Nor any *Excommunicate Perfon*, taken at the Bifhop's Requeft ; fc. upon his Cer- Excommuni-
tificate into the Chancery by the Writ of *Excom. capiend.* F. N. B. 66. c.   cate.

And yet when the Party is fo taken, if he will conform himfelf to the Laws of
Holy Church, and give Surety for his Obedience, he fhall have a Writ *de Cautione ad-*
mittenda, directed to the Bifhop ; and if the Bifhop will not, then he fhall have a Writ
to the Sheriff to deliver him. See *Fitz.* 63. *c. d.*

(*d*) 6. Nor any *Felon* taken with the *Manner*, * or taken for a manifeft Offence. Felon taken
                                                                                                             with the
Manner.   * Manner *may be derived from the French*, Manœuvre, *or* Main-avoir, *which laft anfwers to the* Saxon Hand-habbend *ufed by*
Bracton, *for* furtum Manifeftum.   *See* 2 Hawk. P. C. 98.   Not. [28] *of the third Edition, and* 1 H.H.P.C. 187, 348, 349 and
2 H. H. P. C. 133, 156.

7. Nor a *Thief openly defamed* and known.   Thief openly
                                                                                                             defamed.

8. Nor he which is *Outlawed in Cafe of Felony* ; and yet in fome Cafes, fuch as be Outlawed in
Outlawed may be bailed by the Court, &c. See *Stamf.* 74.   Felony.

                                                                                                  9. Nor

Prifon-breaker.   9. Nor he who hath *broken the King's Prifon.* *Vide antea Felony by Statute.*

Treafon.   10. Nor he which is taken for *Treafon* touching the King himfelf.

Coining.   11. Nor he which is taken for *falfifying the King's Money.*

Counterfeiteth the King's Seal.   12. Nor he which counterfeiteth the King's Seal. *Br. Mainp.* 59.

(*a*) In all thefe Cafes, if the Caufe for which the Party is imprifoned be Treafon or Felony, or otherwife toucheth Life or Member, then fhall he not be bailable ; otheiwife he may be bailed.

Manifeft Offence.   Nor fhall he which is taken for a manifeft Offence be bailed ; as if a Man be indicted and imprifoned for a Riot, or other great Offence, before Juftices, by Force of the King's Commiffion of Oyer and Terminer, this (and the like) are the manifeft Offences whereof the Statute fpeaketh. See *Fitz.* 250. *f.*

Perfons bailable.   (*d*) But by the fame Statute of *Weft.* 1. fuch Perfons are bailable, which be taken in any of thefe fix Cafes following,

Weft. 1. 15.   1. *Perfons fufpected.*   Firft, He that is taken (or indicted) for light Sufpicion of Felony, is bailable. See *Lamb.* 335. *F. N. B.* 249. *g.* 250. *cap.* 251. *f.*

P. Main. 2.   *Stamf.* 74. *c.*   He that is taken upon Sufpicion of Burglary, Robbery or Theft, if he be not of evil Fame, nor that there be any ftrong Prefumption againft him, is bailable.

16 E. 4. 7.   *Br. Main.* 95.   A Man had ftolen certain Hogs, and (for that he was of evil Fame) he was committed without Bail ; yet if he could have brought Proof or Witnefs that he bought them, he fhould have been bailed.

Cro. 154.   A Man is arrefted for Sufpicion of Felony, and brought before the Juftice ; if it fhall appear that there is no fuch Felony committed, the Party may he fet at Liberty without Bail : But if there be a Felony committed, though the Prifoner can clear himfelf, yet the Juftices may either commit or bail him. *Vide antea,* Tit. *Felony by Statute.*

2. *Petty Larceny.*   Secondly, he that is taken (or indicted) for petty Larceny, that amounteth not above the Value of 12 *d.* if he were not guilty of fome Larceny before, is bailable.

P. Main. 2.   *Fitz.* 250. 6.   3. *Perfons indicted by Inqueft of Office.*   Thirdly, fuch as be indicted of Larceny by Inqueft of Office before the Sheriff, or before Coroners or Bailiffs, *&c.* or in any bafe Court, they fhall be fet at Liberty upon fufficient Surety.

P. Main. 2.   *Stamf.* 74.   *Fitz.* 247. & 250. *c.*   *B.* Mainp. 97.   And yet they fhall not be bailed, if they be not alfo of good Fame ; but if they be of good Fame they are to be bailed, though they be indicted as aforefaid (before Sheiiffs, Bailiffs, Coroners, or before any other fuch Officers, by their Office, or in any bafe Court) : Yet *Quære,* if the Juftices of Peace out of their Seffions may fafely bail fuch Perfons ; for being indicted, they are more than vehemently fufpected, *&c.*

(*a*) One that was indicted before the Coroner, that he had killed another *fe defendendo,* was (by the Juftices of Gaol-delivery) bailed till the next Affifes to purchafe his Pardon 26 *El. Cromp.* 153. See *antea,* Tit. *Mifadventure.*

One that is indicted before the Sheriff for ftealing of a Horfe (which feemeth to have been in his Torn) may be bailed by the Sheriff (if he be of good Fame) by the Writ *de Manucaptione.* *F. N. B.* 249. *g.*

Alfo one that was indicted of Burglary, as Principal, pleaded Not guilty, and was afterwards bailed. 29 *Lib. Aff. Fitz. Mainpr.* 9. See *infra.*

Another that was indicted of Robbery was bailed. 41 *Lib. Aff.* 30. *Br. Mainp.* 61.

If any Murderer being indicted, and after arraigned at the King's Suit, fhall be thereof acquitted within the Year and Day, the Juftices before whom he is acquitted fhall not fuffer him to go at large, but either fhall remit him to Prifon, or elfe may bail him (at their Difcretion) till the Year and Day be paffed, to the End that the Wife, or next Heir to the Party murdered, may have their Appeal of the fame Murder within the Year and Day after the fame Murder done, *&c.* 3 *H.* 7. *cap.* 1. *Fitz.* 151. *g.*

Perfons attaint or convict.   *Stamf.* 74. *d.*   *F. Cor.* 297.   354.   (*d*) But fuch as are attainted or convicted of Felony are not bailable. For although it doth not appear by any Words of the faid Statute of *Weft.* 1. that it doth prohibit the Bailment of fuch as be attainted by Verdict, yet it is to be intended, that the Statute doth as well prohibit the Bailment of thofe attainted by Verdict, as it doth of them who are attainted by Outlawry : And therefore if a Prifoner, after he hath pleaded not guilty, be attainted by Verdict, That he killed a Man *fe defendendo,* or by Misfortune, yet fhall he not be bailed by the Juftice of Peace. *Tamen vide antea,* Tit. *Felonies by Cafualty, & Stamf.* 15. *c. F. N. B.* 246. *c.*   (*a*) That he fhall be bailed by the Juftices of Gaol-delivery before whom he is tried.

4

(*d*) And

(*d*) And if a Man that is arraigned of Homicide doth plead Not guilty, and is found guilty, and doth pray his Clergy, and is reprieved without Judgment, he is not bailable; for being convicted of the Felony, he is more now than vehemently suspected, and the Intendment of the Law in Cases of Bailment is, that it resteth indifferent whether he be guilty or not, until Trial. *Dyer* 179. *See* Br. Mainp. 94.

The same Reason seemeth to hold, if a Man be found guilty of Homicide before the Coroner. (*a*) Yet see 22 *Aff. p.* 94. *Br. Cor.* 90. that such are bailable as are found (before the Coroner) but suspicious.

One *Poynes* was found guilty of Manslaughter before the Coroner, and it was certified in the King's Bench; and *Poynes* at the Bar prayed to be bailed, but it was denied him: For (as *Coke* said) peradventure it may be Murder. And it appears by the Statute of Queen *Mary*, that in Manslaughter the Party is not always bailable, for if he confess the Fact he is not bailable; which *Haughton* granted, and said, that he is not bailable if the Fact be notorious, which the Court granted. *Poyne's Cafe, Mich.* 13 *Jac. Roll's Rep. Part* 1. *p.* 268. *Manflaughter.*

Also a Man convicted of Felony remaineth in Prison, and after obtaineth the King's Pardon; the Justice of Gaol-delivery may bail him till the next Gaol-delivery, that he may then come with his Pardon and plead it. 2 *E.* 6. *Br. Mainp.* 94.

(*d*) 4. Those that be charged with the Receipt of Thieves or Felons, or of Command, or Force, or of Aid (in Felony done) be bailable. 4. *Accefferies.* P. Main. 2. Stamf. 71. Stamf. 71. e.

And it seemeth that *Abettors, Confenters* and *Procurers,* and all other *Accefferies* to *Felonies,* are within the Equity of this Statute, and are bailable: Yea, Accefferies (as well in case of the Death of a Man, although it be Murder, as in Case of other Felonies) are bailable, if they be of good Fame, until the Principal be convict or attaint; but after the Principal is attainted the Acceffary shall not be bailed, but kept in Prison: And yet if (after the Attainder of the Principal) the Acceffary shall appear, and plead Not guilty, or other Plea, he shall be bailed. (*a*) The Reason is, for that when the Acceffary shall make Default, then is it as a *fugam fecit,* and a great Caufe of Sufpicion of the Thing; but when he appeareth, by that the Sufpicion is taken away, and so he is bailable. See more in *Br. Mainp.* 6, 9, 22, 54, 64 & 97. Fitz. 250. c. Br. Main. 11. 39 & 58. 40 E. 3. f. 28. Stamf. 71. c. Br. Main. 58.

(*d*) If a Man be acceffary to two, and the one Principal is attainted, though the other be not, yet the Acceffary shall not be bailed. Stamf. 71. F. Co. 200.

(*a*) In *Felony,* if the Principal die in Prison, or be attainted of another Felony, the Acceffary shall be bailed. *F. Cor.* 378. *Br. Mainp.* 91.

But note, that in cafe of *Treafon* the Principal shall not be bailed.

(*d*) Also the said Statute of *Weft.* 1. *cap.* 15. doth no more reftrain the Principals (to be bailed) than the Accefferies, in those Cafes where the same Statute doth not prohibit to let to Mainprife: And therefore if a Man be indicted of *Burglary* as Principal, yet he may be bailed. *Stamf.* 74. *Br.* 56. 29 *Aff.* Pl. 44. *Principals.* Stamf. 74. B. Mainp. 58, 90. F. Main. 9.

Also the Principal in an *Appeal of Robbery* may be bailed; and so may he be bailed upon an Indictment of Robbery. *Br.* 61. (*a*) 75 & 97. Yet in an Appeal of Robbery the Book 6 *H.* 7. *f.* 1. *b.* seemeth to the contrary. Stamf. 74.

(*d*) But the Principal in the *Death of a Man is not bailable,* either by the Common Law, or by the Statute of *Weft.* 1. yet fee hereof before in this Title, that the Juftices of the King's Bench do ufe to bail them. Alfo fee there for what Homicides the Juftices of Peace may bail one that is a Principal. Stamf. 71. Br. 56,58,97.

5. Fifthly, Those that be charged with (or guilty of) any Trefpafs that toucheth not Lofs of Life nor Member, be bailable by the Statute of *Weft.* 1. 15. But yet let the Juftice of Peace have a Care, that Bail be not prohibited by any other later Statute in fuch Cafes of Trefpafs. 5. *Trefpafs.* Weft 1. 15. P. Main. 2.

If any Perfon be committed to Prifon by Procefs from the Seffions made upon an Indictment upon any penal Statute (not prohibiting Bail, or for any Trefpafs) he may be bailed (out of Seffions) by two Juftices of the Peace, the one being of the Quorum. Fitz. 250. g. Lamb. 337. Br. 97.

Or he may have a Writ out of the Chancery directed to the Juftice of Peace, or to the Sheriff, to take Surety of him for his Appearance before the Juftices at their Seffions, &c. Or he may have a *Certiorari* to the Juftices of Peace, to remove the Record into the King's Bench; and a *Habeas Corpus* to the Sheriff to remove the Body thither alfo. *Fitz.* 250. g. h. i. & 251. c.

If Procefs from the Seffions shall go forth upon an Indictment of Trefpafs, &c. it feemeth that any one Juftice of Peace may take Bail of the Party to appear at the Day, &c. *Seffions Procefs.* Cromp. 197. &c. 234.

5 G

&c. to anſwer to the Indictment: And the ſame Juſtice may thereupon make his *Super-ſedeas de cap. Indictat.* and ſo of the Exigent; for otherwiſe, beſides the Miſchief of Imprifonment, the Party may be outlawed before the Seſſions. See ſome Precedents therein, *poſtea,* Tit. *Precedents.*

Note, That the Juſtices of Peace are not to bail any Priſoner, except he be committed for ſuch Cauſe whereof the ſaid Juſtices of Peace be competent Judges, *ſc.* ſuch Cauſes as they may hear and determine.

Lamb. 337.
Cromp. 152.
And therefore if a Man be taken upon Proceſs of Rebellion iſſuing out of the Chancery, the Juſtices of Peace are not to bail him. And Mr. *Crompton* reporteth of two Juſtices of the Peace who were fined for bailing one in ſuch a Caſe.

If a Man be arreſted by Force of any Proceſs, Writ, Bill or Warrant, in any Action perſonal, the Juſtices of Peace are not to bail him.

(*a*) Perſons condemned in any of the King's Courts, and by virtue thereof committed to Priſon; and Perſons being in Execution upon any Statute or Recognizance, *&c.* at the Suit of any Perſon, the Juſtices of Peace are not to bail any ſuch.

Approver.
Fitz. 250. d.
P. Main. 2.
(*d*) 6. Sixthly, He that is appealed by an *Approver,* being no common Thief, nor defamed, after the Death of the *Approver,* is bailable by the ſaid Statute of *Weſt.* 1.

(*a*) An Approver or Appellor is he who hath committed ſome Felony, which he confeſſeth, and then appealeth others, accuſing them that they were Coadjutors or Helpers with him in doing the ſame. *Et ſic dicti, quia ad hoc probandum, quod in Appello allegarunt, tenentur, idque vel * Duello, vel per Patriam, ſc. Jurat. legalium hominum, juxta reorum electionem.* Cow.

* This is diſ-
uſed.

And this Accuſation by the Approver muſt be done before the Coroner, either aſſigned to the Felon by the Court, to take and record what he ſaith; or elſe may be called by the Felon himſelf, and required, for the good of the King and the State, to record his Accuſation, and what he ſaith. *Ibid. Exceptiones contra Apellum.* Vide Bract. lib. 3. cap. 20. &c.

Stamf. 144. a.
B Peace 1.
Abr. d' Aſſ.
72, 76.
(*d*) Note, That a Man cannot become an *Approver* before Juſtices of Peace (becauſe they have no Authority to aſſign him a Coroner): Neverthelefs it ſeemeth both reaſonable and ſerviceable, that if a Felon will become an *Approver,* that is, will confeſs his Felony, and alſo accuſe others that were Coadjutors with him in doing the ſame Felony, (or other Felonies) before a Juſtice of Peace, that ſuch Juſtice may take his Confeſſion, and commit him to the Gaol, and may alſo grant out his Warrant for the apprehending others that are ſo accuſed.

(*a*) Concerning an Approver obſerve theſe Rules.

1. One cannot be an Approver but in Felony or Treaſon. 9 *H.* 6.

Stamf.
Finch.
2. One cannot be an Approver but upon Indictment only. 1 *H.* 7. 5.

3. An Approver muſt accuſe the other of ſuch an Offence as he himſelf did together with the other. *Stamf.* 143.

Execution.
Again, the Statute of 23 *H.* 6. *cap.* 10. taketh away Bail from all ſuch as be in Priſon by Condemnation, Execution, *Capias utlagatum,* Excommunication, Surety for the Peace, or by the ſpecial Command of any Juſtice, prohibiting that ſuch be not bailed either by the Sheriff or other Officer or Miniſter.

There be divers Statutes which take away Bail from the Offenders, and that not only upon their ſolemn Conviction after publick Hearing, Trial and Judgment, but alſo upon the Record of one or two Juſtices of Peace, or by private Examination and Confeſſion of the Offender, or Proof of Witneſſes, or ſuch other private Trial had before the Juſtices of Peace out of their Seſſions, moſt of which I have here ſet down, leaving the Reſt to the Reader's better Search.

See 2 Hawk. P. C. Chap. 15. *of* Bail.

C H A P. CLXVII.

Where Bailment is taken away by Statute.

Where Bail is
taken away.
NO Perſon being impriſoned or taken for any of the Offences or Cauſes hereunder mentioned, ſhall be bailed or let to Mainpriſe, otherwiſe than as hereafter followeth, *&c.*

1　　　　　　　　　　　　　　　　　　　　　　　　　　Such

Such as have abjured the Realm fhall not be bailed. *Weft.* 1. *cap.* 15.

Abjured.
13 E. 1. St. 1.
c 11.

Accountants found in Arrearages before Auditors fhall be imprifoned (without Bail) until they have fatisfied their Mafter all Arrearages.

Accountants.

Alehoufe-keeper without Licenfe fhall be committed to Prifon for three Days with- out Bail; and before his Delivery fhall enter into Recognizance with two Sureties, that he fhall not keep any common Alehoufe, *&c.* *Vide antea,* 'Tit. *Alehoufes.*

Alehoufe-keeper.

Alehoufe-keeper prohibited by two Juftices of Peace, and notwithftanding continuing his Selling, *&c.* fhall be committed for three Days as aforefaid. *Ibid.*

Alehoufe-keepers without Licenfe, for their fecond Offence, fhall be committed to the Houfe of Correction for one Month: And for every fuch their Offence after fhall be committed to the Houfe of Correction, there to remain till they be delivered by Order from the General Seffions. *Ibid.*

See antea Tit. Alehoufes.

Alehoufe-keepers, Inn-keepers, and Victuallers, which fhall fuffer Townfmen to continue drinking in their Houfes contrary to the Statute of 1 *Jac.* 1. *cap.* 9.

Or which fhall fell lefs than one full Ale-quart of their beft Beer or Ale for 1 *d.* and of the fmall two Quarts for 1 *d.*

Such Offenders, not having fufficient whereby to be diftrained for the Forfeiture, fhall be committed to Prifon until they have paid the Penalty.

Aliens conveying Bows and Arrows into any Parts beyond the Seas, without Licenfe, fhall be committed until they have made Fine (by Difcretion of the Juftices of the Peace in their Seffions) and give Surety for the Payment thereof.

Aliens.
33 H. 8. c. 9.
P. Arch. 6.

. Appellors or Approvers fhall not be bailed. *Weft.* 1. *cap.* 15.

Nor he which is appealed by an Approver. *Ibid.*

Approvers.

Armor : Perfons going or riding armed, contrary to the Statute of *Northampton,* and being thereof convict, fhall be imprifoned until they have payed fuch Fine as fhall be therefore impofed upon them. See *poftea fub Loc tit.*

Armor.

Arreft : If any Perfon fhall procure one to be arrefted in another Man's Name, he not knowing thereof, or without his Confent, fuch Offender being convicted thereof, fhall fuffer fix Months Imprifonment without Bail; and before his Delivery fhall pay to the Party fo arrefted treble Cofts, Damages, and Expences; and alfo fhall pay unto the Perfon, in whofe Name he procureth fuch Arreft, ten Pounds for every fuch Offence.

Arreft in the Name of another.
8 El. c. 2.
P. Dam. 3.

(a) If any of a petty Jury in *London* fhall be attainted by the Verdict of a Grand Jury, and therefore committed to Prifon; or if any of a petty jury in *London* fhall receive any Money or Reward, or Promife thereof, of the Defendants in the Attaint, for the Intent to give fuch his or their Verdict.

Attainted by Verdict.

As alfo the Defendant's giving or promifing fuch Reward, *&c.* every fuch Offender being therefore committed to Prifon, fhall there remain without Bail, *&c.* 12 H. 7. *cap.* 21.

(d) *Baftard :* The Mother or reputed Father of a Baftard Child, that fhall not perform the Juftice's Order, after Notice thereof, fhall be imprifoned until they fhall put in Sureties according to the Statute. See before, Tit. *Baftardy.*

Baftardy.
Where Bail is taken away.

The Mother of a Baftard Child, committed to the Houfe of Correction for her firft Offence, fhall there remain for one whole Year; and for her fecond Offence for one whole Year, and farther, until fhe can put in good Sureties for her good Behaviour not to offend fo again. See *Ibid.*

Breakers of Prifon are not bailable. *Weft.* 1. *cap.* 15.

Bridges : Surveyors and Collectors appointed for the Repairing of Bridges, if they refufe to account for the Money by them received, they fhall be imprifoned until they have truly accounted. 22 *H.* 8. *cap.* 5. P. *Bridges* 4. '

Where the Bail is taken away.

Burners of Houfes felonioufly are not bailable. *Weft.* 1. *cap.* 15.

Burning Houfes.

Perfons confpiring to indict another of Felony, are not Mainpernable or Bailable. 27 *Aff.* Pl. 12. *Fit. Mainp.* 7.

Confpirators.

Conftables and Church-wardens, neglecting to levy the Forfeitures for Abufes in Alehoufes, *&c.* not having fufficient whereby to be diftrained for their Forfeiture of forty Shillings, they fhall be committed to Prifon until they have paid the fame Forfeiture. See *antea,* Tit. *Alehoufes.* 1 *Jac.* 1. *cap.* 9.

Conftables.

(a) Conftables neglecting to execute the Juftice's Warrant concerning Alehoufes unlicenfed, the Conftable fhall be committed to the County Gaol, there to remain without Bail, until he hath punifhed the Alehoufe-keeper, or until the Conftable fhall pay forty Shillings to the Ufe of the Poor. 3 *Caroli Regis.*

(d) Con-

(*d*) Conftables neglecting to whip Trefpaffers in Corn, Wood, Orchards, &c. (at the Juftices Command) fhall be imprifoned until they have caufed the Offender to be whipped. See Tit. *Trefpafs.*

Perfons condemned in any of the King's Courts, and by virtue thereof committed to Prifon, they fhall not be bailed until they have agreed with the Plaintiff.   1 R. 2. cap 12.   2 H. 5. cap. 2.   Fitz. N. B. 121. a.

Counterfeiters of the King's Seal or Money are not bailable. *Weft.* 1. cap. 5.

Cloth : Refufers to be Overfeers of Cloth fhall be imprifoned until they have paid the Forfeiture. See *antea,* Tit. *Cloth.*

(*a*) Such Perfons as fhall be convicted for making of deceivable Cloth, if two Juftices of Peace fhall make Certificates thereof, and make their Warrant to the Church-wardens, &c. for the Levying of the Forfeitures, and if the faid Offenders fhall not have whereby they may be diftrained for the fame Forfeitures, the faid two Juftices of Peace may commit the Offenders to the common Gaol, there to remain without Bail, until Payment fhall be made of the Sums fo forfeited, &c. *hic antea,* Cloth.

Deer.

(*d*) *Deer :* Perfons committed to Prifon for committing any Offence prohibited by the Statute, 5 Eliz. cap. 21. concerning unlawful Hunting or Killing of Deer, fhall remain there three Months and farther, until they fhall find fufficient Sureties for their Good Behaviour for feven Years, &c. See *hic antea.*

Where Bail is taken away.
Excommunicated.
Weft. 1. 15.
5 El. 23.
See 23 H. 6.
c. 10.

Excommunicated Perfons, taken by a Writ *de Excommunicato capiendo,* or yielding their Bodies to the Sheriff or other Officer, upon any Writ of *Capias* awarded, and Proclamation thereupon made, according to the Statute of 5 El. cap. 23. provided for the due Execution of the faid Writ *de Excommunicato capiendo,* fuch Perfons fhall not be bailed.

Execution : Such Perfons as are in Execution upon any Statute or Recognizance, or upon Judgment given in the King's Court at the Suit of any Perfon, they fhall not be bailed until they have agreed with the Plaintiff.   1 R. 2. cap. 12.   23 H. 6. cap. 10. *Fitz. Na. Br. fol.* 93. c. & 121. a.   And yet then the Juftices of Peace are not to bail them.

Pheafants. See *Partridges.*

1. Felons taken for the Death of a Man are not bailable; and yet if it be not Murder, and their Offence not apparent, it feemeth they may be bailed.   See *hic antea.*

2. Felons taken with the Manner are not bailable. *Weft.* 1. cap. 15.

3. Nor if it be apparently known that they did the Felony. *Ibid.*

4. Nor if they confefs the Felony upon their Examination before the Juftices of Peace. *Cromp.* 152. b.

5. Nor if it be a Thief openly known. *Weft.* 1. 15.

6. Nor if he be of evil Fame by credible Report. *Br. Mainp.* 75.

Yet in thefe former Cafes of Felony, if the Theft be not above the Value of twelve Pence the Juftice of Peace may bail the Prifoner, it being no Felony of Death.

7. Nor is he which is convict or attaint of Felony bailable.   See before *fub hoc tit.*

(*a*) Acceffaries in Felony fhall not be bailed, after that the Principal (or any one Principal) is attainted. But before the Principal is attainted the Acceffary is bailable by the Common Law. *Stamf.* 71.

(*d*) *Fifh :* Deftroyers of Ponds, Pools or Moats, wherein any Fifh are; or unlawfully to fifh in any feveral Pond, Pool or Moat, to the Intent to take, kill or deftroy any Fifh there; every fuch Offender being thereof lawfully convicted fhall have three Month's Imprifonment, and then fhall find fufficient Sureties for the Good Behaviour for feven Years after, or elfe fhall remain in Prifon without any Bail, until they have found Sureties accordingly.

2. Gaugers, Packers or Searchers of Fifh, that fhall take any Extortion for doing their Office, fhall have forty Days Imprifonment without Bail.

3. Eaters of Flefh upon any Fifh-day fhall forfeit and pay for every Time 20 s. or elfe fuffer one Month's Imprifonment without Bail, (after any lawful Conviction in that Behalf.)   5 El. cap. 5.

Forcible Entry or Detainer; Perfons convict thereof fhall not be bailed until they have paid their Fine, or have found Sureties by Recognizance for Payment thereof. See *antea,* Tit. *Forcible Entry.*

Foreftallers, Regrators and Ingroffers, being thereof convicted, fhall be imprifoned for *Foreftallers.* two Months without Bail. *5 E. 6. cap.* 14. *P.* 4.

Forgers of any Deed, Writing fealed, Will, or Court-Roll : *Forgery.*

    2. And the Affenters thereto :

    3. And the Publifhers thereof, knowing the fame, *&c.*

Every of the Offenders aforefaid, (in Cafes of Forgery) being thereof convicted, fhall *5 El. c.* 14. fuffer perpetual Imprifonment during their Lives, where any Man's Eftate of Inheritance, *P. 1, 2.* Freehold or Copyhold, fhall be defeated, charged or molefted thereby : Otherwife the Offender fhall fuffer one Year's Imprifonment without Bail.

Fowl : Deftroyers of any Pheafant, Partridge, Pigeon or Houfe-dove, or of any *Fowl.* Heron, Mallard, Duck, Teal, or other Fowl ; or Shooters at any fuch Fowl, and the Offence proved before any two Juftices of Peace ; every fuch Offender fhall be committed for three Months without Bail, unlefs the Offender fhall forthwith pay to the Ufe of the Poor there 20 *s.* for every fuch Fowl fo deftroyed, *&c.* See *antea*, Tit. *Partridge.*

Fraudulent Conveyances, Gifts, Bonds or Suits, *&c.* *Fraud.*

    1. The Parties thereto.

    2. The Defenders or Juftifiers thereof, or Putters thereof in Ure, knowing the fame. *13 El. c. 5.*

    3. And thofe who fhall affign over any Lands, Leafes or Goods, fo to them con- *P. 1, 2.* veyed, knowing the fame.

Every Perfon being of any of thefe laft Offences lawfully convicted, fhall fuffer Imprifonment one half Year without Bail. See more Statute 14 *Eliz.* 11 *& 27. cap.* 4.

Games unlawful. *Games.*

    1. The Maintainers of Houfes or Places for any unlawful Game. *33 H. 8. c. 9.*

    2. Players in common Houfes or Places at any fuch Game.

    3. Players elfewhere at any unlawful Game.

Every Juftice of Peace, feeing or finding any fuch Offence, may imprifon the Offenders till they find Sureties by Recognizance no more to offend in the Premiffes, *&c.* See *antea*, Tit. *Games unlawful.*

Guns : Such Perfons as fhall fhoot in, keep, carry, or ufe any Gun, Dag, Crofs- *Guns.* bow or Stone-bow, contrary to the Statute of 33 *H. 8. cap.* 6. (upon Proof thereof made before any Juftice of Peace) fhall be imprifoned until they have paid 10 *l.* for every fuch Offence. See *antea*, Tit. *Guns.*

No Perfon under the Degree of a Lord fhall fhoot in any Hand-gun within any City or Town at any Fowl, or other Mark upon any Church, Houfe or Dove-Cote : Neither fhall any Perfon fhoot in any Place any Hail-fhot, or any more Pellets than one at one Thing, upon Pain to forfeit 10 *l.* and to have three Month's Imprifonment. 2 *& 3 E.* 6. *cap.* 14.

    1. *Hares :* Every Perfon which fhall fhoot at, kill or deftroy, with any Gun or Bow, *Hares.* any Hare.

    2. Or fhall trace or courfe any Hare in the Snow.

    3. Or fhall take or deftroy any Hare with Cords, or any other Engine. *Where Bail is* Any of thefe laft Offences being proved before any two Juftices of Peace, the Offen- *taken away.* der fhall be committed for three Months without Bail, unlefs the Offender fhall forthwith pay to the Ufe of the Poor there 20 *s.* for every Hare fo deftroyed or taken. See *antea*, Tit. *Partridges.*

    1. *Hatters :* Which fhall take above two Apprentices. *Hatters.*

    2. Or which fhall take an Apprentice for lefs Time than feven Years.

The Offenders in either of the fame Cafes fhall fuffer one Month's Imprifonment without Bail. 8 *El. cap.* 11. *P.* Hats 3.

Hawks : Takers (unlawfully) of any Hawks, or of their Eggs, out of another Man's *Hawks.* Ground, and being thereof lawfully convicted, fhall have three Months Imprifonment, *5 El.* 2. and then fhall find Sureties for their Good Behaviour for feven Years after; or elfe fhall *P.* Hawks 1. remain in Prifon without Bail until they find Sureties accordingly. *See* 11 H. 7. *c.* 7. hic poftea *Partridges.*

Hawkers between the 1ft of *July* and the 31ft of *Auguft*, the Offence being proved before any two Juftices of Peace, the Offenders fhall be committed to the Common Gaol for one Month without Bail, unlefs they pay forthwith 40 *s.* for every fuch Hawking, and 20 *s.* for every Pheafant or Partridge that they fhall fo kill or take. 7 *Jac.* 11. See *antea*, Tit. *Partridges.*

Highways.

Highways : Bailiffs and High Conftables, who fhall not pay the Forfeitures by them collected, fhall be imprifoned until they have paid the fame. See before, Tit. *Highways.* 2 *Ph. & M. cap.* 8. *P.* 11.

Honey.

Honey. See *Wax.*

Hoftlers.

Hoftlers or Innholders which fhall make any Horfe-bread, (contrary to the Statute 21 *Jac.* 1. *cap.* 21.) or which fhall not fell their Horfe-bread, Hay, Oats, Beans, Peafe, Provender, or other Kind of Victual (for Man or Beaft) for reafonable Gain, and be thereof lawfully convicted, &c. the fecond Time, fhall be imprifoned by the Space of one Month without Bail.

So of fuch Hoftlers and Innholders, as are allowed by the faid Statute to make Horfe-bread within their Houfes, if the Horfe-bread which any of them fhall make be not fufficient, lawful, and of due Affife, &c. and that they be thereof lawfully convicted the fecond Time, they fhall be imprifoned one Month without Bail. *Ibid.*

Hunting.

(*d*) *Hunting :* If any Layman, not having in Land 40 *s. per Annum,* or if any Prieft or Clerk, not having 10 *l.* Living *per Annum,* fhall have or keep any Hound, Greyhound, or other Dog for to hunt, or any Ferrets, Hays, Hare-pipes, Cords, Nets, or other Engines, to take or deftroy Deer, Hares, Conies, or other Gentlemens Game, and fhall be thereof convicted at the Seffions of Peace, every fuch Offender fhall be imprifoned for one whole Year. 13 *R.* 2. *cap.* 13. *P.* 1.

If any Perfon fhall keep any Greyhound for Deer or Hare, not having fufficient Living, and fhall be thereof convicted before any two Juftices of Peace, he fhall be committed for three Months without Bail, unlefs he forthwith pay 40 *s.* for having fuch Greyhound. See before, Tit. *Partridge,* 1 *Jac.* 1. *cap.* 27.

Hunters, and Takers of the King's Deer. See the Statute of *Charta de Forefta, cap.* 10.

Where Bail is taken away.

Hunters or Killers of any Deer or Conies (in the Night or Day-time) in any Park or Warren, or in any other inclofed Grounds, being thereof lawfully convicted, every fuch Offender fhall fuffer three Months Imprifonment, and find fufficient Sureties for his Good Behaviour for the Space of feven Years after, or elfe continue ftill in Prifon without Bail, until he fhall find Sureties accordingly. 5 *El. cap.* 21. 3 *Jac.* 1. *cap.* 13. *P. Foreft* 9. *& 7 Jac.* 1. 13.

The Statute of *Weftm.* 1. 20. provideth, That Trefpaffers in Parks and Ponds, being thereof attainted, fhall yield to the Party wronged great Damages, and fhall have three Years Imprifonment, making Fine at the King's Pleafure ; and at the End of three Years find good Sureties not to commit the like Trefpafs afterwards, or for Want of fuch Sureties fhall abjure the Realm, or be outlawed. See *Fit.* 67. *d. & Dyer* 238. 5 *H.* 5. *f.* 1. *Fit. Judgment* 62.

But note, That this Statute *de Malefactoribus in Parcis* extendeth only to Hunting or Killing of Beafts there, and not to other Trefpafs. 34 *E.* 3. *f.* 11. *Fitz. Judgment* 144. And if a Man hunts there, or fhall but come into a Park for that Purpofe, yet he fhall be punifhed according to this Statute. *Fitz. Judgment* 62.

The Statute of 19 *H.* 7. 11. ordaineth, That if any Perfon having no Park, &c. of his own, fhall keep any Deer-hays or Buck-ftalls ; or if any Perfon fhall ftalk at any Deer without Licenfe, the Offenders being thereof convicted, fhall be committed to Prifon, till they have found Surety for the Payment of the Forfeiture of the Statute.

King.

King : Speakers of Falfe News, which may Caufe difcord between the King and his People, &c.

And Speakers of Falfe News or Lies of any of the Peers or great Officers of the Realm.

The Offenders in either of the former Cafes fhall be imprifoned until they have brought him into the Court who was firft Author of the Tale. 3 *E.* 1. *cap.* 33. 2 *R.* 2. *cap.* 5. *P. News* 1. See *Dyer* 155. *&* 285. and the Statute of 1 *& 2 P. & M. cap.* 3. 1 *El. cap.* 6. *& 23 El. cap.* 2.

3. No Perfon committed by the fpecial Command of the King, or by the Command of his Privy Council, fhall be bailed. See *antea fub hoc tit.*

4. No Perfon committed by the fpecial Command of any of the King's Juftices fhall be bailed. *P. Mainp.* 1 *& 23 H.* 6. *cap.* 10. See *Ibid.*

Stamf. 7. b. *Br. Mainpr.* 40.

5. So in all Cafes where a Statute ordaineth, That an Offender fhall be imprifoned at the King's Will or Pleafure, there the Prifoner cannot be bailed or delivered, until the King hath fignified his Pleafure of him (as if one be imprifoned for going or riding armed,

armed, contrary to the Statute of *Northampton*, made *Ann.* 2 *E.* 3. *cap.* 3. 24 *E.* 3. *f.* 3. *Br. Contempts* 6.

And in such Cases the Prisoner is to redeem his Liberty with some Portion of Money, *Lamb.* 556. as he can best agree with the King or his Justice for the same : And the Justices before whom such an Offender shall be convict, may assess such Fine or Ransom according to their Discretions, and upon Payment thereof may bail the Prisoner ; for the King therein signifieth his Pleasure by the Mouths of his Justices. See the first Tit. of *Forcible Entry.*

Inn-keepers or Inn-holders : See *hic antea*, Tit. *Alehouse-keeper, and Hostler.* *Inn-keepers.*

Labourers and *Artificers*, departing from their Work before it is finished, shall have 5 *El.* 4. one Month's Imprisonment without Bail. 5 *Eliz. cap.* 4. *P. Labour* 10.

2. Servants departing before their Term be ended, unless it be for some Cause to be al- *Servants.* lowed by some Justice of Peace.

3. Servants departing at the End of their Term, without any Quarter's Warning given before two lawful Witnesses.

4. Persons (compellable to serve) that upon Request made shall refuse to serve for the Wages rated and appointed by Proclamation, *&c.*

5. Persons (compellable to serve) that have promised or covenanted to serve, and do not serve accordingly.

Every of these four last recited Offenders (upon Proof of the Offence before any two 5 *Eliz.* 4. Justices of Peace, *&c.* shall be committed to Ward, there to remain without Bail, until *P. Lab.* 6. he shall be bound, to the Party offended, to serve and continue with him according to the Statute.

6. Persons refusing to be bound Apprentices, according to the Statute, upon Complaint *Apprentices.* thereof made to any Justice of the Peace, he may commit such Offenders to Ward, who *P. Lab.* 24. shall there remain until they will be bound to serve according to the Statute 5 *Eliz.* 4.

7. Women (of the Age of twelve Years, and under forty, and unmarried) that shall *Women Ser-* refuse to serve, shall be committed to Ward, there to remain until they shall be bound *vants.* to serve according to the Statute 5 *Eliz.* 4. *P. Lab.* 14.

8. Masters giving Wages, and Servants, Workmen or Labourers, taking Wages (or other Commodity) contrary to the Rates assessed by Proclamation, *&c.* every such Master shall have ten Days Imprisonment without Bail ; and every such Servant, Workman or Labourer, shall have twenty-one Days Imprisonment without Bail. 5 *Eliz.* 4. *P. Lab.* 4.

9. Masters retaining or hiring a Servant for less Time than for one whole Year, shall have ten Days Imprisonment without Bail : But *quære*, whether this extends to Servants in Husbandry, or only to Servants to Artificers and Tradesmen. *P. Lab.* 1.

10. Masters retaining a Servant that is departed out of Service without shewing a Testimonial according to the Statute, it seemeth such Master shall have ten Days Imprisonment without Bail. 5 *El.* 4.

11. Masters taking Apprentices contrary to the Statute, it seemeth by the general Words of the Statute, that such Masters shall have ten Days Imprisonment without Bail.

Liveries : Such Persons as at their proper Costs shall buy or wear any Livery, Clothes *Liveries.* or Hats, to have Maintenance, and be thereof convicted, shall have one whole Year's Im- 8 *H.* 6. 4. prisonment without Bail. But this Statute is now repealed by the Statute 3 *Car.* 1. 4. *P. Liver.* 2.

In an Appeal of *Maihem*, where upon Evidence the Act shall appear to be heinous, the Offender or Defendant shall not be bailed. 6 *H.* 7. *f.* 1.

Melting notwithstanding Restraint ; but this is repealed. See Tit. *Malt supra.* *Malting.*

Money : Persons taken for falsifying the King's Money shall not be bailed. *West.* 1. *Money.* *cap.* 15.

Musters : Persons absenting themselves from Musters, being commanded to muster be- *Musters.* fore any having Authority for the same, and having no lawful Impediment.

2. And Persons, being commanded to muster as aforesaid, that shall not bring with them their best Furniture and Armour, which they have for their own Person.

The Offender in either of the former Cases shall for every such Offence suffer ten Days *Where Bail is* Imprisonment without Bail, unless they agree with two of the said Commissioners to pay *taken away.* to the King's Use 40 *s.* a Time for every such Offence. *P. Captains* 12. 4 & 5 *P &* M. 3

(a) To muster is to make a Shew of Soldiers well armed and trained before the King's Commissioners in some open Field, *Ubi se ostendentes præludunt prælio.* Co. L. 71.

And it is worthy of Observation, that by the Law before the Conquest, the Musters and Shewing of Armour should be *uno eodemq; die per universam regnum, ne aliqui possint arma familiaribus & notis accommodare, &c.* Ibid.

News :

News : See before, *King.*

Oath of Allegiance.
(d) *Oath :* Refusers to take the Oath of Allegiance (being lawfully tendred to them) shall be committed to the common Gaol; there to remain without Bail until the next Assizes or Quarter-Sessions. See before, Tit. *Oath and Recusants.*

Parliament, and Knights of the Parliament. See *hic postea, Sheriffs.*

Park. Hunting therein. See *Hunting and Hunters.*

Partridges.
Partridges : If any Person shall shoot at, kill or destroy (with any Gun or Bow) any Partridge, Pheasant, or other Fowl, &c.

2. Or shall take, kill or destroy any Partridge, Pheasant or Pigeon, with Setting-dogs and Nets, or with any Manner of Nets, Engines or Instruments;

3. Or shall take out of their Nest, or willingly destroy in the Nest, Eggs of any Partridge, Pheasant or Swan;

4. Or shall have or keep any Setting-dog or Net, or take Partridges or Pheasants, except they have Sufficiency of Estate, &c.

1 Jac. 1. 27.
Every of these four last recited Offenders (upon Proof of the Offence before any two Justices of Peace) shall be committed to the common Gaol, there to remain for three Months without Bail, unless the Offender shall forthwith pay 20 s. for every such Fowl and Egg so taken and destroyed; and 40 s. for having such Setting-dog or Net. See Tit. *Partridges.*

7 Jac. 1. 11.
5. Hawkers at Partridge or Pheasant in *July* or *August,* upon Proof of the Offence before any two Justices of Peace, shall be committed to the common Gaol, there to remain for one Month without Bail, unless the Offender shall forthwith pay 40 s. for every such Hawking, and 20 s. for every Pheasant or Partridge so killed or taken. See *Ibid.*

13 El. 10.
6. Persons convicted according to the Stat. of 23 *El. cap.* 10. for destroying or taking of Pheasants or Partridges in the Night-time, shall have one Month's Imprisonment without Bail, unless they pay the Penalty of that Statute within ten Days; and farther become bound with good Sureties, for the Space of two Years not to offend so again.

**11 H. 7. 17.
Co. 7. 18.**
7. Persons convicted according to the Stat. of 11 *H. 7. cap.* 17. for taking the Egg of any Hawk or Swan, out of their Nests, shall be imprisoned for a Year and a Day, and fined at the King's Will. See *Hawks.*

**Perjury.
Eliz. c. 9.**
Perjury : Persons committing Perjury by his, or their Deposition in any Court of Record or Court-Baron, being thereof lawfully convicted, shall have six Months Imprisonment without Bail. *P. Per.* 1, 2. & 14 *Eliz. cap.* 11.

2. So of Procurers of such Perjury, they being thereof lawfully convicted, and having not to pay the Penalty of the Statute, they shall have one Year's Imprisonment without Bail.

Physicians.
(a) *Physicians :* He which is committed to Prison by the President of the College of the Faculty of Physick of *London,* &c. shall there remain without Bail, until he shall be discharged by the same President, or by such as he shall authorize. 1 *M. cap.* 9.

**Plague.
1 Jac. 1. 31.
P. 1, 2, 3.**
(d) *Plague :* Refusers to pay the Rates for the Relief of Persons infected with the Plague, and not having whereon to be distrained for such their Rate, they shall be committed to the Gaol, there to remain without Bail until they satisfy the same, and the Arrearages. See Tit. *Plague.*

**Poor.
43 Eliz. 2.
P. 2, 4.**
Poor : Refusers to pay their Rates towards the Relief of their Poor, Setting them on Work, or Putting out of poor Children to be Apprentices, and not having whereon to be distrained for such their Rates, they shall be committed to the Gaol, there to remain without Bail until they shall pay the same and the Arrearages.

P. 2.
2. Overseers of the Poor refusing to make their Account, or refusing to pay to the new Overseers, such Arrearages, Sums of Money, or Stock as shall remain in their Hands upon their Account made, they shall be committed to the Gaol, until they have performed the same. See *antea,* Tit. *Poor.*

P. 2.
3. Overseers, negligent (or otherwise failing in their Office, shall forfeit for every Default 20 s. and not having whereon to be distrained for such Forfeiture, they shall be committed to the Gaol, there to remain without Bail until the said Forfeiture shall be paid. See *ibidem.*

P. 8. 12.
4. The Grandfather or Grandchild, or the Parents or Children, refusing to relieve one the other, in such Manner as shall be assessed by the Justices of Peace at their Sessions, shall forfeit for every such Default 20 s. for every Month: And not having whereon to be distrained for such Forfeiture, they shall be imprisoned, as aforesaid, until the said Forfeiture shall be paid. See *Ibid.*

5. Re-

5. Refufers to pay their Rates towards the Relief of the Prifoners in the *King's Bench* P. 13. or *Marfhalfea*, and not having whereon to be diftrained for fuch Rates, they fhall be imprifoned without Bail, until they fhall pay the fame. See *antea*, Tit. *Stock of the Shire.*

Prayers : Such as offend againft the Statute 1 *Eliz. cap.* 2. concerning Uniformity of *Prayers.* Common Prayer and Service in the Church, being thereof lawfully convicted by Verdict of P. Sacra 2. twelve Men, or by their own Confeffion, or by the notorious Evidence of the Fact, they fhall be committed without Bail : See the Statute 1 *Eliz.* 2. for in fome Cafes the Offender fhall fuffer fix Months Imprifonment, in other Cafes one whole Year's Imprifonment, in other Cafes Imprifonment during Life.

Preachers : Difturbers of Preachers in the Time of their Sermons, and their Aiders and *Preachers.* Procurers. 1 *Mar.* 3.

2. Such as fhall difturb the Arrefting of any fuch Offender ;

3. Such as fhall refcue any fuch Offender being apprehended ;

Every fuch Offender, being thereof convicted before any two Juftices of Peace, fhall be 1 M. 1. c. 3. committed to the Gaol, there to remain without Bail for three Months, and farther till P. 1. 2. the Quarter-Seffions, &c.

Prifon : Breakers thereof fhall not be bailed. *Weft.* 1. *cap.* 15. *Prifon-Breakers.*

Prophefiers : To the Intent to make Difturbances within the King's Dominions, every *Prophefiers.* fuch Offender being thereof lawfully convict for his firft Offence fhall fuffer one Year's 5 El. ca. 5. Imprifonment without Bail ; and for the fecond Offence fhall fuffer Imprifonment with- P. Prophef. 1. out Bail during his Life.

Recufants : Perfons fufpected to be Jefuits, Seminaries, or Maffing-Priefts, and being *Recufants.* examined thereof, by any having lawful Authority in that Behalf, if they fhall refufe to 15 El. anfwer directly thereto, they fhall be imprifoned without Bail, until they fhall make di- 35 El. c. 2. rect Anfwer thereto.

2. Perfons fufpected, if they fhall refufe to anfwer the Juftice of Peace upon Oath, 2 Jac. 1. 4. whether they be Recufants or no, they fhall be committed to the common Gaol, there to remain without Bail, until the next Affizes or Quarter-Seffions. See *antea*, Tit. *Recufants.*

3. Popifh Recufants refufing to take the Oath of Allegiance, (being lawfully tendred them) they fhall be imprifoned till the next Affizes or Quarter-Seffions as aforefaid. See *Ibid.*

4. Every other Perfon of the Age of eighteen Years, refufing to take the Oath of Al- 7 Jac. 1. 6. legiance, fhall be committed until the next Affizes or Quarter-Seffions as aforefaid. See *antea*, Tit. *Oath.*

5. A Woman Recufant convicted, and not conforming her felf, being therefore com- Ibid. mitted to Prifon, fhall there remain without Bail, until fhe fhall conform herfelf, &c. See *antea*, Tit. *Recufants.*

6. A Woman covert refufing in the open Affizes, or at the Quarter-Seffions of the 8 Jac. 1. 4. Peace, to take the Oath of Allegiance, fhe fhall be committed to the common Gaol 7 Jac. 1. 6. without Bail, until fhe will take the faid Oath.

7. If any Woman or Child under the Age of 21 Years, fhall pafs over the Sea with- 1 Jac. 1. 4. out lawful Licence, the Mafter of any Ship permitting the fame, fhall fuffer Imprifon- §. 8. ment 12 Months without Bail.

8. Recufants refufing to declare what Armour, &c. they have, or if they, or any P. Rec. 75. other Perfon, fhall hinder or difturb the Delivery of fuch Armour to any Perfon lawfully authorized to feize the fame ; every fuch Offender fhall have three Months Imprifonment without Bail. 3 *Jac.* 1. *cap.* 5.

9. Recufants and Sectaries which fhall impugn the King's Authority, in Caufes Ec- P. Rec. 18. clefiaftical : 35 El. 1.

10. Or that fhall perfuade others thereto, or from coming to Church, to that End and Purpofe :

11. Or fhall meet at any Conventicles, under Colour of any Exercife of Religion, contrary to his Majefty's Laws :

12. Or fhall perfuade any other to meet at any fuch Conventicles or Meetings.

Every Perfon which fhall be lawfully convicted of any of thefe four Offences fhall be committed to Prifon, there to remain without Bail, until they conform themfelves to come to Church, and make open Submiffion and Declaration of their faid Conformity.

13. Perfons abfent from Church upon any Sunday, and not having whereon to be di- 3 Jac. 1. 4. ftrained for the Forfeiture, fhall be committed until Payment be made thereof. See *antea*, §. 27. Tit. *Recufants.*

Perfons

Perfons above the Age of fixteen Years, which fhall abfent themfelves from the Church by the Space of one Month, and fhall be thereof lawfully convicted, fhall forfeit for every Month 20 *l.* And if he fhall not be able, or fhall fail to pay the fame within three Months after Judgment thereof given, he fhall be committed to Prifon, there to remain until he hath paid the faid Sum, or conform himfelf to go to Church, &c. 23 *Eliz.* 1.

So of fuch Perfons as fhall keep any School-mafters, which fhall abfent themfelves from the Church as aforefaid, or which fhall not be allowed by the Ordinary ; if fuch Perfons fhall not be able, or fhall fail to pay the Penalty, (*fc.* 10 *l.* for every Month) within three Months, &c. he fhall be committed without Bail, as aforefaid. *Ibid.*

Perfons convicted for Redifleifin are not bailable. *Merton, cap.* 3. *Fitz.* 66. *e.*

Rioters.
2 H. 5. 8.   Rioters attainted of great Riots, fhall have one Year's Imprifonment, without Bail. *P. Riots* 11.

All Perfons convicted by the View of the Juftices, or upon their Inquiry, or otherwife, of any Riot, fhall be committed until they have paid their Fine. See before, Tit. *Riots.*

Rogues.   Rogues incorrigible, committed to the Gaol or Houfe of Correction, fhall remain there until the next Quarter-Seffions. But fee *antea,* Tit. *Rogues* and 13 *Geo.* 2. *cap.* 23. infra *Chap.* 196.

Servants. See *Labourers.*

Schoolmafter that is a Recufant.

23 El. 1.
P. Recuf. 2.   2. Or that is not allowed by the Ordinary, and being of either of the faid Offences convicted, fhall be imprifoned for one whole Year without Bail.

Sheriffs.
8 H. 6. 7.   Sheriffs not making their Election of Knights for the Parliament in their full County,
23 H. 6. 15. between the Hours of Eight and Eleven in the Forenoon.
P. Parl. 4.   2. Or returning Knights for the Parliament contrary to the Statute, and being of either of the faid Offences attainted before the Juftices of Affize, they fhall be imprifoned for one whole Year without Bail.

Sheriffs, Under-Sheriffs, or other Perfons, making any Warrant for the Summons, arrefting or attaching of any Perfon to appear in any Court, not having the original Procefs or Writ warranting the fame, upon Examination or Proof thereof before the Judges of Affize, or Judges of the Court, &c. fuch Offenders and their Procurers fhall be committed to the Gaol, there to remain without Bail, until they have paid among them 10 *l.*
Where Bail is to the Party grieved, and his Cofts and Damages, and alfo 20 *l.* apiece to the King.
taken away. 43 *El. cap.* 6.

Soldiers.
2 E. 6. 2.   Soldiers, who have purloined their Horfes or Harnefs, fhall be committed without Bail, until they have fatisfied the Party grieved, his Executors, or Adminiftrators, for fuch Horfe or Harnefs. See before, Tit. *Soldier.*

Stock of the
Shire.   Stock of the Shire : Refufers to pay their Rates thereto, and not having whereon to be
43 El. 2. diftrained, &c. fhall be committed till they have paid it. *Vide antea,* Tit. *Stock.*

Tithes.   Tithes: The Defendant in a Suit for Tithes that difobeyeth the Judge's Sentence, fhall
27 H. 8. 20. be committed without Bail, until he fhall find fufficient Sureties by Recognizance, &c. to
32 H. 8. 7. obey and perform that Sentence. *Vide* Tit. *Tithes.*

Tranfportation.   Tranfportation : The Mafters or Mariners tranfporting any Corn, Beer, Herring, Whitage, or Wood, without Licence.
P. Corn 1.   2. The Owners of fuch Things tranfporting more than they are licenfed.
2, 3.
1 & 2 P. & M. 3. The Mariners carrying fuch Things into any Ship to be tranfported.
3, 5.   Every fuch Offender fhall be imprifoned one whole Year without Bail; and yet fee *antea,* Tit. *Tranfport,* that every Man may tranfport Corn without Licence, (or Danger, as it feems) it being at the Price there mentioned.

18 El. 8.   4. The Mafter or Mariners tranfporting or fhipping to that Intent, any Leather, Tal-
P. Leather 50. low, or Raw Hides, and being thereof convicted, fhall have one Year's Imprifonment without Bail.

5. Tranfporters of live Sheep.
8 Eliz. 8.   6. And every Perfon that fhall bring, deliver, fend, receive, take or procure any live Sheep
P. Sheep 1. to be conveyed out of any of the King's Dominions, their Aiders, Procurers and Comforters.

The Offenders in either of the former Cafes, being thereof convicted, fhall for the firft Offence fuffer one whole Year's Imprifonment without Bail.

1 Jac. 1. 4.   7. The Mafter of any Ship permitting any Woman or Children under 12 Years of Age to pafs over the Seas without Licence, fhall fuffer 12 Months Imprifonment without Bail.

8. Aliens tranfporting Bows or Arrows. See *Aliens*

I

                                            Treafon :

Treafon : Perfons committed for Treafon touching the King are not bailable.   *Weft.* 1. *Treafon. Where Bail is taken away.*
cap. 15.

Counterfeiters of Money, or of the King's Seal, are not bailable.   *Weft.* 1. *cap.* 15.
Br. Mainp. 59.

Vagabonds : See before *Rogues.*

Outlawed Perfons, taken for the fame, are not bailable.   *Weft.* 1. 6. 15. & 26 H.   *Outlawed.*
6. *cap.* 10.

(*a*) *Wards :* By the Statute of *W.* 2. *cap.* 25. if any Perfon fhall ravifh, (*fc.* fhall   *Wardi.*
take and carry away) any Ward, the Offender fhall have two Years Imprifonment ;
and if he do not reftore, or do marry the Child after the Years of Confent, and
be not able to fatisfy for the Marriage, he fhall abjure the Realm, or have perpetual
Imprifonment.   And it is faid, that it is at the Election of the Juftices to award the Offender to abjure the Realm, or to have perpetual Imprifonment ; and that if the Juftices
fhall award him to perpetual Imprifonment, that the King cannot pardon him that Imprifonment, for that is in lieu of Damages to the Plaintiff, and that Imprifonment is an Execution thereof, the which the King cannot pardon without the Affent of the Party Plaintiff.

(*d*) *Wax,* and Veffels of Honey; if any Perfon fhall counterfeit any the Marks   *Wax.*
thereof, or fhall mark them with any other Man's Mark, and fhall be thereof convicted,   23 El. 8. P. Wax, 7.
he fhall fuffer three Months Imprifonment without Bail.

Weights : Falfifiers or Counterfeiters thereof, fuch Offenders (after they be indicted   *Weights.*
thereof) fhall be taken and imprifoned without Bail, until they be acquitted or attaint-   P. Juft. of Peace 61.
ed; and if they be attainted, they fhall remain in Prifon until they have made Fine and   P. Weights 13.
Ranfom, according to the Juftices Difcretion. 9 *H.* 5. 8. *Parl.* 2.   *Quære* whether   * *It is expired, according to the*
this Statute be now in Force. *   *laft Edition of the Statutes at Large.*

Women : Taking of Women (unmarried, and under the Age of 16 Years) out of the   *Women.*
Poffeffion of their Parents, or other Perfon having lawfully the Keeping, &c. of them,   P. Women 7.
and againft their Wills, the Offender being thereof convict, fhall be two Years imprifoned without Bail, &c.

2. Taking away and Deflowring fuch Maid or Woman Child, as aforefaid :   P. Women 8.

3. Contracting of Marriage with fuch a Maid, againft the Will of, or unknown
to the Father of fuch a Maid, (if he be living) or againft the Will, &c. of the Mother, having the Cuftody and Governance of fuch Child :

The Offenders in thefe two laft Cafes, being thereof lawfully convicted, fhall have
five Years Imprifonment without Bail, &c.

See more concerning Women *antea,* *Recufants.*

(*a*) There be divers other Statutes made fince the Publication of the Author, which
take away Bail, but they being abridged in the firft Part of this Book under their proper Titles, I forbear to repeat them.

See alfo 2 Hawk. P. C. Chap. 15. of Bail.

C H A P. CLXVIII.

Recognizance.

A Recognizance is a Bond of Record, teftifying the Recognizor to owe a certain Sum
of Money to fome other ; and the Acknowledging of the fame is to remain of
Record ; and none can take it but only a Judge or Officer of Record.

And thefe Recognizances, in fome Cafes, the Juftices of Peace are inabled to take,
by the exprefs Words of certain Statutes : But in other Cafes (as for the Peace and good
Behaviour, and the like) it is rather in Congruity, than by an exprefs Authority given
them, either by their Commiffion or by Statute.

Note ; Wherefoever any Statute giveth them Power to take a Bond of any Man, or   Cromp. 197.
to bind over any Man to appear at the Affifes or Seffions, &c. or to take Sureties for   *See Fitz.* 82.
any Matter or Caufe, they may take a Recognizance.   Yea, wherefoever they have Authority given them to caufe a Man to do a Thing, there it feemeth they have (in Congruity) Power given them to bind the Party by Recognizance to do it.   And if the Party
fhall refufe to be bound, that then the Juftice may fend him to the Gaol ; for it is   Co. 11. 52. a.
Rule in Law, *Conceffo uno aliquo, etiam id concedi videtur fine quo prius conceffum haberi*
nequit.

nequit. But yet inquire of this laſt Caſe, for there is alſo another Rule, *In general: conceſſione non veniunt ea, quæ quis non eſſet verifimiliter in ſpecie conceſſurus.*

I will here ſet down only ſome Particulars where the Juſtices of Peace (out of their Seſſions) may take a Recognizance.

One Juſtice of Peace may take Recognizance for the Peace.

Alſo one Juſtice of the Peace may take a Recognizance for the Good Behaviour (by the Commiſſion): And theſe the Juſtice of Peace may take either upon Diſcretion, or upon Complaint made to him, or upon a *Supplicavit* delivered to him.

1 H. H. P. C.
586. One Juſtice of Peace may bind by Recognizance ſuch as do declare any Thing againſt a Felon, to appear at the Aſſizes or Seſſions, there to give Evidence againſt the Offender: And ſo in divers other Caſes.

One Juſtice of Peace may bind by Recognizance ſuch as keep any common Houſe or Places for unlawful Games, that they keep the ſame no longer. See *antea*, Tit. *Games, &c.*

And alſo ſuch as play at unlawful Games, contrary to the Statute of 33 *H.* 8. *cap.* 9 that they uſe the ſame no more.

One Juſtice may bind by Recognizance Takers of Partridges, *&c.* and Hawkers in Corn, to appear at the next Seſſions, to anſwer their ſaid Offences. See *antea*, Tit. *Partridges.*

One Juſtice of Peace may bind by Recognizance any Perſons convicted for taking or deſtroying any *Pheaſants, Partridges, Fowl, or Hare*, that they offend not thereafter, in any the Particulars any more.

Alſo they uſe (by way of Prevention) to bind *Tramellers for Larks*, that they ſhall deſtroy no Partridges, *&c. Quære* of this, how it is warranted. See *poſtea*, Tit. *Warrants.*

(*a*) But the Binding of *Tramellers* in this ſort ſeemeth rather to do hurt than good, in that it doth enable to tolerate the Uſe of Tramelling in the Night-time, whereby many Partridges are ſecretly taken and killed; whereas any two Juſtices of Peace may more legally prevent that Night-taking and Deſtroying of Partridges, by taking away all ſuch Nets, where they ſhall ſee Cauſe; the which they may do by Force of the Statute 7 *Jac.* 1. *cap.* 11. which ſee here before, Tit. *Partridges.*

I have known ſundry Proclamations, authorizing and commanding the Juſtices of Peace (at or before the Beginning of the Lent-time) to convene and call before them all Taverners, Inn-holders, Alehouſe-keepers, Keepers of ordinary Tables, and other Victuallers within the Precinct and Rule of the ſaid Juſtices; and to take Bonds (by Recognizance) with ſufficient Sureties of every of them, and in good Sums of Money, to the King's Uſe, that they ſhall not dreſs any Fleſh in their Houſes in the Lent-time, for any Reſpect, nor ſuffer it to be eaten there.

(*d*) One Juſtice of Peace may bind by Recognizance the Maſter that ſhall miſuſe his Apprentice, *&c.* to appear at the next Seſſions, *&c.* See *antea*, Tit. *Apprentices.*

Two Juſtices, *&c.* may take Recognizance of Alehouſe-keepers for keeping good Orders, *&c.* See before.

They may bind by Recognizance an Alehouſe-keeper (committed for Victualling without Licence,) that he ſhall keep no more an Alehouſe. See *antea*, Tit. *Alehouſes.*

Two Juſtices, *&c.* may bail Priſoners, and upon ſuch Bailment they are to cauſe the Priſoners to find Sureties for their Appearance, *&c.* which muſt be done by their Recognizance. See here, Tit. *Bailment.*

They may bind the Overſeers of Cloth by Recognizance, to ſee the Statute obſerved. See hereof *antea*, Tit. *Cloth.*

Alſo two Juſtices of Peace may bind by Recognizance the Defendant in a Suit of Tithes, to obey the Sentence of the Judge. See *antea*, Tit. *Tithes.*

Whether the Juſtices of Peace may bind an Offender againſt a penal Statute, to appear and anſwer his Fault at the Seſſions; ſee hereof *poſtea*, Tit. *Warrants.*

To whom. *Note,* That every Obligation and Recognizance taken by Juſtices of Peace muſt be made to the King, and ſhall be made by theſe Words, *Domino Regi*, upon Pain of Impriſonment of any Perſon that ſhall take it otherwiſe: And all ſuch Bonds or Recognizances ſhall be in the Nature of a *Statute-Staple* to all Intents. See hereof *poſtea*, Tit. *Recognizance.*

A Juſtice of Peace can take no Recognizance, but only for ſuch Matters as concern his Office. See hereof Tit. *Surety for the Peace, antea.*

       I   *Note*

Note alfo, That a Recognizance taken by a Juftice of Peace is a Matter of Record ^{33 H. 8. 39.} prefently, fo foon as it is taken and acknowledged, although it be not made up, but ^{Br. Rec. 58.} only entred into his Books ; nay, although it be not entred, as it feemeth. See *Stamf.* 77. *a.* fuch a Matter.

If a Juftice of Peace fhall take a Recognizance where he hath no Authority, it feemeth void.

And thefe Recognizances taken by the Juftices of Peace, are to be certified by them at their Quarter-Seffions : Except Recognizances taken of fuch as fhall inform againft Felons, and upon Bailment of Felons, which by Statute they are appointed to certify at their next General Gaol-delivery. See *antea*, Tit. *Felony.*

For the Forms of Recognizances fee hereafter, Tit. *Recognizances.*

CHAP. CLXIX.

Warrants.

NOW concerning the Precepts or Warrants to be made by the Juftices of Peace : ^{*By Parol.*} The Juftice of Peace, (feeing that he is a Judge of Record) his Precept or Com- ^{Lamb. 87.} mand by Word of Mouth (in fome Cafes) is as ftrong as his Precept in Writing.

And therefore the Juftice of Peace, upon any Riot done in his Prefence, may ^{14 H. 7. 8, 9.} command the Rioters to be arrefted, and caufe them to find Sureties for their good Behaviour.

So upon an Affray, Affault, Threatning, or other Breach of the Peace done in his Prefence, the Juftice of Peace may command by Word, the Officer being prefent, or his own Servant, to arreft fuch Offenders to find Sureties for the Peace. See before, Tit. *Surety for the Peace.*

And where the Juftice of Peace commandeth one being prefent to arreft another that ^{1 H. H. P. C.} is alfo in his Prefence, though that Command be by Word only, it is good, and it is re- ^{587.} puted as an Arreft made by the Juftice himfelf, he being prefent when the Arreft is ^{B. Faux Im-} made. ^{prif. 33.}

(*a*) One in falfe Imprifonment juftified that the Plaintiff being in the Prefence of a Ju- ^{Moor's Rep.} ftice of Peace, the Juftice not having Opportunity to examine him, commanded the Defen- ^{408.} dant to take him into Cuftody, and keep him fafely until next Day, the which he being ^{585.} Conftable did fo ; and this was a good Juftification without fhewing the Caufe the Ju- ftice of Peace had to imprifon him, and without fhewing the Warrant, becaufe it was done in the Prefence of a Juftice of Peace. *Broughton v. Mulfhor*, T. 37. *El.*

(*d*) But the Juftices of Peace cannot command by Word to arreft another being out of ^{14 H. 7. 8.} their Prefence ; neither may one in the Abfence of the Juftice arreft another upon his ^{Br. Peace 7.} Command by Parol, but it muft be by a Precept or Warrant in Writing, by the greater Opinion of the Juftices.

And yet in Cafe of Rioters, the Juftice of Peace may by Word command his Ser- ^{14 H. 7. 9, 10.} vants to arreft them in the Abfence of the Juftice ; by the Opinions of *Fincux* and *Tre-* ^{1 H. H. P. C.} *male* Juftices : See hereof *antea*, Tit. *Riots.* ^{587.}

Next their Warrant or Precept by Writing ought to be under their Hand and Seal, or ^{*By Writing*} under their Hand at leaft. See *hic infra.*

And if it be for the *Peace or Good Behaviour*, or the like, where Sureties are to be ^{*The Form.*} found or required, there the Warrant ought to contain the *Special Caufe* and Matter whereupon it is granted, to the Intent that the Party (upon whom it is to be ferved) may provide his Sureties ready, and take them with him to the Juftice of Peace to be bound for him : But if the Warrant be for *Treafon, Murder* or *Felony*, or other Capital Offence, or for great Confpiracies, Rebellious Affemblies, or the like, it needs not contain any fpecial Caufe, but there the Warrant of the Juftice of Peace may be, to bring the ^{Cromp. 148.} Party before him, to make Anfwer to fuch Things or Matters generally as fhall be ob- jected againft him on the King's Behalf : And this is now the common Ufage, by the Report of Mr. *Crompton.*

And I once received a Warrant, brought me by one *Thomas Evans*, (a Purfivant or ^{An. Dom.} Meffenger of his Majefty's Chamber) under the Hand of the Right Honourable *Thomas* ^{1607.} Lord *Ellefmere*, late Lord Chancellor of *England*, for the apprehending one *James Malin*,

for

for a Matter of Contempt ; and the said Warrant was in general Words, *scil.* to answer to such Matters as were objected against him, without any special Cause therein mentioned.

3 Jac. 1.
2 H. H. P.C.
111, 112.
Also I saw another Warrant granted under the Hand of *Popham,* Chief Justice, to bring one *Edmonds* (of *Barnwel* by *Cambr.*) before him to answer to such Matters as he had to object against him on the King's Behalf, without any special Cause or Matter therein set down.

(a) The like Form you shall find in the Book of *Entries,* Tit. *Attachment : Non omittas, &c. quin attach.* E. H. &c. *ita quod habeas corpus ejus coram Justic. nostris ad Assisas in Com. tuo capiend. assign. apud W. in Octab. Sanct. Mich. ad respond. nobis de his quæ sibi ex parte nostra tunc ibidem objicientur, & ad faciendum ulterius & recipiend. quod Curia nostra de eo consider. in hac parte, &c.*

Blank War-
rant.
1 H. H. P.C.
577.
But it is not safe for a Justice of Peace to grant out his Warrant with a Blank: For about 30 *Eliz.* one wrote to Sir *I. R.* a Justice of Peace, to send him a Precept or Warrant with a Blank, that he might put therein one whom he would attach upon Suspicion of Felony; and the Justice of Peace did so, (granting a Warrant with a Blank, where he neither knew the Party's Name nor the Matter) : And for this the Justice was fined in the Star-Chamber, as Mr. *Crompton* reporteth, *Author. de. Courts* 34.

Sealed.
Also the Warrant of the Justice of Peace should be under the Seal of the said Justice : For every Justice of Peace (being a Judge of Record) hath a Seal of his Office and when he maketh a Warrant under his Seal to the Officer, then the Officer ought to give Credence to the Seal, for that is his Authority; *per Brudenel.* 14 *H.* 8. 16.

14 H. 8. 16.
Lamb. 90.
(d) Again, the Warrant of the Justice of Peace is the better, if it bear Date of the Place where it was made, and it must express the Year and Day when it was made See 21 *H.* 7. 22.

Out of the
County.
Plow. 37.
A Justice of Peace who is dwelling out of the County granteth his Warrant to be served within the County ; the Officer cannot carry the Party out of the County to the Justice of Peace who made the Warrant, but must carry him before some other Justice within the County.

Vide supra
c. 6. p. 19.
Quære whether such a Warrant be good or no.

First, for that a Justice of Peace hath no Authority but in the County where he is a Justice, and in Commission. See *antea.*

And again, for the Date of the Place seemeth to be material by the Books 14 *H.* 8. aforesaid, & 21 *H.* 7. 22. *Br. Fx. Imp.* 12.

Return.
Br. Peace 9.
Co. 5. 59.
The Justice of Peace may make his Warrant to bring the Party *before himself,* and then the Officer needs not to carry the Party before any other Justice. And yet upon a Warrant for the Peace granted *ex officio,* the usual Manner is otherwise. See *antea,* Tit. *Sureties for the Peace.*

Also the Justice of Peace may in some Cases make his Warrant to attach the Offender to be at the next Sessions of the Peace, there to answer his said Offence, &c. See *antea,* Tit. *Counterfeiters, & postea Warrants.*

(a) If a Justice of Peace shall make his Warrant to the Sheriff to attach one, and to bring him to the next Sessions, there to find Sureties for the Peace, &c. it is good. *Cromp.* 135, 136.

So if the Justice shall make his Warrant to warn a Man to appear at the next Sessions, there to give in Evidence for the King; and where the Justice shall command one by his Warrant to be or appear at the next Sessions, &c. if the Party do not appear, then from that Sessions there shall go out a Precept to attach him for such his Contempt. *Cromp.* 123.

For what
Cause.
(d) A Justice of Peace (*ex officio* by the first *Assign.* in the Commission) may grant his Warrant to arrest or attach one that hath broken the Peace, or committed other Misdemeanour against the Peace, to find Sureties for the Peace or Good Behaviour, as the Cause shall require.

Also the Justices of Peace in divers Cases may grant their Warrant against a Man for his Neglect or other Default, as for refusing to pay *Town-Rates,* and the like : And such Warrant may be either to attach the Offender to be at the next Sessions, there to answer, &c. or else to bring him before the said Justice, or any other Justice, who, finding Cause, may bind him to appear at the next Sessions to answer the said Default.

Also where any Statute doth give Authority to the Justices of the Peace to cause another Person to do a Thing, there it seemeth they have Power given them (of Congruity)

gruity) to grant their Warrant to bring such Persons before them, that so they may take Order therein. *Quære.* See *antea*, Tit. *Recognizance.*

But I find it much controverted, whether a Justice of Peace may grant a Warrant _{*Where not be-fore indicted.*} to attach Persons suspected of Felony, or against Offenders upon a penal Statute, unless _{14 H. 8. 16.} such Persons or Offenders be first thereof indicted : For that the Justice of Peace, as he _{Br. Peace 6.} is a Judge of Record, so it is said he must have a Record, whereupon he doth award See_{Br.Com.3.} his Process or Precept. Some hold that the Justice of Peace may grant his Warrant to 4 *Inst*: 177. attach Persons suspected of Felony, *&c.* for that it seems by the first *Assignavimus* in the Commission, and by the Statute of 5 *Ed.* 3. 14. that any one Justice of Peace may cause the Constables to arrest and imprison Offenders suspected of Felony, *&c.* and how shall the Justices of Peace cause this to be done, but by his Warrant or Command ?

Again, if a Felony be done, there is no Doubt but that every private Man without a Warrant may arrest whomsoever he suspecteth of it, being a Man of evil Fame, *&c.* See hereof Tit. *Arrest.* But if the Offender being pursued shall resist, *quære* who shall _{See antea Tit.} be aiding to a private Man, whose Goods are stolen, and who suspected another to have _{Exam. & 2 H.} stolen them, either to search for his Goods, or to apprehend the Party suspected, if the _{7. 15, 16 pro} Justice of Peace (by his Warrant) shall not command the Constable to aid him therein ? _{& contra.} If it be objected, that the Constable may do all this of his own Authority, (upon Request to him made by the Party robbed) it is true; yet we find by common Experience that the Constables, without the Justice's Warrant, are fearful and remiss herein, as neither knowing their own Authority, nor the Danger.

Besides, this is no new Thing, for there is such a Precedent in the old Book of Ju- _{Lamb. 193.} stices of Peace, *impress.* 1561. *fol.* 41. *a.* yea, it is the common Practice at this Day, _{1 H. H. P. C. 579.} and it seemeth to be very serviceable; and of two Evils the less is to be chosen, *sc.* that an Offender or suspected Person, should be imprisoned for a Time, (though sometimes wrongfully) rather than one which hath committed Felony should escape unpunished.

And yet by the Opinion of the Court 14 *H.* 8. a Justice of Peace cannot make a _{14 H. 8. 16.} Warrant to arrest a Felon, unless he be indicted of Felony, (or that the Justice him- _{Br. Peace 6.} self hath Suspicion of the Felon). But if the Constable, or other Officer, shall serve _{Br. Faux Imp. 8 & 9.} such a Warrant, he shall justify the same, though the Justice did err in the awarding _{Co. 10. 76.} thereof. See 24 *E.* 3. 9.

Next, for the Justices of Peace to bind over, or to grant a Warrant against Offenders _{Lamb. 191.} upon any penal Statute, to appear at the Sessions to answer to their Offence or Fault, _{Cro. 197.} though such Statute be within the Power of the Justice of Peace, yet such War- _{*The Inconveni-ence thereof.*} rant or Binding over of such Offenders may seem not warranted, unless it be specially _{See_{Lamb. 197.}} so appointed in the Statute, as it is by the Statutes of 5 *El. cap.* 4. 23 *El.* 10. 39 *El.* 11. See *antea*, Tit. *Counterfeiters, Dying,* and *Labourers.*

But such Offenders ought first *to be indicted*, and thereupon Process from the Sessions is to be awarded against them until they come in, *&c.*

(a) No one or more Justices of Peace can make a Warrant upon a bare Surmise to _{*Breaking a House.*} break any Man's House to search for a Felon, or for stolen Goods; for they are consti- tuted by Acts of Parliament, which Acts give them no such Authority. It would be inconvenient if they might so do. But if a Man be indicted for Felony, the Sheriff upon Process may demand him ; and if he render not himself, may break the House. *Co.* 4. *Inst. p.* 176.

(d) And yet there are several Precedents of Attachments made from one Justice of _{Cro. 238. Lamb. 151.} Peace against Labourers and Servants that shall refuse to serve, or that shall depart out of their Service, contrary to the Statute, to be before the Justices at their Sessions, to answer to their said Defaults. But these may seem also to have been warranted, and so appointed by the Statute of Labourers, made *An.* 25 *E.* 3. *cap.* 6. which Statute is now repealed by the Statute of 5 *El.* 4.

Also it is usual (by Way of Prevention) to bind by Recognizance such as do trammel for Larks, that they shall destroy no Partridges. And for these Purposes the Justices of Peace do grant out their Warrants to convene the said Persons before them, for Victuallers, (*sc.* Taverners, Inn-keepers, Alehouse-keepers, Keepers of ordinary Tables, and other Victuallers) I have known sundry Proclamations which seem to warrant the Justices of Peace therein. But for the other, what Law or Warrant there is for it, I know not, until the Offender is convicted. See *hic* Tit. *Partridges.* Yet see *antea*, where the Justices may in some Cases grant their Warrants against Offenders upon penal Statutes. (*a*) But there the Justices have Power to hear and determine out of the Sessions.

Also

Also where the Offence prohibited by fuch a Statute amounteth to the Breach of th Peace or Good Behaviour, there the Juftice may (either upon Difcretion or Complaint o fuch an Offence and Breach of the Statute) grant out his Warrant, and bind over th Offender to the next Quarter-Seffions, &c. to anfwer his faid Default, and in the mean Time to be of the Good Behaviour. See *hic, Servants affaulting their Mafter*.

To whom directed.
14 H. 8. 16.
Br. Peace 6.
1 H. H. P. C.
581.
Cromp. 147.

(d) The Juftice of Peace may direct his Warrant to the Sheriff, Bailiff, Conftable o other Officer, or to any other indifferent Perfon by Name, though he be no Officer, ye. to any Perfon that he fhall think meet; but yet the fafeft Way is to direct it to the Conftable, or to fome other fworn Officers.

A Warrant directed by the Juftice of Peace to the Conftable, or other fworn Officer and to a Stranger, who is no Officer, and the Warrant is made *conjunctim & divifim* and is delivered to the Stranger, who executeth it; all this is good.

Lamb. 91.
A Warrant directed by the Juftice of Peace to *two Men jointly*, to arreft another, &c yet any one of them alone may do it.

A Warrant directed by the Juftice of Peace to the Sheriff, he may by Word command his Under-Sheriff, Bailiff, or other known or fworn Officer, to ferve it, withou any Precept by Writing.

And fo the Sheriff's Servant, or other Perfon by the Sheriff's Command, and as Servant to the Sheriff, may ferve or execute fuch Warrant without any Precept by Writing See *Br. Fx. Impr. 43. & Trefpafs 339.*

But if the Sheriff will command another Man (that is a Stranger) to ferve it, he muf deliver him a Precept in Writing; otherwife a Writ of Falfe Imprifonment will lie fo the Arreft.

A Warrant directed by the Juftice of Peace to the *Sheriffs, Bailiff*, or to the *Conftable*, or to the *Juftice's Servant*, or to a *Stranger*, to arreft one, &c. fuch Perfon (to whom the Warrant is made) muft ferve it himfelf, for thefe can command none other to do it neither by Word nor Writing, nor make any Deputy.

The Officer's Duty.
8 E. 4. 14.
14 H. 7. 9. b.
20 H. 7. 13.
21 H. 7. 24.
Co. 9. 69.

The Officer to whom any Warrant fhall be directed and delivered, ought with all Speed and Secrecy to find out the Party, and then to execute the faid Warrant.

A fworn and known Officer, (be he Sheriff, Under-Sheriff, Bailiff, or Conftable, &c.) needs not fhew his Warrant to a Man whom he cometh to ferve it upon, although he demandeth it: But if the Juftice will direct his Warrant to his Servant or to another (who is no fworn Officer) to ferve it, they muft fhew their Warrant to the Party if he demand it, or otherwife the Party may make Refiftance, and needs not to obey it. *Br. Fx. Impr. 23.*

Co. 6. 54. & 9. 68.
But a fworn and known Officer, if he will not fhew his Warrant to the Party, yet he ought (upon the Arreft) to declare the Contents of his Warrant, &c.

Co. 9. 69.
And an Officer giveth fufficient Notice what he is, when he faith to the Party, *I arreft you in the King's Name*, &c. and in fuch Cafe the Party at his Peril ought to obey him, though he knoweth him not to be an Officer; and if he have no lawful Warrant, the Party grieved may have his Action of Falfe Imprifonment againft him.

Dyer 244.
F. Bar. 248.
Lamb. 93.

If an Officer do arreft a Man *for the Peace*, or the like, before he hath any Warrant, and then afterwards doth procure a Warrant, (or a Warrant cometh after to him) to arreft the Party for the fame Caufe, yet the firft Arreft was wrongful, and the Officer is fubject to an Action of Falfe Imprifonment. See the Statute 43 *El. cap.* 6.

(a) Where there be two or three known by the Name of *I. S.* of *D.* Yeoman, and upon a Warrant (or other Procefs) granted out againft one of them, another of them is arrefted, an Action of Falfe Imprifonment will not lie againft the Officer for this; for he is not bound at his Peril to take Notice which of them is the Offender, &c. And perhaps no particular Offence is mentioned in the Warrant. *Tamen vide L. 5 E. 4. fol. 51. & 48. pro & contra, & 11 H. 4. fol. 90. contra. Ideo quære.*

Where a Warrant is granted out againft *I. N.* the Son of *W. N.* and the Officer arrefteth *I. N.* the Son of *T. N.* although in Truth he be the fame Perfon that offended, and againft whom the Complaint was made, yet this Arreft is tortious, and the Officer fubject to an Action of Falfe Imprifonment. See the like Matter, 10 *E.* 4. *f.* 12. *Br. Faux Imp.* 38.

Break open an Houfe.
*Tho' the Party be not indicted, and this Forcible Entry.
is the conftant

(d) The Officer, upon any Warrant from a Juftice, either for the Peace, or Good Behaviour, or in any other Cafe where the King is a Party, may by Force break open a Man's Houfe, to arreft the Offender *, &c. See hereof *antea*, in the former Title, *Forcible Entry*.

is the conftant Practice, againft the Opinion of Lord Coke. 4 Inft. 177. *See* 1 H. H. P. C. 582.

If any Officer or other Perfon hath arrefted a Man by virtue of his Warrant, which *How to be* he hath from a Juftice of Peace, and then taketh his Promife that he will come again *executed.* to him fuch a Day, to go to the Juftice with him according to his Warrant, (and fo *See Cromp.* letteth the Party go) who comes not again at the Day appointed, the Officer cannot after 214.a. & 148. arreft or take him again by Force of his former Warrant; for that this was by the Con- Co. 3. 44, 52. fent of the Officer: But if the Party arrefted had efcaped (of his own Wrong) without the Confent of the Officer, now upon frefh Suit the Officer may take him again and again, fo often as he efcapeth, although he were out of View, or that he fhall fly into another Town or County. See more *poftea*, Tit. *Imprifonment, & L. 5 E. 4. fol. 12. Br. Faux Imp. 18.*

(a) Where an Officer hath received a Warrant, he is bound to purfue the Effect of it in every Behalf, or otherwife his Warrant will not excufe him of that which he hath done. See *antea*, Tit. *Surety for the Peace.*

(d) If an Officer, having a lawful Warrant to arreft another, fhall be refifted or af- *Refiftance.* faulted by the Party, or by any other Perfon, then may that Officer juftify the Beating or 21 H. 7. 39. Hurting of fuch Perfons; and other Perfons (upon his Prayer) may and ought to aid the Officer.

If a Juftice of Peace fhall make any Warrant for a Matter wherein he hath Jurif- *Officer not to* diction, although it be beyond his Authority, yet it is not difputable by the Conftable, *queftion the* or other fuch Officer, but muft be obeyed and executed by the Officer; as if the Juftice 14 H. 8. 16. of Peace fhall make his Warrant to arreft one for the Peace or Good Behaviour, &c. E. Faux without Caufe, the Officer fhall not be punifhed for executing this: But if a Juftice of Imp. 8. Peace fhall make his Warrant to do a Thing out of his Jurifdiction, or in a Caufe where- Lamb. 67, 94. of the Juftice of Peace is no Judge, if the Officer fhall execute fuch a Warrant, here he 579, 580, is punifhable; for the Officer is not bound to obey him who is not Judge of the Caufe, 583. no more than a meer Stranger: And fo note, That the Officer is bound to take Notice 79, 80, 107 to of the Authority and Jurifdiction of the Judge. See fuch a Matter, 22 *Aff.* 64. 110. *Plo.* 394. *b.*   Co. 10. 76.
                                                                    Cromp. 147.
                                             2 Hawk. P. C. c. 13. §. 10.

If any Man fhall abufe the Juftice of Peace his Warrant, as by cafting of it into the *Contempt.* Dirt, or treading it under his Feet, &c. he may be bound to his Good Behaviour, and Cromp. 149. may alfo be indicted and fined, for it is the King's Procefs.

When any Perfon cometh before a Juftice of Peace, by Force of any Warrant for the Peace, Good Behaviour, or for a Riot, or the like, the Party muft offer Sureties, or elfe the Juftice may commit him. See *antea*, Tit. *Sureties for the Peace.*

If a Juftice of Peace fhall grant his Warrant to one to apprehend another for Mur- der, Robbery or Felony, it fhall be fafe for the Juftice, upon the Delivery of his faid Warrant, to take (upon Oath) the Examination of the faid Party that requireth the Warrant, or at leaft to bind him over by Recognizance to give Evidence at the next Gaol-delivery, &c. againft the Offender, left that afterwards, when the Offender fhall be brought (by the Officer) before the Juftice upon his faid Warrant, or elfe happen to yield himfelf to the faid Juftice, then the Party that procured the Warrant be gone: For by credible Report I am informed, That one having procured a Warrant from a Juftice of Peace in *Suff.* againft another for a Robbery done upon the Highway, and the Juftice upon the Delivery of his Warrant not having bound over the Complainant to give Evi- dence, nor taken his Examination, as aforefaid, that at the next Affifes and Gaol-delive- ry, the Party charged with the Robbery came and offered himfelf to the faid Juftice of Peace, who immediately acquainted Sir *Tho. Flemming* (then Lord Chief Juftice, and *See* 1 H. H. Judge of Affife there) with the whole Matter; but the faid Judge much blamed the P. C. 582 faid Juftice of Peace for not having bound over the faid Complainant at the firft when he granted him the Warrant, and charged the faid Juftice of Peace, at his Peril, pre- fently to fend for the Party Complainant to come to give Evidence, &c. and farther di- rected the faid Juftice of Peace to bind over the Party charged with good Sureties for his Attendance and Appearance.

CHAP. CLXX.

Arreſt and Impriſonment.

What.

AN *Arreſt* is the Apprehending and Reſtraining of a Man's Perſon, and may be call-ed the Beginning of Impriſonment.

Impriſonment is where a Man is arreſted againſt his Will, or is reſtrained of his Li-berty, by putting him into the Gaol, Cage or Stocks, or into ſome Houſes, or other-wiſe by keeping him in the High Street, or open Field, ſo as he cannot freely go at Liberty, when and whither he would.

If the *Conſtable* or other *Officer* (upon a Warrant received from a Juſtice of Peace) ſhall come unto the Party, and require or command him to go or come before the Juſtice, *&c.* this is no Arreſt or Impriſonment. And upon a Warrant for the Peace, the Officer ought firſt to require the Party to go before the Juſtice before he may ar-reſt him. See hereof *antea,* Tit. *Surety for the Peace.*

(*a*) A Bailiff or Sheriff ſays to a Man being preſent, I arreſt you, altho' he touch him not; this is a good Arreſt, and if the Party go away it is a Reſcue. 8 *Car.* 1. *B. R. Sir James Wingfield's Caſe.*

(*d*) But this Arreſt (being in Execution of the Command of ſome Court, or of ſome Offi-cer of Juſtice) is expreſſed in their Writs, Precepts or Warrants, by theſe Words or the like, *ſc. Capias, Attachias, &c.* To attach, arreſt, take, bring or convey, or cauſe to be attached or arreſted, *&c.* All which Words do imply the Taking or Laying hold of the Perſon.

What Perſons.

To this Arreſt all Lay Perſons (under the Degree of Barons or Peers of the Realm) are ſubject, and that by Warrant from the Juſtices of Peace, as you may ſee here before, Tit. *Surety for the Peace.*

But the Juſtices of the Peace are not to grant their Warrants for the Peace, or the like, againſt any Nobleman; and yet if a *Capias* or Attachment ſhall be awarded againſt a Baron or Peer of the Realm from the King's Juſtices at *Weſtminſter* for a Contempt, or in Caſe of Debt or Treſpaſs, the Officer without any Offence of Law may execute the ſame, for that the Officer is not to diſpute the Authority of the Court.

Eccleſiaſtical Perſons.
See P. Arreſt 1.

Eccleſiaſtical Perſons may alſo be arreſted, and that by Warrant from the Juſtices of Peace, in ſome Caſes. See hereof, Tit. *Surety for the Peace.*

Feme Covert.

(*a*) A *Woman Covert* may be impriſoned by the Juſtice of Peace for a Force or a Riot committed by her. See *antea,* Tit. *Forcible Entry* and *Riots.*

But otherwiſe of *Infants* in ſuch Caſes. See *Ibid.*

Yet if an *Infant cannot find Sureties for the Peace,* being demanded againſt him, he ſhall be committed until he hath found Sureties. See *antea.*

Infant.

An *Infant,* though of Years of Diſcretion, yet he ſhall ſuffer no Impriſonment, nor other corporal Pain, for any Offence committed or done by him againſt any Statute, ex-cept an Infant be expreſſed by Name in the Statute. *Br. Impriſ.* 101. *Covert.* 68. *Plo.* 364. *Doct. & Stud.* 147, 148.

For what Cauſe, and by whom.
Co. 9. 56.

(*d*) The Liberty of a Man is a Thing ſpecially favoured by the Common Law; and therefore if any the King's Subjects ſhall impriſon another without ſufficient Warrant, the Party grieved may have his Action, and ſhall recover Damages againſt the other; and the King alſo ſhall have a Fine of him. For Impriſonment of another without Offence of the Law, is one of the King's Royal Prerogatives, and only annexed to the Crown.

P. Accuſ. 1.
5 E. 3. c. 9.
See Pet. Anno
3 Car. Regis,
& Stat. 5 Ed.
3. c. 9.
Co. 10. 74.

Alſo by the Statute *Magna Charta,* made 9 H. 3. *cap.* 29. no Freeman ſhall be taken or impriſoned, *&c.* but by the lawful Judgment of his Equals, *ſc.* upon his Conviction for ſome Offence, by the Verdict of a Jury of twelve good and lawful Men, or by the Law of the Realm.

And by this Statute of *Magna Charta,* every Arreſt or Impriſonment, and every Op-preſſion againſt the Law of the Land, is forbidden; and if any Judge, Officer, or other Perſon, againſt the Law, ſhall uſurp any Juriſdiction, and by Colour thereof ſhall arreſt, impriſon or oppreſs any Man, it is puniſhable by the Statute. See *Co.* 10. 75.

Magna Charta confirmed.

(*a*) This Grand Charter is a Declaration of the antient Common Law. *Co.* 10. 48. And the Statute of *Magna Charta, & Charta Foreſtæ,* for their Excellency have ſince been confirmed by the Authority of above 30 ſeveral Parliaments. See *Co. Preface* to the 8*th Report.*

1

(*d*) Note.

(*d*) Note, That all Juriſdiction ought to be either by Charter or Preſcription. *Co. Juriſdiction.* 11. 99.

(*a*) Alſo by the Statutes of 25 *E.* 3. *cap.* 4.   28 *E.* 3. *cap.* 3. & 42 *E.* 3. *cap.* 3. no Perſon ſhall be *taken or impriſoned*, nor put to anſwer, unleſs it be by *Indictment or Preſentment* of a Jury, before Juſtices, or by Matter of Record, or by due Proceſs made by Writ Original at the Common Law. See *P. Accuſation* 1. & 42 *Aſſ.* 5. And *Br. Faux Impriſ.* 30. 2 *H.* 4. the Body of a Man ſhall not be taken but by Proceſs out of a Court of Record.

A Commiſſion to arreſt or take a Man (and his Goods) was holden to be againſt Law, for that this ought to be either upon Indictment, or Suit of the Party, or other due Proceſs of Law. *Br.* 15, 16. & *Faux Impriſ.* 9. & *Indictment* 38.   42 *Aſſ.* 5. 12.   24 *E.* 3. 9.   *Co.* 5. 64.

(*d*) Alſo note, that no Man ſhall be arreſted for Debt, Detinue, Treſpaſs, or other Cauſe of Action, but only by Virtue of a Precept or Command out of ſome Court of Record.

Neither ſhall any Man commit another to Priſon, except he is a Judge of Record. *Co.* 10. 103.

But yet for *Miſdemeanors done againſt the King's Peace,* (as for *Treaſon, Felony,* or *See Co.* 3. *breaking of the Peace, &c.*) the Offenders as well by the *Common Law,* as by *divers Sta-* ¹² ᵃ· *tutes,* may be arreſted and impriſoned by the Officers of Juſtice, and ſometimes by *private Perſons,* as hereunder followeth; (*a*) without either *Preſentment, Proceſs, Precept, Warrant,* or other Command. And theſe being by the Law of the Realm, are warranted by the aforeſaid Statute of *Magna Charta.*

And Mr. *Bracton* (*l.* 5. *in fine*) ſaith thus; *In criminalibus cauſis, ubi ſequi debet By a private capitale judicium, vita viz. vel mutilatio membrorum, non ſequitur Attachiamentum ali-* Man. *quod, ſed corpus tale (quicunque fuerit ille) ab omnibus arreſtatur qui ſunt ad fidem Domini Regis, ſive inde Præceptum habuerint, ſive non habuerint.*

And yet you muſt obſerve, that for arreſting the Body of a Man in ſuch Caſes there muſt be ſome juſt Cauſe, or ſome lawful and juſt Suſpicion at the leaſt. And therefore where a Man is indicted of Felony, that is a good Cauſe to arreſt him. But if an Appeal of Felony be commenced againſt another, that is no ſufficient Cauſe, for it is but private Suſpicion, *&c.*

Every private Man may arreſt another, whom he knoweth or ſeeth to have com- 10 *E.* 4. 17. mitted a Robbery, Manſlaughter, or other Felony, and may deliver him to the Conſtable of the Town where ſuch an Offender is apprehended, or in the Conſtable's Abſence may impriſon and ſet him in the Stocks; and if there be no Stocks there, it ſeemeth he *Fitz Bar.* 101 may carry the Offender to the next Town, and deliver him to the Conſtable there. See 9 *E.* 4. 28. or elſe he may carry him before a Juſtice of Peace, by him to be examined and ſent to the Gaol, there to abide until the next Aſſizes, or Seſſions of the Peace, *&c.*

Alſo when a Felony is committed, every Man may arreſt ſuſpicious Perſons that be of evil Fame, *&c.* and if ſuch Perſon ſhall make Reſiſtance, the other may juſtify to beat him.

But for the Arreſting of ſuch ſuſpicious Perſons, note, that there muſt be ſome Felony committed indeed.

Alſo the Party that ſhall arreſt ſuch ſuſpected Perſon muſt have a Suſpicion of him him- 9 *E.* 4. 28. ſelf, and for the ſame Felony, or otherwiſe Suſpicion generally is no Cauſe to arreſt another. See *antea,* Tit. *Examination.*   5 *H.* 7. 4. & *Libr. Intr. Faux Impr. div.* 5.

(*a*) So that when any Felony is done, every Man that ſhall ſuſpect another to be guilty thereof may arreſt him. See 5 *H.* 7. 4. *b. Br. Faux Impriſ.* 16.

Any Man ſuſpecting another of a Felony committed, or only intended, may arreſt *Cauſe* him, ſo as thereupon he commits him to the Gaol, or carries him before a Juſtice of Peace. 9 *E.* 4. 26. 20 *E.* 4. 6. *Vide Finch* 127.

Alſo when a Felony is committed, the common Voice and Fame that *I. S.* did the Felony, is ſufficient Cauſe for any Man to ſuſpect him, and to arreſt him. *Ibid.*

Alſo Hue and Cry after *I. S.* for Felony, ſeemeth to be ſufficient Cauſe to arreſt him, though there be no Felony committed. *Ibid.*

Alſo Hue and Cry is ſufficient Cauſe to arreſt any ſuſpicious Perſon. *Br. Faux Impriſ.* 25.

So when a Felony is done, to be in Company of the Offenders, is ſufficient Cauſe to arreſt him.

So to live idly and vagrant. *Br. Faux Impriſ.* 22. See *antea.*

(*d*) Alſo

9 E. 4. 28.
Finch 127.

(*d*) Alſo every Man may arreſt ſuch as apparently go about to commit any Felony, and may impriſon them.

29 E. 3. 39.
5 H. 7. 4.

Alſo upon Hue and Cry for ſtolen Goods, (ſc. for a Horſe or Bullock, &c. of ſuch Colour, &c.) if *A.* be taken driving or leading, &c. ſuch a Horſe, or ſuch a Bullock, or having ſuch other ſtolen Goods about him, though he be a Man of good Name and Cre-

10 H. 7. 28.

dit, yet every Man may apprehend and ſtay *A.* hereupon, and may deliver him to the Conſtables, by them to be ſet in the Stocks, or ſafely kept, until they carry him before a Juſtice of Peace, that ſo he may be delivered by Courſe of Law.

If any Man ſhall be dangerouſly hurt in Affray, or otherwiſe, every Man may arreſt and impriſon the Offender, &c. What every private Man may further do in Affray, ſee before, Tit. *Affray.*

Juſtification.

(*a*) Unlawful Hunters in Parks, the Keepers, or their Servants, may for ſuch Offence juſtify to arreſt the Offenders, and to cauſe them to depart, &c. *Libr. Intr.* Tit. *Faux Impr. div.* 12.

(*d*) Every Man knowing of any that keepeth or uſeth any Gun, &c. contrary to the Statute, may arreſt him, and bring him to the next Juſtice of Peace, &c. See *antea,*

Co. 9. 63. b.

Tit. *Guns.*

4 H. 7 18.
Br. Faux
Impr. 15.
* But there
ought to be pro-

Night-walkers, being Strangers or ſuſpected Perſons, Watchmen may arreſt them, and may ſtay them till the Morning, &c. See hereof Tit. *Watch antea.* Yea, every Man may arreſt ſuch Night-walkers, for it is for the Good of the Kingdom. *

bable Cauſes of Suſpicion, otherwiſe (according to Ch. Juſt. Holt) it is not lawful even for a Conſtable to take up a Perſon, having been guilty of no Breach of the Peace, nor any unlawful Act. See 2 H. H. P. C. *89. in notis.*

(*a*) But in all theſe Caſes before, where a private Man ſhall arreſt another, he ought thereupon to commit the Priſoner to the Gaol, or to carry and deliver him to the Conſtable, or to ſome other Officer, &c. See 20 E. 4. 6. *Finch* 127.

Officer.

(*d*) The Sheriff, Bailiff, Conſtables and other the King's Officers, may arreſt and impriſon Offenders in all Caſes where a private Perſon may, and without any Writ or Warrant.

Where a Conſtable may arreſt one, &c. See hereof *antea,* Tit. *Conſervators of the Peace, Affray, Forcible Entry,* and *Examination.*

A Conſtable, being informed of a lewd Man and Woman that are together in Incontinency, may take with him ſo many of his Neighbours as he will to arreſt the ſaid Man and Woman, to find Sureties for their Good Behaviour. 1 *H.* 7. 7. 13 *H.* 7. 10.

(*a*) If any Man makes an Aſſault upon the Conſtable, he may juſtify to arreſt him that makes the Aſſault, and to carry him to the Gaol for the Breach of the Peace, although the Conſtable be the Party upon whom the Aſſault was made. 5 *H.* 7. 6. *Br. Faux Imp.* 41.

(*d*) The Juſtice of Peace may arreſt and impriſon Offenders in all Caſes where a private Man may. See *hic antea.*

(*a*) The Juſtice of Peace, upon his own Motion and Diſcretion, or upon Complaint, may alſo grant out his Warrant for the Arreſting, or convening before him, of all ſuch Perſons as ſhall break, or go about to break the Peace, or as he ſhall ſuſpect to be inclined to break the Peace, and may commit them to Priſon, if they ſhall refuſe to find, or cannot find Sureties to keep the Peace.

The Juſtice of Peace, in divers Caſes, may in like Sort grant out his Warrant for the Good Behaviour againſt Offenders, (as you may ſee before) and may commit them to Priſon for not finding Sureties accordingly.

And theſe Things the Juſtices of Peace may do by Force of the Commiſſion, and of the Statutes 18 *E.* 3. *cap.* 2. & 34 *E.* 3. *cap.* 1.

(*d*) If one cometh before the Juſtice of Peace upon his Warrant for the Peace, Good Behaviour, or for a Riot, or the like, the Juſtice needeth not to demand Sureties of him, but may commit him if he do not offer it. *Br. Peace* 7.

Alſo the Juſtices of Peace upon their own View, &c. of the Offence, may impriſon the Offender againſt divers penal Laws; as namely ſuch as keep common Alehouſes without Licence, Offenders for unlawful Games, Rioters, ſuch as ſhall make any Forcible Entries or Holdings of Poſſeſſions, &c. See for theſe before under their particular Titles.

There be divers other Offences which by the Statute are committed to the Juſtices of Peace, out of their Seſſions, to hear and determine, and of which the Offenders ſhall be convicted, ſometimes upon their own Confeſſion before the Juſtices, and ſometimes upon Examination and Proof of Witneſſes; in all which Caſes the ſaid Juſtices of Peace may

convene

convene the ſaid Offenders before them, by their Proceſs or Warrant; and after ſuch Examination and Conviction, they may impriſon or otherwiſe puniſh the Offenders, according as they are limited by the ſaid Statutes. See before.

Whereſoever the Juſtice hath Authority given him by any Statute to bind over any Man, or cauſe him to do any Thing, if ſuch Perſon, being in his Preſence, ſhall refuſe to be bound, or to do ſuch Thing, the Juſtice may ſend him to the Gaol, there to remain till he ſhall perform the ſame. See hereof *antea*, Tit. *Recognizance.*

In what Caſes the King's Officer may break open a Man's Houſe for to arreſt an Offender. See hereof, Tit. *Forcible Entry.* ^{*Break open an Houſe.*}

All Men being required ought to aſſiſt the King's Officers, to purſue and arreſt Offenders againſt the Peace, &c.

If the Party againſt whom any Warrant is granted ſhall make *Reſiſtance*, or ſhall make an Aſſault upon the Officer, or ſhall fly; the Officer may juſtify the Beating and Hurting of him, and may alſo impriſon him in the Stocks for the ſame; but if the Party reſiſteth or flieth before he be arreſted, the Officer cannot juſtify the Beating of him. 2 *Ed.* 4. 7. *a. Br. Treſp.* 296. ^{*Reſiſt.* 2 E. 4. 7. 21 H. 7. 39.}

(*a*) If the Warrant was to arreſt one who is indicted of Felony, then may the Officer juſtify the Killing of ſuch a Perſon, if he ſhall reſiſt or fly, or that he cannot otherwiſe be taken. See *hic antea, Homicide tolerated.*

(*d*) None ſhall be impriſoned by any Juſtice of Peace, but only in the common Gaol, by the Statute of 5 *H.* 4. & 23 *H.* 8. *cap.* 2. ^{*Gaols.* 5 H. 4. 10.}

And therefore Juſtices of Peace cannot commit Felons to any of the Counters in *London*, nor to other Priſons which be not common Gaols; nor make a Gaol of their own Houſes. ^{*The Place.* Co. 9. 119. b.}

And yet Juſtices of Peace may commit to the Stocks ſome Offenders againſt certain Penal Statutes, as Townſmen tippling in Alehouſes, &c. See hereof *antea*, Tit. *Alehouſes.* ^{*Impriſonment.*}

Perſons refuſing to work in Hay and Harveſt-time. See *antea*, Tit. *Labourers.*

And in ſome Caſes the Juſtice may commit an Offender to ſafe Cuſtody by his Diſcretion. *Vide antea*, Tit. *Preachers.*

Alſo in ſome Caſes the Juſtices may ſend Offenders to the Houſe of Correction, there to be continued for any reaſonable Time, at the Diſcretion of the Juſtice. *Vide antea*, Tit. *Rogues.*

The Sheriff or Gaoler may impriſon a Felon or other Priſoner in their own Houſe, or in the common Gaol, at their Pleaſure. (*a*) *Tamen quære & vide Cromp.* 184. that the Gaol is the *King's Priſon*, and that for Cauſes touching the King, Offenders ſhall be ſent thither. ^{Lam. 136. Cromp. 169.}

(*d*) The Conſtable, or other ſuch Officer, cannot impriſon any Man in his Houſe, but in the Stocks; and that not above ſuch a reaſonable Time, as he may provide convenient Aid ſafely to convey the Priſoner to the Juſtice or Gaol. ^{20 E. 4. 6. 22 E. 4. 35. 3 H. 4. 9. Finch.}

(*a*) And yet in Caſe of an Affray, &c. the Conſtable may for a Time impriſon the Offender, being a Man of Quality, in the Conſtable's own Houſe, or may commit him to ſome other ſafe Cuſtody. *Vide hic cap.* 1.

(*d*) If a Man commit Felony in one County, and be arreſted for the ſame in another County, he ſhall be impriſoned in that County where he is taken. *Vide antea*, Tit. *Felony.* ^{*County.* Br. FauxImp. 25.}

The Juſtice of Peace, Conſtable, or other Officer, purſuing a Felon into another County, takes him there; the Felon ſhall be committed to the Gaol of the County where he was taken: For the Juſtice of Peace or Officer, being out of his County, hath no more Authority than a private Man. *Vide antea*, Tit. *Acceſſaries & Felony.* ^{13 E. 4. 9. Br. Freſh Suit. 3. & Plow. 37. a.}

Alſo if the Conſtable, or other Officer, ſhall ſee an Affray, and he coming to arreſt them, the Affrayers do fly into another County, the Officer, as every other private Perſon, may purſue them into the other County, and may arreſt them there; but the Officer cannot bring them out of that County, but muſt carry the Affrayers before ſome Juſtice of Peace of the ſame County where they were taken, &c. But if the Affray be in one Town, and the Affrayers do fly into another Town, or into a Franchiſe or Liberty within the ſame County, the Officer may purſue them, and take them out of the Franchiſe, &c. by freſh Suit. *Vide antea*, Tit. *Affray.*

But if the Conſtable hath arreſted one upon a Warrant from a Juſtice of Peace, and after the Arreſt the Party eſcapeth (of his own Wrong), and flieth into another County, the Conſtable may purſue and take him in the other County by freſh Suit, and bring him ^{*See* 2 E. 4. 6. Br. Treſp. 296.}

before

before the Juſtice of Peace upon whoſe Warrant he was firſt arreſted. See *Cromp.* 172, 173. *& antea,* Tit. *Felony by Statute.*

If a Priſoner taken in Execution ſhall make an *Eſcape of his own Wrong,* and ſhall fly out of Sight, and into another County, where the Sheriff hath no Power, yet the Sheriff *&c.* upon freſh Suit, may take him again in any other County, and he ſhall be ſtill ſaid to be in Execution ; yea, without freſh Suit, the Sheriff, *&c.* may take him again, and keep him until he hath agreed with him: Otherwiſe, if the Eſcape were by the Conſent of the Sheriff, *&c. Co.* 3. 52. *Br. Eſcape* 4. 12.

Charges.
3 Jac. 1. c. 10.
P. Priſ. 7, 8.
21 Jac. 1. c. 28.

Now for the Conveying of Priſoners to the Gaol, it muſt be at the proper Charge of the Priſoners, if they have Means or Ability thereto ; otherwiſe it muſt be at the Charge of the Town where they are taken.

(a) And if the Priſoner ſhall refuſe to bear the Charge, the Juſtice, by his Warrant under his Hand and Seal, may cauſe the *High Conſtable of the Hundred, or Petty Conſtable of the Town,* where he hath any Goods, to ſell ſo much thereof as will ſatisfy the Charges; and if the Priſoner have no Goods known, then the Pariſhioners of the Town, where he was apprehended, refuſing to pay their Rate towards that Charge, may by like Warrant be diſtrained to pay the ſame. *Vide Stat.* 3 *Jac.* 1. *cap.* 10.

10 H. 4. 7.
F. Eſc. 8.

(d) And if a Man be arreſted for Felony, and the Conſtable ſhall carry him to the Gaol, and the Gaoler will not receive him, the Conſtable muſt bring him back to the Town where he was taken, and that Town ſhall be charged with the Keeping of him until the next Gaol-delivery, by the Opinion in the Book 10 H. 4. (a) or the Conſtable or other Party that arreſted him may in ſuch a Caſe keep the Priſoner in his own Houſe. See 1 E. 4. *Br. Faux Impr.* 25. *fine.*

P. Priſ. 6.
4 E. 3. c. 10.

(d) But the *Gaoler denying to receive a Felon* by the Delivery of any Conſtable or Town-ſhip, or taking any Thing for receiving ſuch, ſhall be puniſhed for the ſame by the Juſtices of Gaol-delivery.

The Time.
Co. 8. 119.
Plow. 17. b.

When a Statute doth appoint Impriſonment, but limits no Time when the Offender ſhall be impriſoned, then he is to be impriſoned preſently; as in Caſe of a Force, the Juſtices of Peace, upon View thereof, ought to commit the Offenders preſently, (a) for after they may not commit them.

Cromp. 171.

(d) Alſo when a Statute doth appoint Impriſonment, but limits no Time how long, in ſuch Caſe the Priſoner muſt remain at the Diſcretion of the Court.

Where a Statute doth ordain that an Offender ſhall be impriſoned at the King's Plea-ſure. *Vide antea,* Tit. *Bailment.*

Where a Statute ordaineth that a Priſoner ſhall not be delivered without the King's ſpecial Command, and that upon a Fine to be made to the King; who may aſſeſs the ſame Fine, and deliver him. See 18 *H.* 8. 1.

Br. Impr. 100.
Co. 11. 43.

But Impriſonment to be inflicted by the Juſtice of Peace, almoſt in all Caſes, (except for the Peace, the Good Behaviour, or for Felony, or higher Offences) is but to retain the Party until he hath made Fine to the King for his Contempt or Offence ; and therefore if he ſhall offer to pay his Fine, or ſhall find Sureties by Recognizance to pay it, he ought to be delivered preſently. 2 *Mar.* 1.

The Manner.
Co. 8. 100.
& 9. 87.

Now for the Manner of Impriſonment, it ſeemeth generally in all Caſes where a Man is committed to Priſon, eſpecially if it be for Felony, or upon an Execution, (or but for a Treſpaſs, or other Offence) every Gaoler ought to keep ſuch Priſoner *in ſalva & arcta cuſtodia : Salva, ſc.* that he ought to be impriſoned ſo ſurely as that he cannot eſcape ; *Arcta,* in reſpect that he ought to be kept cloſe, without Conference with others, or In-telligence of Things abroad.

Eſcapes.
Co. 3. 44.

And therefore if the Gaoler ſhall licence his Priſoner to go abroad for a Time, and then to come again, or to go abroad with a Keeper, though he come again ; yet theſe are Eſcapes : And if the Priſoner were in for Felony, this is fineable in the Gaoler at leaſt, and ſo it is if it be not Felony ; and if the Priſoner were in upon an Execution, this is ſo penal to the Officer, as that he ſhall be charged for the Debt ; and if the Priſoner were in but for a Treſpaſs, yet the Officer is fineable : For Impriſonment was ordained for

1 R. 2. c. 12.
7 H. 4. c. 4.

Puniſhment of Offenders, and in Terror of all others; *ut pœna ad paucos, metus ad omnes perveniat. Vide antea* Tit. *Felony by Statute.*

(a) And yet ſee *Co. L.* 260. That *Impriſonment* muſt be *Cuſtodia, & non pœna :* For *Carcer ad homines cuſtodiendos, non ad puniendos, dari debet :* But 'tis juſt that it ſhould be *pœna* as well as *cuſtodia, ſc.* for Malefactors, that it ſhould be a Puniſhment to them, and a Terror to others ; and for Debtors, that they may the ſooner pay their Creditors.

For,

I

For, as one ſaith, *Maxima illecebra peccandi impunitatis ſpes,* A great impulſive Cauſe of Offence is the Hope to eſcape unpuniſhed: And ſo a great Cauſe that Debtors care not to pay their Creditors, is their Hope to eſcape Impriſonment, or of too much Favour and Liberty in Priſon.

(*d*) Alſo (by the Law) thoſe which are in Execution ought not to go at Liberty within the Priſon, nor abroad with their Keeper, 24 *H.* 8. much leſs in Caſes of Felony, or of higher Offences. *In Execution.* *Dyer* 249. *Co.* 3. 44.

Alſo by the Statute of *Weſtm.* 2. *cap.* 11. Accountants, and ſuch as are in Execution, the Sheriff or Gaoler may put Irons or Fetters upon them: And yet if the Gaoler ſhall impriſon a Man ſo ſtraightly, by putting him in the Stocks, or putting more Irons upon him than is needful, or keepeth his Victual from him, whereby the Priſoner becometh decrepit, lamed, or otherwiſe diſeaſed, he ſhall have an Action of the Caſe againſt the Gaoler; and if the Gaoler ſhall keep his Priſoner more ſtraight than of Right he ought to do, ſo that the Priſoner dieth thereof, this is Felony in the Gaoler. *Co.* ibid. *P. Accom.* 2. *Fitz.* 93. h.

Alſo the Conſtable or ſuch other Officer, that ſhall impriſon in the Stocks any Offender for Felony or Suſpicion thereof, may lock the Stocks, and if Need be, may alſo put Irons on him; and when he conveyeth him to the Gaol, or to the Juſtice, may pinion him, or otherwiſe make him ſure, ſo that he cannot eſcape. *Irons.*

It ſeemeth by *Britton, fol.* 17. that by the Common Law (before the Statute of *Weſtm.* 2.) none ſhould have Irons put on them but ſuch Offenders as were taken for Felony, or Treſpaſſers in Parks. But the Words of the Statute of *Weſtm.* 2. *cap.* 11. are general, *quod carceri manucipentur in ferris*; which Word *Carceri* ſeemeth to ſignify any Perſons impriſoned for any Cauſe, (or any Perſons worthy of the Priſon) and is not to be reſtrained to Accountants only. See *Coke* 3. 44. *Kit.* 69.

Alſo by the Statute 7 *Jacobi Regis,* all Rogues, Vagabonds, ſturdy Beggars, and other idle and diſorderly Perſons, ſent to the Houſe of Correction, may (by the Maſter of ſuch a Houſe) be puniſhed by putting Fetters or Gives upon them. *7 Jac.* 1. 4.

(*a*) A Perſon under Arreſt muſt not be carried to a Victualling-houſe without his Conſent, ſo as to charge him with any Sum of Money for Meat or Drink, nor more to be taken for an Arreſt than required by Law; nor any Reward exacted for keeping him out of Gaol till he find Bail or agree, or take more for a Night's Lodging, or other Expences, than what ſhall be allowed by the next Juſtice, or by the Seſſions. *22 & 23 Car.* 2. c. 20.

See 2 *Hawk. P. C. Chap.* 12 & 13. *of Arreſts by private Perſons and publick Officers.*

C H A P. CLXXI.

Poſſe Comitatus.

WHERE the Juſtice of Peace, Sheriff, or other Officer, is enabled to take the Power of the County, it ſeemeth they may command, and ought to have the Aid and Attendance of all *Knights, Gentlemen, Yeomen, Husbandmen, Labourers, Tradeſmen, Servants* and *Apprentices,* and of all other Perſons being above the Age of fifteen Years, and able to travel. *Wh.* *Lamb.* 309.

But Women, Eccleſiaſtical Perſons, and ſuch as be decrepit or diſeaſed, ſhall not be compelled to attend them.

And in ſuch Caſes it is referred to the Diſcretion of the Juſtice of Peace (or Sheriff, &c.) what Number they will have to attend on them, and how and after what Manner they ſhall be armed, or otherwiſe furniſhed.

But it is not juſtifiable for the Juſtice of Peace, Sheriff, or other Officer, to aſſemble the *Poſſe Comitatus,* or raiſe a Power or Aſſembly of People (upon their own Heads) without juſt Cauſe. *Vide antea,* Tit. *Riots.*

C H A P. CLXXII.

What Perfons may take Poffe Comitatus, *and in what Cafes.*

And Part 2. p. 67. **A** NY Juftice of Peace or Sheriff, may take (of that County where he is a Juftice or Sheriff) any Number that he fhall think meet, to purfue, apprehend, arreft and imprifon *Traitors, Murderers, Robbers* and *other Felons*; or fuch as do break, or go about to break, or difturb the King's Peace: And every Man (being required) ought to affift and aid them. *Vide antea,* Tit. *Forcible Entry and Felony.*

14 H. 7. 8. The Juftices of Peace (and Sheriff or Under-Sheriff) may take the *Poffe Comitatus* for fuppreffing Riots; and all Sorts of Perfons (being able and required) ought to affift them therein. *Vide antea,* Tit. *Riots.*

Yea, any Juftice of Peace may take the Power and Aid of the County to fupprefs Rioters, and need not to ftay for the coming of another Juftice, or of the Sheriff.

In what Cafes. Alfo in Cafes of *Forcible Entry,* any Juftice of Peace may take *Poffe Comitatus* to remove fuch Perfons as by his View, or by Inquifition taken before him, fhall be found to have made any Forcible Entry (into other Mens Poffeffions) or to detain them with Force. *Vide antea,* Tit. *Forcible Entry.*

P. Rec. 52. Alfo the Sheriff, or other Officer, upon any lawful Warrant for the apprehending any Popifh Recufants, &c. may take the *Poffe Comitatus,* &c. See the Statute of 3 *Jac.* 1. 4.

3 H. 7. 1, 10. Co. 5. 115. P. Diftr. 4. P. Retor. 5. Br. Fin. P. 37. Br. Riots 2, 3. The Sheriff, Under-Sheriff or Bailiff, &c. if Need be, may by the Common Law take the Power of the County (what Number they fhall think good) to execute the King's Procefs or Writ, be it a Writ of *Execution, Replevin, Eftretment, Capias,* or other Writ, it being the King's Command. See alfo the Statute *Weftm.* 1. 17. *Weftm.* 2. 39.

And fuch as fhall not affift them therein (being required) fhall pay a Fine to the King. See *hic antea.*

3 H. 7. 1. Br. Tref. 266. & Riots 2. The Sheriff's Bailiff, to execute a Replevy, took with him three Hundred Men armed (*modo guerrino, &c.*) with Guns; and it was holden lawful: For the Sheriff's Officer hath Power to take Affiftance as well as the Sheriff himfelf, for that is all one Office, and one Authority.

A Man demands the Peace in the Chancery againft a *great Lord,* and hath a *Supplicavit* directed to the Sheriff: There, if Need fhall be, the Sheriff may take the *Poffe Comitatus* to aid him to arreft fuch a Lord, &c. *Vide antea,* Tit. *Surety for the Peace.*

So if a *Supplicavit* be directed to a Juftice of Peace, he or the Officer to whom the Juftice of Peace fhall make his Warrant in this Behalf, (upon Refiftance made) may (if need be) take the *Poffe Comitatus* to aid him to arreft the Party: *Quia quando aliquid mandatur, mandatur & omne per quod pervenitur ad illud.* Co. 5. 115.

But every Sheriff is inabled befides by his Writ of Affiftance, whereby there is Command under the Great Seal, to all *Archbifhops, Dukes, Earls, Barons,* and all other the King's Subjects within the fame County, to be aiding to him in whatfoever belongeth to his Office, &c.

The Sheriff may take the *Poffe Comitatus* to apprehend *Felons,* &c. or Difturbers of the Peace. *Vide antea,* Tit. *Forcible Entry.*

So he may take the *Poffe Comitatus* to execute the *Precept of the Juftice of Peace.* Ibid.

5 H. 7. 10. 13 H. 7. 10. Br. Trefp. 432. The *Conftable* (of a Town) upon a *Felony* committed, or upon any *Affray,* or the like, may take the Aid of his Neighbours, or other Perfons being prefent, to apprehend the Felons, or to caufe the Peace to be kept, and to carry the Offenders before the Juftice, &c. See *Br. Riot* 3.

One that hurt another, whereby he is in Peril of Death, the Conftable may take Power or Aid to arreft him, &c.

So may the Conftable take the Aid of his Neighbours for executing the Juftice's Warrant directed to him.

28 E. 3. 8. (a) Yea all and every fuch Perfons as are *Confervators of the Peace* by the Common Law, (*fc.* every *Petty Conftable, High Conftable, Coroner, Sheriff, Steward of a Leet,* or *of a Court of Piepowders, Steward of the Sheriff's Torn,* and other *Judge in any Court of Record*) may command and take the Help, Aid and Force of others, to arreft all fuch who

I   in

in their Preſence, and within their Juriſdiction, ſhall go about to break the Peace by Word or Deed.

Every Man may aſſemble his Friends and Neighbours to defend his Perſon, *&c.* (being Co. 11. 82. in his Houſe) againſt Violence, *&c.* but not to go abroad with him to a Fair or Market, 21 H. 7. 39. *&c. Vide antea,* Tit. *Forcible Entry.*

C H A P. CLXXIII.

Certain Advices to the Juſtices of Peace.

(*a*) THIS being ſuch a Form of ſubordinate Government for the Quiet of the Realm, as no Part of the Chriſtian World hath the like, as ſaith my Lord *Coke,* 4 *Inſt.* 170. if the ſame be duly executed ; much of the Happineſs of this Nation depends on our Juſtices of the Peace well and faithful Diſcharge of their Duty ; and their due or ill Adminiſtration of the Authority given them, muſt needs add to the Reputation of our Government, or the Defamation thereof, eſpecially ſince their Authority is ſo much enlarged by ſeveral Statutes : It will concern them therefore for their Direction and Security, to peruſe the Statute 4 *H.* 7. 12. where they may find their Duty to give juſt Relief, and the Danger of Neglect. And therefore (*d*) I thought it not amiſs here ſhortly to admoniſh the Juſtices of Peace again of ſome few Things mentioned before, for their better Memory.

1. Firſt, That they exerciſe not the Office of a Juſtice of Peace before they have taken *Oath of Office.* the *Oath of their Office,* and the *Oath of Supremacy. Vide antea, cap.* 4.

2. That they execute not this their Office *in their own Caſe,* but cauſe the Offenders to *Not to be* be convened or carried before ſome other Juſtice, or deſire the *Aid of ſome other Juſtice* *Judges in their* being preſent ; *quia iniquum eſt aliquem ſuæ rei eſſe judicem. Coke* 8. 118. And ſome *Crom. f. 68.* late Statutes have taken ſpecial Care to prevent this, as you may ſee *hic* Tit. *Treſpaſs, &c.* Lit. 212. Co. L. 141.

(*a*) Beſides, *idem non poteſt eſſe agens & patiens.* 14 *H.* 8. 13. And when a Man is a 9 H. 6: 21. 1 Party, he cannot be a Judge indifferent. 8 *H.* 6. 19. Alſo it has been often ſeen, that 11 H. 6. 49. a Juſtice of Peace who had executed that Office in his own Caſe, has been puniſhed for it in the Star-chamber. *Cromp.* 68.

(*d*) And yet if the Juſtice ſhall deal in his own Caſe, it ſeems good and juſtifiable in many Caſes ; as when a Juſtice of Peace ſhall be aſſaulted, or in the doing his Office eſpecially, ſhall be abuſed to his Face, and no other Juſtice of Peace preſent with him ; then it ſeems he may commit ſuch an Offender, until he ſhall find Sureties for the Peace or the Good Behaviour, as the Caſe ſhall require : And the ſaid Juſtice in ſuch Caſe may himſelf bind the Offender, and take his Security ; but if any oth r Juſtice be preſent, it were fitter to deſire his Aid.

3. That they be careful for the Execution of the Statute of *Riots. Vide antea,* Tit. *Riots.* *Riots.*

(*a*) And that neither in the Caſe of *Riots,* or any Part of their Office they meddle, if *Moor's Rep.* they can avoid it, where any *Relation* is concerned ; for it brings a Suſpicion upon their p. 628. Proceedings ; but if they muſt needs meddle, as it is not always in their Choice, that they carry themſelves uprightly herein : For one *Carew* (a Juſtice of Peace of *Devon*) was cenſured, he going to view a Riot, and the Rioters being eſcaped before his Coming, he refuſed to go to the Place where they were, although but a little Way off ; and the Peace being required againſt them, he took Recognizances to keep the Peace againſt others that demanded it not, and granted *Superſedeas,* and procured the Peace to be releaſed the next Day. And all this in Favour of his Brother.

(*d*) If upon their Inquiry of a Riot the Truth cannot be found, by Reaſon of any Maintenance, *&c.* that they certify the ſame within one Month. *Ibid.*

4. That upon *Forcible Entry* they make no *Reſtitution* without *Enquiry. Vide antea,* *Forcible Entry.* Tit. *Forcible Entry.*

5. That upon Notice of any *Treaſon,* or of any Seminaries, *&c.* or of any *Agnus Dei,* *Treaſon.* *&c.* offered, they diſcover the ſame to ſome of the Privy Council. *Vide* Tit. *Treaſon.*

6. That they be circumſpect in bailing of Priſoners, *viz.* that they neither deny it to *Bail.* ſuch as are bailable, nor yield it where it is not grantable. *Vide hic Bailment.*

7. If any *Felony* be committed, and one is brought before a Juſtice of Peace upon Suſ- *Not to let ſuſ-* picion for the ſame, though it ſhall appear to the Juſtice that the Priſoner is not guilty of *pected Perſons go.*

5 N   that

that Offence, or that it is not Felony of Death, yet he may not ſet him at Liberty, but ſo as he may come to his Trial. *Vide antea,* Tit. *Felony by the Statute, and Evidence againſt Felons.*

Recognizance. 8. That all Recognizances taken by them be in the King's Name.

9. That all Recognizances taken by them be certified at their next Quarter-Seſſions, or Gaol-Delivery, according as the Caſe ſhall require.

Eaſter-Seſſions. 10. That they meet at every *Eaſter* Seſſions at the leaſt. *Vide* 5 *Eliz.* cap. 4. P. *Juſt.* 67. And yet their Preſence and Attendance at every general Seſſions is very requiſite.

Miſentring Plaints in Sheriffs Courts. 11. That their *Examinations taken concerning the Miſ-entring of Plaints in County Courts,* or the Defaults of gathering the Shire Amerciaments, be certified into the Exchequer, &c. *Vide antea,* Tit. *Sheriffs.*

Highways. 12. That ſuch Offences as the *Surveyors of Highways* ſhall preſent to them, they again preſent at their next Quarter-Seſſions. *Vide antea,* Tit. *Highways.*

Recuſants. 13. That the *Oaths,* taken by them upon the *Submiſſion of any Recuſant,* be certified at their next Quarter-Seſſions. *Vide antea,* Tit. *Recuſants.*

To do Juſtice. 14. Alſo that they do Juſtice, and give Remedy to every Party grieved in any Thing that lieth within their Power to hear, determine, or execute, and that without Reſpect of Perſons, and according to the Laws and Statutes of this Realm. *Vide antea, cap.* 4.

(*a*) 15. He muſt ſuffer the *Law to have its Courſe,* and not privately ſtay Proceedings, contrary to the Duty of his Place. *Latch* 48.

To conſider ſuch Statutes which are in Force. 16. Where they have *Juriſdiction by any Statute,* which at firſt was Temporary, they are to conſider whether the ſame be continued or made perpetual, and ſo be not expired.

(*d*) *Note,* that all theſe former Matters are penal to the Juſtices of Peace, if they ſhall offend in any of them, and therefore it is likely they will be the more careful therein. But there are certain other Things principally tending to the publick good, and lately commended from his Majeſty (by the Judges of Aſſize) to the Care of the Juſtices of Peace; in all which they are to imploy their ſpecial Care and Diligence: And they are ſhortly theſe ten Articles following.

Alehouſes. 1. *Alehouſes;* the Abuſes there to be reformed, and ſuch as are unlicenſed to be ſuppreſſed.

Highways. 2. *Highways* and Bridges to be amended.

Hue and Cry. 3. *Hue and Cry* and freſh Suit to be duly made and purſued after Robbers and other Felons.

Labourers. 4. *Labourers, ſc.* idle Perſons meet to ſerve, to be compelled to go to Service.

Poor Apprentices. 5. *Poor,* their Children to be placed *Apprentices;* ſuch as are able of Body, to be holden or ſet to Work.

6. *Recuſants*: Firſt, Popiſh Recuſants, (eſpecially ſuch as have been reconciled to the Pope, or drawn to the Popiſh Religion ſince the Gunpowder-Treaſon, for theſe are by his Majeſty accounted moſt dangerous) that theſe be certified into the King's Bench, and farther to be dealt withal (by the Juſtices of Peace) according to the ſeveral Statutes in that Behalf made.

Alſo negligent Recuſants, which ſhall not reſort every *Sunday* to Church, that ſuch be puniſhed according to the Statute. For the firſt and beſt Means to bring Men to God, is to bring them to Church.

Rogues and Vagabonds. 7. *Rogues* and Vagabonds are to be duly puniſhed.

Houſes of Correction. 8. *Houſes* of Correction to be maintained.

Watch. 9. *Watch* to be duly kept.

Weights. 10. *Weights* and *Meaſures,* the Abuſes therein to be reformed.

Farther, the Juſtices of Peace are to be careful that they ſuffer not any Thing to the Diſadvantage of the King, where it lieth lawfully in their Power to prevent it. *Vide Lamb.* 521.

Alſo that they remember not to exerciſe the Judgments of Men only, but of God himſelf, (whoſe Power they do participate, and who is always preſent with them) and therefore muſt take heed that in all their Actions they ſet God before their Eyes.

But ſince moſt of the Buſineſs of the Juſtices of Peace (out of Seſſions) conſiſteth in the Execution of divers Statutes committed to their Charge, which Statutes cannot be ſufficiently abridged, but that they will come ſhort of the Subſtance and Body thereof; therefore it ſhall be ſafeſt for the Juſtice of Peace not to rely over much upon theſe fhort Colletions thereof, but to have an Eye to the *Abridgment of Statutes*, or rather to the *Book of Statutes at large*, and thereby to take their farther and better Directions for their whole Proceedings: For (as Sir *Ed. Coke* obferveth) Abridgments are of good and neceffary Ufe to ferve as Tables, but not to ground any Opinion, much lefs to proceed judicially upon them. *Ideo* (faith he) *tutius eft petere fontes quam fectari rivulos. Coke* 10. 117.

And laftly, for the better Encouragement of Juftices of Peace, Conftables, and other Officers, and of all others who in their Aid or Affiftance, or by their Command fhall do any Thing touching his or their Office, who by cauflefs Suits commenced by contentious Perfons againft them for executing their Offices, have lately been difcouraged from doing their Offices with that Courage, Care and Diligence which is required at their Hands; now for their Eafe in pleading, they are by the Statute 7 & 21 *Jacobi* allowed to plead the general Iffue of Not guilty, and give the fpecial Matter in Evidence, and for their wrongful Vexation double Cofts. (*a*) And for all Actions, *&c.* to be brought againft any Juftice of Peace, or other Officer, (or other Perfon which in their Aid, *&c.* fhall do any Thing concerning their Office) the faid Action, *&c.* fhall be laid within the County where the Fact fhall be done, and not elfewhere, *&c.* 21 *Jac. Reg. cap.* 12.

7 Jac. 1. c. 5.
21 Jac. 1. 12.
3 Car. c. 1.

Et nota, quicquid Juftic. fecerit de Recordo ignoranter, & pro defectu fcientiæ, non erit pro eo punitus: Nec pro re per ipfum facta judicialiter. 2 *R.* 3. *fol.* 10. But the Juftices of Affife may hear and punifh the Default of Juftices of Peace, *&c.* their Contempts, Omiffions, Negligences, Favours, Affections, Corruptions, and other Faults whatfoever.

And laftly, where a Juftice makes a Conviction in a fummary way, a Summons is neceffary, and therefore upon Complaint made, the Juftice muft fummon the Party to appear, and if he makes Default, then he may proceed.

1 Salk. 181.
Mod. Ca. 41.

C H A P. CLXXIV.

Warrants and Precedents.

THE Warrants of the Juftice of Peace may be ftiled and made after divers Manners: As,

1. Firft in the Name of the King; and yet the *Tefte* may be under the Name of the Juftice (or Juftices) of Peace, that grant them out.

2. Or they may be ftiled and made only in the Names of the Juftices.

3. Or they may be made without any fuch Style, and only under the *Tefte* of the Juftice of Peace, or only fubfcribed by the Juftice, as followeth.

In the King's Majefty's Name.

GEORGE, by the Grace of God, King, *&c.* To our Sheriff of our County of Cambridge, the High Conftables of the Hundred of *Redfield*, the petty Conftables of the Town of *Balfham*, and to all and fingular our Bailiffs and other Minifters in the faid County, as well within Liberties as without, Greeting. Forafmuch as *A. B.* of, *&c.* hath come before Sir *E. P.* Knight and Baronet, one of our Juftices of Peace within the faid County, and hath, *&c.* (concluding it in the Juftice's Name, as thus) Witnefs the faid *E. P.* at *Ifcham*, the   Day of   *&c.*

Cambridge.
The Stile.
The Tefte.

Note, That wherefoever the Warrant is made in the King's Name, (as before) there it ought to be directed to all Minifters as well within Liberties as without, for that the King is made a Party: And fo it may be done in all other Warrants, (efpecially for Felony, or for the Peace, or the Good Behaviour, *&c.*) becaufe it is the Service of the King; and no Liberty or Franchife fhall be allowed, or hold Place againft the King. *Br. Franch.* 31. Yet fee before, that the Juftices of Peace of the County may not intermeddle in any City, Town, or Liberty, which have their proper Juftices. *Hic cap.* 6.

Direct on.

Or

Or thus in the Name of the Justice himself.

Cambridge.

MILES *Sandys,* Knight and Baronet, one of the Justices of the Peace of our Sovereign Lord the King, within the said County ; to the Sheriff of the said County, to the Bailiff or Constables of the Hundred of, *&c.* to the petty Constables of the Town of *P.* within the said Hundred, and to all other the Ministers and Officers of our Sovereign Lord within the said County, and to every of them, Greeting. Forasmuch as, *&c.* Given under my Hand and Seal, at the Day of *&c.*

Or they may be directed to any of these Officers (above named) particularly, or else to any other indifferent Person or Persons.

A Warrant for the Peace.

Cambridge.
A Warrant for
the Peace.
* Any one of
these Causes is
sufficient.

GEORGE by the Grace of God, *&c.* To our Sheriff, *&c.* Forasmuch as *A. B.* of, *&c.* Yeoman, hath personally come before Sir *J. C.* Baronet, one of our Justices of the Peace within the said County, and hath taken a corporal Oath, that he is afraid that one *C. D.* of in the said County, Yeoman, will * beat, (*wound, maim, or kill him, or burn his Houses*;) and hath prayed Surety of the Peace against the said *C. D.* therefore we command and charge you jointly and severally, that (immediately upon the Receipt hereof) you cause the said *C. D.* to come before the said Sir *J. C.* or some other of our Justices of the same County, to find sufficient Surety, as well for his Appearance at the next Quarter-Sessions of our Peace, to be holden at the Castle of *Cambridge,* or elsewhere, for or in the said County, as also for our Peace to be kept towards us and all our Liege People, and chiefly towards the said *A. B.* that is to say, that he the said *C. D.* shall not do, nor by any Means procure or Cause to be done, any of the said Evils to any of the said People, and especially to the said *A. B.* And if the said *C. D.* shall refuse thus to do, that then immediately (without expecting any farther Warrant) you him safely convey, or cause him to be conveyed safely, to our next Prison in the said County, there to remain until he shall willingly do the same : (So that he may be before our said Justices, at the said next general Sessions of the Peace to be holden at *Cambridge* aforesaid, then and there to answer unto us for his Contempt in this Behalf.) And see that you certify your Doings in the Premisses to our said Justices at the said Sessions, bringing then thither this Precept with you. Witness the said *J. C.* at aforesaid, the Day of *&c.*

Or thus, in the Name of the Justice himself, mutatis mutandis.

Cambridge.
For the Peace.

THomas *Jermy* Knight, one of the Justices of the Peace of our Sovereign Lord the King within the said County, to the Sheriff, *&c.* Greeting. Forasmuch as *A. B. &c.* hath personally come before me, and hath taken a corporal Oath, *&c. ut supra.* These shall be therefore on the Behalf, and in the Name of our Sovereign Lord, to command you jointly, *&c.* that you cause the said *C.* to come before me, or some other of his Majesty's said Justices of Peace, in the said County, *&c. ut supra.* Given under my Seal at aforesaid, *&c.*

Another for the Peace.

To the Constables of, &c. And to either of them.

Cambridge.

See before Tit.
Arrest.

WHereas *B. A.* the Wife of *W. A.* of your said Town, Labourer, hath required Sureties of the Peace against *T. B.* of your said Town, Butcher, and withal hath taken her corporal Oath before me, that she required the same not for any private Malice, Hatred, or ill Will, but that she is afraid of her Life, (or the Hurting or Maiming of her Body, or the Burning of her Houses): These are therefore to require you, and in his Majesty's Name to charge and command you, that immediately upon Sight hereof, you, or any of you, require the said *T. B.* to come before me, or some other of his Majesty's Justices within the said County, to find sufficient Sureties, as well for his Appearance at the next general Quarter-Sessions of the Peace to be holden for this County, as also that the said *T. B.* shall in the mean Time keep his Majesty's Peace, as well towards his said Majesty, as towards all his Liege People, and especially towards

2 the

the faid *B. A.* and if he fhall refufe fo to do, that then immediately you do convey the faid *T. B.* or caufe him to be conveyed unto the Common Gaol at the Caftle of *Cambridge*, there to remain until he fhall willingly do the fame. And fee that you certify your Doings in the Premiffes to the Juftices at the faid Seffions; and have you there this Warrant, dated at, *&c.*

Or thus.

WHereas *B.* the Wife of *W. A.* of your faid Town hath perfonally come before me (*I. C.* Knight, one of the Juftices of the Peace for the faid County of *C.*) and hath taken her corporal Oath, that one *T. B.* of your Town hath already affaulted, beaten and bruifed her the faid *B.* and farther hath *threatned her* in fuch Sort, that fhe is afraid that the faid *T. B.* will beat, wound, maim or kill her, or do her fome other bodily Harm; and thereupon fhe the faid *B.* hath prayed Security of the Peace to be had or granted to her againft the faid *T. B.* Thefe are therefore to will and require you, (*&c. ut fupra*) to find fufficient Sureties (or to be bound with two fufficient Sureties) for his perfonal Appearance at the next general Quarter-Seffions of the Peace to be holden for this County, then and there to anfwer the Premiffes; and in the mean Time that he the faid *T. B.* keep the Peace towards our faid Sovereign Lord the King, and all other his Liege People, and efpecially towards the faid *B.* And if he fhall refufe thus to do, that then (*ut fupra.*)

A Warrant for the Peace upon a Supplicavit.

CHriftophorus Hatton Knight, one of the Juftices of the Peace within the County of *Cambridge*, to the Sheriff of the faid County, the High Conftables of the Hundred of *R.* the petty Conftables of the Town of *B.* and to all and fingular the King's Bailiffs and other Minifters, as well within Liberties as without in the faid County, and to every of them, Greeting. Know ye, that I have received the Command (or Writ) of our faid Sovereign Lord (in thefe Words, reciting the whole Writ of *Supplicavit*; or only reciting the Effect of the *Supplicavit*, thus, to compel *A. B.* of, *&c.* to find fufficient Surety for the Peace, by him to be kept towards, *&c.*) And therefore on the Behalf of our faid Sovereign Lord, I command and charge you, jointly and feverally, that immediately upon the Receipt hereof you caufe the faid *A. B.* to come before me at my Houfe in *Chevely*, to find fufficient Surety for the Peace, to be kept towards our faid Sovereign Lord, and all his Liege People, and efpecially towards the faid *C. D.* and if the faid *A. B.* fhall refufe thus to do, that then you him fafely convey, or caufe to be fafely conveyed to his Majefty's Gaol at the Caftle of *Cambridge*, (or to the next Gaol of his Majefty in the faid County) there to remain until that he fhall willingly do the fame; fo that he may be before the Juftices of the Peace of our faid Sovereign Lord within the faid County, at the next General Seffions of the Peace, to be holden for the faid County, there to anfwer to our faid Sovereign Lord for his Contempt in this Behalf. And fee that you certify your Doings in the Premiffes to the faid Juftices at the faid Seffions, bringing then thither this Precept with you. Given at   aforefaid, under my Hand and Seal, the fourth Day of, *&c.*

The Return of this Writ, and Certificate of the Juftices Doings herein, fee here before in the Title of *Surety for the Peace.*

A Warrant for the Good Behaviour.

WHereas *A. B.* of your faid Town is not of good Name or Fame, nor of honeft Converfation, (but an Evil Doer, a Rioter, Barrator, and Difturber of the Peace, of our faid Sovereign Lord) as we are given to underftand by the Complaint of fundry credible Perfons: Therefore on the Behalf of our fovereign Lord we command you, and every of you, that immediately, *&c.* you caufe the faid *A. B.* to come before us, or fome other of our Fellow-Juftices, to find fufficient Surety, as well for his good Behaviour towards our faid Sovereign Lord and all his Liege People, until the next Quarter-Seffions of the Peace to be holden in the faid County, as alfo for his Appearance then and there. And if he fhall refufe fo to do, that then, *&c.* (as in the Warrant for the Peace.)

Cambridge.

Cambridge.
For the Good Behaviour.
Any one of thefe is fufficient, or any other like Caufe.

Or thus,

Cambridge.

WHereas we have been credibly informed that *S. W.* of your Town, *&c.* is a Man of evil Behaviour, one that daily moveth Difcord, Strife, and Diffenfion among his Neighbours, and a common Difturber of his Majefty's Peace: Thefe are therefore in the King's Name to command you, *&c.*

A general Warrant for a Mifdemeanor.

Cambridge.
Mifdemeanor.

THomas *Chichely* Efq; one of the Juftices, *&c.* to the Conftables of, *&c.* and to every of them. Thefe are to will and require you, and in his Majefty's Name to charge and command you, and either of you, that immediately upon the Sight hereof, (or upon *Monday* next by Eight of the Clock in the Forenoon) you bring *I. H.* of your faid Town, Butcher, before me, to anfwer to fuch Matters of Mifdemeanor as on his Majefty's Behalf fhall be objected againft him. And hereof fail you not at your Perils. Dated at, *&c.*

Another for Mifdemeanor.

Cambridge.

THESE are to will and require you, *&c.* that immediately upon the Receipt hereof, you apprehend and take *A. B.* and *C. D. &c.* (or all and every the Perfons here under-named) and to bring them forthwith before me, to anfwer unto fuch Matters of Mifdemeanors as on his Majefty's Behalf fhall be objected againft them. And hereof fail you not at your Perils. Dated, *&c.*

To attach one for Felony.

Cambridge.
For Felony.

WHereas Complaint hath been made unto me by *C. D.* of, *&c.* that of late he hath had certain Goods felonioufly taken from him, and that he hath in Sufpicion one *R. G.* of your faid Town: Thefe are therefore to will and require you *&c.* prefently upon the Receipt hereof, to apprehend the faid *R. G.* and to bring him before me, to anfwer to the Premiffes. And hereof fail you not at your Perils. Dated, *&c.*

Another.

Cambridge.

THESE are to will and require you, *&c.* prefently upon the Receipt hereof, to apprehend *A. B.* of, *&c.* and bring him before me, to anfwer unto fuch Matters o. *Sufpicion of Felony* as on his Majefty's Behalf fhall be objected againft him. And hereo fail you not at your Perils. Dated, *&c.*

Another.

THESE are to will and require you, *&c.* to apprehend, *&c.* to anfwer unto the felonious Taking of certain Goods, wherewith he is charged by *J. S.* And hereof fail you not, *&c.*

To fearch for ftolen Goods.

Cambridge.
To fearch for ftolen Goods.

WHereas Complaint hath been made unto me by *N. O.* that of late he hath had felonioufly taken from him certain Goods, and that he hath in Sufpicion divers lewd and evil-difpofed Perfons within your Parifh: Thefe are to will, *&c.* that immediately upon the Receipt hereof you make diligent *Search in all and every fuch fufpected Houfes* and Places within your Parifh, as you and this Complainant fhall think convenient: And if upon your Search you find any of the faid Goods, or other juft Caufe o Sufpicion, that then you bring all fuch fufpected Perfons as you fhall find, before me, to anfwer unto the Premiffes. And hereof fail you not, *&c.*

Another.

WHereas Complaint hath been made unto me *Robert Hatton* Knight, one of the Cambridge. Juftices, &c. by *J. S.* of, &c. that upon *Monday* Night laft he had felonioufly taken from him certain Goods [they fhould be named] and that he is informed, that there are divers Parcels of fuch Goods in the Hands or Houfes of certain fufpected Perfons within your Town : Thefe are to will, &c. that you be aiding to and affift the faid *I. S.* (the Bearer hereof) whereby he may come to the Sight of the fame Goods, that fo he may the better know whether thofe Goods, or any Part of them, are his ; and if he fhall find the fame Goods, or any of them, that were ftolen from him ; or if he fhall claim any of the faid Goods in the Poffeffion of any of the faid fufpected Perfons, that then you do prefently apprehend all fuch fufpected Perfons within whofe Cuftody, Houfe or Poffeffion, you or he the faid *I. S.* fhall fo find the fame, and them (together with the faid Goods) forthwith bring before me, or fome other of his Majefty's Juftices of Peace for this County, to make Anfwer thereto. And hereof fail you not, &c. Dated, &c.

To bind Men to give in Evidence.

THESE are in his Majefty's Name to charge and command you, &c. that prefent- Cambridge. ly upon the Sight hereof, you, or fome of you, do caufe to come before me, (or *To give Evi-* fome other of his Majefty's Juftices of Peace of this County) the Perfons here under *dence*. named, to the End that they and every of them may be bound to make their perfonal Appearance at the next general Gaol-Delivery, (or Quarter-Seffions) to be holden for this County, then and there to teftify their and every of their Knowledges concerning certain felonious Acts committed by one *A. B.* now a Prifoner in the Caftle of *C. &c.* And hereof fail you not, &c.

A Warrant for a Search after a Robbery committed, directed to the High Conftables.

WHereas there have been many Robberies lately committed about, &c. Now for the better Difcovery thereof, We whofe Names are here underwritten being his Majefty's Juftices of Peace (for the County of *Cambridge*) have thought good, and do hereby will and require you in his Majefty's Name, forthwith to direct your Precepts to every Petty Conftable within your feveral Hundreds, (commanding them) to fearch in all Inns, Alehoufes, and other fufpected Houfes within your Precincts, for all fuch Per- fons as are out of Service ; as alfo for all idle, vagrant or wandering Rogues, Beggars, or other Perfons: And farther, That they the faid Petty Conftables within your Precincts do take Examination and Account of all thofe, and fuch other Perfons as are common Alehoufe-haunters, or which fpend their Money in *Riot*, or which do not labour for their Living, and have not whereon to maintain them: And that the fame Searches be holden all over in your Hundreds in one Night, and at fuch other feveral Times as to your Difcretion fhall feem meet. And if any fuch Perfons fhall be found in the fame Searches, and that upon your or the Petty Conftable's Examination taken of them, or any of them, there fhall be found any Caufe of Sufpicion in them, or any of them, that then they bring the fame Perfons fo fufpected before us, or fome one of us, or fome other of the Juftices of Peace of this County, to be farther examined in the faid Caufes, and to be farther dealt withal according to Law and Juftice. And for the better Doing here- of we require you to command in his Majefty's Name, that every Petty Conftable with- in their Precinct do require (and charge) two chief difcreet Headboroughs in every Parifh to affift them the Petty Conftables in this Service. And hereof fail you not.

A Hue and Cry after Robbery, &c.

To all Conftables and other his Majefty's Officers, as well within the County of Cambridge, at elfewhere within the Realm of England.

WHereas Complaint hath been made unto me *M. D.* Vice-Chancellor of the Uni- Hue and Cry. verfity of *Cambridge*, one of his Majefty's Juftices of Peace within the faid County of *Cambridge*, by *I. S.* of, &c. Hufbandman, that upon *Tuefday* at Night laft (being the 15th Day of this inftant *November*) he was robbed of certain Linen taken

out

They should be named. out of his Houfe, with fome otherThings, and that he hath manifeft Caufe of Sufpicion of one *A. B.* a lewd Rogue, (here defcribe his Perfonage and Apparel) : Thefe are to require you, and every of you, to fearch within your feveral Precincts for the faid *A. B.* and alfo to make Hue and Cry after him from Town to Town, and from County to County, and that as well by Horfemen as Footmen : And if you fhall find him the faid *A. B.* that then you carry him before fome one of the Juftices of Peace within the County where he fhall be taken, by him to be dealt withal according to Law, *&c.*

A Warrant for one who hath dangeroufly hurt another.

Cambridge.
Hurting and Wounding.

WHereas I am credibly informed that *I. B.* of your Town, Blackfmith, hath lately and dangeroufly hurt one *T. G.* of your faid Town, Hufbandman, by a Blow which he hath given the faid *T.* on the Face, and another on the Back; fo as the faid *T.* is in Danger of Death thereby : Thefe are therefore in his Majefty's Name to charge and command you, that immediately upon the Sight hereof, you, or any of you, do bring the faid *I. B.* before me, or fome other of his Majefty's Juftices of the Peace of this County, to find fufficient Sureties, as well for his Appearance before his Majefty's Juftices at the next general Gaol-Delivery to be holden for this County, then and there to anfwer unto the Premiffes, and to do and receive that which by the Court fhall be injoined him : As alfo that the faid *I. B.* fhall in the mean Time keep the Peace towards his Majefty and all his Liege People, and efpecially towards the faid *T. G.* And hereof fail you not at your Perils. Dated, *&c.*

For the reputed Father of a Baftard Child.

Cambridge.
Baftard Child.

WHereas Complaint hath been made unto me *H. B.* Serjeant at Law, one of his Majefty's Juftices, *&c.* by *K. I.* of your faid Town, fingle Woman, that fhe is gotten with Child by one *T. S.* alfo of your faid Town, Butcher : Thefe are therefore to will and require you, and in his Majefty's Name to charge and command you, and either of you, that prefently upon the Receipt hereof you apprehend the faid *T. S.* and bring him before me, or fome other of his Majefty's Juftices of the Peace for this County, to find fufficient Sureties, as well for his Appearance at the next General Seffions of the Peace to be holden for this County, as alfo for his Good Behaviour towards his Majefty and all his Liege People in the mean Time. And hereof fail you not, as you will anfwer the contrary at your Peril. Dated, *&c.*

(a) An Order for a Baftard Child.

Bulftr. Part 2.
p. 341.

IF the Juftices make an Order, from which the reputed Father appeals, and gives Security to abide the Order of Seffions, and the Seffions make another Order, which he refufing to obey, they commit him ; this is illegal, for they ought to profecute him on his Security. *Hammond's* Cafe, *M.* 3 *Car.*

Ib. p. 342, 343.

And an Appeal being made to Seffions from the firft Order, the Seffions ought to confirm or quafh the firft Order ; and if the Seffions repeal the firft Order, they may refer it back again to the Juftices ; but if they neither quafh nor affirm it, they cannot refer it back. *Smith's* Cafe. And if the Juftices at Seffions repeal the firft Order, then it is *res integra*, and the Recognizance ought to be in the Disjunctive, to perform the Order, or to appear at Seffions ; and for not obeying the Order one Juftice of Peace may commit.

Ib. p. 348.

One hath a Baftard, and is not punifhed for it by 7 *Jac.* 1. 4. and fhe hath another Baftard, fhe fhall not be punifhed for this laft as for a fecond Offence by 7 *Jac.* 4. unlefs fhe had been punifhed for the firft. *Jones* Juftice at *Salop*, Lent 7 *Car.*

Ib. p. 349.

A Servant Maid is begot with Child at *T.* but by an Artifice fhe is conveyed to a Hovel upon the Confines of that Parifh, but in Truth within another Parifh where a Child is born. *Jones* Juftice of Affife declared, that in cafe fuch Practice be proved, the Child fhall not be kept by the Parifh where it was born, but where fhe was got with Child.

Ib. p. 350.

One *B.* a Servant Maid was begot with Child by one *R.* at *D.* and the Child born there ; *R.* takes it from the Mother, and puts it to nurfe, and marries another Woman, and keeps the Child with him 10 or 11 Years together, and died, leaving a Wife and divers Children, which fhe was not able to maintain, but they were relieved by the Parifh. The Mother of the Baftard for the moft part lived in Service, and had 3 *l. per Annum* left her by her Friends, but was not in her own Hands : She was ftill able to do

4

some

fome Work, but was a Woman of weak Underftanding. *Jones* and *Whitlock* at *Salop* Lent Affifes 7 *Car.* refolved, that the Child is to be fent to the Mother, if fhe be able to maintain it, if not, to the Place where it was fettled ten Years with the Father.

The Order of Sir I. M. *Knight, and* M. D. *Efquire, two of the Juftices of Peace of the* Wilts ff. *County of* C. *and one of Us of the* Quorum, *and both refiding within the Limits where the Parifh Church of* C. *now ftands in the faid County, the* 6th *Day of* Auguft 1725, *according to the Statute in that Cafe made and provided, concerning a male Baftard Child lately born in the faid Parifh, of the Body of* A. B. *fingle Woman, which Baftard Child, ever fince its Birth, hath been, and is ftill chargeable to that Parifh, and likely fo to continue.*

IMprimis, upon the Examination of the faid *K.* duly by us taken, we do find that the faid *T. S.* is charged to have had divers Times bodily and carnal Knowledge of her (between fuch Times) and to be the only Father of the faid Baftard Child, *&c.* and therefore we do adjudge him to be the reputed Father of the faid Child.

We do farther order as followeth : Firft, That the faid *K.* fhall keep her faid Child until it come to eight Years of Age.

Secondly, That the faid *T. S.* upon Notice of this Order, fhall, after fuch Notice, pay into the Hands of one of the Overfeers of the Poor of *W.* (for the Time being) after the Rate of 3 *s.* every Week, to be paid Monthly every Year, towards the Relief of the faid Child, until it comes to eight Years of Age.

Thirdly, That after the faid Child fhall come to Eight, *&c.* that the faid *T. S.* pay to the Overfeers, *&c.* 5 *l.* toward the putting out of the fame Child to be Apprentice, *&c.*

Fourthly, That the faid *T. S.* prefently give good Security to one of the Overfeers, *&c.* to perform this our Order.

Touching the Order of the Juftices next the Place, according to 18 El. 3. *obferve :*

1. **T**HAT if the Party appeal to the next Seffions, and the Juftices there make an Order thereupon, it is final, and cannot be altered by any after Seffions. And this is exprefly refolved in *Pridgion's* Cafe, *Jones* 330. *& Cro. Car.* 1.

2. It muft appear by the Order that the Juftices of Peace making the Order, are the next Juftices of Peace to the Parifh Church where the Child was born, and that one of them is of the *Quorum.* Style 154.

3. It muft appear that the Child was a Baftard, and born in the Parifh, towards whofe Relief Provifion is made thereby, and an Order for that Caufe was quafhed. H. 1652. B. R. *Style, p.* 368.

4. The Payment muft be made to continue fo long Time as the Child fhall be *chargeable to the Parifh,* and if not fo made it is void. *Style* 154. For the Party may take it and keep it himfelf : And where the Mother is able, the Juftices have nothing to do in the Cafe.

5. The Juftices of Peace may adjudge a *reafonable Sum in grofs to be paid to the Parifh* for the Charge of the Woman's Lying in ; and this I have known often ruled good.

6. None elfe can be made chargeable to the Keeping of it, but the reputed Father or Mother, and the Mafter for fuffering it to be begot in his Houfe.

7. It muft be pofitively declared and adjudged who is the reputed Father, and not to repeat what Witneffes fay, or what the Mother faith ; but the Order muft be pofitive and abfolute ; for it is a Judgment in the Cafe, and every Judgment muft be pofitive and certain.

By 3 *Car.* 1. the Juftices of Peace in Seffions have the fame Authority given them, as was given the two next Juftices by 18 *El.* 3. and the fame Rules are to be obferved in Drawing their Order *mutatis mutandis.*

Where a Maid Servant is gotten with Child, and from thence fent to her Place of Birth.

WHereas I. M. fingle Woman, for the Space of   Years now laft paft hath dwelt in the Parifh of *W.* (in the County of *E.*) and being there fettled in Service with *T. B.* of *W.* aforefaid, was gotten with Child, and being fo with Child is now

5 P

fent

fent or conveyed to your Town of *B.* under Colour that fhe was there born, and contrary to Law: Thefe are in his Majefty's Name to charge and command you fafely to convey the faid *I.* to *W.* aforefaid, there to be fet on Work, or otherwife to be provided for according to Law. And that you deliver and leave, or offer to leave, the faid *I.* to and with fome one of the Church-wardens or Overfeers for the Poor of the Parifh of *W.* aforefaid. And hereof fail you not, *&c.*

Note, That fuch Maid Servant cannot be fent from the Place where fhe is (or was laft) in Service to the Place of her Birth, but muft fet herfelf to labour where fhe laft dwelt or ferved, being able of Body: Or being impotent, fhe is to be relieved by the Town where fhe laft dwelt or ferved. See *hic antea,* Tit. *Poor.*

A Warrant for Overfeers to give up their Accounts.

To the High Conftables of the Hundred of, &c.

Cambridge. Overfeers to account.

THESE are in his Majefty's Name to charge and command you, forthwith to give Warning to the Church-wardens, and other the Overfeers of the Poor of every Parifh within your Hundred, that they do perfonally appear before us at *New Market,* at the Sign of the Greyhound there, upon *Tuefday* the Tenth of *June* next coming, by Nine of the Clock in the Forenoon of the fame Day, to yield up, and to make a true and perfect Account in Writing, fubfcribed with their Names or Marks, of all fuch Sums of Money as they have received, or rated and affeffed and not received, for and towards the Relief of the Poor of their feveral Parifhes, and alfo of fuch Stock (to fet their Poor on Work) as is in their Hands, or in the Hands of any their faid Poor ** See what they be in the Title Poor.* to work, and of all * other Things concerning their faid Office: And hereof that you fail not at your and every of your Perils. And farther we require you, that you give Warning to the Petty Conftables of every Town within your faid Hundred, that they or one of them be alfo then and there prefent before us, to infoim and certify us of the Names of fuch other Perfons as are meet and fitting to be Overfeers of the Poor within their feveral Towns, for this Year next enfuing. And hereof fail you not, *&c.*

This Warrant muft be under the Hands and Seals of two Juftices at the leaft, the one of the *Quorum.* Vide Tit. Poor.

A Warrant to new Overfeers to take their Charge.

New Overfeers to take the Charge.

BY virtue of the Statute made in the three and fortieth Year of the Reign of our late Sovereign Lady Queen *Elizabeth,* (intituled, *An Act for the Relief of the Poor*): Thefe are to will and require you whofe Names are here underwritten, that you, together with the Church-wardens of your Parifh for the Time being, do (according to the fame Statute) take order from Time to Time, for this Year to come, for the Setting to Work of the Poor within your Parifh, and for the Raifing of a convenient Stock of fome Ware or Stuff in your Town to that Purpofe; and for the Providing of neceffary Relief for fuch as be lame and impotent amongft you; and for the Placing as Apprentices fuch Children whofe Parents are not able to maintain them: And hereof fee that you fail not at your Perils. Dated under the Hands and Seals of us *I. S.* and *I. D.* two of his Majefty's Juftices of Peace within the faid County of *Cambridge.*

This Warrant muft be under the Hands and Seals of two Juftices. *Vide antea,* Tit. *Poor.*

A Warrant to diftrain fuch as refufe to pay their Rates for the Poor.

(*a*) But firft the Juftices fhall do well to fend their Warrant for the Offenders to make Anfwer to the Complaint, and after to grant their Warrant, if they find Caufe. See *hic cap.* 2. *&* 7.

Or elfe the Juftices may make their Warrant after this Manner.

(*d*) To

(*a*) *To the Church-wardens, and other the Overseers for the Poor within the Parish of* W. *and every of them.*

WHereas we are credibly informed, that the Persons here under named do refuse to Cambridge. pay the Sums of Money here under mentioned, being assessed and rated upon *To distrain for* them severally, for and towards the necessary Relief of the Poor of your said Town, ac- *the Poors Rate.* cording to the Form of the Statute in that Behalf provided: These are therefore in his Majesty's Name to charge and command you, and every of you, forthwith to require and cause the said Persons (so refusing) to be before us, to shew Cause of their said Refusal: And if they or any of them shall refuse to come before us, that then immediately you do levy all and every the said several Sums of Money unpaid, and all the Arrearages thereof, of all and every the said Persons so refusing, by Distress and Sale of the Offender's Goods, you rendring unto the Parties the Overplus that shall remain upon the Sale of the said Goods. And this shall be your sufficient Warrant therein. Dated, &c. *Vide antea,* Tit. *Poor.*

Another.

To the Church-wardens, &c.

THESE are in his Majesty's Name to charge and command you, and every of you, Cambridge. to demand of all and every the Persons here under named, all and every the *Another to di-* several Sums of Money here under severally written, being assessed and rated upon *strain,* &c. them for and towards the necessary Relief of the Poor of your said Town, according to the Form of the Statute in that Behalf provided: And if they or any of them shall refuse to pay the said several Sums of Money so rated upon them, that then you levy the same by Distress and Sale of the Offender's Goods, rendring to the Parties the Overplus that shall remain upon the Sale of their said Goods. And this shall be your sufficient Warrant therein. Dated, &c.

These two last Warrants must also be under the Hands and Seals of two Justices, &c.

(*a*) And in all Cases of Distraining and Sale of an Offender's Goods, and rendring the Party the Overplus, the Appraisement of such Goods should be made by four of the honest Inhabitants of the Parish where such Goods remain and be, according to the Statute of 3 *Jac.* 1. *cap.* 10. in like Case.

(*d*) *A Warrant for a general Search for Rogues.*

To the High Constable of the Hundred of, &c.

THESE are in the King's Majesty's Name to charge and command you, that toge- Cambridge. ther with the petty Constables of the several Towns, Parishes and Hamlets within *Search for* your Hundred, (taking sufficient Assistance out of the said Towns) you make a general *Rogues.* Privy Search within every of the said several Towns, Parishes and Hamlets, upon *Tues-day* at Night next coming, for the finding out and apprehending all Rogues, Vagabonds, and wandring and idle Persons, in or about your said several Towns, Parishes or Hamlets, and that such as shall be found and apprehended, you do cause them to be brought before us the next Day unto *L.* by nine of the Clock. At which Time and Place we *What the Ju-* farther require you, together with the said Petty Constables to appear before us, and *stice shall do* there to give an Account upon Oath, in writing, and under the Hands of the Mini- *with them see* *infra.* ster of every several Parish within your Hundred, what Rogues, Vagabonds, wandring and disordered Persons have been there apprehended, as well in the same Search, as also since the last Meeting that was made for this Purpose, being upon or about the 20 Day of *July* last past. And hereof fail you not, &c.

Note, That all Rogues which shall be brought before the Justices upon such Search *See the Title of* (after Examination of their idle Life taken by the Justices) are either to be whipped by *Rogues.* the Constables of the Town where the Justices sit, or rather the Constables of the Town where the Justices sit may procure some other to inflict the Punishment of Whipping on all such Rogues as are brought thither; and the Constables that brought those Rogues from other Towns are to satisfy such Persons as shall whip them; or else such Rogues are from thence to be sent to the House of Correction, and to be conveyed thither by
the

the Conftables that brought them, and yet at the Charge of the Hundred: Which Services impofed upon the Conftables are fome Caufe of their Neglect; and therefore I have fet down another Method and Precedent, perhaps no lefs ferviceable, which alfo may be performed and done every Month, or at every Meeting of the Juftices: Or if the Juftices cannot, or fhall not meet, yet fuch Warrant may be granted by any Juftice of Peace, as followeth.

Cambridge.
To fearch for Rogues.

THESE are in the King's Majefty's Name to charge and command you, that, together with the Petty Conftables of the feveral Towns, Parifhes and Hamlets within your Hundred, (taking fufficient Affiftance out of the faid Towns) you do make a general privy Search within every of the faid feveral Towns, Parifhes and Hamlets, upon *Thurf-day* at Night next coming, for the finding out and apprehending all Rogues, Vagabonds, and wandring and idle Perfons, in or about your faid feveral Towns; and that fuch as fhall be found and apprehended, you do caufe them to be punifhed in every feveral Town or Parifh where they fhall be fo apprehended, by the petty Conftables of every feveral Parifh refpectively, and by them alfo farther to be conveyed according to the Statute: And if any of the faid Rogues fhall appear to be dangerous or incorrigible, that then you caufe fuch to be brought before me, or any other of his Majefty's Juftices of the Peace of this Divifion, to be farther dealt withal according to the Statute in fuch Cafes provided. Dated, &c.

38 El. 8.
1 Jac. 1. 7.
P. Vag. 4.

Afterwards any one of thefe Juftices may take the Examination of, or Proof againft fuch dangerous Rogue, and finding that he hath offered any Violence, or ufed any threatning Speeches, or other like Mifdemeanor towards any Perfon; or that he hath been formerly punifhed, and fent home; or that he affirms untruly where he was born, or will not be known, or knows not where he was born or laft dwelt; (for then it is apparent that he hath been and continued a Rogue of a long Time) in every fuch Cafe the Juftice may then join with any other Juftice of Peace of that Limit, being of the *Quorum,* and commit fuch Rogue to the Houfe of Correction or Gaol, as an incorrigible Rogue, although the faid two Juftices fhall not meet together about it.

See the Statute 13 Geo. 2. cap. 24. infra Chap. 196.

A Warrant for a fugitive Servant.

To the Sheriff of, &c.

Servant departing from his Mafter.

WHereas I. E. being lawfully retained in Service with N. A. of, &c. is departed from his faid Mafter's Service before the End of his Term, without his Mafter's Leave, (or without any reafonable Caufe) contrary to the Laws and Statutes of this Realm in this Behalf provided: Thefe are therefore to command you, and every of you, that you, or fome one of you, do apprehend the faid I. E. and bring him before me, or fome other Juftice of Peace, &c.) to find fufficient Sureties, well and faithfully to ferve his faid Mafter, according to the Covenant between them made: And if he fhall refufe thus to do, that then you caufe him to be conveyed fafely to the common Gaol, &c. as before, in a Warrant for the Peace). Given under the Hand of me T. S. one of his Majefty's Juftices of Peace within the faid County.

Or thus; That the faid I. E. to his faid Mafter to ferve him again you do caufe to be delivered: And if that to do he fhall refufe, that then you caufe him to be conveyed to the Gaol, &c.

A Warrant for one refufing to ferve.

Cambridge.
Servant re-fufing to ferve.
Cromp. 238.

MIchael Dalton Efquire, one of the Mafters of the Court of Chancery, and one of the Juftices, &c. to R. L. Bailiff of S. in the County aforefaid, Greeting: On the Behalf of our faid Lord the King, I command you that you attach R. A. of S. aforefaid, Labourer; fo that you have him before me, or my Companions Juftices of our faid Lord the King, affigned to keep the Peace in the faid County, and alfo to hear and determine divers Felonies, Trefpaffes, and other Mifdeeds committed in the faid County, at the next General Seffions of the Peace to be held in the County aforefaid, to anfwer as well to our faid Lord the King, as to B. C. of A. &c. Yeoman, wherefore he the faid R. A. altho' he was often by the aforefaid B. C. requefted to ferve him in Service fit for his Station, yet hath altogether refufed

4

fufed to ferve him the faid *B. C.* in Contempt of our faid Lord the King, and to the grievous Damage of him the faid *B. C.* and againſt the Form of the Statute of Servants lately made and provided: And have you there this Warrant.   Witneſs, *&c.*

And yet ſee the Statute 5 *El. cap.* 4. whereby the Departure of a Servant, and refuſing to ſerve, *&c.* are referred to two Juſtices of Peace, by them to be firſt examined, and then the Offenders to be committed if they be faulty therein.   See *antea,* Tit. *Labourers* and *Warrants.*

For *Alehouſe-keepers to renew their Recognizances.*

JOHN St. *George* Eſquire, one of his Majeſty's Juſtices, *&c.* Theſe are in his Majeſty's Name to require you, to direct your Precepts to every *Cambridge.* petty Conſtable within your Hundred, requiring them, that they warn all Alehouſe- *Alehouſe-* keepers and Victuallers in their ſeveral Towns within your ſaid Hundred, to be and per- *keepers to re-* ſonally appear before us at *Linton* upon *Thurſday, &c.* then and thither bringing with them *cognizances.* their former Licences: And farther, that every of them bring with them a Certificate of their Fitneſs and honeſt Behaviour, to keep their Alehouſes and Victualling-houſes, un- der the Hands of four, at the leaſt, of the moſt ſubſtantial Inhabitants of the Pariſhes where they ſo keep or dwell.   And hereof fail you not, *&c.*

A Warrant for the *ſuppreſſing of an Alehouſe.*

TAlbot *Pepis* and *Iſaac Barrow* Eſquires, two of his Majeſty's Juſtices of Peace for *Alehouſe to* the ſaid County of *Cambridge,* to the Conſtables of *B.* and either of them, Greet- *ſuppreſs.* ing.   Whereas we are credibly informed, that *R. D.* of your Town, Victualler, is him- ſelf a Man of evil Behaviour, and beſides doth ſuffer Diſorders to be kept in his Houſe, contrary to the Laws and Statutes of this Realm: Theſe are therefore to will and command you forthwith to go to the Houſe of the ſaid *R. D.* and to charge him to ſurceaſe from keeping any longer any Alehouſe, or Tippling-Houſe, and from ſelling of Ale or Beer at his Peril ; and withal that you cauſe his Sign to be pulled down.   Hereof fail you not, as you and either of you will anſwer to the contrary at your Peril.   Given under our Hands and Seals at *B.* the 20th Day of *Auguſt,* and in the Year of our Lord *George,* &c.

A Warrant to levy *Money forfeited by Alehouſe-haunters.*

JOhn Gill Eſq; one of his Majeſty's Juſtices of the Peace for the ſaid County of *Cam-* *Cambridge.* *bridge,* to the Conſtables and Church-wardens of the Pariſh of *W.* and to every of *Alehouſe* them, Greeting.   Whereas it hath been duly proved before me, according to the Statute *Haunters.* in that Behalf provided, that all and every the Perſons hereunder named, being Inhabi- tants within your Pariſh of *W.* upon the twelfth Day of this inſtant Month of *November,* have been and continued drinking and tippling in the Houſe of *G. IV.* of your ſaid Town ✻ ✻ *Or Alehouſe-* (Inn-keeper) contrary to the Form of the ſaid Statute : Theſe are therefore in his Ma- *keeper.* jeſty's Name to charge and command you, and every of you, forthwith to levy by Di- ſtreſs and Sale of the Goods of every the ſaid Perſons hereunder named, the Sum of three Shillings and four Pence a-piece, if they ſhall refuſe or neglect forthwith to pay the ſame; (which ſeveral Forfeitures ſhall be beſtowed and employed by you to the Uſe of the Poor of your ſaid Pariſh) and that you render to every of the ſaid Offenders the Overplus that ſhall remain upon your Sale of their ſaid Goods: And if the ſaid Offenders, or any of them, ſhall refuſe or neglect to pay their ſaid ſeveral Forfeitures, and that you can find no ſufficient Diſtreſs whereon to levy the ſame, that then you the Conſtables, or one of you, ſhall commit every ſuch Offender or Offenders (refuſing or neglecting to pay the ſaid Sum or Forfeiture, and not having ſufficient whereon to be diſtrained for the ſame) to the Stocks, there to remain by the Space of four Hours.   And this ſhall be your ſufficient Warrant herein.   Dated, *&c.*

But before the Juſtice of Peace ſhall grant theſe two laſt Warrants, or the like, he ſhall do well firſt to ſend for the Offenders, and to examine them of the Offence; *&c.*   See *hic antea.*

Againſt

Against Alehouse-keepers.

ALSO a Warrant, (like unto the laſt) may be made to ·levy the Forfeiture of Inn-keepers or Alehouſe-keepers, for ſuffering Townſmen or others to continue drinking in their Houſe, ·ſaving that the Diſtreſs taken of ſuch Inn-keepers and Alehouſe-keepers is not to be ſold till after ſix Days; and then for Default of Satisfaction, the ſame are preſently to be appriſed and ſold, and therefore ſuch Warrant muſt herein be made accordingly. See 1 *Jac.* 1. *cap.* 9. P. 7, 8.

A Warrant for the Removing of a Petty Conſtable, and for the Swearing of another.

To remove a Petty Conſtable.

GEORGE, by the Grace of God, &c. to the Sheriff of *Cambridge,* and to the Chief Conſtable of the Hundred of *R.* and to each of them, Greeting : Whereas for certain Cauſes us thereunto moving, we have cauſed *W. P.* and *R. S.* Under-Conſtables of the Towns *C.* and *K.* to be removed and diſcharged : We therefore injoin and command you, and each of you, jointly and ſeverally, that you cauſe *J. F.* and *R. M.* to ſwear well and truly to exerciſe and execute all and every Thing and Things incumbent on the ſaid Office, as they will thereof anſwer unto us; in like Manner injoining the ſaid *W. P.* and *R. S.* that they noways intermeddle in the further exerciſing and executing of the ſaid Office, until they have another Command from us. And that whatever you ſhall do therein, you certify to our Juſtices aſſigned to keep our Peace, at the next General Seſſions of the Peace, to be held at *C.* for the ſaid County, then and there returning this our Precept. Witneſs *Robert Lawrence,* Eſq; one of our Juſtices of the Peace aforeſaid. Dated, &c.

Lam. yy. 3. *'Tis a very unuſual Precedent to begin in the Name of the King, and the Teſte to be in the Name of a Juſtice, &c.*

You ſhall find this former Precedent in M. *Lamb.* But upon ſuch Warrant, *quære* who ſhall give the Oath to the new Conſtables, whether the High Sheriff, or High Conſtable that ſhall execute ſuch Warrant, or the Juſtice of Peace that granted out ſuch Warrant.

But for this Authority of removing Petty Conſtables, and of chuſing and ſwearing new, it is reputed properly to belong to the Leet, (it being one of the ancienteſt Courts in the Realm. *Br. Leet* 14). And if the new Elect be not preſent at the Leet to take his Oath accordingly, then upon Certificate or Notice thereof to any Juſtice of Peace of that County, the Juſtice doth uſe to ſend his Warrant for the Parties ſo choſen, and to give them their Oath.

Alſo in Default of the Leet, or otherwiſe, where there ſhall be juſt Cauſe to remove a Petty Conſtable for his Inſufficiency, or for any Miſdemeanor, or other, every Juſtice of Peace, *ex Officio,* may remove the old Conſtables, and may chuſe and ſwear new : Which alſo we ſee warranted by common Experience. See *Lamb.* of the Duties of Conſtables, *Page* 19.

And I have ſeen ſome Precedents to ſuch Purpoſe, as followeth.

To our loving Friend A. B. of W. Yeoman.

* If they were not choſen at the Leet, this Clauſe is to be left out.

THESE are in his Majeſty's Name to charge and command you to come before us, or ſome other Juſtice of Peace of this County, to take the Oath of a Conſtable, to ſerve his Majeſty within the Town of *W.* (* according to the Choice made of you by the Jury at the laſt Leet holden in your Town) : And hereof fail you not. Dated under the Hands of *M. N.* and *N. O.* Eſquires, two of his Majeſty's Juſtices of Peace, &c.

The Form of the Oath concerning the Office of a Conſtable.

YOU ſhall ſwear, that you ſhall well and truly ſerve our Sovereign Lord the King in the Office of a Conſtable. You ſhall ſee and cauſe his Majeſty's Peace to be well and duly kept and preſerved, according to your Power. You ſhall arreſt all ſuch Perſons as in your Sight and Preſence ſhall ride or go armed offenſively, or ſhall commit or make any Riot, Affray, or other Breach of his Majeſty's Peace. You ſhall do your beſt Endeavour, upon Complaint to you made, to apprehend all Felons, Barrators and Rioters, or Perſons riotouſly aſſembled : And if any ſuch Offenders ſhall make Reſiſtance with Force, you ſhall levy Hue and Cry, and ſhall purſue them until they be taken. You ſhall do your beſt Endeavour that the Watch in and about your Town be duly kept for

the apprehending of Rogues, Vagabonds, Night-Walkers, Eves-Droppers, and other fufpected Perfons, and of fuch as go armed, and the like: And that Hue and Cry be duly
raifed and purfued, according to the Statute of *Winchefter,* againft Murderers, Thieves,
and other Felons: And that the Statutes made for the Punifhment of Rogues and Vagabonds, and fuch other idle Perfons, coming within your Bounds and Limits, be duly put
in Execution. You fhall have a watchful Eye to fuch Perfons as fhall maintain or keep
any common Houfe or Place where any unlawful Crime is or fhall be ufed: As alfo to
fuch as fhall frequent or ufe fuch Places, or fhall ufe or exercife any unlawful Games
there or elfewhere, contrary to the Statutes. At your Affizes, Seffions of the Peace, or
Leet, you fhall prefent all and every the Offences done contrary to the Statutes made
(1 *Jac.* 1. 4. and 21 *Jac.* 1.) to reftrain the inordinate Haunting and Tippling in
Inns, Alehoufes, and other Victualling Houfes, and for repreffing of Drunkennefs. You
fhall there likewife true Prefentment make of all Blood-fheddings, Affrays, Out-cries
Refcous, and other Offences committed or done againft the King's Majefty's Peace within your Limits. You fhall once every Day during your Office prefent at the Quarter-
Seffions, all Popifh Recufants within your Parifh, and their Children above nine, and
their Servants, (*fc.* their monthly Abfence from the Church) 3 *Jac.* 1. 4. And you
fhall have a Care for the Maintenance of Archery according to the Statute. You fhall
well and duly execute all Precepts and Warrants to you directed from the Juftices of Peace
of this County, or higher Officers. You fhall be aiding to your Neighbours againft unlawful Purveyances. In the Time of Hay or Corn Harveft (upon Requeft) you fhall
caufe all Perfons meet to ferve by the Day for the Mowing, Reaping, or getting in of
Corn or Hay. You fhall in *Eafter* Week caufe your Parifhioners to chufe Surveyors for
the Mending of the Highways in your Parifh. You fhall have a Care that the Malt made
or put to Sale in your Town, be well and fufficiently made, trodden, formed and dreffed.
And you fhall well and duly according to your Knowledge, Power and Ability, do and
execute all other Things belonging to the Office of a Conftable, fo long as you fhall continue in this Office. *So help you God.*

 This Oath I have fet down the more largely, whereby to fhew the principal Matters
whereof the Conftables are chiefly to have Care.

C H A P. CLXXV.

The Form of a Superfedeas *by a* Juftice *of Peace.*

Richard Love Doctor of Divinity, and Vice-chancellor of the Univerfity of *Cambridge,* Cambridge.
one of the Juftices of Peace of our Sovereign Lord the King's Majefty within the
County of *Cambridge,* to the Sheriff, Bailiffs, Conftables, and other the faithful Minifters of our Sovereign Lord within the faid County, and to every of them, fendeth Greeting. Forafmuch as *A. B.* of, *&c.* Yeoman, hath perfonally come before me at *W.* &c. and
found fufficient Surety, that * is to fay, *C. D.* and *E. F.* &c. Yeomen, either of the * *The* Super-
which hath undertaken for the faid *A. B.* under the Pain of 20 *l.* and he the faid *A. B.* *fedeas is good,*
hath undertaken for himfelf under the Pain of 40 *l.* that he the faid *A. B.* fhall well and *though it name*
truly keep the Peace towards our Sovereign Lord and all his liege People, and efpecially to- *Sureties nor*
wards *G. H.* of, *&c.* Yeoman, and alfo that he fhall perfonally appear before the *the Sum.*
Juftices of the Peace of our faid Sovereign Lord, at the next general Seffions of the Peace
to be holden for this County of *Cambridge.* Therefore on the Behalf of our Sovereign
Lord I command you and every of you, that you utterly forbear and furceafe to arreft,
take, imprifon, or otherwife by any Means (for the faid Occafion) to moleft the faid
A. B. and if you have (for the faid Occafion, and none other) taken or imprifoned him,
that then you do caufe him to be delivered and fet at Liberty without further Delay.
Given at *Cambridge* aforefaid, under my Seal, this laft Day of *July,* &c.

Otherwife.

Henry Bing Serjeant at Law, one of the Juftices of our Lord the King, *&c.* to the
Sheriff, and all and fingular the Bailiffs, Minifters, and Lieges of the faid Lord the
King in the fame County, and to every of them, Greeting: Whereas *J. S.* hath found
before me fufficient Surety of the Peace, and of his good Behaviour, toward our faid Lord
the

the King, and efpecially towards *W. T.* Therefore on the Behalf of our faid Lord the King, I order and command you and every of you, firmly injoining, that you altogether

Superfedeas. furceafe to take or arreft the faid *J. S.* for the finding fuch Security of the Peace: And if you have taken or imprifoned the faid *J. S.* on the faid Occafion, then you do caufe him to be delivered, if he be detained on that Occafion, and none other. Witnefs, &c.

If the Prifoner be in the Gaol, fee another Form, *hic poftea,* Tit. *Liberate.*

Note, that fuch *Superfedeas* is good, though it name neither the Sureties nor the Sums wherein they are bound: But yet it is the better Form to exprefs them both, for then if it fhall appear that the Sureties are not fufficient Men, or not bound in fufficient Sums, better Sureties may be taken. And accordingly all the *Superfedeas's* iffuing out of the Chancery, King's Bench, and Court of Common Pleas, do rehearfe the Names of the Sureties and the Sums: And thofe Things which the higher Courts do ufe, are the Rules and Orders for others to follow, &c. 2 *H.* 7. *f.* 1. *Fitz. Superfedeas* 4.

The Form of a Superfedeas (*by a Juftice of Peace*) *upon a Writ of* Supplicavit *againft an Infant.*

Cambridge. Superfedeas *upon a Supplicavit.*

S C. Doctor of Divinity, one of the Juftices of our Lord the King affigned to keep the Peace in the faid County, to the Sheriff of the faid County, and to all and fingular the Bailiffs, Conftables and other Minifters of our faid Lord the King, as well within Liberties as without, in the faid Connty, Greeting. Know ye, that I have received a Writ of our faid Lord the King, in thefe Words, *George,* &c. (*reciting here all the Writ* verbatim)

* Manucepe- runt.

and becaufe *J. B.* of, &c. *J. S.* of, &c. and the aforefaid *C. A.* have perfonally appeared before me the faid *S. C.* and the faid *J. B.* and *J. S.* have undertaken for * the faid *C. A.* who

† Manucaptor.

is within the Age of twenty-one Years, to wit, each Surety † aforefaid, in 20 *l.* which they have acknowledged themfelves to owe to our faid Lord the King, and have granted to be levied of their Lands and Tenements, Goods and Chattels, to the Ufe of our faid Lord the King, to wit, that the faid *C. A.* fhall not do, nor caufe to be done any Damage or Evil to any of the People of our faid Lord the King, in their Bodies, or in burning of their Houfes: Therefore on the Behalf of our faid Lord the King, I command you and every of you, that you altogether furceafe or caufe to be furceafed from the reftraining or attaching the faid *C. A.* for the finding Security of the Peace by him to be kept toward our faid Lord the King, and all his People, or any of his faid People. And if you have taken, or commanded to be taken before you or any of you, him the faid *C. A.* on the faid Occafion, and have detained him in the Prifon of our faid Lord the King under your Cuftody, that then you or one of you caufe him to be delivered from the Prifon in which he is detained, without Delay. Witnefs me the faid *S. C.* &c.

Otherwife.

Cambridge.

H S. Doctor of Divinity, &c. one of the Juftices, &c. to the Sheriff, &c. Greeting, Be it known unto you, that I have received a Command (or Writ) of our Lord the King, in thefe Words, *George,* &c. (*reciting all the Writ*) And becaufe *J. B.* of, &c. and *J. S.* of, &c. and the faid *T. C.* have appeared perfonally before me the faid *H. S.* and the faid *J. B.* and *J. S.* have undertaken for the faid *T. C.* each Surety under the Penalty of 20 *l.* and the faid *T. C.* hath undertaken for himfelf, under the Penalty of 40 *l.* to be levied on their Lands and Chattels, to the Ufe of our faid Lord the King, that the faid *C. A.* fhall not, &c. as before.

A Superfedeas *for the Good Behaviour.*

Superfedeas *for the Good Behaviour.* Crom. 237.

NOTE, that upon good Sureties taken for the Good Behaviour, a *Superfedeas* of the Good Behaviour may be granted as for the Peace, *mutatis mutandis.*

Note alfo, that a *Superfedeas de Capias indictatum de Tranfgreffion',* and fo of an *Exigent,* may be granted by the Juftice of Peace out of Seffions: For otherwife it were mifchievous for the Party, as well by Reafon of his Imprifonment, as alfo for that he may be out-lawed before the Seffions, if the Juftice of Peace might not take Sureties of him for his Appearance; and all is but to anfwer to the Indictment.

Crom. 235. H.w 275. Lib Intr. 601. *l. m.* 508.

And Mr. *Crompton* is of Opinion, that thefe may be granted by any one Juftice of Peace; with whom agreeth the *Book of Entries.* But Mr. *Lambard* thinketh it not in the Power of any one Juftice of Peace to grant fuch *Superfedeas* at this Day, but that it muſt be done by two Juſtices at the leaſt, and the one being of the *Quorum*; neverthelefs for that I find the old Precedents to run in the Name of one Juſtice of Peace alone, I have drawn thefe accordingly, perfuading notwithſtanding the Joining of two Juſtices herein, and the one of the *Quorum*, if they may conveniently.

A Superfedeas *of one indicted of Trefpafs.*

T. B. &c. one of the Juſtices, &c. to the Sheriff, &c. Greeting. Forafmuch as Cambridge. C. D. of A. Yeoman, hath come before me, and hath found fufficient Sureties Superfedeas *to* to be before the Juſtices of our faid Lord the King affigned to keep the Peace in the faid *a* Capias *upon* County, as alfo to hear and determine divers Felonies, &c. at the next General Seſſions of *for a Trefpafs.* the Peace to be held at *C.* in the faid County, to anſwer to our faid Lord the King of certain Trefpaſſes, Contempts, and Offences of which he is indicted. Therefore on the Behalf of our faid Lord the King I command you, that you altogether forbear to take or impriſon, or otherwife to moleſt the faid *C. D.* and if you have taken him for this Caufe and none other, that then you caufe him to be delivered without further Delay. Witneſs, &c.

Otherwife ; *for him who hath found Pledges for a Fine.*

T. W. one of the Juſtices, &c. to the Sheriff, and all and fingular the Bailiffs, Con- Cambridge. ſtables, &c. Greeting. Altho' lately by a Writ (or Precept) of our faid Lord the *A* Superfedeas King, it was commanded you or one of you, that you fhould take, or that one of you *upon putting in* fhould take *A. B.* of *S.* in the faid County Yeoman, if he was found within the fame, a *Fine.* and him fafely keep, fo that you or one of you fhould have his Body before the Keepers Crom. 233. of the Peace, and Juſtices of our faid Lord the King affigned to keep the Peace, as alfo to hear and determine divers Felonies, &c. in the faid County, at *Cambridge* (on fuch a Day) to anfwer to our faid Lord the King, of a Contempt and Trefpafs of which he is indicted before the faid Juſtices. Which faid *A. B.* hath come before me, and hath found fufficient Pledges for making his Fine with our faid Lord the King for the Premiſſes: Therefore on the Behalf of our faid Lord the King, I command you jointly and feverally, that you altogether furceafe from any farther executing of the faid Writ. And if you have taken the faid *A. B.* on the faid Occaſion and none other, and have detained him in the Perfon of our faid Lord the King, that then without Delay you or one of you caufe him to be delivered from the fame. And you or one of you have this Precept at the Seſſions aforefaid. Given, &c.

A Superfedeas *of a* Capias *for a Fine.*

J. St. G. Efq; one of the Juſtices, &c. to the Sheriff, &c. Greeting. Forafmuch as Cambridge. C. D. of A. in the faid County Yeoman, hath come before me, and hath found Crom. 234. fufficient Sureties to be at the next General Seſſions of the Peace to be holden in the faid County, to make Fine with our faid Lord the King, for certain Trefpaſſes, Contempts and Offences, of which he is indicted : Therefore I command you, that you altogether furceafe to take, impriſon, or otherwife moleſt the faid *C. D.* on the faid Occaſion. And have you there this Precept. Witneſs, &c.

Superfedeas of a Capias *of one indicted for Felony.*

T. P. Efq; one of the Juſtices of our Lord the King, &c. To the Sheriff, and all Cambridge. and fingular the Bailiffs, Conſtables, &c. Greeting : Forafmuch as *A. B.* of *C.* in Crom. 234. the faid County, Hufbandman, hath come before me, and hath found fufficient Security to be before the Juſtices, &c. affigned to keep the Peace, &c. as alfo to hear and determine divers Felonies, &c. at the next general Seſſions of the Peace to be held in the faid County to anfwer to our faid Lord the King, of divers Felonies and Trefpaſſes of which he is indicted before them. Therefore on the Behalf of our faid Lord the King, I command you and every of you, that you altogether furceafe to take the faid *A. B.* for that Caufe, and if you have taken or impriſoned him on that occaſion and no other, that then you caufe him to be delivered without delay. Given, &c.

A Superfedeas of an Exigent of Felony.

Cambridge.
Cromp. 234.

GEORGE, &c. To the Sheriff, &c. Greeting: Forafmuch as *C. D.* of *A.* in your County, Yeoman, hath come before *E. F.* and hath found fufficient Sureties to be before the Keepers of our Peace, and our Juftices affigned, &c. at the general Seffions of our Peace, &c. to be held (fuch a Day) to anfwer to us of certain Felonies of which he is indicted. Therefore we command you that you altogether furceafe from demanding the aforefaid *C. D.* at any your County Court or imprifoning him, or otherwife molefting him on that occafion. And have you there this Writ. Witnefs *William Marche* at *H.* &c.

A Superfedeas to deliver a Prifoner taken for a Trefpafs or the like.

M. D. Efq; one of the Juftices, &c. To the Conftables of the Town of *B.* and alfo to the Keeper of the Gaol of our faid Lord the King in the faid County Greeting: Forafmuch as *W. C.* of *B.* Labourer, hath come before me, and found fufficient Surety to be before the Juftices of our faid Lord the King, at the next general Seffions of the Peace to be held in the faid County, to anfwer as well to our Lord the King as to *B. C.* of certain Trefpaffes or Contempts, &c. by him the faid *W. C.* perpetrated. Therefore I command you and every of you that you caufe the faid *W. C.* to be delivered out of your Cuftody, and that without delay in the mean Time you fuperfede from my Mandate thereupon directed. And this my Mandate fhall be to you and every of you a fufficient Warrant. Given, &c.

C H A P. CLXXVI.

Recognizance.

A fingle Recognizance taken before Juftices of the Peace.

Cambridge.
Single Recogni-
zance.

BE it remembered, that upon the   Day of *February* in the   Year of the Reign of our Sovereign Lord, &c. *J. S.* of *B.* in the County of *C.* Yeoman, *W. S.* of the fame Place, Weaver, and *R. D.* of *S.* in the faid County, Taylor, came before *M. D.* and *J. B.* Efquires, Juftices of our faid Lord the King, affigned to keep the Peace in the faid County of *C.* and acknowledged themfelves to owe to our faid Lord the King, to wit, each of the faid Sureties five Pounds, and the faid *J. S.* ten Pounds of good and lawful Money of *Great Britain,* to be paid to our faid Lord the King on the Feaft of the Purification of the bleffed Virgin *Mary* next enfuing after the Date of thefe Prefents, and unlefs they fhall fo do, they have granted for themfelves, their Heirs, Executors and Adminiftrators by thefe Prefents, that the faid feveral Sums fhall be levied and recovered of the Manors, Lands, Tenements, Goods, Chattels and Hereditaments of the faid *J. S. W. S.* and *R. D.* their Heirs, Executors and Affigns, wherever they fhall be found. Given, &c.

Another fingle Recognizance.

Another fingle
Recognizance,
and the moft
ufual.

BE it remembered, That on the twentieth Day of *January* in the   Year of the Reign, &c. *D. E.* of *B.* in the faid County, Yeoman, perfonally came before me *M. D.* Efq; one of the Juftices of the faid Lord the King, affigned to keep the Peace in the faid County, and acknowledged himfelf to be owing to the faid Lord the King, ten Pounds of good and lawful Money of *Great Britain,* to be made and levied of his Goods and Chattels, Lands and Tenements, to the Ufe of the faid Lord the King, his Heirs and Succeffors, if he fail in the Condition indorfed.

Otherwife.

Otherwise.

B E it remembered, That on the tenth Day of *December* of the ⟨ ⟩ Year of the Cambridge.
Reign, *&c. T. H.* of *W.* in the faid County, Yeoman, and *J. S.* of the fame *Another with*
Town and County, Hufbandman, came before me *M. C.* one of the Juftices affigned, *&c. two Sureties,*
and did undertake and each of them feverally did undertake under the Penalty of five Pounds *and this is the*
of lawful Money of *Great Britain,* for *W. St.* of *W.* aforefaid, † and the faid *W. St.* *ufual Form.*
did undertake for himfelf under the Penalty of ten Pounds of the like Money ; which
feveral Sums they and each of them did acknowledge himfelf to owe to the faid Lord the
King, to be made and levied of their Lands Tenements, Goods and Chattels, if the
faid *W. St.* fhall fail in performing the * Condition within written. * *See the Con-*
dition on the
other Side, and this is now the Common Practice.

If the Party to be bound be within Age, then he fhall be bound by Sureties only, *Infant.*
(but he himfelf fhall not be bound) and then fhall the Recognizance be *ut fupra* to this
Mark, † and then as followeth :

Who is under the Age of 21 Years, which feveral Sums they did acknowledge, and
each of them as aforefaid, did acknowledge himfelf to owe, *&c.* as above.

A Recognizance for the Peace.

B E it remembred, That on the ⟨ ⟩ Day of ⟨ ⟩ in the ⟨ ⟩ Year of the *Recognizance*
Reign, *&c. R. P.* of *E.* in the faid County, Yeoman, did come perfonally before *for the Peace*
me *T. T.* Efq; one of the Juftices affigned, *&c.* and did undertake for himfelf, under the *dition in it.*
Penalty of twenty Pounds, and *H. J.* of *L.* in the faid County, Yeoman, and *N. A.*
of, *&c.* and *P. Q.* of *&c.* Hufbandman, then and there likewife did perfonally come and
did undertake for the faid *R. P.* to wit, each of them feverally under the Penalty of one
hundred Shillings, that the faid *R. P.* fhall perfonally appear before the Juftices of the
Peace of the faid Lord the King, at the next general Seffions of the Peace to be held
for the faid County, to do and receive that which by the Court fhall be then and there
injoined him, and that he in the mean Time fhall keep the Peace of our faid Lord the
King towards our Lord the King himfelf and all his People, and efpecially towards
M. N. of *A.* aforefaid, Yeoman, that he fhall not do nor procure to be done, any
corporal Damage or Evil or any Grievance to the faid *M. N.* or to any of the People
of our faid Lord the King, which may any way be to the Hurt or Difturbance of the
Peace of our faid Lord the King or of the aforefaid *M.* Which Sum of twenty Pounds Lib.Intr. 453.
the aforefaid *R. P.* and each and every of the faid Sureties the faid feveral Sums of one
hundred Shillings, have acknowledged themfelves to owe to the faid Lord the King,
to be made and levied of the Lands and Tenements, Goods and Chattels of each and
every of them into whofe Hands foever they fhall come, to the Ufe of our faid Lord
the King, if it fhall happen that the faid *R. P.* fhall break the Premiffes in any Thing,
and be thereof lawfully convicted. In Witnefs whereof I the faid *T. T.* have fet my
Seal. Given, *&c.*

And if the Juftice fhall only fubfcribe his Name to the Recognizance without his Seal,
it is well enough ; and fo is the ufual Courfe and Form with us, and that in either of
thefe Sorts, *fc. acknowledged before me T. T.* or only to fubfcribe the Juftice's Name
thus, *T. T.*

Or thus for the Peace.

B E it remembered, That the ⟨ ⟩ Day of, *&c. A. B.* of *&c.* and *W. D.* of *&c.* did Cambridge.
come before me *J. L.* Efq; one of the Juftices, *&c.* and did undertake for *J. S.* *For the Peace.*
late of *L. &c.* that he fhall perfonally appear before me the faid *J. L.* and my Com- Lamb. 106.
panions Juftices of the Peace of our Lord the King at the next general Seffions, *&c.*
and that he the faid *J. S.* in the mean Time fhall keep the Peace towards all the People of our Lord the King, and efpecially towards *R. B. &c.* to wit, each of the faid
Sureties under the Penalty of twenty Pounds, and the faid *J. S.* did undertake for himfelf
under the Penalty of forty Pounds, which Sum of forty Pounds the faid *J. S.* and
. each

each of the faid Sureties the faid Sum of twenty Pounds did acknowledge themfelves to owe to, &c.

And this may be well done alfo by a fingle Recognizance *ut fupra*, with a Condition added or indorfed for the Keeping of the Peace, and for the Day and Place in the Party's Appearance at the Quarter-Seffions, as followeth.

A Condition to keep the Peace.

The Condition of a Recognizance for the Peace.

THE Condition of this Recognizance is fuch, That if the within bounden *I. S.* fhall perfonally appear before the Juftices of our faid Sovereign Lord the King at the next general Seffions of the Peace, to be holden in the faid County of *Cambridge*, to anfwer to fuch Matters as fhall be objected againft him by *R. B.* within named, to do and receive that which by the Court fhall be then and there injoined him, and that he in the mean Time do keep the Peace of our Sovereign Lord the King, towards the King's Majefty and all his Liege People, and efpecially towards the faid *R. B.* of *C.* aforefaid, Yeoman : That then, &c.

A Recognizance for the Good Behaviour.

Recognizance for the good Behaviour.

BE it remembered, That on the　　　Day, &c. in the　　　Year of the Reign, &c. *R. L.* of, &c. and *H. C.* and *J. S.* of the fame, &c. in their proper Perfons did come before us *J. B.* and *R. H.* Efquires, Juftices, &c. And the faid *H. C.* and *J. S.* did undertake for the faid *R. G.* and the faid *R. G.* then did undertake for himfelf, that the faid *R. G.* fhall perfonally appear before the Juftices of the faid Lord the King, affigned,

* See the Recognizance for the Peace.

&c. at the next general * Seffions, &c. And that he in the mean Time fhall bear himfelf well towards our Lord the King and all his People, and efpecially towards *J. B.* of *C.* &c. to wit, That he fhall not do nor caufe to be done by himfelf nor by others, any Damage or Grievance to the faid *J. B.* or to any of the King's People in their Bodies, by Waylaying, Affaults, or in any other Manner, which may be to the Hurt or Difturbance of the Peace of our faid Lord the King in any wife ; to wit, each of the faid *H. C.* and *J. S.* under the Penalty of one hundred Pounds, and the faid *R. G.* under the Penalty of two hundred Pounds, which feveral Sums of one hundred Pounds each

Lib. Intr. 463.

of them the faid *H. C.* and *J. S.* by themfelves as aforefaid, and the faid *R. C.* the faid Sum of two hundred Pounds for himfelf, did acknowledge themfelves to owe to the faid Lord the King, to be made and levied of their and each of their Lands and Tenements, Goods and Chattels, to the Ufe of the faid Lord the King, if it happens that the faid *R. G.* fhall make Default in any of the Premiffes, and fhall be thereof lawfully convicted. Given, &c.

Or thus for the Good Behaviour.

Cambridge.
Another for the Good Behaviour.

BE it remembered, That on the　　　Day of　　　in the　　　Year of the Reign, &c. *N. G.* of, &c. did perfonally come before us *J. B.* and *R. H.* Efqs, Juftices of our faid Lord the King, affigned, &c. and did undertake for himfelf under the Penalty of two hundred Pounds, and *H. C.* and *J. S.* of the fame, &c. likewife did perfonally come and undertake for the faid *N. G.* to wit, each of them feverally, under the Penalty of one hundred Pounds, that the faid *N. G.* fhall perfonally appear before the Juftices, &c. at the next general Seffions of the Peace to be held in the faid County, to do and receive what fhall be then and there injoined him by the Court : And that in the mean Time he fhall well bear himfelf (or be of good Behaviour) towards our Lord the King and all his People, and efpecially towards *J. B.* of *C.* &c. to wit, that he fhall not do nor caufe to be done, by himfelf nor by others, any Damage or Grievance to the faid *J. B.* or to any of the People of the Lord the King unto their Bodies, by Waylaying, Affaults, or any other Means, which may be to the Breach or Difturbance of the Peace of the faid Lord the King ; which feveral Sums, &c. as above.

Or by a Recognizance, with this Condition subscribed or indorsed.

THE Condition of this Recognizance is such, That if the above bounden *R. G.* shall *Condition of a Recognizance.* personally appear before the Justices of our Sovereign Lord the King at the next General Sessions of the Peace to be holden in the County of *C.* to do and receive that which by the Court shall be then and there injoined him, and that in the mean Time he be of Good Behaviour, and do keep the Peace of our said Sovereign Lord the King, towards his Majesty and all his Liege People, that then, *&c.*

Or thus :

THE Condition of the said Recognizance is, That if the said *N. G.* shall for the *Another Condition.* Future be of Good Behaviour, and shall keep the Peace toward our said Lord the King, and all his People, that then the said Recognizance shall be void, or else remain in its Force.

Or thus :

THE Condition of the aforesaid Recognizance is, that if the said *N. G.* shall for the *Another Condition.* Future well bear himself, and shall keep the Peace of our Lord the King, and all his People, and especially towards *J. B.* of, *&c.* and shall no way do any corporal *Lamb 125.* Damage, nor any Thing that may be to the Breach of the King's Peace to the said *J. B.* *Lib. Intr.454.* or to any of the King's People, then the aforesaid Recognizance shall be held void, otherwise it shall remain in its force.

Note, That all Bonds, Obligations and Recognizances, that shall be taken by any Ju- *33 H.8. c.39.* stice of Peace (or any other Person) for any Cause touching the King, must be made and taken in his Name, and by these Words, *Domino Reg', &c.* See hereof *antea,* Tit. *Surety for the Peace, and Recognizances.*

Also note, That the Recognizance runneth, *Of Lands, Tenements, Goods and Chattels,* &c. *to be made and levied,* &c. and yet the King may be at his Election, to take the Execution of the Bodies of the Recognisors (as well of the Principal as of the Sureties) or of their Lands and Chattels, (for the Sum in the Recognizance contained.) *Per Curiam 7 Hen.* 4. 34. *a. Vide antea,* Tit. *Surety for the Peace.*

And it seemeth by the Common Law, before the Statute of 33 *H.* 8. 39. in all Cases where a Man is a Debtor to the King, as well his Body as his Lands and Goods are liable to the King's Execution : For *Thesaurus Regis est Pacis vinculum, & Bellorum nervi :* And therefore the Law doth give to the King full Remedy for it. See *Coke* 3. 12. *b. & Coke* 11. 93. *a.*

A Recognizance to give in Evidence against a Prisoner.

THAT the   Day of   in the   Year of the Reign, *&c. R. T.* of *C.* in *Cambridge.* the said County Yeoman, did come before me *M. D.* Esq; one of the Justices of the *Recognizance* said Lord the King, assigned to keep the Peace in the said County, and did acknowledge *to appear and* himself to owe to the said Lord the King five Pounds of lawful Money of *Great Bri-* *give Evidence.* *tain,* under Condition, that if he should personally appear before the Justices of our said Lord the King at the next general Gaol-Delivery to be holden in the said County, then and there to give Evidence according to the Form of the Statute against *D. F.* late of *W.* in the said County, who being attached, and suspected of Felony, is now committed to the Gaol of our said Lord the King in the said County ; That then, *&c.* otherwise, *&c.*

Or this may be done by a single Recognizance, with a Condition indorsed, as followeth, which is the most usual Course.

A Condi-

A Condition to prefer a Bill of Indictment, and to give in Evidence against a Prisoner.

Condition of a Recognizance to appear and give Evidence against a Felon.

THE Condition of this Recognizance is such; That whereas one *A. B.* of *G.* Labourer, was this present Day brought before the Justice by the within bounden *D. E.* and was by him charged with the felonious Taking of twenty Sheep of the Goods of him the said *D.* and thereupon was committed by the said Justice to the Common Gaol: If therefore he the said *D. E.* shall and do at the next general Gaoldelivery (to be holden in the said County) prefer, or cause to be preferred, one Bill of Indictment of the said Felony against the said *A. B.* and shall then also give Evidence there concerning the same, as well to the Jurors that shall then inquire of the said Felony, as also to them that shall pass upon the Trial of the said *A. B.* that then, &c. or else to stand in full Force for the King.

Or thus, to give in Evidence.

Another.

THE Condition of, &c. That if the above-bounden *D. E.* do at the next general Sessions, &c. pursue and give such Evidence as he knoweth, against *A. B.* now Prisoner in the Castle of *C.* concerning certain felonious Acts by him committed: Then, &c.

A Condition to appear before the Justices of Peace at their next Sessions.

Condition of a Recognizance to appear at next Sessions.

THE Condition of this Obligation is such, That if *A. W.* of, &c. Spinster, shall personally appear before the Justices of our Lord the King, assigned to keep the Peace in the County of *C.* (as also to, &c.) at the next general Sessions of the Peace of our said Lord the King, to be holden in the said County, to answer as well to our said Lord the King, as to *G. S.* of a Plea of Trespass and Contempt, against the Form of the Statute, that then this present Obligation be holden for void and null; and if the said *A.* shall for the Future do any Thing against the Premisses, that then this present Obligation shall stand in all its Force and Effect.

Or thus:

Another Condition to appear at the Sessions.

THE Condition of this Recognizance is such, That if the within bounden *A. W.* shall make his personal Appearance before his Majesty's Justices of the Peace at the next Quarter-Sessions of the Peace to be holden for the said County of *Cambridge*, then and there to answer unto such Matters as on his Majesty's Behalf shall be objected against him (by *A. B.* of, &c. or concerning, &c.) and shall also stand to and abide such farther Orders as the said Court shall award therein; that then, and from thenceforth this present Recognizance shall be void, or else to remain in full Force and Virtue.

Another for him that hath dangerously hurt one.

Condition for one to appear who hath wounded another.

THE Condition of this Recognizance is such; That whereas the within bound *R. W.* hath now lately dangerously hurt one *J. T.* of *F.* within the said County of *Cambridge*, Yeoman, giving him divers Blows on the Head, Face, and left Side, with a Bill, so as the said *J. T.* is in Danger thereby: If therefore the said *R. W.* shall personally appear before his Majesty's Justices at the next general Gaol-Delivery to be holden in the said County of, &c. then and there to answer unto the Premisses, and to do and receive that which by the Court shall be then and there injoined him, and that he the said *R. W.* in the mean Time do keep the Peace of our said Sovereign Lord the King, towards the King's Majesty, and all his Liege People, that then, &c.

A Condition for Alehouse-keepers.

This or the like Form hath heretofore been allowable for Keeping a common Alehouse.

THE Condition of this Recognizance is such; Whereas the within bounden *A. B.* is admitted and allowed by the within named *I. Reynolds* and *Michael Dalton* Esquires, (two of his Majesty's Justices of Peace within the County of *Cambridge* within written) to keep a common Alehouse or Tipplinghouse, and to use common Selling of

5   Ale

Ale or Beer, only within the now Houfe of him the faid *A. B.* (and not elfewhere) fituate in the High Street of the Town of *M.* within written, and called *The Sign of the Hart*: If therefore he the faid *A. B.* during fuch Time as he fhall keep fuch common Alehoufe there, fhall not fuffer any unlawful Play at Tables, Dice, Cards, Tennis, Bowls, Quoits, Loggets, or other unlawful Games to be ufed in his faid Houfe, or in his Garden, Orchard, or other his Ground or Place (efpecially by Men Servants, Apprentices, common Labourers, or idle Perfons;) nor willingly admit or receive into his faid Houfe, or any Part thereof, any Perfon notorioufly defamed of or for Theft, Incontinency or Drunkennefs, or that fhall be beforehand notified to him the faid *A. B.* by the Conftable of *M.* aforefaid, for the Time being, or by his Deputy, to be an un-meet Perfon to be received into a common Alehoufe; nor fhall keep or lodge there any ftrange Perfon above the Space of one Day and one Night together, without Notice thereof firft given to the Conftable or his Deputy there; and finally, if he the faid *A. B.* during all the Time that he fhall keep common Selling of Ale or Beer in the faid Houfe, fhall and do there ufe and maintain good Order or Rule: Then this prefent Recognizance to be void, &c. or elfe, &c.

Or where the Juftices of Peace at their Meeting take divers fuch Recognizances, they were made fhortly, as followeth:

THAT on the   Day of   in   Year of the Reign, &c. before us *E. P.* *This is now the most ufual Form.* Knt. and Baronet, and *H. V.* Efquire, two of the Juftices, &c. did come *A. B.* of *N.* in the faid County Victualler, and did acknowledge himfelf to owe to our faid Lord the King 10 *l.* and *C. D.* of, &c. and *E. F.* of, &c. and each of them, did acknowledge themfelves to owe to our faid Lord the King 5 *l.* of good and lawful Money of *Great Britain*, to be made and levied of their Goods and Chattels, Lands and Tenements, to the Ufe, &c. if he (the faid *A. B.*) fhall make Default in the following Condition.

The Condition of this Recognizance is fuch; That if, &c. (and write the Condition at large.)

G. H. of *N.* in the faid County Victualler, alfo did acknowledge himfelf to owe to our faid Lord the King 10 *l.* and *J. K.* of, &c. and *L. M.* of, &c. and each of them did acknowledge themfelves to owe to our faid Lord the King, 5 *l.* &c.
With Condition as above.

N. O. of *N.* in the faid County Victualler, alfo did acknowledge himfelf to owe to our faid Lord the King 10 *l.* and *P. Q.* of, &c. and *R. S.* &c. and each of them, did acknowledge himfelf to owe to our faid Lord the King 5 *l.* &c.
With Condition as above.

T. F. of *S.* in the faid County Victualler, alfo did acknowledge himfelf to owe to our faid Lord the King 10 *l.* and *W. W.* of, &c. and *J. S.* of, &c. and each of them ac-knowledged themfelves to owe to our faid Lord the King 5 *l.* &c.
With Condition as above.

And fo of the reft.

For the Matter of this Condition for Alehoufe-keepers, it is (by the Statute) partly re-ferred to the Difcretions of fuch Juftices of Peace as take fuch Recognizance or Bond, as you may fee before in Tit. *Alehoufes.*

And in fome Shires the Juftices of Peace did condefcend, and agree upon certain Ar-icles framed by their Difcretions, and generally to be propounded to all common Ale-fellers, taking their Bond for the Performance of the fame Articles; a Copy whereof they did ufe to deliver to every of them: Which Manner was alfo allowed.

Amongft Articles of this Kind I fhould commend to the Juftice's Care thefe Three efpecially.

Firft, That no Alehoufe-keeper upon the Sabbath-day fhould receive or fuffer to re-main any Perfon whatfoever (as their Guefts) in any their Houfes, or other Places, to tipple, eat or drink; other than Travellers, and fuch as come upon neceffary Bufinefs.

Secondly, That they fuffer no Perfon whatfoever, reforting to their Houfes only to eat or drink, to remain there after Nine of the Clock in the Evening, from *Michaelmas* till *Lady-day*; or from *Lady-day* till *Michaelmas*, after Ten of the Clock at Night.
Thirdly,

Thirdly, That they fuffer no Perfon, reforting to their Houfes only to eat and drink to remain Tippling there above one Hour, other than Travellers.

(*a*) But note, That now there be divers Articles of far better Directions, publifhe (touching Alehoufes) by Proclamation given by the King's Majefty at *New-Market,* th 19th Day of *January* in the 16th Year of his Majefty's Reign of *Great Britain, Franc* and *Ireland, Anno Dom.* 1618. in Manner and Form following:

I. That the Juftices of Peace of every County, City, or Town Corporate within thi Kingdom, and the Dominion of *Wales,* do once every Year, in the Months of *Apri* and *May,* affemble themfelves, either at a fpecial Seffions, or fuch other Meeting as the fhall appoint for that Purpofe, (refpecting the Eafe and Convenience of the People of th County) and there call before them, or any Two of them, (whereof one to be of th *Quorum*) all fuch Perfons as do fell Ale or Beer by Retail in any Place (as well withi Liberties as without) within fuch County, City or Town Corporate; and then and ther to take true Certificate and Information from Men of Truft, who be Perfons of honeſ Converfation, and who not; and to give Licenfe to fuch Perfons as they in their Difcre tions fhall think meet to keep common Alehoufes or Victualling-houfes, within the Place where fuch Perfons fhall dwell.

II. That in the Licenfing of the faid Victuallers and Alehoufe-keepers, the Form of th Recognizance hereafter following, and the Condition thereunto annexed, be ufed, an none other.

B E it remembred, That on the   Day of   in the   Year of the Reign *&c.* before *T. P.* and *H. D.* Efquires, Juftices of our faid Lord the King, affigned *&c. A. B.* of, *&c.* and *C. D.* of, *&c.* did undertake for *W. St.* of, *&c.* Victualler, t wit, each of the faid Sureties, under the Penalty of 5 *l.* and the faid *W. St.* undertook fo himfelf under the Penalty of 10 *l.* which they did acknowledge themfelves to owe to ou faid Lord the King under the following Condition.

T HE Condition of this Recognizance is fuch: That whereas the above (or within bounden *A. B.* is allowed by the faid Juftices to keep a common Alehoufe an Victualling-houfe for the Space of one whole Year next enfuing the Date hereof, and n longer, in the Houfe where he now dwelleth, at *C.* in the County of *S.* and not elfe where in the faid County: If therefore the faid *A. B.* fhall not, during the Time afore faid, permit or fuffer, or have any Playing at Dice, Cards, Tables, Quoits, Loggets Bowls, or any other unlawful Game or Games, in his Houfe, Yard, Garden or Back fide; nor fhall fuffer to be or remain in his Houfe any Perfon or Perfons (not being his ordinary houfhold Servants) upon any Sabbath-day or Holy-day, during the Tim of Divine Service or Sermon; nor fhall fuffer any Perfon to lodge or ftay in his Houf above one Day and one Night, but fuch whofe true Name and Surname he fhall deli ver to fome one of the Conftables, or in his Abfence to fome one of the Officers of th fame Parifh the next Day following (unlefs they be fuch Perfon and Perfons as he o the well knoweth, and will anfwer for his or their forth-coming); nor fuffer any Per fon to remain in his or her Houfe tippling or drinking contrary to Law, nor yet to b

there tippling or drinking after Nine of the Clock in the Night-time; nor buy or tak to pawn any ftolen Goods, nor willingly harbour in his faid Houfe, or in his Barns Stables, or otherwhere, any Rogues, Vagabonds, fturdy Beggars, mafterlefs Men, o other notorious Offenders whatfoever; nor fuffer any Perfon or Perfons to fell or utte any Beer or Ale, or other Victual, by Deputation, or by Colour of his or her Licenfe And alfo, if he fhall keep the true Affife and Meafure in his Pots, Bread, and other wife, in his Uttering his Ale, Beer and Bread, and the fame Beer and Ale fell by feal ed Meafure, and according to the Affife, and not otherwife; and fhall not utter or fel any ftrong Beer or ftrong Ale above a Penny the Quart, and fmall Beer or fmall Al above a Halfpenny the Quart, and fo after the fame Rates; and alfo fhall no utter, nor willingly fuffer to be uttered, drunk, taken or tippled, any Tobaccc within his faid Houfe, Shop, Cellar, or other Place thereunto belonging; Tha then, *&c.*

Note, That the whole Sabbath-day being holy, Tippling at the Alehoufe at an Time of the Day muft needs be a Prophanation of the Day, and therefore meet to be in ferted into this Condition.

III. Tha

III. That every Alehouse-keeper and Victualler, so to be licensed, do enter into Recognizance with two able Sureties, to be bound in 5 *l.* a-piece, and the Principal 10 *l.* at the least, for the Performance of the Condition of the said Recognizance, which shall endure but for one whole Year, and then determine, unless it shall seem fit to the Justice of Peace to renew the same again, by Taking a new Recognizance of the same Condition: And whatever Date the Recognizance shall have, it is to endure but until the said Months of *April* and *May*, or one of them.

IV. That the Clerks of the Peace, Town-Clerks, or other Deputies respectively, be called to attend the Justices of Peace at such their Meetings or Assemblies; and that they do there take the Recognisance aforesaid of every Victualler or Alehouse-keeper licensed, and do duly enter them amongst the Records of the Sessions of the Peace in their Charge, whereby his Majesty may be duly answered of the Forfeitures that shall be made of the Parties so bound.

V. That the Clerks of the Peace, and Town-Clerks aforesaid, or their Deputies, shall, within some convenient Time after the Taking of the said Recognizance, fairly ingross the Recognizance and Condition in Parchment, which they shall keep as the Original, and send a true Copy of the said Recognizance, examined with the said Original, to every Alehouse-keeper allowed, whereby he may the better inform himself what he and his Sureties are bound to observe.

VI. That the Clerks of the Peace, and Town-Clerks, or their Deputies, do write out, and bring with them to every Sessions of the Peace or other Meeting of the Justices, a Register-book containing the true Names, Surnames and Places where every Alehouse-keeper or Victualler that is licensed, doth dwell, to the End it may appear to the Justices of the Peace who be licensed, and by whom, and who be not, and what other Alterations have been from Time to Time, for the Placing of Men of honest and good Conversation, and Displacing of others of ill Behaviour.

VII. That the Clerks of the Peace, and Town-Clerks, and their Deputies, may take of every Alehouse-keeper for their Fee, for performing of the Services aforesaid, at the Time of the Acknowledgment of the said Recognizance, the Fee of 18 *d.* and no more, over and above the Fee of 12 *d.* allowed for the Justices Clerks by the Statute, which shall be paid to the said Justices Clerks.

VIII. That in Case the Alehouse-keeper, not knowing of the Justices Meeting, or being hindred by Sickness, or other such like Impediment, shall fail of Admittance at the general or publick Assemblies, and shall notwithstanding be admitted or licensed by two Justices of the Peace, (whereof one to be of the *Quorum*) the Recognizance with the Condition fair ingrossed in Parchment in the Form prescribed, as aforesaid, shall forthwith, or at the next Sessions at the farthest, be returned to the Clerks of the Peace, or the Town-Clerks respectively, under the Hands of the Justices before whom such Recognizance was taken, together also with the said Fee of eighteen Pence for the Entring, Registring, Making and Delivering a Copy under his Hand to the Alehouse-keeper, as aforesaid.

IX. That none be licensed or allowed to keep an Alehouse that hath not one convenient Lodging at least in his or their Houses, for the Lodging of any Passenger or Traveller, and hath not always in his or their House good and wholsome small Beer or Ale, for the Relief of the Labourer, Traveller, or others that call for the same.

X. That the Justices of Peace within their several Precincts do not permit or suffer any unlicensed Alehouse-keeper or Victualler to sell Beer or Ale, but that they proceed against them by all due and lawful Means whatsoever; and that they be very careful, from Time to Time, to cause the Brewers to be proceeded against in their General and Quarter-Sessions, for delivering Beer or Ale to such unlicensed Persons, according to the Statute in that Case provided.

XI. That the Clerks of the Peace, or Town-Clerks respectively, do once every Year, in *Trinity Term*, make and bring in a Brief of all such Recognizances as shall be taken within every County, City and Town Corporate, into the Office of the * Patentees, (appointed by them for that Purpose) to the End all Concealments of Recognizances taken in that Behalf may be discovered, and the Benefit accruing to his Majesty, by such as wilfully break the same, may be more duly prosecuted; of which that his Highness be not defrauded, order is given to the Patentees, that with the Allowance of the Chief Justice of the King's Bench there be appointed Committees in every County for the Recovery thereof from Time to Time.

* *This is now disused.*

XII. That the Juſtices of Aſſize in their Circuits, and Juſtices of Peace at their general Seſſions of the Peace, do from Time to Time, inquire of the due Execution of theſe Preſents, and of all other Abuſes, Diſorders, and Miſdemeanors whatſoever, committed or ſuffered againſt the Proviſions aforeſaid, and the true Meaning of them.

And yet the Means (as I conceive), to reduce them both to a more competent Number, and to better Order, would be by a Law to be made, that none ſhould be licenſed to keep any Alehouſe, unleſs they did find two good ſufficient Sureties (one of them at leaſt to be a Subſidy-man) to be bound for Performance of the Condition of their ſaid Recognizance.

But no Licences are now to be granted but at a General Meeting of the Juſtices. *Vide ſupra*, Chap. 7.

C H A P. CLXXVII.

A Licence to keep an Alehouſe.

Cambridge.
Licence to keep
an Alehouſe.

JOHN *Cutts* Knight, and *Michael Dalton* Eſq; two Juſtices of the Peace of our Sovereign Lord the King for the County of *C*. ſend Greeting. Know ye, that we the ſaid Juſtices, of good and credible Report to us made by divers credible and honeſt Perſons, &c. that *J. W.* of, &c. is a Man fit to keep a common Alehouſe in the Houſe where he now dwelleth, have licenſed, allowed, and admitted, and by theſe Preſents do licence, allow and admit the ſaid *J. W.* to keep a common Alehouſe or Tippling-houſe at *L*. for one whole Year next enſuing the Date hereof, ſo that the ſaid *J. W.* ſuffer not any unlawful Games to be uſed in his ſaid Houſe, nor any Diſorder to be kept within the ſame, during the Time of his ſaid Licence: For the uſing of which Licence accordingly, we have bound the ſaid *J. W.* in 10 *l.* and two other ſufficient Sureties in an Hundred Shillings apiece by Recognizance to the King's Majeſty's Uſe. In Witneſs whereof we have hereunto ſet our Hands and Seals. Dated, &c.

Or thus.

Cambridge.
Another.

J. C. and *M. D.* two Juſtices of the Peace of our Sovereign Lord, &c. to all Bailiffs Conſtables, and other the King's Majeſty's Officers, Greeting. Know ye, that we the ſaid Juſtices have licenced, and by theſe Preſents do licence *J. W.* of, &c. to keep a common Alehouſe in *L*. aforeſaid for one whole Year next enſuing the Date hereof; and have bound the ſaid *J. W.* by Recognizance with Sureties to his Majeſty's Uſe, that he ſhall maintain good Order, and farther to do and behave himſelf therein in all Things according to the Laws and Statutes of this Realm, &c.

Or thus.

Cambridge.
Another, and
the moſt com-
mon and uſual
Form.

WE whoſe Names are here underwritten, Juſtices of the Peace of our Sovereign Lord the King within the County of *Cambridge*, do licence and allow *J. W.* of *L*. in the ſaid County to keep a common Alehouſe or Tippling-houſe in *L*. aforeſaid, for and during one whole Year next enſuing the Date hereof, ſo as he doth not ſuffer any unlawful Games to be uſed in his Houſe, nor any evil Rule to be kept there, but doth behave himſelf therein according to the Laws and Statutes of this Realm in that Behalf made and provided. In Witneſs, &c.

A Licence to brew and keep an Alehouſe.

Cambridge.
Another.
Weſt. 554.

WHereas *A. M.* of *W.* in the County of *C*. Husbandman, hath come before us, *John Cutts* Knight, and *Tho. Chicheley* Eſq; two of his Majeſty's Juſtices of Peace for the ſaid County, and bound himſelf in a Recognizance with ſufficient Sureties, to brew and ſell, and, keep a common Alehouſe, according to the Statute made in the fifth Year of the Reign of our late Sovereign Lord King *Edward* 6. Now know ye, that we the ſaid *John Cutts* and *T. Chicheley*, have licenced the ſaid *A. M.* to brew, ſell, and keep a common Alehouſe according to the ſaid Statute. Given under our Hands the 13th of *July* in the, &c.

                                                               A Li-

A Licence for a Recusant to travel.

WHereas R. C. of L. in the County of C. being a Recusant (convicted) hath con- Cambridge. fined himself to L. aforesaid, being the usual Place of his Abode, according to *Licence for a* the Statute made in the 35th Year of the Reign of our late Sovereign Lady Queen *Eliz.* *Papist to tra-* know ye, that we, &c. four of the King's Majesty's Justices of the Peace within the said *Miles from* County, do, by the Consent of the Right Reverend Father in God, *Nicholas* Lord Bishop *home.* of *Ely*, at the Request of the said R. C. for the Dispatch of his urgent and necessary Busineſs, grant and give Licence to the said R. C. to travel out of the Precincts or Compaſs of five Miles limited by the same Statute, at all Times until the first Day of *November* next coming; and at the first Day of *November* to return again to L. aforesaid. In Witneſs, &c. See *hic antea*, Tit. *Recusants.*

A Testimonial or Paſs-port to travel.

SIR *Roger Millisent* Knight, and Sir *James Reynolds* Knight, two of the King's Ma- Cambridge. jesty's Justices of Peace within the said County, to all Justices of Peace, Mayors, *The Form of a* Bailiffs, Constables, and all other his Majesty's Officers and Ministers whatsoever, send *Paſs.* Greeting. Forasmuch as the Bearer hereof *E. P.* (*here shew the Cause of his Travel*) hath desired our Testimonial, or Licence, for his safe Travel unto the City of *B.* where (*here shew whither he is to go*): In Consideration thereof, know ye, we the said Sir *Roger Millisent* and Sir *James Reynolds*, so far as in us lieth, have licensed the said *E. P.* to paſs and travel the direct Way from *H.* within the said County of *C.* where he lately dwelt, unto the said City of *B.* so as his Journey be not of longer or farther Continuance than twenty Days next after the Date hereof; desiring you and every of you not to moleſt or trouble the said poor Man in his Travel, but to permit and suffer him peaceably to paſs, so as he shew himself in no Respect offensive to his Majesty's Laws. In Witneſs, &c.

But upon such Licence, the Persons thus licensed to travel may neither beg, nor wander *Directions con-* idly, out of their direct Way. Besides, the Justices must be sparing to grant such Li- *cerning such* cences, except in Cases of Neceſſity. (*a*) For except the Person so licensed be one that *Paſſes.* hath suffered Shipwreck, or a Soldier, or a Mariner coming from the Seas, &c. or be a Labourer, and only for Hay or Harveſt Time, or else be a Servant departing from his Maſter, the Justices of Peace are to make no such Licence or Testimonial. And as for the Manner of such Testimonial or Licence for the Persons suffering Shipwreck, and Soldiers coming from Sea, and in what Manner such Persons may travel, see *hic antea*, Tit. *Rogues.*

But in other Cases where any Persons shall become poor, lame, blind, or otherwise diseased, or decayed, and shall have just Cause to travel, they must be provided of Money or Maintenance for their Travel: Otherwise the Justices ought to forbear to grant any such Licence, and must rather cause them to be sent to, and settled in the Town where they laſt dwelt.

Also it is fit that such Person do get the Allowance of such his Paſsport under the Hand of a Justice of Peace in every County where he is to paſs.

(*d*) *The Form of a Testimonial for the conveying of a Rogue that hath been punished according to the Statute of* Vagrants.

JOHN *a-Stile*, a ſturdy vagrant Beggar, (of low Perſonage, red-haired, having the Cambridge. Nail of his right Thumb cloven) aged about 25 Years, was the sixth Day of *April* *Testimonial for* in the tenth Year of the Reign of our Sovereign Lord, &c. openly whipped at *W.* in the *conveying a* said County (according to the Law) for a wandring Rogue, and is ordered to paſs forth- *hath been* with from Pariſh to Pariſh by the Officers thereof, the next ſtraight Way to *P.* in the *punished.* County of *W.* where (as he confeſſeth) he was born, (*or dwelled laſt by one whole Year*, &c. *if the Case be such*) and he is limited to be at *P.* aforesaid within ten Days now next enſuing, at his Peril. Given at *Weſt-Wratting*, under the Hand and Seal of *M. D.* Eſquire, one of his Majesty's Justices of Peace in the said County of *Cambridge.*

Note, by the Words of the Statute 39 *El.* 4. such Testimonial muſt be under the Hand *Directions* and Seal of the Justice of Peace, Conſtable, Headborough, and of the Minister of the *thereon.* Pariſh,

See *the* Stat.13
Geo. 2. c. 24.
infra Chap.
196.

Parifh, or any one of them; and yet it is taken that the Juftice of Peace alone under his Hand and Seal may make fuch Teftimonial. *Lamb.* 206.

Note alfo, that it is needful both in this and in all other Teftimonials, Certificates, and Pafs-ports whatfoever, to note and fpecify exprefsly fome *affured Marks of the Party*, as his Stature, Colour of Hair, Complexion, (if it may be) fome apparent Scar, or other Note, by which he may be infallibly diftinguifhed and known from others; left (as is often found) both himfelf take the Benefit thereof, and he alfo communicate the Ufe of the fame to others, in Abufe of him that made it, and of the Law in that Behalf provided.

A Teftimonial for fuch as have fuffered Shipwreck.

Norfolk.
Teftimonial for
Shipwreck.

A B. of C. in the County of *Norf.* Efquire, one of his Majefty's Juftices, &c. to all &c. Forafmuch as the Bearer hereof *J. S.* aged about, &c. having lately been a Sea, in a Ship called, &c. hath fuffered Shipwreck, and got to Land at *Y.* in the faid County of *Norf.* upon the 20th Day of *July* laft paft, as I am credibly informed, as well by the Report of the faid *J. S.* as alfo by the Teftimony of divers the Inhabitants of *Y.* aforefaid, and for that the faid *J. S.* hath not wherewith to relieve himfelf in his Travel homeward to *D.* in the County of *H.* where he faith he was born, (*or hath a Dwelling*, &c.) Thefe are therefore to defire you, and every of you, to whom thefe Prefent fhall come, not to moleft or trouble the faid *J. S.* in his Travel to *D.* aforefaid, where he is limited to be within 20 Days next after the Date hereof; but to defire you rather to relieve him in his Neceffity, as to you fhall feem meet: And withal, you the Conftable of every Town where he fhall come, to help him with Lodging in convenient Time, fo that he travelleth the direct Way to *D.* aforefaid, not doing any Thing contrary to the Laws and Statutes of this Realm. In Witnefs whereof, &c.

Mariner or
Soldier.

The like (with very little Alteration) may be for a poor Mariner, or a poor Soldier coming from the Seas, or from beyond the Sea. *Vide antea*, Tit. *Rogues.*

But thefe two laft Teftimonials muft be made by fome Juftice of Peace dwelling near where fuch Perfons do land.

C H A P.   CLXXVIII.

Warrants.

A Warrant to the Keeper of a Gaol to receive a Prifoner for Felony.

Cambridge.
To a Gaoler to
receive a Pri-
foner.

E P. Knight and Baronet, one of the Juftices, &c. to the Keeper of the Gaol of our faid Lord the King in the faid County, or to his Deputy, and to each of them Greeting. Whereas *R. T.* late of *F.* in the faid County Labourer, has been arrefted by the Conftable of the Vill of *R.* in the faid County, for Sufpicion of a Felony by him, as it is faid, committed: Therefore on the Behalf of our faid Lord the King, I command you and each of you, that you or one of you receive the faid *R.* into your Cuftody, there to remain till he be delivered from your Cuftody by the Law and Cuftom of *England*. Given, &c.

Otherwife.

Cambridge.

J D. &c. to the Keeper of the Common Gaol at the Caftle of *Cambridge*, or to his Deputy there: Thefe are in his Majefty's Name to charge and command you, that you receive into your faid Gaol the Body of *R. S.* late of, &c. taken by *F. C.* and *J. S.* Conftables of the Town of *W.* and by them brought before me for Sufpicion of Felony, &c. and that you fafely keep the faid *R. S.* in your faid Gaol until the next General Gaol-delivery for the faid County, [if he be not bailable; or if bailable, then thus] until he fhall thence be delivered by due Courfe of Law. And hereof fail you not, &c.

A Mittimus *of a Felon after his Examination taken.*

JOHN *Cotton* Knight, one of the Juftices, *&c.* to the Keeper of the common Gaol at *Mittimus of a* the Caftle of *Cambridge* in the faid County, *&c.* I fend you herewithal the Body of *Felon.* *A. B.* late of *C.* Labourer, brought before me this prefent Day, and charged with the fe-lonious taking of twenty Sheep, *(which alfo he hath * confeffed upon his Examination be-* * *This Claufe* *fore me :)* And therefore thefe are, on the Behalf of our Sovereign Lord to command you, *maketh the* that immediately you receive the faid *A. B.* and him fafely keep in your faid Gaol, until *be bailable.* that he fhall be thence delivered by the due Order of Law. Hereof fail you not, as you will anfwer for your Contempt at your Peril. Given at *Cheveley* the firft Day of *Decem-* *ber* in the   Year of the Reign, *&c.*

Otherwife.

Or thefe Warrants or *Mittimus,* whereby a Prifoner fhall be fent to the Gaol, may be made in the King's Name, and the *Tefte* may be made under the Name of the Juftice of Peace as followeth.

GEORGE, by the Grace of God, *&c.* to the Keeper of our Gaol of *Cambridge,* or *This is now* to his Deputy, Greeting. Whereas *R. S.* late of *B.* in the County of *E.* Labourer, *difufed.* is now arrefted for Sufpicion of Felony by him, as it is faid, committed : We therefore command you, and each of you, that you receive him the faid *R.* into your Cuftody of our faid Gaol, or that one of you receive him, there to remain till he be delivered from your Cuftody, according to the Law of our Kingdom of *England.* Witnefs *E. P. &c.*

A Mittimus *to fend to the Gaol an Alehoufe-keeper that victualleth contrary to the Com-mand, &c.*

H. *E.* and *R. T.* Efquires, two of his Majefty's Juftices of the Peace within the faid Cambridge. County of *Cambridge,* to the Keeper of the common Gaol at *C.* Whereas *R. D.* *Commitment of* of *B.* in the County of *Camb.* (upon Complaint lately made unto us of the evil Rule kept *an Alehoufe-* and fuffered by him in his Houfe, and other Mifdemeanors) by Warrant under both our *ing an Alehoufe* Hands and Seals was difcharged of his Alehoufe-keeping, and was commanded from us *after he was* that he fhould thenceforth ufe no more common Selling of Ale or Beer; and whereas we are credibly informed that the faid *R. D.* (notwithftanding our faid Warrant and Com-mand given him to the contrary, as aforefaid) hath ever fince obftinately, and upon his own Authority, taken upon him to * keep a common Alehoufe or Tippling-houfe, and * *Or to ufe* ftill continues the fame: We do therefore fend you herewithal the Body of him the faid *ling Ale or* *R. D.* commanding you in his faid Majefty's Name to receive him into your faid Gaol, *Beer.* and there fafely to keep him, until fuch Time as he fhall be from thence delivered by due Order of Law. And hereof fail you not at your Peril. Dated at, *&c.*

Or thus.

WHereas by Warrant from divers Juftices of the Peace of this County *J. S.* of, *&c.* *Another Form* hath been fuppreffed for keeping an Alehoufe, *&c.* and forafmuch as Complaint *for the like* hath notwithftanding been made to us (this prefent Day) that the faid *J. S.* hath and *a fuppreffed* doth, contrary to the faid Warrant, and contrary to the Statute in that Behalf provided, *Alehoufe-* ftill keep a common Alehoufe : Therefore we do fend you herewithal the Body of the faid *keeper.* *J. S.* commanding you, *&c.* to receive the faid *J. S.* into the common Gaol, and there fafely to keep him for three Days without Bail or Mainprife ; and afterwards until he fhall with two Sureties enter into Recognizance, that he fhall not keep any common Alehoufe, or ufe common Selling of Ale or Beer, and pay his Fine of 20 *s.* according to the Sta-tute in that Cafe made and provided. Hereof fail you not, *&c.*

A Mittimus *(to the Gaol) of the reputed Father of a Baſtard-child*, &c.

Cambridge.
Commitment of the reputed Father of a Baſtard.

I Send you herewithal the Body of *R. C.* of *B.* in the County of *C.* Labourer, brought before me this preſent Day, and charged by *F. S.* of the ſame Town to have gotten her with Child: And for that the ſaid *R.* refuſeth to put in Security for his Appearance at the next Quarter-Seſſions, to the End he may be forthcoming when an Order ſhall be taken for the Relief and Diſcharging of the ſaid Town of *B.* and for the keeping of the ſaid Child (when it ſhall happen to be born) according to the Statute in that Caſe provided : Theſe are therefore on his Majeſty's Behalf to charge and command you, that immediately you receive the ſaid *R. C.* and him ſafely keep in your ſaid Gaol, until ſuch Time as he ſhall be from thence delivered by due Order of Law. And hereof fail you not as you will anſwer your Contempt at your Peril. Dated, &c.

Directions about Mittimus.

In every *Mittimus* the Cauſe of the Commitment is to be ſet down, to the End it may appear whether the Priſoner be bailable or not. See hereof before in the Title *Bailment*, &c.

Alſo where the Juſtice of Peace out of their Seſſions may hear and determine, and ſo may commit Offenders for the Offence or Fine, it is neceſſary that in their *Mittimus* there be contained the Manner of the Offence, and how long Time the Offender is to be kept in Priſon for it. See the *Mittimus* for Guns afterwards.

A Mittimus *to the Houſe of Correction of a dangerous Rogue.*

Cambridge.
Commitment of a Rogue to the Houſe of Correction.
Or ſuch Rogue may be ſent to the Gaol.
See before Tit. Rogues.

I *R.* Knight, and *Michael Dalton,* Eſquire, two of his Majeſty's Juſtices of Peace within the ſaid County of *Cambridge,* to the Maſter or Governor of the Houſe of Correction at *Bottiſham,* (for the *Eaſt*-ſide of the ſaid County) or to his Deputy there Whereas *I. S.* a ſturdy vagrant Beggar, was the 20th Day of *September* in the Year &c. brought before us, and charged as well with Begging and idle wandring abroad, as alſo with other lewd and diſorderly Behaviour, ſo as he appeareth to us to be dangerous to the inferior Sort of People, *(or ſuch an one as will not be reformed of his roguiſh*

See Stat. 7 Jac. 1. c. 4. 13 G. 2. 24.

Life) contrary to his Majeſty's Laws in ſuch Behalf provided : Theſe are therefore to will and require you to receive the ſaid *I. S.* and him ſafely keep in your ſaid Houſe, until the next Quarter-Seſſions, to be holden in the ſaid County ; and during all that Time (that he ſhall continue with you) that you hold him to Work and Labour, and to puniſh him by putting Fetters and Gyves upon him, and by moderate Whipping him, as in good Diſcretion you ſhall find Cauſe, yielding him for his Maintenance only ſo much as he ſhall deſerve or earn by his Labour and Work ; and that at the ſaid next Quarter-Seſſions you have the ſaid *I. S.* there, together with this our Warrant. And hereof ſee that you fail not, &c. Dated, &c.

A Mittimus *to the Houſe of Correction of a diſorderly Servant, or other diſorderly Perſon.*

Cambridge.
Commitment of a diſorderly Servant.
* Or by the Space of three Days next after the Date of this Warrant.

I Have ſent you herewithal the Body of *E. C.* of *W.* in the ſaid County of *C.* being an idle and diſſolute and diſorderly Fellow : (Or one that will not keep his Service, nor follow any honeſt Courſe of Life.) Theſe are therefore to will and require you to receive the ſaid *E. C.* and him ſafely to keep, (* until he ſhall be thence delivered by Warrant from my ſelf, or ſome other of his Majeſty's Juſtices of Peace for this County of *Cambridge*) and in the mean Time to hold him to Work, and to puniſh him by moderate Whipping, or otherwiſe, according to the Law in ſuch Caſes provided. And hereof fail not at your Peril. Dated, &c. See the Statute 7 *Jac.* 1. *cap.* 4.

Another for one that runneth away, leaving her Charge to the Town.

Cambridge.
Commitment of a Mother that runneth away, and leaves a Charge to the Pariſh.

WE have ſent you herewithal the Body of *I. R.* of *W.* ſingle Woman, being lately delivered of a Child, and one that is able to labour, and thereby to relieve her ſelf and her Child, and hath notwithſtanding lately run away, and left her Child upon the Pariſh, to the Charge of the ſame Pariſh, contrary to the Statute in that Behalf provided : Theſe are therefore to will and require you to receive the ſaid *I. R.* and her ſafely to keep, until the next Quarter-Seſſions to be holden for this County ; and in the mean Time to hold her to ſuch Work, and to give her ſuch due Correction, by moderate

4   Whip-

Whipping or otherwife, as fhall be fitting in your Difcretion, and according to the Law *Or elfe fuch* in that Behalf provided ; yielding her for her Maintenance, *&c. ut fupra.* And hereof *Party muft be delivered at* fail not at your Peril. Dated, *&c.* See the Statute 7 *Jac.* 1. *cap.* 4. *& vide antea,* Tit. *the Meeting of* Rogues. *the Juftices*

upon privy
Note ; If any mean Perfons fhall but threaten to run away, and leave their Family (as *Search made* aforefaid) any two Juftices of Peace of that Divifion may fend them to the Houfe of *for Rogues, and* Correction, as aforefaid, but fuch their Threatning muft be proved by two fufficient Wit-*not otherwife.* neffes upon Oath before the faid Juftice of Peace. *Vide antea,* Tit. *Rogues.* *Direction.,*

A Mittimus *to the Houfe of Correction of the Mother of a Baftard Child.*

WE have fent you herewithal the Body of *I. C.* of *W.* in the faid County, fingle *Commitment* Woman, being lately delivered of a Baftard-child, like to be chargeable to the *of the Mother* Parifh of *W.* aforefaid : And for that the faid *I. C.* is able to labour, and that thereby *of a Baftard.* fhe may the better relieve her felf and her faid Child ; thefe are therefore to will and require you to receive the faid *I.* into your faid Houfe, there to be punifhed, and fet on Work during the Term of one whole Year, according to the Statute in that Behalf provided. And hereof fail you not, *&c.*

(a) Rogues and Vagabonds, fturdy Beggars, and other idle and diforderly Perfons fent to *Houfe of Cor-* the Houfe of Correction, are there to be punifhed by putting Fetters and Gyves upon *rection.* them, and by moderate Whipping. 7 *Jac.* 1. *cap.* 4. *Directions a-*

bout the Pu-
So Perfons running, or threatning to run away, and leave their Family to the *nifhment.* Parifh. *Ibid.*

The Mother of a Baftard-child, *&c.* fhall be fet on work, and punifhed. *Ibid.*

But where by the plain Letter of the Law there is not Authority given to whip or punifh Offenders, (fent to the Houfe of Correction,) there let the Juftices of Peace forbear to appoint or order any Whipping, except it be in open Seffions, or by the Order of the Quarter-Seffions.

Note, That the greater Part of the Juftices of Peace affembled at the Quarter-Seffions may fet down Orders for the Correction and Punifhment of Offenders committed to the Houfe of Correction.

And the Houfes of Correction are to be ufed and employed for the keeping, correcting and fetting to work of fuch Perfons as fhall be fent thither. See Statute 13 *Geo.* 2. *cap.* 24. infra, *Chap.* 196. generally for Rogues, Vagabonds, fturdy Beggars, and other diforderly Perfons.

CHAP. CLXXIX.

A Mittimus *to fend to the Gaol fuch as fhoot,* &c. *in Guns.*

To the Keeper of his Majefty's Gaol at the Caftle of Cambridge, and to his Deputy or Deputies there, and to every of them.

WHereas this prefent Day *A. B.* and *C. B.* of *B.* in the fame County, Yeoman, *Canterbury.* did arreft and bring before me at *C.* aforefaid one *I. S.* in the faid County Ma-*Commitment of* riner, whom they had feen and found the fame Day fhooting in a Hand-gun, charged *thofe who fhoot* with Powder and Pellet, at a Coney in a certain Place in *C.* within the faid County *being qualified.* called the *Churchfield,* contrary to the Laws of the Realm, and thereupon prayed that Juftice may be done in that Behalf ; I *John Cutts,* Knight, being the next Juftice of the Peace in the faid County to the Place aforefaid, did then at *C.* aforefaid, upon the faid Requeft, take the Examination of the faid *I. S.* and did alfo then and there hear the Proofs of them the faid *A. B.* and *C. D.* touching the faid Offence ; And for that it did manifeftly appear unto me, as well by the Teftimonies of them the faid *A. B.* and *C. D.* as alfo by the plain Confeffion of him the faid *I. S.* that he had not *then Lands,* Tenements, *Fees, Annuities or Offices, to the clear yearly Value of* 100 *l.* and that he had *Qualification.* fhot in the faid Hand-gun in Manner and Form as aforefaid ; I do fend you herewithal the Body of him the faid *I. S.* as lawfully convicted of the faid Offence before me, re-
qniring

quiring you in his Majefty's Name to receive him into your faid Gaol, and him there

Forfeiture 10 l. fafely to keep, until he fhall have truly paid the Pain and Forfeiture of 10 *l.* of lawfu
Money of *Great Britain*, laid upon him for his faid Offence by the Statute made in
*To the King
and the Infor-
mer.* the three and thirtieth Year of the Reign of the late King *Henry* the Eighth, that is to
fay, the one Moiety thereof to our faid Sovereign Lord, and the other Moiety to
them the faid *A. B.* and *C. D.* the firft Bringers of him before me. And this fhal
33 H. 8. be your fufficient Warrant in this Behalf. Hereof fail not, as you will anfwer for you
Contempt at your own Peril. Given at *C.* aforefaid, the third Day of *March* in th
tenth Year of the Reign of our faid Sovereign Lord, *&c.*

By me the faid *John Cutts*

The Juftice's Record thereof.

Canterbury.
Record of the
Conviction. **B**E it remembered, That on the   Day of   in the   Year of the Reign
&c. A. B. and *C. D.* of *E.* in the faid County, Yeoman, found one *I. S.* of
E. in the faid County, Mariner, and faw him at *D.* in the faid County, the Day and
Year aforefaid, with a Hand-gun charged with Gun-powder and a Leaden Bullet, fhoot
ing and difcharging the faid Gun at a Coney then being in a certain Place there called
Churchfield, againft the Form of a Statute in a Parliament held the thirty-third Yea
of the Reign of our Lord *Henry* the Eighth, late King of *England*, made and provided
and therefore they did arreft the faid *I. S.* the Day and Year aforefaid, and brought him
with them to *D.* to the faid *J. C.* one of the Juftices (being next to the faid Place
of our faid Lord the King, affigned to keep the Peace in the faid County, as alfo to
hear and determine divers Trefpaffes and other Mifdemeanours in the faid County com
mitted, requefting Juftice thereof to be done, which requeft being heard, I the faid *J*
C. at *D.* aforefaid, the Day and Year aforefaid, have thereupon duly examined the faid
J. S. and taken the Proofs of the faid *A. B.* and *C. D.* in this Behalf. And becaufe
as well by the faid Proofs as by the Confeffion of the faid *I. S.* it hath then and there
manifeftly appeared to me, that the faid *I. S.* (not having in his own Right, nor in the
Right of his Wife, to his own Ufe, nor any other having to the Ufe of the faid *I. S*
Lands, Tenements, Fees, Annuities, or Offices to the clear yearly Value of one
hundred Pounds) did fhoot with the faid Hand-gun in the Manner and Form aforefaid
againft the Form of the faid Statute: I the faid *J. C.* have committed the above
named *I. S.* convicted of the faid Trefpafs before me, the Day and Year aforefaid, to
the neareft Gaol of our faid Lord the King at *Cambridge* in the faid County, there to
remain until he fhall truly pay the Penalty and forfeiture of ten Pounds of lawful Mo
ney of *Great Britain*, to wit, one Half to our faid Lord the King, the other Half to
the faid *A. B.* and *C. D.* who firft brought the faid *I. S.* before me. In Witnefs of al
which, I the faid *John Cutts*, have to thefe Prefents put my Seal. Given at *D.* afore
faid, the Day and Year above written.

By me the faid *J. C*

C H A P. CLXXX.

Bailment.

Canterbury.
Bail for Felony.
Lamb. 341. **B**E it remembered, That on the   Day of   in the   Year of the
Reign, *&c.* before us *J. C.* Knt. and *R. C.* Efq; two of the Juftices, *&c.* at *H*
in the faid County, did come *A. B.* and *C. D.* of *E.* in the faid County, Yeoman, and
took in Bail until the next Gaol-delivery to be held for the faid County, one *F. G. &c*
Labourer, taken and detained in Prifon for Sufpicion of a certain Felony, *&c.* and took
upon themfelves each of the faid *A. B.* and *C. D.* under the Penalty of twenty Pounds
of good and lawful Money of *Great Britain*, and the faid *F. G.* undertook for himfelf,
under the Penalty of forty Pounds of the like Money, of the Goods and Chattels
Lands and Tenements of them and each and every of them, to the Ufe of our faid
Lord the King, his Heirs and Succeffors, to be levied, if the faid *F. G.* fhall not
perfonally appear at the faid next Gaol-delivery, before the Juftices of the faid
Lord the King, affigned to deliver the faid Gaol, to ftand to right concerning the Felony

afore-

aforefaid, and then and there to anfwer to our faid Lord the King, of and upon all that fhall be objected to him.   Given, &c.

Otherwife, fc. if the Gaoler can conveniently bring the Prifoner before the Juftices.

BE it remembered, That upon the   Day of   &c. *A. B.* of *D.* &c. and *E. F.* of *G.* &c. did come before Us *M. D.* and *J. B.* Efqrs; two of the Juftices, &c. and did become Bail for *J. S.* of, &c. each of them under the Penalty of twenty Pounds, &c. and the faid *J. S.* then and there likewife did undertake for himfelf under the Penalty of forty Pounds of the like Money, of their and each and every of their Goods and Chattels, Lands and Tenements, to the Ufe of our faid Lord the King, his Heirs and Succeffors, to be made and levied, if the faid *J. S.* fhall make Default in the Condition indorfed. *Another Form of Bail.*

THE Condition of this Recognizance is fuch, That if the within-bounden *A. B.* fhall make his perfonal Appearance before the King's Majefty's Juftices of the Peace at the next General Seffions to be holden for this County, then and there to make Anfwer to our Sovereign Lord the King, for and concerning the Sufpicion of ftealing certain Corn, where withal he ftandeth charged, that then, &c. *For Sufpicion of ftealing, &c.*

Otherwife.

BE it remembered, that upon the   Day, &c. before us, &c. did come *A. B.* of, &c. *D. E.* of, &c. and *F. G.* of, &c. and did become Bail for *R. B.* of *L.* in the faid County, &c. to wit, each of them Body for Body, that the faid *R. B.* fhall perfonally appear before the faid Juftices, and their Companions, Juftices of the faid Lord the King, at the next General Seffions of the Peace to be held in the faid County, to ftand to Right in the Court (if any one againft him will implead) of divers Felonies and Trefpaffes whereof the fame *R. B.* is indicted (as is faid) and to anfwer to the faid King of the faid Things, as he ought, &c. *Vide antea,* Tit. *Bailment,* that it muft be upon a certain Sum of Money. *Cambridge. Another Form of Bail. Cromp. 235. 21 H. 7. 20. Br. Main. 44.*

And here *Stare recte in Curia* is, when he that ftandeth at the Bar hath no Man to object againft him.

Yet Note, upon this laft Manner the Bail fhall be only fined if the Prifoner maketh Default. 21 *H.* 7. 20. *Cromp. 153.*

Before the Statute of *Marl. cap.* 27. if one arrefted or in Prifon for Felony had been bailed, and at the Day the Prifoner would not at anfwer, but betook himfelf to his Clergy, &c. then his Mainpernors, were amerced, &c. But now by the Statute, if they have the Body at the Day, they fhall not be amerced ; although the Prifoner will not anfwer, &c. Neither fhall they forfeit their Recognizance, if they have the Body of the Prifoner there, although the Prifoner fhall not anfwer, &c. and yet the Words of the Recognizance or Bailment are ufually, to anfwer to our faid Lord the King, &c. as before. But thefe Words feem to be of Courfe.

Otherwife, to bail a Prifoner for the Peace.

BE it remembered, &c. *A. B.* of, &c. *D. E.* &c. of, and *E. F.* of, &c. have come before me *M. D.* of, &c. and become Bail for *R. B.* of, &c. that he fhall keep the Peace towards all the People of our Lord the King, and efpecially towards *J. S.* under the Penalty for each Surety of twenty Pounds, and the faid *R. B.* under the Penalty of forty Pounds, that the faid *R. B.* fhall appear before the Juftices of our Lord the King at the next General Seffions of the Peace to be held for the faid County, &c.

The Liberate to deliver a Prifoner committed for Felony.

EF. and *D. E.* Efquires, two of the Juftices, &c. to the Keeper of his Majefty's Gaol in *C.* &c. Forafmuch as *F. G.* &c. Labourer, hath before us found fufficient Bail to appear before the Juftices of Gaol-delivery, at the next General Gaol-delivery to be holden in the faid County, there to anfwer to fuch Things as fhall be then on the Behalf of our faid Sovereign Lord objected againft him, and namely to the felonious Taking of two Sheep, (for the Sufpicion whereof he was taken and committed to *Canterbury. A Liberate to deliver one committed for Felony. Lamb. 342.*

your faid Gaol :) We command you on the Behalf of our Sovereign Lord, that if th faid *F. G.* do remain in your faid Gaol for the faid Caufe, and for none other, then yo forbear to detain him any longer, but that you deliver him thence, and fuffer him to g at large, and that upon the Pain which will fall thereon. Given under our Seal this, &

A Warrant to deliver a Servant out of Gaol.

Cambridge.
Cromp. 238.

F. *B.* Efq; one of the Juftices, &c. to the Keeper of the Gaol of the faid Lord th -King, in the faid County, Greeting : Forafinuch as *W. K.* of *N.* Labourer, be fore me, hath found fufficient Surety to be before the Juftices of our faid Lord the King &c. at the next General Seffions, &c. to anfwer as well to our faid Lord the King, : to *E. F.* of, &c. of his Trefpaffes and Contempts, contrary to the Form of the Statute c *Labourers*, lately made and provided, I therefore command you on the Behalf of ou faid Lord the King, that without delay you caufe the faid *IV. K.* to be delivered fror his faid Prifon, if he be detained on that Occafion, and none other. Given, &c.

Wherefoever a Juftice of Peace upon his own Motion and Difcretion hath committe one to the Gaol or Houfe of Correction, for want of Sureties for the Peace or Goo Behaviour, or for being a Vagrant or idle Perfon, or the like, it feemeth the fame Ju ftice of Peace may in like Difcretion afterwards difcharge him again, and make his *Li berate* or Warrant to deliver fuch Prifoner. See 14 *H.* 6. *fol.* 8. *Br. Impr.* 27.

(a) To deliver a Prifoner committed for the Peace or Good Behaviour.

Liberate to
difcharge one
committed for
Breach of
Peace, or
Good Behavi-
our.

F. *B.* Efq; one of the Juftices, &c. to the Sheriff (or Keeper of the Gaol) &c. For afmuch as *I. S.* in the Prifon of our Lord the King, in your Cuftody, at th Suit of one *A. S.* for his good Abearing (or for keeping the Peace towards the King an all his People, and efpecially towards the faid *A. S.*) hath found fufficient Surety (o four Sureties) to wit, *A. B. D. E. F. G.* and *H. I.* who have undertaken for the fai *I. S.* that the faid *I. S.* fhall not do nor caufe to be done, neither by himfelf nor b others, any Damage or Grievance to the faid *A. S.* or to any of the People of our fai Lord the King, in their Bodies by Menaces, Waylaying, Affaults or any other Manne that may any way be to the Breach or Difturbance of the Peace of our faid Lord th King, to wit, each of the faid Sureties under the Penalty of twenty Pounds. I there fore command you on the Behalf of our faid Lord the King, that you without Delay caufe to be delivered, the faid *I. S.* being in the Prifon of our faid Lord the King i your Cuftody on that Occafion and no other. Given, &c.

C H A P. CLXXXI.

Releafes of the Peace.

The Releafe of the Juftice of Peace.

Releafe of the
Peace.

I the faid *H. M.* who of my Difcretion have compelled the above-named *A. B.* to find the faid Security of the Peace, have of my Difcretion (as much as in me lies) remifed and releafed the faid Security of the Peace. In Witnefs whereof I have to this prefent Releafe fet my Seal. Given, &c.

The Releafe of the Party before the fame Juftice that took it.

Cambridge.
Another Form.

B E it remembered, that on the   Day of, &c. the faid *E. F.* hath come before me *R. T.* and freely remifed and releafed (as much as in him lies) the faid Secu rity of the Peace, by him prayed before me againft the above named *A. B.* In Witnefs whereof, I the faid *R. T.* have hereunto fet my Seal. Given, &c.

Thefe two former Releafes are to be written under the Recognizance it felf: And if the Juftice fhall only fubfcribe his Name to the Releafe without his Seal, it is well enough, efpecially where the Recognizance is without Seal).

2   *Or*

Or the Releafe of the Party may be by itfelf in this Form, fcil.

BE it remembred, that *E. F.* of *S.* in the faid County Yeoman, on the   Day of Cambridge. in the   Year of the Reign, &c. came before me *I. B.* Efq; one of the *Another Foreft.* Juftices, &c. at *W.* in the faid County, and there remifed and freely releafed to *R. W.* of *S.* in the faid County, Labourer, the Security of the Peace by him the faid *E. F.* before me prayed againft the faid *R. W.* Given, &c.

And if the Releafe be made before another Juftice which took not, or hath not the Recognizance, it may be thus :

BE it remembred, that *A. B.* of *E.* in the faid County, Yeoman, on the   Day of, Cambridge. &c. came before me *R. H.* Efq; one of the Juftices, &c. at *W.* in the faid County, and wholly remifed and releafed the Security of the Peace which he has againft *I. S.* of, &c. Given, &c.

(*a*) But note, that none of thefe Releafes will difcharge the Recognifance, or the Appearance of the Party bound thereby, but that he muft appear according to the Condition of the Recognizance for the Safeguard of the Recognizance.

Releafe for the Good Abearing.

MR. *Lambard* feemeth to doubt whether the Surety of Good Abearing may be re- *Releafe of the* leafed by the Party, (becaufe it feemeth more popular than the Surety of the Peace.) *Good Beha-* But others do hold that it may be releafed; and then may the Form of fuch Releafe be *viour.* eafily made by thofe which are before concerning the Peace, ufing the Words *Security of* P. R. 22. *Good Abearing,* or *of the Good Behaviour,* inftead of the Words *Security of the Peace.* But notwithftanding fuch Releafe, it fhall be fafe alfo for the Party bound to appear according to the Recognizance.

(a) Indentures for Apprentices.

THIS Indenture made the 20th Day of *February,* &c. witneffeth that *A. B. C. D. Indentures of* and *E. F.* Overfeers for the Poor in the Town of *H.* in the County of *C.* and *Poor Appren- J. S.* Church-warden of the fame Town, by and with the Confent of Sir *J. M.* Knight *tices.* and *M. D.* Efquire, two of his Majefty's Juftices of the Peace for the County of *Cambridge,* have by thefe Prefents put, placed and bound *J. H.* (being a poor fatherlefs and motherlefs Child) as an Apprentice with *R. W.* of *H.* aforefaid, Baker, &c. and as an Apprentice with him the faid *R. W.* to dwell, from the Day of the Date of thefe Prefents, until the faid *J. H.* fhall come to be of the Age of 24 Years (if it be a Woman, then until her Age of 21 Years, or the Time of her Marriage,) according to the Statute in that Behalf provided. By and during all which Time and Term the faid *J. H.* fhall the faid *R. W.* his Mafter; well and faithfully ferve in all fuch lawful Bufinefs as the faid *J. H.* fhall be put unto, according to his Power; Wit, and Ability ; and honeftly and obediently in all Things fhall behave himfelf towards his faid Mafter, his Wife and Children, and orderly and honeftly towards all the reft of the Family of the faid *R. W.* And the faid *R. W.* for his Part promifeth, &c. the faid *J. H.* in the Craft, Myftery and Occupation the which he ufeth, after the beft Manner that he can or may, to teach and inform, or caufe to be taught and informed, as much as thereunto belongeth, or in any ways appertaineth : And alfo during all the faid Term to find unto the faid Apprentice Meat, Drink, Linen, Woollen; Hofe, Shoes, and other Things needful or meet for an Apprentice, &c. In Witnefs whereof, &c.

In this Indenture may alfo be added the other ufual Covenants for Apprentices; which fee *Lib. Intr.* verbo *Covenant,* in *Apprentices,* and *Weft.* 581.

CHAP.

CHAP. CLXXXII.

Forcible Entry.

The Form of the Record of a Forcible Entry by the Justice upon his View.

BE it remembred, that *A. B.* of *W. &c.* on the   Day of   in the Year of the Reign, *&c.* complained to me *J. C. &c.* one of the Justices of our said Lord the King assigned to keep the Peace in the said County, that *C. D.* of *W.* aforesaid Yeoman and others unknown Disturbers of the Peace of our said Lord the King with a strong Hand entered into the Dwelling-house of the said *A. B.* at *W.* aforesaid, and disseised the said *J. B.* thereof, and with strong Hand and armed Power do yet hold, and therefore he requested of me to appoint a Remedy on this Behalf. Which Complaint and Request being heard, I the said *J. C.* did immediately go in Person to the said Dwelling-house, and then found the said *C. D.* and others *E. F. G. H. &c.* holding the said House with Force and Arms, a strong Hand and armed Power, that is to say, Swords, Staves and Guns, *&c* against the Form of the Statute made and provided in a Parliament held in the fifteenth Year of the Reign of our Lord *Richard* the second late King of *England*, and against the Form of divers other Statutes: And therefore I the said *J. C.* did then and there arrest the said *C. D. E. F.* and *G. H.* and caused them to be carried to the next Gaol of our said Lord the King at the Castle of *Cambridge* in the said County, as of the said holding with strong Hand and Detainer upon my View and Record convicted, there to abide until they shall make Fines to our said Lord the King for their Trespasses aforesaid. Given at *W.* aforesaid, under my Seal the Day and Year aforesaid.

The Form of the Mittimus *(to the Gaol) of such as hold Land by Force.*

JOHN *Cotton* Knight, one of the Justices of the Peace of our Sovereign Lord the King within his said County of *Cambridge*, to the Keeper of the Common Gaol at, *&c.* in the said County, and to his Deputy and Deputies there, and to every of them. Whereas upon Complaint made unto me this present Day by *A. B.* of *Weston* in the said County Yeoman, I went immediately to the Dwelling-house of the said *J. B.* of *Weston* aforesaid, and there found *C. D. E. F.* and *G. H.* of *D.* aforesaid, Labourers, forcibly and with strong Hand and armed Power holding the said House, against the Peace of our Sovereign Lord, and against the Form of the Statute of Parliament thereof made in the fifteenth Year of the late King *Richard* the second: Therefore I send you (by the Bringers hereof) the said *C. D. E. F.* and *G. H.* convicted of the said forcible Holding by mine own View, Testimony and Record; commanding you in his Majesty's Name to receive them into your said Gaol, and there safely to keep them, until such Time as they shall make their Fines to our said Sovereign Lord for their said Trespasses, and shall be thence delivered by the Order of Law. Hereof fail you not, upon the Peril that may follow thereof. Given at *Weston* aforesaid, under my Seal, the Day and Year abovesaid.

The Form of a Precept (to the Sheriff) to return a Jury for an Inquiry.

J. C. one of the Justices, *&c.* to the Sheriff of the said County, Greeting: On the Behalf of our said Lord the King, I command you that you cause to come before me at *B.* in the said County, on the   Day of   twenty-four honest, sufficient and lawful Men of the Neighbourhood of *W.* in the said County, each of whom shall have at least 40 *s.* of Lands, Tenements or Rents by the Year above Reprises, to inquire upon their Oath for our said Lord the King of a certain Entry with strong Hand made into a Messuage of one *A. B.* at *W.* aforesaid, against the Form of the Statute made in a Parliament holden in the eighth Year of the Reign of *Henry* the Sixth late King of *England*; and see that you return at the said Day 20 *s.* of Issues upon every one of the Jurors by you to be impanelled on this Behalf; And that you no ways omit this, under the Penalty of twenty Pounds, which you know you will incur, if in the Execution of the Premisses you be remiss. And then have you there this Precept. Witness me the said *J. C. &c.*

Note; When the Juftices of Peace are to inquire upon the Statute of 8 *H.* 6. (or any ⟨8 H. 6.⟩ other Statute) they make their Precept to the Sheriff, to return before them Panels to in- ⟨Directions.⟩ quire for the King (generally) of fuch Things as fhall be injoined them on the King's Ma-jefty's Behalf, without faying, to inquire of a Forcible Entry, or of a Riot, &c. *Cromp.* 123.

The Form of the Inquiry, Prefentment, or Verdict of the Jury.

AN Inquifition for our Lord the King taken at *B.* in the County aforefaid, on the ⟨Cambridge.⟩ the   Day of   in the   Year of the Reign, &c. by the Oath of *A. B. C. D. E. F.* &c. before *I. C.* one of the Juftices of our Lord the King affigned, &c. who fay upon their Oath aforefaid, that *A. B.* of *W.* aforefaid, Yeoman, for a long Time was lawfully and peaceably feifed in his Demefne as of Fee, of and in one Meffuage, &c. with the Appurtenants in *W.* aforefaid, and fo continued his Poffeffion and Seifin aforefaid, un-til *C. D.* of, &c. and other Malefactors unknown, did on the   Day of   ⟨* Yet thefe⟩ laft paft, with Force and Arms *, that is, with Swords, Staves, Clubs, and other Wea- ⟨Words, With⟩ pons defenfive and offenfive, enter into the faid Meffuage, and him the faid *A. B.* there- ⟨Force and Arms, here⟩ of did diffeife, and with a ftrong Hand put out, and the fame *A. B.* thus diffeifed and ⟨feem to be need-⟩ put out of the faid Meffuage, &c. from the aforefaid   Day of   until the Day ⟨lefs, being ne-⟩ of taking this Inquifition, by the fame Force and armed Power have kept out, and at this ⟨ceffarily im-plied in the⟩ Time do keep out, to the great Difturbance of the Peace of our faid Lord the King, and ⟨Words, With⟩ againft the Form of the Statute in fuch Cafe made and provided in a Parliament of our ⟨a ftrong Hand.⟩ Lord *Henry* the Sixth, King of *England*, held in the eighth Year of his Reign, † where ⟨Vide antea⟩ none of them nor any other, whofe Eftate they or any of them had, any Thing in the ⟨Tit. *Forcible* Entry.⟩ faid Meffuage or any Parcel thereof had, within three Years next before their Entry ⟨† This laft Claufe may be⟩ aforefaid, nor at any Time preceding, to the Knowledge of the Jurors aforefaid. ⟨omitted.⟩

Otherwife upon the Statute 8 Henry 6.

THE Jurors for our Lord the King prefent *, That whereas in a Statute made in a ⟨* And yet it⟩ Parliament of our Lord *Henry* the Sixth late King of *England*, held at *Weftminfter* ⟨feems not beft to recite the⟩ in the eighth Year of his Reign, it is among other Things contained, that if any Perfon or ⟨Stat. but fhew⟩ Perfons be expelled or diffeifed of any Lands or Tenements with a ftrong Hand, or peace- ⟨the Forcible⟩ ably put out, and afterwards kept out with a ftrong Hand, or that after fuch Entry any ⟨Entry, &c.⟩ Feoffment or Difcontinuance be any way made to defraud and take away the Right of the ⟨and to conclude againft the⟩ Poffeffor, the Party grieved fhall on this Behalf have an Affife or Action of Trefpafs ⟨Form of the Statute, &c.⟩ againft fuch Diffeifor; and if the Party grieved fhall recover by Affife or by Action of ⟨Vide poft 't it.⟩ Trefpafs, or it be found by Verdict, or any other way in due Form of Law, that the ⟨Indictments.⟩ Party defending thus entered into the Lands and Tenements, or held them by Force after fuch his Entry, the Plaintiff fhall recover his treble Damages againft fuch Defendant; and farther, that the fame Defendant fhall make Fine and Ranfom to our faid Lord the King, as in the faid Statute it is more fully contained: Yet one *W. W.* late of *W.* in the County aforefaid Husbandman, and *G. D.* of the fame, Labourer, no ways regarding the Statute aforefaid, nor any way fearing the Penalty in the fame Statute contained, on the Day of   in the   Year of the Reign, &c. in the faid County, into one Barn, being the Freehold of *R. W.* Dean of the Cathedral Church of *W.* with ftrong Hand, and Force and Arms, that is, Swords, &c. did enter, and make Entry, and the faid Dean of the Church aforefaid of his Freehold, with a ftrong Hand and Force and Arms, did put out and diffeife without Judgment, and then and there did put out and eject Sir *L. P.* Knight, Farmer of the faid Dean, of the Barn aforefaid; and the Dean aforefaid being thus expelled and diffeifed, from the   Day of   until the Day of taking this Inqui-fition, they with Force and Arms aforefaid, and with a ftrong Hand kept out, and at this Time do keep out, in Contempt of our Lord the King that now is, and to the grievous Damage of him *R.* and againft the Peace of our Lord the King, and againft the Form of the Statute aforefaid, &c.

Another, wherein the Statute is not recited.

LET it be inquired for our Lord the King, if *A. B.* and *C. D.* late of, &c. having ⟨This is the beft⟩ taken with them other Malefactors and Difturbers of the Peace of our Lord the ⟨Form.⟩ King, and being arrayed in a warlike Manner to the Number of twelve Perfons, whofe

Names

Names the Jurors at prefent do not know, on the   Day of, &c. at *D. &c.* with Force and Arms, that is, &c. into one Meffuage with the Appurtenants, on the peaceable Pof-feffion of *M. L.* did enter, and the faid *M.* from his faid Poffeffion did expel and diffeife; and the fame *M.* being thus expelled and diffeifed from the faid Meffuage with the Appur-tenants, with Force and Arms, and a ftrong Hand, did keep out, and yet keep out, againft the Peace of our faid Lord the King, and againft the Form of the Statute of our Lord *Henry* the Sixth, late King of *England*, in the eighth Year of his Reign, thereof made and provided.

Otherwife upon the Statute 5 R. 2.

* *For fuch Re-cital of the Stat. fee after in the Title Indictments.*

BE it inquired for our Lord the King, &c. * That whereas in a Statute in a Parlia-ment of our Lord *Richard* the fecond after the Conqueft, late King of *England*, made at *Weftminfter* in the fifth Year of his Reign, it is among other Things ordained thus, that none fhould make Entry into any Lands or Tenements, but in the Cafe where Entry is given by Law, and in that Cafe not with a ftrong Hand, nor with a Multitude of People, but in a lawful and quiet Manner only; and if any fhall do to the contrary, and fhall be thereof duly convicted, he fhall be punifhed by Imprifonment of his Body, and fhall make Fine at the Will of our Lord the King, as in the fame Statute among other Things is more fully contained: Neverthelefs a certain *T. H.* of *J.* in the County aforefaid Yeoman, and others, &c. no ways regarding the Statute aforefaid, on the Day of   in the   Year of the Reign, &c. with Force and Arms, that is, with Swords, Staves, &c. into one Clofe of Sir *J. C.* Knight, lying at, &c. in the County aforefaid, in a Place there called *H.* on the Poffeffion of the faid Sir *J. C.* where Entry is not given to them, or to any of them by Law, did make Entry, and root up, pluck up, and fpoil one hundred Poles of the Quick-hedges of him the faid Sir *J. C.* then and there growing, in Contempt of our faid Lord the King that now is, and to the grievous Damage of him Sir *J. C.* and againft the Form of the Statute aforefaid, &c.

(*a*) The Lord *Cromwel* was indicted for a Forcible Entry upon *Andrews*, and in the later End they conclude thus, *Et fi domus pred' non fuit in poffeffione Domine Regine*, they find it *billa vera:* This was adjudged a void Indictment, for it is *quafi a Conditione pred'*. Yelv. p. 15.

Fenton and others indicted, *quod unum meffuag', &c. exiftens folum & liberum tenem'* I. S. *ingreffum fecerunt*, and adjudged good.   1. *Ingreffum fecer.* without faying *in mef-fuag.* is good.   2. *Exiftens* without *adtunc* relates to the Time of the Entry. *Yelv. p.* 27. Yet *Latch* 109. is contrary.

Ford was indicted for a Forcible Entry and Detainer, and the Jury found as to the For-cible Entry *Ignoramus*, and as to the Forcible Detainer *Billa vera*, the Indictment be-ing removed by *Certiorari*, and adjudged naught. *Hill.* 4 *Jac. B. R. Yelv. p.* 99.

Shillet and feven others were indicted for a Forcible Entry upon the Poffeffion of *B.* Farmer *de C.* and diffeifing *C.* but lay no Expulfion of *B.* and adjudged naught: But if it had not been alledged that *B.* was Farmer *de C.* but generally that they entred *fuper pof-feffionem B.* and diffeifed *C.* it had been good enough. *M.* 7 *Jac. B. R. Yelv. p.* 195.

An Indictment was endeavoured to be quafhed, becaufe it is not faid that he entred *ma-nu forti;* but the Court faid it was good, if it be faid, *quod extratenuit manu forti.*   2. Exception, becaufe a Forcible Entry cannot be *in medietat. manerii;* but the Court held it good. *Latch p.* 224.

Indictment. Note, That upon Indictments, &c. the Jury are only charged with the Effect of the Bill, *fc.* whether the Parties be guilty of the Forcible Entry, (or other Fact) or not; and not whether they be guilty in or under fuch Manner and Form as the Indictment or Bill fpecifieth, or not, (*fc.* not whether it were with Staves and Swords, &c. which is but Matter of Form, and muft be kept in every Indictment, though the Parties had nei-ther Staff, Sword, nor other Weapon). And fo when the Jury fay *Billa vera*, they fay True, as they take the Effect of the Bill to be. And if there be falfe *Latin* in the Bill of Indictment, and the Jury find it *Billa vera*, yet their Verdict is True, *fc.* as to the Fact; and their Verdict doth not go to the Form of Words, but to the Effect of the Matter, and to the Fact, *fc.* they are to inquire whether there were any fuch Fact done by the Parties, or not.   And fo though the Bill vary from the Day, from the Year, and from the Place, and the Jury find *Billa vera*, yet they have given a true Verdict *Doctor and Student* 162, 163.

Anc

And therefore the Juſtices of Peace, before whom ſuch Indictments of Forcible Entry or of Riots, &c. ſhall be taken, ſhall do well to inform the Jury, that they are bound to regard the Effect of the Bill of Indictment, or the Fact, and not the Form.

(d) The Warrant to the Sheriff for making of Reſtitution, (if the Juſtice himſelf will not make it.)

SIR J. C. Knight, one of the Juſtices, &c. to the Sheriff of the ſaid County, Greet- Cambridge. ing: Whereas by a certain Inquiſition of the Country before me, at B. in the Coun- Reſtitution. ty aforeſaid, on the   Day of   &c. upon the Oath of A. B. C. D. E. F. &c. and by the Form of the Statute of Entries made with a ſtrong Hand in ſuch Caſe provided, it was found, That C. D. &c. and others, &c. on the   Day of   &c. in a certain Meſ-ſuage of A. B. &c. in W. aforeſaid, did enter, and him A. B. thereof then with a ſtrong Hand did diſſeiſe and drive out, and A. B. aforeſaid thus driven out of the ſaid Meſſuage, &c. from the   Day of   , &c. aforeſaid, to the Day of the Taking of the ſaid Inquiſi-tion, with a ſtrong Hand, and with Force did keep out, as by the Inquiſition aforeſaid more fully appears of Record; therefore on the Behalf of our ſaid Lord the King I com-mand you, that (being hereunto duly required) you go with the Power of your County (if it be needful) to the ſaid Meſſuage, and the other Premiſſes, and that you cauſe the ſame, with the Appurtenants, to be reſeiſed, and that you cauſe the ſaid A. B. to be re-ſtored and put to and in his full Poſſeſſion thereof, according as he, before the Entry aforeſaid, was ſeiſed, according to the Form of the ſaid Statute. And this you ſhall no ways omit, on the Penalty thereon incumbent. Witneſs, &c.

This Warrant to the Sheriff to make Reſtitution ſhall be under the *Teſte* of one of the Juſtices only, as it ſeemeth. *Dyer* 182.

A Certificate of the Preſentment or Verdict of the Jury in the King's Bench, whereof *vide antea*, Tit. *Forcible Entry.*

A Certificate into the King's Bench of the Record of a Force viewed by the Juſtice, whereof *vide antea*, Tit. *Forcible Entry.*

Theſe two former Certificates (and the like) may be done and made by the Juſtices of Peace by Way of a Letter (as it ſeemeth) incloſing therein the ſaid Preſentment of the Jury, or the ſaid Record of the Juſtices; except the ſame be removed thither by a *Cer-tiorari*, and then may the Juſtices return them in ſuch Manner as appeareth hereafter, Tit. *Certiorari*, with ſome little Alteration.

Or the Juſtice of Peace may himſelf deliver into the King's Bench ſuch Preſentment 8 El. 4. 18. found before him, or ſuch Record made by him, and the like, and that without any Br. Cor. 152. *Certiorari*, for that he is a Judge of Record.

The Form of a Certificate (or the Manner of the Return) of the Writ upon the Statute of The Return. Northampton into the Chancery.

Upon the Writ itſelf theſe Words may be indorſed, The Execution of this Writ appears by a Schedule to the ſame Writ annexed. *And the Schedule may be thus.*

I Sir J. C. Knt. one of the Keepers of the Peace of our Lord the King in the County of The Certificate. Cambridge, do certify into the Chancery of our ſaid Lord the King, that by virtue of the Writ firſt delivered to me, on the   Day of   in the   Year, &c. I did (on the Behalf of our ſaid Lord the King) publickly cauſe to be proclaimed at B. of which in the ſaid Writ mention is made, according as it is commanded in the ſaid Writ: And becauſe certain A. B. and D. E. of F. in the County aforeſaid, Labourers, little regarding the Proclamation aforeſaid, after the ſaid Proclamation there ſo made, did go armed, and an armed Force there did lead; that is, two Helmets, one Bow and ten Arrows, two Swords, and as many Daggers, to the Diſturbance of the Peace of our ſaid Lord the King, and Terror of his People, as alſo to the manifeſt Contempt of the Statute in the ſaid Writ ſpecified; and therefore I did arreſt the ſaid A. B. and D. E. together with their Armor aforeſaid, and did cauſe their Bodies to be carried to the next Priſon of our ſaid Lord the King in the County aforeſaid, there to remain until I ſhall have ſome other Command of our ſaid Lord the King for their Delivery. I alſo cauſed their ſaid Armor to be appraiſed by A. B. D. E. and F. G. of B. aforeſaid, Yeomen, hereunto ſworn, who ſay, upon their Oath aforeſaid, that the two Helmets are worth 10 s. and that the ſaid Bow and ten Arrows are worth

worth 6 *s.* and that the Swords aforesaid are worth 20 *s.* and that the said Daggers are worth 5 *s.* and so the Armors aforesaid are upon the Whole worth 41 *s.* of the which I am ready to answer according to the Tenor of the said Writ. In Witness whereof I have to this present Certificate set my Seal. Given, *&c.*

J. C.

(*a*) *The Form of a Certificate to be made by him which shall take the Oaths of a Justice of Peace by Commission or* Dedimus Potestatem.

Upon the Commission (*or* Dedimus Potestatem) *indorse these or the like Words,* The Execution of this Writ appears by a Schedule to this Writ annexed. *And the Certificate may be thus.*

I *M. D.* do certify into the Chancery of our Lord the King, that by virtue of a Writ of our Lord the King to this Schedule annexed, I did, on the   Day of   in the   Year of the Reign, *&c.* at *W. W.* in the County of *C.* receive the Oaths of *J. M.* Knight, in the Writ aforesaid named, as well of the Office of Keeper of the Peace, to be well and truly performed, according to the Forms in the Schedule annexed to the Writ aforesaid, as the Oaths specified in an Act of Parliament made in the first Year of the Reign of our Lord *George* the first, late King of, *&c.* according to the Tenor of the Writ, and Schedule to the Writ aforesaid likewise annexed, and in all Thing as in the said Writ is commanded. In Witness whereof, *&c.*

M. D.

C H A P. CLXXXIII.

Riot.

(*a*) AN unlawful Assembly, and an unlawful Act make a Riot; but if the Assembly was lawful, without an ill Intent, and an Affray happen, the Actor only are guilty: But if the Assembly was unlawful originally, then the Fact will be imputed to all who were present. 2 *Salk.* 594. 6 *Mod.* 43. 141.

(*d*) *The Form of a Record of a Riot viewed by the Justices and Sheriff, or Under Sheriff.*

Cambridge. BE it remembered, That on the   Day of   in the   Year of the Reign *&c.* We *J. C.* and *J. K.* two of the Justices assigned, *&c.* And *W. W.* then Sheriff of the said County, upon the grievous Complaint and humble Petition of *A. B.* of *D.* in the said County, Yeoman, have in our proper Persons come to the Dwelling house of him *A. B.* in *D.* aforesaid, and then and there found *D. E. F. G.* and *H. J.* of *D.* Labourers, and other unknown Malefactors and Disturbers of the Peace of our said Lord the King, to the Number of ten Persons, arrayed in a warlike Manner, that is with Swords, *&c.* unlawfully and riotously assembled, and besetting the same House many Evils to him *A. B.* threatning, to the great Disturbance of the Peace of our said Lord the King, and Terror of his People, and against the Form of a Statute in a Parliament

13 H. 4. of our Lord *Henry* the Fourth, late King of *England,* holden in the thirteenth Year of his Reign, made and provided. And therefore we *J. C. J. K.* and *W. W.* aforesaid, have caused the said *D. E. F. G. H. J. &c.* then and there to be arrested, and carried to the next Gaol of our said Lord the King in the County aforesaid, being convicted by our View and Record of the unlawful Assembly and Riot aforesaid, there to remain until they shall make Fine thereof to our said Lord the King. In Witness whereof we have to this present Record set our Seals. Given at *D.* aforesaid, *&c.*

Lamb. 312. And if a Man be slain or maimed, or a Rescous be done to the Officer by the Rioters, then the Record ought to be *they did riotously kill,* or *riotously maim,* or *riotously rescue,* but not *feloniously,* nor simply *rescue,* because their Authority is in this Case restrained to the Riot only; so as notwithstanding that Record the Parties may plead Not guilty to the Felony or the Rescous, howsoever for the Riot they are estopped.

5

Th

The *Mittimus* for conveying the Rioters to the Gaol may (with some few Words of *Mittimus.* Change) be made out of that which is here before for such as hold by Force. See hereof before amongst the Precedents in *Forcible Entry.*

The Precept to the Sheriff to return a Jury for an Inquiry upon a Riot.

J C. &c. and *J. K.* &c. Two of the Justices assigned, &c. to the Sheriff of the same Cambridge. County, Greeting : On the Behalf of our said Lord the King we require you, that you cause to come before us at *J.* in the County aforesaid, on the ___ Day of ___ next, twenty-four honest, sufficient and lawful Men, of the County aforesaid, whereof every of them have Lands and Tenements within the said County of Freehold, by Charter, of the yearly Value of *twenty* Shillings, or by Copy of Roll of Court to the yearly Value of *twenty-six* Shillings and *eight* Pence, or by both, beyond all Reprises, to inquire upon their Oath for our said Lord the King, and for our Indemnity in this Behalf, of certain unlawful Assemblies and Riots, lately committed at *D.* in the County aforesaid, as it is said. And this you are no ways to omit under the Penalty of *twenty* Pounds, which you will incur, if you make Default in the Execution of the Premisses. And have you there the Names of the Jurors aforesaid, and this Precept. Given, &c.

The Form of the Inquiry, Indictment or Presentment of the Jury.

A N Inquisition for our Lord the King, &c. (as before in *Forcible Entry*) before *J. C.* &c. and *J. K.* &c. two of the Justices, &c. who say upon their Oaths aforesaid, that *D. E. F. G.* and *H. J.* of, &c. Labourers, together with other Malefactors and Disturbers of the Peace of our said Lord the King, unknown, to the Number of ___ Persons, arrayed in a warlike Manner with Force and Arms, that is, with Swords, &c. did on the ___ Day of ___ at *D.* in the County aforesaid, between the Hours of eight and nine after Noon of the same Day, riotously break and enter the Dwelling-house of *A. B.* of *D.* aforesaid, Yeoman, situated in *D.* aforesaid, and did then and there assault him *A. B.* and there and there him did beat, wound, and ill *(unworthily)* treat, so Indignis ma- that his Life was despaired of, to the great Disturbance of the Peace of our said Lord dis. the King, and Terror of his People, and against the Form of the Statute of Riots, Routs, and unlawful Assemblies of People, in a Parliament of our Lord *Henry* the fourth, late King of *England*, held in the thirteenth Year of his Reign, made and provided.

Note, That all Indictments of Riots or Forcible Entries, &c. taken before Justices of *Directions.* the Peace must be after this Form, *sc.* An Inquisition, &c. taken, &c. before *J. C.* and *R. T.* &c. (if out of the Sessions ; or if at the Sessions, then before *J. C.* and his Companions) Justices of our Lord the King, to keep the Peace in the said County, as also to hear and determine divers Felonies, &c. as here before in *Forcible Entry.*

Otherwise.

A N Inquisition, &c. who say, &c. that *A. B. C. D.* and *E. F.* of, &c. having ga- *Another Form* thered to themselves many other unknown Malefactors and Disturbers of the Peace *of the Inquiry* of our Lord the King, to the Number of ___ Persons, arrayed in a warlike Manner, by the Instigation and Procuration of *J. S.* did, on the ___ Day of ___ with Force and Arms, that is, Swords, Clubs, &c. and other Arms, as well offensive as defensive, at *A.* in the County of *Cambridge*, unlawfully, riotously, and routously assemble, and the Close of *W. H.* &c. at *A.* aforesaid, then and there unjustly break and enter, and ten Parcels of quick Hedges of him *W. H.* then and there growing did root out, pluck up and spoil, to the grievous Damage of him *W. H.* and against the Peace of our said Lord, and against the Form of divers Statutes in such Case made and provided.

As for the Certificate (which ought to be made to the King and the Council, in case *Certificate* that by this Inquiry the Truth of the Fault and Riot be not found) such Certificate may be done in *English* by way of a Letter, comprehending the Truth of the whole Matter, with the Certainty of the Time, Place, and other Circumstances of the Fact or Riot, together with the Certainty of the Names of the Rioters ; as also of the Names of such who by Maintenance, Embracery, or otherwise, were any Impediment to the Finding thereof, with their several Misdemeanors : Which Certificate or Letter is to be directed and sent by the said Justices of Peace and Sheriff, or Under Sheriff, into the King's Bench, &c. within one Month. See *antea*, Tit. *Riot.*

A Traverse to an Indictment of a Riot, and the Record thereupon.

Cambridge.
The Style of the Sessions.
HEretofore, to wit, at the Sessions of the Peace held at the Castle of *Cambridge* in the County aforesaid, on the *Tuesday* next before the Feast of St. *Matthew the Apostle* in the fourteenth Year of the Reign of our Lord *George* the Second, by the Grace of God, of *Great Britain, France* and *Ireland* King, Defender of the Faith, and so forth, before *A. B. C. D.* and others their Companions (or Brethren) Justices of our said Lord the King, assigned to keep the Peace in the County aforesaid, as also to hear and determine divers Felonies, Trespasses, and other Offences (Misdeeds) in the same

The Indictment.
County committed, by the Oath of twelve Jurors it is presented, that *J. L.* of *R. M.* of and *T. L.* of with divers others unknown, Malefactors and Disturbers of the Peace of our said Lord the King, in a warlike Manner arrayed, joined and assembled, on the Day of in the Night of the same Day, in the Year, &c. with Force and Arms, that is, Swords, Staves, Clubs, Guns, and other Arms, as

Routose.
well offensive as defensive at *C.* &c. riotously and routously broke and enter'd, and then and there unjustly and unlawfully took and carried off eight Waggons of Hay, to the Value of then and there being, of the Goods and Chattels of the said against

Process.
Traverse.
Jury.
the Peace of our said Lord the King, and against the Force of the Statute thereof made and provided ; whereby the Sheriff was commanded that he should not omit, &c. And afterwards, that is to say, on *Tuesday* next before the Feast of Saint *Matthew the Apostle* aforesaid in the fourteenth Year aforesaid, before the Justices aforesaid came the said *J. L. R. M.* and *T. L.* in their proper Persons, and having had the Hearing of the Indictment

Not guilty,
aforesaid, severally say, that they are not thereof Guilty, and of this they put themselves upon the Country ; and *A. M.* who prosecutes for our Lord the King in this Behalf likewise, &c. Therefore let a Jury thereof come before the Justices of the said Lord the King, assigned to keep the Peace in the County aforesaid, &c. at the Sessions of the Peace at *G.* &c. to be holden upon *Tuesday* next after the Epiphany of our Lord then next to be, and who, &c. to recognize, &c. because as well, &c. The same Day is

Day given.
given as well to *A. M.* aforesaid who prosecutes, &c. as to *J. L. R. M.* and *L. T.* &c. to which Sessions holden at *G.* aforesaid in the County aforesaid, on the Day, &c. before Sir *T. P.* Knight, and his Companions, Justices of our said Lord the King, assigned to keep the Peace in the County aforesaid, and also to hear and determine divers Felonies, Trespasses, and other Offences in the said County committed, as well the said *A. M.* who prosecutes, &c. as the said *J. L. R. M.* and *T. L.* in their proper Persons did come, and the Jurors aforesaid, being by the Sheriff aforesaid for this impanelled, and demanded, to wit, *J. F. J. G.* &c. did also come; who being tried and sworn, to say the Truth

The Verdict.
of the Premisses, say upon their Oath, that the aforesaid *J. L. R. M.* and *T. L.* are Guilty, and every of them is guilty of the Trespass, Contempt and Riot aforesaid, specified in the Indictment aforesaid, in the Manner and Form as against them it is above supposed.

The Judgment.
It is therefore considered by the Court, that the aforesaid *J. L. R. M.* and *T. L.* be taken to satisfy our said Lord the King of their Fines, by occasion of the Trespass, Contempt and Riot aforesaid. Which *J. L. R. M.* and *T. L.* then and there present in Court prayed to be admitted to a Fine with our said Lord the King on the said Occasion ; and

Fine assessed.
thereof they severally put themselves in the Mercy of our Lord the King. And the Fine of the same *J. L.* is by the Justices aforesaid assessed, at three Pounds six Shillings and eight Pence; and the Fine of the same *R. M.* is assessed at twenty Shillings; and the Fine of the same *T. L.* is assessed at five Pounds of good and lawful Money of *Great Britain,* to the Use and Behoof of our said Lord the King.

I have inserted this former Precedent, for that it discovereth much Matter worthy the Justices Observation.

CHAP. CLXXXIV.

Indictments.

FOR the Form of Indictments in Cafes of Forcible Entry and Riots, I have here before fet down certain Precedents; neverthelefs for that thefe Indictments are the
chief Foundation whereupon the whole Trial is after to be grounded, I thought it not
amifs to obferve here thefe few general Rules, as well concerning the Matter as the
Form of thefe and all other Indictments or Prefentments to be taken before the Juftices
of Peace.

Firft, In thefe Indictments of Forcibly Entry and Riots (as alfo in all other Indict- *Forcible Entry.*
ments of Felony or Trefpafs) it is good to fay, *Againft the Peace*, or other Words to
that Effect.

Thefe Words, *With Force and Arms*, (viz.) *with Swords, &c.* are not of Neceffity, Lamb. 484.
yet it is good to ufe them, efpecially if the Circumftances of the Fact do require them; 18 H. 8. c. 8.
for thefe Circumftances do either aggravate or diminifh the Offence. *Stamf.* 94.

But thefe Words [*with Force and Arms*] are needlefs in an Indictment of *Forcible Entry*, becaufe they are implied in the Word *Force*.

Yet Note, That in all the Indictments of *Treafon, Murder, Felony*, or *Trefpaffes*, *Treafon, Mur-
thefe Words *with Force and Arms* are neceffary to be put in: (Otherwife it feemeth *der, and Fe-
of Offences which are againft the Peace only, as Confpiracies, Deceits, Slanders, Efcapes *lony.*
for Debt, and the like). *Finch.*

Alfo in Indictments found upon Statutes it is not needful, nay, it is not fafe to recite *Indictments on
the Statute at all: For as the Recital is not neceffary, fo the Mifrecital thereof in the *Statutes.*
Matter, or in the Year, Day or Place, is fatal to the Indictment, and maketh it void. Co. 4. 48.
But it is fafe and fure to draw the Indictment with this Conclufion. Br. Parl. 87.

Againft the Form of the Statute in fuch Cafe made and provided, (if the Indictment Co. 4. 48.
be founded upon the *Statute:*) Or *againft the Form of feveral Statutes in fuch Cafe made Dyer 363.
and provided*, (without naming any fpecial Statute, where many Statutes do concern one
Offence). *Cromp.* 104.

Yet the Offence againft the Statute muft be certainly defcribed in the Indictment, and Plo. 1. & 79.
the Subftance and material Words in fuch Statute muft be fully fet down therein.
Plow. 1 & 79. *Lamb.* 485. *Co. L.* 98. *b.*

Alfo all Indictments and Prefentments (being in the Nature of Declarations for the Lamb. 463,
King againft the Offenders) ought to contain Certainty, and fhall not be fupplied or &c.
maintained by Implication, Intendment or Argument, *Co.* 5. 120. *Plow.* 84. 122. and Br. Indict. 6,
therefore fix principal Things are requifite in all Prefentments before the Juftices of 24, 34, 46, &
Peace, *viz.* 47.
Stamf. 96.

1. The Names and Surnames, as well of the Parties indicted, as of the Parties offended; with the Addition of the Degree, Myftery, and the Dwelling-place of the Party indicted, (*fc.* both the Town and County.)

Yet in fome Cafes an Indictment, that he did procure unknown Perfons, or that he
did take the Goods of an unknown Perfon, *&c.* or the like, may be good. See *plus
Lamb.* 470, 476. *Br. Indictment* 6, 10, 11. *Dyer* 99. & *Plow. fol.* 85. *b.*

2. The Time, *fc.* the Day and Year when the Offence was done.

3. The Place, *fc.* the Town and Country where it was done, as at *B.* in the Coun- Br. Indict. 24,
ty of *C.* 41, 42.
Lamb. 471.

4. The Name or Quality of the Thing in which the Offence is committed, *viz.* of
dead Things, it may be the Goods and Chattels, expreffing them certainly; of live
Things, Horfe, Ox, Sheep, *&c.* but not Goods and Chattels. So of *Entry, &c.* to exprefs certainly whether it be Houfe, Land, Meadow, Pafture, Wood, *&c.*

5. Alfo the Value or Price of the Thing is commonly to be fet down to aggravate the Fault.

6. The Manner of the Fact, *fc.* the Manner and Nature of the Offence; as whe- Lamb 480.
ther it be Felony, or Trefpafs. See *Lamb.* 480. *Br. Indict.* 7. 36.

And yet for the Form of Indictments the Jury are not ftrictly tied thereunto, (*fc.*
to the Day, Year or Place, *&c.*) but chiefly to the Manner of Fact. *Vide hic antea.*

Alfo

Verity.   Alſo Indictments ought to be framed ſo near the Truth as may be, and the rather, for that they are to be found by the Jury upon their Oaths. *Co.* 9. 119. *Plo.* 84.

Yea, an Indictment being *verdictum, id eſt, dictum veritatis,* and a Matter of Record, ought to ſet forth all the Truth that by Law is requiſite; for *de non apparentibus & non exiſtentibus eadem eſt ratio:* And every Part of the Indictment material ought to be found by the Oath of the Jurors, and it is not to be ſupplied by Averment; otherwiſe the Indictment will be inſufficient.

(*a*) All Law Proceedings are to be in *Engliſh,* by 4 *Geo.* 2. *cap.* 26.

See 2 Hawk. P. C. Chap. 25. *Of* Indictment.

C H A P. CLXXXV. (*a*)

Seſſions.

Deſcription.   THE Seſſions of the Peace are a Court of Record holden before two or more Juſtices of the Peace, whereof one is of the *Quorum,* for Execution of the Authority given them by Commiſſion of the Peace, and certain Statutes and Acts of Parliament.

Time.   2. The Seſſions of the Peace were anciently uncertain and undertermined as to the Times, for that ſo few Perſons being in Commiſſion, as 4 or 6, and thoſe for the moſt part Men of Law, they thought it burthenſome to attend; and therefore 36 *E.* 3. 12. a Law was made, that in the Commiſſion of the Peace expreſs Mention ſhould be made, that the ſaid Juſtices make their Seſſions four Times in the Year, *viz.* one Seſſions within one Week after the *Epiphany;* the ſecond within the ſecond Week of Lent, the third between the Feaſts of *Pentecoſt* and *St. John Baptiſt;* the fourth within eight Days of *St. Michael.* But that Courſe proving inconvenient, by the Statute of 12 *R.* 2. *cap.* 10. it is ordained,

3. The Juſtices ſhall hold their Seſſions in every Quarter of the Year at leaſt, and that by three Days at the leaſt, upon Pain to be puniſhed by the Diſcretion of the King's Counſel. And becauſe thoſe Times were uncertain, it is ordained,

Four Seſſions in   4. By the Statute of 2 *H.* 5. 4. the Juſtices of Peace ſhall make their Seſſions four
the Year.   Times in the Year, *viz.* in the *firſt Week after the Feaſt of* St. Michael, *the firſt Week after the* Epiphany, *the firſt Week after the Cloſe of* Eaſter, *and the firſt Week after the Tranſlation of* St. Thomas *the Martyr;* and more often if need be. And becauſe the Penalty and Danger of every Juſtice in Commiſſion for not appearing there was by the ſaid Statute of 12 *R.* 2. *cap.* 10. to be puniſhed at the Diſcretion of the King's Council, the Juſtices of the one Bench and the other, and Serjeants, were exempted herefrom by the ſaid Statute, as alſo by the ſaid Statute of 2 *H.* 5. 4.

5. But in as much as the King's Court ſitting in the Term-Time, did frequently call before them the Inhabitants of the County of *Middleſex,* and thereby moſt of the Buſineſs in that County was diſpatched, and the Juſtices of Peace were compelled to hold their Seſſions four Times in the Year, to avoid Penalties of former Statutes; by the
Juſtices of   Statute of 14 *H.* 6. *cap.* 4. it is provided, That the Juſtices of Peace in *Middleſex* be diſ-
Middleſex.   charged of theſe Penalties, provided they hold their Seſſions twice a Year, and oftner if need be, for Forcible Entries or Riots. But the Juſtices of Peace may yet hold their Seſſions four Times in the Year if they ſee Cauſe, as formerly they might have done; and if they do hold them but twice a Year, yet thoſe Times muſt be ſome of the Times mentioned in the Statute of 2 *H.* 5. 4. for they are ſuch Times as were judged moſt convenient for the Eaſe of the Subject.

See more touching the Times of theſe Seſſions before, *cap.* 4.

Place   As to the Place, there is no Determination thereof by any Statute Law: But certain it is, they muſt be holden in ſome Place within the County for which they are holden, for that the Juſtices of Peace their Authority is ſo circumſcribed. And therefore if the King ſhall make a Place within a County of it ſelf, and give them all Privileges of Juriſdiction, it will not be ſafe for the Juſtices of the ancient County to hold their Seſſions there, unleſs the King by his Letters Patent reſerve ſuch Power. But if a Place within the County
11 *R.* 2. 11.   be incorporated by the King, and Juſtices be there appointed; yet the ſame remains ſtill Parcel of the County, and the Juſtices of the Peace of the County may hold their Seſſions

there, but may not intermeddle with Matters arising there, saving such as happen in their Sessions, or with Relation thereunto; for the making such Corporation, and giving them such Power, carries with it an Exclusion of other Commissioners to be appointed by the King, as to Matters arising in such Corporation, so long as such Corporation execute their Authority duly and justly. But in Case of any great Miscarriage in, or Default of, the Execution of Justice there by such Incorporation, as their Liberties may be seised, and restored to the Crown by a *Quo Warranto*; so notwithstanding such Grant there is a Construction of Law left in the King, a Power to provide for the Execution of Law and Justice there, and he may grant a concurrent Commission to worthy and able Persons, who shall see Justice there done. And such Power, as it is honourable for the King, so it is safe for the Subject.

And although the Place be not otherwise determined than as aforesaid by any Statute Law, yet may the Common Law have some Influence on such Authorities and delegated Powers, to confine them to what is reasonable and safe: And therefore could it be supposed that Justices of Peace would appoint their Sessions at a Place known publickly, and to them too, to be infected with the Plague, or on the Confines of a County, or near some publick Dangers by Enemies or otherwise, and their so doing be accompanied with other Circumstances of Wilfulness or worse; such Justices would for the same be punishable by Information and Fine in the King's Bench.

Mr. *Lambard* puts a Case from Mr. *Marrow*, that if two or more Justices appoint the Sessions to be holden in one Town, and so many more appoint a Sessions in another Town the same Day, and holds they may be so held, and that the Presentments in both are good; but that Appearance at one is a Discharge of Service at the other. But with his Favour it may be well questioned whether they are not both void; for they make two Courts of that which ought to be intire and but one: For I do not find the Justices are required or enabled to hold more than one Sessions at a Time; and so their Authority being equal, and seeing no Preference can be made by the Priority of Time, or Nature of the Service, they may be taken to be both void. However certainly the Justices, by whose Frowardness such Division happens, or on whom such Miscarriage is chargeable, on Consideration of their Circumstances of the Matter, are punishable for the same by Information and Fine, or putting out of Commission, as the Cause shall require.

So also (which is another Case put by Mr. *Lambard*) if the Justices appoint a Sessions in one Town, and hold it then in another, without timely Notice of their Alteration of such Appointment, it is punishable in them, for it tends to the Hindrance of the Service, and Trouble and Charge for the Subject.

These Sessions may be, and are usually warned by a Warrant under the Hands and Seals of two or more Justices of the Peace, *Quorum unus*, which may be thus.

G. H. and R. C. &c. two of the Justices assigned, &c. to the Sheriff of the same County, Greeting: On the Behalf of our Lord the King, we require and command you, that you do not omit by Reason of any Liberty in your Bailiwick, but that you enter therein, and cause to come before us, or our Companions Justices of the Peace, &c. on the   Day next, at E. in the County aforesaid, as well twenty-four honest and lawful Men of each Hundred in your Bailiwick, as twenty-four Knights, and other honest and lawful Men of the Body of your County, as well within Liberties as without, each of which shall have at least 40 s. by the Year, of Lands and Tenements of Freehold, to inquire then and there of such Things as on the Behalf of our said Lord the King shall be injoined them: Make it known also to all Coroners of your County, to the Stewards, Constables, Petty Constables, Bailiffs of Liberties within the Hundreds and Liberties aforesaid, that they then be there to do and fulfil such Things as by Reason of their Offices are to be done. Cause you therefore to be proclaimed in proper Places throughout your whole Bailiwick, that the Sessions of the Peace aforesaid are to be holden on the Day, and at the Place aforesaid; and you your self be you there, to do and exercise those Things which unto your Office belong. And have you there as well the Names of the Jurors, Coroners, Stewards, Constables, Petty Constables, and Bailiffs aforesaid, as this Precept. Given, &c.

The Persons that ought to appear at these Sessions are as follow.

First, The *Justices of Peace*. For as a Sessions cannot be held without a competent Number; so the Business of the Sessions cannot be well done without their Appearance, not only in the returning thither such Recognizances and Examinations as they have taken,

and

and feeing the Parties profecuted and convicted, or acquitted of the Crimes charged or them; but alfo for deciding and determining fuch Difficulties as fhall arife, and alfo to give Information touching Perfons and Things that fall within their Knowledge refpective-ly; for *In the Multitude of Counfellors there is Safety.*

Clerk of the Peace.   2. The *Cuftos Rotulorum,* who by Virtue of his Place hath the Cuftody of the Rolls o Seffions, ought to be there by himfelf or his Deputy, who is the Clerk of the Peace.

The Sheriff.   3. The *Sheriff by himfelf or his Deputy,* to receive the *Fines,* to return *Jurors,* to execute *Procefs,* and what elfe to his Office doth appertain : For by Virtue of the Com-miffion he is commanded to be attendant on the Juftices of Peace at all Times, efpecially in Seffions.

Conftables of Hundreds.   4. The Conftables of Hundreds ought there to be, and all other Officers to whom any Warrant hath been directed in Order to make Return thereof.

The Gaoler.   5. *The Gaoler,* to bring thither fuch as have been fent by *Mittimus* to him, there to remain until Seffions; and fuch as are fent thither for *Larcenies* and fuch Offences of like Nature, of which the Seffions do ufually deliver the Gaol; and to give a Kalendar of fuch as are in Prifon, and to receive fuch as may be there committed for any Contempt o Offence.

The Keeper of the Houfe of Correction.   6. The *Governor of the Houfe of Correction,* to give in a Kalendar of fuch Rogues and diforderly Perfons as have been committed to his Cuftody, and an Account of them ; or in Default thereof he is finable by 7 *Jac.* 1. 4.

The Jury.   7. *All Jurors* returned by the Sheriff by Virtue of the faid Precept.

  8. All Perfons bound by *Recognizance* to anfwer, or to profecute and give Evidence.

Bailiffs of Hundreds.   9. All Bailiffs of Hundreds and Liberties, in Refpect they are bound to give an Account of all Seffions Procefs.

Coroners.   10. All Coroners, &c.

That the Juftices of Peace are compellable to appear at the Seffions is out of Doubt; for without their Appearance the Seffions cannot be holden. And in this Cafe no one is more bound than another to attend, unlefs fome great Men, and Men of the Law, who are exempted by 12 *R.* 2. 10. & 2 *H.* 5. 4. and thofe Statutes requiring the Seffions to be held. For Default thereof all Perfons in Commiffion (unlefs exempted by the Statute) are equally punifhable ; and if two, three or more, fhall hold the Seffions, why the reft fhould not appear to perform the Duty, and to bear the Burden, or neglecting fhould not be punifhed, there can be no Reafon given. And therefore I conceive, 1. That fuch as do not appear are within the Danger of 12 *R.* 2. 10. whereby for Defaults by them in not holding the Seffions, or not fo long as is thereby appointed, they are to be punifhed by the King's Council in their Difcretion ; which whether it be the King's Privy Coun-cil, or the King's Learned Council, *i. e.* the Judges of the Law, or who elfe it be, 'tis not for me to determine ; for that every one that is abfent is guilty of not holding the Seffions. Or, 2. Such Juftice of Peace may be indicted or informed againft in the King's Bench for fuch Default, it being a Neglect of his Office, and fined for the fame ; efpe-cially if thofe Omiffions are frequent and ufual. Or, 3. There is great Reafon to put him out of the Commiffion of the Peace for fuch Neglect. Or, 4. I fee no Reafon but the Juftices of Peace in Seffions may proceed by Information or Indictment againft fuch Defaulter, and proceed to Fine or Imprifonment : And the Reafon given by Mr. *Lambard* (*lib.* 4. *p.* 3. *fol.* 383.) I think will not hold here ; for what they do in Seffions they do as a Court, and not as particular Perfons, as was lately holden in the Cafe of Sir *Nicholas Stoughton* in the King's Bench, who being a Juftice of Peace in *Surry,* was required by the Court of Sef-fions there to find Sureties for the Good Behaviour, upon the Complaint of one *Gilham,* for threatning a Juror for prefenting a Matter there, and for not giving Security was com-mitted : And this was refolved to be well done for the Reafon aforefaid ; which Reafon to my Obfervation will alfo hold in Cafe of any Neglect or Mifcarriage againft the Court of Seffions, even by a Juftice of Peace ; or otherwife againft any Law whereof they as a Court have Cognizance.

The Jurors not appearing according to their Summons are punifhable by Lofs of Iffues, which ufually make Part of the Eftreats of Seffions. As are alfo the Conftables, by Fine to be fet on them.

The Juftices being met to hold the Seffions, the ufual Courfe is with three *Oyes* to pro-claim the Seffions, and then read the Commiffion of the Peace; which done, to call the Conftables, and out of them to make one or more Juries for Grand Juries, or Juries of Prefentment ; who being fworn, the Charge is given them to call the Recognizances, efpecially fuch as are to profecute and give Evidence, that fo Bills may be drawn and prepared. To which Purpose an able Clerk is requifite, that fo Labour, Time and Charge may not be fpent in vain ; which Bills being ready, the Parties bound over for that Purpofe are fworn to give Evidence upon the Bills : And the Courfe is to bid the Evidence go with the Jury, where they confider of the Matter of the Bill, and either find it or not find it, as the Evidence appears to them credible and fufficient, or otherwife, and then they return it ; but it may be very reafonable, if the Matter be weighty or difficult, and the Jury be not very able, or the Profecution be too flack or over violent, to hear the Evidence given in Court, that fo the Jury may be the better affifted in doing their Duty.

Whilft the Juries are gone out of Court, the ufual way is to hear Motions touching Settlements of poor Perfons, and other Things relating thereunto ; and to call Perfons bound over to the Peace or the Good Behaviour : But it may not be beft to difcharge them until the End of the Seffions, for fear Perfons may come to prefer Bills againft them, or to complain of them when the Birds are flown.

And becaufe the Arraignment and Trial of Prifoners is a great Part of the Bufinefs of Seffions, I will take Notice of fome Parts thereof, and Proceedings thereupon.

Towards the End of the Seffions, when it appears what Bills are come in againft the *Arraignment.* Prifoners, the Gaoler being called to fet his Prifoners to the Bar, and the Crier being called to make a Bar, that is, to difpofe of the Company that a Way be made open from the Court to the Prifoners, that the Court, Jury and Prifoners may fee each other ; one of the Prifoners is called to : *A. B.* hold up thy Hand ; (this is done to notify him to the Court, the Jury and Standers by.) Thou *A. B.* ftandeft indicted by the Name of *A. B.* of, &c. (Name him as he is named in the Indictment, &c.) for that thou, or that thou with others, &c. (and fo recite the whole Indictment in *Englifh* ; which done) How fayft thou *A. B.* art thou guilty of this Felony and Burglary, or Felony and Robbery, or Felony and Murder, (as the Cafe is) whereof thou ftandeft indicted, or not guilty ? If the Prifoner fay Guilty, then the Confeffion is recorded, and no more done as to him till Judgment ; but if he fay Not guilty, then the Clerk fays, *Culp. prift.* (*i. e.* Guilty already.) How wilt thou be tried ? It is ufual to fay, By God and the Country ; but if the Prifoner ftand mute, and will not plead, 'tis beft to ask him three or more Times, and to tell him the Danger of ftanding Mute, and the Grievoufnefs of the Judgment *de peine fort & dure :* And if yet he will ftand Mute, nothing more can be done concerning him, but to record it. But if he plead Not guilty, fo record it ; and in like Manner all the Reft of the Prifoners. And if two, three or more, they being called to feverally, thus ; you *A. B.* hold up your Hand ; you *C. D.* &c. and fo of the Reft. Then fay, you *A. B.* by the Name of *A. B.* of, &c. and you *C. D.* by the Name of, *C. D.* of, &c. and fo the reft ; for that you, &c. and fo recite the Subftance of the Indictment. Then call to them feverally to plead, &c. (The Word *Arraign* cometh from the *French* Word *Arranger, ordine collocare, quia rei ordine vocantur ad Roftra feu Cancellos, quæ nos Barram vocamus,* faith *Skinner.*) Which done, the Profecutors are called on the Recognizances to give Evidence ; then the Jury are called on their Panel, (for a Return cannot be made upon a *Venire facias* made the fame Seffions, and a Trial had there- *Trial the fame* upon in the fame Seffions, as is held 22 *E.* 4. *Fitz. Coron. p.* 44. and *Stamf. l.* 3. *c.* 5. *Seffions.* f. 156. in cafe of Juftices of Peace in their Seffions ; much lefs can they nominate or direct the immediate Return of By-ftanders. But otherwife it is in Cafe of the Juftices *The Clerk* of Gaol-delivery : Therefore confider whether a Trial can be had of a Felon the fame *fpeaks to the* Seffions he pleads, unlefs he confents thereunto) thus, You good Men that are returned *Jury.* and impanelled, to try the Iffue joined between our Sovereign Lord the King and the *The Proclama-* Prifoners at the Bar, anfwer to your Names. Which done, and they appearing a full *tion.* Jury, make Proclamation thus : If any Man can inform the King's Attorney, or this Court, of any Treafons, Murders, Felonies, or other Mifdemeanours, againft *A. B.* &c. the Prifoners at the Bar, let them come forth, for the Prifoners ftand upon their Deliverance. Then fay to the Prifoners, You Prifoners at the Bar, the Perfons that *The Clerk* you fhall now hear called, are to pafs upon your feveral Lives and Deaths ; (or if it be *fpeaks to the* Petit Larceny, are to pafs on your Trial ;) if you will challenge them, or any of *Prifoners.* them, you muft challenge them as they come to the Book to be fworn, and before they be fworn. Then call the Foreman of the Jury, and fay to him, Lay your Hand on *The Jury ca-* the Book, and look upon the Prifoner ; You fhall well and truly try, and true Deli- *led over and* verance make, between our Sovereign Lord the King and the Prifoner or Prifoners at *fworn.* the Bar, whom you fhall have in Charge : You fhall true Verdict give according to your *The Oath.* Evidence. So help you God. Then call the Second, and fwear him in like Manner, and

and fo.on to 12 ; and neither more nor lefs muft be fworn. Then count them 12, and fay: You good Men that are fworn, you fhall underftand, that *A. B.* now Prifoner at the Bar, ftands indicted, for that he, (or if more than one in one Indictment), that they, *&c.* And having recited the Indictment fay, to which Indictment he hath pleaded Not guilty, and for his Trial hath put himfelf upon God and the Country, which Country you are ; fo that your Charge is to inquire whether he be guilty of the Felony, or Petit Larceny, or Felony and Burglary, whereof he ftands indicted, or Not guilty : If you find him guilty, you fhall inquire what Goods and Chattels he had at the Time of the faid Felony and Petit Larceny committed, or at any Time fince : (Or if it be for Felony) then what Goods and Chattels, Lands and Tenements, he had at the Time of the faid Felony committed, or at any Time fince. If you find him guilty, you fhall inquire whether he did fly for it ; if you find he fled for it, you fhall inquire what Goods and Chattels he had at the Time of fuch Flight. If you find him Not guilty, and that he did not fly for it, you fhall fay fo and no more ; and fo hear your Evidence. Then call the Witneffes, and fwear them one by one thus : The Evidence that you fhall give on the Behalf of our Sovereign Lord the King againft *A. B.* Prifoner at the Bar, fhall be the Truth, the whole Truth, and nothing but the Truth. So help you God. And the Evidence being given, fet another Prifoner to the Bar, and fay, You fhall likewife underftand, that *C. D.* ftands likewife indicted before you this Time, for that he, *&c.* (and fo recite the Indictment) for which he hath been arraigned, and hath pleaded thereto Not guilty, and for his Trial hath put himfelf upon God and the Country, which Country you are ; you are therefore to inquire of him as of your firft Prifoner, (that is, where the Offence is of the fame Degree) ; and fo hear your Evidence, *&c.* After the Evidence given a Bailiff muft be fworn to keep the Jury thus, You fhall fwear, that you fhall keep this Jury without Meat, Drink, Fire or Candle ; you fhall fuffer none to fpeak to them, neither fhall you fpeak to them your felf, but only to ask them whether they are agreed. So help you God.

The Jury charged.

The Oath of the Witneffes.

The Oath of him who keeps the Jury.

The Jury coming back within the Bar, or near, the Prifoners are brought to the Bar, call the Jury ; they appearing, fay, Set *A. B.* to the Bar, who being there, fay, Look upon the Prifoner ; how fay you, is *A. B.* guilty of the Felony (or as the Cafe is) whereof he ftands indicted, or Not guilty ? If they fay Not guilty, bid him down upon his Knees. If they fay Guilty, record it, and bid him be taken away. Then fay, Gaoler, fet *C. D.* to the Bar, *&c.* and do as before. And when the Verdicts are given, fay, hearken to the Verdict as the Court hath recorded it ; you fay *A. B.* is not guilty of the Felony whereof he ftands indicted ; you fay that *C. D.* is guilty of the Felony whereof he ftands indicted ; and fo onwards for the reft *mutatis mutandis.*

Sentence.

Then make a Proclamation and fay, All Manner of Perfons keep Silence whilft Sentence is giving, upon Pain of Imprifonment. Then fet the firft Prifoner to the Bar, and give the Sentence ; and fo for the reft.

I have been the more particular herein, to fhew the great Care and Solemnity the Law hath in the Trial of Man's Life.

Counfel.

And upon Trials of this Nature Counfel is not to be allowed to the Party, unlefs he can fhew to the Court fome Matter of Law, fo that it may appear Counfel is neceffary : But otherwife the Court is to be of Counfel with the Prifoner, and ought to advife him for his Good, and ought not to take Advantages too ftrictly againft him. The Court may alfo receive Information from any By-ftander, efpecially a Man of Law, who may offer any Thing, as *amicus Curiæ,* relating to the Trial or Manner of it.

Witneffes.
* This is now altered by the Statute 1 Ann. c. 19. that the Witneffes muft be on Oath.

No Witneffes are to be produced and examined upon * Oath againft the King, but the Prifoner may offer what Witneffes he pleafes, and they fhall be examined, but not upon Oath ; but ought to be ferioufly admonifhed to fpeak the Truth as if they were upon Oath.

Trial the fame Seffions.
See Roll's 2 Part of A-bridment, p. 96.

Although I know it is in many Places ufed to try a Man for Felony the fame Seffions the Indictment is found ; yet it feems to me highly reafonable (if the Prifoner defire it) to be deferred, and fhew Caufe probable, to defer it ; for that, 1. The Seffions are holden oftner than the Affizes : 2. The fpeedy Trials feem to be in Favour of the Prifoner : And *Volenti non fit injuria :* 3. If a Traverfe upon an Indictment of Nufance be not triable the fame Seffions that it is joined, but a Man fhall have Time to provide for it ; much more in Matter of Life, where ufually the Party is in Prifon, and may well be fuppofed lefs able to provide for it, and in the Nature of it requires greater Confideration.

Many Things (according to the Rules and Reaſon of the Common Law) cannot, or ought not, to be done by Juſtices of the Peace but at their Seſſions; for that the Exerciſing of their great Authority doth require a Court and publick Meeting for the Doing thereof; and the Holding ſuch a Court doth ariſe out of the Authority given them by their Commiſſion for the due Execution of it: For the Law requires, that Things of great Import be ſolemnly done, as the Matters of Trial of Offenders.

Many Things there be, that by ſeveral Statutes yet in Force cannot be executed but only in the Seſſions after *Eaſter*, or ſome other particular Seſſions; as the Taking the Accounts of the Treaſurers for maimed Soldiers and Charitable Uſes, and the appointing new Treaſurers, by the Statutes of 43 *El.* 3. and 43 *El.* 2. muſt be done in *Eaſter* Seſſions. And ſo alſo muſt the Rates of Wages by the Statute of 5 *El.* 4. be made and publiſhed in *Eaſter* Seſſions yearly, or within ſix Weeks after; and every Juſtice of the Peace not preſent thereat (being not let by Sickneſs) ſhall forfeit 10 *l.* with others of like Nature.

Divers other Things there be that muſt be done in ſome Seſſions, and not out of the *ſame*; as an Apprentice ill uſed by his Maſter muſt be diſcharged by four Juſtices of Peace in Seſſions under their Hands and Seals; by 5 *El.* 4. *Badgers* muſt be licenſed in open Seſſions under the Hands and Seals of three Juſtices of Peace, *Quorum unus*. Every Perſon having any Office or Place of Truſt of the King's Gift or Grant, ſhall in the next Seſſions after his being admitted into that Office, after receiving of the Sacrament, in open Seſſions (between the Hours of nine and twelve in the Morning) prove the Doing thereof by two Witneſſes, and take the Oaths preſcribed by 1 *El.* 1. and 3 *Jac.* 4. and make a Declaration againſt Tranſubſtantiation, according to 25 *Car.* 2. And many other Particulars there be of that Nature. *{margins: Apprentice. Badgers. Vide chap. 67. ſupra.}*

This alſo I would obſerve, that the Manner in ſome Counties is to make Orders in the Chamber after the Adjournment of the Seſſions, touching ſeveral Matters of great Importance; which is a very ill Uſage, and contrary to the Honour and Dignity of the Imployment: And ſuch Doings are for the moſt part to promote ſome private Deſign, and to ſerve Turns and By-ends, but not the Publick, and are neither valid nor ſafe, ſhould they be complained of. *{margin: Private Orders.}*

Another Thing cenſurable in our Juſtices of Peace is, their over eaſy Diſcharging and Setting aſide Orders made in open and publick Seſſions; whereas be it an Order made by them upon an Appeal from the Order of other Juſtices, as from the Order of two Juſtices of Peace in Caſe of Baſtard-Children, by and upon 18 *Eliz.* 2. or be it an Order made upon Appeal from the Order of two Juſtices upon 14 *Car.* 2. touching Settlements: In theſe Caſes the ſame nor any other Seſſions can repeal theſe Orders, according to *Pridgeon's* Caſe. Nay, be it an Order made by themſelves, intended to be final and made abſolute, without any Time to ſhew Cauſe; I ſee not how another Seſſions can repeal it: For ſuch Order is in the Nature of a Judgment on Record, as all Things are that are done in Seſſions, and may be reverſed by a ſuperior Court, but not by themſelves. *{margin: Reverſing Orders.}*

By the Statute of 14 *R.* 2. *cap.* 11. none above the Degree of a Knight ſhall take the King's Wages for Service at the Seſſions, nor above eight Knights at one Time. *Quære*, Whether a Knight ſhall take Wages, whereas a Banneret ſhall not, for ſo is the Original, not a Baronet. *{margin: Wages.}*

The Eſtreats of Seſſions are a great Part of the Juſtice of Peace his Duty; and they are to be doubled, and one Part thereof unto the Juſtice's Hands is to be delivered to the Sheriff to levy by them, and thereout to pay the Juſtices of Peace their Wages by the Hand of the Sheriff, by Indenture between them to be made; and the Juſtices Names are to be put in thoſe Indentures, that the Sheriff may know whom to pay, and for whom to have Allowance made. 14 *R.* 2. 11. *{margin: Eſtreats.}*

The ſame Seſſions may alter their own Orders, but then the firſt Order muſt be ſet aſide, and the ſecond entered. 6 *Mod.* 287.

They have Power only to quaſh or affirm, but not to ſuſpend or ſuperſede an original Order made by two Juſtices, to remove a poor Perſon. 2 *Salk.* 472.

See *Chap.* 195. Tit. *Certiorari*, infra.

C H A P.

CHAP. CLXXXVI. (a)

Jurors, and Challenges to them.

Trial by Ju-
rors. THIS is that happy Way of Trial, that notwithstanding all Revolutions of Times hath been continued beyond all Memory to this present Day, the Beginning whereof no History specifies, it being contemporary with the Foundation of this State and one of the Pillars of it both as to Age and Consequence : That Maxim, *Ad quæ-stionem facti respondent Juratores*, being as antient and fundamental as that other *Ad quæstionem Juris respondent Judices* ; the one being as liable to be controlled by a Writ of Error as the other by an Attaint, both essential to the Justice of this Nation. And although Jurors are in other Things subject to his Majesty's Judges, yet they are not so in Point of Judgment, which after some Disputes was happily asserted in the Case of the *Habeas Corpora* prosecuted by *Bushel* and others, by a nigh unanimous Opinion of all the Judges.

This Trial is the Birth-right of every Subject of *England*, and is put to him by Way of Question, *How wilt thou be tried?* Which is thought to be so just and equal for him to chuse, that the Waiver of it is revenged with *paine forte & dure* ; no Punishment being judged too severe for one that refuseth so just a Trial.

So happy is our Condition, that every *Englishman* (in Matters of Crime and Forfeitures) passes a double Jury ; neither to my Apprehension doth the Care of the first Inquest differ from the last, but only in Consequence brought on by Custom, the Indictment being as much found to be true by the one as the other.

Challenge. These Jurors are returned by the Sheriff by Virtue of a Precept to that Purpose against which at the Common Law both the King and the Party had two lawful Challenges, one peremptory, the other upon Cause shewed.

By the King. But because Life, Liberty and Estate are all at Stake in Cases of Felony, it is provided by 33 *E.* 1. that the King shall not challenge peremptorily, but must shew his Cause, which shall be inquired and tried, if true, as alledged, and if found otherwise shall be rejected.

By the Party. Yet the peremptory Challenge remaineth for the Party, although not so amply as at Common Law, according to which he might challenge thirty-five without Cause shewed, and as many more as he could upon Cause shewn : But now by the Statute of 32 *H.* 8. 3. this peremptory Challenge is reduced to twenty ; to challenge peremptorily beyond which Number, is to waive his Trial ; and to stand unto which is a great Offence, and grievously punished in our Law, that Person being judged unworthy of Life whose Innocency is not clear to endure an *English* Trial.

Who good Ju-
rors. The Jurors ought to be fairly impanelled, and duly returned, by the Sheriff or other sworn Bailiff, and not at the Nomination of the Juror himself, or any other, by 11 *H.* 4. 9. or else the Indictment is void by that Statute. And they are to be *liberi & legales homines* : For first they must be *liberi*, not Villeins born : 2. *Legales*, not convicted or attainted, and so Slaves to Punishment as well as to their own Vices ; and an Outlawry in a personal Action seems to be not only a good Challenge, but also good Cause to set aside the Indictment. *Jones Rep.* 196.

* By 2 H. 5.
st. 2. c. 3. in-
creased to 4 l.
per Stat. 27
Eliz. c. 6.
and farther
increased by
later Statutes.
Vid. infra.
† By Stat
23 H. 8. c. 13.
Vide infra. They must also be sufficient ; 1. *Respectu census*, every one must have * forty Shillings of Lands or Tenements by the Year ; but for this Cause he must be challenged, or else if the Party omit to challenge him, the Trial is well made by such a Juror. 2. *Respectu rationis*, he must be no Ideot, Lunatick, *&c.*

And because many Times by such Challenges to Jurors for Want of Freehold upon Trials of Offences in Cities, Boroughs, or Towns corporate, such Trials were deferred ; it is † provided, that every Person being the King's natural-born Subject, that useth or enjoyeth the Freedom of such Place, and dwelleth there, having in Moveables and Substance to the Value of 40 *l.* clear, may be admitted on such Trials, except Knights and Esquires.

Medietas Lin-
guæ. There is a Way of Trial also peculiar to Foreigners, called *De medietate linguæ* ; which ought to consist of six *English* and six Foreigners, if so many be in the Place ; if not, then so many as can be found there : But it Matters not whether they be of the same Nation the Prisoner is of, for they may be of another Nation ; and the Party must pray

I
                                                                    it,

it, and shew the Matter to the Justices. Yet where Persons calling themselves *Ægyptians* are to be tried for such their Offence, they are ousted of this Benefit by 1 & 2 *P. & M. cap.* 4.

It is also a good Challenge to a Juror, that he was one of the *Party's Indictors*, for *Indictor.* having been of that Mind that the Prisoner was guilty, he shall not be presumed to change his Mind : This is declared by 25 *E.* 3. 3. to be good Cause of Challenge, for it was so also by the Common Law, and therefore is good Cause of Challenge as well in Felony as Treason.

Many other Causes of Challenge there are, as well for the King as the Party, which you may find very largely and learnedly handled by Justice *Staundeforde* in his Pleas of the Crown, *lib.* 3. *cap.* 7. which relate to criminal Matters only ; and a most excellent Scheme you may find touching Challenges between Party and Party in my Lord *Coke,* 1 *Inst. fol.* 156. many whereof may by a discerning Reader be easily adapted to this present Purpose, and therefore I forbear to mention them.

And because Jurors are too apt to be favourable to their Neighbours or Friends, in not *Concealments.* presenting Offences, the Statute of 3 *H.* 7. *cap.* 1. hath provided, that Justices of Peace may inquire of such *Concealments* by another Jury, and punish them by Amercement by their Discretions ; touching which these Things are considerable.

1. The Matters which they may be thus punished for the Concealment of, must be such as by the Commission of the Peace or Statutes may be inquired of and presented before such Justices.

2. Where Inquests have been taken before Coroners, or some particular Justices out of Sessions, yet the Justices of Peace may inquire thereof, for the Words are Concealments of Inquests taken afore them or afore others. The like seems to me of Inquests in Leets or the Sheriff's Turn, in Matters whereof the Justices of Peace have also Cognisance.

3. Every Juror that shall be impanelled to inquire of such Concealments must have 40 *s. per Annum* of Lands or Tenements.

4. There must be Complaint before them made by Bill or Bills of such Concealment, if the Word Bill or Bills in that Act do refer unto the Proceedings against such Concealments ; or otherwise such Concealments must be in Matters that have been complained of by Bill or Bills, and not for not presenting Things not so first complained of, but in not finding Bills drawn up and presented to them to find ; for the Words are doubtful.

Such Inquiry or Concealment must be made within the Year after such Concealment.

6. Such Amercement must be reasonable, although directed to be by Discretion, which must be *sana & legalis* ; and see *F. N. B.* 175. in the Writ *De moderata misericordia.*

7. It seemeth reasonable the Inquest ought to consist of as many more as the first Inquest did ; for this is a Way of Attainting a Jury which is *criminis accusare, vel suspicione criminis attingere.*

8. Notwithstanding any trivial Complaint, the Justices of Peace may take or not take such Inquests as they see Cause ; for it is left to their Discretion by the Statute.

9. Such Amercement on Jurors for Concealment must be set in *plein* Sessions, not *plain* (as I take it) as the printed Book is.

If any Jurors shall, either upon an Issue of a Traverse in any Thing not Felony, or *SpecialVerdict.* which is Felony, doubt upon the Evidence what the Law is, they may (as it seems) give a special Verdict in Sessions as in the Courts of Gaol-Delivery or Assises, and that by the Common Law before the Statute of *West.* 2. *cap.* 3. for that Statute is but declaratory of the Common Law. *Co.* 2 *Inst.* 425.

Jurors, by the 4 *W. & M. cap.* 24. *sect.* 15. to be returned for Trials of Issues joined 4 W. & M. in the Courts of King's Bench, &c. or before Justices of Assise, &c. or Quarter-Sessions c. 24. §. 15. in any County of *England,* shall have within the County 10 *l.* by the Year of Freehold or Copyhold, or Ancient Demesne, or in Rents in Fee-simple, Fee-tail, or for Life ; and in every County of *Wales* every such Juror shall have 6 *l.*

This Act was continued by 7 & 8 *W.* 3. *cap.* 32. and afterwards continued along with the said Act of 7 & 8 *W.* 3. which see in the next Chapter.

By 3 *Geo.* 2. *cap.* 25. *sect.* 18. it is enacted, That any Person having Land in his own 3 Geo.2.c.25. Right of the yearly Value of 20 *l.* over and above the reserved Rent, being held by Lease §. 18. for the absolute Term of 500 Years or more, or for 99 Years, or any other Term determinable on one or more Lives, may be summoned to serve on Juries as a Freeholder.

By Statute 3 & 4 *Ann. cap.* 18. Justices at *Midsummer* Sessions yearly, are to issue out 3 & 4 Ann. Warrants under the Hands and Seals of two or more of them, to the High Constables of c. 18. §. 5. each

each Hundred, requiring them to iffue out their Precepts to the Petty Conftables, &c. to meet them within fourteen Days after the Date of fuch Precept, to prepare a Lift of Freeholders * according to the Statute 7 & 8 *W.* 3. *cap.* 32. which Lifts they muft fign and return the firft Day of *Michaelmas* Seffions.

* See here the next Chapter.

Any Head Conftable failing to iffue fuch Precept, &c. fhall forfeit 10 *l.* and the Petty Conftables not meeting and returning the Lifts, forfeit 5 *l.* And every fuch high Conftable, Conftable and Tithingman fo offending, fhall be profecuted at the Affifes, Seffions of *Oyer* and *Terminer,* or general Gaol-Delivery, or Seffions of the Peace. And the Juftices of Peace at the Quarter-Seffions after the 24th of *June* yearly, fhall caufe the faid feveral Acts (*viz.* 4 *W.* & *M. cap.* 24. and 7 & 8 *W.* 3. *cap.* 32.) to be read in Court.

3 Geo. 2. c 25.
§. 2. made perpetual
6 Geo. 2. c. 37.

By Statute 3 *Geo.* 2. *cap.* 25. it is enacted, That if any Perfons required by the Statute 7 & 8 *W.* 3. *cap.* 32. and 3 & 4 *Ann. cap.* 18. to give in, or by this Act to make up true Lifts of the Names of Perfons qualified to ferve on Juries, fhall wilfully omit out of any Lift, any Name which ought to be inferted, or take Money for omitting or inferting any Perfon, he fhall forfeit 20 *l.* on Conviction before one or more Juftices; one Half to the Informer, and the other to the Poor of the Parifh; and if not paid in five Days fhall be levied by Diftrefs, by Warrant from one Juftice of Peace.

Ib. §. 7.

It fhall be fufficient for any Conftables, &c. after they have compleated the Lifts for their Precincts, according to 7 & 8 *W.* 3. *cap.* 32. and 3 & 4 *Ann. cap.* 18. and this Act, to fubfcribe the fame in the Prefence of one Juftice for each County, &c. and at the fame Time to atteft the Truth of fuch Lifts upon Oath, to the beft of their Knowledge or Belief; and the Lifts fhall (being figned by the Juftices) be delivered by the Conftables, &c. to the High Conftables, who are to deliver in fuch Lifts to the Quarter-Seffions, attefting upon Oath the Receipt of fuch Lifts from the Conftables, &c. and that no Alteration hath been made fince their Receipt thereof.

Ib. §. 19.

Jurors for the Seffions of the Peace, &c. to be held for the City of *London,* fhall be Houfe-keepers, and have Lands, &c. or perfonal Eftate to the Value of 100 *l.*

Ib. §. 20.

The Sheriff, &c. fhall not return any Perfon to ferve on a Jury for the Trial of any Capital Offence, who would not be qualified to ferve as a Juror in Civil Caufes.

Ib. §. 21.

This Act to be read at every *Midfummer* Quarter-Seffions.

C H A P. CLXXXVII. (a)

Trial.

Scotland.
7 Jac. 1. c. 1.
§. 3. revived by 13 & 14
Car. 2. c. 22. for Suppreffion of Mofs-Troopers flying out of England into Scotland, or out of Scotland into England.
Quære, How far it is in Force fince the Union.

IF any commit in *Scotland* an Offence, which by the Laws of *England* is or fhall be declared or adjudged to be Petty Treafon, Murder, Manflaughter, felonious Burning of Houfes and Corn, Burglary, Robbing of Houfes by Day, Robbery, Theft or Rape, and fhall fly into *England,* and be apprehended in the Counties of *Northumberland, Cumberland, Weftmorland,* or within the Parts or Places lying on the North-fide of the River *Tine* called *Bedlingtonfhire, Northamptonfhire* and *Iflandfhire,* the Town and County of *Newcaftle upon Tine,* and Town of *Berwick upon Tweed,* or Liberties thereof: It fhall and may be lawful for the Juftices of Peace in their general Quarter-Seffions, or any four of them, upon due Examination and pregnant Proofs, by Warrant under their Hands and Seals to remand and fend fuch Offenders into *Scotland,* there to receive Trial, &c.

County.

The Trial of an Offender ought regularly to be in that County where the Offence was committed; unlefs any Statute doth otherwife provide, as fome do, *viz.* 1 & 2 *Ph.* & *M. cap.* 4. and divers others. But if one fteal Goods in the County of *A.* and carry them with him into the County of *B.* and be there apprehended, he may be tried and punifhed for the fame in the County of *B.* for in this Cafe *Facinus fequitur perfonam.* 1 *Jac.* 11. Bigamy fh. ll be tried where the Party is apprehended.

The fame Seffions.

The Trial of Felonies, and of Things and Offences, for which a Perfon is not bailable, or the Party cannot get Bail, but lies in Prifon, ought to be as fpeedy as may be *in favorem libertatis :* And therefore it is ufual to indict them and try them at the fame Seffions. See before in *Seffions.* But in other Caufes of Indictment for Breach of Penal Statutes, or for Nufances, or for other Mifdemeanors not made Felony, they cannot try the Caufe the

fame

fame Seffions the Indictment is, as was refolved in *Bampfted's* Cafe, *Hill.* 11 *Car. i. Cro.* where a Perfon was indicted of Extortion, and proceeded againft to Conviction the fame Seffions, and adjudged not good : And fo was alfo refolved *Trin.* 23 *Car.* 1. upon an Indictment for Words fpoken of the Queen Mother : So likewife of Juftices of *Oyer* and *Terminer.* But otherwife it is of Juftices of Gaol-Delivery ; and by the Cafe of 22 *E.* 4. *Fitz. Coron.* 44. it appeareth, that the Juftices of Peace in their Seffions cannot proceed in a Caufe criminal the fame Seffions, efpecially where the Party requires Time to be advifed.

By the Statute 22 *H.* 8. 14. made perpetual by 32 *H.* 8. the Trial againft the Party indicted fhall be in the County where he is indicted for Murder or Felony, notwithftanding any foreign Plea. *Foreign Plea.*

All Conftables, &c. of Towns in each County, fhall at the general Quarter-Seffions of the Peace yearly, in the Week after the Feaft of *Saint Michael,* give a Lift of the Names and Abodes of all Perfons, within the refpective Places for which they ferve, qualified to ferve on Juries, between the Age of twenty-one and feventy Years, which Lift they fhall deliver to the Juftices, who fhall caufe the Clerk of the Peace to deliver a Duplicate thereof to the Sheriff of the County before the firft of *January* next following, to be enter'd among the Records of the Seffions. And no Sheriff fhall impanel any Perfon to ferve in any Jury at the Affifes, Gaol-Delivery or Seffions of the Peace, who is not named in the Lift. Conftable failing to make fuch Return to forfeit 5 *l.* to the King.

Juries. 7 & 8 W. 3. c. 32. continued for 11 Years by 10 Ann. c. 14. and farther continued for 7 Years by 9 Geo. 1. c. 8. and referred to by 3 Geo. 2. c. 25. which laft Act is made perpetual by 6 Geo. 2. c. 37.

The Juftices Return fhall excufe the Sheriff if he fummons one not qualified. And in an Action brought thereon the Sheriff may plead the General Iffue, and give this Act in Evidence, and upon Nonfuit, Difcontinuance or a Verdict for the Defendant, the Plaintiff fhall pay treble Cofts. *Juftices Excufe.*

The Inhabitants of *Weftminfter* fhall be exempted from ferving in any Jury at the Seffions of the Peace for the County of *Middlefex.* *Weftminfter exempted from Middlefex.*

This Act fhall not extend to the City of *London,* nor to any other County of City or Town within this Realm ; nor to any Corporation that hath Power by Charter to hold Seffions of Gaol-Delivery, or of the Peace. *Not to extend to London, &c.*

See 3 Geo. 2. cap. 25. here, in the preceding Chapter.

CHAP. CLXXXVIII. (a)

Judgment.

A Woman convicted of taking Goods above the Value of 12 *d.* and under the Value of 10 *s.* or as Acceffary to any fuch Offence, for which a Man might have his Clergy, fhall for the firft Offence be branded and marked in the Hand, upon the Brawn of the left Thumb, with an hot burning Iron, with a T upon the Iron, openly in Court ; and be farther punifhed by Whipping, Imprifonment, Stocking, or fending to the Houfe of Correction, in fuch Manner and for fuch Time (not exceeding one Year) as the Judge fhall think fit, and then be delivered out of Prifon. *Woman. 21 Jac. 1. 6.*

But if fhe offend again, fhe is to have Judgment of Death, as fhe was to have had at Common Law.

For the Judgment in Treafon and Petty Treafon, the Juftices not meddling therewith, I refer you to the Books, and efpecially to Mr. Juftice *Staundeforde,* who hath written learnedly and largely of the Pleas of the Crown, *lib.* 3. *c.* 19. and alfo *Coke,* Tit. *Pleas of the Crown.*

In Cafe of Felony the Judgment is ufually pronounced thus : You fhall be carried back to the Prifon from whence you came, and from thence to the Place of Execution, and there be hanged by the Neck until you be dead, and the Lord have Mercy upon your Soul. *Felon.*

In Cafes of Petit Larceny the Juftices of Peace may award the Party either to be whipped at the Cart's Tail, or at the Whipping-Poft, as they fhall judge convenient. But Whip- *Petit Larceny.*

ping

ping is grown the ufual and ordinary Punifhment, although formerly it was uncertain, and punifhed by Pillory or cutting off the Ears. *Co.* 4 *Inft.* 218.

Altering the Judgment. By many Statutes peculiar Punifhments are appointed for feveral Offences, as *Pillory, Stocks, Imprifonment, Binding to the Good Behaviour, &c.* But in all thefe Cafes no Room is left for the Juftices Difcretion, for they ought to give Judgment, and to inflict the Punifhment in all the Circumftances thereof as fuch Statutes do direct. For if the King cannot alter the Manner of Execution, as to direct a Perfon to be beheaded that hath Judgment to be hanged; much lefs can an inferior Court alter a Judgment and Sentence directed by Act of Parliament. And therefore the Courfe taken up in fome Counties, to admit the Party indicted for Breach of Penal Laws to fubmit with a Proteftation of Not guilty, and therefore forbear to inflict the Penalty impofed, and fo mitigate the Penalty, is an Offence for which they are punifhable: For thereby, 1. The Sentence impofed by Act of Parliament is quite altered. 2. The Mifchiefs intended to be remedied go unredrefled. 3. Many Times the Poor, who are by Direction of feveral Acts to have the Penalty, are thereof defrauded.

CHAP. CLXXXIX. [a]

How Juftices of Peace may defend themfelves againft Suits.

General Iffue. **I**F any Action, Bill, Plaint, or Suit upon the Cafe, Trefpafs, Battery, or Falfe Im-
7 Jac. 1. 12. prifonment, fhall be brought any where againft a Juftice of Peace, *&c.* for any Thing done *virtute officii*, it fhall be lawful for them, or any other that act in their Aid, Affiftance or Command, to plead the General Iffue, and to give the Special Matter in Evidence. If the Verdict pafs for the Defendant, or the Plaintiff be Nonfuit or difcontinue, the
Cofts. Judge fhall allow double Cofts.
County. Which Statute was to continue but for feven Years, but is made perpetual by 21 *Jac.1.*
21 Jac. 1. 12. 12. and it is thereby enacted, That all Actions upon that Statute fhall be laid in the proper County where the Fact was done; and if upon the Trial the Plaintiff fhall not prove the Fact done in that County where the Action is laid, the Jury fhall find the Defendant Not guilty: And in cafe of fuch Verdict, Nonfuit or Difcontinuance, the Defendant fhall have his double Cofts.
Conftable. A Conftable may make a Deputy, and may plead the General Iffue, and thereby take Benefit of 7 *Jac.* 1. 5. as was refolved *Mich.* 13 *Jac. B. R. Phillips* contra *Winchcombe,*
* Vide fupra *Moor's Rep. p.* 845. *Bulftr. Part* 3. *p.* 77. *
c. 1.

CHAP. CXC. [a]

Clergy.

What. **W**HAT Clergy is, with the Beginning and Ufe thereof, fee *Hobart Rep. Searle* and
William's Cafe, *p.* 288.
By Common Law. By the Common Law one committing Sacrilege fhall not have his Clergy: *Fruftra enim petit auxilium Ecclefiæ, qui peccat contra Ecclefiam.*
Alfo for High Treafon no Clergy was allowed at Common Law. 1 *Inft.* 150, 336 But in all other Cafes the Offender might; and fome fay in all Treafons but thofe againft the King's Perfon.
By the Common Law every Perfon in Holy Orders might have the Benefit of the Clergy, and fo might others alfo, by 4 *H.* 7. 13. But as to all, except thofe in Holy Orders, it is reftrained to *once* by that Statute: And every Perfon fo convicted for
* Formerly the * *Murder* to be marked with an M. in the Brawn of the left Thumb, and for other
Clergy was al- Felony with a T. and thefe Marks to be made by the Gaoler in open Court before
lowed for Mur- the Judge.
der.
By the Statute of 28 *H.* 8. *cap.* 1. Perfons in Holy Orders fhall be burnt in the Hand and ufed as others be. See 32 *H.* 8. *cap.* 3.
2   . And

And by the Statute of 23 *H*. 8. 1.   28 *H*. 8. 1.   32 *H*. 8. 3. Clergy is taken away in *Where taken away.*
thefe Cafes.

1. Perfons found Guilty after the Laws of the Land for *Petit Treafon.*

2. For *wilful Murder* of Malice prepenfed or *Poifoning.*   1 E. 6 12.

3. Or for *Robbing of Churches* or Chapels, or other Holy Places.   Ibid.

4. *Robbing* any Perfons in their * Dwelling-houfe, or Dwelling-place, or any Parcel   Ibid.
thereof, the Owner or Dweller of the fame Houfe, his Wife, Children, or Servants then   5 E. 6. 11.
being within the fame, or within the Precinct thereof, and put in Fear or Dread by it,   * *In the Day-time, and ta-*
or whether they be waking or fleeping.   . *king from thence to the*

  Value of 5 s. tho' no Perfon is in it.   3 & 4 W. & M.

5. Or for robbing any Perfon in or near the *Highway.*   1 E. 6. 12.

6. Or for wilful *Burning any Dwelling-houfe,* or *Barn* wherein Grain or Corn fhall
happen to be.

7. Any found guilty of Abetment, Procuring, Helping, Maintaining, or Counfelling   4 & 5 P. & M.
to fuch Offences, by 25 *H*. 8. 5. and 5 *El.* 17.   4.

8. No Perfon convicted of *Buggery* fhall have his Clergy.

9. Or of *breaking any Houfe by Day or by Night,* and any Perfon being therein, and   1 E. 6. 12.
put to Fear or Dread.

10. Or for the felonious Stealing of *Horfes, Geldings,* or *Mares.*   1 E. 6. 12.

But by 1 *E*. 6. 12. Clergy was allowed in all other Cafes of Felony; yet fince that   2 & 3 E. 6.
Time Clergy hath been taken away from feveral Perfons; as,   33.

11. Such as fhall *command, hire, or counfel another* to commit or do any *Petit Trea-*   *Acceffaries.*
fon, or *Murder,* or *Robbery* in any Dwelling-Houfe or Houfes; or to commit or do   4 & 5 P. & M.
any Robbery in or near any *Highway* in the Realm of *England,* or any the Queen's   c. 4.
Dominions; or to commit or do any Robbery in the Marches of *England* againft *Scot-*   3 & 4 W. & M.
land; or to burn any Houfe or Barn having Corn in it.

12. If any rob any Perfon in any *Booth or Tent,* in any Fair or Market, the Owner,   8 E. 6. 11.
his Wife, Children, or Servant then being therein.

13. All Perfons being tranfported into *England* called *Egyptians,* ftaying here above a   1 & 2 P. & M.
Month.   13.

14. Any Perfon feen or found in the Company or Fellowfhip of Vagabonds, calling   5 E. 1. 4. 20.
themfelves, or called *Egyptians,* or counterfeiting or difguifing themfelves by their Appa-   5 E. 20.
rel, Speech, or Behaviour like them, and fo remaining a Month at one Time or feveral Times.

15. All Perfons convicted of the felonious Taking away of Money, Goods or Chattels   39 El. 15.
to 5 s. or upwards, in any Dwelling-Houfe, or Part thereof, or any Out-Houfe belong-   3 & 4 W. & M.
ing to and ufed with any Dwelling-Houfe, although no Perfon be in the Houfe.

16. Nor for the felonious Taking of any Money, Goods, or Chattels from another   8 El. 4.
Perfon *privily.*

17. Or he that doth ftab or thruft any Perfon that hath not a Weapon drawn, or that   1 Jac. 1. 8.
hath not firft ftricken him, if the Party die within fix Months.

18. Popifh Recufants or Schifmaticks commanded to abjure, and do not depart, or do   25 El. 1. & 2.
return again.

19. Or any Perfons receiving, &c. a Jefuit, Seminary Prieft, or other Prieft born in   27 El. 2.
England, ordained by any Authority from *Rome.*

20. Or any convicted or attainted for any Offence made Felony by 3 *H*. 7. 2. *viz.*   3 H. 7. 2.
taking any Maid, Widow or Wife of Subftance in Lands or Goods, or after Marrying her
or Affenting to it, or Defiling and Receiving her, knowing it.

21. After Conviction of Forgery the fecond Time committing that Offence.   5 El. 14.

22. Nor any committing Rape or Burglary.

23. Exercifing Conjuration or Invocation, whereby any Perfon is killed or lamed.   18 El. 7.

24. Nor a Soldier departing without Licenfe from his Captain.   1 Jac. 12.

25. Nor a wandering Solder or Marriner that offendeth againft 39 *El.* 17.   2 Ed. 6. 2.   39 El. 17.

26. Or fuch as fteal Cloth from the Tenters.   22 Car. 2.

27. Nor fuch as imbezil his Majefty's Stores.   22 Car. 2.

28. Nor fuch as malicioufly maim any Perfon.   And by many other Statutes.   22 & 23 Car. 2.

Every Perfon having his Clergy fhall be forthwith delivered out of Prifon, and not to   18 El. 7.
the Ordinary; yet the Juftices may detain him in Prifon as a further Punifhment for any
Time not exceeding one Year, and he fhall (notwithftanding his Admiffion to his Clergy)
anfwer any other Offences.

  A Tran-

A Tranfcript certified by the Clerk of the Crown, of the Peace, or of the Affizes concerning the Tenor of the Indictment, and of the Perfon's having had the Benefit o' his Clergy or of this Act, to the Judges or Juftices in any other County, fhall be a fufficient Proof that fuch a Perfon hath had the Benefit of his Clergy, or of this Act.

On this Head of Clergy, *fee* 2 Hawk. P. C. Chap. 33.

C H A P. CXCI. (*a*)

Informations. Actions Popular.

Kinds.

THE Civil Law hath two Sorts of Informers; 1. *Voluntarius*, as our common Informer. 2. *Neceffarius, qui invitus facit propter publici officii neceffitatem*; as with us the King's Attorney, the Clerk of the Crown in the King's Bench, who is *Capitalis Coronator Domini Regis*, which they call *Delator ftationarius, fifcalis*, which with us is Honorary.

The *Delator voluntarius* is with us more neceffary than creditable; for great have been the Complaints againft them, and many and fevere Laws have been made againft them; yet fuch as govern themfelves well are to be encouraged as Furtherers of the publick Good.

How Informa-
tions may be
exhibited,
when, and by
whom.
18 El. 5.
19 El. 5.

1. Every Informer fhall exhibit his Information in Perfon, or by Attorney, and not by Deputy.

2. None fhall be admitted to purfue againft any Perfon upon any Penal Statute, but by Information or Original Action, and not otherwife.

3. Upon every fuch Information a Note fhall be made of the Day, Month and Year of the Exhibiting thereof into any Office, or to any Officer, without antedating thereof, and to be accounted of Record from that Time and not before.

4. No Procefs fhall iffue until the Information be exhibited in Form aforefaid; and upon fuch Procefs fhall be indorfed as well the Perfon's Name that purfueth, as the Statute on which it is brought.

5. The Clerk that maketh out Procefs contrariwife fhall forfeit 40 *s*. a Moiety to the Queen, the other Moiety to the Party againft which fuch Procefs is made, to be recovered in any Court of Record, *&c*.

6. No Informer fhall agree with the Offender before Plea pleaded, nor after, without Leave from the Court.

7. Every Perfon (except Clerks in Court) offending againft the Act, or making any Compofition, or taking any Money, Reward or Promife of Reward, without Confent of fome of the King's Courts at *Weftminfter*, the Party convicted fhall ftand two Hours in the Pillory in fome Market next adjoining, and be difabled to be an Informer, and forfeit 10 *l*. a Moiety to the Queen, and the other Moiety to the Party grieved, to be recovered in any Court of Record.

8. If any Informer fhall willingly delay his Suit, or fhall difcontinue, or be nonfuited, or a Verdict pafs againft him, and Judgment, he fhall pay the Defendant his Cofts, and have ufual Executions.

But that Act fhall not extend,

1. To Officers of Record, who in Refpect of their Offices have ufed to exhibit Informations.

2. Nor to Informations upon the Statutes of Maintenance, Champerty, buying of Titles, or Embracery, as to the Parties grieved.

3. Nor to Perfons to whom any Penalty or Forfeiture is given certainly, and not generally to him that will fue.

Juftices of Peace in their Seffions have Authority to hear and determine Offences againft that Act. This Act was made temporary, but is made perpetual by 27 *El.* 10.

No Perfon fhall be admitted to be an Informer, that by any of the Queen's Courts is difabled for any Mifdemeanor.

In every Informer's Declaration the County fhall be alledged where the Offence was done; and the Defendant may traverfe the County, except in *Champerty, Buying of Titles,* or *Extortion*, and Offences againft 1 *El.* 11. & 1 *El.* 10. for *Tunnage and Poundage*, or for *Ufury*, or for *Regrating, Forestalling*, or *Ingroffing*, where the Penalty exceeds 20 *l*.

2

Any

Any Suit for any Offence whereof the Forfeiture is given to the King alone, fhall be *Time.* brought within *two Years after the Offence,* and not after. And where the Forfeiture is given *to the King and any other, within one Year after the Offence.* Except upon the Statute of Tallage by the Party that will fue, or in his Default within two Years after that by the Queen. And any Suit brought otherwife is void.

All Suits for ufing any *unlawful Game,* or not ufing any lawful Game, or not having Bows or Arrows, or ufing a Trade not having been an *Apprentice,* fhall be heard and determined in the Seffions or Affizes of the County, &c. and not out of it.

If any Perfon fue any Action Popular, and the Defendant plead a Recovery in an *Covin.* Action Popular in Bar, or that before that Time he had barred the Plaintiff in fuch Ac- 4 H. 7. 20. tion, the Plaintiff may aver fuch Recovery or Bar was by *Covin;* and upon fuch Covin found the Plaintiff fhall have Judgment, and the Defendant fo attainted or condemned of Covin fhall have Imprifonment for two Years by Procefs of *Capias* or Outlawry, as well at the King's Suit as at any other; and the Releafe of the Party fhall not avail the Defendant.

All Offences to be committed againft any penal Statute, for which any Informer or *County.* Promoter may ground any Suit, &c. before Juftices of Affize, *Nifi Prius,* Gaol-delivery, 21 Jac. 4. *Oyer and Terminer,* or of the Peace in their General Seffions, fhall be commenced, fued, profecuted, tried, recovered and determined, by Action, Bill, Plaint, Information, or Indictment, before the Juftices of Affize, &c. or before the Juftices of Peace of the County, City, Borough, or Town Corporate and Liberty in any the Courts, Judicatures or Liberties, at the Choice of the Profecutor, and not elfewhere.

Like Procefs in every Popular Action, Bill, Plaint, Information, or Suit to be profe- *Procefs.* cuted according to the Purport of this Act, be had and awarded as in Actions of Trefpafs 21 Jac. 4. *vi & armis* at the Common Law.

Excepted, &c. all Offences for Recufancy againft thofe that fhall not frequent the 21 Jac. 4. Church, for *Champerty, Maintenance,* buying of Titles, or for tranfporting of Gold or Silver, Ordnance, Powder, Shot, Munition, Wool, Woolfels or Leather, or for Tunnage, Poundage, Impoft, Prifage, Subfidy, &c.

No Officer fhall file any Information, Bill or Plaint, Count or Declaration, grounded *Oath.* upon any penal Statute, which by that Act are to be tried in the proper Counties, until 21 Jac. 4. the Informer hath made Oath before fome Judge of the Court, that the Offences were not committed in other Counties than where the Information, &c. is laid.

The Defendant to any Information, &c. to be exhibited on the Behalf of the King, or *General Iffue.* by any other, or on the Behalf of the King and any other, may plead the General Iffue, 21 Jac. 4. and give the fpecial Matter in Evidence.

Now. touching Informations take thefe Rules.

1. One Perfon cannot exhibit two Informations in the fame or in feveral Courts; if he *Rules.* do, the Defendant may plead the firft in Bar of the Second. Hob. 209.

2. If two Informers exhibit Informations againft the fame Perfon, for the fame Offence Hob. 128. on the fame Day, they are both void, and they may be pleaded the one in Bar of the other, for as much as there is no Right of Priority.

3. Informations and Suits on penal Statutes are *ftricti juris,* and excepted out of all the Statutes of Jeofails.

4. The Statute of 21 *Jac.* 4. gives no Jurifdiction to Juftices of Peace where they had none before; but only appoints, that where Informations might have been brought in the Courts at *Weftminfter,* and before Juftices of Peace, they fhall now be brought before Juftices of Peace only. *Farington's* Cafe, *Trin.* 4 *Car.* 1. *Cro.* *Green's* Cafe, *Mich.* 4 *Car.* 1. *Cro.*

5. The Statute of 31 *El.* 5. extends not to an Action or Information by the Party grieved; for he may bring it in any County. *Allen's* Cafe, *Mich.* 40. *El. Cro.* 645.

6. If Jurifdiction be given to the Seffions to hear and determine, and doth not fay by Information, this fhall be by Indictment and not Information. *Jones Rep. p.* 133.

7. Where the Suit is directed to be in any Court of Record, or in any the King's Courts of Record, that is intended the Courts at *Weftminfter. Jones Rep.* 193.

8. Where an Information is *tam pro Dom' Rege quam pro feipfo,* if the Informer die, yet the Attorney General may profecute for the King; and altho' the Ufe is that the Attorney General only join the Iffue, yet he cannot hinder the Profecutor for his Part. 3 *Inft. cap. Informers.*

Informa-

Informations.

4 & 5 W. c. 18. THE Clerk of the Crown in the King's Bench fhall not without exprefs Order of that Court, exhibit, receive, or file any Information, for any *Trefpafs, Battery, or* other *Mifdemeanors*; or iffue out any *Procefs* thereon before he fhall have a * Recogni zance from the Profecutor in the Sum of 20 *l.* effectually to profecute the Informa tion, and to abide the Order of the Court; and the faid Clerk fhall record and file a *Me morandum* thereof in fome publick Place in his Office, for all Perfons to fee without any Fee.

* Which the Clerk of the Crown, or any Juftice of the Peace of the County where the Caufe of the Informa tion doth arife, may take.

If the Informer fhall delay the Profecution, or a Verdict pafs againft him, the Court fhall award Cofts, unlefs the Judge fhall certify on the Record that there was a reafonable Caufe for the Information.

This Act doth not extend to any other Informations than fuch as are exhibited in the Name of the King, Coroner, or Attorney in the Court of King's Bench, called the Mafter of the Crown-Office.

1 Salk. 376. Upon a Motion to file an Information in Nature of a *Quo Warranto* againft the Mayor and Aldermen of *Hertford*, to fhew Caufe by what Authority they admitted Perfons to be Freemen of that Corporation, who did not dwell therein; it was granted, but it was afterwards moved to fet afide the Procefs, becaufe no Recognizance was given purfuant to the faid Statute above mentioned; and the Queftion was, whether this Matter was within the Statute, becaufe it was to try a Right, when the Statute mentions *Batteries, Trefpaffes* and other *Mifdemeanors*, which muft be intended Mifdemeanors of an inferior Nature, but adjudged that this Power ufurped by the Mayor, *&c.* was a *Mifdemeanor*, and the Infor mation for it might be vexatious, for the Procefs was fet afide, but the Information ftood.

4 & 5 W. c. 18. Upon Informations, for Trefpaffes, Batteries, and other Mifdemeanors, one Juftice may take a Recognizance of 20 *l.* of the Informer, that he will profecute the Caufe with Effect, and abide fuch Order as the Court fhall direct.

See 2 Hawk. P. C. Chap. 26. *of* Information.

C H A P. CXCII. (*a*)

Mayor or Magiftrate, where he may act as a Juftice of Peace by fome particular Statutes.

Cuftoms.
14 Car. 2.
c. 11. Parl. 2.

THE next Magiftrate may commit to Prifon until next Seffions fuch as fhall abufe an Officer of the Cuftoms.

Preachers.
14 Car. 2.
c. 14. Parl. 1.

Mayor or Chief Magiftrate of any City or Town Corporate may commit any preach ing a Sermon or Lecture difabled by the Act fo to do.

Cuftom.
12 Car. 2.
c. 19.

The Chief Magiftrate of the Port or Place next adjoining may (upon Complaint) grant a Warrant to fearch for uncuftomed Goods.

Alehoufes.
5 Car. 1. c. 3.

Mayors and Head Officers may convict unlicenfed Alehoufe-keepers, and levy the Penalties.

Sunday.
3 Car. 1. c. 1.

The Mayor or Head Officer may put in Execution the Statute of 3 *Car.* 1. *cap.* 1. for Breach of Sunday.

Swearing.
1 Jac. 9.
21 Jac. c. 20.

The Mayor, *&c.* may punifh Offenders for profane Swearing or Curfing.

Armour.
2 E. 3. 3.

Mayor and Bailiffs of Cities and Boroughs may execute the Statute againft riding armed.

Beer.
23 H. 8. 4.

Mayors, *&c.* in Corporations may affefs the Prices of Ale and Beer.

Games.
23 H. 3. 9.

Mayors, *&c.* may commit Perfons they find playing at unlawful Games.

Weights.
11 H. 7. c. 4.

Mayors, *&c.* may punifh Offenders touching falfe Weights.

Mayors and Head Officers may hear and determine Matters touching Servants and Apprentices. *Servants.*
5 El. 4.

The Mayor and Head Officers may inquire of Offences againſt 1 *El.* 2. 1 El. 2.

Mayors, *&c.* may make a Tax for Relief of Perſons and Places viſited with the Plague. *Plague.*
1 Jac. 31.

Mayors, *&c.* and Head Officers may infpect and affefs the Affize of Talewood, Billet and Faggot. *Wood.*
43 El. 14.

Mayors, *&c.* may punifh the Offenders againſt 43 *El.* 7. for robbing Orchards, *&c.* *Orchards.*
43 El. 7.

Mayors, Bailiffs, *&c.* may inquire of Offences of Artificers and Victuallers. *Artificers.*
2 E. 6. 15.

Mayors, Bailiffs, and Head Officers may affefs the Prices of Beer Veffels. *Veffels.*
8 El. 9.
23 H. 8. 4.

Mayors, Bailiffs and Governors of Cities, Towns and Markets, may ſearch and gauge all Veffels for Salmon, Herrings and Eels. *Veffels.*
11 H. 7. 23.
22 E. 4. 2.

Mayors, Bailiffs and Miniſters of the Port, *&c.* may arreſt Soldiers departing without Licence. *Soldiers.*
18 H. 6. 19.

Mayors, Bailiffs, *&c.* may hear and determine Matters touching Leather, and examine, *&c.* *Leather.*
1 Jac. 1. 22.

And ſee the Statutes under their ſeveral Heads ſupra.

C H A P. CXCIII.

Procefs.

*The Forms of Procefs upon Indictment of Trefpafs, which alfo the Juſtices of Peace out of
their Seffions may in ſome few Cafes make out againſt Offenders.*

NOTE, That as the Authority of making Procefs upon Indictments is given by exprefs
Words in the Commiffion to the Juſtices of Peace in their Seffions; ſo it is given by
exprefs Words in ſome Statutes to the Juſtices of the Peace (yea to one Juſtice of the Peace)
out of their Seffions, to make out Procefs upon Indictments found (before them) againſt
Offenders, or upon Information againſt them, as if they were indicted of Trefpafs in Seffions, as you may ſee here Tit. *Forcible Entry,* and Tit. *Sheriffs, antea.*

Alfo in other Cafes, and by ſome other Statutes, this Authority of making out Procefs Lamb. 317.
501.
(againſt Offenders) by the Juſtices of Peace out of their Seffions is implied of Neceffity:
As where any Statute doth give Power to the Juſtices or Juſtice of Peace out of their Seffions to inquire, hear and determine, (as *hic* Tit. *Riots,* Tit. *Tranfportation,* Tit. *Tyle,*
and Tit. *Weights;*) in thefe and in all other ſuch Cafes, where the Juſtices may inquire,
hear and determine, there after Indictment or Prefentment of the Offence, the ſaid Juſtices
may make out Procefs againſt ſuch Offenders, to caufe them to come and anſwer; for
unlefs the Offenders do come in, either *gratis* or by Procefs, the Juſtices cannot proceed
to hear and determine. Again, in the former Cafes of Tranfportation, Tyle and Weights,
as alfo in all other Cafes where any Statute doth give Power to the Juſtices of Peace out of
their Seffions to hear and determine, either upon the Confeffion of the Offenders, or
upon Examination of the Witneffes, (whereof ſee *antea,* Tit. *Hear and Determine,* &c. and
ſee 5 *E.* 6. 14. againſt Foreſtallers) in all ſuch Cafes it ſeemeth the Juſtices of Peace may
grant out their Procefs or Warrant againſt ſuch Offenders, to appear before them, to anſwer to their ſaid Offences: And thereupon may proceed to examine, hear and determine
the Offence, as being convicted thereof upon ſuch Confeffion or Examination, without any
Indictment or Procefs.

(*a*) The Difference between Procefs and the Precept or Warrant of the Juſtices of
Peace, ſeems to be this:

The Precept or Warrant of the Juſtice is only to attach and convene the Party before
any Indictment or Conviction, and may be made either in the Name of the King or of
the Juſtice, as is before ſhewed.

Procefs

Proceſs is always in the Name of the King, and uſually after an Indictment found, or after other Conviction.

Now theſe Proceſſes ſeem to be as followeth.

27 El. 12.   THE Juſtices of Peace for the Offences mentioned in 27 *El.* 12. for Sheriffs, &c. not taking the Oaths upon Conviction, may award Execution for the Forfeitures by *Fi. fa.* Attachment, *Capias,* or Extent.

4 & 5 P. & M. c. 3.   Proceſs upon 4 & 5 *P. & M.* 3. touching Soldiers, &c. ſhall be as upon Indictments of Treſpaſs at Common Law.

1 E. 6. 1.   The Juſtices of Peace before whom any Perſon ſhall be indicted for depraving or ſpeaking irreverently of the Sacrament contrary to 1 *E.* 6. 1. may award two *Capias* and an Exigent, as well into the County where the Party is indicted, as into any other County.

1 *Venire fac.*   (*d*) Firſt, If the Offender be abſent, a *Venire facias* ſhall be awarded by the Juſtice or Juſtices of the Peace under his or their own *Teſte.* And if thereupon the Offender be

2. *Diſtringas* or *Capias.*   returned ſufficient, (and maketh a Default) then *Diſtringas* is awarded, which *Diſtringas* ſhall go forth *infinite* till the Offender come in. But if a *Nihil habet,* &c. be at the firſt returned, then after the *Venire facias* a *Capias,* then an *Alias,* and after a *Pluries,* ſhall go forth, and after that an *Exigent,* till the Party be taken, or yield himſelf, or elſe be outlawed.

And theſe are the ordinary Proceſſes upon all Indictments of Treſpaſs againſt the Peace, or of other Offences againſt penal Statutes, not being Felony, or a greater Offence. But the Proceſs is commonly grounded upon an Indictment, and is only to cauſe the Offender to come in, and to make his Anſwer ; and therefore if the Offender be preſent, and confeſs ſuch Indictment, Information, or Offence, there needeth no Proceſs at all, for he ſhall be forthwith committed to Priſon, there to remain until he hath paid Fine, or given Security for it. 1 *H.* 7. 20. and *Br. Imp.* 100.

Alſo theſe Proceſſes ſhall be always directed to the Sheriff, (who is the immediate Miniſter and Officer of the King to execute all Proceſs) except the Sheriff himſelf or his Officers be Parties : But if the Juſtice of Peace be to grant out Proceſs againſt the Sheriff, Under-Sheriff, or their Officers, offending contrary to the Statute 8 *H.* 6. *cap.* 9. or 11 *H.* 7. *cap.* 15. which you may ſee here before ; it ſeemeth ſuch Proceſs ſhall be directed to the Coroners of the County, and ſhall be ſerved by them. And ſo are divers Books, as 2 *H.* 6. 12.   8 *H.* 6.   30.   9 *H.* 6. 11. and 18 *Ed.* 4. 7. and others. And ſo alſo the Oath of the Juſtices of Peace ſeemeth to bind them.

Br. Franc. 18.   Note alſo, that this Proceſs ought always to be made in the Name of the King : And for that the King is Party, it muſt be with a *Non omittas propter aliquam libertatem,* &c. But the *Teſte* thereof may be under the Name of the Juſtices of Peace.

(*a*) If the Offender be within any Liberty or Franchiſe, the Sheriff is to enter the Franchiſe, and execute the Proceſs himſelf, (and not to write to the Bailiff of the Franchiſe, becauſe the King is a Party.) See 41 *Aſſ.* 17.   *Br. Franch.* 18. 31.

(*d*) The Forms of theſe Proceſſes to be made by the Juſtice of Peace out of the Seſſions, ſeem to be as followeth :

The Venire Facias *thus.*

Venire Facias.   GEORGE by the Grace of God, &c. King, &c. To the Sheriff of the County of *Cambridge,* Greeting : We command you, that you omit not, by Reaſon of any Liberty in your Bailiwick, but that you Cauſe *A. B.* of *D.* in your ſaid County, Yeoman, to come before *R. M.* &c. and *D. M.* &c. two of our Juſtices aſſigned to keep the Peace, as alſo to hear and determine, &c. at *L.* in your County on the   Day of next to be, to anſwer to us upon certain Articles preſented againſt him *A. B.* And have you there this Precept. Witneſs *R. M.* and *M. D.* at, &c.

The Diſtringas *thus.*

Diſtringas.   GEORGE by the Grace of God, &c. To the Sheriff, &c. We command you, that you omit not by Reaſon of any Liberty in your Bailiwick, but that you enter the ſame, and diſtrain *A. B.* of *D.* &c. by all his Lands and Tenements, &c. and that

2   you

you anfwer for the Iffues of the fame, &c. and that you have his Body before, &c. the Juftices, &c. to anfwer, &c. Witnefs, &c.

The *Writ of* Capias *thus.*

GEORGE by the Grace of God, &c. to the Sheriff, &c. We command you that Cæter you omit not by Reafon of any Liberty in your Bailiwick, but that you enter the fame and take *J. D.* of *A. &c.* if he be found in your Bailiwick, and him caufe to be fafely kept, fo that you have his Body before, &c. two of our Juftices affigned, &c. at *L.* in your County, on the   Day of   next to be, to anfwer to us of divers Trefpaffes and Offences of which he is indicted. And have you then there this Writ. Witnefs, &c.

At which Day *W. W. &c.* Sheriff of the County aforefaid, made a Return that he is not found in his Bailiwick, and he did not come. Therefore it is commanded as before, &c.

The Alias Capias.

GEORGE, &c. To the Sheriff, &c. We command you as we before command- *Alias.* ed you, that you omit not, &c. (as before.

At which Day, &c. (as before) and he did not come. Therefore it is commanded as we have often commanded, &c.

The Party may appear *Gratis,* and fo avoid the Attachment or Arrefting of his Body ; and that is the Caufe that the Entry is, *Et ipfe non venit* (he did not come).

The Pluries Capias.

GEORGE, &c. To the Sheriff, &c. We command you as we often have com- *Pluries.* manded you, that you omit not (as before).

At which Day *W. W.* and the Sheriff aforefaid did make return that *G. F.* is not found in, &c. and he did not come. It is therefore commanded that you caufe to be demanded, &c.

The Exigent.

GEORGE, &c. To the Sheriff, &c. We command you that you caufe *E. F.* of *Exigent.* *A.* in your County, Yeoman, to be demanded, until, by the Law and Cuftom of our Kingdom of *England,* he be outlawed, if he fhall not appear, and if he fhall appear, that you take him and caufe him to be fafely kept, fo that you have his Body before *R. M. &c.* and *M. D. &c.* two of the Juftices affigned, &c. at *L.* in your County, on the   Day of   next to be, to anfwer to us of divers Trefpaffes, Contempts and Offences, of which he is indicted. And have you then there this Writ. Witnefs *R. M.* and *M. D.* at *L. &c.*

At which Day *W. W. &c.* the Sheriff of the faid County did make Return that at the County held at *Cambridge,* the   Day of   in the   Year of the Reign of our Lord the King that now is, and fo at four other Counties then next following, there holden, the aforefaid *E. F.* was demanded, and did not appear. Therefore he was outlawed.

Thefe Proceffes are fent out, to the End that either the Party fhall come or be brought Lamb. 502. in to make his Anfwer, and to be juftified by the Law ; or elfe that for his Contumacy he fhall be outlawed, and fo be deprived of the Benefit of the Law. But the Power of 2 H. H. P C the Juftices of Peace ended with the Outlawry, for they can make no *Capias Utlagatum,* 52. but muft certify the Outlawry into the King's Bench.

Alfo all fuch Proceffes (as well of *Capias, &c.* as of Outlawry) may be ftaid by a *Su-* Lamb. 500. *perfedeas* iffuing from other Juftices of Peace (out of Seffions) teftifying that the Party hath come before them, and hath found Sureties for his Appearance to anfwer to the In- dictment, or to pay his Fine, &c. See before.

Note, That this Authority of the Juftices of Peace in fending out their Proceffes *The Comm* (being out of their Seffions) is beyond the Bounds of their Commiffion. And again, *fion,* by the Commiffion one Juftice of Peace alone cannot grant a *Capias,* nor other Procefs, 14 H. - Br P 5.

6 E   but

but two Juſtices of Peace at the leaſt muſt do it, and that ſitting the Court, and in their Seſſions ; and yet neverthelefs in theſe former Cafes the Statutes (expreſly, or by necef-fary Implication) giving ſuch Authority to the Juſtices of Peace, or to one Juſtice alone and that out of the Seſſions, are ſufficient Warrant and Commiſſion to the Juſtices of Peace therein, as it ſeemeth.

See 2 Hawk. P. C. *Chap.* 27. *on this Head.*

CHAP. CXCIV.
Traverſe.

Lamb. 325.

AFTER that ſuch Proceſs (or other Proceſs *ad refpond*) is awarded againſt the Party, it ſeems he may come in and yield himſelf to pay his Fine : Or elſe he may offer his Traverſe to the Indictment found againſt him before the Juſtices of Peace and the Juſtices ought to allow him his Traverſe againſt it ; which Traverſe is to take Iſſue upon the chief Matters of the Indictment, or to deny the Point of the Indictment The formal Words of the Traverſe are in Latin, *Abſque hoc, &c.*

See Lamb. 522, 523.

But although the Juſtices of Peace have Power in diverſe Cafes as aforeſaid, (out of their general Seſſions,) to take Indictments, and after ſuch Indictments found to award a Proceſs *ad reſpondendum* againſt Offenders, and to hear and determine thereof ; and the Offenders alſo have Liberty to come in and to ſpeak, and may anſwer for themſelves and may offer their Traverſe, and that the Juſtices of Peace are to allow of and to re-ceive them ; yet *Quære,* whether the Juſtices of Peace (out of their General Seſſions may try ſuch Traverſe being tendred to them, (except in Cafes of Riots and Forcible Entries) without which Trial all the reſt may ſeem idle. Or upon the Traverſe tendred they muſt certify or ſend the Inquiſition of the Indictment ſo found before them into the King's Bench, or unto their Quarter or General Seſſions of the Peace, there to be tried and determined. Howſoever it is ſafeſt in all Cafes, (after ſuch Traverſe tendred) to certify or deliver ſuch Inquiſition or Indictment into the King's Bench, or to their next Quarter-Seſſions, and ſo to refer the Trial of the Traverſe, and farther Pro-ceedings therein, to them.

CHAP. CXCV.
Certiorari.

THE Return of a *Certiorari* ſent to remove an Indictment may be thus : Firſt upon the Backſide of the Writ of *Certiorari* indorſe theſe or the like Words : The Execution of this Writ appears in a Schedule to the ſame Writ annexed. And that Schedule may be thus.

Canterbury.

I M. D. Eſq; one of the Keepers of the Peace and Juſtices of our Lord the King aſſigned to keep the Peace, as alſo to hear and determine divers Felonies, Tref-paſſes and other Offences in the ſame County committed, by Virtue of this Writ to me delivered, I do diſtinctly and openly under my Seal certify into the Chancery of our ſaid Lord the King, the Indictment, of which mention is made in the ſaid Writ, to-gether with all Things touching the ſame Indictment. In Witneſs whereof I M. D. a-foreſaid have to theſe Preſents ſet my Seal. Given at, &c. the   Day of in the   Year of the Reign, &c.

Then take the Record of the Indictment, and cloſe it within the Schedule, and ſea and ſend them up both together with the *Certiorari.*

Now to ſhew what is farther meet for the Juſtice of Peace to know concerning this Writ of *Certiorari,* and their Certifying or Return thereof ;

After an Indictment found before Juſtices of Peace, a *Certiorari* is procured by the Means of ſome Party indicted or grieved, thereby to remove ſuch Indictment from the

ſaid

aid Juſtices, and to convey it to Juſtices of a higher Authority, to the End the Party may either traverſe ſuch Indictment above, or may there avoid it for Inſufficiency of Form or Matter.

(*a*) Although the *Cuſtos Rotulorum* keep the Records, yet muſt the Juſtices return Hob. 135. he *Certiorari* ; for the Writ is directed to them, and not to him ; and the Record it elf muſt be returned, and not *Tenorem Recordi*.

(*d*) And this *Certiorari* is the King's Writ, iſſuing ſometimes out of the Chancery, ind ſometimes out of the King's Bench, and may be directed to any inferior Court of Record, or Officer of Record, (as to a Juſtice of Peace, Sheriff, Coroner or Eſcheator) o be certified of any Record which is before any of them.   And firſt an *Alias*, then a *Pluries*, and laſtly an Attachment lieth againſt them that ſhould ſend it, if the Record Fitz. 245. a. be not certified accordingly.   Or it ſeemeth a *Subpœna* is uſed at this Day.

If it be returnable into the Chancery, then the Words are, *In our Chancery* ; and if nto the King's Bench, then the Words are, *Nobis mittatis* ; and if into the Court of Common Pleas, then *Coram Juſt' noſtris de Banco*.

(*a*) This Wiit is not to be ſlighted, nor are any Proceedings to be after the Delivery hereof, although the Return be paſt ; for by the Delivery the Hands of the Juſtices are cloſed.   A Forcible Entry was found, and Reſtitution awarded, but not executed.   A Writ of *Certiorari* comes to a Juſtice of Peace, and he refuſes to open it till he had poke with his Companions.   Reſtitution was in the King's Bench prayed and granted, ind the Juſtice of Peace much chid.   *Yelv.* 32.

(*d*) The *Certiorari* may be ſometimes to remove and ſend up the Record it ſelf, and Plow. 393. ſometimes but only the Tenor of the Record, (as the Words therein be) and it muſt be obeyed accordingly.

If there be *Variance* between the *Certiorari* and the Record removed, the Juſtices Fitz. 245. b. need not to certify ſuch Record.   *Lamb.* 500.

A Juſtice of Peace may deliver or ſend into the King's Bench an Indictment found Cro. 130. a. before him, or a Recognizance of the Peace taken by him, or a Force recorded by & 133. b. him, without any *Certiorari* : But if he having a Record in his Hands be diſcharged of ais Office, now he cannot certify it without a *Certiorari*, although he be made a Juſtice of Peace again.   See 8 *H.* 4. *f.* 5.   *Br. Record* 64.

If a *Certiorari* be to ſend up the Indictment of *A.* in which Indictment ſome others 6 Ed. 4. 5. be indicted with the ſame *A.* yet need not the Juſtices of Peace to make any Certifi-cate concerning any but *A.*   For although they be named jointly, yet they be indicted ſeverally, and the King may pardon *A.* without forgiving the other.   6 *Ed.* 4. 5.

If a *Certiorari* ſhall come to the Juſtices of the Peace to remove an Indictment, and 6 H. 7. 16. the Party ſueth not to have it removed, but ſuffereth it to lie ſtill after the Day of the Br. Jud. 17. Return of the *Certiorari* ; yet the Juſtices of Peace ought *ex officio* to ſend it away, becauſe the Writ containeth in it ſelf a Command to them ſo to do ; and ſo is a *Su-perſedeas* of it ſelf to the Juſtices of Peace to ſtay their Proceedings.   See *antea*, Tit. *Forcible Entry*.

(*a*) And yet by others the Juſtices may proceed upon the Indictment. *Vide Crom.* 132, 133. & 166. *Dyer* 245.

(*d*) And albeit the *Certiorari* be a *Superſedeas* of it ſelf, yet may the Party upon the Lamb. 497. *Certiorari* purchaſed, have a *Superſedeas* alſo directed to the Sheriff, commanding him F.N.B.237.c. that he arreſt him not upon that Record before the Juſtices of Peace.   *Fitz. f.* 237.   In which Place alſo he doubteth whether the Juſtices of Peace themſelves ought not of Duty to award their own *Superſedeas* to the ſame Effect, after that the Writ of *Cer-tiorari* is brought to their Hands.

If a *Certiorari* come to the Juſtices of Peace to remove an Indictment, and in Truth Lamb. 438. it was not taken till after the Date of the *Certiorari* ; yet if the Indictment be remo-ved thereby, it is good enough, for that they be both the King's Courts.   (1 *R.* 3. 4.) and in ſuch a Caſe it is now uſual to remove it.   *Vide Fitz.* 71. *d.*

(*a*) But all Writs of *Certiorari* being to remove any Indictment of Forcible Entry, or Riot, or of Aſſault and Battery, found before the Juſtices of Peace, ſhall now be delivered at ſome Quarter-Seſſions of the Peace in open Court, &c. 21 *Jac.* 1. *cap.* 8.   See *hic antea*, Tit. *Forcible Entry.* And the Perſons ſo proſecuting the ſame ſhall (before the Allowance thereof) become bound unto the Proſecutor in 10 *l.* Bond with Sureties, as the Juſtices ſhall think fit, with Condition to pay to the Proſecutor (within one Month af-ter Conviction) ſuch reaſonable Coſts and Damages, as the Juſtices of the Peace of the
County

County (where the Bill fhall be found) fhall affefs and allow; and in Default thereof the Juftices may proceed.

Lamb. 501.   (*d*) All the higher Courts at *Weftminfter* may write to the Juftices of Peace, to certify their Records for the Trial of Caufes depending before them, as you may read 19 *H.* 6. 19. where they of the Common Pleas did fend to the Juftices of Peace for an Indictment, becaufe in a Writ of Confpiracy (brought or depending before them) it was material to have it.

In fome Cafes the Juftice of Peace may certify a Record (by him made or found before him out of Seffions) without any Writ of *Certiorari* therefore to him directed. *Vide antea,* Tit. *Forcible Entry.*

In other Cafes he muft of Duty certify his Proceedings, but may fpare to certify the Record, until a *Certiorari* come to him for it. See hereof *antea,* Tit. *Surety for the Peace.*

For the Manner of the Writ of *Certiorari* to remove Records from one Court to another, or from the Juftices of Peace, or other Officers of Record, to any of the higher Courts at *Weftminfter, &c.* there are divers Forms and Sorts thereof, as you may fee *F. N. B.* 242. *&c.*

I will only fet you down here one Form for all, and fo conclude.

The Form of Certiorari *out of the Chancery to certify a Recognizance taken by a Juftice of Peace in the County for the Keeping of the Peace,* &c.

* *Certiorari*
of the Good
Behaviour, as
the Cafe is.
F.N.B. 18.c.
Cromp. 148.

GEORGE, *&c.* To the Keepers of our Peace in the County of *Cambridge,* and each of them, Greeting : We being willing * for certain Reafons, to be [certified up on the Tenor of a certain Security of the Peace, which *A. P.* Efq; lately found before you, or fome one of you, of that that he fhould not do nor procure to be done any Damage or Hurt to *R. S.* or to any other of our People, of their Bodies ; we command you that without Delay you do diftinctly and openly, under your Seals or the Seal of one of you, to us into our Chancery, in eight Days of the Purification of the bleffed *Mary,* wherever we fhall then be, fend the Tenor of the Security of the Peace aforefaid And that this you or any of you no ways omit under the Penalty of one hundred Pounds Witnefs my felf at *Weftminfter* the   Day of   in the   Year of our Reign.

The Return hereof fee *antea,* Tit. *Surety for the Peace.*

(*a*) But if the *Certiorari* be with thefe Words, We command that you fend all and fingular the Recognizances aforefaid, with all Matters concerning the fame, as fully and wholly as before you, *&c.* they were late taken, *&c.* Here the Juftice of Peace, together with the Recognizance, muft certify and fend his Examinations taken, or the Warrant whereby the Party was brought before him to find fuch Surety, and fuch other Matter or Caufe as he knoweth, why fuch Surety was required againft the Party that fo the Court above may proceed againft the Party (if Caufe be required) according to Law and Juftice. And the Certificate may be thus.

I *M. D.* one of the Juftices of the Peace in the County of *Cambridge* do certify his Majefty in his Court of Chancery (or King's Bench) That I by Virtue of a certain Warrant (the Tenor of which is here under written) did compel *R. C.* in the fame Writ named, to find Surety according to the Form of the faid Warrant. And I the faid *M. D.* by Virtue of the faid Writ, the faid Recognizance in the faid Writ mentioned, and all Things touching the fame, to his Majefty (under my Seal) do hereby diftinctly fend, as in the faid Writ is of me required. In Witnefs whereof, *&c.*

The Tenor of the above-mentioned Warrant followeth. Then underneath write the Warrant, *&c. Verbatim.*

Note, That a Record fhall not be removed but by *Certiorari* or *Corpus cum Caufa.* Fitz. Record 3.

Note alfo, That upon a *Certiorari* to remove an Indictment of a *Riot* or *Forcible Entry, &c.* the Return muft have thefe Words, *as alfo to hear and determine divers Felonies,* &c. For if the Return mentions only that they are Juftices of the Peace without fuch Words, according to the Commiffion, the Return is infufficient. 12 *H.*7 25. 2 *R.* 3. 9. *Br. Indictment* 32, 50.

Alfo note, that no *Certiorari* fhall be granted to remove any Recognizance, except the fame Writ be fignified with the proper Hand of the Chief Juftice, or (in his Abfence

4   fence

fence) of one of the Justices of that Court out of which the said Writ shall be awarded or made. 1 & 2 *P. & M. cap.* 14.

Certioraries shall be delivered in open Sessions, and before they are allowed, the Parties indicted shall become bound to the Prosecutor in 10 *l.* with such Sureties as the Sessions shall think fit, with Condition to pay within one Month after Conviction, such Costs and Damages as the Sessions shall allow; and in Default of such Payment the Sessions may proceed. *In what Cases Certiorari's shall not be granted, and upon what Conditions.*
21 Jac. 1. c. 8.

Two or more Justices residing near the Place where Offences and Forfeitures relating to the Duties of Excise, shall be done or made, are appointed to judge and determine the same, and no *Certiorari* shall be allowed to supersede the Execution of any of their Orders or Proceedings. 12 Car. 2.
c. 23.

By this Statute the Justices of Peace have Power to hear and determine Offences relating to the Highways, and no *Certiorari* shall be allowed to remove their Proceedings, unless the Person indicted shall before such Allowance, be bound to the Prosecutor in 40 *l.* with Sureties conditioned to pay him, within one Month after Conviction, full Costs and Damages to be ascertained on Oath of the Prosecutor; and in Default thereof, the Sessions may proceed. *Highways.*
13 & 14 Car. 2.
c. 6.

No *Certiorari* shall be allowed to remove any Proceedings concerning Deer-stealing, unless the Person prosecuted become bound to the Prosecutor in 50 *l.* with such Sureties as the Justice before whom convicted shall think fit, with a Condition to pay the Prosecutor his full Costs and Damages, if the Conviction is affirmed, or a *Procedendo* allowed; and in Default thereof the Justice may proceed to Execution. *Deer-stealing.*
3 & 4 W. 3.
c. 10.

All Matters concerning Highways, Causeys, Pavements and Bridges, mentioned in this Act, shall be heard and determined in the proper County, and not elsewhere; and no Proceedings made by Virtue thereof shall be removed by *Certiorari* out of the proper County into any other Court. 3 & 4 W. 3.
c. 12.

No *Certiorari* shall be allowed to remove Convictions or Proceedings of Justices concerning the Game, by virtue of this Act, unless the Party desiring it shall, before such Allowance, become bound to the Prosecutor in 50 *l.* with Sureties to be approved by the Justices, to pay the full Costs and Damages, on Oath of the Prosecutor, within a Month after Conviction, or a *Procedendo* granted; and in Default thereof the Justice may proceed, &c. *The Game.*
4 & 5 W. 3.
c. 23.

Certiorari shall not be granted in Term-Time at the Instance of any Person indicted or presented for a Trespass or Misdemeanor before a Trial is had at the Sessions, unless upon Motion in Court of B. R. and a Rule made for that Purpose, and afterwards, and before it shall be allowed, the Party must enter into a Recognizance of 20 *l.* with two sufficient Sureties, before a Justice of the County, conditioned to appear at the Return of the Writ, and plead to such Indictment or Presentment, and procure Issue to be joined at his own Costs, and to be tried at the next Assises for the County, after the Return of the Writ; and if in *London* or *Middlesex*, then to be tried the next Term after the Writ granted, &c. and to give due Notice of such Trial. *Term-Time.*
5 & 6 W. 3.
c. 11.
This Act was made perpetual by 8 & 9 W. 3.
c. 33.
See postea.

And this Recognizance must be certified into B. R. together with the *Certiorari* and Indictment, there to be filed, and the Name of the Prosecutor, &c. indorsed on the Indictment; and if the Defendant shall not enter into such Recognizance, the Justices may proceed to Trial.

And if he who procures the *Certiorari* is convicted, B. R. must give reasonable Costs to the Prosecutor, and to be taxed according to the Course of that Court; and if the Party doth not pay it within ten Days after Demand, then Oath being made of his Refusal to pay, &c. an Attachment shall be granted against him, and the Recognizance shall not be discharged till the full Costs are paid.

Any of the Judges of B. R. may grant a *Certiorari* in * Vacation, but then his Name, and also the Name of the Party at whose Instance it was granted, must be indorsed on the Writ, and the like Recognizance entered into before 'tis allowed. *Vacation Time.*
* *If 'tis Teste of the precedent Term, the Fiat*

for it must be signed by some Judge before the Essoin-day of the subsequent Term; otherwise a Procedendo will be granted; but he need not sign the Certiorari itself, unless 'tis required by Statute.

And on every *Certiorari* granted in Counties Palatine, the same Rules shall be observed. *Counties Palatine.*

But where the Right of repairing Highways or Bridges, &c. is in Question, in such Case, upon an *Affidavit* made of the Truth thereof, a *Certiorari* may be *Highways, &c. Bridges.*

6 F   granted

granted, the Party procuring it entring into fuch Recognizance with Sureties, as aforefaid.

8 & 9 W. 3. c. 33.   The aforefaid Statute 5 & 6 *Will.* which was only temporary, was made perpetual; and it was farther enacted, that the Party at whofe Inftance a *Certiorari* fhall be granted to remove any Proceedings from the Seffions, may enter into a Recognizance with two fufficient Sureties before a Judge, with the fame Condition as in the aforefaid Statute, which fhall be mentioned on the Back of the Writ, under the Hand of the Judge who took it; and this fhall be as effectual to fuperfede any farther Proceedings below, for the Removal whereof a *Certiorari* fhall be granted, as if the Recognizance had been taken by a Juftice of the Peace of the County, according to the faid Act; only if 'tis taken before a Judge, it muft be added to the Condition of the Recognizance, that the Party profecuting the *Certiorari* fhall appear from Day to Day in the Court of *B. R.* and not to depart without Leave of the Court.

Tithes. 7 & 8 W. 3 c. 6.   Two Juftices have Power to hear and determine Differences concerning fmall Tithes under the Value of 40 s. an Appeal lies to the next Quarter-Seffions, but no *Certiorari* muft be granted to remove any Proceedings by Virtue of that Act, unlefs the Title of the Tithes come in Queftion.

Game. 5 Ann. c. 14.   No *Certiorari* muft be allowed to remove any Proceeding of the Juftices againft Perfons deftroying the Game, unlefs the Party accufed fhall, before the Allowance thereof, become bound to the Profecutor in 50 l. with fuch Sureties as the Juftice fhall think fit, conditioned to pay him, within four Days after *Conviction* or a *Procedende* granted, *full Cofts* and Charges on Oath; and in Default of fuch Security the Juftice may proceed as if no *Certiorari* had been.

'Tis a Superfedeas as foon as 'tis delivered.   A *Certiorari* being delivered is a *Superfedeas* to all fubfequent Proceedings on the Record; but then it muft be delivered before the Jury who are to try the Caufe are fworn, for if afterwards, they may proceed.

Falfe Return.   And the Perfon to whom 'tis delivered may make what Return he thinks proper; which if falfe, yet the Court will not ftay the Filing it, on *Affidavits* made that 'tis falfe, except in publick Cafes, as in Cafes of Commiffioners of Sewers, or for not repairing Highways, or for fome fuch fpecial Caufes, becaufe the Remedy for a Falfe Return is either an Action on the Cafe at the Suit of the Party grieved, or an Information at the Suit of the King.

Cinque Ports, Counties Palatine and Wales. Cro. Car. 252, 264.   It hath been doubted whether a *Certiorari* would lie to remove Indictments found in the Cinque Ports, Counties Palatine and *Wales.* But 'tis now fettled, and it hath been awarded to the Mayor and Juftices of *Dover*, and not to the Lord Warden, to remove an Indictment for Felony found there.

Mich. 8 W. 3. Rex werf. Bird.   So it was granted to remove the like Indictment out of the Court at *Romney*, upon a Suggeftion, that the Defendant could not have an indifferent Trial before the Steward there, though it was infifted againft the *Certiorari*, that they had a very antient Charter to exempt them from the Jurifdiction of the Court of King's Bench, and of Juftices of Affife.

Counties Palatine. March Rep. 165.   It hath been granted to remove Indictments out of Counties Palatine; for though they have Grants of *Jura Regalia*, yet the King never intended to exclude himfelf, and all Indictments are at his Suit.

Wales. 34 H.8. c.26. 26 H. 8. c. 6.   It hath been granted to remove an Indictment of Murder found in a *Welfh* County, for though by the Statute 34 *H.* 8. the Juftices in *Wales* have Power to hold Pleas of the Crown, as the Chief Juftice of *England* may do, yet that is not a Repeal of the Statute 26 *H.* 8. which allows Indictments for Felony found in *Wales*, to be tried in the adjoining *Englifh* Counties; befides, *B. R.* is not excluded by any negative Words in the Statute 34 *H.8.*

But laftly, Where-ever a Statute gives an *Appeal* from the Order of the Juftices to the next Seffions, in fuch Cafe the Granting a *Certiorari* before the Matter upon the Appeal is determined, is altogether irregular; therefore if an Order fhould be removed, then before 'tis filed, the Party may, upon Motion, object againft the *Certiorari*; and then the Order thus removed will be fent down again, but not after the Time of *Appeal* is expired, for then it will be too late to object againft the *Certiorari* thus granted.

5 Geo 2. c. 19. §. 1.   Upon Appeals to the General Seffions for any County or Precinct within *England*, againft Orders made by Juftices of Peace, fuch Juftices affembled at any General Seffions fhall caufe any Defects of Form in fuch Orders to be amended without Cofts, and proceed to hear the Merits of fuch Orders, and to make fuch Determinations thereupon as by Law they ought, in cafe there had not been fuch Defect of Form.

I

No *Certiorari* shall be allowed to remove any Order, unless the Party prosecuting shall ^{Ib. §. 2.} enter into a Recognizance with Sureties before one Justice of Peace where such Order shall have been made, or before one of his Majesty's Justices of the King's Bench, in the Sum of 50 *l.* with Condition to prosecute without wilful Delay, and to pay the Party, in whose Favour such Order was made, within one Month after the said Order shall be confirmed, his Costs to be taxed; and in case the Party prosecuting such *Certiorari* shall not enter into such Recognizance, or shall not perform the Conditions aforesaid, it shall be lawful for the Justices to proceed and make further Orders, as if no *Certiorari* had been granted.

The Recognizances to be taken as aforesaid shall be certified into the King's Bench, ^{Ib. §. 3.} and filed with the *Certiorari*, and Order removed thereby; and if the Order shall be confirmed, the Persons intitled to such Costs, within ten Days after Demand made, upon Oath made of the making such Demand and Refusal of Payment, shall have an Attachment for Contempt, and the Recognizance shall not be discharged until the Costs shall be paid, and the Order complied with.

No Writ of *Certiorari* shall be allowed to remove any Conviction, Judgment, Order, ^{13 Geo. 2.} or other Proceedings before any Justice or Justices of Peace of any County, City, Bo- ^{c. 18. §. 5.} rough, Town Corporate, or Liberty, or the respective General or Quarter-Sessions thereof, unless such *Certiorari* be moved or applied for within six Kalendar Months next after such Conviction, &c. and unless it be duly proved upon Oath, that the Party suing forth the same has given six Days Notice thereof in Writing to the Justice or Justices before whom such Conviction, &c. shall be made, to the End that such Justice or Justices, or the Parties therein concerned may shew Cause, if he or they shall think fit, against the granting such *Certiorari*.

C H A P. CXCVI.

Of the Powers given to Justices of the Peace by several late Statutes.

ALL Actions, Suits, and Informations to be commenced upon this, or any other ^{Wool-Bill.} Acts for preventing the Exportation of Wool, Wool-fells, Wool-flocks, Mort- ^{12 Geo. 2.} lings, Shortlings, Worsted, Bay or Woollen Yarn, Crewels, or Wool slightly manufactu- ^{c. 21. §. 18.} red, or Matresses, or Beds stuffed with combed Wool, or Wool fit for Combing, Fullers Earth, Fulling Clay, Tobacco-Pipe Clay, or any other Scouring Earth or Clay from *Great Britain* or *Ireland*; or for Preventing the Exportation from *Ireland* into foreign Parts, of Cloth, Serges, Bays, Kerseys, Frizes, Druggets, Shalloons, Stuffs, Cloth-Serges, or any other Drapery made of, or mixed with Wool manufactured in *Ireland*, may be enter'd and prosecuted, (except where it is in this Act otherwise directed) at the Quarter-Sessions of the Peace, or before any two Justices of the Peace, for any County, City or Place in this Kingdom, in a summary Way, at the Election of the Seisor or Informer. The *Onus probandi* shall lie on the Claimer of the Property, and not on the Officer or Seisor.

If any Officer of the Customs, Excise or Salt, or Person assisting any such Officer, ^{Ib. §. 26.} shall be hindred, opposed, obstructed, molested, wounded or beaten, in seising any Wool or other Goods before enumerated, by any Person, by Day or Night, by Land or Water; the Person so hindring, &c. or any other Person armed with offensive Weapons, or wearing any Mask or other Disguise, who shall Rescue, or attempt to Rescue any Wool or other Goods aforesaid, seised by any such Officer, every such Offender being convicted may be transported for any Time not exceeding seven Years; and returning from Transportation before the Expiration of the Time for which he is transported, shall suffer as a Felon, without Benefit of Clergy.

The Act 4 *Geo.* 1. *cap.* 11. * shall be construed to extend to all Persons who act as ^{Ib. §. 27.} Aiders and Abettors to Exporters of Wool or Wool-fells. ^{* Vide supra c. 113.}

The Justices of Peace in *England*, at their Quarter-Sessions, shall have Power to make ^{County Rates.} one general Rate for such Sums of Money as they shall think sufficient to answer all the ^{12 Geo. 2.} Ends and Purposes of the several Acts before recited (*viz.* 22 *H.* 8. *cap.* 5. 1 *Ann.* St. 1. ^{c. 29. §. 1.} *cap.* 18.

cap. 18.   11 & 12 *W.* 3. *cap.* 19.   7 *Jac.* 1. *cap.* 4.   43 *El. cap.* 2.   14 *El. cap.* 5. 19 *Car.* 2. *cap.* 4.   12 *Ann. St.* 2. *cap.* 23.) inſtead of the ſeparate and diſtinct Rates thereby directed to be levied; which Rate ſhall be aſſeſſed upon every Pariſh or Place within the Limits of their Commiſſions, in ſuch Proportions, as the Rates made in purſuance of the ſaid Acts, have been uſually aſſeſſed; and the Sums ſo aſſeſſed ſhall be collected by the High Conſtables of the reſpective Hundreds and Diviſions in which any Pariſh or Place lies, in the Manner and at the Times herein after directed.

Ib. §. 2.   The Church-wardens and Overſeers of the Poor of every Pariſh and Place, are required, out of the Money collected for Relief of the Poor, to pay to the High Conſtables of the reſpective Diviſions, the Money ſo rated and aſſeſſed, within thirty Days after Demand thereof in Writing, to be given to the ſaid Church-wardens or Overſeers, or left at their Dwelling-houſes, or affixed on the Church-doors of the Pariſhes to which they belong, by the ſaid High Conſtables; which Demand the High Conſtables are to make, at ſuch Times as the Juſtices ſhall in Seſſions direct; and the Receipts of ſuch High Conſtables ſhall be a ſufficient Diſcharge to ſuch Church-wardens, &c. paying the ſame, and ſhall be allowed in their Accounts. And in caſe the Church-wardens and Overſeers ſhall neglect to pay the Money hereby aſſeſſed, after Demand, the High Conſtables are to levy the ſame by Diſtreſs and Sale of the Goods of ſuch Church-wardens, &c. by Warrant under the Hands and Seals of two Juſtices of the County or Place reſiding in or near ſuch Pariſh, rendering the Overplus (if any) after deducting the Money aſſeſſed, and the Charges of Diſtreſs and Sale, to the Owners.

Ib. §. 3.   In caſe no Rate be made for Relief of the Poor in any Pariſh or Place, the Juſtices may direct the Sum aſſeſſed on ſuch Pariſh or Place for the Purpoſes of this Act, to be levied by any Petty Conſtables, or other Peace-Officer belonging to the ſame, in ſuch Manner as Money for Relief of the Poor is by Law to be rated and levied; which Sum ſo levied ſhall be paid to the High Conſtable for the Diviſion or Liberty wherein ſuch Place lies; and ſhall be demanded of, or levied on ſuch Peace-Officer, in the ſame Manner as the Rates are herein before directed to be demanded of, and levied on the Church-wardens and Overſeers of the Poor: And if ſuch Peace-Officer ſhall pay ſuch Sum, before the ſame ſhall be by him rated, and levied, he may afterwards rate and levy the ſame, or ſhall be reimburſed the ſaid Sum out of any Conſtable's or other Rate made on any Pariſh or Place which the ſaid Juſtices ſhall in Seſſions direct.

Ib. § 4.   The Juſtices of the Peace for the Counties of *York*, *Derby*, *Durham*, *Lancaſter*, *Cheſter*, *Weſtmorland*, *Cumberland*, and *Northumberland*, may order the Sum directed to be aſſeſſed on any Pariſh or Place within the ſaid Counties, for the Purpoſes of this Act, to be paid by the Petty Conſtable of any ſuch Pariſh, in ſuch Manner as the ſame is directed to be paid and levied where no Rate is made for Relief of the Poor.

Ib. §. 5.   Nothing herein contained ſhall extend to make any Perſons or Places liable to pay any Rate to be made in purſance of this Act, to which ſuch Perſon or Place was not liable to contribute before the paſſing thereof; but the Juſtices may aſcertain what Proportion of any Rate to be made by virtue of this Act, ſhall be aſſeſſed on the ſeveral Perſons and Places who have uſually contributed only to one or more of, and not to all the Rates hereby intended to be raiſed, and thrown into one general Aſſeſſment.

Ib. §. 6.   The High Conſtables, at or before the next General or Quarter-Seſſions, after they ſhall have received ſuch Sums of Money, ſhall pay the ſame to ſuch Perſons (being reſident in any ſuch County or Place, where the Rates ſhall be made) as the Juſtices ſhall appoint to be Treaſurers (whom they are hereby impowered to nominate) ſuch Treaſurers firſt giving Security to be accountable for the Money which ſhall be paid to them, and to pay ſuch Sums as ſhall be ordered by the Juſtices in their Quarter-Seſſions, and for the faithful Execution of the Truſts repoſed in them; and all Money paid into their Hands by virtue of this Act, ſhall be deemed the publick Stock; and they are to pay ſo much of the ſame to ſuch Perſons as the Juſtices ſhall direct, for the Purpoſes of the ſaid Acts, and for any other Uſes, to which the publick Stock of any County, City, or Liberty, is applicable by Law.

Ib. §. 7.   The Treaſurers are to keep Books of Entries of the Sums received and paid by them; and alſo to deliver in true Accounts upon Oath, if required, of all the Money received and paid by them, diſtinguiſhing the particular Uſes to which the ſame has been applied, to the Juſtices at every General or Quarter-Seſſions held within the Limits of their Commiſſions; and ſhall lay before the Juſtices at ſuch Seſſions the proper Vouchers for the ſame.

       I   The

The High Conftables are to demand and levy fuch Affeffments in Manner before di- Ib. §. 8. rected, and to account for the fame before the Juftices, if required, in like Manner as the Treafurers are directed to account; and if any High Conftable fhall neglect fo to do; or if he fhall refufe to pay any Money remaining in his Hands, which ought to be paid to the refpective Treafurers at the Times limited by this Act, in order to be applied to the Ufes aforefaid, the Juftices may commit fuch High Conftable to the common Gaol, there to remain without Bail or Mainprize, till he fhall have caufed fuch Affeffment to be demanded and levied, and fhall have rendered a true Account in Manner directed, and made full Payment of the Money that fhall appear to be due on fuch Account; and all the Accounts and Vouchers of the faid Treafurers and High Con- ftables, after having paffed by the Juftices at the Quarter-Seffions, fhall be depofited with the Clerk of the Peace of each County, or the Town-Clerk, or other chief Officer of any City or Liberty, who is to keep them among the Records of fuch County, &c. to be infpected by any of the Juftices, within the Limits of their Commiffions, without Fee or Reward.

The Treafurers Receipts fhall be fufficient Difcharges to all High Conftables; and the Ib. §. 9. Difcharges of the Juftices, made at the Quarter-Seffions to fuch Treafurers, fhall be al- lowed as good and fufficient Releafes in any Court of Law or Equity.

No new Rate fhall be made, until it appear to the Juftices, by the Accounts of their Ib. §. 10. Treafurers, or otherwife, that three Fourths of the Money collected by the preceding Rates have been expended for the Purpofes aforefaid.

The Juftices may continue or remove the Treafurers at their Pleafure, and may allow Ib. §. 11. every of them, infifting on the fame, fuch reafonable Sums of Money for their Pains in the Execution of fuch Truft, not exceeding 20 *l. per Ann.* as they fhall think fit, which they are impowered to direct the Payment of out of the Monies arifing by the Rates.

If the Church-wardens and Overfeers of any Parifh fhall have Reafon to believe the Ib. §. 12. faid Parifh is over-rated, they may appeal to the Quarter-Seffions againft fuch Part of the Rate only as affects the Parifhes in which they ferve fuch Offices, who are to hear and finally determine the fame; but the faid Rate fhall not, upon fuch Appeal, be quafhed in regard to any other Parifhes affeffed thereby.

No Part of the Money to be raifed by this Act, fhall be applied to the Repair of any Ib. §. 13. Bridges, Gaols, or Houfes of Correction, till Prefentments be made by the refpective Grand Juries at the Affife, Great Seffions, general Gaol-Delivery, or Quarter-Seffions held for any County, City, or Liberty of the Infufficiency, or want of Reparation of their Bridges, &c.

When any publick Bridges, or other Works are to be repaired at the Expence of any Ib. §. 14. County, &c. the Juftices of the Peace at their Quarter-Seffions, after Prefentment to be made, as aforefaid, may contract with any Perfons for Rebuilding and Repairing of fuch Bridges, &c. as fhall be within their refpective Counties, &c. and all other Works which are to be repaired, and done by Affeffment on the refpective Counties, &c. for any Term of Years not exceeding feven Years, at a certain annual Payment for the fame, fuch Contractors giving Security for the due Performance thereof, to the Clerk of the Peace, or chief Officer of any City or Liberty; and fuch Juftices fhall 'give publick No- tice of their Intention of contracting with any Perfons for Rebuilding and Repairing the Bridges, and other Works aforefaid; and fuch Contracts fhall be made at the moft rea- fonable Prices which fhall be propofed by fuch Contractors; and all Contracts and Orders relating thereto, fhall be enter'd in a Book to be kept by the Clerk of the Peace, or chief Officer of any City or Liberty amongft the Records of fuch County, City, or Liberty, to be infpected at all feafonable Times by any of the Juftices within the Limits of their Commiffions; and by any Perfons employed by any Parifh or Place contributing to the Purpofes of this Act, without Fee or Reward.

There fhall be but one Rate made by the Juftices *Com' Middlefex* in the faid County, Ib. §. 15. City, and Liberty of *Weftminfter*, for the Purpofes aforefaid, and for Repair of the Gaol called *New Prifon*, in the faid County.

Provided, That the Juftices for the City and Liberty of *Weftminfter*, at the Quarter- Ib. §. 16. Seffions, fhall have power to appoint the Governor of the Houfe of Correction in the faid City, who fhall have fuch Sum of Money yearly, for the Maintenance of the Prifo- ners in his Cuftody, who fhall be fick, or unable to work, not exceeding the prefent Al- lowance of 50 *l. per Ann.* and direct the Repairs and Management thereof, as they have heretofore done; and the Treafurers of the Money arifing by the Rates collected in the faid County of *Middlefex*, and City of *Weftminfter*, fhall obey all Orders made by the Ju-

6 G ⸱ ftices

ftices at the Quarter-Seffions, for the Payment of any Money for the Allowance allotted to. fuch Governor of the Houfe of Correction, and the Repairs thereof, which Orders fhall be fufficient Difcharges to fuch Treafurers.

Ib. §. 17.   The Juftices may oblige the High Conftables, or any other Perfons, who are or have been impowered to levy any Money for the Purpofes aforefaid, and who have any Money in their Hands, to account at the Quarter-Seffions, in fuch Manner as High Conftables are directed to account by this Act; and in cafe fuch high Conftables, or other Perfons fhall refufe to account, or pay the Money remaining in their Hands, when required; the Juftices fhall have the like Remedy againft them, as they have againft the High Conftables by this Act, for not accounting, or paying as aforefaid; and the faid Juftices are impowered to order the Payment of the Money not difpofed of, into the Hands of the Treafurers to be appointed by this Act; which fhall be deemed Part of the Stock of the faid Counties, &c. and to inquire what Sums of Money are owing for the Purpofes aforefaid; and then to order 'the Payment of fuch Sums as fhall appear, upon fuch Inquiry, to be due.

Ib. § 18.   No Suit fhall be commenced againft any Perfon imployed in collecting any Money in Purfance of the faid recited Acts, or this Act, or any Rate which has been or fhall be quafhed on a *Certiorari* brought, or to be brought in any Court of Record at *Weftminfter*, or otherwife, for any Money collected, or to be collected on any fuch Rate, before fuch Writ of *Certiorari* was or fhall be brought and allowed; but the feveral Sums of Money which appear to have been paid by any Perfons on fuch Rate, more than they ought to have paid, fhall be repaid, or allowed in the next Rate which fhall be made purfuant to this Act, as if the fame had been paid on fuch new Rate.

Ib. §. 19.   Provided, That all Perfons fo employed fhall account for, and pay the Money by them received, in the fame Manner, and under the like Penalties for any Neglect or Refufal, as are to be inflicted on Perfons refufing to account for, or pay over any Money which they have received in purfuance of this Act.

Ib. §. 20.   The Juftices *Com' Middlefex*, at their General Seffions of the Peace, fhall have the fame Powers to put this Act in Execution, as are given them at their General Quarter-Seffions.

Ib. §. 21.   No Writ of *Certiorari*, to remove any Rates made in purfuance of this Act, or any Orders made by the General or Quarter-Seffions touching fuch Rates, fhall be granted, but upon a Motion to be made in the firft Week of the next Term after the Time for Appealing from fuch Rates or Orders is expired; and upon making it appear to the Court that the Merits of the Queftion will by fuch Removal come properly in the Judgment of the faid Court; nor till 100 *l.* Security be given to profecute fuch Writ with Effect, and to pay the Cofts to be afcertained by the Court, to which fuch Rates or Orders fhall be removed, in cafe the fame are confirmed; nor fhall any fuch Rates or Orders be vacated for want of Form only; and all Charges attending fuch Removal fhall be defrayed out of that, or any fubfequent Rate.

Ib. §. 22.   So much of the Act 14 *Eliz.* as relates to the Method of taxing Parifhes for the Relief of Prifoners; and of the Act 43 *Eliz.* as relates to the Method of Raifing Money for the *King's Bench* and *Marfhalfea* Prifons, Hofpital, and Alms-Houfes; and of the Act 19 *Car.* 2. as relates to the Method of rating Parifhes for providing Materials for fetting poor Prifoners on work, is repealed.

Ib. §. 23.   Provided, That fuch Sums as have been annually paid to the *King's Bench* and *Marfhalfea* Prifon, fhall be paid out of the Money arifing by this Act, at the Times, and in

11 G.2. c.20. the Manner prefcribed by an Act 11 *Geo.* 2. *For the more effectual fecuring the Payments of certain Sums of Money directed by an Act made in the forty-third Year of the Reign of Queen* Elizabeth, *for Relief of the Poor*, &c. and fuch Money as fhall be judged neceffary by the Juftices in Seffions to be applied, in purfuance of the faid Acts 14 *Eliz.* and 19 *Car.* 2. fhall be paid out of the Money arifing by this Act.

Ib. §. 24.   Suits commenced againft Perfons for Things done in purfuance of this Act, fhall be brought within three Months after the Facts are committed, and fhall be laid in the County wherein the Caufe of Action fhall arife; and the Defendant may plead the General Iffue, &c. and if Judgment fhall be given againft the Plaintiff, &c. the Defendant may recover treble Cofts.

Juftices of Peace for Liberties.   Where any Franchifes in *England* have Commiffions of Peace within themfelves, and are not fubject to the County Juftices; the Juftices of fuch Franchifes fhall exercife the

13 Geo. 2 c. 18. §. 7.   fame Powers and Authorities within the Limits of their Commiffions as the Juftices of Counties are impowered to do by the faid Statute 12 *Geo.* 2. *cap.* 29.

l   It

It having been enacted by 1 *Ann. ſtat.* 2. *cap.* 18. that Perſons employed in Woollen, Linen, Fuſtian, Cotton, or Iron Manufactures, imbezilling any Waſts, Ends of Yarn, or other Materials with which they were intruſted, ſhould forfeit double the Value of the Damages done, for the Uſe of the Poor: And in caſe the Offenders ſhould refuſe to pay their Forfeitures, that then any Juſtice of Peace of the County where the Offence was committed, might ſend ſuch Offenders to the Houſe of Correction, until Satisfaction ſhould be made. And if it ſhould appear to the Juſtice, that any ſuch Offender was not able to make Satisfaction, then he might be publickly whipped, and kept to hard Labour, not exceeding fourteen Days. And it being by the ſaid Act further enacted, that Perſons buying or receiving ſuch Waſts, Ends of Yarn, *&c.* ſhould ſuffer the like Penalties and Forfeitures as Perſons convicted for imbezilling of the ſaid Materials; which Act was made perpetual by an Act of 9 *Annæ* : And Doubts having ariſen whether theſe Clauſes extend to the imbezilling Woollen, Linen, Fuſtian, Cotton, and Iron Manufactures, actually made up into merchantable Wares, and whether the ſaid Forfeitures ſhould be applied for the Uſe of the Poor of the Pariſh where the Perſons injured ſhall reſpectively live, or for the Uſe of the Poor of the Pariſh where the Offence is committed; to explain and amend the ſaid Act, it is enacted by 13 *Geo.* 2. *cap.* 8. That if any Perſons hired to work on any Woollen, Linen, Fuſtian, Cotton, or Iron Manufactures, ſhall imbezil, or any ways illegally diſpoſe of any Materials they were intruſted to work up, or ſhall reel ſhort or falſe Yarn ; the Perſons ſo offending, and convicted as preſcribed by the ſaid recited Act, ſhall forfeit double the Value of the Damages, which the Owners of ſuch Goods (whether manufactured or not) ſhall ſuſtain, with Coſts of Proſecution for every Offence, as ſhall be judged reaſonable by the Juſtice of the Peace before whom ſuch Offenders reſpectively ſhall be convicted : And if immediate Payment of the Forfeitures, with Coſts of Proſecution, ſhall be refuſed, that then the ſame Juſtice, before whom the Offenders were convicted, ſhall commit them to the Houſe of Correction, to be whipt and kept to hard Labour for any Time not exceeding fourteen Days; and for every ſecond or other ſubſequent Offence, to forfeit four Times the Value of the Damages, and Coſts of Suit, to be ſettled by the Juſtice : And if immediate Payment be refuſed, then any Juſtice for the County, Riding, *&c.* ſhall commit ſuch Offenders to the Houſe of Correction, there to be kept to hard Labour for any Time not exceeding three Months, nor leſs than one Month, and publickly whipp'd at the Market-croſs, once or oftner, at the Diſcretion of the Juſtice.

All Perſons who ſhall buy, receive, take in Pawn, *&c.* from any the afore mentioned Perſons, any Woollen, Linen, Fuſtian, Cotton, or Iron Manufactures, whether before wrought or after, knowing the ſame to be purloined, *&c.* and being lawfully convicted, ſhall ſuffer the ſame Penalties as the ſaid Purloiners or Imbezilers ſhall ſuffer by any former or this preſent Act.

The Forfeitures incurred by this Act, ſhall be divided, Half to the Uſe of the injured Party, and Half to the Poor of the Pariſh where the Offence is committed.

Perſons employed in manufacturing Gloves, Breeches, Leather, Skins, Boots, Shoes, Slippers, Wares, or other Materials made uſe of in any of the ſaid Trades, who ſhall imbezil, ſell, pawn, or exchange any the aforeſaid Goods or Materials which they are intruſted with, wrought or unwrought, and convicted on the Oath of the Maſter or Owner, or any other credible Witneſs, or Confeſſion of the Party, before any Juſtice of the Peace of the County, *&c.* where ſuch Offence is committed, or where the Party charged inhabits, the Offender ſhall pay double the Value of the Goods ſo imbeziled, *&c.* one Half to the Party grieved, and the other Half to the Uſe of the Poor of the Pariſh, together with full Charges attending ſuch Conviction, to be levied by Diſtreſs and Sale of the Offender's Goods, returning the Overplus on Demand ; but if there be no Goods ſufficient to defray all Damages, or the Party refuſe immediately to pay, then the Offender to be committed to Priſon, and kept to hard Labour 14 Days, and be whipp'd at the Direction of the Juſtice ; and for the ſecond or any ſubſequent Offence, the Party offending ſhall forfeit four Times the Value of the Damage, with Coſts, to be ſettled by the Juſtice, or be impriſoned and kept to hard Labour for any Time not exceeding three Months, or leſs than one, and publickly whipp'd once or oftner, at the Direction of the Juſtice.

Receivers ſhall be ſubject to the ſame Penalties and Puniſhments as the Offenders.

Workmen ſhall be paid for their Labour in Money, and not in Truck, (except at their own Requeſt) and all Goods delivered out to be wrought, ſhall be delivered with a Declaration, at the ſame Time, of the true Weight, Quantity or Tale, on Forfeiture of double

the

the Value, to the Workman of the Work to be done; and the Workman guilty of Fraud, Neglect, &c. fhall forfeit double the Damages to the Owner.

Ib. §. 7.   All Difputes relating to Wages, Frauds, Neglects, &c. as above, fhall be heard and determined by any two Juftices of the County, &c. where the Controverfy fhall arife, who have Power to examine Witneffes on Oath or Affirmation.

Ib. §. 8.   Any Journeyman employed in making up Gloves, Breeches, Boots, Shoes, Slippers, &c. for any Mafter, neglecting the Performance, by working for any fubfequent Mafter, before he fhall have compleated the Work he firft undertook, fuch Offender being convicted on Oath or Affirmation of one or more credible Witneffes, before one or more Juftices where the Offence fhall be committed, fhall be fent to the Houfe of Correction, for any Time not exceeding a Month.

Ib. §. 9.   If any Perfons think themfelves aggriev'd by any Order of the Truftees, they may appeal to the Juftices at their next General Quarter-Seffions (giving eight Days Notice of fuch Appeal to the Perfons againft whom fuch Appeal fhall be brought) who fhall hear and finally determine the fame, and award the Cofts as they fhall think fit; but no Order of the Juftices fhall be appealed from, for Want of Form only.

Ib. §. 10.   No Perfon fhall fuffer twice for one and the fame Fact.

Ib. §. 11.   The recited Act of 1 *Annæ*, (made perpetual, as aforefaid) and this prefent Act fhall extend to *Scotland*, in as ample a Manner as in *England*.

Vagrants.
13 Geo. 2.
c. 24. §. 1.   The Number of Rogues, Vagabonds, Beggars, and other idle and diforderly Perfons daily increafing, to the great Scandal, Lofs and Annoyance of the Kingdom, it is enacted by 13 *Geo.* 2. *cap.* 24. that Perfons threatning to leave their Wives and Children to the Parifh, returning to a Parifh from which they have been legally removed, without a Certificate from the Place or Parifh to which they belong, living idly, and refufing to work for common Wages, or begging from Door to Door, or placing themfelves in Streets, &c. to beg Alms in the Parifh where they dwell, fhall be deemed idle and diforderly Perfons, and any Juftice of the Peace may commit them to the Houfe of Correction, to be kept to hard Labour, not exceeding one Month. Any Perfon may apprehend and take before a Juftice, People going from Door to Door, or placing themfelves in Streets, &c. to beg in Places where they dwell; and if they refift or efcape, they fhall be fubject to Punifhment by this Act, as Rogues and Vagabonds; and 5 s. for every Offender fo apprehended, fhall be paid by the Overfeer, and allowed him in his Account; but if the Overfeer refufe to pay the faid Sum, it may be levied (by Juftice's Warrant) by Diftrefs and Sale of his Goods, and he fhall not be allowed the fame in his Account.

Ib. §. 2.   All Patent Gatherers, or Gatherers of Alms, under falfe Pretences of Lofs by Fire, &c. Collectors for Prifons or Hofpitals, Fencers and Bearwards, Players of Interludes, &c. (having no legal Settlement at the Place where they act) without Letters Patent, (as by
10 Geo. 2.
c. 28. *Vide fupra*, Chap. 46. Act made 10 *Geo.* II. intitled, *An Act to explain and amend fo much of an Act made in the twelfth Year of the Reign of Queen* Anne, *intitled, An Act for reducing the Laws relating to Rogues*, &c.) or without Licence from the Lord Chamberlain; all Minftrels, Jugglers, Gypfies, Pretenders to Phyfiognomy, Palmeftry, or the like, Fortune-tellers, or Perfons playing at unlawful Games, Perfons run away from their Wives and Children, whereby they become chargeable to the Parifh; all Petty Chapman or Pedlars, without Licence or other Authority, all Wanderers lodging in Barns or Out-houfes, or pretending to be Soldiers, Mariners, or Seafaring Men, or pretending to go to Work in Harveft, and all wandering Beggars, fhall be deemed Rogues and Vagabonds.

Ib. §. 3.   This Act fhall not extend to Soldiers wanting Subfiftence, having Certificates from their Officers, or the Secretary at War, or Mariners or Seafaring Men licenced by fome Juftice of Peace, fetting down their Time and Place of Landing, or Difcharge, whither going, and limiting the Time of their Paffage, and keeping in the direct Way to the Place whither they are going, or to any Perfons going with Certificates abroad to work at Harveft, or otherwife.

Ib. §. 4.   All End-gatherers offending againft the Act 13 *Geo.* 1. intitled, *An Act for the better Regulation of the Woollen Manufactures*, &c. all Perfons apprehended as Vagabonds, and efcaping, or refufing to go before a Juftice, or giving a falfe Account of themfelves, after Warning of their Punifhment, all Perfons breaking Prifon before the Expiration of the Term, or having been punifhed and difcharged, commit a fecond Offence, fhall be deem'd incorrigible Rogues.

Ib. §. 5.   Vagabonds, as above defcribed, may be apprehended by any Parifh-officer, or other Perfon dwelling near where the Offence is committed, to be conveyed before a Juftice;
and

and if any Officer refufe to ufe his beft Endeavours to take fuch Offenders, he fhall be punifhed as after directed: And if any other Perfon, being charged by any Juftice fo to do, fhall refufe to apprehend and deliver fuch Offender to the Conftable, &c. or to carry the fame before a Juftice, if an Officer cannot be found, being convicted on Oath, fhall forfeit for every Offence ten Shillings, to be levied by Diftrefs and Sale, and applied to the Ufe of the Poor: And if any fuch Inhabitant (not being an Officer) fhall apprehend fuch Offenders, and deliver him or her to an Officer, or caufe him or her to be conveyed to fome Juftice, as directed by this Act, the faid Juftice may make an Order in Writing upon fuch Conftable, &c. where the Offender fhall be apprehended, to pay ten Shillings to the Perfon who apprehended the Offender, within a Week after Demand, producing fuch Order, and giving his Receipt, which Money fhall be repaid by the High Conftable, who fhall be allowed the fame in his Account, by the Treafurer of the County, Riding, or Divifion; and the Juftices at General or Quarter-Seffions fhall allow it in the Treafurer's Accounts; and in Places where there are no High Conftables, the Petty Conftables and other Officers fhall be allowed in their Accounts what they fhall fo pay, by Virtue of this Act: And if any Petty Conftable or other Officer fhall refufe to pay the ten Shillings, as aforefaid, then any fuch Juftice may by Warrant levy twenty Shillings, by Diftrefs and Sale of fuch Offender's Goods, ten Shillings to be paid to the Perfon intitled to the fame, and fuch other Recompence for his Trouble, Lofs of Time and Expences, as the faid Juftice fhall think fit; and the Overplus (if any) to be returned to fuch Petty Conftable, &c. on Demand: And if any fuch Petty Conftable or other Officer, fhall pay the faid Ten Shillings to the Perfon intitled, and the High Conftable fhall refufe to pay him again, then the Sum of twenty Shillings fhall be levied on his Goods, to be difpofed of to the Petty Conftables, &c. in Manner as is juft before directed.

The Juftices for every County, &c. or any two, fhall meet four Times in the Year (or ⟨Ib. §. 6.⟩ oftner, if Need be) in their refpective Divifions, and by Warrant command the Conftables or other Officers, with proper Affiftance, to make a general privy Search in one Night throughout their feveral Limits, for apprehending of Vagabonds, which fhall be brought before any Juftice of the fame County, Riding, &c.

Whenever Vagabonds are apprehended, they fhall be taken before a Juftice, and exa- ⟨Ib. § 7.⟩ mined on Oath, or by the Oath of any other Perfon, of the Circumftances of the Perfons fo apprehended, and the Parifh to which they belong, which Examinations fhall be written and figned by the Juftice, and the Perfons examined and tranfmitted to the next General or Quarter-Seffions, to be filed on Record; and if any legal Settlement is made appear, the Juftice fhall pafs them thither, taking Notice of their Age, and the Reafon of their being apprehended; but if no legal Settlement can be found, then they fhall be conveyed to the Place of their Birth, if under 14 Years of Age, and have a Father or Mother living, then to the Place of their Abode; and if the Place of Birth or Parent's Abode cannot be known, then to the Parifh or Place where they were laft found Begging, and paffed unapprehended, there to be delivered to fome Officer of fuch Parifh or Place: The Form of the Pafs fhall be as follows.

*To the Conftable of the Parifh of   in the County of   or to the Tything-
man or other Officer (as the Cafe fhall be) and alfo to the Governor or Mafter of the
Houfe of Correction at   within the faid County; and likewife to all Governors or Mafters of all Houfes of Correction, whom it may concern to receive and convey, and to the Church-wardens, Chapel-wardens, or Overfeers of the Poor of the
Parifh, Place or Precinct (as the Cafe fhall be) of   in the County of
or either of them, to receive and obey.*

WHereas   was or were apprehended in the Parifh of   or in the
Town of   or other Place (*defcribing it*) as a Rogue and Vagabond, or as Rogues and Vagabonds, and brought before me, or us, one, two, or more of his Majefty's Juftices of the Peace for this County, Riding, City, Borough, Town Corporate, Divifion or Liberty; and upon Examination of the faid   taken before me (*or us*) upon Oath, it doth appear, that he, fhe, or they, is a Rogue and Vagabond, or are Rogues and Vagabonds, within the true Intent and Meaning of the Statute in that Cafe made and provided; and that his, her, or their laft legal Settlement is at in this County, or the County of   or that the faid   was or were born in the Parifh of   and hath not fince obtained any legal Settlement, or that the faid   is or are under the Age of fourteen Years, and hath or have a Father or Mo-

ther

ther living or abiding in the Parifh or Town of   or other Place (*defcribing it*) or that the faid   was or were laft found Begging or Mifordering him, herfelf or themfelves, in the Parifh or Town of   or other Place, (*defcribing it*) and pafs'd through the fame unapprehended, and the Place of his, her, or their legal Settlement Birth, or Parents Abode, cannot be difcovered: Thefe are therefore to require you the faid Conftable, or other Officer, (*as the Cafe fhall be*) to convey the faid   in the next direct Way to the faid Parifh or Town of   or other Place within the faid County, or next adjacent County (*as the Cafe fhall happen, defcribing it*) and there deliver him, her, or them, to fome Church-warden, Chapel-warden, or Overfeer of the Poor of the fame Parifh Town or Place, to be there provided for according to Law; and you the faid Church-wardens, Chapel-wardens, and Overfeers of the Poor, are hereby required to receive the faid Perfon or Perfons, and provide for him, her or them, as aforefaid; or in Cafe the faid Place be not within the fame, or next adjacent County, Riding, City, Borough Town Corporate, Divifion or Liberty, then to convey the faid   to the Houfe of Correction at   in the faid County or Place: And you the faid Governor, or Mafter of the faid Houfe of Correction, to receive the faid   into your Cuftody, and him her or them to convey, or caufe to be conveyed to the firft Houfe of Correction in the next County or Place, in the direct Way to the faid Parifh or Town of   or other Place; (*defcribing it*) and in like Manner every other Governor or Mafter of every Houfe of Correction to whom it may belong, to convey the faid   from Houfe of Cor- rection to Houfe of Correction, until he, fhe or they fhall arrive at the Houfe of Cor- rection belonging to the County, Riding, City, Borough, Town Corporate, Divifion or Liberty to which the faid Parifh, Town or Place doth belong; and the Mafter or Gover- nor of the faid Houfe of Correction to convey and deliver, or caufe to be conveyed and de- livered the fame to fome Church-warden, Chapel-warden, or Overfeer of the Poor of the faid Parifh or Town of   or other Place (*defcribing it*) to be there provided for according to Law: And you the faid Church-wardens, Chapel-wardens, and Overfeers of the Poor, are hereby required to receive the faid Perfon or Perfons, and provide for him, her or them, as aforefaid.

Ib. §. 8.   The Juftice fhall fign a Duplicate of fuch Pafs, and tranfmit it to the next General or Quarter-Seffions, there to be filed on Record; and the faid Duplicate, or a Copy thereof may be read as Evidence in any Court of Record.

Ib. §. 9.   Any Perfons herein before defcribed to be Vagabonds being apprehended, the Juftice before whom they are brought may commit them to the Houfe of Correction till the next General or Quarter-Seffions, or any lefs Time as he fhall think fit, according to the Na- ture of the Offence, and then pafs them away as aforefaid.

Ib. §. 10.   Where any incorrigible Rogue, as before defcribed, fhall be taken before a Juftice, he may be fent to the Houfe of Correction, and kept to hard Labour till the next General or Quarter-Seffions; and if the Juftices in General or Quarter-Seffions affembled, fhall ad- judge the Perfon fo committed to the Houfe of Correction to be an incorrigible Rogue, they may order him to be detained for any Time not exceeding fix Months, to be kept to hard Labour, and corrected by Whipping in fuch Manner, Times and Places within their Jurifdiction, as they fhall think fit; and the faid Offender fhall be afterwards paffed away as before directed: And if fuch Offender fhall break Prifon, or make his Efcape before the Time of his Confinement fhall be expired, and being duly convicted, he fhall be judged guilty of Felony, and be tranfported for any Time not exceeding feven Years, according to an Act made 4 *Geo.* 1. intitled, *An Act for the further preventing Robbery, Burglary. and other Felonies, and for the more effectual Tranfportation of Felons*: And if any Offen- der to be tranfported fhall efcape before Tranfportation, or return from Tranfportation before his Time fhall be expired (being convicted thereof) he fhall be guilty of Felony, and fuffer Death without Benefit of Clergy.

Ib. §. 11.   If any Offender being deemed an incorrigible Rogue, and fent to any Parifh or Place, fhall afterwards be found Begging or Mifordering himfelf in another Place, fuch Offender may be committed to the Houfe of Correction to hard Labour for three Months, and to be publickly whipp'd in fuch Manner, and as often as fuch Juftice fhall think fit; and afterwards be pafs'd to the Place to which he was firft fent.

Ib. §. 12.   The Juftice who fhall make any Pafs, fhall at the fame Time give the Conftable or other Officer a Certificate, afcertaining how they are to be conveyed, and what Recom- pence fuch Conftable, *&c.* is to have, as follows.

5

Whereas

WHereas by a Pass (*reciting the Substance or Effect of the said Pass*) I (*or we*) do hereby order and direct the said Person or Persons to be conveyed on Foot (or in a Cart or by Horse, &c. to the said Parish or Town of   in   or other Place (*describing it*) or to the House of Correction at   in the Way to such Parish, Town or Place (*as the Case shall be*) in   Days Time, for which the said Constable, &c. is to be allowed the Sum of   and no more.

  Given under my Hand (or our Hands) this   Day of, &c.

The Constable or other Officer having such Pass and Certificate, shall convey the Per- Ib. §. 13. sons named therein, in such Manner and Time as the Pass shall direct, the nearest Way to the Place where they are ordered to be sent, if such Place shall be in the same County, Riding or Division where the Persons were apprehended, or next adjoining thereto ; but if the Place lies in some distant County, &c. the Constable or other Officer shall deliver them to the Governor or Master of the next House of Correction where they dwell, together with the Pass and Certificate, taking his Receipt for the same : And the said Master of such House of Correction is required to receive them, and give a Receipt, and convey them forward with all convenient Speed, and deliver them, with the Pass, to the Master of some House of Correction in the next County, &c. that lies nearest in the Way to the Place where such Persons are to be sent, who is hereby obliged to receive them, and give a Receipt, and shall without Delay apply to some Justice in the same County, &c. who shall make the like Certificate as before (*mutatis mutandis*) and deliver it to the Master of the last House of Correction, who shall convey the Persons named in the Pass, together with the former Pass, unto the House of Correction in the next County, &c. in the Way to the Place where such Persons are to be conveyed ; and so in like Manner from the House of Correction in one County to the House of Correction in another, till they come to some House of Correction in the County, &c. wherein the Place is where they are to be sent, there to be kept to hard Labour, not exceeding one Month ; and then such Persons shall be conveyed to such Place, and delivered to some Parish Officer, who is required to receive them and the Pass, and provide for them accordingly, and give the like Receipt on their Delivery.

All Constables and other Officers within the Counties of *Cumberland, Northumberland,* Ib. §. 14. *Durham,* or Town of *Berwick* upon *Tweed,* and all Masters of Houses of Correction within the said Counties or Town, shall (upon any Person's being delivered to them by Pass, apprehended within the said Counties or Town, or brought to them, according to the Direction of this Act, whose Settlement is in *Scotland*) convey such Persons to the next adjoining Shire, Stewartry or Place, in that Part of the United Kingdom, and deliver them to any Officer of the next Parish, District or Place, within the said Shire, Stewartry or Place, taking his Receipt ; and such Officer is to receive such Persons, give such Receipt, and dispose of them according to Law.

Any Justice of Peace in *Scotland* next adjoining to the Counties of *Cumberland, Nor-* Ib. §. 15. *thumberland, Durham* or Town of *Berwick* upon *Tweed,* may cause any Constable or other Officer, to convey any Persons apprehended within their Jurisdictions, or brought to them from that Part of the United Kingdom, as Vagabonds, &c. whose Place of Settlement shall appear to be in *England,* to the first House of Correction in the said Counties or Town, and deliver them to the Master of the said Workhouse, taking his Receipt, who is required to receive such Persons, give such Receipt and apply to some Justice in the same County or Town, who shall cause such Persons to be conveyed to the Place of their legal Settlement (if within the said Counties or Town) or else to be conveyed to the House of Correction in the next County in the most direct Way to the Place of their legal Settlement.

In case any Master of a Vessel shall bring into this Realm from *Ireland,* the Isle of Ib. §. 16. *Man,* the Isles of *Jersey, Guernsey* or *Scilly,* or any of the Foreign Plantations any Vagabond or Person likely to live by begging, being a Native of the said Islands or Plantations, and they shall be apprehended wandering and begging, such Master shall forfeit 5 *l.* for every Vagabond so brought over, besides the Charges of apprehending and reconveying them back, and any Officer where such Persons shall be found wandering and begging, may cause them to be apprehended and openly Whipped and put on board any Vessel to be reconveyed to the same Island or Place from whence they were brought, paying such Rate *per* Head for their Passage back as the Justices at their Quarter-Sessions shall appoint, and if such Constable or other Officer, shall make appear on Oath before

a

a Juftice for the fame County or Place what Expence he has been at, the Juftice fhall direct Payment of the Money, and the Penalty of 5 *l.* and if the Mafter refufe to pay the fame on Demand, the Juftices by Warrant fhall levy the fame by Diftrefs and Sale of the faid Veffel, or any of the Goods therein while within the Jurifdiction of fuch Juftice, and if the faid Mafter or the Veffel be gone out of the faid Juftice's Jurifdiction, the faid order may be removed by *Certiorari* into the King's Bench and there filed, and the Judges of the faid Court fhall direct Procefs for arrefting the faid Veffel till the Money mentioned in fuch order and the Charges of fuch Procefs be fully fatisfied, or otherwife to award Procefs for levying the fame by *Capias. Fieri Facias,* or *Elegit,* againft the Mafter or Owners of the faid Veffel, as the Court fhall think proper.

But if the Mafter or Owners of the faid Veffel fhall fhew in the faid Court any ground of Grievance by the faid Order, they may be permitted to traverfe the fame, giving Security in the Penalty of 50 *l.* to anfwer the Charges of fuch Traverfe, if it be determined againft them.

Ib. §. 18.   All Mafters of Ships bound for *Ireland,* the Ifle of *Man, Jerfey, Guernfey* or *Scilly,* fhall, on Warrant of a Juftice of the County, Town or Place where fuch Ship fhall be, take on board fuch Vagrants as fhall be named in the Warrant, and convey them to fuch Place in *Ireland,* the Ifle of *Man, Jerfey, Guernfey* or *Scilly,* as fuch Ship fhall be bound to or arrive at, and the Perfon who ferves him with the Warrant fhall pay him fuch Rate *per* Head as the Juftices at their Quarter-Seffions fhall appoint for every Vagrant delivered to him, and the Mafter fhall fign a Receipt on the Back of the Warrant for the Money fo paid and the Vagrants fo delivered, which Warrant fhall be returned to the Juftice who figned it, and upon his Allowance thereof under his Hand, the Money fhall be repaid by the County in the Manner as this Act directs for paffing Vagrants from County to County, and every Mafter of a Ship refufing to receive on board, or to tranfport fuch Vagrants or fign fuch Receipt as aforefaid, fhall forfeit 5 *l.* to the Ufe of the Poor, to be levied by Diftrefs and Sale of the faid Ship or Goods by Warrant of any Juftice of the County, City or Town Corporate, returning the Overplus on Demand, after deducting the Penalty and Charges.

Ib. §. 19.   The Juftices of Peace of any County, *&c.* at the General or Quarter-Seffions fhall direct, what Rates *per* Mile or otherwife fhall be made for paffing Vagabonds, alfo make fuch Orders for the more regular acting therein, within their Limits as they fhall think proper, and all Perfons within the faid Limits are to give due Obedience to the fame.

Ib. §. 20.   If any Petty Conftable or other Officer bring to the High Conftable a Certificate given him by a Juftice, afcertaining how, and for what Rates he fhall be required to convey Vagabonds as aforefaid, with a Receipt from the Church-wardens, Overfeers of the Poor or Mafter of any Houfe of Correction, to whom the Perfons fo to be conveyed were delivered, the High Conftable fhall pay the Rates fo certified and no more, taking the Certificate and a Receipt, and the High Conftable fhall be allowed the fame in his Accounts by the Treafurer of the County, *&c.* delivering up the Certificate and Receipt and giving his own Receipt to the Treafurer, and the Juftices at their General or Quarter-Seffions fhall allow the fame to the Treafurer in his Accounts on his producing the Vouchers aforefaid, and if any High Conftable refufe to pay the Petty Conftable the Rates aforefaid on Demand, any Juftice may by Warrant levy double the Sum on his Goods by Diftrefs and Sale, and thereout allow the faid Petty Conftable the Sum fo certified, and other Expences and Lofs of Time as the faid Juftice fhall think fit, returning the Overplus on Demand, and in fuch Places where there is no High Conftable the Petty Conftable or other Officer fhall be allowed what they fhall fo pay in their refpective Accounts on producing their Vouchers.

Ib § 21.   The Treafurer of the County, *&c.* fhall pay out of the publick Money in his Hands to the Mafter of the Houfe of Correction within the faid County, *&c.* all his Expences in paffing Vagabonds, the faid Mafter producing the Certificate with a Receipt from the Mafter of the Houfe of Correction, or the Church-warden or Overfeer to whom fuch Perfons are delivered, and giving his own Receipt for the fame, and the Juftices in General or Quarter-Seffions fhall allow the fame to the Treafurer on producing his Vouchers.

Ib. §. 22.   If any Petty Conftable or other Officer or Mafter of any Houfe of Correction counterfeit any Certificate, Receipt or Note, or permit any Alteration in the fame he fhall forfeit 50 *l.* and if they do not convey the Perfons to the Place where they ought to be conveyed, or fhall refufe to receive any Perfons fent to them, or give a Receipt as directed; in every fuch Cafe they fhall forfeit the Sum of 20 *l.* to be levied by Diftrefs

5   and

and Sale of the Offender's Goods, by Warrant of the Juſtices at their General or Quar-ter-Seſſions, one Half to the Informer, and the other to the Treaſurer, to be made Part of the publick Stock, the Overplus to be returned on Demand.

The Place where ſuch Vagabonds ſhall be paſſed to, ſhall employ them in ſome Work-houſe or Alms-houſe, till they betake themſelves to ſome Employment, and if they re-fuſe to Work, or betake themſelves to ſome Employment, the Pariſh Officers may take them before a Juſtice to be ſent to the Houſe of Correction to hard Labour. *Ib. § 23.*

Lunaticks ſhall be apprehended by Warrant of two or more Juſtices, and locked up in ſome ſecure Place, or chained if Occaſion be, if the laſt legal Settlement of ſuch Lunaticks be within the County, but if ſuch Settlement be not there, then the Lunatick ſhall be paſſed to their laſt Settlement, there to be locked up or chained as aforeſaid ; and the Charges of maintaining ſuch Lunaticks ſhall be paid out of their Eſtates, if they have any over and above what ſhall be ſufficient to maintain their Families (if any) ; and if they have no Eſtate, they ſhall be provided for as other Poor are, by the Laws in Being. *Ib. §. 24.*

If any Conſtable or other Officer, or Maſter of any Houſe of Correction, ſhall re-fuſe to apprehend or paſs Vagabonds, or ſhall be otherwiſe remiſs in his Duty, or if any Perſons ſhall hinder the Execution of this Act, or reſcue any Perſon apprehended or paſſing from Place to Place by Virtue thereof, or ſhall be adviſing or aſſiſting in their E-ſcape, and ſhall be thereof convicted on Oath of one or more credible Witneſſes, before one or more Juſtices, they ſhall forfeit any Sum not exceeding 5 *l.* or leſs than 10 *s.* to the Uſe of the Poor, to be levied by Diſtreſs and Sale of the Offender's Goods, for want of which the Offender ſhall be committed to the Houſe of Correction to hard La-bour, for any Time not exceeding two Months. *Ib. §. 26.*

If any Perſon permits Vagabonds to Lodge in their Houſes, Barns or Outhouſes, and ſhall not apprehend and carry them before ſome Juſtice, or give Notice to ſome Conſtable or other Officer ſo to do, ſuch Perſon upon Conviction, on Oath before two or more Juſtices, ſhall forfeit, not exceeding 40 *s.* or leſs then 10 *s.* Half to the Informer, and Half to the Poor to be levied by Diſtreſs and Sale, rendring the Overplus on Demand, and if any Charge be brought on any Place by Means of ſuch Offence, it ſhall be levied by Diſtreſs and Sale as aforeſaid, and for want of ſuch Diſtreſs the Offen-der ſhall be committed to the Houſe of Correction to hard Labour, not exceeding three Months. *Ib. §. 27.*

Church-wardens and Overſeers may relieve Perſons whilſt in their Pariſhes, who by ſudden Sickneſs, or other accidental Misfortune, may not be removed without Danger of their Lives, and their Expences ſhall be allowed in their Accounts, and all Maſters of Hoſpitals may Provide for Sick and Impotent Perſons according to their reſpective Foun-dations, or give Money for Relief of ſuch caſual Poor. *Ib. §. 28.*

Perſons aggrieved by any Juſtice's Paſs, may appeal to the next General or Quarter-Seſſions. *Ib. §. 29.*

All Cities and Towns, where by ſpecial Acts of Parliament the Charge of paſſing Va-grants is to be otherwiſe defrayed than by this Act directed, or Paſſes managed other-ways, ſuch Rules ſhall be followed as if this Act had never been made. *Ib. §. 30.*

If the Grand Jury at the Aſſizes held for any County or Liberty preſent, that there is no Houſe of Correction, or not a ſufficient Number, or that thoſe already erected ought to be enlarged, or made more convenient ; the Juſtices at their General or Quar-ter-Seſſions may build or enlarge ſuch Houſes, to make them more convenient, and may raiſe Money ſufficient for building, enlarging or purchaſing Houſes or Land for that Purpoſe. *Ib. §. 32.*

The Juſtices for any County, *&c.* are to take effectual Care that the Houſes of Cor-rection provided within their Juriſdictions (except they are erected and maintained by any particular Founders) ſhall be duly fitted up, and ſupplied with all Neceſſaries for relieving, ſetting to Work, and correcting all idle and diſorderly Perſons who ſhall be ſent to the ſame, and any two Juſtices appointed at the General or Quarterly Seſſions ſhall viſit the ſame twice or oftner in every Year, and make their Report to the next General or Quarter-Seſſions, that what is amiſs may be reformed, and the ſaid Juſtices ſhall have the ſame Power over the Houſes newly erected, as they have over other Houſes erected under former Laws, and if the Maſters of Houſes of Correction do not ſet to Work and puniſh ſuch Vagabonds, or are otherwiſe negligent in their Duty, they may be fined by the Juſtices in their General or Quarter-Seſſions as by the Act 7 *Jac.* 1. *cap.* 4. which Fines ſhall be paid to the Treaſurer to be accounted for as Part of the publick Stock, *Ib. §. 33.*

6 I

and

and the said Justices may appoint or remove any Masters or other Officers of Houses o Correction, and make such Orders as they shall think fit for the better governing the said Houses, and for employing, relieving and punishing the Persons therein, or sending them to or from thence, and if any Persons shall refuse to quit Possession of such House o. Correction, after having an Order so to do from the General or Quarter-Sessions for the Space of ten Days, any two Justices may by their Warrant to the Sheriff remove them out of such House in like Manner as upon a Writ of *Habere facias Possessionem.*

Ib § 54.   If Offenders are committed to Prison, and the Time and Manner of their Punishmen is not limited by any Law in Being, the Justice shall commit them to the House of Correction to hard Labour, till the next General or Quarter-Sessions or till discharged by due Course of Law, and two Justices (one being the Justice who committed them) may discharge them before Sessions if they see Cause; but if they be not so discharged the Sessions may discharge them, or continue them if they think fit, not exceeding three Months.

Ib. § 35.   All Money raised by Virtue of this Act, whether to pass or maintain Vagrants Houses or Lands, or defray any other Expences concerning them, shall be paid to the Treasurer of the County, by an Act made last Sessions of Parliament, intitled an Ac for the more easy Assessing, Collecting and Levying of County Rates.

Ib. §. 36.   The Defendant in any Actions prosecuted for Things done in pursuance of this Act may plead the General Issue, &c. and if the Judgment be given against the Plaintiff, &c may recover double Costs: And the 12 *Ann. cap.* 23. is hereby repealed, and all Act: therein mentioned to be repealed, are to continue repealed.

Foundlings.   By the 13 Geo. 2. cap. 29. *For confirming and inlarging the Powers granted by his Ma-*
13 G. 2.   c. *jesty to the Corporation of the Governors and Guardians of the Hospital for the Maintenance*
29. §. 5.   *and Education of exposed and deserted young Children,* it is enacted that no Church-warden, Overseer or other Person shall by Virtue of any Law in Being, for the Provision of the Poor, or for Bastard Children, Stop, Molest or Disturb any Person in bringing any Child to any Hospital or House provided by the said Corporation for the Reception of such Children, or in returning from the same; under the Penalty of 40 s. for every such Offence, Half to the Informer, and Half to the Use of the said Hospital, which Forfeiture shall be levied under the Hands and Seals of any two Justices of the Peace for the County or Liberty where such Offence shall be committed.

Ib. §. 6.   No Parish Officer shall have any Authority in any such Hospital or House to inquire about the Birth or Settlement of any such Child therein Maintained and Educated, or to place them out Apprentices, or to do any other Thing within such Hospital, &c. save only to collect such Taxes as they shall be empowered to do by Act of Parliament.

Ib. §. 6.   Children, Nurses or Servants, maintained or employed within any such Hospital or Place, shall not gain any Settlement thereby.

Ib. §. 14.   Inferior Officers or Servants refusing to account, or to produce Papers, Books, Vouchers, or other Effects which they shall be intrusted with by the said Corporation, any two Justices of the County, &c. where the Servant shall be found, may, on Complaint made on the Part of the said Corporation, commit any such inferior Officer or Servant to Gaol, without Bail, until they make a true Account and pay the Ballance in their Hands, and deliver up such Papers, &c.

Houses of Cor-   The Justices of Peace of any County, City, &c. at their General Sessions or General
rection.   Quarter-Sessions assembled, or the major Part of them, where there shall be no Assizes, Great
14 G. 2. c.   Session or General Gaol-delivery held, upon the Presentment of the Grand Jury to such
33. §. 2.   Justices at their General Sessions, or General Quarter-Sessions, shall have as full Power to repair and enlarge any House of Correction already built, or to purchase any Houses for Houses of Correction, or to build any Houses of Correction, or to purchase Land to erect such Houses of Correction upon, and to make convenient Backsides or Outlets thereto, as if such Presentment had been made at the Assizes, Great Session or General Gaol-delivery, in such Manner as is directed by 13 *Geo.* 2. *cap.* 24.

Ib. §. 3.   Justices may send any Person who shall be apprehended as a Rogue, Vagabond, &c. to the House of Correction in the County, Riding or Division where they dwell, or to any other House of Correction in the next County, &c. as shall be most convenient for passing such Persons.

Waggons not   By 15 & 16 *Geo.* 2. *cap.* 2. the Clause of 14 *Geo.* 2. *cap.* 42. which obliges Persons
travelling for   not travelling for Hire to make use of Waggons with Wheels bound with Streaks or
Hire.   Tyre of a certain Breadth, or the said Streaks to be fastened with Nails of a certain
15 & 16 G. 2.   Size, is repealed.
c. 2. vid. supra
c. 21 & 50.   I

By

By 15 & 16 Geo. 2. cap. 13. fect. 12. it is enacted, That if any Perfon fhall forge, *Forging Bank* counterfeit, or alter any Bank Note, Bank Bill of Exchange, Dividend Warrant, or any *Bills, &c.* Bond or Obligation under the common Seal of the faid Company, or any Indorfement 15 & 16 G.2. thereon, or fhall offer or difpofe of, or put away any fuch forged, counterfeit, or al- c. 13. §. 12.. tered Note, Bill, Dividend Warrant, Bond or Obligation, or the Indorfement thereon, or demand the Money therein contained or pretended to be due thereon, or any Part thereof, of the faid Company, or any their Officers or Servants, knowing fuch Note, B.ll, Dividend Warrant, Bond or Obligation, or the Indorfement thereon, to be forged, counterfeited, or altered, with Intent to defraud the faid Company, or their Succeffors, or any other Perfon, every Perfon fo offending, and being thereof convicted, fhall be guilty of Felony without Benefit of Clergy.

Alfo if any Officer or Servant of the faid Company being entrufted with any Note, *Imbezilling,* Bill, Dividend Warrant, Bond, Deed, or any Security, Money, or other Effects be- &c. longing to the faid Company, or having any Bill, Dividend Warrant, Bond, Deed, or Ib, §. 13. any Security or Effects of any Perfon lodged or depofited with the faid Company, or with him as an Officer or Servant of the faid Company, fhall fecrete, imbezil, or run away with any fuch Note, Bill, Dividend Warrant, Bond, Deed, Security, Money, or Effects, or any Part of them, every Officer or Servant fo offending, and being thereof convicted in due Form of Law, fhall be deemed guilty of Felony, and fhall fuffer Death as a Felon without Benefit of Clergy.

By 15 & 16 Geo. 2. cap. 24. it is enacted, That in all Cafes where any Perfon liable *Juftices of* by Law to be committed to the Houfe of Correction, fhall be apprehended within any *Peace of Cities,* Liberty, City or Town Corporate, whofe Inhabitants are contributory to the Suppor- &c. when to and Maintenance of the Houfe or Houfes of Correction of the County, Riding, or Di- *Houfe of* vifion, in which fuch Liberty, City, or Town Corporate is fituate, it fhall be lawful *rection of the* for the Juftices of the Peace of fuch Liberty, City, or Town Corporate, to commit fuch *County.* Perfon to the Houfe of Correction of the County, Riding, or Divifion, in which fuch 15 & 16 G.2. Liberty, City, or Town Corporate is fituate; which Perfon fo committed, fhall and c. 24. may be received, dealt with, and be fubject to the fame Correction and Punifhment to all Intents and Purpofes, as if committed by any Juftice of the Peace of the fame County, Riding, or Divifion.

By 15 & 16 Geo. 2. cap. 27. it is enacted, That in Cafe any Cloth or Woollen Goods *Stealing* remaining upon the Rack, or Tenters, or any Woollen Yarn, or Wool left out to dry, *Woollen Goods* fhall be ftolen or taken away in the Night-time, it fhall be lawful for any one Juftice *off the Tenters* of the Peace of the fame County or Place, upon Complaint made within ten Days after *in the Night-* fuch Cloth, &c. fhall have been fo ftolen, by the Owner of fuch Cloth, &c. by War- 15 & 16 G.2. rant under his Hand and Seal, to authorize any Conftable, or other Peace-Officer in the c. 27. §. 1. Day-time, to enter into and fearch the Houfes, Out-houfes, Yards, Gardens, or other Places belonging to the Houfes of all and every Perfon whom the Owner of fuch Cloth, &c. fhall, upon his Oath, declare to fuch Juftice he fufpects to have ftolen or received the fame; and in Cafe fuch Conftable, &c. fhall find any Cloth, &c. which he fhall, from the Information of the Perfon making fuch Oath, have reafon to fufpect to be fo ftolen or received, he fhall forthwith apprehend the Perfon in whofe Cuftody or Pof- feffion fuch Cloth, &c. fhall be found, and carry him before fome Juftice of the Peace of the fame County, &c. and if the faid Perfon fo fufpected, and carried before the faid Juftice, fhall not then and there give a fatisfactory Account how he acquired the Pro- perty or Poffeffion of fuch Cloth, &c. or fhall not, within fome convenient Time to be fct by the faid Juftice, produce the Party or Parties of whom he received the fame, or fome other credible Witnefs, to depofe upon Oath fuch Property or Right to the Pof- feffion of the faid Cloth, &c. that the faid Perfon fo fufpected, nor producing any fuch Witnefs upon Oath to teftify as aforefaid, fhall be deemed convicted of the faid Offence of ftealing or taking away the faid Cloth, &c. and fhall for the firft Offence forfeit to he Owner of fuch Cloth, &c. treble the Value thereof; and in Default of Payment thereof, fuch Juftice of the Peace may iffue forth his Warrant to levy the fame by Di- trefs and Sale of the Offender's Goods, returning the Overplus, if any be; and in De- ault of fuch Diftrefs, fhall commit the Offender to the common Gaol of the County, &c. where the faid Offender fhall be apprehended, there to remain for the Space of three Months without Bail, or until he pay the fame; and if fuch Perfon fhall again commit he faid Offence, and be thereof convicted as before, then he fhall, over and above the Forfeiture of treble the Value of the Cloth, &c. fo found, to be recovered and levied as aforefaid, be committed to the common Gaol, there to remain for the Space of fix

Months

Months without Bail; and if ſuch Perſon ſhall again commit the ſaid Offence, and be thereof convicted as before, the Juſtice of the Peace, before whom ſuch Perſon ſhall be ſo convicted, ſhall forthwith iſſue his warrant to commit the ſaid Offender to the common Gaol as aforeſaid, there to remain till the next Aſſiſes or Great Seſſion, where the ſaid Offender ſhall be tried for the ſaid Offence; and in Caſe ſuch Offender ſhall not, by producing the Party of whom he acquired the Property of ſuch Cloth, &c. or otherwiſe, prove, to the Satisfaction of the Jury, that he lawfully obtained the Property of the ſame, he ſhall be adjudged to be guilty of Felony, and ſuffer Tranſportation for the Space of ſeven Years, and ſhall be liable to the ſame Puniſhment, &c. for returning from ſuch Tranſportation as other Felons tranſported are liable unto by Virtue of the Laws now in Force.

Ib. §. 2.   Perſons apprehending themſelves aggrieved may Appeal to the General Quarter-Seſſions, whoſe Judgment ſhall be final.

Ib. §. 3.   This Act ſhall not alter or repeal any Law now in Force, for the Puniſhment of any Perſon Stealing or Receiving ſuch Cloth, &c. except in ſuch Caſes where the Proof is laid upon the Offender as aforeſaid.

Counterfeiting the Coin. 15 & 16 G. 2. c. 28. §. 1.   By 15 & 16 *Geo.* 2. *cap.* 28. it is enacted, That if any Perſon ſhall waſh, gild, or colour any *Shilling* or *Sixpence*, or any counterfeit or *falſe Shilling* or *Sixpence*, or add to or alter the Impreſſion, or any Part of the Impreſſion, of either Side of ſuch lawful or counterfeit *Shilling* or *Sixpence*, with Intent to make ſuch *Shilling* look like, or paſs for a Guinea, or to make ſuch Sixpence look like, or paſs for an Half Guinea; or ſhall file, or any ways alter, waſh or colour any *Halfpence* or *Farthings*, or add to or alter the Impreſſion, or any Part of the Impreſſion of either Side of an *Halfpenny* or *Farthing*, with an Intent to make an *Halfpenny* look like, or paſs for a *Shilling*, or to make a *Farthing* look like, or paſs for a *Sixpence*, the Perſon ſo offending in any of the Matters aforeſaid, their Counſellors, Aiders, Abettors and Procurers, ſhall be adjudged to be guilty of High Treaſon.

Ib. §. 2.   And if any Perſon ſhall utter or tender in Payment any falſe or counterfeit Money, knowing the ſame to be falſe or counterfeit, to any Perſon, and ſhall be thereof convicted, ſuch Offender ſhall ſuffer ſix Months Impriſonment, and find Sureties for his good Behaviour for ſix Months more, to be computed from the End of the ſaid firſt ſix Months; and if the ſame Perſon ſhall afterwards be convicted a ſecond Time of the like Offence, he ſhall ſuffer two Years Impriſonment, and find Sureties for his good Behaviour for two Years more, to be computed from the End of the ſaid firſt two Years; and if the ſame Perſon ſhall afterwards ſo offend a third Time, he ſhall be guilty of Felony without Benefit of Clergy.

Ib. §. 3.   And if any Perſon ſhall utter or tender in Payment any falſe or counterfeit Money, knowing the ſame to be falſe or counterfeit, to any Perſon, and ſhall either the ſame Day, or within the Space of ten Days then next, utter or tender in Payment any more falſe Money, knowing the ſame, to the ſame Perſon, or to any other Perſon, or ſhall at the Time of ſuch uttering or tendering have about him in his Cuſtody one or more Piece or Pieces of counterfeit Money, beſides what was ſo uttered or tendered, then ſuch Perſon ſo uttering or tendering the ſame, ſhall be deemed and taken to be a common Utterer of falſe Money, and being thereof convicted, ſhall ſuffer a Year's Impriſonment, and ſhall find Sureties for his good Behaviour for two Years more, to be computed from the End of the ſaid Year; and if any Perſon having been once ſo convicted, ſhall afterwards again utter or tender in Payment any falſe or counterfeit Money, &c. ſuch Offender ſhall be adjudged guilty of Felony without Benefit of Clergy.

Ib. §. 4.   The Blood of the Heirs of ſuch Offender ſhall not be corrupted, nor ſhall his Wife loſe her Dower.

Ib. §. 5.   The Perſon guilty as aforeſaid, ſhall be indicted, &c. in ſuch Manner as is now uſed againſt any Offenders for Counterfeiting the lawful Coin; Provided that there ſhall be no Proſecution for any of the Offences made Treaſon or Felony by this Act, unleſs ſuch Proſecution be commenced within ſix Months next after ſuch Offence ſhall be committed.

Counterfeiting for Half-pence, &c.   If any Perſon ſhall make, coin, or counterfeit any Copper Halfpenny, or Farthing, ſuch Offender and his Aiders, Abettors and Procurers, being thereof convicted, ſhall ſuffer two Years Impriſonment, and find Sureties for his Good Behaviour for two Years more, Ib. §. 6.   to be computed from the end of the ſaid firſt two Years.

Ib. §. 7.   And whoever ſhall apprehend any Perſon who hath committed any of the Offences hereby made High Treaſon or Felony, or who ſhall have made or counterfeited any of the Copper Money aforeſaid, and ſhall proſecute ſuch Offender until Conviction, ſuch

Proſecutor

Proſecutor ſhall have from the Sheriff of the County or City where ſuch Conviction ſhall be made, for every ſuch Offender ſo convicted of any of the Treaſons or Felonies aforeſaid, the Sum of Forty Pounds; and for every Perſon convicted of Counterfeiting any of the ſaid Copper Money, the Sum of Ten Pounds, without paying any Fee for the ſame, within one Month after ſuch Conviction, and Demand thereof made, by tendering a Certificate to the ſaid Sheriff for the Time being, or his Under-Sheriff, under the Hands of the Judge or Juſtices before whom ſuch Conviction ſhall have been made, certifying ſuch Conviction, and that the Offenders were apprehended and proſecuted by the Perſons claiming the ſaid Reward, and thereby directing in what Shares and Proportions the ſaid Reward ſhall be paid and divided to and amongſt ſuch Proſecutors; which Certificate the ſaid Judge or Juſtices are to give without Delay or Fee.

Any Offender being out of Priſon, diſcovering two or more who have committed any *Ib. §. 8.* of the ſaid Offences, ſo as ſuch two or more be thereof convicted, ſuch Diſcoverer ſhall be intitled to the King's Pardon.

And if any Perſon ſhall be convicted of uttering or tendering any falſe or counterfeited *Ib. §. 9.* Money as aforeſaid, and ſhall afterwards be guilty of the like Offence in any other County or City, the Clerk of the Aſſiſe, or Clerk of the Peace for the County or City where ſuch firſt Conviction was ſo had, ſhall, at the Requeſt of the Proſecutor, or any other on his Majeſty's behalf, certify the ſame by a Tranſcript in few Words, containing the Effect and Tenor of ſuch Conviction; for which Certificate two Shillings and Six-pence, and no more, ſhall be paid: And ſuch Certificate being produced in Court, ſhall be ſufficient Proof of ſuch former Conviction.

By the 15 & 16 Geo. 2. cap. 32. it is enacted, That no Perſon, not being a Dealer *Keeping dangerous Quantities of Gunpowder.* in Gunpowder, ſhall within the Cities of *London* or *Weſtminſter*, or the Suburbs thereof, or within three Miles of the Tower of *London*, or within three Miles of the Palace of St. *James's*, or within two Miles of any Magazine of Gunpowder belonging to his Ma- *15&16Geo.2.* jeſty, for the Uſe of the Publick, keep more than fifty Pounds of Gunpowder; and no *c. 32. §. 1.* Dealer in Gunpowder ſhall keep within the Limits aforeſaid, for any longer Time than twenty-four Hours, more than two hundred Pounds of Gunpowder in any Houſe, Yard, &c. or Houſes, Yards, &c. or other Place or Places, either under the ſame Roof, or by dividing the ſame under divers Roofs, &c. or upon the River *Thames*, within the Limits aforeſaid, except in Veſſels paſſing or repaſſing, or detained by Tides or bad Weather, and except alſo in Carts or other Carriages, actually loading or unloading, or paſſing or repaſſing on the Highway, upon Pain of Forfeiture of all ſuch Gunpowder, and the Value thereof with full Coſts of Suit, to any who will ſue for the ſame in any of his Majeſty's Courts of Record at *Weſtminſter*.

Any Juſtice of the Peace reſiding within the Limits aforeſaid, upon Demand made by *Ib. §. 2* any Pariſh Officer, or by any one Houſeholder, Inhabitant within the ſaid Limits, aſſigning a reaſonable Cauſe for the ſame, may iſſue his Warrant, for Searching in the Day-time, for dangerous Quantities of Gunpowder, within the Limits aforeſaid, any Houſes, or other Places whatſoever, or any Ships, or other Veſſels on the River of *Thames*, (except as herein before is excepted) and for that Purpoſe to break open any ſuch Houſes, or other Places, or any Ships, or other Veſſels, if there ſhall be Occaſion; and upon any ſuch Search, the Searchers may immediately ſeize, and at any Time within twelve Hours after ſuch Seizure, amove all ſuch Gunpowder ſo found within the ſaid Limits, exceeding the Quantity allowed by this preſent Act, and may detain the ſame until it be determined in one of his Majeſty's Courts of Record at *Weſtminſter*, whether the ſame be forfeited by Virtue of this Act.

Perſons not being the Owners of Gunpowder, who ſhall permit others to lodge their *Ib. §. 5.* Gunpowder with them, contrary to the Meaning of this Act, ſhall forfeit 1 s. for every Pound thereof, to be recovered as before.

The 5 Geo. 1. cap. 26. and 11 Geo. 1. cap. 23. are to remain in Force. See the *Ap- Ib. §. 7.* pendix*, Tit. Gunpowder.*

By the 15 & 16 Geo. 2. cap. 33. the 5 Geo. 2. cap. 33. and the 8 Geo. 2. cap. 20. men- *Laws continued* tioned before in *Chap. 50. p. 123* of this Book, are revived, and are to continue in Force *15&16Geo.2.* until the firſt Day of *June* 1747. The Act of 8 Geo. 1. cap. 18. (for which ſee here *c. 33.* *Chap. 33. p. 70.*) is alſo continued to the ſaid firſt of *June* 1747.

By the ſame Act of 15 & 16 Geo. 2. it is alſo provided, That if any Perſon without *Cutting Starr* the Conſent of the Owner of *Starr* or *Bent* Hills, ſhall cut, pull up, or carry away any *or Bent.* Starr or Bent, planted or ſet on the Sand-Hills or Banks, on the North-weſt Coaſts of *15&16Geo.2.* *England*, in order to preſerve and to prevent the ſame from being blown upon the ad- *c. 33. §. 6.* jacent

jacent Lands, it shall be lawful for any of his Majesty's Justices of the Peace of the County, Riding, City, Town Corporate, Liberty, or Division, where such *Starr* or *Bent* shall be cut, pulled up, or carried away, and such Justice is hereby impowered upon Complaint or Information, upon Oath made of such Offence, to summon the Party so complained of, and in Default of Appearance thereon, to issue out his Warrant to apprehend and bring before him the Person so complained of; and upon Proof thereof made, either by Confession of the Party, or upon the Oath of one Witness, to convict the Offender and every Person offending, being thereof convicted as aforesaid, shall forfeit the Sum of Twenty Shillings, one Moiety thereof to the Informer, and the other Moiety to the Lord or Owner of such Starr, Bent, or Sand-Hills; the same to be levied by Distress and Sale of the Offender's Goods and Chattels, by Warrant, &c. of such Justice, together with the Charges of such Distress and Sale, rendering the Overplus, if any be, to the Owner and for Want of sufficient Distress, the said Justice shall commit the Person convicted as aforesaid to the House of Correction, to hard Labour for three Months; and if any Person so convicted shall afterwards be guilty of a second Offence, and thereof lawfully convicted by such Justice, either by Confession, or upon the Oath of one Witness, such Person shall be committed to the House of Correction for the Space of one Year, there to be whipt, and kept to hard Labour.

Ibid. §. 7.   And if any *Starr* or *Bent* shall be found in the Custody or Possession of any Person within five Miles of any such Starr, Bent or Sand-Hills as aforesaid, such Person being convicted thereof before one or more such Justice or Justices, in Manner aforesaid, shall be deemed, adjudged and taken to be the Cutter and Puller of such Starr or Bent from such Sand-Hills, and shall forfeit and pay the Sum of Twenty Shillings, one Moiety thereof to the Lord or Owner of such Starr, Bent, or Sand-Hills; the same to be levied by Distress, &c. in Manner aforesaid; and for Want of sufficient Distress, such Person shall be committed in Manner aforesaid to the House of Correction, there to remain and be kept to hard Labour for the Space of three Months.

Word Cattle *explained.*   By the 14 *Geo*. 2. *cap*. 6. (which see before in *Chap*. 160. *p*. 364.) it was enacted, That
15&16Geo.2. Driving away or Stealing of Sheep, or other Cattle, should be Felony, without Benefit
c. 34.   of Clergy: And it being doubtful to what Sorts of Cattle besides Sheep this Act was meant to extend, it is now enacted by the 15 & 16 *Geo*. 2. *c*. 34. that the said Act shall extend to any Bull, Cow, Ox, Steer, Bullock, Heifer, Calf and Lamb, and to no other Cattle whatsoever.

A

TABLE

OF THE

GENERAL HEADS

Contained in the following

APPENDIX,

BEING

A Compleat Summary of all the Acts of Parliament, ſhewing the various Penalties of Offences by *Statute*, and the particular Power of 𝕺𝖓𝖊, 𝕿𝖜𝖔, 𝕿𝖍𝖗𝖊𝖊, or more Juſtices, in their Proceedings and Determinations, under ſeveral diſtinct HEADS.

A.

ABjuration, *fee* Oaths.
  Agnus Dei, fee Papiſts.
Alamodes and Luſtrings.
Ale and Beer (Retailers of) fee Exciſe.
Alehouſes.
Alms-houſes, fee. Rates *in Title* Poor.
Annuitant and Annuity.
Apprentices.
Arms.
Arms and Horſes of Papiſts, fee Papiſts and Popiſh Superſtition.
Arrack, fee Brandy *in* Exciſe.
Artificers.
Attornies and Solicitors.

B.

BAdgers.
  Bail.
Bailiffs, fee County-Courts.
Bakers and Bread.
Bankrupts.
Banks or other Incloſures, fee Wood.
Bark, fee Foreſtallers, *and* Ingroſſers, *and* Wood.
Baſtards.
Bedford Level.
Beer and Ale.
Beer and Ale (Retailers of) fee Exciſe.
Beggar, fee Vagabonds and Vagrants.
Billets, fee Fuel.
Blaſphemous Words.
Boats, fee Keels.

Bone-Lace, fee Hawkers and Pedlars.
Books.
Boots, fee Shoemakers and Tanners.
Bows, fee Game.
Boys bound to Sea, fee Apprentices.
Brandy and Spirits.
Braſs.
Brewers, fee Exciſe.
Bricks and Tiles.
Bridle-Cutters, fee Tanner.
Bridges.
Buggery.
Buildings, fee Fire.
Bullion.
Burials.
Burglars, fee Watchman.
Burglary, fee Stolen Goods.
Butcher.
Butter and Cheeſe.
Buttons and Button-holes.

C.

CArds and Dice, *fee Titles* Stamp-Duty, *and* Games not lawful.
Callicoes.
Carriers *and* Carriages.
Cattle.
Cheeſe, fee Butter and Cheeſe.
Certiorari.
Church.
Church-wardens, fee Poor.

A Table of the General Heads.

Clerk of the Market, see Bakers, Bread, and Weights and Measures.
Clothes.
Clothes, Caps, or other Furniture of Soldiers and Deserters, see Officers and Soldiers.
Cloth and Clothier.
———— Woollen.
———— Linen.
Clothiers and Cloth-workers Servants, see Servants.
Coaches and Chairs, and Coach-horses, see Hackney-Coaches and Chairs.
Coals.
Coin and Coining.
Collar-makers, see Tanners.
Collectors for Prisons, see Vagabonds and Vagrants.
Commission of the Peace.
Conies, and Cony-Dogs, see Game.
Conformity.
Conspiracies.
Constables.
Conventicles.
Convicts.
Coopers.
Coppices, see Wood.
Corn.
Coroner.
Costs.
Cottages.
County-Courts.
Counterfeit Letters, see False Tokens.
Currier.
Curriers Company, see Shoemakers.
Cursing, see Swearing and Cursing.
Custom-house Officers.
Cyder-makers, see Excise.

D.

DEER.
  Deer-stealers.
Deserters, see Soldiers and Mariners.
Dissenters.
Dissenting Teachers, see Oath of Allegiance in Papists, &c.
Distillers, see Brandy in Excise.
Dogs, see Game.
Drunkenness.
Duty on Houses, see Windows.
Dyers.

E.

EStreats, see Sheriffs.
  Examination.
Excise.
  Brandy.
  Brewers.
  Cyder-makers.
  Distillers.
  Gaugers.
  Makers of Mead, Vinegar, Metheglin and Sweets.
  Inn-keepers and Victuallers.
  Low-wines.
  Malt.
  Retailers of Beer, Ale, Cyder, Perry, and Metheglin.

F.

FAirs.
  False Tokens.
Fellers of Oak-Trees.
Felons, see Transportation.

Felony.
Fences, see Orchards and Wood.
Fencers, see Vagabonds and Vagrants.
Fines.
Fire.
Fireworks, see Squibs.
Fish.
Fish-ponds, see Title Fish.
Flesh.
Forcible Entry and Detainer.
Forestallers and Ingrossers.
Fortune-tellers, see Vagabonds and Vagrants.
Fruit-trees, see Orchards.
Fuel.
Fullers Earth and Fullers Clay, see Brandy in Excise.

G.

GAmes not lawful.
  Game.
  Conies.
  Deer, Hare, Partridge, and Pheasant.
  Deer-Hayes, or Buckstalls.
  Eggs of Falcon, Goshawk, Lanner, or Swan.
  Game-keeper.
  Greyhounds, Bows, Setting-Dogs, Ferrets, and Snares.
  Guns.
  Hawks.
  Heron.
  Pigeon,
  Wild Duck, Teal, Widgeon, and Water Fowl.
Gaol.
Gaolers, see Sheriff.
Gilding and Goldsmiths.
Guns, see Guns in Title Game.
Gunpowder.
Gypsies, or Egyptians, see Vagabonds and Vagrants.

H.

HAckney Coaches and Chairs.
  Hare, see Game.
Harvest-Workmen.
Hawkers and Pedlars.
Hawks, Hawkers, and Hawking, see Game.
Hay.
Hay and Oates.
Hay and Straw.
Hay-Market.
Headboroughs, see Jurors.
Heath, Furze and Fern.
Hedges and Hedge-wood, see Highways, Orchards, and Wood.
Hemp and Flax.
Hides.
High Constables, see Constables and Surveyors in Titles Highways, Jurors, and Vagabonds and Vagrants.
Highway-men.
Highways.
Hops.
Horses.
Hospitals, see Rates in Title Poor.
House-breakers, see Watchman.
House of Correction.
Hue and Cry, see Robbery.

I.

JEsuit and Priest, see Papists, &c.
  Informers.
Ingrossers, see Forestallers and Ingrossers.

4

A Table of the General Heads.

Inn-keepers, *see* Alehouse-keepers, *and* Excise.
Journeymen Taylors.
Jurors.
Justices of Peace.

K.

KEels.
Knights *of the Shire, see* Wages.

L.

LAbourers, *see* Servants *and* Wages.
Lamps, *see* Lights.
Land-Carriage *of Goods, see* Waggon *and* Waggoner.
Leather.
Lights.
Linen Manufactures, *see* Cloth *and* Clothier, *and* Wages.
London.
Lotteries.
Low Wines, *see* Distillers *in Title* Excise.
Lunaticks.

M.

MALT.
Manufactures.
Markets, *see* Fairs.
Master *and* Mistress, *see* Servants *and* Apprentices.
Matts.
Measures, *see* Weights and Measures.
Misdemeanors, *see* Informers.
Money.
Murder.

N.

NETS, *see* Fish *and* Game.
News-Papers, *see* Stamp-Duty.
Nonconformity.
Norwich Stuffs.
Nusances *in or upon the Highways, see* Constables *and* Surveyors *in Title* Highways.

O.

OATH.
Oath *of Allegiance, see* Papists, *&c. and Title* Recusancy.
Oats, *see* Hay and Oats.
Officers *and Corporations, see* Oath.
Officers and Soldiers.
Orchards.
Overseers *of the Poor, see* Poor.
Overseers *of Cloth, see* Cloth.

P.

PAles, *see* Orchards *and* Wood.
Pamphlets, *see* Stamp-Duty.
Panels of Juries.
Paper, *see* Stamp-Duty, *and* Vellum and Parchment.
Papists and Popish Superstition.
    Agnus Dei, Crosses, Beads, and Pictures.
    Arms and Horses.
    Books and Relicts.
    Crucifix.
    Feme Coverts.
    Jesuit and Priest.
    Impugning Supremacy.
    Licence.
    Maintaining the Pope's Jurisdiction.
    Mass.
    Oath of Allegiance.

Reconciler *and* reconciled, *see* Oath of Allegiance *supra.*
Recusancy.
Reputed Papists.
Parliament.
Partition of Lands.
Partridge, *see* Game.
Party-Walls, *see* Fire.
Paste-board, *see* Vellum and Parchment.
Paving *the Streets, and Pavements, see* Constables *and* Surveyors, *in* Highways, *and* Scavengers.
Perjury.
Perry *(Retailers of) see* Excise.
Petty Chapmen, *see* Hawkers and Pedlars.
Petty Constables, *see* Jurors, *and* Vagabonds and Vagrants.
Pewter and Brass.
Pheasants, *see* Game, *and* Officers and Soldiers.
Physicians.
Pigeons, *see* Game.
Pilchards.
Plague.
Players of Interludes.
Poor.
    Badge.
    Boys bound to Sea, *see* Apprentices.
    Costs.
    Father, &c. *to maintain Poor Children.*
    Overseers.
    Rates.
    Refusing *to work.*
    Registring Notice.
    Relief and Settlement.
    Setting them to Work.
    Settlement and Removal.
Popish Books and Relicts, and Pictures, *see* Papists, *&c.*
Post and Post-master.
Posts, *see* Wood.
Preachers.
Pretended privileged Places.
Prison, *see* Gaol.
Prisoners, *see* Rates or Tax, *in Title* Poor.
Prison-Collectors, *see* Vagabonds and Vagrants.
Process.
Proclamation *against Rioters, see* Riots and Rioters.
Prophecies.
Purveyors.

Q.

QUakers.
Quarentine.
Quartering Soldiers, *see* Officers and Soldiers.
Quarter-Sessions *of the Peace, see* Justices.
Quicksets, *see* Wood.

R.

RAkers, *see* Scavenger.
Recognizances, *see* Justices of the Peace.
Recusancy.
Rents.
Riots and Rioters.
Robberies.
Robbing Orchards, *see* Orchards.
Rockets, *see* Squibs.
Rogues, *see* Vagabonds and Vagrants.
Rum, *see* Brandy, *in* Excise.
Runaways.
Runners *of foreign Goods, see* Smuglers, *&c.*

S. Sacra-

A Table of the General Heads.

S.

SAcrament.
Sadlers Company, see Shoemakers.
Salt.
Scavenger.
Seamen, see Boys bound to Sea, in Apprentices.
Searchers and Sealers of Leather, see Leather.
Servants.
Sessions of the Peace, see Justices of the Peace.
Setting-Dogs, see Game.
Sewers.
Sheep, see Cattle.
Sheep-Skins, see Tanner.
Sheermen, see Cloth and Clothier.
Sheriff.
Ships.
Shoes, see Tanners.
Shoemakers.
Silk.
Silk-throwers.
Smuglers or Runners of foreign Goods.
Snares, see Game and Fish.
Soldiers and Mariners.
South-Sea Company, see Felony.
Spirits.
Squibs.
Stamp-Duty.
Starch and Hair-powder.
Stewards of Franchises, see Sheriff.
Stolen Goods.
Strong-Waters, see Brandy in Title Excise.
Strong-Waters (Retailers of) see Excise.
Sub-Commissioners of the Excise, see Weights and Measures.
Subornation of Perjury.
Sunday.
Surveyors of Highways, see Highways.
Swans Eggs, see Game.
Swearing and Cursing.
Sweets, see Excise.
Swine, see Cattle.

T.

TAnner.
Tavern, see Alehouses.
Tawers, see Tanners.
Taylors, see Journeymen Taylors, Buttons and Button-holes, and Cloth and Clothier.
Timber Trees, see Wood.
Tiplers, see Alehouses.
Tobacco.
Tobacco-pipe Clay, see Brandy in Title Excise.
Toll, see Hay-market.

Toll-Takers, see Fairs.
Transportation.
Travelling on the Lord's Day by Water, see Sunday.
Treasurer of the County.
Trees, see Wood.
Trespasses, see Informers.
Trophy-Money.
Turnpikes.
Tythes.

V.

VAgabonds and Vagrants.
Vellam and Parchment, see Stamp-Duty.
Victuallers, see Alehouses, and Brewers, Inn-keeper. and Victuallers, in Title Excise.
Vinegar-makers, see Excise.
Vintners, see Alehouses.
Under-Sheriffs.
Under-woods, see Orchards and Wood.
Unlawful Games or Plays, see Vagabonds and Vagrants

W.

WAges.
Wages of Knights of the Shire.
Wages of Burgesses.
Walnut-tree Leaves, see Tobacco.
Warren, see Game.
Watch.
Water-courses, see Highways,
Water-Fowl, see Game.
Water-Measure, see Weights and Measures.
Watermen.
Ways, see Highways.
Weavers, see Cloth and Clothier.
Weavers of Norwich Stuffs, see Norwich Stuffs.
Weights and Measures.
White Herrings, see Salt.
Widening or enlarging Highways, see Sessions, in Title Highways.
Wild-Fowl, see Game.
Windows.
Wood.
Wool, see Brandy in Title Excise.
Woollen Manufactures, see Cloth and Clothier, and Wages.
Words spoken against the Queen's Title.
Work, see Poor, and Vagabonds.
Workmen, see Harvest Workmen.
Wrecks.
Wrought Plate.

Y.

YArn, see Brandy, in Title Excise, and Wool.

N. B. Wherever the Words **One, Two, Three,** appear in the black Letter, it signifies that the Business is to be performed by One Justice, Two Justices, &c.

AN APPENDIX.

AN
APPENDIX.

Offences.	Alamodes and Luftrings.	Penalties.

[One] TO grant a Warrant to fearch for, and feife, prohibited Alamodes and Luftrings, upon Oath of one or more credible Perfon or Perfons, that they have Reafon to fufpect, or believe, that there are fome of the faid Silks fraudulently imported.

Stat. 9 & 10 W. 3. c. 43. §. 5.

Offences.	Alehoufes.	Penalties.

[One] A Lehoufe-keepers, Inn-keepers, Vintners, or Victuallers, fuffering any of the fame Parifh to fit tippling in their Houfes.
Stat. 1 Jac. 1. c. 9. §. 2.
    21 Jac. 1. c. 7. §. 2.
    1 Car. 1. c. 4. §. 1.
One Witnefs, View or Confeffion; and after Confeffion his Oath may convict others.

Ten Shillings to be levied by Diftrefs and Sale after Six Days, and for Want of Diftrefs, to be committed until Payment.
Difabled for Three Years to keep any Alehoufe.
If the Conftables or Church-wardens do not levy the Penalty, or fhall not certify the Want of Diftrefs within Twenty Days, he forfeits 40 s. to be levied, ut fupra, for the Poor.

Alehoufe-keepers, Inn-keepers or Victuallers, felling lefs than one Quart for a Penny.
Stat. 1 Jac. 1. c. 9. §. 3.
    21 Jac. 1. c. 7. §. 1.
Conviction ut fupra.

Twenty Shillings, to be levied ut fupra, and fo employed.
And difabled ut fupra.
Conftable, &c. punifhed ut fupra.
Sufpended during the Continuance of the additional Excife.
Stat. 1 W. & M. c. 24. §. 8.

Alehoufe-keepers, Inn-keeper, Vintner or Victualler, fuffering any Perfon whatfoever to fit tippling in his Houfe.
Stat. 1 Jac. 1. c. 9. §. 2.
    21 Jac. 1. c. 7. §. 2.
    1 Car. 1. c. 4. §. 1.
View, or Two Witneffes.

Ten Shillings to be levied, employed and difabled, ut fupra.

Parifhioners, or others, who fit tippling in any Alehoufe, Inn, Tavern, or Victualling-houfe.
Stat. 4 Jac. 1. c. 5. §. 5.
    21 Jac. 1. c. 7. §. 2.
View, or One Witnefs.

Three Shillings and four Pence, to be levied and employed ut fupra, to be paid in a Week; if not able, to fit in the Stocks four Hours.
Alehoufe-keepers, &c. difabled Three Years.
Conftables, &c. neglect, 10 s. to be levied ut fupra, and fo employed.

Alehoufe-keeper, convicted of Drunkennefs.
Stat. 21 Jac. 1. c. 7. §. 4.
Conviction ut fupra.
Profecution to be in Six Months.

Difabled to keep an Alehoufe for Three Years. Befides the Forfeiture of 5 s. &c. and Penalties inflicted on others.

Keeping an Alehoufe without Licence.
Stat. 3 Car. 1. c. 3. §. 2.
View, Confeffion, or Two Witneffes.
The Offender punifh'd by this Act, not to be punifhed by 5 & 6 Ed. 6. c. 25.

N. B. Sub-Commiffioners, or Collectors of Excife, are to provide a fubftantial Ale-Quart and Pint Winchefter Meafure, in their Divifions, on Pain of 5 l.
Mayors of Towns, &c. refufing to ftamp Ale-Quarts and Pints, are liable to the Penalty of 5 l. by the Stat. 11 & 12 W. 3. c. 15.

Twenty Shillings to the Poor, to be levied ut fupra, and for Want of Diftrefs, to be whipp'd, for the firft Offence.
For the Second, to be committed to the Houfe of Correction for a Month.
For the Third, not to be inlarged there, but by Order of Seffions.
The Officer neglecting his Duty, to be imprifoned without Bail, or pay 40 s. for the Poor.

Perfons

Not

Offences.	**Alehouses.**	*Penalties.*

Offences.	**Alehouses.**	*Penalties.*
Perſons ſelling Ale and Beer in any Veſſel not ſign'd and mark'd with W. R. *and a Crown,* according to the Standard in the *Exchequer,* or City of *London,* and not full Meaſure. Stat. 11 *&* 12 *W.* 3. *c.* 15. §. 1. And Perſons ſelling Brandy or other diſtill'd Liquors, without Licence. Stat. 12 *&* 13 *W.* 3. *c.* 15. §. 1. One Witneſs.	Not above Forty Shillings, nor under Ten, to be levied by Diſtreſs and Sale. One Moiety to the Poor, the other to the Proſecutor.
[**Two**] To licenſe Alehouſes, and take Recognizances, with two Sureties, for good Order in the ſame; for which take 12 *d.* and no more. Stat. 5 *&* 6 *Ed.* 6. *c.* 25. §. 1. *Quorum* 1.	To certify ſuch Recognizances the next Quarter-Seſſions. But no new Licences are now to be granted, but at a General Meeting of the Juſtices by Stat. 2 *Geo.* 2. *c.* 28. §. 10.
All Mayors, Town-Clerks, and other Perſons whom it may concern, ſhall make, or cauſe to made out Ale-Licences duly ſtamp'd before new Recognizances are taken. Stat. 6 *Geo.* 1. *c.* 21. §. 54.	Ten Pounds for every Offence.

To remove, diſcharge, and put away any Alehouſe, as they ſhall think fit and convenient. Stat. 5 *&* 6 *Ed.* 6. *c.* 25. §. 1. *Quor.* 1.

Perſons keeping Alehouſes, or ſelling Beer and Ale without Licence. Stat. 5 *&* 6 *Ed.* 6. *c.* 25. §. 4. *Quorum* 1. This extends not to Fairs.	To be committed for Three Days without Bail, and to enter into a Recognizance, with Two Sureties, before they be diſcharged, not to offend again. This to be certified to the Quarter-Seſſions, which is ſufficient Conviction to fine him 20 *s.*
[**Qu. Seſſ.**] Perſons ſelling Ale or Beer to an un-licenſed Alehouſe-keeper, ſave only for the Expence of his Houſhold. Stat. 4 *Jac.* 1. *c.* 4. §. 1.	Six Shillings and eight Pence a Barrel. One Moiety to the Proſecutor, the other to the Poor.
The Officer who levies the Poor's Moiety, and does not deliver it to the Church-wardens and Overſeers, and they not diſtributing it among the Poor. Stat. 4 *Jac.* 1. *c.* 4. §. 5.	Double the Value of the Moiety. *See* Title **Exciſe.**

No Inn-keeper or Victualler in *London* or *Weſtminſter,* and the Weekly Bills of Mortality, ſhall ſell any Beer or Ale by Retail, to be conſumed out of their Houſes, in any Pot, Cup, or other drinking Veſſel belonging to ſuch Retailer, which ſhall contain leſs than one Gallon in Ale-Meaſure, on Forfeiture of 40 *s.*

But Beer or Ale may be drank at the Door, or in any Out-houſe, Shed, Arbour, Garden, or Yard belonging to ſuch Houſe.

If any Inn-keeper or Victualler ſhall not take out a Permiſſion, or not pay his Compoſition, he ſhall forfeit 20 *l.* 12 *Geo.* 1. *c.* 12. §. 7, 8, 9.

All Fines are to be levied according to the Laws of Exciſe. *Ibid.* §. 11.

Offences.	**Annuitant, &c.**	*Penalties.*

[**One**] TO take an Oath, that the Nominee of the Annuitant was alive on the Day the Payment became due. Stat. 2 *Ann.* *c.* 3. §. 23.

To take an Affidavit of the due Execution of an Aſſignment, or a Will made of an Annuity, purſuant to Statute 4 *Ann.* *c.* 6. §. 28. 5 *Ann.* *c.* 19. §. 22. 6 *Ann.* *c.* 5. §. 15.

Offences.	**Apprentices.**	*Penalties.*

[**One**] PErſons fit to make Apprentices, refuſing to ſerve upon Demand. Stat. 5 *Eliz.* *c.* 4. §. 35.

To be committed till they ſhall be willing to ſerve.

To reconcile Differences between Maſters and Apprentices: And if he cannot. Stat. 5 *Eliz.* *c.* 4. §. 35.

To bind over the Maſter to the Quarter-Seſſions.

I   An   To

Offences.	**Apprentices.**	*Penalties.*
An Apprentice departing from his Master's Service into another Country. Stat. 5 *Eliz. c.* 4. §. 47.	To direct a *Capias* to the Sheriff, or Chief Officer, for his Apprehenſion ; and being taken, to commit him till he gives good Security, that he will honeſtly ſerve out his Time.	

To convey poor Pariſh-Boys bound Apprentices, or turned over to Seamen, to the Port to which their Maſter belongs, as Vagrants are to be ſent by 11 & 12 *W.* 3. *c.* 18. Stat. 2 *Ann. c.* 6. §. 10.

[**Two**] To conſent to the Binding Boys Apprentices till Twenty-four, or Girls till Twenty-one, or Marriage. Stat. 43 *Eliz. c.* 2. §. 5. *Quorum* 1.

Perſons truſted with Monies to put out Apprentices, to account in *Eaſter-Week* yearly, before the Two next Juſtices. Stat. 7 *Jac.* 1. *c.* 3. §. 6.

Perſons refuſing to take an Apprentice put out by the Conſent of Two Juſtices, according to 43 *Eliz.* Stat. 8 & 9 *W.* 3. *c.* 30. §. 5.	Ten Pounds to be levied by Diſtreſs and Sale to the Uſe of the Poor. An Appeal lies to the Quarter-Seſſions.

To conſent to Church-wardens and Overſeers of the Poor, binding and putting out to Sea-Service any Boy of ten Years of Age, who is chargeable, or whoſe Parents are chargeable to the Pariſh, or who ſhall beg for Alms, till he comes to Twenty-one, his Age to be mentioned in the Indenture, and Fifty Shillings to be given with him. Stat. 2 *Ann. c.* 6. §. 1.

Collectors of the Cuſtoms not entering the Indentures of Pariſh-Boys, bound to Sea, in a Book kept for that Purpoſe. Stat. 2 *Ann. c.* 6. §. 6.	Five Pounds to the Uſe of the Poor of the Pariſh whence the Boy was bound, to be levied by Diſtreſs and Sale.

To conſent to the Turning over Pariſh-Boys, bound Apprentices, according to 43 *Eliz.* to Maſters and Owners of Ships, by Indenture of Aſſignment. Stat. 2 *Ann. c.* 6. §. 6.

Every Maſter or Owner of a Ship of the Burden of Thirty to Fifty Tun, not taking one ſuch poor Boy Apprentice, one more for the next Fifty Tun, one more for every 100 Tun above the firſt 100. Stat. 2 *Ann. c.* 6. §. 8.	Ten Pounds, for the Uſe of the Poor of the Pariſh whence ſuch Boy was bound Apprentice, to be levied by Diſtreſs and Sale.

To inquire into, examine, hear and determine all Complaints of hard or ill Uſage, from Maſters to Pariſh-Boys bound Apprentice to Sea. Stat. 2 *Ann. c.* 6. §. 12.

Collectors of Cuſtoms not keeping an exact Regiſter, containing the Number and Burden of all Ships and Veſſels, and Maſters and Owners Names, and the Names of Apprentices in each Ship, and from what Pariſhes and Places ſent, and not tranſmitting true Copies thereof to the Quarter-Seſſions, as often as they ſhall be required. Stat. 2 *Ann. c.* 6. §. 13.	Five Pounds, to be levied and diſpoſed *ut ſupra.*

[**Three**] To certify, That Parents have 40 *s. per Ann.* and 3 *l. per Ann.* Freehold, to qualify their Children to be Apprentices to Merchants. Stat. 5 *Eliz. c.* 4. §. 27.

[**Four**] To diſcharge Apprentices under their Hands and Seals ; and if the Maſter be in Fault, or the Apprentice be in Fault, to inflict ſuch Puniſhment as they, in their Diſcretions, ſhall think fit. Stat. 5 *Eliz. c.* 4. §. 35. *Quorum* 1.

Note ; The Practice now is, for one Juſtice to bind over the Maſter, at the Complaint of the Apprentice, to the next Seſſions, and then Four Juſtices to diſcharge, under their Hands and Seals ; and upon Complaint of the Maſter againſt the Apprentice, to ſend the Apprentice to the Houſe of Correction, if he will not agree to appear at the Seſſions ; and at the Seſſions ſuch Order is to be made, under the Hands and Seals of Four Juſtices, as is juſt.

[**Qu. Seſſ.**] Perſons taking Apprentices, otherwiſe than is limited by 5 *Eliz. c.* 4. except in *London* and *Norwich.* Stat. 5 *Eliz. c.* 4. §. 40.	Ten Pounds, and the Indentures void.

Offences.	**Arms.**	*Penalties.*
[**One**] ONE going or riding armed offenſively, before the King's Juſtices, or other his Officers or Miniſters, or elſewhere, by Night or Day. Stat. 2 *Ed.* 3. *c.* 3. §. 3. 7 *R.* 2. *c.* 13. §. 1. 20 *R.* 2. *c.* 1. §. 4. View or Complaint.	To be apprehended and bound to the Peace or Good Behaviour, and for Want of Sureties, to be committed, and his Arms to be taken away.	

Artificers.

APPENDIX.

Offences.	*Penalties.*
[**One**] MAY bind over to Affifes, or Seffions, Artificers, about to go beyond Sea, and thofe who endeavour to withdraw them thither. One Witnefs or Confeffion. Stat. 5 *Geo.* 1. *c.* 27. §. 4.	For Want of Sureties to be committed to Gaol.
[**Qu. Seff.**] Perfons contracting with, enticing, endeavouring to perfuade, or folicit any Manufacturer or Artificer in *Wool, Iron, Steel, Brafs,* or any other *Metal, Clock-maker, Watch-maker,* or any other Artificer of *Great Britain,* to go out of his Majefty's Dominions. On Conviction. Stat. 5 *Geo.* 1. *c.* 27. §. 1.	To be fined not exceeding 100 Pounds for the firft Offence, Three Months Imprifonment, and until fuch Fine be paid. For the fecond Offence to be fined at the Difcretion of the Court, Twelve Months Imprifonment, and until fuch Fine be paid. Profecution in Twelve Months.
Artificer convicted of any Promife or Contract, or Preparation to go abroad beyond the Seas. Stat. 5 *Geo.* 1. *c.* 27. §. 4.	To find Sureties not to depart out of his Majefty's Dominions, as the Court fhall think fit. And for Want of Sureties to be committed *Quoufque.*

Offences.   **Attornies and Solicitors.**   *Penalties.*

[**Qu. Seff.**] NOTE; the Forfeitures and Penalties of the Statute 2 *Geo.* 2. *c.* 23. (*i. e.* 50 *l.* on any who fhall fue or defend in any Caufe as an Attorney or Solicitor, not being admitted and inrolled according to the Act) may be fued for and recovered, not only in *Weftminfter-Hall, &c.* but alfo at the Affifes and *General Quarter-Seffions* where the Offence was, by any who fues within twelve Months, with treble Cofts of Suit ; and no Effoin, Protection or Wager of Law, and but one Imparlance ; and not to be removed before Judgment, or ftayed by *Certiorari, &c.* Stat. 2 *Geo.* 2. *c.* 23. §. 23, 24.

And by 12 *Geo.* 2. *c.* 13. acting as an Attorney or Solicitor in any County Court, not being legally admitted according to 2 *Geo.* 2. *c.* 23. forfeits 20 *l.* to be recovered within twelve Months in any Court of Record.

Offences.   **Badgers.**   *Penalties.*

[**Two**] PUrveyor, Badger, *&c.* bargaining for any Victual or Grain, in the Markets of *Oxford* or *Cambridge,* or in Five Miles of them. Stat. 2 *& 3 P. & M. c.* 15. §. 2. 13 *Eliz. c.* 21. §. 2.	Quadruple the Value thereof, and Three Months Imprifonment without Bail. Except when the Queen is there, or within Seven Miles.
[**Three**] To licenfe a married Man, Houfholder, and of Thirty Years of Age at leaft, to be a Badger, Lader, Kidder, Carrier, Buyer or Tranfporter of Corn, Grain, Butter and Cheefe. Stat. 5 *Eliz. c.* 12. §. 1. *Quorum* 1.	
[**Qu. Seff.**] Badger, Lader, Kidder, Carrier, Buyer or Tranfporter of Corn, or Grain, Butter and Cheefe without Licence granted in open Seffions of the County, where he hath dwelt Three Years, under the Hands and Seals of (at leaft) Three Juftices. *Quorum* 1. Stat. 5 *Eliz. c.* 12. §. 7. Inquifition, or Verdict, or upon Oath of Two Witneffes.	Five Pounds between the Queen and the Profecutor. The Queen's Moiety to be eftreated according to the ufual Manner, and the Profecutor's levied, by *Fieri facias,* or *Capias* ; but when the Suit is wholly the Queen's, the Whole to be eftreated,
Badger, *&c.* buying of Grain out of open Fair or Market (to fell again) unlefs there be fpecial Words in his Licence to warrant the fame. Stat. 5 *Eliz. c.* 12. §. 7. The Conviction *ut fupra.*	Five Pounds, to be divided *ut fupra.*

At their Difcretions, to take Recognizances of Badgers, *&c.* that they fhall not foreftall, or ingrofs, or put in Practice any Act contrary to 5 *& 6 Ed.* 6. *c.* 14. Stat. 5 *Eliz. c.* 12. §. 6. *Vide* **Purveyor.**

Offences.   **Bail.**   *Penalties.*

[**Two**] TO Bail for Manflaughter, or Felony, or Sufpicion thereof (being bailable by Law) and being both prefent at the Time of fuch Bailment: But they muft firft take the Examination of the Accufed, and the Informations of the Accufers, and Witneffes. *London* and *Middlefex* Juftices may bail, as before the Statute. Stat. 1 *& 2 P. & M. c.* 13. §. 6. *Quorum* 1.

Offences.   𝔅ail.   *Penalties.*

Criminals for Offences under Felony, one Juſtice may bail; and the Sureties and Sum are left to the Diſcretion of the Juſtice, where no certain Sum is appointed by Law; but if the Crime be Felony, they muſt take ſufficient Perſons for the Appearance of the Offender, and bind them in a large Sum.

𝔅ailiffs.   Vide Tit. 𝔠ount𝔶 𝔠ourt𝔰.

Offences.   𝔅aker𝔰 and 𝔅read.   *Penalties.*

[𝔇ne] BAkers, and others, making, baking, or expoſing to Sale, Bread, not obſerving the Aſſiſe, or under Weight, or not duly marked, or breaking ſuch Regulations and Orders as are made by the Juſtices from Time to Time. Stat. 8 *Ann. c.* 18. §. 3. Confeſſion or one Witneſs. Proſecution within Three Days. §. 5.	40 *s.* to be levied by Diſtreſs and Sale, to be given to the Informer. The Convictions to be certified to the next Quarter-Seſſions. §. 4. There lies an Appeal to the next Quarter-Seſſions. §. 6. *Vide* The Table of the Aſſiſe of *Bread*, annex'd to the Statute at large.
Bakers, or Sellers of Bread, putting into any Bread, ſold or expoſed to Sale, any Mixture of any other Grain, than what ſhall be appointed by the Aſſiſe. Stat. 8 *Ann. c.* 18. §. 7.	20 *s.* to be had and recovered *ut ſupra.* Mayor, Alderman, Juſtice, on any Information made to him of any Offence againſt this Act, wilfully omitting the Performance of his Duty, forfeits 20 *s.* to be recovered by Action of Debt, Bill, Plaint, or Information.

In the Day-time, to enter into any Houſe, Shop, Stall, Bake-houſe, Ware-houſe or Out-houſe of any Baker or Seller of Bread, to ſearch for, view, weigh and try all or any the Bread there found; and if the Bread be wanting in the Goodneſs of the Stuff, or deficient in due Baking or Working, or wanting in Weight, or not truly marked, or any other Sort than what is allowed, the ſame Bread to be ſeiſed, and given to the Poor. Stat. 8 *Ann. c.* 18. §. 8.

Any Baker, or others, not permitting or ſuffering a Search; or oppoſing, hindring, or refiſting the ſame. Stat. 8 *Ann. c.* 18. §. 8.	Forty Shillings, to be recovered and given *ut ſupra.*
The Penalty of 40 *s.* by 8 *Ann. c.* 18. on Bakers, for Want of Weight of Bread, is reduced to 5 *s. per* Ounce, for every Ounce wanting in Weight, and 2 *s.* 6 *d.* if under. The Bread to be weighed before a Magiſtrate or Juſtice in 24 Hours after baked or expoſed to Sale in *London* and *Weſtminſter*, and *Bills of Mortality*, and in three Days every where elſe. Stat. 1 *Geo.* 1. *c.* 26. §. 5.	Forfeiture to the Informer, to be adjudged, levied, and recovered as the 40 *s.* Penalty is by 8 *Ann. c.* 18.

Note; By this Statute no Mark ſeems now neceſſary; and Bakers may make and ſell Peck, Half-peck, Quartern, and Half-quartern Loaves, if in Proportion to the Aſſiſe-Table in Weight and Price. Stat. 1 *Geo.* 1. *c.* 26. §. 6.

And the *Clerk of the Market* is to certify upon Oath to the chief Magiſtrate or Juſtices, the Price of Grain, Meal and Flour, every Time the Aſſiſe is altered. Stat. 1 *Geo.* 1. *c.* 26. §. 7.

Note; The Act 8 *Ann. c.* 18. was continued by an Act 12 *Geo.* 2. *c.* 13. to 24 *June* 1748. and to the End of the next Seſſions, and ſhall extend to *Scotland.*

[𝔗wo] In Towns and Places where there is no Mayor, Bailiffs, Aldermen or Chief Magiſtrates, from Time to Time, to ſet, aſcertain, and appoint the Aſſiſe and Weight of all Sorts of Bread, having Reſpect to the Price Grain, Meal or Flour, bears in the publick Markets, and to make a reaſonable Allowance to the Bakers, for Charges, Pains and Livelihoods: The Aſſiſe according to Avoirdupois, and not Troy-Weight. Stat. 8 *Ann. c.* 18. §. 1.

May licenſe and allow the Bakers to bake and ſell ſuch Sorts of Bread as they ſhall think fit. Stat. 8 *Ann. c.* 18. §. 1.

To direct and appoint how, and in what Manner, each Sort of Bread ſhall be marked, for knowing the Baker, or Maker, Price, Weight, and Sort thereof; and to make, and ſet down any other reaſonable Rules and Orders, for the better regulating the Myſtery of baking Bread, and the Sorts, Aſſiſe, Price and Weight thereof, and all Things concerning the ſame, as in their Judgments they ſhall find neceſſary and convenient. Stat. 8 *Ann. c.* 18. §. 3.

[𝔔u. 𝔖eſſ.] Upon an Appeal by Bakers, or others, convicted for Making, Baking, or Expoſing to Sale, Bread, contrary to Statute 8 *Ann. c.* 18. the Seſſions to hear, and finally determine the ſame; and if the Appellant be not relieved, to pay reaſonable Coſts, and be committed to the common Gaol, till he pay the

Penalty

APPENDIX.

Offences.   **Bakers and Bread.**   *Penalties.*

Penalty and the Costs. If he be relieved upon his Appeal, the Informer to pay reasonable Costs. Stat. 8 *Ann.* c. 18. §. 6.

Note; The Stat. 8 *Ann. c.* 18. does not extend to prejudice any Right or Custom of *London*, or the Practice there used, nor Lords of Leets, nor *Clerk of the Market*. §. 10.

And the Justices in their Charges are to inforce and press the Execution of the said Statute. §. 12.

Offences.   **Bankrupt.**   *Penalties.*

[One] UPON Application may grant his Warrant for the Taking and Apprehending a Person certified a Bankrupt, and may commit such Person to the common Gaol of the County where apprehended. Stat. 5 *Geo.* 2. *cap.* 30. §. 14. Continued by 9 *Geo.* 2. *c.* 18. to 29 *Septem.* 1743, &c.

May take the Oath of a Bankrupt, who is to deliver all his Books of Accounts and Writings not seised by the Messenger of the Commission, or not before delivered to the Commissioners.

A Bankrupt not surrendring himself upon Notice given, and within the Time limited by the Act, or not delivering up to the Commissioners all his Goods, Wares, Books, &c. (necessary wearing Apparel of himself, his Wife and Children, excepted) or concealing or imbezilling to the Value of 20 *l.* or any Books of Account, with Intent to defraud his Creditors, (and being thereof convicted by Indictment or Information) is guilty of Felony without the Benefit of Clergy. *Ibid.* §. 1.

Offences.   **Bastards.**   *Penalties.*

[One] ONE who is suspected, or charged to be the Father of a Bastard-Child, which is likely to become chargeable to the Parish. The Woman to be examined, and her Examination put in Writing.	Is either before or after the Birth to be bound to the Good Behaviour, till Order be made by Two Justices, according to 18 *Eliz. c.* 3.
Such Person as shall have any Hand by Persuasion, Procurement, or otherwise, in conveying or sending away a putative Father.	To be bound to the Good Behaviour, and so to the next Gaol-Delivery, (before the Judges of Assise) or to the next Quarter-Sessions.
[Two] After a Bastard-Child is born, which is, or is likely to become chargeable to the Parish. Stat. 18 *Eliz. c.* 3. §. 2. 7 *Jac.* 1. *c.* 4. §. 7. Two next Justices. *Quorum* 1.	In or next to the Limits of such Parish-Church, to examine the Cause and Circumstances, and to make an Order for the Relief of the Parish, in Part, or in all, and Keeping the Child, by charging the Father or Mother with weekly Payments, or other Relief, as also for Punishment of Father and Mother.
Leud Women having Bastard-Children which may be chargeable to the Parish. Stat. 7 *Jac.* 1. *c.* 4. §. 7.	To be committed to the House of Correction, there to be punished, and set to Work one whole Year; for the second Offence, to be committed, till they find good Security for their Good Behaviour, not to offend again.

To order Church-wardens and Overseers, to seise Goods and Profits of Lands of a putative Father, and leud Mother of a Bastard-Child, towards Discharge of the Parish, to be confirmed at the Sessions. Stat. 13 & 14 *Car.* 2. *c.* 12. §. 19.

[Qu. Sess.] To do all Things concerning a Bastard, begot out of lawful Matrimony, that by Justices of Peace, in their several Counties, are by the Stat. of 18 *Eliz. c.* 3. limited to be done. Stat. 3 *Car.* 1. *c.* 4. §. 15. See 6 *Geo.* 2. *Chap.* 31. In *Dalton, Chap.* 11. Tit. *Bastardy.*

Offences.   **Bedford Level.**   *Penalties.*

[Two] BReaking down, or any ways hindring, or laying open the Inclosures in *Bedford* Level. Stat. 15 *Car.* 2. *c.* 17. §. 13. Two Witnesses. | Twenty Pounds, to be levied by Distress and Sale.

Offences.   **Beer and Ale.**   *Penalties.*

[Qu. Sess.] THE Rates and Prices of Beer and Ale to be set by the Justices, at their Discretions. Stat. 23 *H.* 8. *c.* 4. §. 5.

Brewers

APPENDIX.

Brewers felling their *Beer* at other Prices than fet by Juftices. Stat. 23 *H.* 8. *c.* 4. §. 5.

Six Shillings for every Barrel, 3 *s.* 4 *d.* for every Kilderkin, 2 *s.* for every Firkin, and 10 *s.* for every larger Veffel, and leffer 1 *s.* to be divided between the King and Profecutor.

Offences.   𝕭𝖑𝖆𝖋𝖕𝖍𝖊𝖒𝖔𝖚𝖘 𝖂𝖔𝖗𝖉𝖘.   *Penalties.*

[**One**] TO take an Information of Blafphemous Words, within Four Days after the Words fpoken, and not afterwards.

The Profecution to be in Three Months after the Information. Stat. 9 & 10 *W.* 3. *c.* 32. §. 2.

Offences.   𝕭𝖔𝖓𝖊-𝕷𝖆𝖈𝖊.   *Penalties.*

[**One**] UPON Information given, to iffue his Warrant to Conftables, &c. to fearch for foreign Bone-Lace, Cut-work, Embroidery, Fringe, Band-ftrings, Buttons, or Needle-work of Thread or Silk, and to feife them.

The Perfon felling or offering them to Sale, forfeits 50 *l.* and the Goods: And the Perfon importing, 100 *l.* and the Goods; one Moiety to the King, the other to him that fues in any Court of Record. Stat. 13 & 14 *Car.* 2. *c.* 13. §. 3.

Repealed as to Lace made of Thread in all Places, but the Dominion of the *French* King and the Duke of *Anjou*, by Stat. 5 *Ann.* *c.* 17.

Offences.   𝕭𝖔𝖔𝖐𝖘.   *Penalties.*

[**One**] TO grant a Warrant to fearch for any Book, taken out of any Parochial Library, and, if found, to reftore it. Stat. 7 *Ann.* *c.* 14. §. 10.

Offences.   𝕭𝖗𝖆𝖓𝖉𝖞 and 𝕾𝖕𝖎𝖗𝖎𝖙𝖘.   *Penalties.*

[**One**] OFficers of Cuftoms neglecting to feife Veffels, Horfes, &c. forfeited for running of Brandy. 6 *Geo.* 2. *c.* 17. §. 10.

50 *l.* between the King and Informer, to be levied by Diftrefs and Sale.

For want of Diftrefs, to be committed for fix Months.

None to fell, or expofe to Sale, Brandy, Strong-Waters, &c. about the Streets, or on the Water, or on any Bulk, &c. or any where but in the Party's Dwelling-houfe. *Ibid.* §. 11.

And on Refufal of Payment

10 *l.* Oath of one Witnefs.
Complaint within one Month.

Commitment to the Houfe of Correction for three Months.

[**Two**] Brandy imported without Entry, is forfeited by 15 *Car.* 2. and may be adjudged againft the Importer, or Proprietor, by two Juftices. Stat. 15 *Car.* 2. *c.* 11. §. 17.

To take the Oaths of Diftillers, and others, That Brandy or Strong-Waters, intended to be exported, was drawn from Drink brewed from malted Corn, without any Mixture; and that the fame is not mixed with Low-Wines, nor drawn a fecond Time, nor with any other Spirits, or Brandy, made from any other Materials; and that the Duties of the fame are enter'd and paid; and that the fame are exported for Merchandize. Stat. 2 *W.* & *M. c.* 9. §. 6.

May take the Oath of Exporters of Spirits, that the fame are drawn from Corn of *Great Britain*, without any Mixture with other Materials, and that the Duties are paid, and that the fame are Merchandize to be fpent beyond the Seas. 6 *Geo.* 2. *c.* 17. §. 7.

[**Qu. Seff.**] Sellers of Brandy, &c. to be licenfed, and fubject to the fame Penalties as Alehoufe-keepers. 2 *Geo.* 2. *c.* 28. §. 10.

See 9 *Geo.* 2. *Chap.* 23. commonly call'd the *Gin-Act*; as alfo 11 *Geo.* 2. *Chap.* 26. in *Dalton, Chap.* 38. Tit. *Brandy.*

See alfo Title 𝕭𝖗𝖆𝖓𝖉𝖞 in Title 𝕰𝖝𝖈𝖎𝖋𝖊 *infra.*

Offences.   𝕭𝖗𝖆𝖋𝖘.   *Penalties.*

[**Qu. Seff.**] AT their *Michaelmas* Seffions, yearly to appoint Searchers of Brafs and Pewter. Stat. 19 *H.* 7. *c.* 6. §. 15.

APPENDIX.

THE Juftices of Peace have Power to hear and determine Offences againft the Statute 17 *Edw.* 4. *c.* 4. intitled, *The Preparation of Earth for making Tile.* They may fine the Offender for every 1000 Plain Tile 5 *s.* for 100 Roof Tile 6 *s.* 8 *d.* for 100 Corner Tile or Gutter Tile 2 *s.* if fold contrary to the Act.

    N. B. The 12 *Geo.* 1. *c.* 35. & 2 *Geo.* 2. *c.* 15. are expired.

Offences.   𝕭𝖗𝖎𝖉𝖌𝖊𝖘.   *Penalties.*

JUftices in their Seffions may inquire, hear and determine the Annoyances of *Bridges*, and of Highways adjoining within 300 Foot, and may charge thofe who ought to repair the fame. Stat. 22 *H.* 8. *c.* 5.

[**Qu. Seff.**] To affefs towards the Repair of Bridges, every Town, Parifh, and Place, as they have been ufually affeffed, to be collected by the Conftables, or fuch Treafurer, and in fuch Manner as the Juftices fhall appoint. The Affeffments to be levied by Diftrefs and Sale, upon Perfons not paying in ten Days after Demand. Stat. 1 *Ann. Seff.* 1. *c.* 18. §. 2.

    But fee 12 *Geo.* 2. *c.* 29. for the more eafy levying County Rates, in *Dalton,* Chap. 196.

    The Juftices may purchafe Lands not exceeding one Acre, for enlarging or more convenient Rebuilding County Bridges. See 14 *Geo.* 2. *c.* 33. in *Dalton,* Chap. 16.

Conftable, &c. neglecting to collect Monies affeffed for Repair of Bridges : Or to pay the Money collected to the High Conftable in Six Days after Receipt of the fame. Stat. 1 *Ann. c.* 18. §. 5.	Forty Shillings.
Treafurer, paying Money affeffed for Repair of Bridges, except by Order of Seffions. Stat. 1 *Ann. Seff.* 1. *c.* 18. §. 6.	Five Pounds.

    Have Power to allow Perfons concerned in the Execution of the Stat. 1 *Ann. Seff.* 1. *c.* 18. Three Pence *per* Pound. *Ibid.* §. 9.

    Note; No Fine for not repairing Bridges and Highways fhall be returned into the Exchequer, *&c.* But to be returned to the Treafurer, and applied by the Juftices towards the Repair of Bridges and Highways.

Offences.   𝕭𝖚𝖌𝖌𝖊𝖗𝖞.   *Penalties.*

[**One**] BUggery, by Stat. 25 *H.* 8. *c.* 6. Revived and made perpetual 5 *El. c.* 17.   Felony without Clergy.

𝕭𝖚𝖎𝖑𝖉𝖎𝖓𝖌𝖘.   See Tit. 𝕱𝖎𝖗𝖊.

Offences.   𝕭𝖚𝖑𝖑𝖎𝖔𝖓.   *Penalties.*

[**One**] PErfons having unlawful Bullion, if they cannot prove on Oath, that the faid Bullion before the Melting thereof, was not current Coin, or Clippings.   To be committed to Prifon, in order to be tried upon an Indictment for Melting the Current Coin of this Realm. And in Cafe they do not make fuch Proof, to be committed for Six Months.

[**Two**] To enter the Houfe, *&c.* of any Perfon fufpected, and to fearch for unlawful Bullion, and, with the Affiftance of a Conftable, to break open the Door, Box, Trunk, Cheft, *&c.* to fearch for, and difcover the fame, which if they find, they are to feife ; and to carry the Perfon in whofe Cuftody it is found before the next Juftice. Stat. 6 & 7 *W.* 3. *c.* 17. §. 8.

Offences.   𝕭𝖚𝖗𝖎𝖆𝖑𝖘.   *Penalties.*

[**One**] WHEN any Perfon is buried, if no Perfon doth, within Eight Days after Interment, bring an *Affidavit* to the Minifter, *&c.* that the Perfon was buried in Woollen, upon a Certificate of this from the Minifter. Stat. 30 *Car.* 2. *c.* 3. §. 4.   Five Pounds, to be levied by Diftrefs and Sale of the Party's Goods ; if he has none, of the Perfon where the Party died, or of any other who put the Party into the Coffin.
    Mafter's Goods liable for the Servants.
    Parents for Children.
    One Moiety to the Poor, the other to the Informer.

APPENDIX.

Offences.	Burials.	Penalties.

Affidavits of Burying in Woollen to be taken by one Juftice of the Peace; but where no Juftice of Peace fhall refide, or be to be found in any Parifh where the Party is to be interred, there the Parfons, Vicars, and Curates, (other than of the Parifh or Place where the Party is interred) may take fuch Affidavits. Stat. 30 *Car.* 2. *c.* 3. §. 5. 32 *Car.* 2. *c.* 1. §. 3.

[**Qu. Seff.**] To give in Charge the Act for Burying in Woollen. Stat. 30 *Car.* 2. *c.* 3. §. 8.

Offences.	Butcher.	Penalties.

[**One**] BUtcher killing or felling any Victual upon the *Lord's Day.* View, Confeffion, or Two Witneffes. Stat. 3 *Car.* 1. *c.* 1. §. 3.

Six Shillings and eight Pence, to be levied by Diftrefs, &c. A Third to the Informer, the Reft to the Poor.

Butchers are not allow'd by Law to buy fat Cattle and fell them again alive: And if they fell Swines Flefh meafled, or Cattle dying with the Murrain, &c. they fhall for the firft Offence be fubject to the Amercement; for the fecond, ftand in the Pillory; and for the third be fined. Stat. 15 *Car.* 2. *c.* 8.

[**Two**] Butcher, or other Perfon, wilfully or negligently gafhing, flaughtering, or cutting the raw Hide of any Ox, Bull, Steer, or Cow, or the Skin of any Calf, or being fo gafh'd, &c. offering the fame to Sale.
To fummon the Party accufed, and the Witneffes on either Side, Party appearing or not, to examine Witneffes on Oath, and determine.
Profecution in Three Months.
An Appeal lies to next Seffions.
No *Certiorari* to be allowed, but Juftices Determination to be final.
Stat. 9 *Ann.* *c.* 11. §. 11, 36.

2 *s.* 6 *d.* for every Hide, 1 *s.* for every Calf's Skin.
One Moiety to the Poor, the other to the Informer, to be levied by Diftrefs and Sale, if not redeemed in Six Days, rendring the Overplus, if any.
Juftices may mitigate, fo as the reasonable Cofts and Charges in profecuting be allowed over and above fuch Mitigation, and fo as the Penalty be not reduced to lefs than one fourth Part.

[**Qu. Seff.**] If any Butcher in *London,* or *Weftminfter,* or in Ten Miles thereof, buy fat Cattle, and fell them again, alive or dead, to another Butcher. Stat. 22 & 23 *Car.* 2. *c.* 19. §. 3.
Profecution in Six Months.

Forfeits the Value of fuch Cattle, to be divided between the King and Profecutor; the King's Moiety to be eftreated, the Profecutor's to be levied by *Fieri fac'* or *Cap'.*
May proceed, notwithftanding any *Certiorari.*

Butcher gafhing any Hides. Stat. 1 *Jac.* 1. *c.* 22. §. 2.

20 *d.* for every Hide, to be divided; one Third to the King, one to the Profecutor, and the other to the City, Borough, Town, or Lord of the Liberty where the Offence is committed.

Butcher watering of Hides, except in *June, July* or *Auguft,* or putting them to Sale, being putrified. Stat. 1 *Jac.* 1. *c.* 22.

3 *s.* 4 *d.* a Hide, to be divided *ut fupra.*

Vide Tanner.

Offences.	Butter and Cheefe.	Penalties.

[**One**] IMporters of Butter and Cheefe out of *Ireland.* Stat. 32 *Car.* 2. *c.* 2. §. 9.

Liable to the Seifure and Penalties, as Importers of Cattle.
Vide Title Cattle.

Perfons exchanging, or opening a Cafk of Butter, fealed or marked by the Factor, or Buyer, or the Cafk exchanged, or bad Butter packed up and mixed with good; and every Fraud committed by the Seller.
Confeffion, or one Witnefs. Stat. 4 & 5 *W.* & *M.* *c.* 7. §. 3.

Twenty Shillings for every Firkin, and Offence, to be levied by Diftrefs and Sale.
One Half to the Poor, the other to the Informer.

Warehoufe-keepers, Weighers, Searchers, or Shippers, in any Port, refufing to receive Butter or Cheefe, or to take Care thereof, or to fhip the fame fucceffively. *Ibid.* §. 4.
Conviction *ut fupra.*

Ten Shillings for every Firkin of Butter, and Two Shillings for every Weigh of Cheefe.
To be levied by Diftrefs and Sale, and employed *ut fupra.*

Butter and Cheefe.

Offences.	Penalties.
Warehoufe-keepers, &c. not keeping Books, and making Entries of Butter and Cheefe, or making un-true Entries, or refufing in the Day-time to produce the Books to be fearched. Stat. 4 & 5 W. & M. c. 7. §. 5. Conviction ut fupra.	2 s. 6 d. for every Firkin of Butter. The fame for every Weigh of Cheefe, and every other Offence. To be levied by Diftrefs and Sale, and employed ut fupra. For Want of Diftrefs to be committed till Pay-ment.
Mafters of Veffels coming to lade Butter and Cheefe, or their Servants refufing to take on Board any Butter and Cheefe, as fhall be tender'd to be fhipped, by any Warehoufe-keeper, &c. before their Veffels be laden. Stat. 4 & 5 W. & M. c. 7. §. 6.	Five Shillings for every Firkin of Butter, and Two Shillings and fix Pence for every Weigh of Cheefe. To be levied and employed ut fupra. Note; This extends not to the Counties of Chefter and Lancafter, or the City of Chefter.

Upon an Appeal, the Appellant is to give Bond of Twenty Pounds, with one or more Sureties, to the Liking of a Juftice, to pay fuch Cofts as the Court fhall award, in one Month, after the Appeal is heard. Ibid. §. 10.

[Qu. Seff.] May reftrain the Retailers of Butter and Cheefe. Stat. 21 Jac. 1. c. 22. §. 7.	The Retailer, during the Time of that Reftraint, is under the Penalties of 3 & 4 Ed. 6. c. 21. and 5 & 6 Ed. 6. c. 14. againft Foreftallers, &c.
Where the Kilderkin of Butter weighs lefs than One hundred and twelve Pounds, 16 Ounces to the Pound; Firkin lefs than 56, Pot lefs than 14, befides Cafks and Pots, or where old and corrupt Butter is put up with new and found, or Whey-Butter with Butter made of Cream, or Butter is falted with great Salt, or more Salt than will preferve it. Stat. 13 & 14 Car. 2. c. 26. §. 2. Profecution in Four Months.	The Value of the Butter falfe pack'd, and fix Times the Value of every Pound wanting. One Moiety to the Poor where the Offence is com-mitted, the other to the Informer, befides his double Cofts.
[Qu. Seff.] Sellers of Butter, not delivering the Quantities aforefaid in every Kilderkin, &c. Ibid. §. 3.	To make Satisfaction at the Price for which it was fold. Profecution in Four Months.
Repackers of Butter for Sale. Stat. 13 & 14 Car. 2. c. 26. §. 4. Profecution ut fupra.	Double the Value to be divided ut fupra. And to pay Cofts ut fupra.
If Butter for Sale be not pack'd in Cafks of found, dry, well-feafon'd Timber, mark'd with the Weight of the empty Cafk, and the firft Letters of their Chriftian Names, and Surnames at length, with an Iron Brand. Stat. 13 & 14 Car. 2. c. 26. §. 5. Profecution ut fupra.	Ten Shillings for every 100 Weight, and fo for greater or leffer Quantities. To be divided, and pay Cofts ut fupra.
[Qu. Seff.] Potters expofing to Sale Pots for pack-ing Butter without the Weight of it, and without the firft Letter of the Chriftian Name, and Surname at length. Stat. 13 & 14 Car. 2. c. 26. §. 6. Profecution ut fupra.	One Shilling for every Pot. To be divided and pay Cofts ut fupra.
Perfons expofing Butter to Sale in Pots not mark'd ut fupra. Stat. 13 & 14 Car. 2. c. 26. §. 6. Profecution ut fupra.	Two Shillings for every Pot. To be divided and pay Cofts ut fupra.

For the Power of Juftices of Peace, relating to the Sale of Butter within the City of York, fee 8 Geo. 1. c. 27.

Buttons and Button-holes.

Offences.	Penalties.
[One] Importers, Barterers, Sellers, or Exchangers of foreign Buttons, made of Hair, or other foreign Buttons whatfoever. Stat. 4 & 5 W. & M. c. 10. §. 2.	Forfeit them, and are liable to the Penalties in 14 Car. 2. c. 13. for importing Bone-lace. Vide Title Bone-lace.
Taylors, or others, making, felling, fetting on, ufing, or binding, on any Clothes, Buttons, or Button-holes, made, ufed, or bound with Cloth, Serge, Drugget, Frize, Camlet, &c.	Forfeit Forty Shillings for every Dozen of fuch Buttons and Button-holes fo made, &c. or in Propor-tion for any leffer Quantity.

4   One   Between

APPENDIX.

Offences	Penalties
One Witness. Stat. 4 *Geo.* 1. *c.* 7. §. 1. Not to extend to Clothes made of Velvet. §. 2.	Between the Poor, where, *&c.* and the Informer. And if not paid in fourteen Days, to be levied by Distress. And if no Distress, to be committed to hard Labour for Three Kalendar Months. §. 5.
Persons being in Gaol, or within the Rules or Liberties of any Gaol, or House of Correction, or inhabiting in privileged Places, or Liberties of the same, committing any Offence against Stat. 4 *Geo.* 1. *c.* 7. §. 3.	Subject to the same Penalties *ut supra.*
Clothes made with Buttons and Button-holes of the same Cloth, *&c.* exposed to Sale in Fairs, Markets, Shops, Warehouses, or Dwelling-houses.	Forfeited, and may be seised and applied *ut supra.* Stat. 4 *Geo.* 1. *c.* 7. §. 8.
Taylor, or others, causing his or their Apprentice, or Servant, to make any Clothes with Cloth-Buttons and Button-holes, if intitled to the Monies for making them. Stat. 4 *Geo.* 1. *c.* 7. §. 9.	Liable to the same Penalties *ut supra.*

Note; All Offences against the Stat. 4 *Geo.* 1. *c.* 7. to be prosecuted in Three Months after committed or discovered. §. 4.

No Person whatsoever in *Great Britain*, to use or wear on any Clothes, Garments, or Apparel whatsoever, any Buttons or Button-holes made of or bound with Cloth, Serge, Drugget, Frize, Camlet, or any Stuffs whereof Clothes or wearing Garments are usually made. One or more credible Witnesses, or Confession. Stat. 7 *Geo.* 1. *c.* 12. §. 1. *Note*; One or more Justices to summon the Party accused, and upon his Appearance or Confession to proceed to examine the Matter of Fact, and determine the same. *Ibid.* §. 2.	On Forfeiture of Forty Shillings for every Dozen of such Buttons or Button-holes so used or worn; or in Proportion for every lesser Quantity. §. 1. To be levied by Distress and Sale: One Moiety to the Person on whose Oath any Person shall be convicted, the other to the Poor where the Offence was committed. §. 2.

The Prosecution must be in one Month after Offence is committed. §. 4.

Note; An Appeal lies to the next General Quarter-Sessions, (giving Eight Days Notice at least to the Prosecutor) whose Judgment is final. *Ibid.* §. 3.

The above Statute does not extend to Velvet. §. 5.

[Two] Taylor, or other Person making, selling, setting on, using, or binding, on any Clothes, Buttons, or Button-holes, made with Serge, Stuff, Drugget, or any other Stuff, or causing them so to be made. Stat. 8 *Ann. c.* 6. §. 1. May appeal to Quarter-Sessions.	Five Pounds for every Dozen so made, *&c.* to be levied; one Moiety to the Queen, the other to him who sues by Action of Debt, *&c.* But *Quære*, For that Act says only, That they shall levy the Penalty, but does not direct the Manner.

[Qu. Sess.] Upon an Appeal against the Order of Two Justices upon Complaint made against Taylors for making, *&c.* Cloth-Buttons, *&c.* to order the Appellant to pay reasonable Costs, if he be not relieved upon his Appeal. Stat. 8 *Ann. c.* 6. §. 2.

Persons aggrieved by the Order of one Justice, on Conviction for Offences against the Stat. 4 *Geo.* 1. *c.* 7. may on giving sufficient Notice, appeal, *&c.* §. 6.	Sessions to allow such Costs and Charges to the Party grieved, as they shall think reasonable, to be levied and paid as in other Cases of Appeals. Their Award is final.

[One] TO take the Affidavit of any Person or Persons, declaring the Grounds of his or their Knowledge, or Suspicion, That playing Cards or Dice are made, or caused to be made, in any House or Place in *Great Britain*, without Notice thereof in Writing given to the Commissioners of the Stamp-Duties at their head Office. Stat. 6 *Geo.* 1. *c.* 21. §. 57.

Upon Affidavit, as aforesaid, to grant his Warrant, directed to an Officer of the Duties on Cards and Dice, to impower him in the Day-time, and in Presence of a Constable, to break open the Door, or any Part of such House or Place where Cards or Dice are so as aforesaid	Cards, Dice, Tools, and Materials, are forfeited, unless claimed or replevied by the Owner in Five Days after Seisure. To be sold by Direction of the Commissioners.

One

Cards and Dice.

Offences.

foresaid suspected to be made, or making, and to enter such House or Place, and to seise all such Cards, Dice, Tools or Materials for making the same ; and to detain and keep the same in such House or Place as the Commissioners of the Stamps shall direct. Stat. 6 *Geo.* 1. *c.* 21. §. 57.

Penalties.

One Moiety to the King, the other to the Party who discovers the same.

Callicoes.

Offences.

[**One**] NO Person whatsoever to use or wear in *Great Britain*, in any Garment or Apparel whatsoever, any printed, painted, stained, or died Callico.

Confession, or one or more credible Witnesses.

Prosecution in Six Days. Stat. 7 *Geo.* 1. *st.* 1. *c.* 7. *sess.* 1. §. 1.

Persons wearing or using in Apparel, Houshold-Stuff, or Furniture, any Stuff made of Cotton, or mixed therewith, which shall be printed with any Colour or Colours, or any Callico chequered or striped, or any Callico stitched or flowered in foreign Parts with any Colour or Colours, or with coloured Flowers made there, Muslin Neckcloths and Fustians excepted. *Ibid.* §. 10.

Penalties

Five Pounds for every Offence to the Informer.

To be levied by Distress and Sale, &c.

Are liable to the Penalties for using or wearing printed, painted, stained, or dyed Callicoes.

[**Qu. Sess.**] An Appeal lies to the next Quarter-Sessions, (giving the Prosecutor Six Days Notice) whose Judgment is final. *Ibid.* §. 1.

Carriers and Carriage.

Offences.

[**One**] TRavelling with *Waggon, Wain, Cart,* or *Carriage,* with above Six Horses, Oxen, or Beasts. Stat. 6 *Ann. c.* 29. §. 3.

This extends not to such as carry Hay, Straw, Corn, Coal, Chalk, Timber, Materials for Building, Stone of all Sorts, Ammunition, or Artillery.

Penalties

Five Pounds, to be levied by Distress and Sale of any of the said Beasts, in Three Days.

One Moiety to the Highways, the other Moiety to the Prosecutor, so as he be an Inhabitant of the Town Village, or Place.

Any Person or Persons may discover and prosecute Persons drawing with more than Six Horses, &c. contrary to Stat. 6 *Ann. c.* 29. and seise and distrain all or any the Horses, &c. the same to be deliver'd to the Surveyor of the Highways, or other Officer of the Place, where, &c. and if the Five Pounds be not paid in Three Days, the Distress to be sold, and the Money to be delivered to the Justice, to be distributed, as by the said Act is directed. Stat. 9 *Ann. c.* 18. §. 1.

Persons refusing or neglecting to carry Horse, &c. distrained for Driving with above Six Horses, to the Surveyor, or other Parish-Officer. Stat. 9 *Ann. c.* 18. §. 2.

20*l.* to be levied by Distress and Sale ; for Want of Distress, to be committed to the common Gaol, till Payment.

One Moiety to the Informer, the other to be laid out in the Repair of the Highways.

Surveyors of the Highways, or other Parish-Officer, refusing or neglecting to deliver the Sum of Money, or Penalty by him received, to the Justice. Stat. 9 *Ann. c.* 18. §. 2.

Twenty Pounds, to be levied and dispos'd *ut supra.*

Persons employed by any Carrier, or other Person subject to the Penalties in the said Acts of 6 & 9 *Ann.* driving, or assisting in the Driving, with more than Six Horses, &c. Stat. 9 *Ann. c.* 18. §. 3.

Five Pounds, to be levied and disposed *ut supra.*

No travelling Waggon, Wain, Cart, or Carriage, wherein Goods shall be carried, other than according to the Stat. 6 *Ann. c.* 29. to be drawn, or go in any publick Highway or Road, with above five Horses, Oxen, or Beasts, at length. Stat. 1 *Geo.* 1. *c.* 11. §. 1.

Upon the like Forfeitures, in the 6 *Ann. c.* 29. or in the 9 *Ann.*

Carter, Drayman, Carman, Waggoner, or other Person, riding in any Cart, &c. not having another on Foot to guide it in the Streets of *London* and *West-*

Forfeit 10 *s.* to be levied by Distress and Sale.

One Moiety to the Informer, the other to the Poor of the Parish where, &c.

4

Carriers and Carriage.

Offences.		Penalties.
Weſtminſter, *Southwark*, or other Streets within the Bills of Mortality. One Witneſs. Stat. 1 *Geo.* 1. *Seſſ.* 2. *c.* 57. §. 8.		In Default of Payment to be committed to the Houſe of Correction, for Three Days, to hard Labour.
No Waggon travelling for Hire ſhall go, or be drawn with more than Six Horſes, either at Length, or in Pairs, or Sideways. Stat. 5 *Geo.* 1. *c.* 12. §. 1.		Owner or Driver forfeits all the Horſes above Six, and all Geers, Bridles, &c. to the Uſe of the Perſon who ſhall ſeiſe the ſame.

The Horſe or Horſes, or other Thing ſo ſciſed or diſtrained, to be delivered to the Conſtable, or other Pariſh-Officer of the Place where, &c. till Proof upon Oath be made before ſome Juſtice, of the Offence, who is to iſſue his Precept to ſuch Conſtable, &c. to deliver the Horſe or Horſes ſo forfeited, to the Perſon who ſeiſed or diſtrained the ſame, and to allow reaſonable Charges for keeping and ſecuring the Horſe, &c. 5 *Geo.* 1. *c.* 12. §. 2.

Offences.	Penalties.
No *Cart* travelling for Hire ſhall go, or be drawn with more than Three Horſes. 5 *Geo.* 1. *c.* 12. §. 1.	Owner, or Driver, forfeits all the Horſes above Three, and all Geers, &c. and to be ſeiſed, diſtrained, and applied *ut ſupra*.
No *Waggon travelling for Hire*, having the Wheels bound with Streaks, or Tire of leſs Breadth than Two Inches and an Half, when worn; or being ſet or faſtned on with Roſe-headed Nails, ſhall go or be drawn with more than Three Horſes. 5 *Geo.* 1. *c.* 12. §. 3.	Forfeits *ut ſupra*.
Perſons hindring, or with Force attempting to hinder or obſtruct the Seiſures, &c. made by Virtue of this Act, or who ſhall reſcue, or uſe any Violence to Perſons concerned in making ſuch Seiſure, &c. 5 *Geo.* 1. *c.* 12. §. 4. One Witneſs.	To be committed to the common Gaol for Three Months, without Bail or Mainpriſe. And alſo forfeit Ten Pounds for every Offence. To be levied by Diſtreſs and Sale, if the Penalty be not paid within Three Days.

Note; This Act extends not to Waggons, Wains, Carts, or Carriages, employed in and about Huſbandry, or manuring Land, and carrying of Cheeſe, Butter, Hay, Straw, Corn unthreſhed, Coals, Chalk, or any one Tree, or Piece of Timber, or any one Stone, or Block of Marble, Carravans, and covered Carriages of Noblemen and Gentlemen, for their own private Uſe, or Timber, Ammunition, or Artillery for the King's Uſe. 5 *Geo.* 1. *c.* 12. §. 5.

Offences.	Penalties.
Perſons carrying at any one Load, in the Cities of *London* and *Weſtminſter*, or within Ten Miles thereof, in *Waggons* or *Carts*, having their Wheels ſhod or bound with Tire or Streaks of Iron, more than twelve Sacks of Meal, each containing five Buſhels, and no more; or more than twelve Quarters of Malt, or more than ſeven Hundred and an Half of Bricks; or more than one Chalder of Coals. Stat. 6 *Geo.* 1. *c.* 6. §. 1. One Witneſs.	Forfeit one of the Horſes, together with the Geers, Bridles, &c. to any Perſon that ſhall ſeiſe or diſtrain the ſame: In ſuch Manner, and to ſuch Uſes, as the Penalties and Forfeitures are to be levied and applied by the Stat. 5 *Geo.* 1. *c.* 12.
Waggoners or Carriers, taking more for Land-Carriage of Goods than the Juſtices have aſſeſſed. Stat. 3 & 4 *W. & M. c.* 12. §. 24. Proſecution in Six Months.	Five Pounds, to be levied by Diſtreſs and Sale, for the Uſe of the Party grieved.

[Qu. Seſſ.] To aſſeſs yearly at *Eaſter* Seſſions, within their Juriſdiction, the Prices of Land-Carriage of Goods, by Waggoner or Carrier. Stat. 3 & 4 *W. & M. c.* 12. §. 24.

Juſtices of *Wilts*, *Glouceſter*, &c. to aſſeſs yearly at *Eaſter* Seſſions the Carriage of Goods upon the *Thames* and *Iſis*. See *Dalton*, Chap. 21.

Cattle.

Offences.		Penalties.
[One] Cattle, dead or alive, imported, except for Proviſion for the Veſſel, to be made appear in 48 Hours. Stat. 18 *Car.* 2. *c.* 2. §. 1. Two Witneſſes.		Forfeited; one Moiety to the Poor, the other to him who ſeiſes.
Maſter and Mariner of the Veſſel wherein Cattle are imported. Stat. 20 *Car.* 2. *c.* 7. §. 5.		To be committed for Three Months.

Seiſors

d

40 s.

A P P E N D I X.

Offences.   **Cattle.**   *Penalties.*

Seifors of Cattle, Sheep, and Swine, imported out of *Ireland*, not giving Notice in Six Days after Conviction to Church-wardens and Overfeers of fuch Seifure, and they not diftributing all but the Hides and Tallow to the Poor. Stat. 32 *Car.* 2. *c.* 2. §. 6.
   View, Confeffion, or one Witnefs.

40 *s.* for every of the great Cattle.
Ten Shillings for every Sheep or Swine.
One Moiety to the Poor, the other to the Informer, to be levied by Diftrefs and Sale.
   And in Default, to be committed for three Months without Bail or Mainprife.

[**Three**] To enquire by the Oaths of Twelve Men, Examination of Witneffes, or any lawful Means, of the malicious Maiming, or otherwife Hurting any *Horfes, Sheep,* or other Cattle. And for that Purpofe to iffue Warrants to fummon Jurors, fufpected Perfons, and fuch as give Evidence. Stat. 22 & 23 *Car.* 2. *c.* 7. §. 6.
Quorum 1.

Offences.   **Certiorari.**   *Penalties.*

[**Qu. Seff.**] NO *Certiorari* is to be allowed, unlefs the Indicted will become bound with fufficient Sureties (fuch as the Juftices of the Peace in Seffions fhall like of) to pay to the Profecutor, in a Month after Conviction, fuch Cofts and Damages as the Juftices fhall affefs. Stat. 21 *Jac.* 1. *c.* 8. §. 2.

See 5 *Geo.* 2. *c.* 19. in *Dalton,* Chap. 195. Tit. *Certiorari.*
Cheefe. *Vide* Title **Butter** and **Cheefe.**

Offences.   **Church.**   *Penalties.*

[**One**] PErfons not repairing to Church according to the 1 *Eliz. c.* 2. Stat. 23 *Eliz. c.* 1. §. 5.
   This is not to be extended to Proteftant Diffenters, by Stat. 1 *W. & M. Seff.* 1. *c.* 18.

Twenty Pounds a Month, and if forbear for Twelve Months after Certificate made by the Ordinary into the Queen's Bench.
   To be bound with Two fufficient Sureties in 200 Pounds at leaft, to be of the Good Behaviour, until they fhall repair to Church.

Church-wardens to fee that the Parifhioners come to *Church* every Sunday; and if they find any in an Alehoufe, &c. Stat. 1 *Jac.* 1. *c.* 5.

The Perfon to forfeit 3 *s.* 4 *d.* and the Mafter of the Houfe 10 *s.* as in Cafe of Tippling.

Making a Difturbance in a Church or Congregation, or mifufing the Preacher. Stat. 1 *W. & M.*
Two Witneffes.

The Offender to enter into a Recognizance with Two Sureties, in 40 *l.* Penalty for his Appearance at the next Quarter-Seffions: In Default thereof, may be committed 'till then, and upon Conviction fhall forfeit 20 *l.*

Perfons not repairing to fome Church or Chapel. Stat. 3 *Jac.* 1. *c.* 4. §. 27.
   Confeffion, or one Witnefs.
   This is not to be extended to Proteftant Diffenters, by Stat. 1 *W. & M. Seff.* 1. *c.* 18.

Twelve Pence for the Poor.
To be levied by Diftrefs and Sale.
In Default of Diftrefs to be committed.
The Profecution to be in one Month.

Perfons above Sixteen, abfenting from Church above one Month, impugning the Queen's Authority in Caufes Ecclefiaftical, *frequenting Conventicles,* or perfuading others fo to do, under Pretence of Exercife of Religion. Stat. 35 *Eliz. c.* 4. §. 1.
   This is not to be extended to Proteftant Diffenters, by Stat. 1 *W. & M. seff.* 1. *c.* 18.

To be committed till they conform themfelves, and make Submiffion: He may require them to conform and fubmit, and if they refufe, they muft abjure the Realm in open Affife or Seffions.

Every Perfon not reforting to their Parifh-Church, or upon Let thereof, to fome other, every *Sunday* and Holy-Day. Stat. 1 *Eliz. c.* 2. §. 14.
This affects not Proteftant Diffenters.

Twelve Pence for the Poor.
To be levied by the Church-wardens by Diftrefs and Sale.

[**Two**] Incumbents not reading Divine Service once a Month. Stat. 13 & 14 *Car.* 2. *c.* 4. §. 3.
Confeffion, or Two Witneffes.

Five Pounds for every Offence.
To be levied in Ten Days by Diftrefs and Sale.

Perfons difturbing Epifcopal Congregations in *Scotland,* or mifufing, &c. any Minifter or Paftor thereof, on Proof by Two Witneffes. 10 *Ann. c.* 7. §. 9.

To be bound in a Recognizance of 50 *l.* for their Appearance at the next Affifes, &c. or to be committed to Prifon in Default.

1   [**Qu.**   Twenty

APPENDIX.

Offences.	Church.	Penalties.
[**Qu. Seff.**] Every Perfon not repairing to Church according to 1 *Eliz. c.* 2. Stat. 23 *Eliz. c.* 1. §. 5. This extends not to Proteſtant Diſſenters, nor where Divine Service is read in their Houfes.	Twenty Pounds a Month ; Two Thirds to the Queen, one to her own Ufe, the other for the Poor, the Third to the Profecutor.	
Perfons above Sixteen, convicted of Abfence from Church for above a Month, without lawful Caufe, impugning the Queen's Authority in Caufes Eccleſiaſtical, or *frequenting Conventicles*, or perſuading others fo to do, under Pretence of Exercife of Religion. Stat. 35 *Eliz. c.* 1. §. 1. This extends not to Proteſtant Diſſenters.	To be committed to Prifon, till they conform themfelves, and fubmit. And if within Three Months after they refufe to conform and fubmit, being requir'd by a Juſtice of Peace, they ſhall in open Seſſions abjure the Realm, and the Juſtices are to certify the fame at the next Aſſife or Gaol-Delivery.	
Keeping a School-maſter, who abſents himfelf from Church, or is not allowed by the Biſhop or Ordinary. Stat. 23 *Eliz. c.* 1. §. 6.	Ten Pounds a Month, to be divided *ut fupra.*	
Perfons keeping or retaining any Perfon in their Houfe (Servant, or other) which ſhall forbear to come to Church for a Month together. Stat. 3 *Jac.* 1. *c.* 4. §. 32. This extends not to Proteſtant Diſſenters.	Ten Pounds a Month. Children may relieve their Father or Mother, and Guardians their Wards or Pupils.	

Note ; None ſhall be puniſhed for any of his Wife's Offences againſt Stat. 3 *Jac.* 1. *c.* 4. Neither ſhall any married Woman be chargeable with any Penalty or Forfeiture of that Act.

To receive the Letters of Orders of Epifcopal Miniſters in *Scotland*, before they officiate as Paſtors of Congregations, and to order the fame to be entred on Record by the Regiſter or Clerk of the Peace, whofe Fee is 1 *s.* Stat. 10 *Ann. c.* 7. §. 2.	Perfons diſturbing fuch Congregations, &c. and convicted by Two Witneſſes. Forfeit One Hundred Pounds, Half to the Informer, and Half to the Poor.	
And if any Magiſtrate having or pretending Authority in *Scotland*, ſhall forbid or hinder their Meeting or Aſſembling within their Jurifdiction, or caufe the Doors of the Houfe where they meet to be ſhut up. *Ibid.* §. 9.	On Conviction, *ut fupra*, he forfeits One Hundred Pounds. To be difpofed *ut fupra.*	

Offences.	Clothes.	Penalties.
[**One**] Wilfully and maliciouſly to aſſault any Perfon in the publick Streets or Highways, with an Intent to tear, fpoil, cut, burn, or deface, and who ſhall tear, fpoil, cut, burn, or deface the Garments or Clothes of any Perfon. If convicted. Stat. 6 *Geo.* 1. *c.* 23. §. 11.	Felony, and to be tranſported for Seven Years.	

Offences.	Cloth and Clothiers.	Penalties.
(*Woollen*) [**One**] Clothiers not paying their Workfolks their Wages in ready Money. Stat. 4 *Ed.* 4. *c.* 1. §. 6.	Treble Damages, and to be committed till Payment.	
Carders, Spinſters, Weavers, Fullers, Sheermen, and Dyers, not performing their Duty. Stat. 4 *Ed.* 4. *c.* 1. §. 6.	Double Damages, and to be committed till Payment.	
The Juſtice not doing his Duty, about feifing Ropes, and other Things, ufed for unlawful Stretching Northern Cloths, and other Matter, according to Stat. 39 *Eliz. c.* 20. §. 9.	Five Pounds, to be divided into Three Parts : One to the Queen, another to the Informer, and the Third to the Poor.	
Mix'd or *Medley Broad-Cloth* (after 'tis milled, &c.) to be meafured at the Fulling-Mill by the Maſter or Occupier thereof, who is to make Oath, *That he will well and truly perform fuch Meafuring* (before fome neigh-	If the Buyer refufe to take the Cloth according to the Meafure fo mark'd on the Seal, he forfeits 20 *s.* for each Cloth. As doth the Maſter for refuſing or neglecting to fix fuch Seal. <div align="right">And</div>	

APPENDIX.

Offences	Penalties
neigbouring Juſtice, who is to give him a Certificate thereof) and affix a Seal to each Cloth, with his Name, and (in Figures) the Length and Breadth, before 'tis ſold. Stat. 10 *Ann.* c. 16. §. 1, 2. One Witneſs, &c. *Vide infra.*	And every Perſon who ſhall alter ſuch Seal before the Cloth is ſold, forfeits 20 s.
Clothiers, &c. ſtretching or ſtraining any ſuch Cloth above a Yard in Twenty Yards Length, or above One Nail in a Yard in Breadth. Stat. 10 *Ann.* c. 16. §. 3. One Witneſs, &c. *Vide infra.*	Forfeits 20 s. for every Offence, if convicted before 'tis ſold, or expoſed to Sale.
Mill-men, Owners or *Occupiers* of *Fulling-Mills*, to have a Table twelve Foot long, and three Foot wide, whereon the Cloth ſhall be doubled, or creſſed, and laid plain, and one Inch more inſtead of a Thumb's Breadth, *viz.* 37 Inches, to prevent any Diſpute in reſpect of Meaſuring by the Yard. Stat. 10 *Ann.* c. 16. §. 4. One Witneſs, &c. *Vide infra.*	In Default of ſuch Table provided, and conſtantly kept and uſed, every Perſon forfeits 10 l.
Clothiers, or others, concerned in the Woollen Manufacture, ſhall make Payment in Money to the Perſons employed for all Work done in relation thereto, and not (in Lieu of Payment) impoſe or deliver any Sort of Goods, or Wares for ſuch Work. Stat. 10 *Ann.* c. 16. §. 6. One Witneſs, &c. *Vide infra.*	To forfeit for every Offence 20 s.

Note; All Offences againſt this Act may be heard and determined by *one Juſtice*, not concerned in the Matter of the Complaint, and upon the Oath of one Witneſs; and all the Penalties, &c. are Half to the Informer, and Half to the Poor. And if not paid within fourteen Days after Conviction, the Juſtice may cauſe it to be levied by Diſtreſs, &c. And if no Diſtreſs, *commit* to the *Gaol*, or *Houſe of Correction*, to hard Labour, not exceeding Three Months for each Offence; and all Offences to be proſecuted within thirty Days after committed, or Diſcovery made.

But an Appeal lies to the Seſſions. §. 9. Alſo this Act is not to extend to *Yorkſhire*, or to invalidate the Act 7 *Ann.* c. 13. for the Length and Breadth of Cloths made there. Stat. 10 *Ann.* c. 16. §. 7, 8, 11.

Offences	Penalties
Mixed and Medley Broad-Cloths to contain the Quantity mentioned in the Seals ſet by the Maſter or Occupier of the Fulling-Mill. Stat. 1 *Geo.* 1. c. 15. §. 1.	Or Seller forfeits a ſixth Part of the Value of every Cloth under Meaſure to the Poor of the Pariſh. To be paid by the Buyer, and deducted out of the Price of the Cloth.
Owners and Occupiers, &c. refuſing the Oath, *That he will well and truly perform ſuch Meaſuring,* or not fixing a Seal, or others taking off, defacing or counterfeiting it. One Witneſs. Stat. 1 *Geo.* 1. c. 15. §. 2.	Twenty Pounds in Lieu of Twenty Shillings *per* Cloth, by 6 *Ann.* c. 29.
Clothier, Cloth-worker, Cord-maker, and all Perſons concerned in the Woollen Manufacture, not paying their Servants, Labourers, &c. Wages in Money, or impoſing on them Goods, &c. in Lieu thereof.	40 s. for every Offence. Stat. 1 *Geo.* 1. c. 15. §. 12. See 12 *Geo.* 1. c. 34. *infra.*
Mixed or Medley Broad-Cloths, to be ſealed and ſtamped with the Watch-Meaſure on the Seal of the Maſter, Owner, Occupier, or Mill-man, by whom wetted, fulled, and milled; and every Clothier, ſelling or putting to Sale ſuch Broad-Cloth before ſealed. Stat. 1 *Geo.* 1. c. 15. §. 5.	Forfeits a ſixth Part of ſuch Cloth.

Note; All Offences againſt this Act may be heard and determined by One Juſtice, not concerned in the Matter of the Complaint, upon the Oath of one or more Witneſs or Witneſſes. And all the Penalties, &c. are in *London* to *Chriſt's Hoſpital*; and in all other Places to the Poor. And if not paid in thirty Days after Conviction and Demand, or in Caſe the Owner, &c. refuſe or neglect to pay the Forfeiture for Want of ſufficient Length or Breadth of Admeaſurement, the Juſtice may cauſe the Penalties, &c. to be levied by Diſtreſs, &c. And if no Diſtreſs, commit to the Gaol, or Houſe of Correction to hard Labour for Three Kalendar Months. Stat. 1 *Geo.* 1. c. 15. §. 7.

Offences.   **Cloth** and **Clothiers.**   *Penalties.*

All Offences againſt the Stat. 1 *Geo.* 1. *c.* 15. (ſaving where Owner, *&c.* refuſe Repayment of the Forfeitures for Want of ſufficient Length or Breadth in Admeaſurement) to be proſecuted within forty Days after committed or diſcovered. Stat. 1 *Geo.* 1. *c.* 15. §. 8.

[One] On Information on Oath, that any Perſon is guilty, or ſuſpected of the ill Practices in the Cloathing Trade, (mentioned §. 1, 2, 3.) may authorize Conſtable, *&c.* to enter Houſes, *&c.* by Day, and ſearch for and examine Warping-Bars, Weights, *&c.* Stat. 13 *Geo.* 1. *c.* 23. (See Two Juſtices *infra.*)

End-Gatherers buying or carrying Ends of Yarn, Thrums, Refuſe, *&c.* a Conſtable, or other Peace Officer, may by a Warrant ſearch them ; and if he finds any Ends, Thrums, *&c.* carry him before a Juſtice. *Ibid.* §. 8.	On Conviction by Oath of one, or Confeſſion, to be adjudged an incorrigible Rogue, and puniſhed as 12 *Ann.* directs. *Ibid.* §. 8.

(*Linen*)

Linen-Cloth made in *Scotland*, to be of well ſorted Yarn, and equally wrought, and fine from one End of the Piece to the other, and made by the *Standard Yard-Wand.* And all St. *Johnſtons*, or other Plain, Brown, or Green Cloth, made for Whitening, one Yard and a Nail, or Three Quarters and a Nail broad, that when whited, it may be a full Yard, or full Three Quarters broad; and in Length the whole Piece 84 Yards, the Half-Piece 42 Yards, *&c.* that ſo whited it may be 80, or 20 Yards, *&c.* and all other Sorts of plain Cloth a full Yard in Breadth, and in Length 40 Yards the Piece, 20 Yards the Half-Piece, *&c.* And ſee, *ibid.* other Meaſures appointed for Linen Checks, ſtriped Linen, Neckcloths, Ticken, *&c.* Stat. 10 *Ann. c.* 21. §. 1. And for Dornick, Towelling, or Plain Linen, ſee 12 *Ann. Seſſ.* 1. *c.* 20. §. 1, 2. And all Cloth to be ſold in *Scotland* to be made up in Folds of One Yard and Half each Fold, and not rolled or battered. Stat. 10 *Ann. c.* 21. §. 1.	If any make Linen Cloth in *Scotland* otherwiſe, and thereof convicted by Oath of any Overſeer or Searcher, or Two credible Witneſſes, He forfeits for every Inch leſs than Meaſure in Breadth, and every Yard leſs in Length, Five Shillings. And for every Piece not made of well-ſorted Yarn, and equally wrought, and fine, Five Shillings. And if any ſhall buy or expoſe to Sale, or bring to any Town or Place in *Scotland* for Sale, any Linen Cloth not made or not folded as aforeſaid, if convicted within Six Months, forfeits for each Piece Five Shillings. See alſo 13 *Geo.* 1. *c.* 26. relating to the Linen and Hempen Manufacture in *Scotland.*
The Owners of *Scotch* Linen Cloth, before expoſed to Sale, to bring it to ſome Borough-Town, or Place, where Stamps are appointed, there to be ſtamped. Stat. 10 *Ann. c.* 21. §. 3.	And if expoſed to Sale, or carried to the Water-ſide for Exportation before ſtamp'd, and thereof convicted *ut ſupra,* Forfeits for each Piece Five Shillings.
And if any other Perſon ſhall in *Scotland*, buy, export, tranſport, or carry to the Water-Side for that Purpoſe, *Scotch* Linen Cloth not ſtamped as aforeſaid. *Ibid.* §. 4.	If convicted, *ut ſupra,* in *Scotland*, He forfeits for each Piece 5 *s.*
If any Perſon counterfeits any Stamp, or affix it without Authority. *Ibid.* §. 4.	He forfeits 50 *l.* Sterling, or a Year's Impriſonment, if inſolvent.
No Stamp-Maſter, for himſelf, or any other, to buy or diſpoſe of any Linen Cloth, or ſtamp any that is not made of well-ſorted Yarn, equally wrought, and of equal Fineneſs, from one End to the other, and of the ſaid Lengths, Breadths and Foldings. *Ibid.* §. 4.	On Forfeiture of Five Shillings for each Piece, and incapacitated of his Office for the future.
Making uſe of Lime or Pigeons Dung for whitening or bleaching Linen Cloth in *Scotland*, and convicted by Two Witneſſes, or Confeſſion. *Ibid. ſtat.* 10 *Ann. c.* 21. §. 5.	Forfeits for each Piece 20 *l.* and in Default of Payment, to levy it by Diſtreſs, *&c.* And if no Diſtreſs, commit to the Houſe of Correction, or Gaol, to hard Labour, not exceeding twelve Months.

Note; All the Forfeitures and Penalties of this Act are Half to the Informer, and Half to the Poor.

(*Woollen*)

[Two] To appoint once a Year Overſeers for the well-ordering of Cloth. Stat. 3 & 4 *Ed.* 6. *c.* 2. §. 9.

Faulty Cloths expoſed to Sale by Retail. Stat. 5 & 6 *Ed.* 6. *c.* 6. §. 43.	To be divided into three Parts, one to the King, another to the Juſtice, the third to the Proſecutor.

Logwood may be imported and used in Dying. 13 & 14 *Car.* 2. *c.* 1 *pr.* §. 26.

To appoint Overseers to make Search once a Month, at least, for Defects of Northern Cloths. Stat. 39 *Eliz. c.* 20. §. 4.

Offences	Penalties
Sorters, Carders, Kembers, Spinsters, or Weavers of Wool or Yarn, who shall imbezil, or detain any Part from the Owner. Stat. 7 *Jac.* 1. *c.* 7. §. 2.	Either to make Satisfaction, or be whipp'd, and pu in the Stocks.
Makers of deceitful Cloth. Stat. 21 *Jac.* 1. *c.* 18. §. 3. Confession, or Two Witnesses.	Five Pounds, to be certified under Hand and Sea to the Church-wardens and Overseers of the Poor o the Parish where the Offence is committed. To be levied by Distress and Sale, &c. And for Want of Distress, Imprisonment.
[**Three**] If any Means be used whereby Linen Cloth shall be deceitful, or made worse for Use. Stat. 1 *Eliz. c.* 12. §. 1. *Quorum* 1.	The Cloth is forfeited, and the Person to be com mitted for a Month, and fined.
[**Qu. Sess.**] Persons stretching or straining any Cloths made on the North-side of *Trent.* Stat. 39 *El. c.* 20. §. 12. *Vide* Stat. 10 *Ann. c.* 16.	Five Pounds; one Third to the Queen, another t the Informer, and another to the Poor of the Plac where the Offence is committed.
Persons using any Engine, or stretching or straining Cloths. Stat. 39 *Eliz. c.* 20. §. 2.	Twenty Pounds, to be divided *ut supra.*
If a Seal of Lead be not set on Northern Cloths. Stat. 39 *Eliz. c.* 20. §. 3.	The same is forfeited, and 4 s. for every Yard i wants of due Length; and 2 s. for every Pound i wants of due Weight, to be divided *ut supra.*
If any, save the Overseers, set or take away a Seal, to or from the said Cloths, without Warrant. Stat. 39 *Eliz. c.* 20. §. 7. Two Witnesses.	Ten Pounds for the first Offence, Twenty Pound for the Second. To be divided *ut supra.* And besides suffer the Pillory.
Servants to Clothiers, &c. refusing to serve for the Wages limited, according to the Statute; and being retained, departing his or their Service, without a Quarter's Warning, or some lawful Cause. Stat. 5 *Eliz. c.* 4. §. 9.	To be imprisoned, without Bail; but upon Sub mission to perform the Service, to be enlarged withou Fee.
Woollen Cloth Weavers taking an Apprentice, or teaching any their Art, save their own Children, or such whose Parents have three Pounds *per Annum* Free-hold. Stat. 5 *Eliz. c.* 4. §. 29.	Twenty Pounds for every Month.
Every *Cloth-worker, Fuller, Sheerman, Weaver, Taylor,* and *Shoemaker,* who does not keep one Journeyman for every Three Apprentices; and for every Apprentice above Three, another Journeyman. Stat. 5 *Eliz. c.* 4. §. 33.	Ten Pounds. Not to extend to *Norwich* and *Norfolk.*
Persons aggrieved by the Order of one Justice, on a Conviction touching *Mixed Broad-Cloth,* may, on giving sufficient Notice, appeal to the Quarter-Sessions, whose Determination is final. Stat. 10 *Ann. c.* 16. §. 9. 1 *Geo.* 1. *c.* 15. §. 10.	If the Sessions confirm or disannul the Order, they shall allow such *Costs* and *Charges* to the Party grieved, as they think reasonable. To be levied and paid as in other Cases of Appeal.

Note; Stat. 1 *Geo.* 1. *c.* 15. does not extend to any Factor or his Agent imployed in Selling of *Mixed* or *Medley Broad-Cloth.* §. 11.

Nor to any Cloth made in *Yorkshire,* or to invalidate the Act 7 *Ann. c.* 13. for the Length and Breadth of Cloths made there. §. 14.

In *Scotland,* to appoint *Stamps,* to be kept at proper Places, where Linen Cloth is sold, for the Stamping or Marking thereof, and to appoint qualified Persons for Stamping it, who are to take an Oath *de Fideli,* and find Sureties for the faithful Execution of the Office in such Sum as the Sessions shall appoint. Stat. 10 *Ann. c.* 21. §. 4.

Offences	Penalties
Persons aggrieved by the Order of one Justice on a Conviction touching *Mixed Broad-Cloth,* on the Stat. 1 *Geo.*	To allow such Costs and Charges to the Party grieved, as they think reasonable.

Offences.	Cloth and Clothiers.	Penalties.
1 *Geo*. 1. *c*. 15. may, on giving sufficient Notice, appeal, &c. to the Quarter-Sessions, whose Determination is final. §. 10.		To be levied and paid as in other Cases of Appeals.

See the Act for the better regulating the Manufacture of Cloth in the West-Riding of the County of *York*. 11 *Geo*. 1. *c*. 24.

All Contracts, Covenants, or Agreements, and all By-Laws, Ordinances, or Orders in unlawful Clubs and Societies made between Persons brought up in the Mystery of a Wool-comber or Weaver, for Regulating the Trade, or Settling the Prices of Goods, or for Advancing their Wages, or lessening their usual Hours of Work, shall be illegal and void; and if any Wool-comber or other Person concerned in the Woollen Manufactures, shall keep up any Contract or Combination by this Act declared illegal, being convicted on Oath before any Two or more Justices, on Information within Three Kalendar Months after the Offence committed, shall be committed either to the House of Correction not exceeding Three Months, or to the common Gaol without Bail.

If any Person retained as a Wool-comber or Weaver shall depart from his Service before the End of the Term for which he shall be hired, or shall return his Work before it is finished according to Agreement, unless it be for some reasonable Cause, he shall be committed to the House of Correction not exceeding Three Months; and if any Person hired shall wilfully damnify his Work, he shall forfeit to the Owner double the Value, or be committed to the House of Correction.

Every Clothier shall pay the full Prices agreed on in Money, and not in Goods; and any Two Justices, on Complaint, may summon the Party offending, and for Non-payment of Wages may issue their Warrants for Levying thereof by Distress, and for Want of Distress may commit the Party to the common Gaol for Six Months, or till he shall pay the Wages.

If any Clothier shall pay the Persons imployed by him either in Goods, or by Way of Truck, he shall forfeit 10 *l*. Moiety to the Informer, Moiety to the Party aggrieved.

Persons aggrieved by Order of the Justices may appeal to the next Quarter-Sessions, giving reasonable Notice of such Appeal; and if it shall appear to them that reasonable Notice was not given, they shall adjourn the Appeal to the next Quarter-Sessions, and then finally determine the Matter, and may award reasonable Costs to either Party.

If any Persons shall assault a Master Wool-comber or Weaver, whereby he shall receive any bodily Hurt, for not submitting to any illegal By-Laws; or shall write or send any Letter or Message threatning Hurt to a Master, or to burn, or pull down his House, or to cut down his Trees, or maim his Cattle, for not complying with their Demands, being thereof convicted upon any Indictment to be found within Twelve Kalendar Months next after the Offence, he shall be adjudged guilty of Felony, and shall be transported for Seven Years to one of the Plantations in *America*.

If any Person shall break into a Shop by Day or Night to destroy any Woollen Goods in the Loom, or any Tools imployed in making thereof, or shall cut or destroy any such Goods in the Loom, or on the Rack, or shall destroy any Rack, or Tools, he shall be adjudged a Felon, and suffer Death without Benefit of Clergy.

This Act and all the Provisoes therein shall extend to Combers of Jersey and Wool, to Frame-work Knitters or Makers of Stockings, and to all Persons concerned in any of the said Manufactures. 12 *Geo*. 1. *c*. 34.

[Two] No Maker of Mixed or Medley Woollen Broad-Cloth, shall use any long Warping-Bars, but such as are three Yards and three Inches in Length. And round ones to be four Yards and four Inches round, and no more; and the Thrums at each End of the said Bars, are not to exceed 18 Inches long. Stat. 13 *Geo*. 1. *c*. 23. §. 1.	Ten Pounds, to be levied by Distress and Sale; one Moiety to the Informer, the other to the Poor; and if no Distress, Commitment for three Months, or till Payment, &c. *Ibid*. §. 1.

And *Note*; All Disputes relating to Work, Wages, &c. betwixt Clothiers, Combers, Weavers, &c. are to be heard by two or more Justices, who are to summon the Parties, examine on Oath, adjudge such Satisfaction, and give such Costs to the Party grieved, as in their Discretion shall seem reasonable, and levy the same by Distress, &c. or in Default, commit, &c. not exceeding three Months. An Appeal lies to the Quarter-Sessions. Proceedings not removable by *Certiorari*. Stat. 13 *Geo*. 1. *c*. 23. §. 5, 6.

All Wool, Yarn, &c. for making such Cloth, to be given out and received by Weight, at 16 Ounces to the Pound. Stat. 13 *Geo*. 1. *c*. 23. §. 2.	On Penalty of 5 *l*.

Clothiers, &c. interrupting the Search of Constables on a Justice's Warrant. *Ib*. §. 7.	Forfeit 5 *l*.

Clothiers to pay their Weavers according to the Number of Yards that Chains are laid on the Warping-Bar. *Ibid*. §. 9.	Forfeit 5 *l*.

Owners of Tenters or Racks in *Gloucestershire*, *Wilts* and *Somerset*, to measure such Tenters, &c. and mark in	On Forfeiture of 5 *l*. for every Tenter or Rack not so numbred and marked.

Inspectors

A P P E N D I X.

in large Figures their Length of Yards, (beginning N° 1. on the Foreside of the Top Bar) each Yard to contain 36 Inches, and one Inch more for the over Measure usually allowed in Cloths. *Ibid.* §. 10.	
[**Qu. Sess.**] After *Easter*, are yearly to appoint Inspectors, and may allow each not exceeding 30 *l. per Ann.* who are to take an Oath, well and truly to execute their Office, and at all seasonable Times enter and inspect every Mill, Shop, Out-house, and Tenter-ground of Clothiers, Mill-men, &c. and Measure the Length of Tenters, and the Length and Breadth of Cloth there, stamp their Names on a Lead Seal furnished by the Maker, and affix it at the Head of every Cloth ; keep a Register of the Clothier or Milman's Name, and Number, Length and Breadth of every Cloth, and deliver a true Copy of such Register at every Quarter-Sessions. Stat. 13 *Geo.* 1. *c.* 23. §. 10.	Inspectors acting against their Oath, &c. forfeit 20 *l. Ibid.* §. 12.
A Clothier or Mill-man, &c. refusing an Inspector Entrance, &c. *Ibid.* §. 11.	Forfeits 40 *l.*
A Mill-man sending home Cloths before inspected, &c. for every Piece of Cloth so sent. *Ibid.* §. 14.	Forfeits 40 *s.*

Every Maker of such Broad-Cloth to pay the Inspector 2 *d.* for every Cloth he makes before sent from the Mills ; and Inspectors are every three Months to pay the Money to the County-Treasurer, to be applied by Direction of the Justices at their Sessions, towards the Salaries of Inspectors, &c. *Ibid.* §. 13.

Coaches. Vide Hackney-Coaches.

[**One**] PErsons having a Hand in removing or altering the Marks upon Keels and other Boats, Carts and Wains for Carriage of Coals, in the Port of *Newcastle upon Tine.* Stat. 30 *Car.* 2. *c.* 8. §. 6. 6 & 7 *W.* 3. *c.* 10. §. 7. One Witness.	Ten Pounds, to be levied by Distress and Sale ; and on Default to be committed for Three Months.

See *Dalton*, Chap. 24. Tit. *Coals* for 3 *Geo.* 2. *c.* 26.

Coffee. See *Chap.* 20. 10 *Geo.* 1. *c.* 10. 11 *Geo.* 1. *c.* 30. 5 *Geo.* 2. *c.* 24. in *Dalton.*

[**One**] SHeriff or other Officer refusing any lawful Coin in Payment. Stat. 19 *H.* 7. *c.* 5. §. 6.	May compel him to take it, and otherwise punish him at Discretion.
Where any Tools or Instruments for Coining, or counterfeiting Gold or Silver Monies, are found. Stat. 8 & 9 *W.* 3. *c.* 26. §. 5.	The Instruments and the Persons in whose Custody they are found, to be seised and carried before a Justice. And the Persons' and Instruments to be secured, and Instruments to be produced as Evidence, and afterward defaced and destroyed. Counterfeit Money given in Evidence to be cut in Pieces afterwards, and then given to the Party.

[**Qu. Sess.**] IN every Commission of the Peace this Clause is to be inserted, *viz.* That the Justices of Peace in their Sessions shall have Power to inquire of Watches, and to punish them who shall be found in Default, according to the Statute of *Winchester.* Stat. 5 *H.* 4. *c.* 3.

See Justices of the Peace.

APPENDIX.

<table>
<tr><td>*Offences.*</td><td>**Conformity.**</td><td>*Penalties.*</td></tr>
</table>

[Qu. Seff.] TO take the Oath of Perfons having Offices, &c. convicted of *Non-Conformity,* That they have *conformed for a Year paft,* and received the Sacrament Three Times within the Year. Stat. 10 *Ann. c.* 2. §. 4 & 5.

None to fuffer, unlefs Oath be made of the Offence within ten Days, before a Juftice.

And Profecution thereupon within Three Months after the Offence committed.

And Conviction by the Oath of Two Witneffes.

<table>
<tr><td>*Offences.*</td><td>**Conspiracies.**</td><td>*Penalties.*</td></tr>
</table>

[Qu. Seff.] BUtchers, Brewers, Bakers, Poulter-ers, Cooks, Cofter-Mongers or Fruiterers, who confpire, or promife together, that they will not fell their Victuals but at certain Prices. Stat. 2 & 3 *Ed.* 6. *c.* 15. §. 1.

Firft Offence, 10 *l.* to the King, and if not paid in fix Days after Conviction, twenty Days Imprifonment, with Bread and Water.

Second Offence, 20 *l.* and if not paid in fix Days, Pillory.

Third Offence, 40 *l.* and if not paid in fix Days, Pillory again, Lofs of an Ear, and infamous.

<table>
<tr><td>*Offences.*</td><td>**Constables.**</td><td>*Penalties.*</td></tr>
</table>

[One] COnftables, &c. neglecting their Duty in putting the Vagrant Act in Execution, &c. Stat. 13 *Geo.* 2. *c.* 24.

Forfeit for every Offence not exceeding 5 *l.* or lefs than 10 *s.* for the Ufe of the Poor, to be levied by Diftrefs.

[Two] *Conftables* neglecting to put the Acts of Par-liament in Force againft unlicenfed Alehoufe-keepers. Stat: 3 *Car.* 1. *c.* 3.

To forfeit 40 *s.* for the Ufe of the Poor.

If Conftables, Headboroughs, or Tithing-men die, or go out of the Parifh, may fwear new ones, till the Lord of the Manor holds a Court-Leet, or till the next Quarter-Seffions. Stat. 13 & 14 *Car.* 2. *c.* 12. §. 9.

See 13 *Geo.* 2. *c.* 24. in *Dalton,* Chap. 196.

<table>
<tr><td>*Offences.*</td><td>**Conventicles.**</td><td>*Penalties.*</td></tr>
</table>

[One] PErfons of the Age of Sixteen or upwards, Subjects of this Realm, who fhall be pre-fent at any Conventicle, under Pretence of Exercife of Religion, in other Manner than according to the Church of *England,* to the Number of Five, or more, befides thofe of the Houfhold.

Confeffion, Two Witneffes, or notorious Evidence of the Fact. Stat. 22 *Car.* 2. *c.* 1. §. 1.

Proteftant Diffenters are exempt from the Penalties of this Act, by Stat. 1 *W.* & *M. c.* 18. §. 4.

To record the Offence, which is a Conviction, and fet a Fine of Five Shillings, for the firft Offence; which Record muft be certified to the next Quarter-Seffions.

Second Offence Ten Shillings, to be levied by Di-ftrefs, &c. or in Cafe of Poverty, on the Goods of others then convicted of the like Offence at the fame Conventicle, not exceeding Ten Pounds on any one Perfon.

Penalties to be levied by Conftables, &c. per War-rant of a Juftice; and delivered to the Juftice, and he to pay one Third for the King's Ufe into the Quarter-Seffions.

Another Third to the Poor of the Parifh where, &c.

The other Third to the Informer, and to fuch as he fhall think fit.

Perfons convicted of Preaching at any fuch Meeting. Stat. 22 *Car.* 2. *c.* 1.

Not to extend to Proteftant Diffenters, by Stat. 1 *W.* & *M. c.* 18. §. 8.

Forfeit for firft Offence 20 *l.*

And if a Stranger, and his Name or Habitation not known, or he can't be found, or unable to pay.

Penalty to be levied on any Perfons that were pre-fent.

Second Offence 40 *l.* to be levied and difpofed *ut fupra.*

Perfon convicted of wittingly fuffering any fuch Meeting to be held in his Houfe, Yard, &c. Stat. 22 *Car.* 2. *c.* 1. §. 4.

Twenty Pounds, to be levied and difpofed *ut fupra.* And in Cafe of Poverty upon Perfons prefent.

Conftables, &c. knowing, or being informed of fuch Meetings within their Precinct, and who fhall not inform

Forfeit Five Pounds, to be levied and difpofed *ut fupra.*

f

A P P E N D I X.

Offences.   **Conventicles.**   *Penalties.*

inform a Juſtice or Chief Magiſtrate, &c. but ſhall wilfully omit their Duty, on Conviction. Stat. 22 *Car.* 2. *c.* 1. §. 12.

Note ; Juſtices and Chief Magiſtrates, &c. omitting their Duty, forfeit One hundred Pounds : One Moiety to the Informer, to be recovered in any of the Courts at *Weſtminſter*. *Ibid.*

[**Two**] Or Conſtables, &c. by Warrant from them, may with what Aſſiſtance they think fit, break and enter any Houſe where they ſhall be informed any ſuch Conventicle is, within Liberties and without, and take into Cuſtody the Perſons ſo aſſembled : And the Lieutenants, Deputy-Lieutenants, or any commiſſionated Officer of the Militia, or other the King's Forces with Horſe and Foot, and the Sheriffs and other Miniſters of Juſtice, with ſuch Aſſiſtance as they ſhall think fit, on Certificate under Hand and Seal of any Juſtice of Peace or Chief Magiſtrate, of ſuch Meeting, that he is not able to ſuppreſs, may diſſolve ſuch Meetings, and take the Perſons preſent into Cuſtody. Stat. 22 *Car.* 2. *c.* 1. §. 9.

Not to extend to Proteſtant Diſſenters.

No Dwelling-houſe of a Peer, where he or his Wife ſhall be reſident, to be ſearched but by Warrant under the Sign Manual, or in the Preſence of the Lieutenant, or one Deputy-Lieutenant, or Two Juſtices of Peace. *Quorum* 1. Stat. 22 *Car.* 2. *c.* 1. §. 10.

[**Qu. Seſſ.**] To deliver the King's Third of the Penalties incurred by this Act to the Sheriff, and to make a Record of ſuch Payment and Delivery, which ſhall diſcharge the Juſtices, and charge the Sheriff, both which are to be certified into the *Exchequer*. Stat. 22 *Car.* 2. *c.* 1. §. 2.

Where the Sum charged upon any Offender exceeds Ten Shillings, he may, within a Week, appeal in Writing to the Quarter-Seſſions, to whom the Juſtices, &c. ſhall return the Money levied, and certify under Hand and Seal the Evidence, with the whole Record and the ſaid Appeal, whereupon ſuch Offender may plead, and have his Trial by a Jury, and if he proſecute not with Effect, or be not acquitted, or Judgment paſs not for him, he ſhall pay treble Coſts ; ſuch Appeal is final. Stat. 22 *Car.* 2. *c.* 1. §. 6.

Note ; All Proſecutions upon the Stat. 22 *Car.* 2. *c.* 1. to be within Three Months after the Offence.

Vide Title **Church.**

Offences.   **Convicts.**   *Penalties.*

[**Two**] ANY Perſon having the Benefit of his Clergy, and being committed to the Houſe of Correction, and eſcaping out of Priſon, and being retaken. Stat. 5 *Ann. c.* 6. §. 3. *Quorum* 1.

To be committed to ſome Houſe of Correction, or publick Workhouſe, in the Place where retaken, without Bail or Mainpriſe, for not leſs than twelve Months, and not exceeding four Years, to be ſet to work, and kept to hard Labour.

Offences.   **Coopers.**   *Penalties.*

BRewers not putting their Drink in a Veſſel marked by a *Cooper*. Stat. 23 *H.* 8. *c.* 4.

Three Shillings and four Pence a Barrel.

[**Qu. Seſſ.**] The Rates and Prices which *Coopers* are to ſell their Veſſels at, to be ſet in Seſſions after *Eaſter* yearly. Stat. 8 *Eliz. c.* 9. §. 5.

Offences.   **Corn.**   *Penalties.*

[**Qu. Seſſ.**] AFTER *Michaelmas* and *Eaſter*, yearly, they are, by the Oaths of Two or more Perſons of the reſpective Counties, where foreign Corn or Grain ſhall be imported, not concerned in importing it, and of 20 *l. per Annum* Freehold, or 50 *l. per Annum* Leaſehold, or by ſuch other Means as they ſhall think fit, to determine the Market-Prices of midling *Engliſh* Corn, and to certify the ſame with Two ſuch Oaths to the Officer of the Cuſtoms, to be hung up in the Cuſtom-houſe there. Stat. 1 *Jac.* 2. *c.* 19. §. 3.
To be done in *London*, in *October* and *April*, by the Lord Mayor, Aldermen, and Juſtices of Peace there.

Vide Title **Orchard.**

See 2 *Geo.* 2. *c.* 18.   5 *Geo.* 2. *c.* 12.   11 *Geo.* 2. *c.* 22. in *Dalton*, Chap. 27. Tit. *Corn.*

Offences.   **Coroner.**   *Penalties.*

[**Qu. Seſſ.**] COroner not doing his Duty without Fee, where a Perſon is ſlain by Miſadventure. Stat. 1 *Hen.* 8. *c.* 7. §. 1.

Forty Shillings.

APPENDIX.

Offences. ..... **Costs.** ..... *Penalties.*

WHERE *Costs* are given upon an Appeal, from an Order of Settlement of the Poor determin'd; or where Notice is given, and the Person order'd to pay such Costs, dwells out of the Jurisdiction of the Court, which gave the Costs. Stat. 8 & 9 *W.* 3. *c.* 30.

Producing a true Copy of the Order for Costs, on Oath of one Witness.

The Costs to be levied by Warrant of one Justice of the County where the Party dwells, by Distress and Sale; and for Want of Distress, the Party to be committed to the common Gaol for Twenty Days.

Note; Upon an Appeal, the Appellant is to give Bond of 20 *l.* with one or more Sureties to the Liking of a Justice, to pay such Costs as the Court shall award, in one Month after the Appeal is heard. Stat. 4 & 5 *W.* & *M. c.* 7.

Offences. ..... **Cottages.** ..... *Penalties.*

[**Qu. Sess.**] ERecting a Cottage for Habitation, without Four Acres of Freehold.
Continuance of it. Stat. 31 *Eliz. c.* 7. §. 1.

Ten Pounds to the Queen.

Forty Shillings a Month to the Queen.

Owner or Occupier of a Cottage, suffering any more Families than one to dwell there. Stat. 31 *Eliz. c. 7.* §. 3.

Ten Shillings a Month to the Lord of the Leet.

Note; The Stat. 31 *Eliz. c.* 7. extends not to Cottages in Cities, Boroughs, or Markets-Towns, or provided for Labourers in Mines or Quarries, within one Mile of them; or for Sea-faring Men within a Mile of the Sea, or a navigable River; or for Keeper, Warrener, Shepherd, or Herdsman; or an impotent Person; or to Cottages, which by Order of Justices of Assise, or Justices of Peace in Sessions, shall be decreed to continue for Habitation. Stat. 31 *Eliz. c.* 7. §. 4.

Offences. ..... **County-Courts.** ..... *Penalties.*

[**One**] SHeriff, Under-Sheriff, or Sheriff's Clerk, entring in the *County-Court*, any Plaint in the Absence of the Plaintiff or his Attorney, or having above one Plaint for one Cause. Stat. 11 *H.* 7. *c.* 15.

Forty Shillings, to be divided between the King and the Prosecutor.

To examine this Matter; and if the Party be found guilty, to certify the Examination into the *Exchequer* within three Months, on Pain of Forty Shillings.
The Certificate is a Conviction.

The Officer who collects the Estreats out of the *County-Court*, if he levies more than is contain'd in them. *Ibid.*

Forty Shillings; the Matter to be examined and certified *ut supra.*

The Defendant in the *County-Court* not having lawful Summons, the Bailiff being found Faulty.

Forty Shillings, upon Examination, &c. *ut supra.*

[**Two**] To view the Estreats of Sheriffs before they issue them out of the *County-Court*; and there are to be Two Parts of them indented and sealed by the Justices and Sheriff; and one Part is to remain with the Justices, and the other with the Sheriff. Stat. 11 *H.* 7. *c.* 15.

Vide Title **Sheriffs.**

Offences. ..... **Currier.** ..... *Penalties.*

[**Qu. Sess.**] CUrrier currying Hide or Skin insufficiently tann'd and dried, or out of his own House, in some Corporate or Market-Town, or gashing or spoiling them. Stat. 1 *Jac.* 1. *c.* 22. §. 22.

Six Shillings and eight Pence a Skin or Hide, besides the Value of the same.

To be divided; one Third to the King, one to the Prosecutor, and the other to the City, Borough, Town, or Lord of the Liberty where the Offence is committed.

And to the Party grieved, twice so much as he impairs.

Persons in *London*, or Three Miles, putting any Leather to be curried to any but Freemen of the Curriers Company. *Ibid.* §. 23.

Forfeit the same, or the Value.

To be divided in Thirds; one to the Seisor, another to the Chamber of *London*, the Third to the Poor.

Within the Jurisdiction of *London*, Persons putting into made Wares any curried Leather, before it be searched and sealed. *Ibid.* §. 24.

Six Shillings and eight Pence a Hide or Skin, and the Value of every such Hide or Skin, to be divided in *London*, *ut supra.*

Currier ..... Six

APPENDIX.

Currier.

Offences. — *Penalties.*

Currier úfing the Art of a *Tanner, Cordwainer, Shoemaker, Butcher,* or any other who ufeth cutting of Leather. *Ibid.* §. 25.

Six Shillings and eight Pence for every Hide or Skin he cutteth during the Time. To be divided *ut fupra.*

Currier (fufficient Stuff being tender'd unto him) refufing fufficiently to curry Leather within Eight Days in Summer, and Sixteen in Winter, after he takes it in Hand. *Ibid.* §. 24.

Ten Shillings for every Hide or Piece not curried.

Currier in *London* not currying his Leather fufficiently, other Artificers (ufing tanned and curried Leather) putting into his Wares Leather infufficiently tanned or curried. *Ibid.* §. 44.

The Wares, and, the juft Value, to be divided in Thirds in *London, ut fupra.*

See Tit. **Leather, Shoemakers,** and **Tanners.**

Curfing. *Vide* Title **Swearing** and **Curfing.**

Custom-house Officer.

Offences. — *Penalties.*

[One] Perfons refifting, abufing, beating, &c. *Cuftom-houfe* Officers, or their Deputies, in the Execution of their Office. Stat. 13 & 14 *Car.* 2. c. 11. §. 6.

To be committed till the next Quarter-Seffions, and fined then, not exceeding One hundred Pounds, and to remain in Prifon till difcharged by Order of *Exchequer,* or difcover who fet them on Work.

Carman, or other Perfon, affifting in taking up, landing, fhipping, or carrying away any Goods, &c. without a Warrant, or in the Prefence of one or more *Officers of the Cuftoms.* Stat. 13 & 14 *Car.* 2. c. 11. §. 7.

Two Witneffes.

Firft Offence, to be committed till he find Sureties for the Good Behaviour, or be difcharged by the Lord Treafurer, Chancellor, Under-Treafurer, or Barons of the *Exchequer.*
Second Offence, to be committed for Two Months, or till he pay five Pounds to the Sheriff, for the King's Ufe, or be difcharged by the Lord Treafurer, &c.

Perfons armed with Clubs, or any Manner of Weapon, tumultuoufly affembled in the Day or Night, to the Number of Eight or more, their Aiders and Affiftants forcibly hindring, wounding or beating *Cuftom-houfe Officers* in the due Execution of their Office. Stat. 6 *Geo.* 1. c. 21. §. 33.

Being convicted, fhall by Order of Court be *tranfported* for fuch Term as the Court fhall think fit, not exceeding feven Years, in the fame Manner as Felons are by 4 *Geo.* 1. c. 11.

Such Offender returning into *Great Britain* or *Ireland,* before the Expiration of the faid Term. Stat. 6 *Geo.* 1. c. 21. §. 34.

Felony without Benefit of Clergy.

See Tit. **Smuglers,** and *Dalton,* Chap. 33.

Cyder-maker. *Vide* Title **Excife.**

Deer.

Offences. — *Penalties.*

[One] Perfons courfing, killing, hunting or taking away *Red* or *Fallow Deer,* in any Ground where Deer are kept, without Confent of the Owner, or Perfons chiefly intrufted therewith, or are aiding therein. Stat. 13 *Car.* 2. c. 10. §. 2.
Confeffion, or one Witnefs.
Profecution within Six Months.

20 l. to be levied by Diftrefs and Sale; for Want of Diftrefs, to be committed to the Houfe of Correction for Six Months, or to the common Gaol for a Year, not to be difcharged but upon Security for the Good Behaviour for a Year, after Enlargement.

Perfons unlawfully courfing, hunting, taking in Toils, killing, wounding, or taking away any *Red* or *Fallow Deer,* in any Foreft, &c. without the Confent of the Owner, or be aiding therein. Stat. 3 & 4 *W. & M.* c. 10. §. 2.
Confeffion, or Oath of one Witnefs.
Profecution to be in Twelve Months; and where the Offence is committed, or Party apprehended.

Twenty Pounds for the Offence of Hunting, &c.
And for every Deer taken or killed 30 l. to be levied by Diftrefs and Sale.
One Third to the Informer, the other to the Poor, and the Reft to the Owner.
For Want of Diftrefs twelve Months Imprifonment, and to be fet in the Pillory for an Hour, in fome Market-Town next to the Place.

4

To

APPENDIX.

Offences.	Deer.	Penalties.

To grant a Warrant to Constables, Headboroughs and Tithing-men, when Deer are stolen, to search as for stolen Goods. Stat. 3 & 4 W. & M. c. 10. §. 3. See Stat. 9 Geo. 1. c. 22. §. 11.

Offences	Penalties
If upon Search any Venison, or Skins of Deer, or Toils be found, and the Persons can give no good Account how they came by them, nor in some convenient Time produce the Person of whom they bought them, or prove such Sale upon Oath. Stat. 3 & 4 W. & M. c. 10. §. 3. Confession, or Oath of one Witness.	The same Penalties with the Deer-Stealer. And to be levied and employed *ut supra*.
Persons in the Night-time, pulling down or destroying the Pales or Walls of any Park, Forest, &c. or other Ground inclosed, where Red or Fallow Deer shall be kept. Stat. 3 & 4 W. & M. c. 10. §. 9. Oath of one Witness.	Three Months Imprisonment.
[Qu. Sess.] Unlawfully entring into any Park, Woods, or other Grounds inclosed, and there killing or chasing the Deer. Stat. 5 Eliz. c. 21. §. 7.	Three Months Imprisonment, to be bound to the Good Behaviour for Seven Years. Treble Damages to the Party grieved. Upon the Offender's Acknowledgment in Sessions, and Satisfaction to the Party, the Behaviour may be released.

Vide Title **Deer**, &c. in Title **Game.**

Offences.	Deer-Stealers.	Penalties.

Offences	Penalties
[One] KEepers or other Officers of any Forest, Chase, Purlieu, Paddock, Wood, Park, or Place where Deer are usually kept, convicted of Killing or Taking away any Red or Fallow Deer, or being aiding therein without the Consent of the Owner, or Person chiefly intrusted with the Custody of such Forests, &c. Stat. 5 Geo. 1. c. 15. §. 5.	50 l. for each Deer. To be levied by Distress, and distributed as Forfeitures are, by 3 & 4 W. & M. c. 10. For Want of Distress Three Years Imprisonment, without Bail or Mainprise, and to be set in the Pillory for Two Hours on the Market-Day.
Persons pulling down, or destroying, or causing to be pulled down or destroyed, the Pales or Walls of any Park, Forest, &c. where Red or Fallow Deer shall be then kept without the Owner's Consent. One Witness. Stat. 5 Geo. 1. c. 15. §. 6.	Subject to the like Forfeitures and Penalties as for killing Deer.

May on Confirmation of any Conviction of Deer-stealing, by Superior Courts at Westminster, and Delivery of the Rule, proceed against the Party convicted in the same Manner as if a Procedendo had been granted. Stat. 5 Geo. 1. c. 15. §. 2.

Offences	Penalties
Convicts before discharged, to be bound to the Person offended in Fifty Pounds for their Good Behaviour, and not to offend in like Manner, and on Failure or Refusal, to be committed to the County-Gaol till so bound. And if afterwards convicted on the Stat. 3 & 4 W. & M. c. 10. the Penalty of the Bond is forfeited, to be recovered with full Costs of Suit in any of the Courts at Westminster, and likewise liable to the Penalties and Forfeitures in the said Statute. Stat. 5 Geo. 1. c. 15. §. 4.	Penalties to be distributed in the same Manner as Forfeitures are by 3 & 4 W. & M.
No Certiorari for removing Convictions of Deer-stealing, or other Proceedings upon the Stat. 3 & 4 W. & M. c. 10. to be allowed, unless he first give Securities to the Justices who convicted him in Sixty Pounds for each Offence, to prosecute it, and to pay the Justice the Forfeitures due, &c. or render the Party convicted to the Justice in a Month after Conviction confirmed, or Procedendo granted. Stat. 5 Geo. 1. c. 15. §. 1.	In Default of Rendring, &c. the Justice may proceed to execute the Conviction, as if no Certiorari had been.

[Qu. Sess.] Justices of Gaol-Delivery by Order of Court to transport, for Seven Years to his Majesty's Plantations in America, Persons convicted upon Indictment of Entring Parks, &c. with armed Force, and wilfully wounding or killing Red or Fallow Deer there. Stat. 5 Geo. 1. c. 28. §. 1.

Offenders punished by this Act, not punishable by any other.

Persons

APPENDIX.

Perfons being armed with Swords, &c. and having their Faces blacked, or otherwife difguifed, fhall appear and unlawfully hunt, kill, or fteal any *Red* or *Fallow Deer*, &c. being thereof lawfully convicted, fhall fuffer Death as a Felon. 9 *Geo.* 1. *c.* 22. §. 1.

Where any Venifon or Skin of a Deer fhall be found in the Cuftody of a Perfon, and it fhall appear the Perfon bought it of One who might be juftly fufpected to come by it unlawfully, and he doth not produce the Party of whom he bought it, or prove on Oath his Name and Place of his Abode, then the Perfon who bought it fhall be convicted of fuch, by One or more Juftices.	Shall be fubject to the Penalties inflicted for killing a Deer, by the Act 3 & 4 *W.* Offences againft the Act 3 & 4 *IV.* fhall be commenced within Three Years from the Time of the Offence, but not after. 9 *Geo.* 1. *c.* 22. §. 13. This Act, commonly called the *Black-Act*, is continued by 10 *Geo.* 1. *c.* 32. to 1ft of *Septem.* 1744, &c.

Deferters. *Vide* **Soldiers** and **Mariners.**

(*Proteftant.*)

[One] Diffenters refuling to make and fubfcribe the Declaration in 30 *Car.* 2. and to take the Oaths, which came in the Room of the Oaths of Allegiance and Supremacy. Stat. 1 *W. & M. feff.* 1. *c.* 18. §. 12. *Vide* 10 *Ann. c.* 2. §. 7, 8.	To be committed without Bail, and their Names to be certified to the Quarter-Seffions.
Perfons refuling the Oath when tender'd. Stat. 1 *W. & M. feff.* 1. *c.* 18. §. 12. *Vide* 10 *Ann. c.* 2. §. 7, 8.	To enter into a Recognizance with two Sureties of 50 *l.* for their producing a Certificate under the Hands of Six of the Proteftant Congregation, whereof he is one ; Two Proteftant Witneffes, or a Certificate under the Hands of Four Church of *England* Proteftants, that he is a Proteftant.

May require Diffenting Teachers, preaching in any Congregation in fuch Counties where they have not qualified themfelves as the Toleration-Act directs, to take the Oath and Declaration of Allegiance and Fidelity. Stat. 10 *Ann. c.* 2.

[Qu. Seff.] Difturbing any Proteftant Diffenting Teacher. Stat. 1 *W. & M. c.* 18. Two Witneffes.	Twenty Pounds.

The Acts of 10 *Ann. c.* 2. in Part, and 12 *Ann. c.* 7. excluding Diffenters from Offices, repealed by 5 *Geo.* 1. *c.* 4. But Magiftrates knowingly or willingly reforting to, or being prefent at Meetings in *England*, *Wales*, *Berwick* upon *Tweed*, or the Ifles of *Jerfey* or *Guernfey*, with the *Infignia* or Habits of Office, are difabled, &c. §. 2.

[One] ONE convicted for being drunk. Stat. 4 *Jac.* 1. *c.* 5. §. 2. 21 *Jac.* 1. *c.* 7. §. 3. View, one Witnefs, or Confeffion. The Profecution to be within Six Months.	Five Shillings, for the Poor, where, &c. for the Firft Offence, within a Week, or to be levied by Diftrefs and Sale after fix Days. And for Want of Diftrefs, to fit in the Stocks Six Hours. For the Second Offence, to be bound in Two Sureties in Ten Pounds to the Good Behaviour.
Alehoufe-keeper convicted of Drunkennefs. Stat. 21 *Jac.* 1. *c.* 7. §. 4. Conviction *ut fupra.*	Difabled to keep an Alehoufe for Three Years.

Dyers. See 13 *Geo.* 1. *c.* 24. *Dalton*, Chap. 35.

[One] ONE accufed of Manflaughter or Felony, who for Want of Bail is to be fent to the Gaol, muft be *examined* before he fend him ; and the Accufers muft be bound over to give Evidence, whofe Information muft be taken in Writing. Stat. 2 & 3 *Phil. & Mar. c.* 10.

I

A P P E N D I X.

Examinations muſt be ſeveral, and given in Writing; and if it be a large Felony, they are to be certified to the next Aſſiſes; and if a ſmall Felony, then to the Seſſions; or the Juſtice may be fined by the Judge. If a Felon upon Examination confeſſeth the Fact, the Juſtice muſt take his Name ſubſcrib'd to his Confeſſion.

Offences.　　　　　　　　**Excise.**　　　　　　　　*Penalties.*

[One] ALL Informations, Complaints, and other Proceedings before Juſtices, by Virtue of the Stat. 6 *Geo.* 1. *c.* 21. or any other Act or Acts whatſoever, relating to the Duties of Excife, or any other Duty under the Management of the Commiſſioners of Excife, to be entred and inrolled in *Engliſh.* §. 23.

[Two] Perfons oppoſing, moleſting, or obſtructing the *Officers* of *Excife* in the due Execution of the Powers or Authorities given by the Stat. 6 *Geo.* 1. *c.* 21. or any other Act or Acts relating to the Duties of Ex- cife. §. 7.	Forfeit Ten Pounds, to be ſued for, recovered and levied, or mitigated by ſuch Ways and Means and Methods, as Penalties, *&c.* may by any Law of Ex- cife.

(Brandy.)

All Diſtillers, Makers or Sellers of, or Dealers in Brandy, Arrack, Rum, Strong-Waters, or Spirits, by Wholeſale or Retail, to make true Entry in Writing of all Ware-houſes, Store-houſes, Rooms, Shops, Cel- lars, and Vaults, made Uſe of for keeping Brandy, *&c.* for Sale, at the next Excife-Office. Stat. 6 *Geo.* 1. *c.* 21. §. 11.	On Penalty of forfeiting 20 *l.* for every ſuch Ware- houſe, *&c.* ſo made Uſe of without Entry. To be ſued for, recovered and levied, or mitigated, in the ſame Manner as any Penalty or Forfeitures may by any the Laws of Excife. One Moiety to the King, the other to the Informer. §. 14. *Vide* Title **Brewers.**
All Perſons who ſhall become Diſtillers, Makers or Sellers of, or Dealers in Brandy, *&c.* to make like Entry of Warehouſes, *&c.* before they take into their Cuſtody or Poſſeſſion any Brandy, *&c.* Stat. 6 *Geo.* 1. *c.* 21. §. 12.	On the like Penalty of 20 *l.* for every ſuch Ware- houſe, *&c.* ſo made Uſe of without Entry. To be levied, mitigated and divided, *ut ſupra.*
No Brandy, *&c.* to be brought into ſuch Warehouſe, *&c.* by Diſtillers, *&c.* without firſt giving Notice to Excife-Officer, and producing to, and leaving with him, an Authentick Certificate, that the Duties of ſuch Brandies, *&c.* have been actually paid or condemned as forfeited, or was Part of the Stock of ſome Im- porter, Diſtiller or Maker, who paid the Duty. Stat. 6 *Geo.* 1. *c.* 21. §. 13.	On Penalty of forfeiting the Brandy, *&c.* ſo brought in without Notice or Certificate, together with the Caſk and Veſſel.
Diſtiller, Maker, Seller or Dealer in Brandy, *&c.* hindring or refuſing Officers of Excife to enter into their Warehouſes, *&c.* to take an Account of Brandy, *&c.* or ſhall let, hinder or obſtruct Officers in exe- cuting Powers given them by the Stat. 6 *Geo.* 1. *c.* 21. Stat. 6 *Geo.* 1. *c.* 21. §. 14.	50 *l.* for every Offence. To be ſued for, levied, mitigated and divided, *ut ſupra.*
No Brandy, *&c.* to be ſold, uttered, or expoſed to Sale by Wholeſale or Retail, but when the ſame ſhall be in ſome or one of the ſaid Warehouſes, *&c.* ſo entred. Stat. 6 *Geo.* 1. *c.* 21. §. 15.	On Penalty of 40 *s.* for every Gallon, *&c.* To be levied, mitigated and divided, *ut ſupra.*
No Brandy, *&c.* exceeding a Gallon, to be removed or carried from any Part of *Great Britain* to another, by Land or Water, without a Permit or Certificate from one of the Officers of Excife. Stat. 6 *Geo.* 1. *c.* 21. §. 17.	On Penalty of forfeiting the Brandy, *&c.* ſo re- moved, together with the Caſk or Veſſel.

Note; Perſons who ſhall have in their Cuſtody any Brandy, *&c.* exceeding the Quantity of Sixty-three Gallons, are deemed Sellers of Brandy, *&c.* and are ſubject to the Survey of the Officers of Excife. Stat. 6 *Geo.* 1. *c.* 21. §. 18.

Juſtices reſiding near the Place where a Seiſure of Brandy, *&c.* clandeſtinely imported, ſhall be made, to ſummon the Perſon in whoſe Cuſtody ſuch Brandy, *&c.* was found, to appear before them, and upon the Appearance or Default of ſuch Perſon ſo ſummoned, may in a ſummary Way proceed upon, hear, examine into, determine, and give Judgment for the Condemnation of ſuch Brandy, *&c.* And if it ſhall be found to be for- feited,

(Brandy.)

feited, to iffue out their Warrant for Sale of fuch Brandy, &c. together with the Cafk or Veffel. Stat. 6 *Geo.* 1. *c.* 21. §. 20.

Judgment of the Juftices is final, and not liable to *Appeal* or *Certiorari.*

When Brandy, &c. is feifed as aforefaid, and no Claim made in twenty Days, the Officer muft caufe publick Notice to be given by Proclamation the next Market-Day after the faid twenty Days, of the Day and Place when and where the Juftices will proceed to examine into the Caufe of fuch Seifure, and to give Judgment for the Condemnation of fuch Brandy, &c. fo feifed.

Judgment final, and not liable to Appeal or *Certiorari.* Stat. 6 *Geo.* 1. *c.* 21. §. 21.

Note; In both the laft Cafes, Juftices have no Jurifdiction within the Limits of the Chief Excife-Office in *London.* Nor in Cafes where the Seifure is made for unlawful Importation, and the whole Quantity of Brandy, &c. at any one Time for that Caufe feifed, doth exceed 63 Gallons. Stat. 6 *Geo.* 1. *c.* 21. §. 20.

Offences	Penalties
Mafter and Purfer of any Ship who fhall fuffer any *Brandy, &c.* or other uncuftomed or prohibited Goods, to be put out of his Ship or Veffel into any Hoy, Lighter, Boat, or Bottom, to be laid on Land; or fhall fuffer any *Wool, Woolfells, Mortlings, Shortlings, Yarn made of Wool, Woolftocks, Fullers-Earth, Fulling-Clay, or Tobacco-pipe Clay,* to be put on board fuch Ship to be carried beyond Sea. Stat. *6 Geo.* 1. *c.* 21. §. 32.	If convicted, fhall (befides the Penalties and Forfeitures to which they will be liable by any Law now in Being) fuffer fix Months Imprifonment without Bail or Mainprife.

(Brewers.)

[**One**] To take the Oath of two able Artifts to compute the Contents and Gauge of all Brewing-Veffels. Stat. 15 *Car.* 2. *c.* 11. §. 7.

Offences	Penalties
[**Two**] Brewers not making true Entries once a Week. Stat. 12 *Car.* 2. *c.* 23 & 24. §. 16, 17. 1 *W.* & *M. Seff* 1. *c.* 24. One Witnefs, or Confeffion. The Profecution muft be within three Months.	Five Pounds; and ten Pounds more, to be levied by Diftrefs and Sale, if not redeemed in fourteen Days; and for want of Diftrefs, to be imprifoned till Satisfaction made. The Forfeiture may be mitigated, fo as it be not lefs than double the Duty of Excife, befides Cofts and Charges. Three Fourths to the King, and one to the Informer, after Charges deducted. *Note*; The firft Warrant muft be returned, that there is no Diftrefs, before a fecond Warrant can iffue, to take the Body.
Brewers not paying within a Week, and Retailers within a Month after making their Entries. Stat. 12 *Car.* 2. *c.* 23. §. 17. *c.* 24. §. 31. Profecution and Conviction *ut fupra.*	Double the Duty, to be levied and mitigated *ut fupra.*
Brewers, Victuallers, and Diftillers, refufing Gaugers to enter; and being forbid by Gaugers to fell, felling, or delivering out any Liquors, not having paid the Duty. Stat. 12 *Car.* 2. *c.* 23. §. 19. *c.* 24. §. 32. 1 *W.* & *M. Seff.* 1. *c.* 24. Profecution and Conviction *ut fupra.*	Five Pounds; and ten Pounds more, over and above the double Value. To be levied, mitigated and divided, *ut fupra.*
Brewers making falfe Entries. Stat. 12 *Car.* 2. *c.* 23. §. 23. Profecution and Conviction *ut fupra.*	Over and above the faid Penalties, forfeits his Allowance for Wafte and Leakage for fix Months.
Brewer, or Retailer, without giving Notice at the next Excife-Office, fetting up, altering or enlarging any Tun, Fat, Back, Cooler, or Copper, and ufing them, or keeping any private Store-houfe for laying fuch Liquors in Cafk. Stat. 15 *Car.* 2. *c.* 11. §. 1. 1 *W.* & *M. Seff.* 1. *c.* 24. Two Witneffes. Informations to be brought in three Months, and Notice given in a Week after Information brought.	Fifty Pounds for every Tun, &c. to be levied by Diftrefs and Sale; and for want, to be committed to the County-Gaol for three Months. One Third to the King, one Third to the Poor, and one Third to the Informer. Two hundred Pounds by Stat. 8 *W.* 3. *c.* 19. §. 8.

Offences.	Excise.	Penalties.
	(*Brewers.*)	

Offences.	Penalties.
Perfons in whofe Occupation the Houfe, &c. is, where a concealed Tun, &c. fhall be difcovered. Stat. 15 *Car.* 2. *c.* 11. §. 1. Profecution and Conviction *ut fupra.* *Note* ; There muft be an Adjudication of this fpecifick Forfeiture before the Juftices, before a Sale for the Ufe of the Poor, or a Diftribution amongft them.	Fifty Pounds, to be levied and employed *ut fupra.* Or he to be punifhed *ut fupra* ; and alfo fuch Tun, &c. with the Beer, &c. to be feifed and delivered to the Overfeers of the Poor, to be fold for their Ufe, or diftributed amongft them.
Brewers delivering, or carrying out Ale, or Beer, to his Cuftomers in any City, &c. before Notice, unlefs between three in the Morning and nine in the Evening, from *March* 25 to *September* 29, unlefs between five in the Morning and feven in the Evening, from 29 *Sept.* to 25 *March.* Stat. 15 *Car.* 2. *c.* 11. §. 11. Conviction, and Profecution, *ut fupra.*	Twenty Shillings a Barrel, to be levied and employed, and the Party punifhed *ut fupra.*
Brewers converting fmall Drink into ftrong, by Mixture, after the Gauge taken, without Notice to a Gauger, or hiding, or concealing Drink ungauged. Stat. 15 *Car.* 2. *c.* 11. §. 12. Conviction, and Profecution, *ut fupra.*	Twenty Shillings a Barrel, to be levied and employed, and the Party punifhed *ut fupra.*
Brewers not fhewing to the Gaugers all the Beer, Ale, or Worts of every Guile. Stat. 1 *W. & M. Seff.* 1. *c.* 24. §. 10. Conviction, and Profecution, *ut fupra.*	To have no Benefit of the *Provifo* in 15 *Car.* 2. touching Mif-entry, and incurs all the Penalties impofed by the former Acts.
Brewers or Victuallers cleanfing before the whole Guile is brewed off. Stat. 7 *W.* 3. *c.* 30. §. 21.	Forty Shillings a Barrel, to be recovered and employed *ut fupra.*
Brewers or Victuallers, refufing Gauger to enter and ftay in his Brewhoufe, to fee the Guile brewed off. Stat. 7 *W.* 3. *c.* 30. §. 22.	Twenty Pounds, to be recovered and employed *ut fupra.*
Brewer or Inn-keeper, upon carrying out Drink, or after carried out, mixing any Small with Strong, upon the Dray, or in the Victualler's Cellar. Stat. 7 *W.* 3. *c.* 30. §. 23.	Five Pounds, to be recovered and employed *ut fupra.*
Brewer, Diftiller, or any other, obftructing the Officer in fearching for private Tun, Back, Cafk, &c. Stat. 7 *W.* 3. *c.* 30. §. 27.	Twenty Pounds, to be recovered and employed *ut fupra.*
Brewer refufing to declare his Length. Stat. 8 & 9 *W.* 3. *c.* 18. §. 2.	Twenty Shillings a Barrel for the whole Guile ; to be recovered and employed *ut fupra,* and to be charged ftrong.
Brewer making any Increafe, or found laid off, after the Length declared. Stat. 8 & 9 *W.* 3. *c.* 18. §. 2.	Five Pounds a Barrel, to be recovered and employed *ut fupra.*
Brewer's Servant concerned in making fuch Increafe. Stat. 8 & 9 *W.* 3. *c.* 18. §. 2.	Twenty Shillings, to be recovered and employed *ut fupra.*
Brewer keeping any private Pipe or Conveyance, &c. or Hole in any Tun, &c. Stat. 8 & 9 *W.* 3. *c.* 18. §. 4.	One Hundred Pounds, to be recovered and employed *ut fupra.*
Brewer, or other Perfon obftructing the Officer in fearching for fuch Pipes. Stat. 8 & 9 *W.* 3. *c.* 18. §. 6.	Fifty Pounds, to be recovered and employed *ut fupra.*
Brewers carrying out, and delivering any Wafh, Tilts, &c. to any Diftiller, or Vinegar-Maker, without Notice. Stat. 8 & 9 *W.* 3. *c.* 18. §. 9.	Twenty Shillings a Barrel, to be recovered and employed *ut fupra.*

A P P E N D I X.

Offences.	€rcife.	*Penalties.*

(Brewers.)

Brewer, Innkeeper, &c. ufing or mixing any Sugar, Honey, foreign Grains, *Guinea* Pepper, *Effentia Binæ, Coculus Indiæ,* or any other unwholefome Ingredients in brewing Beer, or Ale, &c. Stat. 1 *Ann. Seff.* 2. *c.* 3. §. 29.	Twenty Pounds, to be recovered and difpofed *ut fupra.*

Brewers who confpire to fell their Drink but at certain Prices. *Vide* Title **Confpiracies.**

Cyder-Makers.

[**Two**] Makers of *Cyder* concealing it. Stat. 7 *W.* 3. *c.* 30. §. 16.	40 *s.* a Hogfhead, and fo proportionably, to be levied and employed *ut fupra.*
Makers of *Cyder, &c.* refufing Gauger to enter and take Account. Stat. 7 *W.* 3. *c.* 30. §. 16.	Fifteen Pounds, to be levied and employed *ut fupra.*
Makers of *Cyder* delivering any Wafh, or Cyder to any Diftiller, or Vinegar-Maker, without Notice. Stat. 8 & 9 *W.* 3. *c.* 18. §. 9.	Twenty Shillings a Barrel, to be recovered and employed *ut fupra.*

(Diftillers.)

[**One**] Perfons making or keeping any Wafh, Cyder, or other Materials fit for Diftillation; and having in his or their Poffeffion or Occupation any Still, or Stills, containing twenty Gallons or upwards, fhall be deemed a common Diftiller. Stat. 8 & 9 *W.* 3. *c.* 18. §. 11. Conviction upon the Oath of one or more credible Witneffes.	Liable to the feveral Rates and Duties of Excife, and fubject to the Penalties and Forfeitures of this and all other Acts in Force.
When any Perfon is fufpected to conceal any Still, Back, or other Veffels, Spirits, Low-Wines, or other Materials for Diftillation. Stat. 10 & 11 *W.* 3. *c.* 4. §. 7.	Upon an Affidavit declaring the Grounds of fuch Sufpicion, to grant a Warrant to fearch for, and feife fuch Still, &c. And if not claimed by the Owner in 20 Days, to be fold by the Commiffioners of Excife.
[**Two**] Diftillers of Low-Wines, removing them after Account taken by the Gauger without drawing them off a fecond Time. Stat. 1 *W.* & *M. feff.* 1. *c.* 24. §. 3. Conviction by two Witneffes. Profecution in three Months; Notice in a Week, as againft Brewers: And fo for all other Offences.	Five Shillings a Gallon, to be levied by Diftrefs and Sale.
Diftillers, on Requeft of a Gauger in the Day-time, or in the Night, in Prefence of a Conftable, refufing to permit Gauger to enter his Dwelling-houfe. Stat. 1 *W.* & *M. feff.* 1. *c.* 24. §. 9. Conviction *ut fupra.*	Double the Value, and Five Pounds and Ten Pounds, and no Need of proving Sale, &c. before Duty paid, &c. to be levied and employed *ut fupra.*

To hear and determine Complaints of Over-charges upon Oath, or other due Proof. Stat. 1 *W.* & *M. feff.* 1. *c.* 24. §. 13.

Diftillers fetting up, making ufe of, or altering any Tun, Cafk, &c. for the Brewing, or making any Wafh, Low-Wines, or Spirits for Sale; or making ufe of any private Warehoufe, Cellar, or other Place for laying any Wafh, &c. without firft giving Notice at the next Office of Excife: And the Perfons in whofe Occupation fuch Tun, &c. fhall be found. Stat. 3 & 4 *W.* & *M. c.* 15. §. 1.	Twenty Pounds, to be levied *ut fupra.* One Moiety to the King, the other to the Informer.
Diftillers hiding, concealing, or conveying any Low-Wines, Spirits, or Strong-Waters, from the Sight of the Gauger. Stat. 3 & 4 *W.* & *M. c.* 15. §. 2.	Five Shillings a Gallon. To be recovered, as by 12 & 15 *Car.* 2. and employed *ut fupra.*
Diftillers preparing any Wafh, or other Material, before he has drawn off all the Liquors made from Corn. Stat. 7 *W.* 3. *c.* 30. §. 8.	Five Pounds a Barrel, to be levied *ut fupra.* One Moiety to the King, the other to the Informer.

I   Diftillers   Twenty

Offences.	Excise.	Penalties.

(Distillers.)

Distillers refusing Gaugers to stay in the Still-house, to see the Stills wrought off, &c. Stat. 7 W. 3. c. 30. §. 12.		Twenty Pounds, to be levied and employed *ut supra.*
Distillers carrying out Spirits, or working Stills, at other Hours than from *Michaelmas* to *Lady-Day*, between five in the Morning and eight at Night; and from *Lady-Day* to *Michaelmas*, between three in the Morning and nine at Night. Stat. 7 W. 3. c. 30. §. 15.		Ten Pounds, to be levied and employed *ut supra.*
Distiller, or any other, obstructing the Officer in Searching for private Tun, Back, Cask, &c. Stat. 7 W. 3. c. 30. §. 27.		Twenty Pounds, to be recovered and employed *ut supra.*
Distiller keeping any private Pipe, Hole, or other Conveyance, &c. from one Vessel to another. Stat. 10 & 11 W. 3. c. 4. §. 3.		One hundred Pounds, to be recovered and disposed *ut supra.*
Distiller, or other Person, obstructing the Officer in Searching for private Pipe, &c. Stat. 10 & 11 W. 3. c. 4. §. 5.		One hundred Pounds, to be recovered and disposed *ut supra.*
Distiller keeping any private Still, or other Vessel, he or other hindering the Officer in Searching for the same; and Person in whose Custody such Still or Vessel shall be found. Stat. 10 & 11 W. 3. c. 4. §. 7.		Two hundred Pounds, to be recovered and disposed *ut supra.*

Distiller receiving Cyder or Perry into his Custody, and not giving Notice to the proper Officer 48 Hours before he puts it into the Still, &c. forfeits 5 l. Stat. 11 Geo. 2. c. 1. §. 12. See *Dalton*, Chap. 61. Tit. *Malt.*

(Gaugers.)

[**Two**] Gaugers who do not weekly deliver to Brewers a true Copy, under their Hands, of the Return he charges them with. Stat. 15 Car. 2. c. 11. §. 5. Two Witnesses. Informations to be brought in three Months, and Notice given in a Week after Information brought.		40 s. for every Neglect, to be levied by Distress and Sale; and for Want, to be committed to the County-Gaol for three Months. One Third to the King, one Third to the Poor, one Third to the Informer.
Gauger taking a Bribe to make a false Return, and the Party who gives the Bribe. Stat. 15 Car. 2. c. 11. §. 16.		Ten Pounds for every Offence, to be levied and employed, or the Party punished, *ut supra.*
Gaugers not leaving Notes with Brewers of the last Gauges. Stat. 1 W. & M. sess. 1. c. 24. §. 12.		Forty Shillings, to be levied *ut supra.*

To adjudge what Satisfaction the Gaugers and Officers of the Excise shall make, where any Door or House is broken open, and no private or concealed Back, Still, or other Vessel, Spirits, Low-Wines, Wash, or other Materials for Distillation shall be found. Stat. 10 & 11 W. 3. c. 4. §. 8. *Quorum* 1.

(Makers of Mead, Vinegar, Metheglin, and Sweets.)

[**Two**] Makers of *Vinegar, Mead, Metheglin,* or *Sweets* for Sale, concealing them. Stat. 7 W. 3. c. 30. §. 16.		Forty Shillings for every Barrel of Vinegar or Sweets so hid, and so proportionably. And Five Shillings for every Gallon of Mead or Metheglin. To be levied *ut supra.* One Moiety to the King, the other to the Informer.
Makers of *Vinegar,* &c. refusing Gauger to enter and take Account. Stat. 7 W. 3. c. 30. §. 17.		15 l. to be levied and employed *ut supra.*
Makers of *Vinegar* and *Sweets,* carrying them out without Notice, at other Hours than from *Michaelmas* to *Lady-Day*, between five in the Morning and eight at Night; and from *Lady-Day* to *Michaelmas*, between three in the Morning and nine at Night. Stat. 7 W. 3. c. 30. §. 18.		40 s. a Barrel, to be recovered and employed *ut supra.*

Sweet-

APPENDIX.

(Makers of Vinegar, &c.)

Sweet-makers fetting up, or ufing any private Steeping-Tub, Tun, &c. without Notice, &c. Stat. 8 *W.* 3. *c.* 21. §. 12.	50 *l.* to be recovered and employed *ut fupra*.
Vinegar-makers receiving Liquors in, or delivering Vinegar out at other Hours than from 29 *September* to 25 *March*, between feven in the Morning and five in the Evening ; and from 25 *March* to 29 *September* between five in the Morning and feven in the Evening. Stat. 10 & 11 *W.* 3. *c.* 21. §. 12.	50 *l.* to be recovered and difpofed *ut fupra*.
Vinegar-maker taking in Liquors, and mixing them with other Liquors, before he fhews them to the Gauger. Stat. 10 & 11 *W.* 3. *c.* 21. §. 13.	Twenty Pounds, to be recovered and difpofed *ut fupra*.
Vinegar-maker keeping a private Store-houfe, Cellar, &c. Stat. 10 & 11 *W.* 3. *c.* 21. §. 14.	Fifty Pounds, to be recovered and difpofed *ut fupra*.
Sweets made for Sale, for which the Duty is paid, or charged by the Excife-Officer, not to be removed from one Place to another, without Certificate under the Hand of the Officer of Excife of the Place from whence fuch Sweets are fo to be fent or removed. The Maker who fhall fend or remove fuch Sweets, and Vintner who fhall receive or take them without Certificate. Stat. 6 *Geo.* 1. *c.* 21. §. 22. The Judgment is final, and liable to no *Appeal* or *Certiorari*.	Forfeit refpectively 10 *s. per* Gallon, together with the Cafks and Veffels containing the fame. To be feifed by Officers of *Excife*. And to be proceeded upon, heard and examined into, adjudged and determined by the fame Ways and Means, and in the fame Manner and Form as is prefcribed to be done upon Seifures of Brandy, &c. *Vide* Title 𝔅𝔯𝔞𝔫𝔡𝔶 and 𝔅𝔯𝔢𝔴𝔢𝔯𝔰 *antea*.

Note ; Juftices have no Jurifdiction within the Limits of the chief Office of *Excife* in *London*. Stat. 6 *Geo.* 1. *c.* 21. §. 22.

(Inn-keeper or Victualler.)

[**Two**]　*Inn-keepers,* not making true Entries once a Month. Stat. 12 *Car.* 2. *c.* 16, 23, 24. §. 30.　1 *W.* & *M. Seff.* 1. *c.* 24. One Witnefs, or Confeffion. The Profecution muft be within three Months.	Five Pounds, and Five Pounds more, to be levied. mitigated and divided in the fame Manner as the Penalty on Brewers, not making true Entries once a Week. *Vide* 𝔅𝔯𝔢𝔴𝔢𝔯𝔰 *antea.*
Inn-keeper or *Victualler* refufing Gauger to enter their Cellars and tafte the Drink. Stat. 7 *W.* 3. *c.* 30. §. 23.	Five Pounds, to be levied by Diftrefs and Sale One Moiety to the King, the other to the Informer.

(Low-Wines.)

[**Two**]　Low-Wines or Spirits brought by Sea coaftwife from any Port or Place in this Kingdom to another, without a Certificate from the Officer of Excife, that the Duty has been paid. Stat. 3 *Geo.* 1. *c.* 4. §. 17.	Forfeited, and may be feifed by the Officers of the Cuftoms of Excife. To be fued for, recovered, determined and mitigated, as Penalties may by any the Laws of Excife. One Moiety to the King, the other to the Perfon that fhall fue or inform.

(Malt.)

[**Two**]　*Maltfter* or *Maker of Malt* for Sale, or Exportation, who fhall caufe, or permit any Barley, or other Corn or Grain making into Malt, to be *fteeped, wetted,* or *watered,* upon the Couch or Floor, or in any other Place, but in Cifterns or Uting-Vats duly entred at the Office of Excife of the Divifion or Place where fuch Malt fhall be wetted. Stat. 6 *Geo.* 1. *c.* 21. §. 1.	Forfeits 2 *s.* 6 *d.* for every Bufhel of Malt *fo fteeped wetted,* or *watered.* To be fued for, recovered, and levied or mitigated by fuch Ways, and Means and Methods, as Penalties or Forfeitures may by any Laws of Excife. §. 9.
Maltfter or *Maker of Malt* for Sale, or Exportation, who fhall caufe, or permit any Corn or Grain by him making into Malt, to be worked or made in fuch Manner, that the fame fhall acrefpire, that is to fay, run	Forfeits 5 *s.* for every Bufhel. To be recovered, levied or mitigated, *ut fupra.*

run out, grow, or sprout at that End of the Corn or Grain from which the Blade proceeds. Stat. 6 Geo. 1. c. 21. §. 2.

Excise-Officer discovering such acrespired Corn, or Grain making into Malt, to give Notice thereof in Writing within 48 Hours to the Malster, or Maker of such Malt, or his Servant. Stat. 6 Geo. 1. c. 21. §. 3.	On Penalty of 40 s. for every Neglect of such Notice ut supra.
Person or Persons shipping, or who shall cause, or p ocure to be shipped, Malt mixed with unmalted Oats or Barley. Stat. 6 Geo. 1. c. 21. §. 4.	Forfeits 5 s. for every Bushel ut supra.
Exporter of Malt to give 48 Hours Notice in Writing to the Officer of Excise, of the Day and Hour when Malt intended to be shipped, or put on Board for Exportation, shall begin to be put on Board. Stat. 6 Geo. 1. c. 21. §. 6. And also of the Name of the Ship, &c. by 12 Geo. 1. c. 4. §. 57.	5 s. for every Bushel of Malt, shipped or put on Board without Notice, ut supra.
Every Maltster or Maker of Malt (other than Compounder for the Duty on Malt) where Corn in any Cistern or Uting-Vat is steeping, or steeped, in order to be made into Malt, shall be found so hard, close, and compact, as it could not be, unless it had been forced together, to prevent the Rising and Swelling thereof. Stat. 6 Geo. 1. c. 21. §. 8.	2 s. 6 d. for every Bushel of such Corn steeping or steeped, which shall be found so hard, close, and compact, ut supra. See 11 Geo. 2. c. 1. in Dalton, Chap. 61. Tit. Malt.

[**Qu. Sess.**] Upon Appeals against original Judgments, given by particular Justices, upon Information for Offences committed contrary to the Acts relating to the Duties upon Malt, the Duties upon Hides, &c. and upon Vellum and Parchment, to rehear, examine, and consider the Truth and Merits of the Facts in Question, and to re-examine the Witnesses upon Oath, and finally determine; and may rectify and amend Defects of Form in Proceedings before the Justices, who gave such Original Judgments. Stat. 6 Geo. 1. c. 21. §. 10.

See Tit. Malt post.

(Retailers of Beer, Ale, Cyder, Perry, Metheglin, &c.

[**Two**] Retailers of Beer, Ale, Cyder, Perry, Metheglin, or Strong-Waters, not making true Entries once a Month. Stat. 12 Car. 2. c. 23. §. 15. c. 24. §. 29. 1 W. & M. sess. 1. c. 24. One Witness, or Confession. The Prosecution must be within Three Months.	20 s. and 20 s. more, to be levied, mitigated and divided in the same Manner as the Penalty on Brewers, not making true Entries once a Month. Vide Brewers antea.
Retailers of Beer, &c. after Receipt from Brewer, mixing Beer, &c. of extraordinary Strength, with any Small Beer, &c. in a Vessel that holds Three Gallons, or more. Stat. 22 & 23 Car. 2. c. 5. §. 11.	Double the Duty of Strong so mixed; to be levied by Distress and Sale. One Third to the King, one Third to the Poor, and one Third to the Informer.
Witnesses refusing to appear. Stat. 22 & 23 Car. 2. c. 5. §. 11.	40 s. to be levied and disposed ut supra. Increased to 10 l. by 7 & 8 W. 3. c. 30. §. 19.

Offences.   Fairs.   Penalties.

[**Qu. Sess.**] OWNER of a Fair or Market, not appointing a Toll-taker (where Toll is taken) or a Book-keeper (where Toll is paid) to sit there from Ten of the Clock in the Forenoon, till Sunset. Stat. 2 & 3 P. & M. c. 7. §. 2.	40 s. for every Default, to be divided between the King and Prosecutor.
The Toll-taker or Book-keeper not delivering, in one Day after, unto the Owner, a Note of all Horses sold there. Stat. 2 & 3 P. & M. c. 7. §. 2.	40 s. to be divided ut supra.

APPENDIX.

Every Seller or Exchanger of an Horfe, in a Fair or Market, which being unknown to the Toll-taker or Book-keeper, doth not procure one credible Witnefs, that is well known unto him, to vouch the fame Sale of the fame Horfe, and every falfe Voucher, and the Toll-taker or Book-keeper who fuffers fuch Sale or Exchange to pafs. Stat. 31 *Eliz. c.* 12. §. 2. | Five Pounds, to be divided between the Queen and the Profecutor ; and the Sale void.

Offences.   𝔉𝔞𝔩𝔰𝔢 𝔗𝔬𝔨𝔢𝔫𝔰.   *Penalties.*

[**Two**] TO convene by Procefs, or otherwife, Perfons fufpected to have gotten Money or other Thing by Falfe Tokens, or counterfeit Letter. Stat. 33 *H.* 8. *c.* 1. §. 3. *Quorum* 1. | To commit or bail till Affifes or Seffions, or otherwife to order them at their Difcretion.

[**Qu. Seff.**] Perfons obtaining any Money, or other Thing, by Colour of any Falfe Token, or counterfeit Letters. Stat. 33 *H.* 8. *c.* 1. §. 2. Confeffion, or Witneffes. | To fuffer fuch Punifhment as the Court fhall adjudge, Death only excepted.

Offences.   𝔉𝔢𝔩𝔩𝔢𝔯𝔰 𝔬𝔣 𝔒𝔞𝔨-𝔗𝔯𝔢𝔢𝔰.   *Penalties.*

[**Qu. Seff.**] FEllers of Oak-Trees apt for Barking, where Bark is worth 2 *s.* a Cart-Load (except Timber for Repair of Houfes, Ships and Mills) but only between the firft of *April* and the laft of *June.* Stat. 1 *Jac.* 1. *c.* 22. §. 20. | Forfeit the Trees, or the double Value of them, to be divided ; one Third to the King, one to the Profecutor, and the other to the City, Borough, Town, or Lord of the Liberty, where the Offence is committed.

𝔉𝔢𝔩𝔬𝔫𝔰. *Vide* Title 𝔗𝔯𝔞𝔫𝔰𝔭𝔬𝔯𝔱𝔞𝔱𝔦𝔬𝔫.

𝔉𝔢𝔩𝔬𝔫𝔶. See *Dalton,* Chap. 159, 160.

Offences.   𝔉𝔦𝔫𝔢𝔰.   *Penalties.*

ALL Fines fet by Virtue of the Stat. 7 *Jac.* 1. *c.* 4. are to be paid to the Treafurer of the County, and by him accounted for. Stat. 7 *Jac.* 1. *c.* 4.

Offences.   𝔉𝔦𝔯𝔢.   *Penalties.*

[**Two**] CHurch-wardens of every Parifh, within the *Weekly Bills of Mortality*, not making, placing, fixing, and continuing Stop-blocks or Firecocks on Mains and Pipes, and not having and keeping in Repair a large Engine, Hand-Engine, and Leather-Pipe and Socket. Stat. 6 *Ann. c.* 31. §. 1. | Ten Pounds, to be levied by Diftrefs and Sale. One Moiety to the Informer, the other to the Poor of the Parifh.

Church-warden, where Fire happens, not paying to the Turn-Cock, whofe Water fhall be found on, or firft come into the Main or Pipe, Ten Shillings. Stat. 6 *Ann. c.* 31. §. 1. | Ten Shillings, to be levied by Diftrefs and Sale.

Church-warden, where Fire happens, not paying to the firft Engine-keeper, who brings in a Parifh-Engine, 30 *s.* to the Second 20 *s.* and to the Third 10 *s.* Stat. 6 *Ann. c.* 31. §. 1. | The 30 *s.* 20 *s.* and 10 *s.* to be levied by Diftrefs and Sale.

Menial, or other Servants, firing any Dwelling-houfe or Out-houfe, through Negligence or Carelefnefs. Stat. 6 *Ann. c.* 31. §. 3. | One hundred Pounds, to be paid to the Church-wardens, to be given to Sufferers by Fire ; in Cafe of Default, or Refufal, to be committed to the Workhoufe or Houfe of Correction, to hard Labour, as the Juftices fhall think fit.

The Owner, or Head-builder or Workman, who fhall build any new Houfe without a Party-Wall between Houfe and Houfe, wholly of Brick or Stone ; and | Fifty Pounds a-piece, to be levied by Diftrefs and Sale ; and for Want of Diftrefs, to be imprifoned till Payment.

                                                      One

4.

Offences.	Fire.	Penalties.

and Two Bricks thick in the Cellar and Ground-Stories; and if it be not 13 Inches thick upwards, and 18 Inches above the Roof: And if any Mundillion, or Cornice of Timber or Wood, under the Eaves, shall be made, or suffer'd in any such new House and Houses; and if all Front and Rear Walls of every House and Houses, shall not be built of Brick or Stone, to be carried a Foot and half above the Garret and Floor, and coped with Stone or Brick. Stat. *6 Ann. c. 31. §. 4.*

One Moiety to the Informer, the other to the Poor. Actions against Persons where the Fire accidentally begins, taken away for Three Years.

This Act was made perpetual, 10 *Ann. c.* 14.

All Persons who shall erect any House on an old or new Foundation, in *London* or *Westminster*, or the *Weekly Bills of Mortality*, or in *Mery le Bone* and *Paddington*; in the Parishes of *Chelsea* and *St. Pancras*, (except Houses on *London-Bridge*, and on the *Thames* below Bridge) and who shall think it necessary to pull down any Partition-Wall between that and the adjoining House, shall (if the Owner of the adjoining House will not agree) give Three Months Notice in Writing of their Intention, that before the Party-Wall be pull'd down, it may in a Month after Notice be viewed by Four able Workmen, Two to be nam'd by the first Builder, and Two by the Owner of the next House; and if either Party shall not name, in Three Weeks, such Workmen, then the other shall name Four to view the Party-Wall; and (without Consent) the same shall not be pulled down, unless the major Part of the Workmen shall certify to the Quarter-Sessions, that the Party-Wall is defective and ruinous, and ought to be pulled down; and if any Person shall think himself aggrieved by such Certificate, the Justices are to summon before them, one or more of the Workmen, and such others as they think fit, and examine them on Oath, and thereon the Justices are to make Orders in the Premises, which shall be conclusive to all Parties without Appeal.

If within Three Days after such Certificate, and there be no Appeal from the same, and the Owner of the next House shall not shore and support it in Six Days after the Time allowed for Appeal, then the first Builder may shore and support the same at the Charges of the Owner, and build up a new Party-Wall; and in Ten Days after the Party-Wall shall be built, he shall leave with the Owner of the next House, an Account of the Rods in the Party-Wall; and one half Part of the Expence, at 5 *l. per* Rod, shall be paid by such Owner; and the Tenant shall pay to the first Builder for the same, and for shoring, and deduct it out of the next Rent; and the first Builder, if not paid in 21 Days after Demand, may sue for his Proportion of the Expence.

It shall not be lawful to have in any Party-Wall, which shall be erected in the said Limits, any Door-case, Window, Lentil, Breast-summer, or Story-Posts or Plates, unless where Two or more Houses shall be laid together, and used as one House, during such Usage, on Forfeiture of 50 *l.* but such Door-case, Window, *&c.* may be affixed in the Front for Conveniency of Shops only.

First Builder, giving Three Months Notice, may pull down the old Timber-Walls or Partitions, and build a new Brick Party-Wall, and be paid for the same as afore directed, and subject to such Appeal, *&c.*

The Water falling from the Tops of the Houses built after 24 *June* 1725. in the said Limits, and Water falling from Balconies and Penthouses, shall be conveyed into the Chanels by Party-Pipes, on the Sides of the Houses, on Forfeiture of 10 *l.*

All Penalties imposed by this Act shall be sued for in Manner before-mentioned, and one Moiety shall be to the Informer, and the other to the Poor of the Parish.

Where Houses are built on new Foundations, no second Builder shall take Benefit of such Party-Wall and Fence-Wall, nor lay any Timber, or cut any Hole for Cup-boards, Presses, or other Uses in the Party-Wall, on Forfeiture of 10 *l.*

The Conviction for the said Forfeitures shall be before Two Justices of the Peace at the least. 11 *Geo.* 1. *c.* 28.

Offences.	Fish.	Penalties.
[One] ERectors of Wear or Wears along the Sea-Shore, or in any Haven or Creek, *&c.* wilfully destroying the Spawn or Fry of Fish. Stat. 3 *Jac.* 1. *c.* 12. §. 2.	Ten Pounds, to be levied by Distress, *&c.* and divided between the Poor and the Prosecutor.
Fishers in any Haven or Creek, or within Five Miles of them, with any Net of a less Mesh than Three Inches and an Half between Knot and Knot, (except for the taking Smoulds in *Norfolk* only) or with a Canvas Net, or other Engine, whereby the Spawn or Fry of Fish may be destroyed. Stat. 3 *Jac.* 1. *c.* 12. §. 2.	The Net or Engine to be forfeited, and 10 *s.* to be levied and divided *ut supra.*
Persons taking Fish by any Device, in any several Water or River, or assisting therein, without the Owner's Consent. Stat. 22 *&* 23 *Car.* 2. *c.* 25. §. 7. Confession, or one Witness. Prosecution to be in a Month.	Such Recompence, and in such Time as the Justice shall appoint, not exceeding treble Damages, such Sum to the Overseers of the Poor as he shall appoint, not exceeding 10 *s.* In Default, to be levied by Distress and Sale; and for Want of Distress, to be committed, not exceeding a Month, unless he gives Bond, with one or more Sureties to the Party injured, not exceeding Ten Pounds, not to offend again.

Persons

APPENDIX.

Offences.	Fiſh.	Penalties.

Perſons keeping any Net, Angle, Leap, Piche, or other Engine for taking Fiſh, other than Makers and Sellers of them, and Owners or Occupiers of Rivers or Fiſheries. Stat. 4 & 5 *W. & M.* c. 23. §. 5.

— Such Engines may be ſeiſed, and kept by the Owners and Occupiers of ſuch Rivers and Fiſheries, or ſuch as they ſhall authorize.

Inferior Tradeſmen, Apprentices, and other diſſolute Perſons fiſhing or fowling, unleſs in Company with the Maſter of ſuch Apprentice qualified by Law. Stat. 4 & 5 *W. & M.* c. 23. §. 10.

— Subject to the ſame Penalties as Perſons are where Game is found; and to be levied and employed in the ſame Manner.
Vide Title **Deer**, &c. in Title **Game**.

To grant his Warrant to ſearch the Houſes of Perſons prohibited, and ſuſpected to have Engines for taking Fiſh, and to ſeiſe or deſtroy the ſame. Stat. 4 & 5 *W. & M.* c. 23. §. 5.

By Warrant to order Nets of leſs Meſh or Moke than three Inches and an half, or of falſe or double Bottom, Cod or Pouch, forfeited, to be publickly burnt. Stat. 1 *Geo.* 1. c. 18. §. 6.

Selling, offering, or expoſing to Sale, or exchanging for any other Goods, *Bret* or *Turbot* under 16 Inches long, *Brill,* or *Pearl* 14, *Codlin* 12, *Whiting* 6, *Baſs* and *Mullet* 12, *Sole, Place,* or *Dab* 8, and *Flounder* 7, from the Eyes to the utmoſt Extent of the Tail. Stat. 1 *Geo.* 1. c. 18. §. 7.

— Forfeit the Fiſh to the Poor, where, &c. and twenty Shillings by Diſtreſs.
One Moiety to the Informer, the other to the Poor, where, &c. In Default of Payment, or want of Diſtreſs, to be ſent to the Houſe of Correction to be whipt, and put to hard Labour, not longer than fourteen Days, nor leſs than ſix.

Note; Perſons impriſoned by this Act not liable to pay the Penalty. §. 8.

No Proſecution for any Offence againſt the Stat. 1 *Geo.* 1. c. 18. unleſs commenced in one Month after committed. §. 9.

Laying or drawing any Kind of Nets, Engines, or Devices, in the Rivers *Severn, Dee, Wye, Thame, Were, Tees, Ribble, Merſey, Dun, Air, Onze, Swaile, Caldor, Wharf, Eure, Darwent,* and *Trent,* whereby the Spawn, or ſmall Fry of *Salmon,* or any Kepper or Sheddler-Salmons, or Salmons under 18 Inches long, from the Eye to the middle of the Tail, ſhall be taken, killed, or deſtroyed; or making, erecting, or ſetting any Bank, Dam, or Hedge, or Stank, or Nets, croſs the ſaid Rivers, to take the Salmon, or to hinder them from going up to ſpawn, or killing Salmon in the ſaid Rivers, between the laſt of *July* and 12 *November;* or fiſhing for Salmon with unlawful Nets, after the 12th of *November.*
View, Confeſſion, or one or more Witneſſes. Stat. 1 *Geo.* 1. c. 18. §. 14.

— Five Pounds for every Offence, beſides the Fiſh taken, and all Nets, &c.
One Moiety of the ſaid Sum to the Informer, the other to the Poor where, &c. to be levied by Diſtreſs and Sale, &c.
And for want of Diſtreſs, Commitment to the Houſe of Correction to hard Labour, not exceeding three, nor leſs than one Month. And to ſuffer ſuch other corporal Puniſhment, as the Juſtice ſhall think fit.
Nets, &c. to be ſeiſed and cut to Pieces in the Preſence of the Juſtice.
To cauſe Banks, Dams, &c. to be demoliſhed at the Charge of Offenders, and ſuch Charges to be levied *ut ſupra.*

No Salmon to be ſent to *London* to Fiſhmongers, or their Agents, that ſhall weigh leſs than ſix Pounds each Fiſh. And every Perſon buying, ſelling, or ſending Salmon under ſix Pounds Weight.
View, Confeſſion, or one or more Witneſſes. Stat. 1 *Geo.* 1. c. 18. §. 15.

— Five Pounds for every Offence, beſides the Fiſh, between Informer and Poor, to be levied *ut ſupra.*
And for want of Diſtreſs, Commitment to the Houſe of Correction to hard Labour for three Months, unleſs paid in the mean Time.

Note; An Appeal lies upon any Branch of the Statute 1 *Geo.* 1. c. 18. to Quarter-Seſſions. §. 17.

Maſters, or Commanders of Smacks, Hoys, Boats, Ships, or other Veſſels, importing Fiſh taken by Foreigners or Strangers, except Proteſtants inhabiting in this Kingdom; to be ſummoned, and if convicted.
Two Witneſſes.
Stat. 1 *Geo.* 1. c. 18. §. 2.

— Forfeit for every Offence twenty Pounds by Diſtreſs, and for want thereof, twelve Months Impriſonment.
Not to extend to the Importing, Buying, or Selling any Eels, Stockfiſh, Anchovies, Sturgeon, Botarge, or Cavear. §. 3.
Or Lobſters and Turbots. §. 10.

None to uſe Nets for fiſhing at Sea upon the Coaſt of *England,* (except for Herrings, Pilchards, Sprats, or Lavidnian) with a Meſh or Moke leſs than three Inches and an half, from Knot to Knot, or with any falſe or double Bottom, Cod, or Pouch, or ſhall put Nets of legal Size or Meſh, upon or behind one another. Stat. 1 *Geo.* 1. c. 18. §. 4.

— Liable to the ſame Penalties as Maſters of Veſſels importing Fiſh contrary to this Act, and the Nets forfeited.

APPENDIX.

Offences.	Fish.	Penalties.

Two] To iſſue out Warrants upon their own Knowledge, or upon Information, of unlawful fiſhing in the River *Severn*, to ſearch all ſuſpected Places for unlawful Inſtruments, and to ſeiſe them, and bring them to the Quarter-Seſſions to be deſtroyed. Stat. 30 *Car.* 2. *c.* 9. §. 3.

Offences.	Fish.	Penalties.
Qu. Seſſ.] Uſing any Net or Engine to deſtroy the Spawn or Fry of Fiſh, or take Salmons or Trouts out of Seaſon, or Pikes ſhorter than 10 Inches, Salmon than 16, Trouts than 8, and Barbels than 12, or uſing any Engine to take Fiſh, other than Angle or Net, or a Trammel of 2 Inches and a half Meſh. Stat. 1 *Eliz.* *c.* 17. §. 5.	Twenty Shillings a Fiſh, and the Net, or Engine.
Unlawfully breaking down Fiſh-Ponds, or fiſhing there without the Owners Licence. Stat. 5 *Eliz.* *c.* 21. §. 7.	Three Months Impriſonment, and to be bound to the Good Behaviour for Seven Years. Treble Damages to the Party grieved. Upon the Offender's Acknowledgment in Seſſions, and Satisfaction to the Party, the Behaviour may be releaſed.
Fiſhing in the River *Severn* with, or making uſe of any Engine or Device, whereby any Salmon, Trout, or Barbel, under the Length appointed by 1 *Eliz.* *c.* 17. ſhall be taken or killed, or ſhall fiſh with any Net for Salmon, Peale, Pike, Carp, Trout, Barbel, Chub, or Grayling, the Meſh whereof ſhall be under 2 Inches and an half ſquare from Knot to Knot, or above 20 Yards in Length, and 2 in Breadth ; or above 50 Yards in Length, and 6 in Breadth in the Wing of the Net, from *Ripple-Lock* Stake to *Glouceſter* Bridge, or above 60 Yards in Length below *Glouceſter* Bridge, and 6 Yards in Breadth in the Wing of the Net, or ſhall fiſh with more than one of thoſe Nets at once, or ſhall uſe any Device for taking the Fry of Eels. Stat. 30 *Car.* 2. *c.* 9. §. 1.	Five Pounds for every Offence, and the Fiſh ſo taken, and the Inſtruments. One Moiety to the Poor, the other to the Proſecutor.
Every Perſon who, between the firſt of *March* and the laſt of *May*, ſhall do any Act whereby the Spawn of Fiſh ſhall be deſtroyed. Stat. 30 *Car.* 2. *c.* 9. §. 2.	Forty Shillings, and the Inſtrument, to be divided *ut ſuprn.*

See 9 *Geo.* 2. Chap. 33. in *Dalton*, Chap. 42. Tit. *Fiſh.*

Offences.	Fleſh.	Penalties.
[Qu. Seſſ.] Perſon preaching, or otherwiſe avouching, or notifying, that any Eating of Fleſh, or Forbearing of Fleſh, is neceſſary for the Service of God, otherwiſe than as other political Laws be. Stat. 5 *Eliz.* *c.* 5. §. 40.	To be puniſhed as Spreaders of falſe News.

Offences.	Forcible Entry and Detainer.	Penalties.
[One] Entring into Lands and Tenements by Force, and *detaining* them by Force. Stat. 5 *R.* 2. *c.* 7. 15 *R.* 2. *c.* 2. §. 2. 8 *H.* 6. *c.* 9. §. 1. Upon View.	Impriſonment, and Ranſom at the King's Pleaſure. *Note* ; The Statute of 8 *H.* 6. *c.* 9. ſhall indamage none, where peaceable Poſſeſſion hath been enjoyed three Years. Stat. 31 *Eliz.* *c.* 11.

Upon Complaint of a *Forcible Entry* or *Detainer*, by Precept to command the *Sheriff* to return a Jury to inquire of the Force committed, and to cauſe the Tenements to be ſeiſed. Stat. 8 *H.* 6. *c.* 9. §. 4.

Jurors returned to inquire of a Forcible Entry, making Default. Stat. 8 *H.* 6. *c.* 9. §. 4.	Iſſue 20 Shillings upon the firſt Precept, 40 Shillings upon the ſecond, 5 Pounds upon the third ; and every Default after, double.

To give Reſtitution upon *Force* or *Detainer* to Tenants for Years, by *Elegit*, Statute Merchant or Staple ; and Copyholders, as well as thoſe who claim Freehold or Inheritance : And may fine or commit. Stat. 21 *Jac.* 1. *c.* 15. By Inquiry.

k

[Qu. Seſſ.]

APPENDIX.

[𝔔u. 𝔖eff.] The *Sheriff* or *Bailiff* negle&ting his Duty in the Cafe of *Forcible Entry* or *Detainer.* Stat. 8 *H.* 6. *c.* 9. §. 5.

Twenty Pounds, to be divided between the King and the Profecutor.

Offences. 𝔉o𝔯eftallers and 𝔍ng𝔯offers. *Penalties.*

[𝔔u. 𝔖eff.] INgroffers of Bark, to the Intent to fell the fame again. Stat. 1 *Jac.* 1. *c.* 22. §. 19.

Forfeit the Bark, or the Value of it, to be divided; one Third to the King, the other to the Profecutor, and the other to the City, Borough, Town, or Lord of the Liberty where the Offence is committed.

Foreflallers, Regrators, Ingroffers of Merchandizes, Vi&uals, &c. Stat. 5 & 6 *Ed.* 6. *c.* 14. §. 4, 5.

By Inquifition, Prefentment, Bill, or Information, or two Witneffes.

Extends not to buying Barley, or Oats to make Malt or Oatmeal, nor Provifion of any Town Corporate, Ship, &c. or any Fifhmonger, Innholder, Vi&tualler, Butcher, Poulterer, or People living within a Mile of the Sea, which are to buy or fell Fifh; they retailing the fame at reafonable Prices. Nor to any Badger, Kidder, or Carrier, licenfed by three Juftices, and felling in one Month.; nor to taking any Thing referved on a Leafe, fo as all be done without Fraud and Foreftalling; nor to reftrain Tranfportation of Corn, or Cattle, allowed by three Juftices. Nor to Wines, Oil, &c. or other Vi&tuals brought from beyond Sea, Fifh and Salt only excepted. Stat. 13 *Eliz. c.* 25. §. 20.

Firft Offence, the Value of the Goods, and two Months Imprifonment, without Bail.

Second Offence, double Value, and fix Months Imprifonment, without Bail.

Third Offence, all his Goods, to be fet in the Pillory, and Imprifonment during the King's Pleafure.

One Moiety of the Forfeitures to the King, the other to the Profecutor, by *Fieri fa'* or *Capias.*

If the Profecution be at the King's Suit only, the whole to the King.

Not to be punifhed twice for the fame Offence.

Note; A *Foreftaller* is one that fhall buy or contra&t for any Merchandize, Vi&tual, or other Thing whatfoever, in the Way, before it fhall be brought by Land or by Water, unto any City, Port, Road, Fair or Market, where it fhall be fold; or fhall caufe the fame to be fo bought; or fhall diffuade People from bringing any fuch Commodity to any fuch Place; or being brought, fhall perfuade them to inhance the Price thereof. Stat. 5 & 6 *Ed.* 6. *c.* 14.

A *Regrator* is one that buys any Grain, Wine, Fifh, Butter, Cheefe, Candles, Tallow, Sheep, Lambs, Calves, Swine, Pigs, Geefe, Capons, Hens, Chickens, Pigeons, Conies, or other dead Vi&tual whatfoever, brought to a Fair or Market to be fold there, and does fell the fame in the fame Fair or Market, or in fome other Fair or Market within four Miles. *Ibid.*

An *Ingroffer* is he that gets into his Hands by Buying, Contra&t or Promife (other than by Demife, Grant, or Leafe of Land or Tithes) any Corn growing in the Fields, or other Grain, Butter, Cheefe, Fifh, or other dead Vi&tual whatfoever, with Intent to fell it again. Stat. 5 & 6 *Ed.* 6. *c.* 14.

𝔉𝔯uit-𝔗𝔯ees. *Vide* 𝔒𝔯cha𝔯ds.

Offences. 𝔉uel. *Penalties.*

[𝔒ne] OFfenders againft the Statute for the Affife of Fuel, if they be not able to fatisfy the Forfeitures. Stat. 7 *Ed.* 6. *c.* 7. §. 6. 43 *Eliz. c.* 14. One Witnefs, or otherwife. Profecution to be within a Year.

To be fet upon the Pillory in the next Market-Town, on the Market-Day at Eleven of the Clock, having a Billet or Faggot bound to fome Part of his Body.

Where *Billet* is expofed to Sale, and not affifed and marked, or cut, as is dire&ted by Stat. 9 *Ann. c.* 15. §. 2. which fee.

This extends not to Owners or Proprietors of Trees, who make Billet for their own private Ufe only.

The Juftice, upon Information, is to call before him Six good lawful Men of the Parifh, &c. where the faid Billet is expofed to Sale, and fwear them to inquire into the Truth; and if they find the Billet not truly affifed and marked, the faid Juftice fhall deliver the fame to the Overfeer of the Poor, to be given to the Poor there.

Offences. 𝔊ames not 𝔏a𝔴ful. *Penalties.*

[𝔒ne] TO enter into any common Houfe or Place, where Playing at Dice, Tables, Cards, Bowls, Coits, Cates, Logats, Shove-groat, Tennis, cafting the Stone, Foot-ball, or other unlawful Game is fufpe&ted to be ufed. Stat. 33 *H.* 8. *c.* 9. §. 14.

APPENDIX.

Offences.	Games not Lawful.	Penalties.
The Keepers of Houfes or Places where unlawful Games are ufed. Stat. 33 *H. 8. c.* 9. §. 14.	To be taken and imprifoned, till they find Sureties by Recognizance, no longer to keep fuch Houfe or Place.	
Artificers, Hufbandmen, Labourers, Apprentices at Hufbandry, Journeymen, or Servants of Artificers, Mariners, Fifhermen, or Serving-men, playing at any unlawful Game. Stat. 33 *H. 8. c.* 9. §. 16.	To be committed without Bail, till he be bound in fuch Sum as the Juftice fhall think reafonable, not to offend again.	
[Two] To caufe to come, or be brought before them, fuch Perfons whom they fhall have juft Caufe to fufpect to have no vifible Eftate, or Calling, to maintain themfelves by ; but do for the moft part fupport themfelves by Gaming; and if they appear to be fuch. Stat. 9 *Ann. c.* 14. §. 6.	To be bound to the Good Behaviour for twelve Months : And if they cannot find Sureties, to be committed to the common Gaol, till they find Sureties.	

Note ; If fuch Perfon fo bound to the Good Behaviour, fhall afterwards at any one Time play or bet for more than 20 Shillings, it is a Breach of his Good Behaviour, and the Recognizance becomes forfeited. *Ib.* §. 7.

Offences.	Games not Lawful.	Penalties.
[Qu. Seff.] Keeping a Houfe of unlawful Games. Stat. 33 *H. 8. c.* 9. §. 11.	Forty Shillings a Day.	
· Reforting to, or Playing in an Houfe of unlawful Games. Stat. 33 *H. 8. c.* 2. §. 12.	Six Shillings and eight Pence a Time.	
Mayor, Sheriffs, Conftables, and Head-Officers, not fearching Places fufpected for unlawful Gaming. Stat. 33 *H. 8. c.* 9. §. 15.	Forty Shillings.	
Artificers, Apprentices, &c. *ut fupra*, ufing unlawful Games out of *Chriftmas* Time. Stat. 33 *H. 8. c.* 9. §. 16.	Twenty Shillings.	

The Statute 33 *H. 8. c.* 9. againft unlawful Games, to be proclaimed Four Times a Year in the Market, and every Quarter-Seffions in open Seffions.

See 2 *Geo.* 2. *c.* 28. §. 9. in *Dalton*, Chap. 46. Tit. *Games and Plays.*

Offences.	Game.	Penalties.
(Conies.)		
[One] PErfons entring *wrongfully into* Ground kept for breeding *Conies,* tho' not inclofed ; and chafing, taking or killing any againft the Owner's Will. Stat. 22 & 23 *Car.* 2. *c.* 25. §. 4. Confeffion, or one Witnefs. Profecution to be in a Month.	Treble Damages and Cofts, and three Months Imprifonment, and till they find Sureties for their Good Behaviour.	
Perfons killing or taking in the Night, *Conies* upon the Borders of Warrens, or on other Grounds, ufed for keeping Conies, except Owners. They who ufe Snares, Hair-pipes, and other Engines. Stat. 22 & 23 *Car.* 2. *c.* 25. §. 5. Conviction *ut fupra*.	Such Recompence, in fuch Time as the Juftice fhall appoint, and pay fuch Sum to the Overfeers of the Poor, as he fhall think fit, not exceeding Ten Shillings ; and in Default to be committed to the Houfe of Correction.	
(Deer, Hare, Partridge and Pheafant.)		
[One] Killers or Takers of *Pheafants* or *Partridges* in the Night. Stat. 23 *Eliz. c.* 10. §. 2.	Being convicted, he is to take Bond (for Two Years only) with good Sureties, not to offend in the like Kind. To examine and bind over all Offenders againft the faid Statute.	

To grant a Warrant to fearch the Houfes of fufpected Perfons for *Hare, Partridge,* and other Game. Stat. 4 & 5 *W. & M. c.* 23. §. 3.

Offences.	Game.	Penalties.
Perfons where *Game* is found, not giving a good Account how they came by it, or not producing the Party of whom they bought it, in fome convenient Time,	Not under 5 *s.* nor exceeding 20 *s.* for every Hare, Partridge, or other Game, to be levied by Diftrefs and Sale ; and in Default, to be committed to the Houfe of Cor-	

Offences.   **Game.**   **Penalties.**

(*Deer, Hare, Partridge and Pheasant.*)

Offences	Penalties
Time, or some credible Person, to prove such Sale upon Oath. Stat. 4 & 5 W. & M. c. 23. §. 3.	Correction, not exceeding a Month, nor less than ten Days, to be whipp'd and kept to hard Labour. One Moiety of the Penalties to the Informer, the other to the Poor.
Higlers, Chapmen, Carriers, Inn-keepers, Victuallers or Alehouse-keepers, having in his or their Custody or Possession, any *Hare, Pheasant, Partridge, Moore, Heath-Game,* or *Grouse*; or shall buy, sell, or offer to sell any Hare, &c. except Carriers who carry for Persons qualified. Stat. 5 *Ann.* c. 14. §. 2. View, or one Witness. Conviction to be in Three Months.	Five Pounds for every Hare, &c. to be levied by Distress and Sale. One Moiety to the Informer, the other to the Poor. For Want of Distress, to be committed to the House of Correction for Three Months, without Bail or Mainprise, for the first Offence, and Four Months for every other Offence.
Persons offending against 5 *Ann.* c. 14. having Game in Custody, and bringing a *Certiorari* to remove the Conviction. Stat. 5 *Ann.* c. 14. §. 2. *Note*; The Stat. 5 *Ann.* c. 14. is made perpetual by 9 *Ann.* c. 25.	To enter into a Recognizance for 50 l. with Sureties, conditioned to pay the Prosecutor full Costs, to be ascertained upon Oath within fourteen Days after Conviction or *Procedendo* granted. In Default, Justices may proceed to execute such Conviction.

If any *Hare, &c.* shall be found in the Shop, House, or Possession of any Person not qualified in his own Right to kill Game, or intitled thereto under some Person qualified, the same shall be adjudged exposing the same to Sale. Stat. 9 *Ann.* c. 25. §. 2.

Offences	Penalties
Persons taking, killing, or destroying *Hare, &c.* in the Night-time. Stat. 9 *Ann.* c. 25. §. 3.	Incur the same Forfeitures, Pains, and Penalties; and to be recovered, as by Stat. 5 *Ann.* c. 14.
[Two] Killers or Takers of any *Pheasant, Partridge, Pigeon, Duck, Heron, Hare,* or other Game; and Takers or Destroyers of the Eggs of Pheasants, Partridges, or Swans. Stat. 1 *Jac.* 1. c. 27. §. 2. Confession, or Two Witnesses.	To be committed without Bail, unless they pay to the Poor where the Offence was committed, or they apprehended, 20 s. for every Fowl, Hare or Egg. After they have been committed a Month, to be bound with Two sufficient Sureties in twenty Pounds a-piece, not to offend again.
Sellers, or Buyers to sell again of *Deer, Hare, Pheasant* or *Partridge*, (except reared up or brought from beyond Sea.) Stat. 1 *Jac.* 1. c. 27. §. 4.	*Deer*, 40 s. *Hare*, 10 s. *Pheasant*, 20 s. *Partridge*, 10 s. Between the Poor and the Prosecutor. Extends not to one licensed in open Sessions to kill Hawks-Meat; but then he must be bound in a Recognizance of 20 l. not to kill any of the same Game, nor to shoot within 200 Yards of an Heronry, within 100 Paces of a Pigeon-house, or in a Park, Forest or Chase, whereof his Master is not Owner.
Hawkers at, or Destroyers of *Pheasants* or *Partridges*, between the first of *July* and the last of *August*. Stat. 7 *Jac.* 1. c. 11. §. 2. Confession, or Two Witnesses. Prosecution in Six Months.	One Month's Imprisonment, without Bail, unless he pays to the Poor of the Parish where the Offence was committed, 40 s. for every Time he hawked, and 20 s. for every Pheasant or Partridge destroyed or taken.
[Qu. Sess.] Taking *Pheasants* or *Partridges* with Engines, in another's Ground, without Licence. Stat. 11 *H.* 7. c. 17. §. 2.	Ten Pounds, to be divided between the Owner of the Ground and the Prosecutor.
Killing or taking any *Pheasants* or *Partridges* with any Net or Engine, in the Night-time. Stat. 2 *Eliz.* c. 10. §. 2.	20 s. for every Pheasant, and 10 s. for every Partridge. If not paid in ten Days, a Month's Imprisonment without Bail. The Money to be divided between the Lord and the Prosecutor; but if the Lord, &c. shall dispense with it, then his Moiety to the Poor.

(*Deer-Hayes,* or *Buck-Stalls.*)

Offences	Penalties
[Two] Keepers of *Deer-Hayes* or *Buck-Stalls,* save in his own Forest or Park. Stat. 19 *H.* 7. c. 11. §. 3.	40 s. a Month, the Offender to be examined and committed til Payment. Justices to have the 10th Part.

(*Deer-*

APPENDIX.

Offences.	Game.	Penalties.

(Deer-Hayes, or Buck-Stalls.)

Stalkers, with any Bush or Beast to any *Deer*, except in his own Forest or Park. Stat. 19 *H.* 7. *c.* 11. §. 4.

Ten Pounds, Proceedings against him *ut supra*.

(Eggs of Falcon, Goshawk, Lanner or Swan.)

[**Qu. Sctt.**] Taking out of the Nest any Eggs of *Faulcon, Goshawk, Lanner* or *Swan.* Stat. 11 *H.* 7. *c.* 17. §. 4.

A Year and Day's Imprisonment; a Fine, one Moiety to the King, the other to the Owner of the Ground. But where they are Swans Eggs, to the Owner of the Swans.

Vide Title **Deer** *supra*.

(Game-keeper.)

[**One**] *Game-keepers* selling or disposing of Game without the Consent or Knowledge of the Lord. Stat. 5 *Ann. c.* 14. §. 4.
One Witness.

To be committed to the House of Correction for three Months, to be kept to hard Labour.

No Lord or Lady of a Manor to make above one Person to be a *Game-keeper* within any one Manor, whose Name must be entred with the Clerk of the Peace, who is to grant a Certificate thereof. And *Game-keepers*, whose Names are not so entred, and not otherwise qualified, who shall kill any Hare, *&c.* or who shall sell or expose to Sale any Hare, *&c.* Stat. 9 *Ann. c.* 25. §. 1.

Incur like Forfeitures, Pains and Penalties, as are inflicted on Higlers, *&c.* for Buying or Selling of Game, by 5 *Ann. c.* 14.
Forfeitures to be recovered by such Means as are prescrib'd in the said Act 5 *Ann.*

Game-keepers not qualified, or not Servants to Lords of Manors, or immediately employed by them to take and kill Game for their sole Use or Benefit, killing Hare, . Pheasant, *&c.* or keeping Greyhounds, *&c.* Stat. 3 *Geo.* 1. *c.* 11. §. 1.

Incur the Penalties in the Acts 5 *&* 9 *Ann.*

Note; The Acts 5 *&* 9 *Ann.* and all other Laws now in Force for the better Preservation of the Game, are continued and enforced by 3 *Geo.* 1. *c.* 11. §. 2.

(Greyhounds, Bows, Setting-Dogs, Ferrets and Snares.)

[**One**] Persons, not qualified by Law, keeping or using any *Bows, Greyhounds, Setting-Dogs, Ferrets, Coney-Dogs, Hayes, Lurchers, Tunnels, Low-bells, Hare-pipes, Snares,* or other Instruments for destroying of Game. Stat. 4 *&* 5 *W. &* M. *c.* 23. §. 3.
Confession, or one Witness.

Subject to the same Pains and Penalties as Offenders are liable to, on whom Game shall be found, and who do not give a good Account how they came by it; which *vide supra*, in Title *Deer, &c.* under Title **Game**.
To be levied and employed in the same Manner.

Before the Allowance of a *Certiorari*, to remove any Conviction upon the Stat. 4 *&* 5 *W. &* M. *c.* 23. the Party is to become bound to the Prosecutor in 50 *l.* with *Sureties,* to be approved by a Justice, to pay Costs, upon Oath, in a Month after Conviction is confirmed. Stat. 4 *&* 5 *W. &* M. *c.* 23. § 7.

Persons not qualified, keeping, or using any *Greyhounds, Setting-Dogs, Hayes, Lurchers, Tunnels,* or any other Engine, to kill and destroy the Game. Stat. 5 *Ann. c.* 14. §. 4.
One Witness.

Five Pounds, to be levied by Distress and Sale; and for Want, to be committed to the House of Correction for Three Months, for the first Offence, and Four Months for every other Offence.

[**Two**] Keepers of *Greyhound, Dog* or *Net,* to kill or take *Deer, Hare, Pheasant* or *Partridge,* by any who have not an Inheritance of Ten Pounds *per Ann.* or Lease for Life of Thirty Pounds *per Ann.* or be worth 200 Pounds in Goods, or be Son of a Baron, or Knight, or Heir apparent of an Esquire. Stat. 1 *Jac.* 1. *c.* 27. §. 3.
Confession, or Two Witnesses.

To be committed without Bail, unless they pay 40 *s.* to the Poor where the Offence was committed.

Persons of mean Condition, killing or taking any *Pheasant* or *Partridge,* with Dogs, Nets, or Engines. Stat. 7 *Jac.* 1. *c.* 11. §. 8.
Confession, or one Witness.

To be committed without Bail, unless he pays 20 *s.* for every Pheasant and Partridge so killed, or taken; and also be bound in a Recognizance of 20 *l.* never to offend again.

To

1

The

APPENDIX.

(Greyhounds, Bows, Setting-Dogs, Ferrets and Snares.)

Offences	Penalties
To grant a Warrant for any Constable, or Head-borough, to search the Houses of Persons suspected to have any Setting-Dogs or Nets. Stat. 21 *Jac.* 1. *c.* 11. §. 9.	The Dogs to be killed, and the Nets cut in Pieces.

(Guns.)

[**One**]. To grant his Warrant to *Game-keepers*, and others, to search the Houses of Persons prohibited to keep Guns, &c. for such Guns, &c. and to seise them for the Use of the Lord of the Manor, or destroy them. Stat. 22 & 23 *Car.* 2. *c.* 25. §. 2.	

(Hawks.)

[**Qu. Seff.**] Bearing any *Hawk* of *English* Breed, called a Nyesse, Goshawk, Tassel, Lanner, Lanneret, or Faulcon. Stat. 11 *H.* 7. *c.* 17. §. 4.	Forfeited to the King, and to be at his Disposal.
Killing or scaring away any of the said *Hawks* from the Coverts where they used to breed. Stat. 11 *H.* 7. *c.* 17. §. 9, 10.	Ten Pounds, to be divided between the King and Prosecutor.
Unlawfully taking any *Hawk*, or Hawk's Eggs. Stat. 5 *Eliz. c.* 21. §. 7.	Three Months Imprisonment; to be bound to the Good Behaviour for Seven Years. Treble Damages to the Party grieved. Upon the Offender's Acknowledgment in Sessions, and Satisfaction to the Party, the Behaviour may be released.

(Hawking and Hunting.)

[**One**] Hunters in Forests, Parks or Warrens, in the Night-time, or disguised. Stat. 1 *H.* 7. *c.* 7. §. 3.	To be examined, and bound over, or committed. Rescous of the Execution of the Justice's Warrant, Felony.
Inferior Tradesmen, Apprentices, and other dissolute Persons, hunting or hawking, unless in Company with the Master of such Apprentice qualified by Law. Stat. 4 & 5 *W. & M. c.* 23. §. 10.	Subject to the same Penalties as Persons are where Game is found, and to be levied and employed in the same Manner.
[**Qu. Seff.**] Hunters in Forests, Parks, or Warrens, in the Night-time, or disguised. Stat. 1 *H.* 7. *c.* 7. §. 5, 6.	If the Fact be concealed, Felony. If confessed, fineable.
Hawking or *Hunting* with Spaniels in standing Corn, except on his own Ground, or with the Owner's Consent. Stat. 23 *Eliz. c.* 10. §. 4.	Forty Shillings to the Owner of the Ground.

(Heron.)

[**Two**] Takers of any old *Heron*, without their Grounds.	Six Shillings and eight Pence.
A young *Heron*. Stat. 19 *H.* 7: *c.* 11. §. 6.	Ten Shillings. The Offender to be examined, and committed till Payment.

Pigeon. *Vide* Title *Deer*, &c. supra.

(Wild-Duck, Teal, Widgeon and Water-Fowl.)

[**One**] Persons, between *July* 1 and *Sept.* 1. as they shall yearly happen, by Hayes, Tunnels, or other Nets, driving and taking any *Wild-Duck*, *Teal*, *Widgeon*, or any other Water-Fowl, in Fens, &c. or other Places of Resort for Wild Fowl in the Molting Season. Stat. 9 *Ann. c.* 25. §. 4. One Witness on Oath. The Time limited by 10 *Geo.* 2. *c.* 32. §. 10. is between 1 *June* and 1 *October*.	5 s. for every Wild-Duck, Teal, or other Water-Fowl. One Moiety to the Informer, the other to the Poor: To be levied by Distress and Sale, rendring the Overplus, if any be, above the Penalty and Charge of Distress. For Want of Distress, to be committed to the House of Correction for any Time not exceeding one Month, nor less than fourteen Days, there to be kept to hard Labour. The Justice to order the Hays, Nets, or Tunnels, to be seised and destroyed in his Presence.

4 [**Qu.** Forfeits

APPENDIX.

(Wild-Duck, Teal, Widgeon and Water-Fowl.)

[**Qu. Seff.**] Deſtroying or taking away any Wild-Fowl. Stat. 25 *H.* 8. *c.* 11. §. 5.	Forfeits for every Egg of a Crane or Buſtard, 20 *d.* of a Bittern, Heron, or Shovelard, 8 *d.* of a Mallard, Teal, or other Wild-Fowl, 1 *d.* To be divided between the King and Proſecutor.

Whereſoever any Perſon ſhall, for any Offence hereafter to be committed againſt any Law now in Being, for the better Preſervation of the Game, be liable to pay any pecuniary Penalty, upon Conviction before any Juſtice or Juſtices of Peace; it ſhall be lawful for any other Perſon whatſoever, either to proceed to recover the ſaid Penalty by Information or Conviction before a Juſtice, or to ſue for the ſame by Action of Debt, &*c.* in any Court of Record; and the Plaintiff, if he recover, ſhall have double Coſts.

Provided, That all Suits and Actions to be brought by Force of this Act, ſhall be brought before the End of the next Term after the Offence committed, and no Offender ſhall be proſecuted for the ſame Offence both by the Way preſcribed by this Law, and by the Way preſcribed by any of the former Laws. 8 *Geo.* 1. *c.* 19. §. 1, 2.

Offences.	*Gaol.*	*Penalties.*

[**One**] CAN commit Murderers and Felons to no other Priſon but to the common Gaol. Stat. 5 *H.* 4. *c.* 10. 11 & 12 *W.* 3. *c.* 19. §. 3.	

[**One** or **Qu. Seff.**] To ſettle what Perſons under Arreſt ſhall pay for each Night's Lodging, and other Expences. Stat. 22 & 23 *Car.* 2. *c.* 20, §. 9.

[**One**] An Offender, who is to be conveyed to Gaol, if he does not bear all the Charges. Stat. 3 *Jac.* 1. *c.* 10. §. 2.	His Goods (if he has any) are by Warrant, to be ſold by the Conſtable, the Appraiſement thereof to be made by the Neighbours, and the Overplus returned. If he has no Goods, the Conſtables, Church-wardens, and two or three honeſt Inhabitants, may, with the Allowance of a Juſtice under his Hand, tax every Inhabitant, to be levied by Diſtreſs and Sale.
Perſons not paying Monies charged for Repair of Gaols. Stat. 11 & 12 *W.* 3. *c.* 19. §. 2. Continued for ſeven Years by 10 *Ann. c.* 14.	To be diſtrained; and if not paid in four Days, the Diſtreſs to be ſold.

Act 10 *Ann. c.* 14. made perpetual as to ſo much of the ſaid Act as relates to the Building and Repairing County-Gaols, by Stat. 6 *Geo.* 1. *c.* 19. §. 1.

May commit Vagrants, and other Criminals, Offenders, and Perſons charged with ſmall Offences, or for Want of Sureties, to the common Gaol, or Houſe of Correction, as he in his Judgment ſhall think fit. Stat. 6 *Geo.* 1. *c.* 19. §. 2.

[**Three**] May conſent, that Keepers of Gaols, upon emergent Occaſions, may provide other Places for the Removal of Sick, or other Perſons, out of the uſual Gaols, but not againſt the good Will of the Owner. Stat. 19 *Car.* 2. *c.* 4. §. 2. *Quorum* 1.

To ſettle Gaolers Fees for Commitment, Diſcharge and, Chamber-Rent, within their ſeveral Precincts, except *London, Middleſex,* and *Surry,* which are to be ſettled by the two Chief Juſtices, and the Chief Baron, or two of them, and the Juſtices of Peace, in their ſeveral Juriſdictions. Stat. 22 & 23 *Car.* 2. *c.* 20. §. 10.

Note, That the ſeveral Rates of Fees, and the Rates for the Government of Priſons, are to be ſigned by the Chief Juſtices, and Chief Baron, or two of them, and the Juſtices of Peace of *London, Middleſex,* and *Surry;* and by the Judges for the Circuits, and the Juſtices in their Precincts, in the other Counties; to be regiſtred by the Clerk of the Peace, and hung in a Table in each Priſon.

See the Stat. 2 *Geo.* 2. *c.* 22. §. 4, 7.

[**Qu. Seff.**] Upon Preſentment of the Grand Jury at the Aſſiſes or Great Seſſions, of the Inſufficiency of the Priſons or Gaols, may upon Examination of Workmen agree on a Sum for Building or Repairing thereof, and equally levy the ſame on the ſeveral Diviſions of the County, by Warrant iſſued at the Quarter-Seſſions to the High Conſtable, &*c.* and may make a Receiver. Stat. 11 & 12 *W.* 3. *c.* 19. §. 1, 2.

Made perpetual by 6 *Geo.* 1. *c.* 19.

Vide Title **Houſe of Correction.**

Offences.	*Gilding and Goldſmiths.*	*Penalties.*

[**Qu. Seff.**] Gilding Sheaths, or any Metal, but Silver, and the Ornaments of Holy Church; and ſilvering any Metal but Knights Spurs, and	Ten Times the Value of the Thing ſo gilt, and a Year's Impriſonment.

One

APPENDIX.

and the Apparel belonging to a Baron, or above. Stat. 8 *H.* 5. *c.* 3. §. 4.	One Third Part of the Forfeiture to the Profecutor.

To hear and determine all Offences about Goldsmiths, felling Silver, contrary to Stat. 2 *H.* 6. *c.* 14. §. 8.

Offences.   **Gunpowder.**   *Penalties.*

[**Two**] MAY fummon and examine Dealers in Gunpowder upon their Oath, if 600 Pounds is kept in any Place within *London* and *Weftminfter*, or three Miles of the Tower, or St. *James's*, or two Miles of any the Magazines of the Crown. Stat. 5 *Geo.* 1. *c.* 26. §. 2.	And commit fuch as refufe to be examined, to the County-Gaol without Bail, till he conform, &c.
If on Examination, or Oath of two Witneffes, it fhall appear he has more than 600 Pounds, *ut fupra.* Stat. 5 *Geo.* 1. *c.* 26. §. 2.	May by Order caufe him to remove it, and if he does not within 24 Hours after Notice of fuch Order, he forfeits Twenty Shillings for every 100 Pounds, to any that fues within fix Months.
May by Warrant order Store-houfes, or Places ufed for keeping Gunpowder, to be fearched in the Day-time, and to break open Doors, if Occafion.	Oppofers hereof forfeit Five Pounds to any that fues in fix Months. And if more than 600 Pounds be found, to caufe it to be removed at the Owner's Charge, to be levied by Diftrefs. Stat. 5 *Geo.* 1. *c.* 26. §. 3.
None to carry thro' *London, Weftminfter,* or Suburbs, above twenty Hundred Pounds of Gunpowder at a Time, and to be carried in Carriages and Barrels clofe jointed, and hooped and cafed with Canvas or Leather. And Gunpowder carried by Man or Horfe, to be put in Cafes of Canvas or Leather, intirely covered. Stat. 5 *Geo.* 1. *c.* 26. §. 4.	On Forfeiture of all the Gunpowder, on Conviction before two Juftices. To Perfon feifing the fame.

Note; This Act does not extend to any Store-houfe or Magazine belonging to the King, or to the proving Gunpowder by his Majefty's Officers, or to the carrying of Gunpowder to or from his Majefty's Magazines, or with Forces in their Marches. Stat. 5 *Geo.* 1. *c.* 26. §. 5.

[**Qu. Seff.**] The Seffions for *Effex, Kent,* and *Surry*, to appoint Places not exceeding two Acres in a Place, for erecting Warehoufes for *Gunpowder*; and if the Land-Owners difagree, fend Warrants to the Sheriff to return a Jury to inquire the Value: Such Inquifitions to be kept among the Seffions Records, and their Judgment final: To which End they may examine on Oath, and order the Sum not exceeding 30 Years Purchafe to be paid the Owner; which if he refufes, they may receive for his Ufe, and thereon the Inheritance to be vefted in the Purchafer. Stat. 5 *Geo.* 1. *c.* 26. §. 8.

By the 11 of *Geo.* 1. *c.* 23. The Quantity of Gunpowder kept in any one Houfe, is not to exceed 200 *lb.* weight, on Forfeiture of the Gunpowder, or Value, with Cofts.

[**One**] Perfons ufing any Iron Hammer, or Hammer plated with Iron or Steel, in any Warehoufe or Place while any Gunpowder is there, if convicted within one Month after, on Oath of one Witnefs. Stat. 11 *Geo.* 1. *c.* 23. §. 3.	Twenty Shillings to the Informer, by Diftrefs, &c. and if none, to the Houfe of Correction, for not lefs than 14 Days, nor above a Month.
[**Two**] On Demand of a Parifh-Officer (or two Houfholders affigning reafonable Caufe) to iffue Warrants *gratis* for a Search, &c. The Searchers are immediately to feife, and in twelve Hours amove the Gunpowder, except the Quantity allowed to be kept. *Ib.* §. 2.	Obftructing Seifure or Amoval 5 *l.* to the Informer, &c. *ut fupra.*

Note; This does not extend to any Magazine, &c. of the Crown. *Ib.* §. 4. and 5 *Geo.* 1. *c.* 26. fhall be in Force. *Ib.* §. 6.

Offences.   **Hackney Coaches and Chairs.**   *Penalties.*

NO Perfon fhall drive or let to hire by the Hour or Day, or otherwife, any Hackney-Coach, or Coach-Horfes, within the Cities of *London* or *Weftminfter,* or Suburbs,	Upon Pain to forfeit five Pounds, for every Offence. To be levied by Diftrefs, and to be fold in ten Days, and the Overplus to be returned to the Owner. The.

Offences.	Hackney Coaches and Chairs.	Penalties.
Suburbs, or within the *Bills of Mortality*, without Leave or Licence from the Commiffioners appointed by Virtue of the Stat. 9 *Ann. c.* 23. *Ibid.* §. 4.	The Charges of the Diftrefs to be firft deducted, if not paid upon feven Days Notice. In Default to be committed till Payment, without Bail. §. 12, 17.	
No Perfon fhall carry for Hire, in any Hackney-Chair, any Perfon whatfoever in the Cities of *London*, &c. without a Licence from the Commiffioners. *Ibid.* §. 4.	Upon Pain to forfeit Forty Shillings for every Offence. To be levied *ut fupra*, and in Default, to be committed *ut fupra*.	
No Horfe, Gelding, or Mare, to be ufed with any Hackney-Coach, to be under the Size of 14 Hands high, according to the Standard. *Ibid.* §. 4.	Five Pounds, to be levied *ut fupra*, and in Default, to be committed *ut fupra*.	
No Perfon fhall put the fame Figure or Mark of Diftinction upon his Coach or Chair, that is appointed for any other Coach or Chair, or fhall blot out, obliterate, alter, or deface the Figure appointed by the Commiffioners for his Coach or Chair. *Ibid.* §. 4.	Under the Forfeiture of five Pounds for every Offence. To be levied *ut fupra*, and in Default, to be committed *ut fupra*. One Moiety of the above Penalties to be to the Informer, the other to the Queen, her Heirs and Succeffors. §. 12, 17.	

No Hackney-Coachman, nor Driver, fhall take for his Hire, in and about *London* and *Weftminfter*, or within ten Miles thereof, above the Rate of ten Shillings for a Day, reckoning twelve Hours to the Day; and by the Hour, not above eighteen Pence for the firft Hour, and twelve Pence for every Hour after.

From any of the *Inns of Court*, or thereabouts, to any Part of St. *James's* or City of *Weftminfter* (except beyond *Turtle-Street*) above twelve Pence; and the fame Prices from the fame Places to the *Inns of Court*, or Places thereabouts.

From any of the *Inns of Court*, or thereabouts, to the *Royal Exchange*, twelve Pence; and if to the *Tower*, *Bifhopfgate*, or *Aldgate*, or thereabouts, one Shilling and fix Pence, and the like Rates from and to any Place of the like Diftance. *Ibid.* §. 6.

No Perfon to pay above twelve Pence for any Diftance, not exceeding one Mile and four Furlongs; and if above that Diftance, and not exceeding two Miles, eighteen Pence: The Commiffioners to caufe the feveral Diftances between the moft noted Places within the *Weekly Bills of Mortality* to be admeafured, and publifhed. *Ibid.* §. 7.

No Perfon to pay Chairmen for an Hackney-Chair, carried any Diftance within the faid Limits, more than the Rate by this Act allowed for an Hackney-Coach, driven two Thirds of the fame Diftance; and Commiffioners to publifh in Writing the feveral Rates of Chairmen. Stat. 9 *Ann. c.* 23. §. 8.

Hackney Coachman or Chairman refufing to go at, or exacting more for his Hire than the Rates limited by the Stat. 9 *Ann. c.* 23. *Ibid.* §. 8.	Forfeits for every Offence Forty Shillings. To be levied *ut fupra*, and in Default, to be committed *ut fupra*.

All the Offences againft the Stat. 9 *Ann. c.* 23. are to be heard and determined in a fummary Way upon the Oath of one or more credible Witneffes (the Party accufed being fummoned to make his Defence) or upon Confeffion of the Party offending.
One Moiety of all the Forfeitures and Penalties to the Queen, her Heirs, &c. the other to the Informer. *Ibid.* §. 13.

The Breach of any of the Rules and Orders appointed by the Stat. 5 & 6 *W.* & *M. c.* 22. and 9 *Ann. c.* 23. and the Penalties thereupon; and the Rules, Orders, and By-Laws made by the Commiffioners, and allowed and approved by the Lord Chancellor, &c. are punifhable, and to be inflicted and put in Execution by any Juftice, &c. where fuch Offence fhall be committed, in as full and ample Manner as by the Commiffioners. *Ibid.* §. 17.
No Perfon to be twice punifhed for the fame Offence.

The Penalties levied by any Juftice of the Peace, &c. by Virtue of the Stat. 9 *Ann. c.* 23. or By-Laws: The Queen's Part to be tranfmitted to the Receiver General of the Hackney Coaches and Chairs, and to be certified to the Commiffioners within ten Days after levied. *Ibid.* §. 18.	Upon Pain to forfeit double the Value of the Sum which fhould be tranfmitted and certified. Two Thirds to the Queen, the other to him that will inform or fue for the fame.

Hackney Coachman, Driver, or Chairman, may ply and drive on the *Lord's Day*, within the *Weekly Bills of Mortality*, notwithftanding the Act 29 *Car.* 2. *Ibid.* §. 20.

APPENDIX.

Offences	Penalties
Persons refusing or neglecting to pay Coachman or Chairman the Money justly due to him, or wilfully cutting, defacing, or breaking any Coach or Chair, upon Complaint thereof. *Ibid.* §. 22.	To grant a Warrant to bring the Offender before him, and upon Proof on Oath, to award reasonable Satisfaction for Damages and Costs; and on Refusal, to pay or make Satisfaction, to bind over to the Quarter-Sessions.
Persons *driving* a Coach, or *carrying* a Chair for Hire, *not being interested himself in the Licence so to do,* but acting under the Licence of another, as his or her Servant, or otherwise, being guilty of any Misbehaviour in his Employment, by demanding more than his Fare, or by giving abusive Language, or any other rude Behaviour. *Ibid.* §. 56. If convicted by the Oath of one or more credible Witnesses before one Justice of *London, Middlesex,* or *Surry.*	Forfeits a Sum not exceeding 20 s. to the Poor; if not able, or refuse to pay, to be committed to the *House of Correction,* to be kept to hard Labour for seven Days, and receive the Correction of the House before he be discharged.
Hackney Coachman or Driver, refusing to go at, or exacting more for his Hire than according to the Stat. 9 *Ann. c.* 23. or By-Laws made pursuant thereto. Stat. 1 *Geo.* 1. *c.* 57. §. 2, 7.	Forfeit not exceeding three Pounds, nor under 10 s. Offences to be determined, and Penalties and Forfeitures to be recovered, levied and applied, as the 40 s. Penalty may by 9 *Ann. c.* 23.
Justices have the same Power to inflict Penalties, as the Commissioners.	
[**Qu. Sess.**] Finally to hear and determine the Matter of Complaint between Persons refusing to pay Coachmen or Chairmen, what is justly due; and cutting, defacing or breaking Coach or Chair, where the Party is bound over by a Justice, for not paying or making such Satisfaction as is awarded. *Ibid.* §. 22.	The Court is to award Satisfaction for Damages and Costs to the Party grieved; and for Non-payment, to levy the same by Distress.

[**Two**] TO convey back Harvest or other Workmen who are licensed, and do not return when their Work is finished, or shall become impotent. Stat. 13 & 14 *Car.* 2. *c.* 12. §. 3.

Offences	Penalties
[**One**] HAwkers, Pedlars and Petty-Chapmen, trading without or contrary to Licence. Stat. 8 & 9 *W.* 3. *c.* 24. §. 3. 9 & 10 *W.* 3. *c.* 27. §. 3. Confession, or due Proof upon Oath, of one or more Witnesses.	For every Offence twelve Pounds: One Moiety to the Informer, the other to the Poor, to be levied by Distress and Sale.
Persons so trading, and upon Demand, refusing to shew to a Justice, &c. a Licence. Stat. 8 & 9 *W.* 3. *c.* 24. §. 3. 9 & 10 *W.* 3. *c.* 27. §. 3. Conviction *ut supra.*	Five Pounds to the Use of the Poor, and for Non-payment, shall suffer as a common Vagrant, and be committed to the *House of Correction.*
Constables, or other Officers, refusing, or neglecting upon due Notice, to aid or assist in the Execution of Stat. 8 & 9 *W.* 3. *c.* 24. §. 7. 9 & 10 *W.* 3. *c.* 27. §. 7.	40 s. One Moiety to the Poor, the other to the Informer, to be levied by Distress and Sale.

Note; Any Person may seise and detain any Hawker, &c. till such Time as he or she shall produce a Licence, if they have any; if not, till they give Notice to the Constable or some other Parish-Officer, who shall carry such Offender before a Justice, who is by Warrant to levy the Penalty out of the Offender's Goods and Wares, with reasonable Charges. *Ibid.* §. 8.

Persons trading as Hawkers, &c. who shall not, upon Demand, have their Licence ready to be produced. Stat. 3 & 5 *Ann. c.* 4. §. 4.	Forfeits as one trading without Licence, and may be committed, and the Forfeitures levied and employed *ut supra.*

Makers and Wholesale Traders in *English* Bone-lace, and selling the same by Wholesale, are not *Hawkers, &c.* within the Stat. 8 & 9 *W.* 3. *c.* 24. And 9 & 10 *W.* 3. *c.* 27. And they, their Children, Apprentices, Servants or Agents, (selling by Wholesale only) may go from House to House, or Shops, to their Customers, without being liable to the Penalties against *Hawkers.* Stat. 4 *Geo.* 1. *c.* 6. §. 1.

2

APPENDIX.

Offences.	Hay.	Penalties.

[One] PErſons offering any old *Hay* to be ſold within the *Weekly Bills of Mortality*, be-:ween the laſt of *Auguſt* and firſt of *June*, which does not weigh 56 Pounds a Truſs at leaſt ; and between the firſt of *June* and the laſt of *Auguſt*, weighs not 60 Pounds a Truſs new, and old 56. Stat. 2 *W. & M. Geſſ. 2. c.* 8. §. 16.

View, Confeſſion, or one Witneſs.

One Shilling and ſix Pence for every Truſs, to be levied and employed, as the Penalties for not ſweeping the Streets ; which ſee in Title **Scavenger.**

Offences.	Hay and Oats.	Penalties.

THE Statutes 13 *Car. 2. c.* 8. 1 *Jac. 2. c.* 10. and 5 *& 6 W. & M. c.* 22. (inſerted in Edition of 1727 of this Book under this Title, and in ſeveral late Books relating to Juſtices of Peace) are all expired.

Offences.	Hay and Straw.	Penalties.

[One] PErſons ſuffering their Waggon, Cart, *&c.* to ſtand in any Place within the *Weekly Bills of Mortality*, laden with *Hay* or *Straw* to be ſold, from *Michaelmas* to *Lady-Day*, after Two a-Clock in the Afternoon, and from *Lady-Day* to *Michaelmas* after Three. Stat. 2 *W. & M. c.* 8. §. 17.

View, Confeſſion, or one Witneſs.

Five Shillings, to be levied and employed, as the Penalties for not ſweeping the Streets ; which ſee in Title **Scavenger.**

Offences.	Hay-Market.	Penalties.

[One] PErſons refuſing to pay three Pence a Cart-Load of *Hay*, and one Penny a Cart-Load of *Straw*, that ſhall ſtand to be ſold in the *Hay-Market*, in the Pariſh of St. *Martin* and St. *James*, in Eaſe of the Pariſhioners of the ſaid Pariſhes, for and towards the Paving and Amending the Street. Stat. 8 *& 9 W.* 3. *c.* 17. §. 3.

The ſame to be levied by Warrant, under the Hand and Seal of one Juſtice of *Middleſex* or *Weſtminſter*, by Diſtreſs, to be ſold, if not paid in Three Days.

One Juſtice of the *Quorum* of *Middleſex* or *Weſtmin-ſter*, may take the Complaint againſt ſuch as ſtand longer in the ſaid *Hay-Market* than they ought, where-by they forfeit. Stat. 8 *& 9 W.* 3. *c.* 17. §. 3.

Five Shillings, to be levied, as by 2 *W. & M. c.* 8.

[Qu. Seſſ.] The Collectors of the Toll gathered in the *Hay-Market*, are yearly, at every *Eaſter* Seſſions, to give to the Juſtices of the Peace of the County of *Middleſex* and City of *Weſtminſter*, a particular Account, upon Oath, of their Receipts and Diſburſements, and the Overplus is to go to the County of *Middleſex*. Stat. 8 *& 9 W.* 3. *c.* 17. §. 7.

Offences.	Heath, Furze, and Fern.	Penalties.

[One] PErſons on Mountains, Hills, Heaths, Moors, Foreſts, Chaſes, or other Waſtes, burning between 2 *Feb.* and 24 *June*, any *Grig, Ling, Heath, Furze, Gors* or *Fern*. Stat. 4 *& 5 W. & M. c.* 23. §. 11.

To be committed to the Houſe of Correction, not exceeding one Month, nor under ten Days, to be whipp'd, and kept to hard Labour.

Offences.	Hemp and Flax.	Penalties.

[Qu. Seſſ.] WAtering *Hemp* or *Flax* in the River *Severn*. Stat. 30 *Car.* 2. *c.* 9. §. 1.

Five Pounds for every Offence.
One Moiety to the Poor, the other to the Proſe-cutor.

To adminiſter the Oaths to Foreigners, who ſhall uſe the Trade of *Hemp* or *Flax Dreſſing* for Three Years ; of making and whitening Thread ; Spinning, Weaving, *&c.* Cloth made of Hemp or Flax ; and making Tapeſtry-Hangings, Storing Cordage, Twine or Nets for Fiſhery. Stat. 15 *Car.* 2. *c.* 15.

APPENDIX.

Offences.	Hides.	Penalties
[One] TO administer an Oath to all subordinate Officers for the Duty on *Hides*, &c. who shall receive any Salary or Allowance, in respect of his Office, before he acts, for his due and faithful Execution of his Office; and to give a Certificate *gratis*. Stat. 9 *Ann. c.* 11. §. 45.		
[Qu. Sess.] Putting *Hides* to Sale being putrified, or watering them at any other Times but *June*, *July*, or *August*. Stat. 1 *Jac.* 1. *c.* 22.	Three Shillings and four Pence a Hide; one Third to the King, one to the Prosecutor, and the other to the Town, Place, &c. where the Offence is committed.
Persons Buying rough Hides, or Calves Skins in the Hair, except such as can lawfully tan them. *Ibid.*	Forfeit them, or the Value.
Forestalling *Hides*, or Buying them otherwise than in open Fair or Market. *Ibid.*	Six Shillings and eight Pence a Hide, to be divided *ut supra.*

Offences.	Highway-man.	Penalties.
[Two] IF any Person, endeavouring to apprehend a *Highway-man*, be killed, his Executors or Administrators, upon a Certificate under the Hand and Seal of the Two next Justices, shall receive the Sum of Forty Pounds. Stat. 4 & 5 *W.* & *M. c.* 8. §. 3.	The Sheriff in Failure of Payment forfeits double the Sum. To be recovered by Action of Debt, Bill, Plaint, or Information, &c. with treble Costs.

The Streets of *London* and *Westminster*, and other Cities, Towns and Places, are deemed and taken to be Highways within the Intent and Meaning of the Stat. 4 & 5 *W.* & *M. c.* 8. Stat. 6 *Geo.* 1. *c.* 23. §. 8.

Offences.	Highways.	Penalties.
(Constables and Surveyors.)		
[One] COnstables and Surveyors of the *Highways*, neglecting to put in Execution the Statutes made for repairing the *Highways*. Stat. 22 *Car.* 2. *c.* 12. §. 1. View, or one Witness.	To be fined, not exceeding 40 *s*. To be levied by Warrant, directed to the High Constable, and to be employed in amending the *Highways*. The Penalty is increased to Five Pounds, by 6 *Ann. c.* 29. §. 3.
Resisting any employed in the executing the Acts for Repairing the *Highways* or rescuing Goods distrained by Virtue of them. Stat. 22 *Car.* 2. *c.* 12. §. 3. View, or one Witness.	Forty Shillings, to be employed *ut supra*, and if not paid in Seven Days after Notice, to be committed till Payment.

To take the Returns, which the Surveyors of the *Highways* are to make, of Defaulters, within a Month after every Default, and to present the same at the next Quarter-Sessions. Stat. 22 *Car.* 2. *c.* 12. §. 12.

Surveyors of the *Highways* not viewing the Roads, Water-Courses, Bridges, Causways, &c. and not returning, upon Oath, once in Four Months to a Justice. Stat. 3 & 4 *W.* & *M. c.* 12. §. 8. Prosecution in Six Months.	The same Penalty as for refusing to execute the Office.
Where Notice of Defaults is given in the Church by the Surveyors of the *Highways*, and the Defaulters do not repair and amend in thirty Days, and the Surveyors do. Stat. 3 & 4 *W.* & *M. c.* 12. §. 8. Upon Oath of the Surveyors. Prosecution *ut supra.*	Defaulters to pay to the Surveyors, such Charges as one Justice shall think reasonable, to be levied by Distress and Sale.
Surveyors of the *Highways* neglecting to erect or fix a Stone or Post, where Two or more cross *Highways* meet, with an Inscription thereon in large Letters, containing the Name of the next Market-Town, to which each of the adjoining *Highways* lead, according to the Precept to him to be directed by the Justices, at their Four Months Sessions for the *Highways*. Stat. 8 & 9 *W.* 3. *c.* 15. §. 7.	Ten Shillings, to be levied by Distress and Sale, and employed towards such Stone or Post; if any Overplus, in repairing the *Highways*.

Offences.   **Highways.**   **Penalties.**

(Constables and Surveyors.)

Offences	Penalties
Surveyors of the *Highways* neglecting to put the 6 *Ann. c.* 29. or any former Laws for repairing *Highways*, in Execution. Stat. 6 *Ann. c.* 29. §. 3.	Five Pounds, to be levied by Diftrefs and Sale in Three Days. One Moiety to the *Highways*. The other Moiety to the Profecutor, fo as he be an Inhabitant of the Town, Village or Place.
Juftices of Corporations, &c. are to put in Execution this and all former Statutes relating to *Highways*. Stat. 1 *Geo.* 1. *c.* 52. §. 7.	
[**Two**] Surveyors of the *Highways* elected, and not taking the Office upon them. Stat. 2 & 3 *P. & M. c.* 8. §. 1. *Quorum* 1.	Twenty Shillings a-piece, by Diftrefs and Sale, and employed in the Amendment of the *Highways*. Increafed to Five Pounds, by 3 & 4 *W. & M. c.* 12. §. 3. *Vide infra.*
Bailiff or High Conftable, not accounting for Monies by them received towards the Repair of the *Highways*. Stat. 2 & 3 *P. & M. c.* 8. §. 4. *Quorum* 1.	To be committed till all Arrears are paid, fave eight Pence in the Pound for themfelves, and twelve Pence for the Clerk of the Peace.
Surveyors of the *Highways* not prefenting Defaulters in not Repairing the *Highways*, and all Offenders therein, to the next Juftice. Stat. 5 *Eliz. c.* 13. §. 8.	Forty Shillings, to be levied as the Penalties in 2 & 3 *P. & M. c.* 8.
To nominate on *Jan.* 3. yearly, or within 15 Days after, at a fpecial Seffions, to be held for that Purpofe, out of a Lift, to be to them returned by the Conftables, Headboroughs, Tithing-men, Church-wardens, Surveyors of the *Highways*, and Inhabitants, One, Two, or more to be Surveyor or Surveyors of the *Highways*, under Hand and Seal. Stat. 3 & 4 *W. & M. c.* 12. §. 3.	
Note; Juftices are required to give Notice to Conftables, &c. within the Divifion, Ten Days before the Holding their fpecial Seffions. And none are qualified to be Surveyors who have not an Eftate in Land in their own Right, or their Wife's, of 10 *l. per Ann.* or a perfonal Eftate of 100 *l.* or occupy Lands, &c. of 30 *l. per Ann.* if fuch there be.	
Perfons nominated by the Juftices to be Surveyors of the *Highways*, refufing or neglecting. Stat. 3 & 4 *W. & M. c.* 12. §. 3. One Witnefs. Profecution in Six Months.	Five Pounds, to be levied by Diftrefs and Sale. One Moiety to the Informer, the other to the Repair of the *Highways*.
To name other Perfons in the Room of Surveyors of the *Highways* refufing, *toties queties.* Stat. 3 & 4 *W. & M. c.* 12. §. 3.	
Conftables, &c. who fhall not return Lifts of Names to the Juftices at their fpecial Seffions, out of which they are to nominate Surveyors of the *Highways*. Stat. 3 & 4 *W. & M. c.* 12. §. 3. Conviction and Profecution *ut fupra.*	Twenty Shillings, to be levied and employed *ut fupra.*
The Surveyors, every Four Months, to make their Prefentments on Oath. Stat. 3 & 4 *W. & M. c.* 12. §. 10. Conviction and Profecution *ut fupra.*	Forty Shillings, to be levied and employed as the Penalty for refufing to hold.
Surveyor of the *Highways*, before he be difcharged of his Office, is to account upon Oath, and if they have Money in their Hands, and do not pay it. Stat. 3 & 4 *W. & M. c.* 12. §. 9. Profecution in Six Months.	Double the Value, to be levied and employed *ut fupra.*
Surveyors neglecting their Duty in any Thing required by Stat. 3 & 4 *W. & M. c.* 12. §. 12. Conviction and Profecution *ut fupra.*	Forty Shillings, to be levied and difpofed *ut fupra.* Vide *Rate infra.*
Surveyors of the *Highways* nominated by Virtue of the Stat. 3 & 4 *W. & M. c.* 12. within Fourteen Days after Acceptance of their Office; and fo every Four Months, or oftner, if required thereto by Warrant, to view all the Roads, common *Highways*, Bridges, Caufways, Pavements, Hedges, Ditches, and Water-Courfes appertaining to fuch *Highways*, and Nufances	The like Penalty on Surveyors neglecting to give fuch Account, as on Surveyors refufing to execute the Office. To be levied and difpofed of as the Penalties are by 3 & 4 *W. & M. c.* 12. Juftices, at fuch their fpecial Seffions, may excufe on reafonable Excufe.

n

(*Conſtables* and *Surveyors.*)

Offences.	*Penalties.*
and Incroachments made in or upon them. And to give an Account in Writing upon Oath, of the State and Condition of them, and of Neglects of Labourers, and of thoſe obliged to find Labourers or Teams, to the Juſtices at their ſpecial Seſſions. Stat. 1 *Geo.* 1. *c.* 52. §. 2.	
Juſtices at their ſpecial Seſſions, by Writing under their Hands and Seals, may order Roads out of Repair, within the Hundred or Diviſion, to be amended, and in what Manner the ſame ſhall be performed. Stat. 1 *Geo.* 1. *c.* 52. §. 3.	Surveyors required to proceed according to ſuch Orders.
Surveyors or other Perſons miſapplying any Fine, Penalty, or Forfeiture laid by Virtue of this Act, on Proof upon Oath before Juſtices at their ſpecial Seſſions, who likewiſe may examine upon Oath, Perſons that can give any Account of Monies that ought to be applied to amend *Highways.* Stat. 1 *Geo.* 1. *c.* 52. §. 5.	Forfeit Five Pounds to the Informer. To be levied by Diſtreſs.

Note ; Juſtices Clerks not to take any Fee for Surveyor's Oath, or Accounts, on Pain of Ten Pounds, to be recovered in any Court of Record. Stat. 1 *Geo.* 1. *c.* 52. §. 11.

Offences.	*Penalties.*
[𝕼𝖚. 𝕾𝖾𝖋𝖋.] Surveyors neglecting their Duty. Stat. 1 *Geo.* 1. *c.* 52. §. 10.	Forfeit Forty Shillings, to be levied by Diſtreſs and Sale, if not paid in Eight Days.

(*Obſtructions.*)

Offences.	*Penalties.*
[𝕿𝖜𝖔] Perſons laying in any *Highways,* not 20 Foot broad, any Thing whereby the ſame may be obſtructed or annoyed. Stat. 3 & 4 *W.* & *M. c.* 12. §. 4. One Witneſs. Proſecution in Six Months.	Five Shillings, to be levied by Diſtreſs and Sale. One Moiety to the Informer, the other to the Repair of the *Highways.*
Poſſeſſors of Lands next adjoining to *Highways,* where Timber, Stone, Hay, Straw, Stubble, or other Matter for making Dung is laid, ſhall remove and diſpoſe of the ſame to their own Uſe ; and if they neglect to clear the Way, or cleanſe their Ditches, and carry away the Earth; to lay ſufficient Trunks or Bridges, where there are Cart-ways into Grounds, by the Space of Ten Days after Notice given by Surveyors. Stat. 3 & 4 *W.* & *M. c.* 12. §. 6. Conviction and Proſecution *ut ſupra.*	Five Shillings for every Offence, to be levied and employed *ut ſupra.*
Owner of Tree, Buſh or Shrub, growing in any *Highway,* not cutting it down in 10 Days after Notice by the Surveyor. Stat. 3 & 4 *W.* & *M. c.* 12. §. 6. Conviction and Proſecution *ut ſupra.*	Five Shillings for every Offence, to be levied and employed *ut ſupra.*
Perſons neglecting or delaying to ſcour and keep open Ditches and Water-Courſes adjoining to *Highways,* and to remove ſuch Annoyances to the *Highways* 30 Days after Notice by Surveyors. Or ſhall leave the Earth of Ditches ſcoured in the *Highways,* for the Space of Eight Days, Oath thereof being made by Surveyors. Stat. 1 *Geo.* 1. *c.* 52. §. 8.	Forfeit two Shillings and ſix Pence for every eight Yards of Ditching ſo not ſcoured. And not exceeding Five Pounds, nor under Twenty Shillings for each other Offence. To be levied by Diſtreſs and Sale, and applied to the Amending the *Highways.*
[𝕼𝖚. 𝕾𝖾𝖋𝖋.] Not ſcouring Ditches, or keeping low Hedges, Trees and Buſhes, according to 5 *Eliz. c.* 13. Stat. 18 *Eliz. c.* 10. §. 8.	Ten Shillings, to be levied by Diſtreſs and Sale.
Not ſcouring the Ditches in the Ground next the *Highway.* Stat. 18 *Eliz. c.* 10. §. 6.	Twelve Pence for every Rod unſcoured, to be levied *ut ſupra.*
Caſting the Scouring of Ditches into the *Highway,* and ſuffering it to lie there Six Months. Stat. 18 *Eliz. c.* 10. §. 7.	Twelve Pence for every Load, to be levied *ut ſupre.*

I

Offences. **Highways.** **Penalties.**

(Presentment and Certificate.)

[**One**] To certify the Prefentments made by the Surveyors of the *Highways* the next Seffions; and his Prefentment of the *Highways*, upon his own Knowledge, is a good Conviction. Stat. 5 *Eliz. c.* 13. §. 9.

(Rates.)

[**Two**] At Four Months Seffions, upon Oath made by the Surveyors of the *Highways* what Sum or Sums they have expended for Materials to repair the *Highways*, the Juftices are, by Warrant to order a Rate to be made, according to 43 *Eliz.* for Relief of the Poor, to reimburfe Surveyors. Stat. 3 & 4 *W.* & *M. c.* 12. §. 17.

Perfons refufing to pay the above-mentioned Rate for re-imburfing the Surveyors. Stat. 3 & 4 *W.* & *M. c.* 12. Profecution in Six Months.	The Rate to be levied by Diftrefs and Sale.

If any Fine, &c. impofed upon a Parifh for not repairing the *Highways*, fhall be levied on one or more of the Inhabitants; the Juftices, at Four Months Seffions, fhall caufe a Rate to be made to re-imburfe them, which is to be levied and paid by the Surveyors in a Month. Stat. 3 & 4 *W.* & *M. c.* 12. §. 14.

[**Qu. Seff.**] To order Rates to be made for repairing the *Highways*, but not to exceed Six Pence in the Pound upon Land, and Six Pence for 20 *l.* in Perfonal Eftate, where they cannot be repaired by any former Law in Force. Stat. 3 & 4 *W.* & *M. c.* 12. §. 17, 18.

To order a Rate for Repair of *Highways* in the Parifhes in *Middlefex* within the Bills of Mortality, not exceeding Four Pence in the Pound for Land, and Eight Pence for Twenty Pounds Perfonal Eftate. Stat. 2 & 3 *W.* & *M. c.* 8. §. 23.

On the Surveyor's Application to the Quarter-Seffions, if the Juftices there find the *Highways*, &c. fo far out of Order, that they cannot be repaired without a further Power than the Laws have appointed, they may caufe Affeffments to be made not exceeding what is limited by 3 & 4 *W.* & *M.* tho' the Six Days Work have not been performed. But raifing Money by fuch Affeffments, not to excufe the working of Teams, or Labourers, by Law appointed to work, &c. Stat. 1 *Geo.* 1. *c.* 52. §. 6.

To make fuch Order for Relief of Perfons aggrieved as they fhall think convenient. The fame to conclude and bind all Perfons, except fuch who neglect to fcour their Ditches, and carry away the Earth taken out of the fame; or who fhall not carry away Stone, Timber, Straw or Dung, left in *Highways*; or who fhall not remove Annoyances to *Highways* by Water-Courfes. Stat. 1 *Geo.* 1. *c.* 52. §. 12.

Note; No Perfon is liable to be punifhed for any Offence againft the Stat. 1 *Geo.* 1. *c.* 52. unlefs profecuted in Six Months. And no Perfon who fhall be punifhed for any Offence by this Act, to be punifhed for the fame Offence by Virtue of any other Act or Law whatfoever. §. 14. *Ibid.*

(Seffions.)

[**Two**] To hold a fpecial Seffions for the *Highways*, every Four Months, and fummon thereunto all the Surveyors of the *Highway*, and declare to them what they are obliged to do by Virtue of this, or any former Act. Stat. 3 & 4 *W.* & *M. c.* 12. §. 10.	Juftices neglecting or refufing to do what is required of them by this Act, forfeit Five Pounds, to be recovered by Action of Debt, &c. One Moiety to the Profecutor, the other in Amending the *Highway*. Profecution in Six Months.

[**Five**] After Summons, to fhew Caufe why *Highways* fhould not be enlarged; at the Quarter-Seffions to order the Enlarging or Widening any *Highway*: But the Ground taken in muft not exceed Eight Yards; nor muft any Houfe be pull'd down, or Garden, Orchard, Court or Yard, taken away; and Satisfaction muft be made, by Jury, for the fame, not exceeding 25 Years Purchafe. Stat. 8 & 9 *W.* 3. *c.* 15. §. 1.

An Appeal to the Judge of Affife.

[**Five**] To order Affeffments upon Land not exceeding Six Pence in the Pound; and upon Perfonal Eftate, not exceeding Six Pence for every 20 Pounds, upon fuch as are to pay to the *Highways*, towards Payment of the Owners of the Land taken away. Stat. 8 & 9 *W.* 3. *c.* 15. §. 2.

Appeal *ut fupra.*

[**Qu. Seff.**] To inquire of Breaches of 2 & 3 *P.* & *M. c.* 8. concerning *Highways*, and fet fuch Fines as they, or any Two (*Quorum* 1.) fhall think fit, to be levied by way of Diftrefs; and if no Diftrefs, or not paid in 20 Days after Demand, double fo much, to be employed in mending the *Highways*. Stat. 2 & 3 *P.* & *M. c.* 8. §. 10.

To affefs a Fine upon a Juftice of Peace his Prefentment of the *Highways*, upon his own Knowledge, to be eftreated, levied, accounted, and employed, as by 2 & 3 *P.* & *M. c.* 8. Stat. 5 *Eliz. c.* 13. §. 9.

(Who to work.)

[**Two**] Perfons having a Team, or Plough-Land, either in Arable or Pafture, and a Subfidy-Man of Nine Pounds in Goods, or Forty Shillings in Lands,	Ten Shillings for every Day, to be levied by Diftrefs and Sale, and employed in the Amending of the *Highways.*

APPENDIX.

Offences.	**Highways.**	*Penalties.*

(Who to work.)

Offences	**Highways**	*Penalties*
not fending Two able Men with Team and Tools convenient, to work for Six Days, Eight Hours in a Day. Stat. 2 & 3 *P. & M. c.* 8. §. 2. 5 *Eliz. c.* 3. §. 2. 18 *Eliz. c.* 16. §. 2, 3. *Quorum* 1.		
Cottagers not working themselves, or finding a sufficient Labourer. Stat. 2 & 3 *P. & M. c.* 8. §. 2. *Quorum* 1.	Twelve Pence for every Day, to be levied *ut supra*.	
Labourers neglecting to work in the *Highways*. Others, neglecting to fend a Man and a Horfe. Others neglecting to fend a Cart with Two Men. Stat. 22 *Car.* 2. *c.* 12. §. 9. Upon Surveyor's Complaint, and one Witnefs.	One Shilling and Six Pence. Three Shillings. Ten Shillings. To be levied by Diftrefs and Sale.	

Two or more Juftices of the Peace for the County of *Middlefex*, at any Petty Seffions, or Special Seffions of the Peace, upon Application made to them by any Five of the Truftees for repairing the *Highways* between *Kilburn-Bridge* in *Middlefex*, and *Sparrows-Herne* in *Hertford*, to adjudge and determine what Part and Proportion of the Statute-Work fhall be done in the faid Roads, by and in each Parifh. 8 *Geo.* 1. *c.* 9. §. 3.

See **Carriers**, **Scavenger** and **Turnpikes.** As alfo 7 *Geo.* 2. *c.* 9. & 14 *Geo.* 2. *c.* 42. in *Dalton*, Chap. 50. Tit. *Highways*.

Offences.	**Hops.**	*Penalties.*
[**One**] TO adminifter an Oath to every Officer, who fhall be empowered to make a Charge on *Hops*, for the due and faithful Execution of his Office, and fhall give to fuch Officer a Certificate thereof. Stat. 9 *Ann. c.* 12. §. 12.		
Pickers or Gatherers of *Hops*, and others privately conveying any Hops from the Place of their Growth, or where put to be cured, bagged or weighed. Stat. 9 *Ann. c.* 12.	Five Shillings for every Pound, to be levied by Diftrefs; and if no Diftrefs can be found, the Offenders to be committed to the Houfe of Correction, not exceeding a Month.	
Perfons obftructing, beating, or abufing the Officer in the Execution of his Office, concerning the Duty on Hops. Stat. 9 *Ann. c.* 12.	Five Pounds, to be levied *ut supra*.	

Offences.	**Horfes.**	*Penalties.*
[**One**] TO take the Oaths of two Witneffes to prove a ftolen Horfe to be the Owner's, and on the Buyer's Oath what he paid for the Horfe, the Owner is to have him again, paying the Buyer: But this muft be done in fix Months after the Sale. Stat. 31 *Eliz. c.* 12. §. 4.		
[**Qu. Seff.**] Have Power to hear and determine all Offences againft 32 *H.* 3. *c.* 13. for putting ftoned Horfes to feed upon Forefts or Common Ground, above two Years old, and not 15 Hands high, according to the Standard, and for refufing to meafure them. Stat. 32 *H.* 8. *c.* 13. §. 3.		

Vide Titles **Cattle** and **Fairs.**

Offences.	**Houfe of Correction.**	*Penalties.*
[**Qu. Seff.**] TO give Orders for erecting Houfes of Correction, and for Maintenance and Government of the fame, and for the Punifhment of Offenders committed thither; and to appoint Governors and their Salaries, which are to be paid Quarterly by the Treafurers. Stat. 39 *Eliz. c.* 4. §. 1. 7 *Jac.* 1. *c.* 4. §. 6.		
Governors of Houfes of Correction, not yielding a true Account every Quarter-Seffions, of Perfons committed, or fuffering any to efcape, or to be troublefome to the County by going abroad. Stat. 7 *Jac.* 1. *c.* 4. §. 9.	Fineable, as Juftices fhall think fit. *Vide* Title **Gaol.**	

See 13 *Geo.* 2. *c.* 24. & 14 *Geo.* 2. *c.* 33. in *Dalton*, Chap. 196.

Hue and Cry. See Title **Robbery.**

X

Informers.

APPENDIX.

Offences.	Informers.	Penalties.

[One] UPON Information for Trefpaffes, Batteries, and other Mifdemeanors, to take the Informer's Recognizance in 20 *l.* That he will profecute with Effect, and abide by fuch Order as the Court fhall direct. Stat. 4 & 5 *W.* & *M. c.* 18. §. 2.

Offences.	Journeymen Taylors.	Penalties.

[Two] ANY Perfon brought up in, or profeffing, ufing, or exercifing the Art or Myftery of a Taylor, or Journeyman Taylor, in making up Mens or Womens Work in the Cities of *London* and *Weftminfter*, or *Weekly Bills of Mortality*, who fhall at any Time keep up, continue, act in, make, enter into, fign, feal, or be knowingly interefted or concerned in any Contract, Covenant, or Agreement, in Writing, or not in Writing, for advancing their Wages, or for leffening their ufual Hours of Work.

One or more credible Witneffes.

Profecution in three Months after the Offence was committed. Stat. 7 *Geo.* 1. *feff.* 1. *c.* 13. §. 1.

To be committed either to the Houfe of Correction, to hard Labour, not exceeding *two Months*, or to the common Gaol, there to remain without Bail or Mainprife, not exceeding two Months, at the Difcretion of the Juftices before whom convicted.

Journeymen Taylors, Servants, and Apprentices to Taylors, and others, employed or retained as Taylors, in making up Mens or Womens Work within the Cities of *London* and *Weftminfter*, or *Weekly Bills of Mortality*, to work from Six of the Clock in the Morning, until Eight at Night. The Mafter to allow one Penny Halfpenny a Day for Breakfaft, and one Hour for Dinner. And for the Time or Hours of Work aforefaid, to pay them not exceeding *two Shillings per Diem*, from the 25th Day of *March* to the 24th Day of *June*; and for the *Reft* of the *Year*, 1 *s.* and 8 *d. per Diem*. Stat. 7 *Geo.* 1. *feff.* 1. *c.* 13. §. 2.

Taylor or others, acting as fuch within the Limits aforefaid, hiring, retaining, or employing any Journeyman Taylor, or other Perfon, not being an Apprentice, to pay them after the *Rates aforefaid* for the full Time for which they hire them. *Ibid.* §. 3.

Upon Complaint thereof to fummon before them the Party offending, and for Non-payment of the Wages directed by this Statute, to iffue their Warrant for levying fuch Wages by Diftrefs and Sale, &c. *Ibid.* §. 4.	For Want of Diftrefs to commit the Party offending to the common Gaol without Bail or Mainprife, till Payment or Satisfaction made.	

Journeyman Taylor, &c. departing from his Service before the End of the Term for which he is hired, or until the Work for which he is hired be finifhed; or not being retained or employed, fhall refufe to work after Requeft made for that Purpofe by any Mafter Taylor, for the Wages and Hours limited, unlefs fome reafonable Caufe to be allowed by two Juftices. And being thereof convicted. *Ibid.* §. 6.	To be committed to the Houfe of Correction to hard Labour, not exceeding two Months.	

Taylor, &c. within the Limits aforefaid giving, allowing, or paying any more, or greater Wages than limited by this *Statute* or the *Qu. Seff.* for the Hours of Work aforefaid, to any Journeyman Taylor, &c. being lawfully convicted. Profecution in three Months. *Ibid.* §. 7.	Five Pounds. One Moiety to the Informer or Profecutor. The other to the Poor of the Parifh where, &c.	

Journeymen Taylors, &c. taking more or greater Wages for the Hours of Work aforefaid than limited by this *Statute* or *Qu. Seff. Ibid.* §. 7.	To be fent to the Houfe of Correction to hard Labour, not exceeding two Months.	

Note; All Wages, Pay or Allowances contrary to this Act or Order of Qu. Seff. are null and void. *Ibid.* §. 7.

This Act does not extend to Wages or Allowances agreed upon for Working before or after the Hours of Work limited, or to be limited. *Ibid.* §. 8.

[Qu. Seff.] An Appeal lies to the next General Quarter-Seffions, giving Six Days Notice, whofe Judgment is final. And may award reafonable Cofts to either Party, as to them fhall feem juft. *Ibid.* §. 9.

Within the Limits aforefaid, upon Application to be made to them for that Purpofe, may from Time to Time	To be imprifoned, not exceeding Two Months.	

o

APPENDIX.

Offences.

Journeymen Taylors.

Penalties.

Time take into their Confideration the Plenty or Scarcity of the Times, &c. and alter the Wages and Hours of Work directed by this Statute. *And* may order and appoint what *Wages* and *Allowances* fhall be paid or made to Journeymen Taylors, &c. *and* what *Hours* they fhall work, which Rates and Alterations the Seffions muft caufe to be printed and publifhed in Fourteen Days next after fuch General Quarter-Seffions, at the reafonable Expence of the Perfons defiring the fame. And from and after Publication thereof, All Taylors and their Journeymen, &c. not obferving the fame, and being thereof convicted. *Ibid.* §. 5.

Profecution in Six Days after Offence committed.

Offences.

Jurors.

Penalties.

[**Qu. Seff.**] TO take the Return of the Conftables and Headboroughs, of their Lift of Names and Places of Abode, of Perfons qualified to ferve on Juries, between the Age of 21 and 70; which they are to make at *Michaelmas*-Seffions yearly; and to caufe the Clerk of the Peace to deliver a Duplicate thereof to the Sheriff, before the firft of *January* after, and to enter the fame fairly in a Book. Stat. 7 & 8 *W.* 3. *c.* 32. §. 4.

Note; The foregoing Act was continued for 11 Years, by 10 *Ann. c.* 14. And farther continued for 7 Years, by 9 *Geo.* 1. *c.* 8. and referred to by 3 *Geo.* 2. *c.* 25. which laft Act is made perpetual by 6 *Geo.* 2. *c.* 37. See *Dalton*, Chap. 186.

At *Midfummer*-Seffions yearly to iffue Warrants, under the Hands and Seals of Two or more, to the High Conftables, to iffue out their Precepts to prepare a Lift of Freeholders, according to 7 & 8 *W.* 3. *c.* 32. which the Conftables are to return the firft Day of *Michaelmas*-Seffions.

Note; The Act of the 10 *Ann. c.* 14. and the Act 7 & 8 *W.* 3. *c.* 32. are to be read publickly in open Court. Stat. 3 & 4 *Ann. c.* 18. §. 5.

The High Conftables not iffuing their Precepts to the Conftables, to prepare their Lifts of Perfons to ferve on Juries. Stat. 3 & 4 *Ann. c.* 18. §. 5.	Ten Pounds.
The Petty Conftables not returning the Lift of Perfons to ferve on Juries. Stat. 3 & 4 *Ann. c.* 18. §. 5.	Five Pounds.

Vide Title Panels of Juries.
And fee 3 *Geo.* 2. *c.* 25. in *Dalton.* Chap. 186. Tit. *Jurors, &c.*

Offences.

Justices of Peace.

Penalties.

JUftices have Power to arreft and chaftife *Rioters, Barrators,* and other Offenders; and alfo to imprifon and punifh them according to Law, and by Difcretion and good Advifement; alfo to bind People of evil Fame to the Good Behaviour, to hear and determine Felonies and Trefpaffes done in the fame County, according to Law. And to *impofe Fines* for Trefpaffes, which muft be reafonable and juft. Stat. 34 *Eliz.* 3. 1.

Juftices muft keep their Seffions Four Times in the Year, and by Three Days, if need be, *viz.* in the firft Week after *Michaelmas, Epiphany, Eafter,* and the *Tranflation* of St. *Thomas* the Martyr, *viz. Becket,* being the 7th of *July.* And oftner, if need require. Stat. 12 *R.* 2. *c.* 10. 2 *H.* 5.

Juftices of Peace of *Middlefex* are not compellable to keep their Seffions above twice in the Year, notwithftanding the Stat. 12 *R.* 2. *c.* 10. yet they may keep them oftner at their Difcretion. Stat. 14 *H.* 6.

None (except Men learned in the Law, or inhabiting Corporations) to be Juftices, unlefs their Lands be worth Twenty Pounds *per Annum.* Stat. 18 *H.* 6. 11.

If any be put into the Commiffion, not having Lands, *ut fupra,* and do not within one Month after Notice thereof acquaint the Lord Chancellor therewith, or do fit or make any Warrant by Force of fuch Commiffion. *Ibid.*	Forfeits Twenty Pounds. To be divided betwixt the King and the Profecutor.

Juftices muft certify Recognizances to the next General or Quarter-Seffions, where, if the Party bound, being called, do not appear, the Recognizance muft be certified into the *Chancery, King's Bench,* or *Exchequer.* Stat. 3 *H.* 7. 1.

I

Offences.   **Justices of Peace.**   *Penalties.*

A new Commiſſion of the Peace, or Gaol-Delivery of the whole County, does not ſuperſede a Commiſſion granted to a City or Town Corporate. Stat. 2 & 3 *P. & M.* 18.

If a Juſtice for any County at large ſhall dwell in a City, that is a County of itſelf, and within the County at large for which he ſhall be appointed a Juſtice, though not within the ſame County, he may grant Warrants, take Examinations, &c. at his own Dwelling-houſe, though it be out of that County where he is authorized to act as a Juſtice, and in ſome City or Precinct adjoining, that is a County of itſelf; and ſuch Acts of the Juſtice, and of the Peace-Officers in Obedience to any ſuch Warrant, ſhall be good in Law, though it happen to be out of his Limits.

Provided, That nothing in this Act ſhall give Juſtices of the County Power to hold their Quarter-Seſſions in Cities that are Counties of themſelves; nor Peace-Officers of the County at large, to intermeddle in any Matters ariſing within ſuch Cities or Towns. 9 *Geo.* 1. *c.* 7. §. 3.

Juſtices of Peace in *England* or *Wales* muſt have 100 *l. per Annum* in Free, Copy or Leaſehold. See 5 *Geo.* 2. *c.* 18. in *Dalton,* Chap. 2.

Offences.   **Keels.**   *Penalties.*

[One] Perſons removing or altering the Marks of Keels, Boats, &c. Stat. 6 & 7 *W.* 3. *c.* 10. §. 7. One Witneſs.	Ten Pounds, to be levied by Diſtreſs and Sale; for Default, three Months Impriſonment. The Penalty between the King and the Diſcoverer.

Lamps. See Lights.

Offences.   **Leather.**   *Penalties.*

[Qu. Seſſ.] THE Mayor and Aldermen of *London* to chuſe and ſwear Eight expert Men out of ſome of the Four Companies of *Shoemakers, Curriers, Girdlers* and *Sadlers,* to be Searchers and Sealers of all tanned Leather there, whereof one to be aſſigned to keep the Seal. Stat. 1 *Jac.* 1. *c.* 22. §. 31.	Forty Shillings, to be divided between the King and Proſecutor.
Head Officers in Corporate and Market-Towns, and Lords of Liberties, to appoint and ſwear yearly Two, Three, or more honeſt and ſkilful Men to be Searchers and Sealers of Leather. *Ibid.* §. 32.	Forty Shillings, to be divided *ut ſupra.*
The Mayor of *London,* and the Head Officer, or Lord aforeſaid, to appoint Six Triers of inſufficient Leather and Leather-Wares. *Ibid.* §. 35.	Five Pounds, to be divided *ut ſupra.*
Triers not doing their Duty without Delay. *Ibid.* §. 35.	5 *l.* to be divided *ut ſupra.*
A *Trier* in *London* continuing Two Years together. *Ibid.* §. 36.	Incapable of being choſen for three Years after, on Pain to forfeit for every Month he continues otherwiſe in that Office 10 *l.* to be divided in Thirds. One to the King, one to the Proſecutor, and the other to the City, Borough, Town, or Lord of the Liberty where the Offence is committed.
Searcher or *Sealer* refuſing in convenient Time to do his Office, or allowing inſufficient Wares. *Ibid.* §. 37.	40 *s.* to be divided in Thirds *ut ſupra.*
Searchers or *Sealers* taking Bribes, or exacting more than due Fees. *Ibid.* §. 37.	20 *l.* to be divided in Thirds *ut ſupra.*
Searcher or *Sealer* being lawfully elected, and refuſing the Office. *Ibid.* §. 37.	10 *l.* to be divided in Thirds *ut ſupra.*
Selling tanned Leather in *London* before it is ſearched and ſealed. *Ibid.* §. 39.	Forfeited, or the Value thereof, to be divided in Thirds *ut ſupra.*

With-

APPENDIX.

Offences	Penalties
Withstanding the *Searchers* and *Sealers* in the Execution of their Office, or their seising insufficient Wares. *Ibid.* §. 40.	5 *l.* to be divided in Thirds *ut supra*
Persons selling any tann'd Leather (red or unwrought) before it is registred. *Ibid.* §. 42.	The Value thereof to be divided in Thirds *ut supra*.
Persons Buying any tanned Leather before it be searched and sealed ; or carrying it out of the Fair or Market before it be registred. *Ibid.* §. 44.	The same, or the Value thereof, to be divided in Thirds *ut supra*.
Artificers in *London* using tanned and curried Leather, putting into his Wares Leather insufficiently tanned or curried. *Ibid.* §. 44.	The Wares, and the just Value, to be divided in Thirds *ut supra*.
Such Artificers selling any where but in open Shop, Fair or Market, where due Search may be had. *Ibid.* §. 45.	The Wares, and Ten Shillings for every Offence, to be divided in Thirds *ut supra*.
Buying forfeited Wares to sell again. *Ibid.* §. 47.	3 *s.* 4 *d.* for every Parcel, to be divided in Thirds *ut supra*.

Note ; The Stat. 1 *Jac.* 1. *c.* 22. is not to prejudice the Authority of the Universities, so as their Officers observe the Provision of the same ; and Hides or Skins of Ox, Steer, Bull, Cow, Calf, Deer, Goats and Sheep, being tanned or tawed, and salt Hides are reputed Leather within this Act.

Vide Titles **Currier, Shoemaker** and **Tanner.**

See more in *Dalton*, Chap. 59.

Offences	Penalties
[One] HOuse-keepers, within the *Weekly Bills of Mortality*, whose Houses adjoin to or near the Street, from *Michaelmas* to *Lady-Day*, not hanging out Lights every Night from the Time it is dark, till twelve at Night, or paying to the Lamps. Stat. 2 *W. & M. c.* 8. §. 15. View, Confession, or one Witness.	Two Shillings every Default, to be levied and employed as the Penalties for not sweeping the Streets.

[Two] To approve the Distances which one Lamp is to be set from the other. Stat. 2 *W. & M. c.* 8.

See 9 *Geo.* 2. *c.* 20. in *Dalton*, Chap. 60. Tit. *London*.

FOR the Rules of Buildings to be erected in the City and Liberties, see 19 *Car.* 2. *c.* 3. And the Powers of the Lord Mayor, or any two Justices in Relation thereto, *ibid.* §. 3. in *Dalton*, Chap. 60. Tit. *London*, & *vide supra*, Tit. **Fire.**

Offences	Penalties
[Two] EVERY Person who shall erect, set up, continue, or keep any Office or Place under the Denomination of Sales of Houses, Lands, Advowsons, Presentations to Livings, Plate, Jewels, Ships, Goods, or other Things, for the Improvement of small Sums of Money, or shall sell or expose to Sale any Houses, &c. by Way of *Lottery*, or by Lots, Tickets, Numbers, or Figures ; or who shall make, print, advertise, or publish, or cause to be made, advertised, or published Proposals or Schemes for advancing small Sums of Money by several Persons, amounting in the Whole to large Sums, to be divided amongst them by the Chances of the Prizes in some publick Lottery or Lotteries, or shall deliver out, or cause, or procure to be delivered out Tickets to Persons advancing such Sums, to intitle them to a Share	500 *l.* over and above any former Penalties inflicted by any former Act or Acts of Parliament. One Third to his Majesty, one other Third to the Informer, and the remaining Third to the Poor of the Parish where the Offence is committed. To be levied by Distress and Sale ; and also to be committed for every such Offence to the County-Gaol, without Bail for one whole Year, and from thence till full Payment be made of the 500 *l.* forfeited as aforesaid. Conviction by one Witness.

1   of

Lotteries.

Offences.

of the Money fo advanced, according to fuch Propofals or Schemes; or fhall make, print or publifh, or caufe to be made, &c. any Propofal or Scheme of the like Nature, under any Denomination or Title whatfoever. One or more credible Witneffes. Stat. 8 *Geo.* 1. *c.* 2. §. 36.

See 12 *Geo.* 2. *c.* 28. and 13 *Geo.* 2. *c.* 19. in *Dalton*, Chap. 46. Tit. *Games and Plays.*

Penalties.

Setting up any Lottery under Colour of Authority from any foreign Prince, or felling Tickets in foreign Lotteries.
One Witnefs.
Appeal to Quarter-Seffions.
9 *Geo.* 1. *c.* 19. §. 4, 5. 6 *Geo.* 2. *c.* 35. §. 29.

200 *l.* The Crown, Informer, and Poor, one Third each, to be levied by Diftrefs, &c. and Offender *committed* to the County Gaol for *one Year*, and till Satisfaction of fuch Sum.

Note; An Appeal lies to the next General Quarter-Seffions, whofe Judgment is final. *Ibid.*

Lunaticks.

Offences. *Penalties.*

[**Two**] MAY by their Warrant directed to the Conftables, Church-wardens and Overfeers of the Poor, of the County or Place where *Lunaticks* or mad Perfons fhall be found, caufe fuch *Lunaticks* and Perfons *furioufly mad* to be locked up, and, if neceffary, chained, &c. (but not whipp'd) during their Lunacy, &c. and charge their Eftate (if any) for their Maintenance; or (if none) provided for as the Poor of the Parifh. 12 *Ann. feff.* 2. *c.* 23. §. 22.

Malt.

Offences. *Penalties.*

[**One**] COnftable may fearch for Malt which is faulty or mingled, and being found, may with the Advice of a Juftice of Peace, make Sale thereof. The Profecution muft be within a Year; and not to be againft Perfons who make their own Malt. Stat. 2 *E.* 6. *c.* 10. §. 44.

Note; The 39 *Eliz. c.* 16. inferted in former Editions of this Book, is repealed by 9 & 10 *W.* 3. *c.* 22.

[**Qu. Seff.**] Every Perfon employing lefs Time in making and drying of Malt (except in *June*, *July* and *Auguft*) than Three Weeks, and in thofe Months lefs than 17 Days; and putting to Sale Malt mingled of good and bad. Stat. 2 & 3 *Ed.* 6. *c.* 10. §. 2.

Two Shillings for every Quarter.
To be divided between the King and Profecutor.

Putting any Malt to Sale before (by Treading, Rubbing and Fanning it) he fhall have taken out of every Quarter, Half a Peck of Duft, or more. Stat. 2 & 3 *Ed.* 6. *c.* 10. §. 3.

Twenty Pence for every Quarter, to be divided *ut fupra.*

Malt entred and made for Exportation only, (as the Act directs) not to be charged with any of the Duties impofed on Malt made in *Great Britain*, and no Drawback to be allowed on any Malt exported. Stat. 12 *Geo.* 1. *c.* 4. §. 48.

Makers of Malt for Exportation are, before they begin to fteep it, to leave Notice in Writing of the Quantities intended to be made, &c. which fhall be kept feparate from what is intended for home Confumption. *Ibid.* §. 49.

5 *s.* for every Bufhel found mixed with what is intended for home Confumption.

Maltfters fhall not begin to wet any Grain to make into Malt for Exportation, for above fix Days before the Corn, &c. intended for home Confumption be dried off; nor wet any Grain for home Confumption above fix Days before the Malt for Exportation be dried and locked up *ut infra.* Ib. §. 50.

5 *s.* for every Bufhel fo wet, &c.

Notice in Writing is to be given by the Exporter to the Port Officer, of the Day and Hour when the putting fuch Malt on board is to be begun, and of the Ship's Name, &c. *Ibid.* §. 57.

5 *s.* for every Bufhel put on Board without fuch Notice. *Ibid.*

If fuch Malt be not exported within nine Months after made and put into Rooms or Store-houfes *ut infra.* *Ibid.* §. 57.

5 *s.* for every Bufhel.

Maltfters

5 *s.*

𝔐alt.

Offences.	Penalties.
Maltsters (other than Compounders for the Duties) not to mix their Corn or Grain of one wetting or steeping, or any Part thereof, or of their Couches or Floors, with Corn or Grain of a former wetting or steeping before it be put on the Kiln for drying. Stat. 2 *Geo.* 2. *c.* 1. §. 11, 12.	5 *s.* for every Bushel so mixed, &c. recoverable by any Laws of Excise. One Moiety to the King, the other to the Informer. *Vide* **Excise** *antea.*
Malt for Exportation when fully dried, &c. shall in the Presence of the Officer where made, be measured and carried thence directly on Shipboard, or into Store-houses or Rooms provided by the Maker, and there kept from other Malt under two Locks and Keys, one to be kept by the Officer, &c. Stat. 12 *Geo.* 1. *c.* 4. §. 51.	Not entring such Corn *ut supra*, or not providing Rooms or Store-houses with Locks, &c. or not giving Notice, or not causing it to be measured and locked up within six Days after it is dried, forfeits 50 *l.* *Ibid.* §. 58.
The said Officers may gauge such Malt in all its Operations, till it be fully dried, &c. and on Notice are to attend at Store-houses, &c. on the Delivery out of Malt for Exportation; as also to keep an Account thereof, and give out Certificates, &c. *Ibid.* §. 52, 53, 54.	Opposing and hindring an Officer, forfeits 50 *l.* *Ibid.* §. 58. Proprietor neglecting to deliver such Certificate, forfeits 50 *l.* *Ibid.* §. 54.
The Port Officers are to attend the Measuring of Malt, and to continue on board till the Ship be cleared. *Ibid.* §. 55.	
The Hatches of the Ship are to be locked down when it is not loading, &c. *Ibid.* §. 56.	Breaking open the Hatches after locked down, 50 *l.* *Ib.* §. 58.

See also *Malt* in Title **Excise.**

See 11 *Geo.* 2. *c.* 1. in *Dalton,* Chap. 61. Tit. *Malt.*

𝔐anufactures.

Offences.	Penalties.
[**Two**] TO hear and determine all Wages, Frauds, &c. of Labourers imployed in *Manufactures* of Woollen, Linen, Fustian, Cotton and Iron, concerning any Work done in the same Manufactures. Stat. 1 *Ann. c.* 10. And see 13 *Geo.* 2. *c.* 8. in *Dalton,* Chap. 196.	

𝔐ariners. See 1 *Geo.* 1. *c.* 25. and 2 *Geo.* 2. *c.* 36. in *Dalton,* Chap. 64. under this Title.

𝔐ats.

Offences.	Penalties.
[**Four**] TO licence Persons to make Mats, Coverlets, and Dornicks, in *Norwich,* or *Norfolk.* If a Reward be taken for such Licence, the Forfeiture is five Pounds. Stat. 5 & 6 *Ed.* 6. *c.* 24. §. 5.	
Qu. Sess.] Making any Mats, Dornicks, or Coverlets, in *Norfolk,* without Licence, except in a corporate Town. Stat. 5 & 6 *Ed.* 6. *c.* 24. §. 3.	Every six Fells 10 *s.* every Coverlet 3 *s.* 4 *d.* every six Yards of Dornicks 6 *s.* 8 *d.* Not to extend to *Pulham* in *Norfolk.*

𝔐oney.

Offences.	Penalties.
[**One**] TO hear and determine, upon Oath, whether any Piece of Money cut be counterfeit or not. Stat. 9 & 10 *W.* 3. *c.* 21. §. 1. *Vide* Title **Coin.**	

𝔐urder.

Offences.	Penalties.
[**Qu. Sess.**] IN Case of Murder, may inquire of Escapes, and certify them into the *King's Bench.* Stat. 3 *H.* 7. *c.* 1. §. 21.	

2

APPENDIX.

Offences.	Non-conformity.	Penalties.

[One] TO take Information of the *Non-conformity* of Perfons in publick Offices, or Imployments, Places of Truft, &c. who receive Salaries or Wages, by reafon of any Patent or Grant, or are of the King's Houfhold, or bear Office in any Corporation. Stat. 10 *Ann. c.* 2.

Forty Pounds recoverable in *Weftminfter-Hall*, and the Perfon incapable of any Office, &c. for the future; except he conforms for a Year, and receives the Sacrament three Times within the fame.

Offences.	Norwich Stuffs.	Penalties.

[One] TO convict Counterfeits of the Seal for *Norwich* Suffs, or fealing them with a counterfeit Seal, or removing the Seal from one Piece to another. Stat. 13 & 14 *Car.* 2. *c.* 5. §. 14. Confeffion, or two Witneffes.

Twenty Pounds.

Buyers of Stuffs unfealed, and they in whofe Poffeffion they are found, other than the firft Owner or Maker, and the Maker or Seller delivering them unfealed. Stat. 13 & 14 *Car.* 2. *c.* 5. §. 13. Two Witneffes.

Four Shillings for the Poor of the Trade, to be levied by Diftrefs, &c.

Weavers weaving without their proper Mark at the Head of the Piece. Stat. 13 & 14 *Car.* 2. *c.* 5. §. 16.

Three Shillings, to be levied and difpofed *ut fupra.*

Perfons refufing to appear on any Jury to be returned, by Virtue of the Stat. 13 & 14 *Car.* 2. *c.* 5. §. 20.

Five Shillings, to be levied and difpofed *ut fupra.*

[Two] Two Juftices of the County of *Norfolk*, fhall join with the Mayor, and one Juftice of the City of *Norwich*, in taking the Account of the Wardens of the Weavers of *Norwich* Stuffs quarterly, and applying one Half of the Fines and Forfeitures for the Poor of the faid Trade. Stat. 13 & 14 *Car.* 2. *c.* 5. §. 22.

[Three] Three Juftices of the County of *Norfolk*, with the Mayor of *Norwich*, and two Juftices of the City, to confirm By-Laws made by the Wardens and Affiftants there chofen, for the regulating the Making of *Norwich* Stuffs. Stat. 13 & 14 *Car.* 2. *c.* 5. §. 3. *Quorum* 1.

Offences.	Oath.	Penalties.

[One] IF any, who maintain that the Taking of an Oath in any Cafe whatfoever is unlawful, do refufe to take an Oath, where by Law they are bound; or do endeavour to perfuade others to refufe; or maintain that the Taking an Oath in any Cafe whatfoever is unlawful. Stat. 13 & 14 *Car.* 2. *c.* 1. §. 2.

To be committed to Gaol, or be bound over with Sureties to the Quarter-Seffions, in order to Conviction.

Note; Quakers are exempted from the Penalties of this Act, *per* Stat. 1 *W. & M. c.* 18. §. 13.

Perfons refufing the Oaths when tendered. Stat. 1 *W. & M. feff.* 1. *c.* 18.

To enter into a Recognizance with two Sureties of 50 *l.* for his producing a Certificate under the Hands of fix of the Proteftant Congregation, whereof he is one, &c. that he is a Proteftant.

[Two] In Default of Juftices in Corporations, two Juftices of the County are to adminifter the Oaths required to be taken by Officers in Corporations. Stat. 13 *Car.* 2. *c.* 1. §. 10.

To adminifter the *Oath* of Allegiance to any Perfon of the Age of eighteen, or above, and not a Peer. Stat. 7 *Jac.* 1. *c.* 6. *Quorum* 1.

To take the Oath and Declaration of Allegiance and Fidelity of Diffenters profecuted contrary to 1 *W. & M. c.* 18. And the folemn Affirmation of Quakers, with their Subfcription to the Confeffion of the Chriftian Faith, and to certify the fame to the Seffions. Stat. 10 *Ann. c.* 2.

Two next Juftices, *Quorum unus*, to adminifter an Oath to the *Sheriff* or *Returning Officer*, upon his delivering over to the Clerk of the Peace the *Poll-Books* of the *Election of Knights of the Shire*, within twenty Days after the *Election*, *That he has delivered over all the faid Books without Imbezilment or Alteration.* Or where there are more Clerks of the Peace than one, the Original Books to one, and attefted Copies to the Reft. 10 *Ann. c.* 23. §. 5.

APPENDIX.

Offences.	Oath.	Penalties

[Qu. Seff.] To difcharge Perfons certified by two Juftices to have refufed to take the Oath, and fubfcribe the Declaration, upon their doing it in open Seffions. Stat. 1 *W. & M. c.* 15. §. 8.

See the Statute 1 *Geo.* 1. *ftat.* 2. *c.* 13. and *Dalton,* Chap. 4. for the Oaths to be taken by all Perfons bearing any Office Civil or Military, *&c.*

The Time limited for taking fuch Oaths is fix Kalendar Months after Admiffion. 9 *Geo.* 2. *c.* 26.

Juftices in Seffions to take the *Oaths,* of Perfons having Offices, *&c.* convicted of Non-conformity; on their conforming, that they have conformed for a Year paft, and received the Sacraments three Times within that Time. Stat. 10 *Ann. c.* 2.

Officers and Soldiers. See the Annual Act for punifhing Mutiny and Defertion, *&c.*

Offences.	Orchards.	Penalties.

[One] PErfons unlawfully cutting and taking Corn growing, robbing Orchards, and taking away any Fruit-Trees; breaking any Hedges, Pales, or other Fences, cutting or fpoiling any Woods or Underwoods, ftanding and growing, or the like, and the Acceffaries thereunto. Stat. 43 *Eliz. c.* 7. §. 1.

Confeffion, or one Witnefs.

Profecution to be in Six Weeks, by 15 *Car.* 2. *c.* 2. (which fee in Title **Wood**) it alters the Punifhment.

First Offence, To pay to the Perfon grieved fuch Damages as the Juftice fhall appoint. If he be thought not able to pay, to be committed to the Conftable, to be whipp'd, and for every other Offence to be whipp'd.

The Conftable refufing or neglecting to do his Duty, to be committed till he does.

In the Juftice's own Cafe, he is to affociate one or more Juftices.

Offences.	Panels of Juries.	Penalties.

[Qu. Seff.] JUftices before whom Panels of Juries are returned by the Sheriff, to inquire for the King, *Quorum* 1. may reform fuch Panels, and the Sheriff muft return the Panel fo reformed, on the Penalty of Twenty Pounds, to be divided between the King and the Profecutor. Stat. 3 *H.* 8. *c.* 12. §. 6.

Offences.	Papifts and Popifh Superftition.	Penalties.

(*Agnus Dei,* &c.)

[One] PErfons bringing into any of the Queen's Dominions any *Agnus Dei,* Croffes, Pictures, Beads, or any fuch vain or fuperftitious Thing; or delivering, or offering the fame to any Perfon to be ufed. Stat. 13 *Eliz. c.* 2. §. 7.

A *Præmunire.* A Juftice may receive Notice hereof, and is to difclofe the fame to the Privy Council in 14 Days after, in Pain of a *Præmunire.*

[Qu. Seff.] Perfons receiving any *Agnus Dei,* Croffes, Pictures, Beads, *&c.* Stat. 13 *Eliz. c.* 2. §. 17. 23 *Eliz. c.* 1. §. 2.

A *Præmunire.*

(*Arms and Horfes.*)

[One] A Popifh Recufant refufing to declare what *Armour* or *Munition* he hath, or to deliver it to fuch Perfon as hath Power to feife it. Stat. 3 *Jac.* 1. *c.* 5. §. 28.

Forfeits the fame, and fhall be imprifoned, by Warrant, for Three Months, without Bail.

[Two] Papift, or reputed Papift, refufing to make the Declaration in 30 *Car.* 2. *c.* 1. or neglecting to appear before Two Juftices, upon Notice. Stat. 1 *W. & M. feff.* 1. *c.* 15. §. 4, 5.

His Arms, Weapons, Gunpowder, or Ammunition, to be feifed, by Warrant, to the Ufe of the Crown, to be delivered at the next Quarter-Seffions, in open Court.

If he does not difcover his Arms, or hinders Search for them, to be committed for Three Months without Bail, forfeits his Arms, and to pay treble Value, to be fet at next Quarter-Seffions.

Perfons concealing, or privy to concealing Arms of Papifts, or reputed Papifts; or hindring Search for, and Seifing the fame. Stat. 1 *W. & M. feff.* 1. *c.* 15. §. 6.

To be committed to the common Gaol for Three Months, without Bail, and forfeit treble the Value of the Arms.

Papifts concealing, or Aiders in concealing Horfes of Papifts, or reputed Papifts. Stat. 1 *W. & M. c.* 15. §. 10.

To be committed for Three Months, without Bail, and forfeit the treble Value of the Horfes.

[Four]

[Four] To take away from a Popiſh Recuſant convict, all his Armour, Gunpowder and Munition, but what they allow him. Stat. 3 *Jac.* 1. *c.* 5. §. 27.

(*Books and Relicks.*)

[Two] To ſearch the Houſes and Lodgings of Popiſh Recuſants convict, and of every Perſon whoſe Wife is a Popiſh Recuſant convict, for Popiſh Books and Relicks. Stat. 3 *Jac.* 1. *c.* 5. §. 26.	The Books and Relicks are to be burnt and defaced.

(*Crucifix.*)

[Qu. Seſſ.] A Crucifix, or other Popiſh Relick, of any Price. Stat. 3 *Jac.* 1. *c.* 5. §. 26.	To be defaced in open Seſſions, and then returned to the Owner.

(*Feme Coverts.*)

[Two] Feme Coverts being convicted Recuſants (under Peerage) not conforming within Three Months after Conviction. Stat. 7 *Jac.* 1. *c.* 6. §. 28. *Quor* 1.	To be committed till they conform, unleſs their Huſbands pay 10 s. a Month to the King, or the Third Part of his Lands.

Vide Titles **Abjuration** and **Church.**

(*Jeſuit and Prieſt.*)

[One] To take an Information of a Jeſuit or Prieſt's remaining in any of the Queen's Dominions, and in 28 Days to diſcloſe it to ſome of the Privy Council, or forfeits. Stat. 27 *Eliz.* c. 2. §. 13.	Two hundred Marks.

(*Impugning Supremacy.*)

[One] Perſons above 16 abſenting from Church above one Month, impugning the Queen's Authority in Cauſes Eccleſiaſtical, or frequenting *Conventicles*, or perſuading others ſo to do, under Pretence of Exerciſe of Religion. Stat. 35 *Eliz.* c. 4. §. 1. This is not to be extended to Proteſtant Diſſenters, by Stat. 1 *W. & M. ſeſſ.* 1. *c.* 18.	To be committed till they conform themſelves, and make Submiſſion. He may require them to conform and ſubmit; and if they refuſe, they muſt abjure the Realm in open Aſſiſe or Seſſions.

(*Licence.*)

[Four] To licence a Popiſh Recuſant to go about his neceſſary Occaſions, with the Aſſent in Writing of the Biſhop, Lord Lieutenant, or Deputy Lieutenant, upon Oath of the true Reaſon of his Journey, and that he will make no cauſeleſs Stays. Stat. 3 *Jac.* 1. *c.* 5. §. 7.

(*Maintaining the Pope's Juriſdiction.*)

[Two] Perſons who maintain the Juriſdiction of the Biſhop, or See of *Rome*, and their Acceſſaries. Stat. 5 *Eliz.* c. 1.	Incur a *Præmunire*, which Two Juſtices are to hear and determine, and certify their Preſentments into the Queen's Bench, if in Term-time, within 40 Days; if not, the firſt Day of the next Term, on Pain of 100 *l. Quorum* 1.
[Qu. Seſſ.] Perſons affirming or maintaining the Power or Juriſdiction of any foreign Prelate or Potentate within the Queen's Dominions. Stat. 5 *Eliz.* c. 1. §. 2. 23 *Eliz.* c. 1. §. 2. The Proſecution to be in Twelve Months; but if by Preaching, Teaching, or Words only, in Six Months. Two, or more Witneſſes.	Firſt Offence, Forfeiture of all Goods and Chattels; and if not worth 20 *l.* at the Time of Conviction, all, and one Year's Impriſonment, without Bail. Second Offence, *Præmunire.*

The Statute of 5 *Eliz.* c. 1. againſt maintaining the Pope's Juriſdiction, is to be openly read by the Clerk of the Peace every Quarter-Seſſions. Stat. 5 *Eliz.* c. 1. §. 15.

The Comforters and Maintainers of ſuch as obtain, or put in Uſe any Bull of Abſolution or Reconciliation from the Biſhop of *Rome*, or abſolve, or be abſolved thereby. Stat. 13 *Eliz.* c. 2. §. 4. 23 *Eliz.* c. 1. §. 2.	A *Præmunire*, unleſs within ſix Weeks they diſcover them to ſome of the Privy Council.

APPENDIX.

Offences. **Papists and Popish Superstition.** Penalties.

(Mass.)

Offences	Penalties
Saying or finging Mafs. Stat. 23 *Eliz. c. 1. §. 4.*	200 Marks, and one Year's Imprifonment, and not to be enlarged till the Fine be paid. Two Thirds to the Queen, one to her own Ufe, the other for the Poor, the Third to the Profecutor.
Hearing *Mafs.* Stat. 23 *Eliz. c. 1. §. 4.*	100 Marks, and one Year's Imprifonment, the Fine to be divided *ut fupra.*

(Oath of Allegiance.)

[One] May require *Diffenting Teachers*, Preaching in any Congregation in fuch Counties where they have not qualified themfelves, as the Toleration-Act directs, to take the Oath and Declaration of Allegiance and Fidelity. Stat. 10 *Ann. c. 2. §. 9.*

[Two] To tender the Oath of Allegiance to any Perfons of 18, or above, convicted or indicted of Recufancy, who have not received the Sacrament twice in the Year next before, and to certify the Name and Dwelling of Perfons taking the Oath, to the next Seffions, to be recorded by the Clerk of the Peace, or Town-Clerk. Stat. 3 *Jac. 1. c. 4. §. 13.*
Note; This extends not to Noblemen or Noblewomen.

Jointly or feverally, to adminifter the Oaths of Allegiance and Supremacy to any Perfon reconciled to the Church of *Rome*, and returning into the Realm, to be certified the next Seffions, on the Penalty of 40 *l.* If fuch Perfon takes the Oaths, in Six Days after he fhall return, he fhall not be profecuted for the Treafon. Stat. 3 *Jac. 1. c. 4. §. 24.*

To adminifter the Oath of Allegiance to any Perfon of the Age of 18, or above, and not a Peer. Stat. 7 *Jac. 1. c. 6. §. 26. Quorum* 1.

To adminifter the Oaths of Allegiance and Supremacy to Foreigners, who fhall ufe for three Years the Trades of Breaking, Hickling, or Dreffing *Hemp* or *Flax*; and of making and whitening Thread; and fpinning, weaving, making, whitening or bleaching Cloth made of Hemp or Flax only; and making Twine or Nets for Fifhery; or ftoring Cordage, or making Tapeftry Hangings. Stat. 15 *Car. 2. c. 15. §. 3.*

To take the Oath and Declaration of Allegiance and Fidelity of *Diffenters*, profecuted contrary to 1 *W. & M. c.* 18. (and *folemn Affirmation* and Declaration of *Quakers*) and their Subfcription to the Confeffion of the Chriftian Faith, and to certify the fame to the Seffions. Stat. 10 *Ann. c. 2. §. 8.*

To adminifter and tender the Oaths directed by 1 *Geo.* 1. *c.* 13. to be taken, to Perfons whom they fhall fufpect to be dangerous or difaffected to his Majefty or his Government. On Neglect or Refufal. Stat. 1 *Geo.* 1. *c.* 13. §. 1?	To certify the Refufal to the Quarter-Seffions, to be recorded, and from thence to be certified by the Clerk of the Peace into Chancery or King's Bench. Perfon fo refufing or neglecting, is a Popifh Recufant convict, and forfeits as fuch.
May fummon any Perfon to appear at a Day and Place, to take the Oaths directed by 1 *Geo.* 1. *c.* 13. And on Oath made that the Summons was left at his Houfe, and the Party not appearing. Stat. 1 *Geo.* 1. *c.* 13. §. 12.	To certify the Default to the Seffions; and if he neglects or refufes to take the Oaths at the Seffion; his Name to be proclaimed at the firft Meeting of the Seffions. Then to be adjudged a Popifh Recufant convict, and this to be certified *ut fupra.*

No Manors, Lands, &c. to be fold or bequeathed by Papifts, &c. refufing to take the Oaths, by any Deed or Will, unlefs fuch Deed within fix Months after the Date, and fuch Will within fix Months after the Teftator's Death, be inrolled in one of the Courts of Record at *Weftminfter*, or by the *Cuftos Rotulorum*, and Two Juftices, and the Clerk of the Peace, or Two of them at the leaft, whereof the Clerk of the Peace to be one. Stat. 3 *Geo.* 1. *c.* 18. §. 6.

Note; No Action or Suit for the Penalties or Forfeitures, by 1 *Geo.* 1. *c.* 13. or 3 *Geo.* 1. *c.* 18. for wilfully neglecting or refufing to regifter, to be commenced or brought after Two Years. Stat. 3 *Geo.* 1. *c.* 18. §. 2.

[Qu. Seff.] A Papift of the Age of 21 Years, having an Eftate in Lands, and not taking the Oaths, and alfo repeating and fubfcribing the Declaration 13 *Car.* 2. at the Quarter-Seffions, or Courts at *Weftminfter*, between the Hours of Nine and Twelve in the Forenoon; or in Default thereof not regiftring his Name and Lands, &c. *what Eftate he has in them, the yearly Rents*, &c. within fix Months, and not fubfcribing fuch Regifter in Prefence of Two Juftices in open Seffions, or by Warrant of Attorney, under Hand and Seal executed in the Prefence of Two Witneffes, who are to make Proof thereof at the Seffions, upon Oath. On Neglect or Refufal,	Forfeits the Fee-fimple of his Land, not regiftred, or fraudulently regiftred, and the full Value of other Lands, whereof he has not the Fee-fimple. Two Thirds thereof to the Crown, and the other to any Proteftant that will fue.

I   Two   Ir

(Oath of Allegiance.)

Two of the Justices then present to sign as Witnesses) such Entry. Stat. 1 *Geo.* 1. *c.* 55. §. 1.

In Default, each forfeits Twenty Pounds to the King.

All Officers Civil and Military, Ecclesiastical Persons, Heads of Colleges, *&c.* Serjeants at Law, Counsellors, Attornies, Solicitors, *&c.* practising in Courts, re within three Months to take the Oaths at Quarter-essions, or one of the Courts at *Westminster.* Stat. *Geo.* 1. *c.* 13. §. 3, 9.

Neglecting are disabled to execute any Offices or Employments, or to sue any Action, or to be a Guardian, Executor or Administrator, not capable of any Legacy, or voting for a Member of Parliament, and forfeit 500 *l.* to be recovered by Action of Debt, *&c.* to the Person who sues for the same.

But by 2 *Geo.* 2. *c.* 31. §. 2. this Clause is repealed. See *Dalton,* Chap. 67. Tit. *Oaths.*

(Reconciler and Reconciled.)

One] Aiders and Maintainers of Persons reconciling nd reconciled to the *Romish* Religion, if they do not n 20 Days discover the Reconciling and Reconciled to Justice or higher Officer. Stat. 23 *Eliz. c.* 8. §. 3.

Misprision of Treason.

(Recusancy.)

Qu. Sess.] A Recusant, who conforms, not receiving the Sacrament within a Year after, and so once every Year at the least. Stat. 3 *Jac.* 1. *c.* 4. §. 3.

For the first Year, 20 *l.* for the second, 40 *l.* and every Default after, 60 *l.* And if after he hath received it, he maketh Default therein by the Space of a Year, 60 *l.* to be divided between the King and Prosecutor.

The *Church-wardens* and *Constables* of every Parish, or one of them, or (if there be none such) then the High Constable of the Hundred there, not presenting once every Year at the Quarter-Sessions, the Monthly Absence from Church of every Popish Recusant, and their Children, being nine Years of Age, and their Servants with the Childrens Age, as near as they can know them. Stat. 3 *Jac.* 1. *c.* 4. §. 4.

20 *s.* for every Default. The Clerk of the Peace to record it on 40 *s.* Penalty. If upon such Presentment (being the first) the Recusant be convicted, the Officer who presents him, shall have 40 *s.* to be levied on the Reculant's Goods and Estate, by Warrant, as the Justices shall think fit.

To cause Proclamation to be made, that Popish Recusants shall render themselves to the Sheriff, or Bailiff of the Liberty, where they are before the next Assise, Gaol-Delivery, or Sessions respectively. If they do not, the Default being recorded, shall be taken as a sufficient Conviction. Stat. 3 *Jac.* 1. *c.* 4. §. 7.

Every Conviction of a Popish Recusant is, before the End of the Term next following, to be certified into the Exchequer, in such Certainty, that Process may issue. Stat. 3 *Jac.* 1. *c.* 4. §. 9.

Note ; No Indictment against a Recusant shall be reversed for Want of Form, other than by direct Traverse to the Point of not coming to Church, or not receiving the Sacrament. Stat. 3 *Jac.* 1. *c.* 4. §. 16.

(Reputed Papists.)

[One] Justice of *London, Westminster* and *Southwark,* and of the Counties of *Middlesex, Surrey, Kent* and *Sussex,* to cause to be brought before him every Person (not being a Merchant Foreigner within the Cities of *London* and *Westminster)* or within ten Miles of the same, as are *reputed to be Papists,* and tender them the Declaration mentioned in the Statute 30 *Car.* 2. intituled, *An Act for more effectual preserving the King's Person and Government,* &c. Stat. 1 *W. & M. sess.* 1. *c.* 9. §. 1.

Every such Person after Refusal to make and subscribe the same, who shall continue to be within the said City or Cities, or within ten Miles of the same, he or she shall forfeit or suffer as a *Popish Recusant* convict.

Justices of *Essex* have like Jurisdiction by Stat. 1 *W. & M. sess.* 1. *c.* 17. §. 1.

Offences.   **Parliament.**   *Penalties.*

THREE Justices may consent to, and have Power to order a Petition to the King or *Parliament.* Stat. 13 *Car.* 2. *c.* 5.

Persons endeavouring to procure above Twenty Hands to any *Petition* to the King or *Parliament,* for any Alterations in the Church or State, unless by Consent of Three or more Justices, the Grand Jury at the Assises, *&c.* and repairing to the King, *&c.* to deliver it, with above Ten Persons. Stat. 13 *Car.* 2. *c.* 5.

Forfeit a Sum not exceeding 100 *l.* and to be imprisoned for Three Months,

APPENDIX.

| Offences. | Parliament. | Penalties |

[Two] To administer the Oaths to Candidates to serve after the Determination of this present Parliament for County, City, Borough, or Cinque Port in *England, Wales,* or *Berwick upon Tweed.* He who stands so for the County, that he has 600 *l. per Annum* of or in Lands, Tenements, or Hereditaments, above Reprizes; and for City, Borough, or Cinque Port, of 300 *l. per Annum* above Reprizes. Stat. 9 *Ann. c.* 5. §. 6.

[One] To administer the Oath required by 2 *Geo.* 2. *c.* 24. for preventing Bribery and Corruption in Elections for Parliament, to the Sheriff or other Returning Officer. *Ibid.* §. 3.

Note; This Act for preventing Bribery and Corruption in the Election of Members to serve in Parliament, is to be openly read every Year at the General Quarter-Sessions after *Easter,* in every County, &c. Stat. 2 *Geo.* 2 *c.* 24. §. 9.

| Offences. | Partition of Lands. | Penalties |

[Two] TO be present at the Under-Sheriff's Executing a Writ of Partition, when the High Sheriffs, by Reason of Distance, Infirmity, or any other Hindrance, cannot be present. Stat. 8 & 9 *W.* 3 *c.* 31. §. 4.

See *Dalton*, Chap. 67. Tit. *Partition of Lands.*

| Offences. | Perjury. | Penalties |

[Qu. Sess.] ONE who commits wilful Perjury. Stat. 5 *Eliz. c.* 9. §. 4.

Forfeits 20 *l.* and shall suffer Six Months Imprisonment without Bail, and is disabled to give Evidence until the Judgment be reversed.

If he be not able to pay the Fine, to be set in the Pillory in the publick Market, and his Ears to be nailed.

Note; One Justice may bind the Offender over to Sessions.
See the 2 *Geo.* 2. *c.* 25. in *Dalton*, Chap. 70. Tit. *Perjury.*

Petition to King or Parliament. See Tit. Parliament.

Pewter. See Brass.

| Offences. | Physicians. | Penalties. |

[One] TO assist the President, and all Persons authorized by the College of Physicians, for the due Execution of the several Acts of Parliament, which concern the said College. Stat. 1 *Mar. Parl.* 1 *Sess.* 2. *c.* 9. §. 6.

| Offences. | Pilchards. | Penalties. |

[One] SUspicious Persons, flocking together about the Boats, Nets and Cellars, belonging to the *Pilchard Craft* upon the Coast of *Cornwal* and *Devon,* being warned to be gone, and refusing. Stat. 13 & 14 *Car.* 2. *c.* 28. §. 5.
Warning to be by the Company, or Owner of the Boats and Cellars.

Five Shillings to the Poor, or to be set in the Stocks.

Masters of Vessels, &c. importing *Pilchards, Herrings, Salmon,* &c. or selling the same in *England,* taken by Foreigners (except Protestants dwelling here). Stat. 1 *Geo.* 1. *c.* 18. §. 1, 2.
Oath of two credible Witnesses.

Twenty Pounds, to be levied by Distress; one Moiety to the Poor, the other to the Informer.
For want of a Distress, the Offender to be committed to the common Gaol for a Twelvemonth.

| Offences. | Plague. | Penalties. |

[One] TO command any Person infected with the Plague, residing in an infected House, not to go out; and if he does afterwards go out. Stat. 1 *Jac.* 1. *c.* 31. §. 7.

The Watchman may resist him; and if any Hurt happen thereupon, the Watchman shall not be impeached for the same.

If any Person being infected with the Plague, who has no Sore upon him, go abroad, and converse in Company. Stat. 1 *Jac.* 1. *c.* 31. §. 7.

To be openly whipped as a Vagabond, according to Stat. 39 *Eliz. c.* 4.
But 39 Eliz. c. 4. *is repealed.*

I   **[Two]**   To

APPENDIX

Offences.	𝔓lague.	*Penalties.*
[**𝕿wo**] The Mayor, Bailiffs, Head-Officers and Juſtices of Peace; and where there are none, two Juſtices of the County may tax the Inhabitants towards Relief of ſuch as have the Plague. Stat. 1 *Jac.* 1. *c.* 31. §. 2. Theſe Taxes to be certified to the Quarter-Seſſions.	To be levied by Diſtreſs and Sale; and upon Refuſal, to be committed till Payment. *Vide* 𝔔uarentine.	

𝔓layers of 𝔍nterludes. See 10 *Geo.* 2. *c.* 28. in *Dalton*, Chap. 46. Tit. *Games* and *Plays.*
See alſo Tit. 𝔙agabonds and 𝔙agrants *infra.*

Offences.	𝔓oor.	*Penalties.*
(Badge.)		
[**𝕺ne**] E Very Perſon receiving Relief of any Pariſh or Place, and the Wife and Children of any ſuch Perſon, cohabiting in the ſame Houſe (except one Child to attend an impotent or helpleſs Parent) refuſing or neglecting to wear their *Badge*, in an open and viſible Manner. Stat. 8 & 9 *W.* 3. *c.* 30. §. 2. Upon Complaint.	His or her Allowance to be abridged, or withdrawn, or to be committed to the Houſe of Correction to be whipped, and kept to hard Labour, not exceeding 21 Days.	
Church-wardens, or Overſeers, relieving any ſuch Poor, not having and wearing ſuch *Badge*. Stat. 8 & 9 *W.* 3. *c.* 30. §. 2. One, or more Witneſſes.	Twenty Shillings, to be levied by Diſtreſs and Sale. One Moiety to the Informer, the other to the Poor.	

𝔅oys bound to 𝔖ea. Vide 𝔄pprentice.

(Coſts.)

[**𝕺ne**] Where *Coſts* are given upon an Appeal, from an Order of Settlement of the Poor determined, or where Notice was given, and the Perſon, ordered to pay ſuch Coſts, dwells out of the Juriſdiction of the Court, which gave the Coſts. Stat. 8 & 9 *W.* 3. *c.* 30. §. 3.
Upon Requeſt, and producing a true Copy of the Order for Coſts, on Oath of one Witneſs. | The *Coſts* to be levied by Warrant of one Juſtice of the County where the Party dwells, who is to pay the *Coſts*, by Diſtreſs and Sale; and for Want, to be committed to the common Gaol for 20 Days.

The Overſeers to be reimburſed their reaſonable Charges to be aſcertained by one Juſtice. 3 *Geo.* 2. *c.* 29. §. 9. See *Dalton*, Chap. 73. Tit. *Poor.*

(Father, &c. to maintain poor Children.)

𝔔u. 𝔖eſſ.] Father, Grandfather, Mother, Grandmother, and Children of Poor who cannot work, to be aſſeſſed towards their Relief. Stat. 43 *Eliz. c.* 2. §. 7.

(Overſeers.)

[**𝕿wo**] The Church-wardens, and four, three or two Houſholders of every Pariſh (according to the Greatneſs of the Pariſh) to be nominated in *Eaſter-Week*, or in a *Month* after, under their Hands and Seals, are *Overſeers* of the Poor. Stat. 4 *Eliz. c.* 2. §. 1. *Quorum* 1. | Juſtices neglecting to nominate, forfeit 5 *l.*

Overſeers of the *Poor*, not meeting once a Month in the Church upon *Sunday* after Evening Prayer. Stat. 43 *Eliz. c.* 2. §. 2. *Quorum* 1. | Twenty Shillings to the Uſe of the Poor, to be levied by Diſtreſs and Sale.

To allow of the *Overſeers* Excuſe, for not meeting once a Month, or not, as they ſee Cauſe. Stat. 43 *Eliz. c.* 2. §. 2. *Quorum* 1.

Overſeers not accounting in four Days after the End of their Year. Stat. 43 *Eliz. c.* 2. §. 2. *Quorum* 1. | To be committed without Bail, till they account.

May upon Application by Warrant or Order authorize the Church-wardens or *Overſeers* of the Poor, where any Wife, Child, &c. is left to the Pariſh, to ſeiſe ſo much of the Husband, Father or Mother's Goods, Chattels, Rents, &c. as may diſcharge the Pariſh, and provide for ſuch Wife, Child, &c. Stat. 5 *Geo.* 1. *c.* 8. §. 1.

(Overfeers.)

[𝔔u. 𝔖𝔢𝔰𝔰.] If fuch Warrant of two Juftices be confirmed at the next Seffions, the Seffions may order the Church-wardens or Overfeers to fell the Goods, &c. or receive the Rents, &c. as fhall be neceffary to difcharge the Parifh, &c. And they to account at the Seffions for what Money they receive on fuch Warrant. Stat. 5 *Geo.* 1. *c.* 8. §. 1, 2.

(Rates.)

[𝔗𝔴𝔬] To confent to the fetting poor People to work ; to the raifing by Taxation a convenient Stock to work upon ; and alfo Monies for relieving the Aged and Impotent, and putting forth Apprentices. Stat. 43 *Eliz.* c. 2. §. 1. *Quorum* 1.

Parfon, and all Inhabitants who are able, are taxable to the Relief of the Poor. Stat. 43 *Eliz.* c. 2. §. 1. *Quorum* 1.	Such Tax is to be levied by Diftrefs and Sale of Goods, and in Default to be committed without Bail, till it be difcharged.

Where any Parifh is not able to relieve themfelves, may tax other Parifhes and Places, and the Hundred, if need be. Stat. 43 *Eliz.* c. 2. §. 3. *Quorum* 1.

The *Rates* fet upon every Parifh, at *Eafter*-Seffions. Stat. 43 *Eliz.* c. 2. §. 13. *Quorum* 1.	To be levied by Diftrefs and Sale, and Commitment *ut fupra.*
The Conftable not paying the Monies rated at *Eafter*-Seffions, to the High Conftable. Stat. 43 *Eliz.* c. 2. *Quorum* 1.	Ten Shillings, to be levied by Diftrefs and Sale of Goods ; and in Default, to be committed without Bail, till it be difcharged.
The High Conftable not paying the Monies above mentioned to the Treafurers. Stat. 43 *Eliz.* c. 2. *Quorum* 1.	Twenty Shillings, to be levied *ut fupra.*

[𝔔u. 𝔖𝔢𝔰𝔰.] To *tax* every Parifh in the County, not above 6 *d.* or 8 *d.* a Week for every Parifh, towards Relief of *Prifoners* in the Common Gaol ; to be levied by the Church-wardens, and paid to the High Conftables, and the High Conftables to pay it to the Collector appointed by the Juftices, upon the Penalty of 5 *l.* a-piece. Stat. 14 *Eliz.* c. 5. §. 2.

To provide a Stock to fet poor *Prifoners* committed for Felony, and other Mifdemeanors, to work, in fuch Manner as other County-Charges are levied ; and to appoint Overfeers, and order their Accounts, and punifh Abufes. No Parifh to be rated above 6 *d.* a Week. Stat. 19 *Car.* 2. c. 4. §. 1.

Where the whole Hundred is not able to relieve the Poor, the Juftices, in Seffions, may tax the County in Part, or in Whole, at their Difcretions. Stat. 43 *Eliz.* c. 2. §. 3.

At *Eafter*-Seffions, yearly to *rate* every Parifh at a certain Sum, to be paid weekly : No Parifh to pay more than 6 *d.* nor lefs than a Halfpenny, towards Relief of poor *Prifoners* in the *Queen's* Bench, *Marfhalfea, Hofpitals* and *Alms-houfes* in their Jurifdictions, every one refpectively, to receive out of every County 20 *s.* yearly. Stat. 43 *Eliz.* c. 2. §. 14.

(Refuſing to work.)

[𝔗𝔴𝔬] Such Perfons as refufe to work. Stat. 43 *Eliz.* c. 2. § 4. *Quorum* 1.	To be fent to the Houfe of Correction. One Juftice may do this, as well as two.

(Regiſtring Notice.)

[𝔒𝔫𝔢] Church-wardens and Overfeers, refufing to regifter Notice of poor Perfons coming into a Parifh, and not reading, or caufing to be read fuch Notice. Stat. 3 & 4 *W.* & *M.* c. 11. §. 5. Two Witneffes upon Oath.	Forty Shillings, to be levied by Diftrefs and Sale ; and for want, to be committed for a Month.

(Relief and Settlement, &c.).

[𝔒𝔫𝔢] No Juftice to order *Relief* to a poor Perfon, before Oath made before him, of a reafonable Caufe for it, and that the Party had applied to the Parifhioners at a Veftry, or to two Overfeers, and was by them re-fufed to be relieved ; nor till he has fummoned the two Overfeers, to fhew Caufe why the Party fhould not be relieved, and the Perfon fummoned heard, or made Default to appear. Stat. 9 *Geo.* 1. c. 7. §. 1.

Perfons ordered to be relieved by fuch Juftice, are to be regiftred in the Parifh Books as other Poor, only as long as the Caufe for Relief continues, and no longer.

Two or more Parifhes (if fmall) may with Approbation of *one Juſtice*, under his Hand and Seal, unite in hiring a Houfe, and for Lodging, Employing and Maintaining their Poor ; and the Church-wardens, &c. of one Parifh may contract with thofe of other Parifhes for fuch Lodging, Maintenance, &c. *Ib.* §. 4. *Vide infra.*

(Relief and Settlement, &c.)

[Two] No Officer of any Parish, (except on emergent Occasions) shall bring to the Parish Account, any Money he shall give to any Poor not regiftred *ut fupra*. *Ibid.* §. 2.	5 *l.* to the Poors Ufe, to be levied by Diftrefs, &c. by Warrant of two Juftices after Examination, &c.

Note; By the faid Statute Church-wardens and Overfeers of any Parish or Place may, with Confent of the major Part of the Inhabitants at a Veftry or Meeting, purchafe or hire any Houfe or Houfes in fuch Parish or Place, and contract with Perfons for Lodging, Keeping, or Employing the Poor, who are to have the Benefit of their Work and Labour for their better Maintenance. *Ibid.* §. 4.

A poor Perfon refufing to be lodged or kept in fuch Houfe. *Ibid.* §. 4.	To be ftruck out of the Parish Books, and have no Relief.

[Settlement] But no Poor, or their Children, Apprentices, &c. to gain any Settlement in the Parish or Place to which they are removed by Virtue of this Act. *Ibid.* §. 4.

None to acquire a Settlement in any Parish by reafon of any Purchafe therein, where the Confideration does not amount to 30 *l.* for any longer than he dwells in the Eftate purchafed; but fhall be liable to be removed to the Place laft fettled. *Ibid.* §. 5.

And Perfons taxed to the Scavengers Rates, or Repairs of Highways, and paying the fame, gain not thereby any Settlement. *Ibid.* §. 6.

[Qu. Seff.] No Appeal from any Order for Removal fhall be proceeded on in any Court or Quarter-Seffions, unlefs reafonable Notice be given by the Church-wardens, or Overfeers making the Appeal to the Church-wardens, &c. from whence fuch Poor are to be removed; and if due Notice be not given, the Juftices fhall adjourn the Appeal to the next Quarter-Seffions, and then finally determine it. *Ibid.* §. 8.

If the Appeal be determined in favour of the Appellants, the Quarter-Seffions are to order the Money expended for Relief of the poor Perfon, between the Time of his Removal and the Determination of the Appeal, to be paid to the Appellants; recoverable as prefcribed by the Act of the 9 *W.* 3. (which fee before.) *Ib.* §. 9.

(Setting them to work.)

[One] Where there is but one Juftice of the Peace, he may confent to the Church-wardens and Overfeers of the Poors fetting up, ufing and occupying any Trade, Myftery or Occupation, only for the fetting on Work, and better Relief of the Poor of the Parish where they bear Office. Stat. 3 *Car.* 1. *c.* 4. §. 22.

(Settlement and Removal.)

[One] Complaint is to be made to one Juftice, by the Church-wardens or Overfeers of the Poor, within Forty Days, of Perfons like to be become chargeable to the Parish, who come to fettle in a Tenement under 10 *l. per Ann.* Stat. 13 & 14 *Car.* 2. *c.* 12. §. 1.

Note; The Stat. 13 & 14 *Car.* 2. *c.* 12. is now made perpetual by 12 *Ann. feff.* 1. *c.* 18. §. 1.

Perfons returning to the Parish whence they were removed. Stat. 13 & 14 *Car.* 2. *c.* 12. §. 3.	To be fent to the Houfe of Correction.

Church-wardens or Overfeers refufing to receive any Perfon removed, and to provide for them. Stat. 13 & 14 *Car.* 2. *c.* 12. §. 3.	To be bound to the Affifes or Seffions, to be indicted for their Contempt.

Church-wardens or Overfeers refufing to receive any Perfon removed by two Juftices. Stat. 3 & 4 *W.* & *M.* *c.* 11. §. 10. Two Witneffes upon Oath.	Five Pounds for the Poor of the Parish from which he fhall be removed, to be levied by Diftrefs and Sale: For want, to be committed for Forty Days. The Warrant, by the Juftice of the Place to which the Removal is directed, to the Conftable where the Offender dwells.

[Two] Where any Poor come to fettle in any Tenement under 10 *l. per Annum*, they may remove fuch Perfon, who is likely to be chargeable to fuch Parish where he or they were laft legally fettled, either as a Native, Houfholder, Sojourner, Apprentice or Servant, for the Space of 40 Days at leaft, unlefs Security be given to difcharge the Parish, to be allowed by the Juftices. An Appeal lies to the next Quarter-Seffions.
Stat. 13 & 14 *Car.* 2. *c.* 12. §. 1, 2.
——— 1 *Jac.* 2. *c.* 17. §. 3.
——— 3 & 4 *W.* & *M.* *c.* 11. §. 3.
——— 12 *Ann. feff.* 1. *c.* 18. §. 2. *Quorum* 1.

To allow Certificates under the Hands and Seals of the Church-wardens or Overfeers of the Poor, attefted by two or more Witneffes, owning the Perfon mentioned in the Certificate to be an Inhabitant legally fettled, which Certificate is not good without their Allowance. Stat. 8 & 9 *W.* 3. *c.* 30. §. 1.

But

APPENDIX.

(Settlement and Removal.)

But if the Perfon, who hath fuch Certificate, rents 10 *l. per Annum*, or bears an Office in any other Parifh afterwards, that will gain a Settlement in that Parifh, notwithstanding fuch Certificate. Stat. 9 & 10 *W.* 3. *c.* 11. §. 1.

And *Note*; Perfons removing to other Parifhes by Virtue of fuch Certificates, and taking Apprentices, or hiring Servants there, fuch Apprentices or Servants do not thereby acquire any legal Settlement in fuch Parifhes. S.at. 12 *Ann. feff.* 1. *c.* 18. §. 2.

[**Qu. Seff.**] Upon an Appeal concerning the Settlement of the Poor, or upon Proof of Notice given of an Appeal, (though the Appeal was not afterwards profecuted) to award reafonable Cofts to the Party, for whom fuch Notice had been given. Stat. 8 & 9 *W.* 3. *c.* 30. §. 3.

Appeals againft an Order for the Removal of poor Perfons, to be heard and determined at the Quarter-Seffions in the County where the Place is, from whence fuch Perfon is removed, and not elfewhere. Stat. 8 & 9 *W.* 3. *c.* 30. §. 6.

See this Statute explained by the 12 *Ann. feff.* 1. *c.* 18. *antea.*

See 3 *Geo.* 2. *c.* 29. in *Dalton,* Tit. *Poor.*

Offences.   **Poft and Poft-Mafter.**   *Penalties.*

[**One**] **N**O Perfon fhall be capable of having, ufing or exercifing the Office of *Poft-Mafter General,* or any Part thereof, or any other Employment relating to the Poft-Office or any Branch thereof, or be any Way concerned in receiving, forting or delivering Letters or Packets, unlefs fuch Perfon fhall have taken the Oath prefcribed before one Juftice for the County or Place where fuch Perfon refides. Stat. 9 *Ann. c.* 10. §. 41.

[**Two**] *Poft-Mafter General,* or any other Officer relating to the Poft-Office, not taking the Oaths of Allegiance and Supremacy before two Juftices of the County where they are refident. Stat. 12 *Car.* 2. *c.* 35. §. 13.	Not capable to hold.

All Sums not exceeding 5 *l.* due for Poftage of Letters, to be recovered before them in the fame Manner, and under the fame Rates, as fmall Tithes are. See Title *Tithes,* where you will fee how fmall Tithes are to be recovered. Stat. 9 *Ann. c.* 10. §. 30.

Bill of Exchange wrote on one and the fame Piece of Paper with a Letter, and Letters to feveral and diftinct Perfons wrote upon one and the fame Piece of Paper, to be rated by the Poft-Mafter General, and to pay as fo many feveral and diftinct Letters, according to the Rates mentioned in the Stat. 9 *Ann. c.* 10. Stat. 6 *Geo.* 1. *c.* 21. §. 50.	To be recovered as fmall Tithes are by 7 & 8 *W.* 3. *c.* 6.

For 4 *Geo.* 2. *c.* 33. relating to the Penny-Poft, fee *Dalton,* Chap. 74. Tit. *Poft-Office.*

Offences.   **Preachers.**   *Penalties.*

[**One**] **A** Difturber of a Preacher lawfully licenfed. Stat. 1 *Mar. feff.* 2. *c.* 3. §. 5. *Vide* 10 *Ann. c.* 7.	To be committed.
[**Two**] Difturbers of Preachers lawfully licenfed. Stat. 1 *Mar. feff.* 2. *c.* 3. §. 6. *Vide* Title **Church,** touching Preachers in *Scotland.*	In fix Days after Commitment by a fingle Juftice. he and one other are to examine the Fact, and if they find Caufe, to commit him to the common Gaol for three Months, and thence to the next Quarter-Seffions.

[**Qu. Seff.**] If a Difturber of a Preacher lawfully licenfed, who has been committed to the County-Gaol by two Juftices, fhall at the Seffions be reconciled, and enter into Bond for his good Behaviour for a Year, he fhall be difcharged; but if he perfifts in his Obftinacy, he is to be committed without Bail, till he be reconciled, and be penitent for his Offence. Stat. 1 *Mar. feff.* 2. *c.* 3. §. 6.

He that refcues a Difturber of a licenfed Preacher. Stat. 1 *Mar. feff.* 2. *c.* 3. §. 7.	To be imprifoned and fined 5 *l.*
The Inhabitants of a Town, who fuffer a Difturber of a licenfed Preacher to efcape. Stat. 1 *Mar. feff.* 2. *c.* 3. §. 8.	Five Pounds.

I

[**One**

APPENDIX.

Prisons. See Gaols.

Offences.	Process.	Penalties.

[One] TO commit to the County-Gaol, without Bail or Mainprize, till the next Assises, Sessions of *Oyer* and *Terminer*, and General Gaol-Delivery, Persons opposing or resisting any Officer or Officers, or any aiding and assisting in the Execution of any Process in *White-Fryars, Savoy, Salisbury-Court, Ram-Alley, Mitre-Court, Fuller's Rents, Baldwyn's Gardens, Mountague-Close,* or the *Minories, Mint, Chink,* or *Deadman's Place.* Stat. 8 & 9 *W.* 3. *c.* 27. §. 15.

Offences.	Prophecies.	Penalties.

[Qu. Sess.] PUblisher or Setter forth of any fantastical, or false Prophecy, with an Intent to raise Sedition. Stat. 5 *Eliz. c.* 15. §. 2, 3.
Prosecution to be within six Months.

First Offence 10 *l.* and one Year's Imprisonment.
Second, forfeits all his Goods, and Imprisonment during his Life.
The Forfeitures to be divided between the Queen and the Prosecutor.

Offences.	Purveyors.	Penalties.

[One] PErsons making Purveyance, or impressing Carriages, or other Things, by Colour of any Warrant under the Great Seal, or otherwise. Stat. 12 *Car.* 2. *c.* 24. §. 14.
At the Request of the Party grieved.

To be committed to Gaol till next Sessions.

[Two] *Purveyor, Badger,* &c. bargaining for any Victual or Grain, in the Markets of *Oxford* or *Cambridge,* or in five Miles of them. Stat. 2 & 3 *P. & M. c.* 15. §. 2. 13 *Eliz. c.* 21.

Quadruple the Value thereof, and three Months Imprisonment without Bail.
Except when the Queen is there, or within seven Miles.

Offences.	Quakers.	Penalties.

[One] INstead of the Declaration of Fidelity appointed to be made and subscribed by *Quakers,* by 1 *W. & M. c.* 18. they are to make and subscribe the Declaration of Fidelity, mentioned in 8 *Geo.* 1. *c.* 6.
And instead of the solemn Affirmation or Declaration prescribed by 7 & 8 *W.* 3. *c.* 34. they are to make the solemn Declaration or Affirmation following:

I A. B. do solemnly, sincerely, and truly declare and affirm.

And instead of the Form prescribed by 1 *W. & M. c.* 18. for the Effect of the Abjuration Oath, they are to take that mentioned in 8 *Geo.* 1. *c.* 6.

Note; All Persons authorized to administer or tender either the said former Declaration, or the said solemn Affirmation or Declaration, or the said Effect of the Abjuration Oath aforesaid, are authorized and required to administer and tender the same respectively to *Quakers* in the Words appointed by the Stat. 8 *Geo.* 1. *c.* 6. §. 4.

If any *Quaker,* making such Affirmation or Declaration, shall be lawfully convicted of wilfully, falsly and corruptly affirming or declaring any Matter or Thing, which if sworn in the common or usual Form, would have amounted to wilful and corrupt Perjury. 8 *Geo.* 1. *c.* 6. §. 5.

Offender to suffer such and the same Pains, Penalties and Forfeitures, as are against Persons convict of wilful and corrupt Perjury.

Note; Quakers or reputed Quakers are disabled to give Evidence in any criminal Cause, to serve on a Jury, or bear Office or Place in the Government, by 7 & 8 *W.* 3. *c.* 34. And 8 *Geo.* 1. *c.* 6. §. 6.

Offences.	Quarentine.	Penalties.

NOTE; The 7 *Geo.* 1. *stat.* 1. *c.* 3. inserted under this Title in the Edition of this Book 1727. is expired.

A P P E N D I X.

[**One**] IF the Minifter, Petty Conftables, or Church-wardens of any Parifh, or any Two, complain of any Perfon (under the Peerage) fufpected for Recufancy. Stat. 7 *Jac.* 1. *c.* 6. §. 26.

To tender the Oath of Allegiance, and upon Refufal, to commit till next Affife or Seffions, where if he refufeth again, he incurs a *Præmunire*; but Feme Coverts fhall be imprifoned only, to remain there, till they take the Oath.

[**Two**] To fummon and convene before them all fuch Perfons within their Jurifdictions, *&c.* fufpected to be dangerous, or difaffected to the Government, and tender the Oath of Abjuration.
Upon Refufal. Stat. 6 *Ann. c.* 14. §. 7. *Quorum* 1.

To certify the Chriftian Name, Surname, and Place of Abode to the next Quarter-Seffions; if he takes it not next Term, or Seffions after Certificate, is a Popifh Recufant convict.

Vide *Recufancy* in Title **Papifts.**

Rents. See the Stat. 11 *Geo.* 2. *c.* 19. for the Powers of Juftices of Peace in Relation to Rents, in *Dalton,* Chap. 81. under this Title.

Offences.   **Riots and Rioters.**   *Penalties.*

[**One**] IF twelve or more Perfons are riotoufly and tumultuoufly affembled, he may by Proclamation require and command them to difperfe themfelves, and peaceably to depart to their Habitations, or to their lawful Bufinefs. Stat. 1 *Geo.* 1. *c.* 5. §. 1.

And if they continue together an Hour after, it is Felony without Clergy.

The Form of the *Proclamation.*

OUR Sovereign Lord the King chargeth and commandeth all Perfons, being affembled, immediately to difperfe themfelves, and peaceably to depart to their Habitations, or to their lawful Bufinefs, upon the Pains contained in the Act made in the Firft Year of King George, for preventing Tumults and riotous Affemblies.

God fave the King.

Every Juftice within his Jurifdiction is required on Notice or Knowledge of any riotous and tumultous Affembly, to refort to the Place, and there to make or caufe to be made Proclamation in Manner aforefaid. 1 *Geo.* 1. *c.* 5. §. 2.

Rioters demolifhing, or pulling down, or beginning to demolifh or pull down any Church or Chapel, or any Building for religious Worfhip, certified and regiftred according to the Stat. 1 *W. & M. c.* 18. or any Dwelling-houfe, Barn, Stable, or other Out-houfe. Stat. 1 *Geo.* 1. *c.* 5. §. 4.	Felony without Clergy.
Knowingly to let, hinder or hurt any Perfon beginning to make Proclamation, whereby fuch Proclamation fhall not be made; and the Rioters, to whom it fhould have been made, if not hindred, not difperfing themfelves, but continuing together an Hour after fuch Let or Hindrance. Stat. 1 *Geo.* 1. *c.* 5. §. 5.	Felony without Clergy.

The Stat. 1 *Geo.* 1. *c.* 5. againft Rioters, to be read openly at every Quarter-Seffions. §. 7.

Note; All Profecutions upon the Stat. 1 *Geo.* 1. *c.* 5. to be commenced in twelve Months. §. 8.

[**Two**] With the Sheriff or Under-Sheriff, fhall by the Power of the County, fupprefs Riots, Routs, and unlawful Affemblies, upon View to record it, commit the Offenders, and return the Record into the *King's Bench,* by which they fhall be convict: If the Offenders be gone, Inquiry to be made in a Month, and the Matter determined according to Law. The Penalty of not doing this, 100 Pounds. Stat. 13 *H.* 4. *c.* 7. §. 4.

Riots, *&c.* fhall be fupprefs'd and inquired of, at the King's Charge, which the Sheriff is to difburfe, by Indenture, between the Juftices and him. Stat. 2 *H.* 5. *c.* 8. §. 2.

Perfons guilty of heinous Riots. Stat. 2 *H.* 5. *c.* 8. §. 2.	One Year's Imprifonment, without Bail.

Together with the Sheriff, under their Hands and Seals to certify a Riot to the Lord Chancellor, to the End he may fend out a *Capias* againft the Rioters. Stat. 2 *H.* 5. *c.* 9. §. 2.

A P P E N D I X.

| *Offences.* | **Riot and Rioters.** | *Penalties.* |

To testify, That the common Fame runs in the same County of the same Riot, before a *Capias* shall be awarded, upon 6 *H.* 5. *c.* 9. Stat. 8 *H.* 6. *c.* 14. §. 2.

| If a Riot, &c. by Maintenance, or Embracery of the Jurors, be not found. Stat. 19 *H.* 7. *c.* 13. §. 11. | They, with the Sheriff, or Under-Sheriff, are to certify the Names of such Maintainers and Embracers, which shall be a Conviction; and they shall forfeit 20 *l.* a-piece, and to remain in Prison, at the Discretion of the Justices. |

| *Offences.* | **Robberies.** | *Penalties* |

[**One**] TO take the Oath of the Person robbed, whether he knows the Persons who robbed him, or any of them; and if he knows any of them, he is to enter into sufficient Bond to prosecute the Person or Persons, so by him known, by Indictment, or otherwise, according to Law. Stat. 27 *Eliz. c.* 13. §. 11.

To grant a Warrant to make Hue and Cry from Town to Town, and County to County, where a Robbery is committed. Stat. 28 *Ed.* 3. *c.* 11.

See the Statute of *Hue and Cry,* 8 *Geo.* 2. *c.* 16. in *Dalton,* Chap. 84. Tit. *Robbery.*

[**Two**] Two Justices dwelling within, or near the Hundred, where the Robbery is committed, shall set a Tax upon every Parish within the Hundred, for the Payment of the Money, whereof the Party is robbed. Stat. 27 *Eliz. c.* 13. §. 5. *Quorum* 1.

| *Offences.* | **Runaways.** | *Penalties.* |

[**Two**] PErsons running away and leaving their Charge to the Parish. Stat. 7 *Jac.* 1. *c.* 4. §. 8. *Vide* Stat. 12 *Ann. sess.* 2. *c.* 4. | To be punished as incorrigible Rogues.

| Persons, who threaten to run away, and leave their Charge to the Parish. Stat. 7 *Jac.* 1. *c.* 4. §. 8. | To be sent to the House of Correction, there to be punished as sturdy Rogues, (unless they put in sufficient Sureties to discharge the Parish) and not to be delivered, but at a Meeting of the Justices, or in open Sessions. |

Vide Title **Vagabonds.**

| *Offences.* | **Sacrament.** | *Penalties.* |

[**Three**] TO take Informations upon Oath, of two lawful Persons at least, against any Person, who shall speak or do any Thing in Contempt of the most Holy Sacrament; and to bind over by Recognizance, every Accuser and Witness in five Pounds a-piece, to appear at the next Sessions, and prosecute. Stat. 1 *Ed.* 6. *c.* 1. §. 1.

To send out two Writs, *Capias Exigend'* and *Capias Utlegat',* against Contemners of the Holy Sacrament, in all Counties and Liberties; and upon their Appearance to fine and imprison them, or to take Bail for their Appearance, to be tried at Sessions. Stat. 1 *Ed.* 6. *c.* 1. § 3.

To direct a Writ in the King's Name to the Bishop of the Diocese, where the Contemner of the Sacrament committed the Offence, by which Writ he shall be required to be present himself (or some for him sufficiently learned) at the Arraignment of the Offender, to give Advice concerning the Offence committed. Stat. 1 *Ed.* 6. *c.* 1. §. 4.

| *Offences.* | **Salt.** | *Penalties.* |

[**One**] OWners of *Salt* seised, not making it appear before the next Justice, within ten Days after Seisure, by the Oath of one or more Witnesses, That the *Salt* was duly entred, and that there was a Warrant for carrying away the same. Stat. 5 & 6 *W.* & *M. c.* 7. §. 7. | The *Salt* shall be forfeited; one Moiety to the King, the other to him who seised, and the Owner shall forfeit double the Value.

| *Salt* not measured by a Bushel of Eight Gallons *Winchester* Measure, by fit Measurers, sworn and admitted by a Justice without Fee. Stat. 5 & 6 *W.* & *M. c.* 7. §. 18. | Double the Value of the Salt so measur'd.

APPENDIX.

To take the *Affidavit* of the Quantity of *Rock-Salt*, melted and refined. Stat. 5 & 6 *W.* & *M. c.* 7. §. 26.

Offences.	*Penalties.*
Perfons removing or conveying any *Salt* from any Salt-Works, or Place thereunto belonging, without due Entry of the fame, and Payment or Security, or without Warrant, Ticket or Licence, for removing the fame. Stat. 1 *Ann. feff.* 1. *c.* 21. §. 4. Due Proof.	To be feifed, and if not able to pay the Penalties, and no fufficient Diftrefs, to be committed to the Houfe of Correction, to be whipp'd and kept to hard Labour, not exceeding one Month.
Perfons hindring or obftructing any Officer or Officers, for the Salt-Duties, in the Execution of his or their Offices, or fhall beat or abufe them. Stat. 1 *Ann. feff.* 1. *c.* 21. §. 4. Due Proof.	Twenty Pounds; and for Non-payment, and in Default of Diftrefs, to be committed to the Houfe of Correction, to be whipp'd, and kept to hard Labour, not exceeding a Month.
No Salt to be brought out of *Scotland* by Land. Stat. 2 & 3 *Ann. c.* 14. §. 7.	The Salt forfeited, and 20 *s.* a Bufhel; and if not paid, to be committed to the next Gaol, for fix Months, without Bail or Mainprife.
[**Two**] Officer having due Notice, and neglecting or refufing to attend weighing Salt, which is entred, to be put on Board any Ship or Veffel, or carried by Land, and the Duty paid or fecured, and all other Monies due on Account of Salt delivered. Stat. 9 & 10 *W.* 3. *c.* 6. §. 3. Party to be fummoned. Confeffion, or Two Witneffes.	Forty Shillings, to the Informer. To be levied by Diftrefs and Sale, unlefs redeemed in Six Days; and for Want of Diftrefs, Imprifonment till Satisfaction be made. An Appeal lies to the Quarter-Seffions.
Every Maker or Curer of White Herrings in that Part of *Great Britain* called *England, Wales,* and *Berwick upon Tweed,* before he remove any White Herrings (except for Exportation) from the Office or Place where cured, muft enter them at the next Salt-Office, and pay the Duty. And the Quantity muft be marked on the Cafk, and upon the Entry and Payment of the Duty the Salt-Officer to give a Permit. Stat. 8 *Geo.* 1. *c.* 16. §. 2.	The White Herrings removed or carried away before Entry and Duty paid, or Cafk mark'd, forfeited; and 40 Shillings for every Cafk or Veffel removed. One Moiety to his Majefty, the other to the Officer who fhall feife the fame. To be recovered, levied and mitigated in fuch Manner, as Penalties by any Law of Excife are recoverable.
[**Three**] *Badger, Retailer,* or other Perfon, making, or dealing in Salt, or buying Salt to fell again, otherwife than by Weight, after the Rate of 56 Pounds Weight to the Bufhel. Stat. 9 & 10 *W.* 3. *c.* 6. §. 1. Party to be fummoned, Confeffion, or Two Witneffes.	Five Pounds to the Informer, to be levied by Diftrefs and Sale, unlefs redeemed in Six Days; and for Want of Diftrefs, Imprifonment, till Satisfaction be made. An Appeal lies to the Quarter-Seffions.

[**Qu. Seff.**] To certify the Proof of Salt taken by the Enemy, or perifhed at Sea, in order for the Owners to have the Duty repaid, or Security delivered up. Stat. 12 *Ann. feff.* 2. *c.* 2. §. 7.

Offences.	*Penalties.*
[**One**] Houfe-keepers in the County of *Middlefex,* and City of *Weftminfter,* which are within the *Weekly Bills of Mortality,* and in *Kenfington,* not fweeping the Streets before their Houfes, on *Wednefdays* and *Saturdays.* Stat. 2 *W.* & *M. c.* 8. §. 2. View, Confeffion, or one Witnefs.	Three Shillings and four Pence a Day, to be levied by Diftrefs and Sale; if not paid within Six Days, to be committed till Payment. This Penalty enlarged to 10 *s.* by Statute 8 & 9 *W.* 3. *c.* 37. To be employed, if upon Conviction, by the Evidence; one Moiety to the Poor, the other to the Informer. If upon View, one Moiety to the Poor, the other to the Repair of the Highways.
Perfons laying, or fuffering to be laid any Sea-coal-Afhes, Duft, Dirt, &c. in any open Street, Lane or Alley, before their own Houfes, or any publick Places. Stat. 2 *W.* & *M. c.* 8. §. 2. View, Confeffion, or one Witnefs.	Five Shillings, to be levied and employed *ut fupra.*

APPENDIX.

Offences.	Scavenger.	Penalties.
Persons laying any Ashes, Dirt, or Soil, before the Houses or Walls of Inhabitants, or any Church-yard Wall, or the Queen's Palace; or throwing, or causing to be thrown into any common Sewer or Highway, or any private Vault, any noisome Thing whatsoever. Stat. 2 W. & M. c. 8. §. 2. Conviction ut supra.	Twenty Shillings, to be levied and employed ut supra.	
The respective Church-wardens, and the House-keepers, and other Keepers of Whitehall, Somerset-house, St. James's House and Park, the Guard-houses and Stables, &c. the Ushers, Porters, or Keepers of Courts of Justice. Ibid.	To suffer the like Penalties for the like Offences, and to be levied and employed ut supra.	
Persons hooping, washing, or cleansing any Vessels in Streets, Lanes, or open Passages; or setting any Dung, Soil, Rubbish, or empty Coaches to make or mend, or rough Timber, or Stones to be saw'd or wrought. Stat. 2 W. & M. c. 8. §. 4. Conviction ut supra.	Twenty Shillings for every Offence, to be levied and employed ut supra.	
Rakers, Scavengers, &c. not bringing Carts, and by a Bell, or otherwise, giving Notice of their Coming, and not daily (except Sundays and Holidays) carrying away the Dirt, &c. Stat. 2 W. & M. c. 8. §. 5. Conviction ut supra.	Forty Shillings for every Offence, to be levied and employed ut supra.	
Inhabitants, and Owners of Houses unoccupied, not Paving the Streets, before their Doors. Stat. 2 W. & M. c. 8. §. 8. Conviction ut supra.	Twenty Shillings a Rod or Perch for every Default, and Twenty Shillings a Week, till amended, to be levied and employed ut supra.	
Owners and Inhabitants of Houses new built, not paving, or otherwise amending the Ground before their Houses and Buildings. Stat. 2 W. & M. c. 8. §. 7. Conviction ut supra.	Forty Shillings for every Perch, and the like for every Week, till amended, to be levied and employed ut supra.	
Scavengers duly chosen, and refusing. Stat. 2 W. & M. c. 8. §. 9. Conviction ut supra.	Ten Pounds, to be levied ut supra, and employed in Mending and Repairing the Highways and Streets of the same Parish.	

[Two] Scavengers Tax to be made, after a Pound-Rate, by Constables, &c. and other antient Inhabitants, for a Year, to be allowed by Two Justices, payable quarterly; and in Case of Refusal, to be levied by Distress and Sale; and for Want of Distress to be imprisoned till Payment. Stat. 2 W. & M. c. 8. sess. 2. §. 10.

Scavengers refusing to account within 28 Days after the Election of new Scavengers. Stat. 2 W. & M. c. 8. sess. 2. §. 11.	To be committed till they account, and pay over the Money in their Hands to the new Scavengers.

To appoint vacant Places, near the Streets, for the Scavengers, to lay the Dirt, &c. in giving Satisfaction to the Owners, and in Case of unreasonable Demand, to moderate the Price. Stat. 2 W. & M. c. 8. §. 12.

Note; If any Conviction upon the Stat. 2 W. & M. c. 8. or on the Stat. 8 & 9 W. 3. c. 37. shall be by View or Knowledge of a Justice of Peace, then one Half of the Penalty shall be to the Poor, the other towards repairing Highways, and cleansing the Streets, to be paid to the Scavenger, otherwise to the Relief of the Poor. Stat. 8 9 W. 3. c. 37. §. 2.

[Qu. Sess.] Justices of the Peace in any City or Market-Town (not having already Provision made for them by any former Law) at their General or Quarter-Sessions, may appoint Scavengers, and order the Repairing and Cleansing the Streets; and may appoint Persons, or make Assessments on Owners and Occupiers of Lands and Houses equally, not exceeding Six Pence in the Pound, to defray the Charges of such Scavengers, to be levied in Eight Days, by Distress and Sale. Stat. 1 Geo. 1. c. 52. §. 9.

This Clause is extended to Justices of Peace in Corporate Towns, by 9 Geo. 2. c. 18.

Offences.	Servants.	Penalties.
[One] Servants to Clothiers, Woollen-Weavers, Tuckers, Fullers, Cloth-workers, Sheermen, Dyers, Hosiers, Taylors, Shoemakers, Tanners, Pewterers,	To be bound over to the Sessions. The Cause to excuse, must be proved by Two Witnesses.	

t

| *Offences.* | Servants. | *Penalties.* |

terers, Bakers, Brewers, Glovers, Cutlers, Smiths, Far-
riers, Curriers, Sadlers, Spurriers, Turners, Cappers,
Hat or Felt-makers, Fletchers, Arrowhead-makers,
Butchers, Cooks, Millers, refusing to serve for Statute-
Wages, and departing (being retained) without a Quar-
ter's Warning, or lawful Cause, to be allowed by a
Justice. Stat. 5 *Eliz. c.* 4. §. 9.

Masters, being Clothiers, or any of the Trades a-
bovementioned, putting away his Servant without a
Quarter's Warning, and good Cause to be allowed by
a Justice, and proved by two Witnesses. Stat. 5 *Eliz.
c.* 4. §. 8. | Forty Shillings, to be inflicted at Sessions, and they
to be bound over.

One retained in Service to work, and departing
without Licence. Stat. 5 *Eliz. c.* 4. §. 11. | One Month's Imprisonment.

To give a *Testimonial* under his Hand to Labourers, that they had not sufficient Work in the Place, where
they dwelt, that they might get Work in other Shires in the Time of Harvest, for which he may take one
Penny. Stat. 5 *Eliz. c.* 4. §. 23.

[**Two**] Servants assaulting Master, Mistress, Dame,
or Overseer. Stat. 5 *Eliz. c.* 4. §. 21. | One Year's Imprisonment, or less, or to be bound
over to the Sessions, there to receive such open Punish-
ment, as shall be thought convenient, Life and Member
excepted.

Unmarried Women fit to serve, being above 12, and
under 43, refusing to serve for convenient Time and
Wages. 5 *Eliz. c.* 4. §. 24. | Imprisonment.

To hear and determine the Breach of 5 *Eliz. c.* 4. upon Indictment, or otherwise, and award Process and
Execution accordingly. The Forfeitures (except those otherwise limited) to be divided between the Queen and
Prosecutor. Stat. 5 *Eliz. c.* 4. §. 39.

[**Qu. Sess.**] Servants to Clothiers, &c. refusing to
serve for the Wages limited, according to the Statute;
and being retained, departing his or their Service without a Quarter's Warning, or some lawful Cause. Stat.
5 *Eliz. c.* 4. §. 9. | To be imprisoned without Bail, but upon Submission
to perform the Service, to be enlarged without Fees.

A Servant having served in one City or Town, and
getting to serve in another, without a Testimonial.
Stat. 5 *Eliz. c.* 4. §. 11. | To be imprisoned till he procure one; if he procure
it not in 20 Days, to be whipped as a Vagabond.

A Master taking a Servant without a Testimonial.
Stat. 5 *Eliz. c.* 4. §. 11.
Vide Wages. | Five Pounds.

| *Offences.* | Sewers. | *Penalties.* |

[**Sir**] After the End of ten Years, all Laws, Ordinances, and Constitutions, made by Virtue of any Commission of *Sewers*, shall be in Force for one Year; and *Six* Justices may execute such Commission,
and Law, &c. unless in the Interim a new Commission issues. Stat. 13 *Eliz. c.* 9. §. 2. *Quorum* 2.

[**Qu. Sess.**] To swear the Commissioners of *Sewers.* Stat. 23 *H.* 8. *c.* 5. §. 5.

| *Offences.* | Sheep. | *Penalties.* |

[**Qu. Sess.**] HE that keeps in his own Possession
at any one Time above 2000
Sheep. Stat. 25 *H.* 8. *c.* 13. §. 1.
The Prosecution for the King to be within three
Years; for a Subject, within one. | Three Shillings and four Pence a-piece.
Lambs not to be accounted Sheep till *Midsummer*
twelve Months after their Fall.
1000 Sheep to be reckoned after the Rate of 120
to the 100.
Executors, Infants, Spiritual Persons, or Temporal
Persons, for House-Provisions, exempted.

APPENDIX.

Offences.	**Sheep.**	*Penalties.*
Transporting Sheep beyond Sea. Stat. 8 *Eliz. c.* 3. §. 2.	First Offence, Forfeiture of Goods, to be divided between the Queen and the Profecutor. To be imprifoned for a Year, and to have his Hand cut off in fome open Market. Second Offence, Felony.

Offences.	**Sheriff.**	*Penalties.*
[**One**] SHeriff, Under-Sheriff, or Sheriff's Clerk, entring in the County-Court any Plaint in the Abfence of the Plaintiff, or his Attorney, or having above one Plaint for one Caufe. Stat. 11 *H.* 7. *c.* 15.	Forty Shillings, to be divided between the King and the Profecutor. To examine this Matter, and if the Party be found guilty, to certify the Examination into the *Exchequer*, within three Months, on Pain of 40 *s.* The Certificate is a Conviction.
[**Qu. Seff.**] Sheriffs, Under-Sheriffs Clerks, Bailiffs, Gaolers, Coroners, Stewards, Bailiffs of Franchifes, and all other Officers, who act contrary to Stat. 23 *H.* 6. *c.* 10. §. 1.	40 *l.* to be divided between the King and the Profecutor *ut fupra.*

The Juftices, who are to have the Controlment of the Sheriff, and his Eftreats, are to be named in *Michaelmas* Seffions, by the *Cuftos Rotulorum,* or (in his Abfence) by the Eldeft of the *Quorum.* Stat. 11 *H.* 7. *c.* 15.

Sheriffs, Coroners, and other Perfons having Return of Writs, not returning Jurors, and not levying Iffues, according to Stat. 27 *Eliz. c.* 7. §. 2.	Five Marks to the Queen, upon Conviction, Procefs to iffue for the Levying of it.
Every Bailiff of a Franchife, Deputy, or Clerk of a Sheriff, or Under-Sheriff, intermeddling with their Offices before they are fworn. Stat. 27 *Eliz. c.* 12. §. 4.	40 *l.* to be divided between the King and the Profecutor; upon Conviction to award Procefs.

Note; The *Original Poll-Books, &c.* of Elections of Knights of the Shire, are to be delivered on Oath by the Sheriffs, or Returning Officers, to the Clerk of the Peace, and by him kept among the Records of the Seffions of the Peace. Stat. 10 *Ann. c.* 23. §. 5.

Vide Title **Forcible Entry** and **Detainer**, Title **Oath**, and Title **Wages of Knight of the Shire.**

Offences.	**Ships.**	*Penalties.*
[**Two**] PErfons entring Ships in Diftrefs, without Leave of the Commander, (except Officers of the Cuftoms, Conftables, or others by their Order) or fhall moleft the Affiftants, or endeavour to hinder the Saving of the Ships or Goods, or when faved, deface the Marks of any Goods before taken down in a Book. Stat. 12 *Ann. feff.* 2. *c.* 18. §. 3.	Shall within twenty Days after make double Satisfaction to the Party grieved, at Difcretion of two next Juftices; or in Default, be by them fent to the next Houfe of Correction to hard Labour for twelve Months enfuing.
[**Three**] Perfons affifting Ships in Diftrefs, and preferving the fame, or their Cargoes, to be paid by the Commander, Mafter or Owner, within 30 Days after, a reafonable Reward for their Service. Stat. 12 *Ann. feff.* 2. *c.* 18. §. 2.	In Default, the Ship, *&c.* to remain in Cuftody of the Officer of the Cuftoms, till all Affiftants be reafonably gratified; and in Cafe of Difagreement, three near Juftices named by the Officer, fhall adjuft the *Quantum* to be paid each Affiftant.

And if no Perfon claims the Goods, the chief Officer of the neareft Port to apply to Three of the neareft Juftices, who are to put him, or fome other refponfible Perfon, in Poffeffion of the Goods, taking an Account in Writing thereof, to be figned by the faid Officer, and if *perifhable,* fold prefently, or elfe kept a Year. 12 *Ann. feff.* 2. *c.* 18. §. 2.
Made perpetual 4 *Geo.* 1. *c.* 12.

Offences.	**Shoemakers.**	*Penalties.*
[**Qu. Seff.**] SHoemakers not making their Boots, *&c.* of good and fufficient Stuff, nor fewing them well, and felling on *Sunday.* Stat. 1 *Jac.* 1. *c.* 22. §. 28.	3 *s.* 4 *d.* for every Offence, and the Value of the Wares made and fold, to be divided one Third to the King, one to the Profecutor, and the other to the City, Borough, Town or Lord of the Liberty, where the Offence is committed.

A P P E N D I X.

In *London*, the Mafter and Wardens of the Company of *Shoemakers, Curriers, Girdlers* and *Sadlers*, to fearch every Quarter at leaft, and view all Wares made of tanned Leather, and to feife all infufficient Wares. Stat. 1 *Jac.* 1. *c.* 22. §. 29.

Forty Shillings for every Year's Default, to be divided between the King and Profecutor.

See 9 *Geo.* 1. *c.* 27. in *Dalton,* Chap. 58. Tit. *Labourers.*

Offences. **Silk.** *Penalties.*

[**One**] Silk-winders, and Doublers, unjuftly purloining, imbezilling, pawning, felling, or detaining Silk, delivered by Silk-throwers, and the Buyers and Receivers of fuch Silk. Stat. 13 & 14 *Car.* 2. *c.* 15. §. 7. 20 *Car.* 2. *c.* 6. §. 3.

Confeffion, or one Witnefs.

This extends to all Perfons, who fhall imbezil, pawn, fell, or detain any Silk delivered to any Silk-Manufacturers, Agents, Journeymen, Warpers, and Winders, by Stat. 8 & 9 *W.* 3. *c.* 36. §. 6.

To pay fuch Recompence and Satisfaction for Damage, Lofs, and Charges, as he fhall order, not exceeding what the Party proves: If the Party be not able to make Satisfaction, or if he be, and do it not in 14 Days, to be whipped and fet in the Stocks.

To be committed to Prifon, or Houfe of Correction, till Satisfaction be made, or Punifhment inflicted.

Offences. **Silk-thrower.** *Penalties.*

Qu. Seff.] Exercifing the Trade of a Silk-thrower, not having ferved feven Years. Stat. 13 & 14 *Car.* 2. *c.* 15. §. 2.

40 *s.* a Month; one Moiety to the King, the other to the Profecutor.

Offences. **Smugglers or Runners of Foreign Goods.** *Penalties,*

[**One**] Perfons who fhall be found paffing (knowingly and wittingly) with any Foreign Goods or Commodities landed from any Ship or Veffel, without due Entry, and Payment of the Duties in their Cuftody, from any of the Coafts of this Kingdom, or within 20 Miles of any of the faid Coafts; and fhall be more than five Perfons in Company, or fhall carry any offenfive Arms or Weapons, or wear any Vizard, Mafk, or other Difguife, when paffing with fuch Goods, or fhall forcibly hinder or refift any Officer of the *Cuftoms* or *Excife,* in the Seifing Run-Goods, are, Stat. 8 *Geo.* 1. *c.* 18. §. 6.

Guilty of Felony, and to be tranfported for feven Years, to fome of his Majefty's Plantations or Colonies in *America.*

Returning into *Great Britain* or *Ireland,* before the Expiration of Seven Years.

Felony without Benefit of Clergy.

Perfons Receiving or Buying any Goods, Wares, or Merchandizes, clandeftinely run or imported, before the fame fhall have been legally condemned, knowing the fame to be fo clandeftinely run or imported.

One or more credible Witneffes, or Confeffion. Stat. 8 *Geo.* 1. *c.* 18. §. 10.

Forfeit Twenty Pounds, to be levied by Diftrefs and Sale, &c.

And for Want of Diftrefs, to be committed to Prifon without Bail or Mainprife for three Months.

One Moiety of the above Penalty to the Informer, the other to the Poor of the Parifh where the Offence committed.

[**Two**] All Seifures of Veffels or Boats of 15 Tuns, or under, which fhall be made by Virtue of the Act 8 *Ann. For granting to her Majefty new Duties of Excife,* &c. And of an *Act for Continuing feveral Impofitions,* &c. *to raife Money by Loan for the Service of the Year* 1710. or of any other Act relating to the Revenue of Cuftoms, for carrying uncuftomed or prohibited Goods from Ships, inwards, or for relanding Certificate or Debentur Goods from Ships, outwards: And all Seifures of Horfes, or other Cattle, or Carriages whatfoever, for being ufed in the Removing, Carriage, or Conveyance of fuch Goods contrary to the faid Acts. Stat. 8 *Geo.* 1. *c.* 18. §. 16.

To be examined into, proceeded upon, heard, adjudged, and determined by two or more Juftices, refiding near the Place where fuch Seifure fhall be made, whofe Judgment is final, and not liable to *Appeal,* or *Certiorari.*

1

Note;

Offences.   **Smugglers or Runners of Foreign Goods.**   Penalties.

Note; Juftices of *London* and *Weftminfter* have the like Power in Summoning, Examining, &c. fuch Seifures, made in the faid Cities, as Juftices of any other County or Place have. *Ibid.* §. 17.

See 12 *Geo.* 1. *c.* 28. and 9 *Geo.* 2. *c.* 35. in *Dalton*, Tit. *Cuftoms*, Chap. 33.

Offences.   **Soldiers and Mariners.**   Penalties.

[**Qu. Seff.**] A Soldier lifted *departing* without Licence. Stat. 7 *H.* 7. *c.* 1. §. 2. Stat. 2 & 3 *Ed.* 6. *c.* 2. §. 6. The Trial to be in the County where he is apprehended.	Felony without Benefit of Clergy.

To charge every Parifh towards a weekly Relief of maimed *Soldiers* and *Mariners*, fo as no Parifh pay weekly above 10 *d.* nor under 2 *d.* nor any County, which confifts of above 50 Parifhes, pay above 6 *d.* one Parifh with another. Stat. 43 *Eliz. c.* 3. §. 6.

Upon a Certificate under the Hand and Seal of the chief Commander, or of the Captain under whom a *Soldier* or *Mariner* ferved, a quarterly Penfion is to be allowed him, till revoked or altered; he who hath not born Office, not to exceed 10 *l.* An Officer under a Lieutenant 15 *l.* A Lieutenant 20 *l.* Stat. 43 *Eliz. c.* 3. §. 8.

A Perfon commanded to mufter, abfenting himfelf without lawful Excufe, or not bringing his beft Arms. Stat. 4 & 5 *P.* & *M. c.* 3. §. 2.	Ten Days Imprifonment without Bail, unlefs he agrees to pay 40 *l.* to be eftreated into the *Exchequer*.
Any Perfon authorized to mufter or levy Soldiers, exacting or taking any Reward to difcharge, or fpare any from the Service. Stat. 4 & 5 *P.* & *M. c.* 3. §. 3.	Ten Times fo much as he fhall exact, or take; one Moiety to the Crown, the other to the Profecutor.
A *Captain*, or other Officer, after he fhall have (for a Reward) licenfed a Soldier to depart, not paying him his Wages, and Coat, and Conduct-Money. Stat. 4 & 5 *P.* & *M. c.* 3. §. 4.	Ten Times fo much as he fhall take, to be divided between the Crown and the Profecutor, and to the Soldier three Times fo much as he fhould have paid him.

See the annual Act for punifhing Mutiny and Defertion, &c.

Offences.   **Spirits.**   Penalties.

[**Qu. Seff.**] SErvants and others wittingly and willingly affifting in making Spirits, &c. contrary to Stat. 10 & 11 *W.* 3. *c.* 4. §. 1.	Six Months Imprifonment, without Bail or Mainprife.

See **Brandy and Spirits.**

Offences.   **Squibs.**   Penalties.

[**One**] NO Perfon of what Age, Sex, Degree or Quality foever, to make, fell, or utter, or offer, or expofe to Sale any *Squibs*, *Rockets*, *Serpents* or other *Fireworks*; or to permit or fuffer any Squibs, &c. to be caft, thrown, or fired out of, or in their Houfes or Lodgings, or any Part or Place thereto adjoining, into any publick Street, &c. or to throw, caft, or fire, or to be aiding and affifting in Throwing, &c. any Squibs, &c. in or into any Street, &c. is a common Nufance. Stat. 9 & 10 *W.* 3. *c.* 7. §. 1.

Perfons making, or caufing to be made, giving, felling or uttering, or offering, or expofing to Sale any Squibs, &c. Stat. 9 & 10 *W.* 3. *c.* 7. §. 2. Confeffion, or two Witneffes.	Five Pounds, to be levied by Diftrefs and Sale, one Half to the Poor, the other to the Profecutor.
Perfons permitting, or fuffering any Squibs, &c. to be caft, thrown, or fired from out of, or in his, her, or their Houfe or Houfes, Shops, Dwelling or Habitation, or any Part thereof, into any Street, &c. Stat. 9 & 10 *W.* 3. *c.* 7. §. 2. Conviction *ut fupra.*	Twenty Shillings, to be levied and employed *ut fupra.*
Perfons throwing, cafting or firing, or being aiding and affifting in Throwing, &c. any Squibs, &c. Stat. 9 & 10 *W.* 3. *c.* 7. §. 3. Conviction *ut fupra.*	Twenty Shillings, to be employed *ut fupra*; and if not paid immediately to the Juftice, the Party to be committed to the Houfe of Correction, to hard Labour, not exceeding a Month, unlefs the Offender fhall fooner pay the Money.

Note; This Act extends not to the Mafter of the Ordnance, nor to the Artillery Company.

                     Stamp-

A P P E N D I X.

Offences	Stamp-Duties	Penalties
[One] Counterfeiting or forging Stamps made in Pursuance of the several Statutes.	Felony without Benefit of Clergy.	
To cause or procure to be forged or counterfeited any *Stamp* or *Mark*, to resemble any Mark or Stamp, provided, made, or used in Pursuance of this, or any Act, relating to the Stamp-Duties ; or to cause or procure any Vellum, Parchment, Paper, Cards, or Dice, to be marked or stamped, with such counterfeit Stamp, or Mark. Stat. 6 *Geo.* 1. *c.* 21. §. 60.	Felony without Benefit of Clergy.	
[Two] If any Person shall write or print any Surrender or Admittance of or to any Copyhold Estate in *Great Britain* or *Wales*, or any Grant or Lease by Copy of Court-Roll, *&c.* (except the Surrender to the Use of a Will) or any Matter directed to be stamp'd, by 10 *Ann. c.* 19. or shall sell or expose to Sale any Pamphlet or News-paper (excepting Pamphlets exceeding one whole Sheet) before the same shall be stamped, the Offender forfeits. 10 *Ann. c.* 19. §. 105.	Ten Pounds, with full Costs for every Offence. One Moiety to the Crown, the other Moiety, with full Costs, to the Prosecutor. §. 119, 120.	
Every Steward, or his Deputy, offending, and being convicted. *Ibid.*	Over and above the said Forfeiture, shall lose his Place ; and such Writing is not good, and shall not be given in Evidence, until five Pounds together with the Ten, be paid, and a Receipt be produced under the Hand of the Receiver General of the Stamp-Duties, or his Deputy, and until the Vellum, *&c.* be stamped.	
Persons writing or printing any Thing on stamped Paper, after the Crown shall think fit to alter or renew the Stamps, after the Expiration of sixty Days, after such Intention of Altering or Renewing shall be published by Proclamation. 5 *& 6 W. & M. c.* 21. §. 16.	Forfeit as Persons writing on Paper not stamped.	
Printer and Publisher of any Pamphlet of more than one Sheet, and the Duty not paid, and the Title of it registred, and one Copy not stamped within the Time limited by the said Statute. 10 *Ann. c.* 19. §. 112.	Twenty Pounds, with full Costs. One Moiety to the Crown, the other Moiety, with full Costs, to the Prosecutor. §. 119, 120. And the Author, Printer and Publisher to lose the Property in the Copy, though the Title thereto be registred in *Stationers Hall* ; and any Person may freely print and publish the same, paying the Duty, without being liable to a Prosecution.	
All Pamphlets must have the Printer's or Publisher's Name printed thereon. *Ibid.* §. 113.	Twenty Pounds for every Offence *ut supra.*	

Two or more Justices, residing near the Place where any Pecuniary Forfeiture, not exceeding Twenty Pounds, upon this or any of the Acts of Parliament, touching the Duties under the Management of the Commissioners for managing the Duties on stamped Vellum, Parchment and Paper, shall be incurred, to hear and determine the same, within one Year after Seizure made, or Offence committed in a summary Way. And to award and issue out Warrants for levying the Penalties, adjudged on the Offender's Goods, and to cause them to be sold, unless redeemed within six Days, rendring the Overplus. *Ibid.* §. 172.

2. Whether the Party offending may not be committed (if he has no Goods whereon to levy) till he pay the Penalty.

In their Discretions.

Justices may mitigate Penalties as they shall think fit, the reasonable Costs and Charges of the Officers and Informers being first allowed over and above such Mitigation, and so as it does not reduce the Penalties to less than double the Duties, over and above the Costs and Charges. *Ibid.* §. 173.

[Qu. Sess.] Persons aggrieved by the Sentence of two Justices, may appeal to the next Quarter-Sessions, who may examine Witnesses on Oath, and finally determine the same, and issue Warrants to levy. *Ibid.* §. 173.

Note ; No *Writ* or *Certiorari* lies to supersede Execution or other Proceedings upon any Order made in Pursuance of the above Statute. *Ibid.* § 174.

Journals, Mercuries and News-papers, printed on one Sheet and Half-Sheet of Paper, shall not for the future be deemed or taken as Pamphlets, to be entred, and pay only three Shillings for each Impression thereof.

There

APPENDIX.

Offences.   **Stamp-Duty.**   *Penalties.*

There shall be paid for every Sheet of Paper, on which any Journal, Mercury, or other News-paper whatsoever shall be printed, a Duty of one Penny; and for every Half-Sheet, one Halfpenny, during the Term mentioned in the Act 10 *Ann.*

These Duties shall be levied in the same Manner, and subject to the same Penalties, &c. as are contained in the said Act 10 *Ann.* or any other Act relating to those Duties. 11 *Geo.* 1. *c.* 8. §. 13, 14, 15.

Offences.   **Starch and Hair Powder.**   *Penalties.*

NOTE; The Penalties in relation to the Duties on Starch and Hair Powder, shall be recovered or mitigated, by such Ways as any Penalty may be by any Law of Excise, or by Action in any Court at *Westminster,* &c. And one Moiety of such Penalties (not otherwise directed by the Acts) shall be to the Crown, the other Moiety to him that shall sue. See the Statutes 10 *Ann. c.* 26. 12 *Ann. stat.* 2. *c.* 9. 4 *Geo.* 2. *c.* 14.

Offences.   **Stolen Goods.**   *Penalties.*

[One] Taking Money or Reward, directly or indirectly, under Pretence, or upon Account of helping any Person to any stolen Goods or Chattels, unless such Person doth apprehend, or cause to be apprehended such Felon who stole the same, and bring him to Trial, and give Evidence against him. Stat. 4 *Geo.* 1. *c.* 11. §. 4.

> Guilty of Felony, and to suffer in the same Manner, as if he had stole such Goods himself.

[Two] Whoever shall discover, apprehend, and prosecute to Conviction of Felony without Benefit of Clergy, any Person for taking Money, or other Reward, directly or indirectly, to help any Person to stolen Goods (such Offender not having apprehended the Felon who stole the same, and brought him to Trial for the same, and given Evidence against him) upon a Certificate under the Hand and Seal of the two next Justices, shall receive the Sum of 40 *l.* to be paid by the Sheriff. Stat. 6 *Geo.* 1. *c.* 23. §. 9

> Penalty of Forty Pounds, to be recovered by Action of Debt, &c. on any Person taking more than five Shillings for a Certificate.
>
> *Note*; The Reward of Forty Pounds for apprehending and convicting any Person for Burglary, to be paid without any Deduction as aforesaid. §. 10.

Offences.   **Subornation of Perjury.**   *Penalties.*

[Qu. Sess.] Suborning a Witness to give Testimony in any Court of Record, concerning any Lands, Goods, Debts, or Damages. Stat. 5 *Eliz. c.* 9. §. 3.

> Forty Pounds, and if he has not wherewith to satisfy the same, six Months Imprisonment, without Bail, to stand upon the Pillory in the same or next Market-Town where the Offence was committed, and disabled to give Testimony in any Court of Record, till the Judgment be reversed by Attaint, or otherwise.

Note; One Justice may bind over, or commit the Offender.

See 2 *Geo.* 2. *c.* 25. in *Dalton*, Chap. 70. Tit. *Perjury.*

Offences.   **Sunday.**   *Penalties.*

[One] Persons being present at Bear-baitings, Bull-baitings, Interludes, common Plays, and any other unlawful Pastimes on the Lord's Day. Stat. 1 *Car.* 1. *c.* 1. §. 4.
View, Confession, or one Witness.
Prosecution in one Month.

> Three Shillings and four Pence for the Poor, to be levied by Distress, &c. in Default, to sit in the Stocks three Hours.

Carrier, Waggoner, Carman, Wainman, or Drover, travelling on the Lord's Day about their respective Business. Stat. 3 *Car.* 1. *c.* 1. §. 2.
View, Confession, or two Witnesses.
Prosecution in six Months.

> Twenty Shillings for every Offence, to be levied and employed *ut supra.*
> Third Part may be allowed to the Prosecutor.

Persons of the Age of 14 Years, and upwards, doing any worldly Labour or Business on the Lord's Day, Works

> Five Shillings to the Poor, to be levied by Distress and Sale; if not able, to be set in the Stocks two Hours. The

A P P E N D I X.

Offences.	𝖘𝖚𝖓𝖉𝖆𝖞.	*Penalties.*
Works of Charity and Neceffity only excepted. Stat. 29 *Car.* 2. *c.* 7. §. 1. View, Confeffion, or one Witnefs.		
Perfons publickly crying, or expofing to Sale any Wares, except Milk. Stat. 29 *Car.* 2. *c.* 7. §. 1. Conviction *ut fupra.* View, Confeffion, or one Witnefs.	The Wares to be feifed, and fold for the Poor.	
Drovers, Horfe-Courfers, Waggoners, Butchers, Higlers, or their Servants, travelling on the Lord's Day. Stat. 29 *Car.* 2. *c.* 7. §. 2. Conviction *ut fupra.*	Twenty Shillings, to be employed *ut fupra;* to be levied by Diftrefs and Sale ; if not able, to be fet in the Stocks two Hours.	
Perfons ufing or travelling on the Lord's Day, with Boat, Wherry, &c. except allowed by a Juftice, &c. Stat. 29 *Car.* 2. *c.* 7. §. 2. Conviction *ut fupra.*	Five Shillings, to be levied and employed *ut fupra* ; and if not able, punifhed *ut fupra.* A Part of the Penalties in this Act, not exceeding a Third, may be given to the Informer.	

Vide 𝖘𝖍𝖔𝖊𝖒𝖆𝖐𝖊𝖗𝖘 and 𝕭𝖚𝖙𝖈𝖍𝖊𝖗.

Offences.	𝖘𝖜𝖊𝖆𝖗𝖎𝖓𝖌 𝖆𝖓𝖉 𝕮𝖚𝖗𝖘𝖎𝖓𝖌.	*Penalties.*
[𝕺𝖓𝖊] Perfons profanely Swearing or Curfing. Stat. 21 *Jac.* 1. *c.* 20. §. 1. Hearing of a Juftice, Confeffion, or two Witneffes.	Twelve Pence for the Poor, to be levied by Diftrefs, &c. or in Default, to be fet in the Stocks three Hours, if the Offender be above 12 Years old ; but if under, and not paying, to be whipped by the Conftable, or the Parent or Mafter, in the Conftable's Prefence.	
Servants, Labourers, common Soldiers, common Seamen, profanely fwearing and curfing in the Prefence or Hearing of a Juftice of Peace. Every other Perfon. Stat. 6 & 7 *W.* 3. *c.* 11. §. 1. Confeffion, or one Witnefs. Profecution to be in ten Days.	One Shilling for the firft Offence, for the Second double, for the Third treble, to the Ufe of the Poor. Two Shillings firft, fecond and third, *ut fupra,* to the fame Ufe, to be levied by Diftrefs and Sale ; if no Diftrefs, to be fet in the Stocks one Hour for one Offence, two Hours for more, if above 16 Years of Age ; if under, to be whipped.	
Juftice omitting or neglecting to put in Execution the Act immediately above mentioned. Stat. 6 & 7 *W.* 3. *c.* 11. §. 3. Profecution *ut fupra.*	Five Pounds.	
Parfon not reading the laft mentioned Act, the next *Sunday* after every Quarter-Day, yearly, immediately after Morning Prayer. Stat. 6 & 7 *W.* 3. *c.* 11. §. 6. Profecution *ut fupra.*	Twenty Shillings for every Omiffion.	

To regifter in a Book all Convictions upon Stat. 6 & 7 *W.* 3. *c.* 11. and the Time, and certify the fame to the Quarter-Seffions. Stat. 6 & 7 *W.* 3. *c.* 11. §. 7.

Offences.	𝕮𝖆𝖓𝖓𝖊𝖗𝖘.	*Penalties.*

[𝕺𝖓𝖊] To adminifter an Oath to Tanners, and Dreffers of Hides in *England,* That they did, within two Days after taking Hide, or Skin, or Pieces thereof, or Vellum, or Parchment, out of Wooze, Mill, Liquor, or other Materials, make a true Entry, with the proper Officer, of the Number and Quality of the Hides, &c. fo taken out to be dried. Stat. 9 *Ann. c.* 11. §. 16.

To adminifter an Oath to Tanners, &c. that they give Notice to the proper Officer two Days before Removal of Hides, &c. Stat. 9 *Ann. c.* 11. §. 16.

[𝕿𝖜𝖔] Tanner, or other Perfon, fhaving, or caufing to be fhaved, Hide or Calf-Skin before tanned, whereby it fhall be impaired, or Duty diminifhed. Profecution in three Months.	Every fuch Hide, or Skin, or the Value, forfeited. One Moiety to the Queen, the other to the Informer. Juftices may mitigate, fo as the reafonable Cofts and Charges in Profecution be allowed over and above fuch	

2   An   Miti-

APPENDIX.

Offences	Penalties
An Appeal to the next Quarter-Seffions. Stat. *9 Ann.* *c.* 11. §. 11.	Mitigation, fo as the Penalty be not reduced to lefs than one fourth Part. §. 37. To continue for 32 Years.

Vide the Definition of tanned Hides or Skins, Pieces of Hides or Skins, Leather dreffed in Oil, &c. and tawed Leather, in Stat. *9 Ann. c.* 11. §. 3.

Offences	Penalties
Tanners, Bazil-Tanners, Curriers, Tawers, *Spanish* Leather-Dreffers, and all other Dreffers of Hides or Skins, or Pieces of Hides or Skins, and all Makers of Vellum and Parchment, neglecting to give Notice in Writing to the proper Officer, of their refpective Names and Places of Abode, and Tan-houfes, Yards, Work-houfes, Mills, or other Places for Tanning, Tawing, or Dreffing any fuch Hides, or Skins, or Pieces thereof. Profecution and Appeal *ut fupra.* Stat. *9 Ann. c.* 11. §. 15.	Fifty Pounds; one third Part to the Queen, the other two Thirds to the Informer.
Owners, or Occupiers of Tan-Yards, &c. refufing the proper Officer to enter. Profecution and Appeal *ut fupra.* Stat. *9 Ann. c.* 11. §. 17.	Ten Pounds, to be divided *ut fupra.* Mitigation *ut fupra.*
Tanners, Tawers, Curriers, or Dreffers of any Hides, or Skins, or Pieces thereof; or any Makers of Vellum or Parchment, ufing any private Tan-yard, &c. or not giving timely Notice of taking the Hides, &c. out of the Wooze, &c. or Removing, Sending, or Carrying away the fame, or any Part thereof; or hiding or concealing any Skins, &c. or caufing the fame to be hid or concealed. Profecution and Appeal *ut fupra.* Stat. *9 Ann. c.* 11. §. 17.	Twenty Pounds, and the Forfeiture of the Skins, &c. or the Value thereof; one Moiety to the Queen, the other to the Informer. Mitigation *ut fupra.*
Tanners, &c. not paying the Duties, with which Hides, Skins, &c. are chargeable. Sending, delivering, or carrying out any Hides, &c. before the Duty is paid. Profecution and Appeal *ut fupra.* Stat. *9 Ann. c.* 11. §. 25.	Double the Duty. Double the Value of fuch Hides fo delivered, or carried out. To be divided *ut fupra.* Mitigation *ut fupra.*
Tanners, &c. not keeping juft Scales and Weights, or not permitting Hides, &c. to be weighed, or neglecting to bring the fame to the Scale; or to affift at the Weighing, or removing Hides, &c. or caufing them to be removed, before the Duties be charged, and the Skins, &c. marked. Profecution and Appeal *ut fupra.* Stat. *9 Ann. c.* 11. §. 26.	Fifty Pounds, to be divided *ut fupra.* Mitigation *ut fupra.*
Tanners, &c. not accounting with the proper Officer once in Three Months. Profecution and Appeal *ut fupra.* Stat. *9 Ann. c.* 11. §. 27.	Fifty Pounds, to be divided *ut fupra.* Mitigation *ut fupra.*

Note; Collar-makers, Glovers, Bridle-Cutters, and others, who drefs any Skins or Hides, or Pieces of Skins or Hides, in Oil, Allom and Salt, or Meal, or with other Ingredients, and who cut and make the fame into Wares, are Tawers and Dreffers within the Act, and fubject to the Penalties and Forfeitures in the fame. Stat. *9 Ann. c.* 11. §. 28.

Offences	Penalties
Officer taking any Fee or Reward for any Entries, Accounts, Permiffions, Certificates, Marks, or Receipts. Profecution and Appeal *ut fupra.* Stat. *9 Ann. c.* 11. §. 35.	Five Pounds to the Party grieved, for every fuch Offence.

To hear and determine all Offences againft the Statute of 1 *Jac.* 1. *c.* 22. concerning Tanners, within the Time, and in the Manner, and fubject to Mitigation and Appeal *ut fupra.* Stat. *9 Ann. c.* 11. §. 36, 37.

Offences.   **Tanners.**   *Penalties.*

Offences	Penalties
Relanding, or putting on Shore again, within *Great Britain*, any Hides, Calve-Skins, Boots, Shoes, Gloves, or other Manufactures of Leather, shipp'd to be exported. Profecution and Appeal *ut fupra*. Stat. 9 *Ann. c.* 11. §. 42.	Forfeiture of the fame, and the treble Value. One Moiety to the Queen, the other to the Informer. Mitigation *ut fupra*.

Note ; The Judgment of the Juftices is final, and no *Certiorari* to be brought or allowed to remove any the Proceedings of the Juftices of Peace, relating to Offences committed againft Stat. 9 *Ann. c.* 11. *Ibid.* §. 47.

Offences	Penalties
[**Qu. Seff.**] Butcher exercifing the Myftery of a Tanner. 1 *Jac.* 1. *c.* 22. §. 4.	Six Shillings and eight Pence a Day, to be divided. One Third to the King, one to the Profecutor, and the other to the City, Borough, Town, or Lord of the Liberty, where the Offence is committed.
Perfons exercifing the Myftery of a Tanner, not having ferved Seven Years as an Apprentice or hired Servant, except the Widow or Children of a Tanner, and having been brought up in that Profeffion Four Years. 1 *Jac.* 1. *c.* 22. §. 5.	Forfeit all the Leather they tan, or the Value thereof, to be divided *ut fupra*.
Perfons buying rough Hides or Calves-Skins in the Hair, except fuch as can lawfully tan them. 1 *Jac.* 1. *c.* 22. §. 7.	Forfeit them, or the juft Value, to be divided *ut fupra*.
Perfons foreftalling Hides, or buying them otherwhere than in open Fair or Market. 1 *Jac.* 1. *c.* 22. §. 7.	Six Shillings and eight Pence a Hide, to be divided *ut fupra*.
Tanner who over-limes his Hides, or ufeth in Tanning any Thing fave Afh-Bark, Tapwork, Malt, Meal, Lime, Culver-dung or Hen-dung, or fuffers them to be frozen, or parched with Fire or Sun ; or tans rotten Hides, or works them in other Sort than is by the Statute limited. 1 *Jac.* 1. *c.* 22. §. 11.	Forfeits every Hide fo tann'd, and put to Sale, or the full Value thereof, to be divided *ut fupra*.
Tanner, who by Mixtures raifes any Hide for Sole-Leather not fit for that Ufe. 1 *Jac.* 1. *c.* 22. §. 14.	Forfeits it, to be divided *ut fupra*.
Perfons putting to Sale tanned Leather, red and unwrought, but in Fair or Market, unlefs fearched and fealed before, or offering to fell fuch Leather before it be parched and fealed. 1 *Jac.* 1. *c.* 22. §. 14.	Six Shillings and eight Pence a Hide, and for every Dozen of Calf-Skins or Sheep-Skins, 3 *s.* 4 *d.* befides the Hides and Skins themfelves, or the full Value thereof, to be divided *ut fupra*.
Perfons putting to Sale any Leather infufficiently tanned or dried. 1 *Jac.* 1. *c.* 22. §. 15.	Forfeit the Whole, to be divided *ut fupra*.
Tanner haftening the Tanning of his Leather, by giving it unkind Heats with hot Wooze, or otherwife. 1 *Jac.* 1. *c.* 22. §. 17.	Ten Pounds, to be divided *ut fupra*, and to ftand upon the Pillory Three Days in the next Market.

Tithes. See **Tythes.**

Offences.   **Tobacco.**   *Penalties.*

Offences	Penalties
[**Two**] MAY grant a fpecial Warrant to fearch for, and feife Walnut-Tree-Leaves, Hop-Leaves, *&c.* cut, mixed, or manufactured to, refemble Tobacco, and the Engines, *&c.* And if feifed within Six Miles of any Sea-Port, fuch Leaves, *&c.* to be brought to the next Cuftom-houfe Warehoufe ; and if at any greater Diftance. Stat. 1 *Geo.* 1. *feff.* 2. *c.* 46. §. 4.	To fecure them at the King's Coft, till the Caufe of Seifure be determined by the Quarter-Seffions, who are to hear and determine the fame at the fartheft at the fecond Quarter-Seffions after Seifure made. After Condemnation, to be openly burnt or deftroyed, by Order of Seffions, at the King's Charge.
Servants and Labourers employed in Cutting, Colouring, Curing, or Manufacturing any fuch Leaves, *&c.*	To be committed to the common Gaol, or Houfe of Correction, to hard Labour, not exceeding Six Months,

I   to

Offences.	Tobacco.	Penalties.
to refemble Tobacco, or making a Mixture thereof, or knowingly vending the fame. One Witnefs. Stat. 1 *Geo.* 1. *c.* 46. §. 5.	Months, without Bail or Mainprife.	

[**Qu. Seff.**] Two Juftices of Peace may, at the Quarter-Seffions, prefent any Perfons for fowing, planting, or making Tobacco; which Prefentment is a Conviction in Law; and the Party forfeits 40 *s.* for every Rod, unlefs he, having Notice in Writing ten Days before, fhall traverfe fuch Prefentment, and find Sureties to profecute next Quarter-Seffions. Stat. 22 & 23 *Car.* 2. *c.* 6. §. 3.

Offences.	Tobacco-pipe Clay.	Penalties.
[**Qu. Seff.**] EXporting Tobacco-pipe Clay. Stat. 13 & 14 *Car.* 2. *c.* 18. §. 7.	Three Shillings a Pound, to be divided between the King and the Profecutor.	

Offences.	Tranfportation.	Penalties.
[**One**] TO refcue fuch Felon or Offenders, as are order'd for Tranfportation; and the Perfon aiding or affifting them in making their Efcape. Stat. 6 *Geo.* 1. *c.* 23. §. 5.	Felony without Benefit of Clergy.	
A Felon ordered for Tranfportation, who fhall be afterwards at large within the Kingdom of *Great Britain*, without fome lawful Caufe, before the Expiration of the Term, for which fuch Felon was order'd to be tranfported, being lawfully convicted. Stat. 6 *Geo.* 1. *c.* 23. §. 6. Certificate of the Clerk of the Peace, containing the Effect and Tenor of the Indictment, and Conviction of fuch Felon, produced in Court, is a fufficient Proof. §. 7.	Felony without Benefit of Clergy. And may be tried either in the County where apprehended, or from whence ordered for Tranfportation.	

Vide Smugglers or Runners of Foreign Goods.

[**Two**] The Lord Mayor of *London*, or one Juftice of the Peace of the City of *London*, and in all other Places Two Juftices, may allow of Contracts by Perfons above 15 and under 21 Years of Age, with Merchants or others, for ferving in the Plantations, not exceeding Eight Years. Stat. 4 *Geo.* 1. *c.* 11. §. 5.	Contracts to be certified to the next Quarter-Seffions, and there regiftred without Fee, by the Clerk of the Peace.	
The Court before whom Felons are convicted, may nominate and appoint, if they fhall think fit, Two or more Juftices, to contract for the Performance of the Tranfportation of fuch Felons, to any of the Colonies and Plantations in *America*: And to order fuch fufficient Security, as directed by 4 *Geo.* 1. *c.* 11. And alfo to caufe fuch Felons to be delivered by the Gaolers to the Perfons contracting for them. Stat. 6 *Geo.* 1. *c.* 23. §. 2.	Contracts and Security to be certified by the Juftices to the next Court, held for the County, &c. to be filed and kept amongft the Records of fuch Court.	

[**Qu. Seff.**] To order the Treafurer of the County, &c. for which the Court was held that ordered fuch Felons to be tranfported, to pay all fuch Charges and Expences to fuch Perfon or Perfons, as fhall be imployed for the Purpofes aforefaid. Stat 6 *Geo.* 1. *c.* 23. §. 3.

All Securities for Tranfportation of Felons to be by Bond in the Name of the Clerk of the Peace of the County, &c. which faid Clerks of the Peace, and their Succeffors, fhall profecute fuch Bonds in their own Names, (to which Purpofe they are a Body Corporate) and to be paid fuch Cofts, Charges and Expences, as the Quarter-Seffions fhall direct, out of the publick Stock by the Treafurer of the County, &c. Stat. 6 *Geo.* 1. *c.* 23. §. 4.	The Monies recovered on fuch Securities, to the Ufe of the County, &c. and paid to the Treafurer, to be Part of the County Stock.	

Note; The Perfons contracting, and to whom fuch Felons are delivered, in order to be tranfported; or the Perfons directed by the Juftices, may carry and fecure them in and thro' any County of *Great Britain*. Stat. 6 *Geo.* 1. *c.* 23. §. 5.

Treafurer

APPENDIX.

Offences.	Treasurer of the County.	Penalties.
[Qu. Seff.] THE Treasurer (or his Executors, &c.) who hath been negligent to execute his Office, or render an Account. Stat. 43 *Eliz.* c. 3. §. 7.	Five Pounds at leaft.	
Treasurers wilfully refufing to give Relief. Stat. 43 *Eliz.* c. 3. §. 12.	Fineable, to be levied by Diftrefs and Sale of Goods, by a Warrant of any Two to be appointed by the Reft.	

Two Treafurers for the County are to be chofen yearly at *Eafter*-Seffions, by the more Part of the Juftices, out of fuch Subfidy-Men as were taxed in the laft Tax of Subfidies, at Five Pounds Lands, or Ten Pounds Goods. Stat. 43 *Eliz.* c. 2. §. 14.

Treafurer for the County refufing to execute the Office, diftribute Relief, or to account to their Succeffors, and pay the Monies in their Hands to the Lord Chief Juftice of the *King's Bench*, and the Knight Marfhal, by equal Portions. Stat. 43 *Eliz.* c. 2. §. 16.	Three Pounds at leaft, to be levied by Diftrefs and Sale, and to be profecuted by any Two Juftices, authorized by the Reft.	

Offences.	Trophy-Money.	Penalties.
[Three] TO certify under their Hands and Seals, the Examination, Stating, and Allowance by the Quarter-Seffions, of *Trophy-Money* raifed, levied and collected for any precedent Year. Stat. 12 *Ann.* feff. 1. c. 10. §. 2. and feff. 2. c. 8. §. 2.		
[Qu. Seff.] The Lieutenancy fhall not iffue out any Warrants for levying *Trophy-Money*, till the *Juftices of Peace*, or the major Part of them at their Quarter-Seffions, fhall have examined, ftated, and allowed the Accounts of the *Trophy-Money* laft raifed, levied, and collected for any preceding Year, and certified fuch Examination of the faid Accounts under the Hands and Seals of Three or more of them, to the refpective Lieutenants, or their Deputies. Stat. 12 *Ann.* feff. 1. c. 10. §. 2. and feff. 2. c. 8. §. 2.		

Turnpikes. See 1 *Geo.* 2. *ftat.* 2. c. 19. in *Dalton*, Chap. 50. Tit. *Highways.*

Offences.	Tythes.	Penalties.
[One] PErfons fubftracting, or with-holding fmall Tythes. Stat. 7 & 8 *W.* 3. c. 6. §. 3.	Shall levy the Sum adjudged by Two Juftices, upon their Certificate, where the Party fubftracting, or with-holding, removes out of the County.	
Where Two Juftices have adjudged what Sum any *Quaker* is to pay for great or fmall Tythes. Stat. 7 & 8 *W.* 3. c. 6. §. 3.	To be levied by Warrant, under either of their Hands and Seals, by Diftrefs and Sale.	
[Two] Defendants in the Ecclefiaftical Court, againft whom the Judge complains for any Contumacy or Mifdemeanor, or any Suit there depending for Tythes. Stat. 27 *H.* 8. c. 20. §. 1. 2 & 3 *Ed.* 6. c. 13. §. 13. *Quorum* 1. This extends not to *London*.	To be committed to Prifon, till they find fufficient Sureties to be bound by Recognizance, or otherwife, to obey the Procefs, Proceedings, Decrees, and Sentences of the faid Court.	
Perfons after a Sentence for Tithes in the Ecclefiaftical Court, refufing to pay Tithes, or Sums of Money adjudged, upon a Certificate thereof from the Judge. Stat. 32 *H.* 8. c. 7. §. 4. 2 & 3 *Ed.* 6. c. 13. §. 1. *Quorum* 1. This extends not to *London*.	To be committed to the next Gaol, till they find Surety by Recognizance, to perform the Sentence.	

Upon Complaint made, within Two Years, againft any Perfon for Subftraction, or with-holding of fmall Tythes, under Hand and Seal, to fummon the Perfon, and after Appearance, or Default (Summons being proved) to examine and determine the fame ; by Evidence upon Oath, and in Writing under Hand and Seal, to adjudge fuch reafonable Allowance for Tythes and Cofts, not exceeding 10 s. as they fhall think fit, except in Cafe of Prefcription, or *Modus Decimandi.* Stat. 7 & 8 *W.* 3. c. 6. §. 2.

Perfons refufing or neglecting for ten Days after Notice to pay the Sum adjudged for Subftraction of Tythes.	The Sum to be levied by Diftrefs, and Sale in Three Days after the Diftrefs, unlefs paid before : All Charges to be deducted out of the Money raifed by the Sale.	

1

Where

Offences.   **Tythes.**   *Penalties.*

Where any Person makes a false and vexatious Complaint for Subtraction, or with-holding of small Tythes, to give Costs not exceeding 10 *s.* to the Party prosecuted.

Neither of the Justices, who put this Act in Execution, must be Patron. Stat. 7 *&* 8 *W.* 3. *c.* 6. §. 12.

Quaker refusing to pay, or compound for great or small Tythes, or to pay any Church-Rates. Stat. 7 *&* 8 *W.* 3. *c.* 34. §. 4.	To be convened before Two Justices, who are to examine, upon Oath, the Truth and Justice of the Complaint, and by Order under their Hands and Seals direct the Payment thereof, not exceeding 10 *l.*

If not Patrons, or interested in the Tythes, are on Complaint of any Parson, *&c.* to summon in Writing *Quakers,* and determine on Appearance, or in Default, and Summons proved upon Oath, to hear and determine the Complaint, and make such Order as directed by Stat. 7 *&* 8 *W.* 3. And also to order such Costs and Charges, as they shall think reasonable, not exceeding Ten Shillings. Stat. 1 *Geo.* 1. *c.* 6. §. 2.

An Appeal lies.

[**Qu. Sess.**] May reverse the Judgment of Two Justices, relating to Tythes on an Appeal ; but if they affirm it, are to give Costs against the Appellant, to be levied, as provided by 7 *&* 8 *W.* 3. *c.* 34. unless the Title of such Tythes, *&c.* be in Question. 1 *Geo.* 1. *c.* 6. §. 2.

Vagabonds and Vagrants. See 13 *Geo.* 2. *c.* 24. in *Dalton,* Chap. 196.

Offences.   **Under-Sheriffs.**   *Penalties.*

[**Two**] EVERY Under-Sheriff before he inter-meddles with his Office, not taking the *Oath of Supremacy,* and also the following *Oath.* Stat. 27 *Eliz. c.* 12. §. 2. *Quorum* 1.	Forfeits 40 Pounds, to be divided between the King and Prosecutor, and treble Damages to the Party grieved, if he commits any Act contrary to his Duty.

I A. B. *will not use, nor exercise the Office of Under-Sheriff corruptly, during the Time that I shall remain therein ; neither shall or will accept, receive, or take by any Colour, Means or Device whatsoever, or consent to the Taking of any Manner of Fee or Reward of any Person or Persons, for the Impanelling or Return of any Inquest, Jury, or Tales, in any Court of Record for the King, or betwixt Party and Party, above two Shillings, or the Value thereof, and such Fees as are allowed and appointed for the same by the Laws and Statutes of this Realm, but will according to my Power, truly and indifferently, with convenient Speed impanel all Jurors, and return all such Writ or Writs touching the same, as shall appertain to be done by my Duty or Office, during the Time I shall remain in the said Office.*

So help me God.

Bailiffs of *Franchises, Deputies,* or *Clerk of a Sheriff,* or *Under-Sheriffs* intermeddling with their several Offices, before they have taken the said Oaths. *Ibid.*	Forfeit Forty Pounds *ut supra.*

[**Qu. Sess.**] Have Power to hear and determine the Defaults and Offences aforesaid. *Ibid.*

See **Sheriffs.**

Offences.   **Wages.**   *Penalties.*

[**Two**] Givers of greater Wages, than are set by the Justices in *Easter*-Sessions yearly. Stat. 5 *Eliz. c.* 4. §. 18.	Five Pounds, and ten Days Imprisonment, without Bail.
Takers of more Wages, than are set by the Justices. Stat. 5 *Eliz. c.* 4. §. 19.	One and twenty Days Imprisonment, without Bail.

To hear and determine all Wages, Demands, Frauds, and Defaults of Labourers in the *Woollen, Linen, Fustian, Cotton,* and *Iron Manufactures,* for or concerning any Work done in the same Manufactures. Stat. 1 *Ann. sess.* 2. *c.* 18. §. 4.

Witnesses to be summoned. An Appeal lies to the Quarter-Sessions.

Vide Title **Servants.**

Wages of the Knights of the Shire.

[**Qu. Sess.**] *Sheriffs, Coroners, Chief Constables,* and *Bailiffs,* not being present at assessing the Wages of Knights of the Shire, which is 4 *s.* a Day. Stat. 23 *H.* 6. *c.* 11. §. 1.	Forty Shillings.

The

Y

Twenty

APPENDIX.

Offences.   **Wages.**   *Penalties.*

Wages of the Knights of the Shire.

The Sheriff, or other Officer, who levies more than is affessed for the Knights of the Shires Wages. Stat. 23 *H.* 6. *c.* 11. §. 1.	Twenty Pounds to the King, ten Pounds to the Profecutor.

Wages of Burgeffes.

[**Two**] To tax every City and Borough in the feveral Counties in *Wales*, where they inhabited refpectively, towards the Wages of the Burgeffes, which is 2 *s.* a Day. Stat. 35 *H.* 8. *c.* 11. §. 4.

Waggons and Waggoners. See Carriers and Carriage.

Offences.   **Watch.**   *Penalties.*

[**Two**] TO certify that a Watchman, or other Perfon, endeavouring to apprehend a Burglar, or Houfe-breaker, was killed, which intitles the Executors or Adminiftrators of the Perfon killed to forty Pounds. Stat. 5 *Ann. c.* 31. §. 2.

Sec 5 *H.* 4. *c.* 3. in *Dalton*, Chap. 104. Tit. *Watch.*

Watermen. See *Dalton*, Chap. 105.

Offences.   **Weights and Meafures.**   *Penalties.*

[**One**] ONE felling, buying or keeping any Weight, or Meafure, which is not according to the Standard of the *Exchequer.* Stat. 16 *Car.* 1. *c.* 19. §. 2. One Witnefs.	Five Shillings for the Poor, to be levied by Diftrefs and Sale; in Default of Diftrefs, to be committed till Payment.
[**Two**] *Clerk of the Market,* or any other Officer, who feals any Weight or Meafure, not agreeable to the Standard, or refufing to feal fuch as are agreeable thereto. Stat. 16 *Car.* 1. *c.* 19. §. 4. One Witnefs.	Five Pounds for the Poor, to be levied *ut fupra.*
If they take any other Fine, Fee, Reward, or Sum of Money, than are allowed by Statute or ancient Cuftom, for Signing or Examining Weights and Meafures, or otherwife mifdemean themfelves. Stat. 16 *Car.* 1. *c.* 19. §. 5. One Witnefs.	Firft Offence 5 *l.* fecond 10 *l.* and 20 *l.* for every other, for the Poor, to be levied *ut fupra.*
Selling Corn or Salt by other Bufhel, or Meafure, than according to the Standard ftruck even by the Brim. Stat. 22 *Car.* 2. *c.* 8. §. 2.	Forty Shillings, to be levied by Diftrefs and Sale.
Selling or buying Corn without Meafuring, or in other Manner, than according to 22 *Car.* 2. *c.* 8. and that without fhaking the Meafure by the Buyer. Stat. 22 & 23 *Car.* 2. *c.* 12. §. 2.	Befides the Penalties of the former Act, all the Corn or Salt, or the Value thereof, forfeited to the Perfon complaining.
The Sub-Commiffioners, or Collectors of the Excife, not providing or procuring within their refpective Circuits or Divifions, a fubftantial Ale-Quart and Ale-Pint, *Winchefter* Meafure. Stat. 11 & 12 *W.* 3. *c.* 15. §. 3.	Five Pounds, to be levied and employed *ut fupra.*
The Mayor or Chief Officer of every City, Town Corporate, Borough, or Market-Town, neglecting, or refufing, upon Requeft to him made, to ftamp and mark Ale-Quart, and Ale-Pint. Stat. 11 & 12 *W.* 3. *c.* 15. §. 5. One or more Witneffes. Profecution to be within 30 Days.	Five Pounds, to be levied and employed *ut fupra.*

Note; This Act extends not to the Univerfities, by Stat. 12 & 13 *W.* 3. *c.* 11. §. 19.

APPENDIX.

Offences.	Weights and Measures.	Penalties.
Selling in any other Water-Measure, than is according to Stat. 1 *Ann. sess.* 1. *c.* 15. §. 1. One Witness. *Note* ; This extends not to *London.*	Ten Shillings, to be levied by Distress and Sale. One Half to the Informer, the other to the Poor.	
[**Two**] Persons buying and selling with any other Weights and Measures than such as are marked, except on Shipboard. Stat. 11 *H.* 7. *c.* 4. §. 12. *Quor'* 1.	First Offence 6 *s.* 8 *d.* Second 13 *s.* 4 *d.* and Pillory ; and the Weights and Measures to be broke, and burnt.	
[**Qu. Sess.**] Any Person buying or taking any Corn by any other Measure, than eight Bushels striked for the Quarter. Stat. 1 *H.* 5. *c.* 10. §. 2.	Five Pounds to the King, and as much to the Party grieved, and a Year's Imprisonment.	
Importing or making any Tun of Wine less than 252 Gallons *English* Measure, the Pipe 126, the Barrel of Herrings and Eels 30 Gallons, the Butt of Salmon 84 Gallons. Stat. 2 *H.* 6. *c.* 11. §. 3, 4.	Forfeits the Commodities therein contained to the Lord of the Town, where they are found ; the Prosecutor to have the fourth Part.	
Every City, Borough, and Town within *England,* that has not a common Balance, with common Weights sealed, according to the Standard of the *Exchequer,* at the Costs of the City, &c. in the Keeping of the Head Officer, or Constable there. Stat. 8 *H.* 6. *c.* 5. §. 9.	The City forfeits 10 *l.* to the King, the Borough 5 *l.* and every other Town 40 *s.* The Inhabitants to weigh *gratis.* Foreigner to pay for under 40 *lb.* a Farthing, for between 40 and 100 *lb.* a Half-penny ; for between 100 and 1000 *lb.* one Penny, towards maintaining the Weights. Restrained to Market-Towns, by 11 *H.* 7. *c.* 4.	
In every City, Borough, and Town, there shall be a common Bushel sealed. Stat. 11 *H.* 6. *c.* 8. §. 10.	Upon the Penalties in 8 *H.* 6. *c.* 5.	

Measures and Weights of Brass shall be sent to every City and Borough, there to be kept, as their Treasure, according to which all Measures and Weights in every County shall be reformed. Stat. 11 *H.* 7. *c.* 4.

The Mayor, or Chief Officer, in Cities and Boroughs, shall have a special Mark, wherewith he shall seal the Measures and Weights, and shall take for Sealing a Bushel one Penny, every other Measure an Half-penny ; 100 Weight one Penny, half 100 an Half-penny, every less Weight a Farthing, refusing or delaying to Seal, or doing any Thing contrary to Stat. 11 *H.* 7. *c.* 4.	Forty Shillings, to be divided between the King and the Party grieved.	

Justices of the Quarter-Sessions are to give in Charge the Statute for ascertaining the Measures of Ale and Beer. Stat. 11 & 12 *W.* 3. *c.* 15. §. 9.

Offences.	Windows.	Penalties.
[**Two**] TO put in Execution the Statute of 7 & 8 *W.* 3. *c.* 18. for laying a Duty on Houses ; and also 8 & 9 *W.* 3. *c.* 20. and 5 *Ann. c.* 13. concerning the same Duty. Stat. 8 *Ann. c.* 4.		
[**Three**] May annually appoint two such Persons, as they shall think able, and responsible to be Collectors of the Duties on Houses, whether the Names be or be not presented by the preceding Collectors. Stat. 6 *Geo.* 1. *c.* 21. §. 61.		
Where there shall be any Arrears of the Duty on Houses, by the Failure of any Collector, for which any Parish or Place shall be answerable, to cause such Arrears to be raised by Re-assessment, and to be paid to the Receiver General, or into the Exchequer. *Ibid.*	To be levied by such Ways and Means, as the Duties on Houses are raised and levied.	

Offences.	Wood.	Penalties.
[**One**] PErsons suspected for having or conveying any *Wood, Under-wood, Poles* or *young Trees, Bark* or *Bast of Trees,* or any *Gates, Stiles, Posts, Pales, Rails, Hedge-wood, Broom* or *Furze,* found by a Search-Warrant, and can give no good Account how they came by the same ; or if they do not, in con-	First Offence, convicts within 43 *Eliz. c.* 7. and accordingly punished ; and shall make such Recompence, and in such Time, as Justice shall appoint ; and a Sum not exceeding 10 *s.* as Justice shall direct for the Poor ; in Default to be committed to the House of Correction, not to exceed a Month, or be whipped.	

Second

Offences. **Wood.** *Penalties.*

convenient Time, produce the Person, of whom they bought the same, or some Witness to prove Sale on Oath, Constables or any other Person may apprehend them. Stat. 15 *Car.* 2. *c.* 2. §. 3.

See 43 *Eliz. c.* 7. in Title **Orchards.**

Second Offence, to be sent to the House of Correction for a Month, to be kept to hard Labour.	
Third, to be deemed incorrigible Rogues.	

Maliciously setting on Fire, or burning Wood, Under-wood, or Coppice. Stat. 1 *Geo.* 1. *c.* 48. §. 4.

Felony.

[**Two**] When appointed by the Sessions, shall summon twelve Commoners to set out the fourth Part of Woods, or Coppices, where they have Common, for the Lord, Owner of the Soil, to fell, or cut down. Stat. 35 *H.* 8. *c.* 17. §. 7.

If any Person shall either *by Day or Night*, maliciously and in a clandestine and private Manner, cut, take, destroy, break, throw down, bark, pluck up, burn, deface, spoil, or carry away any Wood-Springs, or Springs of Wood, Trees, Poles, Wood, Tops of Trees, Under-woods, or Coppice-woods, Thorns, or Quicksets, without the Consent of the Owner, or Person intrusted with the Care and Custody thereof; or shall break open, throw down, level, or destroy any Hedges, Gates, Posts, Stiles, Railings, Walls, Fences, Dikes, Ditches, Banks, or other Inclosures of Woods, Wood-grounds, Parks, Chases or Coppices, Plantations, Timber-Trees, Fruit-Trees, or other Trees, Thorns, or Quicksets. Stat. 6 *Geo.* 1. *c.* 16. §. 1.

Lords of Manors, Owners and Proprietors, that are damaged, shall recover such Damages against the Parish, as the Stat. 13 *Ed.* 1. directs, if the Parish do not convict the Offender in six Months.

May upon Complaint of any Inhabitant of the Parish, where Wood, Wood-Springs, &c. are in a riotous, open, tumultuous, or in a secret and clandestine Manner, forcibly or wrongfully, and without Consent of the Proprietor, &c. cut down, destroyed, broke, barked, thrown down, burned, took, defaced, spoiled, or carried away: Or where any Hedges, Gates, Posts, Stiles, Rails, Fences, Ditches, Banks, or Inclosures are maliciously broke open, thrown down, levelled, or destroyed, cause Offenders to be apprehended, if convicted. Stat. 6 *Geo.* 1. *c.* 16. §. 2.

Liable to the Penalties and Punishments in the Stat. 1 *Geo.* 1. *sess.* 2. *c.* 48.

Or Justices in open Sessions, upon Complaint of any Inhabitant of the Parish where Timber, Trees, &c. are maliciously cut, &c. may cause the Offenders to be apprehended, and finally hear, determine, and adjudge such Offenders; and after Conviction. Stat. 1 *Geo.* 1. *c.* 48. §. 2.

Commit them to the House of Correction to hard Labour, for three Months, without Bail; and to be whipped once a Month in the next Market-Town, on the Market-Day, between Eleven and Two. And not to be discharged, till Security given for their good Behaviour for two Years, §. 3. Where there is no House of Correction, to be committed to the common Gaol for four Months, and to be whipped by the common Hangman once a Month.

Offences. **Wool.** *Penalties.*

[**Alt. Sess.**] PErsons pressing together with Screws, Presses, or other Engines into any Sack, Bag, &c. or putting or pressing any *Wool* or *Yarn* made of Wool, into any Cask or Vessel, or causing to be laid near the Shore, or Coasts of the Sea, or any navigable River; or into any House or Place adjoining, any Wool, Wool-fells, or Yarn made of Wool, to export the same. Stat. 13 & 14 *Car.* 2. *c.* 18. §. 7.

Forfeit the same, or to the Value, to be divided between the King and the Prosecutor.

Conveying of Packs, Bags, or Casks of Wool, &c. to or from any Place in *England*, &c. but at seasonable Times, *viz.* from *March* 1. to *September* 29. between the Hours of Four in the Morning and Eight

The Loss of all such Goods, or the Value, to be divided *ut supra.*

APPENDIX.

in the Evening, and from *September* 29. to *March* 1. between Seven in the Morning and Five in the Evening. Stat. 13 & 14 *Car.* 2. *c.* 18. §. 9.

The Transportation or Conveying the Wool, &c. mentioned in Stat. 13 & 14 *Car.* 2. *c.* 18. §. 11. | A common Nusance.

See Title 𝔠𝔩𝔬𝔱𝔥, and 12 *Geo.* 2. *c.* 21. in *Dalton*, Chap. 196.

Offences.   𝔚𝔬𝔯𝔡𝔰 𝔣𝔭𝔬𝔨𝔢 𝔞𝔤𝔞𝔦𝔫𝔰𝔱 𝔱𝔥𝔢 𝔔𝔲𝔢𝔢𝔫'𝔰 𝔗𝔦𝔱𝔩𝔢.   *Penalties*

[𝔒𝔫𝔢] TO take the Information of Words spoken against the Queen's Title to the Crown, &c. in three Days after they were spoken, but not after. Stat. 4 *Ann. c.* 8. §. 3. 6 *Ann. c.* 7. §. 3. Two Witnesses.

Offences.   𝔚𝔯𝔢𝔠𝔨𝔰.   *Penalties*

[𝔒𝔫𝔢] OWner of, or Captain, Master, Mariner or other Officer, belonging to any Ship, who shall wilfully cast away, burn, or otherwise destroy the Ship, of which he is Owner, or to which he belongeth, or in any wise direct or procure the same to be done, if to the Prejudice of Persons underwriting Policies of Insurance, or Merchants loading Goods thereon. Stat. 4 *Geo.* 1. *c.* 12. §. 3. | To suffer Death.

Note; The Stat. 12 *Ann. sess.* 2. *c.* 18. enforced and made perpetual by 4 *Geo.* 1. *c.* 12. §. 1.

See 𝔖𝔥𝔦𝔭𝔰.

Offences.   𝔚𝔯𝔬𝔲𝔤𝔥𝔱 𝔓𝔩𝔞𝔱𝔢.   *Penalties.*

[𝔒𝔫𝔢] EVERY Officer for the Duties on *Wrought Plate* or Manufactures of Silver, who shall be impowered to make a Charge on the Maker or Worker of Plate, &c. shall in the first Place be sworn for the due and faithful Execution of his Office by any Justice of the Peace, who shall give such Officer a Certificate thereof. Stat. 6 *Geo.* 1. *c.* 11. §. 11.

A TABLE of the PRINCIPAL MATTERS contained in this Book.

A.

ABjuration, the Oath to be adminiftred to Recufants *Page* 197
Acceffary, who 367
There is none in Treafon *ibid.*
In Felony before and after the Fact *ibid.*
In Petty Treafon there are Principals and Acceffaries 368
In Felony, there are Acceffaries before and after the Fact *ibid.*
Who fhall be a Principal *ibid.*
Acceffary, none before the Fact in Manflaughter 370
All are Principals in Forgery, made Felony by the Statute *ibid.*
Who are Acceffaries after the Fact, who not *ibid.*
By buying ftolen Goods, and at an Undervalue 371
By receiving his own Goods being ftolen *ibid.*
Acceffary of an Acceffary 372
Where a Man is convicted of Felony, the Profecutor may proceed againft the Acceffary *ibid.*
Acre of Land, is 40 Pole in Length, and 4 in Breadth, or 160 Pole 262
Actions Popular. See *Informations.*
Ad quod damnum, a Highway inclofed by the Writ, an Appeal lies to the next Seffions 120
Affray, what 28
What may be done by a private Man in fuch Cafe *ibid.*
What by Conftable and Juftice of Peace *ibid.* 161
What, if 'tis made in his Prefence 267
Agnus Dei 320
Alehoufe-keeper, fuffering Tippling 20
Muft be licenfed by the Seffions 28
Two Juftices may put down any Alehoufe 23
Selling Ale without Licenfe, how to be punifhed 23, 27
The Wife keeping an Alehoufe without Confent of her Hufband, how to be punifhed 24
Selling Ale after he is put down, how to be punifhed *ibid.*
Brewers delivering Beer or Ale to any unlicenfed Alehoufe-keeper *ibid.*
What Perfons, and in what Places, Alehoufekeepers and Alehoufes are to be 25
Bailiffs not to keep Alehoufes *ibid.*
Nor Tradefmen, and others *ibid.*
Ale and Beer muft be fold in Pots ftamp'd or mark'd 26
Ale or Beer fold within the Bills of Mortality, the Seller muft pay no lefs than 20 s. nor more than fix Pounds for one Year 27

Ale-Quart and Ale-Pint muft be provided by the Collectors of Excife *Page* 262
Alehoufe-keepers, the Recognizance, Condition and Licenfe to keep an Alehoufe 436, 438
Mittimus of an Alehoufe-keeper felling Ale after prohibited 441
Alms; a Regifter fhall be kept in every Parifh, of thofe who receive Alms 178
Amicus Curiæ 381
Anabaptift Preachers 190
Annuity Orders, counterfeiting them Felony 359
Appeals. See *Orders.*
Shall be determined at the Quarter-Seffions of the County from whence the poor Perfon is removed 182
Notice of the Appeal muft be given to a Parifh Officer *ibid.* 188
Appeal ought to be to the next Seffions 183
Appellant, where Seffions may award his Charges 188
Apprentice, who may be bound 135
What he is *ibid.*
Who may take an Apprentice *ibid.*
Mifufed by the Mafter, the Seffions may difcharge him *ibid.* & 142, 143
If the Fault be in the Apprentice, he may be fent to the Houfe of Correction *ibid.*
Apprentice purloining his Mafter's Goods above the Value of 12 d. fhall be fent to Gaol; if under that Value, to the Houfe of Correction 135, 136
Apprentice being an Infant 139, 140
Apprentices to Trades *ibid.*
Apprenticing poor Boys to Hufbandry 137
This muft be done by the Parifh Officers, and the Mafter refufing forfeits 10 l. 143
Inticing him to leave his Service; inticing him to purloin his Mafter's Goods, Indictments for thofe Facts *ibid.*
What he gains is for the Ufe of his Mafter *ibid.*
Overfeers may put out poor Children to be Apprentices 164
Apprentices, putting them forth, Confiderations to be had 166
Apprentice being diforderly, may be fent to the Houfe of Correction 143
Apprentice, where to be fettled 174
Charity given to put out Apprentices 177
Apprentice bound and dwelling in a Parifh, makes a Settlement without Notice 180
Apprentice affigned, fhall be fettled in the laft Parifh *ibid.*
Apprenticefhip Indentures, the Form 447
Approver, what 362

Armcur,

A Table of the Principal Matters.

Armour, wearing it offensively — Page 30
Armour, imbeziling it. See *Ordinance*.
Arrack; Entry muſt be made where 'tis kept — 78
Arraignment, in what Manner to be made — 459
Arreſt, what it is — 406
What Perſons, and for what Cauſe — *ibid.*
Shall not be carried to a Victualling-Houſe without his Conſent — 411
Artificers, going beyond Sea — 31
Aſſurers of Ships, the Corporation Seal being counterfeited, or any Policy altered, Felony without Clergy — 359
Attainder, how it differs from Conviction — 376

B.

Badge, muſt be worn by the Poor — 183
Bail, who are bailable, who not, and by whom — 39, 83, 377
Bail, perſonating, Felony — 359
Bailment defined — 384
The Juſtices are Judges of the Sufficiency of the Sureties — *ibid.*
Bail taken where the Perſon is not bailable by Law — *ibid.* 385
Perſons not bailable by Law — 386, 388
Bail taken by particular Statutes for Offences — 392
Suſpected of Felony not to be bailed — 413
The Form of Bail for Felony and Suſpicion, &c. — 444
Bailiff, his Fees for Arreſt — 82
Bailiff of the Hundred, the Juſtices may examine his Defaults — 229
Bailiff ſhall not take more for Lodging or Expences than the next Juſtice or Seſſions ſhall appoint — 411
Baker, making Bread not full Weight, how to be puniſhed — 41
Baker and Bread — 258
Bank Bills, counterfeiting any ſealed Bill, or Note, or altering or razing it, Felony — 353
Bankrupt — 40
Shall not be diſcharged, or receive any Benefit by the Statute 5 *Geo.* 2. *cap.* 30. who hath loſt in one Day 5 *l.* or 100 *l.* in a Year, before he became a Bankrupt — 105
Bark of Oak, how to be preſerved — 253
Barrator, who he is — 31
In Courts and in Country — *ibid.*
How to be puniſhed — 32
A Feme Covert cannot be a common Barrator *ibid.*
Of the Indictment — *ibid.*
Sueing in the Name of another — *ibid.*
Baſtard, where the Mother muſt prove it was born alive — 367
Baſtardy, where the two next Juſtices cannot agree about the Order, what is to be done — 20, 33
What it is — 32
Putative Father may be bound to the Good Behaviour before the Child is born — 33

If he be ſent away by the Practice of another that Perſon ſhall be bound to his Good Behaviour — Page 33, 42
Two Juſtices muſt make the Order — 3.
Appeal to the next Seſſions, and that is final *ibid.*
The Mother may be examined on Oath — 3.
She may be ſent to the Houſe of Correction after ſhe is delivered — *ibid.*
But not to be whipped before — *ibid.*
Not performing the Order upon Notice thereof — *ibid.*
The Child is not to be ſent to the Houſe of Correction with the Mother — *ibid.*
Leaving a Child to the Pariſh, what is to be done — 34, 35
The Order of two Juſtices — 42
Rules concerning the Order — 35, 42
Orders good — *ibid.*
Orders quaſhed — 3
Mittimus of the reputed Father — 44
Appeals from Orders, Caſes adjudged therein 36
Whether the Seſſions can make an Original Order — *ibid.*
And commit for not obeying it — 37
Who ſhall be a Baſtard — *ibid.* 38
Battery. See *Beating.*
Beating, where juſtifiable — 281
In Defence of his Perſon — 282
In Defence of others — *ibid.*
In Defence of his Goods or Poſſeſſion — 283, 300, 301
In Execution of Juſtice — 283
Beer, the Meaſure thereof — 259
Beggars. See *Vagabonds.*
Begging, not allowed by Law. — 168
Benefices, how many in *England* — 195
Blackmail, what it is, and how puniſhable — 362
Blacks, appearing with black Faces, and Hunting, &c. Felony — 359
Blaſphemy — 40
Boots, may be tranſported — 149
Bows, keeping them to deſtroy Game, not being qualified — 107
Brandy, muſt not be ſold, nor diſtilled Liquors, by Retail, without Licenſe — 26
Is declared to be Strong Water — 74
Entry muſt be made where 'tis kept — 78
Brandy exported — *ibid.*
Breach, of the Peace, what is, and what is not a Breach of the Peace — 281
Bread. See Baker, the Aſſiſe thereof — 258
Breaking open an Houſe, when lawful — 29, 46, 98, 403, 404
By the King's Officers, to apprehend a Felon — 374
Brewers, Forfeiture for making falſe Entry — 80
There lies an Appeal — *ibid.*
Juſtices may mitigate the Forfeitures — *ibid.*
Brewers, Offences relating to them — *ibid.*
Bridges, who ſhall repair them — 42
Who ſhall be charged — 43
By Preſcription — *ibid.*

5

By

A Table of the Principal Matters.

By Tenure   Page 43
What the Quarter-Sessions may do in such Cases
                                                        44
Certiorari doth not lie for removing Indictments
                                                      ibid.
Lying in two Counties   117
Buggery, Felony   45, 359
Bullion, unlawful   46
Burglary, by breaking a Chamber in the Inns of
   Court   88
By breaking Barns and Out-houses adjoining to
   Dwelling-houses   ibid.
Servant opening a Door, and the Thief entring,
   Burglary   ibid.
Stealing Money or Goods to the Value of 40 s.
   being in a Dwelling-house or Out-house, tho'
   not actually broke open, and tho' no Person
   therein, Burglary without Clergy   89
Burglary defined   340
The Time and Manner of committing it   341
The Place where 'tis done   342
The Intent for which a Burglar enters   343
Burials, must be in Woollen   45
Overseers must give Account of Burials   165
Burning Ricks or Stacks of Corn or Hay, Felo-
   ny   354, 359, 367
Accessary before the Fact, no Clergy   370
Bushel, the Measure   255
Butchers, Offences committed by them, how pu-
   nishable   46, 47
Butter, the Packing, Casking, Marking it, &c.
   and Offences, how punishable   48
Butter, the Measure   260
Buttons, and Buttonhole-makers, Offences rela-
   ting thereunto, how punishable   49

                     C.

CAlves-Skins, must not be gashed   149
   Cards and Dice, Offences relating thereunto,
   how punishable   49, 50
Are not prohibited by Law   104
Carriages, Waggons travelling for Hire shall not
   be drawn with more than six Horses in length,
   &c. See Waggon   51, 121
The Sessions at Easter yearly may assise the Prices
   of all Land-Carriage of Goods   50
Carts standing in Streets at irregular Hours   124
Carve of Land. See Plough Land and Hide of
   Land, 'tis the same
Casual Death, as by the Fall of an House   336
Cattle, buying them alive and selling them again.
   See Butchers.   52
Killing or destroying them, Felony, in the Night-
   Time   87, 359
Certificate, shall be given by the Judge to him
   who apprehends a Felon, stealing above the
   Value of 5 s. &c. and the Effect thereof   88
Executor or Administrator hath a Right to the
   Certificate, if the Party is killed   ibid.
The like for discovering Burglars   89
The like for taking a Highwayman   123

Certiorari, not to be allowed to remove Convi-
   ction of Offences in destroying the Game Page
                                                108, 132
Shall not be allowed for Offences about Hides and
   Leather   150
Certificate given to a poor Man   184
Certificate Man cannot be removed, unless he is
   chargeable   ibid.
The giving a Certificate makes a Settlement   185
But not of the Children, unless named in the
   Certificate, if they do not live with their Pa-
   rents   ibid.
Certiorari, not to be allowed to supersede Pro-
   ceedings on the Salt Act   225
Certiorari doth not lie to supersede Execution on
   the Stamp Act   236
Nor Proceedings about Tithes   245
Certiorari, Returns thereof to remove an Indict-
   ment   474
If there is a Variance between the Certiorari and
   the Record, the Justices need not return it   475
The Form of a Certiorari   476
In what Cases they shall not be granted   477
May be granted in Vacation, signed by one Judge
                                                  ibid.
'Tis a Supersedeas as soon as delivered   478
Challenge, to Jurors. See Juries.
Challenge. See Duel.
Challenging another for Money won at Play   105
Chancemedley. See Misadventure and Casual Death.
Cheating, at Play, forfeits five Times the Value
   got   105
Cheese, the Measure or Weigh must contain 32
   Cloves   260
Children, must be settled where their Parents were
   settled   184
Children of Recusants must not be sent beyond
   Sea   207
Church and Church-yard   52
Striking there.   53
Who must come to Church   ibid.
Church-warden committed for refusing to account
   for Poors Money   186
Church, absenting from it   196
Cinque Ports, Sureties of Peace against one there
                                                   271
Certiorari may be granted to them   478
Clergy, what it is, and where taken away   466,
                                                   467
Clergymen, liable to repair Highways   123
And to be taxed to the Poor   186
Surety of the Peace against him   270
Clerk of the Peace, by whom chosen   53
By whom, and for what to be removed   ibid.
Drawing an insufficient Indictment   54
Must have but 2 s. for drawing a good one   ibid.
He, or the Clerk of Assise, or his Deputy, draw-
   ing a defective Indictment, must draw a new
   one gratis   ibid.
Clipping and Coining. See Money.
Cloth, Justices may search   ibid.

                                        a a   Cloth,

A Table of the Principal Matters.

Cloth, Juſtices may appoint Overſeers   Page 54
The Duty of Overſeers   ibid.
Conviction of Offenders   55
Forfeitures   56
Spinſters imbezling   57
Their Wages muſt be paid in Money   58
Linen Cloth, ſtretching it   ibid.
No Importation of foreign Wool Card   ibid.
Mixed or Medley Broad Cloth, where and how to be meaſured   ibid.
Offences, how to be determined   ibid.
Cloths, defacing them, Felony   87, 360
Cloth, ſtealing it from the Tenters, Felony   ibid.
Clove is 8 Pounds Averdupois Weight   260
Coaches. See *Carriages.* For the better Regulating Hackney Coaches the Commiſſioners may make By-Laws   51
Coach-Houſe, ſtealing Goods out of it to the Value of 5 s. though not broke open, Felony; and likewiſe in him who aſſiſts   88, 364
Coals, how to be meaſured at *Newcaſtle*   59
Muſt be 36 Buſhels to the Chaldron   262
Coffee, the new Duties on Coffee, Tea and Chocolate, to be paid by the Maker or Seller   60
Coining and Clipping. See *Money.*
Commiſſion of the Peace, the Form thereof   12
Commitment, by the Juſtices, muſt be to the Common Gaol   409
Common Prayer, how often to be read   60
Common Prayer Book eſtabliſhed   194
Coney Dogs, keeping them to deſtroy Game not being qualified   107
Conviction for keeping them to deſtroy Conies 109
Deſtroying them in the Night-time upon Borders of Warrens, or other Grounds uſed for keeping Conies, the Puniſhment   131
Coney Skins, black, ſhall not be dreſſed by any Perſon but a Skinner   233
No leſs than 1000 black Coney Skins, or 3000 grey, ſhall be contracted for by any Merchant at one Time   ibid.
Confeſſion, of a Crime, is good Evidence 162, 383
The Party confeſſing may accuſe others   378
Confeſſion of the Party   377
Conformity, Quarter-Seſſions may take the Oath of Perſons having Offices, and who have been convicted for not conforming; that they have now conformed for a Year laſt paſt   81
Conjuration, by 1 *Jac.* 1. is Felony, but this is repealed   360
Conſervators of the Peace, at Common Law   1
The King   ibid.
The Lord Chancellor or Keeper   ibid.
The Lord High Steward   ibid.
The Lord Marſhal   ibid.
The Lord Treaſurer   ibid.
Judges of the King's Bench   ibid.
Maſter of the Rolls   ibid.
Judges of the Common Pleas ⎱ within their Precincts
Barons of the Excheqier ⎰
Juſtices of Aſſiſe

Steward of Sheriffs Turn   Page 2
Steward of Leets   ibid.
Sheriffs by the Common Law   ibid.
Coroners by the Common Law   ibid.
High Conſtables   ibid.
Petty Conſtables   ibid.
They are only to meddle with Affrays, Aſſaults and Batteries, &c. but not with Riots or Forcible Entries   4
Conſpiracy, amongſt Traders and Artificers   65
Conſpiracy to deſtroy the King or Peer, or the Steward, Treaſurer, or any of the Privy Counſellors, Felony   355
Conſtable, may make a Deputy   3, 64
He is no Officer of Record   3
He cannot take Surety of the Peace by Recognizance or Bail   4
Nor take an Oath of the Party that is in Fear ibid.
He may arreſt an Affrayer, and put him in the Stocks, or in his own Houſe, as his Quality requireth   ibid.
This Office began not long before the Juſtices   ibid.
Neglecting to apprehend Vagabonds, the Forfeiture   489
High Conſtable, how to be choſen   63
When firſt made   ibid.
How to be removed   ibid. 175
Petty Conſtables, why made   ibid.
When to be choſen and removed   64
Their Qualifications   ibid.
Upon the Death or Removal of a Conſtable out of the Pariſh, two Juſtices may appoint another   65
How to be reimburſed, if out of Purſe in Relieving or Paſſing Vagabonds, &c.   ibid.
Who are exempted from being a Conſtable   ibid.
Oath of a Conſtable   426
Conventicles, Proteſtant Diſſenters are exempted from Penalties of 17 *Car.* 2. by 1 *W. & M.* cap. 18.   67
Conviction, in a ſummary Way, the Party muſt be ſummoned   415
Conviction, what it is   376
Convicts. See *Eſcape.*
Cooper, how big he muſt make his Veſſels for Beer and Ale to be ſold   259
Copper, blanching it for Sale, Felony   88
Corn, when to be tranſported   61
See *Tranſportation*   241
Corn growing, cut and taken away, the Puniſhment   242
Coroner is Conſervator of the Peace   2
Their Authority not determined by the Demiſe of the King   10
His Fees   82
Coſts, the Seſſions may give Coſts on an Appeal   182
Cottages and Inmates   68
Who may erect a Cottage   ibid.
Cottage, what 'tis   114
Counties

I

A Table of the Principal Matters.

Counties and Shire Towns   *Page* 262

Counterfeiters, by getting Money or Goods by *False Tokens*, or Letters in another Perfon's Name   68

He who knowingly fends a Letter to another with a fictitious Name, demanding any valuable Thing, is a Felon without Benefit of Clergy; and fo is he who refcues one in Cuftody for that Offence   69

Crown, oppofing the Succeffion of it, &c. is High Treafon   321

Currier, muft not buy and fell by Wholefale 145

Shall not ufe the Trade of a Tanner   *ibid.*

Where and when he fhall curry   *ibid.*

Muft not curry Leather ill tanned   148

Cuftoms, refifting a Cuftom-houfe Officer, how punifhable   69, 70, 233

'Tis Felony   70, 71, 360

May enter a Houfe to fearch for Goods concealed   69

Cuftom-houfe Officers of the Out-Ports fhall take an Oath   *ibid.*

Cuftos Rotulorum, by whom, and how to be appointed   71

Cutting out a Tongue, or putting out the Eye with Malice prepenfed, Felony   360

D.

Declaration of Recufants to be fubfcribed 204

Deer. See *Game.*

Unlawfully Courfing, Killing, Hunting, or Taking Deer, &c. forfeits 20 *l.* formerly, and then 30 *l.* and now 50 *l.* where taking them is Felony 350

Deodand, what   336

Forfeiture   *ibid.*

It muft be found on Record   *ibid.*

Inquiry by the Coroner   337

Difcharge, of a Prifoner committed for Felony   445

Difcharge of a Servant committed   446

Difcharge of one committed for the Breach of the Peace or Good Behaviour   *ibid.*

Difcovering Felons and Burglars, the Reward   89

Difcretion, what is left to the Difcretion of Juftices   16, 23, 30

Diffenters, refufing to take the Oaths when tendred, what is to be done   72

Not excluded from Offices   *ibid.*

Muft not be at Conventicles with the *Infignia* of Offices   *ibid.*

Diffenting Preachers taking the Oaths, and fubfcribing the Declaration   190

Shall not ferve on Juries, and fhall be exempt from Parifh Offices   *ibid.*

Difcharged from the Penalties of the Acts made againft Recufants   205

Their Meeting Houfes muft be certified to the Bifhop of the Diocefe, or to the Archdeacon, or to the Seffions   206

Diftringas, the Form of it   472

Ditches, neglected to be fcower'd after 30 Days Notice given by the Surveyors, forfeits for every Yard, 2 *s.* 6 *d.*   *Page* 120

Dogs. See *Game.*

May be taken from Perfons not qualified, for the Ufe of the Juftice or Lord of the Manor   108

Dog, of any Kind, not Felony to fteal them 351

Drunkennefs, Conviction by a Juftice   21

After Conviction the Forfeiture is not to be difcharged   172

Durham, Bifhop and his Chancellor are Juftices of Peace by Statute 27 *H.* 8.   8

Dying and Logwood   72

Dwelling-houfe, breaking it in the Day-time, and removing Goods from one Room to another, Felony   87

Taking away Goods out of a Dwelling-houfe, any Body being *put in Fear*, robbing it in the Day-time, Shop or Warehoufe, and taking to the Value of 5 *s.* tho' no Perfon is therein, Felony without Clergy   88, 344, 364

Entring without breaking it, or being within and breaking it to get out, Felony without Clergy   89

Stealing to the Value of 40 *s.* out of a Dwelling-houfe or Out-houfe, tho' not broke open, and tho' no body was therein, the Aider and Affifter are Burglars   344

E.

Eggs of Wild-Fowl   159, 251

Egyptians, how to be punifhed, and thofe in their Company   73, 361

Ell is 3 Foot 9 Inches   261

Efcape, and breaking Prifon. See *Cap.*   159

Suffering a Felon to efcape voluntarily, Felony   357

Efcape is either voluntary or negligent   *ibid.*

He who hath the Benefit of Clergy, and is committed to the Houfe of Correction and efcapes, and is retaken, fhall be committed to the Houfe of Correction where retaken, for not lefs than one Year, and not exceeding four Years   358

Efcape, by giving Leave to a Prifoner to go Abroad for a Time   409

Eftreats, Clerks of the Peace muft deliver to the Sheriff an Eftreat of all Fines, Iffues, Amerciaments, Recognizances, Monies and Forfeitures   73

Evidence againft Felons. See *Cap.*   164

He who refufes to be bound to give Evidence, what is to be done   86

Confeffion is good Evidence   162

Examination of a Felon, what the Juftice is to do therein   377

He is to be examined   380

The Information being on Oath, if the Witnefs fhould die before Trial, and not appear on his Recognizance, it may be given in Evidence as a Matter of Credit   *ibid.*

Exchequer-Bills, Counterfeiting them, &c. Felony without Clergy   Page 361

Excife, fettled on the King for Life   74

Head Office muft be kept in *London*   75

Duties of Excife laid on Beer   77

Forcibly refifting any Officer of Excife in feizing Run Goods, is Felony   233

Who fhall pay Excife   74

Entries, common Brewers muft make Entries and pay the Duty   *ibid.*

Gaugers may be appointed by Commiffioners   *ibid.*

Allowance of one out of 23 Barrels to common Brewers   75

Of Compounding and Farming   *ibid.*

Appeal lies   *ibid.*

Juftices may mitigate the Forfeiture   *ibid.*

Oath of Officers of Excife   75

Veffels fhall not be altered without giving Notice to the next Officer of Excife   *ibid.*

Forfeitures, how to be difpofed   77

Time of Appeal   *ibid.*

Wafte and Leakage   *ibid.*

Farmers of Excife   *ibid.*

Retailer of Beer fhall not mix it   *ibid.*

Gaugers muft deliver to common Brewers a Copy of their Return   74

Commiffioner muft not farm the Excife   76

Nor act as a Juftice of Peace   *ibid.*

May appoint Deputies   *ibid.*

Time of delivering out Beer   *ibid.*

Mingling Beer, or concealing it from the Gauger   *ibid.*

Veffels and Utenfils fhall be fubject to the Forfeiture   *ibid.*

Bribing Officer to make a falfe Report   *ibid.*

No Appeal if the Appellant doth not lay down in the Hands of the Commiffioners the fingle Duty   *ibid.*

Extortion, what it is   82

In the Under-Sheriff   90

Taking more than their Fees for Poundage   231

Extraparochial Places   186, 187

F.

FAIRS. See *Markets.*

Fairs, Horfes fold therein, and the Sale good, and where not   125

Fathom, is 7 Foot   261

Fees   89

Three Juftices may fettle the Fees any Perfon fhall pay for his Commitment, Difcharge and Chamber-Rent   191

The next Juftice may adjudge what is fitting to be taken by Bailiffs, Under-Sheriffs, &c. *ibid.*

Fees of Gaolers   *ibid.*

Fees of the Sheriffs and Under-Sheriffs for Poundage   231

Felo de fe   327

The Forfeiture   *ibid.*

The Coroner muft inquire into the Fact   328

Felony, the Forfeiture of one attainted for Felony   Page 375

Felonies, by Common Law   325

Felony in one County, and flying into another 373, 409

Felons, the Juftice muft take the Examination and put it into Writing   82

And bind by Recognizance the Witneffes to give Evidence   83

Felonies, not to be tried by the Seffions   84

Felony, where the Party had a lawful Poffeffion   87

By taking out Execution on a Judgment in Ejectment where the Party had no Title, and breaking the Houfe, and taking away Goods, Felony   *ibid.*

Breaking a Copper fixed to a Freehold, and carrying it away at the fame Time, Felony *ibid.*

Stealing Goods, which by Agreement the Party is to ufe, Felony   *ibid.*

Felon out of Prifon difcovering two others, fhall have a Pardon after Conviction of the Perfons difcovered   88

Fences, breaking or cutting   242, 244

Feræ naturæ, what   350

Ferrets, keeping them to deftroy Game not being qualified   107

Fine, upon Conviction for a Forcible Entry cannot be fet afide on a Motion   97, 98

Fines certain not to be mitigated   172

Fines fet on Rioters   215, 217

Fine acknowledged in the Name of another, &c. Felony   361

Fire, Servant firing a Dwelling-houfe or Outhoufe thro' Negligence, forfeits 100*l.*   96

Fifh, the Juftice may burn the Nets, &c. for the firft Offence   91

May commit for a Quarter of a Year for the fecond Offence, and for a whole Year for the third Offence   *ibid.*

Deftroying the Brood of Sea-Fifh, the Juftice by Warrant may caufe the Forfeiture to be levied by Diftrefs   *ibid.*

Fifhmongers Company, the Court of Affiftants may make By-Laws   93

Fifh, the Size thereof from the Eye to the Extent of the Tail   94

Fifh exported, the Rates thereof   95

Stealing Fifh armed and difguifed, or breaking down the Head of a Fifh-pond, Felony without Clergy   96

Flax, fhall not be water'd where Cattle drink 156

Forcible Entry, the Juftices are to execute the Statutes   96

Cannot make Reftitution without Inqueft of the Force by a Jury   96, 98

Entring peaceably, and holding with Force   292

What is a Forcible Entry   293

Force, where lawful   294, 299

Forcible Detainer, what   295

Where there is no Fact there is no Force   296

Forcible

I

A Table of the Principal Matters.

Forcible Defence, how far lawful   *Page* 300
Force, what Remedy againſt the Offender   302
The Record of it   448
The Precept to return a Jury   *ibid.*
The Inquiry, Preſentment, and Verdict   449
Forging Writings, Court-Roll or Will, ſecond Offence, Felony   361
Forging Stamps on Indentures of Apprenticeſhip, Felony   87
Foreſtaller, who he is   100
Who may inquire of him   101
Penalties   *ibid.*
Foundling Hoſpital, Penalty of 40 *s.* for moleſting any one in bringing any Child to it   490
Servants of the Hoſpital refuſing to account, &c. may be committed by two Juſtices   *ibid.*
Fowl, Wild, when not to be taken   109
Freſh Purſuit for Felony   357
Fruit-Trees, digging up and carrying away   242, 243
Fullers Earth, exporting, the Puniſhment   263
Furlong is 40 Pole   261
Furze, not to be burnt on Hills or Waſtes   108
Fuſtian, Perſons employed in working it, and purloining it, forfeit double the Value to the Poor   264

G.

Gauger may enter into the Brewing Places   74
Games unlawful   103
Juſtices may ſearch the Places   *ibid.*
And commit the Players   104
What Games are lawful, what not   *ibid.*
The Penalties for *uſing Games* unlawful   103
Thoſe who live by Gaming may be bound to Good Behaviour   105
Securities for Money won by Gaming are void *ibid.*
Loſing above 10 *l.* may be recovered of the Winner within three Months   *ibid.*
The Winner muſt anſwer a Bill of Diſcovery on Oath   *ibid.*
Winning above the Value of 10 *l.* at one Time, forfeits five Times the Value to the Informer *ibid.*
Game, Apprentices, Tradeſmen and others neglecting their Trades and following the Game, may be ſued as Treſpaſſers, and ſhall pay full Coſts as well as Damages   107
Conſtables may ſearch the Houſes of ſuſpected Perſons for Game   *ibid.*
How the Perſon is to be convicted if any Game is found   *ibid.*
He who is liable to any pecuniary Puniſhment for an Offence againſt the Laws of the Game, may be ſued for the Penalty in an Action of Debt   109
Conviction for killing four Hares   *ibid.*
Laws in Force for Preſervation of Game are enforced   160
Gardens, robbing, the Puniſhment   242
Gaol, Priſoner to be conveyed thither, who muſt be at the Charge   410

Gaoler denying to receive a Priſoner   *Page* 410
Gaol, Children born in common Gaols and Houſes of Correction, their Parents being Priſoners 175
Gaol, when out of Repair, what is to be done 191
Gaoler, made by Conſent of four Juſtices, *Quorum unus*, may provide other ſafe Places to remove the Sick   *ibid.*
Uſing a Priſoner very ſtrictly, ſo that he dieth, Felony   362, 411
Good Behaviour. See Sureties for the Good Behaviour.
Greg, not to be burnt on Hills or Waſtes, &c. 108
Greyhounds, keeping them to deſtroy Game not being qualified   107, 130
Guns, who may ſhoot in Hand-Guns, who not 111
Indictments for keeping and ſhooting in Guns *ibid.*
Mittimus of him who ſhoots in Guns not being qualified, and thereof convicted   443
The Record of the Conviction   444

H.

Hare-Pipes, keeping them to deſtroy Game not being qualified   107, 131, 159
Hare found in the Cuſtody of Alehouſe-keeper, Carrier, Chapman, Inn-keeper, or Victualler, forfeits 5 *l.* for every Hare   108
Diſcoverer of a Hare ſold to an Alehouſe-keeper, ſhall be diſcharged of the Penalties   *ibid.*
Found in the Shop, Houſe or Poſſeſſion of one not qualified, is an Expoſing to Sale   109
Hare traced in Snow   130, 159
Harveſt and Hay-time, Juſtices may compel Labourers to work   134, 139
Hayes, keeping them to deſtroy Game not being qualified   107
Hay, wanting Weight   124
Hawkers and Pedlars, trading without Licenſe 111
Hawking, when lawful   112
Hawks and their Eggs   *ibid.*
Concealing a Hawk, Felony   *ibid.*
Hawking in Corn prohibited   130
Hawks, to take away, ſteal or conceal them, Felony   350, 362
Heath, not to be burnt on Hills or Waſtes 108
Hedges, Breaking or Cutting   242
Hemp, ſhall not be watered where Cattle uſually drink   158
The Stone is 20 Pound Weight   260
Hide of Land. See Plough Land   119
Hides, Raw, muſt not be gaſhed   149
Additional Duties laid on Hides   *ibid.*
High Treaſon, in Compaſſing the Death of the King   314, 315
In levying War, and adhering to the King's Enemies   315
In counterfeiting the Great Seal and Money 316
Concealing the Treaſon is High Treaſon, in which all are Principals   317

He

A Table of the Principal Matters.

He who is indicted for High Treafon fhall have a true Copy of his Indictment, fhall be allowed Counfel, and make his Defence on Oath *Page* 320

Muft be two Witneffes to the fame Treafon *ibid.*
Prifoner fhall have a Copy of the Panel *ibid.*
Judgment in High Treafon 322
Highways, taxing to Repairs, no Settlement 187
Highways, how many Sorts 113
What is a Highway *ibid.*
Juftices may caufe it to be enlarged *ibid.*
Juftice may prefent the Want of Reparation *ibid.*
Surveyors, when to be chofen 114
Forfeits 5 *l.* for not taking the Office 115
Indictment for not working fix Days *ibid.*
Ploughland, Occupier is to be charged in the Parifh where he lives *ibid.*
Whofe the Soil is 114
Inclofure 115
Who is to repair it *ibid.*
Why called the King's Highway *ibid.*
The Surveyors Authority *ibid.*
Eftreats and Levies of Forfeitures *ibid.*
He who ufeth feveral Teems muft fend them all out 117
Fines and Forfeitures levied upon one, two Juftices may caufe a Rate to be made for their Reimburfement 118
None to remove Pofts for fecuring Highways 119
Highways may be enlarged by Seffions, and impanel a Jury to give Damages to the Owner of any Ground taken in *ibid.*
Indictment for not Repairing 122, 123
Highways to be enlarged 221
Highwaymen. See *Robber.*
Taker of a Highwayman fhall have 40 *l.* paid by the Sheriff in producing a Certificate from the Judge before whom convicted 123
Hired, for a Year, and ferving that Year is a Settlement, without Notice 178, 180
Hiring where it doth not make a Settlement *ibid.*
Holy Days 196
Homicide, what 325
The different Kinds of it 326
Who are chargeable with it, who not 334
Homicide of Neceffity, what it is 337
In Execution of Juftice *ibid.*
Who fhall inquire of it *ibid.*
Neceffity, three Sorts of it 338
Hops, five Score and twelve Pounds make the Hundred 260
Horfes, Sheep or other Cattle, killing or deftroying them in the Night-time, Felony 87
Horfes fold in Fairs or Markets, where the Sale is good, where not 125
Sold by the Thief by a wrong Name *ibid.*
What Horfes may be put in Commons 126
Horfes, where to be exported 242
Horfe-ftealer, no Clergy 370
Hofpitals, who may erect them 127
Their Lands are chargeable to the Poors Rate 186

Houfe of Correction, who may erect it *Page* 127, 490
Perfons fent thither muft live by their Labour, unlefs impotent 176
Rogue not to be fent to the Houfe of Correction, but by a Pafs, to the Place of his Birth 219
Directions about fending Perfons thither 443
Hue and Cry, where and how to be made 128, 221, 373
Juftices refufing to take the Examination of the Perfon robbed 128
He acts as a Minifter in taking the Examination, and not as a Judge of Record *ibid.*
There muft be a Certainty of the Hundred, tho' not of the Parifh *ibid.*
Where the Robbery was done, in what Cafes the Hundred is liable 129
Servant robbed, who muft make Oath, he or his Mafter, and who muft bring the Action *ibid.*
Hue and Cry levied without any Caufe how to be punifhed 374
Hundreds, when firft made 63
How to be charged with a Robbery 220
Contribution to be made where levied upon one Inhabitant *ibid.*
Any other Hundred neglecting to make frefh Purfuits, forfeits a Moiety *ibid.*
Hundred excufed, if Robbing is done in an Houfe, or in the Night, or if any of the Robbers are taken 221
Hundred in Tale, what fhall be fold at five Score, and what at five Score and Ten to the Hundred 260
Hunting in Vizards 129, 362
In Standing Corn prohibited 130
Hufband and Wife, fhe ftealing Goods with him, or by his Command, not Felony 87, 352
Binding themfelves to ferve, fhall do it according to Covenant 139
He may demand Sureties of the Peace againft her, and fhe againft him ; *fed quære* 271
The Wife may be guilty of a Forcible Entry, for which fhe fhall be committed 297
Married Women may be guilty of a Riot 314
Wife, killing her Hufband, is Petty Treafon *ibid.* 324
If by the Command of her Hufband fhe committeth Murder, this is Felony in both 352
If fhe fteal Goods without the Compulfion of her Hufband, fhe is guilty of Felony *ibid.*
If they both join in committing Treafon, both are punifhable 353
If both join in ftealing Goods, this fhall be imputed to the Hufband *ibid.*
If both join in Trefpafs, fhe fhall be punifhed *ibid.*
The Wife, without the Knowledge of the Hufband, may be guilty of Felony *ibid.*
She fhall not be charged as a Felon, for ftealing her Hufband's Goods *ibid.*

The

A Table of the Principal Matters.

The Wife relieving her Husband, knowing him to be a Felon, is not acceffary, and where she is acceffary **Page 370**

If she receiveth another Felon, she is acceffary 371

She shall not be produced as Evidence against her Husband 377

Unlefs she is the Party grieved 378

I.

IDLE and Diforderly Perfons, who 484
  Reward for taking them 5 s. ibid.

Jefuit, apprehending him, and profecuting him to Conviction of faying Mafs, shall have 100 l. 207

Jefuit, or other Ecclefiaftical Perfon born in the King's Dominions, coming and remaining here, is guilty of High Treafon 319

Imprifonment, when appointed by any Statute, and no Time limited 410

The Manner of it is, that the Party may not efcape ibid.

Indictment for a Forcible Entry, the Form of it. 305, 455

For High Treafon, shall not be quashed for Infufficiency, unlefs Exception is made in Court before Evidence given 320

Indictments for Forcible Entry, good and not good 450

Indictments, how to be drawn, and in what Form 455

Infant, ftealing Goods, no Felony 87
See poftea contra.

Shall be bound by his Covenant to ferve in Hufbandry 139

Infant Apprentice ibid.

Infant may be guilty of a Forcible Entry 296

Infant may commit Homicide 334

Infant of 14, convicted of Felony, had his Clergy 354

Infants allowed to be good Evidence 378

Informations, there are two Sorts of Informers 468

How they shall be exhibited, and by whom ibid.

The Defendant may traverfe the County ibid.

Shall not be filed in the Crown-Office, without a Recognizance of the Profecutor 470

Ingroffer, who he is 101

Who may inquire of him ibid.

Penalty ibid.

Inn-keeper, refufing to lodge a Traveller, how to be punished 22

Traveller must firft pay, or tender the Money for Lodging 23

Inns, Common, their Ufe 24

How and for what to be fuppreffed 25

Gueft rifing in the Night and removing Goods, Felony 87

Inn-keeper shall not make Horfe-Bread 132

Every Man may erect an Inn that will or can 133

Inn-keeper ufing the Trade of an Alehoufe, is within the Statutes about Alehoufes ibid.

Where an Inn-keeper is liable to make Satisfaction for a Robbery done in his Inn, where not ibid.

Who shall be a Gueft **Page 133**

What are Inns for quartering Soldiers ibid.

Inrollment of Bargain and Sale ibid.

The Fees ibid.

Journeymen Taylors 65

Iron Works, prohibited to be fet up in particular Places 253

Iffues, eftreated of Jurors 230

Judgment in High Treafon 322

In Mifprifion of Treafon ibid.

In Felony 465

In Petit Larceny ibid.

Judgment in Treafon may be reverfed by Writ of Error 320

Judgment in Petit Treafon 325

Judgment in a Præmunire 323

Judgment cannot be altered 466

Juryman must have a fufficient Addition to his Name 229

Must have 10 l. per Annum 463

The Precept of the Juftices to the Sheriff to return a Jury 457

To inquire of a Riot 453

Juries, the Trial by them commended 462

Challenge to them ibid.

What is a good Caufe of Challenge, what not ibid.

Conftables at Michaelmas Seffions must return the Names of Perfons qualified to ferve on Juries 465

Juftices of Peace, their Beginning 4

They are Judges of Record 5

Their Qualifications 6

Their Number in each County 7

Their Office, in what it confifts 8

By whom made ibid.

Made by Grant or Patent void ibid.

Made by Commiffion under the Great Seal 9

How their Authority doth determine ibid.

What he may do at his Difcretion 17

They have a larger Authority than the Confervators had 18

They are not to exercife their Power in Corporations, tho' no County of itfelf ibid.

He may grant Warrants tho' out of the County ibid.

He cannot take a Recognizance, or examine Witneffes out of the County 19

Where Authority is given to one, two, or more of them ibid.

Why Lawyers must be Juftices 83

Their Fees in Seffions 90

Where they have Power to hear and determine out of Seffions they ought to make a Record of the Conviction, if they commit the Offender 265

If they fine him, then they ought to Eftreat the Fine ibid.

Where one Juftice may hear and determine out of Seffions ibid.

Where he may convict upon Confeffion ibid.

Where upon the Oath of one Witnefs ibid.

Where two Juftices may hear and determine out of Seffions 266

And

A Table of the Principal Matters.

And by Indictment taken before them Page 266
Juflices Precept to the Sheriff to return a Jury, the Form 453
In what Cafes he may grant a Warrant to bring the Offender before himfelf 273
A good Form of fubordinate Government is by Juflices 413
They muft take the Oaths ibid.
Muft not execute their Office in their own Cafe ibid.
How they may defend themfelves where Suits are brought againft them for doing any Thing *Virtute Officii* 466

L.

Larceny, what 346
Grand Larceny is, where 'tis above a Shilling ftolen ibid.
Petty Larceny, under a Shilling ibid.
There muft be an actual Taking away ibid.
Where a Man hath the Goods by Delivery, yet if he carry them to another Place, *animo furandi*, 'tis Felony ibid. 347
But there muft be a carrying away to make it Felony 349
Of what Things it may be committed ibid.
Of what it cannot be committed, (*viz.*) of Chattels real, Trees, Writings, &c. 351
Larceny of his own Goods 352
Laths, muft be five Foot long, two Inches broad, and half an Inch thick 260
Leather, Butcher his Duty 145
Who may be a Tanner ibid.
Red and unwrought Leather fhall not be put to Sale without Searching 146
Searchers and Sealers of Leather, when to be nominated 147
Leather muft not be tranfported 149
Leather unwrought fhall not be bought by any one but he who fhall make it into Wares ibid.
Leets, choofing unfit Conftables 64
Libels and Libellers may be bound to the Good Behaviour 289
The feveral Ways of Libelling ibid.
Liberate. See *Difcharge*.
Licenfe for a Badger, Drover, &c. the Fees 90
Muft be in Seffions 102
Licenfe to travel 177
Licenfe to a Soldier fuffering Shipwreck 233
To keep an Alehoufe 436
Lights, &c. Houfholders to hang out Lights 124
Ling, not to be burnt on Hills or Waftes, &c. 108
Linen, Perfons employed in working Linen and purloining it, forfeit double the Value to the Poor 264
London and *Weftminfter*, no Carts carrying more than 12 Sacks of Meal, or 12 Quarters of Malt, or 700 and half of Bricks, or a Chaldron of Coals, having their Wheels bound with Iron, fhall be fuffered there, or within ten Miles thereof 52, 122

London, new Ways Page 124
Waggons travelling in *London* 151
Buildings prohibited ibid.
Lottery Tickets, forging or counterfeiting them, Felony 363
Lowbels, keeping them to deftroy Game not being qualified 107
Lunaticks muft be locked up 489
Charges of conveying them to the Place of Settlement, how to be raifed ibid.
Lurchers, keeping them to deftroy Game not being qualified 107

M.

Magna Charta, how often confirmed 406
Maid Servant, got with Child 172
How to be difcharged 173
Mainprife, what 384
Malt, decitfully made 152
Damaged after the Duty paid ibid.
Manor, Lord thereof may appoint a Game-keeper 108
But it muft be a Perfon qualified by Law ibid.
Manflaughter defined 333
Where Death enfues by doing an unlawful Act 335
Manufactures 483, 484
Markets, Sale of Horfes therein good, and not good 125
Markets and Fairs, whence derived 153
Their Privileges ibid.
Time of Continuance ibid.
On what Days, and where to be held ibid.
Marriage by Juflices confirmed 154
Married, a Servant Woman marrying muft ferve out her Time 139
Marrying in Service, cannot be removed to the laft Place of Settlement, if the Mafter doth not complain 179
Marriage of a Popifh Recufant 203
Marriage a fecond Time, the firft Hufband or Wife living, Felony 363
Mariner, Fifhermen ufing the Sea fhall be taken as Mariners 154
Who are to be Apprentices to the Sea-Service ibid.
Mafons, Congregations and Confederacies holden by them, whether 'tis Felony 360
Mafter and Servant, Mafter cannot difcharge his Servant but for fome reafonable Caufe, unlefs the Servant confent 140
Mafter being dead, where his Apprentice fhall be fent to the Adminiftrator, where not 143
The Mafter affigning an Apprentice, and he confenting, will not make him an Apprentice to the Affignee ibid.
Mafter refufing to take an Apprentice, forfeits 10 l. 166
He may ftrike his Servant 281
Mafter delivering Goods to his Servant to keep, and he runs away with them, if under the Value of 40 s. no Felony 348

4

But

But if the Goods were not delivered to him, yet tho' under 40 s. Value, and he run away, 'tis Felony   Page 348

Servant may be acceffary to a Felony done by his Mafter   371

Mayors are Juftices of Peace by Grant   8

Mayor or Magiftrate, where he may act as a Juftice of Peace by particular Statutes   470

Meafures. See *Weights.*

Medietas linguæ   462

Mile is 8 Furlongs, or 320 Poles   261

Millers Toll-difh muft be according to the Standard   259

Muft take but a Quart for grinding a Bufhel of hard Corn   *ibid.*

If he fetch and carry the Grift, then he may take two Quarts   *ibid.*

And half as much for Malt   *ibid.*

Muft not be common Buyer of Corn   *ibid.*

Mifadventure, what it is   335

Mifprifion of Treafon, what it is   322

The Judgment therein   *ibid.*

Mifprifion of Felony, what it is, and how punifhable   370

Mittimus, the Caufe of the Commitment muft be mentioned   386

Mittimus for a Felon, the Form   441

Money, Coining it is High Treafon   317

Coining Farthings is a Mifdemeanor   *ibid.*

Uttering falfe Money coined here is Mifprifion of Treafon   *ibid.*

Coining Inftruments bought and fold, making Grainings round the Edges of Money, gilding or plating the Coin, is High Treafon   320

He who apprehends a Coiner or Clipper, and profecutes to Conviction, fhall have 40 l.   321

Making or mending any Coining Tools, or concealing, or having them in Cuftody, is a Traitor   *ibid.*

Conveying Tools out of the Mint is High Treafon   *ibid.*

Maker of Letters for Grainings, Gilding, or Cafing over Coin, refembling the Current Coin, is High Treafon   *ibid.*

Blanching Copper for Sale, or mixing it with Silver, or knowingly buying or felling it, or putting off counterfeit Mill'd Money, Felony   360

Month, how to be computed   134

Murder, muft be tried at the Affifes   84

Definition of Murder   328

The Malice muft be forethought   *ibid.*

Killing an Officer or a Magiftrate, the Law implies Malice   329

Beaft killing a Man   *ibid.*

What fhall not be a Provocation   330

Rules in judging Murder   331

Principals in Murder, tho' not prefent   *ibid.*

Mufters, abfenting from Mufters, or not bringing their beft Armour, muft pay 40 s. or be committed for ten Days   395

N.

Naval Stores, where imbeziling them to the Value of 20 s. is Felony   Page 361

Nets, to catch Fifh, muft be 3 Inches and an half from Knot to Knot   94

Keeping Nets to deftroy Game not being qualified   107

Nets to catch Fifh, who may keep them, who not   *ibid.*

Newgate, by what Commiffion the Juftices fit there   175

Nobility, Surety of the Peace is not to be required of them by a Juftice. See the Method of getting it in Chancery   270

Trial of a Peer for High Treafon   320

Peer may not be arrefted   406

Northampton, the Method of Proceeding on that Statute   99

Who may have a Writ on that Statute   303

Certificate, the Form thereof on the Statute of Northampton   451

Notice in Writing, when 'tis neceffary in the Cafes of poor People removing from one Parifh to another   179

Notice muft be given of an Appeal from an Order of Removal   188

Nufances on Highways, any Body may remove, but cannot convert the Materials to their own Ufe   122

Indictments for Nufances   *ibid.*

Exporting or importing Leather, is a common Nufance   149

What are Nufances   156

What are private Nufances for which an Indictment will not lie   *ibid.*

Never admitted to a Fine till the Nufance is removed   *ibid.*

Importing Cattle is a Nufance   241

O.

Oaks fhall not be fell'd which are fit to be barked, but at fuch Times   253

Oath, of a Juftice of Peace   11

Oath of two Witneffes to convict one for felling Ale without Licenfe   23

Of the Commiffioners of Excife   75

Oath, who may adminifter, and who muft take it   157

Oath of Supremacy, who muft take it   196

Oath of Commiffioners of Sewers   227

Oath of him who requires Sureties of the Peace 268

Oath, Directions for thofe who take an Oath   380

Oath of a Conftable   426

Oath of a Juftice taken by *Dedimus*, and the Return thereof   452

Oath of a Sheriff   230

Who fhall take the Oath of the Under-Sheriff, his Bailiffs, Deputies, and Clerks, and other Officers   231

c c   *Office,*

A Table of the Principal Matters.

Office, the Executing a publick Office in a Parish for a Year makes a Settlement *Page* 178, 179

Orchards, robbing, the Punishment 242

Order of two Justices to remove a poor Man, is binding till reverfed by an Appeal 179

The Appeal muft be in due Time 181

Orders quafhed *ibid.*

Order muft be made upon Complaint of the Church-wardens and Overfeers of the Poor *ibid.*

It muft fet forth, that the Perfon removed was laft legally fettled in the Parifh of, &c. *ibid.*

It muft appear that the Party was chargeable to the Parifh *ibid.*

It muft be directed to the Parifh Officers of both Parifhes 182

Order upon an Appeal reverfed, is conclufive as to the contending Parifhes *ibid.*

Order upon an Appeal confirmed, is conclufive to all Parifhes *ibid.*

Order for an Overfeer to take upon him the Office 187

Warrant for Overfeers to give up their Accounts, and for new Overfeers to take the Charge 422

To diftrain for the poor Tax *ibid.*

Ordinance, Armour, Shot, Powder, Habiliments of War, or Victuals for Soldiers, imbeziling it, Felony 361

They may make what lawful Proof they can by Witneffes to difcharge themfelves 381

Out-houfe, ftealing to the Value of 40s. tho' not broke open, and tho' no Body in it, Burglary 344

Overfeers, of the Poor, when to be chofen, and by whom 164

Their Duty *ibid.*

May raife Money by Tax to fet the Poor on Work 165

They muft account, and what is to be done if they refufe 167

New Overfeers muft levy the Forfeitures for not paying Poor Tax *ibid.*

Overfeer not bound to lay out his own Money for the Relief of the Poor 186

Old Overfeer muft pay over Money in his Hands to the new one *ibid.*

Overfeers are to account before two Juftices *ibid.*

They may be indicted for refufing 187

Mandamus to them to account, not good *ibid.*

Outlawry, Proceedings to it 472, 473

Oxgang is 13 Acres 261

P.

PALES, Breaking or Cutting 242

Paper, a Bale is ten Ream 260

Papifts, having not taken the Oaths, muft regifter their Names and Lands, and fubfcribe the Regifter 208, 209

Papift, Sale of his Lands to a Proteftant Purchafer fhall not be void 210

Parchment, a Roll is five Dozen, or 60 Skins 260

Pardon for Murder 332

Parents, of Ability, muft relieve their poor Children *Page* 167, 183

Parents, who are Papifts, muft allow competent Maintenance to Proteftant Children 207

Parifh, what is a Parifh 165, 183

Parifh extending into two Counties 167

Parks, inclofed for keeping Deer, broke down 129, 130

Park Pales pulled down in the Night-Time 131

Park muft be fo many Foot from the Highway 221

Partridge, found in the Poffeffion of the Alehoufe-keeper, forfeits 5l. and the Juftice may take it away 108

Deftroying and difcovering a Partridge bought and fold, fhall be difcharged of the Penalties *ibid.*

Partridges, Forfeiture of taking them 158

Shooting, killing or deftroying them, or deftroying their Eggs *ibid.*

Pafs, the Form of it 439

Directions about it *ibid.*

Pafs for conveying Vagabonds by 13 Geo. 2. 24. 485

Pafture Lands for Cows, Sheep, &c. 160

Peace, what it is 7, 160

Breach thereof, what it is 161

Recognizance to keep the Peace 276

What fhall not be a Breach of the Peace 281

Perch is 16 Foot and an half 261

Peer. See *Nobility*.

Perjury, an Offence at Common Law 161

And by the Statute *ibid.*

Petitions, to redrefs Grievances 162

Petty Treafon, what it is 323

What Perfons may be guilty of it 324

The Forfeiture and Judgment 325

Petty Larceny may be tried at Seffions 83

What it is 87

Pheafant, Difcoverer of one fold to an Alehoufe-keeper, &c. fhall be difcharged of the Penalties 108

Found in the Cuftody of Alehoufe-keeper, forfeits 5l. and may be taken away by Juftice, or Lord of a Manor *ibid.* 159

Forfeiture of taking them 158

Shooting, killing or deftroying them *ibid.*

Pick-Pocket. See *Privately Stealing*.

Pigeon, deftroying one *ibid.*

Pillory and Tumbril, in every Market 258

Plague 163

Play. See *Games and Gaming*.

Plough-Land, how much it is 116

'Tis now by Statute 50l. per Annum *ibid.*

Plough-Land 261

Poifon, the Party muft die within a Year and a Day, Felony 363

Pole is 16 Foot and an half 261

Poor, what 164

Parifh not able to provide for their own Poor, two Juftices may tax the Hundred 167

4

He

A Table of the Principal Matters.

He who brings Poor into a Parish without their Consent, may be raised in his Rates *Page* 167
Poor Children, whose Parents are dead, where to be relieved 168
Who may be removed not renting 10 *l. per Ann.* 169
Poor, three Sorts of them 176
Popish Bishop, apprehending him, and prosecuting him to Conviction of saying Mass, &c. 207
Popish Priest, teaching School, to be committed for Life *ibid.*
Post-Office 189
Post-Master may appoint a Surveyor *ibid.*
Postage of Letters under 5 *l.* shall be recovered before Justices *ibid.*
Post-Master sued where Letters are opened *ibid.*
Posse Comitatus, what, and when to be raised 411
Powdike 360
Poundage Money 231
Præmunire, for refusing to take the Oath of Supremacy 197
To purchase a Bull from *Rome* 319
Judgment on a *Præmunire* 323
Presentation to a Benefice, Recusant is disabled 207, 208
The Universities shall present 207
Trustee for a Recusant must give Notice to the University of the next Avoidance *ibid.*
The Ordinary must tender the Declaration against Transubstantiation, to him who brings the Presentation 208
Pretender. See *Wales*.
Priest, Popish, apprehending him and prosecuting to Conviction of saying Mass 207
Printers and Printing, an Act relating to them expired 190
Prison, who must be at the Charge of sending an Offender to Prison 191, 410
Prisoners for Debt, Gifts made for their Benefit, Justices may send for Persons and Writings 191
Person committed for a Crime shall not be removed into the Custody of another Officer, unless by Writ 192
Prison Breaking, the Punishment. See *Escape* 355
Irons, when to be put on them 411
Privately Stealing, the Punishment 345
The Person being put in Fear *ibid.*
Privy Search 485
Probate of Wills, and Administration granted, the Fees 90
Process upon Indictments 471
How it differs from a Warrant *ibid.*
To whom directed 472
Proclamation for dispersing a Riot 219
Property, how many Sorts in a Thing 350
Prophecies 190
Purchase, doth not make a Settlement, unless the Money be 30 *l.* truly paid 179, 188
Purveyors prohibited 192
How punishable, and for what 364

Q.

Quakers, subscribing the Declaration of Fidelity and the Christian Belief, before two Justices *Page* 193
Shall not be a Witness in Criminal Causes, nor serve on Juries; and their solemn Affirmation goes for an Oath *ibid.*
Refusing to pay or compound for Great or Small Tithes 194
Qualifications, for keeping Guns, Nets, Dogs, &c. 100 *l. per Annum* Lands of Inheritance, either in his own or his Wife's Right 130
Or for Term of Life *ibid.*
Or 150 *l. per Annum* for 99 Years *ibid.*
The Son and Heir of an Esquire *ibid.*

R.

RAILS, Breaking or Cutting 242
Ranfom, what 214, 217
Rape, Felony 343, 366
What it is 366
The Complaint ought to be made presently *ibid.*
Rate, General 479
What Parishes; Places and Things shall be rated to the Poor 185
Rates, how to be made *ibid.*
Farmer not to be rated for his State on the Land *ibid.*
The Pound-Rate is the most equal for Land *ibid.*
The personal Estate must be rated in Proportion to the Land *ibid.*
Rate, a Distress for a Quarter's Rate cannot be made till the Quarter is ended 186
Rates, unequally made, quashed *ibid.*
Ream of Paper is 20 Quire 260
Recognizance, what it is 399
Who may take it *ibid.*
To whom it may be made 400
'Tis Matter of Record as soon as taken by the Justice 401
Recognizance, for keeping an Alehouse 23
The Fees thereof 90
Recognizance of the Peace 276
The Proceedings, if forfeited 277
What shall discharge it 278
By the Release of the Justice 279
By the Release of the Party *ibid.*
By the Death of the King 'tis discharged 280
By the Death of the Cognizor or Cognizee *ibid.*
What is a Forfeiture of the Recognizance *ibid.*
What is no Breach of it 283
Recognizance single, the Form 430
Recognizance for the Peace *ibid.*
The Condition 432
For the Good Behaviour *ibid.*
The Condition 433
To give Evidence against a Prisoner *ibid.* 434
To prefer an Indictment *ibid.*

Recogni,

A Table of the Principal Matters.

Record imbeziled, by Reason whereof a Judgment is reversed, Felony   *Page* 361

Record, rasing it, Felony   *ibid.*

Recusants, who   194

Register, the Poor must be registred in the Parish Book   183

See *Alms.*

Papists must register their Names and Lands, and subscribe the Register   208, 209

Neglecting to register, or fraudulently registring, forfeits the Inheritance   *ibid.*

Regrater, who he is   100

Who may inquire of him   101

Penalty   *ibid.*

Relation, where 'tis to be had to the Fact   376

Release of the Peace   446

Of the Good Behaviour   447

Relief to the Poor, where the Justice may order it, where not   183

Removal, a poor Man removed must be received by the Parish Officers to whom removed   178

Rents, Power of Justices in relation thereto   210, 211

Rescuing a Man in Custody for Felony, is a principal Felon, and not an Accessary   371

Rescuing a Felon carrying to Execution, is Felony   88, 355, 356

Resolutions of the Judges so called, of no great Authority   171

Restitution, not to be made before Inquest   413

Restitution on Forcible Entry, how to be made, and by whom   298, 304

The Form of the Indictment for the Force   304

Who shall award and make Restitution   305

To whom it shall be made   306

Causes for not granting Restitution   307

Pardon is a good Bar to *Restitution*   309

Where Restitution shall be granted   *ibid.*

Restitution of stolen Goods, how and when to be made   379

Restitution, the Warrant on a Forcible Entry   451

Retainer, of a Servant, good and not good   139

Riot, the Form of a Precept to return a Jury   453

Riot, what it is   452

The Record on the View of the Justice   *ibid.*

Riot, one Justice may prevent it   211

What the Justices may do without the Sheriff   212

Traverse to an Indictment for Riot   454

Riotous Assembly, of 12 or more, and being commanded by Proclamation to disperse   218

The Form of the Proclamation   219

Continuing together afterwards, &c. Felony, without Benefit of Clergy   *ibid.*

Pulling down, or demolishing a Place of Religious Worship, Felony without Clergy   *ibid.*

Obstructing the Reading the Proclamation, Felony   *ibid.*

Riots, Statutes against them   310

What shall be a Riot within the Meaning of these Statutes   *Page* 310

The Intent of meeting together must appear   311

Of the Lawfulness or Unlawfulness of the Act, and the Manner and Circumstances of it   312, 313

What the Justice is to do in suppressing Riots   413

Robbing, to the Value of a Penny, if put in Fear, Felony   88

Robbery by threatning to murder one, unless he swear to bring Money to such a Place, and 'tis brought accordingly   *ibid.*

Robbing a Dwelling-house in the Day-time, and taking to the Value of 5 s. tho' no body within   344, 364

Robbery, is the felonious Taking any Thing from the Person of another putting him in Fear   344

What shall be a Taking   *ibid.*

What shall be the Person   *ibid.*

What shall be putting in Fear   *ibid.*

Rogue, is to be sent to the Place of Birth   219

His Description   484

He who takes him shall have 10 s.   *ibid.*

May be sent to the House of Correction   486

Must be sent to the Place of his last Settlement; if not known, then by a Pass to the Place of his Birth; if not known, then to the Place where he was last found begging   485

Rogue incorrigible, who   484

Rogue coming from *Ireland* may be put in any Vessel to be sent back   487

Master of a Ship bringing a Rogue from the Plantations, and found Begging, how to be punished   *ibid.*

Rogue incorrigible, transported, and returning, &c. Felony without Benefit of Clergy   486

Testimonial that he hath been punished   439

Rome, Bishop thereof, maintaining his Authority   86, 195, 318

Rout, what it is   311

Rum, Entry must be made where 'tis kept   78

Running away, and leaving his Wife and Children to the Parish   183, 484

Mittimus, the Form   443

S.

SAbbath-Day, no Games on that Day   103

No Resort to Fairs or Markets on that Day   126

Driving Cattle on that Day   173

Travelling on that Day prohibited   224

Arresting on that Day, unless for Treason, Felony, or Breach of the Peace, void   225

Sacraments, depraving them, how to be punished   223

Salmon, destroying them in *Hampshire* and *Wiltshire,* the Penalty   93

When to be caught   95

Salt shall be seized which is conveyed away before Entry   225

Prices of Salt to be set at Sessions   *ibid.*

4

Must

Muſt be ſold by Weight, (*viz.*) after the Rate of
  56 Pounds the Buſhel, and not by Meaſure
  Page 225
Salt loſt after Payment of the Duty, *&c.* *ibid.*
Scavengers in Cities and Market-Towns muſt be
  appointed by the Quarter-Seſſions   120, 124
Taxing and paying to a Scavenger, no Settlement
  187
Schoolmaſter muſt have a Licenſe   226
Search, a Privy Search to be made in one Night
  485
Sea Trouts   93
Seamen, Regiſters, *&c.*   155
Sectaries, when firſt in *England*   195
Se defendendo   339
Servant. See *Maſter*.
Departing or putting away before the End of his
  Term   136, 140
Who is compellable to ſerve, who not   *ibid.*
Shall not be hired for leſs than a Year   137
Aſſaulting his Maſter, ſhall be committed for a
  Year   *ibid.*
Servant retained for a Year and falling ſick, or
  being hurt or lame in his Service, ſhall not be
  put away, or his Wages abated   141
Shall not be put away before the End of his Term
  without reaſonable Cauſe   136
What ſhall be a Departure   141
Servants going away with their Maſters Goods
  Felony   144
Servant imbeziling his Maſter's Goods to the Va-
  lue of 40 s. is Felony without Clergy   *ibid.*
Service, Perſons able, and not putting themſelves
  to Service after Warning   173
Servant killing his Maſter is Petty Treaſon   323
Mittimus of a diſorderly Servant   442
Seſſions, Fees therein   90
May puniſh by Fine all Nuſances in Highways 118
Special Seſſions may order the Highways to be re-
  paired   120
Seſſions may cauſe an Houſe of Correction to be
  erected   127
May examine a Perſon ſuſpected for ſtealing Deer
  131
Seſſions cannot delegate their Power   181
Seſſions upon an Appeal may give Coſts   182
Muſt either affirm or reverſe the Order   *ibid.*
Have no Juriſdiction but on Appeal   183
Seſſions need not give the Reaſon of their Judg-
  ment   *ibid.*
May appoint Rates for paſſing Vagrants   488
Seſſions are to ſet the Prices on Salt   225
Seſſions, what it is   456
How many in a Year   *ibid.*
In what Place to be kept   457
Seſſions, the Precept to return a Jury   *ibid.*
Who ought to be preſent   *ibid.*
Settlement of Poor, what makes a Settlement 178,
  179
Renting 10 *l. per Annum*   169
Purchaſing to the Value of 30 *l.*   170

The 40 Days to be accounted from the Publicati-
  on of Notice in Writing, to be delivered to the
  Pariſh Officers   *Page* 178, 179
Executing any publick Office in a Pariſh for a
  Year   178
Paying to the publick Taxes   *ibid.*
Hired for a Year, and ſerving that Year   *ibid.*
Servant ſhall be ſettled where the Maſter was a
  Lodger or Viſitor   181, 188
Setting Dogs, keeping them to deſtroy Game not
  being qualified   107, 130, 158
Sewers, Commiſſioners, their Oath   227
Who they may tax, *&c.* and in what Manner
  ibid. 228
Sheep, Horſes, or other Cattle, killing or deſtroy-
  ing them, Felony   87
Sheep muſt not be tranſported   228, 366
No Farmer ſhall keep above 2000 Sheep at one
  Time   228
Six Score ſhall go to the Hundred   *ibid.*
Sheriff, his Fees   82, 89, 230, 231
One Juſtice to overſee the Sheriff's Courts   229
One Juſtice may examine him about taking and
  entring Plaints   *ibid.*
May examine the Defaults of Collectors, Bailiffs,
  and other Gatherers of Amerciaments   *ibid.*
And upon Complaint of the Party grieved may
  make Proceſs   *ibid.*
Sheriff taking any Reward for ſparing a Juror,
  forfeits 5 *l.*   230
Shall not be a Juſtice of Peace in that Year where-
  in he was Sheriff   *ibid.*
Oath of a Sheriff   *ibid.*
Sherwood Foreſt, Heath ſhall not be burnt there to
  Aſhes   108
Ships in Diſtreſs, and hindering them from being
  ſaved   231
Ship wilfully burnt or deſtroyed by the Captain,
  Mariner, *&c.* Felony   364
Making Holes in the Bottom of it   *ibid.*
Teſtimonial for a Shipwreck   440
Shoemakers, Journeyman accuſed by his Maſter
  for fraudulently ſelling, pawning, exchanging
  any Boots, Leather, *&c.* and being convicted,
  ſhall make Satisfaction   144
He who buys or takes Boots to pawn, ſhall make
  Satisfaction   *ibid.*
Shoemaker employed by one, and retained by
  another before the Work done, muſt be ſent to
  the Houſe of Correction   145
Shoemakers muſt uſe Leather well tanned   *ibid.*
Muſt not uſe Leather not well tanned and curried   148
Shoes and Slippers may be tranſported   149
Shop, breaking it open in the Day-time   89,
  343
And tho' not broke open, if he take to the Value
  of 5 s. Felony   364
Silk, imbeziling, pawning, ſelling, or detaining
  it by any to whom 'tis delivered to manufacture   232

d d   *Skinner,*

A Table of the Principal Matters.

Skinner, none shall use the Trade unless he has served Apprentice for seven Years *Page* 232

Smuglers, their Punishment 233

Snares, using them to destroy Game not being qualified 107, 131

Soap, the Barrel, how much it must contain 260

Soldiers and Mariners, &c. deserting, or begging and counterfeiting a Certificate from the Captain, or making any Mutiny in the Army, Felony 365

See the annual Act for punishing *Mutiny* and *Desertion*, &c.

South-Sea, Forging any Warrant or Dividend, or any Endorsement or Writing, Felony 365

Spices, what are garbleable 235

Spirits, Entry must be made where they are kept 78

Squibs, selling them, or suffering them to be cast out of Houses 235

Stabbing, the Statute made against it 328

Stalking any Deer without License of the Owner, forfeits 40 *l.* 131

Stamps, Felony to counterfeit them without Benefit of Clergy 235, 365

Pamphlets above a Sheet must be stamped 236

Stocks, the Offender not able to pay the Forfeiture for being drunk 21

The Constable may put a Prisoner in the Stocks for a reasonable Time, till he can get Help to convey him to Gaol 409

Stock of the Shire, to what Uses to be employed, and how to be assessed 236, 237

Rules for making Assessments *ibid.*

Remedy, where wrongfully charged *ibid.*

Stock of any Company, or Share thereof, forging or procuring to be forged, Felony 365

Stolen Goods, taking Money or Reward to help the Person to them, unless the Felon is taken and brought to Trial, is Felony 349

Buying and receiving them, knowing them to be stolen is a Misdemeanor, to be punished by Fine and Imprisonment, tho' the principal Felon is not convicted 373

Strong Waters, Entry must be made where they are kept 78

Summons, necessary where the Offender is to be convicted in a summary Way 415

Superfedeas, the Form of it 427

Superfedeas of the Peace out of the King's Bench or Chancery 274

Must be granted upon Motion in Court 275, 285

Superfedeas by a Justice of Peace 427

For the Good Behaviour 428

To a *Capias* upon an Indictment for a Trespass 429

To an Indictment for Felony *ibid.*

To an Exigent for Felony 430

Superfedeas on a *Supplicavit* 428

Supplicavit for the Peace, to whom directed 284

The Execution of it *ibid.*

In what Cases to be granted 285

In what Manner a *Superfedeas* must be got *Page* 285

How the *Supplicavit* must be returned 286

The Return of the *Certiorari* *ibid.*

Sureties of the Peace, for whom, and against whom to be granted 267, 269

The Oath of him who requires it 268

Where the Justice may deny to take Sureties 269

Against a Knight 270

Against a Justice of Peace *ibid.*

How to be commanded 272

How to be executed 273, 274

How to be discharged either by Death or Release 273

Sureties for Good Behaviour 287

Peace and Behaviour, how they differ *ibid.*

Granted by one Justice, and by *Supplicavit* 288

For what Cause to be granted *ibid.*

Release, *Superfedeas, Certiorari* 292

Surveyors of Highways nominated, when and by whom 118

Penalty of refusing *ibid.*

Must view the Roads, and once in four Months present upon Oath to a Justice what Condition they are in 120

Must set up a Stone where two Cross-ways meet *ibid.*

Neglecting their Duty, forfeits 40 *s.* 121

Suspected of Felony, not to be bailed 413

Suspicion, What shall be the Causes of it 381

There must be Felony committed 384

Swans, where taking them is Felony 350

Swearing and Cursing prophanely, the Punishment 238

Swine, must not be kept on the Backside of any paved Streets 125

T.

Aylors, Journeymen, all Contracts made by them for advancing their Wages, &c. void 144

Departing before the End of the Term agreed on, and before the Work is finished, or refusing to work, must be sent to the House of Correction *ibid.*

Taylor giving, or Journeyman taking greater Wages than *per* Statute, forfeits 5 *l.* *ibid.*

Tanner, what he is to do 146

Must not shave upper Leather Hides 149

Must make a true Entry of Hides 150

Must not use any private Tan-yard *ibid.*

Must pay the Duties on Hides *ibid.*

Must keep just Scales and Weights *ibid.*

Task-Work 140

Tawers, who are Tawers 150

Taxes, where paying the Publick Taxes makes a Settlement, or not 178, 179, 180, 188

Taxes, to the Poor, how to be made 165, 173

Who to be taxed, and where *ibid.*

See *Rates*.

Testimonial of a Servant 140

Theftbote, what it is 371

2

Theft,

A Table of the Principal Matters.

Theft, what it is   Page 344
'Tis of two Sorts, (*viz.*) either Robbery or Larceny   ibid.
Tile-making, Juftices may inquire therein   246
Muft be fix-Score to the Hundred   260
Timber fquared, 50 Foot makes a Load   ibid.
Time, Computation thereof   154
Tithes, fhall be fet out   245
Juftices fhall determine Complaints   ibid.
Tobacco, Penalty of planting it   239
Who may deftroy it   ibid.
Refifting the Execution of the Act   ibid.
Refufing to affift in the Execution of the Act 240
Cutting Leaves and Plants refembling Tobacco   ibid.
Tobacco-Pipe Clay not to be exported   263
Toll-taker, upon Sale of Horfes in Fairs and Markets, what he is to do   125
Toll fhall be taxed to the Poor   165
Trades mentioned in the Statute, 5 *Eliz.*   137
Trade may be ufed by any Man at Common Law   138
But by the Statute he muft be Apprentice to it for 7 Years   ibid.
Indictments for ufing Trades not being Apprentices   142
What fhall be Exercifing a Trade within the Statute   143
Tramellers for Larks   400
Traverfe to an Indictment of Forcible Entry 309
Traverfe, the Method of Traverfing   474
Trees, barking or breaking down   244
Trial, the Manner of Trials   459
In what Cafes it may be the fame Seffions, and in what not   460, 464
Trial regularly, muft be in the fame County where the Offence was committed   ibid.
Trial. See *medietas linguæ*   462
Tunnels, keeping them to deftroy Game not being qualified   107

V.

Vagabond, what he is.   484
May be apprehended by any one   ibid.
Reward for taking fuch Offender 10 s.   485
Penalty on Officer refufing to take fuch Offenders   ibid.
Penalty for refufing to pay the faid 10 s. to the Taker   ibid.
Vagabonds, how to be examined and conveyed, &c.   ibid.
May be committed to the Houfe of Correction   486
See *Idle and Diforderly Perfons and Rogues.*
Vagrant. See *Vagabond.*
Vellum, Hides made into Vellum, the Maker muft give Notice to a proper Officer of his Tan-houfe, Warehoufe, &c.   149
Venire facias, the Form it   472
Under Sheriff, his Oath   230
His Fees for Poundage   231

Underwoods, Cutting or Spoiling   Page 242
Shall not be converted into Tillage or Pafture 253
Univerfities, what they may do in relation to Purveyors   192
They may file a Bill in Equity to difcover fecret Trufts made by Recufants about Prefentations   208
And if the Patron is only a Truftee, his Anfwer fhall be good Evidence   ibid.
Colleges and Halls exempted from paying Excife of Beer   76

W.

Wages of Servants, Confiderations thereon 136
Mafter putting away a Servant, he fhall have Wages to the Time he ferved   140
Servant wilfully departing, lofes his Wages   141
Mafter dying, his Executor fhall pay the Wages   ibid.
Wages exceffive giving or taking   137
Waggon, for Hire, except for Hufbandry, fhall not be drawn with more than fix Horfes, the Owner or Driver forfeits all above, to the Ufe of the Seizor   51
What the Seizor muft do   ibid.
Hindring the Seizure, fhall be fent to Gaol ibid.
Wales, the pretended Prince of *Wales* attainted, and correfponding with him, or with any Perfon employed by him, or remitting Money, knowing it to be for his Ufe, is High Treafon   320
Maintaining his Title, High Treafon   321
Warding in the Day-time to apprehend Rogues 175
Warehoufe, robbing it in the Day-time to the Value of 5 s. tho' no Perfon is in it, Burglary without Benefit of Clergy   89, 343, 364
Warrant, what the Juftice may do by Word without Warrant   401
Warrant in writing, where it may be General without mentioning the Crime, where it muft be Special   ibid.
May be granted before the Party is indicted   403
To whom to be directed   404
The Officers Duty, and how to be executed ibid.
  405
Contempt of it, how to be punifhed   ibid.
Warrant, where granted to apprehend a Felon, the Juftice at the fame Time ought to take a Recognizance of the Profecutor to appear and give Evidence   405
Refifting the Executing a Warrant, the Officer may juftify the Beating and Wounding   409
The Stile and Tefte of a Warrant, and to whom it muft be directed   415
How it differs from Procefs   471
Warren, entring it, being ufed to keep Conies, and taking, chafing or killing, them   130
Watch, where to be kept   246, 374
Who may be compelled to watch   247
How to be punifhed for Neglect   ibid.
Watch and Ward, what   ibid.
Watch-

A Table of the Principal Matters.

Watchman killed in taking a Burglar, &c. his Administrator is intitled to 40 l. Page 247

Watermen offending against the Statute ibid.

Must not hide themselves from Pressing ibid.

Water-Measure 262

Wax, Justice may examine Sellers of Wax and Wax-Candles 249

Wears, the Penalty for erecting them ibid.

And of taking Fish in them ibid.

And fishing with unlawful Nets ibid.

Weavers, what Looms they may keep 250

What Apprentices they may take ibid.

Weights and Measures, Faults of Officers in great Towns punishable by Justices 254

False Weights, what is to be done with them ibid.

One Weight and one Measure thro' the Kingdom ibid.

Yet two Weights allowed, (viz.) Troy and Averdupois, the one is by Law, the other by Custom 255

Measure of Corn, Beer, Ale, &c. 256

Clerk of the Market, his Office 257

Standards of Brass Weights in every Shire-Town 261

Scales, Bushel and Weights sealed in every Market-Town 262

Wild-Fowl, at what Time they may not be taken 251

Who may hunt them with Spaniels ibid.

When their Eggs may not be taken ibid.

Wine, not to be sold in a Town not Corporate without a Licence from the Justices 250

Nor in a Corporation without the Licence of the Mayor ibid.

But Wine Licenses are now vested in the Crown, and the Price of a Licence ibid.

Mingling or corrupting Wine 251

Witchcraft, Enchantment, &c. 360

Witnesses, who shall be good Witnesses, who not 378

Witnesses in Criminal Cases must be on Oath 380

Women, unmarried, and under the Age of sixteen, Takers of them out of the Possession of Parents or Guardians, and against their Wills, shall be committed for two Years without Bail 399

Taking away and Deflowering them, or Marrying them against their Will, shall be committed for five Years without Bail ibid.

Forcibly taking away a Maid or Widow of Substance against their Consent, and marrying or deflowering her, Felony by the Statute 3 H. 7. cap. 2. Page 366

Taking away a Child under the Age of sixteen, from Parents or Guardians, and against her Consent, and marrying her, is Fine and Imprisonment by the Statute 4 & 5 Ph. & Mar. cap. 8. In such Case the next of Kin, to whom the Inheritance would descend, shall enjoy the Lands during the Life of the married Woman 367

Woods, Cutting and Spoiling 242

Cutting and carrying it away 251

Buying Wood suspected to be stole 252

Standels to be left in felling Coppice Wood ibid.

How to be inclosed and preserved after Felling ibid.

Wool, 14 Pound is a Stone, and 28 Pound is a Todd 260

Pressing it in order to Exportation 263

Times of carrying it from Place to Place ibid.

Exporting Sheep or Wool ibid.

Shall not be transported from Ireland to any Place but to England 264

Persons employed in working Wool, and purloining it, forfeits double the Value to the Use of the Poor ibid.

Wool designed to be exported may be seised by any Person ibid.

Where to be prosecuted ibid.

He who is in Gaol for unlawful Exportation of Wool, how to be proceeded against; must pay the Condemnation Money, or be transported ibid.

Wool, to pull it from the Sheep's Back, Felony 351

To transport it, Felony 366

Wool-Bill of 12 Geo. 2. 21. See here Chap. 196. 479

Words, evil Words punishable 264

Words of Contempt to a Magistrate 290, 291

Work-houses, who may erect them 188

Sessions may provide Materials to set poor People to work 191

Y.

YARD-Land is either 20 or 30 Acres 261

Year, when it begins 154

Of the Julian Account ibid.

F I N I S.

A D D E N D A.

C H A P. CXCVII.

Containing the Statutes 16, 17, 18 & 19 Geo. 2.

BY 16 Geo. 2. cap. 8. two Juſtices of the Peace for the County or Place from whence ſpirits 16 Geo. 2. are intended to be exported, may adminiſter an Oath, that the Duties were duly enter'd and c. 8. §. 7. paid, and that the Spirits are exported for Merchandize to be ſpent beyond the Seas. Spirits.

Perſons retaling ſpirituous Liquors without Licenſe, and not renewing as directed by the Act, forfeit Ib. §. 9. 10 l. for each Offence, and upon Nonpayment, when lawfully demanded, any one Juſtice, on Oath made of ſuch Neglect, ſhall commit the Offenders to the Houſe of Correction, to be kept to hard Labour for two Months, not to be diſcharged till Payment of 10 l. or the expiration of the ſaid two Months.

No Licenſes ſhall be granted to any Perſon whatſoever, for retaling ſpirituous Liquors, but to Ib. §. 10. thoſe only, who ſhall keep Taverns, victualling Houſes, Inns, Coffee-Houſes, or Ale-Houſes, and all Licenſes granted to any other Perſons, are void.

Perſons ſelling ſpirituous Liquors, by retale, muſt be licenſed by two or more Juſtices for the Ib. §. 11. County, &c. wherein ſuch Perſons ſhall ſell the ſaid Liquors.

By 16 Geo. 2. cap. 15. it is enacted, That if any Felon, or other Offender, ordered for Tranſpor- 16 Geo. 2. tation, or agreed to tranſport him or herſelf on certain Conditions, to any of his Majeſty's Colo- cap. 15. nies in America, either for Life, or any Number of Years, ſhall be afterwards at large in any Part Tranſpor- of Great Britain, without ſome lawful Cauſe, before the Expiration of the Term for which he or ſhe tation. were to be tranſported, and being thereof lawfully convicted, ſhall ſuffer Death, as in Caſes of Fe- lony, without Benefit of Clergy.

Whoever ſhall diſcover, apprehend and proſecute to Conviction of Felony, without Benefit of Ib. §. 3. Clergy, any ſuch Offenders, ſhall be intitled to a Reward of 20 l. and ſhall have the like Certifi- cate, and like Payments made without Fee or Reward, as any Perſons may be intitled to for the apprehending, proſecuting, and convicting of Highwaymen, by any Law for that Purpoſe.

By 16 Geo. 2. cap. 18. it is enacted, That all Juſtices of the Peace, within their reſpective Ju- 16 Geo. 2. riſdictions, may do all things belonging to their Office as Juſtices, ſo far as the ſame relates to the cap. 18. §. 1. Laws for the Relief, Maintenance, and Settlement of poor Perſons; for paſſing and puniſhing Va- Juſtices of the grants; for Repair of the Highways; or to any other Laws concerning Parochial Taxes, Levies, Peace. or Rates, notwithſtanding thoſe Juſtices are chargeable with the Taxes, Levies or Rates, within any ſuch Pariſh or Place affected by the Acts of ſuch Juſtices.

No Actions of any Juſtices of the Peace, performed before the making this Act, ſhall hereafter Ib. §. 2. be made void, becauſe the Juſtices themſelves are chargeable with the Rates as aforeſaid.

This Act ſhall not impower any Juſtice of the Peace for any County or Riding at large, to act Ib. §. 3. in the Determination of any Appeal to the Quarter-Seſſions for ſuch County or Riding, from any Order relating to the Pariſh or Place where ſuch Juſtice of the Peace is ſo charged as aforeſaid.

By 16 Geo. 2. cap. 26. it is enacted, That if any Perſon ſhall ſell, or expoſe to ſale, any News 16 Geo. 2. Paper, or any Book, Pamphlet, or Paper, deemed to be a News Paper, within the Meaning of cap. 26. §. 5. any of the Acts of Parliament, relating to the Stamp-Duties now in Force, not being ſtampt or Unſtamped marked, as in the ſaid Acts are directed, any Juſtice of the Peace may commit every ſuch Offender, News Papers. being thereof convicted before him, to the Houſe of Correction, for three Months; and any Perſon may apprehend and carry the Offender before a Juſtice of the Peace of the County or Place where ſuch Offence ſhall be committed; and on producing a Certificate of ſuch Conviction, under the Hand of ſuch Juſtice (which Certificate ſuch Juſtice ſhall give without Fee) he ſhall be intitled to the Reward of 20 s. to be paid by the Receiver General of his Majeſty's Stamp-Duties.

By 16 Geo. 2. cap. 29. the confining the drawing of Carts to three Horſes only, being found incon- 16 Geo. 2. venient to Farmers and others, and highly detrimental to the Markets of this Kingdom; it is there- cap. 29. fore enacted, That the ſaid Number of Three Horſes ſhall be enlarged to Four Horſes, under all Carriages. the Proviſions, Exceptions, and Limitations in the Acts of 5 Geo. 1. and 14 Geo. 2.

By 16 Geo. 2. cap. 31. it is enacted, That if any Perſon ſhall any ways aſſiſt any Priſoner to at- 16 Geo. 2. tempt his Eſcape from any Gaol, tho' no Eſcape be actually made, if ſuch Priſoner then was at- cap. 31. §. 1. tainted Reſcue.

tainted or convicted of Treason or Felony, except petty Larceny, or lawfully committed to, or detained in any Gaol for Treason or Felony, except petty Larceny, expressed in the Warrant of Commitment or Detainer, every such Offender, being lawfully convicted, shall be adjudged guilty of Felony, and shall be transported to *America*, for seven Years; and if such Prisoner then was convicted of, committed to, or detained in any Gaol for any Crime, not being Treason or Felony, or then was in Gaol upon any Process for Debt, &c. amounting to 100 l. every Person so offending, and being lawfully convicted, shall be adjudged guilty of a Misdemeanor, and be liable to a Fine and Imprisonment.

Ib. §. 2.

If any Person shall convey, or cause to be convey'd, any Disguise, Instrument, or Arms, to any Prisoner in Gaol, or to any other Person for his Use, without the Consent or Privity of the Keeper or under Keeper; such Person, altho' no Escape or Attempt be actually made, shall be deem'd to have delivered such Disguise, &c. with an Intention to assist such Prisoner to escape or attempt to escape; and if such Prisoner then attainted, or convicted of Treason or Felony, except petty Larceny, or lawfully committed to, or detained in any Gaol for Treason, or Felony, except petty Larceny, expressed in the Warrant of Commitment or Detainer, every such Offender being lawfully convicted, shall be adjudged guilty of Felony, and shall be transported to *America* for seven Years; but if the Prisoner then was convicted, committed, or detained for any Crime, not being Treason or Felony, or upon any Process for Debt, &c. amounting to 100 l. every such Person so offending, and being lawfully convicted, shall be adjudged guilty of a Misdemeanor, and be liable to a Fine and Imprisonment.

Ib. §. 3.

If any Person shall assist any Prisoner to attempt to escape from any Constable, or other Officer or Person who shall then have the lawful Charge of such Prisoner, in order to carry him to Gaol, by Virtue of a Warrant of Commitment for Treason or Felony, except petty Larceny, or if any Person shall assist any Felon, to attempt his Escape from any Boat or Vessel carrying Felons for Transportation, or from the Contractor for the Transportation of such Felons, or his Agents, &c. the Offender being lawfully convicted, shall be adjudged guilty of Felony, and shall be transported to *America* for seven Years.

Ib. §. 4.

All Prosecutions for any of the said Offences, shall be commenced within a Year after the Offence committed.

Ib. §. 5.

If any Person who shall be order'd for Transportation, shall return, or be at large in any Part of *Great Britain*, without some lawful Cause, before the Expiration of the Term for which he was ordered to be transported, he shall be liable to the same Punishment, and to the like Methods of Prosecution, as other Felons transported, or ordered to be transported, are liable unto by Virtue of the Laws now in Force.

17 Geo. 2. cap. 3. §. 1. Poor.

By the 17 *Geo. 2. cap. 3.* it is enacted, That the Church-wardens and Overseers of the Poor, or other Persons authorized to take care of the Poor, shall cause publick Notice to be given in the Church, of every Rate for Relief of the Poor, allowed by the Justices, the next *Sunday* after such Allowance is obtained; and no Rate shall be reputed sufficient to be collected, till after such Notice given.

Ib. §. 2.

The Church-wardens and Overseers, or other Persons authorized, shall permit any Inhabitant to inspect such Rate at all seasonable Times, paying one Shilling; and shall give Copies on Demand, being pay'd Sixpence for every 24 Names.

Ib. §. 3.

If any Church-wardens, &c. shall not permit any Inhabitant to inspect, or refuse to give Copies, as aforesaid, he shall for every such Offence forfeit 20 Pounds to the Party aggrieved; to be sued for and recovered in any of his Majesty's Courts of Record, wherein no Essoin, &c. or more than one Imparlance shall be allowed.

17 Geo. 2. cap. 5. Vagrants.

By the 17 *Geo. 2. cap. 5.* the Statute of 13 *Geo. 2. cap. 24.* inserted Page 484 *supra*, is repealed. As there are many Clauses common to both Acts, we shall here chiefly take notice of the Sections wherein they differ.

§. 1, 2, 3.

Sect. 1. A Justice may convict Offenders by his own View; the rest of this Clause as also §. 2 and 3, are to the same effect, as in the said 13 *Geo. 2.*

§. 4.

Sect. 4. The same in effect as §. 4. pag. 484 *supra*, and Persons refusing to be conveyed by Pass, according to the Act, shall be deemed incorrigible Rogues.

Sect. 5. Any Person may apprehend Offenders, and the Penalty on Officers &c. neglecting their Duty; the Reward for taking up Vagabonds, and the Penalty on not paying the Reward, are to the same Effect as in §. 5. pag. 485 *supra*.

Sect. 6. Directs privy Search as in §. 6. pag. 485, and also that every Justice shall, on receiving Information that Rogues and Vagabonds are within his Jurisdiction, issue his Warrant to the proper Officer to apprehend them, and such Rogues, &c. may be brought before any Justice of the same County, &c.

Sect. 7. Rogues, &c. thus apprehended, are to be examined by such Justice upon Oath, as in §. 7. pag. 485, *supra*, and such Examination is to be signed by the Person examined, as well as by the Justice, to be transmitted to the next General or Quarter Sessions, &c. All such Persons apprehended, shall be publickly whipt, or sent to the House of Correction to remain until the next General or Quarter Sessions, or less time, as the Justice shall think proper; after Whipping or Confinement, the Justice may, by Pass under Hand and Seal, in the Form hereafter directed, cause such Persons to be conveyed to the Place of their last legal Settlement; but if that cannot be found, then to the Place of their Birth; or if they be under 14 Years, and have Father or Mother living, then to their Abode, there to be delivered to some Church-warden, &c. The Form of the Pass is as follows.

I

To the Conftables of　　　　in the County of　　　　or to the Tythingman, or other Officer (as the Cafe fhall be, or if the Offender is committed to the Houfe of Correction, then to the Governor or Mafter thereof) *and alfo to all Conftables and other Officers, whom it may concern, to receive and convey; and to the Church-wardens, Chapel-wardens, or Overfeers of the Poor of the Parifh, Town, or Place (as the Cafe fhall be) of　　　　in the County of or either of them, to receive and obey.*

WHEREAS　　　　was (*or were*) apprehended in the Parifh of　　　　(*or in the Town of　　　　or other Place, defcribing it*) as a Rogue and Vagabond, or as Rogues and Vagabonds, *videlicet,* wandering and begging there *(or as the Cafe fhall be)* and upon Examination of the faid　　　　taken before　　　　upon Oath (which Examination is hereunto annexed) it doth appear, that his, her, or their laft legal Settlement is at　　　　in this County (or in the County of　　　　) or that the faid　　　　was (*or were*) born in the Parifh of in this County (or in the County of　　　　and hath (*or have*) not fince obtained any legal Settlement; or that the faid　　　　is (*or are*) under the Age of fourteen Years, and hath (*or have*) a Father or Mother living, or abiding in the Parifh (*or Town*) of　　　　(*or other Place, defcribing it*) : Thefe are therefore to require you the faid Conftable, or other Officer (*or Governor, or Mafter of the Houfe of Correction (as the Cafe fhall be*) to convey the faid　　　　in the next direct Way to the faid Parifh (*or Town*) of　　　　(*or other Place*) within the faid County, and there to deliver him (*her or them*) to fome Church-warden, Chapel-warden, or Overfeer of the Poor of the fame Parifh (*Town or Place*) to be there provided for according to Law, (*or in cafe the faid Parifh, Town, or Place, to which fuch Perfon or Perfons is or are to be fent, lies in fome other County, Riding, Divifion, Corporation, or Franchife, having Separate General or Quarter-Seffions of the Peace, then the Form fhall be as followeth,* videlicet, To convey the faid　　　　to the Parifh (*or Town*) of 　　　　that being the firft Parifh (*or Town*) in the next Precinct through which he (*fhe or they*) ought to pafs in the direct way to the faid Parifh (or Town) of　　　　to which he (*fhe or they*) is (*or are*) to be fent, and to deliver him (*her or them*) to the Conftable, or other Officer of fuch firft Town (*or Parifh*) in fuch next Precinct, together with this Pafs, and the Duplicate of the Examination of the faid　　　　taking his Receipt for the fame; and the faid　　　　is (*or are*) to be thence conveyed on in like manner to the faid Parifh (*or Town*) of　　　　there to be delivered to fome Church-warden, Chapel-warden or Overfeer of the Poor of the fame Parifh (*Town or Place*) to be there provided for according to Law; and you the faid Church-wardens, Chapel-wardens, and Overfeers of the Poor, are hereby required to receive the faid Perfon (*or Perfons*) and provide for him, her (*or them*) as aforefaid.

Sect. 8. A Duplicate of the Pafs and Examination are to be filed at the next General or Quarter Seffions as in §. 8. pag. 486 *fupra.*

Sect. 9. Where Offenders fhall be committed to the Houfe of Correction as before, and the Juftices of the Seffions adjudge fuch Perfon a Rogue, a Vagabond or an incorrigible Rogue; they may order fuch Rogue or Vagabond to hard Labour, for any farther time, not exceeding fix Months, and fuch incorrigible Rogue, for any time not exceeding two Years, nor lefs than fix Months, from the time of fuch Order of Seffions, and fuch Offender may be corrected by Whipping, &c. as in §. 9. pag. 486 *fupra.*

Sect. 10. The Form of the Pafs, for paffing or conveying Rogues, &c. is as follows.

WHEREAS by a Pafs (*reciting the Subftance or Effect of the faid Pafs*) I (*or we*) do hereby order and direct the faid Perfon (or Perfons) to be conveyed on Foot (or in a Cart, or by Horfe, &c.) to the faid Town (*or Parifh*) of　　　　in　　　　(*or other Place, defcribing it*) in the way to fuch Parifh (*Town or Place, as the Cafe fhall be*) in　　　　Days time; for which the faid Conftable, &c. is to be allowed the Sum of　　　　and no more.

Given under my Hand (or our Hands) *this Day,* &c.

Sect. 11. The Officer receiving fuch Pafs, fhall convey the Perfon therein named, according to the Directions thereof, the next direct way to the Place where fuch Perfon is ordered to be fent, if in the fame County where he was apprehended ; but if the Place, to which fuch Perfon is to be fent, lies in fome other County, &c. the Officer fhall deliver him to the Conftable, &c. of the firft Town, Parifh, or Place in the next County, in the direct way to the Place to which fuch Perfon is to be conveyed, together with the Pafs and Duplicate of Examination, taking a Receipt for the fame ; and fuch Conftable, &c. fhall apply to a Juftice of the Peace in the fame County, &c. who fhall make the like Certificate as before (*mutatis mutandis*) and deliver it to the Conftable, who fhall convey the Perfon to the firft Parifh, &c. in the next County, &c. in the direct way to the Place where fuch Perfon is to be conveyed, and fo from one County to another, till they come to the Place where fuch Perfon is to be fent, and the Conftable, &c. fhall deliver fuch Perfon to the Church-warden or other, ordered to receive him by the Pafs, together with the Duplicate of Examination, taking a Receipt for the fame. And if the Church-warden, &c. fhall think the Examination falfe, he is to carry the Perfon fo fent, before fome Juftice of the Peace, who may commit fuch Perfon to the Houfe of Correction, till the next Quarter-Seffions, where the Juftices may deal with fuch Perfon as an incorrigible Rogue. The Perfon fo fent fhall not be removed from the Place to which fent but by Order of two Juftices, as other poor Perfons are removed to the Place of their Settlement.

Sect. 12. Perfons committing Acts of Vagrancy, fhall pay for their own Paffage, in part or in whole, if found able.

Sect. 13. Vagrants, whofe legal Settlement is in *Scotland*, are to be fent thither as in §. 14 pag. 487 *fupra*, and if any Perfon, after being fo fent, be found wandering, begging or mifbehaving, in *England*, fuch Offender fhall be deemed an incorrigible Rogue, and punifhed accordingly.

Sect. 14. The Regulations for paffing Vagrants into *Ireland*, the Ifles of *Man*, *Jerfey*, *Guernfy* or *Scilly*, are to the fame Effect as in §. 18. pag. 488 *fupra*.

Sect. 15. No Mafter of a Veffel fhall be compelled to take on board more than one Vagrant for every 20 Tons Burden.

Sect. 16. Juftices to make Rates, &c. as in §. 19. pag. 488 *fupra*.

Sect. 17. is to the fame Effect as §. 20 pag. 488 *fupra*.

Sect. 18. Any Perfon counterfeiting or altering a Certificate, &c. forfeits five Pounds; the reft as in §. 22 pag. 488, 489 *fupra*.

Sect. 19. See §. 23 pag. 489 *fupra*.

Sect. 20. See §. 24 *ibid*.

Sect. 21. This not to abridge the Power of the Lord Chancellor, &c. concerning Lunatics.

Sect. 22. See §. 26 pag. 489 *fupra*.

Sect. 23. See §. 27 *ibid*. but the time of Commitment to the Houfe of Correction is limited to *one* Month.

Sect. 24. If Perfons having Children with them, are found offending againft this Act, fuch Child being above feven Years old, may be fent to the Houfe of Correction; and the Juftices may place them out to Service, or Apprentices to any that will take them, within their Jurifdictions, till they come to the Age of 21 Years, or lefs time, as the Juftices think fit; and any Offender found again with the fame Child, fo placed out, fhall be deemed an incorrigible Rogue.

Sect. 25. If any Woman wandering and begging, fhall be delivered of any Child, and become thereby chargeable; the Church-wardens or Overfeers may detain fuch Woman till fhe can be taken before a Juftice, who fhall examine her, and commit her to the Houfe of Correction till the next General or Quarter Seffions; and the Juftices there may order her to be publickly whipp'd, and detained in the Houfe of Correction for any farther time, not exceeding fix Months; and on Application of the Church-wardens or Overfeers, the faid Juftices fhall order the Treafurer of the County or Diftrict, to pay a reafonable Satisfaction, as they fhall fettle, for the Charges fuch Place has been at on the Woman's Account; and if the Woman be detained and taken before a Juftice, the Child, if a Baftard, fhall not be fettled on the Place where born, but the Woman's Settlement fhall be a Settlement for the Child.

Sect. 26. Any Perfon aggrieved for the Act of any Juftice, may appeal to the General or Quarter Seffions, giving timely Notice, whofe Order fhall be final.

Sect. 27. See §. 30 pag. 489 *fupra*, and if any Perfons be delivered to a Bedel or Conftable, within the City or Liberties, that Bedel or Conftable fhall not deliver them to any other Precinct, but in the next County.

Sect. 28. When Offenders againft this Act are examined at Seffions, and no Place is found to pafs them to, the Juftices may order them to be detained and employed in the Houfe of Correction, till they can be placed out as Servants, Apprentices, Soldiers, Mariners or otherwife, within this Realm, or in any of his Majefty's Colonies in *America*.

Sect. 29. This Act not to prejudice the Heirs, &c. of *John Dutton*.

Sect. 30. See §. 32 pag. 489 *fupra*.

Sect. 31. See §. 33 pag. 489, 490 *fupra*.

Sect. 32. See §. 34 *ibid*.

Sect. 33. Sums to defray the Expences arifing in the Execution of this Act, are to be raifed as Rates are directed to be raifed by 12 *Geo.* 2. fee pag. 479 *fupra*.

Sect. 34. Perfons fued for any thing done in Execution of this Act, may plead the General Iffue, &c. and if a Verdict pafs for the Defendant, or the Plaintiff be nonfuited or difcontinue, &c. the Defendant may recover treble Cofts; and the 13 *Geo.* 2. *cap.* 24. is hereby repealed, but all Acts thereby repealed continue fo.

17 Geo. 2.
cap. 8.
§. 2.
Butter.

By 17 *Geo.* 2. *cap.* 8. To prevent the committing of Abufes in the weighing and packing of Butter in the Town of *New Malton* in the County of *York*, Offenders againft that Act are to be convicted by Proof, on Oath of one or more credible Witnefs or Witneffes, before any Juftice of Peace of any of the Ridings of the County of *York*, where the Offence fhall be committed; and in default of Payment of the Forfeiture upon Demand (being 3 s. 4 d. for every Cafk, Pot or Veffel of Butter fold or tranfported, without being firft brought to the Market at *New Malton*, to be there viewed, fearched, weighed and fealed, as by the Act is more particularly directed) the faid Forfeiture fhall be levied by Diftrefs and Sale of the Offender's Goods, by Warrant under the Hand and Seal of any one or more Juftice or Juftices of the Peace of the faid Ridings. One half of the Forfeiture fhall be to the Ufe of the Poor, and the other half to the Informer.

Ib. §. 5.

Perfons aggrieved by any Determination of the Juftices of Peace, may appeal to the next General Quarter-Seffions for the Riding where the Offence was committed.

17 Geo. 2.
cap. 17.
Spirits.

Some Doubts having arifen on the Act of 16 *Geo.* 2. about the Power of Juftices in feveral Cafes relating to the Forfeitures for retaling fpirituous Liquors, it is therefore enacted by the 17 *Geo.* 2. cap. 17. That all Penalties and Forfeitures impofed by the faid Act, and alfo by this Act, may be recovered, levied and mitigated, by the fame Methods as are practifed by any Laws of Excife.

Juftices,

Justices, if they think proper, instead of levying the Penalty, may commit the Offender to the Ib. §. 17.-
House of Correction to hard Labour for two Months; and the Persons so committed, before they
are discharged, shall be stripped naked from the Middle upwards, and be whipp'd till their Bodies
are bloody.

No Licenfe shall be granted for retaling spirituous Liquors, except to such Persons only who keep Ib. §. 18.
Taverns, Victualling-Houfes, Inns, Coffee-Houfes, or Ale-Houfes; and all other Licenfes shall be
void; and if any Perfon having a lawful Licenfe, shall afterwards, during the Continuance of such
Licenfe, exercife the Trade of a Diftiller, Grocer, or Chandler, or keep a Brandy Shop, for Sale of
spirituous Liquors, the Licenfe in every fuch Cafe shall be void, and the Retalers shall forfeit 10 *l.*
for every Offence.

All Perfons who by themfelves, or Servants, shall retale spirituous Liquors, mixt or unmixt with Ib. §. 19.
any Ingredients, to be drank or confumed in any Quantity whatfoever, in any Places to them belonging; or shall retale or fend the fame abroad in lefs Quantity than two Gallons, without firft taking
out a Licenfe, and renewing the fame, as in the Act 16 *Geo.* 2. is particularly directed, shall be
deemed a Retaler of spirituous Liquors within the Meaning of the faid Act, and shall forfeit 10 *l.*
for every Offence.

No Licenfe for retaling spirituous Liquors, shall impower any Perfon to fell the fame in any Places, Ib. §. 21.
except in the Houfes or Places thereto belonging, wherein they shall inhabit at the time of granting
such Licenfe.

By 17 *Geo.* 2. *cap.* 29. for the making more effectual Provifion for enlightening the Streets of the 17 Geo. 2.
City of *London*, it is enacted, That if any Perfon shall wilfully break, throw down, or extinguish cap. 29.
any Lamp fet up to light the Streets, or damage the Pofts, Irons, or other Furniture thereof, such *Lamps.*
Offender being convicted by the Oath of one or more credible Witnefs or Witneffes, before any
one Juftice of the Peace for the City of *London*, shall for the firft Offence, forfeit the Sum of 40 *s.*
and for the fecond, the Sum of 50 *s.* and for the third Offence, the Sum of Three Pounds.

By the 17 *Geo.* 2. *cap.* 30. for the more effectual preventing of the affixing counterfeit Stamps to 17 Geo. 2.
foreign or other Linens, it is enacted, That if any Perfon shall affix, or caufe or procure to be af- cap. 30.
fixed, any Stamp in Imitation of thofe put upon the Linen Manufactures of *Scotland* or *Ireland*, *Linen.*
on any foreign Linens imported into this Kingdom, fuch Offender shall forfeit the Sum of 5 *l.*
for each Piece of Linen fo ftamped. And if any Perfon shall expofe to Sale, or pack up for Sale,
any foreign Linens, knowing them to be fo ftamped as aforefaid, as the Manufacture of *Scotland* or
Ireland, fuch Offender shall forfeit the faid Linens, and the Sum of 5 *l.* for each Piece thereof fo
fold, expofed to Sale, or packed up as aforefaid. And if any Perfon shall affix any counterfeit Stamp
or Stamps, upon any Linens of the Manufactures of *Great Britain* or *Ireland*, in order to vend the
fame as Linens duly ftamped, fuch Offender shall forfeit the Sum of 5 *l.* for every Piece of Linen
fo ftamped. And if any Perfon shall fell, expofe to, or pack up for Sale, any fuch Linens, knowing the fame to be ftamped as aforefaid, fuch Offender shall forfeit the Linens, and 5 *l.* for each
Piece fo fold, *&c.*

Any Juftice of the Peace, for the Place where any Offence shall be committed againft this Act, Ib. §. 2.
may convict the Party offending, upon the Oath of one Witnefs, and upon Conviction, the Juftice
may grant his Warrant under his Hand and Seal, to levy the Penalty by Diftrefs and Sale of the
Offender's Goods and Chattels *&c.* And in cafe Goods and Chattels of the Offender fufficient to
pay fuch Penalty cannot be found, fuch Juftice shall, upon Proof thereof made upon Oath before
him, by the Perfon who shall have the Execution of the Warrant for levying fuch Diftrefs, commit
the Offender to the Gaol of the County, *&c.* without Bail for fix Months, unlefs the Penalty be
fooner paid, which Penalty shall be applied to the Ufe of the Informer, deducting two Shillings in
the Pound for the Conftable or Officer executing the Warrant.

By the 17 *Geo.* 2. *cap.* 35. it is enacted, That the Juftices of the Peace, in the feveral Counties 17 Geo. 2.
in the kingdom of *England*, Dominion of *Wales*, and of the Town of *Berwick* upon *Tweed*, or any cap. 35 §. 1.
three or more of them, whereof one to be of the *Quorum*, are hereby impowered to fet the Rates *Coals.*
and Prices of all fuch Coals called Sea Coals, as shall be brought by Sea into any other Rivers,
Creeks, Havens, or Ports, and fold by Retale, after landed, in any other Cities, *&c.* within the
Kingdom of *England*, Dominion of *Wales*, and Town of *Berwick* upon *Tweed*, to which the Act of
the 17 *Car.* 2. recited doth not extend, as they from time to time shall judge reafonable, allowing a competent Profit to the Retaler, beyond the Price paid by him to the Importer, and the
ordinary Charges thereupon accruing; and if any Ingroffer or Retaler of fuch Coals, shall refufe to
fell as aforefaid, then the Juftices of the Peace refpectively, are hereby authorized to appoint and
impower fuch Officers, or other Perfons, as they shall think fit, to enter into any Wharf, or other
Place, where fuch Coals are ftored up; and in cafe of Refufal, taking a Conftable, to force Entrance,
and to fell the faid Coals at fuch Rates, as the Juftices refpectively shall judge reafonable, rendering to
fuch Ingroffer or Retaler the Money for which the Coals shall be fo fold, neceffary Charges being
deducted; and if any Action shall be commenced againft the Juftice of Peace, Conftable, or any
Officer, or Perfon, for any thing to be done in Purfuance of this Act, the Defendant may plead the
General Iffue, and give the fpecial Matter in Evidence; and if the Verdict be found for him, or the
Plaintiff become Nonfuited, fuch Defendant shall recover his Damages, and Treble Cofts of Suit,
for his unjuft Vexation in that Behalf.

Provided, that no Perfon, having Intereft in any Wharf, ufed for the receiving and uttering of Ib §. 2.
Coals, or that trades by himfelf or others, in his own or any other Name, in the Sale of Coals, or
the ingroffing, in order to fell the fame, and not for his own private Ufe only, shall Act, or otherwife intermeddle in the fetting the Price of Coals.

By

17 Geo. 2.
cap. 37. §. 1.
Rates.

By 17 *Geo.* 2. *cap.* 37. it is enacted, That where there shall be any Dispute, in what Parish or Place improved or drained Lands lie, and ought to be rated; the Occupiers of such Lands, or Houses built thereon, Tenements, Tithes arising therefrom, Mines therein, and saleable underwoods, shall be rated to the Relief of the Poor, and to all other Parochial Rates within such Parish and Place which lies nearest to such Lands, as all other Lands within such Parish and Place, are by Law liable to be rated; and if on Application to the Officers of such Parish or Place, any Dispute shall arise, the Justices for the County, &c. where such Lands lie, at their next General Quarter-Sessions, after such Application made, and after Notice given to the Officers of the several Parishes and Places adjoining to such Lands, and to all other Persons interested therein, to hear and determine the same on the Appeal of any Person interested, and to cause such Lands or Hereditaments to be equally assessed, and such Determination shall be final and conclusive.

Ib. §. 2.

No Allotment to be made by the Justices, shall determine the Boundaries of any Parishes or Places, other than for the Purpose of rating such Lands, &c. to the Relief of the Poor, and to all other Parochial Rates within such Parish or Place, to which they shall be so allotted.

17 Geo. 2.
cap. 38. §. 1.
Poor.

By reason of some Defects in the Act 43 *Eliz.* the Money raised for Purposes therein mentioned, is liable to be misapplied, and there is often great Difficulty and Delay in raising of the same; for Remedy whereof, it is therefore enacted, by 17 *Geo.* 2. *cap.* 38. That the Church-wardens and Overseers of the Poor shall Yearly, within 14 Days after other Overseers shall be appointed, deliver in to the succeeding Overseers, a just account in Writing, fairly entered in a Book to be kept for that Purpose, and signed by the Church-wardens and Overseers, of all Sums of Money by them received, or rated and not received; and also of all Materials that shall be in their Hands, or in the Hands of any of the Poor to be wrought, and of all Monies paid by such Church-wardens and Overseers so accounting, and of all other things concerning their Office; and shall also pay all Sums of Money, &c. as shall be in their Hands, to the succeeding Overseers; which Account shall be verified by Oath, or Affirmation of Quakers, before one or more Justices, which said Oath, or Affirmation, such Justices are hereby authorized and required to administer, and to sign the same, without Fee, and the said Books shall be preserved by the Church-wardens and Overseers; to be inspected at all seasonable Times, paying 6 d. for such Inspection, and shall, upon Demand, give Copies, at the Rate of 6 d. for every 300 Words, and so in Proportion for any greater or lesser Number.

Ib. §. 2.

If the Church-wardens and Overseers of the Poor shall neglect to make up their Account within the Time herein before limited, or shall neglect to pay over the Money, and other things in their Hands, any two Justices may commit them to the common Gaol, till they shall have accounted and paid as aforesaid.

Ib. §. 3.

If any Overseer shall die, or remove, or become insolvent, before the Expiration of his Office, any two Justices may appoint another Overseer in his stead, who shall continue in Office till new Overseers are appointed; and every Overseer shall, before such Removal, deliver his Accounts on Oath, with all Rates, and other things, concerning his Office, under the like Penalties as are inflicted on an Overseer refusing to do the same, after the Expiration of his Office; and if any Overseer shall die, his Executors or Administrators shall, within forty Days after his Decease, deliver over all things concerning his Office, to some Church-warden, or other Overseer of the same Place; and shall pay out of the Assets left by such Overseer, all Sums of Money remaining due, which he received by Virtue of his Office, before any of his other Debts are paid.

Ib. §. 4.

If any Person shall find himself aggrieved, by any Assessment made for Relief of the Poor, or shall have any material Objection to any Person's being put on, or left out of such Assessment, or to the Sum charged on any Persons therein, or shall have any material Objection to such Account, or any Part thereof, or shall find himself aggrieved by any thing done or omitted by the Church-wardens and Overseers, or by any of his Majesty's Justices, they may, giving reasonable Notice, appeal to the next General or Quarter-Sessions; where the same shall be heard, and finally determined; but if reasonable Notice be not given, then they shall adjourn the Appeal to the next Quarter-Sessions; and the Justices may award to the Party, for whom such Appeal shall be determined, reasonable Costs, as they are impowered to do in case of Appeals concerning the Settlement of poor Persons, by an Act made 8 & 9 *Will.* 3.

Ib. §. 5.

In all Corporations or Franchises, who have not four Justices, any Person may appeal to the next General or Quarter-Sessions of the Peace, for the County, &c. wherein such Corporation or Franchise is situate.

Ib. §. 6.

On all Appeals from Rates and Assessments, the Justices (where they shall see just Cause) shall amend the same, in such manner only as shall be necessary for giving Relief, without altering such Rates, with respect to other Persons mentioned in the same; but if upon an Appeal from the whole Rate, it shall be found necessary to set aside the same, then the Justices shall order the Church-wardens and Overseers to make a new equal Rate, and they are hereby required to make the same accordingly.

Ib. §. 7.

The Goods of any Person assessed, and refusing to pay, may be levied by Warrant of Distress, in any Part of the County; and if sufficient Distress cannot be found within the said County, on Oath made thereof before some Justice of any other County (which Oath shall be certified on the said Warrant) the Goods may be levied in such other County or Precinct, by virtue of such Warrant and Certificate; and if any Person shall find himself aggrieved by such Distress, he may appeal to the next General Quarter-Sessions for the County or Precinct where such Assessment was made, and the Justices there are hereby required to hear and finally determine the same.

2

Where any Diftrefs fhall be made for Money juftly due for Relief of the Poor, the Diftrefs itfelf Ib. §. 8. fhall not be deemed unlawful, nor the Parties making it, be deemed Trefpaffers, on account of any Defect, or Want of Form in the Warrant for the Appointment of fuch Overfeers, or in the Rate, or in the Warrant of Diftrefs thereupon; nor fhall the Parties diftraining, be deemed Trefpaffers *ab initio*, on account of any Irregularity, which fhall be afterwards done by the Parties diftraining; but the Parties aggrieved by fuch Irregularity, may recover full Satisfaction for the fpecial Damage, and no more, in an Action of Trefpafs, or on the cafe, at the Election of the Plaintiffs.

Provided always, that where the Plaintiffs fhall recover in fuch Action, they fhall be paid their Ib. §. 9. full Cofts of Suit, and have all the like Remedies for the fame, as in other Cafes of Cofts.

No Plaintiff fhall recover in any Action for any fuch Irregularity, if tender of Amends hath been Ib. §. 10. made by the Parties diftraining, before fuch Action brought.

If any Perfon fhall neglect to pay to fuch Overfeers, any Sum of Money that fhall be legally rated, Ib. §. 11. the fucceeding Overfeers fhall levy fuch Arrears, and reimburfe their Predeceffors all Sums of Money which they have expended for the Ufe of the Poor, and which are allowed to be due to them in their Accounts.

Where Perfons fhall come into, or occupy any Premiffes, out of which any other Perfon affeffed Ib. §. 12. fhall be removed, or which, at the time of making fuch Rate, was unoccupied, then every Perfon, fo removing from, or coming into, or occupying the fame, fhall be liable to pay to fuch Rate, in Proportion to the time that fuch Perfon occupied the fame refpectively, under the like Penalty of Diftrefs, as if fuch Perfon fo removing, had not removed, or the Perfon coming in or occupying, had been originally affeffed in fuch Rate; which Proportion, in cafe of Difpute, fhall be afcertained by any two or more Juftices.

True Copies of all Rates, hereafter to be made for Relief of the Poor, fhall be fairly entered in a Ib §. 13. Book, by the Church-wardens and Overfeers of the Poor, within 14 Days after all Appeals from fuch Rates are determined, and fhall atteft the fame by putting their Names thereto; and all fuch Books fhall be preferved by the Church-wardens and Overfeers for the Time being, or one of them, in every fuch Parifh, &c. whereto all Perfons liable to be affeffed may freely refort, and fhall be delivered over from time to time, to the new Church-wardens and Overfeers, as foon as they enter into their Offices, to be preferved, and produced at the General or Quarter-Seffions, when any Appeal is to be heard.

Any Parifh-Officer neglecting to obey the Directions of this Act, for the Space of two Calendar Ib §. 14. Months, being convicted on Oath before any two Juftices, fhall forfeit a Sum not exceeding 5 l. or lefs than 20 s. for the Ufe of the Poor, to be levied by Diftrefs and Sale of the Offender's Goods.

Overfeers in every Townfhip or Place where there are no Church-wardens, fhall perform all Acts Ib. §. 15. relating to the Poor, as Church-wardens and Overfeers may do by this or any other Statute concerning the Poor; and fhall fuffer all fuch Penalties for Neglect thereof, as Church-wardens and Overfeers are liable to, by virtue of this or any former Statute concerning the Poor.

By the 18 *Geo.* 2. *cap.* 10. for the fpeedy and effectual recruiting of his Majefty's Regiments of 18 Geo. 2. Foot ferving in *Flanders, Minorca, Gibraltar* and the Plantations, and the Regiments of cap. 10. Marines, Juftices of Peace among others, are appointed Commiffioners for putting this Act in Exe-Recruits. cution; but as this Act expires *April* 12, 1746. we think it needlefs to infert it here.

By 18 *Geo. 2. cap.* 20. for the further Qualification of Juftices of the Peace, it is enacted, That 18 Geo. 2. no Perfon fhall be capable of being or acting as a Juftice of the Peace, for any County or Divifion cap. 20. of *England* or *Wales*, who fhall not have in Law or Equity, for his own Ufe, in Poffeffion, a Free-Peace. hold, Copyhold, or Cuftomary Eftate for Life, or for fome greater Eftate, or an Eftate for fome long Term of Years, determinable upon one or more Life or Lives, or for a certain Term originally created for 21 Years, or more, in Lands, &c. in *England* or *Wales*, of the clear yearly Value of 100 l. above what will difcharge all Incumbrances affecting the fame, and all Rents and Charges payable out of the fame; or who fhall not be intitled to the immediate Reverfion of Lands, &c. leafed for One, Two, or Three Lives, or for any Term of Years, determinable on the Death of One, Two, or Three Lives, upon referved Rents of the Yearly Value of 300 l. and who fhall not, before he takes upon him to act as a Juftice, at fome General or Quarter-Seffions for the County or Divifion for which he intends to act, firft take and fubfcribe the Oath following, *viz.*

I A. B. *do fwear, That I truly and* bona fide *have fuch an Eftate, in Law or Equity, to and for my own Ufe and Benefit, confifting of* (fpecifying the Nature of fuch an Eftate, whether Meffuage, Land, Rent, Tithe, Office, Benefice or what elfe) *as doth qualify me to act as a Juftice of the Peace for the County, Riding, or Divifion of according to the true Intent and Meaning of an Act of Parliament, made in the eighteenth Year of the Reign of his Majefty King* George the Second, *intituled,* An Act to amend and render more effectual an Act paffed in the fifth Year of his prefent Majefty's Reign, intituled, *An Act for the further Qualification of Juftices of the Peace; and that the fame* (except where it confifts of an Office, Benefice, or Ecclefiaftical Preferment, which it fhall be fufficient to afcertain by their known and ufual Names) *is lying, or being, or iffuing out of Lands, Teuements, or Hereditaments, being within the Parifh, Townfhip, or Precinct of or in the feveral Parifhes, Townfhips, or Precincts of in the County of or in the feveral Counties of* (as the Cafe may be)

Which Oath taken and fubfcribed, fhall be kept by the Clerk of the Peace of the County, &c. Ib. §. 2. among the Records for the Seffions of the fame.

The

Ib. §. 3. The Clerk of the Peace, on Demand, shall forthwith deliver an attested Copy to any Person, paying 2 s. for the same; which being proved to be a true copy of such Oath, shall be admitted in Evidence on any Issue in any Action, &c. to be brought on this Act.

Ib. §. 4. Any Person who shall act as a Justice of the Peace, for any County or Division within *England* or *Wales*, without having taken and subscribed the said Oath, or without being qualified according to the Intent of this Act, shall, for every Offence, forfeit 100 l. one Moiety to the Poor of the Parish in which he most usually resides, and the other to the Person who shall sue for the same; to be recovered with full Costs of Suit, by Action of Debt, &c. in any Court of Record at *Westminster*, in which no Essoin, &c. or more than one Imparlance shall be allowed; and in every such Action, &c. the Proof of his Qualification shall lie on the Person against whom it is brought.

Ib. §. 5. If the Defendant in any such Suit, &c. shall intend to insist on any Lands, &c. not contained in such Oath, as his Qualification to act as a Justice, in Part, or in the whole, at the Time of the supposed Offence, wherewith he is charged, he shall, at or before the Time of his pleading, deliver the Plaintiff or his Attorney a Notice in Writing, specifying such Lands, &c. (other than those contained in the Oath) and the Parish or Place, or Parishes or Places, and the County or Counties wherein the same are respectively situate (Offices and Benefices excepted, which it shall be sufficient to ascertain by their usual Names); and if the Plaintiff in such Suit shall think fit thereon not to insist further, he may, with Leave of the Court, discontinue such Suit, on Payment of Costs to the Defendant, as the Court shall award.

Ib. §. 6. Upon Trial of the Issue in any Suit to be brought, no Lands, &c. which are not contained in the Oath and Notice, or one of them, shall be allowed to be insisted on by the Defendant, as any Part of his Qualification.

Ib. §. 7. Where the Lands contained in the said Oath or Notice, are, together with other Lands, belonging to the Person taking such Oath, or delivering such Notice, liable to any Charges or Incumbrances, within the Intent, and for the Purposes of this Act, the Lands, &c. contained in the Oath or Notice, shall be deemed to be chargeable only so far, as the other Lands, &c. jointly charged, are not sufficient to discharge the same.

Ib. §. 8. Where the Qualification required, or any Part of it, consists of Rent, it shall be sufficient to specify in the Oath or Notice, so much of the Lands, &c. out of which such Rent is issuing, as shall be of Value to answer such Rent.

Ib. §. 9. If the Plaintiff, or Informer in any such Suit, shall discontinue the same, otherwise than aforesaid, or be Nonsuit, or Judgment be otherwise given against him, then the Person against whom the Action shall have been brought, shall recover treble Costs.

Ib. §. 10. Only one Penalty of 100 l. shall be recovered from the same Person by this, or an Act of 5 *Geo.* 2. *cap.* 18. for the same, or any other Offence committed by the same Person, upon which one Penalty of 100 l. shall have been recovered, and due Notice given to the Defendant, of the Commencement of such Action.

Ib. §. 11. Where an Action shall be brought, and due Notice given thereof, no Proceedings shall be had on any subsequent Action, &c. against the same Person, for any Offence committed before the Time of giving such Notice; but the Court, where such subsequent Action shall be brought, may, on the Defendant's Motion, stay Proceedings thereon, so as such first Action be prosecuted without Fraud, and with Effect; for no Action which shall not be so prosecuted, shall be deemed an Action within the Intent of this Act.

Ib. §. 12. Every Action, &c. given by this or the said former Act, shall be commenced within six Months after the Fact, on which the same is grounded, shall have been committed.

Ib. §. 13. This Act shall not extend to any City or Town, being a County of itself, or to any other City, Town, Cinqueport, or Liberty, having Justices within their respective Precincts, by Charter, Commission, or otherwise; but in every such City, &c. such Persons may be Justices of the Peace, and in such manner as they might have been if this Act had never been made.

b §. 14, 15 and 16. These Sections contain the like Proviso's and Exceptions, as the 5 *Geo.* 2. *cap.* 18, *vide supra* pag. 7.

8 Geo. 2. ap. 27. §. 1. *Linen*, &c. *Felony.* By 18 *Geo.* 2. *cap.* 27. it is enacted, That every Person who shall, by Day or Night, feloniously steal any Linen, Fustian, Callico, Cotton, Cloth, or Cloth worked, woven, or made of any Cotton or Linen-Yarn mixed, or any Thread, Linen, or Cotton-Yarn, Linen, or Cotton-Tape, Incle, Filleting, Laces, or any other Linen, Fustian, or Cotton Goods, or Wares, laid or exposed to be printed, whitened, bowked, bleached, or dried, in any whitening or bleaching Croft, or Grounds, Bowking-House, &c. or other Building, or Place made Use of by any Callico-Printer, Whitster, Crofter, Bowker, or Bleacher, for printing, whitening, bowking, bleaching or drying the same, to the Value of 10 s. or shall aid, hire, or procure any other Person to commit such Offence, or shall buy or receive any such Wares so stolen, knowing them to be stolen, being convicted, shall be declared guilty of Felony, and shall suffer Death as in Cases of Felony, without Benefit of Clergy.

b. §. 2, 3. The Court may transport the Offender for 14 Years, and if he break Gaol, escape before Transportation, or return into, or be at large, in *Great Britain*, before the Expiration of the Term, he shall suffer Death as a Felon, without Benefit of Clergy.

b. §. 4. 8 Geo. 2. ap 33. art. The Act of 4 *Geo.* 2. *cap.* 16. *supra* pag. 363, is repealed.

The 18 *Geo.* 2. *cap.* 33. repeals a Clause of the Statute 3 & 4 *Will.* & *Mar.* whereby it is declared lawful for any Inhabitant within the Bills of Mortality, who dwells off from the Pavement, or uses his Carts, as well off as upon the Pavement, and for any Brewer, or Scavenger, to use any Cart, Car or Dray, with Wheels shod with Iron, and narrower than six Inches in the fellies, and drawn with more than two Horses.

By

By *Sect.* 2. it is enacted, That any Perſon whatſoever may make uſe of any Cart, Car or Dray, 13 Geo. 2. with Wheels of ſix Inches in the fellies, and not wrought about with Iron, drawn by three Horſes. cap. 33.

But he that uſes any ſuch Cart, &c. drawn by more than three Horſes, is liable to the Penalties Ib. §. 3. of the Statute 2. *Will. & Mar.*

The Name of the Owner of every Cart is to be placed thereon, and numbred, and regiſtered with Ib. §. 4, 5. the Commiſſioners for Licenſing hackney Coaches.

By 18 *Geo.* 2. *cap.* 34. the Statutes 12 *Geo.* 2. *cap.* 28. and 13 *Geo.* 2. *cap.* 19. *vide ſupra* pag. 106, 18 Geo. 2. 107, are explained, amended, and made more effectual. cap. 34. Gaming.

By 18 *Geo.* 2. *cap.* 36. the wearing of Cambrick, and *French* Lawn, is prohibited after *June* 24 18 Geo. 2. 1748, under the Penalty of 5 *l.* upon Conviction on Oath of one Witneſs, before any Juſtice of Peace. cap. 36.

By 19 *Geo.* 2. the king is impowered to ſecure and detain ſuch Perſons as he ſhall ſuſpect are con- French Cam ſpiring againſt his Perſon and Government, for which Purpoſe it is enacted, That Perſons impriſoned *brick and* by Warrant ſigned by ſix of the privy Council, for Suſpicion of High Treaſon, or treaſonable Prac- *Lawn.* tices, or by Warrant ſigned by any of the Secretaries of State for ſuch Cauſes, may be detained in 19 Geo. 2. ſafe Cuſtody without Bail or Mainprize until the 19th of *April* 1746, and till then no Judge or Ju- *Treaſon.* ſtice of Peace ſhall Bail or try any ſuch Perſon ſo committed, without an Order ſigned by ſix of the privy Council.

CHAP. CXCVIII.

Caſes relating to the Juriſdiction of Juſtices of the Peace; abſtracted from the Reports of Lord Raymond *and Chief Baron* Comyns.

THE Juſtices in Seſſions have a Power by the Stat. 5 & 6 *Ed.* 6. *c.* 25. to ſuppreſs Alehouſes, and *Alehouſes.* need not proceed by Information or Conviction; but they have thereby a diſcretionary L*d* Raym. Power to ſuppreſs them, without ſhewing any Cauſe or Miſdemeanor : And where the Act ſpeaks of 1303. a Conviction, that is only intended where the Juſtices proceed for the Penalty, which ought to be by *Scire Facias.*

The Court of King's Bench were unanimouſly of Opinion, that an Apprentice letting himſelf to *Apprentices.* Service without his Maſter's Conſent, gained no Settlement by ſuch Service, altho' his Maſter was L*d* Raym. broke : for this would not determine the Apprenticeſhip; for the Apprentice continued not *ſui juris* : 1352. And though in the Caſe before the Court, the Maſter had afterwards delivered up the Indenture, yet this was not looked upon as a ſubſequent Conſent, and will not make the Apprentice's letting himſelf to a third Perſon good, ſo as to gain a Settlement. But if the letting had been with the Maſter's Conſent, the Service would have been a Settlement.

Upon a ſpecial Order of Seſſions removed into the King's Bench by *Certiorari*, for diſcharging L*d* Raym. an Apprentice, who appeared by the Order to have been bound to a Glazier, a Freeman of *London*, 1410. before the Chamberlain ; it was moved to quaſh the Order, for that the Apprentice being bound before the Chamberlain of *London*, the Juſtices of Peace had no Power to diſcharge him, the Liberties and Privileges of the Citizens of *London*, as to having and retaining Apprentices, being expreſly ſaved by the Stat. 5 *Eliz. cap.* 4. §. 40. But the Court held, that the Apprentice being out of *London* and ſerving his Maſter out of the City, there can be no Proceedings againſt him before the Chamberlain ; but the Juſtices of Peace have a Juriſdiction to diſcharge him, notwithſtanding he was bound in *London.*

An Exception was alſo taken to the Order in this Caſe, becauſe the Trade to which the Apprentice was bound, *viz.* a Glazier, was not within the Statute of 5 *Eliz.* But though it was formerly held, the Trade ought to be a Trade within the Statute ; yet the latter Reſolutions have been otherwiſe.

An Order was made by Juſtices of Peace, that the Church-wardens and Overſeers of the Poor *Baſtard.* ſhould ſeize of the Goods of a putative Father of a Baſtard, what they ſhould judge proper to ſe- L*d* Raym. cure the Pariſh from the Maintenance of the Child. Upon a Removal of this Order into the King's 858. Bench it was quaſhed, becauſe by the 13 & 14 *Car. cap.* 12. they have only Authority to make an Order to impower the Church-wardens and Overſeers, &c. to ſeize what the Juſtices ſhould judge proper, and not what the Church-wardens, &c. ſhould judge proper. Part of the Order was alſo quaſhed, becauſe it ordered that the Defendant ſhould give Security for Payment of the Sum impoſed for the Maintenance of the Child ; when it did not appear that the Defendant had diſobeyed the Order in Point of Payment. And by 18 *Eliz. cap.* 3. an Order for Security cannot be made, till after Contempt.

If a Man is adjudged by two Juſtices the reputed Father of a Baſtard, and ordered to pay, and L*d* Raym. on Appeal the Order is confirmed, the Juſtices at the Seſſions cannot commit for Non-payment, but 1157. muſt proceed on the Recognizance taken by the two Juſtices.

Juſtices of Peace may order Payment of Money for Maintenance of a Baſtard on a Day certain, L*d* Raym. weekly, and before the Week is quite up. If the Money be ordered to be paid to the Overſeers of 1197. the Poor, it is well enough.

[7 M]   An

L.ᵈ Rayᵐ.
1363.

An Order made upon the Defendant to maintain a Baſtard Child, was quaſhed, becauſe though in the Complaint it was alledged the Child was born in the Pariſh of *Hitchin* in *Hertfordſhire,* yet there was no Adjudication by the Juſtices, nor no Words of the Juſtices from whence it could be collected, in what Pariſh the Child was born.

Lᵈ Raym.
1423.

An Order was made by two Juſtices of the Peace upon the Defendant, to keep a Baſtard, as being the reputed Father. This Order was appealed from to the Quarter-Seſſions, where upon full Hearing of the Merits, the Order was diſcharged ; but the Defendant was bound to appear at the next Quarter-Seſſions, under Apprehenſion that better Evidence might be procured. After this the two Juſtices made a new Order upon the Defendant for keeping this Baſtard : But the Court of King's Bench quaſhed this laſt Order ; for their firſt Order being regularly diſcharged upon an Appeal, the Defendant was legally acquitted, and cannot be drawn in Queſtion again for the ſame Fact.

Bridges.
Comyns 86.

A *Certiorari* lies to remove an Order made by the Juſtices of the Peace, concerning the Repair of a Bridge and Wear, purſuant to a private Act of Parliament ; and the Juſtices ought to return the private Act upon which their Order is founded.

Lᵈ Raym.
1175.
Certiorari.

An Indictment for not repairing a Bridge ought to ſhew what ſort of Bridge it is, whether for Carts and Carriages, or for Horſes, or for Footmen only.

Lᵈ Raym.
1199.
Conſtable.

A *Certiorari* to return all Orders againſt *A.* and *B.* will not remove Orders only againſt *A.*

Lᵈ Raym.
736.

A Conſtable may execute the Warrant of a Juſtice of Peace out of his Liberty, but he is not compellable to execute it there.

Lᵈ Raym.
1189.

A Conſtable of a Hundred being indicted for not returning the Warrant of two Juſtices, for levying a Forfeiture on Conviction of Deer-ſtealing ; the Defendant pleaded Not Guilty, and was tried and convicted at the Aſſizes. The Record was removed into the King's Bench by *Certiorari,* where, after ſeveral Arguments, Judgment was given for the Queen, and the Defendant fined 200 *l.* by the Opinion of three Judges againſt *Holt,* Chief Juſtice. They held that the Conſtable is obliged to execute the Juſtices Warrant on a Conviction of Deer-ſtealing, and that a Conſtable of a Hundred is as much an Officer of the Juſtices, as a Conſtable of a Pariſh : That it not being ſaid in the Act who ſhould execute the Warrant, the Conſtable muſt execute it, he being the proper Officer attendant on the Juſtices of Peace. That there being ſeveral Things appointed by the Act of Parliament to be done by the Conſtables ; as detaining the Offender in Cuſtody till a Return may be made to the Warrants ; ſearching for Veniſon, Skins of Deer, and Toils ; which ſhews that the Legiſlature looked upon him as the proper Perſon in this Caſe. *Holt* made no Queſtion but that an Indictment would lie in this Caſe, and that the Conſtable was a proper Officer to execute the Warrant ; but his Objection was to the Warrant, as not mentioning Time nor Place, nor when and where it ſhould be returned ; whereas there ought to be both ; and all Proceſs in the ſuperior Courts are ſo.

Lᵈ Raym.
1195, 1196.

Upon the Arguments in this Caſe, the Court held, that in Caſe an Offender was but once convicted, and had Goods only ſufficient to ſatisfy Part of the Sum forfeited, that his Goods could not be taken, but he muſt be impriſoned for a Year, and ſet in the Pillory. But in Caſe he were twice convicted, and had Goods ſufficient to ſatisfy one Conviction, but not both ; he ſhould pay one, and ſuffer corporal Puniſhment for the other : But the Law never intended he ſhould ſuffer both Ways upon one Conviction, to pay Part, and be ſet in the Pillory for the Reſidue.

Lᵈ Raym.
1196.

Upon the Return of Want of Diſtreſs, the Juſtice of Peace ſhould make a Record of it, and give Judgment for the corporal Puniſhment.

The Conſtable is not obliged to return the Warrant itſelf to the Juſtice, but may keep it for his own Juſtification, in Caſe he ſhould be queſtioned for what he had done ; but only give him an Account what he had done upon it.

Deer-ſtealing.
Lᵈ Raym.
545.

A Man convict upon the Statute of Deer-ſtealing, 3 & 4 *W.* & *M. cap.* 10. cannot be committed, if he have ſufficient Diſtreſs.

Lᵈ Raym.
581, 582.

In Convictions by Juſtices of Peace, in a ſummary Way, where the ancient Courſe of Proceeding by Indictment and Trial by Jury is diſpenſed with, the Court may more eaſily diſpenſe with Forms ; and it is ſufficient for the Juſtices, in the Deſcription of the Offence to purſue the Words of the Statute ; and they are not confined to the legal Forms requiſite in Indictments for Offences by the Common Law. For though all Acts which ſubject Men to new and other Trials, than thoſe by which they ought to be tried by the Common Law, being contrary to the Rights and Liberties of *Engliſhmen,* as they were ſettled by *Magna Charta,* ought to be taken ſtrictly ; yet when ſuch a Statute is made, one ought to purſue the Intent of the Makers, and expound it in ſo reaſonable a Manner as that it may be executed. But it is alſo incumbent upon Judges, to take great Care that in the Execution of this Law they do not go beyond the Act of Parliament. Said by Chief Juſtice *Holt,* in pronouncing the Opinion of the Court upon a Conviction for Deer-ſtealing by a Juſtice of Peace, upon the 3 & 4 *W.* & *M. cap.* 10. the Conviction being removed into the King's Bench by *Certiorari.*

Lᵈ Raym.
583, 584.

Upon a Conviction for Deer-ſtealing on this Statute, exception was taken that *illicite occidit* is not ſufficient, but that it ought to be *furtive,* or *cum animo furandi,* or ſomething reſembling it ; for every unlawful killing is not within the Act. But *per Holt* Chief Juſtice ; if there is a Pretence of Right, we ought to ſuppoſe that the Juſtice would do Right, and acquit the Defendant ; becauſe he is intruſted with the Execution of the Law. The Intent of the Act was to prevent killing in a clandeſtine Manner by Stealth ; but it is enough to lay the Fact in the Words of the Act of Parliament, and that ought to be admitted upon Evidence. The Title of the Act is againſt Deer-ſtealers, but there is not any ſuch Word in the Body of the Act : And therefore if there was a Diſpute concerning the Limits of a Walk in a Foreſt, and one claims, as Part of his Walk, what is, in Fact, Part

2

of

of the Divifion of another, and accordingly kills Deer there, the Cafe is out of the Intent of the Act, but is plainly within the Words. The Intent of the Act was to punifh Rogues and Vagabonds; not to punifh Perfons, who by Miftake in the Execution of their Trufts exceed what the Law warrants. If the Keeper of a Walk gives Leave to a Perfon to kill a Deer, though this Licence does not give him fufficient Authority to kill it, yet it will not be an unlawful killing within the Statute, becaufe there is a Colour of Right.

Three Men were convicted upon the 3 & 4 *W. & M. cap.* 10. made againft Deer-ftealers, *viz.* L⁴ Raym. two of them for killing five Deer in a Park, and the third for aiding and affifting, by inciting and 842. perfwading the others to kill the faid Deer, and by lending them a Horfe and a Dog for that Purpofe. This Conviction was moved into the King's Bench by *Certiorari*, and Exceptions were taken to it. The grand Queftion was, whether the third Defendant was convict of any Offence within the faid Act of Parliament? And three Juftices, againft *Holt* Chief Juftice, held the Conviction good.

A Conviction againft the Defendant for killing Deer, was removed into the King's Bench by *Cer-* L⁴ Raym. *tiorari*; and quafhed, becaufe it faid only, that he killed Deer *in quodam loco*, where they had been 791. ufually kept, and did not fay inclofed.

Upon an Information before two Juftices of the Peace, the Defendant was convicted on 8 *Ann. Excife. cap.* 9. for not permitting, and refufing to affift an Officer of the Excife to weigh Candles. By this L⁴ Raym. Statute an Excife Officer may by Day or Night, but if in the Night, it muft be with a Conftable, 1375. enter into a Houfe, *&c.* It was laid in the Information, that the Officer entered into the Houfe lawfully, and not faid, whether it was in the Day or Night. Hence an Exception was taken for the Defendant; but the Court affirmed the Conviction: For it is laid in the Information to have been *lawfully*, and it does not appear upon the Face of the Information, that it was wrong; and therefore the Court will not intend it was fo. If it had been unlawfully, the Defendant would have had the Benefit of it, in his Defence before the Juftices.

Where a Fact is made Felony by a Statute, it is not indictable as a Trefpafs.   *Felony.*

An Inquifition of forcible Detainer, taken before two Juftices of the Peace, being removed into L⁴ Raym. the King's Bench by *Certiorari*, was quafhed, becaufe it did not appear that the Jury, before whom 712. the Inquifition was taken, were of that Neighbourhood, nor of the County.   *Forcible Detainer.*

Some Perfons being convicted, upon View of three Juftices of the Peace, of a Forcible Detainer, L⁴ Raym. were by them committed to Gaol, till they fhould pay a Fine to the King; but the Juftices did 926. affefs no Fine. The Court of King's Bench held this Conviction naught, and it was quafhed, and L⁴ Raym. the Defendants difcharged.   1514.

A Man indicted of Forcible Entry may hinder the Juftices from awarding Execution, either by *Forcible Entry.* traverfing the Force (though the Books heretofore have been *pro* and *con*, as to that Opinion) or by L⁴ Raym. Plea of Poffeffion of three Years.   440.

By the 15 *Rich.* 2. *cap.* 2. Commitment by a Juftice of Peace for a Forcible Entry ought to be L⁴ Raym. forthwith: And there is no Difference in Reafon, why Reftitution upon the 8 *Hen.* 6. fhould not be 483. immediately, as well as the Commitment upon the 15 *Rich.* 2. There is rather greater Reafon, becaufe the Conviction upon the 15 *Rich.* 2. is not traverfable, as the Inquifition upon 8 *Hen.* 6. is. And it would be a great Mifchief, and againft the Reafon of the Common Law, if it fhould be otherwife; becaufe the Title in fo long Time might be altered: And the Poffeffion intimates, that the Perfon poffeffed is the rightful Owner, and fo fome Reafon for Reftitution; yet where a long Space of Time intervenes, this Reafon is not of Force.

An Inquifition of Forcible Entry ought to fhew what Eftate the Tenant has, and ought to fhew L⁴ Raym. an exprefs Diffeifin.   610.

An Indictment upon the Stat. 8 *H.* 6. for a Forcible Entry, was found before the Juftices of the Comyns 61. Peace; but no Reftitution awarded at the Time of the Conviction. At the End of two Years and a Half, Reftitution of the Poffeffion upon this Indictment was awarded to the Party oufted; and upon a Motion in the King's Bench (after Deliberation) Reftitution was granted by the whole Court, and it was held that Reftitution ought to have been awarded immediately; the Intent of the Statute being to give a prefent Remedy, and for that Reafon does not delay it till the Quarter-Seffions; but impowers a private Juftice to put the Act in Execution, which is not done, if he does not reftore the Party oufted.

A Conviction *fuper præmiffis*, for three Penalties of 5 *l.* each, for killing three Hares, where it *Game.* appears it was done the fame Time, is bad, for the Statute does not give 5 *l.* for every Hare, it be- Comyns 274. ing but one Offence.

Upon a Conviction upon the 5 *Ann. cap.* 14. for killing of Hares, it ought to be made out be- Comyns 525. fore the Juftice, that the Defendant had no fuch Qualification as the Law requires; therefore the Juftice ought to return, that he had no Manner of Qualification, before he can convict the Defendant.

Juftices of Peace cannot affefs a Fine certain, for killing of Rabbits in a private Warren; for the L⁴ Raym. Stat. 22 & 23 *Car.* 2. *cap.* 25. gives treble Cofts and Damages, but no Fine.   151.

A Conviction before a Juftice of Peace for unlawfully keeping a Lurcher, and a Gun, to kill and L⁴ Raym. deftroy the Game, was quafhed; becaufe it only averred generally that he was not qualified, and 1415. did not aver that the Defendant had not the particular Qualifications mentioned in the Statute, as to Degree, Eftate, *&c.*

A Man being convicted by a Juftice of Peace, for killing a fallow Deer of the King's in *Cran-* L⁴ Raym. *born Chace*; the Conviction was quafhed, becaufe the Informer was a Witnefs; divers Convictions 1545. having been quafhed for the fame Reafon before.

The

Highways.
Ld Raym.
725.

The Inhabitants of every Parifh of Common Right ought to repair the Highways; and therefore if particular Perfons are made chargeable to repair the faid Ways, by a Statute lately made, and they become infolvent, the Juftices of Peace may put that Charge upon the reft of the Inhabitants.

Ld Raym.
858.

An Indictment found for not working in the Repair of the Highways in *London*, upon the 22 & 23 *Car.* 2. *cap.* 17. §. 6. was held bad; becaufe that fix Days were appointed between fuch and fuch Days for the Work, but the particular Days were not mentioned; for the Appointment ought to be of fuch Days in particular, *viz.* the 20th of *April*, &c. and Notice ought to be given accordingly.

Ld Raym.
922.

A Man was indicted for not repairing the Pavement before his Houfe in *Old-Street*; and the Indictment was quafhed, becaufe it was not faid how he was obliged to repair it; and this was not within the late Act of Parliament for paving the Streets.

Indictment.
Ld Raym.
991.

A Man was indicted for affaulting and beating a Cuftom-Houfe Officer, in the Execution of his Office; and the Indictment was quafhed, becaufe the Stat. 13 & 14 *Car.* 2. *c.* 11. §. 6. inflicts a Penalty, and prefcribes the particular Method of punifhing that Offence, *viz.* by the Juftices of Peace, by Fine and Imprifonment; and therefore no Indictment lies for this Offence.

Ld Raym.
1116.

An Indictment does not lie againft a Man for enticing away the Apprentice of another; for it is a private Injury, for which an Action upon the Cafe will lie; but it is not of fuch a public Nature, as to maintain an Indictment.

Ld Raym.
1197.

A Woman was convicted at the Seffions, for being a common Bawd, and fined 100 *l*. but the Judgment was reverfed, upon a Writ of Error in the King's Bench; for the Judgment ought to have been, for keeping a common Bawdy-Houfe.

It was agreed by the Court in this Cafe, that if a Perfon was only a Lodger in a Houfe, yet if fhe made Ufe of her Room for the entertaining and accommodating People in the Way of a Bawdy-Houfe, it would be keeping of a Bawdy-Houfe, as much as if fhe had the whole Houfe.

Ld Raym.
1210.

An Indictment for affembling *riotofe ad quoddam illicitum faciendum*, was quafhed for being too general; the Act ought to be fhewn, that the Court may judge whether the Act be unlawful or not.

Ld Raym.
1368.

The Defendant was indicted at the general Quarter-Seffions, for fecreting a Woman with Child by him, to hinder her Evidence, and to elude the Execution of the Law for the Crime aforefaid. The Indictment being removed into the King's Bench by *Certiorari*, the Defendant demurred, and Judgment was given for him, that this Indictment was not maintainable; it being no Offence for which an Indictment would lie, as this Fact was charged.

Juftices of Peace.
Ld Raym.
426.

Where Authority is given to two Juftices of Peace to do any Act, the Seffions may do it in all Cafes, except where Appeal is directed to the Seffions.

Ld Raym.
481.

Juftices of Peace at their Seffions may adjourn an Appeal upon Debate, for farther Confideration.

Ld Raym.
676.

An Attachment is not grantable for Non-performance of an old Order of Juftices, confirmed in the King's Bench; the proper Remedy is to apply to the Juftices for a new Order.

Ld Raym.
871.

An Order made at the general Quarter-Seffions, that the Defendant fhould be profecuted as a common Barrator, and that the Profecution fhould be at the Charge of the County, being removed into the King's Bench by *Certiorari*, was quafhed; becaufe the Juftices have not Power to charge the County with the Cofts of fuch a Profecution.

Ld Raym.
1369.

Mr. *A.* is a Rafcal, a Villain, and a Lyar, fpoken of a Juftice of Peace in the Execution of his Office, were held actionable by the Court of King's Bench, they being laid to have been fpoken of the Plaintiff in the Execution of his Office, and fo found; fo that it is the fame as if the Defendant had faid, that the Plaintiff is a Villain in the Execution of his Office, a Rafcal in the Execution of his Office, and a Lyar in the Execution of his Office; which carry with them a great Scandal, and in common Underftanding import a great Imputation againft the Plaintiff's Integrity and Behaviour in that Office; and therefore Judgment was given for the Plaintiff, although it had been infifted on for the Defendant, that the Words were not actionable, and fome ftrong Cafes cited; but none of them came up to the prefent.

Ld Raym.
1407.

In fummary Convictions before Juftices of the Peace, the Party ought to be heard, and for that Purpofe ought to be fummoned in Fact; and if the Juftices proceed againft a Perfon without fummoning him, it would be a Mifdemeanor in them, for which an Information would lie againft them. See the Cafe of *The King* and *Venables*, Ld Raym. 1405 to 1407.

Labourers.
Ld Raym.
767.

An Indictment was found at the Seffions of the Peace of the Corporation of *Wells* in *Somerfetfhire*, againft the Defendant, for having ufed a Trade, not having ferved an Apprentice for feven Years: and being moved into the King's Bench by *Certiorari*, it was quafhed; becaufe the Juftices at fuch Seffions have not Jurifdiction to take fuch Indictments.

Ld Raym.
1305.

The Statute of Labourers was firft intended to extend only to Servants who had the rated Wages, and not to covenant Servants; and then if the Servant had proved how long he had ferved, it appeared how much was due: but now the Act has been extended to covenant Servants, and that mafters the Mifchief in this Cafe; for it will be difficult, perhaps, for the Servant to prove how much he had agreed for; but however he ought not, againft a Rule of Law, to be admitted to prove it himfelf. An Order of Seffions made upon a Mafter, to pay his Servant 7 *l*. for Wages in Hufbandry, was quafhed, for this Reafon.

Murder.
Ld Raym.
1485.

A. throws a Bottle at *B.* and the blow is returned, they are parted, and an Hour after they fight without any Reconciliation intervening, and *A.* kills *B.* it is Murder. See *Oneby's* Cafe in *Ld Raym. Rep. peg.* 1485. *& feq.*

2   The

The Building of a Houfe in a larger Manner than it was before, whereby the Street becomes *Nufance.* darker, is not any publick Nufance by Reafon of the Darkning. 1.⁴ Raym.

The Defendant was indicted for keeping of Hogs in *London*, in fome of the back Streets, *contra* 737. *formam ftatuti* ; and a Motion was made in the King's Bench to quafh the Indictment, becaufe L⁴ Raym. there was a particular penalty appointed for this Offence, *viz.* Forfeiture of the Swine, to the Ufe 1163. of the Poor of the Parifh where they are kept ; and therefore an Indictment would not lie, at leaft not upon the Statute as this was, by concluding *contra, formam ftatuti.* But it was agreed by the Court, that where a new Penalty is appointed by Act of Parliament, for a Matter that was an Offence at Common Law, there you may either take the Remedy which is given by Statute, or proceed by way of Indictment, as you might have done before ; and therefore keeping Swine in the City being a Nufance at Common Law, the Profecutor is at Liberty either to proceed by Way of Indictment for the Nufance, or to take the more expeditious Remedy, which is given him by the Act of Parliament, by Sale of the Swine. But where the Statute makes the Offence, there you muft purfue that. As to the *contra formam ftatuti,* the Offence being an Offence at Common Law, that was but Surplufage, and would do no Harm. The Court farther faid, that if the Defendant had any Hopes in his Exception, he fhould demur ; for that it was a Rule, never to quafh Indictments for Nufances.

An Order of two Juftices made for the Removal of a Man and his Children, was, upon a *Poor. Certiorari* into the King's Bench, quafhed ; for the Removal of a Man and his Family has been Comyns 86. judged uncertain ; and the Children ought to be removed to the Place of their Settlement, which may be diftinct from that of the Father.

It has been faid, that the Juftices of Peace out of Seffions could not make an Order for an exprefs L⁴ Raym. Sum for the Maintenance of a poor Man ; but that they might fign a Rate made by the Parifhioners. 42. But the Court of King's Bench, in the Cafe of *Waltham* and *Sparkes*, faid, that all the Juftices of Peace in *England* did fo ; and therefore though they have not an Authority to do it in ftrictnefs of Law, yet *communis error jus facit.*

An Order for the Removal of a poor Woman was held ill, becaufe fhe was thereby fent to her Comyns 97. Mafter, and not to the Parifh where fettled.

An Order was made to remove three Perfons and their Families, and it was quafhed, becaufe too L⁴ Raym. general ; for it might be that fome of their Families were not removable. If a Man marries a poor 395. Woman who is fettled in *B.* and had Children by a former Husband, and he is fettled in *A.* his Wife fhall be removed to him to *A.* but fuch of her Children as are more than feven Years of Age fhall not be removed, thofe under feven Years of Age may, for Caufe of Nurture ; but ought to be maintained at the Charge of the Parifh of *B.*

No Parifh fhall be bound by Order of the Juftices made upon Appeal, which is not Party to it. L⁴ Raym. It is not neceffary that there be an Adjudication in an Order, that a Man is likely to become charge- 513. able to the Parifh.

The Juftices of Peace have no Authority to fettle any Perfon in an extraparochial Place ; for the L⁴ Raym. Statute which gives them Authority, extends only to the Poor within Parifhes ; Parifhes in Reputa- 549. tion are within the Act, but Places extraparochial are out of it.

A poor Infant ought to be maintained by the Parifh where it was born, if it has not obtained L⁴ Raym. another Settlement ; and therefore it is incumbent upon the Parifh where it was born to find another 567. Place of Settlement.

Juftices of Peace make a Warrant to levy a Poors Rate upon *J. S.* which was directed to the L⁴ Raym. Conftables of the Parifh of *A. J. S.* had Land in *A.* upon which he had no Chattles ; but his 735. Houfe ftood in the adjoining Parifh of *B.* in the fame County, in which he had Goods. The Conftables of *A.* levied thefe Goods by Virtue of the faid Warrant ; and *Holt* Chief Juftice ruled upon Evidence at the Trial at *Hertford Summer* Affizes 1698. that the Goods were well levied.

An original Order made at the general Quarter-Seffions for the Weft-Riding of *Yorkfhire* (where- L⁴ Raym. of the Tenor was thus, *viz.* It is ordered that the Church-wardens and Overfeers of the Poor of the 798. Parifh of *Abberford* do make an Affeffment to the Church and Poor, by a Pound Rate ; and in the faid Affeffment do affefs *Grayftonfield* Lands, and all other Lands within the faid Conftabulary, to the Ufe aforefaid, equally by a Pound Rate) was removed, with other Orders, into the King's Bench upon a *Certiorari.* Upon a Motion to quafh this Order, becaufe the Juftices have not any Jurifdiction to make fuch original Order at the Quarter-Seffions ; though it had been otherwife if it had come before them by Appeal ; a Day was given to hear Counfel on both Sides. Nobody then appearing to maintain the Order, it was moved to quafh it next day ; and this was granted, *Powell* Juftice faying it was impoffible to make it good.

No *Mandamus* lies to command Church-wardens and Overfeers of the Poor, to make a Rate to L⁴ Raym. reimburfe former Overfeers. 1009.

If Overfeers lay out Money for the Poor, and then a Rate is made, they may reimburfe them- L⁴ Raym. ib. felves out of that Rate ; but a Rate cannot be made to reimburfe them.

If a Rate is made for the Poor, which by accident falls fhort, the Overfeers lay out Money, and L⁴ Raym. ib. the Parifh make a new rate, if then the Juftices refufe to confirm it, a *Mandamus* will lie.

Church-wardens and Overfeers, with the Confirmation of the Juftices, may order Money to be L⁴ Raym. ib. levied for the Poor, without the Concurrence of the Parifh.

A Farmer is not taxable for the Poor's Rate for his Stock ; but a Tradefman is for his Stock in L⁴ Raym. Trade. 1281.

The Place of the Birth of a poor Child, where the Father has got no Settlement, is the Place of L⁴ Raym. the Settlement of the Child ; yet where the Father has gained a Settlement, his Children, though 1332. born

[7 N]

born in another Parish, shall be looked on as settled at the Place of their Father's last legal Settlement, and shall be removed thither, as well after the Death of their Father, if Occasion requires, as in his Life-time, supposing they have gained no Settlement of their own.

L⁴ Raym.
1394.

An Order of Justices of the Peace, for appointing an Overseer of the Poor, was quashed, because it did not appear by the Order, that the Person appointed was a substantial Householder.

L⁴ Raym.
1454.

A Motion was made in the King's Bench, to quash an Order of the Quarter-Sessions, whereby the Father-in-Law was ordered to maintain his Daughter-in-Law; because he was not by Law obliged to maintain her. A Rule was made to shew Cause, why it should not be quashed; which Rule was made absolute, no Person shewing Cause to the contrary.

L⁴ Raym.
1473.

J. B. rented an House and some Closes at *W.* about 30 *l. per Annum*, and inhabited the said House for several Years, and died insolvent, he left a Widow and one Daughter *E. B.* The Widow, soon after removed to *P.* into a Messuage or Tenement about 40 *s. per Annum* Value, and some Lands about 10 *l. per Annum*, that was her own Estate for Life, both House and Land being Copyhold, and took her Daughter with her, then about the Age of fourteen Years; and the Daughter lived with her Mother at *P.* above two Years in the said Messuage or Tenement; but the Mother let the said Lands to a Tenant; whereupon the general Quarter-Sessions were of Opinion that *E. B.* was settled at *W.* the Place of her Father's Settlement, and not at *P.* where she lived with her Mother; and therefore confirmed the Order of two Justices of Peace, for sending *E. B.* to *W.* but the Court of King's Bench quashed these Orders, and adjudged the Place of *E. B.*'s last legal Settlement to be at *P.* The Reasons alledged by the Counsel in this Case, and approved of by the Court, were, that the Mother being a Widow, and gaining a new Settlement after her Husband's Death, the Daughter gained a Settlement also, as Part of her Family; and there is no Difference between a Father's gaining a Settlement and a Mother's, in such a Case as this; for the Mother is obliged to provide for her Children, after her Husband's Death, as the Father was when living; and she could not leave this Daughter behind her, neither could she be removed from her. But if after her Husband's Death she had married a Man settled in another Parish, though her Children by her former Husband must have gone with her for Nurture, yet they would have been no Part of her second Husband's Family; and therefore would have gained no Settlement thereby in the Parish, where the Father-in-Law was settled.

Orders.
L⁴ Raym.
1304.

Prædicto in Orders or Indictments does not refer to the County mentioned in the Margin, though it does in Declarations, and for this Reason an Order made by two Justices was quashed.

L⁴ Raym.
1198.

If an Order by two Justices of Peace says *doth* adjudge instead of *do*, the singular Number for the Plural, it will be ill, and an Order was quashed upon a *Certiorari* for this Reason.

Riot.
L⁴ Raym.
215.

When a Riot is supprest by the Justices, together with the Sheriff, having the *Posse Comitatus* with them for that Purpose, and they convict the Rioters by a Record of the Force, upon their proper View, the Sheriff ought to be Party in such Inquisition; and so he ought by the 19 *Hen.* 7. *cap.* 13. But if the Rioters disperse of themselves, and after they are parted an Inquisition is made of it by two Justices of Peace, there is no Need that it appear by the Inquisition, that the Sheriff was Party to the Inquiry.

L⁴ Raym. ib.

When the Conviction of a Riot is by Inquisition taken before two Justices of Peace, the Inquisition has no Need to be as taken *pro Domino Rege & corpore Comitatus*, but *pro Domino Rege* is sufficient, or rather better; for their Inquiry is not for the County, but for the King; and so is the Constant Form of such Inquests. But when an Inquisition is by the Grand Jury, then it ought to be *pro Domino Rege & corpore Comitatus.*

L⁴ Raym. ib.

Though the Words of the Statute of 13 *Hen.* 4. *cap.* 7. are, that the Justices shall make Inquiry within one Month after the Riot, yet an Inquiry by them after the Month is good; for the Statute intended only to hasten their Proceedings, by subjecting them to the Penalty in Case they did not make Inquiry within the Month, and not to restrain their Authority to the Month, so as it could not be executed afterwards: The Lapse of the Month makes them incur the Penalty, but does not determine their Power.

L⁴ Raym.
965.

If a Number of People assemble together in a lawful Manner, and upon a lawful Occasion, as for electing a Mayor, or the like, and during the assembly a sudden affray happens; this will not make it a Riot *ab initio*, but only a common affray. But if a Number of People assemble in a riotous Manner to do an unlawful Act, and a Person, who was upon the Place before upon a lawful Occasion, and not privy to their first Design, comes and joins with them, he will be guilty of a Riot equally with the rest.

Robbery.
Comyns 478.

It was held in the Case of *The King* and *Frances and others*, by a Majority of all the Judges at Serjeants-Inn, on a special Verdict on an Indictment for a Robbery on the Highway, that the Words *then* and *there immediately* do not sufficiently ascertain the Time to find the Prisoners guilty. The Case was, that a Man in the Highway holding some Pieces of Gold, *Frances* struck his Hand, whereby the Gold fell to the Ground, the Owner offering to take it up, the Prisoners swore that if he touched it, they would knock out his Brains; the Jury also found that the said Prisoners *then and there immediately* took up the said Pieces of Gold and rode off with them, &c. The Court of King's Bench, pursuant to this Opinion of the Majority of the Judges held that the Defendants ought to be discharged of this Indictment.

Trees.
Comyns 131,
132.

In a Conviction before Justices of the Peace on the 43 *Eliz. cap.* 7. for cutting down Trees, the Number and Quantity of the Trees ought to be mentioned expresly.

Warrant.
L⁴ Raym.
740.

An Officer cannot justify the Imprisonment of a Man for Non-payment of Taxes under the general printed Warrant which the Collectors have, signed by two Justices of Peace; but he ought to have a special Warrant.

F I N I S.